ADVANCES IN NEURAL INFORMATION PROCESSING SYSTEMS 7

ADVANCES IN NEURAL INFORMATION PROCESSING SYSTEMS

Published by Morgan-Kaufmann

NIPS-1
Advances in Neural Information Processing Systems: Proceedings of the 1988 Conference,
David Touretzky, ed., 1989

NIPS-2
Advances in Neural Information Processing Systems: Proceedings of the 1989 Conference,
David Touretzky, ed., 1990

NIPS-3
Advances in Neural Information Processing Systems: Proceedings of the 1990 Conference,
Richard P. Lippmann, John E. Moody, and David S. Touretzky, eds., 1991

NIPS-4
Advances in Neural Information Processing Systems: Proceedings of the 1991 Conference,
John E. Moody, Steve J. Hanson, and Richard P. Lippmann, eds., 1992

NIPS-5
Advances in Neural Information Processing Systems: Proceedings of the 1992 Conference,
Stephen Jose Hanson, Jack D. Cowan, and C. Lee Giles, eds., 1993

NIPS-6
Advances in Neural Information Processing Systems: Proceedings of the 1993 Conference,
Jack D. Cowan, Gerald Tesauro, and Joshua Alspector, eds., 1994

Published by The MIT Press

NIPS-7
Advances in Neural Information Processing Systems: Proceedings of the 1994 Conference,
Gerald Tesauro, David Touretzky, and Todd Leen, eds., 1995

ADVANCES IN NEURAL INFORMATION PROCESSING SYSTEMS 7

Edited by
Gerald Tesauro, David Touretzky, Todd Leen

The MIT Press
Cambridge, Massachusetts
London, England

© 1995 Massachusetts Institute of Technology

All rights reserved. No part of this book may be reproduced in any form by any electronic or mechanical means (including photocopying, recording, or information storage and retrieval) without permission in writing from the publisher.

This book was printed and bound in the United States of America.

ISSN 1049-5258
ISBN 0-262-20104-6

Contents

Preface	*xvii*
Contributors	*xix*

PART I
COGNITIVE SCIENCE

DIRECTION SELECTIVITY IN PRIMARY VISUAL CORTEX USING MASSIVE INTRACORTICAL CONNECTIONS *Humbert Suarez, Christof Koch, Rodney Douglas*	3
ON THE COMPUTATIONAL UTILITY OF CONSCIOUSNESS *Donald Mathis, Michael C. Mozer*	11
CATASTROPHIC INTERFERENCE IN HUMAN MOTOR LEARNING *Tom Brashers-Krug, Reza Shadmehr, Emanuel Todorov*	19
GRAMMAR LEARNING BY A SELF-ORGANIZING NETWORK *Michiro Negishi*	27
PATTERNS OF DAMAGE IN NEURAL NETWORKS: THE EFFECTS OF LESION AREA, SHAPE AND NUMBER *Eytan Ruppin, James A. Reggia*	35
FORWARD DYNAMIC MODELS IN HUMAN MOTOR CONTROL: PSYCHOPHYSICAL EVIDENCE *Daniel M. Wolpert, Zoubin Ghahramani, Michael I. Jordan*	43
A SOLVABLE CONNECTIONIST MODEL OF IMMEDIATE RECALL OF ORDERED LISTS *Neil Burgess*	51

PART II
NEUROSCIENCE

A MODEL FOR CHEMOSENSORY RECEPTION 61
Rainer Malaka, Thomas Ragg, Martin Hammer

THE ELECTRONIC TRANSFORMATION: A TOOL FOR
RELATING NEURONAL FORM TO FUNCTION 69
Nicholas Carnevale, Kenneth Y. Tsai, Brenda J. Claiborne, Thomas H. Brown

A MODEL OF THE HIPPOCAMPUS COMBINING SELF-ORGANIZATION
AND ASSOCIATIVE MEMORY FUNCTION 77
Michael E. Hasselmo, Eric Schnell, Joshua Berke, Edi Barkai

MODEL OF BIOLOGICAL NEURON AS A TEMPORAL NEURAL NETWORK 85
Sean D. Murphy, Edward W. Kairiss

A CRITICAL COMPARISON OF MODELS FOR ORIENTATION AND
OCULAR DOMINANCE COLUMNS IN THE STRIATE CORTEX 93
E. Erwin, K. Obermayer, K. Schulten

A NOVEL REINFORCEMENT MODEL OF BIRDSONG VOCALIZATION
LEARNING 101
Kenji Doya, Terrence J. Sejnowski

OCULAR DOMINANCE AND PATTERNED LATERAL CONNECTIONS IN A
SELF-ORGANIZING MODEL OF THE PRIMARY VISUAL CORTEX 109
Joseph Sirosh, Risto Miikkulainen

ANATOMICAL ORIGIN AND COMPUTATIONAL ROLE OF DIVERSITY IN
THE RESPONSE PROPERTIES OF CORTICAL NEURONS 117
Kalanit Grill Spector, Shimon Edelman, Rafael Malach

REINFORCEMENT LEARNING PREDICTS THE SITE OF PLASTICITY FOR
AUDITORY REMAPPING IN THE BARN OWL 125
Alexandre Pouget, Cedric Deffayet, Terrence J. Sejnowski

MORPHOGENESIS OF THE LATERAL GENICULATE NUCLEUS:
HOW SINGULARITIES AFFECT GLOBAL STRUCTURE 133
Svilen Tzonev, Klaus Schulten, Joseph G. Malpeli

A COMPUTATIONAL MODEL OF PREFRONTAL CORTEX FUNCTION 141
Todd S. Braver, Jonathan D. Cohen, David Servan-Schreiber

A NEURAL MODEL OF DELUSIONS AND HALLUCINATIONS IN
SCHIZOPHRENIA 149
Eytan Ruppin, James A. Reggia, David Horn

SPATIAL REPRESENTATIONS IN THE PARIETAL CORTEX MAY
USE BASIS FUNCTIONS 157
Alexandre Pouget, Terrence J. Sejnowski

GROUPING COMPONENTS OF THREE-DIMENSIONAL MOVING OBJECTS
IN AREA MST OF VISUAL CORTEX 165
Richard S. Zemel, Terrence J. Sejnowski

A MODEL OF THE NEURAL BASIS OF THE RAT'S SENSE OF DIRECTION 173
William Skaggs, James J. Knierim, Hemant S. Kudrimoti, Bruce L. McNaughton

PART III
LEARNING THEORY AND DYNAMICS

ON THE COMPUTATIONAL COMPLEXITY OF NETWORKS OF SPIKING
NEURONS 183
Wolfgang Maass

$H\infty$ OPTIMAL TRAINING ALGORITHMS AND THEIR RELATION
TO BACKPROPAGATION 191
Babak Hassibi, Thomas Kailath

SYNCHRONY AND DESYNCHRONY IN NEURAL OSCILLATOR NETWORKS 199
DeLiang Wang, David Terman

LEARNING IN LARGE LINEAR PERCEPTRONS AND WHY THE
THERMODYNAMIC LIMIT IS RELEVANT TO THE REAL WORLD 207
Peter Sollich

GENERALISATION IN FEEDFORWARD NETWORKS 215
Adam Kowalczyk, Herman Ferra

FROM DATA DISTRIBUTIONS TO REGULARIZATION IN INVARIANT
LEARNING 223
Todd Leen

NEURAL NETWORK ENSEMBLES, CROSS VALIDATION, AND ACTIVE
LEARNING 231
Anders Krogh, Jesper Vedelsby

LIMITS ON LEARNING MACHINE ACCURACY IMPOSED BY DATA QUALITY 239
Corinna Cortes, L. D. Jackel, Wan-Ping Chiang

HIGHER ORDER STATISTICAL DECORRELATION WITHOUT
INFORMATION LOSS 247
Gustavo Deco, Wilfried Brauer

HYPERPARAMETERS, EVIDENCE AND GENERALISATION FOR AN
UNREALISABLE RULE 255
Glenn Marion, David Saad

TEMPORAL DYNAMICS OF GENERALIZATION IN NEURAL NETWORKS 263
Changfeng Wang, Santosh S. Venkatesh

STOCHASTIC DYNAMICS OF THREE-STATE NEURAL NETWORKS 271
Toru Ohira, Jack D. Cowan

LEARNING STOCHASTIC PERCEPTRONS UNDER K-BLOCKING
DISTRIBUTIONS 279
Mario Marchand, Saeed Hadjifaradji

LEARNING FROM QUERIES FOR MAXIMUM INFORMATION GAIN
IN IMPERFECTLY LEARNABLE PROBLEMS 287
Peter Sollich, David Saad

BIAS, VARIANCE AND THE COMBINATION OF LEAST SQUARES
ESTIMATORS 295
Ronny Meir

ON-LINE LEARNING OF DICHOTOMIES 303
N. Barkai, H. S. Seung, H. Sompolinsky

DYNAMIC MODELLING OF CHAOTIC TIME SERIES WITH NEURAL NETWORKS 311
Jose Principe, Jyh-Ming Kuo

A RIGOROUS ANALYSIS OF LINSKER-TYPE HEBBIAN LEARNING 319
Jianfeng Feng, H. Pan, V. P. Roychowdhury

SAMPLE SIZE REQUIREMENTS FOR FEEDFORWARD NEURAL NETWORKS 327
Michael Turmon, Terrence L. Fine

ASYMPTOTICS OF GRADIENT-BASED NEURAL NETWORK TRAINING
ALGORITHMS 335
Sayandev Mukherjee, Terrence L. Fine

PART IV
REINFORCEMENT LEARNING

REINFORCEMENT LEARNING ALGORITHM FOR PARTIALLY OBSERVABLE
MARKOV DECISION PROBLEMS 345
Tommi Jaakkola, Satinder P. Singh, Michael I. Jordan

ADVANTAGE UPDATING APPLIED TO A DIFFERENTIAL GAME 353
Mance E. Harmon, Leemon C. Baird III, A. Harry Klopf

REINFORCEMENT LEARNING WITH SOFT STATE AGGREGATION 361
Satinder Singh, Tommi Jaakkola, Michael I. Jordan

GENERALIZATION IN REINFORCEMENT LEARNING: SAFELY
APPROXIMATING THE VALUE FUNCTION 369
Justin Boyan, Andrew W. Moore

INSTANCE-BASED STATE IDENTIFICATION FOR REINFORCEMENT
LEARNING 377
R. Andrew McCallum

FINDING STRUCTURE IN REINFORCEMENT LEARNING 385
Sebastian Thrun, Anton Schwartz

REINFORCEMENT LEARNING METHODS FOR CONTINUOUS-TIME
MARKOV DECISION PROBLEMS 393
Steven Bradtke, Michael O. Duff

AN ACTOR/CRITIC ALGORITHM THAT IS EQUIVALENT TO Q-LEARNING 401
Robert Crites, Andrew G. Barto

PART V
ALGORITHMS AND ARCHITECTURES

FINANCIAL APPLICATIONS OF LEARNING FROM HINTS 411
Yaser S. Abu-Mostafa (Invited Paper)

COMBINING ESTIMATORS USING NON-CONSTANT WEIGHTING FUNCTIONS 419
Volker Tresp, Michiaki Taniguchi

AN INPUT OUTPUT HMM ARCHITECTURE 427
Yoshua Bengio, Paolo Frasconi

BOLTZMANN CHAINS AND HIDDEN MARKOV MODELS 435
Lawrence K. Saul, Michael I. Jordan

BAYESIAN QUERY CONSTRUCTION FOR NEURAL NETWORK MODELS 443
Gerhard Paass, Jörg Kindermann

USING A SALIENCY MAP FOR ACTIVE SPATIAL SELECTIVE ATTENTION: 451
IMPLEMENTATION & INITIAL RESULTS
Shumeet Baluja, Dean A. Pomerleau

MULTIDIMENSIONAL SCALING AND DATA CLUSTERING 459
Thomas Hofmann, Joachim Buhmann

A NON-LINEAR INFORMATION MAXIMISATION ALGORITHM THAT
PERFORMS BLIND SEPARATION 467
Anthony J. Bell, Terrence J. Sejnowski

PLASTICITY-MEDIATED COMPETITIVE LEARNING 475
Nicol Schraudolph, Terrence J. Sejnowski

PHASE-SPACE LEARNING 481
Fu-Sheng Tsung, Garrison W. Cottrell

LEARNING LOCAL ERROR BARS FOR NONLINEAR REGRESSION 489
David A. Nix, Andreas S. Weigend

DYNAMIC CELL STRUCTURES 497
Jörg Bruske, Gerald Sommer

EXTRACTING RULES FROM ARTIFICIAL NEURAL NETWORKS WITH
DISTRIBUTED REPRESENTATIONS 505
Sebastian Thrun

CAPACITY AND INFORMATION EFFICIENCY OF A BRAIN-LIKE
ASSOCIATIVE NET 513
Bruce Graham, David Willshaw

BOOSTING THE PERFORMANCE OF RBF NETWORKS WITH DYNAMIC
DECAY ADJUSTMENT 521
Michael R. Berthold, Jay Diamond

SIMPLIFYING NEURAL NETS BY DISCOVERING FLAT MINIMA 529
Sepp Hochreiter, Jürgen Schmidhuber

LEARNING WITH PRODUCT UNITS 537
Laurens Leerink, C. Lee Giles, Bill G. Horne, Marwan A. Jabri

DETERMINISTIC ANNEALING VARIANT OF THE EM ALGORITHM 545
Naonori Ueda, Ryohei Nakano

DIFFUSION OF CREDIT IN MARKOVIAN MODELS 553
Yoshua Bengio, Paolo Frasconi

FACTORIAL LEARNING BY CLUSTERING FEATURES 561
Joshua B. Tenenbaum, Emmanuel V. Todorov

INTERIOR POINT IMPLEMENTATIONS OF ALTERNATING MINIMIZATION
TRAINING 569
Michael Lemmon, Peter T. Szymanski

SARDNET: A SELF-ORGANIZING FEATURE MAP FOR SEQUENCES 577
Daniel L. James, Risto Miikkulainen

CONVERGENCE PROPERTIES OF THE K-MEANS ALGORITHMS 585
Léon Bottou, Yoshua Bengio

ACTIVE LEARNING FOR FUNCTION APPROXIMATION 593
Kah Kay Sung, Partha Niyogi

ANALYSIS OF UNSTANDARDIZED CONTRIBUTIONS IN CROSS
CONNECTED NETWORKS 601
Thomas R. Shultz, Yuriko Oshima-Takane, Yoshio Takane

TEMPLATE-BASED ALGORITHMS FOR CONNECTIONIST RULE EXTRACTION 609
Jay A. Alexander, Michael C. Mozer

FACTORIAL LEARNING AND THE *EM* ALGORITHM 617
Zoubin Ghahramani

A GROWING NEURAL GAS NETWORK LEARNS TOPOLOGIES 625
Bernd Fritzke

AN ALTERNATIVE MODEL FOR MIXTURES OF EXPERTS 633
Lei Xu, Michael I. Jordan, Geoffrey E. Hinton

ESTIMATING CONDITIONAL PROBABILITY DENSITIES FOR PERIODIC
VARIABLES 641
Chris M. Bishop, Claire Legleye

EFFECTS OF NOISE ON CONVERGENCE AND GENERALIZATION
IN RECURRENT NETWORKS 649
Kam Jim, Bill G. Horne, C. Lee Giles

LEARNING MANY RELATED TASKS AT THE SAME TIME
WITH BACKPROPAGATION 657
Rich Caruana

A RAPID GRAPH-BASED METHOD FOR ARBITRARY
TRANSFORMATION-INVARIANT PATTERN CLASSIFICATION 665
Alessandro Sperduti, David G. Stork

RECURRENT NETWORKS: SECOND ORDER PROPERTIES AND PRUNING 673
Morten With Pedersen, Lars Kai Hansen

CLASSIFYING WITH GAUSSIAN MIXTURES AND CLUSTERS 681
Nanda Kambhatla, Todd K. Leen

EFFICIENT METHODS FOR DEALING WITH MISSING DATA
IN SUPERVISED LEARNING 689
Volker Tresp, Ralph Neuneier, Subutai Ahmad

AN EXPERIMENTAL COMPARISON OF RECURRENT NEURAL NETWORKS 697
Bill G. Horne, C. Lee Giles

ACTIVE LEARNING WITH STATISTICAL MODELS 705
David Cohn, Zoubin Ghahramani, Michael I. Jordon

LEARNING WITH PREKNOWLEDGE: CLUSTERING WITH POINT AND
GRAPH MATCHING DISTANCE MEASURES 713
Steven Gold, Anand Rangarajan, Eric Mjolsness

DIRECT MULTI-STEP TIME SERIES PREDICTION USING TD(λ) 721
Peter Kazlas, Andreas S. Weigend

PART VI
IMPLEMENTATIONS

ICEG MORPHOLOGY CLASSIFICATION USING AN ANALOGUE VLSI
NEURAL NETWORK 731
Richard Coggins, Marwan Jabri, Barry Flower, Stephen Pickard

A SILICON AXON 739
Bradley A. Minch, Paul Hasler, Chris Diorio, Carver Mead

THE NI1000: HIGH SPEED PARALLEL VLSI FOR IMPLEMENTING
MULTILAYER PERCEPTRONS 747
Michael P. Perrone, Leon N. Cooper

A REAL TIME CLUSTERING CMOS NEURAL ENGINE 755
T. Serrano-Gotarredona, B. Linares-Barranco, J. L. Huertas

Contents

PULSESTREAM SYNAPSES WITH NON-VOLATILE ANALOGUE
AMORPHOUS-SILICON MEMORIES 763
A. J. Holmes, A. F. Murray, S. Churcher, J. Hajto, M. J. Rose

A LAGRANGIAN FORMULATION FOR OPTICAL BACKPROPAGATION
TRAINING IN KERR-TYPE OPTICAL NETWORKS 771
*James E. Steck, Steven R. Skinner, Alvaro A. Cruz-Cabrara,
Elizabeth C. Behrman*

A CHARGE-BASED CMOS PARALLEL ANALOG VECTOR QUANTIZER 779
Gert Cauwenberghs, Volnei Pedroni

AN AUDITORY LOCALIZATION AND COORDINATE TRANSFORM CHIP 787
Timothy Horiuchi

AN ANALOG NEURAL NETWORK INSPIRED BY FRACTAL BLOCK CODING 795
Fernando Pineda, Andreas G. Andreou

A STUDY OF PARALLEL PERTURBATIVE GRADIENT DESCENT 803
D. Lippe, J. Alspector

IMPLEMENTATION OF NEURAL HARDWARE WITH THE NEURAL VLSI
OF URAN IN APPLICATIONS WITH REDUCED REPRESENTATIONS 811
Il-Song Han, Hwang-Soo Lee, Ki-Chul Kim

SINGLE TRANSISTOR LEARNING SYNAPSES 817
Paul Hasler, Chris Diorio, Bradley A. Minch, Carver Mead

PART VII
SPEECH AND SIGNAL PROCESSING

PATTERN PLAYBACK IN THE '90S 827
Malcolm Slaney (Invited Paper)

NON-LINEAR PREDICTION OF ACOUSTIC VECTORS USING
HIERARCHICAL MIXTURES OF EXPERTS 835
S. R. Waterhouse, A. J. Robinson

GLOVE-TALKII: MAPPING HAND GESTURES TO SPEECH USING
NEURAL NETWORKS 843
S. Sidney Fels, Geoffrey Hinton

VISUAL SPEECH RECOGNITION WITH STOCHASTIC NETWORKS 851
Javier Movellan

HIERARCHICAL MIXTURES OF EXPERTS METHODOLOGY
APPLIED TO CONTINUOUS SPEECH RECOGNITION 859
Ying Zhao, Richard Schwartz, Jason Sroka, John Makhoul

CONNECTIONIST SPEAKER NORMALIZATION WITH GENERALIZED
RESOURCE ALLOCATING NETWORKS 867
Cesare Furlanello, Diego Giuliani, Edmondo Trentin

USING VOICE TRANSFORMATIONS TO CREATE ADDITIONAL
TRAINING TALKERS FOR WORD SPOTTING 875
Eric I. Chang, Richard P. Lippmann

A COMPARISON OF DISCRETE-TIME OPERATOR MODELS FOR NONLINEAR
SYSTEM IDENTIFICATION 883
Andrew D. Back, Ah Chung Tsoi

PART VIII
VISUAL PROCESSING

LEARNING SACCADIC EYE MOVEMENTS USING MULTISCALE
SPATIAL FILTERS 893
Rajesh P. N. Rao, Dana H. Ballard

A CONVOLUTIONAL NEURAL NETWORK HAND TRACKER 901
Steven J. Nowlan, John C. Platt

CORRELATION AND INTERPOLATION NETWORKS FOR REAL-TIME
 EXPRESSION ANALYSIS/SYNTHESIS 909
Trevor Darrell, Irfan Essa, Alex Pentland

LEARNING DIRECTION IN GLOBAL MOTION: TWO CLASSES OF
PSYCHOPHYSICALLY-MOTIVATED MODELS 917
V. Sundareswaran, Lucia M. Vaina

ASSOCIATIVE DECORRELATION DYNAMICS: A THEORY OF
SELF-ORGANIZATION AND OPTIMIZATION IN FEEDBACK NETWORKS 925
Dawei W. Dong

JPMAX: LEARNING TO RECOGNIZE MOVING OBJECTS AS A MODEL-
FITTING PROBLEM 933
Suzanna Becker

PCA-PYRAMIDS FOR IMAGE COMPRESSION 941
Horst Bischof, Kurt Hornik

UNSUPERVISED CLASSIFICATION OF 3D OBJECTS FROM 2D VIEWS *949*
Satoshi Suzuki, Hiroshi Ando

NEW ALGORITHMS FOR 2D AND 3D POINT MATCHING:
POSE ESTIMATION AND CORRESPONDENCE *957*
Steven Gold, Chien Ping Lu, Anand Rangarajan,
Suguna Pappu, Eric Mjolsness

USING A NEURAL NET TO INSTANTIATE A DEFORMABLE MODEL *965*
Christopher K. I. Williams, Michael D. Revow, Geoffrey E. Hinton

NONLINEAR IMAGE INTERPOLATION USING MANIFOLD LEARNING *973*
Christoph Bregler, Stephen M. Omohundro

COARSE-TO-FINE IMAGE SEARCH USING NEURAL NETWORKS *981*
Clay D. Spence, John C. Pearson, Jim Bergen

PART IX
APPLICATIONS

TRANSFORMATION INVARIANT AUTOASSOCIATION WITH
APPLICATION TO HANDWRITTEN CHARACTER RECOGNITION *991*
Holger Schwenk, Maurice Milgram

LEARNING PROTOTYPE MODELS FOR TANGENT DISTANCE *999*
Trevor Hastie, Patrice Simard, Eduard Säckinger

REAL-TIME CONTROL OF TOKAMAK PLASMA USING NEURAL NETWORKS *1007*
Chris M. Bishop, Paul S. Haynes, Mike E. U. Smith, Tom N. Todd,
David L. Trotman, Colin G. Windsor

RECOGNIZING HANDWRITTEN DIGITS USING MIXTURES OF LINEAR MODELS *1015*
Geoffrey E. Hinton, Michael Revow, Peter Dayan

OPTIMAL MOVEMENT PRIMITIVES *1023*
Terence Sanger

AN INTEGRATED ARCHITECTURE OF ADAPTIVE NEURAL
NETWORK CONTROL FOR DYNAMIC SYSTEMS *1031*
Liu Ke, Robert L. Tokar, Brian D. McVey

A CONNECTIONIST TECHNIQUE FOR ACCELERATED TEXTUAL INPUT:
LETTING A NETWORK DO THE TYPING *1039*
Dean Pomerleau

PREDICTIVE CODING WITH NEURAL NETS: APPLICATION TO
TEXT COMPRESSION *1047*
Jürgen Schmidhuber, Stefan Heil

PREDICTING THE RISK OF COMPLICATIONS IN CORONARY
ARTERY BYPASS OPERATIONS USING NEURAL NETWORKS *1055*
Richard P. Lippmann, Linda Kukolich, David Shahian

COMPARING THE PREDICTION ACCURACY OF ARTIFICIAL NEURAL
NETWORKS AND OTHER STATISTICAL MODELS FOR BREAST CANCER
SURVIVAL *1063*
Harry B. Burke, David B. Rosen, Philip H. Goodman

LEARNING TO PLAY THE GAME OF CHESS *1069*
Sebastian Thrun

A MIXTURE MODEL SYSTEM FOR MEDICAL AND MACHINE DIAGNOSIS *1077*
Magnus Stensmo, Terrence J. Sejnowski

INFERRING GROUND TRUTH FROM SUBJECTIVE LABELLING OF VENUS
IMAGES *1085*
Padhraic Smyth, Usama Fayyad, Michael Burl, Pietro Perona, Pierre Baldi

THE USE OF DYNAMIC WRITING INFORMATION IN A CONNECTIONIST
ON-LINE CURSIVE HANDWRITING RECOGNITION SYSTEM *1093*
Stefan Manke, Michael Finke, Alex Waibel

ADAPTIVE ELASTIC INPUT FIELD FOR RECOGNITION IMPROVEMENT *1101*
Minoru Asogawa

PAIRWISE NEURAL NETWORK CLASSIFIERS WITH PROBABILISTIC OUTPUTS *1109*
David Price, Stefan Knerr, Léon Personnaz, Gérard Dreyfus

INTERFERENCE IN LEARNING INTERNAL MODELS OF INVERSE
 DYNAMICS IN HUMANS *1117*
Reza Shadmehr, Tom Brashers-Krug, Ferdinando Mussa-Ivaldi

COMPUTATIONAL STRUCTURE OF COORDINATE TRANSFORMATIONS:
A GENERALIZATION STUDY *1125*
Zoubin Ghahramani, Daniel M. Wolpert, Michael I. Jordan

Author Index *1133*
Keyword Index *1137*

Preface

This volume contains the collected papers summarizing the talks and posters presented at the eighth annual conference on Neural Information Processing Systems (NIPS), held in Denver, Colorado, from Nov. 28 to Dec. 1, 1994. The previous six volumes of Advances in NIPS were published by Morgan Kaufmann Publishers, San Francisco, California, while the proceedings of the first NIPS conference in 1987 were published by the American Institute of Physics. These volumes have been influential, and the high quality of papers in them has been matched by the high quality of the production. We are pleased that this volume is being published by MIT Press, which maintains the same exacting standards.

NIPS is the longest running annual meeting devoted to neural networks and neural information processing. Over the years it has consistently presented research that is technically sound as well as topically fresh and exciting. This year's meeting certainly lived up to the standards set by previous meetings. In fact, two major procedural changes were implemented this year which we believe have resulted in even stronger technical presentations. First, the submissions format was changed from extended abstracts to full 8-page papers. This gave the program committee and reviewers a better basis for making their acceptance decisions. Only about 1 out of 3 submitted papers was accepted for presentation at the conference. Second, detailed reviewer comments were returned to the submitting authors. Reviewer feedback was valuable in improving the presentations and final manuscripts of the accepted authors, and for authors whose submissions were not accepted, it indicated how submissions could be improved for future meetings.

This year's papers show continued progress, and the enduring scientific and practical merit of the broad-based, inclusive approach towards neural networks favored by NIPS participants. Papers presented at NIPS freely cross traditional academic boundaries to draw upon many disparate domains such as neuroscience, cognitive science, computer science, statistics, mathematics, engineering and theoretical physics. As usual, the dominant component of NIPS was devoted to the study of a wide variety of learning algorithms and architectures, for both supervised and unsupervised learning. Topics attracting exceptional interest this year were the analysis of recurrent nets (Horne and Giles), connections to HMMs and the EM procedure (Saul and Jordan) and reinforcement learning algorithms and the relation to dynamic programming (Boyan and Moore). On the theoretical front, ample progress was reported in the theory of generalization (Kowalczyk and Ferra), regularization (Leen), combining multiple models (Tresp), and active learning (Cohn et al.). Neuroscience remained a large and vital component of NIPS, with studies ranging from large-scale systems such as visual cortex (Erwin and Obermayer) to single-cell electrotonic structure (Carnevale et al.). Work reported in cognitive science this year seemed to be more closely tied to underlying neural constraints, as seen e.g. in the paper of Brashers-Krug et al. on motor learning. The applications work presented at NIPS continues to grow in prominence and many novel applications were presented, such as tokamak plasma control (Bishop et al.), Glove-Talk (Fels and Hinton), and hand tracking (Nowlan and Platt). A variety of hardware implementations were also presented, with particular focus on analog VLSI (Coggins et al.; Serrano et al.).

In addition to the main conference presentations, NIPS was fortunate to have had a very strong one-day tutorial program preceding the conference, chaired by Steve Hanson and Gerald Tesauro, and a highly popular two-day program of post-conference workshops in Vail, chaired by Todd Leen. The workshop program has grown in scope and significance to the point where it is now a valuable scientific meeting in its own right, and this year's program attracted a record turnout. Topics covered at the workshops spanned the full range of multidisciplinary approaches characteristic of NIPS. Some of the particularly noteworthy topics were: Unsupervised Learning Rules and Visual Processing, Computational Role of Lateral Connections in the Cortex, Neural Networks in Medicine, Time Delay Connections for Nonlinear Signal Processing, and Algorithms for High Dimensional Spaces.

Organizing a conference such as NIPS is an enormous undertaking, and we would like to express our appreciation and gratitude to all those who volunteered their time (collectively totaling several thousand person-hours of labor) to help organize and run the meeting. Thanks go to all the members of the Organizing Committee, the Program Committee, the Publicity Committee, the Board of Directors of the NIPS Foundation, and all the referees who reviewed submissions this year. In particular, we especially thank Lori Pratt for a truly outstanding job organizing both the local arrangements and conference registration, Christy Medina and Denise Hallman, for their superb efforts as conference secretaries, and all the student volunteers from Colorado School of Mines and elsewhere. We are also grateful to Colorado School of Mines for generous financial support of our registration operations. Finally, we thank Barbara Yoon of the Advanced Projects Research Agency, Tom McKenna of the Office of Naval Research, and Captain Steve Suddarth of the Air Force Office of Scientific Research, who once again provided valuable financial support that made it possible for many students and young investigators to attend the meeting.

Gerald Tesauro, IBM
David S. Touretzky, Carnegie Mellon
Todd K. Leen, Oregon Graduate Institute

Contributors

**NIPS-94
ORGANIZING COMMITTEE**

General Chair	Gerald Tesauro, IBM
Program Chair	David Touretzky, Carnegie Mellon University
Workshops Chair	Todd Leen, Oregon Graduate Institute
Publicity Chair	Bartlett Mel, Caltech
Publications Chair	Joshua Alspector, Bellcore
Treasurer	Rodney Goodman, Caltech
Local Arrangements Chair	Lori Pratt, Colorado School of Mines
Government & Corporate Liaison	John Moody, Oregon Graduate Institute
Tutorials Chairs	Stephen Hanson, Siemens and Gerald Tesauro, IBM
Contracts	Steve Hanson, Siemens and Scott Kirkpatrick, IBM

**NIPS-94
PROGRAM COMMITTEE**

Program Chair	David Touretzky, Carnegie Mellon
Program Co-Chairs	Subutai Ahmad, Interval Research
	Chuck Anderson, Colorado State University
	Eric Baum, NEC Research Institute
	Tom Brown, Yale
	Scott Fahlman, CMU
	Terrence Fine, Cornell
	Michael Jordan, MIT
	John Lazzaro, UC Berkeley
	Yann LeCun, AT&T Bell Labs
	Richard Lippmann, MIT
	Paul Munro, University of Pittsburgh
	John Platt, Synaptics

NIPS-94 PUBLICITY COMMITTEE

Publicity Chair   Bartlett Mel, Caltech
Overseas Liaisons
Japan   Bitsuo Kawato, ATR Research Laboratories
Australia, Singapore, India   Marwan Jabri, University of Sydney
United Kingdom   Alan Murray, Edinburgh University
South America   Andreas Meier, Simon Bolivar University

NIPS FOUNDATION BOARD MEMBERS

President   Terrence Sejnowski, The Salk Institute
Vice President for Development   John Moody, Oregon Graduate Institute
Secretary   Scott Kirkpatrick, IBM
Treasurer   Rod Goodman, Caltech
Members   Jack Cowan, University of Chicago
                                   Terrence Fine, Cornell University
                                   Stephen J. Hanson, SIEMENS Research
                                   Richard Lippmann, MIT Lincoln Laboratory
                                   Gerald Tesauro, IBM

NIPS-94 REFEREES

Joshua Alspector	James Anderson	Chris Atkeson
Jonathan Bachrach	Pierre Baldi	Shumeet Baluja
Etienne Barnard	Andrew R. Barron	Peter Bartlett
Andy Barto	Sue Becker	Yoshua Bengio
Uli Bodenhausen	Brian Bonnlander	Léon Bottou
Herve Bourlard	Justin Boyan	Jane Bromley
Tim X. Brown	Tom Brown	Ken Buckland
Joachim Buhmann	Wray Buntine	David J. Burr
William Byrne	N.T. Carnevale	David Chalmers
Tzi-Dar Chieuh	Michael Cohen	David Cohn
Gary Cottrell	Chris Darken	Shawn Day
Thomas Dietterich	George Dorffner	Gérard Dreyfus
Harris Drucker	Richard Duda	Mark Fanty
Bernd Fritzke	Patrick Gallinari	Michael Gasser
Zoubin Ghahramani	Lee Giles	David Gillespie
Gene Gindi	Fererico Girosi	Rodney Goodman
Hans Graf	Patrick Haffner	Dan Hammerstrom
John Hampshire	Catherine Harris	John Harris
Sherif Hashem	Mike Hasselmo	Babak Hassibi
David Haussler	Simon Haykin	Andreas Herz

Geoffrey Hinton
Nathan Intrator
Chuanyi Ji
B.H. Juang
Michael Kearns
Phil Kohn
Gary Kuhn
Kevin Lang
Tsungnan Lin
Marco Maggini
George Marnellos
Risto Miikkulainen
Eric Mjolsness
Nelson Morgan
Steven Nowlan
Stephen Omohundro
Carsten Peterson
Tony Plate
Mark Plutowski
Lorien Pratt
Anand Rangarajan
Tony Robinson
Philip Saves
Warren S. Sarle
Terry Sejnowski
Hava Siegelmann
K-Y Siu
Steve Smith
Sara A. Solla
David Stork
Rob Tibshirani
Ah Chung Tsoi
Vladimir Vapnik
Alex Waibel
Raymond Watrous
Janet Wiles
Robert Williamson
Lei Xu

Bill Horne
Marwin Jabri
Mark St. John
Stephen Judd
Dan Kersten
Anders Krogh
S.Y. Kung
Harold Levy
Jim Little
Eve Marder
Bimal Mathur
Ken Miller
Martin Moller
Tony Movshon
Alice O'Toole
Kannan Parthasarathy
Jim Peterson
John Platt
Jordan Pollack
Jose C. Principe
David Redish
Vwani Roychowdhury
Eduard Säckinger
Larry Saul
Dan Seligson
Patrice Simard
Massimo Sivilotti
Paul Smolensky
David Standley
Rich Sutton
Naftali Tishby
Micael Trumon
Bert de Vries
Chris Watkins
John Wawrzynek
Chris Williams
Charles Wilson
Richard Zemel

John Houde
Robbie Jacobs
Da Johnston
Visakan Kadirkamanathan
Cristoff Koch
Anthony Kugh
Jyh-Ming Kuo
Long-Ji Lin
Michael Littman
Scott Markel
Bartlett Mel
Melanie Mitchell
Andre Moore
Bob Narendra
Bruno Olshausen
Barak Pearlmutter
Tom Petsche
David Plaut
Dean Pomerleau
Mazim Rahim
Steve Renals
Mike Runick
Terry Sanger
Eric Saund
Jude Shavlik
Stainder Pal Singh
Roger Smith
Padhraic Smyth
Paul Stolorz
Sebastian Thrun
Volker Tresp
Lyle Ungar
Kelvin Wagner
Steve Watkins
Andreas Weigend
Ronald J. Williams
David Wolpert

ADVANCES IN NEURAL INFORMATION PROCESSING SYSTEMS 7

PART I
COGNITIVE SCIENCE

Direction Selectivity In Primary Visual Cortex Using Massive Intracortical Connections

Humbert Suarez
CNS Program 216-76
Caltech
Pasadena, CA 91125

Christof Koch
CNS Program 216-76
Caltech
Pasadena, CA 91125

Rodney Douglas
MRC Anatomical Neuropharmacology Unit
University of Oxford
Oxford
UK

Abstract

Almost all models of orientation and direction selectivity in visual cortex are based on feedforward connection schemes, where geniculate input provides all excitation to both pyramidal and inhibitory neurons. The latter neurons then suppress the response of the former for non-optimal stimuli. However, anatomical studies show that up to 90 % of the excitatory synaptic input onto any cortical cell is provided by other cortical cells. The massive excitatory feedback nature of cortical circuits is embedded in the *canonical microcircuit* of Douglas & Martin (1991). We here investigate analytically and through biologically realistic simulations the functioning of a detailed model of this circuitry, operating in a *hysteretic* mode. In the model, weak geniculate input is dramatically amplified by intracortical excitation, while inhibition has a dual role: (i) to prevent the early geniculate-induced excitation in the null direction and (ii) to restrain excitation and ensure that the neurons fire only when the stimulus is in their receptive-field. Among the insights gained are the possibility that hysteresis underlies visual cortical function, paralleling proposals for short-term memory, and strong limitations on linearity tests that use gratings. Properties of visual cortical neurons are compared in detail to this model and to a classical model of direction selectivity that does not include excitatory cortico-cortical connections. The model explain a number of puzzling features of direction-selective simple cells, including the small somatic input conductance changes that have been measured experimentally during stimulation in the null direction. The model also allows us to understand why the velocity-response curve of area 17 neurons is different from that of their LGN afferents, and the origin of expansive and compressive nonlinearities in the contrast-response curve of striate cortical neurons.

1 INTRODUCTION

Direction selectivity is the property of neurons that fire more strongly for one direction of motion of a bar (the preferred direction) than the other (null direction). It is one of the fundamental properties of neurons in visual cortex and is intimately related to the processing of motion by the visual system. LGN neurons that provide input to visual cortex respond approximately symmetrically to motion in different directions; so cortical neurons must generate that direction specificity. Models of direction selectivity in primary visual cortex generally overlook two important constraints. **1.** at least 80% of excitatory synapses on cortical pyramidal cells originate from other pyramidal cells, and less than 10 % are thalamic afferents (Peters & Payne, 1993). **2.** Intracellular *in vivo* recordings in cat simple cells by Douglas, et al. (1988) failed to detect significant changes in somatic input conductance during stimulation in the null direction, indicating that there is very little synaptic input to direction-selective neurons in that condition, including no massive "shunting" inhibition.

One very attractive solution incorporating these two constraints was proposed by Douglas & Martin (1991) in the form of their *canonical microcircuit*: for motion of a visual stimulus in the preferred direction, weak geniculate excitation excites cortical pyramidal cells to respond moderately. This relatively small amount of cortical excitation is amplified via excitatory cortico-cortical connections. For motion in the null direction, the weak geniculate excitation is vetoed by weak inhibition (mediated via an interneuron) and the cortical loop is never activated. In order to test quantitatively this circuit against the large body of experimental data, it is imperative to model its operation through mathematical analysis and detailed simulations.

2 MODEL DESCRIPTION AND ANALYSIS

The model consists of a retino-geniculate and a cortical stage (Fig. 1). The former includes a center-surround receptive field and bandpass temporal filtering (Victor, 1987). We simulate a 1-D array of ON LGN neurons, with 208 LGN neurons at each of 6 spatial positions in this array. The output of the LGN—action potentials—feeds into the cortical module consisting of 640 pyramidal (excitatory) and 160 inhibitory neurons. Each neuron is modeled using 3-4 compartments whose parameters reflect, in a simplified way, the biophysics and morphology of cortical neurons; the somatic compartment produces action potentials in response to current injection. There are excitatory connections among all pyramidal neurons, and inhibitory connections from the inhibitory population to itself and to the pyramidal population. The receptive field of the geniculate input to the inhibitory cortical neurons is displaced in space from the geniculate input to the pyramidal neurons, so that in the null direction inhibition overlaps with geniculate excitation in the pyramidal neurons, resulting in direction selectivity in the pyramidal neurons. The time courses of the post-synaptic potentials (PSP's) are consistent with physiologically recorded PSP's. The EPSP's in our model arise exclusively from non-NMDA synapses, and the IPSP's originate from both $GABA_A$ and $GABA_B$ synapses.

There are two operating modes of this cortical amplifier circuit, depending on parameter values. In the first mode, the pyramidal neurons' response increases proportionally to the stimulus strength over a substantial range of input values, before saturating. In the second mode, the response increases much faster over a narrow range of stimulus strengths, then saturates. Analytically, one can define a steady-state transfer function for the network of pyramidal neurons; then, in the first mode, the transfer function has a slope that is less than 1, so that the network's firing rate at equilibrium increases proportionally to the input strength and the network dynamics are rather slow. In the second mode the initial slope is larger than 1, so that the network can discharge briskly at equilibrium even without any input, show hysteresis, and has rather fast dynamics. The network does not fire without any input, because of the neuron's threshold. In this paper, we will show responses in that second, hysteretic mode of operation.

We will compare the cortical amplifier model's response properties to a pure feedforward model, that has no excitatory connections between pyramidal neurons. In order to maintain strong responses in that model, the LGN was connected more strongly to the pyramidal neurons, and in order to maintain direction selectivity, the weights of the connections of the inhibitory neurons to the pyramids were increased as well.

3 AMPLIFICATION AND CONDUCTANCE CHANGE IN THE NULL DIRECTION

The input conductance of pyramidal neurons, a measure of total synaptic input, changes by only 50 % in the cortical amplifier model versus 400 % in the feedforward model, and so is more consistent with physiology (Fig. 2). Indeed, most of the current causing firing in the preferred direction originates from other pyramidal neurons, so the connection weight from the LGN is small. Consequently, the inhibitory weight is also small, since it needs only be large enough to balance out the LGN current in the null direction. Since there is little firing in other pyramidal neurons in the null direction, there is also little total synaptic input to the fiducial cell. The cortical amplifier circuit provides substantial amplification of the LGN input. In the preferred direction, excitatory intracortical connections amplify the LGN input, providing a feedback current that is about 2.2 times larger than the

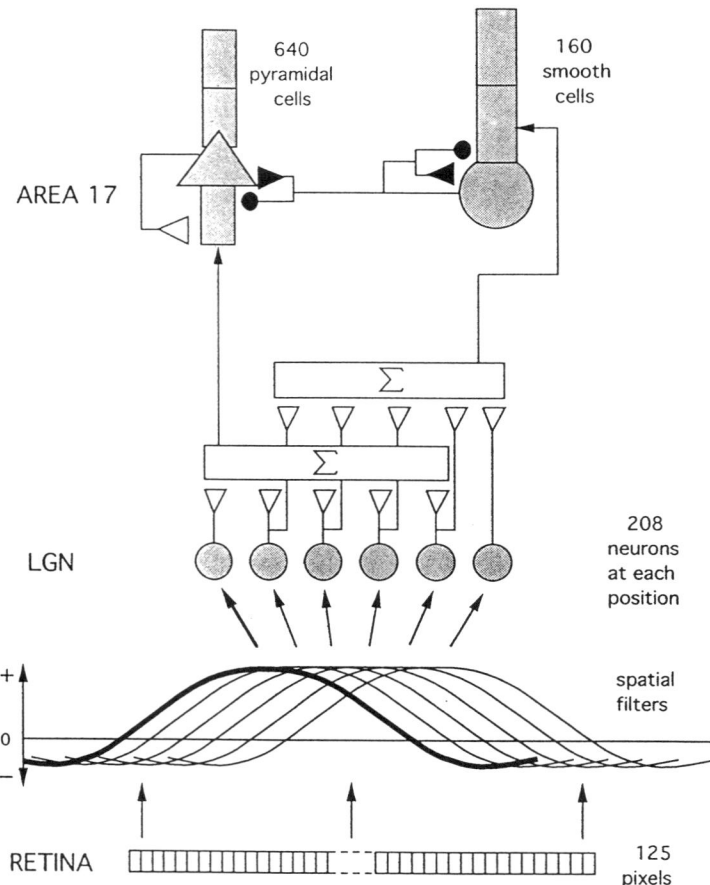

Figure 1: Wiring diagram of the direction selectivity model. Input to LGN neurons comes from a one-dimensional array of retinal pixels. There are 208 LGN neurons at each of six spatial positions. The LGN neurons connect slightly differently with the two populations of cortical neurons (pyramidal and inhibitory) so that as a group the LGN inputs to the pyramids are displaced spatially by 5' from those to the inhibitory neurons. The open triangle symbols denote excitatory connections, the filled triangles inhibitory $GABA_A$-mediated synapses, and the filled circles inhibitory $GABA_B$-mediated synapses. The capital sigma symbol indicates convergence of inputs from many LGN neurons onto cortical neurons.

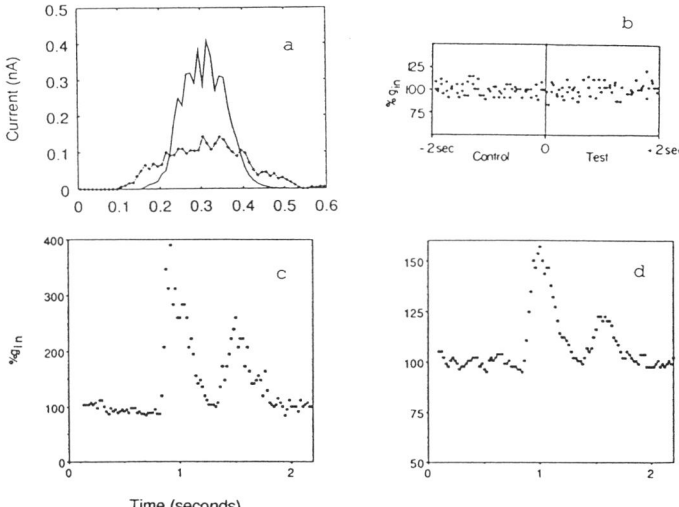

Figure 2: (a) Total synaptic current in a simulated pyramidal cell from the LGN (with symbols) and from other pyramidal cells (continuous without symbols), during stimulation by a bar moving in the preferred direction. For the same stimulus moving in the null direction, somatic input conductance as a function of time, (b) for a direction-selective pyramidal neuron (data from Douglas et al., 1988); (c) feedforward model; (d) cortical amplifier model;

LGN current at 60 % contrast (Fig. 2).

4 CONTRAST-RESPONSE CURVES

Contrast-response curves plot the peak firing rate to a grating moving in the preferred direction as function of its contrast, or stimulus amplitude (Albrecht & Hamilton, 1982). The cortical amplifier's contrast-response curve is very different from the LGN inputs' and is similar to those that have been described experimentally in cortex (Albrecht & Geisler 1991), having a steep power-function portion followed by abrupt saturation (Fig. 3). The network firing saturates at the fixed point of the transfer function mentioned above (see section 2) and the steep portion results from the fast rise to that fixed point when the stimulus has exceeded the neurons' threshold. In contrast, the feedforward model's contrast-response curve is similar to the LGN inputs' and does not match physiology. The response is very small in the null direction, resulting in very good direction selectivity at all contrasts (i.e., the average direction index is above 0.9).

5 VELOCITY-RESPONSE CURVES

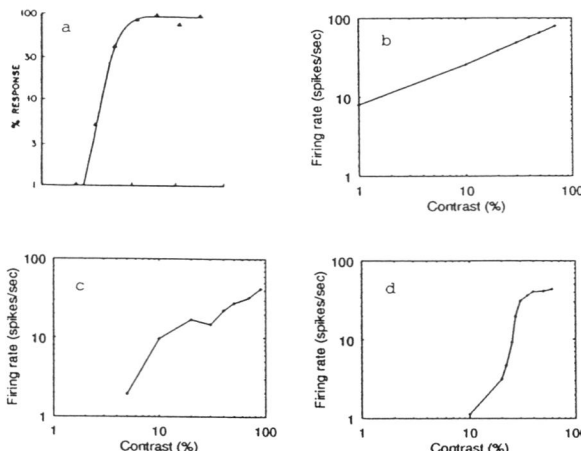

Figure 3: Peak firing rate versus contrast during stimulation by a moving grating. (a) Visual cortical neuron. Data from Albrecht & Hamilton, 1982. (b) LGN model. (c) Feedforward model. (d) Cortical amplifier model.

Velocity-response curves plot the peak response to a bar moving in the preferred direction as a function of its velocity . Again, the cortical amplifier's velocity-response curve is very different from the LGN inputs' and is similar to physiology (Orban, 1984; Fig. 4). The LGN model is firing strongly at high velocities but the model pyramidal neurons are totally silent, due to a combination of $GABA_A$ inhibition, neuron threshold, and membrane low-pass filtering. At low velocities, the LGN model does not fire much, while the cortical neurons respond strongly. Indeed, the network firing has enough time to reach the fixed point of the transfer function and will reach it as long as the input is suprathreshold. In contrast, the feedforward model's velocity-response curve is again similar to the LGN input's and does not match physiology. Also shown in Fig. 4 is the response in the null direction for the cortical amplifier model. There is very good direction selectivity at all velocities, consistent with physiological data (Orban, 1984). The persistence of direction selectivity down to low velocities depends critically on the time constant of $GABA_B$ and the presence of a very small displacement between the LGN inputs to the pyramidal and inhibitory neurons.

6 OTHER PROPERTIES

Recently, direction-selective cortical neurons have been tested for linearity using an intracellular grating superposition test and found to be quite linear (Jagadeesh et al., 1993). Despite that amplification in the present model is so nonlinear, the model is also linear according to that superposition test. An analysis of the test in the context of the model shows that such a test has limited usefulness and suggests improvements.

Given that the network transfer function has a fixed point at high firing without any

Direction Selectivity in Primary Visual Cortex

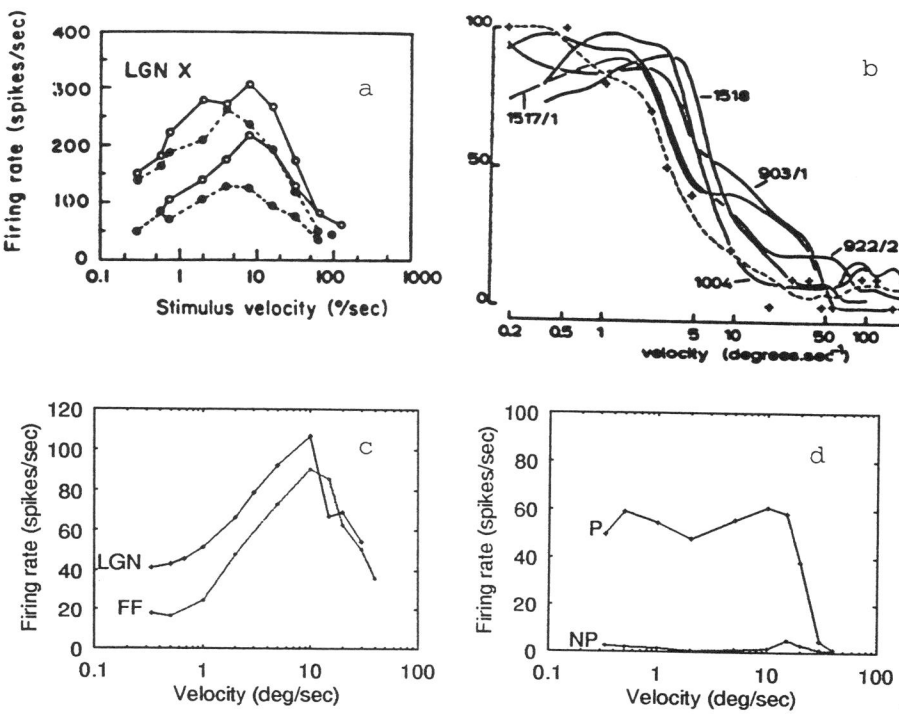

Figure 4: Peak firing rate versus velocity during stimulation by a bar. (a) LGN neuron in cat (Frishman *et al.*, 1983). (b) area 17 visual cortical neuron in cat (Orban, 1984). (c) LGN model neuron (curve labelled "LGN") and feedforward model (FF). (d) Cortical amplifier model in the preferred (curve labelled "P") and null directions (NP).

input (see section 2), *hysteresis* may occur, whereby the network's discharge persists after the initial stimulus is withdrawn. Because of hysteresis, it is imperative to *reset* the network by presenting a negative, or inhibitory, input. A parallel can be drawn to several recent proposals for the mechanisms underlying short-term memory.

7 CONCLUSIONS

From early on, neurophysiologists have proposed that the LGN provides most of the input to visual cortical neurons and shapes their receptive properties (Hubel and Wiesel, 1962). However, direction selectivity and several other stimulus selectivities are not present in LGN neurons, and other important discrepancies have appeared between the receptive field properties of cortical neurons and those of their LGN afferents. Anatomically, synaptic inputs from the LGN account for less than 10 % of synapses to pyramidal neurons in visual cortex; the remaining 90 % could clearly provide a substrate for these receptive field transformations. Although intracortical inhibition has often been invoked to explain various cortical properties, excitation is usually not mentioned, despite that most cortico-cortical synapses are excitatory. In this paper, we show that intracortical excitation can better account for several key properties of cortical neurons than a purely feedforward model, including the magnitude of the conductance change in the null direction, contrast-response curves, and velocity-response curves. Furthermore, surprisingly, other key cell properties that are appear to point to feedforward models, such as linearity measured by superposition tests, are also properties of a model based on intracortical excitation.

Acknowledgements

This research was supported by the Office of Naval Research, the National Science Foundation, the National Eye Institute, and the McDonnell Foundation.

References

Albrecht, D.G., and Geisler, W.S. (1991) *Visual Neuroscience* **7**, 531-546.
Albrecht, D.B., and Hamilton, D.B. (1982) *J. Neurophysiol.* **48**, 217-237.
Douglas, R.J., and Martin, K.A.C. (1991) *J. Physiol.* **440**, 735-769.
Douglas, R.J., Martin, K.A.C., and Whitteridge, D. (1988) *Nature* **332**, 642-644.
Frishman, L.J., Schweitzer-Tong, D.E., and Goldstein, E.B. (1983) *J. Neurophysiol.* **50**, 1393-1414.
Hubel, D.H., and Wiesel, T.N. (1962) *J. Physiol.* **165**, 559-568.
Jagadeesh, B., Wheat, H.S. and Ferster, D. (1993) *Science* **262**, 1901-1904
Orban, G.A. (1984) Neuronal operations in the visual cortex. Springer, Berlin.
Peters, A. and Payne, B. R. (1993) *Cerebral Cortex* **3**, 69-78.
Victor, J.D. (1987) *J.Physiol.* **386**, 219-246.

On the Computational Utility of Consciousness

Donald W. Mathis and Michael C. Mozer
mathis@cs.colorado.edu, mozer@cs.colorado.edu
Department of Computer Science and Institute of Cognitive Science
University of Colorado, Boulder
Boulder, CO 80309-0430

Abstract

We propose a computational framework for understanding and modeling human consciousness. This framework integrates many existing theoretical perspectives, yet is sufficiently concrete to allow simulation experiments. We do not attempt to explain *qualia* (subjective experience), but instead ask what differences exist within the cognitive information processing system when a person is conscious of mentally-represented information versus when that information is unconscious. The central idea we explore is that the contents of consciousness correspond to temporally persistent states in a network of computational modules. Three simulations are described illustrating that the behavior of persistent states in the models corresponds roughly to the behavior of conscious states people experience when performing similar tasks. Our simulations show that periodic settling to persistent (i.e., conscious) states improves performance by cleaning up inaccuracies and noise, forcing decisions, and helping keep the system on track toward a solution.

1 INTRODUCTION

We propose a computational framework for understanding and modeling consciousness. Though our ultimate goal is to explain psychological and brain imaging data with our theory, and to make testable predictions, here we simply present the framework in the context of previous experimental and theoretical work, and argue that it is sensible from a computational perspective. We do not attempt to explain *qualia*—subjective experience and feelings. It is not clear that qualia are amenable to scientific investigation. Rather, our aim is to understand the mechanisms underlying awareness, and their role in cognition. We address three key questions:

- What are the preconditions for a mental representation to reach consciousness?

- What are the computational consequences of a representation reaching consciousness? Does a conscious state affect processing differently than an unconscious state?

- What is the computational utility of consciousness? That is, what is the computational role of the mechanism(s) underlying consciousness?

2 THEORETICAL FRAMEWORK

Modular Cognitive Architecture. We propose that the human cognitive architecture consists of a set of functionally specialized computational modules (e.g., Fodor, 1983). We imagine the modules to be organized at a somewhat coarse level and to implement processes such as visual object recognition, visual word-form recognition, auditory word and sound recognition, computation of spatial relationships, activation of semantic representations of words, sentences, and visual objects, construction of motor plans, etc. Cognitive behaviors require the coordination of many modules. For example, functional brain imaging studies indicate that there are several brain areas used for different subtasks during cognitive tasks such as word recognition (Posner & Carr, 1992).

Modules Have Mapping And Cleanup Processes. We propose that modules perform an associative memory function in their domain, and operate via a two-stage process: a fast, essentially feedforward input-output mapping[1] followed by a slower relaxation search (Figure 1). The computational justification for this two stage process is as follows. We assume that, in general, the output space of a module can represent a large number of states relative to the number of states that are meaningful or *well formed*—i.e., states that are interpretable by other modules or (for output modules) that correspond to sensible motor primitives. If we know which representations are well-formed, we can tolerate an inaccurate feedforward mapping, and "clean up" noise in the output by constraining it to be one of the well-formed states. This is the purpose of the relaxation step: to clean up the output of the feedforward step, resulting in a well-formed state. The cleanup process knows nothing about which output state is the best response to the input; it acts solely to enforce well-formedness. Similar architectures have been used recently to model various neuropsychological data (Hinton & Shallice, 1991; Mozer & Behrmann, 1990; Plaut & Shallice, 1993). The empirical motivation for identifying consciousness with the results of relaxation search comes from studies indicating that the contents of consciousness tend to be *coherent*, or well-formed (e.g., Baars, 1988; Crick, 1994; Damasio, 1989).

Persistent States Enter Consciousness. In our model, module outputs enter consciousness if they persist for a sufficiently long time. What counts as long enough

---

[1] We do not propose that this process is feedforward at the neural level. Rather, we mean that any iterative refinement of the output over time is unimportant and irrelevant.

Figure 1: Modules consist of two components.

is not yet determined, but in order to model specific psychological data, we will be required to make this issue precise. At that time a specific commitment will need to be made, and this commitment must be maintained when modeling further data.

An important property of our model is that there is no hierarchy of modules with respect to awareness, in contrast to several existing theories that propose that access to some particular module (or neural processing area) is required for consciousness (e.g., Baars, 1988). Rather, information in any module reaches awareness simply by persisting long enough. The persistence hypothesis is consistent with the theoretical perspectives of Smolensky (1988), Rumelhart et al (1986), Damasio (1989), Crick and Koch (1990), and others.

2.1 WHEN ARE MENTAL STATES CONSCIOUS?

In our framework, the output of any module will enter consciousness if it persists in time. The persistence of an output state of a module is assured if: (1) it is a point attractor of the relaxation search (i.e., a well-formed state), and (2) the inputs to the module are relatively constant, i.e., they continue to be mapped into the same attractor basin.

While our framework appears to make strong claims about the necessary and sufficient conditions for consciousness, without an exact specification of the modules forming the cognitive architecture, it is lacking as a rigorous, testable theory. A complete theory will require not only a specification of the modules, but will also have to avoid arbitrariness in claiming that certain cognitive operations or brain regions are modules while other are not. Ultimately, one must identify the neurophysiological and neuroanatomical properties of the brain that determine the module boundaries (see Crick, 1994, for a promising step in this regard).

3 COMPUTATIONAL UTILITY OF CONSCIOUSNESS

For the moment, suppose that our framework provides a sensible account of awareness phenomena (demonstrating this is the goal of ongoing work.) If one accepts this, and hence the notion that a cleanup process and the resulting persistent states are required for awareness, questions about the role of cleanup in the model become quite interesting because they are equivalent to questions about the role of the mechanism underlying awareness in cognition. One question one might ask is whether there is computational utility to achieving conscious states. That is, does a system that achieves persistent states perform better than a system that does not?

Does a system that encourages settling to well-formed states perform better than a system that does not? We now show that the answer to this question is yes.

3.1 ADDITION SIMULATION

To examine the utility of cleanup, we trained a module to perform a simple multistep cognitive task: adding a pair of two-digit numbers in three steps.[2] We tested the system with and without cleanup and compared the generalization performance.

The network architecture (Figure 2) consists of a single module. The inputs consist of the problem statement and the current partial solution-state. The output is an updated solution-state. The module's output feeds back into its input. The problem statement is represented by four pools of units, one for each digit of each operand, where each pool uses a local encoding of digits. Partial solution states are represented by five pools, one for each of the three result digits and one for each of the two carry digits.

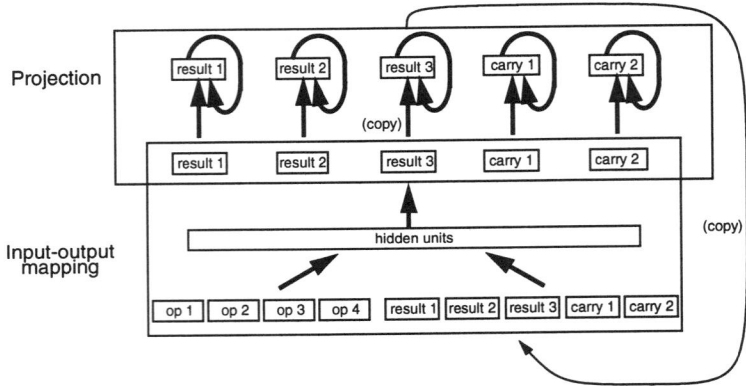

Figure 2: Network architecture for the addition task

Each addition problem was decomposed into three steps (Figure 3), each describing a transformation from one partial solution state to the next, and the mapping net was trained perform each transformation individually.

$$
\begin{array}{c}
?\ ? \\
4\ 8 \\
+\ 6\ 2 \\
\hline
?\ ?\ ?
\end{array}
\xrightarrow{\text{step 1}}
\begin{array}{c}
?\ 1 \\
4\ 8 \\
+\ 6\ 2 \\
\hline
?\ ?\ 0
\end{array}
\xrightarrow{\text{step 2}}
\begin{array}{c}
1\ 1 \\
4\ 8 \\
+\ 6\ 2 \\
\hline
?\ 1\ 0
\end{array}
\xrightarrow{\text{step 3}}
\begin{array}{c}
1\ 1 \\
4\ 8 \\
+\ 6\ 2 \\
\hline
1\ 1\ 0
\end{array}
$$

Figure 3: The sequence of steps in an example addition problem

Step 1 Given the problem statement, activate the rightmost result digit and rightmost carry digit (comprising the first partial solution).

---

[2] Of course, we don't believe that there is a brain module dedicated to addition problems. This choice was made because addition is an intuitive example of a multistep task.

Step 2 Given the first partial solution, activate the next result and carry digits (second partial solution).

Step 3 Given the second partial solution, activate the leftmost result digit (final solution).

The set of well-formed states in this domain consists of all possible combinations of digits and "don't knows" among the pools ("don't knows" are denoted by question marks in Figure 3). Local representations of digits are used within each pool, and "don't knows" are represented by the state in which no unit is active. Thus, the set of well-formed states are those in which either one or no units are active in each pool. To make these states attractors of the cleanup net, the connections were hand-wired such that each pool was a winner-take-all pool with an additional attractor at the zero state.

To run the net, a problem statement pattern is clamped on the input units, and the net is allowed to update for 200 iterations. Unit activities were updated using an incremental rule approximating continuous dynamics:

$$a_i(t) = \tau f(\sum_j w_{ij} a_j(t-1)) + (1-\tau) a_i(t-1)$$

where $a_i(t)$ is the activity of unit i at time t, τ is a time constant in the interval [0,1], and $f(\cdot)$ is the usual sigmoid squashing function.

Figure 4 shows the average generalization performance of networks run with and without cleanup, as a function of training set size. Note that, in principle, it is not necessary for the system to have a cleanup process to learn the training set perfectly, or to generalize perfectly. Thus, it is not simply the case that no solutions exist without cleanup. The generalization results were that for any size training set, percent correct on the generalization set is always better with cleanup than without. This indicates that although the mapping network often generalizes incorrectly, the output pattern often falls within the correct attractor basin. This is especially beneficial in multistep tasks because cleanup can correct the inaccuracies introduced by the mapping network, preventing the system from gradually diverging from the desired trajectory.

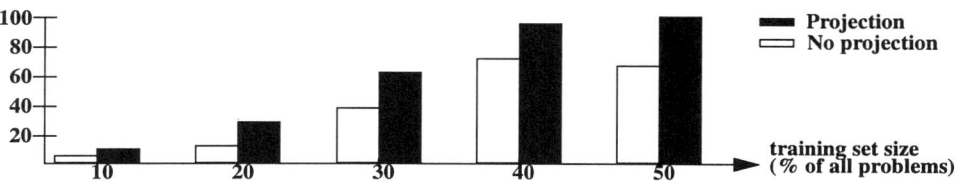

Figure 4: Cleanup improves generalization performance.

Figure 5 shows an example run of a trained network. There is one curve for each of the five result and carry pools, showing the degree of "activity" of the ultimate target pattern, **t**, for that pool as a function of time. Activity is defined to be $e^{-\|\mathbf{t}-\mathbf{a}\|^2}$ where **a** is the current activity pattern and **t** is the target. The network solves the problem by passing though the correct sequence of intermediate states, each of which are temporarily persistent. This resembles the sequence of conscious states a person might experience while performing this task; each step of the problem is performed by an unconscious process, and the *results* of each of step appear in conscious awareness.

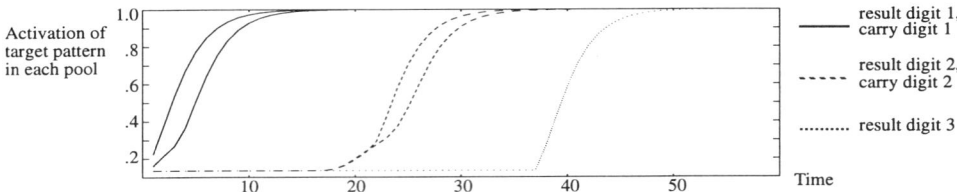

Figure 5: Network solving the addition task in three steps

3.2 CHOICE POINT SIMULATION

In many ordinary situations, people are required to make decisions, e.g., drive straight through an intersection or turn left, order macaroni or a sandwich for lunch. At these choice points, any of the alternative actions are reasonable a priori. Contextual information determines which action is correct, e.g., whether you are trying to drive to work or to the supermarket. Conscious decision making often occurs at these choice points, except when the task is overlearned (Mandler, 1975).

We modeled a simple form of a choice point situation. We trained a module to output sequences of states, e.g., ABCD or EFGH, where states were represented by unique activity patterns over a set of units. If the sequences shared no elements, then presenting the first element of any sequence would be sufficient to regenerate the sequence. But when sequences overlap, choice points are created. For example, with the sequences ABCD and AEFG, state A can be followed by either B or E.

We show that cleanup allows the module to make a decision and complete one of the two sequences. Figure 6 shows the operation of the module with and without cleanup following presentation of an A after training on the sequence pair ABCD and AEFG. There is one curve for each state, showing the activation of that state (defined as before), as a function of time. When the network is run with cleanup, although both states B and E are initially partially activated, the cleanup process maps this ill-formed state to state B, and the network then correctly completes the sequence ABCD. Without cleanup, the initial activation of states B and E causes a blending of the two sequences ABCD and AEFG and the state degenerates.[3]

Although the arithmetic and choice point tasks seem simple in part because we predefined the set of well-formed states. However, because the architecture segre-

---

[3]In this simulation, we are not modeling the role of context in helping to select one sequence or another; we are simply assuming that either sequence is valid in the current context. The nature of the model does not change when we consider context. Assuming that the domain is not highly overlearned, the context will not strongly evoke one alternative action or the other in the feedforward mapping, leading to partial activation of multiple states, and the cleanup process will be needed to force a decision.

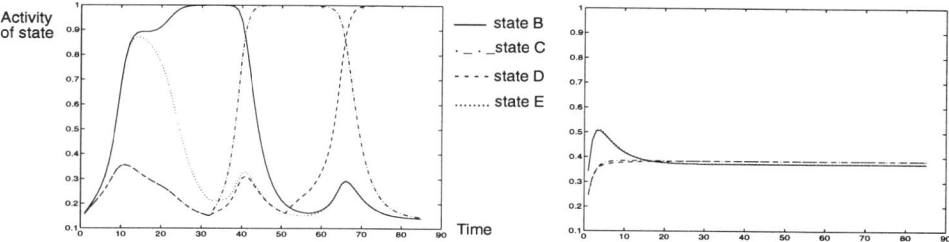

Figure 6: Decision-point task with and without cleanup

gates knowledge of well-formedness from knowledge of how to solve problems in the domain, well-formedness could be learned simultaneously with, or prior to learning the task. One could imagine training the cleanup network to autoassociate states it observes in the domain before or during training using an unsupervised or self-supervised procedure.

4 COMPUTATIONAL CONSEQUENCES OF PERSISTENT STATES

In a network of modules, a persistent well-formed state in one module exerts larger influences on the state of other modules than do transient or ill-formed states. As a result the dynamics of the system tends to be dominated by well-formed persistent states. We show this in a final simulation.

The network consisted of two modules, A and B, connected in a simple feedforward cascade. Each module's cleanup net was trained to have ten attractors, locally represented in a winner-take-all pool of units. The mapping network of module B was trained to map the attractors of module A to attractors in B in a one-to-one fashion. Thus, state α_1 in module A is mapped to β_1 in module A, α_2 to β_2, etc.

Module B was initialized to a well-formed state β_1, and the output state of module A was varied, creating three conditions. In the *persistent well-formed* condition, module A was clamped in the well-formed state α_2 for 50 time steps. In the *transient well-formed* condition, module A was clamped in state α_2 for only 30 time steps. And in the *ill-formed* condition, module A was clamped in an ill-formed state in which two states, α_2 and α_3, were both partially active. Figure 7 shows the subsequent activation of state β_2 in module B as a function of time. Module B undergoes a transition from state β_1 to state β_2 only in the persistent well-formed condition. This indicates that the *conjunction* of well-formedness and persistence is required to effect a transition from one state to another.

5 CONCLUSIONS

Our computational framework and simulation results suggest the following answers to our three key questions:

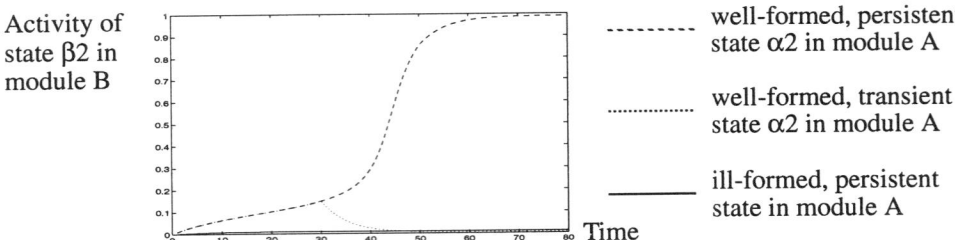

Figure 7: Well-formedness and persistence are both required for attractor transitions.

- In order to reach consciousness, the output of a module must be both persistent and semantically well-formed, and must not initiate an overlearned process.
- The computational consequences of conscious (persistent) representations include exerting larger influences on the cognitive system, resulting in increased ability to drive response processes such as verbal report.
- The computational utility of consciousness in our model lies in the ability of cleanup to "focus" cognition, by keeping the system close to states which are semantically meaningful. Because the system has learned to process such states, performance is improved.

References

Baars, B. J. (1988) *A Cognitive Theory of Consciousness*, Cambridge University Press.

Crick, F. (1994) The astonishing hypothesis: The scientific search for the soul. Scribner.

Crick, F., & Koch, C. (1990) Towards a neurobiological theory of consciousness. *Sem. Neuro.*, 2: 263-275

Damasio, A. (1989) The brain binds entities and events by multiregional activation from convergence zones. *Neural Computation*, 1, 123-132

Fodor, J. A. (1983) *The modularity of mind: An essay on faculty psychology.* Cambridge, MA: MIT Press.

Hinton, G. E., & Shallice, T. (1991) Lesioning an attractor network: Investigations of acquired dyslexia., *Psych. Rev.*, 98: 74-95

Mandler, G. (1975) Consciousness: Respectable, useful and probably necessary. In Information Processing and Cognition, The Loyola Symposium, R. Solso (Ed.). Erlbaum.

Mozer, M. C., & Behrmann, M. (1990). On the interaction of spatial attention and lexical knowledge: A connectionist account of neglect dyslexia. *Cognitive Neuroscience*, 2, 96-123.

Plaut, D. C., & Shallice, T. (1993) Perseverative and semantic influences on visual object naming errors in optic aphasia: A connectionist account. *J. Cog. Neuro.*, 5(1): 89-117

Posner, M. I., & Carr, T. (1992) Lexical access and the brain: Anatomical constraints on cognitive models of word recognition. *American Journal of Psychology*, 105(1): 1-26

Rumelhart, D. E., Smolensky, P., McClelland, J. L., & Hinton, G. E. (1986) Schemata and sequential thought in PDP models. In J. L. McClelland & D. E. Rumelhart (Eds.), *Parallel Distributed Processing*, Vol. 2. Cambridge, MA: MIT Press.

Smolensky, P. (1988) On the proper treatment of connectionism. *Brain Behav. Sci.*, 11: 1-74

Catastrophic Interference in Human Motor Learning

Tom Brashers-Krug, Reza Shadmehr[†], and Emanuel Todorov
Dept. of Brain and Cognitive Sciences, M. I. T., Cambridge, MA 02139
[†]Currently at Dept. of Biomedical Eng., Johns Hopkins Univ., Baltimore, MD 21205
Email: tbk@ai.mit.edu, reza@bme.jhu.edu, emo@ai.mit.edu

Abstract

Biological sensorimotor systems are not static maps that transform input (sensory information) into output (motor behavior). Evidence from many lines of research suggests that their representations are plastic, experience-dependent entities. While this plasticity is essential for flexible behavior, it presents the nervous system with difficult organizational challenges. If the sensorimotor system adapts itself to perform well under one set of circumstances, will it then perform poorly when placed in an environment with different demands (negative transfer)? Will a later experience-dependent change undo the benefits of previous learning (catastrophic interference)? We explore the first question in a separate paper in this volume (Shadmehr et al. 1995). Here we present psychophysical and computational results that explore the question of catastrophic interference in the context of a dynamic motor learning task. Under some conditions, subjects show evidence of catastrophic interference. Under other conditions, however, subjects appear to be immune to its effects. These results suggest that motor learning can undergo a process of consolidation. Modular neural networks are well suited for the demands of learning multiple input/output mappings. By incorporating the notion of fast- and slow-changing connections into a modular architecture, we were able to account for the psychophysical results.

1 Introduction

Interacting physically with the world changes the dynamics of one's limbs. For example, when holding a heavy load, a different pattern of muscular activity is needed to move one's arm along a particular path than when not holding a load. Previous work in our laboratory has shown that humans learn a novel dynamic task by forming an internal model of the new inverse dynamics of thier limbs. (Shadmehr and Mussa-Ivaldi 1994, Shadmehr et al, 1995). Preliminary evidence suggests that subjects can retain one of these internal models over time (Brashers-Krug, et al. 1994). Humans are required, however, to move their limbs effectively under a large number of dynamic conditions. Are people able to learn and store an inverse dynamic model appropriate for each condition, or do they form such models from scratch as they need them? In particular, can learning a new inverse dynamic model overwrite or displace a previous model? We will present evidence that certain conditions must be met before a subject is able to retain more than one inverse dynamic model in a given experimental context. These conditions can be modeled as leading to a process of consolidation, whereby learning is transfered from vulnerable, low-capacity storage to a long-term, high-capacity storage.

2 Experimental Protocol

We have developed a motor learning paradigm that allows us to alter the dynamics of a subject's arm and so to monitor a subject's ability to learn dynamic tasks. A subject moves the handle on the free end of a two-link planar robot arm–called a manipulandum–to guide a cursor to a series of targets displayed on a computer screen (fig 1a). The position and velocity of the handle of the manipulandum are recorded at ten-millisecond intervals and are used to deliver state-dependent forces to the subject's hand. In order to test a subject's ability to learn a novel dynamic task, we present the subject with a viscous force field as s/he moves from one target to the next (fig 1b). Initially, such forces perturb the subject's movements, causing them to depart from the smooth, straight-line trajectories of the baseline condition (i.e., the condition before the viscous forces were presented) (figs 1c,1d). The extent of learning is measured as the degree to which a subject's movements in the force field over time come to resemble that subject's baseline movements. We have shown in previous work that subjects adapt to the imposed force fileds by forming a predictive model of the velocity-dependent forces, and that subjects use this inverse dynamic model to control their arms in what appears to be a feedforward manner (Shadmehr and Mussa-Ivaldi 1994).

3 Psychophysical Findings

3.1 Catastrophic Interference

Here, we employed this paradigm to explore the consequences of learning two different dynamic tasks in a row. In an initial series of experiments, we allowed twelve subjects to learn to move the manipulandum in a first force field (Field A) for approximately 5 minutes. Immediately after this first set of movements, we presented the subjects with an anti-correlated force field (Field B). For example, if we pre-

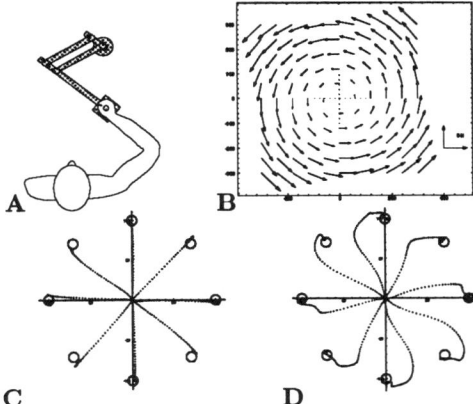

Figure 1: **A:** The experimental setup. **B:** An example of a viscous field, plotted in velocity space (mm/sec). The arrows indicate the direction and magnitude of the forces exerted by the manipulandum on the subject's hand at each location in velocity space. **C:** One subject's trajectories before forces were introduced. Targets are indicated by the open circles. **D:** Trajectories immediately after the force field in (B) was presented.

sented the counter-clockwise curl field depicted in fig. 1B as Field A, we would next present a clockwise curl field as Field B. Half the subjects learned the clockwise curl field first and the counter-clockwise field second; the other half learned the two fields in the reverse order. (The first field will be referred to as Field A and the second field as Field B, whichever field was learned first.) The subjects' mean performance in Field B was worse ($p < 0.0001$, paired t-test) than in Field A. This phenomenon has been called negative transfer in the psychophysical literature. Negative transfer in this motor learning paradigm is explored more fully in a separate paper in this volume (Shadmehr et al, 1995). In that paper, we suggested that this negative transfer could result from the fact that the same neural elements are learning both tasks. We predicted that, if this is the case, learning to move in Field B would interfere with a subject's ability to retain an inverse dynamic model of Field A. Learning to move in Field B would, in effect, cause subjects to "unlearn" Field A, resulting in catastrophic interference.

In order to test this prediction, we compared the improvement in performance from one day to the next of two groups of subjects, with twelve subjects in each group. The subjects in the control group learned to move in one force field on Day One and were then tested on Day Two in the same force field. The subjects in the experimental group learned two separate force fields in a row on Day One and were then tested on Day Two in the first force field they learned. The experimental group retained significantly less of their learning ($p < 0.01$, paired t-test) from Day One to Day Two than the control group (figs 2a,2b). In other words, learning the second force field resulted in catastrophic interference. (The question of whether this represents a storage or a retrieval phenomenon is beyond the scope of this paper.)

3.2 Consolidation

Having found evidence for catastrophic interference, we wanted to know whether there were circumstances under which dynamic motor learning was immune to being functionally erased by subsequent learning. We therefore tested two further groups of subjects. We allowed these subjects to practice longer in one field before they learned the second field. We also allowed 24 hours to pass between the time subjects first learned one field and when they learned the second field. The subjects in the experimental group (n = 10) practiced in one force field for approximately 15 minutes on Day One. They returned on Day Two and practiced in the same force field for five more minutes. They were then allowed to practice in a second force field for 15 minutes. By the end of this fifteen minutes, they were performing in the second field at a level comparable to the level they acheived in the first force field. We had the subjects return on Day Three, when they were tested for their retention of the first field they learned. We compared the difference in performance on Day Two and Day Three of this experimental group with that of a control group (n = 9) who followed the same protocol in all respects except that they never learned a second force field. In this way we could determine whether learning the second field resulted in a decrement in performance for the experimental group when compared with the control group.

Under these conditions, we found no difference in the retention of learning between the experimental and control groups (fig 2c, 2d). That is, learning the second field under these conditions no longer resulted in catastrophic interference. What subjects had learned about the first field had become resistant to such interference. It had become consolidated.

We can not tell from these experiments whether such consolidation is the result of the increased practice in the first field, or whether it is the result of the 24 hours that elapsed between when the first field was first learned and when the second field was learned. There is evidence that increased practice in a motor task can engage different neural circuits than those that are active during initial learning (Jenkins, et al 1994). The shift to "practiced" circuits may represent the neural substrate of consolidation. There is also evidence that time can be an important factor in the consolidation of skill learning. (Karni and Sagi 1993) In the next section, we present a model of our results that assumes that time is the key variable in the consolidation of motor learning. The model could also be applied to a practice-based model of consolidation with minor modifications.

4 Computational Modeling of the Experimental Results

In order to model the results presented above we need a network that learns to compute an appropriate control signal Y given the current state and the desired next state X of the plant. More precisely, it needs to compute a mapping from joint angles θ, joint velocities $\dot{\theta}$, and desired joint accelerations $\ddot{\theta}$ to torques. Several approaches for solving this problem have been proposed. One way to learn a mapping from X into Y is to use direct inverse modeling: apply a control signal, measure the next state of the plant, and use the current state, new state, and control signal as a training pair for the controller. This approach is not suitable for explaining non-

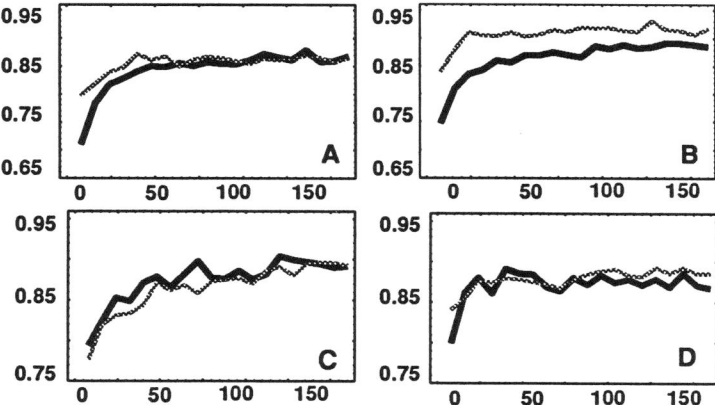

Figure 2: Plots of average learning curves. The correlation of trajectories in the force field to baseline trajectories (before the force field was applied) is plotted as a function of movement number. **A:** Learning curves for the first experimental group. Dark curve: learning curve on Day One in Field A. Light curve: learning curve in Field A on Day Two. This group learned Field B immediately after Field A on Day One (learning curve for Field B not shown). Note minimal improvement from Day One to Day Two. **B:** Learning curves for the first control group. Dark curve: learning curve in Field A on Day One. Light curve: learning curve in Field A on Day Two. Control group never learned Field B. Note significant improvement from Day One to Day Two. **C:** Second experimental group. Dark line: learning curve in Field A on Day Two immediately before learning Field B (Field B curve not shown). Light line: learning curve in Field A on Day Three. **D:** Second control group. Dark and light lines: learning curves in FIeld A on Day Two and Three, respectively. Note the similarity of the curves in C and D. This indicates that learning Field B did not significantly affect the experimental group's retention of Field A. All curves in C and D are significantly higher than curves for the initial learning of Field A on Day One.

convex mappings, however. The learning situation we must model is non-convex: we change the dynamic environment the controller operates in by presenting force fileds, and so there will be different Y values corresponding to any X value. A different approach that solves the nonconvexity problem is distal supervised learning (Jordan and Rumelhart 1992): produce control signals, observe the new state of the plant, and use that information to train a forward model that maps actions into states; then learn a controller, using the forward model to backpropagate error from observable cartesian coordinates to the unknown control space. Distal supervised learning solves the nonconvexity problem by learning one correct value of Y for each X. But that can not explain the consolidation of learning – when the force field changes back to something already learned, our controller should rapidly recover its performance in that old field, meaning that it should retain information about all Ys that a particular X can map into.

An architecture that seems to have most of the desirable properties discussed above is the Mixture of Experts (ME) model (Jordan and Jacobs 1994): several experts learn a mapping from X to Y. A separate gating network selects an expert which is most likely to be correct at each moment. Such a model has been used previously (Jacobs and Jordan 1993) to learn a feedforward controller for a 2-joint planar arm operating under different loads. In their model however they assumed that the identity of the load is known to the controller. The subjects in our study were not given any explicit cues about the identity of the fields they were learning. The mixture of experts cannot be used directly here because it decides which expert to select based on a soft partitioning of the input space, and in our experiment any force field is active over any portion of the input space at different moments in time. Here we propose an extension to the ME architecture that is able to deal with mappings overlapping in X space.

Another aspect of the results that is difficult to model using standard computational architectures is memory consolidation. To account for this effect we introduce two different learning rates (Alverez and Squire 1994). Some connections in the network change faster, as a result of which they can serve as short-term memory. We also introduce an off-line training phase (possibly corresponding to sleep) in which random inputs are generated, the part of the network containing the fast connections is used to produce a target output, and the resulting input-output pair is used to train the slowly changing connections. During the offline phase the faster changing connections are fixed, after that they are randomized.

4.1 Modified Mixture of Experts

The ME model assumes that Y is generated from X by one of N processes $(W_1, ..., W_N)$ and therefore the likelihood function is:

$$L(\Theta|x_t, y_t) = P(y_t|x_t, \Theta) = \sum_i g_i{}^t P(y_t|W_i, x_t, \Theta)$$

$$g_i{}^t = P(W_i|x_t, \Theta),$$

where Θ represents the parameters of the model and g_i is the prior probability. We want to use the posterior probability $P(W_i|x_t, y_t)$ instead, because the processes (different force fields) are separable in XY space, but not in X space. If we want to implement an on-line controller such a term is not available, because at time t, y_t is still unknown (the task of the controller is to produce it). We could approximate $P(W_i|x_t, y_t)$ with $P(W_i|x_{t-1}, y_{t-1})$, because dynamic conditions do not change very often. Now the gating network (which computes $P(W_i|x_t)$ in ME) is going to select expert i based on the previous XY pair. This approach would obviously lead to a single large error at the moment when the force field changes, but so will any model using only x_t to compute y_t. In fact such an error seems to be consistent with our psychophysics data. Thus the learning rule is:

$$\Delta \Theta_i = \nu_i h_i{}^t (y_t - \mu_i(x_t, \Theta_i))$$

$$g_i{}^t = h_i{}^{t-1}$$

$$h_i{}^t = P(W_i^t|x_i^t, y_i^t, \Theta) = \frac{g_i{}^t P(y_t|W_i, x_t, \Theta)}{\sum_j g_j{}^t P(y_t|W_j, x_t, \Theta)},$$

where h_i^t is the posterior probability and μ_i is the output of exper i. μ_i is a linear function of the inputs. In our model we used 4 experts. In order to model the process of consolidation, we gave one expert a learning rate that was 10 times higher than the learning rate of the other 3 experts.

4.2 The Model

We simulated the dynamics of a 2-joint planar arm similar to the one used in our previous work (Shadmehr and Mussa-Ivaldi, 1994). The torque applied to the arm at every point in time is the sum of the outputs of a fixed controller, a PD controller, and an adaptive controller with the architecture described above.

The fixed controller maps $\theta, \dot{\theta}$ (current state), and $\ddot{\theta}$ (desired next state) into a torque τ. The mapping is exact when no external forces are applied. The desired trajectories are minimum-jerk trajectories (Flash and Hogan 1985) sampled at 100Hz. The desired trajectories are 10 cm long and last 0.5 seconds. The PD controller is used to compensate for the troques produced by the force field while the adaptive controller has not yet learned to do that. The adaptive part of the controller consists of a mixture of 4 linear experts (whose initial output is small) and a modified gating network described above. The system operates as follows: $\theta, \dot{\theta}, \ddot{\theta}$ are sent to the fixed controller, which outputs a torque τ_1; the PD controller outputs a torque τ_2 based on the current deviation from the desired joint position and velocity; 8 terms describing the current state of the arm (and chosen to linearize the mapping to be learned) are sent to the mixture model, which outputs a torque τ_3; $\tau_c = \tau_1 + \tau_2 - \tau_3$ is applied to the plant as a control signal; the actual torque $\tau = \tau_c + \tau_f$ is computed. The mixture model is trained to produce the torque τ_f resulting from the force field. In other words, the adaptive part of the controller learns to compensate for the force field exerted by the environment.

The parameters of the mixture model are updated after every movement, so a training pair (x_t, y_t) is actually a batch of 50 points. The input, x_t, consists of the 8 terms describing the current state and the desired next state; the output, y_t, is the torque vector that the force field produces.The compensatory torques for a complete movement are computed before the movement starts. The only processing done during the movement is the computations necessary for the PD controller.

4.3 Results

4.3.1 Negative Transfer

When the network was given two successive, incompatable mappings to learn (this corresponds to learning to move in two opposite force fields), the resulting performance very much resembled that of our human subjects. The performance in the second mapping was much poorer than that in the first mapping. The fast-learning expert changed its weights to learn both tasks. Since the two tasks involved anti-correlated maps, the fast expert's weights after learning the first mapping were very inappropriate for the second task, leading to the observed negative transfer.

4.3.2 Catastrophic Interference

When the network was trained on two successive, opposite force fields, with no consolidation occurring between the two training sessions, the learning in second training session overwrote the learning that occurred during the first training session (fig 3A). Since the expert with the fast-changing weights attempted to learn both mappings, this catastrophic interference is not unexpected.

4.3.3 Consolidation

When the network was allowed to undergo consolidation between learning the first and the second force field, the network no longer suffered from catastrophic inter-

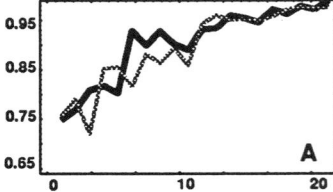 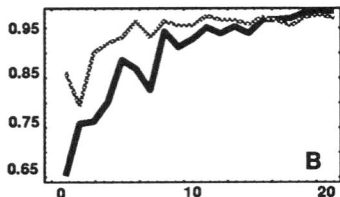

Figure 3: **A:** Learning curves for the ME architecture. Dark line: curve when first learning Field A. light line: curve when given Field A a second time, after learning FIeld B (no consolidation allowed between learning Field A and Field B). Note lack of retention of Field A. **B:** Learning curves for the same architecture in Field A before and after learning Field B. Consolidations was allowed between learning Field A and Field B.

ference (fig 3B). The learning that had initially resided in the fast-learning expert was transfered to one of the slower-learning networks. Thus, when the expert with the fast-changing connections learned the second mapping, the original learning was no longer destroyed. In addition, when the network was allowed to consolidate the second force field, a different slow-learning expert stored the second mapping. In this way, the network stored multiple maps in long-term memory.

5 Conclusions

We have presented psychophysical evidence for catastrophic interference. We have also shown results that suggest that motor learning can undergo a process of consolidation. By adding distinct fast- and slow-changing weights to a mixture of experts architecture, we were able to account for these psychophysical findings. We plan to investigate further the neural correlates of consolidation using both brain imaging in humans and electrophysiological studies in primates.

References

P. Alverez and L. Squire. (1994) Memory consolidation and the medial temporal love: a simple network model, *PNAS* **91:15**:7041-7045. T. Brashers-Krug, et al. (1994) Temporal aspects of human motor learning, *Soc. Neurosci. Abstract* in press.

T. Flash and N. Hogan. (1985) The coordination of arm movements: an experimentally confirmed mathematical model. *J. Neurosci.* **5**:1688-1703.

R. Jacobs and M. Jordan. (1993) Learning piecewise control strategies in a modular neural network architecture. IEEE Trans. on Systems, Man and Cyber. **23:2**: 337-345.

I. Jenkins, et al. (1994) Motor sequence learning: a study with positron emission tomography, *J. Neurosci.* **14**:3775-3790.

M. Jordan and R. Jacobs. (1994) Hierarchical mixture of experts and the EM algorithm, *Neural Computation* **6:2**: 181-214.

M. Jordan and D. Rumelhart. (1992) Forward models: supervised learning with a distal teacher *Cognitive Sci.* **16**:307-354

A. Karni and D. Sagi. (1993) *Nature* **365**:250.

R. Shadmehr and F. Mussa-Ivaldi. (1994) Adaptive representation of dynamics during learning of a motor task, *J. Neurosci.***14:5**:3208-3224.

R. Shadmehr, T. Brashers-Krug, F. Mussa-Ivaldi, (1995) Interference in learning internal models of inverse dynamics in humans, *Adv Neural Inform Proc Syst*vol **7**, in press

Grammar Learning by a Self-Organizing Network

Michiro Negishi
Dept. of Cognitive and Neural Systems, Boston University
111 Cummington Street
Boston, MA 02215 email : negishi@cns.bu.edu

Abstract

This paper presents the design and simulation results of a self-organizing neural network which induces a grammar from example sentences. Input sentences are generated from a simple phrase structure grammar including number agreement, verb transitivity, and recursive noun phrase construction rules. The network induces a grammar explicitly in the form of symbol categorization rules and phrase structure rules.

1 Purpose and related works

The purpose of this research is to show that a self-organizing network with a certain structure can acquire syntactic knowledge from only positive (*i.e.* grammatical) data, without requiring any initial knowledge or external teachers that correct errors.

There has been research on supervised neural network models of language acquisition tasks [Elman, 1991, Miikkulainen and Dyer, 1988, John and McClelland, 1988]. Unlike these supervised models, the current model self-organizes word and phrasal categories and phrase construction rules through mere exposure to input sentences, without any artificially defined task goals. There also have been self-organizing models of language acquisition tasks [Ritter and Kohonen, 1990, Scholtes, 1991]. Compared to these models, the current model acquires phrase structure rules in more explicit forms, and it learns wider and more structured contexts, as will be explained below.

2 Network Structure and Algorithm

The design of the current network is motivated by the observation that humans have the ability to handle a frequently occurring sequence of symbols (chunk) as an unit of information [Grossberg, 1978, Mannes, 1993]. The network consists of two parts : classification networks and production networks (Figure 1). The classification networks categorize words and phrases, and the production networks evaluate how it is likely for a pair of categories to form a phrase. A pair of combined categories is given its own symbol, and fed back to the classifiers.

After weights are formed, the network parses a sentence as follows. Input words are incrementally added to the neural sequence memory called the Gradient Field [Grossberg, 1978] (GF hereafter). The top (*i.e. most recent*) two symbols and the lookahead token are classified by three classification networks. Here a symbol is either a word or a phrase, and the lookahead token is the word which will be read in next. Then the lookahead token and the top symbol in the GF are sent to the right production network, and the top and the second ones are sent to the left production network. If the latter pair is judged to be more likely to form a phrase, the symbol pair *reduces* to a phrase, and the phrase is fed back to the GF after removing the top two symbols. Otherwise, the lookahead token is added to the sequence memory, causing a *shift* in the sequence memory. If the input sentence is grammatical, the repetition of this process reduces the whole sentence to a single "S" (sentence) symbol. The sequence of shifts and reductions (annotated with the resultant symbols) amounts to a parse of the sentence.

During learning, the operations stated above are carried out as weights are gradually formed. In classification networks, the weights record a distribution pattern with respect to each symbol. That is, the weights record the co-occurrence of up to three adjacent symbols in the corpus. An symbol is classified in terms of this distribution in the classification networks. The production networks keep track of the categories of adjacent symbols. If the occurrence of one category reliably predicts the next or the previous one, the pair of categories forms a phrase, and is given the status of an symbol which is treated just like a word in the sentence. Because the symbols include phrases, the learned context is wider and more structured than the mere bigram, as well as the contexts utilized in [Ritter and Kohonen, 1990, Scholtes, 1991].

3 Simulation

3.1 The Simulation Task

The grammar used to generate input sentences (Table 3) is identical to that used in [Elman, 1991], except that it does not include optionally transitive verbs and proper nouns. Lengths of the input sentences are limited to 16 words. To determine the completion of learning, after accepting 200 consecutive sentences with learning, learning is suppressed and other 200 sentences are processed to see if all are accepted. In addition, the network was tested for 44 ungrammatical sentences to see that they are correctly rejected. Ungrammatical sentences are derived by hand from randomly generated grammatical sentences. Parameters used in the simulation are : number of symbol nodes = 30 (words) + 250 (phrases), number of category nodes = 150, $\epsilon = 10^{-9}$, $\gamma = 0.25$, $\rho = 0.65$, $\alpha_1 = 0.00005$, $\beta_1 = 0.005$, $\beta_2 = 0.2$, $\alpha_3 = 0.0001$, $\beta_3 = 0.001$, and $T = 4.0$.

3.2 Acquired Syntax Rules

Learning was completed after learning 19800 grammatical sentences. Tables 1 and 2 show the acquired syntax rules extracted from the connection weights. Note that category names such as Ns, VPp, are not given a priori, but assigned by the author for the exposition. Only rules that eventually may reach the "S"(sentence) node are shown. There were a small number of uninterpretable rules, which are marked "?". These rules might disturb normal parsing for some sentences, but they were not activated while testing for 200 sentences after learning.

3.3 Discussion

Recursive noun phrase structures should be learned by finding equivalences of distribution between noun phrases and nouns. However, nouns and noun phrases have the same contextual features *only when* they are in certain contexts. An examination of the acquired grammar reveals that the network finds equivalence of features not of "N" and "N RC" (where RC is a relative clause) but of "N V" and "N RC V" (when "N RC" is subjective), or "V N" and "V N RC" (when "N RC" is objective). As an example, let us examine the parsing of the sentence [19912] below. The rule used to reduce *FEEDS CATS WHO LIVE* ("V N RC") is P0, which is classified as category C4, which includes P121 ("V N") where V are the singular forms of transitive verbs, and also includes the "V" where V are singular forms of intransitive verbs. Thus, *GIRL WHO FEEDS CATS WHO LIVE* is reduced to *GIRL WHO "VPsingle"*.

```
***[19912]***************************************************
 +---141---+
 |    +---88------+
 |    |    +---206------+
 |    |    |    +----0----+
 |    |    |    |    +-219-+
 |    |    +-41-+    |    +-36-+    |
 BOYS CHASE GIRL WHO FEEDS CATS WHO LIVE .

<<Accepted>> Top symbol was 77
```

4 Conclusion and Future Direction

In this paper, a self-organizing neural network model of grammar learning was presented. A basic principle of the network is that all words and phrases are categorized by the contexts in which they appear, and that familiar sequence of categories are chunked.

As it stands, the scope of the grammar used in the simulation is extremely limited. Also, considering the poverty of the actual learning environment, the learning of syntax should also be guided by the cognitive competence to comprehend the utterance situations and conversational contexts. However, being a self-organizing network, the current model offers a plausible model of natural language acquisition through mere exposures to only grammatical sentences, not requiring any external teacher or an explicit goal.

Table 1. Acquired categorization rules

S	:=	C29 /* NPs VPs */ |			C52	:=	P41 /* Ns R */	
		C30 /* ? */ |			C56	:=	P36 /* Np R */	
		C77 /* NPp VPp */			C58	:=	P28 /* Ns VTs */ |	
C4	:=	LIVES | WALKS |					P34 /* Np VTp */ |	
		P0 /* VTs Np RC */ |					P68 /* Ns RC VTs */ |	
		P74 /* VTs Ns RC */ |					P147 /* Np RC VTp */	= /* N VT */
		P121 /* VTs Ns */ |			C69	:=	P206 /* Ns R VPs */ |	= /* Ns RCs */
		P157 /* VTs Np */	= /* VPs */				P238 /* Ns R N VT */	
C13	:=	GIRL | DOG |			C74	:=	P219 /* Np R VPp */ |	= /* Np RCp */
		CAT | BOY	= /* Ns */				P249 /* Np R N VT */	
C16	:=	CHASE | FEED	= /* VTp */		C77	:=	P141 /* Np VPp */ |	
C18	:=	WHO	= /* R */				P217 /* Np RC VPp */	= /* NPp VPp */
C20	:=	CHASES | FEEDS	= /* VTs */		C119	:=	P148	= /* VTs N VT */
C26	:=	BOYS | CATS |			C122	:=	P243	= /* Ns R VTs N VT */
		DOGS | GIRLS	= /* Np */		C139	:=	P10 /* VTs NPs VPs */ |	= /* VPs' VPp/s ?*/
C29	:=	P93 /* Ns RC VPs */ |					P32 /* VTs NPp VPp */	
		P138 /* Ns VPs */	= /* NPs VPs */		where			
C30	:=	P2 /* VTp NPp VPp */ |			RCs	=	R VPs | R N VT	
		P94 /* VTp N VT */ |			RCp	=	R VPp | R N VT	
		P137 /* ? */	= /* ? */		NPp	=	Np | Np RCp	
C32	:=	WALK | LIVE |			NPs	=	Ns | Ns RCs	
		P1 /* VTp Np RC */ |						
		P61 /* VTp Np */ |						
		P88 /* VTp Ns RC */ |						
		P122 /* VTp Ns */	= /* VPp */					

Table 2. Acquired production rules

P0	:=	C20 /* VTs */		C74 /* Np RCp */		= /* VTs Np RCp */	
P1	:=	C16 /* VTp */		C74 /* Np RCp */		= /* VTp Np RCp */	
P2	:=	C16 /* VTp */		C77 /* NPp VPp */		= /* VTp NPp VPp */	
P10	:=	C20 /* VTs */		C29 /* NPs VPs */		= /* VTs NPs VPs */	
P28	:=	C13 /* Ns */		C20 /* VTs */		= /* Ns VTs */	
P32	:=	C20 /* VTs */		C77 /* NPp VPp */		= /* VTs NPp VPp */	
P34	:=	C26 /* Np */		C16 /* VTp */		= /* Np VTp */	
P36	:=	C26 /* Np */		C18 /* R */		= /* Np R */	
P41	:=	C13 /* Ns */		C18 /* R */		= /* Ns R */	
P61	:=	C16 /* VTp */		C26 /* Np */		= /* VTp Np */	
P68	:=	C69 /* Ns RCs */		C20 /* VTs */		= /* Ns RCs VTs */	
P74	:=	C20 /* VTs */		C69 /* Ns RCs */		= /* VTs Ns RCs */	
P88	:=	C16 /* VTp */		C69 /* Ns RCs */		= /* VTp Ns RCs */	
P93	:=	C69 /* Ns RCs */		C4 /* VPs */		= /* Ns RCs VPs */	
P94	:=	C16 /* VTp */		C58 /* N VT */		= /* VTp N VT */	
P121	:=	C20 /* VTs */		C13 /* Ns */		= /* VTs Ns */	
P122	:=	C16 /* VTp */		C13 /* Ns */		= /* VTp Ns */	
P137	:=	C122 /* Ns R VTs N VT */		C32 /* VPp */		= /* ? */	
P138	:=	C13 /* Ns */		C4 /* VPs */		= /* Ns VPs /	
P141	:=	C26 /* Np */		C32 /* VPp */		= /* Np VPp */	
P147	:=	C74 /* Np RCs */		C16 /* VTp */		= /* Np RCs VTp */	
P148	:=	C20 /* VTs */		C58 /* N VT */		= /* VTs N VT */	
P157	:=	C20 /* VTs */		C26 /* Np */		= /* VTs Np */	
P206	:=	C52 /* Ns R */		C4 /* VPs */		= /* Ns R VPs */	
P217	:=	C74 /* Np RCs */		C32 /* VPp */		= /* Np RCs VPp */	
P219	:=	C56 /* Np R */		C32 /* VPp */		= /* Np R VPp */	
P238	:=	C52 /* Ns R */		C58 /* N VT */		= /* Ns R N VT */	
P243	:=	C52 /* Ns R */		C119 /* VTs N VT */		= /* (Ns R VTs N) VT */	
P249	:=	C56 /* Np R */		C58 /* N VT */		= /* Np R N VT */	

Acknowledgements

The author wishes to thank Prof. Dan Bullock, Prof. Cathy Harris, Prof. Mike Cohen, and Chris Myers of Boston University for valuable discussions.

This work was supported in part by the Air Force Office of Scientific Research (AFOSR F49620-92-J-0225).

References

[Elman, 1991] Elman, J. (1991). Distributed representations, simple recurrent networks, and grammatical structure. *Machine Learning*, 7.

[Grossberg, 1978] Grossberg, S. (1978). A theory of human memory: Self-organization and performance of sensory-motor codes, maps, and plans. *Progress in Theoretical Biology*, 5.

[John and McClelland, 1988] John, M. F. S. and McClelland, J. L. (1988). Applying contextual constraints in sentence comprehension. In Touretzky, D. S., Hinton, G. E., and Sejnowsky, T. J., editors, *Proceedings of the Second Connectionist Models Summer School 1988, Los Altos, CA*. Morgan Kaufmann Publisher, Inc.

[Mannes, 1993] Mannes, C. (1993). Self-organizing grammar induction using a neural network model. In Mitra, J., Cabestany, J., and Prieto, A., editors, *New Trends in Neural Computation : Lecture Notes in Computer Science 686*. Springer Verlag, New York.

[Miikkulainen and Dyer, 1988] Miikkulainen, R. and Dyer, M. G. (1988). Encoding input/output representations in connectionist cognitive systems. In Touretzky, D. D., Hinton, G. E., and Senowsky, T. J., editors, *Proceedings of the Second Connectionist Models Summer School 1988, Los Altos, CA*. Morgan Kauffman Publisher, Inc.

[Ritter and Kohonen, 1990] Ritter, H. and Kohonen, T. (1990). Learning semanto-topic maps from context. *Proceedings of . IJCNN 90, Washington D.C.*, I.

[Scholtes, 1991] Scholtes, J. C. (1991). Unsupervised context learning in natural language processing. *Proceedings of IJCNN Seattle 1991*.

Appendix A. Activation and learning equations

A.1 Classification Network Activities

•*Gradient Field*
$$X0_i(t) = 0.5 X0_i(t-1) + I_i(t) \tag{1}$$

where t is a discrete time, i is the symbol id. and $I_i(t)$ is an input symbol.

•*Input Layer*
$$X1_{Ai}(t) = \theta(2(X0_i(t) - \theta(X0_i(t)))), \quad X1_{Bi}(t) = \theta(X0_i(t)), \quad X1_{Ci}(t) = I_i(t+1)$$

Where the suffix A, B, and C the most recent, the next to most recent, and the lookahead symbols, respectively. Weights in networks A, B, and C are identical.

$$\theta(x) = \begin{cases} 1 & \text{if } x > 1 - 2^{-M} \\ 0 & \text{otherwise} \end{cases}$$

Here M is the maximum number of symbols on the gradient field.

• *Feature Layer*

$$X2^I_{si} = \sum_j X1_{sj} W1_{sji}, \quad X2^{II}_{si}{}' = f(X1^I_{si}/(a+\sum_j X2^I_{sj})), \quad X2_{si} = X2^{II}_{si}/(a+\sum_j X2^{II}_{sj})$$

$$f(x) = 2/(1 + exp(-Tx)) - 1$$

where s is a suffix which is either A, B, or C and T is the steepness of the sigmoid function and a is a small positive constant. Table 4 shows the meaning of above suffix i.

• *Category Layer*

$$X3_{pi} = \begin{cases} 1 & \text{if } i = min\{j| \sum_{ks} X2_{sk} W2_{skj} > \rho\}, \text{ or} \\ & \text{if } \phi = min\{j| \sum_{ks} X2_{sk} W2_{skj} > \rho\} \text{ \& } unref_i =^{max}_j \{unref_j\} \\ 0 & \text{otherwise} \end{cases} \quad (2)$$

Where ρ is the least match score required and $uref_i$ is an unreferenced count.

A.2 Classification Learning

• *Feature Weights*
$$\Delta W1_{sij} = -\alpha_1 W1_{sij} + \beta_1 X1_i(X2_{sj} - W1_{sij})$$
where α_1 is the forgetting rate, and β_1 is the learning rate.

• *Categorization Weights*

$$\begin{cases} \Delta W2_{sij} = \beta_2 X3_{si}(X2_{si} - W2_{sij}) & \text{if the node is selected by the first line of (2)} \\ W2_{sij} = X2_{si} & \text{if the node is selected by the second line of (2)} \end{cases}$$

where β_2 is the learning rate.

A.3 Production Network Activities

• *Mutual predictiveness*

$$\begin{aligned} X4_{ij} &= X3_{Ai} W3_{ij}, & X5_{ji} &= X3_{Bj} W4_{ji}, & X6_{ij} &= X4_{ij} X5_{ji} \\ X7_{ij} &= X3_{Bi} W3_{ij}, & X8_{ji} &= X3_{Cj} W4_{ji}, & X9_{ij} &= X7_{ij} X8_{ji} \end{aligned}$$

The phrase identification number for a category pair (i, j) is given algorithmically in the current version by a cash function $cash(i, j)$.

(i) Case in which $\gamma \sum_{ij} X6_{ij} \geq \sum_{ij} X9_{ij}$: Reduce

$$X10_i = \begin{cases} 1 & \text{if } i = cash(I, J) \text{ where } X6_{IJ} =^{max}_{ij}(X6_{ij}) \\ 0 & \text{otherwise} \end{cases}$$

$$X0_i(t+1) = 0.5 * pop(pop(X0_i(t))) + X10, \quad pop(x) = 2(x - \theta(x))$$

(ii) Case in which $\gamma \sum_{ij} X6_{ij} < \sum_{ij} X9_{ij}$: Shift

The next input symbol is added on the gradient field, as was expressed in (1).

A.4 Production Learning

$$\Delta W3_{ij} = -\alpha_3 W3_{ij} + \beta_3 X3_{Ai}(X3_{Bj} - W3_{ij}), \quad \Delta W4_{ji} = -\alpha_3 W4_{ji} + \beta_3 X3_{Bj}(X3_{Ai} - W4_{ji})$$

where $X3_{Ai}$ and $X3_{Bj}$ are nodes that receive the next to the most recent symbol i and the most recent symbol j, respectively.

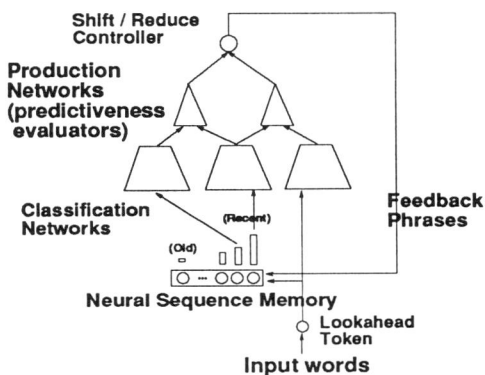

Figure 1. Block diagram of the network

S	→	NP VP .
NP	→	N	N RC
VP	→	V [NP]
RC	→	who NP V	who VP
N	→	boy	girl	cat	dog	boys	girls	cats	dogs
V	→	chase	feed	work	live	chases	feeds	works	lives
Number agreement		
- Agreements between N and V within clause		
- Agreements between head N and subordinate V (where appropriate)		
Verb arguments		
- chase, feed -> require a direct object		
- walk, live -> preclude a direct object (Observed also for head/verb relations in relative clauses)		

Table 3. Grammar for generated sentences

(1)	Left context, words. $s = L, 1 <= i <= N_w$
(2)	Left context, phrases. $s = L, N_w < i <= N_w + N_p$
(3)	Left context, categories. $s = L, N_w + N_p < i <= N_w + N_p + N_c$
(4)	Right context, words. $s = R, 1 <= i <= N_w$
(5)	Right context, phrases. $s = R, N_w < i <= N_w + N_p$
(6)	Right context, categories. $s = R, N_w + N_p < i <= N_w + N_p + N_c$
(7)	Right context, lookahead. $s = R, N_w + N_p + N_c < i <= 2N_w + N_p + N_c$

N_w, N_p, and N_c denotes number of words, phrases, and categories, respectively.

Table 4. Subfields in a feature layer

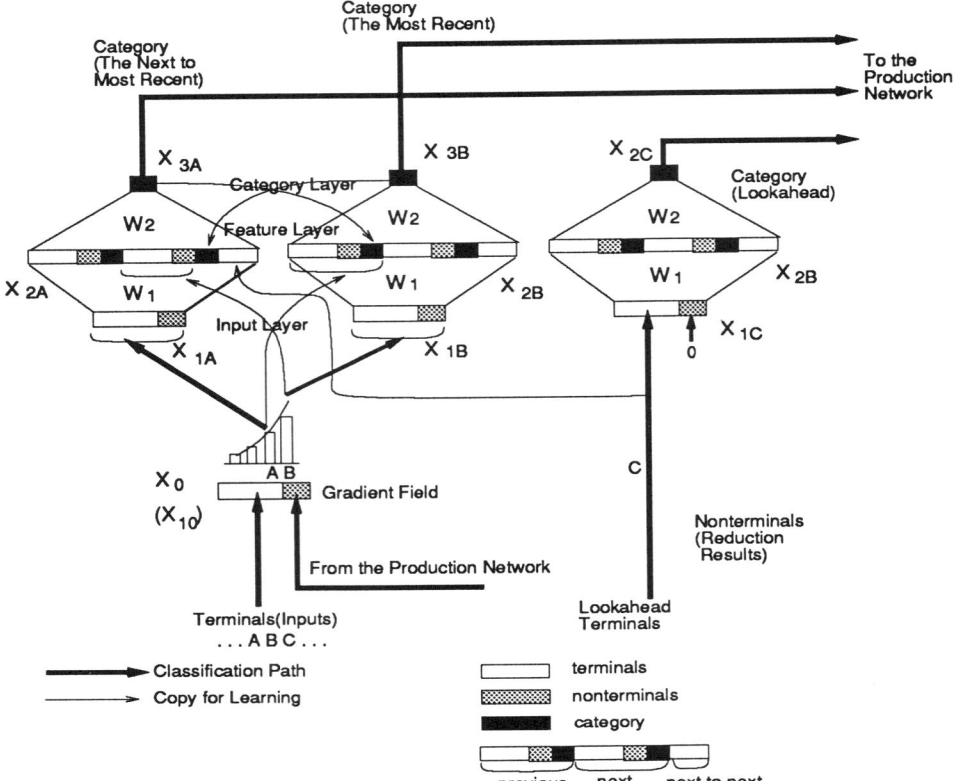

Figure 2. Classification Network

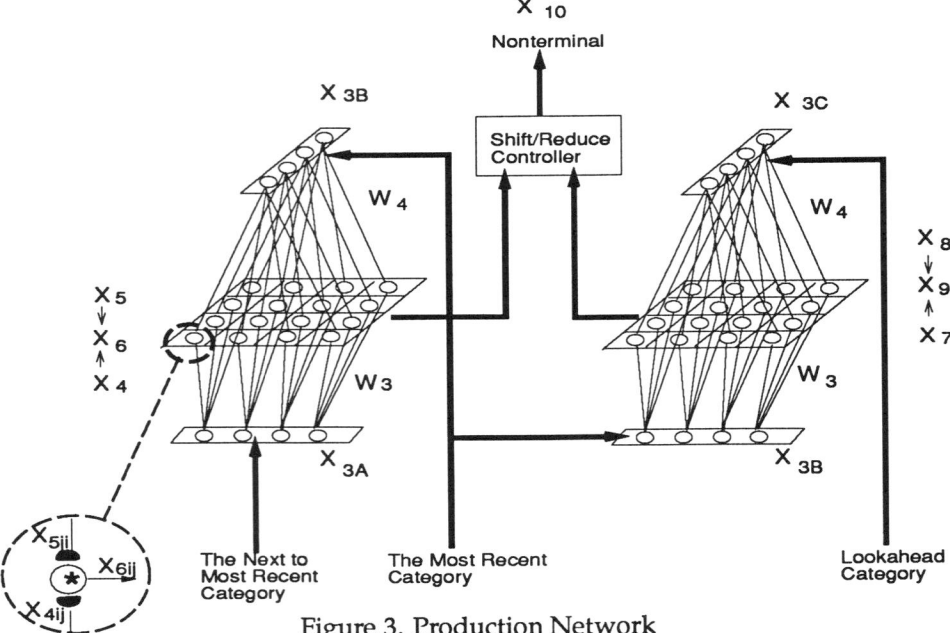

Figure 3. Production Network

Patterns of damage in neural networks: The effects of lesion area, shape and number

Eytan Ruppin and James A. Reggia [*]
Department of Computer Science
A.V. Williams Bldg.
University of Maryland
College Park, MD 20742
ruppin@cs.umd.edu   reggia@cs.umd.edu

Abstract

Current understanding of the effects of damage on neural networks is rudimentary, even though such understanding could lead to important insights concerning neurological and psychiatric disorders. Motivated by this consideration, we present a simple analytical framework for estimating the functional damage resulting from focal structural lesions to a neural network. The effects of focal lesions of varying area, shape and number on the retrieval capacities of a spatially-organized associative memory. Although our analytical results are based on some approximations, they correspond well with simulation results. This study sheds light on some important features characterizing the clinical manifestations of multi-infarct dementia, including the strong association between the number of infarcts and the prevalence of dementia after stroke, and the 'multiplicative' interaction that has been postulated to occur between Alzheimer's disease and multi-infarct dementia.

---

[*]Dr. Reggia is also with the Department of Neurology and the Institute of Advanced Computer Studies at the University of Maryland.

1 Introduction

Understanding the response of neural nets to structural/functional damage is important for a variety of reasons, e.g., in assessing the performance of neural network hardware, and in gaining understanding of the mechanisms underlying neurological and psychiatric disorders. Recently, there has been a growing interest in constructing neural models to study how specific pathological neuroanatomical and neurophysiological changes can result in various clinical manifestations, and to investigate the functional organization of the symptoms that result from specific brain pathologies (reviewed in [1, 2]). In the area of associative memory models specifically, early studies found an increase in memory impairment with increasing lesion severity (in accordance with Lashley's classical 'mass action' principle), and showed that slowly developing lesions have less pronounced effects than equivalent acute lesions [3]. Recently, it was shown that the gradual pattern of clinical deterioration manifested in the majority of Alzheimer's patients can be accounted for, and that different synaptic compensation rates can account for the observed variation in the severity and progression rate of this disease [4]. However, this past work is limited in that model elements have no spatial relationships to one another (all elements are conceptually equidistant). Thus, as there is no way to represent focal (localized) damage in such networks, it has not been possible to study the functional effect of focal lesions and to compare them with that caused by diffuse lesions.

The limitations of past work led us to use spatially-organized neural network for studying the effects of different types of lesions (we use the term lesion to mean any type of structural and functional damage inflicted on an initially intact neural network). The elements in our model, which can be thought of as representing neurons, or micro-columnar units, form a 2-dimensional array (whose edges are connected, forming a torus to eliminate edge effects), and each unit is connected primarily to its nearby neighbors, as is the case in the cortex [5]. It has recently been shown that such spatially-organized attractor networks can function reasonably well as associative memory devices [6]. This paper presents the first detailed analysis of the effects of lesions of various size, form and number on the memory performance of spatially-organized attractor neural networks. Assuming that these networks are a plausible model of some frontal and associative cortical areas (see, e.g., [7]), our results shed light on the clinical progress of disorders such as stroke and dementia.

In the next section, we derive a theoretical framework that characterizes the effects of focal lesions on an associative network's performance. This framework, which is formulated in very general terms, is then examined via simulations in Section 3, which show a remarkable quantitative fit with the theoretical predictions, and are compared with simulations examining performance with diffuse damage. Finally, the clinical significance of our results is discussed in Section 4.

2 Analyzing the effects of focal lesions

Our analysis pertains to the case where in the pre-damaged network, all units have an approximately similar average level of activity [1]. A focal *structural lesion*

---
[1] This is true in general for associative memory networks, when the activity of each unit is averaged over a sufficiently long time span.

(anatomical lesion), denoting the area of damage and neuronal death, is modeled by clamping the activity of the lesioned units to zero. As a result of this primary lesion, the activity of surrounding units may be decreased, resulting in a secondary area of *functional lesion*, as illustrated in Figure 1. We are primarily interested in large focal lesions, where the area s of the lesion is significantly greater than the local neighborhood region from which each unit receives its inputs. Throughout our analysis we shall hold the working assumption that, traversing from the border of the lesion outwards, the activity of units gradually rises from zero until it reaches its normal, predamaged levels, at some distance d from the lesion's border (see Figure 1). As s is large and d is determined by local interactions on the borders of the structural lesion, we may reasonably assume that the value of d is independent of the lesion size, and depends primarily on the specific network characteristics, such as it architecture, dynamics, and memory load.

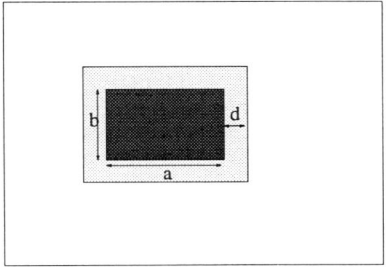

Figure 1: A sketch of a structural (dark shading) and surrounding functional (light shading) rectangular lesion.

Let the intact baseline performance level of the network be denoted as $P(0)$, and let the network size be A. The network's performance denotes how accurately it retrieves the correct memorized patterns given a set of input cues, and is defined formally below. A structural lesion of area s (dark shading in Figure 1), causing a functional lesion of area Δ_s (light shading in Figure 1), will then result in a performance level of approximately

$$P(s) = \frac{P(0)\left[A - (s + \Delta_s)\right] + P_\Delta \Delta_s}{A - s} = P(0) - (\Delta P \Delta_s)/(A - s) , \qquad (1)$$

where P_Δ denotes the average level of performance over Δ_s and $\Delta P = P(0) - P_\Delta$. $P(s)$ hence reflects the performance level over the remaining viable parts of the network, discarding the structurally damaged region. Bearing these definitions in mind, a simple analysis shows that the effect of focal lesions is governed by the following rules.

Consider a symmetric, circular structural lesion of size $s = \pi r^2$. Δ_s, the area of functional damage following such a lesion is then (assuming large lesions and hence $\sqrt{s} > d$)

<u>Rule 1:</u>
$$\Delta_s \cong \sqrt{4\pi} d \sqrt{s} , \qquad (2)$$

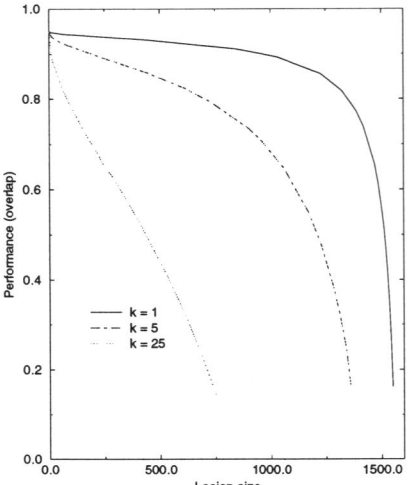

Figure 2: Theoretically predicted network performance as a function of a single focal structural lesion's size (area): analytic curves obtained for different k values; $A = 1600$.

and
$$P(s) \cong P(0) - \frac{k\sqrt{s}}{A-s} , \qquad (3)$$
for some constant $k = \sqrt{4\pi d}\Delta P$. Thus, the area of functional damage surrounding a single focal structural lesion is proportional to the square root of the structural lesion's area. Some analytic performance/lesioning curves (for various k values) are illustrated in Figure 2. Note the different qualitative shape of these curves as a function of k. Letting $x = s/A$ be the *fraction of structural damage*, we have
$$P(x) \cong P(0) - \frac{k\sqrt{x}}{1-x}\frac{1}{\sqrt{A}} , \qquad (4)$$
that is, the same *fraction x* of damage results in less performance decrease in larger networks. This surprising result testifies to the possible protective value of having functional 'modular' cortical networks of large size.

Expressions 3 and 4 are valid also when the structural lesion has a square shape. To study the effect of the structural lesion's shape, we consider the area $\Delta_{s[n]}$ of a functional lesion resulting from a rectangular focal lesion of size $s = a \cdot b$ (see Figure 1), where, without loss of generality, $n = a/b \geq 1$. Then, for large n, we find that the functional damage of a rectangular structural lesion of fixed size increases as its shape is more elongated, following
Rule 2:
$$\Delta_{s[n]} \cong \sqrt{n/4}\Delta_s , \qquad (5)$$
and
$$P(s) \cong P(0) - \frac{k\sqrt{ns}}{2(A-s)} . \qquad (6)$$

To study the effect of the number of lesions, consider the area $\Delta_s{}^m$ of a functional lesion composed of m focal rectangular structural lesions (with sides $a = n \cdot b$), each of area s/m. We find that the functional damage increases with the number of focal sub-lesions (while total structural lesion area is held constant), according to *Rule 3*:

$$\Delta_s{}^m \geq \sqrt{m}\Delta_{s[n]}, \tag{7}$$

and

$$P(s) \cong P(0) - \frac{k\sqrt{mns}}{2(A-s)}. \tag{8}$$

While Rule 3 presents a lower bound on the functional damage which may actually be significantly larger and involves no approximations, Rule 2 presents an upper bound on the actual functional damage. As we shall show in the next section, the number of lesions actually affects the network performance significantly more than its precise shape.

3 Numerical Simulation Results

We now turn to examine the effect of lesions on the performance of an associative memory network via simulations. The goal of these simulations is twofold. First, to examine how accurately the general but approximate theoretical results presented above describe the actual performance degradation in a specific associative network. Second, to compare the effects of focal lesions to those of diffuse ones, as the effect of diffuse damage cannot be described as a limiting case within the framework of our analysis. Our simulations were performed using a standard Tsodyks-Feigelman attractor neural network [8]. This is a Hopfield-like network which has several features which make it more biologically plausible [4], such as low activity and non-zero positive thresholds. In all the experiments, 20 sparse random $\{0, 1\}$ memory patterns (with a fraction of $p \ll 1$ of 1's) were stored in a network of $N = 1600$ units, placed on a 2-dimensional lattice. The network has spatially organized connectivity, where each unit has 60 incoming connections determined randomly with a Gaussian probability $\phi(z) = \sqrt{1/2\pi} \exp(-z^2/2\sigma^2)$, where z is the distance between two units in the array. When σ is small, each unit is connected primarily to its nearby neighbors. As in [4], the cue input patterns are presented via an external field of magnitude $e = 0.035$, and the noise level is $T = 0.005$. The performance of the network is measured (over the viable, non-lesioned units) by the standard *overlap* measure which denotes the similarity between the final state S the network converges to and the memory pattern ξ^μ that was cued in that trial, defined by

$$m^\mu(t) = \frac{1}{p(1-p)N} \sum_{i=1}^{N} (\xi_i^\mu - p) S_i(t). \tag{9}$$

In all simulations we report the average overlap achieved over 100 trials.

We first studied the network's performance at various σ values. Figure 3a displays how the performance of the network degrades when *diffuse* structural lesions of increasing size are inflicted upon it (i.e., randomly selected units are clamped to zero), while Figure 3b plots the performance as a function of the size of a single square-shaped focal lesion. As is evident, spatially-organized connectivity enables the network to maintain its memory retrieval capacities in face of focal lesions of considerable size. Diffuse lesions are always more detrimental than *single* focal lesions of identical size. Also plotted in Figure 3b is the analytical curve calculated via expression (3) (with $k = 5$), which shows a nice fit with the actual performance of the spatially-connected network parametrized by $\sigma = 1$. Concentrating on the study of focal lesions in a spatially-connected network, we adhere to the values $\sigma = 1$ and $k = 5$ hereafter, and compare the analytical and numerical results. With these values, the analytical curves describing the performance of the network as a function of the fraction of the network lesioned (obtained using expression 4) are similar to the corresponding numerical results.

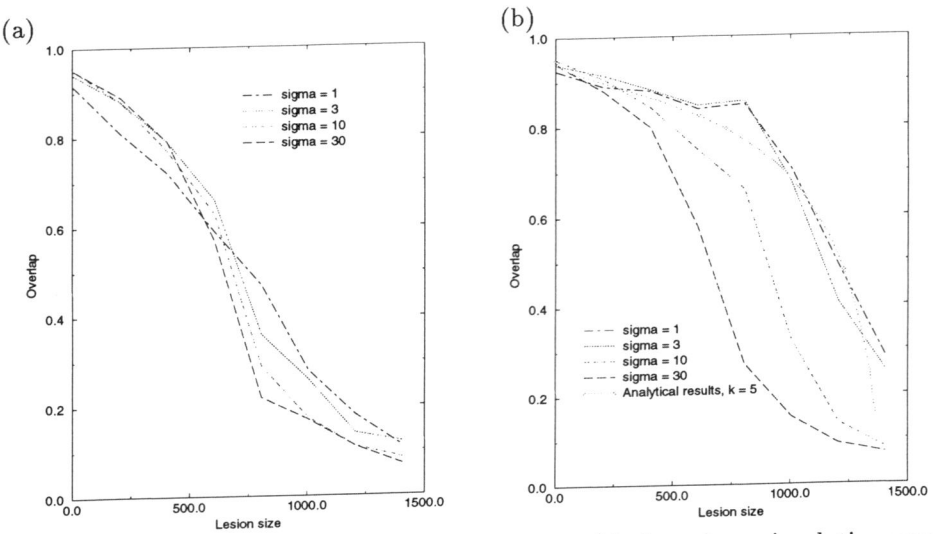

Figure 3: Network performance as a function of lesion size: simulation results obtained in four different networks, each characterized by a distinct distribution of spatially-organized connectivity. (a) Diffuse lesions. (b) Focal lesions.

To examine Rule 2, a rectangular structural lesion of area $s = 300$ was induced in the network. As shown in Figure 4a, as the ratio n between the sides is increased, the network's performance further decreases, but this effect is relatively mild. The markedly stronger effect of varying the lesion number (described by Rule 3) is demonstrated in figure 4b, which shows the effect of multiple lesions composed of $2, 4, 8$ and 16 separate focal lesions. For comparison, the performance achieved with a diffuse lesion of similar size is plotted on the $20'th$ x-ordinate. It is interesting to note that a sufficiently large multiple focal lesion ($s = 512$) can cause a larger performance decrease than a diffuse lesion of similar size. That is, at some point, when the size of each individual focal lesion becomes small in relation to the spread of each unit's connectivity, our analysis looses its validity, and Rule 3 ceases to hold.

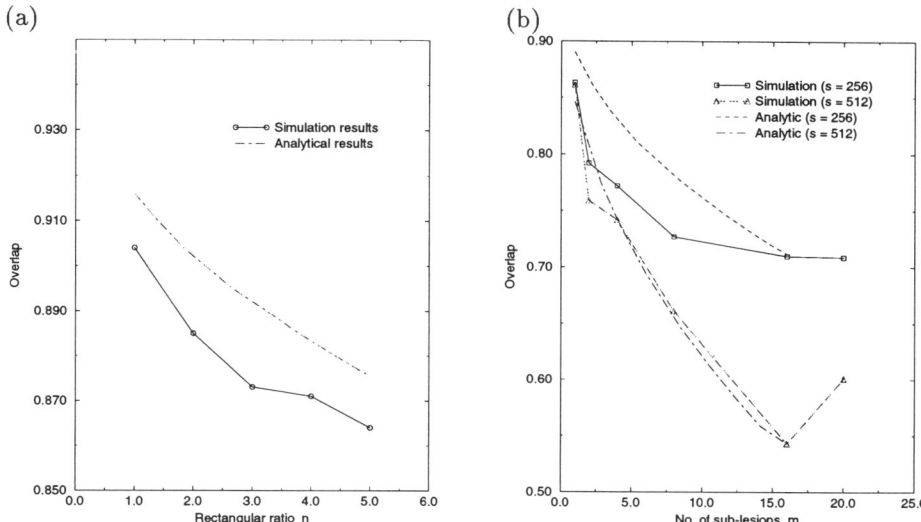

Figure 4: Network performance as a function of focal lesion shape (a) and number (b). Both numerical and analytical results are displayed. In Figure 4b, the x-ordinate denotes the number of separate sub-lesions (1,2,4,8,16), and, for comparison, the performance achieved with a diffuse lesion of similar size is plotted on the $20'th$ x-ordinate.

4 Discussion

We have presented a simple analytical framework for studying the effects of focal lesions on the functioning of spatially organized neural networks. The analysis presented is quite general and a similar approach could be adopted to investigate the effect of focal lesions in other neural models. Using this analysis, specific scaling rules have been formulated describing the functional effects of structural focal lesions on memory retrieval performance in associative attractor networks. The functional lesion scales as the square root of the size of a single structural lesion, and the form of the resulting performance curve depends on the impairment span d. Surprisingly, the same fraction of damage results in significantly less performance decrease in larger networks, pointing to their relative robustness. As to the effects of shape and number, elongated structural lesions cause more damage than more symmetrical ones. However, the number of sub-lesions is the most critical factor determining the functional damage and performance decrease in the model. Numerical studies show that in some conditions multiple lesions can damage performance more than diffuse damage, even though the amount of lost innervation is always less in a multiple focal lesion than with diffuse damage.

Beyond its computational interest, the study of the effects of focal damage on the performance of neural network models can lead to a better understanding of functional impairments accompanying focal brain lesions. In particular, we are interested in *multi-infarct dementia*, a frequent cause of dementia (chronic deterioration of cognitive and memory capacities) characterized by a series of multiple, aggregating focal lesions. Our results indicate a significant role for the number of infarcts in determining the extent of functional damage and dementia in multi-infarct disease. In our model, multiple focal lesions cause a much larger deficit than their simple 'sum', i.e., a single lesion of equivalent total size. This is consistent with clinical studies that have suggested the main factors related to the prevalence of dementia after stroke to be the infarct number and site, and not the overall infarct size, which is related to the prevalence of dementia in a significantly weaker manner [9, 10]. Our model also offers a possible explanation to the 'multiplicative' interaction that has been postulated to occur between co-existing Alzheimer and multi-infarct dementia [10], and to the role of cortical atrophy in increasing the prevalence of dementia after stroke; in accordance with our model, it is hypothesized that atrophic degenerative changes will lead to an increase in the value of d (and hence of k) and increase the functional damage caused by a lesion of given structural size. This hypothesis, together with a detailed study of the effects of the various network parameters on the value of d, are currently under further investigation.

Acknowledgements
This research has been supported by a Rothschild Fellowship to Dr. Ruppin and by Awards NS29414 and NS16332 from NINDS.

References

[1] J. Reggia, R. Berndt, and L. D'Autrechy. Connectionist models in neuropsychology. In *Handbook of Neuropsychology*, volume 9. 1994, in press.

[2] E. Ruppin. Neural modeling of psychiatric disorders. *Network: Computation in Neural Systems*, 1995. Invited review paper, to appear.

[3] J.A. Anderson. Cognitive and psychological computation with neural models. *IEEE Trans. on Systems, Man, and Cybernetics*, SMC-13(5):799–815, 1983.

[4] D. Horn, E. Ruppin, M. Usher, and M. Herrmann. Neural network modeling of memory deterioration in alzheimer's disease. *Neural Computation*, 5:736–749, 1993.

[5] A. M. Thomson and J. Deuchars. Temporal and spatial properties of local circuits in the neocortex. *Trends in neuroscience*, 17(3):119–126, 1994.

[6] J.M. Karlholm. Associative memories with short-range higher order couplings. *Neural Networks*, 6:409–421, 1993.

[7] F.A.W. Wilson, S.P.O Scalaidhe, and P.S. Goldman-Rakic. Dissociation of object and spatial processing domains in primate prefrontal cortex. *Science*, 260:1955–1958, 1993.

[8] M.V. Tsodyks and M.V. Feigel'man. The enhanced storage capacity in neural networks with low activity level. *Europhys. Lett.*, 6:101 – 105, 1988.

[9] T.K. Tatemichi, M.A. Foulkes, J.P. Mohr, J.R. Hewitt, D. B. Hier, T.R. Price, and P.A. Wolf. Dementia in stroke survivors in the stroke data bank cohort. *Stroke*, 21:858–866, 1990.

[10] T. K. Tatemichi. How acute brain failure becomes chronic: a view of the mechanisms of dementia related to stroke. *Neurology*, 40:1652–1659, 1990.

Forward dynamic models in human motor control: Psychophysical evidence

Daniel M. Wolpert
wolpert@psyche.mit.edu

Zoubin Ghahramani
zoubin@psyche.mit.edu

Michael I. Jordan
jordan@psyche.mit.edu

Department of Brain & Cognitive Sciences
Massachusetts Institute of Technology
Cambridge, MA 02139

Abstract

Based on computational principles, with as yet no direct experimental validation, it has been proposed that the central nervous system (CNS) uses an internal model to simulate the dynamic behavior of the motor system in planning, control and learning (Sutton and Barto, 1981; Ito, 1984; Kawato et al., 1987; Jordan and Rumelhart, 1992; Miall et al., 1993). We present experimental results and simulations based on a novel approach that investigates the temporal propagation of errors in the sensorimotor integration process. Our results provide direct support for the existence of an internal model.

1 Introduction

The notion of an internal model, a system which mimics the behavior of a natural process, has emerged as an important theoretical concept in motor control (Jordan, 1995). There are two varieties of internal models—"forward models," which mimic the causal flow of a process by predicting its next state given the current state and the motor command, and "inverse models," which are anticausal, estimating the motor command that causes a particular state transition. Forward models—the focus of this article—have been been shown to be of potential use for solving four fundamental problems in computational motor control. First, the delays in most sensorimotor loops are large, making feedback control infeasible for rapid movements. By using a forward model for internal feedback the outcome of an action can be estimated and used before sensory feedback is available (Ito, 1984; Miall et al., 1993). Second, a forward model is a key ingredient in a system that uses motor outflow ("efference copy") to anticipate and cancel the reafferent sensory effects of self-movement (Gallistel, 1980; Robinson et al., 1986). Third, a forward model can be used to transform errors between the desired and actual sensory outcome of a movement into the corresponding errors in the motor command, thereby providing appropriate signals for motor learning (Jordan and Rumelhart, 1992). Similarly by predicting the sensory outcome of the action, without actually performing it, a forward model can be used in mental practice to learn to select between possible actions (Sutton and Barto, 1981). Finally, a forward model can be used for state estimation in which the model's prediction of the next state is combined with a reafferent sensory correction (Goodwin and Sin, 1984). Although shown to be of theoretical importance, the existence and use of an internal forward model in the CNS is still a major topic of debate.

When a subject moves his arm in the dark, he is able to estimate the visual location of his hand with some degree of accuracy. Observer models from engineering formalize the sources of information which the CNS could use to construct this estimate (Figure 1). This framework consists of a state estimation process (the observer) which is able to monitor both the inputs and outputs of the system. In particular, for the arm, the inputs are motor commands and the output is sensory feedback (e.g. vision and proprioception). There are three basic methods whereby the observer can estimate the current state (e.g. position and velocity) of the hand form these sources: It can make use of sensory inflow, it can make use of integrated motor outflow (dead reckoning), or it can combine these two sources of information via the use of a forward model.

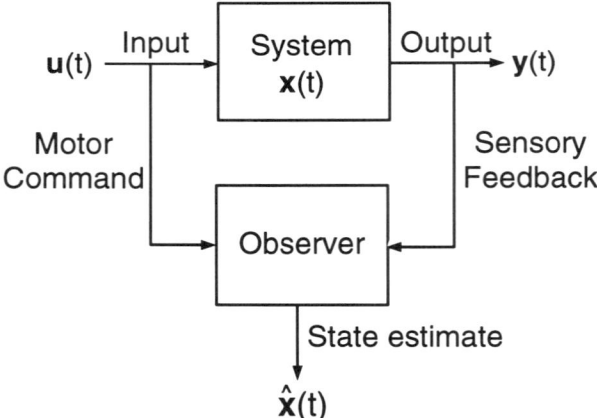

Figure 1. Observer model of state estimation.

2 State Estimation Experiment

To test between these possibilities, we carried out an experiment in which subjects made arm movements in the dark. The full details of the experiment are described in the Appendix. Three experimental conditions were studied, involving the use of null, assistive and resistive force fields. The subjects' internal estimate of hand location was assessed by asking them to localize visually the position of their hand at the end of the movement. The bias of this location estimate, plotted as a function of movement duration shows a consistent overestimation of the distance moved (Figure 2). This bias shows two distinct phases as a function of movement duration, an initial increase reaching a peak of 0.9 cm after one second followed by a sharp transition to a region of gradual decline. The variance of the estimate also shows an initial increase during the first second of movement after which it plateaus at about 2 cm^2. External forces had distinct effects on the bias and variance propagation. Whereas the bias was increased by the assistive force and decreased by the resistive force ($p < 0.05$), the variance was unaffected.

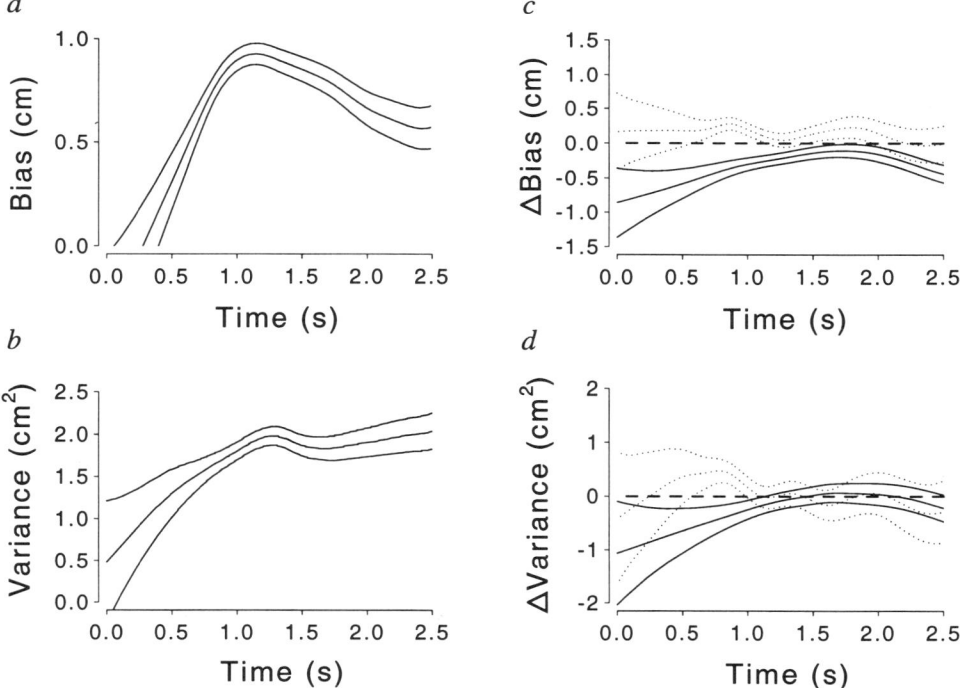

Figure 2. The propagation of the (a) bias and (b) variance of the state estimate is shown, with standard error lines, against movement duration. The differential effects on (c) bias and (d) variance of the external force, assistive (dotted lines) and resistive (solid lines), are also shown relative to zero (dashed line). A positive bias represents an overestimation of the distance moved.

3 Observer Model Simulation

These experimental results can be fully accounted for only if we assume that the motor control system integrates the efferent outflow and the reafferent sensory inflow. To establish this conclusion we have developed an explicit model of the sensorimotor integration process which contains as special cases all three of the methods referred to above. The model—a Kalman filter (Kalman and Bucy, 1961)—is a linear dynamical system that produces an estimate of the location of the hand by monitoring both the motor outflow and the feedback as sensed, in the absence of vision, solely by proprioception. Based on these sources of information the model estimates the arm's state, integrating sensory and motor signals to reduce the overall uncertainty in its estimate.

Representing the state of the hand at time t as $\mathbf{x}(t)$ (a 2×1 vector of position and velocity) acted on by a force $\mathbf{u} = [u_{\text{int}}, u_{\text{ext}}]^T$, combining both internal motor commands and external forces, the system dynamic equations can be written in the general form of

$$\dot{\mathbf{x}}(t) = A\mathbf{x}(t) + B\mathbf{u}(t) + \mathbf{w}(t), \tag{1}$$

where A and B are matrices with appropriate dimension. The vector $\mathbf{w}(t)$ represents the process of white noise with an associated covariance matrix given by $Q = E[\mathbf{w}(t)\mathbf{w}(t)^T]$. The system has an observable output $\mathbf{y}(t)$ which is linked to the actual hidden state $\mathbf{x}(t)$ by

$$\mathbf{y}(t) = C\mathbf{x}(t) + \mathbf{v}(t), \tag{2}$$

where C is a matrix with appropriate dimension and the vector $\mathbf{v}(t)$ represents the output white noise which has the associated covariance matrix $R = E[\mathbf{v}(t)\mathbf{v}(t)^T]$. In our paradigm, $\mathbf{y}(t)$ represents the proprioceptive signals (e.g. from muscle spindles and joint receptors).

In particular, for the hand we approximate the system dynamics by a damped point mass moving in one dimension acted on by a force $\mathbf{u}(t)$. Equation 1 becomes

$$\dot{\mathbf{x}}(t) = \begin{bmatrix} 0 & 1 \\ 0 & -\beta/m \end{bmatrix} \mathbf{x}(t) + \frac{1}{m} \begin{bmatrix} 0 & 0 \\ 1 & 1 \end{bmatrix} \mathbf{u}(t) + \mathbf{w}(t) \tag{3}$$

where the hand has mass m and damping coefficient β. We assume that this system is fully observable and choose C to be the identity matrix. The parameters in the simulation, $\beta = 3.9$ N·s/m, $m = 4$ kg and $u_{\text{int}} = 1.5$ N were chosen based on the mass of the arm and the observed relationship between time and distance traveled. The external force u_{ext} was set to -0.3, 0 and 0.3 N for the resistive, null and assistive conditions respectively. To end the movement the sign of the motor command u_{int} was reversed until the arm was stationary. Noise covariance matrices of $Q = 9.5 \times 10^{-5} I$ and $R = 3.3 \times 10^{-4} I$ were used representing a standard deviation of 1.0 cm for the position output noise and 1.8 cm s^{-1} for the position component of the state noise.

At time $t = 0$ the subject is given full view of his arm and, therefore, starts with an estimate $\hat{\mathbf{x}}(0) = \mathbf{x}(0)$ with zero bias and variance—we assume that vision calibrates the system. At this time the light is extinguished and the subject must rely on the inputs and outputs to estimate the system's state. The Kalman filter, using a model of the system $\hat{A}$, $\hat{B}$ and $\hat{C}$, provides an optimal linear estimator of the state given by

$$\dot{\hat{\mathbf{x}}}(t) = \underbrace{\hat{A}\hat{\mathbf{x}}(t) + \hat{B}\mathbf{u}(t)}_{\text{forward model}} + \underbrace{K(t)[\mathbf{y}(t) - \hat{C}\hat{\mathbf{x}}(t)]}_{\text{sensory correction}}$$

where $K(t)$ is the recursively updated gain matrix. The model is, therefore, a combination of two processes which together contribute to the state estimate. The first process uses the current state estimate and motor command to predict the next state by simulating the movement dynamics with a forward model. The second process uses the difference between actual and predicted reafferent sensory feedback to correct the state estimate resulting from the forward model. The relative contributions of the internal simulation and sensory correction processes to the final estimate are modulated by the Kalman gain matrix $K(t)$ so as to provide optimal state estimates. We used this state update equation to model the bias and variance propagation and the effects of the external force.

By making particular choices for the parameters of the Kalman filter, we are able to simulate dead reckoning, sensory inflow-based estimation, and forward model-based sensorimotor integration. Moreover, to accommodate the observation that subjects generally tend to overestimate the distance that their arm has moved, we set the gain that couples force to state estimates to a value that is larger than its veridical value; $\hat{B} = \dfrac{1}{m} \begin{bmatrix} 0 & 0 \\ 1.4 & 1.6 \end{bmatrix}$ while both $\hat{A}$ and $\hat{C}$ accurately reflected the true system. This is consistent with the independent data that subjects tend to under-reach in pointing tasks suggesting an overestimation of distance traveled (Soechting and Flanders, 1989).

Simulations of the Kalman filter demonstrate the two distinct phases of bias propagation observed (Figure 3). By overestimating the force acting on the arm the forward model overestimates the distance traveled, an integrative process eventually balanced by the sensory correction. The model also captures the differential effects on bias of the externally imposed forces. By overestimating an increased force under the assistive condition, the bias in the forward model accrues more rapidly and is balanced by the sensory feedback at a higher level. The converse applies to the resistive force. In accord with the experimental results the model predicts no change in variance under the two force conditions.

4 Discussion

We have shown that the Kalman filter is able to reproduce the propagation of the bias and variance of estimated position of the hand as a function of both movement duration and external forces. The Kalman filter also simulates the interesting and novel empirical result that while the variance asymptotes, the bias peaks after about one second and then gradually declines. This behavior is a consequence of a trade off between the inaccuracies accumulating in the internal simulation of the arm's dynamics and the feedback of actual sensory information. Simple models which do not trade off the contributions of a forward model with sensory feedback, such as those based purely on sensory inflow or on motor outflow, are unable to reproduce the observed pattern of bias and variance propagation. The ability of the Kalman filter to parsimoniously model our data suggests that the processes embodied in the

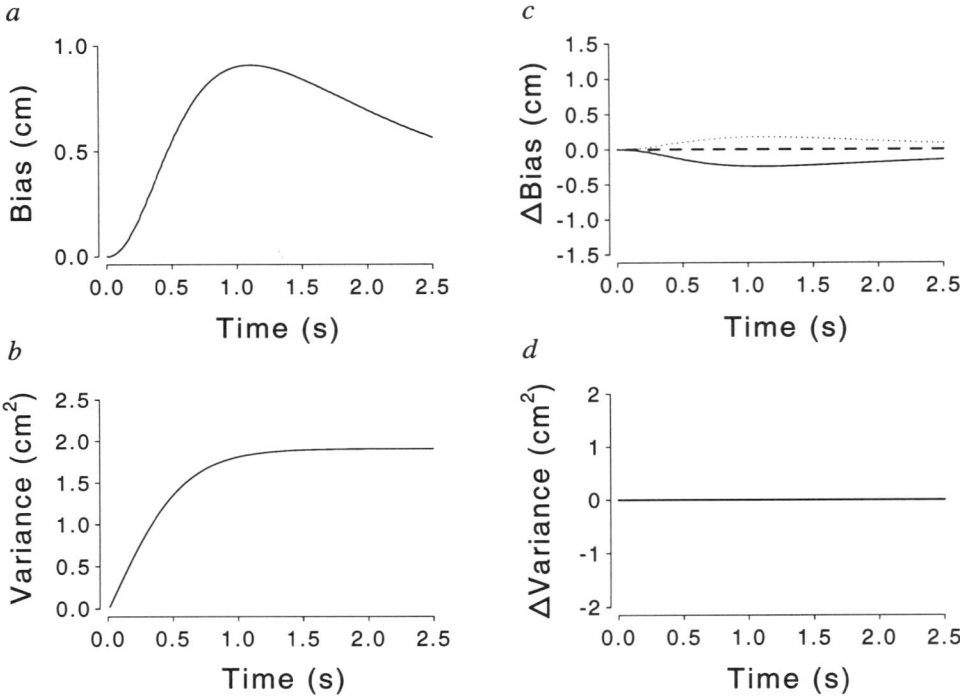

Figure 3. Simulated bias and variance propagation, in the same representation and scale as Figure 2, from a Kalman filter model of the sensorimotor integration process.

filter, namely internal simulation through a forward model together with sensory correction, are likely to be embodied in the sensorimotor integration process. We feel that the results of this state estimation study provide strong evidence that a forward model is used by the CNS in maintaining its estimate of the hand location. Furthermore, the state estimation paradigm provides a framework to study the sensorimotor integration process in both normal and patient populations. For example, the specific predictions of the sensorimotor integration model can be tested in both patients with sensory neuropathies, who lack proprioceptive reafference, and in patients with damage to the cerebellum, a proposed site for the forward model (Miall et al., 1993).

Acknowledgements

We thank Peter Dayan for suggestions about the manuscript. This project was supported by grants from the McDonnell-Pew Foundation, ATR Human Information Processing Research Laboratories, Siemens Corporation, and by grant N00014-94-1-0777 from the Office of Naval Research. Daniel M. Wolpert and Zoubin Ghahramani are McDonnell-Pew Fellows in Cognitive Neuroscience. Michael I. Jordan is a NSF Presidential Young Investigator.

Appendix: Experimental Paradigm

To investigate the way in which errors in the state estimate change over time and with external forces we used a setup (Figure 4) consisting of a combination of planar virtual visual feedback with a two degree of freedom torque motor driven manipulandum (Faye, 1986). The subject held a planar manipulandum on which his thumb was mounted. The manipulandum was used both to accurately measure the position of the subject's thumb and also, using the torque motors, to constrain the hand to move along a line across the subject's body. A projector was used to create virtual images in the plane of the movement by projecting a computer VGA screen onto a horizontal rear projection screen suspended above the manipulandum. A horizontal semi-silvered mirror was placed midway between the screen and manipulandum. The subject viewed the reflected image of the rear projection screen by looking down at the mirror; all projected images, therefore, appeared to be in the plane of the thumb, independent of head position.

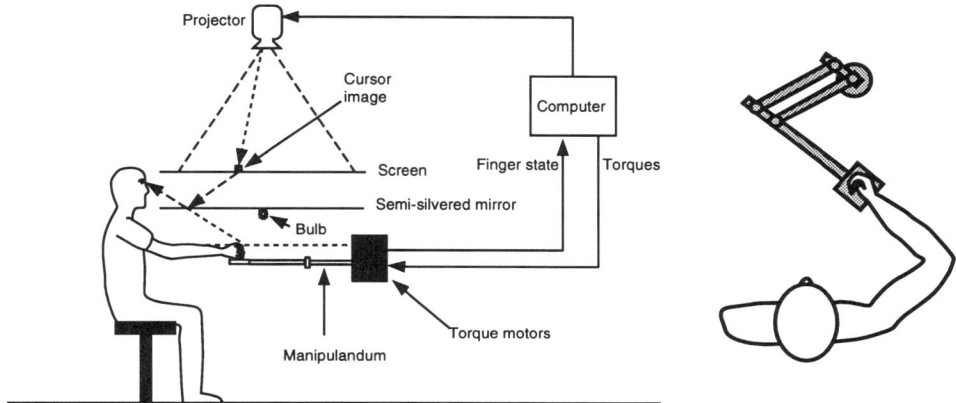

Figure 4. Experimental Setup

Eight subjects participated and performed 300 trials each. Each trial started with the subject visually placing his thumb at a target square projected randomly on the movement line. The arm was then illuminated for two seconds, thereby allowing the subject to perceive visually his initial arm configuration. The light was then extinguished leaving just the initial target. The subject was then required to move his hand either to the left or right, as indicated by an arrow in the initial starting square. This movement was made in the absence of visual feedback of arm configuration. The subject was instructed to move until he heard a tone at which point he stopped. The timing of the tone was controlled to produce a uniform distribution of path lengths from 0–30 cm. During this movement the subject either moved in a randomly selected null or constant assistive or resistive 0.3N force field generated by the torque motors. Although it is not possible to directly probe a subject's internal representation of the state of his arm, we can examine a function of this state—the estimated visual location of the thumb. (The relationship between the state of the arm and the visual coordinates of the hand is known as the kinematic transformation; Craig, 1986.) Therefore, once at rest the subject indicated the visual estimate of his unseen thumb position using a trackball, held in his other hand, to move a cursor projected in the plane of the thumb along the movement line. The discrepancy between the actual and visual estimate of thumb location was recorded as a measure of the state estimation error. The bias and variance propagation of the state estimate was analyzed as a function of movement duration and external forces. A generalized additive model (Hastie and Tibshirani, 1990) with smoothing splines (five effective degrees of freedom) was fit to the bias and variance as a function of final position, movement duration and the interaction of the two forces with movement duration, simultaneously for main effects and for each subject. This procedure factors out the additive effects specific to each subject and, through the final position factor, the position-dependent inaccuracies in the kinematic transformation.

References

Craig, J. (1986). *Introduction to robotics.* Addison-Wesley, Reading, MA.

Faye, I. (1986). *An impedence controlled manipulandum for human movement studies.* MS Thesis, MIT Dept. Mechanical Engineering, Cambridge, MA.

Gallistel, C. (1980). *The organization of action: A new synthesis.* Erlbaum, Hilladale, NJ.

Goodwin, G. and Sin, K. (1984). *Adaptive filtering prediction and control.* Prentice-Hall, Englewood Cliffs, NJ.

Hastie, T. and Tibshirani, R. (1990). *Generalized Additive Models.* Chapman and Hall, London.

Ito, M. (1984). *The cerebellum and neural control.* Raven Press, New York.

Jordan, M. and Rumelhart, D. (1992). Forward models: Supervised learning with a distal teacher. *Cognitive Science*, 16:307–354.

Jordan, M. I. (1995). Computational aspects of motor control and motor learning. In Heuer, H. and Keele, S., editors, *Handbook of Perception and Action: Motor Skills.* Academic Press, New York.

Kalman, R. and Bucy, R. S. (1961). New results in linear filtering and prediction. *Journal of Basic Engineering (ASME)*, 83D:95–108.

Kawato, M., Furawaka, K., and Suzuki, R. (1987). A hierarchical neural network model for the control and learning of voluntary movements. *Biol. Cybern.*, 56:1–17.

Miall, R., Weir, D., Wolpert, D., and Stein, J. (1993). Is the cerebellum a Smith Predictor? *Journal of Motor Behavior*, 25(3):203–216.

Robinson, D., Gordon, J., and Gordon, S. (1986). A model of the smooth pursuit eye movement system. *Biol. Cybern.*, 55:43–57.

Soechting, J. and Flanders, M. (1989). Sensorimotor representations for pointing to targets in three- dimensional space. *J. Neurophysiol.*, 62:582–594.

Sutton, R. and Barto, A. (1981). Toward a modern theory of adaptive networks: expectation and prediction. *Psychol. Rev.*, 88:135–170.

A solvable connectionist model of immediate recall of ordered lists

Neil Burgess
Department of Anatomy, University College London
London WC1E 6BT, England
(e-mail: n.burgess@ucl.ac.uk)

Abstract

A model of short-term memory for serially ordered lists of verbal stimuli is proposed as an implementation of the 'articulatory loop' thought to mediate this type of memory (Baddeley, 1986). The model predicts the presence of a repeatable time-varying 'context' signal coding the timing of items' presentation in addition to a store of phonological information and a process of serial rehearsal. Items are associated with context nodes and phonemes by Hebbian connections showing both short and long term plasticity. Items are activated by phonemic input during presentation and reactivated by context and phonemic feedback during output. Serial selection of items occurs via a winner-take-all interaction amongst items, with the winner subsequently receiving decaying inhibition. An approximate analysis of error probabilities due to Gaussian noise during output is presented. The model provides an explanatory account of the probability of error as a function of serial position, list length, word length, phonemic similarity, temporal grouping, item and list familiarity, and is proposed as the starting point for a model of rehearsal and vocabulary acquisition.

1 Introduction

Short-term memory for serially ordered lists of pronounceable stimuli is well described, at a crude level, by the idea of an 'articulatory loop' (AL). This postulates that information is phonologically encoded and decays within 2 seconds unless refreshed by serial rehearsal, see (Baddeley, 1986). It successfully accounts for (i) the linear relationship between memory span s (the number of items s such that 50% of lists of s items are correctly recalled) and articulation rate r (the number of items that can be said per second) in which $s \approx 2r + c$, where r varies as a function of the items, language and development; (ii) the fact that span is lower for lists of phonemically similar items than phonemically distinct ones; (iii) unattended speech and articulatory distractor tasks (e.g. saying blah-blah-blah...) both reduce memory span. Recent evidence suggests that the AL plays a role in the learning of new words both during development and during recovery after brain traumas, see e.g. (Gathercole & Baddeley, 1993). Positron emission tomography studies indicate that the phonological store is localised in the left supramarginal gyrus, whereas subvocal rehearsal involves Broca's area and some of the motor areas involved in speech planning and production (Paulesu et al., 1993).

However, the detail of the types of errors committed is not addressed by the AL idea. Principally: (iv) the majority of errors are 'order errors' rather than 'item errors', and tend to involve transpositions of neighbouring or phonemically similar items; (v) the probability of correctly recalling a list as a function of list length is a sigmoid; (vi) the probability of correctly recalling an item as a function of its serial position in the list (the 'serial position curve') has a bowed shape; (vii) span increases with the familiarity of the items used, specifically the c in $s \approx 2r + c$ can increase from 0 to 2.5 (see (Hulme et al., 1991)), and also increases if a list has been previously presented (the 'Hebb effect'); (viii) 'position specific intrusions' occur, in which an item from a previous list is recalled at the same position in the current list. Taken together, these data impose strong functional constraints on any neural mechanism implementing the AL.

Most models showing serial behaviour rely on some form of 'chaining' mechanism which associates previous states to successive states, via recurrent connections of various types. Chaining of item or phoneme representations generates errors that are incompatible with human data, particularly (iv) above, see (Burgess & Hitch, 1992, Henson, 1994). Here items are maintained in serial order by association to a repeatable time-varying signal (which is suggested by position specific intrusions and is referred to below as 'context'), and by the recovery from suppression involved in the selection process – a modification of the 'competitive queuing' model for speech production (Houghton, 1990). The characteristics of STM for serially ordered items arise due to the way that context and phoneme information prompts the selection of each item.

2 The model

The model consists of 3 layers of artificial neurons representing context, phonemes and items respectively, connected by Hebbian connections with long and short term plasticity, see Fig. 1. There is a winner-take-all (WTA) interaction between item nodes: at each time step the item with the greatest input is given activation 1, and the others 0. The winner at the end of each time step receives a decaying inhibition that prevents it from being selected twice consecutively.

During **presentation**, phoneme nodes are activated by acoustic or (translated) visual input, activation in the context layer follows the pattern shown in Fig. 1, item nodes receive input from phoneme nodes via connections w_{ij}. Connections

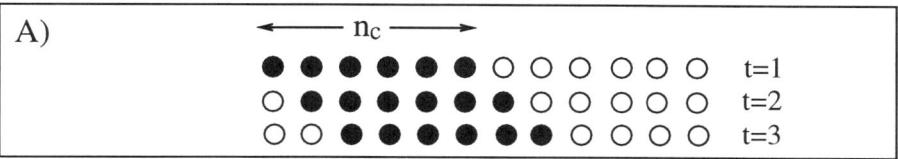

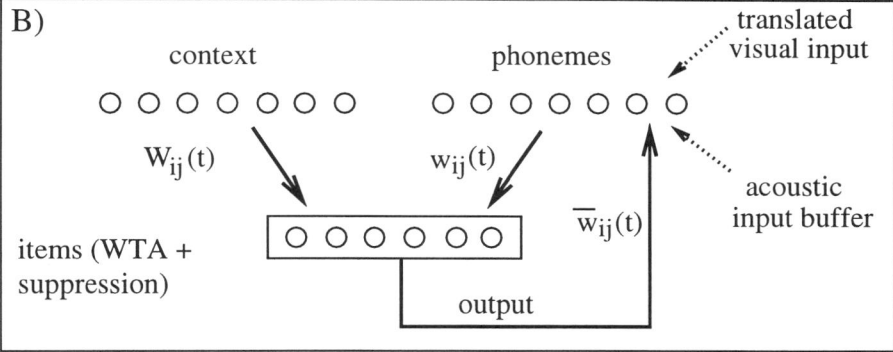

Figure 1: A) Context states as a function of serial position t; filled circles are active nodes, empty circles are inactive nodes. B) The architecture of the model. Full lines are connections with short and long term plasticity; dashed lines are routes by which information enters the model.

$W_{ij}(t)$ learn the association between the context state and the winning item, and w_{ij} and $\bar{w}_{ij}$ learn the association with the active phonemes. During **recall**, the context layer is re-activated as in presentation, activation spreads to the item layer (via $W_{ij}(t)$) where one item wins and activates its phonemes (via $\bar{w}_{ij}(t)$). The item that now wins, given both context and phoneme inputs, is **output**, and then suppressed.

As described so far, the model makes no errors. Errors occur when Gaussian noise is added to items' activations during the selection of the winning item to be output. Errors are likely when there are many items with similar activation levels due to decay of connection weights and inhibition since presentation. Items may then be selected in the wrong order, and performance will decrease with the time taken to present or recall a list.

2.1 Learning and familiarity

Connection weights have both long and short term plasticity: $W_{ij}(t)$ (similarly $w_{ij}(t)$ and $\bar{w}_{ij}(t)$) have an incremental long term component $W_{ij}^l(t)$, and a one-shot short term component $W_{ij}^s(t)$ which decays by a factor Δ per second. The net weight of the connection is the sum of the two components: $W_{ij}(t) = W_{ij}^l(t) + W_{ij}^s(t)$. Learning occurs according to:

$$W_{ij}^s(t+1) = \begin{cases} c_j(t)a_i(t) & \text{if } c_j(t)a_i(t) > W_{ij}(t); \\ W_{ij}^s(t) & \text{otherwise,} \end{cases}$$

$$W_{ij}^{\ell}(t+1) = \begin{cases} W_{ij}^{\ell}(t) + \varepsilon c_j(t)a_i(t) & \text{if } c_j(t)a_i(t) > 0; \\ W_{ij}^{\ell}(t) & \text{otherwise,} \end{cases} \qquad (1)$$

where $c_j(t)$ and $a_i(t)$ are the pre- and post-connection activations, and ε decreases with $|W_{ij}^{\ell}(t)|$ so that the long term component saturates at some maximum value. These modifiable connection weights are never negative.

An item's 'familiarity' is reflected by the size of the long term components w_{ij}^{ℓ} and $\bar{w}_{ij}^{\ell}$ of the weights storing the association with its phonemes. These components increase with each (error-free) presentation or recall of the item. For lists of totally unfamiliar items, the item nodes are completely interchangeable having only the short-term connections $\bar{w}_{ij}^{s}$ to phoneme nodes that are learned at presentation. Whereas the presentation of a familiar item leads to the selection of a particular item node (due to the weights w_{ij}^{ℓ}) and, during output, this item will activate its phonemes more strongly due to the weights $\bar{w}_{ij}^{\ell}$. Unfamiliar items that are phonemically similar to a familiar item will tend to be represented by the familiar item node, and can take advantage of its long-term item-phoneme weights $\bar{w}_{ij}^{\ell}$.

Presentation of a list leads to an increase in the long term component of the context-item association. Thus, if the same list is presented more than once its recall improves, and position specific intrusions from previous lists may also occur. Notice that only weights to or from an item winning at presentation or output are increased.

3 Details

There are n_w items per list, n_p phonemes per item, and a phoneme takes time ℓ_p seconds to present or recall. At time t, item node i has activation $a_i(t)$, context node i has activation $c_i(t)$, C_t is the set of n_c context nodes active at time t, phoneme node i has activation $b_i(t)$ and $\mathcal{P}_i$ is the set of n_p phonemes comprising item i.

Context nodes have activation 0 or $\sqrt{3/2n_c}$, phonemes take activation 0 or $1/\sqrt{n_p}$, so $W_{ij}^{s}(t) \leq \sqrt{3/2n_c}$ and $w_{ij}^{s}(t) = \bar{w}_{ji}^{s}(t) \leq 1/\sqrt{n_p}$, see (1). This sets the relative effect that context and phoneme layers have on items' activation, and ensures that items of neither few nor many phonemes are favoured, see (Burgess & Hitch, 1992). The long-term components of phoneme-item weights $w_{ij}^{\ell}(t)$ and $\bar{w}_{ji}^{\ell}(t)$ are $0.45/\sqrt{n_p}$ for familiar items, and $0.15/\sqrt{n_p}$ for unfamiliar items (chosen to match the data in Fig. 3B). The long-term components of context-item weights $W_{ij}^{\ell}(t)$ increase by $0.15/\sqrt{n_c}$ for each of the first few presentations or recalls of a list.

Apart from the WTA interaction, each item node i has input:

$$h_i(t) = E_i(t) + I_i(t) + \eta_i, \qquad (2)$$

where $I_i(t) < 0$ is a decaying inhibition imposed following an item's selection at presentation or output (see below), η_i is a $(0, \sigma)$ Gaussian random variable added at output only, and $E_i(t)$ is the excitatory input to the item from the phoneme layer during presentation and the context and phoneme layers during recall:

$$E_i(t) = \begin{cases} \sum_j w_{ij}(t)b_j(t) & \text{during presentation;} \\ \sum_j W_{ij}(t)c_j(t) + w_{ij}(t)b_j(t) & \text{during recall.} \end{cases} \qquad (3)$$

During recall phoneme nodes are activated according to $b_i(t) = \sum_j \bar{w}_{ij}(t)a_j(t)$.

One time step refers to the presentation or recall of an item and has duration $n_p \ell_p$. The variable t increases by 1 per time step, and refers to both time and serial position. Short term connection weights and inhibition $I_i(t)$ decay by a factor Δ per second, or $\Delta^{n_p \ell_p}$ per time step.

The algorithm is as follows; rehearsal corresponds to repeating the recall phase.

Presentation
0. Set activations, inhibitions and short term weights to zero, $t = 1$.
1. Set the context layer to state $\mathcal{C}_t : c_i(t) = \sqrt{3/2n_c}$ if $i \in \mathcal{C}_t$; $c_i(t) = 0$ otherwise.
2. Input items, i.e. set the phoneme layer to state $\mathcal{P}_t : b_i(t) = 1/\sqrt{n_p}$ if $i \in \mathcal{P}_t$; $b_i(t) = 0$ otherwise.
3. Select the winning item, i.e. $a_k(t) = 1$ where $h_k(t) = \max_i\{h_i(t)\}$; $a_i(t) = 0$, for $i \neq k$.
4. Learning, i.e. increment all connection weights according to (1).
5. Decay, i.e. multiply short-term connection weights $W_{ij}^s(t)$, $w_{ij}^s(t)$ and $\bar{w}_{ij}^s(t)$, and inhibitions $I_i(t)$ by a factor $\Delta^{n_p \ell_p}$.
6. Inhibit winner, i.e. set $I_k(t) = -2$, where k is the item selected in 3.
7. $t \to t + 1$, go to 1.

Recall
0. $t = 1$.
1. Set the context layer to state $\mathcal{C}_t$, as above.
2. Set all phoneme activations to zero.
3. Select the winning item, as above.
4. Output. Activate phonemes via $\bar{w}_{ji}(t)$, select the winning item (in the presence of noise).
5. Learning, as above.
6. Decay, as above.
7. Inhibit winner, i.e. set $I_k(t) = -2$, where k is the item selected in 4.
8. $t \to t + 1$, go to 1.

4 Analysis

The output of the model, averaged over many trials, depends on (i) the activation values of all items at the output step for each time t and, (ii) given these activations and the noise level, the probability of each item being the winner. Estimation is necessary since there is no simple exact expression for (ii), and (i) depends on which items were output prior to time t.

I define $\gamma(t, i)$ to be the time elapsed, by output at time t, since item i was last selected (at presentation or output), i.e. in the absence of errors:

$$\gamma(t,i) = \begin{cases} (t-i)\ell_p n_p & \text{if } i < t; \\ (n_w - (i-t))\ell_p n_p & \text{if } i \geq t. \end{cases} \quad (4)$$

If there have been no prior errors, then at time t the inhibition of item i is $I_i(t) = -2(\Delta)^{\gamma(t,i+1)}$, and short term weights to and from item i have decayed by a factor $\Delta^{\gamma(t,i)}$. For a novel list of familiar items, the excitatory input to item i during output at time t is, see (3):

$$E_i(t) = 3\Delta^{\gamma(t,i)}||\mathcal{C}_i \cap \mathcal{C}_t||/2n_c + (0.45 + \Delta^{\gamma(t,i)})^2||\mathcal{P}_i \cap \mathcal{P}_t||/n_p, \quad (5)$$

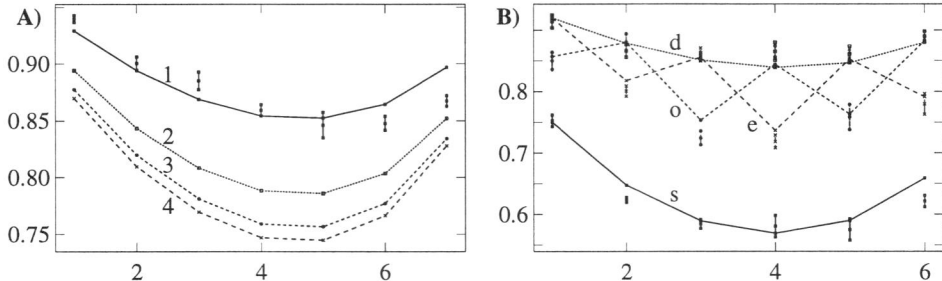

Figure 2: Serial position curves. Full lines show the estimation, extra markers are error bars at one standard deviation of 5 simulations of 1,000 trials each, see §5 for parameter values. A) Rehearsal. Four consecutive recalls of a list of 7 digits ('1',..,'4'). B) Phonemic similarity. SPCs are shown for lists of dissimilar letters ('d'), similar letters ('s'), and alternating similar and dissimilar letters with the similar ones in odd ('o') and even ('e') positions. C.f. (Baddeley, 1968, expt. V).

where $||\mathcal{X}||$ is the number of elements in set $\mathcal{X}$.

The probability $p(t, i)$ that item i wins at time t is estimated by the softmax function(Brindle, 1990):

$$p(t,i) \approx \frac{\exp(m_i(t)/\sigma')}{\sum_{j=1}^{n_w} \exp(m_j(t)/\sigma')}, \qquad (6)$$

where $m_i(t)$ is $h_i(t)$ without the noise term, see (2-3), and $\sigma' = 0.75\sigma$. For $\sigma = 0.5$ (the value used below), the r.m.s. difference between $p(t, i)$ estimated by simulation (500 trials) and by (6) is always less than 0.035 for $-1 < m_i(t) < 1$ with 2 to 6 items.

Which items have been selected prior to time t affects $I_i(t)$ in $h_i(t)$ via $\gamma(t, i)$. $p(t, i)$ is estimated for all combinations of up to two prior errors using (6) with appropriate values of $m_i(t)$, and the average, weighted by the probability of each error combination, is used. The 'missing' probability corresponding to more than two prior errors is corrected for by normalising $p(t, i)$ so that $\sum_i p(t, i) = 1$ for $t = 1, .., n_w$. This overestimates the recency effect, especially in super-span lists.

5 Performance

The parameter values used are $\Delta = 0.75$, $n_c = 6$, $\sigma = 0.5$. Different types of item are modelled by varying (n_p, ℓ_p) : 'digits' correspond to (2,0.15), 'letters' to (2,0.2), and 'words' to (5,0.15-0.3). 'Similar' items all have 1 phoneme in common, dissimilar items have none. Unless indicated otherwise, items are dissimilar and familiar, see §3 for how familiarity is modelled. The size of σ relative to Δ is set so that digit span ≈ 7. n_p and ℓ_p are such that approximately 7 digits can be said in 2 seconds.

The model's performance is shown in Figs. 2 and 3. Fig. 2A: the increase in the long-term component of context-item connections during rehearsal brings stability after a small number of rehearsals, i.e. no further errors are committed. Fig. 2B: serial position curves show the correct effect of phonemic similarity among items.

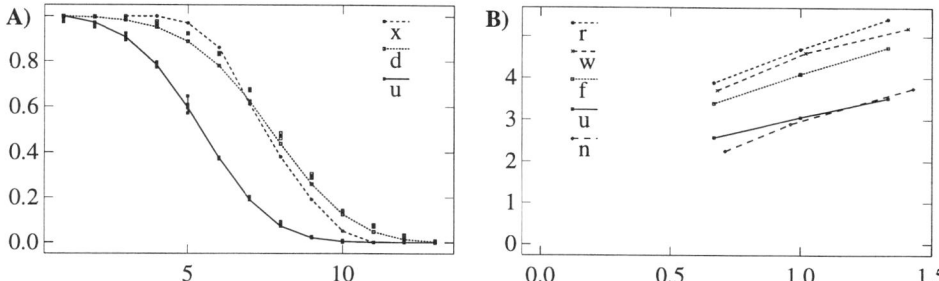

Figure 3: Item span. Full lines show the estimation, extra markers (A only) are error bars at one standard deviation of 3 simulations of 1,000 trials each, see §5 and §3 for parameter values. A) The probability of correctly recalling a whole list versus list length. Lists of digits ('d'), unfamiliar items (of the same length, 'u'), and experimental data on digits (adapted from (Guildford & Dallenbach, 1925), 'x') are shown. B) Span versus articulation rate (rate= $1/\ell_p n_p$, with $n_p = 5$ and ℓ_p =0.15,0.2, and 0.3). Calculated curves are shown for novel lists of familiar ('f') and unfamiliar ('u') words and lists of familiar words after 5 repetitions ('r'). Data on recall of words ('w') and non-words ('n') are also shown, adapted from (Hulme et al., 1991).

Fig. 3A: the probability of recalling a list correctly as a function of list length shows the correct sigmoidal relationship. Fig. 3B: item span shows the correct, approximately linear, relationship to articulation rate, with span for unfamiliar items below that for familiar items. Span increases with repeated presentations of a list in accordance with the 'Hebb effect'. Note that span is slightly overestimated for short lists of very long words.

5.1 Discussion and relation to previous work

This model is an extension of (Burgess & Hitch, 1992), primarily to model effects of rehearsal and item and list familiarity by allowing connection weights to show plasticity over different timescales, and secondly to show recency and phonemic similarity effects simultaneously by changing the way phoneme nodes are activated during recall. Note that the 'context' timing signal varies with serial position: reflecting the rhythm of presentation rather than absolute time (indeed the effect of temporal grouping can be modelled by modifying the context representations to reflect the presence of pauses during presentation (Hitch et al., 1995)), so presentation and recall rates cannot be varied.

The decaying inhibition that follows an items selection increases the locality of errors, i.e. if item $i+1$ replaces item i, then item i is most likely to replace item $i+1$ in turn (rather than e.g. item $i+2$). The model has two remaining problems: (i) selecting an item node to form the long term representation of a new item, without taking over existing item nodes, and (ii) learning the correct order of the phonemes within an item – a possible extension to address this problem is presented in (Hartley & Houghton, 1995).

The mechanism for selecting items is a modification of competitive queuing

(Houghton, 1990) in that the WTA interaction occurs at the item layer, rather than in an extra layer, so that only the winner is active and gets associated to context and phoneme nodes (this avoids partial associations of a context state to all items similar to the winner, which would prevent the zig-zag curves in Fig. 2B). The basic selection mechanism is sufficient to store serial order in itself, since items recover from suppression in the same order in which they were selected at presentation. The model maps onto the articulatory loop idea in that the selection mechanism corresponds to part of the speech production ('articulation') system and the phoneme layer corresponds to the 'phonological store', and predicts that a 'context' timing signal is also present. Both the phoneme and context inputs to the item layer serve to increase span, and in addition, the former causes phonemic similarity effects and the latter causes recency, position specific intrusions and temporal grouping effects.

6 Conclusion

I have proposed a simple mechanism for the storage and recall of serially ordered lists of items. The distribution of errors predicted by the model can be estimated mathematically and models a very wide variety of experimental data. By virtue of long and short term plasticity of connection weights, the model begins to address familiarity and the role of rehearsal in vocabulary acquisition. Many of the predicted error probabilities have not yet been checked experimentally: they are predictions. However, the major prediction of this model, and of (Burgess & Hitch, 1992), is that, in addition to a short-term store of phonological information and a process of sub-vocal rehearsal, STM for ordered lists of verbal items involves a third component which provides a repeatable time-varying signal reflecting the rhythm of the items' presentation.

Acknowledgements: I am grateful for discussions with Rik Henson and Graham Hitch regarding data, and with Tom Hartley and George Houghton regarding error probabilities, and to Mike Page for suggesting the use of the softmax function. This work was supported by a Royal Society University Research Fellowship.

References

Baddeley A D (1968) *Quarterly Journal of Experimental Psychology* **20** 249-264.
Baddeley A D (1986) *Working Memory*, Clarendon Press.
Brindle, J S (1990) in: D S Touretzky (ed.) *Advances in Neural Information Processing Systems 2*. San Mateo, CA: Morgan Kaufmann.
Burgess N & Hitch G J (1992) *J. Memory and Language* **31** 429-460.
Gathercole S E & Baddeley A D (1993) *Working memory and language*, Erlbaum.
Guildford J P & Dallenbach K M (1925) *American J. of Psychology* **36** 621-628.
Hartley T & Houghton G (1995) *J. Memory and Language* to be published.
Henson R (1994) Tech. Report, M.R.C. Applied Psychology Unit, Cambridge, U.K.
Hitch G, Burgess N, Towse J & Culpin V (1995) *Quart. J. of Exp. Psychology*, submitted.
Houghton G (1990) in: R Dale, C Mellish & M Zock (eds.), *Current Research in Natural Language Generation* 287-319. London: Academic Press.
Hulme C, Maughan S & Brown G D A (1991) *J. Memory and Language* **30** 685-701.
Paulesu E, Frith C D & Frackowiak R S J (1993) *Nature* **362** 342-344.

PART II
NEUROSCIENCE

A Model for Chemosensory Reception

Rainer Malaka, Thomas Ragg
Institut für Logik, Komplexität und Deduktionssysteme
Universität Karlsruhe, PO Box
D-76128 Karlsruhe, Germany
e-mail: malaka@ira.uka.de, ragg@ira.uka.de

Martin Hammer
Institut für Neurobiologie
Freie Universität Berlin
D-14195 Berlin, Germany
e-mail: mhammer@castor.zedat.fu-berlin.de

Abstract

A new model for chemosensory reception is presented. It models reactions between odor molecules and receptor proteins and the activation of second messenger by receptor proteins. The mathematical formulation of the reaction kinetics is transformed into an artificial neural network (ANN). The resulting feed-forward network provides a powerful means for parameter fitting by applying learning algorithms. The weights of the network corresponding to chemical parameters can be trained by presenting experimental data. We demonstrate the simulation capabilities of the model with experimental data from honey bee chemosensory neurons. It can be shown that our model is sufficient to rebuild the observed data and that simpler models are not able to do this task.

1 INTRODUCTION

Terrestrial animals, vertebrates and invertebrates, have developed very similar solutions for the problem of recognizing volatile substances [Vogt *et al.*, 1989]. Odor molecules bind to receptor proteins (receptor sites) at the cell membrane of the sensory cell. This interaction of odor molecules and receptor proteins activates a G-protein mediated second

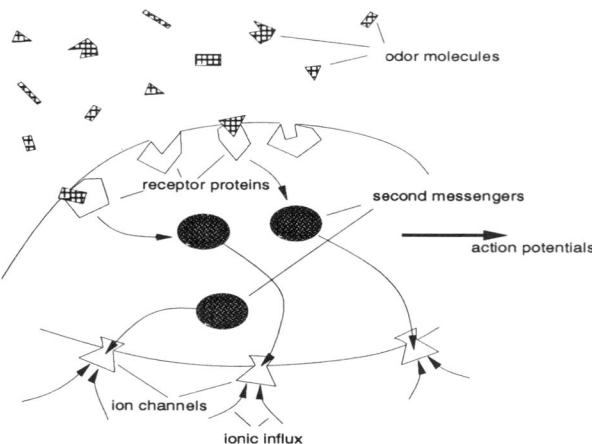

Figure 1: Reaction cascade in chemosensory neurons. Volatile odor molecules reach receptor proteins at the surface of the chemosensory neuron. The odor bound binding proteins activate second messengers (e.g. G-proteins). The activated second messengers cause a change in the conductivity of ion channels. Through ionic influx a depolarization can build an action potential.

messenger process. The concentrations of cAMP or IP_3 rise rapidly and activate cyclic-nucleotide-gated ion channels or IP_3-gated ion channels [Breer et al., 1989, Shepherd, 1991]. As a result of this second messenger reaction cascade the conductivity of ion channels is changed and the cell can be hyperpolarized or depolarized, which can cause the generation of action potentials. It has been shown that one odor is able to activate different second messenger processes and that there is some interaction between the different second messenger processes [Breer & Boekhoff, 1992].

Figure 1 shows schematically the cascade of reactions from odor molecules over receptor proteins and second messengers up to the changing of ion channel conductance and the generation of action potentials.

Responses of sensory neurons can be very complex. The response as a function of the odor concentration is highly non-linear. The response to mixtures can be synergistic or inhibitory relative to the response to the components of the compound. A synergistic effect occurs, if the response of one sensory cell to a binary mixture of two odors A_1 and A_2 with concentrations $[A_1]$, $[A_2]$ is higher than the sum of the responses to the odors A_1, A_2 at concentrations $[A_1]$, $[A_2]$ alone. An inhibitory effect occurs, if the response to the mixture is smaller than either response to the single odors. In bee subplacode and placode recordings both effects can be observed [Akers & Getz, 1993].

Models of chemosensory reception should be complex enough to simulate the inhibitory and synergistic effects observed in sensory neurons, and they must provide a means for parameter fitting. We want to introduce a computational model which is constructed analogously to the chemical reaction cascade in the sensory neuron. The model can be expressed as an ANN and all unknown parameters can be trained with a learning algorithm.

2 THE RECEPTOR TRANSDUCER MODEL

The first step of odor reception is done by receptor proteins located at the cell membrane. There may be many receptor protein types in sensory cells at different concentrations and with different sensitivity to various odors. There is the possibility for different odors ligands A_i to react with a receptor protein R_j, but it is also possible for a single odor to react with different receptor proteins.

The second step is the activation of second messengers. Ennis proposed a modelling of these complex reactions by a reaction step of activated odor-receptor complexes with transducer mechanisms [Ennis, 1991]. These transducers are a simplification of the second messengers processes. In Ennis' model transducers and receptor proteins are odor specific. We generalize Ennis' model by introducing transducer mechanisms T_k that can be activated by odor-receptor complexes, and as with odors and receptor proteins we allow receptor proteins and transducers to react in any combination. Receptor proteins and transducer proteins are not required to be odor specific.

The kinetics of the two reactions are given by

$$\begin{aligned} A_i + R_j &\rightleftharpoons A_i R_j \\ A_i R_j + T_k &\rightleftharpoons A_i R_j T_k \end{aligned} \quad (1)$$

In a first reaction odor ligands A_i bind to receptor proteins R_j and build odor-receptor complexes $A_i R_j$, which can activate transducer mechanisms T_k in a second reaction.

Affinities k_{ij} and l_{jk} describe the possibility of reactions between odor ligands A_i and receptor proteins R_j or between odor-receptor complexes $A_i R_j$ and transducers T_k, respectively. The mass action equations are

$$\begin{aligned}{} [A_i R_j] &= k_{ij}[A_i][R_j] \\ [A_i R_j T_k] &= l_{jk}[A_i R_j][T_k] \end{aligned} \quad (2)$$

The binding of odor-receptor complexes with transducer mechanisms is not dependent on the specific odor which is bound to the receptor protein, i.e. l_{jk} does not depend on i. It is only necessary that the receptor protein is bound.

A sensory neuron can now be defined by the total concentration (or amount) of receptor proteins $[\hat{R}]$ and transducers $[\hat{T}]$. The total concentration of either type corresponds to the sum of the free sites and the bound sites:

$$[\hat{R}_j] = [R_j] + \sum_i [A_i R_j] \quad (3)$$

$$[\hat{T}_k] = [T_k] + \sum_{i,j} [A_i R_j T_k] \,.^1 \quad (4)$$

Activated transducer mechanisms may elicit an excitatory or inhibitory effect depending on the kind of ion channel they open. Thus we divide the transducers T_k into two types: inhibitory and excitatory transducers. With

$$\delta_k = \begin{cases} +1 & \text{, if transducer } T_k \text{ is excitatory} \\ -1 & \text{, if transducer } T_k \text{ is inhibitory} \end{cases} \quad (5)$$

---

[1] We use the simplification $[\hat{R}_j] = [R_j] + \sum_i [A_i R_j]$ instead of $[\hat{R}_j] = [R_j] + \sum_i [A_i R_j] + \sum_{i,k} [A_i R_j T_k]$, which is sufficient for $[\hat{R}_j] \gg [\hat{T}_k]$, see also [Malaka & Ragg, 1993].

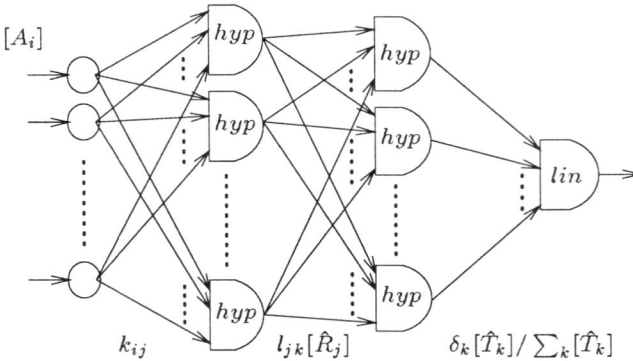

Figure 2: ANN equivalent to the full receptor-transducer model. The input layer corresponds to the concentration of odor ligands $[A_i]$, the first hidden layer to activated receptor protein types, the second to activated transducer mechanisms. The output neuron computes the effect E of the sensory cell.

the effect can be set to the sum of all activated excitatory transducers minus the sum of all inhibitory transducers relative to the total amount of transducers. An additive constant θ is used to model spontaneous reactions. With this the effect of an odor can be set to

$$E = \left(\sum_k \delta_k \sum_{i,j} [A_i R_j T_k] \right) / \left(\sum_k [\hat{T}_k] \right) + \theta . \qquad (6)$$

With Eqs.(2,4) and the hyperbolic function $\mathrm{hyp}(x) = x/(1+x)$ the effect E defined in Eq.(6) can be reformulated to

$$E = \frac{1}{\sum_k [\hat{T}_k]} \sum_k \mathrm{hyp} \left(\sum_{i,j} l_{jk}[A_i R_j] \right) \delta_k [\hat{T}_k] + \theta . \qquad (7)$$

Analogously, we eliminate $[A_i R_j]$ and $[R_j]$:

$$E = \frac{1}{\sum_k [\hat{T}_k]} \sum_k \mathrm{hyp} \left(\sum_j l_{jk}[\hat{R}_j] \mathrm{hyp} \left(\sum_i k_{ij}[A_i] \right) \right) \delta_k [\hat{T}_k] + \theta . \qquad (8)$$

Equation (8) can now be regarded as an ANN with 4 feed-forward layers. The concentrations of the odor ligands $[A_i]$ represent the input layer, the two hidden layers correspond to activated receptor proteins and activated transducers, and one output element in layer 4 represents the effect caused by the input odor. The weight between the i-th element of the input layer to the j-th element of the first hidden layer is k_{ij} and from there to the k-th neuron of the second hidden layer $l_{jk}[\hat{R}_j]$. The weight from element k of hidden layer 2 to the output element is $\delta_k[\hat{T}_k]/\sum_k[\hat{T}_k]$. The adaptive elements of the hidden layers have the hyperbolic activation functions hyp. The network structure is shown in Figure 2.

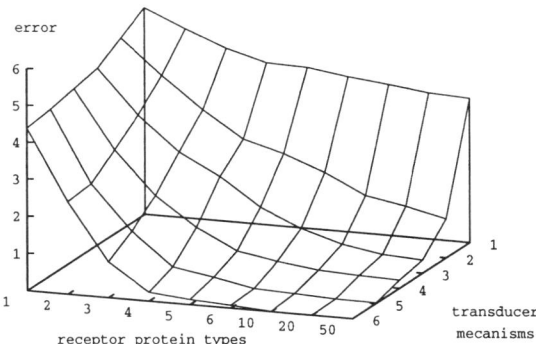

Figure 3: Mean error in spikes per output neuron for the model with different network sizes. Network sizes are varied in the number of receptor protein types and the number of transducing mechanisms.

3 SIMULATION RESULTS

Applying learning algorithms like backpropagation or RProp to the model network, it is possible to find parameter settings for optimal (or local optimal) simulations of chemosensory cell responses with given response characteristics. In our simulations the best training results were achieved by using the fast learning algorithm RProp, which is an improved version of backpropagation [Riedmiller & Braun, 1993].

For our simulations we used extracellular recordings made by Akers and Getz from single sensilla placodes of honey bee workers applying different stimuli and their binary mixtures to the antenna (see [Akers & Getz, 1992] for material and methods). The data set for training the ANNs consists of responses of 54 subplacodes to the four odors, geraniol, citral, limonene, linalool, their binary mixtures, and a mixture of all of four odors each at two concentration levels and to a blank stimulus, i.e. 23 responses to different odor stimulations for each subplacode.

In a series of training runs with varying numbers of receptor protein types and transducer types the full model was trained to fit the data set. The networks were able to simulate the responses of the subplacodes, dependent on the network size. The size of the first hidden layer corresponds to the number of receptor protein types (R) in the model, the size of the second hidden layer corresponds to the number of transducing mechanisms (T).

Figure 3 shows the mean error per output neuron in spikes for all combinations of one to six receptor types and one to six transducer mechanisms and for combinations with ten, twenty and fifty receptor protein types.

The mean response over all subplacode responses is 18.15 spikes. The best results with errors less than two spikes per response were achieved with models with at least three receptor protein types and at least three transducer mechanisms. A model with only two transducer types is not sufficient to simulate the data.

For generalization tests we generated a larger pattern set with our model. This training set

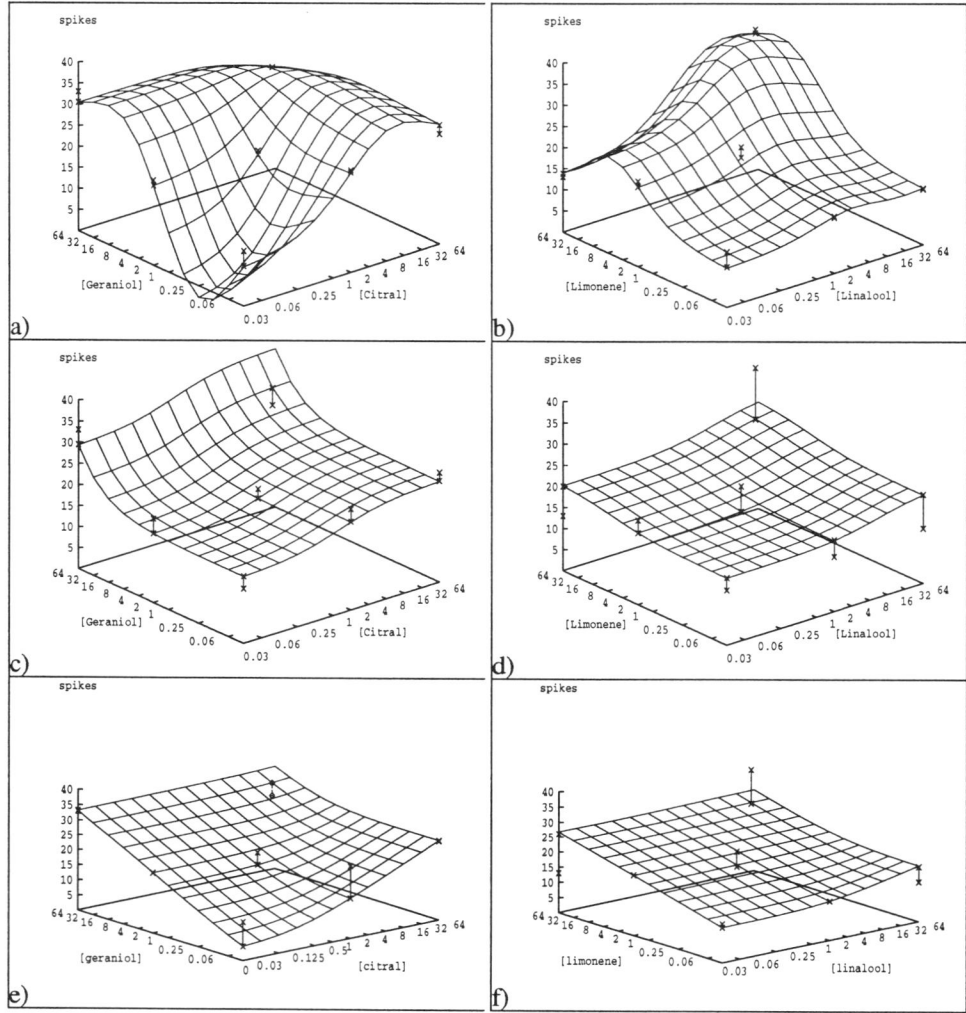

Figure 4: Simulation results of our model (a,b) and the Ennis model (c,d). The responses of simulated sensory cells is given in spikes. The left column (a,c) represents receptor neuron responses to mixtures of geraniol and citral, the right column (b,d) represents sensory cell responses to mixtures of limonene and linalool. The concentrations of the odorants are depicted on a logarithmic scale from 2^{-5} to 2^6 micrograms (0.03 to 64 micrograms). Measurement points and deviations from simulated data are given by crosses in the diagrams.

was divided in a set of 23 training patterns and 88 test patterns. The training set had the same structure as the experimental data. Training of new randomly initialized networks provided a mean error on the test set that was approximately 1.6 times higher than on the training set. An overfitting effect was not observable during the training sequence of 10000 learning epochs.

It is also possible to transform many other models for chemosensory perception into ANNs. We fitted the stimulus summation model and the stimulus substitution model [Carr & Derby, 1986] as well as the models proposed by Ennis [Ennis, 1991]. All of the other models were not able to reproduce the complex response functions observed in honey bee sensory neurons. Some of them are able to simulate synergistic responses to binary mixtures, but none were able to produce inhibitory effects. Figure 4 shows the simulation of a sensory neuron that shows very similar spike rates for the single odors geraniol and citral and to their binary mixture at the same concentration, while the mixture interaction of limonene and linalool shows a strong synergistic effect, i.e. the response to mixture of both odors is much higher than the responses to the single odors. As shown in Figure 4a) and b) our model is able to simulate this behavior, while the Ennis model is not sufficient to show the two different types of interaction for the binary mixtures geraniol-citral and limonene-linalool, as shown in Figure 4c) and d). The error for the Ennis model is greater than four spikes per output neuron and the error for our model with six receptor types and four transducer mechanisms is smaller than one spike per output neuron. The stimulus summation and stimulus substitution model have very similar results as the Ennis model, Figure 4 e) and f) show the simulation of the stimulus summation.

4 CONCLUSIONS

Artificial neural networks are a powerful tool for the simulation of the responses of chemosensory cells. The use of ANNs is consistent with theoretical modelings. Many previously proposed models are expressible as ANNs. The new receptor transducer model described in this paper is also expressible as an ANN. The use of learning algorithms is a means to fit parameters for the simulation with given experimental response data. With this method it is possible to create simulation models of chemosensory cells, that can be used in further modelings of olfactory and chemosensory systems.

Applying data from honey bee placode recordings we could also investigate the necessary complexity of chemosensory models. It could be shown that only the full receptor transducer model is able to simulate the complex response characteristics observed in honey bee chemosensory cells. Most other models can show only low synergistic mixture interactions and none of the other models is able to simulate inhibitory effects in odor perception.

The found parameters of the ANN do not have to correspond to physiological entities, such as affinities between molecules. The learning or parameter fitting optimizes the parameters in a way that the difference between experimental data and simulation results is minimized. If there are several solutions to this task, one solution will be found, which might differ from the actual values. But it can be said, that a model is not sufficient if the learning algorithm is not able to fit the experimental data. This implies that the smallest model, which is able to simulate the given data covers the minimum of complexity necessary. For honey bees this means that a competitive receptor transducer model is necessary with at least two transducer mechanisms and three receptor protein types. Any other model, such as the stimulus summation model, the stimulus substitution model and the Ennis model, is not sufficient.

The model is not restricted to insect olfactory receptor neurons and can also be applied to many types of olfactory or gustatory receptor neurons in invertebrates and vertebrates.

Acknowledgments

We want to thank Pat Akers and Wayne Getz for giving us subplacode response data to train the ANNs used in our model, Heinrich Braun and Wayne Getz for fruitful discussions on our work. This work was supported by grants of the Deutsche Forschungsgemeinschaft (DFG), SPP Physiologie und Theorie neuronaler Netze, and the State of Baden-Württemberg.

References

[Akers & Getz, 1992] R.P. Akers & W.M. Getz. A test of identified response classes among olfactory receptor neurons in the honeybee worker. *Chemical Senses*, 17(2):191–209, 1992.

[Akers & Getz, 1993] R.P. Akers & W.M. Getz. Response of olfactory receptor neurons in honey bees to odorants and their binary mixtures. *J. Comp. Physiol. A*, 173:169–185, 1993.

[Breer & Boekhoff, 1992] H. Breer & I. Boekhoff. Second messenger signalling in olfaction. *Current Opinion in Neurobiology*, 2:439–443, 1992.

[Breer et al., 1989] H. Breer, I. Boekhoff, J. Strotmann, K. Raming, & E. Tareilus. Molecular elements of olfactory signal transduction in insect antennae. In D. Schild, editor, *Chemosensory Information Processing*, pages 75–86. Springer, 1989.

[Carr & Derby, 1986] W.E.S. Carr & C.D. Derby. Chemically stimulated feeding behavior in marine animals: the importance of chemical mixtures and the involvement of mixture interactions. *J.Chem.Ecol.*, 12:987–1009, 1986.

[Ennis, 1991] D.M. Ennis. Molecular mixture models based on competitive and non-competitive agonism. *Chemical Senses*, 16(1):1–17, 1991.

[Malaka & Ragg, 1993] R. Malaka & T. Ragg. Models for chemosensory receptors: An approach using artificial neural networks. Interner Bericht 18/93, Institut für Logik, Komplexität und Deduktionssysteme, Universität Karlsruhe, 1993.

[Riedmiller & Braun, 1993] M. Riedmiller & H. Braun. A direct adaptive method for faster backpropagation learning: The rprop algorithm. In *Proceedings of the ICNN*, 1993.

[Shepherd, 1991] G.M. Shepherd. Computational structure of the olfactory system. In J.L. Davis & H. Eichenbaum, editors, *Olfaction — A Model System for Computational Neuroscience*, chapter 1, pages 3–41. MIT Press, 1991.

[Vogt et al., 1989] R.G. Vogt, R. Rybczynski, & M.R. Lerner. The biochemistry of odorant reception and transduction. In D. Schild, editor, *Chemosensory Information Processing*, pages 33–76. Springer, 1989.

The Electrotonic Transformation: a Tool for Relating Neuronal Form to Function

Nicholas T. Carnevale
Department of Psychology
Yale University
New Haven, CT 06520

Kenneth Y. Tsai
Department of Psychology
Yale University
New Haven, CT 06520

Brenda J. Claiborne
Division of Life Sciences
University of Texas
San Antonio, TX 79285

Thomas H. Brown
Department of Psychology
Yale University
New Haven, CT 06520

Abstract

The spatial distribution and time course of electrical signals in neurons have important theoretical and practical consequences. Because it is difficult to infer how neuronal form affects electrical signaling, we have developed a quantitative yet intuitive approach to the analysis of electrotonus. This approach transforms the architecture of the cell from anatomical to electrotonic space, using the logarithm of voltage attenuation as the distance metric. We describe the theory behind this approach and illustrate its use.

1 INTRODUCTION

The fields of computational neuroscience and artificial neural nets have enjoyed a mutually beneficial exchange of ideas. This has been most evident at the network level, where concepts such as massive parallelism, lateral inhibition, and recurrent excitation have inspired both the analysis of brain circuits and the design of artificial neural net architectures.

Less attention has been given to how properties of the individual neurons or processing elements contribute to network function. Biological neurons and brain circuits have been simultaneously subject to eons of evolutionary pressure. This suggests an essential interdependence between neuronal form and function, on the one hand, and the overall architecture and operation of biological neural nets, on the other. Therefore reverse-engineering the circuits of the brain appears likely to reveal design principles that rely upon neuronal properties. These principles may have maximum utility in the design of artificial neural nets that are constructed of processing elements with greater similarity to biological neurons than those which are used in contemporary designs.

Spatiotemporal extent is perhaps the most obvious difference between real neurons and processing elements. The processing element of most artificial neural nets is essentially a point in time and space. Its activation level is the instantaneous sum of its synaptic inputs. Of particular relevance to Hebbian learning rules, all synapses are exposed to the same activation level. These simplifications may insure analytical and implementational simplicity, but they deviate sharply from biological reality. Membrane potential, the biological counterpart of activation level, is neither instantaneous nor spatially uniform. Every cell has finite membrane capacitance, and all ionic currents are finite, so membrane potential must lag behind synaptic inputs. Furthermore, membrane capacitance and cytoplasmic resistance dictate that membrane potential will almost never be uniform throughout a living neuron embedded in the circuitry of the brain. The combination of ever-changing synaptic inputs with cellular anatomical and biophysical properties guarantees the existence of fluctuating electrical gradients.

Consider the task of building a massively parallel neural net from processing elements with such "nonideal" characteristics. Imagine moreover that the input surface of each processing element is an extensive, highly branched structure over which approximately 10,000 synaptic inputs are distributed. It might be tempting to try to minimize or work around the limitations imposed by device physics. However, a better strategy might be to exploit the computational consequences of these properties by making them part of the design, thereby turning these apparent weaknesses into strengths.

To facilitate an understanding of the spatiotemporal dynamics of electrical signaling in neurons, we have developed a new theoretical approach to linear electrotonus and a new way to make practical use of this theory. We present this method and illustrate its application to the analysis of synaptic interactions in hippocampal pyramidal cells.

2 THEORETICAL BACKGROUND

Our method draws upon and extends the results of two prior approaches: cable theory and two-port analysis.

2.1 CABLE THEORY

The modern use of cable theory in neuroscience began almost four decades ago with the work of Rall (1977). Much of the attraction of cable theory derives from the conceptual simplicity of the steady-state decay of voltage with distance along an infinite cylindrical cable: $V(x) = V_0 e^{-x/\lambda}$ where x is physical distance and λ is the length constant. This exponential relationship makes it useful to define the electrotonic distance X as the logarithm of the signal attenuation: $X = \ln V_0/V(x)$. In an infinite cylindrical cable, electrotonic distance is directly proportional to physical distance: $X = x/\lambda$.

However, cable theory is difficult to apply to real neurons since dendritic trees are neither infinite nor cylindrical. Because of their anatomical complexity and irregular variations of branch diameter and length, attenuation in neurons is not an exponential function of distance. Even if a cell met the criteria that would allow its dendrites to be reduced to a finite equivalent cylinder (Rall 1977), voltage attenuation would not bear a simple exponential relationship to X but instead would vary inversely with a hyperbolic function (Jack et al. 1983).

2.2 TWO-PORT THEORY

Because of the limitations and restrictions of cable theory, Carnevale and Johnston (1982) turned to two-port analysis. Among their conclusions, three are most relevant to this discussion.

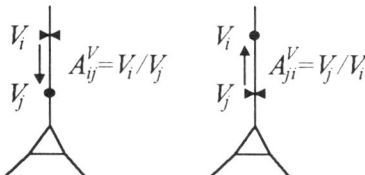

Figure 1: Attenuation is direction-dependent.

The first is that signal attenuation depends on the direction of signal propagation. Suppose that i and j are two points in a cell where i is "upstream" from j (voltage is spreading from i to j), and define the voltage attenuation from i to j: $A_{ij}^V = V_i/V_j$. Next suppose that the direction of signal propagation is reversed, so that j is now upstream from i, and define the voltage attenuation $A_{ji}^V = V_j/V_i$. In general these two attenuations will not be equal: $A_{ij}^V \neq A_{ji}^V$

They also showed that voltage attenuation in one direction is identical to current attenuation in the opposite direction (Carnevale and Johnston 1982). Suppose current I_i enters the cell at i, and the current that is captured by a voltage clamp at j is I_j, and define the current attenuation $A_{ij}^I = I_i/I_j$. Because of the directional reciprocity between current and voltage attenuation, $A_{ij}^I = A_{ji}^V$. Similarly, if we interchange the current entry and voltage clamp sites, the current attenuation ratio would be $A_{ji}^I = A_{ij}^V$.

Finally, they found that charge and DC current attenuation in the same direction are identical (Carnevale and Johnston 1982). Therefore the spread of electrical signals between any two points is completely characterized by the voltage attenuations in both directions.

2.3 THE ELECTROTONIC TRANSFORMATION

The basic idea of the electrotonic transformation is to remap the cell from anatomical space into "electrotonic space," where the distance between points reflects the attenuation of an electrical signal spreading between them. Because of the critical role of membrane potential in neuronal function, it is usually most appropriate to deal with voltage attenuations.

2.3.1 The Distance Metric

We use the logarithm of attenuation between points as the distance metric in electrotonic space: $L_{ij} = \ln A_{ij}$ (Brown et al. 1992, Zador et al. 1991). To appreciate the utility of this definition, consider voltage spreading from point i to point j, and suppose that k is on the direct path between i and j. The voltage attenuations are $A_{ik}^V = V_i/V_k$, $A_{kj}^V = V_k/V_j$, and $A_{ij}^V = V_i/V_j = A_{ik}^V A_{kj}^V$. This last equation and our definition of L establish the additive property of electrotonic distance $L_{ij} = L_{ik} + L_{kj}$. That is, electrotonic distances are additive over a path that has a consistent direction of signal propagation. This justifies using the logarithm of attenuation as a metric for the electrical separation between points in a cell.

At this point several important facts should be noted. First, unlike the electrotonic distance X of classical cable theory, our new definition of electrotonic distance L always bears a simple and direct logarithmic relationship to attenuation. Second, because of membrane capacitance, attenuation increases with frequency. Since both steady-state and transient signals are of interest, we evaluate attenuations at several different frequencies. Third, attenuation is direction-dependent and usually asymmetric. Therefore at every frequency of interest, each branch of the cell has two different representations in electrotonic space depending on the direction of signal flow.

2.3.2 Representing a Neuron in Electrotonic Space

Since attenuation depends on direction, it is necessary to construct transforms in pairs for each frequency of interest, one for signal spread away from a reference point (V_{out}) and the other for spread toward it (V_{in}). The soma is often a good choice for the reference point, but any point in the cell could be used, and a different vantage point might be more appropriate for particular analyses.

The only difference between using one point i as the reference instead of any other point j is in the direction of signal propagation along the direct path between i and j (dashed arrows in Figure 2), where V_{out} relative to i is the same as V_{in} relative to j and vice versa. The directions of signal flow and therefore the attenuations along all other branches of the cell are unchanged. Thus the transforms relative to i and j differ only along the direct path ij, and once the V_{out} and V_{in} transforms have been created for one reference i, it is easy to assemble the transforms with respect to any other reference j.

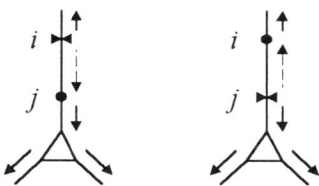

Figure 2: Effect of reference point location on direction of signal propagation.

We have found two graphical representations of the transform to be particularly useful. "Neuromorphic figures," in which the cell is redrawn so that the relative orientation of branches is preserved (Figures 3 and 4), can be readily compared to the original anatomy for quick, "big picture" insights regarding synaptic integration and interactions. For more quantitative analyses, it is helpful to plot electrotonic distance from the reference point as a function of anatomical distance (Tsai et al. 1993).

3 COMPUTATIONAL METHODS

The voltage attenuations along each segment of the cell are calculated from detailed, accurate morphometric data and the best available experimental estimates of the biophysical properties of membrane and cytoplasm. Any neural simulator like NEURON (Hines 1989) could be used to find the attenuations for the DC V_{out} transform. The DC V_{in} attenuations are more time consuming because a separate run must be performed for each of the dendritic terminations. However, the AC attenuations impose a severe computational burden on time-domain simulators because many cycles are required for the response to settle. For example, calculating the DC V_{out} attenuations in a hippocampal pyramidal cell relative to the soma took only a few iterations on a SUN Sparc 10-40, but more than 20 hours were required for 40 Hz (Tsai et al. 1994). Finding the full set of attenuations for a V_{in} transform at 40 Hz would have taken almost three months.

Therefore we designed an O(N) algorithm that achieves high computational efficiency by operating in the frequency domain and taking advantage of the branched architecture of the cell. In a series of recursive walks through the cell, the algorithm applies Kirchhoff's laws to compute the attenuations in each branch. The electrical characteristics of each segment of the cell are represented by an equivalent T circuit. Rather than "lump" the properties of cytoplasm and membrane into discrete resistances and capacitances, we determine the elements of these equivalent T circuits directly from complex impedance functions that we derived from the impulse response of a finite cable (Tsai et al. 1994). Since each segment is treated as a cable rather than an isopotential compartment, the resolution of the spatial grid does not affect accuracy, and there is no need to increase the resolution of the spatial grid in order to preserve accuracy as frequency increases. This is an important consideration for hippocampal neurons, which have long membrane time constants and begin to show increased attenuations at frequencies as low as 2 - 5 Hz (Tsai et al. 1994). It also allows us to treat a long unbranched neurite of nearly constant diameter as a single cylinder.

Thus runtimes scale linearly with the number of grid points, are independent of frequency, and we can even reduce the number of grid points if the diameters of adjacent unbranched segments are similar enough. A benchmark of a program that uses our algorithm with NEURON showed a speedup of more than four orders of magnitude without sacrificing accuracy (2 seconds vs. 20 hours to calculate the V_{out} attenuations at 40 Hz in a CA1 pyramidal neuron model with 2951 grid points) (Tsai et al. 1994).

4 RESULTS

4.1 DC TRANSFORMS OF A CA1 PYRAMIDAL CELL

Figure 3 shows a two-dimensional projection of the anatomy of a rat CA1 pyramidal neuron (cell 524, left) with neuromorphic renderings of its DC V_{out} and V_{in} transforms (middle and right) relative to the soma. The three-dimensional anatomical data were obtained from HRP-filled cells with a computer microscope system as described elsewhere (Rihn and Claiborne 1992, Claiborne 1992). The passive electrical properties used to compute the attenuations were R_i = 200 Ωcm, C_m = 1 μF/cm^2 (for nonzero frequencies, not shown here) and R_m = 30 kΩcm^2 (Spruston and Johnston 1992).

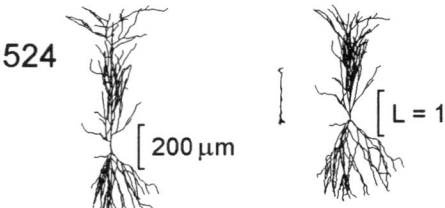

Figure 3: CA1 pyramidal cell anatomy (cell 524, left) with neuromorphic renderings of V_{out} (middle) and V_{in} (right) transforms at DC.

The V_{out} transform is very compact, indicating that voltage propagates from the soma into the dendrites with relatively little attenuation. The basilar dendrites and the terminal branches of the primary apical dendrite are almost invisible, since they are nearly isopotential along their lengths. Despite the fact that the primary apical dendrite has a larger diameter than any of its daughter branches, most of the voltage drop for somatofugal signaling is in the primary apical. Therefore it accounts for almost all of the electrotonic length of the cell in the V_{out} transform.

The V_{in} transform is far more extensive, but most of the electrotonic length of the cell is now in the basilar and terminal apical branches. This reflects the loading effect of downstream membrane on these thin dendritic branches.

4.2 SYNAPTIC INTERACTIONS

The transform can also give clues to possible effects of electrotonic architecture on voltage-dependent forms of associative synaptic plasticity and other kinds of synaptic interactions. Suppose the cell of Figure 3 receives a weak or "student" synaptic input located 400 μm from the soma on the primary apical dendrite, and a strong or "teacher" input is situated 300 μm from the soma on the same dendrite.

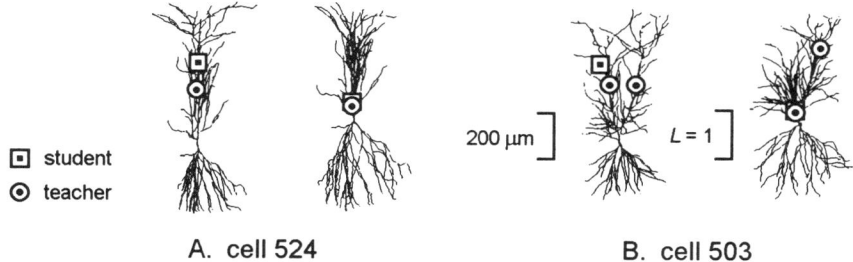

Figure 4: Analysis of synaptic interactions.

The anatomical arrangement is depicted on the left in Figure 4A ("student" = square, "teacher" = circle). The V_{in} transform with respect to the student (right figure of this pair) shows that voltage spreads from the teacher to the student synapse with little attenuation, which would favor voltage-dependent associative interactions.

Figure 4B shows a different CA1 pyramidal cell in which the apical dendrite bifurcates shortly after arising from the soma. Two teacher synapses are indicated, one on the same branch as the student and the other on the opposite branch. The V_{in} transform with respect to the student (right figure of this pair) shows clearly that the teacher synapse on the same branch is closely coupled to the student, but the other is electrically much more remote and less likely to influence the student synapse.

5. SUMMARY

The electrotonic transformation is based on a logical, internally consistent conceptual approach to understanding the propagation of electrical signals in neurons. In this paper we described two methods for graphically presenting the results of the transformation: neuromorphic rendering, and plots of electrotonic distance vs. anatomical distance. Using neuromorphic renderings, we illustrated the electrotonic properties of a previously unreported hippocampal CA1 pyramidal neuron as viewed from the soma (cell 524, Figure 3). We also extended the use of the transformation to the study of associative interactions between "teacher" and "student" synapses by analyzing this cell from the viewpoint of a "student" synapse located in the apical dendrites, contrasting this result with a different cell that had a bifurcated primary apical dendrite (cell 503, Figure 4). This demonstrates the versatility of the electrotonic transformation, and shows how it can convey the electrical signaling properties of neurons in ways that are quickly and easily comprehended.

This understanding is important for several reasons. First, electrotonus affects the integration and interaction of synaptic inputs, regulates voltage-dependent mechanisms of synaptic plasticity, and influences the interpretation of intracellular recordings. In addition, phylogeny, development, aging, and response to injury and disease are all accompanied by alterations of neuronal morphology, some subtle and some profound.

The significance of these changes for brain function becomes clear only if their effects on neuronal signaling are reckoned. Finally, there is good reason to expect that neuronal electrotonus is highly relevant to the design of artificial neural networks.

Acknowledgments

We thank R.B. Gonzales and M.P. O'Boyle for their contributions to the morphometric analysis, and Z.F. Mainen for assisting in the initial development of graphical rendering. This work was supported in part by ONR, ARPA, and the Yale Center for Theoretical and Applied Neuroscience (CTAN).

References

Brown, T.H., Zador, A.M., Mainen, Z.F. and Claiborne, B.J. Hebbian computations in hippocampal dendrites and spines. In: *Single Neuron Computation*, eds. McKenna, T., Davis, J. and Zornetzer, S.F., New York, Academic Press, 1992, pp. 81-116.

Carnevale, N.T. and Johnston, D.. Electrophysiological characterization of remote chemical synapses. *J. Neurophysiol. 47*:606-621, 1982.

Claiborne, B.J. The use of computers for the quantitative, three-dimensional analysis of dendritic trees. In: *Methods in Neuroscience. Vol. 10: Computers and Computation in the Neurosciences*, ed. Conn, P.M., New York, Academic Press, 1992, pp. 315-330.

Hines, M. A program for simulation of nerve equations with branching geometries. *Internat. J. Bio-Med. Computat. 24*:55-68, 1989.

Rall, W.. Core conductor theory and cable properties of neurons. In: *Handbook of Physiology, The Nervous System*, ed. Kandel, E.R., Bethesda, MD, Am. Physiol. Soc., 1977, pp.39-98.

Rihn, L.L. and Claiborne, B.J. Dendritic growth and regression in rat dentate granule cells during late postnatal development. *Brain Res. Dev.* 54(1):115-24, 1990.

Spruston, N. and Johnston, D. Perforated patch-clamp analysis of the passive membrane properties of three classes of hippocampal neurons. *J. Neurophysiol.* 67:508-529, 1992.

Tsai, K.Y., Carnevale, N.T., Claiborne, B.J. and Brown, T.H. Morphoelectrotonic transforms in three classes of rat hippocampal neurons. *Soc. Neurosci. Abst.* 19:1522, 1993.

Tsai, K.Y., Carnevale, N.T., Claiborne, B.J. and Brown, T.H. Efficient mapping from neuroanatomical to electrotonic space. *Network* 5:21-46, 1994.

Zador, A.M., Claiborne, B.J. and Brown, T.H. Electrotonic transforms of hippocampal neurons. *Soc. Neurosci. Abst.* 17:1515, 1991.

A model of the hippocampus combining self-organization and associative memory function.

Michael E. Hasselmo, Eric Schnell
Joshua Berke and Edi Barkai
Dept. of Psychology, Harvard University
33 Kirkland St., Cambridge, MA 02138
hasselmo@katla.harvard.edu

Abstract

A model of the hippocampus is presented which forms rapid self-organized representations of input arriving via the perforant path, performs recall of previous associations in region CA3, and performs comparison of this recall with afferent input in region CA1. This comparison drives feedback regulation of cholinergic modulation to set appropriate dynamics for learning of new representations in region CA3 and CA1. The network responds to novel patterns with increased cholinergic modulation, allowing storage of new self-organized representations, but responds to familiar patterns with a decrease in acetylcholine, allowing recall based on previous representations. This requires selectivity of the cholinergic suppression of synaptic transmission in stratum radiatum of regions CA3 and CA1, which has been demonstrated experimentally.

1 INTRODUCTION

A number of models of hippocampal function have been developed (Burgess et al., 1994; Myers and Gluck, 1994; Touretzky et al., 1994), but remarkably few simulations have addressed hippocampal function within the constraints provided by physiological and anatomical data. Theories of the function of specific subregions of the hippocampal formation often do not address physiological mechanisms for changing dynamics between learning of novel stimuli and recall of familiar stimuli. For example, the afferent input to the hippocampus has been proposed to form orthogonal representations of entorhinal activity (Marr, 1971; McNaughton and Morris, 1987; Eichenbaum and Buckingham, 1990), but simulations have not addressed the problem of when these representations should remain stable, and when they should be altered. In addition, models of autoassociative memory function in region CA3 (Marr, 1971; McNaughton and Morris, 1987; Levy, 1989; Eichenbaum and Buckingham, 1990) and heteroassociative memory function at the Schaffer collaterals projecting from region CA3 to CA1 (Levy, 1989; McNaughton, 1991) require very different activation dynamics during learning versus recall.

Acetylcholine may set appropriate dynamics for storing new information in the cortex (Hasselmo et al., 1992, 1993; Hasselmo, 1993, 1994; Hasselmo and Bower, 1993). Acetylcholine has been shown to selectively suppress synaptic transmission at intrinsic but not afferent fiber synapses (Hasselmo and Bower, 1992), to suppress the neuronal adaptation of cortical pyramidal cells (Hasselmo et al., 1994; Barkai and Hasselmo, 1994), and to enhance long-term potentiation of synaptic potentials (Hasselmo, 1994b). Models show that suppression of synaptic transmission during learning prevents recall of previously stored information from interfering with the storage of new information (Hasselmo et al., 1992, 1993; Hasselmo, 1993, 1994a), while cholinergic enhancement of synaptic modification enhances the rate of learning (Hasselmo, 1994b).

Feedback regulation of cholinergic modulation may set the appropriate level of cholinergic modulation dependent upon the novelty or familiarity of a particular input pattern. We have explored possible mechanisms for the feedback regulation of cholinergic modulation in simulations of region CA1 (Hasselmo and Schnell, 1994) and region CA3. Here we show that self-regulated learning and recall of self-organized representations can be obtained in a network simulation of the hippocampal formation. This model utilizes selective cholinergic suppression of synaptic transmission in stratum radiatum of region CA3, which has been demonstrated in brain slice preparations of the hippocampus.

2 METHODS

2.1. SIMPLIFIED REPRESENTATION OF HIPPOCAMPAL NEURONS.

In place of the sigmoid input-output functions used in many models, this model uses a simple representation in which the output of a neuron is not explicitly constrained, but the total network activity is regulated by feedback from inhibitory interneurons and adaptation due to intracellular calcium concentration. Separate variables represent pyramidal cell membrane potential a, intracellular calcium concentration c, and the membrane potential of inhibitory interneurons h:

$$\Delta a_i = A_i - \eta a_i - \mu c + \sum_j W_{ij} g(a_j - \theta_o) - H_{ik} g(h_k - \theta_h)$$

$$\Delta c_i = \gamma g(a_i - \theta_c) - \Omega c$$

$$\Delta h_k = \sum_j W_{kj} g(a_j - \theta_o) - \eta h_k - \sum_l H_{kl} g(h_l - \theta_o)$$

where A = afferent input, η = passive decay of membrane potential, μ = strength of calcium-dependent potassium current (proportional to intracellular calcium), W_{ij} = excitatory recurrent synapses (longitudinal association path terminating in stratum radiatum), g() is a threshold linear function proportional to the amount by which membrane potential exceeds an output threshold θ_o or threshold for calcium current θ_c, γ = strength of voltage-dependent calcium current, Ω = diffusion constant of calcium, W_{ki} = excitatory synapses inhibitory interneurons, H_{ik} = inhibitory synapses from interneurons to pyramidal cells, H_{kl}= inhibitory synapses between interneurons. This representation gives neurons adaptation characteristics similar to those observed with intracellular recording (Barkai and Hasselmo, 1994), including a prominent afterhyperpolarization potential (see Figure 1).

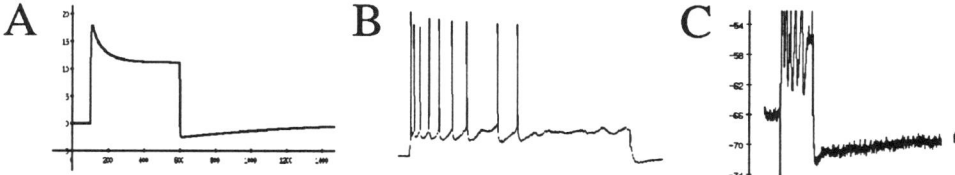

Figure 1. Comparison of pyramidal cell model with experimental data.

In Figure 1, A shows the membrane potential of a modeled pyramidal cell in response to simulated current injection. Output of this model is a continuous variable proportional to how much membrane potential exceeds threshold. This is analogous to the reciprocal of interspike interval in real neuronal recordings. Note that the model displays adaptation during current injection and afterhyperpolarization afterwards, due to the calcium-dependent potassium current. B shows the intracellularly recorded membrane potential in a piriform cortex pyramidal cell, demonstrating adaptation of firing frequency due to activation of calcium-dependent potassium current. The firing rate falls off in a manner similar to the smooth decrease in firing rate in the simplified representation. C shows an intracellular recording illustrating long-term afterhyperpolarization caused by calcium influx induced by spiking of the neuron during current injection.

2.2. NETWORK CONNECTIVITY

A schematic representation of the network simulation of the hippocampal formation is shown in Figure 2. The anatomy of the hippocampal formation is summarized on the left in A, and the function of these different subregions in the model is shown on the right in B. Each of the subregions in the model contained a population of excitatory neurons with a single inhibitory interneuron mediating feedback inhibition and keeping excitatory activity bounded. Thus, the local activation dynamics in each region follow the equations presented above. The connectivity of the network is further summarized in Figure 3 in the Results section. A learning rule of the Hebbian type was utilized at all synaptic connections, with the exception of the mossy fibers from the dentate gyrus to region CA3, and the connections to and from the medial septum. Self-organization of perforant path synapses was obtained through decay of synapses with only pre or post-synaptic activity, and growth of synapses with combined activity. Associative memory function at synapses arising from region CA3 was obtained through synaptic modification during cholinergic suppression of synaptic transmission.

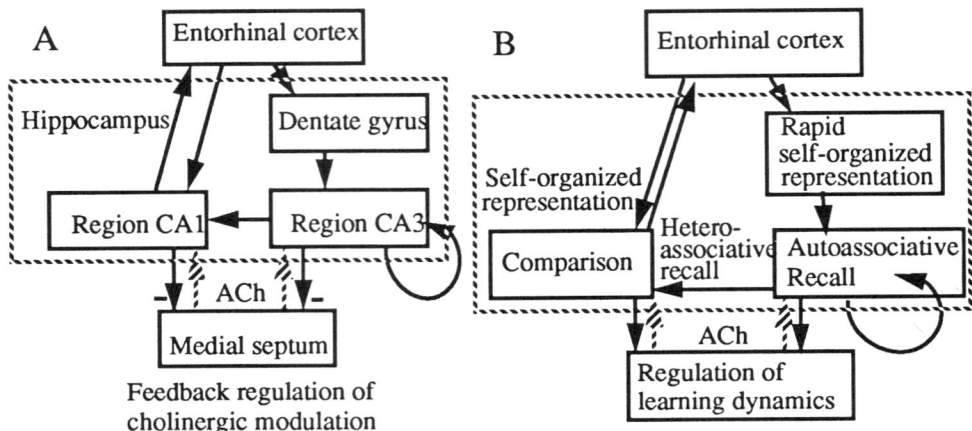

Figure 2. Schematic representation of hippocampal circuitry and the corresponding function of connections in the model.

2.3. CHOLINERGIC MODULATION

The total output from region CA1 determined the level of cholinergic modulation within both region CA3 and CA1, with increased output causing decreased modulation. This is consistent with experimental evidence suggesting that activity in region CA1 and region CA3 can inhibit activity in the medial septum, and thereby downregulate cholinergic modulation. This effect was obtained in the model by excitatory connections from region CA1 to an inhibitory interneuron in the medial septum, which suppressed the activity of a cholinergic neuron providing modulation to the full network. When levels of cholinergic modulation were high, there was strong suppression of synaptic transmission at the excitatory recurrent synapses in CA3 and the Schaffer collaterals projecting from region CA3 to CA1. This prevented the spread of activity due to previous learning from interfering with self-organization. When levels of cholinergic modulation were decreased, the strength of synaptic transmission was increased, allowing associative recall to dominate. Cholinergic modulation also increased the rate of synaptic modification and depolarized neurons.

2.4. TESTS OF SELF-REGULATED LEARNING AND RECALL

Simulations of the full hippocampal network evaluated the response to the sequential presentation of a series of highly overlapping activity patterns in the entorhinal cortex. Recall was tested with interspersed presentation of degraded versions of previously presented activity patterns. For effective recall, the pattern of activity in entorhinal cortex layer IV evoked by degraded patterns matched the pattern evoked by the full learned version of these patterns. The function of the full network is illustrated in Figure 3. In simulations focused on region CA3, activity patterns were induced sequentially in region CA3, representing afferent input from the entorhinal cortex. Different levels of external activation of the cholinergic neuron resulted in different levels of learning of new overlapping patterns. These results are illustrated in Figure 4.

2.5. BRAIN SLICE EXPERIMENTS

The effects in the simulations of region CA3 depended upon the cholinergic suppression of synaptic transmission in stratum radiatum of this region The cholinergic suppression of glutamatergic synaptic transmission in region CA3 was tested in brain slice preparations by analysis of the influence of the cholinergic agonist carbachol on the size of field potentials elicited by stimulation of stratum radiatum. These experiments used techniques similar to previously published work in region CA1 (Hasselmo and Schnell, 1994).

3 RESULTS

In the full hippocampal simulation, input of an unfamiliar pattern to entorhinal cortex layer II resulted in high levels of acetylcholine. This allowed rapid self-organization of the perforant path input to the dentate gyrus and region CA1. Cholinergic suppression of synaptic transmission in region CA1 prevented recall from interfering with self-organization. Instead, recurrent collaterals in region CA3 stored an autoassociative representation of the input from the dentate gyrus to region CA3, and connections from CA3 to CA1 stored associations between the pattern of activity in CA3 and the associated self-organized representation in region CA1.

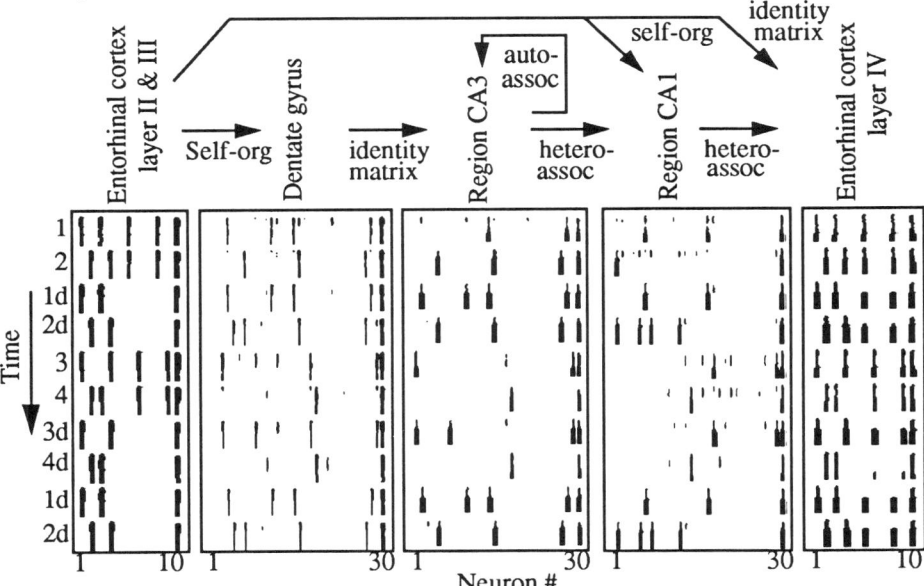

Figure 3. Activity in each subregion of the full network simulation of the hippocampal formation during presentation of a sequence of activity patterns in entorhinal cortex.

In Figure 3, width of the lines represents the activity of each neuron at a particular time step. As seen here, the network forms a self-organized representation of each new pattern consisting of active neurons in the dentate gyrus and region CA1. At the same time, an association is formed between the self-organized representation in region CA1 and the same afferent input pattern presented to entorhinal cortex layer IV. Four overlapping patterns (1-4) are presented sequentially, each of which results in learning of a separate self-organized representation in the dentate gyrus and region CA1, with an association formed between this representation and the full input pattern in entorhinal cortex.

The recall characteristics of the network are apparent when degraded versions of the afferent input patterns are presented in the sequence (1d-4d). This degraded afferent input weakly activates the same representations previously formed in the dentate gyrus. Recurrent excitation in region CA3 enhances this activity, giving robust recall of the full version of this pattern. This activity then reaches CA1, where it causes strong activation if it matches the pattern of afferent input from the entorhinal cortex. Strong activation in region CA1 decreases cholinergic modulation, preventing formation of a new representation and allowing recall to dominate. Strong activation of the representation stored in region CA1 then activates the full representation of the pattern in entorhinal cortex layer IV. Thus, the network can accurately recall each of many highly overlapping patterns.

The effect of cholinergic modulation on the level of learning or recall can be seen more clearly in a simulation of auto-associative memory function in region CA3 as shown in Figure 4. Each box shows the response of the network to sequential presentation of full and degraded versions of two highly overlapping input patterns. The width of the black traces represents the activity of each of 10 CA3 pyramidal cells during each simulation step. In the top row, level of cholinergic modulation (ACh) is plotted. In A, external activation of the cholinergic neuron is absent, so there is no cholinergic suppression of synaptic transmission. In this case, the first pattern is learned and recalled properly, but subsequent presentation of a second overlapping pattern results only in recall of the previously learned pattern. In B, with greater cholinergic suppression, recall is suppressed sufficiently to allow learning of a combination of the two input patterns. Finally, in C, strong cholinergic suppression prevents recall, allowing learning of the new overlapping pattern to dominate over the previously stored pattern.

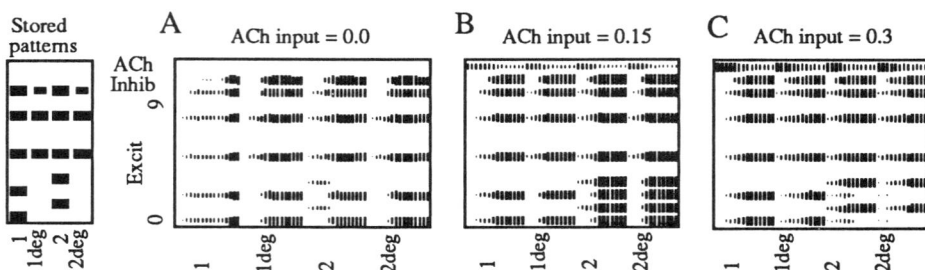

Figure 4. Increased cholinergic suppression of synaptic transmission in region CA3 causes greater learning of new aspects of afferent input patterns.

Extracellular recording in brain slice preparations of hippocampal region CA3 have demonstrated that perfusion of the cholinergic agonist carbachol strongly suppresses synaptic potentials recorded in stratum radiatum, as shown in Figure 5. In contrast, suppression of synaptic transmission at the afferent fiber synapses arising from entorhinal cortex is much weaker. At a concentration of 20μM, carbachol suppressed synaptic potentials in stratum radiatum on average by 54.4% (n=5). Synaptic potentials elicited in stratum lacunosum were more weakly suppressed, with an average suppression of 28%.

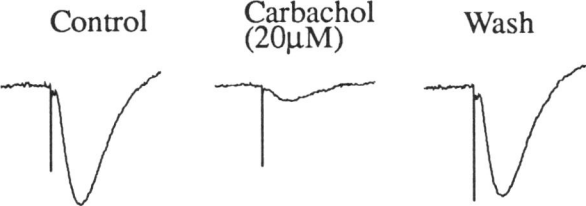

Figure 5. Cholinergic suppression of synaptic transmission in stratum radiatum of CA3.

4 DISCUSSION

In this model of the hippocampus, self-organization at perforant path synapses forms compressed representations of specific patterns of cortical activity associated with events in the environment. Feedback regulation of cholinergic modulation sets appropriate dynamics for learning in response to novel stimuli, allowing predominance of self-organization, and appropriate dynamics for recall in response to familiar stimuli, allowing predominance of associative memory function. This combination of self-organization and associative memory function may also occur in neocortical structures. The selective cholinergic suppression of feedback and intrinsic synapses has been proposed to allow self-organization of feedforward synapses while feedback synapses mediate storage of associations between higher level representations and activity in primary cortical areas (Hasselmo, 1994b). This previous proposal could provide a physiological justification for a similar mechanism utilized in recent models (Dayan et al., 1995). Detailed modeling of cholinergic effects in the hippocampus provides a theoretical framework for linking the considerable behavioral evidence for a role of acetylcholine in memory function (Hagan and Morris, 1989) to the neurophysiological evidence for the effects of acetylcholine within cortical structures (Hasselmo and Bower, 1992; 1993; Hasselmo, 1994a, 1994b).

Acknowledgements

This work supported by a pilot grant from the Massachusetts Alzheimer's Disease Research Center and by an NIMH FIRST award MH52732-01.

References

Barkai E, Hasselmo ME (1994) Modulation of the input/output function of rat piriform cortex pyramidal cells. *J. Neurophysiol.* 72: 644-658.

Barkai E, Bergman RE, Horwitz G, Hasselmo ME (1994) Modulation of associative memory function in a biophysical simulation of rat piriform cortex. *J. Neurophysiol.* 72:659-677.

Burgess N, Recce M, O'Keefe J (1994) A model of hippocampal function. *Neural Networks* 7: 1065-1081.

Dayan P, Hinton GE, Neal RM and Zemel RS (1995) The Helmholtz machine. *Neural computation* in press.

Eichenbaum, H. and Buckingham, J. (1990) Studies on hippocampal processing: experiment, theory and model. In: Learning and computational neuroscience: foundations of adaptive networks, M. Gabriel and J. Moore, eds., Cambridge, MA: MIT Press.

Hagan, JJ and Morris, RGM (1989) The cholinergic hypothesis of memory: A review of animal experiments. In *Psychopharmacology of the Aging Nervous System*, L.L. Iversen, S.D. Iversen and S.H. Snyder, eds. New York: Plenum Press, p. 237-324.

Hasselmo, M.E. (1993) Acetylcholine and learning in a cortical associative memory. *Neural Comp.* 5: 22-34.

Hasselmo ME (1994a) Runaway synaptic modification in models of cortex: Implications for Alzheimer's disease. *Neural Networks* 7: 13-40.

Hasselmo ME (1994b) Neuromodulation and cortical function. *Behav. Brain Res.* in press

Hasselmo ME, Anderson, BP and Bower, JM (1992) Cholinergic modulation of cortical associative memory function. *J. Neurophysiol.* 67(5): 1230-1246.

Hasselmo ME, Bower JM (1992) Cholinergic suppression specific to intrinsic not afferent fiber synapses in rat piriform (olfactory) cortex. *J. Neurophysiol.* 67(5): 1222-1229.

Hasselmo ME, Bower JM (1993) Acetylcholine and memory. *Trends Neurosci* 16:218-222.

Hasselmo ME, Barkai E, Horwitz G, Bergman RE (1993) Modulation of neuronal adaptation and cortical associative memory function. In: Computation and Neural Systems II (Eeckman F, Bower JM, ed). Norwell, MA: Kluwer Academic Publishers.

Hasselmo ME, Schnell E (1994) Laminar selectivity of the cholinergic suppression of synaptic transmission in rat hippocampal region CA1: Computational modeling and brain slice physiology. *J. Neurosci.* 14: 3898-3914.

Levy WB (1989) A computational approach to hippocampal function. In: Computational models of learning in simple neural systems (Hawkins RD, Bower GH, ed), pp. 243-305. Orlando, FL: Academic Press.

Myers CE and Gluck M (1994) Context, conditioning and hippocampal rerepresentation in animal learning. *Behav. Neurosci.* 108: 835-847.

Marr D (1971) Simple memory: A theory for archicortex. *Phil. Trans. Roy. Soc. B* B262:23-81

McNaughton BL (1991) Associative pattern completion in hippocampal circuits: New evidence and new questions. *Brain Res. Rev.* 16:193-220.

McNaughton BL, Morris RGM (1987) Hippocampal synaptic enhancement and information storage within a distributed memory system. *Trends Neurosci.* 10:408-415.

Touretzky DS, Wan HS and Redish AD (1994) Neural representation of space in rats and robots. In Zurada JM and Marks RJ (eds) Computational Intelligence: Imitating life. IEEE Press.

Model of a Biological Neuron as a Temporal Neural Network

Sean D. Murphy and Edward W. Kairiss
Interdepartmental Neuroscience Program, Department of Psychology,
and The Center for Theoretical and Applied Neuroscience,
Yale University,
Box 208205, New Haven, CT 06520

Abstract

A biological neuron can be viewed as a device that maps a multidimensional temporal event signal (dendritic postsynaptic activations) into a unidimensional temporal event signal (action potentials). We have designed a network, the Spatio-Temporal Event Mapping (STEM) architecture, which can learn to perform this mapping for arbitrary biophysical models of neurons. Such a network appropriately trained, called a STEM cell, can be used in place of a conventional compartmental model in simulations where only the transfer function is important, such as network simulations. The STEM cell offers advantages over compartmental models in terms of computational efficiency, analytical tractabililty, and as a framework for VLSI implementations of biological neurons.

1 INTRODUCTION

Discovery of the mechanisms by which the mammalian cerebral cortex processes and stores information is the greatest remaining challenge in the brain sciences. Numerous modeling studies have attempted to describe cortical information processing in frameworks as varied as holography, statistical physics, mass action, and nonlinear dynamics. Yet, despite these theoretical studies and extensive experimental efforts, the functional architecture of the cortex and its implementation by cortical neurons are largely a mystery.

Our view is that the most promising approach involves the study of computational models with the following key properties: (1) Networks consist of large ($>10^3$) numbers of neurons; (2) neurons are connected by modifiable synapses; and (3) the neurons themselves possess biologically-realistic dynamics.

Property (1) arises from extensive experimental observations that information processing and storage is distributed over many neurons. Cortical networks are also characterized by *sparse connectivity*: the probability that any two local cortical neurons are synaptically connected is typically less than 0.1. These and other observations suggest that key features of cortical dynamics may not be apparent unless large, sparsely-connected networks are studied.

Property (2) is suggested by the accumulated evidence that (a) memory formation is subserved by use-dependent synaptic modification, and (b) Hebbian synaptic plasticity is present in many areas of the brain thought to be important for memory. It is also well known that artificial networks composed of elements that are connected by Hebb-like synapses have powerful computational properties.

Property (3) is based on the assumption that biological neurons are computationally more complex than, for example, the processing elements that compose artificial (connectionist) neural networks. Although it has been difficult to infer the computational function of cortical neurons directly from experimental data, models of neurons that explicitly incorporate biophysical components (e.g. neuronal geometry, channel kinetics) suggest a complex, highly non-linear dynamical transfer function. Since the "testability" of a model depends on the ability to make predictions in terms of empirically measurable single-neuron firing behavior, a biologically-realistic nodal element is necessary in the network model.

Biological network models with the above properties (e.g. Wilson & Bower, 1992; Traub and Wong, 1992) have been handicapped by the computationally expensive single-neuron representation. These "compartmental" models incorporate the neuron's morphology and membrane biophysics as a large (10^2 -10^4) set of coupled, non-linear differential equations. The resulting system is often stiff and requires higher-order numerical methods and small time-steps for accurate solution. Although the result is a realistic approximation of neuronal dynamics, the computational burden precludes exhaustive study of large networks for functionality such as learning and memory.

The present study is an effort to develop a computationally efficient representation of a single neuron that does not compromise the biological dynamical behavior. We take the position that the "dynamical transfer function" of a neuron is essential to its computational abstraction, but that the underlying molecular implementation need not be explicitly represented unless it is a target of analysis. We propose that a biological neuron can be viewed as a device that performs a mapping from multidimensional spatio-temporal (synaptic) events to unidimensional temporal events (action potentials). This computational abstraction will be called a Spatio-Temporal Event Mapping (STEM) cell. We describe the architecture of the neural net that implements the neural transfer function, and the training procedure required to develop realistic dynamics. Finally, we discuss our preliminary analyses of the performance of the model when compared with the full biophysical representation.

2 STEM ARCHITECTURE

The architecture of the STEM cell is similar to that found in neural nets for temporal sequence processing (e.g. review by Mozer, in press). In general, these networks have 2 components: (1) a short-term memory mechanism that acts as a preprocessor for (2) a non-linear feedforward network. For example, de Vries & Principe (1992) describe the utility of the gamma net, a real-time neural net for temporal processing, in time series prediction. The preprocessor in the gamma net is the gamma memory structure, implemented as a network of adaptive dispersive elements (de Vries & Principe, 1991). The preprocessor in our model (the "tau layer", described below) is somewhat simpler, and is inspired by the temporal dynamics of membrane conductances found in biological neurons.

The STEM architecture (diagrammed in Figure 1) works by building up a vectorial representation of the state of the neuron as it continuously receives incoming synaptic activations, and then labeling that vector space as either "FIRE" or "DON'T FIRE". This is accomplished with the use of four major components: (1) TAU LAYER: a layer of nodes that continuously maps incoming synaptic activations into a finite-dimensional vector space (2) FEEDBACK TAU NODE: a node that maintains a vectorial representation of the past activity of the cell itself (3) MLP: a multilayer perceptron that functions as a non-linear spatial mapping network that performs the "FIRE" / "NO-FIRE" labeling on the tau layer output (4) OUTPUT FILTER: this adds a refractory period and threshold to the MLP output that contrains the format of the output to be discrete-time events.

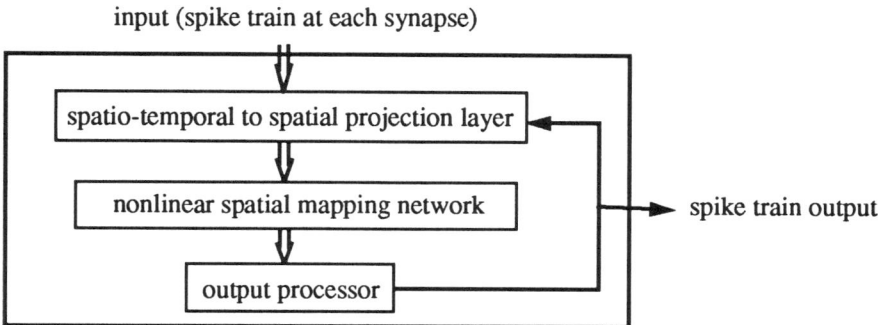

Figure 1: Information Flow in The STEM Cell

The tau layer (Fig. 2) consists of N + 1 tau nodes, where N is the number of synapses on the cell, and the extra node is used for feedback. Each tau node consists of M tau units. Each tau unit within a single tau node receives an identical input signal. Each tau unit within a tau node calculates a second-order rise-and-decay function with unique time constants. The tau units within a tau node translate arbitrary temporal events into a vector form, with each tau-unit corresponding to a different vector component. Taken as a whole, all of the tau unit outputs of the tau node layer comprise a high-dimensional vector that represents the overall state of the neuron. Functionally, the tau layer approximates a one-to-one mapping between the spatio-temporal input and the tau-unit vector space.

The output of each tau unit in the tau layer is fed into the input layer of a multilayer perceptron (MLP) which, as will be explained in the next section, has been trained to label the tau-layer vector as either FIRE or NO-FIRE. The output of the MLP is then fed into an output filter with a refractory period and threshold. The STEM architecture is illustrated in Fig. 3.

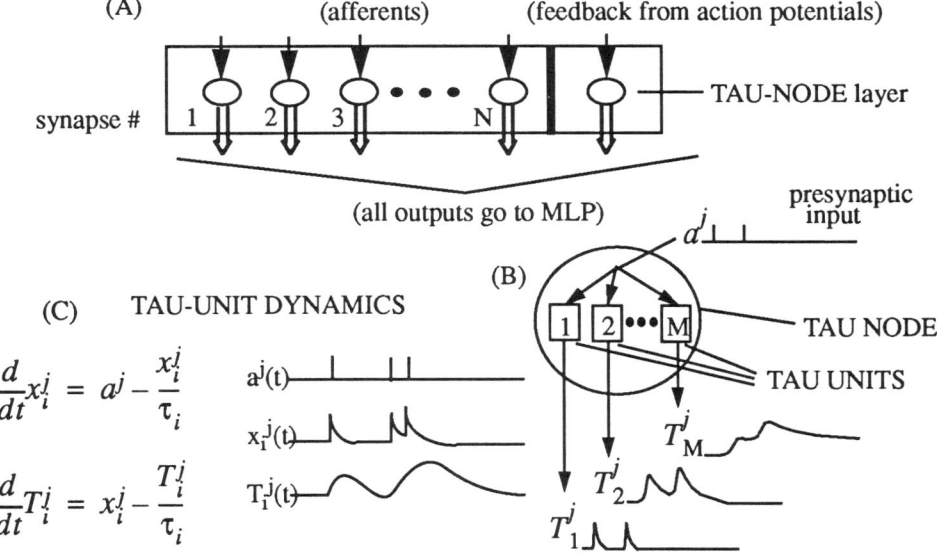

Figure 2: Tau Layer Schematic. (A) the tau layer has an afferent section, with N tau nodes, and a single-node feedback section. (B) Each tau node contains M tau units, and therefore has 1 input and M outputs (C) Each of the M tau units in a tau node has a rise and decay function with different constants. The equations are given for the ith tau unit of the jth tau node. a is input activity, x an internal state variable, and T the output.

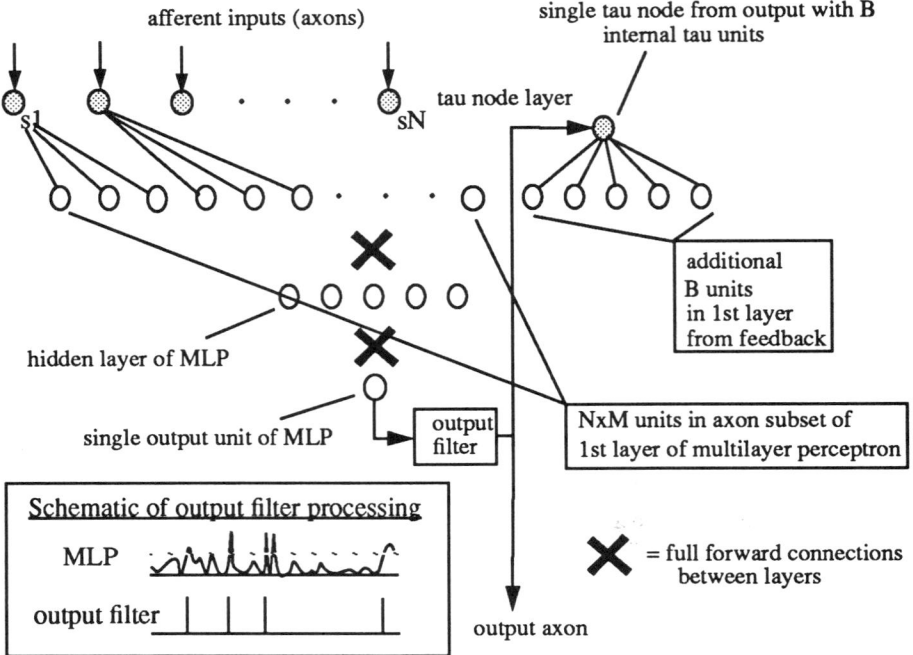

Figure 3: STEM Architecture. Afferent activity enters the tau layer, where it is converted into a vectorial representation of past spaiotemporal activity. The MLP maps this vector into a FIRE/NO-FIRE output unit, the continuous value of which is converted to a discrete event signal by the refractory period and threshold of the output filter.

3 STEM TRAINING

There are six phases to training the STEM cell:

(1) Biology: anatomical and physiological data are collected on the cell to be modeled.

(2) Compartmental Model: a compartmental model of the cell is designed, typically with a simulation environment such as GENESIS. As much biological detail as possible is incorporated into the model.

(3) Transfer Function Trials: many random input sequences are generated for the compartmental model. The firing response of the model is recorded for each input sequence.

(4) Sampling assignments: In the next step, sampling will need to be done on the affect of the input sequences on the STEM tay layer. The timing of the sampling is calculated by separating the response of the compartmental model on each trial into regions where no spikes occur, and regions surrounding spikes. High-rate sampling times are determined for spike regions, and lower rate times are determined for quiet regions.

(5) Tau layer trials: the identical input sequences applied to the compartmental model in step #3 are applied to an isolated tau layer of the STEM cell. The spike events from the compartmental model are used as input for the feedback node. For each input sequence, the tay layer is sampled at the times calculated in step #4, and the vector is labeled as FIRE or NO-FIRE (0 or 1).

(6) MLP training: conjugate-gradient and line-search methods are used to train the multilayer perceptron using the results of step #5 as training vectors.

Training is continued until a minimal performance level is reached, as determined by comparing the response of the STEM cell to the original compartmental model on novel input sequences.

4 RESULTS

The STEM cell has been initially evaluated using Roger Traub's (1991) compartmental model of a hippocampal CA1 cell, implemented in GENESIS by Dave Beeman. This is a relatively simple model structurally, with 19 compartments connected in a linear segment, with the soma in the middle. Dynamically, however, it is one of the most accurate and sophisticated models published, with on the order of 100 voltage- and Ca++ sensitive membrane channel mechanisms. 94 synapses were placed on the model. Each synapse recevied a random spike train with average frequency 10Hz during training. A diagram of the model and the locations of synaptic input is given in Fig. 4.

Inputs going to a single compartment were treated as members of a common synapse, so there were a total of 13 tau nodes, with 5 tau units per node, for a total of 65 tau units, plus 5 additional units from the feedback tau node. These fed into 70 units in the input layer of the MLP. Two STEM cells were trained, one on a passive shell of the CA1 cell, and the other with all of the membrane channels included. Both used 70 units in the hidden layer

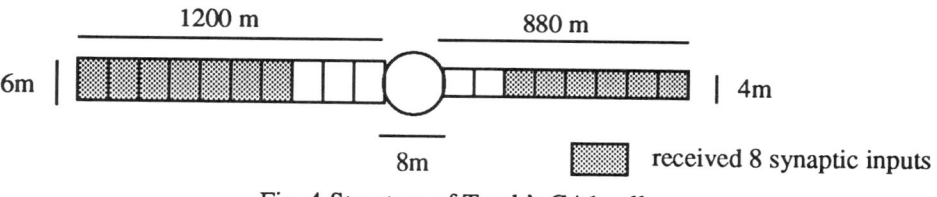

Fig. 4 Structure of Traub's CA1 cell

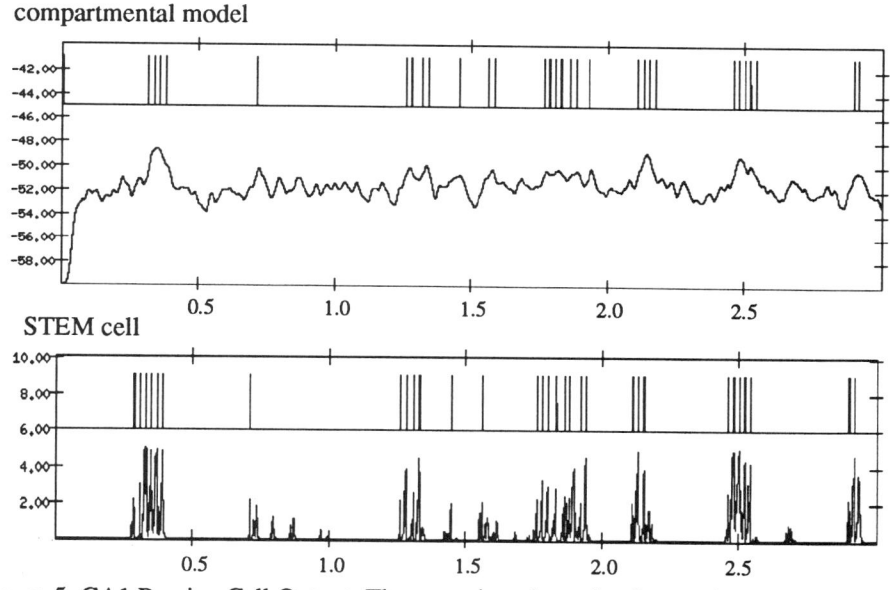

Figure 5: CA1 Passive Cell Output. The somatic voltage for the passive compartmental model and the corresponding output-filtered spike events are given in the upper graph. The lower graph shows the repsonse of the STEM cell to the same input. The upper trace of the lower graph is the output filter response, the lower trace is the raw output of the MLP. Horizontal axes in seconds. Vertical axis: top, mV, and bottom, arbitrary units.

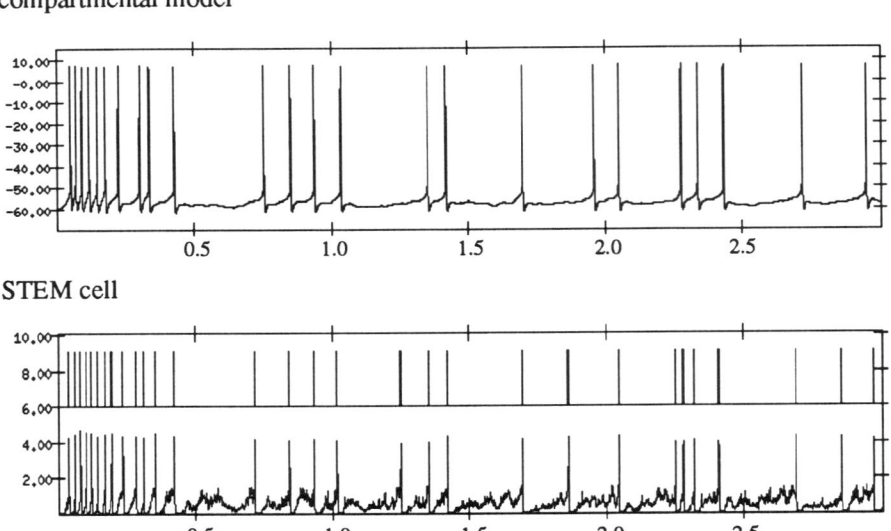

Figure 6: Response of Active CA1 Cell. The upper graph is the somatic voltage of the CA1 cell in response to a random input. The lower graph is the response of the STEM cell to the same input. The upper trace of the STEM graph is the output filter response, and the lower trace is the raw MLP output. Horizontal axes in seconds. Vertical axis: top, mV, and bottom, arbitrary units.

of the MLP. Comparisons of the compartmental model vs. STEM are shown in Fig. 5 and , for the passive and active models, respectively, Fig. 6.

For the active cell model, the STEM cell was approximately 10 times faster, and used 10% of the memory as the compartmental model.

5 DISCUSSION

The STEM cell is a general spatio-temporal node architecture and is similar to many context networks that have been previously developed. Its role as a single node in a large meta-network is unexplored, albeit interesting because of its capacity to mimic the transfer functions of biological neurons. Between the complexity range of connectionist networks to biological networks, there may be a multitude of useful computational schemes for solving different types of problems. The STEM cell is an attempt to efficiently capture some elements of biological neural function in a form that can be scaled along this range.

Characterization of the computational function of the neuron is a topic of considerable interest and debate. STEM cells may be useful as a rough measure of how complex the transfer function of a given biophysical model is. For example, it might be able to answer the question: Which instantiates a more sophisticated nonlinear spatio-temporal map, a single-compartment cell with complex somatic Ca^{++} dynamics, or a cell with active Na^+ channels in a complex dendritic tree?

STEM architecture may also be interesting for theoretical and applied ANN research as a connectionist representation of a biological neuron. The expanding body of work on focused network architectures (Mozer, 1989; Stornetta, 1988) may be an avenue towards the formalization of biological neural transfer functions. Because a VLSI implementation of a STEM cell could be reprogrammed on the fly to assume the transfer function of any pre-trained biophysically-modeled cell, a VLSI STEM network chip is a more versatile approach to artifical implementations of biological neurons than reconstructing compartmental models in VLSI.

Our future plans include using networks with delay lines and hebbian learning rules, both of which the STEM architecture is directly suited for, to investigate the capacity for STEM networks to perform real-time dynamic pattern tracking. The present implementation of the STEM cell is by no means an optimal one. We are experimenting with alternative components for the MLP, such as modular recurrent networks.

Acknowledgements

This work was supported by the Yale Center for Theoretical and Applied Neuroscience.

References

de Vries, B. and Principe, J.C. (1991) A theory for neural networks with time delays. In R.P. Lippmann, J. Moody, & D.S. Touretzky (Eds.), *Advances in Neural Information Processing Systems 3* (pp. 162-168). San Mateo, CA: Morgan Kaufmann.

de Vries, B. and Principe, J.C. (1992) The gamma model - A new neural net model for temporal processing. *Neural Networks*, 5, 565-576.

Mozer, M.C. (1989). A focused back-propagation algorithm for temporal pattern recognition, *Complex Systems*, 3, 349-381.

Mozer, M.C. (in press) Neural net architectures for temporal sequence processing. In A. Weigend & N. Gershenfeld (Eds.), *Predicting the Future and Understanding the Past*. Redwood City, CA: Addison-Wesley.

Stornetta, W.S., Hogg, T., & Huberman, B.A. (1988). A dynamical approach to temporal pattern processing. In Anderson D.Z. (Ed.), *Neural Information Processing Systems*, 750-759.

Traub, R.D. and Wong, R. K. S. (1991). *Neuronal Networks of the Hippocampus*. Cambridge: Cambridge University Press.

Wilson, M. and Bower, J.M. (1992) Cortical oscillations and temporal interactions in a computer simulation of piriform cortex. *J. Neurophysiol.* 67:981-95.

A Critical Comparison of Models for Orientation and Ocular Dominance Columns in the Striate Cortex

E. Erwin	K. Obermayer	K. Schulten
Beckman Institute	Technische Fakultät	Beckman Institute
University of Illinois	Universität Bielefeld	University of Illinois
Urbana, IL 61801, USA	33615 Bielefeld, FRG	Urbana, IL 61801, USA

Abstract

More than ten of the most prominent models for the structure and for the activity dependent formation of orientation and ocular dominance columns in the striate cortex have been evaluated. We implemented those models on parallel machines, we extensively explored parameter space, and we quantitatively compared model predictions with experimental data which were recorded optically from macaque striate cortex.

In our contribution we present a summary of our results to date. Briefly, we find that (i) despite apparent differences, many models are based on similar principles and, consequently, make similar predictions, (ii) certain "pattern models" as well as the developmental "correlation-based learning" models disagree with the experimental data, and (iii) of the models we have investigated, "competitive Hebbian" models and the recent model of Swindale provide the best match with experimental data.

1 Models and Data

The models for the formation and structure of orientation and ocular dominance columns which we have investigated are summarized in table 1. Models fall into two categories: "Pattern models" whose aim is to achieve a concise description of the observed patterns and "developmental models" which are focussed on the pro-

Class	Type	Model	Reference
Pattern Models	Structural Models	1. Icecube	Hubel and Wiesel 1977 [9]
		2. Pinwheel	Braitenberg and Braitenberg 1979 [6]
		3. Götz	Götz 1987 [8]
		4. Baxter	Baxter and Dow 1989 [1]
	Spectral Models	5. Rojer	Rojer and Schwartz 1990 [20]
		6. Niebur	Niebur and Wörgötter 1993 [15]
		7. Swindale	Swindale 1992a [21]
Develop. Models	Correlation Based Learning	8. Linsker	Linsker 1986c [12]
		9. Miller	Miller 1989, 1994 [13, 14]
	Competitive Hebbian	10. SOM-h	Obermayer, et. al. 1990 [19]
		11. SOM-l	Obermayer, et. al. 1992 [17]
		12. EN	Durbin and Mitchison 1990 [7]
	Other	13. Tanaka	Tanaka 1991 [22]
		14. Yuille	Yuille, et. al. 1992 [23]

Table 1: Models of visual cortical maps which have been evaluated.

cesses underlying their formation. Pattern models come in two varieties, "structural models" and "spectral models", which describe orientation and ocular dominance maps in real and in Fourier space, respectively. Developmental models fall into the categories "correlations based learning", "competitive Hebbian" learning and a few miscellaneous models.

Models are compared with data obtained from macaque striate cortex through optical imaging [2, 3, 4, 16]. Data were recorded from the representation of the parafovea from the superficial layers of cortex. In the following we will state that a particular model reproduces a particular feature of the experimental data (i) if there exists a parameter regime where the model generates appropriate patterns and (ii) if the phenomena are robust. We will state that a particular model does not reproduce a certain feature (i) if we have not found an appropriate parameter regime and (ii) if there exists either a proof or good intuitive reasons that a model cannot reproduce this feature.

One has to keep in mind, though, that model predictions are compared with a fairly special set of data. Ocular dominance patterns, e.g., are known to vary between species and even between different regions within area 17 of an individual. Consequently, a model which does not reproduce certain features of ocular dominance or orientation columns in the macaque may well describe those patterns in other species. Interspecies differences, however, are not the focus of this contribution; results of corresponding modelling studies will be reported elsewhere.

2 Examples of Organizing Principles and Model Predictions

It has been suggested that the most important principles underlying the pattern of orientation and ocular dominance are "continuity" and "diversity" [7, 19, 21]. Continuity, because early image processing is often local in feature space, and diversity, because, e.g., the visual system may want to avoid perceptual scotomata. The continuity and diversity principles underlie almost all descriptive and developmental

Figure 1: Typical patterns of orientation preferences as they are predicted by six of the models listed in Table 1. Orientation preferences are coded by gray values, where black → white denotes preferences for vertical → horizontal → vertical. **Top row** (left to right): Models 7, 11, 9. **Bottom row** (left to right) Models 5, 12, 8.

models, but maps which comply with these principles often differ in qualitative ways: The icecube model, e.g., obeys both principles but contains no singularities in the orientation preference map and no branching of ocular dominance bands. Figure 1 shows orientation maps generated by six different algorithms taken from Tab. 1. Although all patterns are consistent with the continuity and diversity constraints, closer comparison reveals differences. Thus additional elements of organization must be considered.

It has been suggested that maps are characterized by local correlations and global disorder. Figure 2 (left) shows as an example two-point correlation functions of orientation maps. The autocorrelation function [17] of one of the Cartesian coordinates of the orientation vector is plotted as a function of cortical distance. The fact that all correlation functions decay indicates that the orientation map exhibits global disorder. Global disorder is predicted by all models except the early pattern models 6, 8 and 9. Figure 2 (right) shows the corresponding power spectra. Bandpass-like spectra which are typical for the experimental data [16] are well predicted by models 10–12. Interestingly, they are not predicted by model 9, which also fails reproducing the Mexican-hat shaped correlation functions (bold lines), and model 13.

Based on the fact that experimental maps are characterized by a bandpass-like power spectrum it has been suggested that orientation maps may be organized

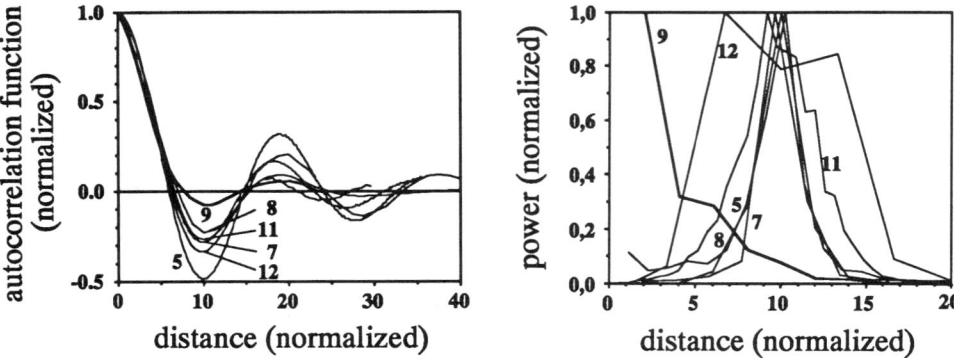

Figure 2: **Left:** Spatial autocorrelation functions for one of the cartesian coordinates of the orientation vector. Autocorrelation functions were averaged over all directions. **Right:** Complex power spectra of orientation maps. Power was averaged over all directions of the wave vector. Model numbers as in Tab. 1.

according to four principles [15]: continuity, diversity, homogeneity and isotropy. If those principles are implemented using bandpass filtered noise the resulting maps [15, 21] indeed share many properties with the experimental data. Above principles alone, however, are not sufficient: (i) There are models such as model 5 which are based on those principles but generate different patterns, (ii) homogeneity and isotropy are hardly ever fulfilled ([16] and next paragraph), and (iii) those principles cannot account for correlations between maps of various response properties [16].

Maps of orientation and ocular dominance in the macaque are anisotropic, i.e., there exist preferred directions along which orientation and ocular dominance slabs align [16]. Those anisotropies can emerge due to different mechanisms: (i) spontaneous symmetry breaking, (ii) model equations, which are not rotation invariant, and (iii) appropriately chosen boundary conditions. Figure 3 illustrates mechanisms (ii) and (iii) for model 11. Both mechanisms indeed predict anisotropic patterns, however, preferred directions of orientation and ocular dominance align in both cases (fig. 3, left and center). This is not true for the experimental data, where preferred directions tend to be orthogonal [16]. Orthogonal preferred directions can be generated by using different neighborhood functions for different components of the feature vector (fig. 3, right). However, this is not a satisfactory solution, and the issue of anisotropies is still unsolved.

The pattern of orientation preference in the area 17 of the macaque exhibits four local elements of organization: linear zones, singularities, saddle points and fractures [16]. Those elements are correctly predicted by most of the pattern models, except models 1–3, and they appear in the maps generated by models 10–14. Interestingly, models 9 and 13 predict very few linear zones, which is related to the fact that those models generate orientation maps with lowpass-like power spectra.

Another important property of orientation maps is that orientation preferences and their spatial layout across cortex are not correlated which each other. One conse-

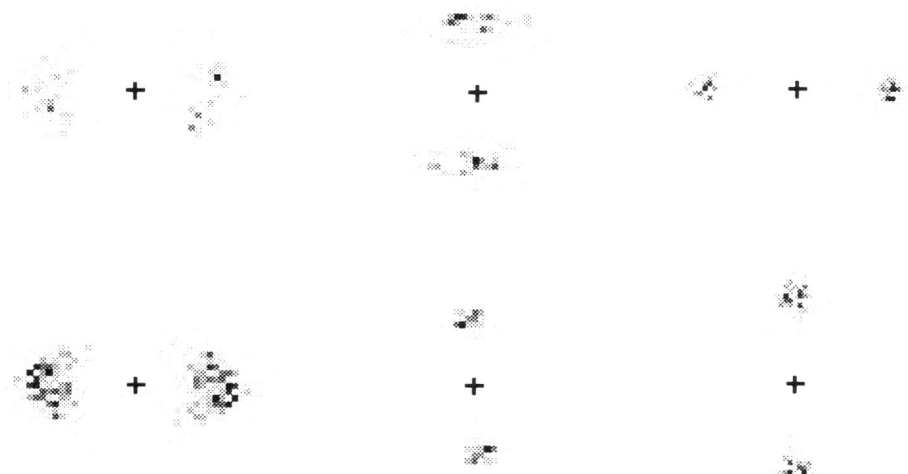

Figure 3: Anisotropic orientation and ocular dominance maps generated by model 11. The figure shows Fourier spectra [17] of orientation (**top row**) and ocular dominance maps (**bottom row**). **Left:** Maps generated with an elliptic neighborhood function (case (ii), see text); **Center:** Maps generated using circular input layers and an elliptical cortical sheet (case (iii), see text), **Right:** Maps generated with different, elliptic neighborhood functions for orientation preference and ocular dominance. '+' symbols indicate the locations of the origin.

quence is that there exist singularities, near which the curl of the orientation vector field does not vanish (fig. 4, left). This rules out a class of pattern models where the orientation map is derived from the gradient of a potential function, model 5. Figure 4 (right) shows another consequence of this property. In those figures cortical area is plotted against the angular difference between the iso-orientation lines and the local orientation preference. The even distribution found in the experimental data is correctly predicted by models 1, 6, 7 and 10–12. Model 8, however, predicts preference for large difference angles while model 9 - over a wide range of parameters - predicts preference for small difference angles (bold lines).

Finally, let us consider correlations between the patterns of orientation preference and ocular dominance. Among the more prominent relationships present in macaque data are [3, 16, 21]: (i) Singularities are aligned with the centers of ocular dominance bands, (ii) fractures are either aligned or run perpendicular, and (iii) iso-orientation bands in linear zones intersect ocular dominance bands at approximately right angles. Those relationships are readily reproduced only by models 7 and 10–12. For model 9 reasonable orientation and ocular dominance patterns have not been generated at the same time. It would seem as if the parameter regime where reasonable orientation columns emerge is incompatible with the parameter regime where ocular dominance patterns are formed.

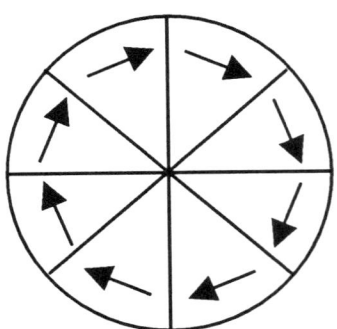 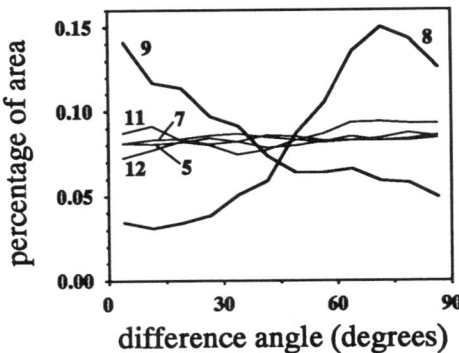

Figure 4: **Left**: This singularity is an example of a feature in the experimental data which is not allowed by model 5. The arrows indicate orientation vectors, whose angular component is twice the value of the local orientation preference. **Right**: Percentage of area as a function of the angular difference between preferred orientation and the local orientation gradient vector. Model numbers as in Table 1.

3 The Current Status of the Model Comparison Project

Lack of space prohibits a detailed discussion of our findings but we have summarized the current status of our project in Tables 2 and 3. Given the models listed in Tab. 1 and given the properties of the orientation and ocular dominance patterns in macaque striate cortex listed in Tables 2 and 3 it is models 7 and 10–12 which currently are in best agreement with the data. Those models, however, are fairly abstract and simplified, and they cannot easily be extended to predict receptive field structure. Biological realism and predictions about receptive fields are the advantages of models 8 and 9. Those models, however, cannot account for the observed orientation patterns. It would, therefore, be of high interest, if elements of both approaches could be combined to achieve a better description of the data.

The main conclusion, however, is that there are now enough data available to allow a better evaluation of model approaches than just by visual comparison of the generated patterns. It is our hope, that future studies will address at least those properties of the patterns which are known and well described, some of which are listed in Tables 2 and 3. In case of developmental models more stringent tests require experiments which (i) monitor the actual time-course of pattern formation, and which (ii) study pattern development under experimentally modified conditions (deprivation experiments). Currently there is not enough data available to constrain models but the experiments are under way [5, 10, 11, 18].

Acknowledgements

We are very much indebted to Drs. Linsker, Tanaka and Yuille for sharing modelling data. E.E. thanks the Beckman Institute for support. K.O. thanks ZiF (Universität Bielefeld) for its hospitality. Computing time on a CM-2 and a CM-5 was made available by NCSA.

no.	Properties of OR Maps									
	dis-order	band-pass	linear zones	saddle points	sing. $\pm 1/2$	fract.	indep. coord.	high spec.	aniso-tropy	OR-bias
1	-	+	+	-	-	-	+	n	+	n
2	-	+	+	+	-	-	-	n	n	n
3	-	+	+	+	+	-	-	n	n	n
4	$+^2$	+	+	+	$+^2$	-	-	n	+	n
5	+	+	+	+	+	$+^1$	-	-	+	n
6	+	+	+	+	+	$+^1$	+	-	+	n
7	+	+	+	+	+	$+^1$	+	+	+	n
8	+	+	-	+	+	+	-	n	n	n
9	+	-	-	+	+	+	-/+	+	n	n
10	+	+	-	+	+	$+^1$	+	+	+	+
11	+	+	+	+	+	$+^1$	+	+	+	+
12	+	+	+	+	+	$+^1$	+	+	+	+
13	+	-	+	+	+	$+^1$	+	+	n	n
14	+	?	?	+	+	+	?	n	n	n

Table 2: Evaluation of orientation (OR) map models. Properties of the experimental maps include (left to right): global disorder; bandpass-like power spectra; the presence of linear zones in roughly 50% of the map area; the presence of saddle points, singularities ($\pm 1/2$ with equal densities), and fractures; independence between cortical and orientation preference coordinates; a distribution favoring high values of orientation specificity; global anisotropy; and a possible orientation bias. Symbols: '+': There exists a parameter regime in which a model generates maps with this property; '-': The model cannot reproduce this property; 'n': The model makes no predictions; '?': Not enough data available. [1]Models agree with the data only if one assumes that fractures are loci of rapid orientation change rather than real discontinuities. [2]One of several cases.

References

[1] W. T. Baxter and B. M. Dow. *Biol. Cybern.*, 61:171–182, 1989.

[2] G. G. Blasdel. *J. Neurosci.*, 12:3115–3138, 1992.

[3] G. G. Blasdel. *J. Neurosci.*, 12:3139–3161, 1992.

[4] G. G. Blasdel and G. Salama. *Nature*, 321:579–585, 1986.

[5] T. Bonhoeffer, D. Kim, and W. Singer. *Soc. Neurosci. Abs.*, 19:1800, 1993.

[6] V. Braitenberg and C. Braitenberg. *Biol. Cybern.*, 33:179–186, 1979.

[7] R. Durbin and G. Mitchison. *Nature*, 343:341–344, 1990.

[8] K. G. Götz. *Biol. Cybern.*, 56:107–109, 1987.

[9] D. Hubel and T. N. Wiesel. *Proc. Roy. Soc. Lond. B*, 198:1–59, 1977.

[10] D. Hubel, T. N. Wiesel, and S. LeVay. *Phil. Trans. Roy. Soc. Lond. B*, 278:377–409, 1977.

[11] D. Kim and T. Bonhoeffer. *Soc. Neurosci. Abs.*, 19:1800, 1993.

[12] R. Linsker. *Proc. Nat. Acad. Sci., USA*, 83:8779–8783, 1986.

no.	Properties of OD Maps					Correlations Between OR and OD			
	segre-gation	dis-order	aniso-tropy	OD-bias	stra-bismus	local orthog.	global orthog.	sing. vs. OD	spec. vs. OD
1	+	-	+	+	n	+[2]	+[2]	-	n
2	n	n	n	n	n	n	n	n	n
3	+	-	+	n	n	+	n	+[2]	n
4	n	n	n	n	n	n	n	n	n
5	+	+	+	-	n	+[1]	-[1]	+[1,2]	-[1]
6	n	n	n	n	n	n	n	n	n
7	+	+	+	+	n	-	+	+	+
8	n	n	n	n	n	n	n	n	n
9	+	+	+	+	+	?[1]	?[1]	?[1]	?[1]
10	+	+	+	+	+	+	n	+	+
11	+	+	+	+	+	+[2]	n	+[2]	+[2]
12	+	+	+	+	+	+[1,2]	n	+[1,2]	+[1,2]
13	+	+	+	+	+	n	n	n	n
14	+	+	+	+	n	n	n	n	n

Table 3: **Left**: Evaluation of ocular dominance (OD) map models. Properties of the experimental maps include (left to right): Segregated bands of eye dominance; global disorder; bandpass-like power spectra; global anisotropy; a bias to the representation of one eye; and OD-patterns in animals with strabismus. **Right**: Evaluation of correlations between OD and OR. Experimental maps show (left to right): Local and global orthogonality between OR and OD slabs; singularities preferably in monocular regions, and lower OR specificity in monocular regions. [1]Authors treated OD and OR in independent models, but we consider a combined version. [2]Correlations are stronger than in the experimental data.

[13] K. D. Miller. *J. Neurosci.*, 14:409–441, 1994.

[14] K. D. Miller, J. B. Keller, and M. P. Stryker. *Science*, 245:605–615, 1989.

[15] E. Niebur and F. Wörgötter. In F. H. Eeckman and J. M. Bower, *Computation and Neural Systems*, pp. 409–413. Kluwer Academic Publishers, 1993.

[16] K. Obermayer and G. G. Blasdel. *J. Neurosci.*, 13:4114–4129, 1993.

[17] K. Obermayer, G. G. Blasdel, and K. Schulten. *Phys. Rev. A*, 45:7568–7589, 1992.

[18] K. Obermayer, L. Kiorpes, and G. G. Blasdel. In J. D. Cowan at al., *Advances in Neural Information Processing Systems 6*. Morgan Kaufmann, 1994. 543-550.

[19] K. Obermayer, H. Ritter, and K. Schulten. *Proc. Nat. Acad. Sci., USA*, 87:8345–8349, 1990.

[20] A. S. Rojer and E. L. Schwartz. *Biol. Cybern.*, 62:381–391, 1990.

[21] N. V. Swindale. *Biol. Cybern.*, 66:217–230, 1992.

[22] S. Tanaka. *Biol. Cybern.*, 65:91–98, 1991.

[23] A. L. Yuille, J. A. Kolodny, and C. W. Lee. TR 91-3, Harvard Robotics Laboratory, 1991.

A Novel Reinforcement Model of Birdsong Vocalization Learning

Kenji Doya
ATR Human Information Processing
Research Laboratories
2-2 Hikaridai, Seika, Kyoto 619-02, Japan

Terrence J. Sejnowski
Howard Hughes Medical Institute
UCSD and Salk Institute,
San Diego, CA 92186-5800, USA

Abstract

Songbirds learn to imitate a tutor song through auditory and motor learning. We have developed a theoretical framework for song learning that accounts for response properties of neurons that have been observed in many of the nuclei that are involved in song learning. Specifically, we suggest that the *anterior forebrain pathway*, which is not needed for song production in the adult but is essential for song acquisition, provides synaptic perturbations and adaptive evaluations for syllable vocalization learning. A computer model based on reinforcement learning was constructed that could replicate a real zebra finch song with 90% accuracy based on a spectrographic measure. The second generation of the birdsong model replicated the tutor song with 96% accuracy.

1 INTRODUCTION

Studies of motor pattern generation have generally focussed on innate motor behaviors that are genetically preprogrammed and fine-tuned by adaptive mechanisms (Harris-Warrick et al., 1992). Birdsong learning provides a favorable opportunity for investigating the neuronal mechanisms for the acquisition of complex motor patterns. Much is known about the neuroethology of birdsong and its neuroanatomical substrate (see Nottebohm, 1991 and Doupe, 1993 for reviews), but relatively little is known about the overall system from a computational viewpoint. We propose a set of hypotheses for the functions of the brain nuclei in the song system and explore their computational strength in a model based on biological constraints. The model could reproduce real and artificial birdsongs in a few hundred learning trials.

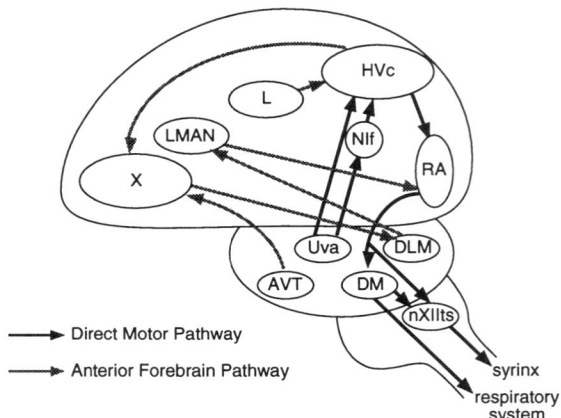

Figure 1: Major songbird brain nuclei involved in song control. The dark arrows show the direct motor control pathway and the gray arrows show the anterior forebrain pathway. Abbreviations: Uva, nucleus uvaeformis of the thalamus; NIf, nucleus interface of the neostriatum; L, field L (primary auditory are of the forebrain); HVc, higher vocal center; RA, robust nucleus of the archistriatum; DM, dorso-medial part of the nucleus intercollicularis; nXIIts, tracheosyringeal part of the hypoglossal nucleus; AVT, ventral area of Tsai of the midbrain; X, area X of lobus parolfactorius; DLM, medial part of the dorsolateral nucleus of the thalamus; LMAN, lateral magnocellular nucleus of the anterior neostriatum.

2 NEUROETHOLOGY OF BIRDSONG

Although songs from individual birds of the same species may sound quite similar, a young male songbird *learns* to sing by imitating the song of a tutor, which is usually the father or another adult male in the colony. If a young bird does not hear a tutor song during a *critical period*, it will sing short, poorly structured songs, and if a bird is deafened in the period when it practices vocalization, it develops highly abnormal songs. These observations indicate that there are two phases in song learning: the sensory learning phase when a young bird memorizes *song templates* and the motor learning phase in which the bird establishes the motor programs using auditory feedback (Konishi, 1965). These two phases can be separated by several months in some species, implying that birds have remarkable capability for memorizing complex temporal sequences. Once a song is *crystallized*, its pattern is very stable. Even deafening the bird has little immediate effect.

The brain nuclei involved in song learning are shown in Figure 1. The primary motor control pathway is composed of Uva, NIf, HVc, RA, DM, and nXIIts. If any of these nuclei is lesioned, a bird cannot sing normally. Experimental studies suggest that HVc is involved in generating syllable sequences and that RA produces motor commands for each syllable (Vu et al., 1994). Interestingly, neurons in HVc, RA and nXIIts show vigorous auditory responses, suggesting that the motor control system is closely coupled with the auditory system (Nottebohm, 1991).

There is also a "bypass" from HVc to RA which consists of area X, DLM, and LMAN called the *anterior forebrain pathway* (Doupe, 1993). This pathway is not directly involved

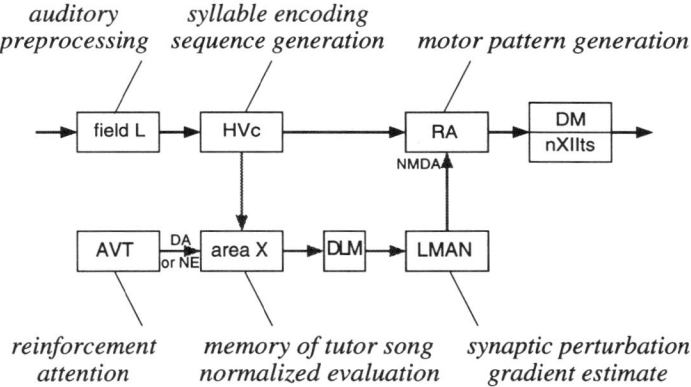

Figure 2: Schematic of primary song control nuclei and their proposed functions in the present model of bird song learning.

in vocalization because lesions in these nuclei in adult birds do not impair their crystallized songs. However, lesions in area X and LMAN during the motor learning phase result in contrasting deficits. The songs of LMAN-lesioned birds crystallize prematurely, whereas the songs of area X-lesioned birds remain variable (Scharff and Nottebohm, 1991). It has been suggested that this pathway is responsible for the storage of song templates (Doupe and Konishi, 1991) or guidance of the synaptic connection from HVc to RA (Mooney, 1992).

3 FUNCTIONAL NEUROANATOMY OF BIRDSONG

The song learning process can be decomposed into three stages. In the first stage, suitable internal acoustic representations of syllables and syllable combinations are constructed. This "auditory template" can be assembled by unsupervised learning schemes like clustering and principal components analysis. The second stage involves the encoding of phonetic sequences using the internal representation. If the representation is sparse or nearly orthogonal, sequential transition can be easily encoded by Hebbian learning. The third stage is an inverse mapping from the internal auditory representation into spatio-temporal patterns of motor commands. This can be accomplished by exploration in the space of motor commands using reinforcement learning. The responses of the units that encode the acoustic primitives can be used to the evaluate the resulting auditory signal and direct the exploration.

How are these three computational stages organized within the brain areas and pathways of the songbird? Figure 2 gives an overview of our current working hypothesis. Auditory inputs are pre-processed in field L. Some higher-order representations, such as syllables and syllable combinations, are established in HVc depending on the bird's auditory experience. Moreover, transitions between syllables are encoded in the HVc network. The sequential activation of syllable coding units in HVc are transformed into the time course of motor commands in RA. DM and nXIIts control breathing and the muscles in syrinx, bird's vocal organ.

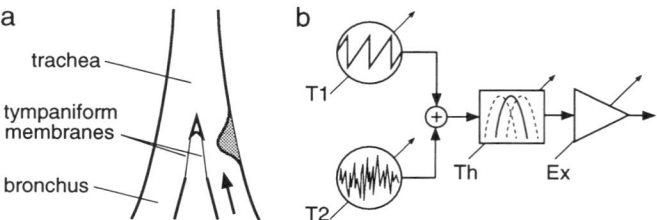

Figure 3: (a) The syrinx of songbirds. (b) The model syrinx.

The consequences of selective lesions of areas in the anterior forebrain pathway (Scharff and Nottebohm, 1991) are consistent with the failures expected for a reinforcement learning system. In particular, we suggest that this pathway serves the function of an adaptive critic with stochastic search elements (Barto et al., 1983). We propose that LMAN perturbs the synaptic connections from HVc to RA and area X regulates LMAN by the song evaluation. Modulation of HVc to RA connection by LMAN is biologically plausible since LMAN input to RA is mediated mainly by NMDA type synapses, which can modulate the amplitude of mainly non-NMDA type synaptic input from HVc (Mooney, 1992).

The assumption that area X provides evaluation is supported by the fact that it receives catecholaminergic projection (dopamine of norepinephrine) from a midbrain nucleus AVT (Lewis et al., 1981). These neurotransmitters are used in many species for reinforcement or attention signals. It is known that auditory learning is enhanced when associated with visual or social interaction with the tutor. Area X is a candidate region where auditory inputs from HVc are associated with reinforcing input from AVT during auditory learning.

4 CONSTRUCTION OF SONG LEARNING MODEL

In order to test the above hypothesis, we constructed a computer model of the birdsong learning system. The specific aim was to simulate the process of explorative motor learning, in which the time course of motor command for each syllable is determined by auditory template matching. We assumed that orthogonal representations for syllables and their sequential activation were already established in HVc and that an auditory template matching mechanism exists in area X.

4.1 The syrinx

The bird's syrinx is located near the junction of the trachea and the bronchi (Vicario, 1991). Its sound source is the tympaniform membrane which faces to the bronchus on one side and the air sac on the other (Figure 3a). When some of the syringeal muscles contract, the lumen of the bronchus is throttled and produces vibration in the membrane. When stretched along one dimension, the membrane produces harmonic sounds, but when stretched along two dimensions, the sound contains non-harmonic components (Casey and Gaunt, 1985).

Accordingly, we provided two sound sources for the model syrinx (Figure 3b). The fundamental frequency of the harmonic component was controlled by the membrane tension in one direction (T1). The amplitude of the noisy component was proportional to the

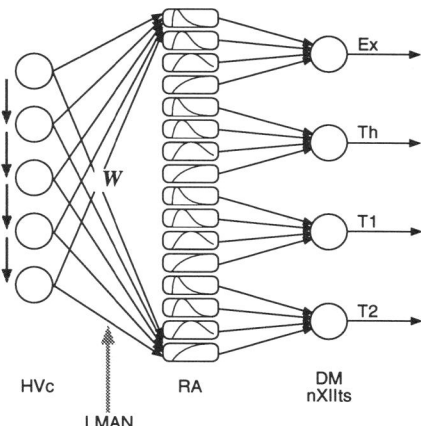

Figure 4: RA units with different spatio-temporal output profiles are driven by locally-coded HVc units. LMAN perturbs the weights W between HVc and RA. The output units in DM and nXIIts drive the model syrinx.

membrane tension in an orthogonal direction (T2). Mixture of these sounds went through a bandpass filter whose resonance frequency was controlled by the throttling of the bronchus (Th). The overall sound amplitude was determined by the strength of expiration (Ex). By controlling the time course of these four variables (Ex,Th,T1,T2), the model could produce wide variety of "bird-like" chirps and warbles.

4.2 Motor pattern generation in RA

RA is topographically organized, each part projecting to different motoneuron pools in nXIIts (Vicario, 1991). Also, RA neurons have complex temporal responses to the inputs from HVc (Mooney, 1992). Therefore, we assumed that RA consists of groups of neurons with specific spatial and temporal output properties, as shown in Figure 4. For each of the four motor command variables, we provided several units with different temporal response kernels. The sequential activation of syllable coding units in HVc drove the RA units through the weights W. Their responses were linearly combined and squashed between 0 and 1 to make the final motor commands.

4.3 Weight space search by LMAN and area X

With the above model of the motor output, the task is to find a connection matrix W that maximizes a template matching measure. One way for doing this is to perturb the output of the units and correlate it with the input and the evaluation (Barto et al., 1983). An alternative way, adopted here, is to perturb the weights and correlate them with the evaluation.

We used the following stochastic gradient ascent algorithm. The weight matrix W is modulated by ΔW, given by the sum of the evaluation gradient estimate G and a random component. The modulated weight persists if the resulting vocalization is better than the recent average evaluation $E[r]$. The evaluation gradient estimate G is updated by the sum of the perturbations ΔW weighted with the normalized evaluation.

$$\Delta W := G + \text{random perturbation}$$

$$r := \text{evaluation of the song generated with } W + \Delta W$$

$$W := W + \Delta W \qquad \text{if } r > E[r]$$

$$G := \alpha \frac{r - E[r]}{\sqrt{V[r]}} \Delta W + (1 - \alpha)G,$$

where $0 < \alpha < 1$ provides a form of "momentum" in weight space similar to that used in supervised learning. The average and the variance of evaluation are also estimated on-line as follows.

$$E[r] := \alpha r + (1 - \alpha)E[r]$$

$$V[r] := \alpha(r - E[r])^2 + (1 - \alpha)V[r].$$

4.4 Spectrographic template matching

We assumed that evaluation for vocalization is given separately for each of the syllables in a song. The sound signal was analyzed by an 80 channel spectrogram. Each output channel was sent to an analog delay line similar to the gamma filter (de Vries and Principe, 1992). The snapshot image of this (80 channels) × (12 steps) delay line at the end of each syllable was stored as the template. The same delay line image of the syllable generated by the model was compared with the template. This allowed some compensation for variable syllable duration. The direction cosine between the two delay line images was used for the reinforcement signal, r.

5 SIMULATION RESULTS

One phrase of a recorded zebra finch song (Figure 5a) was the target. Templates were stored for the five syllables in the phrase. Five HVc units coded the five different syllables and 16 RA units represented the four output variables and four different temporal kernels. Learning was started with small random weights. After 200 to 300 trials, the syllable evaluation by direction cosine reached 0.9 (Figure 5d, solid line). The syllables of the learned song resembled the overall frequency profiles of the original syllables. The complex spectrographic structure of the original syllables were, however, not accurate (Figure 5b).

One reason for this imperfect replication could be the difference between the vocal organs of the real zebra finch syrinx and our model syrinx. In order to check the significance of this difference, we took syllable templates from the model song (Figure 5b) and trained another model with random initial weights. In this case, the direction cosine went up to 0.96 (Figure 5d, dotted line) and they sounded quite similar to human ears (Figure 5c).

We also checked the importance of the gradient estimate G in our algorithm. The dashed line in Figure 5d shows the performance of the model with $G \equiv 0$: a simple random walk learning. The learning was hopelessly slow and resembles the deficit seen after lesion of area X (Figure 2).

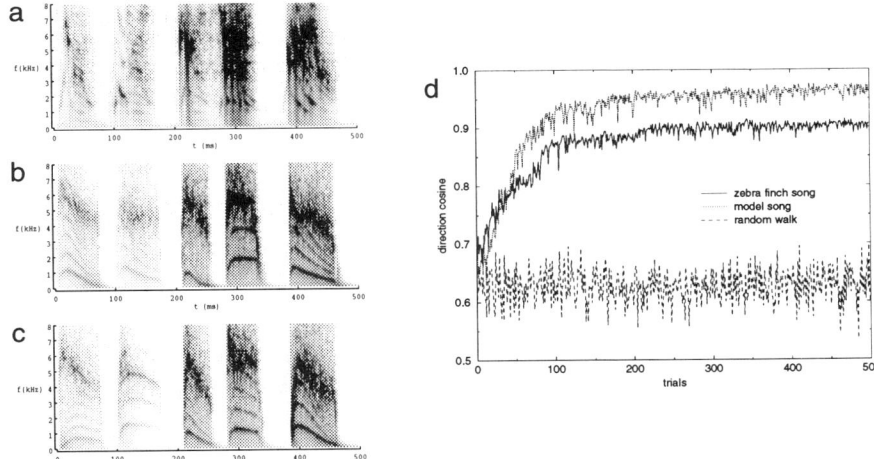

Figure 5: Spectrograms of (a) the original zebra finch song, (b) the learned song based on the tutor in (a), and (c) the second generation learned song based on the tutor in (b). (d) Learning curves for two tutors: a zebra finch song (solid line) and a model song (dotted line) compared with an undirected search in weight space (dashed line). Weight perturbation was given by a Gaussian distribution with $\sigma = 0.1$. The averaging parameter was $\alpha = 0.2$. Simulating 500 trials took 30 minutes on Sparc Station 10.

6 Discussion

We have assumed that each vocalized syllable was separately evaluated. If the evaluation is given only at the end of one song or a phrase, learning can be much more difficult because of the temporal credit assignment problem. If we assume that birds take the easiest strategy available, there should be syllable specific evaluation and separate perturbation mechanisms. In some songbirds, individual syllables are practiced out of order at an early stage, and only later is the sequence matched to the auditory template.

Selectivity of auditory responses in both HVc and area X develop during motor learning (Volman, 1993; Doupe, 1993). We can expect such change in response tuning in area X if the evaluations of syllables or syllable sequences are normalized with respect to recent average performance, as we assumed in our model.

Many simplifying assumptions were made in the present model: syllables were unary coded in HVc; simple spectrographic template matching was used; the number of motor output variables and temporal kernels were fairly small; and the sound synthesizer was much simpler than a real syrinx. However, it is not difficult to replace these idealizations with more biologically accurate models. Since the number of learning trials needed in the present model was much less than in the real birdsong learning (tens of thousands of trials), there is margin for further elaboration.

Acknowledgments

We thank M. Lewicki for the zebra finch song data and M. Konishi, A. Doupe, M. Lewicki, E. Vu, D. Perkel and G. Striedter for their helpful discussions.

References

Barto, A. G., Sutton, R. S., and Anderson, C. W. (1983). Neuronlike adaptive elements that can solve difficult learning control problems. *IEEE Transactions on System, Man, and Cybernetics*, SMC-13:834–846.

Casey, R. M. and Gaunt, A. S. (1985). Theoretical models of the avian syrinx. *Journal of Theoretical Biology*, 116:45–64.

de Vries, B. and Principe, J. C. (1992). The gamma model—A new neural model for temporal processing. *Neural Networks*, 5:565–576.

Doupe, A. J. (1993). A neural circuit specialized for vocal learning. *Current Opinion in Neurobiology*, 3:104–111.

Doupe, A. J. and Konishi, M. (1991). Song-selective auditory circuits in the vocal control system of the zebra finch. *Proceedings of the National Academy of Sciences, USA*, 88:11339–11343.

Harris-Warrick, R. M., Marder, E., Selverston, A. I., and Moulins, M. (1992). *Dynamic Biological Networks—The Stomatogastric Nervous System*. MIT Press, Cambridge, MA.

Konishi, M. (1965). The role of auditory feedback in the control of vocalization in the white-crowned sparrow. *Zeitschrift fur Tierpsychologie*, 22:770–783.

Lewis, J. W., Ryan, S. M., Arnold, A. P., and Butcher, L. L. (1981). Evidence for a catecholaminergic projection to area x in the zebra finch. *Journal of Comparative Neurology*, 196:347–354.

Mooney, R. (1992). Synaptic basis of developmental plasticity in a birdsong nucleus. *Journal of Neuroscience*, 12:2464–2477.

Nottebohm, F. (1991). Reassessing the mechanisms and origins of vocal learning in birds. *Trends in Neurosciences*, 14:206–211.

Scharff, C. and Nottebohm, F. (1991). A comparative study of the behavioral deficits following lesions of various parts of the zebra finch song systems: Implications for vocal learning. *Journal of Neuroscience*, 11:2896–2913.

Vicario, D. S. (1991). Neural mechanisms of vocal production in songbirds. *Current Opinion in Neurobiology*, 1:595–600.

Volman, S. F. (1993). Development of neural selectivity for birdsong during vocal learning. *Journal of Neuroscience*, 13:4737–4747.

Vu, E. T., Mazurek, M. E., and Kuo, Y.-C. (1994). Identification of a forebrain motor programming network for the learned song of zebra finches. *Journal of Neuroscience*, 14:6924–6934.

Ocular Dominance and Patterned Lateral Connections in a Self-Organizing Model of the Primary Visual Cortex

Joseph Sirosh and Risto Miikkulainen
Department of Computer Sciences
University of Texas at Austin, Austin, TX 78712
email: sirosh,risto@cs.utexas.edu

Abstract

A neural network model for the self-organization of ocular dominance and lateral connections from binocular input is presented. The self-organizing process results in a network where (1) afferent weights of each neuron organize into smooth hill-shaped receptive fields primarily on one of the retinas, (2) neurons with common eye preference form connected, intertwined patches, and (3) lateral connections primarily link regions of the same eye preference. Similar self-organization of cortical structures has been observed experimentally in strabismic kittens. The model shows how patterned lateral connections in the cortex may develop based on correlated activity and explains why lateral connection patterns follow receptive field properties such as ocular dominance.

1 Introduction

Lateral connections in the primary visual cortex have a patterned structure that closely matches the response properties of cortical cells (Gilbert and Wiesel 1989; Malach et al. 1993). For example, in the normal visual cortex, long-range lateral connections link areas with similar orientation preference (Gilbert and Wiesel 1989). Like cortical response properties, the connectivity pattern is highly plastic in early development and can be altered by experience (Katz and Callaway 1992). In a cat that is brought up squint-eyed from birth, the lateral connections link areas with the same ocular dominance instead of orientation (Löwel and Singer 1992). Such patterned lateral connections develop at the same time as the orientation selectivity and ocular dominance itself (Burkhalter et al. 1993; Katz and Callaway 1992). Together, these observations suggest that the same experience-dependent process drives the development of both cortical response properties and lateral connectivity.

Several computational models have been built to demonstrate how orientation preference, ocular dominance, and retinotopy can emerge from simple self-organizing processes (e.g. Goodhill 1993; Miller 1994; Obermayer et al. 1992; von der Malsburg 1973). These models assume that the neuronal response properties are primarily determined by the afferent connections, and concentrate only on the self-organization of the afferent synapses to the cortex. Lateral interactions between neurons are abstracted into simple mathematical functions (e.g. Gaussians) and assumed to be uniform throughout the network; lateral connectivity is not explicitly taken into account. Such models do not explicitly replicate the activity dynamics of the visual cortex, and therefore can make only limited predictions about cortical function.

We have previously shown how Kohonen's self-organizing feature maps (Kohonen 1982) can be generalized to include self-organizing lateral connections and recurrent activity dynamics (the Laterally Interconnected Synergetically Self-Organizing Map (LISSOM); Sirosh and Miikkulainen 1993, 1994a), and how the algorithm can model the development of ocular dominance columns and patterned lateral connectivity with abstractions of visual input. LISSOM is a low-dimensional abstraction of cortical self-organizing processes and models a small region of the cortex where all neurons receive the same input vector. This paper shows how realistic, high-dimensional receptive fields develop as part of the self-organization, and scales up the LISSOM approach to large areas of the cortex where different parts of the cortical network receive inputs from different parts of the receptor surface. The new model shows how (1) afferent receptive fields and ocular dominance columns develop from simple retinal images, (2) input correlations affect the wavelength of the ocular dominance columns and (3) lateral connections self-organize cooperatively and simultaneously with ocular dominance properties. The model suggests new computational roles for lateral connections in the cortex, and suggests that the visual cortex maybe maintained in a continuously adapting equilibrium with the visual input by coadapting lateral and afferent connections.

2 The LISSOM Model of Receptive Fields and Ocular Dominance

The LISSOM network is a sheet of interconnected neurons (figure 1). Through afferent connections, each neuron receives input from two "retinas". In addition, each neuron has reciprocal excitatory and inhibitory lateral connections with other neurons. Lateral excitatory connections are short-range, connecting only close neighbors. Lateral inhibitory connections run for long distances, and may even implement full connectivity between neurons in the network.

Neurons receive afferent connections from broad overlapping patches on the retina called anatomical receptive fields, or RFs. The $N \times N$ network is projected on to each retina of $R \times R$ receptors, and each neuron is connected to receptors in a square area of side s around the projections. Thus, neurons receive afferents from corresponding regions of each retina. Depending on the location of the projection, the number of afferents to a neuron from each retina could vary from $\frac{1}{2}s \times \frac{1}{2}s$ (at the corners) to $s \times s$ (at the center).

The external and lateral weights are organized through an unsupervised learning process. At each training step, neurons start out with zero activity. The initial response η_{ij} of neuron (i, j)

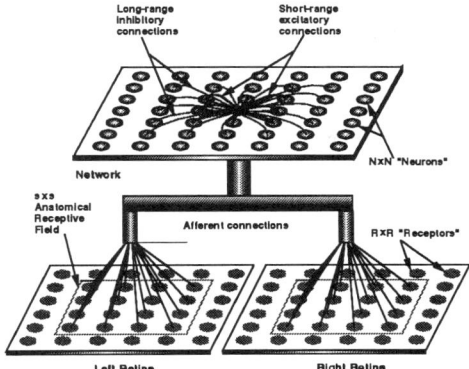

Figure 1: **The Receptive-Field LISSOM architecture.** The afferent and lateral connections of a single neuron in the LISSOM network are shown. All connection weights are positive.

is based on the scalar product

$$\eta_{ij} = \sigma \left(\sum_{a,b} \xi_{ab} \mu_{ij,ab} + \sum_{c,d} \xi_{cd} \mu_{ij,cd} \right), \qquad (1)$$

where ξ_{ab} and ξ_{cd} are the activations of retinal receptors (a,b) and (c,d) within the receptive fields of the neuron in each retina, $\mu_{ij,ab}$ and $\mu_{ij,cd}$ are the corresponding afferent weights, and σ is a piecewise linear approximation of the familiar sigmoid activation function. The response evolves over time through lateral interaction. At each time step, the neuron combines the above afferent activation $\sum \xi\mu$ with lateral excitation and inhibition:

$$\eta_{ij}(t) = \sigma \left(\sum \xi\mu + \gamma_e \sum_{k,l} E_{ij,kl} \eta_{kl}(t-1) - \gamma_i \sum_{k,l} I_{ij,kl} \eta_{kl}(t-1) \right), \qquad (2)$$

where $E_{ij,kl}$ is the excitatory lateral connection weight on the connection from neuron (k,l) to neuron (i,j), $I_{ij,kl}$ is the inhibitory connection weight, and $\eta_{kl}(t-1)$ is the activity of neuron (k,l) during the previous time step. The constants γ_e and γ_i determine the relative strengths of excitatory and inhibitory lateral interactions. The activity pattern starts out diffuse and spread over a substantial part of the map, and converges iteratively into stable focused patches of activity, or activity bubbles. After the activity has settled, typically in a few iterations of equation 2, the connection weights of each neuron are modified. Both afferent and lateral weights adapt according to the same mechanism: the Hebb rule, normalized so that the sum of the weights is constant:

$$w_{ij,mn}(t+\delta t) = \frac{w_{ij,mn}(t) + \alpha \eta_{ij} X_{mn}}{\sum_{mn}[w_{ij,mn}(t) + \alpha \eta_{ij} X_{mn}]}, \qquad (3)$$

where η_{ij} stands for the activity of neuron (i,j) in the final activity bubble, $w_{ij,mn}$ is the afferent or lateral connection weight (μ, E or I), α is the learning rate for each type of connection (α_a for afferent weights, α_E for excitatory, and α_I for inhibitory) and X_{mn} is the presynaptic activity (ξ for afferent, η for lateral).

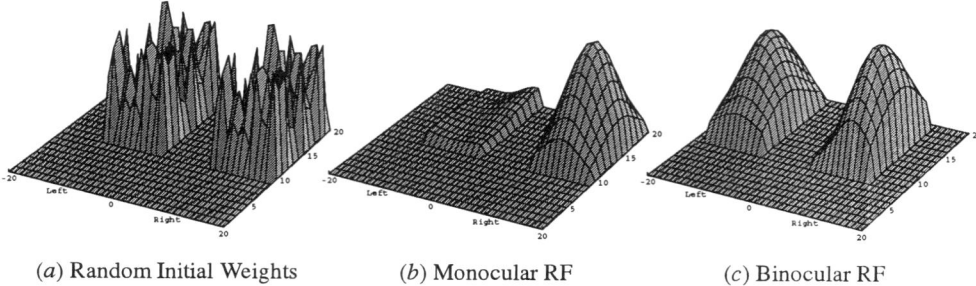

(a) Random Initial Weights (b) Monocular RF (c) Binocular RF

Figure 2: **Self-organization of the afferent input weights into receptive fields.** The afferent weights of a neuron at position $(42, 39)$ in a 60×60 network are shown before (a) and after self-organization (b). This particular neuron becomes monocular with strong connections to the right eye, and weak connections to the left. A neuron at position $(38, 23)$ becomes binocular with appoximately equal weights to both eyes (c).

Both excitatory and inhibitory lateral connections follow the same Hebbian learning process and strengthen by correlated activity. The short-range excitation keeps the activity of neighboring neurons correlated, and as self-organization progresses, excitation and inhibition strengthen in the vicinity of each neuron. At longer distances, very few neurons have correlated activity and therefore most long-range connections become weak. Such weak connections are eliminated, and through weight normalization, inhibition concentrates in a closer neighborhood of each neuron. As a result, activity bubbles become more focused and local, weights change in smaller neighborhoods, and receptive fields become better tuned to local areas of each retina.

The input to the model consists of gaussian spots of "light" on each retina:

$$\xi_{x,y} = exp(-\frac{(x-x_i)^2 + (y-y_i)^2}{u^2}) \qquad (4)$$

where $\xi_{x,y}$ is the activation of receptor (x, y), u^2 is a constant determining the width of the spot, and (x_i, y_i): $0 \leq x_i, y_i < R$ its center. At each input presentation, one spot is randomly placed at (x_i, y_i) in the left retina, and a second spot within a radius of $\rho \times RN$ of (x_i, y_i) in the right retina. The parameter $\rho \in [0, 1]$ specifies the spatial correlations between spots in the two retinas, and can be adjusted to simulate different degrees of correlations between images in the two eyes.

3 Simulation results

To see how correlation between the input from the two eyes affects the columnar structures that develop, several simulations were run with different values of ρ. The afferent weights of all neurons were initially random (as shown in figure 2a), with the total strength to both eyes being equal.

Figures 2b,c show the final afferent receptive fields of two typical neurons in a simulation with $\rho = 1$. In this case, the inputs were uncorrelated, simulating perfect strabismus. In the early stages of such simulation, some of the neurons randomly develop a preference for one eye or the other. Nearby neurons will tend to share the same preference because lateral

 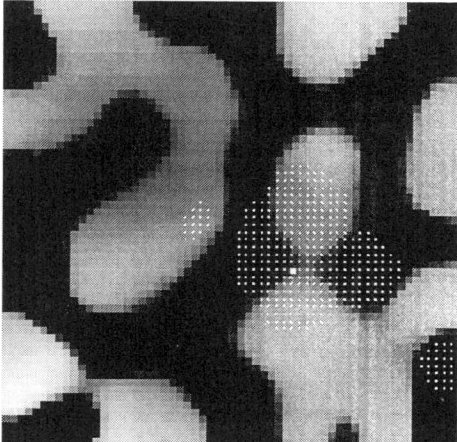

(a) Connections of a Monocular Neuron   (b) Connections of a Binocular Neuron

Figure 3: **Ocular dominance and lateral connection patterns.** The ocular dominance of a neuron is measured as the difference in total afferent synaptic weight from each eye to the neuron. Each neuron is labeled with a grey-scale value (*black* → *white*) that represents continuously changing eye preference from exclusive left through binocular to exclusive right. Small white dots indicate the lateral input connections to the neuron marked with a big white dot. (a) The surviving lateral connections of a left monocular neuron predominantly link areas of the same ocular dominance. (b) The lateral connections of a binocular neuron come from both eye regions.

excitation keeps neural activity partially correlated over short distances. As self-organization progresses, such preferences are amplified, and groups of neurons develop strong weights to one eye. Figure 2b shows the afferent weights of a typical monocular neuron.

The extent of activity correlations on the network determines the size of the monocular neuronal groups. Farther on the map, where the activations are anticorrelated due to lateral inhibition, neurons will develop eye preferences to the opposite eye. As a result, alternating ocular dominance patches develop over the map, as shown in figure 3.[1] In areas between ocular dominance patches, neurons will develop approximately equal strengths to both eyes and become binocular, like the one shown in figure 2c.

The width and number of ocular dominance columns in the network (and therefore, the wavelength of ocular dominance) depends on the input correlations (figure 4). When inputs in the two eyes become more correlated ($\rho < 1$), the activations produced by the two inputs in the network overlap closely and activity correlations become shorter range. By Hebbian adaptation, lateral inhibition concentrates in the neighborhood of each neuron, and the distance at which activations becomes anticorrelated decreases. Therefore, smaller monocular patches develop, and the ocular dominance wavelength decreases. Similar dependence was very recently observed in the cat primary visual cortex (Löwel 1994). The LISSOM model demonstrates that the adapting lateral interactions and recurrent activity dynamics regulate the wavelength, and suggests how these processes help the cortex develop feature detectors at a scale

---

[1] For a thorough treatment of the mathematical principles underlying the development of ocular dominance columns, see (Goodhill 1993; Miller et al. 1989; von der Malsburg and Singer 1988).

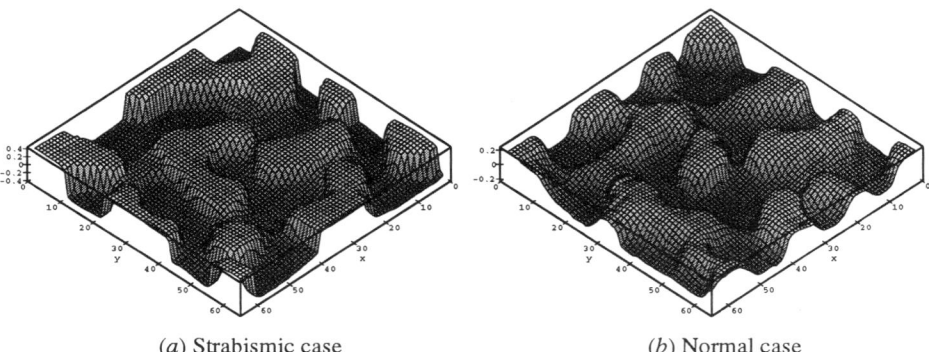

(a) Strabismic case (b) Normal case

Figure 4: **Ocular dominance wavelength in strabismic and normal models**. In the strabismic case, there are no between-eye correlations ($\rho = 1$), and broad ocular dominance columns are produced (a). With normal, partial between-eye correlations ($\rho = 0.45$ in this example), narrower stripes are formed (b). As a result, there are more ocular dominance columns in the normal case and the ocular dominance wavelength is smaller.

that matches the input correlations.

As eye preferences develop, left or right eye input tends to cause activity only in the left or right ocular dominance patches. Activity patterns in areas of the network with the same ocular dominance tend to be highly correlated because they are caused by the same input spot. Therefore, the long-range lateral connections between similar eye preference areas become stronger, and those between opposite areas weaker. After the weak lateral connections are eliminated, the initially wide-ranging connections are pruned, and eventually only connect areas of similar ocular dominance as shown in figure 3. Binocular neurons between ocular dominance patches will see some correlated activity in both the neighboring areas, and maintain connections to both ocular dominance columns (figure 3b).

The lateral connection patterns shown above closely match observations in the primary visual cortex. Löwel and Singer (1992) observed that when between-eye correlations are abolished in kittens by surgically induced strabismus, long-range lateral connections primarily link areas of the same ocular dominance. However, binocular neurons, located between ocular dominance columns, retained connections to both eye regions. The receptive field model confirms that such patterned lateral connections develop based on correlated neuronal activity, and demonstrates that they can self-organize simultaneously with ocular dominance columns. The model also predicts that the long-range connections have an inhibitory function.

4 Discussion

In LISSOM, evolving lateral interactions and dynamic activity patterns are explicitly modeled. Therefore, LISSOM has several novel properties that set it apart from other self-organizing models of the cortex.

Previous models (e.g. Goodhill 1993; Miller et al.1989; Obermayer et al.1992; von der Malsburg 1973) have concentrated only on forming ordered topographic maps where clusters of adjacent neurons assume similar response properties such as ocular dominance or orientation preference. The lateral connections in LISSOM, in addition, adapt to encode correlations between the responses.[2] This property can be potentially very useful in models of cortical function. While afferent connections learn to detect the significant features in the input space (such as ocularity or orientation), the lateral connections can learn correlations between these features (such as Gestalt principles), and thereby form a basis for feature grouping.

As an illustration, consider a single spot of light presented to the left eye. The spot causes disjoint activity patterns in the left-eye-dominant patches. How can these multiple activity patterns be recognized as representing the same spatially coherent entity? As proposed by Singer et al. (1990), the long-range lateral connections between similar ocular dominance columns could synchronize cortical activity, and form a coherently firing assembly of neurons. The spatial coherence of the spot will then be represented by temporal coherence of neural activity. LISSOM can be potentially extended to model such feature binding.

Even after the network has self-organized, the lateral and afferent connections remain plastic and in a continuously-adapting dynamic equilibrium with the input. Therefore, the receptive field properties of neurons can dynamically readapt when the activity correlations in the network are forced to change. For example, when a small area of the cortex is set inactive (or lesioned), the sharply-tuned afferent weight profiles of the neurons surrounding that region expand in size, and neurons begin to respond to the stimuli that previously activated only the lesioned area (Sirosh and Miikkulainen 1994b, 1994c). This expansion of receptive fields is reversible, and when the lesion is repaired, neurons return to their original tuning. Similar changes occur in response to retinal lesions as well. Such dynamic expansions of receptive fields have been observed in the visual cortex (Pettet and Gilbert 1992). The LISSOM model demonstrates that such plasticity is a consequence of the same self-organizing mechanisms that drive the development of cortical maps.

5 Conclusion

The LISSOM model shows how a single local and unsupervised self-organizing process can be responsible for the development of both afferent and lateral connection structures in the primary visual cortex. It suggests that this same developmental mechanism also encodes higher-order visual information such as feature correlations into the lateral connections. The model forms a framework for future computational study of cortical reorganization and plasticity, as well as dynamic perceptual processes such as feature grouping and binding.

Acknowledgments

This research was supported in part by National Science Foundation under grant #IRI-9309273. Computer time for the simulations was provided by the Pittsburgh Supercomputing Center under grants IRI930005P and TRA940029P.

References

Burkhalter, A., Bernardo, K. L., and Charles, V. (1993). Development of local circuits in human visual cortex. *Journal of Neuroscience*, 13:1916–1931.

Gilbert, C. D., and Wiesel, T. N. (1989). Columnar specificity of intrinsic horizontal and corticocortical connections in cat visual cortex. *Journal of Neuroscience*, 9:2432–2442.

---

[2] The idea was conceived by von der Malsburg and Singer (1988), but not modeled.

Goodhill, G. (1993). Topography and ocular dominance: a model exploring positive correlations. *Biological Cybernetics*, 69:109–118.

Katz, L. C., and Callaway, E. M. (1992). Development of local circuits in mammalian visual cortex. *Annual Review of Neuroscience*, 15:31–56.

Kohonen, T. (1982). Self-organized formation of topologically correct feature maps. *Biological Cybernetics*, 43:59–69.

Löwel, S. (1994). Ocular dominance column development: Strabismus changes the spacing of adjacent columns in cat visual cortex. *Journal of Neuroscience*, 14(12):7451–7468.

Löwel, S., and Singer, W. (1992). Selection of intrinsic horizontal connections in the visual cortex by correlated neuronal activity. *Science*, 255:209–212.

Malach, R., Amir, Y., Harel, M., and Grinvald, A. (1993). Relationship between intrinsic connections and functional architecture revealed by optical imaging and in vivo targeted biocytin injections in the primate striate cortex. *Proceedings of the National Academy of Sciences, USA*, 90:10469–10473.

Miller, K. D. (1994). A model for the development of simple cell receptive fields and the ordered arrangement of orientation columns through activity-dependent competition between on- and off-center inputs. *Journal of Neuroscience*, 14:409–441.

Miller, K. D., Keller, J. B., and Stryker, M. P. (1989). Ocular dominance column development: Analysis and simulation. *Science*, 245:605–615.

Obermayer, K., Blasdel, G. G., and Schulten, K. J. (1992). Statistical-mechanical analysis of self-organization and pattern formation during the development of visual maps. *Physical Review A*, 45:7568–7589.

Pettet, M. W., and Gilbert, C. D. (1992). Dynamic changes in receptive-field size in cat primary visual cortex. *Proceedings of the National Academy of Sciences, USA*, 89:8366–8370.

Singer, W., Gray, C., Engel, A., König, P., Artola, A., and Bröcher, S. (1990). Formation of cortical cell assemblies. In *Cold Spring Harbor Symposia on Quantitative Biology, Vol. LV*, 939–952. Cold Spring Harbor, NY: Cold Spring Harbor Laboratory.

Sirosh, J., and Miikkulainen, R. (1993). How lateral interaction develops in a self-organizing feature map. In *Proceedings of the IEEE International Conference on Neural Networks (San Francisco, CA)*, 1360–1365. Piscataway, NJ: IEEE.

Sirosh, J., and Miikkulainen, R. (1994a). Cooperative self-organization of afferent and lateral connections in cortical maps. *Biological Cybernetics*, 71(1):66–78.

Sirosh, J., and Miikkulainen, R. (1994b). Modeling cortical plasticity based on adapting lateral interaction. In *The Neurobiology of Computation: Proceedings of the Annual Computational Neuroscience Meeting*. Dordrecht; Boston: Kluwer. In Press.

Sirosh, J., and Miikkulainen, R. (1994c). A neural network model of topographic reorganization following cortical lesions. In *Proceedings of the World Congress on Computational Medicine, Public Health and Biotechnology* (Austin, TX). World Scientific. In Press.

von der Malsburg, C. (1973). Self-organization of orientation-sensitive cells in the striate cortex. *Kybernetik*, 15:85–100.

von der Malsburg, C., and Singer, W. (1988). Principles of cortical network organization. In Rakic, P., and Singer, W., editors, *Neurobiology of Neocortex*, 69–99. New York: Wiley.

Anatomical origin and computational role of diversity in the response properties of cortical neurons

Kalanit Grill Spector†   Shimon Edelman†   Rafael Malach‡
Depts of †Applied Mathematics and Computer Science and ‡Neurobiology
The Weizmann Institute of Science
Rehovot 76100, Israel
{kalanit,edelman,malach}@wisdom.weizmann.ac.il

Abstract

The maximization of diversity of neuronal response properties has been recently suggested as an organizing principle for the formation of such prominent features of the functional architecture of the brain as the cortical columns and the associated patchy projection patterns (Malach, 1994). We show that (1) maximal diversity is attained when the ratio of dendritic and axonal arbor sizes is equal to one, as found in many cortical areas and across species (Lund et al., 1993; Malach, 1994), and (2) that maximization of diversity leads to better performance in systems of receptive fields implementing steerable/shiftable filters, and in matching spatially distributed signals, a problem that arises in many high-level visual tasks.

1 Anatomical substrate for sampling diversity

A fundamental feature of cortical architecture is its columnar organization, manifested in the tendency of neurons with similar properties to be organized in columns that run perpendicular to the cortical surface. This organization of the cortex was initially discovered by physiological experiments (Mouncastle, 1957; Hubel and Wiesel, 1962), and subsequently confirmed with the demonstration of histologically defined columns. Tracing experiments have shown that axonal projections throughout the cerebral cortex tend to be organized in vertically aligned clusters or patches. In particular, intrinsic horizontal connections linking neighboring cortical sites, which may extend up to $2 - 3\ mm$, have a striking tendency to arborize selectively in preferred sites, forming distinct axonal patches $200 - 300\ \mu m$ in diameter.

Recently, it has been observed that the size of these patches matches closely the average diameter of individual dendritic arbors of upper-layer pyramidal cells

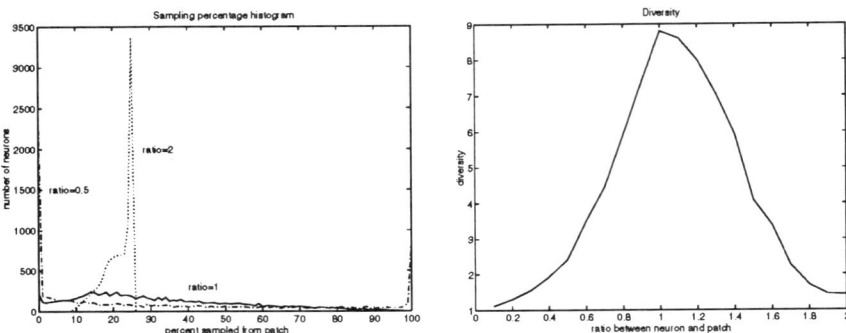

Figure 1: *Left:* histograms of the percentage of patch-originated input to the neurons, plotted for three values of the ratio r between the dendritic arbor and the patch diameter (0.5, 1.0, 2.0). The flattest histogram is obtained for $r = 1.0$ *Right:* the diversity of neuronal properties (as defined in section 1) vs. r. The maximum is attained for $r = 1.0$, a value compatible with the anatomical data.

(see Malach, 1994, for a review). Determining the functional significance of this correlation, which is a fundamental property that holds throughout various cortical areas and across species (Lund et al., 1993), may shed light on the general principles of operation of the cortical architecture. One such driving principle may be the *maximization of diversity* of response properties in the neuronal population (Malach, 1994). According to this hypothesis, matching the sizes of the axonal patches and the dendritic arbors causes neighboring neurons to develop slightly different functional selectivity profiles, resulting in an even spread of response preferences across the cortical population, and in an improvement of the brain's ability to process the variety of stimuli likely to be encountered in the environment.[1]

To test the effect of the ratio between axonal patch and dendritic arbor size on the diversity of the neuronal population, we conducted computer simulations based on anatomical data concerning patchy projections (Rockland and Lund, 1982; Lund et al., 1993; Malach, 1992; Malach et al., 1993). The patches were modeled by disks, placed at regular intervals of twice the patch diameter, as revealed by anatomical labeling. Dendritic arbors were also modeled by disks, whose radii were manipulated in different simulations. The arbors were placed randomly over the axonal patches, at a density of 10,000 neurons per patch. We then calculated the amount of patch-related information sampled by each neuron, defined to be proportional to the area of overlap of the dendritic tree and the patch. The results of the calculations for three

---

[1] Necessary conditions for obtaining dendritic sampling diversity are that dendritic arbors cross freely through column borders, and that dendrites which cross column borders sample with equal probability from patch and inter-patch compartments. These assumptions were shown to be valid in (Malach, 1992; Malach, 1994).

values of the ratio of patch and arbor diameters appear in Figure 1.

The presence of two peaks in the histogram obtained with the arbor/patch ratio $r = 0.5$ indicates that two dominant groups are formed in the population, the first receiving most of its input from the patch, and the second – from the inter-patch sources. A value of $r = 2.0$, for which the dendritic arbors are larger than the axonal patch size, yields near uniformity of sampling properties, with most of the neurons receiving mostly patch-originated input, as apparent from the single large peak in the histogram. To quantify the notion of diversity, we defined it as $diversity \sim < |\frac{dn}{dp}| >^{-1}$, where $n(p)$ is the number of neurons that receive p percent of their inputs from the patch, and $< \cdot >$ denotes average over p. Figure 1, right, shows that diversity is maximized when the size of the dendritic arbors matches that of the axonal patches, in accordance with the anatomical data. This result confirms the diversity maximization hypothesis stated in (Malach, 1994).

2 Orientation tuning: a functional manifestation of sampling diversity

The orientation columns in V1 are perhaps the best-known example of functional architecture found in the cortex (Hubel and Wiesel, 1962). Cortical maps obtained by optical imaging (Grinvald et al., 1986) reveal that orientation columns are patchy rather then slab-like: domains corresponding to a single orientation appear as a mosaic of round patches, which tend to form pinwheel-like structures. Incremental changes in the orientation of the stimulus lead to smooth shifts in the position of these domains. We hypothesized that this smooth variation in orientation selectivity found in V1 originates in patchy projections, combined with diversity in the response properties of neurons sampling from these projections. The simulations described in the rest of this section substantiate this hypothesis.

Computer simulations. The goal of the simulations was to demonstrate that a limited number of discretely tuned elements can give rise to a continuum of responses. We did not try to explain how the original set of discrete orientations can be formed by projections from the LGN to the striate cortex; several models for this step can be found in the literature (Hubel and Wiesel, 1962; Vidyasagar, 1985).[2] In setting the size of the original discrete orientation columns we followed the notion of a point image (MacIlwain, 1986), defined as the minimal cortical separation of cells with non-overlapping RFs. Each column was tuned to a specific angle, and located at an approximately constant distance from another column with the same orientation tuning (we allowed some scatter in the location of the RFs). The RFs of adjacent units with the same orientation preference were overlapping, and the amount of overlap

---

[2] In particular, it has been argued (Vidyasagar, 1985) that the receptive fields at the output of the LGN are already broadly tuned for a small number of discrete orientations (possibly just horizontal and vertical), and that at the cortical level the entire spectrum of orientations is generated from the discrete set present in the geniculate projection.

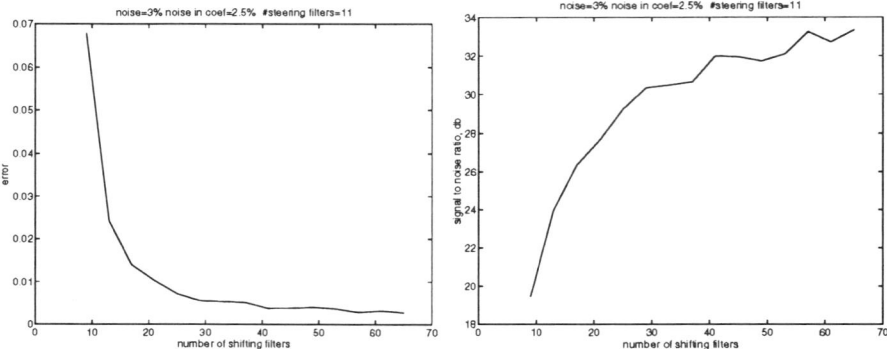

Figure 2: The effects of (independent) noise in the basis RFs and in the steering/shifting coefficients. *Left:* the approximation error vs. the number of basis RFs used in the linear combination. *Right:* the signal to noise ratio vs. the number of basis RFs. The SNR values were calculated as $10\log_{10}(signal\ energy/noise\ energy)$. Adding RFs to the basis increases the accuracy of the resultant interpolated RF.

was determined by the number of RFs incorporated into the network. The preferred orientations were equally spaced at angles between 0 and π. The RFs used in the simulations were modeled by a product of a 2D Gaussian G_1, centered at $\vec{r_j}$, with orientation selectivity G_2, and optimal angle θ_i: $G(\vec{r},\vec{r_j},\theta,\theta_i) = G_1(\vec{r},\vec{r_j})G_2(\theta,\theta_i)$.

According to the recent results on shiftable/steerable filters (Simoncelli et al., 1992), a RF located at $\vec{r_0}$ and tuned to the orientation ϕ_0 can be obtained by a linear combination of basis RFs, as follows:

$$\begin{aligned}G(\vec{r},\vec{r_0},\theta,\phi_0) &= \sum_{j=0}^{M-1}\sum_{i=0}^{N-1}b_j(\vec{r_0})k_i(\phi_0)G(\vec{r},\vec{r_j},\theta,\theta_i) \\ &= \sum_{j=0}^{M-1}b_j(\vec{r_0})G_1(\vec{r},\vec{r_j})\sum_{i=0}^{N-1}k_i(\phi_0)G_2(\theta,\theta_i)\end{aligned} \quad (1)$$

From equation 1 it is clear that the linear combination is equivalent to an outer product of the shifted and the steered RFs, with $\{k_i(\phi_0)\}_{i=0}^{N-1}$ and $\{b_j(\vec{r_0})\}_{j=0}^{M-1}$ denoting the steering and shifting coefficients, respectively. Because orientation and localization are independent parameters, the steering coefficients can be calculated separately from the shifting coefficients. The number of steering coefficients depends on the polar Fourier bandwidth of the basis RF, while the number of steering filters is inversely proportional to the basis RF size (Grill-Spector et al., 1995). In the presence of noise this minimal basis has to be extended (see Figure 2). The results of the simulation for several RF sizes are shown in Figure 3, left. As expected, the number of basis RFs required to approximate a desired RF is inversely proportional to the

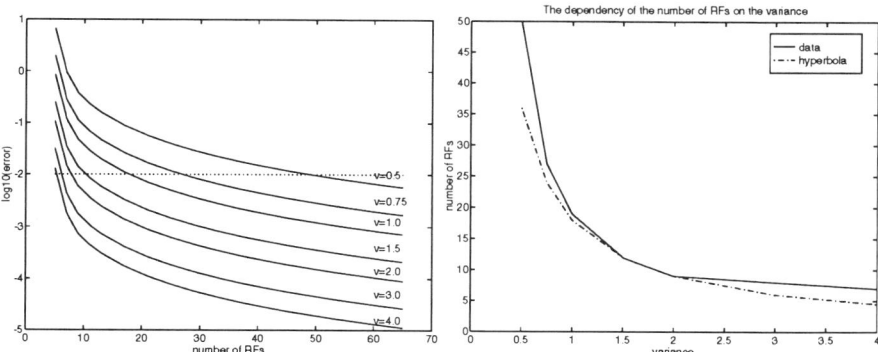

Figure 3: *Left:* error of the steering/shifting approximation for several basis RF sizes. *Right:* the number of basis RFs required to achieve a given error for different sizes of the basis RFs. The dashed line is the hyperbola $num\ RFs \times size = const$.

size of the basis RFs (Figure 3, right).

Steerability and biological considerations. The anatomical finding that the columnar "borders" are freely crossed by dendritic and axonal arbors (Malach, 1992), and the mathematical properties of shiftable/steerable filters outlined above suggest that the columnar architecture in V1 provides a basis for creating a continuum of RF properties, rather that being a form of organizing RFs in discrete bins. Computationally, this may be possible if the input to neurons is a linear combination of outputs of several RFs, as in equation 1. The anatomical basis for this computation may be provided by intrinsic cortical connections. It is known that long-range ($\sim 1mm$) connections tend to link cells with like orientation preference, while the short-range ($\sim 400\ \mu m$) connections are made to cells of diverse orientation preferences (Malach et al., 1993). We suggest that the former provide the inputs necessary to shift the position of the desired RF, while the latter participate in steering the RF to an arbitrary angle (see Grill-Spector et al., 1995, for details).

3 Matching with patchy connections

Many visual tasks require matching between images taken at different points in space (as in binocular stereopsis) or time (as in motion processing). The first and foremost problem faced by a biological system in solving these tasks is that the images to be compared are not represented as such anywhere in the system: instead of images, there are patterns of activities of neurons, with RFs that are overlapping, are not located on a precise grid, and are subject to mixing by patchy projections in each successive stage of processing. In this section, we show that a system composed of scattered RFs with smooth and overlapping tuning functions can, as a matter of fact, perform matching precisely by allowing patchy connections between domains. Moreover, the weights that must be given to the various inputs that feed a RF carrying out the match are identical to the coefficients that would be generated by a learning algorithm required to capture a certain well-defined input-output relationship from pairs of examples.

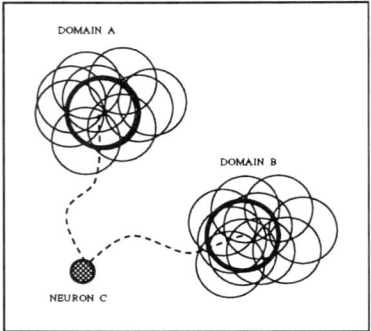

Figure 4: Unit C receives patchy input from areas A and B which contain receptors with overlapping RFs.

Consider a unit C, sampling two domains A and B through a Gaussian-profile dendritic patch equal in size to that of the axonal arbor of cells feeding A and B (Figure 4). The task faced by unit C is to determine the degree to which the activity patterns in domains A and B match. Let ϕ_{jp} be the response of the j'th unit in A to an input $\vec{x_p}$:

$$\phi_{jp} = \exp\{\frac{-(\vec{x_p} - \vec{x_j})^2}{2\sigma^2}\} \qquad (2)$$

where $\vec{x_j}$ be the optimal pattern to which the j'th unit is tuned (the response θ_{jp} of a unit in B is of similar form). If, for example, domains A and B contain orientation selective cells, then $\vec{x_j}$ would be the optimal combination of orientation and location of a bar stimulus. For simplicity we assume that all the RFs are of the same size σ, that unit C samples the same number of neurons N from both domains, and that the input from each domain to unit C is a linear combination of the responses of the units in each area. The input to C from domain A, with $\vec{x_p}$ presented to the system is then:

$$A_{in} = \sum_{j=1}^{N} a_j \phi_{jp} \qquad (3)$$

The problem is to find coefficients $\{a_j\}$ and $\{b_j\}$ such that on a given set of inputs $\{\vec{x}_p\}$ the outputs of domains A and B will match. We define the matching error as follows:

$$E_m = \sum_{p=1}^{P} \left(\sum_{i=1}^{N} a_i \phi_{ip} - \sum_{i=1}^{N} b_i \theta_{ip} \right)^2 \qquad (4)$$

Proposition 1 *The desired coefficients, minimizing E_m, can be generated by an algorithm trained to learn an input/output mapping from a set of examples.*

This proposition can be proved by taking the derivative of E_m with respect to the coefficients (Grill-Spector et al., 1995). Learning here can be carried out by radial basis function (RBF) approximation (Poggio and Girosi, 1990), which is particularly suitable for our purpose, because its basis functions can be regarded as multidimensional Gaussian RFs.

4 Summary

Our results show that maximal diversity of neuronal response properties is attained when the ratio of dendritic and axonal arbor sizes is equal to 1, a value found in many cortical areas and across species (Lund et al., 1993; Malach, 1994). Maximization of diversity also leads to better performance in systems of receptive fields implementing steerable/shiftable filters, which may be necessary for generating the seemingly continuous range of orientation selectivity found in V1, and in matching spatially distributed signals. This cortical organization principle may, therefore, have the double advantage of accounting for the formation of the cortical columns and the associated patchy projection patterns, and of explaining how systems of receptive fields can support functions such as the generation of precise response tuning from imprecise distributed inputs, and the matching of distributed signals, a problem that arises in visual tasks such as stereopsis, motion processing, and recognition.

References

Grill-Spector, K., Edelman, S., and Malach, R. (1995). Anatomical origin and computational role of diversity in the response properties of cortical neurons. In Aertsen, A., editor, *Brain Theory: biological basis and computational theory of vision*. Elsevier. in press.

Grinvald, A., Lieke, T., Frostigand, R., Gilbert, C., and Wiesel, T. (1986). Functional architecture of the cortex as revealed by optical imaging of intrinsic signals. *Nature*, 324:361–364.

Hubel, D. and Wiesel, T. (1962). Receptive fields, binocular interactions and functional architecture in the cat's visual cortex. *Journal of Physiology*, 160:106–154.

Lund, J., Yoshita, S., and Levitt, J. (1993). Comparison of intrinsic connections in different areas of macaque cerebral cortex. *Cerebral Cortex*, 3:148–162.

MacIlwain, J. (1986). Point images in the visual system: new interest in an old idea. *Trends in Neurosciences*, 9:354–358.

Malach, R. (1992). Dendritic sampling across processing streams in monkey striate cortex. *Journal of Comparative Neurobiology*, 315:305–312.

Malach, R. (1994). Cortical columns as devices for maximizing neuronal diversity. *Trends in Neurosciences*, 17:101–104.

Malach, R., Amir, Y., Harel, M., and Grinvald, A. (1993). Relationship between intrinsic connections and functional architecture, revealed by optical imaging and in vivo targeted biocytine injections in primate striate cortex. *Proceedings of the National Academy of Science, USA*, 90:10469–10473.

Mouncastle, V. (1957). Modality and topographic properties of single neurons of cat's somatic sensory cortex. *Journal of Neurophysiology*, 20:408–434.

Poggio, T. and Girosi, F. (1990). Regularization algorithms for learning that are equivalent to multilayer networks. *Science*, 247:978–982.

Rockland, K. and Lund, J. (1982). Widespread periodic intrinsic connections in the tree shrew visual cortex. *Science*, 215:1532–1534.

Simoncelli, E., Freeman, W., Adelson, E., and Heeger, D. (1992). Shiftable multiscale transformations. *IEEE Transactions on Information Theory*, 38:587–607.

Vidyasagar, T. (1985). Geniculate orientation biases as cartesian coordinates for cortical orientation detectors. In *Models for the visual cortex*, pages 390–395. Wiley, New York.

Reinforcement Learning Predicts the Site of Plasticity for Auditory Remapping in the Barn Owl

Alexandre Pouget[†]
alex@salk.edu

Cedric Deffayet[‡]
cedric@salk.edu

Terrence J. Sejnowski[†]
terry@salk.edu

[†]Howard Hughes Medical Institute
The Salk Institute
La Jolla, CA 92037
Department of Biology
University of California, San Diego
and
[‡]Ecole Normale Superieure
45 rue d'Ulm
75005 Paris, France

Abstract

The auditory system of the barn owl contains several spatial maps. In young barn owls raised with optical prisms over their eyes, these auditory maps are shifted to stay in register with the visual map, suggesting that the visual input imposes a frame of reference on the auditory maps. However, the optic tectum, the first site of convergence of visual with auditory information, is not the site of plasticity for the shift of the auditory maps; the plasticity occurs instead in the inferior colliculus, which contains an auditory map and projects into the optic tectum. We explored a model of the owl remapping in which a global reinforcement signal whose delivery is controlled by visual foveation. A hebb learning rule gated by reinforcement learned to appropriately adjust auditory maps. In addition, reinforcement learning preferentially adjusted the weights in the inferior colliculus, as in the owl brain, even though the weights were allowed to change throughout the auditory system. This observation raises the possibility that the site of learning does not have to be genetically specified, but could be determined by how the learning procedure interacts with the network architecture.

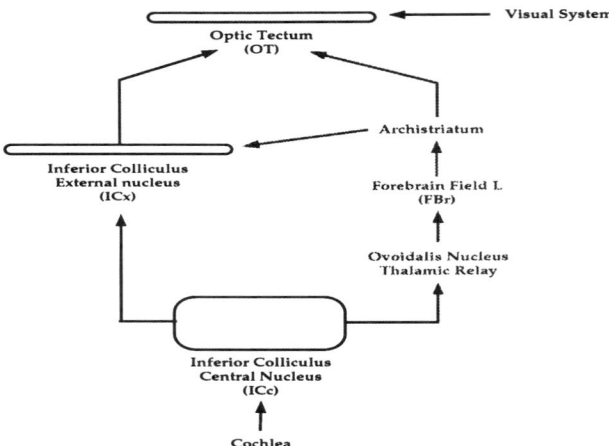

Figure 1: Schematic view of the auditory pathways in the barn owl.

1 Introduction

The barn owl relies primarily on sounds to localize prey [6] with an accuracy vastly superior to that of humans. Figure 1A illustrates some of the nuclei involved in processing auditory signals. The barn owl determines the location of sound sources by comparing the time and amplitude differences of the sound wave between the two ears. These two cues are combined together for the first time in the shell and core of the inferior colliculus (ICc) which is shown at the bottom of the diagram. Cells in the ICc are frequency tuned and subject to spatial aliasing. This prevents them from unambiguously encoding the position of objects. The first unambiguous auditory map is found at the next stage, in the external capsule of the inferior colliculus (ICx) which itself projects to the optic tectum (OT). The OT is the first subforebrain structure which contains a multimodal spatial map in which cells typically have spatially congruent visual and auditory receptive fields.

In addition, these subforebrain auditory pathways send one major collateral toward the forebrain via a thalamic relay. These collaterals originate in the ICc and are thought to convey the spatial location of objects to the forebrain [3]. Within the forebrain, two major structures have been involved in auditory processing: the archistriatum and field L. The archistriatum sends a projection to both the inferior colliculus and the optic tectum.

Knudsen and Knudsen (1985) have shown that these auditory maps can adapt to systematic changes in the sensory input. Furthermore, the adaptation appears to be under the control of visual input, which imposes a frame of reference on the incoming auditory signals. In owls raised with optical prisms, which introduce a systematic shift in part of the visual field, the visual map in the optic tectum was identical to that found in control animals, but the auditory map in the ICx was shifted by the amount of visual shift introduced by the prisms. This plasticity ensures that the visual and auditory maps stay in spatial register during growth and other perturbations to sensory mismatch.

Since vision instructs audition, one might expect the auditory map to shift in the optic tectum, the first site of visual-auditory convergence. Surprisingly, Brainard and Knudsen (1993b) observed that the synaptic changes took place between the ICc and the ICx, one synapse before the site of convergence.

These observations raise two important questions: First, how does the animal knows how to adapt the weights in the ICx in the absence of a visual teaching signal? Second, why does the change take place at this particular location and not in the OT where a teaching signal would be readily available?

In a previous model [7], this shift was simulated using backpropagation to broadcast the error back through the layers and by constraining the weights changes to the projection from the ICc to ICx. There is, however, no evidence for a feedback projection between from the OT to the ICx that could transmit the error signal; nor is there evidence to exclude plasticity at other synapses in these pathways.

In this paper, we suggest an alternative approach in which vision guides the remapping of auditory maps by controlling the delivery of a scalar reinforcement signal. This learning proceeds by generating random actions and increasing the probability of actions that are consistently reinforced [1, 5]. In addition, we show that reinforcement learning correctly predicts the site of learning in the barn owl, namely at the ICx-ICc synapse, whereas backpropagation [8] does not favor this location when plasticity is allowed at every synapse. This raises a general issue: the site of synaptic adjustment might be imposed by the combination of the architecture and learning rule, without having to restrict plasticity to a particular synapse.

2 Methods

2.1 Network Architecture

The network architecture of the model based on the barn owl auditory system, shown in figure 2A, contains two parallel pathways. The input layer was an 8x21 map corresponding to the ICc in which units responded to frequency and interaural phase differences. These responses were pooled together to create auditory spatial maps at subsequent stages in both pathways. The rest of the network contained a series of similar auditory maps, which were connected topographically by receptive fields 13 units wide. We did not distinguish between field L and the archistriatum in the forebrain pathways and simply used two auditory maps, both called FBr.

We used multiplicative (sigma-pi) units in the OT whose activities were determined according to:

$$y_i = \sum_j w_{ij}^{FBr} y_j^{FBr} w_{jk}^{FBr} y_j^{ICx} \tag{1}$$

The multiplicative interaction between ICx and FBr activities was an important assumption of our model. It forced the ICx and FBr to agree on a particular position before the OT was activated. As a result, if the ICx-OT synapses were modified during learning, the ICx-FBr synapses had to be changed accordingly.

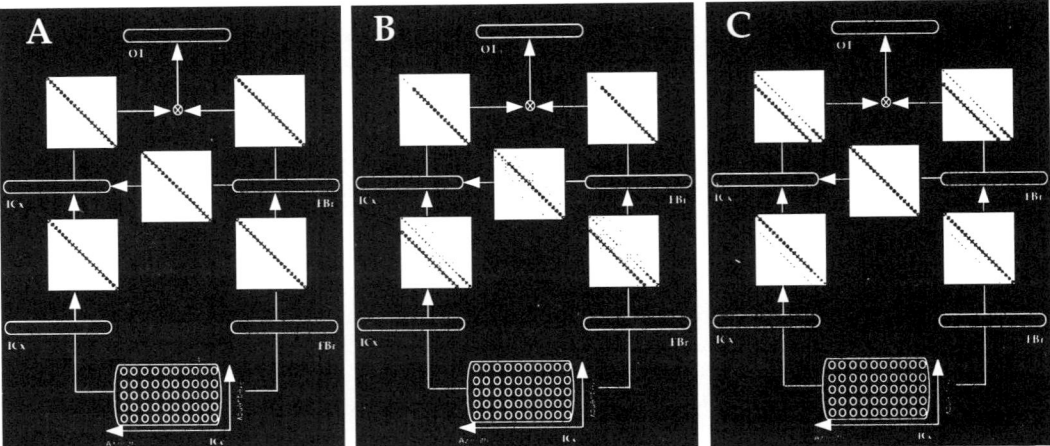

Figure 2: Schematic diagram of weights (white blocks) in the barn owl auditory system. A) Diagram of the initial weights in the network. B) Pattern of weights after training with reinforcement learning on a prism-induced shift of four units. The remapping took place within the ICx and FBr. C) Pattern of weights after training with backpropagation. This time the ICx-OT and FBr-OT weights changed.

Weights were clipped between 5.0 and 0.01, except for the FBr-ICx connections whose values were allowed to vary between 8.0 and 0.01. The minimum values were set to 0.01 instead of zero to prevent getting trapped in unstable local minima which are often associated with weights values of zero. The strong coupling between FBr and ICx was another important assumption of the model whose consequence will be discussed in the last section.

Examples were generated by simply activating one unit in the ICc while keeping the others to zero, thereby simulating the pattern of activity that would be triggered by a single localized auditory stimulus. In all simulations, we modeled a prism-induced shift of four units.

2.2 Reinforcement learning

We used stochastic units and trained the network using reinforcement learning [1]. The weighted sum of the inputs, net_i, passed through a sigmoid, f(x), is interpreted as the probability, p_i, that the unit will be active:

$$p_i = f(net_i) * 0.99 + 0.01 \qquad (2)$$

were the output of the unit y_i was:

$$y_i = \begin{cases} 0 & \text{with probability } 1 - p_i \\ 1 & \text{with probability } p_i \end{cases} \qquad (3)$$

Because of the form of the equation for p_i, all units in the network had a small probability (0.01) of being spontaneously active in the absence of any inputs. This is what allowed the network to perform a stochastic search in action space to find which actions were consistently associated with positive reinforcement.

We ensured that at most one unit was active per trial by using a winner-take-all competition in each layer.

Adjustable weights in the network were updated after each training examples with hebb-like rule gated by reinforcement:

$$\Delta w_{ij} = \epsilon y_i \frac{\partial net_i}{\partial w_{ij}} r \qquad (4)$$

A trial consisted in choosing a random target location for auditory input (ICc) and the output of the OT was used to generate a head movement. The reinforcement, r, was then set to 1 for head movements resulting in the foveation of the stimulus and to -0.05 otherwise.

2.3 Backpropagation

For the backpropagation network, we used deterministic units with sigmoid activation functions in which the output of a unit was given by:

$$y_i = f(net_i) \qquad (5)$$

where net_i is the weighted sum of the inputs as before.

The chain rule was used to compute the partial derivatives of the squared error, E, with respect to each weights and the weights were updated after each training example according to:

$$\Delta w_{ij} = -\epsilon \frac{\partial E}{\partial w_{ij}} \qquad (6)$$

The target vectors were similar to the input vectors, namely only one OT units was required to be activated for a given pattern, but at a position displaced by 4 units compared to the input.

3 Results

3.1 Learning site with reinforcement

In a first set of simulation we kept the ICc-ICx and ICc-FBr weights fixed. Plasticity was allowed at these site in later simulations.

Figure 2A shows the initial set of weights before learning starts. The central diagonal lines in the weight diagrams illustrate the fact that each unit receives only one non-zero weight from the unit in the layer below at the same location.

There are two solutions to the remapping: either the weights change within the ICx and FBr, or from the ICx and the FBr to the OT. As shown in figure 2B, reinforcement learning converged to the first solution. In contrast, the weights between the other layers were unaltered, even though they were allowed to change.

To prove that the network could have actually learned the second solution, we trained a network in which the ICc-ICx weights were kept fixed. As we expected, the network shifted its maps simultaneously in both sets of weights converging onto the OT, and the resulting weights were similar to the ones illustrated in figure 2C. However, to reach this solution, three times as many training examples were needed.

The reason why learning in the ICx and FBr were favored can be attributed to probabilistic nature of reinforcement learning. If the probability of finding one solution is p, the probability of finding it twice independently is p^2. Learning in the ICx and FBR is not independent because of the strong connection from the FBr to the ICx. When the remapping is learned in the FBR this connection automatically remapped the activities in the ICx which in turn allows the ICx-ICx weights to remap appropriately. In the OT on the other hand, the multiplicative connection between the ICx and FBr weights prevent a cooperation between this two sets of weights. Consequently, they have to change independently, a process which took much more training.

3.2 Learning at the ICc-ICx and ICc-FBr synapses

The aliasing and sharp frequency tuning in the response of ICc neurons greatly slows down learning at the ICc-ICx and ICc-FBr synapses. We found that when these synapses were free to change, the remapping still took place within the ICx or FBr (figure 3).

3.3 Learning site with backpropagation

In contrast to reinforcement learning, backpropagation adjusted the weights in two locations: between the ICx and the OT and between the Fbr and OT (figure 2C). This is the consequence of the tendency of the backpropagation algorithm to first change the weights closest to where the error is injected.

3.4 Temporal evolution of weights

Whether we used reinforcement or supervised learning, the map shifted in a very similar way. There was a simultaneous decrease of the original set of weights with a simultaneous increase of the new weights, such that both sets of weights coexisted half way through learning. This indicates that the map shifted directly from the original setting to the new configuration without going through intermediate shifts.

This temporal evolution of the weights is consistent the findings of Brainard and Knudsen (1993a) who found that during the intermediate phase of the remapping, cells in the inferior colliculus typically have two receptive fields. More recent work however indicates that for some cells the remapping is more continuous(Brainard and Knudsen, personal communication), a behavior that was not reproduced by either of the learning rule.

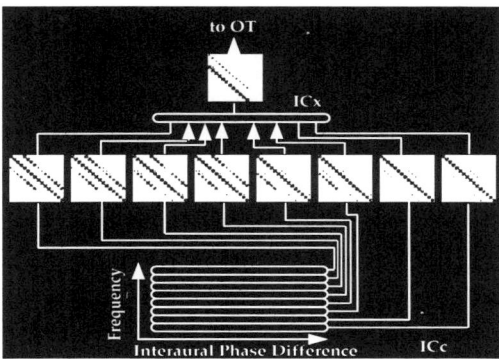

Figure 3: Even when the ICc-ICx weights are free to change, the network update the weights in the ICx first. A separate weight matrix is shown for each isofrequency map from the ICc to ICx. The final weight matrices were predominantly diagonal; in contrast, the weight matrix in ICx was shifted.

4 Discussion

Our simulations suggest a biologically plausible mechanism by which vision can guide the remapping of auditory spatial maps in the owl's brain. Unlike previous approaches, which relied on visual signals as an explicit teacher in the optic tectum [7], our model uses a global reinforcement signal whose delivery is controlled by the foveal representation of the visual system. Other global reinforcement signals would work as well. For example, a part of the forebrain might compare auditory and visual patterns and report spatial mismatch between the two. This signal could be easily incorporated in our network and would also remap the auditory map in the inferior colliculus.

Our model demonstrates that the site of synaptic plasticity can be constrained by the interaction between reinforcement learning and the network architecture. Reinforcement learning converged to the most probably solution through stochastic search. In the network, the strong lateral coupling between ICx and FBr and the multiplicative interaction in the OT favored a solution in which the remapping took place simultaneously in the ICx and FBr. A similar mechanism may be at work in the barn owl's brain. Colaterals from FBr to ICx are known to exist, but the multiplicative interaction has not been reported in the barn owl optic tectum.

Learning mechanisms may also limit synaptic plasticity. NMDA receptors have been reported in the ICx, but they might not be expressed at other synapses. There may, however, be other mechanisms for plasticity.

The site of remapping in our model was somewhat different from the existing observations. We found that the change took place *within* the ICx whereas Brainard and Knudsen [3] report that it is *between* the ICc and the ICx. A close examination of their data (figure 11 in [3]) reveals that cells at the bottom of ICx were not remapped, as predicted by our model, but at the same time, there is little anatomical or physiological evidence for a functional and hierarchical organization within the ICx. Additional recordings are need to resolve this issue. We conclude that for the barn owl's brain, as well as for our model, synaptic plasticity within ICx was favored over changes between ICc and ICx. This supports the hypothesis that reinforcement learning is used for remapping in the barn owl auditory system.

Acknowledgments

We thank Eric Knudsen and Michael Brainard for helpful discussions on plasticity in the barn owl auditory system and the results of unpublished experiments. Peter Dayan and P. Read Montague helped with useful insights on the biological basis of reinforcement learning in the early stages of this project.

References

[1] A.G. Barto and M.I. Jordan. Gradient following without backpropagation in layered networks. *Proc. IEEE Int. Conf. Neural Networks*, 2:629–636, 1987.

[2] M.S. Brainard and E.I. Knudsen. Dynamics of the visual calibration of the map of interaural time difference in the barn owl's optic tectum. In *Society For Neuroscience Abstracts*, volume 19, page 369.8, 1993.

[3] M.S. Brainard and E.I. Knudsen. Experience-dependent plasticity in the inferior colliculus: a site for visual calibration of the neural representation of auditory space in the barn owl. *The journal of Neuroscience*, 13:4589–4608, 1993.

[4] E. Knudsen and P. Knudsen. Vision guides the adjustment of auditory localization in the young barn owls. *Science*, 230:545–548, 1985.

[5] P.R. Montague, P. Dayan, S.J. Nowlan, A. Pouget, and T.J. Sejnowski. Using aperiodic reinforcement for directed self-organization during development. In S.J. Hanson, J.D. Cowan, and C.L. Giles, editors, *Advances in Neural Information Processing Systems*, volume 5. Morgan-Kaufmann, San Mateo, CA, 1993.

[6] R.S. Payne. Acoustic location of prey by barn owls (tyto alba). *Journal of Experimental Biology*, 54:535–573, 1970.

[7] D.J. Rosen, D.E. Rumelhart, and E.I. Knudsen. A connectionist model of the owl's sound localization system. In *Advances in Neural Information Processing Systems*, volume 6. Morgan-Kaufmann, San Mateo, CA, 1994.

[8] D.E. Rumelhart, G.E. Hinton, and R.J. Williams. Learning internal representations by error propagation. In D. E. Rumelhart, J. L. McClelland, and the PDP Research Group, editors, *Parallel Distributed Processing*, volume 1, chapter 8, pages 318–362. MIT Press, Cambridge, MA, 1986.

Morphogenesis of the Lateral Geniculate Nucleus: How Singularities Affect Global Structure

Svilen Tzonev
Beckman Institute
University of Illinois
Urbana, IL 61801
svilen@ks.uiuc.edu

Klaus Schulten
Beckman Institute
University of Illinois
Urbana, IL 61801
kschulte@ks.uiuc.edu

Joseph G. Malpeli
Psychology Department
University of Illinois
Champaign, IL 61820
jmalpeli@uiuc.edu

Abstract

The macaque lateral geniculate nucleus (LGN) exhibits an intricate lamination pattern, which changes midway through the nucleus at a point coincident with small gaps due to the blind spot in the retina. We present a three-dimensional model of morphogenesis in which local cell interactions cause a wave of development of neuronal receptive fields to propagate through the nucleus and establish two distinct lamination patterns. We examine the interactions between the wave and the localized singularities due to the gaps, and find that the gaps induce the change in lamination pattern. We explore critical factors which determine general LGN organization.

1 INTRODUCTION

Each side of the mammalian brain contains a structure called the lateral geniculate nucleus (LGN), which receives visual input from both eyes and sends projections to the primary visual cortex. In primates the LGN consists of several distinct layers of neurons separated by intervening layers of axons and dendrites. Each layer of neurons maps the opposite visual hemifield in a topographic fashion. The cells comprising these layers differ in terms of their type (magnocellular and parvocellular), their input (from ipsilateral (same side) and contralateral (opposite side) eyes), and their receptive field organization (ON and OFF center polarity). Cells in one layer receive input from one eye only (Kaas et al., 1972), and in most parts of the nucleus have the same functional properties (Schiller & Malpeli, 1978). The maps are in register, i.e., representations of a point in the visual field are found in all layers, and lie in a narrow column roughly perpendicular to the layers (Figure 1). A prominent

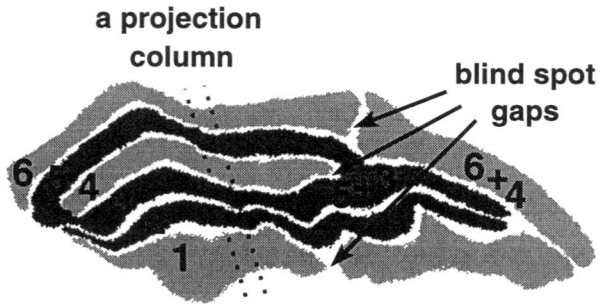

Figure 1: A slice along the plane of symmetry of the macaque LGN. Layers are numbered ventral to dorsal. Posterior is to the left, where foveal (central) parts of the retinas are mapped; peripheral visual fields are mapped anteriorly (right). Cells in different layers have different morphology and functional properties: 6-P/C/ON; 5-P/I/ON; 4-P/C/OFF; 3-P/I/OFF; 2-M/I/ON&OFF; 1-M/C/ON&OFF, where P is parvocellular, M is magnocellular, C is contralateral, I is ipsilateral, ON and OFF refer to polarities of the receptive-field centers. The gaps in layers 6, 4, and 1 are images of the blind spot in the contralateral eye. Cells in columns perpendicular to the layers receive input from the same point in the visual field.

feature in this laminar organization is the presence of cell-free gaps in some layers. These gaps are representations of the blind spot (the hole in the retina where the optic nerve exits) of the opposite retina. In the LGN of the rhesus macaque monkey (*Macaca mulatta*) the pattern of laminar organization drastically changes at the position of the gaps — foveal to the gaps there are six distinct layers, peripheral to the gaps there are four layers. The layers are extended two-dimensional structures whereas the gaps are essentially localized. However, the laminar transition occurs in a surface that extends far beyond the gaps, cutting completely across the main axis of the LGN (Malpeli & Baker., 1975).

We propose a developmental model of LGN laminar morphogenesis. In particular, we investigate the role of the blind-spot gaps in the laminar pattern transition, and their extended influence over the global organization of the nucleus. In this model a wave of development caused by local cell interactions sweeps through the system (Figure 2). Strict enforcement of retinotopy maintains and propagates an initially localized foveal pattern. At the position of the gaps, the system is in a metastable

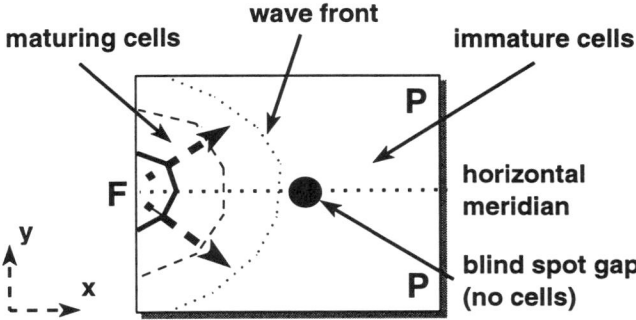

Figure 2: Top view of a single layer. As a wave of development sweeps through the LGN the foveal part matures first and the more peripheral parts develop later. The shape of the developmental wave front is shown schematically by lines of "equal development".

state, and the perturbation in retinotopy caused by the gaps is sufficient to change the state of the system to its preferred four-layered pattern. We study the critical factors in this model, and make some predictions about LGN morphogenesis.

2 MODEL OF LGN MORPHOGENESIS

We will consider only the upper four (parvocellular) layers since the laminar transition does not involve the other two layers. This transition results simply from a reordering of the four parvocellular strata (Figure 1). Foveal to the gaps, the strata form four morphologically distinct layers (6, 5, 4 and 3) because adjacent strata receive inputs from opposite eyes, which "repel" one another. Peripheral to the gaps, the reordering of strata reduces the number of parvocellular eye alternations to one, resulting in two parvocellular layers (6+4 and 5+3).

2.1 GEOMETRY AND VARIABLES

LGN cells c_i are labeled by indices $i = 1, 2, \ldots, N$. The cells have fixed, quazi-random and uniformly distributed locations $r_i \in V \subset \Re^3$, where $V = \{(x,y,z) \mid 0 < x < S_x, 0 < y < S_y, 0 < z < S_z\}$, and belong to one projection column C_{ab}, $a = 1, 2, \ldots, A$ and $b = 1, 2, \ldots, B$, (Figure 3). Functional properties of the neurons change in time (denoted by τ), and are described by eye specificity and receptive-field polarity, $e_i(\tau)$, and $p_i(\tau)$, respectively: $e_i(\tau), p_i(\tau) \in [-1, 1] \subset \Re$, $i = 1, 2, \ldots, N$, $\tau = 0, 1, \ldots, T_{max}$.

The values of eye specificity and polarity represent the proportions of synapses from competing types of retinal ganglion cells (there are four type of ganglion cells — from different eyes and with ON or OFF polarity). $e_i = -1$ ($e_i = 1$) denotes that the i-th cell is receiving input solely from the opposite (same side) retina. Similarly, $p_i = -1$ ($p_i = 1$) denotes that the cell input is pure ON (OFF) center. Intermediate values of e_i and p_i imply that the cell does not have pure properties (it receives

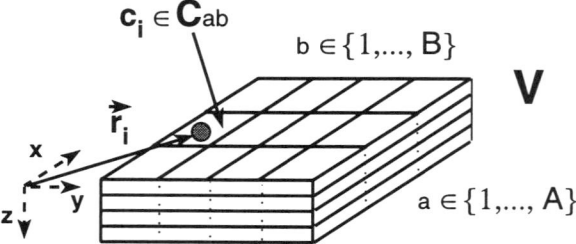

Figure 3: Geometry of the model. LGN cells c_i ($i = 1, 2, \ldots, N$) have fixed random, and uniformly-distributed locations r_i within a volume $V \subset \Re^3$, and belong to one projection column C_{ab}.

input from retinal ganglion cells of both eyes and with different polarities). Initially, at $\tau = 0$, all LGN cells are characterized by $e_i, p_i = 0$. This corresponds to two possibilities: no retinal ganglion cells synapse on any LGN cell, or proportions of synapses from different ganglion cells on all LGN neurons are equal, i.e., neurons possess completely undetermined functionality because of competing inputs of equal strength. As the neurons mature and acquire functional properties, their eye specificity and polarity reach their asymptotic values, ±1.

Even when cells are not completely mature, we will refer to them as being of four different types, depending on the signs of their functional properties. Following accepted anatomical notation, we will label them as 6, 5, 4, and 3. We denote eye specificity of cell types 6 and 4 as negative, and cell types 5 and 3 as positive. Polarity of cell types 6 and 5 is negative, while polarity of types 4 and 3 is positive.

Cell functional properties are subject to the dynamics described in the following section. The process of LGN development starts from its foveal part, since in the retina it is the fovea that matures first. As more peripheral parts of the retina mature, their ganglion cells start to compete to establish permanent synapses on LGN cells. In this sorting process, each LGN cell gradually emerges with permanent synapses that connect only to several neighboring ganglions of the same type. A wave of gradual development of functionality sweeps through the nucleus. The driving force for this maturation process is described by localized cell interactions modulated by external influences. The particular pattern of the foveal lamination is shaped by external forces, and later serves as a starting point for a "propagation of sameness" of cell properties. Such a sameness propagation produces clustering of similar cells and formation of layers. It should be stressed that cells do not move, only their characteristics change.

2.2 DYNAMICS

The variables describing cell functional properties are subject to the following dynamics

$$\begin{aligned} \hat{e}_i(\tau+1) &= e_i(\tau) + \Delta e_i(\tau) + \eta_e \\ \hat{p}_i(\tau+1) &= p_i(\tau) + \Delta p_i(\tau) + \eta_p, \quad i = 1, 2, \ldots, N. \end{aligned} \quad (1)$$

In Eq. (1), there are two contributions to the change of the intermediate variables $\hat{e}_i(\tau)$ and $\hat{p}_i(\tau)$. The first is deterministic, given by

$$\Delta e_i(\tau) = \alpha(r_i) \left[\left(\sum_{j=1}^{N} e_j(\tau) f(|r_i - r_j|) \right) + E_{ext}(r_i) \right] (1 - e_i^2(\tau)) \beta_{ab}^t$$

$$\Delta p_i(\tau) = \alpha(r_i) \left[\left(\sum_{j=1}^{N} p_j(\tau) f(|r_i - r_j|) \right) + P_{ext}(r_i) \right] (1 - p_i^2(\tau)) \beta_{ab}^t. \quad (2)$$

The second is a stochastic contribution corresponding to fluctuations in the growth of the synapses between retinal ganglion cells and LGN neurons. This noise in synaptic growth plays both a driving and a stabilizing role to be explained below. We explain the meaning of the variables in Eq. (2) only for the eye specificity variable e_i. The corresponding parameters for polarity p_i have similar interpretations.

The parameter $\alpha(r_i)$ is the rate of cell development. This rate is the same for eye specificity and polarity. It depends on the position r_i of the cell in order to allow for spatially non-uniform development. The functional form of $\alpha(r_i)$ is given in the Appendix.

The term $E_{int}(r_i) = \sum_{j=1}^{N} e_j f(|r_i - r_j|)$ is effectively a cell force field. This field influences the development of nearby cells and promotes clustering of same type of cells. It depends on the maturity of the generating cells and on the distance between cells through the interaction function $f(\delta)$. We chose for $f(\delta)$ a Gaussian form, i.e., $f(\delta) = \exp(-\delta^2/\sigma^2)$, with characteristic interaction distance σ.

The external influences on cell development are incorporated in the term for the external field $E_{ext}(r_i)$. This external field plays two roles: it launches a particular laminar configuration of the system (in the foveal part of the LGN), and determines its peripheral pattern. It has, thus, two contributions $E_{ext}(r_i) = E_{ext}^f(r_i) + E_{ext}^p(r_i)$. The exact forms of $E_{ext}^f(r_i)$ and $E_{ext}^p(r_i)$ are provided in the Appendix.

The nonlinear term $(1 - e_i^2)$ in Eq. (2) ensures that ± 1 are the only stable fixed points of the dynamics. The neuronal properties gradually converge to either of these fixed points capturing the maturation process. This term also stabilizes the dynamic variables and prevents them from diverging.

The last term $\beta_{ab}^t(\tau)$ reflects the strict columnar organization of the maps. At each step of the development the proportion of all four types of LGN cells is calculated within a single column C_{ab}, and $\beta_{ab}^t(\tau)$ for different types t is adjusted such that all types are equally represented. Without this term, the cell organization degenerates to a non-laminar pattern (the system tries to minimize the surfaces between cell clusters of different type). The exact form of $\beta_{ab}^t(\tau)$ is given in the Appendix.

At each stage of LGN development, cells receive input from retinal ganglion cells of particular types. This means that eye specificity and polarity of LGN cells are not independent variables. In fact, they are tightly coupled in the sense that $|e_i(\tau)| = |p_i(\tau)|$ should hold for all cells at all times. This gives rise to coupled dynamics described by

$$m_i(\tau+1) = \min(|\hat{e}_i(\tau+1)|, |\hat{p}_i(\tau+1)|)$$
$$e_i(\tau+1) = m_i(\tau+1)\,\text{sgn}(\hat{e}_i(\tau+1))$$
$$p_i(\tau+1) = m_i(\tau+1)\,\text{sgn}(\hat{p}_i(\tau+1)),\ i=1,2,\ldots,N. \quad (3)$$

The blind spot gaps are modeled by not allowing cells in certain columns to acquire types of functionality for which retinal projections do not exist, e.g., from the blind spot of the opposite eye. Accordingly, e_i is not allowed to become negative. Thus, some cells never reach a pure state $e_i, p_i = \pm 1$. It is assumed that in reality such cells die out. Of all quantities and parameters, only variables describing the neuronal receptive fields (e_i and p_i) are time-dependent.

3 RESULTS

We simulated the dynamics described by Eqs. (1, 2, 3), typically for 100,000 time steps. Depending on the rate of cell development, mature states were reached in about 10,000 steps. The maximum value of α was 0.0001. We used an interaction function with $\sigma = 1$.

First, we considered a two-dimensional LGN, $V = \{(x,z)|0 < x < S_x, 0 < z < S_z\}$ with $S_x = 10$ and $S_z = 6$. There were ten projection columns (with equal size) along the x axis. An initial pattern was started in the foveal part by the external field. The size of the gaps g measured in terms of the interaction distance σ was crucial for pattern development. When the developmental wave reached the gaps, layer 6 could "jump" its gap and continued to spread peripherally if the gap was sufficiently narrow ($g/\sigma < 1.5$). If its gap was not too narrow ($g/\sigma > 0.5$), layer 4 completely stopped (since cells in the gaps were not allowed to acquire negative eye specificity) and so layers 5 and 3 were able to merge. Cells of type 4 reappeared after the gaps (Figure 4, right side, shows behavior similar to the two-dimensional model) because of the required equal representation of all cell types in the projection columns, and because of noise in cell development. Energetically, the most favorable position of cell type 4 would be on top of type 6, which is inconsistent with experimental observations. Therefore, one must assume the existence of an external field in the peripheral part that will drive the system away from its otherwise preferred state. If the gaps were too large ($g/\sigma > 1.5$), cells of type 6 and 4 reappeared after the gaps in a more or less random vertical position and caused transitions of irregular nature. On the other hand, if the gaps were too narrow ($g/\sigma < 0.5$), both layers 6 and 4 could continue to grow past their gaps, and no transition between laminar patterns occurred at all. When g/σ was close to the above limits, the pattern after the gaps differed from trial to trial. For the two-dimensional system, a realistic peripheral pattern always occurred for $0.7 < g/\sigma < 1.2$.

We simulated a three-dimensional system with size $S_x = 10$, $S_y = 10$, and $S_z = 6$, and projection columns ordered in a 10 by 10 grid. The topology of the system is different in two and three dimensions: in two dimensions the gaps interrupt the layers completely and, thus, induce perturbations which cannot be by-passed. In three dimensions the gaps are just holes in a plane and generate localized perturbations: the layers can, in principle, grow around the gaps maintaining the initial laminar pattern. Nevertheless, in the three-dimensional case, an extended transi-

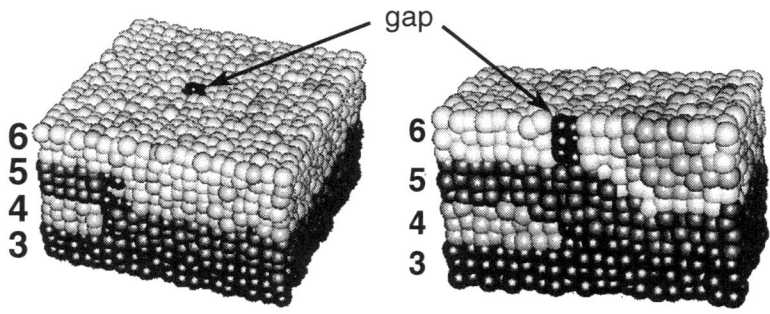

Figure 4: **Left:** Mature state of the macaque LGN — result of the three-dimensional model with 4,800 cells. Spheres with different shades represent cells with different properties. Gaps in strata 6 and 4 (this gap is not visible) are coded by the darkest color, and coincide with the transition surface between 4- and 2-layered patterns. **Right:** A cut of the three-dimensional structure along its plane of symmetry. A two-dimensional system exhibits similar organization. Compare with upper layers in Figure 1. Spatial segregation between layers is not modeled explicitly.

tion was triggered by the gaps. The transition surface, which passed through the gaps and was oriented roughly perpendicularly to the x axis, cut completely across the nucleus (Figure 4).

Several factors were critical for the general behavior of the system. As in two dimensions, the size of the gaps must be within certain limits: typically $0.5 < g/\sigma < 1.0$. These limits depend on the curvature of the wavefront. The gaps must lie in a certain "inducing" interval along the x axis. If they were too close to the origin, the foveal pattern was still more stable, so no transition could be induced there. However, a spontaneous transition might occur downstream. If the gaps were too far from the origin, a spontaneous transition might occur before them. The occurrence and location of a spontaneous transition , (therefore, the limits of the "inducing" interval) depended on the external-field parameters. A realistic transition was observed only when the front of the developmental wave had sufficient curvature when it reached the gaps. Underlying anatomical reasons for a sufficiently curved front along the main axis could be the curvature of the nucleus, differences in layer thickness, or differences in ganglion-cell densities in the retinas.

Propagation of the developmental wave away from the gaps was quite stable. Before and after the gaps, the wave simply propagated the already established patterns. In a system without gaps, transitions of variable shape and location occurred when the peripheral contribution to the external fields was sufficiently large; a weaker contribution allowed the foveal pattern to propagate through the entire nucleus.

4 SUMMARY

We present a model that successfully captures the most important features of macaque LGN morphogenesis. It produces realistic laminar patterns and supports the hypothesis (Lee & Malpeli, 1994) that the blind spot gaps trigger the transition between patterns. It predicts that critical factors in LGN development are the size and location of the gaps, cell interaction distances, and shape of the front of the developmental wave. The model may be general enough to incorporate the LGN organizations of other primates. Small singularities, similar to the blind spot gaps, may have an extended influence on global organization of other biological systems.

Acknowledgements

This work has been supported by a Beckman Institute Research Assistantship, and by grants PHS 2P41 RR05969 and NIH EY02695.

References

J.H. Kaas, R.W. Guillery & J.M. Allman. (1972) Some principles of organization in the dorsal lateral geniculate nucleus, *Brain Behav. Evol.*, **6**: 253-299.

D.Lee & J.G.Malpeli. (1994) Global Form and Singularity: Modeling the Blind Spot's Role in Lateral Geniculate Morphogenesis, *Science*, **263**: 1292-1294.

J.G. Malpeli & F.H. Baker. (1975) The representation of the visual field in the lateral geniculate nucleus of Macaca mulatta, *J. Comp. Neurol.*, **161**: 569-594.

P.H. Schiller & J.G. Malpeli. (1978) Functional specificity of LGN of rhesus monkey, *J. Neurophysiol.*, **41**: 788-797.

APPENDIX

The form of $\alpha(x,y,z)$ (with $\alpha_0 = 0.0001$) was chosen as

$$\alpha(x,y,z) = \alpha_0 \left(0.1 + \exp\left(-(y - S_y/2)^2\right)\right). \tag{4}$$

Foveal external fields of the following form were used:

$$E_{ext}^f(x,y,z) = 10\left[\theta(z-d) - 2\theta(z-2d) + 2\theta(z-3d) - \theta(d-z)\right]\exp(-x)$$
$$P_{ext}^f(x,y,z) = 10\left[2\theta(z-2d) - 1\right]\exp(-x), \tag{5}$$

where $d = S_z/4$ is the layers' thickness and the "theta" function is defined as $\theta(x) = 1, x > 0$ and $\theta(x) = 0, x < 0$. Peripheral external fields (in fact they are present everywhere but determine the pattern in the peripheral part only) were chosen as

$$E_{ext}^p(x,y,z) = 5\left[2\theta(z-2d) - 1\right]$$
$$P_{ext}^p(x,y,z) = 5\left[\theta(z-d) - 2\theta(z-2d) + 2\theta(z-3d) - \theta(d-z)\right]. \tag{6}$$

$\beta_{ab}^t(\tau)$ was calculated in the following way: at any given time τ, within the column C_{ab}, we counted the number $N_{ab}^t(\tau)$ of cells, that could be classified as one of the four types $t = 3, 4, 5, 6$. Cells with $e_i(\tau)$ or $p_i(\tau)$ exactly zero were not counted. The total number of classified cells is then $N_{ab}(\tau) = \sum_{t=3}^{6} N_{ab}^t(\tau)$. If there were no classified cells ($N_{ab}(\tau) = 0$), then $\beta_{ab}^t(\tau)$ was set to one for all t. Otherwise the ratio of different types was calculated: $n_{ab}^t = N_{ab}^t(\tau)/N_{ab}(\tau)$. In this way we calculated

$$\beta_{ab}^t(\tau) = 4 - 12\, n_{ab}, \quad t = 3, 4, 5, 6. \tag{7}$$

If $\beta_{ab}^t(\tau)$ was negative it was replaced by zero.

A Computational Model of Prefrontal Cortex Function

Todd S. Braver
Dept. of Psychology
Carnegie Mellon Univ.
Pittsburgh, PA 15213

Jonathan D. Cohen
Dept. of Psychology
Carnegie Mellon Univ.
Pittsburgh, PA 15213

David Servan-Schreiber
Dept. of Psychiatry
Univ. of Pittsburgh
Pittsburgh, PA 15232

Abstract

Accumulating data from neurophysiology and neuropsychology have suggested two information processing roles for prefrontal cortex (PFC): 1) short-term active memory; and 2) inhibition. We present a new behavioral task and a computational model which were developed in parallel. The task was developed to probe both of these prefrontal functions simultaneously, and produces a rich set of behavioral data that act as constraints on the model. The model is implemented in continuous-time, thus providing a natural framework in which to study the temporal dynamics of processing in the task. We show how the model can be used to examine the behavioral consequences of neuromodulation in PFC. Specifically, we use the model to make novel and testable predictions regarding the behavioral performance of schizophrenics, who are hypothesized to suffer from reduced dopaminergic tone in this brain area.

1 Introduction

Prefrontal cortex (PFC) is an area of the human brain which is significantly expanded relative to other animals. There is general consensus that the PFC is centrally involved in higher cognitive activities such as planning, problem solving and language. Recently, the PFC has been associated with two specific information processing mechanisms: short-term active memory and inhibition. Active memory is the capacity of the nervous system to maintain information in the form of sustained activation states (e.g., cell firing) for short periods of time. This can be distinguished from forms of memory that are longer in duration and are instantiated as modified values of physiological parameters (e.g., synaptic strength). Over the last two decades, there have been a large number of neurophysiological studies focusing on the cellular basis of active memory in prefrontal cortex. These studies have revealed neurons in PFC that fire selectively to specific stimuli and response patterns, and that remain active during a delay between these. Investigators such as Fuster (1989) and Goldman-Rakic (1987) have argued from this data that PFC maintains temporary information needed to guide behavioral responses through sustained patterns of neural activity. This hypothesis is consistent with behavioral findings from both animal and human lesion studies, which suggest that PFC is required for tasks involving delayed responses to prior stimuli (Fuster, 1989; Stuss & Benson, 1986).

In addition to its role in active memory, many investigators have focused on the inhibitory functions of PFC. It has been argued that PFC representations are required to overcome reflexive or previously reinforced response tendencies in order to mediate a contextually appropriate – but otherwise weaker – response (Cohen & Servan-Schreiber, 1992). Clinically, it has been observed that lesions to PFC are often associated with a syndrome of behavioral disinhibition, in which patients act in impulsive and often socially inappropriate ways (Stuss & Benson, 1986). This syndrome has often been cited as evidence that PFC plays an important role inhibiting behaviors which are compelling but socially inappropriate.

While the involvement of PFC in both active memory and inhibition is generally agreed upon, computational models can play an important role in providing mechanisms by which to explain how these two information processing functions arise. There are several computational models now in the literature which have focused on either the active memory (Zipser, 1991), or inhibitory (Levine & Pruiett, 1989) functions of PFC, or both functions together (Dehaene & Changeux, 1989; Cohen & Servan-Schreiber, 1992). These models have been instrumental in explaining the role of PFC in a variety of behavioral tasks (e.g., the Wisconsin Card Sort and Stroop). However, these earlier models are limited by their inability to fully capture the dynamical processes underlying active memory and inhibition. Specifically, none of the simulations have been tightly constrained by the temporal parameters found in the behavioral tasks (e.g., durations of stimuli, delay periods, and response latencies). This limitation is not found solely in the models, but is also a feature of the behavioral tasks themselves. The tasks simulated were not structured in ways that could facilitate a dynamical analysis of processing.

In this paper we address the limitations of the previous work by describing both a new behavioral task and a computational model of PFC. These have been developed in parallel and, together, provide a useful framework for exploring the temporal dynamics of active memory and inhibition and their consequences for behavior. We then go on to describe how this framework can be used to examine neuromodulatory effects in PFC, which are believed to play a critical role in both normal functioning and in psychiatric disorders, such as schizophrenia.

2 Behavioral Assessment of Human PFC Function

We have developed a task paradigm which incorporates two components central to the function of prefrontal cortex – short-term active memory and inhibition – and that can be used to study the dynamics of processing. The task is a variant of the continuous performance test (CPT), which is commonly used to study attention in behavioral and clinical research. In a standard version of the task (the CPT-AX), letters are presented one at a time in the middle of a computer screen. Subjects are instructed to press the target button to the letter X (probe stimulus) but only when it is preceded by an A (the cue stimulus). In previous versions of the CPT, subjects only responded on target trials. In the present version of the task, a two response forced-choice procedure is employed; on non-A-X trials subjects are asked to press the non-target button. This procedure allows for response latencies to be evaluated on every trial, thus providing more information about the temporal dimensions of processing in the task.

Two additional modifications were made to the standard paradigm in order to maximally engage PFC activity. The memory function of PFC is tapped by manipulating the delay between stimuli. In the CPT-AX, the prior stimulus (cue or non-cue) provides the context necessary to decide how to respond to the probe letter. However, with a short delay (750 msec.), there is little demand on memory for the prior stimulus. This is supported by evidence that PFC lesions have been shown to have no effect on performance when there is only a short delay (Stuss & Benson, 1986). With a longer delay (5000 msec.), however, it becomes necessary to maintain a representation of the prior stimulus in order for it to be used as context for responding to the current one. The ability of the PFC to sustain contextual representations over the delay period can be determined behaviorally by comparing performance on short delay trials (50%) against those with long delays (50%).

The inhibitory function of PFC is probed by introducing a prepotent response tendency that must be overcome to respond correctly. This tendency is introduced into the task by increasing the frequency of target trials (A followed by X). In the remaining trials, there are three types of distractors: 1) a cue followed by a non-target probe letter (e.g., A-Y); 2) a non-cue followed by the target probe letter (e.g., B-X); and a non-cue followed by a non-target probe letter (e.g., B-Y). Target trials occur 70% of the time, while each type of distractor trial occurs only 10% of the time. The frequency of targets promotes the development of a strong tendency to respond to the target probe letter whenever it occurs, regardless of the identity of the cue (since a response to the X itself is correct 7 out of 8 times).

The ability to inhibit this response tendency can be examined by comparing accuracy on trials when the target occurs in the absence of the cue (B-X trials), with those made when neither the cue nor target occurs (i.e., B-Y trials, which provide a measure of non-specific response bias and random responding). Trials in which the cue but not the target probe appears (A-Y trials) are also particularly interesting with respect to PFC function. These trials measure the cumulative influence of active representations of context in guiding responses. In a normally functioning system, context representations should stabilize and increase in strength as time progresses. Thus, it is expected that A-Y accuracy will tend to decrease for long delay trials relative to short ones.

As mentioned above, the primary benefit of this paradigm is that it provides a framework in which to simultaneously probe the inhibitory and memory functions associated with PFC. This is supported by preliminary neuroimaging data from our laboratory (using PET) which suggests that PFC is, in fact, activated during performance of the task. Although it is simple in structure, the task also generates a rich set of behavioral data. There are four stimulus conditions crossed with two delay conditions for which both accuracy and reaction time performance can be

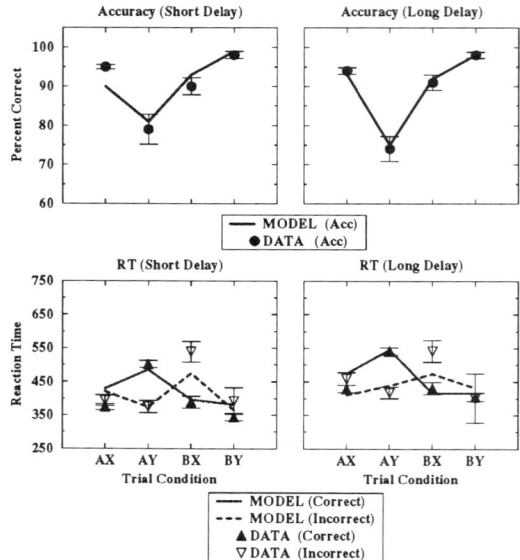

Figure 1: Subject behavioral data with model performance superimposed. **Top Panels:** Accuracy across both delays in all four conditions. **Bottom Panels:** Reaction times for both correct and incorrect responses in all conditions. Bars represent standard error of measurement for the empirical data.

measured. Figure 1 shows data gathered from 36 college-age subjects performing this task.

In brief, we found that: 1) Accuracy was relatively unchanged in the long delays compared to the short, demonstrating that active memory was adequately supporting performance; 2) A-Y accuracy, however, did slightly decrease at long delays, reflecting the normal build-up of context representations over time; 3) Accuracy on B-X trials was relatively high, supporting the assumption that subjects could effectively use context representations to inhibit prepotent responses; 4) A distinct pattern emerged in the latencies of correct and incorrect responses, providing information on the temporal dynamics of processing (i.e., responses to A-Y trials are slow on correct trials and fast on incorrect ones; the pattern is reversed for B-X trials). Taken together, the data provides specific, detailed information about normal PFC functioning, which act as constraints on the development and evaluation of a computational model.

3 A Computational Model of the CPT-AX

We have developed a recurrent network model which produces detailed information regarding the temporal course of processing in the CPT-AX task. The network is composed of three modules: an input module, a memory module, and an output module. The memory module implements the memory and inhibitory functions believed to be carried out by PFC. Figure 2 shows a diagram of the model.

Each unit in the input module represents a different stimulus condition: A, B, X &

A Computational Model of Prefrontal Cortex Function

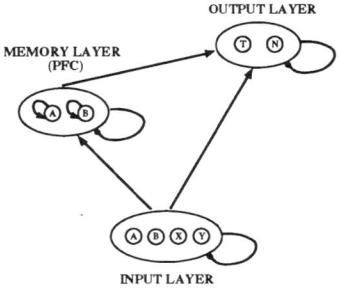

Figure 2: A diagram of the CPT-AX model.

Y. Units in the input module make excitatory connections on the response module, both directly and indirectly through the memory module. Lateral inhibition within each layer produces competition for representations. Activity from the cue stimulus flows to the memory module, which is responsible for maintaining a trace of the relevant context in each trial. Units in the memory module have self-excitatory connections, which allow for the activity generated by the cue to be sustained in the absence of input. The recurrent connectivity utilized by each unit in this module is assumed to be a simpler, but formally equivalent analogue of a fully connected recurrent cell assembly. Further, Zipser (1991) has used this type of connectivity to produce temporal activity patterns which are highly similar to the firing patterns of neurons in memory-associated areas of cortex, such as PFC. Activity from the input and memory modules is integrated in the output module. The output of this module determines whether a target (T) or non-target (N) response is made.

To simulate the CPT-AX task we have purposefully kept the network architecture and size as simple as possible in order to maximize the model's interpretability. We have therefore not attempted to simulate neural information processing in a neuron-by-neuron manner. Rather, the populations of a few units are seen as capturing the information processing characteristics of much larger populations of real neurons. In this way, it is possible to capture the stochastic, distributed, and dynamical properties of real neural networks with small and analytically tractable simulations.

The simulation is run in a temporally continuous framework in which processing is governed by the following difference equation:

$$I_j(t+1) = (\gamma \sum_i w_{ij} y_i + \beta - I_j(t))dt \qquad (1)$$

where

$$y_j = \frac{1}{1 + e^{-I_j}} \qquad (2)$$

is the state of unit j, I_j is the total input to j, dt is the time-step of integration, γ is the gain and β is the bias. The continuous framework is preferable to a discrete event-based one in that it allows for a plausible way to scale events appropriately to the exact temporal specifications of the task (i.e., the duration of stimuli and the delay between cue and probe). In addition, the continuous character of the simulation naturally provides a framework for inferring the reaction times in the various conditions.

4 Simulations of Behavioral Performance

We used a continuous recurrent generalization of backpropagation (Pearlmutter, 1989) to train the network to perform the CPT-AX. All of the connection weights were developed entirely by the training procedure, with the constraint that that all self and between layer weights were forced to be positive and all within layer weights were forced to be negative. Training consisted of repeated presentation of each of the 8 conditions in the task (A-X,A-Y,B-X,B-Y, at both long and short delays), with the presentation frequency of each condition matching that of the behavioral task. Weights were updated after the presentation of each trial, biases (β) were fixed at -2.5, and dt was set at 0.1. The network was trained deterministically; completion of training occurred when network accuracy reached 100% for each condition.

Following training, weights were fixed. Errors and reaction time distributions were then simulated by adding zero-mean Gaussian noise to the net input of each unit at every time step during trial presentation. A trial consisted of the presentation of the cue stimulus, a delay period and then the probe stimulus. As mentioned above, the duration of these events was appropriately scaled to match the temporal parameters of the task (e.g., 300 msec. duration for cue and probe presentation, 750 msec. for short delays, 5000 msec. for long delays). A time constant (τ) of 50 msec. was used for simulation in the network. This scaling factor provided sufficient temporal resolution to capture the relationship between the two task delays while still permitting a tractable way of simulating the events.

Responses were determined by noting which output unit reached a threshold value first following presentation of the probe stimulus. Response latency was determined by calculating the number of time steps taken by the model to reach threshold multiplied by the time constant τ. To facilitate comparisons with the experimental reaction times, a constant k was added to all values produced. This parameter might correspond to the time required to execute a motor response. The value of k was determined by a least mean squares fit to the data. 1000 trials of each condition were run in order to obtain a reliable estimate of performance under stochastic conditions. The standard deviation of the noise distribution (σ) and the threshold (T) of the response units were adjusted to produce the best fit to the subject data. Figure 1 compares the results of the simulation against the behavioral data.

As can be seen in the figure, the model provides a good fit to the behavioral data in both the pattern of accuracy and reaction times. The model not only matches the qualitative pattern of errors and reaction times but produces very similar quantitative results as well. The match between model and experimental results is particularly striking when it is considered that there are a total of 24 data points that this model is fitting, with only 4 free parameters (σ,T,τ,k). The model's ability to successfully account for the pattern of behavioral performance provides convincing evidence that it captures the essential principles of processing in the task. We can then feel confident in not only examining normal processing, but also in extending the model to explore the effects of specific disturbances to processing in PFC.

5 Behavioral Effects of Neuromodulation in PFC

In a previous meeting of this conference a simulation of a simpler version of the CPT was discussed (Servan-Schreiber, Printz, & Cohen, 1990). In this simulation the

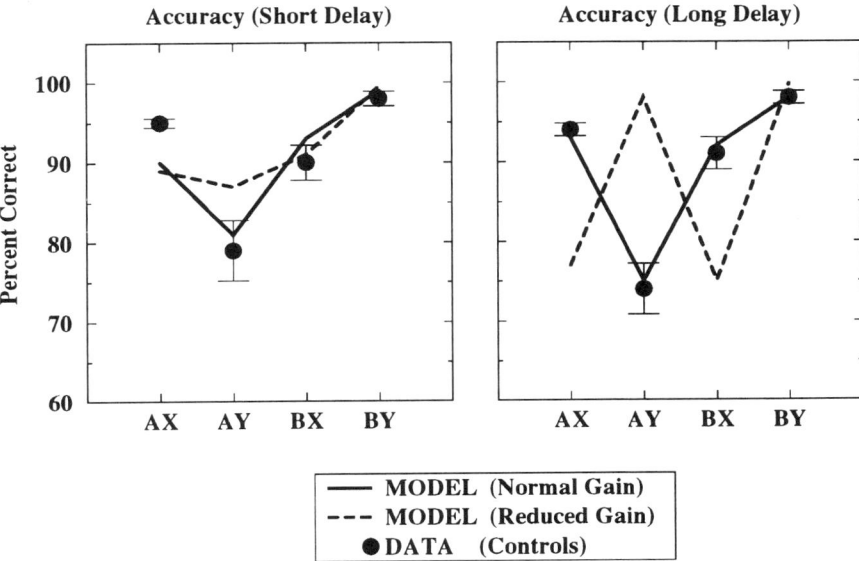

Figure 3: Comparision of of model performance with normal and reduced gain. The graph illustrates the effect of reducing gain in the memory layer on task performance. In the baseline network $\gamma=1$, in the reduced-gain network $\gamma=0.8$.

effects of system-wide changes in catecholaminergic tone were captured by changing the gain (γ) parameter of network units. Changes in gain are thought correspond to the action of modulatory neurotransmitters in modifying the responsivity of neurons to input signals (Servan-Schreiber et al., 1990; Cohen & Servan-Schreiber, 1992).

The current simulation of the CPT offers the opportunity to explore the effects of neuromodulation on the information processing functions specific to PFC. The transmitter dopamine is known to modulate activity in PFC, and manipulations to prefrontal dopamine have been shown to have effects on both memory-related neuronal activity and behavioral performance (Sawaguchi & Goldman-Rakic, 1991). Furthermore, it has been hypothesized that reductions of the neuromodulatory effects of dopamine in PFC are responsible for some of the information processing deficits seen in schizophrenia. To simulate the behavior of schizophrenic subjects, we therefore reduce the gain (γ) of units in the memory module of the network.

With reduced gain in the memory module, there are striking changes in the model's performance of the task. As can be seen in Figure 3, in the short delay conditions the performance of the reduced-gain model is relatively similar to that of control subjects (and the intact model). However, at long delays, the reduced-gain model produces a qualitatively different pattern of performance. In this condition, the model has a high B-X error rate but a low A-Y error rate, a pattern which is opposite to that seen in the control subjects. This double dissociation in performance is a robust effect of the reduced-gain simulation (i.e., it seems relatively uninfluenced by other parameter adjustments).

Thus, the model makes clear-cut predictions which are both novel and highly testable. Specifically, the model predicts that: 1) Differences in performance between control and schizophrenic subjects will be most apparent at long delays; 2) Schizophrenics will perform significantly worse than control subjects on B-X trials at long delays; 3) Schizophrenics will perform significantly *better* than control subjects on A-Y trials at long delays. This last prediction is especially interesting given the fact that tasks in which schizophrenics show superior performance relative to controls are relatively rare in experimental research.

Furthermore, the model not only makes predictions regarding schizophrenic behavioral performance, but also offers explanations as to their mechanisms. Analyses of the trajectories of activation states in the memory module reveals that both of the dissociations in performance are due to failures in maintaining representations of the context set up by the cue stimulus. Reducing gain in the memory module blurs the distinction between signal and noise, and causes the context representations to decay over time. As a result, in the long delay trials, there is a higher probability that the model will show both failures of inhibition (more B-X errors) and memory (less A-Y errors).

6 Conclusions

The results of this paper show how a computational analysis of the temporal dynamics of PFC information processing can aid in understanding both normal and disturbed behavior. We have developed a behavioral task which simultaneously probes both the inhibitory and active memory functions of PFC. We have used this task in combination with a computational model to explore the effects of neuromodulatory dysfunction, making specific predictions regarding schizophrenic performance in the CPT-AX. Confirmation of these predictions now await further testing.

References

Cohen, J. & Servan-Schreiber, D. (1992). Context, cortex, and dopamine: A connectionist approach to behavior and biology in schizophrenia. *Psychological Review, 99*, 45–77.

Dehaene, S. & Changeux, J. (1989). A simple model of prefrontal cortex function in delayed-response tasks. *Journal of Cognitive Neuroscience, 1*(3), 244–261.

Fuster, J. (1989). *The prefrontal cortex*. New York: Raven Press.

Goldman-Rakic, P. (1987). Circuitry of primate prefrontal cortex and regulation of behavior by representational memory. In F. Plum (Ed.), *Handbook of physiology-the nervous system, v*. Bethesda, MD: American Physiological Society, 373–417.

Levine, D. & Pruiett, P. (1989). Modeling some effects of frontal lobe damage: novelty and perseveration. *Neural Networks, 2*, 103–116.

Pearlmutter, B. (1989). Learning state space trajectories in recurrent neural networks. *Neural Computation, 1*, 263–269.

Sawaguchi, T. & Goldman-Rakic, P. (1991). D1 dopamine receptors in prefrontal cortex: Involvement in working memory. *Science, 251*, 947–950.

Servan-Schreiber, D., Printz, H., & Cohen, J. (1990). The effect of catecholamines on performance: From unit to system behavior. In D. Touretzky (Ed.), *Neural information processing systems 2*. San Mateo, CA: Morgan Kaufman, 100–108.

Stuss, D. & Benson, D. (1986). *The frontal lobes*. New York: Raven Press.

Zipser, D. (1991). Recurrent network model of the neural mechanism of short-term active memory. *Neural Computation, 3*, 179–193.

A Neural Model of Delusions and Hallucinations in Schizophrenia

Eytan Ruppin and James A. Reggia
Department of Computer Science
University of Maryland, College Park, MD 20742
ruppin@cs.umd.edu   reggia@cs.umd.edu

David Horn
School of Physics and Astronomy,
Tel Aviv University, Tel Aviv 69978, Israel
horn@vm.tau.ac.il

Abstract

We implement and study a computational model of Stevens' [1992] theory of the pathogenesis of schizophrenia. This theory hypothesizes that the onset of schizophrenia is associated with reactive synaptic regeneration occurring in brain regions receiving degenerating temporal lobe projections. Concentrating on one such area, the frontal cortex, we model a frontal module as an associative memory neural network whose input synapses represent incoming temporal projections. We analyze how, in the face of weakened external input projections, compensatory strengthening of internal synaptic connections and increased noise levels can maintain memory capacities (which are generally preserved in schizophrenia). However, These compensatory changes adversely lead to spontaneous, biased retrieval of stored memories, which corresponds to the occurrence of schizophrenic delusions and hallucinations without any apparent external trigger, and for their tendency to concentrate on just few central themes. Our results explain why these symptoms tend to wane as schizophrenia progresses, and why delayed therapeutical intervention leads to a much slower response.

1 Introduction

There has been a growing interest in recent years in the use of neural models to investigate various brain pathologies and their cognitive and behavioral effects. Recent published examples of such studies include models of cortical plasticity following stroke, Alzheimer's disease and schizophrenia, and cognitive and behavioral explorations of aphasia, acquired dyslexia and affective disorders (reviewed in [1, 2]). Continuing this line of study, we present a computational account linking specific pathological synaptic changes that are postulated to occur in schizophrenia, and the emergence of schizophrenic delusions and hallucinations. The latter symptoms denote persistent, unrealistic, psychotic thoughts (delusions) or percepts (hallucinations) that may at times flood the patient in an overwhelming, stressful manner.

The wealth of data gathered concerning the pathophysiology of schizophrenia supports the involvement of both the frontal and the temporal lobes. On the one hand, there are atrophic changes in the hippocampus and parahippocampal areas including neuronal loss and gliosis. On the other hand, neurochemical and morphometric studies testify to an expansion of various receptor binding sites and increased dendritic branching in the frontal cortex of schizophrenics. Stevens has recently presented a theory linking these temporal and frontal findings, claiming that the onset of schizophrenia is associated with reactive anomalous sprouting and synaptic reorganization taking place in the projection sites of degenerating temporal neurons, including (among various cortical and subcortical structures) the frontal lobes [3].

This paper presents a computational study of Stevens' theory. Within the framework of a memory model of hippocampal-frontal interaction, we show that the introduction of the 'microscopic' synaptic changes that underlie Stevens' hypothesis can help preserve memory function but results in specific 'pathological' changes in the 'macroscopic' behavior of the network. A small subset of the patterns stored in the network are now spontaneously retrieved at times, without being cued by any specific input pattern. This emergent behavior shares some of the important characteristics of schizophrenic delusions and hallucinations, which frequently appear in the absence of any apparent external trigger, and tend to concentrate on a limited set of recurrent themes [4]. Memory capacities are fairly preserved in schizophrenics, until late stages of the disease [5]. In Section 2 we present our model. The analytical and numerical results obtained are described in Section 3, followed by our conclusions in Section 4.

2 The Model

As illustrated in Figure 1, we model a frontal module as an associative memory attractor neural network, receiving its input memory cues from decaying *external* input fibers (representing the degenerating temporal projections). The network's *internal* connections, which store the memorized patterns, undergo synaptic strengthening changes that model the reactive synaptic regeneration within the frontal module. The effect of other *diffuse* external projections is modeled as background noise. A frontal module represents a macro-columnar unit that has been suggested as a basic functional building block of the neocortex [6]. The assumption that memory retrieval from the frontal cortex is invoked by the firing of incoming

A Neural Model of Delusions and Hallucinations in Schizophrenia

temporal projections is based on the notion that temporal structures have an important role in establishing long-term memory in the neocortex and in the retrieval of facts and events (e.g., [7]).

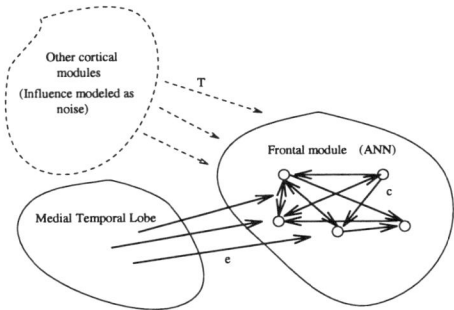

Figure 1: A schematic illustration of the model. A frontal module is modeled as an attractor neural network whose neurons receive inputs via three kinds of connections: internal connections from other frontal neurons, external connections from temporal lobe neurons, and diffuse external connections from other cortical modules, modeled as noise.

The attractor network we use is a biologically-motivated variant of Hopfield's ANN model, proposed by Tsodyks & Feigel'man [8]. Each neuron i is described by a binary variable $S_i = \{1, 0\}$ denoting an active (firing) or passive (quiescent) state, respectively. $M = \alpha N$ distributed memory patterns ξ^μ are stored in the network. The elements of each memory pattern are chosen to be 1 (0) with probability p ($1-p$) respectively, with $p \ll 1$. All N neurons in the network have a fixed uniform threshold θ.

In its initial, undamaged state, the weights of the internal synaptic connections are

$$W_{ij} = \frac{c_0}{N} \sum_{\mu=1}^{M} (\xi^\mu{}_i - p)(\xi^\mu{}_j - p) , \qquad (1)$$

where $c_0 = 1$. The post-synaptic potential (input field) h_i of neuron i is the sum of internal contributions from other neurons and external projections F_i^e

$$h_i(t) = \sum_j W_{ij} S_j(t-1) + F_i^e . \qquad (2)$$

The updating rule for neuron i at time t is given by

$$S_i(t) = \begin{cases} 1, & \text{with prob. } G(h_i(t) - \theta) \\ 0, & \text{otherwise} \end{cases} \qquad (3)$$

where G is the sigmoid function $G(x) = 1/(1+\exp(-x/T))$, and T denotes the noise level. The activation level of the stored memories is measured by their *overlaps* m^μ with the current state of the network, defined by

$$m^\mu(t) = \frac{1}{p(1-p)N} \sum_{i=1}^{N} (\xi_i^\mu - p) S_i(t) \ . \tag{4}$$

Stimulus-dependent retrieval is modeled by orienting the field F^e with one of the memorized patterns (the *cued* pattern, say ξ^1), such that

$$F_i^e = e \cdot \xi^1{}_i \ , \quad (e > 0) \ . \tag{5}$$

Following the presentation of an external input cue, the network state evolves until it converges to a stable state. The network parameters are tuned such that in its initial, undamaged state it correctly retrieves the cued patterns ($e_0 = 0.035$, $c_0 = 1$, $T = 0.005$).

We also examine the network's behavior *in the absence of any specific stimulus*. The network may either continue to wander around in a state of random low baseline activity, or it may converge onto a stored memory state. We refer to the latter process as *spontaneous retrieval*.

Our investigation of Stevens' work proceeds in two stages. First we examine and analyze the behavior of the network when it undergoes uniform synaptic changes that represent the pathological changes occurring in accordance with Stevens' theory. These include the weakening of external input projections ($e \downarrow$) and the increase in the internal projections ($c \uparrow$) and noise levels ($T \uparrow$). In the second stage, we add the assumption that the internal synaptic compensatory changes have an additional Hebbian activity-dependent component, and examine the effect of the rule

$$W_{ij}(t) = W_{ij}(t-1) + \frac{\gamma}{N}(\bar{S}_i - p)(\bar{S}_j - p) \ , \tag{6}$$

where $\bar{S}_k$ is 1 (0) only if neuron k has been consecutively firing (quiescent) for the last τ iterations, and γ is a constant.

3 Results

We now show some simulation and analytic results, examining the effects of the 'microscopic' pathological changes, taking place in accordance with Stevens' theory, on the 'macroscopic' behavior of the network. The analytical results presented have been derived by calculating the magnitude of randomly formed initial 'biases', and comparing their effect on the network's dynamics versus the effect of externally presented input cues. This comparison is performed by formulating a corresponding overlap master equation, whose fixed point dynamics are investigated via phase-plane analysis, as described in [9]. First, we study whether the reactive synaptic changes (occurring in both internal and external, diffuse synapses) are really compensatory, i.e., to what extent can they help maintaining memory capacities in the face of degenerating external input synapses. As illustrated in Figure 2, we find that increased noise levels can (up to some degree) preserve memory retrieval in the face of decreased external input strength. Increased synaptic strengthening preserves

A Neural Model of Delusions and Hallucinations in Schizophrenia 153

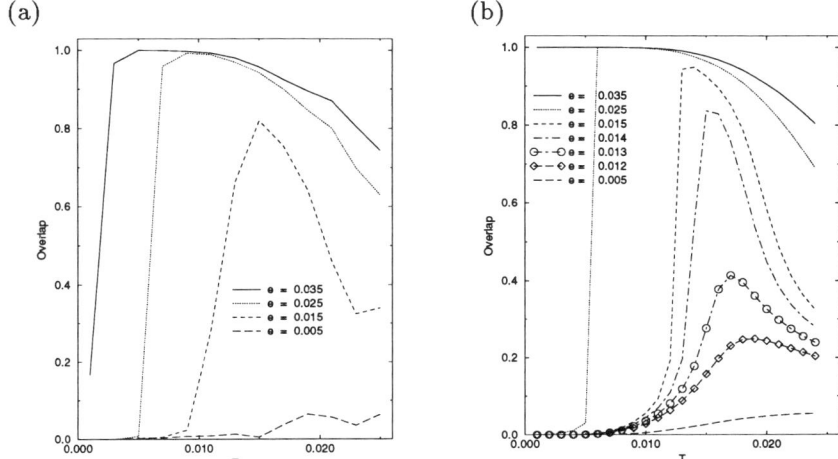

Figure 2: Stimulus-dependent retrieval performance, measured by the average final overlap m, as a function of the noise level T. Each curve displays this relation at a different magnitude of external input projections e. (a) Simulation results. (b) Analytic approximation.

memory retrieval in a similar manner, and the combined effect of these synaptic compensatory measures is synergistic.

Second, although the compensatory synaptic changes help maintain memory retrieval capacities, they necessarily have adverse effects, leading eventually to the emergence of spontaneous activation of non-cued memory patterns; the network converges to some of its memory patterns in a pathological, autonomous manner, in the absence of any external input stimuli. This emergence of pathological spontaneous retrieval, when either the noise level or the internal synaptic strength (or both) are increased beyond some point, is demonstrated in Figure 3.

Third, when the compensatory regeneration of internal synapses has an additional Hebbian component (representing a period of increased activity-dependent plasticity due to the regenerative synaptic changes), a *biased* spontaneous retrieval distribution is obtained. That is, as time evolves (measured in time units of 'trials'), the distribution of patterns spontaneously retrieved by the network in a pathological manner tends to concentrate only on one or two of all the memory patterns stored in the network, as is shown in Figure 4a. This highly peaked distribution is maintained for a few hundred additional trials until memory retrieval sharply collapses to zero as a global mixed-state attractor is formed. Such a mixed attractor state does not have very high overlap with any memorized pattern, and thus does not represent any well-defined cognitive or perceptual item. It is an end state of the Hebbian, activity-dependent evolution of the network. Yet, even after activity-dependent changes ensue, if spontaneous activity does not emerge the distribution of retrieved memories remains homogeneous (see Figure 4b). Eventually, a global

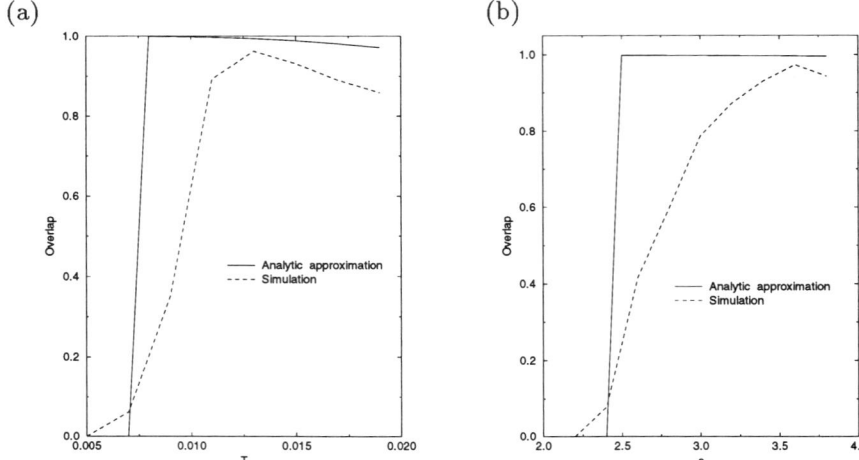

Figure 3: (a) Spontaneous retrieval, measured as the highest final overlap m achieved with any of the stored memory patterns, displayed as a function of the noise level T. $c = 1$. (b) Spontaneous retrieval as a function of internal synaptic compensation factor c. $T = 0.009$.

mixed-state attractor is formed, and the network looses its retrieval capacities, but during this process no memory pattern gets to dominate the retrieval output. Our results remain qualitatively similar even when bounds are placed on the absolute magnitude of the synaptic weights.

4 Conclusions

Our results suggest that the formation of biased spontaneous retrieval requires the concomitant occurrence of both degenerative changes in the external input fibers, and regenerative Hebbian changes in the intra-modular synaptic connections. They add support to the plausibility of Stevens' theory by showing that it may be realized within a neural model, and account for a few characteristics of schizophrenic symptoms:

- The emergence of spontaneous, non-homogeneous retrieval is a self-limiting phenomenon (as eventually a cognitively meaningless global attractor is formed) - this parallels the clinical finding that as schizophrenia progresses both delusions and hallucinations tend to wane, while negative symptoms are enhanced [10].
- Once converged to, the network has a much larger tendency to remain in a biased memory state than in a non biased one - this is in accordance with the persistent characteristic of schizophrenic florid symptoms.
- As more spontaneous retrieval trials occur the frequency of spontaneous retrieval increases - indeed, while early treatment in young psychotic adults

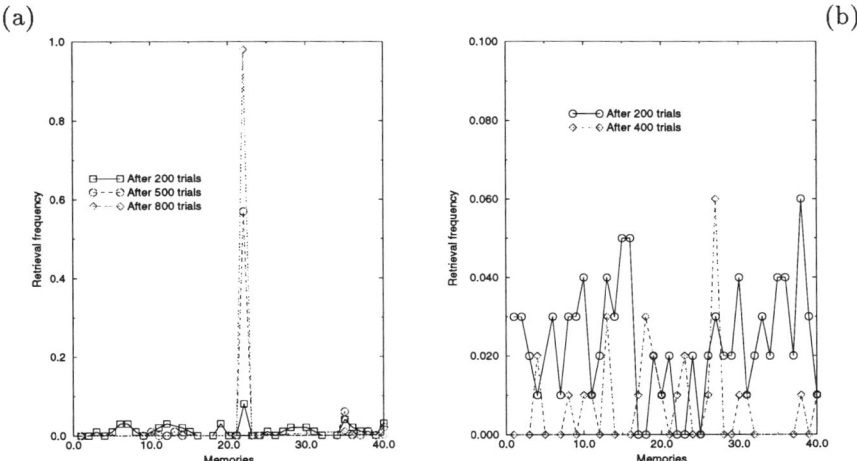

Figure 4: (a) The distribution of memory patterns spontaneously retrieved. The x-axis enumerates the memories stored, and the y-axis denotes the retrieval frequency of each memory. $\gamma = 0.0025$. (b) The distribution of stimulus-dependent retrieval of memories. $\gamma = 0.0025$.

leads to early response within days, late, delayed intervention leads to a much slower response during one or more months [11].

The current model generates some testable predictions:

- On the neuroanatomical level, the model can be tested quantitatively by searching for a positive correlation between a recent history of florid psychotic symptoms and postmortem neuropathological findings of synaptic compensation. (For example, this kind of correlation, between indices of synaptic area and cognitive functioning was found in Alzheimer patients [12]).

- On the physiological level, the increased compensatory noise should manifest itself in increased spontaneous neural activity. While this prediction is obviously difficult to examine directly, EEG studies in schizophrenics show significant increase in slow-wave delta activity which may reflect increased spontaneous activity [13].

- On the clinical level, due to the formation of a large and deep basin of attraction around the memory pattern which is at the focus of spontaneous retrieval, the proposed model predicts that its retrieval (and the elucidation of the corresponding delusions or hallucinations) may be frequently triggered by various environmental cues. A recent study points in this direction [14].

Acknowledgements

This research has been supported by a Rothschild Fellowship to Dr. Ruppin.

References

[1] J. Reggia, R. Berndt, and L. D'Autrechy. Connectionist models in neuropsychology. In *Handbook of Neuropsychology*, volume 9. 1994, in press.

[2] E. Ruppin. Neural modeling of psychiatric disorders. *Network: Computation in Neural Systems*, 1995. Invited review paper, to appear.

[3] J.R. Stevens. Abnormal reinnervation as a basis for schizophrenia: A hypothesis. *Arch. Gen. Psychiatry*, 49:238–243, 1992.

[4] S.K. Chaturvedi and V.D. Sinha. Recurrence of hallucinations in consecutive episodes of schizophrenia and affective disorder. *Schizophrenia Research*, 3:103–106, 1990.

[5] M. Marsel Mesulam. Schizophrenia and the brain. *New England Journal of Medicine*, 322(12):842–845, 1990.

[6] P.S. Goldman and W.J.H. Nauta. Columnar distribution of cortico-cortical fibers in the frontal, association, limbic and motor cortex of the developing rhesus monkey. *Brain Res.*, 122:393–413, 1977.

[7] L. R. Squire. Memory and the hippocampus: A synthesis from findings with rats, monkeys, and humans. *Psychological Review*, 99:195–231, 1992.

[8] M.V. Tsodyks and M.V. Feigel'man. The enhanced storage capacity in neural networks with low activity level. *Europhys. Lett.*, 6:101 – 105, 1988.

[9] D. Horn and E. Ruppin. Synaptic compensation in attractor neural networks: Modeling neuropathological findings in schizophrenia. *Neural Computation*, page To appear, 1994.

[10] W.T. Carpenter and R.W. Buchanan. Schizophrenia. *New England Journal of Medicine*, 330:10, 1994.

[11] P. Seeman. Schizophrenia as a brain disease: The dopamine receptor story. *Arch. Neurol.*, 50:1093–1095, 1993.

[12] S. T. DeKosky and S.W. Scheff. Synapse loss in frontal cortex biopsies in alzheimer's disease: Correlation with cognitive severity. *Ann. Neurology*, 27(5):457–464, 1990.

[13] Y. Jin, S.G. Potkin, D. Rice, and J. Sramek et. al. Abnormal EEG responses to photic stimulation in schizophrenic patients. *Schizophrenia Bulletin*, 16(4):627–634, 1990.

[14] R.E. Hoffman and J.A. Rapaport. A psycholoinguistic study of auditory/verbal hallucinations: Preliminary findings. In David A. and Cutting J., editors, *The Neuropsychology of Schizophrenia*. Erlbaum, 1993.

Spatial Representations in the Parietal Cortex May Use Basis Functions

Alexandre Pouget
alex@salk.edu

Terrence J. Sejnowski
terry@salk.edu

Howard Hughes Medical Institute
The Salk Institute
La Jolla, CA 92037
and
Department of Biology
University of California, San Diego

Abstract

The parietal cortex is thought to represent the egocentric positions of objects in particular coordinate systems. We propose an alternative approach to spatial perception of objects in the parietal cortex from the perspective of sensorimotor transformations. The responses of single parietal neurons can be modeled as a gaussian function of retinal position multiplied by a sigmoid function of eye position, which form a set of basis functions. We show here how these basis functions can be used to generate receptive fields in either retinotopic or head-centered coordinates by simple linear transformations. This raises the possibility that the parietal cortex does not attempt to compute the positions of objects in a particular frame of reference but instead computes a general purpose representation of the retinal location and eye position from which any transformation can be synthesized by direct projection. This representation predicts that hemineglect, a neurological syndrome produced by parietal lesions, should not be confined to egocentric coordinates, but should be observed in multiple frames of reference in single patients, a prediction supported by several experiments.

1 Introduction

The temporo-parietal junction in the human cortex and its equivalent in monkeys, the inferior parietal lobule, are thought to play a critical role in spatial perception. Lesions in these regions typically result in a neurological syndrome, called hemineglect, characterized by a lack of motor exploration toward the hemispace contralateral to the site of the lesion. As demonstrated by Zipser and Andersen [11], the responses of single cells in the monkey parietal cortex are also consistent with this presumed role in spatial perception.

In the general case, recovering the egocentric position of an object from its multiple sensory inputs is difficult because of the multiple reference frames that must be integrated. In this paper, we consider a simpler situation in which there is only visual input and all body parts are fixed but the eyes, a condition which has been extensively used for neurophysiological studies in monkeys. In this situation, the head-centered position of an object, $\vec{A}$, can be readily recovered from the retinal location, $\vec{R}$, and current eye position, $\vec{E}$, by vector addition:

$$\vec{A} = \vec{R} + \vec{E} \qquad (1)$$

If the parietal cortex contains a representation of the egocentric position of objects, then one would expect to find a representation of the vectors, $\vec{A}$, associated with these objects. There is an extensive literature on how to encode a vector with a population of neurons, and we first present two schemes that have been or are used as working hypothesis to study the parietal cortex. The first scheme involves what is typically called a computational map, whereas the second uses a vectorial representation [9].

This paper shows that none of these encoding schemes accurately accounts for all the response properties of single cells in the parietal cortex. Instead, we propose an alternative hypothesis which does not aim at representing $\vec{A}$ *per se*; instead, the inputs $\vec{R}$ and $\vec{E}$ are represented in a particular basis function representation. We show that this scheme is consistent with the way parietal neurons respond to the retinal position of objects and eye position, and we give computational arguments for why this might be an efficient strategy for the cortex.

2 Maps and Vectorial Representations

One way to encode a two-dimensional vector is to use a lookup table for this vector which, in the case of a two-dimensional vector, would take the form of a two-dimensional neuronal map. The parietal cortex may represent the egocentric location of object, $\vec{A}$, in a similar fashion. This predicts that the visual receptive field of parietal neurons have a fixed position with respect to the head (figure 1B). The work of Andersen *et al.* (1985) have clearly shown that this is not the case. As illustrated in figure 2A, parietal neurons have retinotopic receptive fields.

In a vectorial representation, a vector is encoded by N units, each of them coding for the projection of the vector along its preferred direction. This entails that the activity, h, of a neuron is given by:

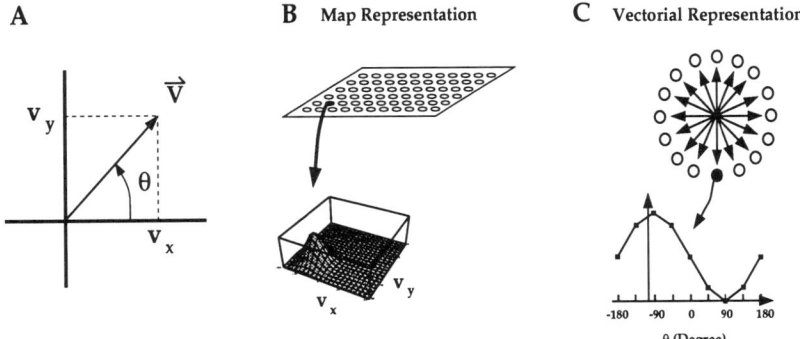

Figure 1: Two neural representations of a vector. A) A vector $\vec{V}$ in cartesian and polar coordinates. B) In a map representation, units have a narrow gaussian tuning to the horizontal and vertical components of $\vec{V}$. Moreover, the position of the peak response is directly related to the position of the units on the map. C) In a vectorial representation, each unit encodes the projection of $\vec{V}$ along its preferred direction (central arrows). This results in a cosine tuning to the vector angle, θ.

$$h = \vec{W}_a^T \vec{A} = \|\vec{W}_a\| \, \|\vec{A}\| \cos \theta \qquad (2)$$

$\vec{W}_a$ is usually called the preferred direction of the cells because the activity is maximum whenever $\theta = 0$; that is, when $\vec{A}$ points in the same direction as $\vec{W}_a$. Such neurons have a cosine tuning to the direction of the egocentric location of objects, as shown also in figure 1C.

Cosine tuning curves have been reported in the motor cortex by Georgopoulos *et al.* (1982), suggesting that the motor cortex uses a vectorial code for the direction of hand movement in extrapersonal space. The same scheme has been also used by Goodman and Andersen (1990), and Touretzski *et al.* (1993) to model the encoding of egocentric position of objects in the parietal cortex. Touretzski *et al.* (1993) called their representation a *sinusoidal array* instead of a *vectorial representation*.

Using Eq. 1, we can rewrite Eq. 2:

$$h = \vec{W}_a^T (\vec{R} + \vec{E}) = \vec{W}_a^T \vec{R} + \vec{W}_a^T \vec{E} \qquad (3)$$

This second equation is linear in $\vec{R}$ and $\vec{E}$ and uses the same vectors, $\vec{W}_a$, in both dot products. This leads to three important predictions:

1) The visual receptive fields of parietal neurons should be planar.

2) The eye position receptive fields of parietal neurons should also be planar; that is, for a given retinal positions, the response of parietal neuron should be a linear function of eye position.

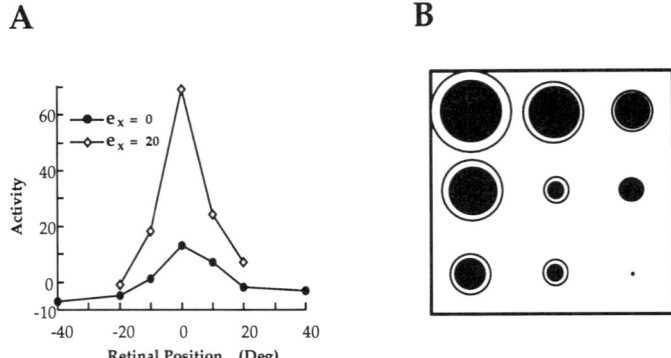

Figure 2: Typical response of a neuron in the parietal cortex of a monkey. A) Visual receptive field has a fixed position on the retina, but the gain of the response is modulated by eye position (e_x). (Adpated from Andersen et al., 1985) B) Example of an eye position receptive field, also called gain field, for a parietal cell. The nine circles indicate the amplitude of the response to an identical retinal stimulation for nine different eye positions. Outer circles show the total activity, whereas black circles correspond to the total response minus spontaneous activity prior to visual stimulation. (Adpated from Zipser et al., 1988)

3) The preferred direction for retinal location and eye position should be identical. For example, if the receptive field is on the right side of the visual field, the gain field should also increase with eye positon to the right side.

The visual receptive fields and the eye position gain fields of single parietal neurons have been extensively studied by Andersen et al. [2]. In most cases, the visual receptive fields were bell-shaped with one or several peaks and an average radius of 22 degrees of visual angle [1], a result that is clearly not consistent with the first prediction above. We show in figure 2A an idealized visual receptive field of a parietal neuron. The effect of eye position on the visual receptive field is also illustrated. The eye position clearly modulates the gain of the visual response.

The prediction regarding the receptive field for eye position has been borne out by statistical analysis. The gain fields of 80% of the cells had a planar component [1, 11]. One such gain field is shown in figure 2B.

There is not enough data available to determine whether or not the third prediction is valid. However, indirect evidence suggests that if such a correlation exists between preferred direction for retinal location and for eye position, it is probably not strong. Cells with *opposite* preferred directions [2, 3] have been observed. Furthermore, although each hemisphere represents all possible preferred eye position directions, there is a clear tendency to overrepresent the contralateral retinal hemifield [1].

In conclusion, the experimental data are not fully consistent with the predictions of the vectorial code. The visual receptive fields, in particular, are strongly nonlinear. If these nonlinearities are computationally neutral, that is, they are averaged out in subsequent stages of processing in the cortex, then the vectorial code could capture the essence of what the parietal cortex computes and, as such, would provide a valid approximation of the neurophysiological data. We argue in the next section that the nonlinearities cannot be disregarded and we present a representational scheme in which they have a central computational function.

3 Basis Function Representation

3.1 Sensorimotor Coordination and Nonlinear Function Approximation

The function which specified the pattern of muscle activities required to move a limb, or the body, to a specific spatial location is a highly nonlinear function of the sensory inputs. The cortex is not believed to specify patterns of muscle activation, but the intermediate transformations which are handled by the cortex are often themselves nonlinear. Even if the transformations are actually linear, the nature of cortical representations often makes the problem a nonlinear mapping. For example, there exists in the putamen and premotor cortex cells with gaussian head-centered visual receptive fields [7] which means that these cells compute gaussians of $\vec{A}$ or, equivalently, gaussians of $\vec{R} + \vec{E}$, which is nonlinear in $\vec{R}$ and $\vec{E}$. There are many other examples of sensory remappings involving similar computations. If the parietal cortex is to have a role in these remappings, the cells should respond to the sensory inputs in a way that can be used to approximate the nonlinear responses observed elsewhere.

One possibility would be for parietal neurons to represent input signals such as eye position and retinal location with basis functions. A basis function decomposition is a well-known method for approximating nonlinear functions which is, in addition, biologically plausible [8]. In such a representation, neurons do not encode the head-centered locations of objects, $\vec{A}$; instead, they compute functions of the input variables, such as $\vec{R}$ and $\vec{E}$, which can be used subsequently to approximate any functions of these variables.

3.2 Predictions of the Basis Function Representation

Not all functions are basis functions. Linear functions do not qualify, nor do sums of functions which, individually, would be basis functions, such as gaussian functions of retinal location plus a sigmoidal functions of eye position. If the parietal cortex uses a basis function representation, two conditions have to be met:

1) The visual and the eye position receptive fields should be smooth nonlinear function of $\vec{R}$ and $\vec{E}$.

2) The selectivities to $\vec{R}$ and $\vec{E}$ should interact nonlinearly

The visual receptive fields of parietal neurons are typically smooth and nonlinear. Gaussian or sum of gaussians appear to provide good models of their response profiles [2]. The eye position receptive field on the other hand, which is represented by the gain field, appears to be approximately linear. We believe, however, that the published data only demonstrate that the eye position receptive field is monotonic,

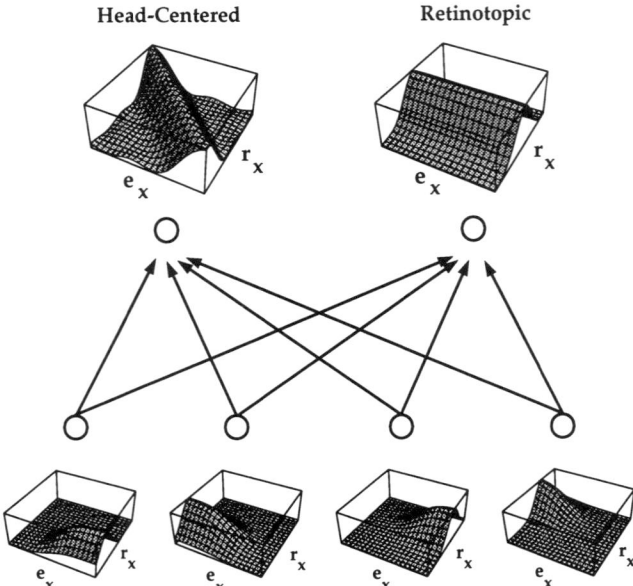

Figure 3: Approximation of a gaussian head-centered (top-left) and a retinotopic (top-right) receptive field, by a linear combination of basis function neurons. The bottom 3-D plots show the response to all possible horizontal retinal position, r_x, and horizontal eye positions, e_x, of four typical basis function units. These units are meant to model actual parietal neurons

but not necessarily linear. In published experiments, eye position receptive fields (gain fields) were sampled at only nine points, which makes it difficult to distinguish between a plane and other functions such as a sigmoidal function or a piecewise linear function. The hallmark of a nonlinearity would be evidence for saturation of activity within working range of eye position. Several published gain fields show such saturations [3, 11], but a rigorous statistical analysis would be desirable.

Andersen *et al.* (1985) have have shown that the responses of parietal neurons are best modeled by a multiplication between the retinal and eye position selectivities which is consistent with the requirements for basis functions.

Therefore, the experimental data are consistent with our hypothesis that the parietal cortex uses a basis function representation. The response of most gain-modulated neurons in the parietal cortex could be modeled by multiplying a gaussian tuning to retinal position by a sigmoid of eye position, a function which qualifies as a basis function.

3.3 Simulations

We simulated the response of 121 parietal gain-modulated neurons modeled by multiplying a gaussian of retinal position, r_x, with a sigmoid of eye position, e_x:

$$h_i = \frac{e^{-\frac{(r_x - r_{xi})^2}{2\sigma^2}}}{1 + e^{-\frac{e_x - e_{xi}}{t}}} \tag{4}$$

where the centers of the gaussians for retinal loction r_{xi} and the positions of the sigmoids for eye postions e_{xi} were uniformly distributred. The widths of the gaussian σ and the sigmoid t were fixed. Four of these functions are shown at the bottom of figure 3.

We used these basis functions as a hidden layer to approximate two kinds of output functions: a gaussian head-centered receptive field and a gaussian retinotopic receptive field. Neurons with these response properties are found downstream of the parietal cortex in the premotor cortex [7] and superior colliculus, two structures believed to be involved in the control of, respectively, arm and eye movements.

The weights for a particular output were obtained by using the delta rule. Weights were adjusted until the mean error was below 5% of the maximum output value. Figure 3 shows our best approximations for both the head-centered and retinotopic receptive fields. This demonstrates that the same pool of neurons can be used to approximate several diffferent nonlinear functions.

4 Discussion

Neurophysiological data support our hypothesis that the parietal cortex represents its inputs, such as the retinal location of objects and eye position, in a format suitable to non-linear function approximation, an operation central to sensorimotor coordination. Neurons have gaussian visual receptive fields modulated by monotonic function of eye position leading to response function that can be modeled by product of gaussian and sigmoids. Since the product of gaussian and sigmoids forms basis functions, this representation is good for approximating nonlinear functions of the input variables.

Previous attempts to characterize spatial representations have emphasized linear encoding schemes in which the location of objects is represented in egocentric coordinates. These codes cannot be used for nonlinear function approximation and, as such, may not be adequate for sensorimotor coordination [6, 10]. On the other hand, such representations are computationally interesting for certain operations, like addition or rotation. Some part of the brain more specialized in navigation like the hippocampus might be using such a scheme [10].

In figure 3, a head-centered or a retinotopic receptive field can be computed from the same pool of neurons. It would be arbitrary to say that these neurons encode the positions of objects in egocentric coordinates. Instead, these units encode a position in several frames of reference simultaneously. If the parietal cortex uses this basis function representation, we predict that hemineglect, the neurological syndrome which results from lesions in the parietal cortex, should not be confined to any particular frame of reference. This is precisely the conclusion that has emerged from recent studies of parietal patients [4]. Whether the behavior of parietal patients can be fully explained by lesions of a basis function representation remains to be investigated.

Acknowledgments

We thank Richard Andersen for helpful conversations and with access to unpublished data.

References

[1] R.A. Andersen, C. Asanuma, G. Essick, and R.M. Siegel. Corticocortical connections of anatomically and physiologically defined subdivisions within the inferior parietal lobule. *Journal of Comparative Neurology*, 296(1):65–113, 1990.

[2] R.A. Andersen, G.K. Essick, and R.M. Siegel. Encoding of spatial location by posterior parietal neurons. *Science*, 230:456–458, 1985.

[3] R.A. Andersen and D. Zipser. The role of the posterior parietal cortex in coordinate transformations for visual-motor integration. *Canadian Journal of Physiology and Pharmacology*, 66:488–501, 1988.

[4] M. Behrmann and M. Moscovitch. Object-centered neglect in patient with unilateral neglect: effect of left-right coordinates of objects. *Journal of Cognitive Neuroscience*, 6:1–16, 1994.

[5] A.P. Georgopoulos, J.F. Kalaska, R. Caminiti, and J.T. Massey. On the relations between the direction of two-dimensional arm movements and cell discharge in primate motor cortex. *Journal of Neuroscience*, 2(11):1527–1537, 1982.

[6] S.J. Goodman and R.A. Andersen. Algorithm programmed by a neural model for coordinate transformation. In *International Joint Conference on Neural Networks*, San Diego, 1990.

[7] M.S. Graziano, G.S. Yap, and C.G. Gross. Coding of visual space by premotor neurons. *Science*, 266:1054–1057, 1994.

[8] T. Poggio. A theory of how the brain might work. *Cold Spring Harbor Symposium on Quantitative Biology*, 55:899–910, 1990.

[9] J.F. Soechting and M. Flanders. Moving in three-dimensional space: frames of reference, vectors and coordinate systems. *Annual Review in Neuroscience*, 15:167–91, 1992.

[10] D.S. Touretzky, A.D. Redish, and H.S. Wan. Neural representation of space using sinusoidal arrays. *Neural Computation*, 5:869–884, 1993.

[11] D. Zipser and R.A. Andersen. A back-propagation programmed network that stimulates reponse properties of a subset of posterior parietal neurons. *Nature*, 331:679–684, 1988.

Grouping Components of Three-Dimensional Moving Objects in Area MST of Visual Cortex

Richard S. Zemel
Carnegie Mellon University
Department of Psychology
Pittsburgh, PA 15213
zemel@cmu.edu

Terrence J. Sejnowski
CNL, The Salk Institute
P.O. Box 85800
San Diego, CA 92186-5800
terry@salk.edu

Abstract

Many cells in the dorsal part of the medial superior temporal (MST) area of visual cortex respond selectively to spiral flow patterns—specific combinations of expansion/contraction and rotation motions. Previous investigators have suggested that these cells may represent self-motion. Spiral patterns can also be generated by the relative motion of the observer and a particular object. An MST cell may then account for some portion of the complex flow field, and the set of active cells could encode the entire flow; in this manner, MST effectively segments moving objects. Such a grouping operation is essential in interpreting scenes containing several independent moving objects and observer motion. We describe a model based on the hypothesis that the selective tuning of MST cells reflects the grouping of object components undergoing coherent motion. Inputs to the model were generated from sequences of ray-traced images that simulated realistic motion situations, combining observer motion, eye movements, and independent object motion. The input representation was modeled after response properties of neurons in area MT, which provides the primary input to area MST. After applying an unsupervised learning algorithm, the units became tuned to patterns signaling coherent motion. The results match many of the known properties of MST cells and are consistent with recent studies indicating that these cells process 3-D object motion information.

1 INTRODUCTION

A number of studies have described neurons in the dorsal part of the medial superior temporal (MSTd) monkey cortex that respond best to large expanding/contracting, rotating, or shifting patterns (Tanaka et al., 1986; Duffy & Wurtz, 1991a). Recently Graziano et al. (1994) found that MSTd cell responses correspond to a point in a multidimensional space of *spiral* motions, where the dimensions are these motion types.

Combinations of these motions are generated as an animal moves through its environment, which suggests that area MSTd could play a role in optical flow analysis. When an observer moves through a static environment, a singularity in the flow field known as the focus of expansion may be used to determine the direction of heading (Gibson, 1950; Warren & Hannon, 1988). Previous computational models of MSTd (Lappe & Rauschecker, 1993; Perrone & Stone, 1994) have shown how navigational information related to heading may be encoded by these cells. These investigators propose that each MSTd cell represents a potential heading direction and responds to the aspects of the flow that are consistent with that direction.

In natural environments, however, MSTd cells are often faced with complex flow patterns produced by the combination of observer motion with other independently-moving objects. These complex flow fields are not a single spiral pattern, but instead are composed of multiple spiral patterns. This observation that spiral flows are local subpatterns in flow fields suggests that an MSTd cell represents a particular regular subpattern which corresponds to the aspects of the flow field arising from a single *cause*—the relative motion of the observer and some object or surface in the scene. Adopting this view implies a new goal for MST: the set of MST responses accounts for the flow field based on the ensemble of motion causes.

An MST cell that responds to a local subpattern accounts for a portion of the flow field, specifically the portion that arises from a single motion cause. In this manner, MST can be considered to be segmenting motion signals. As in earlier models, the MSTd cell responds to the aspects of flow consistent with its motion hypothesis, but here a cell's motion hypothesis is not a heading direction but instead represents the 3-D motion of a scene element relative to the observer. This encoding may be useful not only in robustly estimating heading detection, but may also facilitate several other tasks thought to occur further down the motion processing stream, such as localizing objects and parsing scenes containing multiple moving objects.

In this paper we describe a computational model based on the hypothesis that an MST cell signals those aspects of the flow that arise from a common underlying cause. We demonstrate how such a model can develop response properties from the statistics of natural flow images, such as could be extracted from MT signals, and show that this model is able to capture several known properties of information processing in MST.

2 THE MODEL

The input to the system is a movie containing some combination of observer motion, eye movements, and a few objects undergoing independent 3-D motion. An optical flow algorithm is then applied to yield local motion estimates; this flow field is the input to the network, which consists of three layers. The first layer is designed after monkey area MT. The connectivity between this layer and the second layer is based on MST receptive field properties, and the second layer has the same connectivity pattern to the output layer. The weights on all connections are determined by a training algorithm which attempts to force the network to recreate the input pattern on the output units. We discuss the inputs, the network, and the training algorithm in more detail below.

2.1 STIMULI

The flow field input to the network is produced from a movie. The various movies are intended to simulate natural motion situations. Sample situations include one where all motion is due to the observer's movement, and the gaze is in the motion direction. Another situation that produces a qualitatively different flow field is when the gaze is not in the motion direction. A third situation includes independent motion of some of the objects in the environment. Each movie is a sequence of images that simulates one of these situations.

The images are created using a flexible ray-tracing program, which allows the simulation of many different objects, backgrounds, observer/camera motions, and lighting effects. We currently employ a database of 6 objects (a block of swiss cheese, a snail, a panther, a fish, a ball, and a teapot) and three different backgrounds. A movie is generated by randomly selecting one to four of the objects, and a background. To simulate one of the motion situations, a random selection of motion parameters follows: a). The observer's motion along (x, z) describes her walking; b). The eyes can rotate in (x, y), simulating the tracking of an object during motion; c). Each object can undergo independent 3-D motion. A sequence of 15 images is produced by randomly selecting 3-D initial positions and then updating the pose of the camera and each object in the image based on these motion parameters. Figure 1 shows 3 images selected from a movie generated in this manner.

We apply a standard optical flow technique to extract a single flow field from each synthetic image sequence. Nagel's (1987) flow algorithm is a gradient-based scheme which performs spatiotemporal smoothing on the set of images and then uses a multi-resolution second-order derivative technique, in combination with an oriented smoothness relaxation scheme, to produce the flow field.

2.2 MODEL INPUT AND ARCHITECTURE

The network input is a population encoding of these optical flow vectors at each location in a 21x31 array by small sets of neurons that share the same receptive field position but are tuned to different directions of motion. The values for each input unit is computed by projecting the local flow vector onto the cell's preferred direction. We are currently using 4 inputs per location, with evenly spaced preferred directions and a tuning half-width of 45°.

This population encoding in the input layer is intended to model the response of cells in area MT to a motion sequence. The receptive field (RF) of each model MT unit is determined by the degree of spatial smoothing and subsampling in the flow

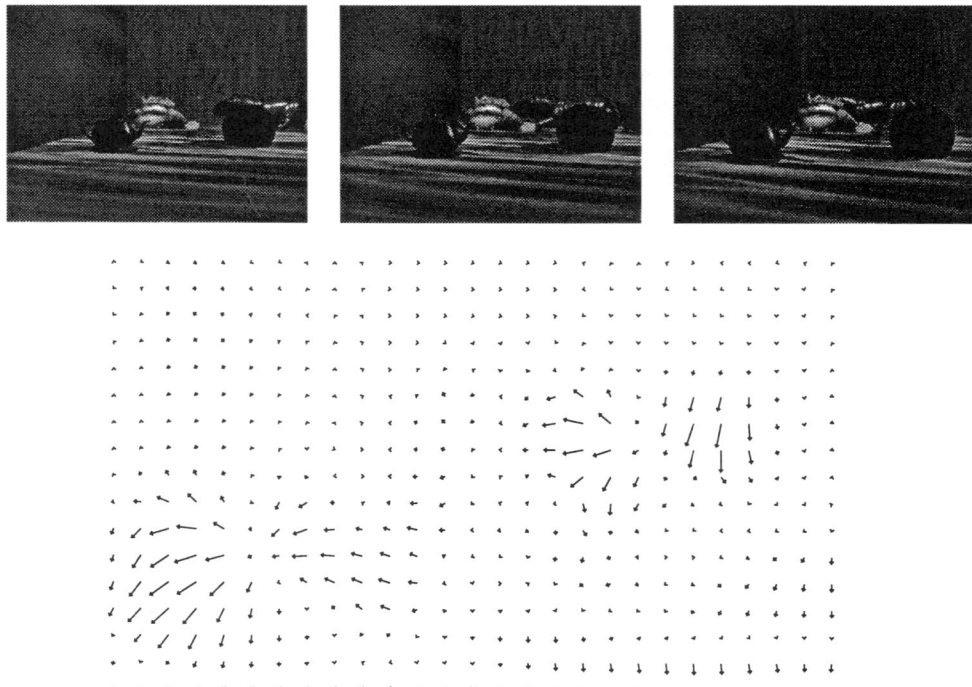

Figure 1: Three images from a movie, and the corresponding flow field. In this movie, the observer is moving into the scene while maintaining his gaze on the fish. The panther is moving independently. Note that the flow field contains spiral subpatterns that describe the independent relative motion of different objects.

algorithm. We have set these so that each input unit in the model is sensitive to a 10° range in the visual field, which approximately matches the RF sensitivity of MT neurons near the fovea.

The connectivity between the input layer and hidden layer of the network is based on the receptive field properties of MST cells. These RFs have always been reported to be large, but the exact size has been controversial. We base our RFs on the recent studies of Lagae *et al.* (1994), who found that most MSTd RFs included the fovea, and the sensitive part of the RF averaged 25°–30° and was relatively independent of eccentricity. Our input images cover approximately a 60°x45° portion of the visual field. We therefore evenly place the centers of the second layer cell's RFs within a region near the image center, and extend the RFs to include approximately 1/3 of the image. There are a total of 20 different RF centers, and ten hidden layer units share each RF; each of these 200 hidden units receives input from a 14x21 unit patch in the input layer.

2.3 LEARNING ALGORITHM

The question that we asked is whether the model would develop MST-like response properties in the second layer of the network under conditions of unsupervised learning. This would provide evidence for our hypothesis that the spiral pattern selectivity of an MST cell derives from the regular occurrence of a set of flow signals caused by the relative motion of an object and the observer. An earlier model (Zhang et al., 1993) showed how simple Hebbian synapses can yield weight patterns resembling the combinations of motion components; the inputs to this model were simple linear combinations of these motion patterns. However, a Hebbian mechanism fails to find the underlying structure—the spiral motion patterns—for the more complicated inputs described above. Other standard unsupervised methods, such as Principal Components Analysis and competitive learning, also fail to achieve the desired selectivity in the MST units.

The network we used for unsupervised learning was an autoencoder, in which the network is trained to reconstruct the input on its output units. This type of network is well-suited for a *generative* view of input examples, in which inputs are seen as random samples drawn from some particular distribution, which it is then the goal of learning to discover. Unsupervised learning methods attempt to invert this process to extract the representations of the underlying causes of the inputs. Zemel (1993) shows that unsupervised techniques contain assumptions about the form of these underlying causes; these different assumptions can be translated into the network architecture, activations, and cost function, and the resulting network tends to learn representations that conform to these assumptions.

In this network we make an assumption about the causes that generated the scene based on our knowledge of the underlying structure in the flow fields. Each input example is assumed to be generated by several independent causes, each of which corresponds to one moving object, or a part thereof. Furthermore, we assume that the value of a single output dimension, here the response of an MT cell, can always be specified as coming from just one cause; that is, local flow is generally the result of the relative motion of the observer and the nearest object along that line-of-sight.

This assumption can be translated into an activation function for the output units which encourages the causes to compete to account for the activity of an input unit while also allowing multiple causes to be present in each image (Dayan & Zemel, 1995). The stochastic activity of an output unit j is given by: $p_j = 1 - (1 + \sum_i \frac{x_i w_{ji}}{1-w_{ji}})^{-1}$, where x_i is the binary output of hidden unit i, sampled from the standard sigmoidal function of its net input.

We use a cross-entropy error measure for each output unit j: $E_j = -t_j \log p_j - (1-t_j)\log(1-p_j)$, where t_j is the value of the corresponding input unit. A second cost in the objective function implements our assumption that only a few causes will account for an input example. This cost is the asymmetric divergence between each hidden unit's expected and actual activity distributions, which encourages the unit's activity to match its expected activity b across the training set. We back-propagate this summed error to determine the network weights.[1]

---

[1] Our activation function is derived from a probabilistic formulation of the image formation process. A biologically plausible learning rule can be applied if the network is run

3 SIMULATION RESULTS

The training set for the network contained 600 flow fields, each computed from a different motion sequence. The network reached a minimum of the cost function after approximately 1000 iterations of a conjugate gradient procedure.

We have tested the generalization ability of the network by presenting 50 flow fields from novel random motion sequences. The network is able to successfully reconstruct these fields using only a few active hidden units. We have examined the selectivity of individual hidden units by simulating the neurophysiological experiments, i.e., presenting various spiral flow patterns in the unit's RF. The speed was held equal for all stimuli, and the pitch of spiral motion systematically varied. Figure 2 shows the result for one unit; like most units, this unit prefers a particular combination of the motion types. To quantify the units' selectivities, we fit a circular normal function to each unit's tuning curve. We found that 68% of the cells (all with $y_{max} > 0.9$) were selective—their tuning half-width was less than 30°.

Another interesting property of some dorsal MST neurons is that they maintain their preference for a motion pattern regardless of the location of the velocity flow center. We tested the position-invariance of the model MST units in our network by shrinking the flow stimuli and placing them in different positions within each unit's RF. Most of the selective units retained their preferences in these experiments.

In this position-invariance test, we discovered another interesting property of the network: 43 of the 200 model MST units that were not selective for a particular motion type on the full-field test were selective when the stimuli were reduced in size; that is, these units responded preferentially to particular flows at specific positions in their RFs. This local flow specificity is a natural consequence of modeling not only observer motion but also independent object motion, as can be seen in Figure 1.

4 DISCUSSION

Many of the hidden units in the model have receptive fields that prefer spiral flow fields and resemble the responses observed in area MST neurons. Several other properties are consistent with this identification. For example, the hidden unit responses are relatively invariant to the object shape. This is clear from the units' flow selectivities, as shown in Figure 2—the units instead respond to localized patches of the flow field undergoing coherent motion. This shape-invariance agrees with the physiological findings of (Lagae et al., 1994), who found that MST cells are less selective for motion types that depend on object structure than they are to types that depend primarily on the relative movement between objects and the observer.

Also, many of the model MST units motion selectivities are unaffected by placing the stimulus in different locations within the RF, which matches the results of (Duffy & Wurtz, 1991b; Graziano et al., 1994) and others. One way that our simulation results diverge from the neurophysiological findings on MSTd is the presence of units that are selective to a particular motion type at specific locations within their RF. This local selectivity suggests that these units may model the response properties of

---

using a stochastic sampling procedure. We use a mean-field approximation, and backpropagation to speed up learning.

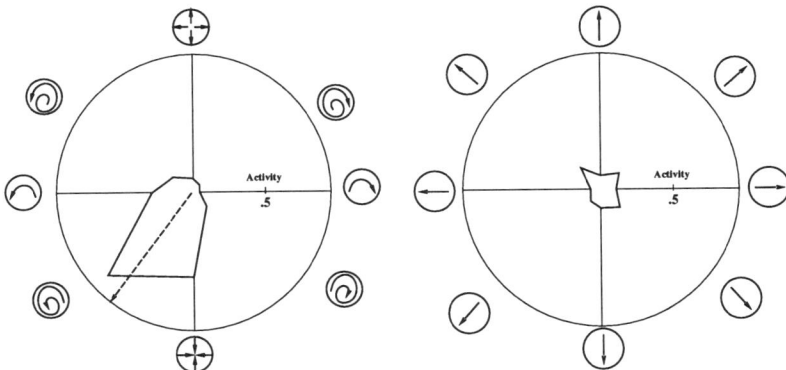

Figure 2: The response selectivity of an individual model MST unit to various motion types. In this polar plot, the angle represents the pitch of spiral motion, and the radius represents the response of the unit. Eight directions were sampled in two continuous spaces, one for translation and the other for rotation-expansion/contraction.

cells that have been described in MSTl, the lateral portion of MST. This leads to a testable prediction concerning these cells—that they would exhibit similar local selectivities on these full-field and within-RF flow selectivity experiments.

We have thus demonstrated that a network constructed to model MT-MST cortical processing is capable of learning (via an unsupervised procedure) to group components of the optical flow field for a variety of images. This grouping is accomplished through the cooperative activity of several model MST units, each of which accounts for a portion of the field indicative of coherent motion. Adopting a novel approach to the question of what MST is encoding has produced an alternative derivation of its response characteristics.

We are currently extending this model in several directions. Recent studies have shown that over 90% of MSTd cells are sensitive to the disparity of the visual stimulus (Roy et al., 1992). This disparity sensitivity provides an additional criteria for making segmentation decisions, as image components at similar depths may be grouped. Furthermore, for some MSTd cells the preferred direction of stimulus motion reversed as the disparity (relative to the plane of fixation) of the stimulus reversed. Adding disparity information to the network input should allow the hidden units to respond to particular combinations of these cues.

We also intend to extend our model to consider the relations between functions carried out in the dorsal and lateral portions of MST. Our current results indicate that it may be possible to construct a model of MST that incorporates both areas. For both areas, evidence exists that many cells are sensitive to an extraretinal input (Newsome et al., 1988), and respond differently to identical flows depending on whether the motion is due to observer or object motion (Erickson & Thier, 1991). Including an extraretinal signal in the network will allow us to tie the model more closely to the animal's behavior. Our current hypothesis is that the two MST areas act in conjunction to allow an observer to track a moving object through a dynamic environment, while maintaining enough information about other objects that may be relevant, either for avoidance or to switch attention.

Acknowledgements

We thank Thomas Albright, Peter Dayan, Alexandre Pouget, Gene Stoner, and Paul Viola for helpful comments, and the developers of the Persistence of Vision Ray Tracer for making this package public. This research was supported by the Office of Naval Research.

References

Dayan, P., & Zemel, R. S. (1995). Competition and multiple cause models. *Neural Computation*. In press.

Duffy, C. J., & Wurtz, R. H. (1991a). The sensitivity of MST neurons to optic flow stimuli. I. A continuum of response selectivity to large field stimuli. *Journal of Neurophysiology*, 65, 1329–1345.

Duffy, C. J., & Wurtz, R. H. (1991b). Sensitivity of MST neurons to optic flow stimuli. II. Mechanisms of response selectivity revealed by small field stimuli. *Journal of Neurophysiology*, 65, 1346–1359.

Erickson, R. G., & Thier, P. (1991). A neuronal correlate of spatial stability during periods of self-induced visual motion. *Experimental Brain Research*, 86, 608–616.

Gibson, J. J. (1950). *The perception of the visual world.* Boston: Houghton Mifflin.

Graziano, M. S. A., Andersen, R. A., & Snowden, R. J. (1994). Tuning of MST neurons to spiral motions. *Journal of Neuroscience*, 14(1), 54–67.

Lagae, L., Maes, H., Raiguel, S., Xiao, D.-K., & Orban, G. A. (1994). Responses of macaque STS neurons to optic flow components: A comparison of areas MT and MST. *Journal of Neurophysiology*, 71(5), 1597–1626.

Lappe, M., & Rauschecker, J. P. (1993). A neural network for the processing of optic flow from ego-motion in man and higher mammals. *Neural Computation*, 5(3), 374–391.

Nagel, H.-H. (1987). On the estimation of optical flow: relations between different approaches and some new results. *Artificial Intelligence*, 33(3), 299–324.

Newsome, W. T., Wurtz, R. H., & Komatsu, H. (1988). Relation of cortical areas MT and MST to pursuit eye movements. II. Differentiation of retinal from extretinal inputs. *Journal of Neurophysiology*, 60, 604–620.

Perrone, J. A., & Stone, L. S. (1994). A model of self-motion estimation within primate extrastriate visual cortex. *Vision Research*, 34(21), 2917–2938.

Roy, J.-P., Komatsu, H., & Wurtz, R. H. (1992). Disparity sensitivity of neurons in monkey extrastriate area MST. *Journal of Neuroscience*, 12(7), 2478–2492.

Tanaka, K., Hikosaka, K., Saito, H.-A., Yukie, M., Fukada, Y., & Iwai, E. (1986). Analysis of local and wide-field movements in the superior temporal visual areas of the macaque monkey. *Journal of Neuroscience*, 6, 134–144.

Warren, W. H., & Hannon, D. J. (1988). Direction of self motion is perceived from optical flow. *Nature*, 336, 162–163.

Zemel, R. S. (1993). *A minimum description length framework for unsupervised learning.* PhD thesis, University of Toronto.

Zhang, K., Sereno, M. I., & Sereno, M. E. (1993). Emergence of position-independent detectors of sense of rotation and dilation with hebbian learning: An analysis. *Neural Computation*, 5(4), 597–612.

A Model of the Neural Basis of the Rat's Sense of Direction

William E. Skaggs
bill@nsma.arizona.edu

James J. Knierim
jim@nsma.arizona.edu

Hemant S. Kudrimoti
hemant@nsma.arizona.edu

Bruce L. McNaughton
bruce@nsma.arizona.edu
ARL Division of Neural Systems, Memory, And Aging
344 Life Sciences North, University of Arizona, Tucson AZ 85724

Abstract

In the last decade the outlines of the neural structures subserving the sense of direction have begun to emerge. Several investigations have shed light on the effects of vestibular input and visual input on the head direction representation. In this paper, a model is formulated of the neural mechanisms underlying the head direction system. The model is built out of simple ingredients, depending on nothing more complicated than connectional specificity, attractor dynamics, Hebbian learning, and sigmoidal nonlinearities, but it behaves in a sophisticated way and is consistent with most of the observed properties of real head direction cells. In addition it makes a number of predictions that ought to be testable by reasonably straightforward experiments.

1 Head Direction Cells in the Rat

There is quite a bit of behavioral evidence for an intrinsic sense of direction in many species of mammals, including rats and humans (e.g., Gallistel, 1990). The first specific information regarding the neural basis of this "sense" came with the discovery by Ranck (1984) of a population of "head direction" cells in the dorsal presubiculum (also known as the "postsubiculum") of the rat. A head direction cell fires at a high rate if and only if the rat's head is oriented in a specific direction. Many things could potentially cause a cell to fire in a head-direction dependent manner: what made the postsubicular cells particularly interesting was that when their directionality was tested with the rat at different locations, the head directions corresponding to maximal firing were consistently parallel, within the experimental resolution. This is difficult to explain with a simple sensory-based mechanism; it implies something more sophisticated.[1]

The postsubicular head direction cells were studied in depth by Taube et al. (1990a,b), and, more recently, head direction cells have also been found in other parts of the rat brain, in particular the anterior nuclei of the thalamus (Mizumori and Williams, 1993) and the retrosplenial (posterior cingulate) cortex (Chen et al., 1994a,b). Interestingly, all of these areas are intimately associated with the hippocampal formation, which in the rat contains large numbers of "place" cells. Thus, the brain contains separate but neighboring populations of cells coding for location and cells coding for direction, which taken together represent much of the information needed for navigation.

Figure 1 shows directional tuning curves for three typical head direction cells from the anterior thalamus. In each of them the breadth of tuning is on the order of 90 degrees. This value is also typical for head direction cells in the postsubiculum and retrosplenial cortex, though in each of the three areas individual cells may show considerable variability.

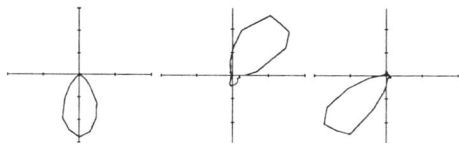

Figure 1: Polar plots of directional tuning (mean firing rate as a function of head direction) for three typical head direction cells from the anterior thalamus of a rat.

Every study to date has indicated that the head direction cells constitute a unitary system, together with the place cells of the hippocampus. Whenever two head direction cells have been recorded simultaneously, any manipulation that caused one of them to shift its directional alignment caused the other to shift by the same amount; and when head direction cells have been recorded simultaneously with place cells, any manipulation that caused the head direction cells to realign either caused the hippocampal place fields to rotate correspondingly or to "remap" into a different pattern (Knierim et al., 1995).

Head direction cells maintain their directional tuning for some time when the lights in the recording room are turned off, leaving an animal in complete darkness; the directionality tends to gradually drift, though, especially if the animal moves around (Mizumori and Williams, 1993). Directional tuning is preserved to some degree even

---

[1] Sensitivity to the Earth's geomagnetic field has been ruled out as an explanation of head-directional firing.

if an animal is passively rotated in the dark, which indicates strongly that the head direction system receives information (possibly indirect) from the vestibular system.

Visual input influences but does not dictate the behavior of head direction cells. The nature of this influence is quite interesting. In a recent series of experiments (Knierim et al., 1995), rats were trained to forage for food pellets in a gray cylinder with a single salient directional cue, a white card covering 90 degrees of the wall. During training, half of the rats were disoriented before being placed in the cylinder, in order to disrupt the relation between their internal sense of direction and the location of the cue card; the other half of the rats were not disoriented. Presumably, the rats that were not disoriented during training experienced the same initial relationship between their internal direction sense and the cue card each time they were placed in the cylinder; this would not have been true of the disoriented rats. Head direction cells in the thalamus were subsequently recorded from both groups of rats as they moved in the cylinder. *All rats were disoriented before each recording session.* Under these conditions, the cue card had much weaker control over the head direction cells in the rats that had been disoriented during training than in the rats that had not been disoriented. For all rats the influence of the cue card upon the head direction system weakened gradually over the course of multiple recording sessions, and eventually they broke free, but this happened much sooner in the rats that had been disoriented during training. The authors concluded that *a visual cue could only develop a strong influence upon the head direction system if the rat experienced it as stable.*

Figure 2 illustrates the shifts in alignment during a typical recording session. When the rat is initially placed in the cylinder, the cell's tuning curve is aligned to the west. Over the first few minutes of recording it gradually rotates to SSW, and there it stays. Note the "tail" of the curve. This comes from spikes belonging to another, neighboring head direction cell, which could not be perfectly isolated from the first. Note that, even though they come from different cells, both portions shift alignment synchronously.

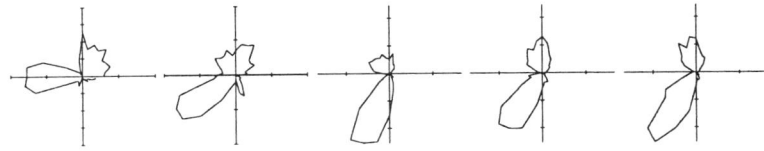

Figure 2: Shifts in alignment of a head direction cell over the course of a single recording session (one minute intervals).

2 The Model

As reviewed above, the most important facts to be accounted for by any model of the head direction system are (1) the shape of the tuning curves for head direction cells, (2) the control of head direction cells by vestibular input, and (3) the stability-dependent influence of visual cues on head direction cells. We introduce here a model that accounts for these facts. It is a refinement of a model proposed earlier by McNaughton *et al.* (1991), the main addition being a more specific account of neural connections and dynamics. The aim of this effort is to develop the simplest possible architecture consistent with the available data. The reality is sure to be more complicated than this model.

Figure 3 schematically illustrates the architecture of the model. There are four groups of cells in the model: head direction cells, rotation cells (left and right), vestibular cells (left and right), and visual feature detectors. For expository purposes it is helpful to think of the network as a set of circular layers; this does not reflect the anatomical organization of the corresponding cells in the brain.

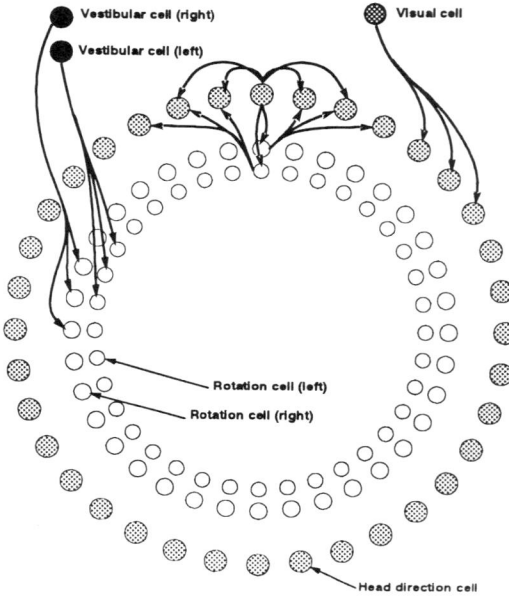

Figure 3: Architecture of the head direction cell model.

The head direction cell group has intrinsic connections that are stronger than any other connections in the model, and dominate their dynamics, so that other inputs only provide relatively small perturbations. The connections between them are set up so that the only possible stable state of the system is a single localized cluster of active cells, with all other cells virtually silent. This will occur if there are strong excitatory connections between neighboring cells, and strong inhibitory connections between distant cells. It is assumed that the network of interconnections has rotation and reflection symmetry. Small deviations from symmetry will not impair the model too much; large deviations may cause it to have strong attractors at a few points on the circle, which would cause problems.

The crucial property of this network is the following. Suppose it is in a stable state, with a single cluster of activated cells at one point on the circle, and suppose an external input is applied that excites the cells selectively on one side (left or right) of the peak. Then the peak will rotate toward the side at which the input is applied, and the rate of rotation will increase with the strength of the input.

This feature is exploited by the mechanisms for vestibular and visual control of the system. The vestibular mechanism operates via a layer of "rotation" cells, corresponding to the circle of head direction cells (Units with a similar role were referred to as "H × H'" cells in the McNaughton et al. (1991) model). There are two groups of rotation cells, for left and right rotations. Each rotation cell receives excitatory input from the head direction cell at the same point on the circle, and from the vestibular system. The activation function of the rotation cell is sigmoidal or threshold linear, so that the cell does not become active unless it receives input simultaneously from both sources. Each right rotation cell sends excitatory projections to head direction cells neighboring it on the right, but not to those that neighbor it on the left, and contrariwise for left rotation cells.

It is easy to see how the mechanism works. When the animal turns to the right, the right vestibular cells are activated, and then the right rotation cells at the current peak of the head direction system are activated. These add to the excitation of the head direction cells to the right of the peak, thereby causing the peak to shift rightward. This in turn causes a new set of rotation cells to become active (and the old ones inactive), and thence a further shift of the peak, and so on. The peak will continue to move around the circle as long as the vestibular input is active, and the stronger the vestibular input, the more rapidly the peak will move. If the gain of this mechanism is correct (but weak compared to the gain of the intrinsic connections of the head direction cells), then the peak will move around the circle at the same rate that the animal turns, and the location of the peak will function as an allocentric compass. This can only be expected to work over a limited range of turning rates, but the firing rates of cells in the vestibular nuclei are linearly proportional to angular velocity over a surprisingly broad range, so there is no reason why the mechanism cannot perform adequately.

Of course the mechanism is intrinsically error-prone, and without some sort of external correction, deviations are sure to build up over time. But this is an inevitable feature of any plausible model, and in any case does not conflict with the available data, which, while sketchy, suggests that passive rotation of animals in the dark can cause quite erratic behavior in head direction cells (E. J. Markus, J. J. Knierim, unpublished observations).

The final ingredient of the model is a set of visual feature detectors, each of which responds if and only if a particular visual feature is located at a particular angle with respect to the axis of the rat's head. Thus, these cells are feature specific and direction specific, but direction specific in the head-centered frame, not in the world frame. It is assumed that each visual feature detector projects weakly to all of the head direction cells, and that these connections are modifiable according to a Hebbian rule, specifically,

$$\Delta W = \alpha(W_{\max} f(\lambda_{\text{post}}) - W)\lambda_{\text{pre}},$$

where W is the connection weight, $W_{\max}$ is its maximum possible value, λ_{post} is the firing rate of the postsynaptic cell, λ_{pre} is the firing rate of the presynaptic cell, and the function $f()$ has the shape shown in figure 4. (Actually, the rule is modified slightly to prevent any of the weights from becoming negative.) The net effect of this rule is that the weight will only change when the presynaptic cell (the visual feature detector) is active, and the weight will increase if the postsynaptic cell is strongly active, but decrease if it is weakly active or silent. Modification rules of this form have previously been proposed in theories of the development of topography in the neocortex (e.g., Bienenstock *et al.*, 1982), and there is considerable evidence for such an effect in the control of LTP/LTD (Singer and Artola, 1994).

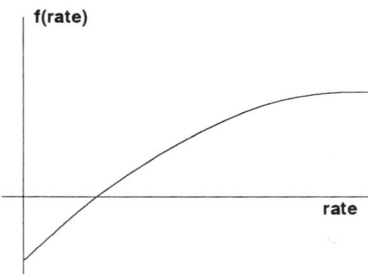

Figure 4: Dependence of synaptic weight change on postsynaptic firing rate for connections from visual feature detectors to head direction cells in the model.

To understand how this works, suppose we have a feature detecting cell that responds to a cue card whenever the cue card is directly in front of the rat. Suppose the rat's motion is restricted to a small area, and the cue card is far away, so that it is always at approximately the same absolute bearing (say, 30 degrees), and suppose the rat's head direction system is working correctly, i.e., functioning as an absolute compass. Then the cell will only be active at moments when the head direction cells corresponding to 30 degrees are active, and the Hebbian learning process will cause the feature detecting cell to be linked by strong weights to these cells, but by vanishing weights to other head direction cells. If the absolute bearing of the cue card were more variable, then the connection strengths from the feature detecting cell would be weaker and more broadly dispersed. In the limit where the bearing of the cue card was completely random, all connections would be weak and equal. Thus the influence of a visual cue is determined by the amount of training and by the variability in its bearing (with respect to the head direction system).

It can be seen that the model implements a competition between visual inputs and vestibular inputs for control of the head direction cells. If the visual cues are rotated while the rat is left stationary, then the head direction cells may either rotate to follow the visual cues, or stick with the inertial frame, depending on parameter values and, importantly, on the training regimen imposed on the network. Both of these outcomes have been observed in anterior thalamic head direction cells (McNaughton *et al.*, 1993).

3 Discussion

Do the necessary types of cells exist in the brain? Cells in the brainstem vestibular nuclei are known to have the properties required by the model (Precht, 1978). The "rotation" cells would be recognizable from the fact that they would fire only when the rat is facing in a particular direction and turning in a particular direction, with rate at least roughly proportional to the speed of turning. Cells with these properties have been recorded in the postsubiculum (Markus et al., 1990) and retrosplenial cortex (Chen et al., 1994a). The visual cells would be recognizeable from the fact that they would respond to visual stimuli only when they come from a particular direction with respect to the animal's head axis. Cells with these properties have been recorded in the inferior parietal cortex, the internal medullary lamina of the thalamus, and the superior colliculus (e.g., Sparks, 1986). The superior colliculus also contains cells that respond in a direction-dependent manner to auditory inputs, thus allowing a possiblility of control of the head direction system by sound sources. There do not seem to be any strong direct projections from the superior colliculus to the components of the head direction system, but there are numerous indirect pathways.

The most general prediction of the model is that the influence of vestibular input upon head direction cells is not susceptible to experience-dependent modification, whereas the influence of visual input is plastic, and is enhanced by the duration of experience, the richness of the visual cue array, and the distance of visual cues from the rat's region of travel.

The "rotation" cells should be responsive to stimulation of the vestibular system. It is possible to activate the vestibular system by applying hot or cold water to the ears: if this is done in the dark, and head direction cells are simultaneously recorded, the model predicts that they will show periodic bursts of activity, with a frequency related to the intensity of the stimulus.

For another prediction, suppose we train two groups of rats to forage in a cylinder containing a single landmark. For one group, the landmark is placed at the edge of the cylinder; for the other group, the same landmark is placed halfway between the center and the edge. The model predicts that in both cases the landmark will influence the head direction sytem, but the influence will be stronger and more tightly focused when the landmark is at the edge.

In some respects the model is flexible, and may be extended without compromising its essence. For example, there is no intrinsic necessity that the vestibular system be the sole input to the rotation cells (other than the head direction cells). The performance of the system might be improved in some ways by sending the rotation cells input about optokinetic flow, or certain types of motor efference copy. But there is as yet no clear evidence for these things.

On a more abstract level, the mechanism used by the model for vestibular control may be thought of as a special case of a general-purpose method for integration with neurons. As such, it has significant advantages over some previously proposed neural integrators, in particular, better stability properties. It might be worth considering whether the method is applicable in other situations where integrators are known to exist, for example the control of eye position.

Supported by MH46823 and O.N.R.

References

Bienenstock, E. L., Cooper, L. N., and Munro, P. W. (1982). Theory for the development of neuron selectivity: orientation specificity and binocular interaction in visual cortex. *J. Neurosci.*, 2:32–48.

Chen, L. L., Lin, L., Green, E. J., Barnes, C. A., and McNaughton, B. L. (1994b). Head-direction cells in the rat posterior cortex. I. Anatomical distribution and behavioral modulation. *Exp. Brain Res.*, 101:8–23.

Chen, L. L., Lin, L., Barnes, C. A., and McNaughton, B. L. (1994a). Head-direction cells in the rat posterior cortex. II. Contributions of visual and ideothetic information to the directional firing. *Exp. Brain Res.*, 101:24–34.

Gallistel, C. R. (1990). *The Organization of Learning*. MIT Press, Cambridge, Massachusetts.

Knierim, J. J., Kudrimoti, H. S., and McNaughton, B. L. (1995). Place cells, head direction cells, and the learning of landmark stability. *J. Neurosci.* (in press).

Markus, E. J., McNaughton, B. L., Barnes, C. A., Green, J. C., and Meltzer, J. (1990). Head direction cells in the dorsal presubiculum integrate both visual and angular velocity information. *Soc. Neurosci. Abs.*, 16:441.

McNaughton, B. L., Chen, L. L., and Markus, E. J. (1991). "Dead reckoning," landmark learning, and the sense of direction: A neurophysiological and computational hypothesis. *J. Cognit. Neurosci.*, 3:190–202.

McNaughton, B. L., Markus, E. J., Wilson, M. A., and Knierim, J. J. (1993). Familiar landmarks can correct for cumulative error in the inertially based dead-reckoning system. *Soc. Neurosci. Abs.*, 19:795.

Mizumori, S. J. and Williams, J. D. (1993). Directionally selective mnemonic properties of neurons in the lateral dorsal nucleus of the thalamus of rats. *J. Neurosci.*, 13:4015–4028.

Precht, W. (1978). *Neuronal operations in the vestibular system*. Springer, New York.

Ranck, Jr., J. B. (1984). Head direction cells in the deep cell layer of dorsal presubiculum in freely moving rats. *Soc. Neurosci. Abs.*, 10:599.

Singer, W. and Artola, A. (1994). Plasticity of the mature neocortex. In Selverston, A. I. and Ascher, P., editors, *Cellular and molecular mechanisms underlying higher neural functions*, pages 49–69. Wiley.

Sparks, D. L. (1986). Translation of sensory signals into commands for control of saccadic eye movements: role of primate superior colliculus. *Physiol. Rev.*, 66:118–171.

Taube, J. S., Muller, R. U., and Ranck, Jr., J. B. (1990a). Head direction cells recorded from the postsubiculum in freely moving rats. I. Description and quantitative analysis. *J. Neurosci.*, 10:420–435.

Taube, J. S., Muller, R. U., and Ranck, Jr., J. B. (1990b). Head direction cells recorded from the postsubiculum in freely moving rats. II. Effects of environmental manipulations. *J. Neurosci.*, 10:436–447.

PART III
LEARNING THEORY AND DYNAMICS

On the Computational Complexity of Networks of Spiking Neurons

(Extended Abstract)

Wolfgang Maass
Institute for Theoretical Computer Science
Technische Universitaet Graz
A-8010 Graz, Austria
e-mail: maass@igi.tu-graz.ac.at

Abstract

We investigate the computational power of a formal model for networks of spiking neurons, both for the assumption of an unlimited timing precision, and for the case of a limited timing precision. We also prove upper and lower bounds for the number of examples that are needed to train such networks.

1 Introduction and Basic Definitions

There exists substantial evidence that timing phenomena such as temporal differences between spikes and frequencies of oscillating subsystems are integral parts of various information processing mechanisms in biological neural systems (for a survey and references see e.g. Abeles, 1991; Churchland and Sejnowski, 1992; Aertsen, 1993). Furthermore simulations of a variety of specific mathematical models for networks of spiking neurons have shown that temporal coding offers interesting possibilities for solving classical benchmark-problems such as associative memory, binding, and pattern segmentation (for an overview see Gerstner et al., 1992). Some aspects of these models have also been studied analytically, but almost nothing is known about their computational complexity (see Judd and Aihara, 1993, for some first results in this direction). In this article we introduce a simple formal model SNN for networks of spiking neurons that allows us to model the most important timing phenomena of neural nets (including synaptic modulation), and we prove upper and lower bounds for its computational power and learning complexity. Further details to the results reported in this article may be found in Maass, 1994a,1994b, 1994c.

Definition of a Spiking Neuron Network (SNN): *An SNN $\mathcal{N}$ consists of*
- *a finite directed graph $\langle V, E \rangle$ (we refer to the elements of V as "neurons" and to the elements of E as "synapses")*
- *a subset $V_{in} \subseteq V$ of input neurons*
- *a subset $V_{out} \subseteq V$ of output neurons*
- *for each neuron $v \in V - V_{in}$ a threshold-function $\Theta_v : \mathbf{R}^+ \to \mathbf{R} \cup \{\infty\}$ (where $\mathbf{R}^+ := \{x \in \mathbf{R} : x \geq 0\}$)*
- *for each synapse $\langle u, v \rangle \in E$ a response-function $\varepsilon_{u,v} : \mathbf{R}^+ \to \mathbf{R}$ and a weight- function $w_{u,v} : \mathbf{R}^+ \to \mathbf{R}$.*

We assume that the firing of the input neurons $v \in V_{in}$ is determined from outside of $\mathcal{N}$, i.e. the sets $F_v \subseteq \mathbf{R}^+$ of firing times ("spike trains") for the neurons $v \in V_{in}$ are given as the input of $\mathcal{N}$. Furthermore we assume that a set $T \subseteq \mathbf{R}^+$ of potential firing times has been fixed.

For a neuron $v \in V - V_{in}$ one defines its set F_v of firing times recursively. The first element of F_v is $\inf\{t \in T : P_v(t) \geq \Theta_v(0)\}$, and for any $s \in F_v$ the next larger element of F_v is $\inf\{t \in T : t > s \text{ and } P_v(t) \geq \Theta_v(t - s)\}$, where the potential function $P_v : \mathbf{R}^+ \to \mathbf{R}$ is defined by

$$P_v(t) := 0 + \sum_{u\, :\, \langle u, v \rangle \in E} \sum_{s \in F_u\, :\, s < t} w_{u,v}(s) \cdot \varepsilon_{u,v}(t - s) .$$

The firing times ("spike trains") F_v of the output neurons $v \in V_{out}$ that result in this way are interpreted as the output of $\mathcal{N}$.

Regarding the set T of potential firing times we consider in this article the case $T = \mathbf{R}^+$ (SNN with continuous time) and the case $T = \{i \cdot \mu : i \in \mathbf{N}\}$ for some μ with $1/\mu \in \mathbf{N}$ (SNN with discrete time).

We assume that for each SNN $\mathcal{N}$ there exists a bound $\tau_{\mathcal{N}} \in \mathbf{R}$ with $\tau_{\mathcal{N}} > 0$ such that $\Theta_v(x) = \infty$ for all $x \in (0, \tau_{\mathcal{N}})$ and all $v \in V - V_{in}$ ($\tau_{\mathcal{N}}$ may be interpreted as the minimum of all "refractory periods" τ_{ref} of neurons in $\mathcal{N}$). Furthermore we assume that all "input spike trains" F_v with $v \in V_{in}$ satisfy $|F_v \cap [0, t]| < \infty$ for all $t \in \mathbf{R}^+$. On the basis of these assumptions one can also in the continuous case easily show that the firing times are well-defined for all $v \in V - V_{in}$ (and occur in distances of at least $\tau_{\mathcal{N}}$).

Input- and Output-Conventions: For simulations between SNN's and Turing machines we assume that the SNN either gets an input (or produces an output) from $\{0, 1\}^*$ in the form of a spike-train (i.e. one bit per unit of time), or encoded into the phase-difference of just two spikes. *Real-valued* input or output for an SNN is always encoded into the phase-difference of two spikes.

Remarks
a) In models for *biological neural systems* one assumes that if x time-units have

passed since its last firing, the current threshold $\Theta_v(x)$ of a neuron v is "infinite" for $x < \tau_{ref}$ (where τ_{ref} = refractory period of neuron v), and then approaches quite rapidly from above some constant value. A neuron v "fires" (i.e. it sends an "action potential" or "spike" along its axon) when its current membrane potential $P_v(t)$ at the axon hillock exceeds its current threshold Θ_v. $P_v(t)$ is the sum of various postsynaptic potentials $w_{u,v}(s) \cdot \varepsilon_{u,v}(t-s)$. Each of these terms describes an *excitatory* (EPSP) or *inhibitory* (IPSP) *postsynaptic potential* at the axon hillock of neuron v at time t, as a result of a spike that had been generated by a "presynaptic" neuron u at time s, and which has been transmitted through a synapse between both neurons. Recordings of an EPSP typically show a function that has a constant value c (c = resting membrane potential; e.g. $c = -70mV$) for some initial time-interval (reflecting the axonal and synaptic transmission time), then rises to a peak-value, and finally drops back to the same constant value c. An IPSP tends to have the negative shape of an EPSP. For the sake of mathematical simplicity we assume in the SNN-model that the constant initial and final value of all response-functions $\varepsilon_{u,v}$ is equal to 0 (in other words: $\varepsilon_{u,v}$ models the *difference* between a postsynaptic potential and the resting membrane potential c). Different presynaptic neurons u generate postsynaptic potentials of different sizes at the axon hillock of a neuron v, depending on the size, location and current state of the synapse (or synapses) between u and v. This effect is modelled by the weight-factors $w_{u,v}(s)$.

The precise shapes of threshold-, response-, and weight-functions vary among different biological neural systems, and even within the same system. Fortunately one can prove significant *upper bounds* for the computational complexity of SNN's $\mathcal{N}$ without any assumptions about the *specific shapes* of these functions of $\mathcal{N}$. Instead, we only assume that they are of a reasonably simple *mathematical structure*.

b) In order to prove *lower bounds* for the computational complexity of an SNN $\mathcal{N}$ one is forced to make more specific assumptions about these functions. All lower bound results that are reported in this article require only some rather weak *basic assumptions* about the response- and threshold-functions. They mainly require that EPSP's have some (arbitrarily short) segment where they increase linearly, and some (arbitrarily short) segment where they decrease linearly (for details see Maass, 1994a, 1994b).

c) Although the model SNN is apparently more "realistic" than all models for biological neural nets whose computational complexity has previously been analyzed, it deliberately sacrifices a large number of more intricate biological details for the sake of mathematical tractability. Our model is closely related to those of (Buhmann and Schulten, 1986), and (Gerstner, 1991, 1992). Similarly as in (Buhmann and Schulten, 1986) we consider here only the deterministic case.

d) The model SNN is also suitable for investigating algorithms that involve *synaptic modulation* at various time-scales. Hence one can investigate within this framework not only the complexity of algorithms for supervised and unsupervised learning, but also the potential *computational* power of rapid weight-changes *within* the course of a computation. In the theorems of this paper we allow that the value of a weight $w_{u,v}(s)$ at a firing time $s \in F_u$ is defined by an *algebraic computation tree* (see van Leeuwen, 1990) in terms of its value at previous firing times $s' \in F_u$ with $s' < s$, some preceding firing times $\tilde{s} < s$ of arbitrary other neurons, and arbitrary real-valued parameters. In this way $w_{u,v}(s)$ can be defined by different rational functions of the abovementioned arguments, depending on the numerical relationship between these arguments (which can be evaluated by comparing first the relative size of arbitrary rational functions of these arguments). As a simple special case one can for example increase $w_{u,v}$ (perhaps up to some specified saturation-value) as long as neurons u and v fire coherently, and decrease $w_{u,v}$ otherwise.

For the sake of simplicity in the statements of our results we assume in this extended abstract that the algebraic computation tree for each weight $w_{u,v}$ involves only $O(1)$ tests and rational functions of degree $O(1)$ that depend only on $O(1)$ of the abovementioned arguments. Furthermore we assume in Theorems 3, 4 and 5 that either each weight is an arbitrary time-invariant real, or that each current weight is rounded off to bit-length poly$(\log p_\mathcal{N})$ in binary representation, and does not depend on the times of firings that occured longer than time $O(1)$ ago. Furthermore we assume in Theorems 3 and 5 that the parameters in the algebraic computation tree are rationals of bit-length $O(\log p_\mathcal{N})$.

e) It is well-known that the *Vapnik-Chervonenkis dimension ("VC-dimension")* of a neural net $\mathcal{N}$ (and the *pseudo-dimension* for the case of a neural net $\mathcal{N}$ with *real-valued* output, with some suitable fixed norm for measuring the error) can be used to bound the number of examples that are needed to train $\mathcal{N}$ (see Haussler, 1992). Obviously these notions have to be *defined differently* for a network with *time-dependent* weights. We propose to define the VC-dimension (pseudo-dimension)of an SNN $\mathcal{N}$ with time-dependent weights as the VC-dimension (pseudo-dimension) of the class of all functions that can be computed by $\mathcal{N}$ with different assignments of values to the real-valued (or rational-valued) parameters of $\mathcal{N}$ that are involved in the definitions of the piecewise rational response-, threshold-, and weight-functions of $\mathcal{N}$. In a biological neural system $\mathcal{N}$ these parameters might for example reflect the concentrations of certain chemical substances that are known to modulate the behavior of $\mathcal{N}$.

f) The focus in the investigation of computations in biological neural systems differs in two essential aspects from that of classical computational complexity theory. First, one is not only interested in single computations of a neural net for unrelated inputs x, but also in its ability to process an interrelated sequence $(\langle x(i), y(i)\rangle)_{i\in\mathbf{N}}$ of inputs and outputs, which may for example include an initial training sequence for learning or associative memory. Secondly, exact timing of computations is all-important in biological neural nets, and many tasks have to be solved within a specific number of steps. Therefore an analysis in terms of the notion of a *real-time computation* and *real-time simulation* appears to be more adequate for models of biological neural nets than the more traditional analysis via complexity classes.

One says that a sequence $(\langle x(i), y(i)\rangle)_{i\in\mathbf{N}}$ is *processed in real-time* by a machine M, if for every $i \in \mathbf{N}$ the machine M outputs $y(i)$ within a constant number c of computation steps after having received input $x(i)$. One says that M' *simulates M in real-time* (with delay factor Δ), if every sequence that is processed in real-time by M (with some constant c), can also be processed in real-time by M' (with a constant $\Delta \cdot c$). For SNN's M we count each spike in M as a computation step.

These definitions imply that a real-time simulation of M by M' is a special case of a linear-time simulation, and hence that any problem that can be solved by M with a certain time complexity $t(n)$, can be solved by M' with time complexity $O(t(n))$

(see Maass, 1994a, 1994b, for details).

2 Networks of Spiking Neurons with Continuous Time

Theorem 1: *If the response- and threshold-functions of the neurons satisfy some rather weak basic assumptions (see Maass, 1994a, 1994b), then one can build from such neurons for any given $d \in \mathbf{N}$ an SNN $\mathcal{N}_{TM}(d)$ of finite size with rational delays that can simulate with a suitable assignment of rational values from $[0,1]$ to its weights any Turing machine with at most d tapes in real-time.*

Furthermore $\mathcal{N}_{TM}(2)$ can compute <u>any</u> function $F : \{0,1\}^* \to \{0,1\}^*$ with a suitable assignment of real values from $\overline{[0,1]}$ to its weights.

The fixed SNN $\mathcal{N}_{TM}(d)$ of Theorem 1 can simulate Turing machines whose tape content is much larger than the size of $\mathcal{N}_{TM}(d)$, by encoding such tape content into the phase-difference between two oscillators. The proof of Theorem 1 transforms arbitrary computations of Turing machines into operations on such phase-differences.

The last part of Theorem 1 implies that the VC-dimension of some finite SNN's is infinite. In contrast to that the following result shows that one can give finite bounds for the VC-dimension of those SNN's that only use a bounded numbers of spikes in their computation. Furthermore the last part of the claim of Theorem 2 implies that their VC-dimension may in fact grow linearly with the number S of spikes that occur in a computation.

Theorem 2: *The VC-dimension and pseudo-dimension of any SNN $\mathcal{N}$ with piecewise linear response- and threshold-functions, arbitrary real-valued parameters and time-dependent weights (as specified in section 1) can be bounded (even for real-valued inputs and outputs) by $O(|E| \cdot |V| \cdot S(\log |V| + \log S))$ if $\mathcal{N}$ uses in each computation at most S spikes.*

Furthermore one can construct SNN's (with any response- and threshold-functions that satisfy our basic assumptions, with fixed rational parameters and rational time-invariant weights) whose VC-dimension is for computations with up to S spikes as large as $\Omega(|E| \cdot S)$.

We refer to Maass, 1994a, 1994c, for *upper bounds* on the computational power of SNN's with continuous time.

3 Networks of Spiking Neurons with Discrete Time

In this section we consider the case where all firing times of neurons in $\mathcal{N}$ are multiples of some μ with $1/\mu \in \mathbf{N}$. We restrict our attention to the biologically plausible case where there exists some $t_\mathcal{N} \geq 1$ such that for all $x > t_\mathcal{N}$ all response functions $\varepsilon_{u,v}(x)$ have the value 0 and all threshold functions $\Theta_v(x)$ have some arbitrary constant value. If $t_\mathcal{N}$ is chosen minimal with this property, we refer to $p_\mathcal{N} := \lceil t_\mathcal{N}/\mu \rceil$ as the *timing-precision of $\mathcal{N}$*. Obviously for $p_\mathcal{N} = 1$ the SNN is equivalent to a "non-spiking" neural net that consists of linear threshold gates, whereas a SNN with continuous time may be viewed as the opposite extremal case for $p_\mathcal{N} \to \infty$.

The following result provides a significant upper bound for the computational power of an SNN with discrete time, even in the presence of arbitrary real-valued parameters and weights. Its proof is technically rather involved.

Theorem 3: *Assume that $\mathcal{N}$ is an SNN with timing-precision $p_\mathcal{N}$, piecewise polynomial response- and piecewise rational threshold-functions with arbitrary real-valued parameters, and weight-functions as specified in section 1.*

Then one can simulate $\mathcal{N}$ for boolean valued inputs in real-time by a Turing machine with $\text{poly}(|V|, \log p_\mathcal{N}, \log 1/\tau_\mathcal{N})$ states and $\text{poly}(|V|, \log p_\mathcal{N}, t_\mathcal{N}/\tau_\mathcal{N})$ tape-cells.

On the other hand any Turing machine with q states that uses at most s tape-cells can be simulated in real-time by an SNN $\mathcal{N}$ with any response- and threshold-functions that satisfy our basic assumptions, with rational parameters and time-invariant rational weights, with $O(q)$ neurons, $\log p_\mathcal{N} = O(s)$, and $t_\mathcal{N}/\tau_\mathcal{N} = O(1)$.

The next result shows that the VC-dimension of any SNN with discrete time is finite, and grows proportionally to $\log p_\mathcal{N}$. The proof of its lower bound combines a new explicit construction with that of Maass, 1993.

Theorem 4: *Assume that the SNN $\mathcal{N}$ has the same properties as in Theorem 3. Then the VC-dimension and the pseudo-dimension of $\mathcal{N}$ (for arbitrary real valued inputs) can be bounded by $O(|E| \cdot |V| \cdot \log p_\mathcal{N})$, independently of the number of spikes in its computations.*

Furthermore one can construct SNN's $\mathcal{N}$ of this type with any response- and threshold-functions that satisfy our basic assumptions, with rational parameters and time-invariant rational weights, so that $\mathcal{N}$ has (already for boolean inputs) a VC-dimension of at least $\Omega(|E|(\log p_\mathcal{N} + \log |E|))$.

4 Relationships to other Computational Models

We consider here the relationship between SNN's with discrete time and recurrent *analog neural nets*. In the latter no "spikes" or other non-trivial timing-phenomena occur, but the output of a gate consists of the "analog" value of some squashing- or activation function that is applied to the weighted sum of its inputs. See e.g. (Siegelmann and Sontag, 1992) or (Maass, 1993) for recent results about the computational power of such models. We consider in this section a perhaps more "realistic" version of such models $\mathcal{N}$, where the output of each gate is rounded off to an integer multiple of some $\frac{1}{a}$ (with $a \in \mathbf{N}$). We refer to a as the *number of activation levels* of $\mathcal{N}$.

It is an interesting open problem whether such analog neural nets (with gate-outputs interpreted as firing rates) or networks of spiking neurons provide a more adequate computational model for biological neural systems. Theorem 5 shows that in spite of their quite different structure the computational power of these two models is in fact closely related.

On the side the following theorem also exhibits a new subclass of deterministic finite automata (DFA's) which turns out to be of particular interest in the context of neural nets. We say that a DFA M is a *sparse DFA of size s* if M can be realized by a Turing machine with s states and space-bound s (such that each step of M corresponds to one step of the Turing machine). Note that a sparse DFA may have exponentially in s many states, but that only $\text{poly}(s)$ bits are needed to describe its transition function. Sparse DFA's are relatively easy to construct, and hence are very useful for demonstrating (via Theorem 5) that a specific task can be carried out on a "spiking" neural net with a realistic timing precision (respectively on an analog neural net with a realistic number of activation levels).

Theorem 5: *The following classes of machines have closely related computational power in the sense that there is a polynomial p such that each computational model from any of these classes can be simulated in real-time (with delay-factor $\leq p(s)$) by some computational model from any other class (with the size-parameter s replaced by $p(s)$):*
- *sparse DFA's of size s*
- *SNN's with $O(1)$ neurons and timing precision 2^s*
- *recurrent analog neural nets that consist of $O(1)$ gates with piecewise rational activation functions with 2^s activation levels, and parameters and weights of bit-length $\leq s$*
- *neural nets that consist of s linear threshold gates (with recurrencies) with arbitrary real weights.*

The result of Theorem 5 is remarkably stable since it holds no matter whether one considers just SNN's $\mathcal{N}$ with $O(1)$ neurons that employ very simple fixed piecewise linear response- and threshold-functions with parameters of bit-length $O(1)$ (with $t_\mathcal{N}/\tau_\mathcal{N} = O(1)$ and time-invariant weights of bit-length $\leq s$), or if one considers SNN's $\mathcal{N}$ with s neurons with arbitrary piecewise polynomial response- and piecewise rational threshold-functions with arbitrary real-valued parameters, $t_\mathcal{N}/\tau_\mathcal{N} \leq s$, and time-dependent weights (as specified in section 1).

5 Conclusion

We have introduced a simple formal model SNN for networks of spiking neurons, and have shown that significant bounds for its computational power and sample complexity can be derived from rather weak assumptions about the mathematical structure of its response-, threshold-, and weight-functions. Furthermore we have established quantitative relationships between the computational power of a model for networks of spiking neurons with a limited timing precision (i.e. SNN's with discrete time) and a quite realistic version of recurrent analog neural nets (with a bounded number of activation levels). The simulations which provide the proof of this result create an interesting link between computations with spike-coding (in an SNN) and computations with frequency-coding (in analog neural nets). We also have established such relationships for the case of SNN's with continuous time (see Maass 1994a, 1994b, 1994c), but space does not permit to report these results in this article.

The Theorems 1 and 5 of this article establish the existence of mechanisms for simulating arbitrary Turing machines (and hence *any* common computational model) on an SNN. As a consequence one can now demonstrate that a concrete task (such as binding, pattern-matching, associative memory) can be carried out on an SNN by simply showing that some arbitrary common computational model can carry out that task. Furthermore one can bound the required *timing-precision* of the SNN in terms of the *space* needed on a Turing machine.

Since we have based our investigations on the rather refined notion of a *real-time* simulation, our results provide information not only about the possibility to implement computations, but also *adaptive behavior* on networks of spiking neurons.

Acknowledgement

I would like to thank Wulfram Gerstner for helpful discussions.

References

M. Abeles. (1991) Corticonics: Neural Circuits of the Cerebral Cortex. *Cambridge University Press.*

A. Aertsen. ed. (1993) Brain Theory: Spatio-Temporal Aspects of Brain Function. *Elsevier.*

J. Buhmann, K. Schulten. (1986) Associative recognition and storage in a model network of physiological neurons. *Biol. Cybern.* 54: 319-335.

P. S. Churchland, T. J. Sejnowski. (1992) The Computational Brain. *MIT-Press.*

W. Gerstner. (1991) Associative memory in a network of "biological" neurons. *Advances in Neural Information Processing Systems, vol. 3, Morgan Kaufmann*: 84-90.

W. Gerstner, R. Ritz, J. L. van Hemmen. (1992) A biologically motivated and analytically soluble model of collective oscillations in the cortex. *Biol. Cybern.* 68: 363-374.

D. Haussler. (1992) Decision theoretic generalizations of the PAC model for neural nets and other learning applications. *Inf. and Comput.* 95: 129-161.

K. T. Judd, K. Aihara. (1993) Pulse propagation networks: A neural network model that uses temporal coding by action potentials. *Neural Networks* 6: 203-215.

J. van Leeuwen, ed. (1990) Handbook of Theoretical Computer Science, vol. A: Algorithms and Complexity. *MIT-Press.*

W. Maass. (1993) Bounds for the computational power and learning complexity of analog neural nets. *Proc. 25th Annual ACM Symposium on the Theory of Computing*, 335-344.

W. Maass. (1994a) On the computational complexity of networks of spiking neurons (extended abstract). *TR 393 from May 1994 of the Institutes for Information Processing Graz* (for a more detailed version see the file *maass.spiking.ps.Z* in the *neuroprose archive*).

W. Maass. (1994b) Lower bounds for the computational power of networks of spiking neurons. *Neural Computation*, to appear.

W. Maass. (1994c) Analog computations on networks of spiking neurons (extended abstract). Submitted for publication.

H. T. Siegelmann, E. D. Sontag. (1992) On the computational power of neural nets. *Proc. 5th ACM-Workshop on Computational Learning Theory*, 440-449.

H^∞ Optimal Training Algorithms and their Relation to Backpropagation

Babak Hassibi[*]
Information Systems Laboratory
Stanford University
Stanford, CA 94305

Thomas Kailath
Information Systems Laboratory
Stanford University
Stanford, CA 94305

Abstract

We derive *global* H^∞ optimal training algorithms for neural networks. These algorithms guarantee the smallest possible prediction error energy over *all* possible disturbances of fixed energy, and are therefore robust with respect to model uncertainties and lack of statistical information on the exogenous signals. The ensuing estimators are infinite-dimensional, in the sense that updating the weight vector estimate requires knowledge of all previous weight esimates. A certain finite-dimensional approximation to these estimators is the backpropagation algorithm. This explains the *local* H^∞ optimality of backpropagation that has been previously demonstrated.

1 Introduction

Classical methods in estimation theory (such as maximum-likelihood, maximum entropy and least-squares) require a priori knowledge of the statistical properties of the exogenous signals. In some applications, however, one is faced with model uncertainties and lack of statistical information, which has led to an increasing interest in minimax estimation (see *e.g.*, Zames 1981, Khargonekar and Nagpal 1991, and the references therein) with the belief that the resulting so-called H^∞ algorithms will be more robust and less sensitive to parameter variations.

---

[*]**Contact author:** Information Systems Laboratory, Stanford University, Stanford CA 94305. Phone (415) 723-1538. Fax (415) 723-8473. E-mail: hassibi@rascals.stanford.edu.

In (Hassibi, Sayed and Kailath, 1994) we have shown that LMS (Widrow and Hoff, 1960) and backpropagation (Rumelhart and Mclelland, 1986), the currently most widely used adaptive algorithms that have long been considered to be approximate H^2 (or least-squares) solutions, are indeed H^∞ optimal and locally H^∞ optimal algorithms, respectively. This, in our view, connects earlier work in learning theory to more recent ideas in robust estimation, and explains why LMS and backpropagation have found wide applicability in such a diverse range of problems.

The local H^∞ optimality of backpropagation implies that backpropagation minimizes the energy gain from the disturbances to the prediction errors, only if the initial condition is close enough to the true weight vector and if the disturbances are small enough. In this paper we derive global H^∞ optimal estimators that minimize the energy gain from the disturbances to the prediction errors for *all* initial conditions and disturbances. The resulting estimator (given by Theorem 1) has growing memory, which we refer to as being infinite-dimensional, since updating the weight vector estimate requires knowledge of all previous weight estimates. When the underlying model is linear, we show that this infinite-dimensional estimator reduces to the finite-dimensional LMS filter. When the underlying model is nonlinear, the infinite-dimensionality of the estimator may prohibit its practical applicablity, and one needs to construct finite-dimensional approximations to this estimator. We consider two such approximations here: one yields the backpropagation algorithm, and the other is a second-order algorithm based on the Newton-Raphson iteration. There are, no doubt, a wide variety of other approximations which should be worthy of further scrutiny.

2 Robust Estimation

In estimation problems one assumes a certain model (say an FIR filter in adaptive filtering, or a neural network), observes a corrupted version of the output of this model, and wants to estimate the parameters associated with this model (say the weights of the FIR filter or neural network). Most estimation algorithms make some *assumption* about the nature of the disturbances, and then proceed to estimate the parameters using some optimality criterion. To be more specific, we shall consider the following two cases.

2.1 The Linear Case

Suppose that we observe an output sequence $\{d_i\}$ that obeys the following linear model

$$d_i = x_i^T w + v_i, \tag{1}$$

where $x_i^T = [\ x_{i1}\ \ x_{i2}\ \ \ldots\ \ x_{in}\ ]$ is a known input vector, w is the unknown weight vector that we intend to estimate, and $\{v_i\}$ is an unknown disturbance sequence. Let $w_i = \mathcal{F}(d_0, d_1, \ldots, d_i)$ denote the estimate of the weight vector given the inputs $\{x_j\}$ and the outputs $\{d_j\}$ from time 0 up to and including time i. The most widely used estimate w_i, is one that satisfies the following H^2 criterion

$$\min_w \left[\mu^{-1}|w - w_{-1}|^2 + \sum_{j=0}^{i} |d_j - x_j^T w|^2 \right], \tag{2}$$

where μ is a positive constant that reflects a priori knowledge as to how close w is to the initial estimate w_{-1}. The *exact* solution to the above criterion is given by the RLS algorithm (Haykin, 1991):

$$w_i = w_{i-1} + k_{p,i}(d_i - x_i^T w), \qquad w_{-1} \tag{3}$$

where w_{-1} denotes the initial value,

$$k_{p,i} = \frac{P_i x_i}{1 + x_i^T P_i x_i}$$

and

$$P_{i+1} = P_i - \frac{P_i x_i x_i^T P_i}{1 + x_i^t P_i x_i}, \qquad P_0 = \mu I.$$

If we assume that in the model (1) the $w - w_{-1}$ and $\{v_i\}$ are zero-mean independent Gaussian random variables with variances μI and 1, respectively, then the cost function in (2) is simply the associated log-likelihood function. Thus the estimate given by minimizing (2) will be the maximum-likelihood estimate of the weight vector w. In particular, it can be shown that under these assumptions, RLS minimizes the expected prediction energy

$$E \parallel e \parallel_i^2 = E \sum_{j=0}^{i} |x_j^T w - x_j^T w_{j-1}|^2.$$

Note that the LMS algorithm is an approximation to RLS where $k_{p,i}$ is replaced by μx_i, so that the estimates are updated along the direction of the instantaneous gradient of (2):

$$w_i = w_{i-1} + \mu x_i (d_i - x_i^T w), \qquad w_{-1}. \qquad (4)$$

2.2 The Nonlinear Case

Suppose now that we observe an output sequence $\{d_i\}$ that obeys the following nonlinear model

$$d_i = g_i(w) + v_i, \qquad (5)$$

where $g_i(.)$ is a known *nonlinear* function (with bounded first and second order derivatives), w is the unknown weight vector we intend to estimate, and $\{v_i\}$ is an unknown disturbance sequence. In a neural network context the index i in $g_i(.)$ will correspond to the nonlinear function that maps the weight vector to the output when the ith input pattern is presented, i.e., $g_i(w) = g(x_i, w)$ where x_i is the ith input pattern. As before we shall denote by $w_i = \mathcal{F}(d_0, \ldots, d_i)$ the estimate of the weight vector using measurements up to and including time i. The H^2 criterion for finding the estimate is

$$\min_w \left[\mu^{-1} |w - w_{-1}|^2 + \sum_{j=0}^{i} |d_j - g_j(w)|^2 \right]. \qquad (6)$$

As in the linear case, if we assume that in the model (5) the disturbances $w - w_{-1}$ and $\{v_i\}$ are zero-mean independent Gaussian random variables with variances μI and 1, respectively, then the cost function in (6) is the log-likelihood function and the weight vector that minimizes it is the maximum-likelihood estimate. However, contrary to the linear case, the solution to (6) will *not*, in general, minimize the expected prediction error energy.

In the nonlinear case exact solutions to (6) do not exist, and the backpropagation algorithm is a generalization of the LMS algorithm where once more the estimates are updated along the negative direction of the instantaneous gradient of the log-likelihood function:

$$w_i = w_{i-1} + \mu \frac{\partial g_i}{\partial w}(w_{i-1})(d_i - g_i(w_i)), \qquad w_{-1}. \qquad (7)$$

Generalizations of the RLS algorithm to the nonlinear setting are the second order Gauss-Newton methods.

2.3 The Question of Robustness

In view of the above discussion we have seen that H^2-optimal estimation strategies (see (2) and (6)) are maximum-likelihood and minimize the expected prediction error energy (in the linear case), if we assume that the disturbances are zero-mean independent Gaussian random variables. However, the question that begs itself is what the performance of such estimators will be if the assumptions on the disturbances are violated, or if there are modelling errors in our model so that the disturbances must include the modelling errors? In other words

- is it possible that *small* disturbances and modelling errors may lead to *large* estimation errors?

Obviously a nonrobust algorithm would be one for which the above is true, and a robust algorithm would be one for which small disturbances lead to small estimation errors. (For example in the adaptive filtering problem, where we assumed an FIR model, the *true* model may be IIR, but we neglect the tail of the filter since its components are small. However, unless one uses a robust estimation algorithm, it is conceivable that this small modelling error may result in large estimation errors.)

The problem of robust estimation is thus an important one, and is worthy of study in its own right. Rather surprisingly, it had not received much attention until quite recently. The H^∞ criterion has been introduced (Zames, 1981) as a means of studying such questions in the contexts of estimation and control. This is the subject of the next section.

3 The H^∞ Problem

The H^∞ estimation formulation is an attempt to address the robustness question raised in the previous section. The idea is to come up with estimators that minimize (or in the suboptimal case bound) the maximum energy gain from the disturbances to the estimation errors. This will guarantee that if the disturbances are small (in energy) then the estimation errors will be as small as possible (in energy), *no matter what the disturbances are*. In other words the maximum energy gain is minimized over *all possible* disturbances. The robustness of the H^∞ estimators arises from this fact. Since they make no assumption about the disturbances, they have to accomodate for all conceivable disturbances, and are thus over-conservative.

We once more assume that we observe an output sequence $\{d_i\}$ that obeys the following nonlinear model
$$d_i = g_i(w) + v_i, \tag{8}$$
where $g_i(.)$ is a known *nonlinear* function, w is an unknown weight vector, and $\{v_i\}$ is an unknown disturbance sequence that includes noise and/or modelling errors. Recall that in a neural network context $g_i(w) = g(x_i, w)$, where x_i is the ith input pattern. As before we shall denote by $w_i = \mathcal{F}(d_0, \ldots, d_i)$ the estimate of the weight vector using measurements up to and including time i, and the prediction error by
$$e_i = g_i(w) - g_i(w_{i-1}).$$

The optimal H^∞ estimation problem may now be stated as follows.

Problem 1 (Optimal H^∞ Estimation Problem) *Find an H^∞-optimal estimation strategy $w_i = \mathcal{F}(d_0, d_1, \ldots, d_i)$ that minimizes the maximum energy gain from the disturbances $w - w_{-1}$ and $\{v_i\}$ to the prediction errors $\{e_i = g_i(w) - g_i(w_{i-1})\}$, and obtain the resulting*

$$\gamma_{opt}^2 = \inf_{\mathcal{F}} \sup_{w,v \in h_2} \frac{\|e\|_i^2}{\mu^{-1}|w - w_{-1}|^2 + \|v\|_i^2} = \inf_{\mathcal{F}} \sup_{w,v \in h_2} \frac{\sum_{j=0}^{i} |g_j(w) - g_j(w_{j-1})|^2}{\mu^{-1}|w - w_{-1}|^2 + \sum_{j=0}^{i} |v_j|^2} \tag{9}$$

where $\mu > 0$ reflects a priori knowledge of how close w is to the initial estimate w_{-1}, and where h_2 is the space of all causal square-summable sequences. γ_{opt} is the so-called minimum H^∞ norm.

Note that the infimum in (9) is taken over all *causal* estimators $\mathcal{F}$. Although the H^∞ estimation problem has been solved in the linear case, to date there does not exist a satisfactory solution for the nonlinear case, and indeed the class of nonlinear functions $g_i(.)$ for which the above problem has a solution is not known (Ball and Helton, 1992).

We have, however, been able to solve Problem 1 in the case where the $g_i(.)$ are bounded functions with bounded first and second order derivatives. These conditions are of course satisfied by multi-layer neural networks with sigmoidal elements. The result is stated below, where we call the column vectors $\{x_i\}$ *exciting* if $\lim_{i \to \infty} \sum_{j=0}^{i} x_j^t x_j = \infty$.

Theorem 1 (H^∞ Optimal Algorithm) *Consider the model (8) where the $g_i(.)$ are bounded and have bounded first and second order derivatives, and suppose we wish to minimize the maximum energy gain from the unknowns $w - w_{-1}$ and $\{v_i\}$ to the prediction errors $\{e_i\}$. If*

$$0 < \mu < \inf_i \inf_w \frac{1}{|\frac{\partial g_i}{\partial w}(w)|^2}, \tag{10}$$

and the $\{\frac{\partial g_i}{\partial w}(w)\}$ are exciting, then the minimum H^∞ norm is

$$\gamma_{opt} = 1.$$

In this case an optimal H^∞ estimator is given by the following sequence of nonlinear equations

$$\begin{cases} \frac{1}{\mu} w_0 = (d_0 - g_0(w_{-1}))\frac{\partial g_0}{\partial w}(w_0) \\ \frac{1}{\mu} w_1 = (d_0 - g_0(w_{-1}))\frac{\partial g_0}{\partial w}(w_1) + (d_1 - g_1(w_0))\frac{\partial g_1}{\partial w}(w_1) \\ \vdots \quad \vdots \\ \frac{1}{\mu} w_i = (d_0 - g_0(w_{-1}))\frac{\partial g_0}{\partial w}(w_i) + (d_1 - g_1(w_0))\frac{\partial g_1}{\partial w}(w_i) + \\ \qquad \ldots + (d_i - g_i(w_{i-1}))\frac{\partial g_i}{\partial w}(w_i) \\ \vdots \quad \vdots \end{cases} \tag{11}$$

Remarks:

(i) The fact that $\hat{g}_i(w) = g_i(w_{i-1})$ implies that the output prediction has the same *structure* as our model (*i.e.* that there exists a weight vector estimate w_{i-1} that yields the desired output prediction).

(ii) Theorem 1 states that $\gamma_{opt} = 1$. While it is not intuitively difficult to convince oneself that γ_{opt} cannot be less than one (simply choose the disturbances v_i so that $v_i = e_i$, whereby the ratio in (9) can be made arbitrarily close to one), the surprising fact is that γ_{opt} is one. What this means is that the estimator of Theorem 1 guarantees that the energy of the prediction errors will never exceed the energy of the disturbances. This is of course not true of other estimators.

(iii) Theorem 1 gives an upper bound on the quantity μ that guarantees $\gamma_{opt} = 1$. As we shall see below, the μ of Theorem 1 is a generalization of the learning rate μ of the LMS and backpropagation algorithms (see (4) and (7)), and this is in accordance with the well-known fact that LMS and backpropagation behave poorly if the learning rate is chosen too large.

(iv) In view of Theorem 1, to obtain the estimate w_i we need to solve a nonlinear equation that involves all previous estimates $w_0, \ldots, w_{i-1}$. This means that the estimator (11) is infinite-dimensional. Although this may prohibit practical applications of this algorithm, it will be very useful to study special cases under which the estimator becomes finite-dimensional, or to find finite-dimensional approximations for (11). This will be done in the next section.

4 Special Cases

4.1 The Linear Case

In the linear case the model we consider has

$$g_i(w) = x_i^T w,$$

so that $\frac{\partial g_i}{\partial w}(w) = x_i$. Although the linear function $g_i(w) = x_i^T w$ does not satisfy the boundedness condition of Theorem 1, let us investigate the consequence of applying algorithm (11) to this case. Thus the $(i+1)$th equation in (11) becomes

$$\frac{1}{\mu} w_i = (d_0 - x_0^T w_{-1})x_0 + (d_1 - x_1^T w_0)x_1 + \ldots + (d_{i-1} - x_{i-1}^T w_{i-2})x_{i-1} + (d_i - x_i^T w_{i-1})x_i.$$

But from the ith equation

$$\frac{1}{\mu} w_{i-1} = (d_0 - x_0^T w_{-1})x_0 + (d_1 - x_1^T w_0)x_1 + \ldots + (d_{i-1} - x_{i-1}^T w_{i-2})x_{i-1}$$

so that

$$\frac{1}{\mu} w_i = \frac{1}{\mu} w_{i-1} + (d_i - x_i^T w_{i-1})x_i, \qquad (12)$$

which is the LMS algorithm (4). Thus in the linear case the estimator of Theorem 1 specializes to the LMS algorithm. This is expected since we have shown in (Hassibi et al., 1994) that the LMS algorithm is H^∞ optimal. The result obtained there is as follows.

Theorem 2 (LMS Algorithm) *Consider the model (1), and suppose we wish to minimize the maximum energy gain from the unknowns $w - w_{-1}$ and v_i to the prediction errors e_i. If the input vectors x_i are exciting and*

$$0 < \mu < \inf_i \frac{1}{|x_i|^2} \qquad (13)$$

then the minimum H^∞ norm is $\gamma_{opt} = 1$. In this case an optimal H^∞ estimator is given by the LMS algorithm with learning rate μ, viz.

$$w_i = w_{i-1} + \mu x_i (d_i - x_i^T w_{i-1}) \qquad , \qquad w_{-1} \qquad (14)$$

Note that in the linear case the estimator is finite-dimensional since to find w_i we only require knowledge of w_{i-1}.

4.2 Backpropagation

As mentioned at the end of Section 3, the H^∞ optimal estimator of Theorem 1 is infinite-dimensional, in the sense that to obtain the estimate w_i we need all previous estimates $w_0, \ldots, w_{i-1}$. We may obtain finite-dimensional approximations to the estimator (11) by constructing approximations to the nonlinear equations appearing in (11). However, the resulting estimators will no longer be H^∞ optimal in a global sense, but will only have local optimality.

The method that we shall use to obtain such approximate estimators is to assume that we have found the estimate w_{i-1}, and to use it as an initial guess to solve the $(i+1)$th equation in (11) whose solution is w_i. Depending on what algorithm we use to solve the $(i+1)$th equation with initial guess w_{i-1}, we shall get a different approximate estimator to (11).

To this end, suppose that we have solved the ith equation in (11) and have obtained w_{i-1}, i.e.

$$\frac{1}{\mu}w_{i-1} = (d_0 - g_0(w_{-1}))\frac{\partial g_0}{\partial w}(w_{-1}) + \ldots + (d_{i-1} - g_{i-1}(w_{i-2}))\frac{\partial g_{i-1}}{\partial w}(w_{i-1}).$$

We now intend to solve the $(i+1)$th equation in (11) for w_i. Note that this equation is of the form $x = f(x)$ (where $x = w_i$). If we use one step of the *fixed-point iteration* method $x_{j+1} = f(x_j)$ with initial condition $x_0 = w_{i-1}$, we have

$$\frac{1}{\mu}w_i = \underbrace{(d_0 - g_0(w_{-1}))\frac{\partial g_0}{\partial w}(w_{-1}) + \ldots + (d_{i-1} - g_{i-1}(w_{i-2}))\frac{\partial g_{i-1}}{\partial w}(w_{i-1})}_{\frac{1}{\mu}w_{i-1}} \quad (15)$$

$$+ (d_i - g_i(w_{i-1}))\frac{\partial g_i}{\partial w}(w_{i-1}) \quad (16)$$

$$= \frac{1}{\mu}w_{i-1} + (d_i - g_i(w_{i-1}))\frac{\partial g_i}{\partial w}(w_{i-1}) \quad (17)$$

which is the backpropagation algorithm (7). Note that since we only use w_{i-1} to compute w_i, backpropagation is a finite-dimensional approximation to the global H^∞ optimal estimator (11). Due to its approximate nature, backpropagation has only *local H^∞* optimality properties, as we have shown in (Hassibi et al., 1994). The result is stated below, where the column vectors $\{x_i\}$ are called *persistently exciting* if, $\lim_{i \to \infty} \frac{1}{i} \sum_{j=0}^{i} x_j x_j^t > \alpha I$, for some $\alpha > 0$.

Theorem 3 (Local H^∞ Optimality) *Consider the model (8) and the backpropagation algorithm (7). Suppose that the $\frac{\partial g_i}{\partial w}(w_{i-1})$ are persistently exciting, and that (10) is satisfied. Then for each $\epsilon > 0$, there exist $\delta_1, \delta_2 > 0$ such that for all $|w - w_{-1}| < \delta_1$ and all $v \in h_2$ with $|v_i| < \delta_2$, we have*

$$\frac{\| e \|^2}{\mu^{-1}|w - w_{-1}|^2 + \| v \|^2} \leq 1 + \epsilon$$

Note that contrary to the global Theorem 1, backpropagation cannot achieve $\gamma_{opt} = 1$, and that it bounds the energy gain by $\sqrt{1+\epsilon}$ only for *small enough* disturbances.

4.3 A Second-Order Algorithm

If instead of using one step of the fixed-point iteration to solve for w_i, as was done in Section 4.2, we use one step of the Newton-Raphson method with initial condition w_{i-1}, we obtain the following algorithm as an approximation to (11).

$$\begin{cases} w_i = w_{i-1} + \mu(d_i - g_i(w_{i-1}))\Phi_i \frac{\partial g_i}{\partial w}(w_{i-1}), & w_{-1} \\ \Phi_i = \Phi_{i-1} + \mu(d_{i-1} - g_{i-1}(w_{i-2}))\frac{\partial^2 g_{i-1}}{\partial w^2}(w_{i-2}), & \Phi_0 = I. \end{cases} \quad (18)$$

As before, (18) has only local optimality properties. However, since the Newton-Raphson method is less crude than the fixed-point iteration, it is expected to have better local properties than backpropagation. The complexity of the algorithm is $O(n^2)$ per iteration which is, of course, higher than backpropagation which requires only $O(n)$ per iteration.

5 Conclusion

We have derived *global* H^∞ optimal estimators for training neural networks. Such H^∞ optimal algorithms will be most applicable in uncertain environments where there may be modelling errors, and where the statistics and/or distributions of the disturbances are not known (or are too expensive to obtain).

The resulting H^∞ optimal algorithm of Theorem 1 is infinite-dimensional, so that computing the most recent weight vector estimate requires knowledge of all previous weight estimates. We considered two finite-dimensional approximations to this estimator (one of which was backpropagation) with the property that constructing the most recent weight estimate required only the immediately preceding weight estimate. However, the estimator of Theorem 1 has a very interesting structure that should allow for a wide variety of approximations, some of which may yield alternatives to the backpropagation algorithm. In particular, it would be interesting to study the possiblity of constructing estimators where updating the weight estimates requires more than one (but only finitely many) previous estimates.

The estimators constructed in this paper used prediction error as their criterion and should therefore have good generalization properties. It is also possible to construct similar estimators using filtered or smoothing error as the criterion, though this was not done due to lack of space.

Acknowledgements

This work was supported in part by the Air Force Office of Scientific Research, Air Force Systems Command under Contract AFOSR91-0060 and by the Army Research Office under contract DAAL03-89-K-0109.

References

J. A. Ball and J. W. Helton. (1992) Nonlinear H^∞ control theory for stable plants. *Math. Control Signals Systems*, 5:233-261.

B. Hassibi, A. H. Sayed, and T. Kailath. (1994) H^∞ optimality criteria for LMS and backpropagation. To appear in *Advances in Neural Information Processing Systems*, Vol. 6, Morgan-Kaufmann.

S. Haykin. (1991) *Adaptive Filter Theory*. Prentice Hall, Englewood Cliffs, NJ.

P. P. Khargonekar and K. M. Nagpal. (1991) Filtering and smoothing in an H^∞ setting. *IEEE Trans. on Automatic Control*, AC-36:831-847.

D. E. Rumelhart, J. L. McClelland and the PDP Research Group. (1986) *Parallel distributed processing : explorations in the microstructure of cognition*. Cambridge, Mass. : MIT Press.

B. Widrow and M. E. Hoff, Jr. (1960) Adaptive switching circuits. *IRE WESCON Conv. Rec.*, Pt.4:96-104.

G. Zames. (1981) Feedback optimal sensitivity: model preference transformation, multiplicative seminorms and approximate inverses. *IEEE Trans. on Automatic Control*, AC-26:301-320.

Synchrony and Desynchrony in Neural Oscillator Networks

DeLiang Wang
Department of Computer and Information Science
and Center for Cognitive Science
The Ohio State University
Columbus, Ohio 43210, USA
dwang@cis.ohio-state.edu

David Terman
Department of Mathematics
The Ohio State University
Columbus, Ohio 43210, USA
terman@math.ohio-state.edu

Abstract

An novel class of locally excitatory, globally inhibitory oscillator networks is proposed. The model of each oscillator corresponds to a standard relaxation oscillator with two time scales. The network exhibits a mechanism of selective gating, whereby an oscillator jumping up to its active phase rapidly recruits the oscillators stimulated by the same pattern, while preventing others from jumping up. We show analytically that with the selective gating mechanism the network rapidly achieves both synchronization within blocks of oscillators that are stimulated by connected regions and desynchronization between different blocks. Computer simulations demonstrate the network's promising ability for segmenting multiple input patterns in real time. This model lays a physical foundation for the oscillatory correlation theory of feature binding, and may provide an effective computational framework for scene segmentation and figure/ground segregation.

1 INTRODUCTION

A basic attribute of perception is its ability to group elements of a perceived scene into coherent clusters (objects). This ability underlies perceptual processes such as figure/ground segregation, identification of objects, and separation of different objects, and it is generally known as scene segmentation or perceptual organization. Despite the fact that humans perform it with apparent ease, the general problem of scene segmentation remains unsolved in the engineering of sensory processing, such as computer vision and auditory processing.

Fundamental to scene segmentation is the grouping of similar sensory features and the segregation of dissimilar ones. Theoretical investigations of brain functions and feature binding point to the mechanism of temporal correlation as a representational framework (von der Malsburg, 1981; von der Malsburg and Schneider, 1986). In particular, the correlation theory of von der Malsburg (1981) asserts that an object is represented by the temporal correlation of the firing activities of the scattered cells coding different features of the object. A natural way of encoding temporal correlation is to use neural oscillations, whereby each oscillator encodes some feature (maybe just a pixel) of an object. In this scheme, each segment (object) is represented by a group of oscillators that shows synchrony (phase-locking) of the oscillations, and different objects are represented by different groups whose oscillations are desynchronized from each other. Let us refer to this form of temporal correlation as *oscillatory correlation*. The theory of oscillatory correlation has received direct experimental support from the cell recordings in the cat visual cortex (Eckhorn et al., 1988; Gray et al., 1989) and other brain regions. The discovery of synchronous oscillations in the visual cortex has triggered much interest from the theoretical community in simulating the experimental results and in exploring oscillatory correlation to solve the problems of scene segmentation. While several demonstrate synchronization in a group of oscillators using local (lateral) connections (König and Schillen, 1991; Somers and Kopell, 1993; Wang, 1993, 1995), most of these models rely on long range connections to achieve phase synchrony. It has been pointed out that local connections in reaching synchrony may play a fundamental role in scene segmentation since long-range connections would lead to indiscriminate segmentation (Sporns et al., 1991; Wang, 1993).

There are two aspects in the theory of oscillatory correlation: (1) synchronization within the same object; and (2) desynchronization between different objects. Despite intensive studies on the subject, the question of desynchronization has been hardly addressed. The lack of an efficient mechanism for desynchronization greatly limits the utility of oscillatory correlation to perceptual organization. In this paper, we propose a new class of oscillatory networks and show that it can rapidly achieve both synchronization within each object and desynchronization between a number of simultaneously presented objects. The network is composed of the following elements: (1) A new model of a basic oscillator; (2) Local excitatory connections to produce phase synchrony within each object; (3) A global inhibitor that receives inputs from the entire network and feeds back with inhibition to produce desynchronization of the oscillator groups representing different objects. In other words, the mechanism of the network consists of local cooperation and global competition. This surprisingly simple neural architecture may provide an elementary approach to scene segmentation and a computational framework for perceptual organization.

2 MODEL DESCRIPTION

The building block of this network, a single oscillator i, is defined in the simplest form as a feedback loop between an excitatory unit x_i and an inhibitory unit y_i:

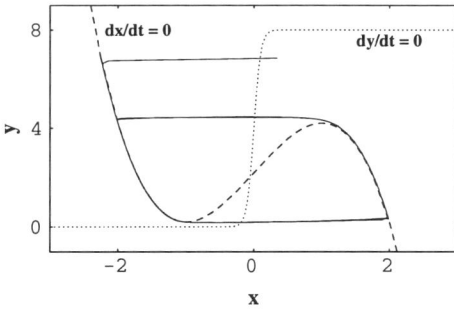

Figure 1: Nullclines and periodic orbit of a single oscillator as shown in the phase plane. When the oscillator starts at a randomly generated point in the phase plane, it quickly converged to a stable trajectory of a limit cycle.

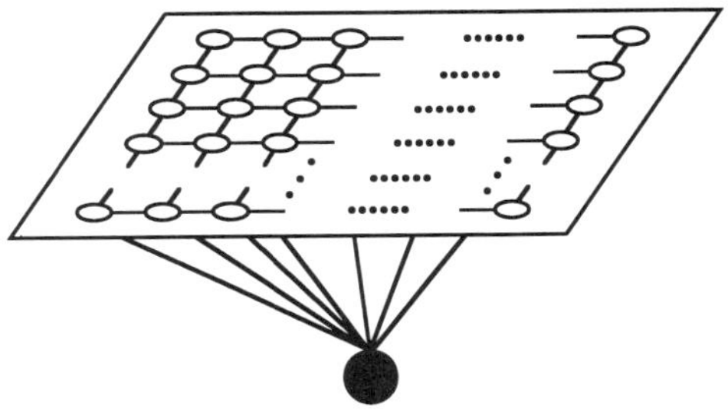

Figure 2: Architecture of a two dimensional network with nearest neighbor coupling. The global inhibitor is indicated by the black circle.

$$\frac{dx_i}{dt} = 3x_i - x_i^3 + 2 - y_i + \rho + I_i + S_i \tag{1a}$$

$$\frac{dy_i}{dt} = \varepsilon \left(\gamma (1 + tanh(x_i/\beta)) - y_i \right) \tag{1b}$$

where ρ denotes the amplitude of a Gaussian noise term. I_i represents external stimulation to the oscillator, and S_i denotes coupling from other oscillators in the network. The noise term is introduced both to test the robustness of the system and to actively desynchronize different input patterns. The parameter ε is chosen to be small. In this case (1), without any coupling or noise, corresponds to a standard relaxation oscillator. The x-nullcline of (1) is a cubic curve, while the y-nullcline is a sigmoid function, as shown in Fig. 1. If $I > 0$, these curves intersect along the middle branch of the cubic, and (1) is oscillatory. The periodic solution alternates between the silent and active phases of near steady state behavior. The parameter γ is introduced to control the relative times that the solution spends in these two phases. If $I < 0$, then the nullclines of (1) intersect at a stable fixed point along the left branch of the cubic. In this case the system produces no oscillation. The oscillator model (1) may be interpreted as a model of spiking behavior of a single neuron, or a mean field approximation to a network of excitatory and inhibitory neurons.

The network we study here in particular is two dimensional. However, the results can easily be extended to other dimensions. Each oscillator in the network is connected to only its four nearest neighbors, thus forming a 2-D grid. This is the simplest form of local connections. The global inhibitor receives excitation from each oscillator of the grid, and in turn inhibits each oscillator. This architecture is shown in Fig. 2. The intuitive reason why the network gives rise to scene segmentation is the following. When multiple connected objects are mapped onto the grid, local connectivity on the grid will group together the oscillators covered by each object. This grouping will be reflected by phase synchrony within each object. The global inhibitor is introduced for desynchronizing the oscillatory responses to different objects. We assume that the coupling term S_i in (1) is given by

$$S_i = \sum_{k \in N(i)} W_{ik} S_\infty(x_k, \theta_x) - W_z S_\infty(z, \theta_{xz}) \qquad (2)$$

$$S_\infty(x, \theta) = \frac{1}{1+ exp[-K(x-\theta)]} \qquad (3)$$

where W_{ik} is a connection (synaptic) weight from oscillator k to oscillator i, and $N(i)$ is the set of the neighoring oscillators that connect to i. In this model, $N(i)$ is the four immediate neighbors on the 2-D grid, except on the boundaries where $N(i)$ may be either 2 or 3 immediate neighbors. θ_x is a threshold (see the sigmoid function of Eq. 3) above which an oscillator can affect its neighbors. W_z (positive) is the weight of inhibition from the global inhibitor z, whose activity is defined as

$$\frac{dz}{dt} = \phi \, (\sigma_\infty - z) \qquad (4)$$

where $\sigma_\infty = 0$ if $x_i < \theta_{zx}$ for every oscillator, and $\sigma_\infty = 1$ if $x_i \geq \theta_{zx}$ for at least one oscillator i. Hence θ_{zx} represents a threshold. If the activity of every oscillator is below this threshold, then the global inhibitor will not receive any input. In this case $z \to 0$ and the oscillators will not receive any inhibition. If, on the other hand, the activity of at least one oscillator is above the threshold θ_{zx} then, the global inhibitor will receive input. In this case $z \to 1$, and each oscillator feels inhibition when z is above the threshold θ_{zx}. The parameter ϕ determines the rate at which the inhibitor reacts to such stimulation.

In summary, once an oscillator is active, it triggers the global inhibitor. This then inhibits the entire network as described in Eq. 1. On the other hand, an active oscillator spreads its activation to its nearest neighbors, again through (1), and from them to its further neighbors. In the next section, we give a number of properties of this system.

Besides boundaries, the oscillators on the grid are basically symmetrical. Boundary conditions may cause certain distortions to the stability of synchrous oscillations. Recently, Wang (1993) proposed a mechanism called *dynamic normalization* to ensure that each oscillator, whether it is in the interior or on a boundary, has equal overall connection weights from its neighbors. The dynamic normalization mechanism is adopted in the present model to form effective connections. For binary images (each pixel being either 0 or 1), the outcome of dynamic normalization is that an effective connection is established between two oscillators if and only if they are neighbors and both of them are activated by external stimulation. The network defined above can readily be applied for segmentation of binary images. For gray-level images (each pixel being in a certain value range), the following slight modification suffices to make the network applicable. An effective connection is established between two oscillators if and only if they are neighbors and the difference of their corresponding pixel values is below a certain threshold.

3 ANALYTICAL RESULTS

We have formally analyzed the network. Due to space limitations, we can only list the major conclusions without proofs. The interested reader can find the details in Terman and Wang (1994). Let us refer to a *pattern* as a connected region, and a *block* be a subset of oscillators stimulated by a given pattern. The following results are about singular solutions in the sense that we formally set $\varepsilon = 0$. However, as shown in (Terman and Wang, 1994), the results extend to the case $\varepsilon > 0$ sufficiently small.

Theorem 1. (*Synchronization*). The parameters of the system can be chosen so that all of the oscillators in a block always jump up simultaneously (synchronize). Moreover, the rate of synchronization is exponential.

Theorem 2. (*Multiple Patterns*) The parameters of the system and a constant T can be chosen to satisfy the following. If at the beginning all the oscillators of the same block synchronize with each other and the temporal distance between any two oscillators belonging to two different blocks is greater than T, then (1) Synchronization within each block is maintained; (2) The blocks activate with a fixed ordering; (3) At most one block is in its active phase at any time.

Theorem 3. (*Desynchronization*) If at the beginning all the oscillators of the system lie not too far away from each other, then the condition of Theorem 2 will be satisfied after some time. Moreover, the time it takes to satisfy the condition is no greater than N cycles, where N is the number of patterns.

The above results are true with arbitrary number of oscillators. In summary, the network exhibits a mechanism, referred to as *selective gating*, which can be intuitively interpreted as follows. An oscillator jumping to its active phase opens a gate to quickly recruit the oscillators of the same block due to local connections. At the same time, it closes the gate to the oscillators of different blocks. Moreover, segmentation of different patterns is achieved very rapidly in terms of oscillation cycles.

4 COMPUTER SIMULATION

To illustrate how this network is used for scene segmentation, we have simulated a 20x20 oscillator network as defined by (1)-(4). We arbitrarily selected four objects (patterns): two **O**'s, one **H**, and one **I**; and they form the word **OHIO**. These patterns were simultaneously presented to the system as shown in Figure 3A. Each pattern is a connected region, but no two patterns are connected to each other.

All the oscillators stimulated (covered) by the objects received an external input $I = 0.2$, while the others have $I = -0.02$. The amplitude ρ of the Gaussian noise is set to 0.02. Thus, compared to the external input, a 10% noise is included in every oscillator. Dynamic normalization results in that only two neighboring oscillators stimulated by a single pattern have an effective connection. The differential equations were solved numerically with the following parameter values: $\varepsilon = 0.02$, $\phi = 3.0$; $\gamma = 6.0$, $\beta = 0.1$, $K = 50$, $\theta_x = -0.5$, and $\theta_{zx} = \theta_{xz} = 0.1$. The total effective connections were normalized to 6.0. The results described below were robust to considerable changes in the parameters. The phases of all the oscillators on the grid were randomly initialized.

Fig. 3B-3F shows the instantaneous activity (snapshot) of the network at various stages of dynamic evolution. The diameter of each black circle represents the normalized x activity of the corresponding oscillator. Fig. 3B shows a snapshot of the network a few steps after the beginning of the simulation. In Fig. 3B, the activities of the oscillators were largely random. Fig. 3C shows a snapshot after the system had evolved for a short time period. One can clearly see the effect of grouping and segmentation: all the oscillators belonging to the left **O** were entrained and had large activities. At the same time, the oscillators stimulated by the other three patterns had very small activities. Thus the left **O** was segmented from the rest of the input. A short time later, as shown in Fig. 3D, the oscillators stimulated by the right **O** reached high values and were separated from the rest of the input. Fig. 3E shows another snapshot after Fig. 3D. At this time, pattern **I** had its turn to be activated and separated from the rest of the input. Finally in Fig. 3F, the oscillators representing **H** were active and the rest of the input remained silent. This successive "pop-out" of the objects continued in a stable periodic fashion. To provide a complete picture of dynamic evolution, Fig. 3G shows the temporal evolution of each oscillator. Since the oscillators receiving no external input were inactive during the entire simulation process, they were excluded from the display in Fig. 3G. The activities of the oscillators stimulated by each object are combined together in the figure. Thus, if they are synchronized, they appear like a single oscillator. In Fig. 3G, the four upper traces represent the activities of the four oscillator blocks, and the bottom trace represents the activity of the global inhibitor. The synchronized oscillations within each object are clearly shown within just three cycles of dynamic evolution.

5 DISCUSSION

Besides neural plausibility, oscillatory correlation has a unique feature as an computational approach to the engineering of scene segmentation and figure/ground segregation. Due to the nature of oscillations, no single object can dominate and suppress the perception of the rest of the image permanently. The current dominant object has to give way to other objects being suppressed, and let them have a chance to be spotted. Although at most one object can dominant at any time instant, due to rapid oscillations, a number of objects can be activated over a short time period. This intrinsic dynamic process provides a natural and reliable representation of multiple segmented patterns.

The basic principles of selective gating are established for the network with lateral connections beyond nearest neighbors. Indeed, in terms of synchronization, more distant connections even help expedite phase entrainment. In this sense, synchronization with all-to-all connections is an extreme case of our system. With nearest-neighbor connectivity (Fig. 2), any isolated part of an image is considered as a segment. In an noisy image with many tiny regions, segmentation would result in too many small fragments. More distant connections would also provide a solution to this problem. Lateral connections typically take on the form of Gaussian distribution, with the connection strength between two oscillators falling off exponentially. Since global inhibition is superimposed to local excitation, two oscillators positively coupled may be desynchronized if global inhibition is strong enough. Thus, it is unlikely that all objects in an image form a single segment as the result of extended connections.

Due to its critical importance for computer vision, scene segmentation has been studied quite extensively. Many techniques have been proposed in the past (Haralick and Shapiro, 1985; Sarkar and Boyer, 1993). Despite these techniques, as pointed out by Haralick and Shapiro (1985), there is no underlying theory of image segmentation, and the techniques tend to be adhoc and emphasize some aspects while ignoring others. Compared to the traditional techniques for scene segmentation, the oscillatory correlation approach offers many unique advantages. The dynamical process is inherently parallel. While conventional computer vision algorithms are based on descriptive criteria and many adhoc heuristics, the network as exemplified in this paper performs computations based on only connections and oscillatory dynamics. The organizational simplicity renders the network particularly feasible for VLSI implementation. Also, continuous-time dynamics allows real time processing, desired by many engineering applications.

Acknowledgments

DLW is supported in part by the NSF grant IRI-9211419 and the ONR grant N00014-93-1-0335. DT is supported in part by the NSF grant DMS-9203299LE.

References

R. Eckhorn, et al., "Coherent oscillations: A mechanism of feature linking in the visual cortex?" *Biol. Cybern.*, vol. 60, pp. 121-130, 1988.

C.M. Gray, P. König, A.K. Engel, and W. Singer, "Oscillatory responses in cat visual cortex exhibit inter-columnar synchronization which reflects global stimulus properties," *Nature*, vol. 338, pp. 334-337, 1989.

R.M. Haralick and L.G. Shapiro, "Image segmentation techniques," Comput. Graphics Image Process., vol. 29, pp. 100-132, 1985.

P. König and T.B. Schillen, "Stimulus-dependent assembly formation of oscillatory responses: I. Synchronization," *Neural Comput.*, vol. 3, pp. 155-166, 1991.

S. Sarkar and K.L. Boyer, "Perceptual organization in computer vision: a review and a proposal for a classificatory structure," IEEE Trans. Syst. Man Cybern., vol. 23, 382-399, 1993.

D. Somers, and N. Kopell, "Rapid synchronization through fast threshold modulation," *Biol. Cybern,* vol. 68, pp. 393-407, 1993.

O. Sporns, G. Tononi, and G.M. Edelman, "Modeling perceptual grouping and figure-ground segregation by means of active reentrant connections," *Proc. Natl. Acad. Sci. USA*, vol. 88, pp. 129-133, 1991.

D. Terman and D.L. Wang, "Global competition and local cooperation in a network of neural oscillators," *Physica D*, in press, 1994.

C. von der Malsburg, "The correlation theory of brain functions," Internal Report 81-2, Max-Planck-Institut for Biophysical Chemistry, Göttingen, FRG, 1981.

C. von der Malsburg and W. Schneider, "A neural cocktail-party processor," *Biol. Cybern.*, vol. 54, pp. 29-40, 1986.

D.L. Wang, "Modeling global synchrony in the visual cortex by locally coupled neural oscillators," *Proc. 15th Ann. Conf. Cognit. Sci. Soc.*, pp. 1058-1063, 1993.

D.L. Wang, "Emergent synchrony in locally coupled neural oscillators," *IEEE Trans. on Neural Networks*, in press, 1995.

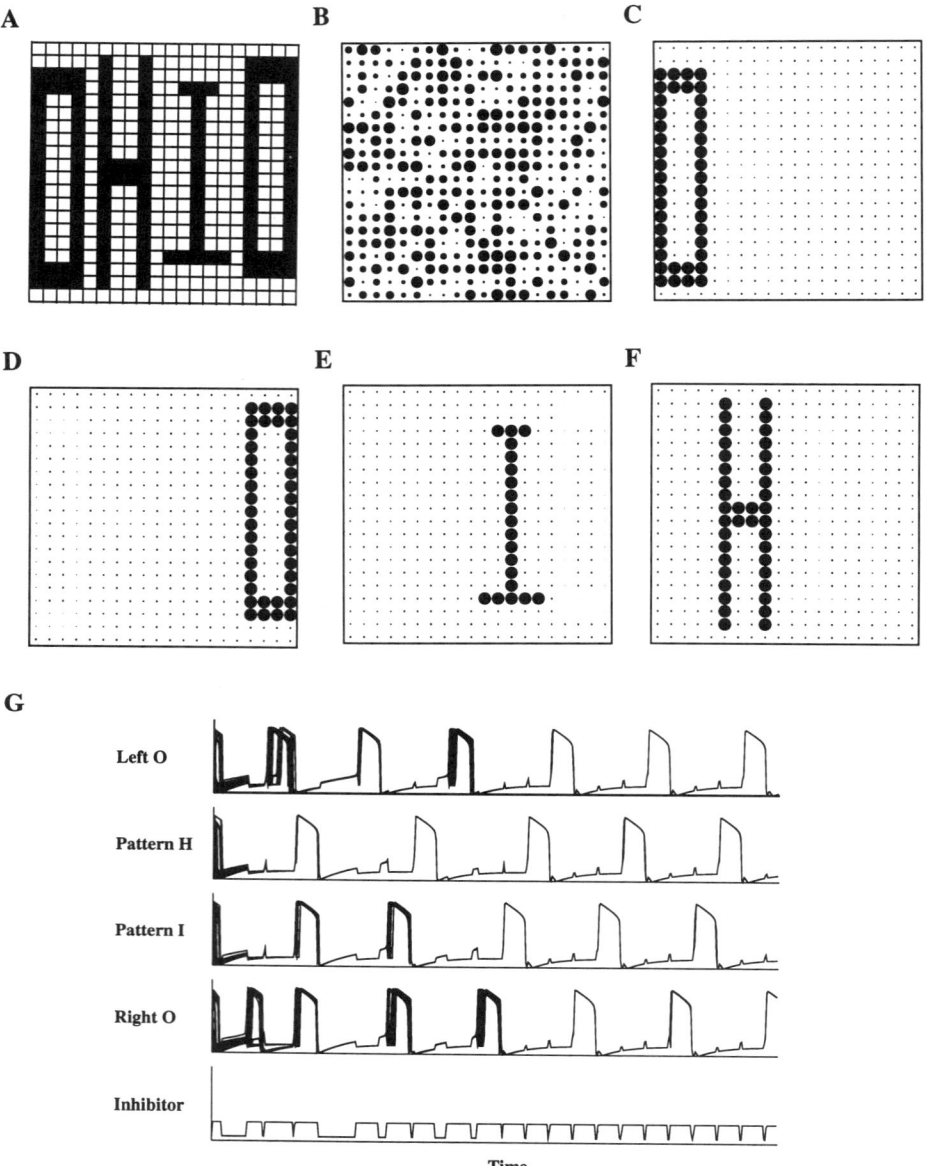

Figure 3. **A** An image composed of four patterns which were presented (mapped) to a 20x20 grid of oscillators. **B** A snapshot of the activities of the oscillator grid at the beginning of dynamic evolution. **C** A snapshot taken shortly after the beginning. **D** Shortly after **C**. **E** Shortly after **D**. **F** Shortly after **E**. **G** The upper four traces show the combined temporal activities of the oscillator blocks representing the four patterns, respectively, and the bottom trace shows the temporal activity of the global inhibitor. The simulation took 8,000 integration steps.

Learning in large linear perceptrons and why the thermodynamic limit is relevant to the real world

Peter Sollich
Department of Physics, University of Edinburgh
Edinburgh EH9 3JZ, U.K.
P.Sollich@ed.ac.uk

Abstract

We present a new method for obtaining the response function $\mathcal{G}$ and its average G from which most of the properties of learning and generalization in linear perceptrons can be derived. We first rederive the known results for the 'thermodynamic limit' of infinite perceptron size N and show explicitly that $\mathcal{G}$ is self-averaging in this limit. We then discuss extensions of our method to more general learning scenarios with anisotropic teacher space priors, input distributions, and weight decay terms. Finally, we use our method to calculate the finite N corrections of order $1/N$ to G and discuss the corresponding finite size effects on generalization and learning dynamics. An important spin-off is the observation that results obtained in the thermodynamic limit are often directly relevant to systems of fairly modest, 'real-world' sizes.

1 INTRODUCTION

One of the main areas of research within the Neural Networks community is the issue of learning and generalization. Starting from a set of training examples (normally assumed to be input-output pairs) generated by some unknown 'teacher' rule $\mathcal{V}$, one wants to find, using a suitable learning or training algorithm, a student $\mathcal{N}$ (read 'Neural Network') which generalizes from the training set, *i.e.*, predicts the outputs corresponding to inputs not contained in the training set as accurately as possible.

If the inputs are N-dimensional vectors $\mathbf{x} \in \mathcal{R}^N$ and the outputs are scalars $y \in \mathcal{R}$, then one of the simplest functional forms that can be assumed for the student $\mathcal{N}$ is the linear perceptron, which is parametrized in terms of a weight vector $\mathbf{w}_\mathcal{N} \in \mathcal{R}^N$ and implements the linear input-output mapping

$$y_\mathcal{N}(\mathbf{x}) = \tfrac{1}{\sqrt{N}} \mathbf{w}_\mathcal{N}^T \mathbf{x}. \tag{1}$$

A commonly used learning algorithm for the linear perceptron is gradient descent on the training error, *i.e.*, the error that the student $\mathcal{N}$ makes on the training set. Using the standard squared output deviation error measure, the training error for a given set of p training examples $\{(\mathbf{x}^\mu, y^\mu), \mu = 1 \ldots p\}$ is $E_\mathrm{t} = \sum_\mu \tfrac{1}{2}(y^\mu - y_\mathcal{N}(\mathbf{x}^\mu))^2 = \tfrac{1}{2} \sum_\mu (y^\mu - \mathbf{w}_\mathcal{N}^T \mathbf{x}^\mu / \sqrt{N})^2$. To prevent the student from fitting noise in the training data, a quadratic weight decay term $\tfrac{1}{2} \lambda \mathbf{w}_\mathcal{N}^2$ is normally added to the training error, with the value of the weight decay parameter λ determining how strongly large weight vectors are penalized. Gradient descent is thus performed on the function $E = E_\mathrm{t} + \tfrac{1}{2} \lambda \mathbf{w}_\mathcal{N}^2$, and the corresponding learning dynamics is, in a continuous time approximation, $d\mathbf{w}_\mathcal{N}/dt = -\nabla_\mathbf{w} E$. As discussed in detail by Krogh and Hertz (1992), this results in an exponential approach of $\mathbf{w}_\mathcal{N}$ to its asymptotic value, with decay constants given by the eigenvalues of the matrix $\mathbf{M}_\mathcal{N}$, defined by (**1** denotes the $N \times N$ identity matrix)

$$\mathbf{M}_\mathcal{N} = \lambda \mathbf{1} + \mathbf{A}, \quad \mathbf{A} = \tfrac{1}{N} \sum_\mu \mathbf{x}^\mu (\mathbf{x}^\mu)^T.$$

To examine what generalization performance is achieved by the above learning algorithm, one has to make an assumption about the functional form of the teacher. The simplest such assumption is that the problem is learnable, *i.e.*, that the teacher, like the student, is a linear perceptron. A teacher $\mathcal{V}$ is then specified by a weight vector $\mathbf{w}_\mathcal{V}$ and maps a given input $\mathbf{x}$ to the output $y_\mathcal{V}(\mathbf{x}) = \mathbf{w}_\mathcal{V}^T \mathbf{x}/\sqrt{N}$. We assume that the test inputs for which the student is asked to predict the corresponding outputs are drawn from an isotropic Gaussian distribution, $P(\mathbf{x}) \propto \exp(-\tfrac{1}{2}\mathbf{x}^2)$. The generalization error, *i.e.*, the average error that a student $\mathcal{N}$ makes on a random input when compared to teacher $\mathcal{V}$, is given by

$$\epsilon_\mathrm{g} = \tfrac{1}{2}\langle (y_\mathcal{N}(\mathbf{x}) - y_\mathcal{V}(\mathbf{x}))^2 \rangle_{P(\mathbf{x})} = \tfrac{1}{2N}(\mathbf{w}_\mathcal{N} - \mathbf{w}_\mathcal{V})^2. \tag{2}$$

Inserting the learning dynamics $\mathbf{w}_\mathcal{N} = \mathbf{w}_\mathcal{N}(t)$, the generalization acquires a time dependence, which in its exact form depends on the specific training set, teacher, and initial value of the student weight vector, $\mathbf{w}_\mathcal{N}(t=0)$. We shall confine our attention to the average of this time-dependent generalization error over all possible training sets and teachers; to avoid clutter, we write this average simply as $\epsilon_\mathrm{g}(t)$. We assume that the inputs $\mathbf{x}^\mu$ in the training set are chosen independently and randomly from the same distribution as the test inputs, and that the corresponding training outputs are the teacher outputs corrupted by additive noise, $y^\mu = y_\mathcal{V}(\mathbf{x}^\mu) + \eta^\mu$, where the η^μ have zero mean and variance σ^2. If we further assume an isotropic Gaussian prior on the teacher weight vectors, $P(\mathbf{w}_\mathcal{V}) \propto \exp(-\tfrac{1}{2}\mathbf{w}_\mathcal{V}^2)$, then the average generalization error for $t \to \infty$ is (Krogh and Hertz, 1992)

$$\epsilon_\mathrm{g}(t \to \infty) = \frac{1}{2}\left[\sigma^2 G + \lambda(\sigma^2 - \lambda)\frac{\partial G}{\partial \lambda}\right], \tag{3}$$

where G is the average of the so-called *response function* over the training inputs:

$$G = \langle \mathcal{G} \rangle_{P(\{\mathbf{x}^\mu\})}, \quad \mathcal{G} = \tfrac{1}{N}\mathrm{tr}\,\mathbf{M}_\mathcal{N}^{-1}. \tag{4}$$

The time dependence of the average generalization error for finite but large t is an exponential approach to the asymptotic value (3) with decay constant $\lambda + a_{\min}$, where $a_{\min}$ is the lowest eigenvalue occurring in the average eigenvalue spectrum of the input correlation matrix $\mathbf{A}$ (Krogh and Hertz, 1992). This average eigenvalue spectrum, which we denote by $\rho(a)$, can be calculated from the average response function according to (Krogh, 1992)

$$\rho(a) = \frac{1}{\pi} \lim_{\epsilon \to 0^+} \operatorname{Im} G|_{\lambda = -a - i\epsilon}, \tag{5}$$

where we have assumed $\rho(a)$ to be normalized, $\int da\, \rho(a) = 1$.

Eqs. (3,5) show that the key quantity determining learning and generalization in the linear perceptron is the average response function G defined in (4). This function has previously been calculated in the 'thermodynamic limit', $N \to \infty$ at $\alpha = p/N = \text{const.}$, using a diagrammatic expansion (Hertz et al., 1989) and the replica method (Opper, 1989, Kinzel and Opper, 1991). In Section 2, we present what we believe to be a much simpler method for calculating G, based only on simple matrix identities. We also show explicitly that $\mathcal{G}$ is self-averaging in the thermodynamic limit, which means that the fluctuations of $\mathcal{G}$ around its average G become vanishingly small as $N \to \infty$. This implies, for example, that the generalization error is also self-averaging. In Section 3 we extend the method to more general cases such as anisotropic teacher space priors and input distributions, and general quadratic penalty terms. Finite size effects are considered in Section 4, where we calculate the $O(1/N)$ corrections to G, $\epsilon_g(t \to \infty)$ and $\rho(a)$. We discuss the resulting effects on generalization and learning dynamics and derive explicit conditions on the perceptron size N for results obtained in the thermodynamic limit to be valid. We conclude in Section 5 with a brief summary and discussion of our results.

2 THE BASIC METHOD

Our method for calculating the average response function G is based on a recursion relation relating the values of the (unaveraged) response function $\mathcal{G}$ for p and $p+1$ training examples. Assume that we are given a set of p training examples with corresponding matrix $\mathbf{M}_\mathcal{N}$. By adding a new training example with input $\mathbf{x}$, we obtain the matrix $\mathbf{M}_\mathcal{N}^+ = \mathbf{M}_\mathcal{N} + \frac{1}{N}\mathbf{x}\mathbf{x}^T$. It is straightforward to show that the inverse of $\mathbf{M}_\mathcal{N}^+$ can be expressed as

$$\left(\mathbf{M}_\mathcal{N}^+\right)^{-1} = \mathbf{M}_\mathcal{N}^{-1} - \frac{\frac{1}{N}\mathbf{M}_\mathcal{N}^{-1}\mathbf{x}\mathbf{x}^T\mathbf{M}_\mathcal{N}^{-1}}{1 + \frac{1}{N}\mathbf{x}^T\mathbf{M}_\mathcal{N}^{-1}\mathbf{x}}.$$

(One way of proving this identity is to multiply both sides by $\mathbf{M}_\mathcal{N}^+$ and exploit the fact that $\mathbf{M}_\mathcal{N}^+\mathbf{M}_\mathcal{N}^{-1} = 1 + \frac{1}{N}\mathbf{x}\mathbf{x}^T\mathbf{M}_\mathcal{N}^{-1}$.) Taking the trace, we obtain the following recursion relation for $\mathcal{G}$:

$$\mathcal{G}(p+1) = \mathcal{G}(p) - \frac{1}{N}\frac{\frac{1}{N}\mathbf{x}^T\mathbf{M}_\mathcal{N}^{-2}\mathbf{x}}{1 + \frac{1}{N}\mathbf{x}^T\mathbf{M}_\mathcal{N}^{-1}\mathbf{x}}. \tag{6}$$

Now denote $z_i = \frac{1}{N}\mathbf{x}^T\mathbf{M}_\mathcal{N}^{-i}\mathbf{x}$ ($i = 1, 2$). With $\mathbf{x}$ drawn randomly from the assumed input distribution $P(\mathbf{x}) \propto \exp(-\frac{1}{2}\mathbf{x}^2)$, the z_i can readily be shown to be random

variables with means and (co-)variances
$$\langle z_i \rangle = \tfrac{1}{N} \operatorname{tr} \mathbf{M}_\mathcal{N}^{-i}, \quad \langle \Delta z_i \Delta z_j \rangle = \tfrac{2}{N^2} \operatorname{tr} \mathbf{M}_\mathcal{N}^{-i-j}.$$
Combining this with the fact that $\operatorname{tr} \mathbf{M}_\mathcal{N}^{-k} \leq N\lambda^{-k} = O(N)$, we have that the fluctuations Δz_i of the z_i around their average values are $O(1/\sqrt{N})$; inserting this into (6), we obtain

$$\begin{aligned}
\mathcal{G}(p+1) &= \mathcal{G}(p) - \frac{1}{N} \frac{\tfrac{1}{N}\operatorname{tr}\mathbf{M}_\mathcal{N}^{-2}}{1 + \tfrac{1}{N}\operatorname{tr}\mathbf{M}_\mathcal{N}^{-1}} + O(N^{-3/2}) \\
&= \mathcal{G}(p) + \frac{1}{N} \frac{\partial \mathcal{G}(p)}{\partial \lambda} \frac{1}{1+\mathcal{G}(p)} + O(N^{-3/2}).
\end{aligned} \quad (7)$$

Starting from $\mathcal{G}(0) = 1/\lambda$, we can apply this recursion $p = \alpha N$ times to obtain $\mathcal{G}(p)$ up to terms which add up to at most $O(pN^{-3/2}) = O(1/\sqrt{N})$. This shows that $\mathcal{G}$ is self-averaging in the thermodynamic limit: whatever the training set, the value of $\mathcal{G}$ will always be the same up to fluctuations of $O(1/\sqrt{N})$. In fact, we shall show in Section 4 that the fluctuations of $\mathcal{G}$ are only $O(1/N)$. This means that the $O(N^{-3/2})$ fluctuations from each iteration of (7) are only weakly correlated, so that they add up like independent random variables to give a total fluctuation for $\mathcal{G}(p)$ of $O((p/N^3)^{1/2}) = O(1/N)$.

We have seen that, in the thermodynamic limit, $\mathcal{G}$ is identical to its average G because its fluctuations are vanishingly small. To calculate the value of G in the thermodynamic limit as a function of α and λ, we insert the relation $\mathcal{G}(p+1) - \mathcal{G}(p) = \tfrac{1}{N}\partial \mathcal{G}(\alpha)/\partial \alpha + O(1/N^2)$ into eq. (7) (with $\mathcal{G}$ replaced by G) and neglect all finite N corrections. This yields the partial differential equation

$$\frac{\partial G}{\partial \alpha} - \frac{\partial G}{\partial \lambda} \frac{1}{1+G} = 0, \quad (8)$$

which can readily be solved using the method of characteristic curves (see, *e.g.*, John, 1978). Using the initial condition $G|_{\alpha=0} = 1/\lambda$ gives $\alpha/(1+G) = 1/G - \lambda$, which leads to the well-known result (see, *e.g.*, Hertz *et al.*, 1989)

$$G = \frac{1}{2\lambda}\left(1 - \alpha - \lambda + \sqrt{(1-\alpha-\lambda)^2 + 4\lambda}\right). \quad (9)$$

In the complex λ plane, G has a pole at $\lambda = 0$ and a branch cut arising from the root; according to eq. (5), these singularities determine the average eigenvalue spectrum $\rho(a)$ of $\mathbf{A}$, with the result (Krogh, 1992)

$$\rho(a) = (1-\alpha)\Theta(1-\alpha)\delta(a) + \frac{1}{2\pi a}\sqrt{(a_+ - a)(a - a_-)}, \quad (10)$$

where $\Theta(x)$ is the Heaviside step function, $\Theta(x) = 1$ for $x > 0$ and 0 otherwise. The root in eq. (10) only contributes when its argument is non-negative, *i.e.*, for a between the 'spectral limits' a_- and a_+, which have the values $a_\pm = (1 \pm \sqrt{\alpha})^2$.

3 EXTENSIONS TO MORE GENERAL LEARNING SCENARIOS

We now discuss some extensions of our method to more general learning scenarios. First, consider the case of an anisotropic teacher space prior, $P(\mathbf{w}_\nu) \propto$

$\exp(-\frac{1}{2}\mathbf{w}_\nu^T \boldsymbol{\Sigma}_\nu^{-1} \mathbf{w}_\nu)$, with symmetric positive definite $\boldsymbol{\Sigma}_\nu$. This leaves the definition of the response function unchanged; eq. (3), however, has to be replaced by $\epsilon_g(t \to \infty) = 1/2\{\sigma^2 G + \lambda[\sigma^2 - \lambda(\frac{1}{N}\text{tr}\,\boldsymbol{\Sigma}_\nu)]\partial G/\partial \lambda\}$.

As a second extension, assume that the inputs are drawn from an anisotropic distribution, $P(\mathbf{x}) \propto \exp(-\frac{1}{2}\mathbf{x}^T \boldsymbol{\Sigma}^{-1}\mathbf{x})$. It can then be shown that the asymptotic value of the average generalization error is still given by eq. (3) if the response function is redefined to be $\mathcal{G} = \frac{1}{N}\text{tr}\,\boldsymbol{\Sigma}\mathbf{M}_\mathcal{N}^{-1}$. This modified response function can be calculated as follows: First we rewrite $\mathcal{G}$ as $\frac{1}{N}\text{tr}\,(\lambda\boldsymbol{\Sigma}^{-1} + \tilde{\mathbf{A}})^{-1}$, where $\tilde{\mathbf{A}} = \frac{1}{N}\sum_\mu (\tilde{\mathbf{x}}^\mu)^T \tilde{\mathbf{x}}^\mu$ is the correlation matrix of the transformed input examples $\tilde{\mathbf{x}}^\mu = \boldsymbol{\Sigma}^{-1/2}\mathbf{x}^\mu$. Since the $\tilde{\mathbf{x}}^\mu$ are distributed according to $P(\tilde{\mathbf{x}}^\mu) \propto \exp(-\frac{1}{2}(\tilde{\mathbf{x}}^\mu)^2)$, the problem is thus reduced to finding the response function $\mathcal{G} = \frac{1}{N}\text{tr}\,(\mathbf{L} + \mathbf{A})^{-1}$ for isotropically distributed inputs and $\mathbf{L} = \lambda\boldsymbol{\Sigma}^{-1}$. The recursion relations between $\mathcal{G}(p+1)$ and $\mathcal{G}(p)$ derived in the previous section remain valid, and result, in the thermodynamic limit, in a differential equation for the average response function G analogous to eq. (8). The initial condition is now $G|_{\alpha=0} = \frac{1}{N}\text{tr}\,\mathbf{L}^{-1}$, and one obtains an implicit equation for G,

$$G = \frac{1}{N}\text{tr}\left(\mathbf{L} + \frac{\alpha}{1+G}\mathbf{1}\right)^{-1}, \qquad (11)$$

where in the case of an anisotropic input distribution considered here, $\mathbf{L} = \lambda\boldsymbol{\Sigma}^{-1}$. If $\boldsymbol{\Sigma}$ has a particularly simple form, then the dependence of G on α and λ can be obtained analytically, but in general eq. (11) has to solved numerically.

Finally, one can also investigate the effect of a general quadratic weight decay term, $\frac{1}{2}\mathbf{w}_\mathcal{N}^T \boldsymbol{\Lambda}\mathbf{w}_\mathcal{N}$, in the energy function E. The expression for the average generalization error becomes more cumbersome than eq. (3) in this case, but the result can still be expressed in terms of the average response function $G = \langle \mathcal{G} \rangle = \langle \frac{1}{N}\text{tr}\,(\boldsymbol{\Lambda} + \mathbf{A})^{-1}\rangle$, which can be obtained as the solution of eq. (11) for $\mathbf{L} = \boldsymbol{\Lambda}$.

4 FINITE N CORRECTIONS

So far, we have focussed attention on the thermodynamic limit of perceptrons of infinite size N. The results are clearly only approximately valid for real, finite systems, and it is therefore interesting to investigate corrections for finite N. This we do in the present section by calculating the $O(1/N)$ corrections to G and $\rho(a)$. For details of the calculations and results of computer simulations which support our theoretical analysis, we refer the reader to (Sollich, 1994).

First note that, for $\lambda = 0$, the exact result for the average response function is $G|_{\lambda=0} = (\alpha - 1 - 1/N)^{-1}$ for $\alpha > 1 + 1/N$ (see, e.g., Eaton, 1983), which clearly admits a series expansion in powers of $1/N$. We assume that a similar expansion also exists for nonzero λ, and write

$$G = G_0 + G_1/N + O(1/N^2). \qquad (12)$$

G_0 is the value of G in the thermodynamic limit as given by eq. (9). For finite N, the fluctuations $\Delta\mathcal{G} = \mathcal{G} - G$ of $\mathcal{G}$ around its average value G become relevant; for $\lambda = 0$, the variance of these fluctuations is known to have a power series expansion in $1/N$, and again we assume a similar expansion for finite λ, $\langle(\Delta\mathcal{G})^2\rangle = \Delta^2/N + O(1/N^2)$, where the first term is $O(1/N)$ and not $O(1)$ because, as discussed in Section 2, the fluctuations of $\mathcal{G}$ for large N are no greater than $O(1/\sqrt{N})$. To calculate G_1 and Δ^2, one starts again from the recursion relation (6), now expanding everything up to second order in the fluctuation quantities Δz_i and $\Delta \mathcal{G}$. Averaging over the training inputs and collecting orders of $1/N$ yields after some straightforward algebra the known eq. (8) for G_0 and two linear partial differential equations for G_1 and Δ^2, the latter obtained by squaring both sides of eq. (6). Solving these, one obtains

$$\Delta^2 \equiv 0, \quad G_1 = \frac{G_0^2(1 - \lambda G_0)}{(1 + \lambda G_0^2)^2}. \tag{13}$$

In the limit $\lambda \to 0$, $G_1 = 1/(\alpha - 1)^2$ consistent with the exact result for G quoted above; likewise, the result $\Delta^2 \equiv 0$ agrees with the exact series expansion of the variance of the fluctuations of $\mathcal{G}$ for $\lambda = 0$, which begins with an $O(1/N^2)$ term (see, e.g., Barber et al., 1994).

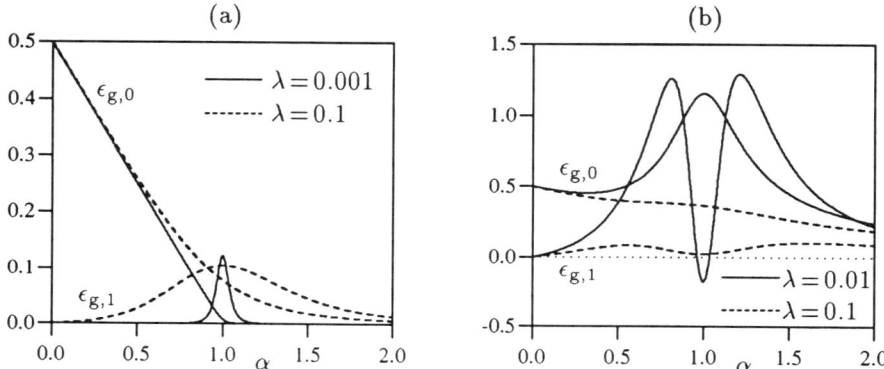

Figure 1: Average generalization error: Result for $N \to \infty$, $\epsilon_{g,0}$, and coefficient of $O(1/N)$ correction, $\epsilon_{g,1}$. (a) Noise free teacher, $\sigma^2 = 0$. (b) Noisy teacher, $\sigma^2 = 0.5$. Curves are labeled by the value of the weight decay parameter λ.

From the $1/N$ expansion (12) of G we obtain, using eq. (3), a corresponding expansion of the asymptotic value of the average generalization error, which we write as $\epsilon_g(t \to \infty) = \epsilon_{g,0} + \epsilon_{g,1}/N + O(1/N^2)$. It follows that the thermodynamic limit result for the average generalization error, $\epsilon_{g,0}$, is a good approximation to the true result for finite N as long as $N \gg N_c = |\epsilon_{g,1}/\epsilon_{g,0}|$. In Figure 1, we plot $\epsilon_{g,0}$ and $\epsilon_{g,1}$ for several values of λ and σ^2. It can be seen that the relative size of the first order correction $|\epsilon_{g,1}/\epsilon_{g,0}|$ and hence the critical system size N_c for validity of the thermodynamic limit result is largest when λ is small. Exploiting this fact, N_c can be bounded by $1/(1 - \alpha)$ for $\alpha < 1$ and $(3\alpha + 1)/[\alpha(\alpha - 1)]$ for $\alpha > 1$. It follows, for example, that the critical system size N_c is smaller than 5 as long as $\alpha < 0.8$ or $\alpha > 1.72$, for all λ and σ^2. This bound on N_c can be tightened for non-zero λ; for $\lambda > 2$, for example, one has $N_c < (2\lambda - 1)/(\lambda + 1)^2 < 1/3$. We have thus shown explicitly that thermodynamic limit calculations of learning and generalization behaviour can be relevant for fairly small, 'real-world' systems of size N of the order of a few tens or hundreds. This is in contrast to the widespread suspicion among non-physicists that the methods of statistical physics give valid results only for huge system sizes of the order of $N \approx 10^{23}$.

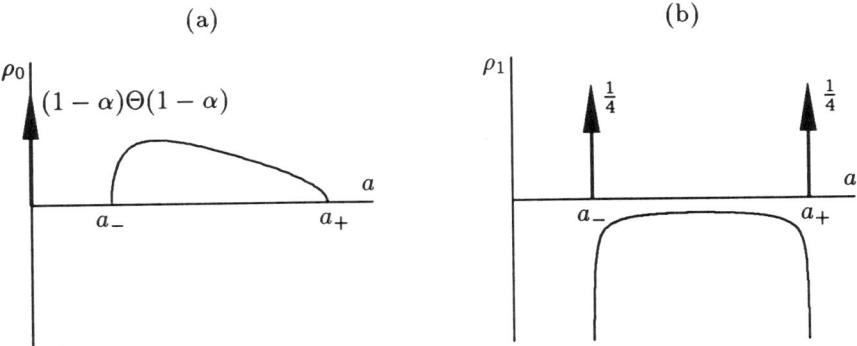

Figure 2: Schematic plot of the average eigenvalue spectrum $\rho(a)$ of the input correlation matrix $\mathbf{A}$. (a) Result for $N \to \infty$, $\rho_0(a)$. (b) $O(1/N)$ correction, $\rho_1(a)$. Arrows indicate δ-peaks and are labeled by the corresponding heights.

We now consider the $O(1/N)$ correction to the average eigenvalue spectrum of the input correlation matrix $\mathbf{A}$. Setting $\rho(a) = \rho_0(a) + \rho_1(a)/N + O(1/N^2)$, $\rho_0(a)$ is the $N \to \infty$ result given by eq. (10), and from eq. (13) one derives

$$\rho_1(a) = \frac{1}{4}\delta(a - a_+) + \frac{1}{4}\delta(a - a_-) - \frac{1}{2\pi} \frac{1}{\sqrt{(a_+ - a)(a - a_-)}}.$$

Figure 2 shows sketches of $\rho_0(a)$ and $\rho_1(a)$. Note that $\int da\, \rho_1(a) = 0$ as expected since the normalization of $\rho(a)$ is independent of N. Furthermore, there is no $O(1/N)$ correction to the δ-peak in $\rho_0(a)$ at $a = 0$, since this peak arises from the $N - p$ zero eigenvalues of $\mathbf{A}$ for $\alpha = p/N < 1$ and therefore has a height of $1 - \alpha$ for any finite N. The δ-peaks in $\rho_1(a)$ at the spectral limits a_+ and a_- are an artefact of the truncated $1/N$ expansion: $\rho(a)$ is determined by the singularities of G as a function of λ, and the location of these singularities is only obtained correctly by resumming the full $1/N$ expansion. The δ-peaks in $\rho_1(a)$ can be interpreted as 'precursors' of a broadening of the eigenvalue spectrum of $\mathbf{A}$ to values which, when the whole $1/N$ series is resummed, will lie outside the $N \to \infty$ spectral range $[a_-, a_+]$. The negative term in $\rho_1(a)$ represents the corresponding 'flattening' of the eigenvalue spectrum between a_- and a_+. We can thus conclude that the average eigenvalue spectrum of $\mathbf{A}$ for finite N will be broader than for $N \to \infty$, which means in particular that the learning dynamics will be slowed down since the smallest eigenvalue $a_{\min}$ of $\mathbf{A}$ will be smaller than a_-. From our result for $\rho_1(a)$ we can also deduce when the $N \to \infty$ result $\rho_0(a)$ is valid for finite N; the condition turns out to be $N \gg a/[(a_+ - a)(a - a_-)]$. Consistent with our discussion of the broadening of the eigenvalue spectrum of $\mathbf{A}$, N has to be larger for a near the spectral limits a_-, a_+ if $\rho_0(a)$ is to be a good approximation to the finite N average eigenvalue spectrum of $\mathbf{A}$.

5 SUMMARY AND DISCUSSION

We have presented a new method, based on simple matrix identities, for calculating the response function $\mathcal{G}$ and its average G which determine most of the properties of learning and generalization in linear perceptrons. In the thermodynamic limit, $N \to \infty$, we have recovered the known result for G and have shown explicitly that $\mathcal{G}$ is self-averaging. Extensions of our method to more general learning scenarios have also been discussed. Finally, we have obtained the $O(1/N)$ corrections to G and the corresponding corrections to the average generalization error, and shown explicitly that the results obtained in the thermodynamic limit can be valid for fairly small, 'real-world' system sizes N. We have also calculated the $O(1/N)$ correction to the average eigenvalue spectrum of the input correlation matrix **A** and interpreted it in terms of a broadening of the spectrum for finite N, which will cause a slowing down of the learning dynamics.

We remark that the $O(1/N)$ corrections that we have obtained can also be used in different contexts, for example for calculations of test error fluctuations and optimal test set size (Barber et al., 1994). Another application is in an analysis of the evidence procedure in Bayesian inference for finite N, where optimal values of 'hyperparameters' like the weight decay parameter λ are determined on the basis of the training data (G Marion, in preparation). We hope, therefore, that our results will pave the way for a systematic investigation of finite size effects in learning and generalization.

References

D Barber, D Saad, and P Sollich (1994). Finite size effects and optimal test set size in linear perceptrons. Submitted to J. Phys. A.

M L Eaton (1983). *Multivariate Statistics - A Vector Space Approach*. Wiley, New York.

J A Hertz, A Krogh, and G I Thorbergsson (1989). Phase transitions in simple learning. J. Phys. A, 22:2133–2150.

F John (1978). *Partial Differential Equations*. Springer, New York, 3rd ed.

W Kinzel and M Opper (1991). Dynamics of learning. In E Domany, J L van Hemmen, and K Schulten, editors, *Models of Neural Networks*, pages 149–171. Springer, Berlin.

A Krogh (1992). Learning with noise in a linear perceptron. J. Phys. A, 25:1119–1133.

A Krogh and J A Hertz (1992). Generalization in a linear perceptron in the presence of noise. J. Phys. A, 25:1135–1147.

M Opper (1989). Learning in neural networks: Solvable dynamics. *Europhysics Letters*, 8:389–392.

P Sollich (1994). Finite-size effects in learning and generalization in linear perceptrons. J. Phys. A, 27:7771–7784.

Generalisation in Feedforward Networks

Adam Kowalczyk and Herman Ferra
Telecom Australia, Research Laboratories
770 Blackburn Road, Clayton, Vic. 3168, Australia
(a.kowalczyk@trl.oz.au, h.ferra@trl.oz.au)

Abstract

We discuss a model of consistent learning with an additional restriction on the probability distribution of training samples, the target concept and hypothesis class. We show that the model provides a significant improvement on the upper bounds of sample complexity, i.e. the minimal number of random training samples allowing a selection of the hypothesis with a predefined accuracy and confidence. Further, we show that the model has the potential for providing a finite sample complexity even in the case of infinite VC-dimension as well as for a sample complexity below VC-dimension. This is achieved by linking sample complexity to an "average" number of implementable dichotomies of a training sample rather than the maximal size of a shattered sample, i.e. VC-dimension.

1 Introduction

A number of fundamental results in computational learning theory [1, 2, 11] links the generalisation error achievable by a set of hypotheses with its Vapnik-Chervonenkis dimension (VC-dimension, for short) which is a sort of capacity measure. They provide in particular some theoretical bounds on the sample complexity, i.e. a minimal number of training samples assuring the desired accuracy with the desired confidence. However there are a few obvious deficiencies in these results: (*i*) the sample complexity bounds are unrealistically high (c.f. Section 4.), and (*ii*) for some networks they do not hold at all since VC-dimension is infinite, e.g. some radial basis networks [7].

One may expect that there are at least three main reasons for this state of affairs: (a) that the VC-dimension is too crude a measure of capacity, (b) since the bounds are universal they may be forced too high by some malicious distributions, (c) that particular estimates themselves are too crude, and so might be improved with time. In this paper we will attack the problem along the lines of (a) and (b) since this is most promising. Indeed, even a rough analysis of some proofs of lower bound (e.g. [1]) shows that some of these estimates were determined by clever constructions of discrete, malicious distributions on sets of "shattered samples" (of the size of VC-dimension). Thus this does not necessarily imply that such bounds on the sample complexity are really tight in more realistic cases, e.g. continuous distributions and "non-malicious" target concepts, the point eagerly made by critics of the formalism. The problem is to find such restrictions on target concepts and probability distributions which will produce a significant improvement. The current paper discusses such a proposition which significantly improves the upper bounds on sample complexity.

2   A Restricted Model of Consistent Learning

First we introduce a few necessary concepts and some basic notation. We assume we are given *a space of samples* X with *a probability measure* μ, a set H of binary functions $X \mapsto \{0,1\}$ called the *hypothesis space* and *a target concept* $t \in H$. For an n-sample $\vec{x} = (x_1, ..., x_n) \in X^n$ and $h : H \to \{0,1\}$ the vector $(h(x_1), ..., h(x_n)) \in \{0,1\}^n$ will be denoted by $h(\vec{x})$. We define two projections $\pi_{\vec{x}}$ and $\pi_{t,\vec{x}}$ of H onto $\{0,1\}^n$ as follows $\pi_{\vec{x}}(h) \stackrel{def}{=} h(\vec{x}) \stackrel{def}{=} (h(x_1), ..., h(x_n))$ and $\pi_{t,\vec{x}}(h) \stackrel{def}{=} \pi_{\vec{x}}(|t-h|) = |t-h|(\vec{x})$ for every $h \in H$. Below we shall use the notation $|S|$ for the cardinality of the set S. The average density of the sets of projections $\pi_{\vec{x}}(H)$ or $\pi_{t,\vec{x}}(H)$ in $\{0,1\}^n$ is defined as

$$\Pr_H(\vec{x}) \stackrel{def}{=} |\pi_{\vec{x}}(H)|/2^n = |\pi_{t,\vec{x}}(H)|/2^n$$

(equivalently, this is the probability of a random vector in $\{0,1\}^n$ belonging to the set $\pi_{\vec{x}}(H)$). Now we define two associated quantities:

$$\bar{\Pr}_{H,\mu}(n) \stackrel{def}{=} \int \Pr_H(\vec{x}) \mu^n(d\vec{x}) = 2^{-n} \int |\pi_{\vec{x}}(H)| \mu^n(d\vec{x}), \qquad (1)$$

$$\Pr_{H,\max}(n) \stackrel{def}{=} \max_{\vec{x} \in X^n} \Pr_H(\vec{x}).$$

We recall that $d_H \stackrel{def}{=} \max\{n \ ; \ \exists_{\vec{x} \in X^n} |\pi_{\vec{x}}(H)| = 2^n\}$ is called the Vapnik-Chervonenkis dimension (VC-dimension) of H [1, 11]. If $d_H \leq \infty$ then Sauer's lemma implies the estimates (c.f. [1, 2, 10])

$$\bar{\Pr}_{H,\mu}(n) \leq \Pr_{H,\max}(n) \leq 2^{-n} \Phi(d_H, n) \leq 2^{-n} (en/d_H)^{d_H}, \qquad (2)$$

where $\Phi(d,n) \stackrel{def}{=} \sum_{i=0}^{d} \binom{n}{i}$ (we assume $\binom{n}{i} \stackrel{def}{=} 0$ if $i > n$).

Now we are ready to formulate our main assumption in the model. We say that the space of hypotheses H is (μ^n, C)-*uniform* around $t \in 2^X$ if for every set $S \subset \{0,1\}^n$

$$\int |\pi_{t,\vec{x}}(H) \cap S| \mu^n(d\vec{x}) \leq C|S|\bar{\Pr}_{H,\mu}(n). \qquad (3)$$

The meaning of this condition is obvious: we postulate that on average the number of different projections $\pi_{t,\vec{x}}(h)$ of hypothesis $h \in H$ falling into S has a bound proportional to the probability $\bar{\mathrm{Pr}}_{H,\mu}(n)$ of random vector in $\{0,1\}^n$ belonging to the set $\pi_{t,\vec{x}}(H)$. Another heuristic interpretation of (3) is as follows. Imagine that elements of $\pi_{t,\vec{x}}(H)$ are almost uniformly distributed in $\{0,1\}^n$, i.e. with average density $\rho_{\vec{x}} \leq C|\pi_{t,\vec{x}}(H)|/2^n$. Thus the "mass" of the volume $|S|$ is $|\pi_{t,\vec{x}}(H) \cap S| \approx \rho_{\vec{x}}|S|$ and so its average $\int |\pi_{t,\vec{x}}(H) \cap S|\mu^n(d\vec{x})$ has the estimate $\leq |S|\int \rho_{\vec{x}}\mu^n(d\vec{x}) \leq C|S|\bar{\mathrm{Pr}}_{H,\mu}(n)$.

Of special interest is the particular case of *consistent* learning [1], i.e. when the target concept and the hypothesis fully agree on the training sample. In this case, for any $\epsilon > 0$ we introduce the notation

$$Q^\epsilon(m) \stackrel{def}{=} \{\vec{x} \in X^m \; ; \; \exists_{h \in H} \; er_{t,\vec{x}}(h) = 0 \; \& \; er_{t,\mu}(h) \geq \epsilon\},$$

where $er_{t,\vec{x}}(h) \stackrel{def}{=} \sum_{i=1}^m |t-h|(x_i)/m$ and $er_{t,\mu}(h) \stackrel{def}{=} \int |t-h|(x)\mu(dx)$ denote error rates on the training sample $\vec{x} = (x_1, ..., x_m)$ and X, respectively. Thus $Q^\epsilon(m)$ is the set of all m-samples for which there exists a hypothesis in H with no error on the sample and the error at least ϵ on X.

Theorem 1 *If the hypothesis space H is (μ^{2m}, C)-uniform around $t \in H$ then for any $\epsilon > 8/m$*

$$\mu^m(Q^\epsilon(m)) \leq \mathcal{E}(m,\epsilon) \stackrel{def}{=} C\bar{\mathrm{Pr}}_{H,\mu}(2m) \sum_{j=\lceil m\epsilon/2 \rceil}^m \binom{2m}{j} 2^{-j} \quad (4)$$

$$\leq C\bar{\mathrm{Pr}}_{H,\mu}(2m)(3/2)^{2m} \leq C(2em/d_H)^{d_H}(3/4)^{2m}. \quad \Box \quad (5)$$

Proof of the theorem is given in the Appendix.

Given $\epsilon, \delta > 0$. The integer $m_L(\delta,\epsilon) \stackrel{def}{=} \min\{m > 0 \; ; \; \mu^m(Q^\epsilon) \leq \delta\}$ will be called *the sample complexity* following the terminology of computational learning theory (c.f. [1]). Note that in our case the sample complexity depends also (implicitly) on the target concept t, the hypothesis space H and the probability measure μ.

Corollary 2 *If the hypothesis space H is (μ^n, C)-uniform around $t \in H$ for any $n > 0$, then*

$$m_L(\delta,\epsilon) \leq max\{8/\epsilon, \min\{m \; ; \; 2C\bar{\mathrm{Pr}}_{H,\mu}(2m)(3/2)^m < \delta\}\} \quad (6)$$

$$\leq max\{8/\epsilon, 6.9\,d_H + 2.4\log_2 \frac{C}{\delta}\}. \quad \Box \quad (7)$$

The estimate (7) of Corollary 2 reduces to the estimate

$$m_L(\delta,\epsilon) \leq 6.9\,d_H$$

independent of δ and ϵ. This predicts that under the assumption of the corollary a transition to perfect generalisation occurs for training samples of size $\leq 6.9\,d_H$, which is in agreement with some statistical physics predictions showing such transition occurring below $\approx 1.5 d_H$ for some simple neural networks (c.f. [5]).

Proof outline. Estimate (6) follows from the first estimate (5). Estimate (7) can be derived from the second bound in (5) (virtually by repeating the proof of [1, Theorem 8.4.1] with substitution of $4\log_2(4/3)$ for ϵ and δ/C for δ). Q.E.D.

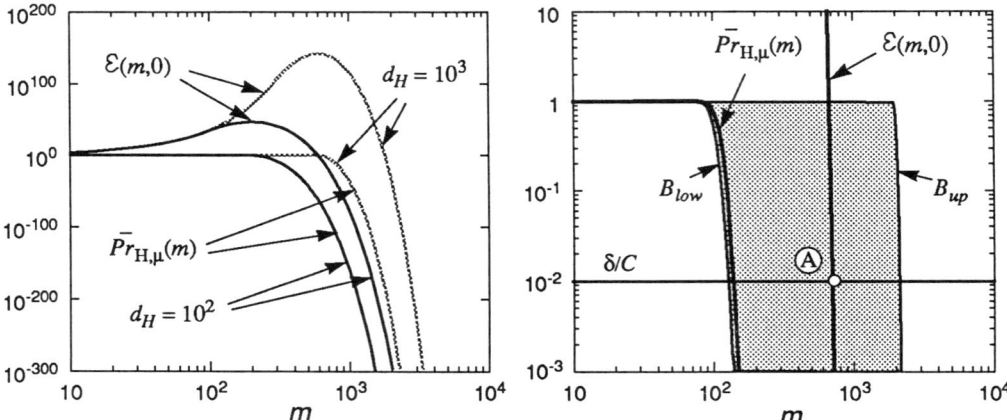

Figure 1: Plots of estimates on $\bar{Pr}_{H,\mu}(m)$ and $\mathcal{E}(m,\epsilon)/C \leq \mathcal{E}(m,0)/C = (3/2)^{2m}\bar{Pr}_{H,\mu}(2m)$ (Fig. a) for the analytic threshold neuron ($\bar{Pr}_{H,\mu}(m) = \Phi(d_H, 2m)(3/4)^{2m}$ and (Fig. b) for the abstract perceptron according to the estimate (11) on $\bar{Pr}_{H,\mu}(m)$ for $m_1 = 50$, $m_2 = 1000$ and $\rho = 0.015$. The upper bound on the sample complexity, $m_L(\epsilon, \delta)$, corresponds to the abscissa value of the intersection of the curve $\mathcal{E}(m, 0)$ with the level δ/C (c.f. point A in Fig.b). In this manner for $\delta/C = 0.01$ we obtain estimates $m_L \leq 602$ and $m_L < 1795$ in the case of Fig. a for $d_H = 100$ and $d_H = 300$ and $m_L \leq 697$ in the case of Fig. b ($d_H = m_2 = 1000$), respectively.

3 An application to feedforward networks

In this section we shall discuss the problem of estimation of $\bar{Pr}_{H,\mu}(m)$ which is crucial for application of the above formalism.

First we discuss an example of an *analytic threshold neuron on* $\mathbf{R}^n$ [6] when H is the family of all functions $\mathbf{R}^n \to \{0, 1\}$, $x \mapsto \theta(\sum_{i=1}^{k} w_i \alpha_i(x))$, where $\alpha_i : \mathbf{R}^n \to \mathbf{R}$ are fixed real analytic functions and θ the ordinary hard threshold. In this case d_H equals the number of linearly independent functions among $\alpha_1, \alpha_2, ..., \alpha_k$. For any continuous probability distribution μ on $\mathbf{R}^n$ we have:

$$\Pr_H(\vec{x}) = \Phi(d_H, m)/2^m \quad (\forall m \text{ and } \forall \vec{x} \in (\mathbf{R}^n)^m \text{ with probability 1}), \quad (8)$$

and consequently

$$\bar{Pr}_{H,\mu}(m) = \Pr_{H,\max}(m) = \Phi(d_H, m)/2^m \quad \text{for every } m. \quad (9)$$

Note that this class of neural networks includes as particular cases, *the linear threshold neuron* (if $k = n+1$ and $\alpha_1, ..., \alpha_{n+1}$ are chosen as $1, x_1, ..., x_n$) and *higher order networks* (if $\alpha_i(x)$ are polynomials); in the former case (8) follows also from the classical result of T. Cover [3].

Now we discuss the more complex case of a *linear threshold multilayer perceptron* on $X = \mathbf{R}^n$, with H defined as the family of all functions $\mathbf{R}^n \to \{0, 1\}$ that such an architecture may implement and μ is any continuous probability measure on $\mathbf{R}^n$. In this case there exist two functions, $B_{low}(m)$ and $B_{up}(m)$, such that $B_{low}(m) \leq \Pr_H(\vec{x}) \leq B_{up}(m)$ for any $\vec{x} \in (\mathbf{R}^n)^m$ with probability 1. In other words, $\Pr_H(\vec{x})$ takes values within a "bifurcation region" similar to the shaded region in Fig. 1.b. Further, it is known that $B_{low}(m) = 1$ for $m \leq nh_1 + 1$, $B_{up}(m) = 1$ for $m \leq d_H$ and, in general, $B_{low}(m) \leq \Phi(nh_1+1,m)$ and $B_{up}(m) \leq \Phi(d_H, m)$, where h_1 is the number of neurons in the first hidden layer. Given this we can say that $\bar{\Pr}_{H,\mu}(m)$ takes values somewhere within the "bifurcation region". It is worth noting that the width of the "bifurcation region", which approximately equals $2(d_H - nh_1)$ (since it is known that values on the boundaries have a positive probability of being randomly attained) increases with increasing h_1 since [9]

$$\Omega(nh_1 \log_2(h_1)) = \max_p p(n-p)(h_1/2 - 2^p) \leq d_H. \qquad (10)$$

Estimate (6) is better than (7) in general, and in particular, if $\bar{\Pr}_{H,\mu}(m)$ "drops" to 0 much quicker than $B_{up} = \Phi(d_H, m)$, we may expect that it will provide an estimate of sample complexity m_L even below d_H; if $\bar{\Pr}_{H,\mu}(m)$ is close to B_{up}, then the difference between both estimates will be negligible. In order to clarify this issue we shall consider now a third, abstract example.

We introduce the *abstract perceptron* defined as the set of hypotheses H on a probabilistic space (X, μ) with the following property for a random $m+1$-tuple $(\vec{x}, x) \in X^m \times X$:

$d_{VC}(\vec{x}, x) = d_{VC}(\vec{x}) + 1$ with probability $= 1$ if $d_{VC}(\vec{x}) < m_1$ and with probability ρ if $m_1 \leq d_{VC}(\vec{x}) < m_2$, and $d_{VC}(\vec{x}, x) = d_{VC}(\vec{x})$, otherwise.

Here $0 \leq m_1 \leq m_2 \leq \infty$ are two (integer) constants, $0 \leq \rho \leq 1$ is another constant and $d_{VC}(x_1, ..., x_m)$ is the maximal n such that $|\pi_{(x_{i_1},...,x_{i_n})}(H)| = 2^n$ for some $1 \leq i_1 < \cdots < i_n \leq m$. It can easily be seen that $d_H = m_2$ in this case and that the threshold analytic neuron is a particular example of abstract perceptron (with $\rho \stackrel{def}{=} 0$ and $m_1 = m_2 = d_H$, $B_{low}(m) = B_{up} = \Phi(m_1, m)/2^m$). Note further, that if $0 < \rho < 1$, then for any $m \geq m_1$, $d_{VC}(\vec{x}) = m_1$ with probability > 0, and for any $m \geq m_2$, $d_{VC}(\vec{x}) = d_H = m_2$ with probability > 0. In this regard the abstract perceptron resembles the linear threshold multilayer perceptron (with m_1 and m_2 corresponding to $nh_1 + 1$ and d_H, respectively). However, the main advantage of this model is that we can derive the following estimate:

$$\bar{\Pr}_{H,\mu}(m) \leq 2^{-m} \sum_{i=0}^{m-m_1} \binom{m - m_1}{i} \rho^{m-m_1-i}(1-\rho)^i \Phi(\min(m-i, m_2), m) \qquad (11)$$

Using this estimate we find that for sufficiently low ρ (and sufficiently large m_2) the sample complexity upper bound (6) is determined by m_1 and can even be lower than $m_2 = d_H$ (c.f. Figure 1.b). In particular, the sample complexity determined by Eqns. (6) and (11) can be finite even if $d_H = m_2 = \infty$ (c.f. the curve $\mathcal{E}(m, 0)$ for $\rho = .05$ in Fig. 1.b which is the same for $m_2 = 1000$ and $m_2 = \infty$).

4 Discussion

The paper strongly depends on the postulate (3) of (μ^n, C)-uniformity. We admit that this is an ad hoc assumption here as we do not give examples when it is satisfied nor a method to determine the constant C. From this point of view our results at the current stage have no predictive power, perchaps only explanatory one. The paper should be viewed as an attempt in the direction to explain within VC-formalism some known generalisation properties of neural networks which are out of the reach of the formalism to date, such as the empirically observed peak generalisation for backpropagation network trained with samples of the size well below VC-dimension [8] or the phase transitions to perfect generalisation below $1.5 \times$ VC-dimension [5]. We see the formalism in this paper as one of a number of possible approaches in this direction. There are other possibilities here as well (e.g. [5, 12]) and in particular other, weaker versions of (μ^n, C)-uniformity can be used leading to similar results. For instance in Theorem 1 and Corollary 2 it was enough to assume (μ^n, C)-uniformity for a special class of sets S ($S = S_{0,j}^{m,\tilde{m}}$, c.f. the Appendix); we intend to discuss other options in this regard on another occasion.

Now we relate this research to some previous results (e.g. [2, 4]) which imply the following estimates on sample complexity (c.f. [1, Theorems 8.6.1-2]):

$$\max\left(\frac{d_H - 1}{32\epsilon}, -\ln(\delta)/\epsilon\right) \leq m_L^*(\delta, \epsilon) \leq \left\lceil \frac{4}{\epsilon}\left(d_H \log_2 \frac{12}{\epsilon} + \log_2 \frac{2}{\delta}\right)\right\rceil, \qquad (12)$$

where the lower bound is proved for all $\epsilon \leq 1/8$ and $\delta \leq 1/100$; here $m_L^*(\delta, \epsilon)$ is the "universal" sample complexity, i.e. for all target concepts t and all probability distributions μ. For $\epsilon = \delta = 0.01$ and $d_H >> 1$ this estimate yields $3d_H < m_L^*(.01, .01) < 4000d_H$. These bounds should be compared against estimates of Corollary 2 of which (7) provides a much tighter upper bound, $m_L(.01, .01) \leq 6.9 d_H$, if the assumption on (μ^m, C)-uniformity of the hypothesis space around the target concept t is satisfied.

5 Conclusions

We have shown that under appropriate restriction on the probability distribution and target concept, the upper bound on sample complexity (and "perfect generalisation") can be lowered to $\approx 6.9\times$ VC-dimension, and in some cases even below VC-dimension (with a strong possibility that multilayer perceptron could be such).

We showed that there are other parameters than VC-dimension potentially impacting on generalisation capabilities of neural networks. In particular we showed by example (abstract perceptron) that a system may have finite sample complexity and infinite VC dimension at the same time.

The formalism of this paper predicts transition to perfect generalisation at relatively low training sample sizes but it is too crude to predict scaling laws for learning curves (c.f. [5, 12] and references in there).

Acknowledgement. The permission of Managing Director, Research and Information Technology, Telecom Australia, to publish this paper is gratefully acknowledged.

References

[1] M. Anthony and N. Biggs. *Computational Learning Theory*. Cambridge Uni-

versity Press, 1992.

[2] A. Blumer, A. Ehrenfeucht, D. Haussler, and M.K. Warmuth. Learnability and the Vapnik-Chervonenkis dimensions. *Journal of the ACM*, **36**:929–965, (Oct. 1989).

[3] T.M. Cover. Geometrical and statistical properties of linear inequalities with applications to pattern recognition. *IEEE Trans. Elec. Comp.*, EC-14:326–334, 1965.

[4] A. Ehrenfeucht, D. Haussler, M. Kearns, and L. Valiant. A general lower bound on the number of examples needed for learning. *Information and Computation*, **82**:247–261, 1989.

[5] D. Hausler, M. Kearns, H.S. Seung, and N. Tishby. Rigorous learning curve bounds from statistical mechanics. Technical report, 1994.

[6] A. Kowalczyk. Separating capacity of analytic neuron. In *Proc. ICNN'94, Orlando*, 1994.

[7] A. Macintyre and E. Sontag. Finiteness results for sigmoidal "neural" networks. In *Proc. of the 25th Annual ACM Symp. Theory of Comp.*, pages 325–334, 1993.

[8] G.L. Martin and J.A. Pitman. Recognizing handprinted letters and digits using backpropagation learning. *Neural Comput.*, 3:258–267, 1991.

[9] A. Sakurai. Tighter bounds of the VC-dimension of three-layer networks. In *Proceedings of the 1993 World Congress on Neural Networks*, 1993.

[10] N. Sauer. On the density of family of sets. *Journal of Combinatorial Theory (Series A)*, **13**:145–147, 1972).

[11] V. Vapnik. *Estimation of Dependences Based on Empirical Data*. Springer-Verlag, 1982.

[12] V. Vapnik, E. Levin, and Y. Le Cun. Measuring the vc-dimension of a learning machine. *Neural Computation*, 6 (5):851–876, 1994).

6 Appendix: Sketch of the proof of Theorem 1

The proof is a modification of the proof of [1, Theorem 8.3.1]. We divide it into three stages.

Stage 1. Let
$$\mathcal{R}^j \stackrel{def}{=} \{(x,y) \in X^m \times X^m \approx X^{2m} \; ; \; \exists_{h \in H} er_x h = 0 \; \& \; er_y h = j/m\} \tag{13}$$
for $j \in \{0, 1, ..., m\}$. Using a Chernoff bound on the "tail" of binomial distribution it can be shown [1, Lemma 8.3.2] that for $m \geq 8/\epsilon$
$$\mu^m(Q^\epsilon(m)) \leq 2 \sum_{j \geq \lceil m\epsilon/2 \rceil}^{m} \mu^{2m}(\mathcal{R}^j) \tag{14}$$

Stage 2. Now we use a combinatorial argument to estimate $\mu^{2m}(\mathcal{R}^j)$. We consider the 2^m-element commutative group G_m of transformations of $X^m \times X^m \approx X^{2m}$ generated by all "co-ordinate swaps" of the form
$$(x_1, ..., x_m, y_1, ..., y_m) \mapsto (x_1, ..., x_{i-1}, y_i, x_{i+1}, ..., x_m, y_1, ..., y_{i-1}, x_i, y_{i+1}, ..., y_m),$$

for $1 \leq i \leq m$. We assume also that G_m transforms $\{0,1\}^m \times \{0,1\}^m \approx \{0,1\}^{2m}$ in a similar fashion. Note that

$$\sigma(\pi_{t,(\vec{x},\vec{y})})(h)) = (\pi_{t,\sigma(\vec{x},\vec{y})}(h) \quad (\text{for } \sigma \in \mathcal{G}_m). \tag{15}$$

As transformation $\sigma \in G_m$ preserve the measure μ^{2m} on $X^m \times X^m$ we obtain

$$2^m \mu^{2m}(\mathcal{R}^j) = |G_m| \mu^{2m}(\mathcal{R}^j) = \sum_{\sigma \in \mathcal{G}_m} \int \mu^{2m}(d\vec{x}d\vec{y}) \chi_{\mathcal{R}^j}(\sigma(\vec{x},\vec{y}))$$

$$= \int \mu^{2m}(d\vec{x}d\vec{y}) \sum_{\sigma \in \mathcal{G}_m} \chi_{\mathcal{R}^j}(\sigma(\vec{x},\vec{y})). \tag{16}$$

Let $S_{0,j}^{m,m} \stackrel{def}{=} \{\tilde{h} = (\tilde{h}_1, \tilde{h}_2) \in \{0,1\}^m \times \{0,1\}^m \ ; \ \tilde{h}_1 = 0 \ \& \ ||\tilde{h}_2|| = j\}$ and $S_j^{2m} \stackrel{def}{=} \{\tilde{h} \in \{0,1\}^{2m} \ ; \ ||\tilde{h}|| = j\}$, where $||\tilde{h}|| \stackrel{def}{=} \tilde{h}_1 + \cdots + \tilde{h}_m$ for any $\tilde{h} = (\tilde{h}_1, ..., \tilde{h}_m) \in \{0,1\}^m$. Then $|S_j^{2m}| = \binom{2m}{j}$, $\sigma(S_{0,j}^{m,m}) \subset S_j^{2m}$ for any $\sigma \in G_m$ and

$$\mathcal{R}^j = \{(\vec{x},\vec{y}) \in X^m \times X^m \ ; \ \exists \tilde{h} \in \pi_{t,(\vec{x},\vec{y})}(H) \cap S_{0,j}^{m,m}\}, \tag{17}$$

Thus from Eqn. (16) we obtain

$$2^m \mu^{2m}(\mathcal{R}^j) \leq \int \mu^{2m}(d\vec{x}d\vec{y}) \sum_{\sigma \in \mathcal{G}_m} \sum_{\tilde{h} \in \pi_{t,(\vec{x},\vec{y})}(H) \cap S_j^{2m}} \chi_{S_{0,j}^{m,m}}(\sigma\tilde{h})$$

$$= \int \mu^{2m}(d\vec{x}d\vec{y}) \sum_{\tilde{h} \in \pi_{t,(\vec{x},\vec{y})}(H) \cap S_j^{2m}} \sum_{\sigma \in \mathcal{G}_m} \chi_{S_{0,j}^{m,m}}(\sigma\tilde{h})$$

$$= \int \mu^{2m}(d\vec{x}d\vec{y}) \sum_{\tilde{h} \in \pi_{t,(\vec{x},\vec{y})}(H) \cap S_{0,j}^{m,m}} |\{\sigma \in G_m \ ; \ \sigma\tilde{h} \in S_j^{2m}\}|$$

$$= \int \mu^{2m}(d\vec{x}d\vec{y}) |\{\pi_{t,(\vec{x},\vec{y})}(H) \cap S_j^{2m}\}| \, 2^{m-j}.$$

Applying now the condition of (μ^{2m}, C)-uniformity (Eqn. 3), Eqn. 17 and dividing by 2^m we get

$$\mu^{2m}(\mathcal{R}^j) \leq C \bar{\Pr}_{H,\mu}(2m) \binom{2m}{j} 2^{-j}.$$

Stage 3. On substitution of the above estimate into (14) we obtain estimate (4). To derive (5) let us observe that $\sum_{j=\lceil m\epsilon/2 \rceil}^{m} \binom{2m}{j} 2^{-j} \leq (1 + 1/2)^{2m}$. Q.E.D.

From Data Distributions to Regularization in Invariant Learning

Todd K. Leen

Department of Computer Science and Engineering
Oregon Graduate Institute of Science and Technology
20000 N.W. Walker Rd
Beaverton, Oregon 97006
tleen@cse.ogi.edu

Abstract

Ideally pattern recognition machines provide constant output when the inputs are transformed under a group $\mathcal{G}$ of desired invariances. These invariances can be achieved by enhancing the training data to include examples of inputs transformed by elements of $\mathcal{G}$, while leaving the corresponding targets unchanged. Alternatively the cost function for training can include a regularization term that penalizes changes in the output when the input is transformed under the group.

This paper relates the two approaches, showing precisely the sense in which the regularized cost function approximates the result of adding transformed (or distorted) examples to the training data. The cost function for the enhanced training set is equivalent to the sum of the original cost function plus a regularizer. For unbiased models, the regularizer reduces to the intuitively obvious choice – a term that penalizes changes in the output when the inputs are transformed under the group. For infinitesimal transformations, the coefficient of the regularization term reduces to the variance of the distortions introduced into the training data. This correspondence provides a simple bridge between the two approaches.

1 Approaches to Invariant Learning

In machine learning one sometimes wants to incorporate invariances into the function learned. Our knowledge of the problem dictates that the machine outputs ought to remain constant when its inputs are transformed under a set of operations $\mathcal{G}^1$. In character recognition, for example, we want the outputs to be invariant under shifts and small rotations of the input image.

In neural networks, there are several ways to achieve this invariance

1. The invariance can be hard-wired by weight sharing in the case of summation nodes (LeCun et al. 1990) or by constraints similar to weight sharing in higher-order nodes (Giles et al. 1988).

2. One can enhance the training ensemble by adding examples of inputs transformed under the desired invariance group, while maintaining the same targets as for the raw data.

3. One can add to the cost function a regularizer that penalizes changes in the output when the input is transformed by elements of the group (Simard et al. 1992).

Intuitively one expects the approaches in 3 and 4 to be intimately linked. This paper develops that correspondence in detail.

2 The Distortion-Enhanced Input Ensemble

Let the input data x be distributed according to the density function $p(x)$. The conditional distribution for the corresponding targets is denoted $p(t|x)$. For simplicity of notation we take $t \in R$. The extension to vector targets is trivial. Let $f(x;w)$ denote the network function, parameterized by weights w. The training procedure is assumed to minimize the expected squared error

$$\mathcal{E}(w) \equiv \int\int dt\,dx\, p(t|x)\,p(x)\,[\,t - f(x;w)\,]^2 \ . \tag{1}$$

We wish to consider the effects of adding new inputs that are related to the old by transformations that correspond to the desired invariances. These transformations, or distortions, of the inputs are carried out by group elements $g \in \mathcal{G}$. For Lie groups[2], the transformations are analytic functions of parameters $\alpha \in R^k$

$$x \to x' = g(x;\alpha) \ , \tag{2}$$

with the identity transformation corresponding to parameter value zero

$$g(x;0) = x \ . \tag{3}$$

In image processing, for example, we may want our machine to exhibit invariance with respect to rotation, scaling, shearing and translations of the plane. These

---
[1] We assume that the set forms a group.
[2] See for example (Sattinger, 1986).

transformations form a six-parameter Lie group[3].

By adding distorted input examples we alter the original density $p(x)$. To describe the new density, we introduce a probability density for the transformation parameters $p(\alpha)$. Using this density, the distribution for the distortion-enhanced input ensemble is

$$p(x') = \int\int d\alpha\, dx\, p(x'|x,\alpha)\, p(\alpha)\, p(x)$$

$$= \int\int d\alpha\, dx\, \delta(\, x' - g(x;\alpha)\,)\, p(\alpha)\, p(x)\ ,$$

where $\delta(\cdot)$ is the Dirac delta function[4]

Finally we impose that the targets remain unchanged when the inputs are transformed according to (2) i.e., $p(t|x') = p(t|x)$. Substituting $p(x')$ into (1) and using the invariance of the targets yields the cost function

$$\tilde{\mathcal{E}} = \int\int\int dt\, dx\, d\alpha\ p(t|x)\, p(x)\, p(\alpha)\ [\, t - f(g(x;\alpha);w)\,]^2\ . \tag{4}$$

Equation (4) gives the cost function for the distortion-enhanced input ensemble.

3 Regularization and Hints

The remainder of the paper makes precise the connection between adding transformed inputs, as embodied in (4), and various regularization procedures. It is straightforward to show that the cost function for the distortion-enhanced ensemble is equivalent to the cost function for the original data ensemble (1) plus a regularization term. Adding and subtracting $f(x;w)$ to the term in square brackets in (4), and expanding the quadratic leaves

$$\tilde{\mathcal{E}} = \mathcal{E} + \mathcal{E}_R\ , \tag{5}$$

where the regularizer is

$$\mathcal{E}_R = \mathcal{E}_H + \mathcal{E}_C$$

$$\equiv \int d\alpha\, p(\alpha) \int dx\ p(x)\ [\, f(x,w) - f(g(x;\alpha);w)\,]^2$$

$$- 2 \int\int\int dt\, dx\, d\alpha\ p(t|x)\, p(x)\, p(\alpha)$$

$$\times [\, t - f(x;w)\,]\, [\, f(g(x;\alpha);w) - f(x;w)\,]\ . \tag{6}$$

---

[3] The parameters for rotations, scaling and shearing completely specify elements of $GL2$, the four parameter group of 2×2 invertible matrices. The translations carry an additional two degrees of freedom.

[4] In general the density on α might vary through the input space, suggesting the conditional density $p(\alpha\,|\,x)$. This introduces rather minor changes in the discussion that will not be considered here.

Training with the original data ensemble using the cost function (5) is equivalent to adding transformed inputs to the data ensemble.

The first term of the regularizer $\mathcal{E}_H$ penalizes the average squared difference between $f(x;w)$ and $f(g(x;\alpha);w)$. This is *exactly* the form one would intuitively apply in order to insure that the network output not change under the transformation $x \to g(x,\alpha)$. Indeed this is the similar to the form of the invariance "hint" proposed by Abu-Mostafa (1993). The difference here is that there is no arbitrary parameter multiplying the term. Instead the strength of the regularizer is governed by the average over the density $p(\alpha)$. The term $\mathcal{E}_H$ measures the error in satisfying the invariance hint.

The second term $\mathcal{E}_C$ measures the correlation between the error in fitting to the data, and the error in satisfying the hint. Only when these correlations vanish is the cost function for the enhanced ensemble equal to the original cost function plus the invariance hint penalty.

The correlation term vanishes trivially when either

1. The invariance $f(g(x;\alpha);w) = f(x;w)$ is satisfied, or
2. The network function equals the least squares regression on t

$$f(x;w) = \int dt\, p(t|x)\, t \equiv E[t|x] \ . \tag{7}$$

The lowest possible $\mathcal{E}$ occurs when f satisfies (7), at which $\mathcal{E}$ becomes the variance in the targets averaged over $p(x)$. By substituting this into $\mathcal{E}_C$ and carrying out the integration over $dt\, p(t|x)$, the correlation term is seen to vanish.

If the minimum of $\tilde{\mathcal{E}}$ occurs at a weight for which the invariance is satisfied (condition 1 above), then minimizing $\tilde{\mathcal{E}}(w)$ is equivalent to minimizing $\mathcal{E}(w)$. If the minimum of $\tilde{\mathcal{E}}$ occurs at a weight for which the network function is the regression (condition 2), then minimizing $\tilde{\mathcal{E}}$ is equivalent to minimizing the cost function with the intuitive regularizer $\mathcal{E}_H$ [5].

3.1 Infinitesimal Transformations

Above we enumerated the conditions under which the correlation term in $\mathcal{E}_R$ vanishes exactly for unrestricted transformations. If the transformations are analytic in the parameters α, then by restricting ourselves to small transformations (those close to the identity) we can show how the correlation term approximately vanishes for unbiased models. To implement this, we assume that $p(\alpha)$ is sharply peaked up about the origin so that large transformations are unlikely.

---

[5] If the data is to be fit optimally, with enough freedom left over to satisfy the invariance hint, then there must be several weight values (perhaps a continuum of such values) for which the network function satisfies (7). That is, the problem must be under-specified. If this is the case, then the interesting part weight space is just the subset on which (7) is satisfied. On this subset the correlation term in (6) vanishes and the regularizer assumes the intuitive form.

We obtain an approximation to the cost function $\tilde{\mathcal{E}}$ by expanding the integrands in (6) in power series about $\alpha = 0$ and retaining terms to second order. This leaves

$$\tilde{\mathcal{E}} = \mathcal{E} + \int\int dx\, d\alpha\, p(x)\, p(\alpha) \left(\alpha_i \left.\frac{\partial g^\mu}{\partial \alpha_i}\right|_{\alpha=0} \frac{\partial f}{\partial x^\mu} \right)^2$$

$$- 2 \int\int\int dt\, dx\, d\alpha\ p(t|x)\, p(x)\, p(\alpha)\, [t - f(x;w)] \times$$

$$\left[\left(\alpha_i \left.\frac{\partial g^\mu}{\partial \alpha_i}\right|_{\alpha=0} + \frac{1}{2} \alpha_i \alpha_j \left.\frac{\partial^2 g^\mu}{\partial \alpha_i \partial \alpha_j}\right|_{\alpha=0} \right) \left(\frac{\partial f}{\partial x^\mu} \right) \right.$$

$$\left. + \frac{1}{2} \alpha_i \alpha_j \left.\frac{\partial g^\mu}{\partial \alpha_i}\right|_{\alpha=0} \left.\frac{\partial g^\nu}{\partial \alpha_j}\right|_{\alpha=0} \left(\frac{\partial^2 f}{\partial x^\nu \partial x^\mu} \right) \right] + \mathcal{O}(\alpha^3) \qquad (8)$$

where x^μ and g^μ denote the μth components of x and g, α_i denotes the ith component of the transformation parameter vector, repeated Greek and Roman indices are summed over, and all derivatives are evaluated at $\alpha = 0$. Note that we have used the fact that Lie group transformations are analytic in the parameter vector α to derive the expansion.

Finally we introduce two assumptions on the distribution $p(\alpha)$. First α is assumed to be zero mean. This corresponds, in the linear approximation, to a distribution of distortions whose mean is the identity transformation. Second, we assume that the components of α are uncorrelated so that the covariance matrix is diagonal with elements σ_i^2, $i = 1\ldots k$.[6] With these assumptions, the cost function for the distortion-enhanced ensemble simplifies to

$$\tilde{\mathcal{E}} = \mathcal{E} + \sum_{i=1}^{k} \sigma_i^2 \int dx\, p(x) \left(\left.\frac{\partial g^\mu}{\partial \alpha_i}\right|_{\alpha=0} \frac{\partial f}{\partial x^\mu} \right)^2$$

$$- \sum_{i=1}^{k} \sigma_i^2 \int\int dx\, dt\ p(t|x)\, p(x) \left\{ \, (f(x;w) - t) \right.$$

$$\left. \times \left[\left.\frac{\partial^2 g^\mu}{\partial \alpha_i^2}\right|_{\alpha=0} \left(\frac{\partial f}{\partial x^\mu} \right) + \left.\frac{\partial g^\mu}{\partial \alpha_i}\right|_{\alpha=0} \left.\frac{\partial g^\nu}{\partial \alpha_i}\right|_{\alpha=0} \left(\frac{\partial^2 f}{\partial x^\nu \partial x^\mu} \right) \right] \right\}$$

$$+ \mathcal{O}(\sigma^4) \, . \qquad (9)$$

This last expression provides a simple bridge between the the methods of adding transformed examples to the data, and the alternative of adding a regularizer to the cost function: The coefficient of the regularization term in the latter approach is equal to the *variance of the transformation parameters* in the former approach.

---

[6] Note that the *transformed patterns* may be correlated in parts of the pattern space. For example the results of applying the shearing and rotation operations to an infinite vertical line are indistinguishable. In general, there may be regions of the pattern space for which the action of several different group elements are indistinguishable; that is $x' = g(x;\alpha) = g(x;\beta)$. However this does not imply that α and β are statistically correlated.

3.1.1 Unbiased Models

For unbiased models the regularizer in $\tilde{\mathcal{E}}(w)$ assumes a particularly simple form. Suppose the network function is rich enough to form an unbiased estimate of the least squares regression on t for the *undistorted* data ensemble. That is, there exists a weight value w_0 such that

$$f(x;w_0) = \int dt \ t \ p(t|x) \equiv E[t|x] \ . \tag{10}$$

This is the *global minimum* for the original error $\mathcal{E}(w)$.

The arguments of section 3 apply here as well. However we can go further. Even if there is only a single, isolated weight value for which (10) is satisfied, then to $\mathcal{O}(\sigma^2)$ the correlation term in the regularizer vanishes. To see this note that by the implicit function theorem the modified cost function (9) has its global minimum at the new weight[7]

$$\tilde{w}_0 = w_0 + \mathcal{O}(\sigma^2) \ . \tag{11}$$

At this weight, the network function is no longer the regression on t, but rather

$$f(x;\tilde{w}_0) = E[t|x] + \mathcal{O}(\sigma^2) \ . \tag{12}$$

Substituting (12) into (9), we find that the minimum of (9) is, to $\mathcal{O}(\sigma^2)$, at the same weight as the minimum of

$$\hat{\mathcal{E}} = \mathcal{E} + \sum_{i=1}^{k} \sigma_i^2 \int dx \ p(x) \left[\left. \frac{\partial g^\mu}{\partial \alpha_i} \right|_{\alpha=0} \frac{\partial f(x,w)}{\partial x^\mu} \right]^2 \ . \tag{13}$$

To $\mathcal{O}(\sigma^2)$, minimizing (13) is equivalent to minimizing (9). So we regard $\hat{\mathcal{E}}$ as the effective cost function.

The regularization term in (13) is proportional to the average square of the gradient of the network function along the direction in the input space generated by the linear part of g. The quantity inside the square brackets is just the linear part of $[f(g(x;\alpha)) - f(x)]$ from (6). The magnitude of the regularization term is just the variance of the distribution of distortion parameters.

This is precisely the form of the regularizer given by Simard et al. in their tangent prop algorithm (Simard et al, 1992). This derivation shows the equivalence (to $\mathcal{O}(\sigma^2)$) between the tangent prop regularizer and the alternative of modifying the input distribution. Furthermore, we see that with this equivalence, the constant fixing the strength of the regularization term is simply the *variance of the distortions* introduced into the original training set.

We should stress that the equivalence between the regularizer, and the distortion-enhanced ensemble in (13) only holds to $\mathcal{O}(\sigma^2)$. If one allows the variance of the

---
[7]We assume that the Hessian of $\mathcal{E}$ is nonsingular at w_0.

distortion parameters σ^2 to become arbitrarily large in an effort to mock up an arbitrarily large regularization term, then the equivalence expressed in (13) breaks down since terms of order $\mathcal{O}(\sigma^4)$ can no longer be neglected. In addition, if the transformations are to be kept small so that the linearization holds (e.g. by restricting the density on α to have support on a small neighborhood of zero), then the variance will bounded above.

3.1.2 Smoothing Regularizers

In the previous sections we showed the equivalence between modifying the input distribution and adding a regularizer to the cost function. We derived this equivalence to illuminate mechanisms for obtaining invariant pattern recognition. The technique for dealing with infinitesimal transformations in section §3.1 was used by Bishop (1994) to show the equivalence between added input noise and smoothing regularizers. Bishop's results, though they preceded our own, are a special case of the results presented here. Suppose the group $\mathcal{G}$ is restricted to translations by random vectors $g(x; \alpha) = x + \alpha$ where α is spherically distributed with variance σ_α^2. Then the regularizer in (13) is

$$\mathcal{E}_R = \sigma_\alpha^2 \int dx \ p(x) \ |\nabla_x f(x; w)|^2 \ . \qquad (14)$$

This regularizer penalizes large magnitude gradients in the network function and is, as pointed out by Bishop, one of the class of generalized Tikhonov regularizers.

4 Summary

We have shown that enhancing the input ensemble by adding examples transformed under a group $x \to g(x; \alpha)$, while maintaining the target values, is equivalent to adding a regularizer to the original cost function. For unbiased models the regularizer reduces to the intuitive form that penalizes the mean squared difference between the network output for transformed and untransformed inputs – i.e. the error in satisfying the desired invariance. In general the regularizer includes a term that measures correlations between the error in fitting the data, and the error in satisfying the desired invariance. For infinitesimal transformations, the regularizer is equivalent (up to terms linear in the variance of the transformation parameters) to the tangent prop form given by Simard et al. (1992), with regularization coefficient equal to the variance of the transformation parameters. In the special case that the group transformations are limited to random translations of the input, the regularizer reduces to a standard smoothing regularizer.

We gave conditions under which enhancing the input ensemble and adding the intuitive regularizer $\mathcal{E}_H$ are equivalent. However this equivalence is only with regard to the optimal weight. We have not compared the training dynamics for the two approaches. In particular, it is quite possible that the full regularizer $\mathcal{E}_H + \mathcal{E}_C$ exhibits different training dynamics from the intuitive form $\mathcal{E}_H$. For the approach in which data are added to the input ensemble, one can easily construct datasets and distributions $p(\alpha)$ that either increase the condition number of the Hessian, or decrease it. Finally, it may be that the intuitive regularizer can have either detrimental or positive effects on the Hessian as well.

Acknowledgments

I thank Lodewyk Wessels, Misha Pavel, Eric Wan, Steve Rehfuss, Genevieve Orr and Patrice Simard for stimulating and helpful discussions, and the reviewers for helpful comments. I am grateful to my father for what he gave to me in life, and for the presence of his spirit after his recent passing.

This work was supported by EPRI under grant RP8015-2, AFOSR under grant FF4962-93-1-0253, and ONR under grant N00014-91-J-1482.

References

Yasar S. Abu-Mostafa. A method for learning from hints. In S. Hanson, J. Cowan, and C. Giles, editors, *Advances in Neural Information Processing Systems, vol. 5*, pages 73–80. Morgan Kaufmann, 1993.

Chris M. Bishop. Training with noise is equivalent to Tikhonov regularization. To appear in *Neural Computation*, 1994.

C.L. Giles, R.D. Griffin, and T. Maxwell. Encoding geometric invariances in higher-order neural networks. In D.Z.Anderson, editor, *Neural Information Processing Systems*, pages 301–309. American Institute of Physics, 1988.

Y. Le Cun, B. Boser, J.S. Denker, D. Henderson, R.E. Howard, W. Hubbard, and L.D. Jackel. Handwritten digit recognition with a back-propagation network. In *Advances in Neural Information Processing Systems, vol. 2*, pages 396–404. Morgan Kaufmann Publishers, 1990.

Patrice Simard, Bernard Victorri, Yann Le Cun, and John Denker. Tangent prop - a formalism for specifying selected invariances in an adaptive network. In John E. Moody, Steven J. Hanson, and Richard P. Lippmann, editors, *Advances in Neural Information Processing Systems 4*, pages 895–903. Morgan Kaufmann, 1992.

D.H. Sattinger and O.L. Weaver. *Lie Groups and Algebras with Applications to Physics, Geometry and Mechanics*. Springer-Verlag, 1986.

Neural Network Ensembles, Cross Validation, and Active Learning

Anders Krogh*
Nordita
Blegdamsvej 17
2100 Copenhagen, Denmark

Jesper Vedelsby
Electronics Institute, Building 349
Technical University of Denmark
2800 Lyngby, Denmark

Abstract

Learning of continuous valued functions using neural network ensembles (committees) can give improved accuracy, reliable estimation of the generalization error, and active learning. The *ambiguity* is defined as the variation of the output of ensemble members averaged over *unlabeled* data, so it quantifies the disagreement among the networks. It is discussed how to use the ambiguity in combination with cross-validation to give a reliable estimate of the ensemble generalization error, and how this type of ensemble cross-validation can sometimes improve performance. It is shown how to estimate the optimal weights of the ensemble members using *unlabeled data*. By a generalization of query by committee, it is finally shown how the ambiguity can be used to select new training data to be labeled in an active learning scheme.

1 INTRODUCTION

It is well known that a combination of many different predictors can improve predictions. In the neural networks community "ensembles" of neural networks has been investigated by several authors, see for instance [1, 2, 3]. Most often the networks in the ensemble are trained individually and then their predictions are combined. This combination is usually done by majority (in classification) or by simple averaging (in regression), but one can also use a weighted combination of the networks.

---

*Author to whom correspondence should be addressed. Email: `krogh@nordita.dk`

At the workshop after the last NIPS conference (December, 1993) an entire session was devoted to ensembles of neural networks ("Putting it all together", chaired by Michael Perrone). Many interesting papers were given, and it showed that this area is getting a lot of attention.

A combination of the output of several networks (or other predictors) is only useful if they disagree on some inputs. Clearly, there is no more information to be gained from a million identical networks than there is from just one of them (see also [2]). By quantifying the disagreement in the ensemble it turns out to be possible to state this insight rigorously for an ensemble used for approximation of real-valued functions (regression). The simple and beautiful expression that relates the disagreement (called the ensemble ambiguity) and the generalization error is the basis for this paper, so we will derive it with no further delay.

2 THE BIAS-VARIANCE TRADEOFF

Assume the task is to learn a function f from R^N to R for which you have a sample of p examples, (x^μ, y^μ), where $y^\mu = f(x^\mu)$ and $\mu = 1,\ldots,p$. These examples are assumed to be drawn randomly from the distribution $p(x)$. Anything in the following is easy to generalize to several output variables.

The ensemble consists of N networks and the output of network α on input x is called $V^\alpha(x)$. A weighted ensemble average is denoted by a bar, like

$$\overline{V}(x) = \sum_\alpha w_\alpha V^\alpha(x). \tag{1}$$

This is the final output of the ensemble. We think of the weight w_α as our belief in network α and therefore constrain the weights to be positive and sum to one. The constraint on the sum is crucial for some of the following results.

The *ambiguity* on input x of a single member of the ensemble is defined as $a^\alpha(x) = (V^\alpha(x) - \overline{V}(x))^2$. The *ensemble ambiguity* on input x is

$$\overline{a}(x) = \sum_\alpha w_\alpha a^\alpha(x) = \sum_\alpha w_\alpha (V^\alpha(x) - \overline{V}(x))^2. \tag{2}$$

It is simply the variance of the weighted ensemble around the weighed mean, and it measures the disagreement among the networks on input x. The quadratic error of network α and of the ensemble are

$$\epsilon^\alpha(x) = (f(x) - V^\alpha(x))^2 \tag{3}$$
$$e(x) = (f(x) - \overline{V}(x))^2 \tag{4}$$

respectively. Adding and subtracting $f(x)$ in (2) yields

$$\overline{a}(x) = \sum_\alpha w_\alpha \epsilon^\alpha(x) - e(x) \tag{5}$$

(after a little algebra using that the weights sum to one). Calling the weighted average of the individual errors $\overline{\epsilon}(x) = \sum_\alpha w_\alpha \epsilon^\alpha(x)$ this becomes

$$e(x) = \overline{\epsilon}(x) - \overline{a}(x). \tag{6}$$

All these formulas can be averaged over the input distribution. Averages over the input distribution will be denoted by capital letter, so

$$E^\alpha = \int dx p(x) \epsilon^\alpha(x) \tag{7}$$

$$A^\alpha = \int dx p(x) a^\alpha(x) \tag{8}$$

$$E = \int dx p(x) e(x). \tag{9}$$

The first two of these are the generalization error and the ambiguity respectively for network α, and E is the generalization error for the ensemble. From (6) we then find for the *ensemble generalization error*

$$E = \overline{E} - \overline{A}. \tag{10}$$

The first term on the right is the weighted average of the generalization errors of the individual networks ($\overline{E} = \sum_\alpha w_\alpha E^\alpha$), and the second is the weighted average of the ambiguities ($\overline{A} = \sum_\alpha w_\alpha A^\alpha$), which we refer to as the ensemble ambiguity.

The beauty of this equation is that it separates the generalization error into a term that depends on the generalization errors of the individual networks and another term that contain *all correlations* between the networks. Furthermore, the correlation term $\overline{A}$ can be estimated entirely from *unlabeled data*, *i.e.*, no knowledge is required of the real function to be approximated. The term "unlabeled example" is borrowed from classification problems, and in this context it means an input x for which the value of the target function $f(x)$ is unknown.

Equation (10) expresses the tradeoff between bias and variance in the ensemble, but in a different way than the the common bias-variance relation [4] in which the averages are over possible training sets instead of ensemble averages. If the ensemble is strongly biased the ambiguity will be small, because the networks implement very similar functions and thus agree on inputs even outside the training set. Therefore the generalization error will be essentially equal to the weighted average of the generalization errors of the individual networks. If, on the other hand, there is a large variance, the ambiguity is high and in this case the generalization error will be smaller than the average generalization error. See also [5].

From this equation one can immediately see that the generalization error of the ensemble is always smaller than the (weighted) average of the ensemble errors, $E < \overline{E}$. In particular for uniform weights:

$$E \leq \frac{1}{N} \sum_\alpha E^\alpha \tag{11}$$

which has been noted by several authors, see *e.g.* [3].

3 THE CROSS-VALIDATION ENSEMBLE

From (10) it is obvious that increasing the ambiguity (while not increasing individual generalization errors) will improve the overall generalization. We want the networks to disagree! How can we increase the ambiguity of the ensemble? One way is to use different types of approximators like a mixture of neural networks of different topologies or a mixture of completely different types of approximators. Another

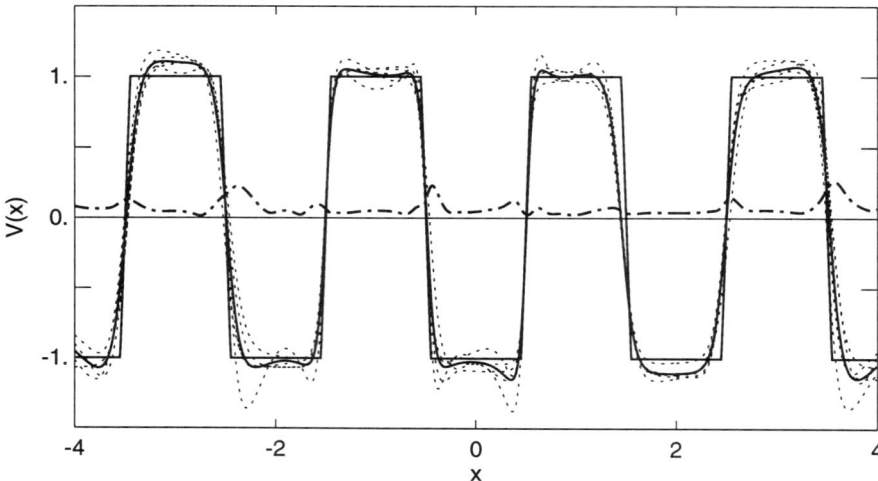

Figure 1: An ensemble of five networks were trained to approximate the square wave target function $f(x)$. The final ensemble output (solid smooth curve) and the outputs of the individual networks (dotted curves) are shown. Also the square root of the ambiguity is shown (dash-dot line). For training 200 random examples were used, but each network had a cross-validation set of size 40, so they were each trained on 160 examples.

obvious way is to train the networks on different training sets. Furthermore, to be able to estimate the first term in (10) it would be desirable to have some kind of cross-validation. This suggests the following strategy.

Chose a number $K \leq p$. For each network in the ensemble hold out K examples for testing, where the N test sets should have minimal overlap, i.e., the N training sets should be as different as possible. If, for instance, $K \leq p/N$ it is possible to choose the K test sets with no overlap. This enables us to estimate the generalization error E^α of the individual members of the ensemble, and at the same time make sure that the ambiguity increases. When holding out examples the generalization errors for the individual members of the ensemble, E^α, will increase, but the conjecture is that for a good choice of the size of the ensemble (N) and the test set size (K), the ambiguity will increase more and thus one will get a decrease in overall generalization error.

This conjecture has been tested experimentally on a simple square wave function of one variable shown in Figure 1. Five identical feed-forward networks with one hidden layer of 20 units were trained independently by back-propagation using 200 random examples. For each network a cross-validation set of K examples was held out for testing as described above. The "true" generalization and the ambiguity were estimated from a set of 1000 random inputs. The weights were uniform, $w^\alpha = 1/5$ (non-uniform weights are addressed later).

In Figure 2 average results over 12 independent runs are shown for some values of

Figure 2: The solid line shows the generalization error for uniform weights as a function of K, where K is the size of the cross-validation sets. The dotted line is the error estimated from equation (10). The dashed line is for the optimal weights estimated by the use of the generalization errors for the individual networks estimated from the cross-validation sets as described in the text. The bottom solid line is the generalization error one would obtain if the individual generalization errors were known exactly (the best possible weights).

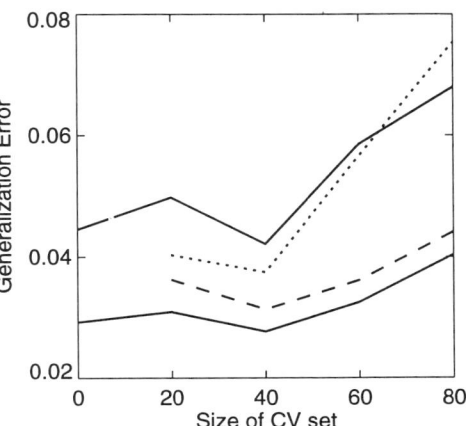

K (top solid line). First, one should note that the generalization error is the same for a cross-validation set of size 40 as for size 0, although not lower, so it supports the conjecture in a weaker form. However, we have done many experiments, and depending on the experimental setup the curve can take on almost any form, sometimes the error is larger at zero than at 40 or vice versa. In the experiments shown, only ensembles with at least four converging networks out of five were used. If all the ensembles were kept, the error would have been significantly higher at $K = 0$ than for $K > 0$ because in about half of the runs none of the networks in the ensemble converged — something that seldom happened when a cross-validation set was used. Thus it is still unclear under which circumstances one can expect a drop in generalization error when using cross-validation in this fashion.

The dotted line in Figure 2 is the error estimated from equation (10) using the cross-validation sets for each of the networks to estimate E^α, and one notices a good agreement.

4 OPTIMAL WEIGHTS

The weights w_α can be estimated as described in e.g. [3]. We suggest instead to use unlabeled data and estimate them in such a way that they minimize the generalization error given in (10).

There is no analytical solution for the weights, but something can be said about the minimum point of the generalization error. Calculating the derivative of E as given in (10) subject to the constraints on the weights and setting it equal to zero shows that

$$E^\alpha - A^\alpha = E \text{ or } w_\alpha = 0. \qquad (12)$$

(The calculation is not shown because of space limitations, but it is easy to do.) That is, $E^\alpha - A^\alpha$ has to be the same for all the networks. Notice that A^α depends on the weights through the ensemble average of the outputs. It shows that the optimal weights have to be chosen such that each network contributes exactly $w_\alpha E$

to the generalization error. Note, however, that a member of the ensemble can have such a poor generalization or be so correlated with the rest of the ensemble that it is optimal to set its weight to zero.

The weights can be "learned" from *unlabeled examples*, e.g. by gradient descent minimization of the estimate of the generalization error (10). A more efficient approach to finding the optimal weights is to turn it into a quadratic optimization problem. That problem is non-trivial only because of the constraints on the weights ($\sum_\alpha w_\alpha = 1$ and $w_\alpha \geq 0$). Define the correlation matrix,

$$C_{\alpha\beta} = \int dx p(x) V^\alpha(x) V^\beta(x). \tag{13}$$

Then, using that the weights sum to one, equation (10) can be rewritten as

$$E = \sum_\alpha w_\alpha E^\alpha + \sum_{\alpha\beta} w_\alpha C_{\alpha\beta} w_\beta - \sum_\alpha w_\alpha C_{\alpha\alpha}. \tag{14}$$

Having estimates of E^α and $C_{\alpha\beta}$ the optimal weights can be found by linear programming or other optimization techniques. Just like the ambiguity, the correlation matrix can be estimated from *unlabeled data* to any accuracy needed (provided that the input distribution p is known).

In Figure 2 the results from an experiment with weight optimization are shown. The dashed curve shows the generalization error when the weights are optimized as described above using the estimates of E^α from the cross-validation (on K examples). The lowest solid curve is for the idealized case, when it is assumed that the errors E^α are known exactly, so it shows the lowest possible error. The performance improvement is quite convincing when the cross-validation estimates are used.

It is important to notice that any estimate of the generalization error of the individual networks can be used in equation (14). If one is certain that the individual networks do not overfit, one might even use the training errors as estimates for E^α (see [3]). It is also possible to use some kind of regularization in (14), if the cross-validation sets are small.

5 ACTIVE LEARNING

In some neural network applications it is very time consuming and/or expensive to acquire training data, *e.g.*, if a complicated measurement is required to find the value of the target function for a certain input. Therefore it is desirable to only use examples with maximal information about the function. Methods where the learner points out good examples are often called active learning.

We propose a query-based active learning scheme that applies to ensembles of networks with continuous-valued output. It is essentially a generalization of query by committee [6, 7] that was developed for classification problems. Our basic assumption is that those patterns in the input space yielding the largest error are those points we would benefit the most from including in the training set.

Since the generalization error is always non-negative, we see from (6) that the weighted average of the individual network errors is always larger than or equal to the ensemble ambiguity,

$$\overline{\epsilon}(x) \geq \overline{a}(x), \tag{15}$$

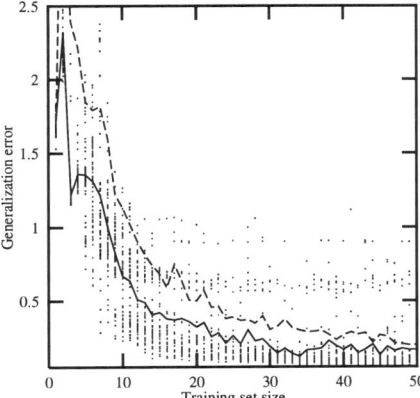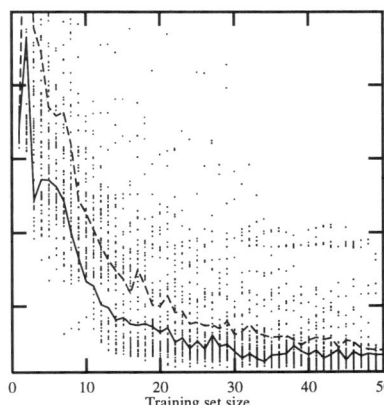

Figure 3: In both plots the full line shows the average generalization for *active learning*, and the dashed line for *passive learning* as a function of the number of training examples. The dots in the left plot show the results of the individual experiments contributing to the mean for the active learning. The dots in right plot show the same for passive learning.

which tells us that the ambiguity is a lower bound for the weighted average of the squared error. An input pattern that yields a large ambiguity will always have a large average error. On the other hand, a low ambiguity does not necessarily imply a low error. If the individual networks are trained to a low training error on the same set of examples then both the error and the ambiguity are low on the training points. This ensures that a pattern yielding a large ambiguity cannot be in the close neighborhood of a training example. The ambiguity will to some extent follow the fluctuations in the error. Since the ambiguity is calculated from unlabeled examples the input-space can be scanned for these areas to any detail. These ideas are well illustrated in Figure 1, where the correlation between error and ambiguity is quite strong, although not perfect.

The results of an experiment with the active learning scheme is shown in Figure 3. An ensemble of 5 networks was trained to approximate the square-wave function shown in Figure 1, but in this experiments the function was restricted to the interval from -2 to 2. The curves show the final generalization error of the ensemble in a passive (dashed line) and an active learning test (solid line). For each training set size 2x40 independent tests were made, all starting with the same initial training set of a single example. Examples were generated and added one at a time. In the passive test examples were generated at random, and in the active one each example was selected as the input that gave the largest ambiguity out of 800 random ones. Figure 3 also shows the distribution of the individual results of the active and passive learning tests. Not only do we obtain significantly better generalization by active learning, there is also less scatter in the results. It seems to be easier for the ensemble to learn from the actively generated set.

6 CONCLUSION

The central idea in this paper was to show that there is a lot to be gained from using unlabeled data when training in ensembles. Although we dealt with neural networks, all the theory holds for any other type of method used as the individual members of the ensemble.

It was shown that apart from getting the individual members of the ensemble to generalize well, it is important for generalization that the individuals disagrees as much as possible, and we discussed one method to make even identical networks disagree. This was done by training the individuals on different training sets by holding out some examples for each individual during training. This had the added advantage that these examples could be used for testing, and thereby one could obtain good estimates of the generalization error.

It was discussed how to find the optimal weights for the individuals of the ensemble. For our simple test problem the weights found improved the performance of the ensemble significantly.

Finally a method for active learning was described, which was based on the method of query by committee developed for classification problems. The idea is that if the ensemble disagrees strongly on an input, it would be good to find the label for that input and include it in the training set for the ensemble. It was shown how active learning improves the learning curve a lot for a simple test problem.

Acknowledgements

We would like to thank Peter Salamon for numerous discussions and for his implementation of linear programming for optimization of the weights. We also thank Lars Kai Hansen for many discussions and great insights, and David Wolpert for valuable comments.

References

[1] L.K. Hansen and P Salamon. Neural network ensembles. *IEEE Transactions on Pattern Analysis and Machine Intelligence*, 12(10):993–1001, Oct. 1990.

[2] D.H Wolpert. Stacked generalization. *Neural Networks*, 5(2):241–59, 1992.

[3] Michael P. Perrone and Leon N Cooper. When networks disagree: Ensemble method for neural networks. In R. J. Mammone, editor, *Neural Networks for Speech and Image processing*. Chapman-Hall, 1993.

[4] S. Geman, E. Bienenstock, and R Doursat. Neural networks and the bias/variance dilemma. *Neural Computation*, 4(1):1–58, Jan. 1992.

[5] Ronny Meir. Bias, variance and the combination of estimators; the case of linear least squares. Preprint (In Neuroprose), Technion, Heifa, Israel, 1994.

[6] H.S. Seung, M. Opper, and H. Sompolinsky. Query by committee. In *Proceedings of the Fifth Workshop on Computational Learning Theory*, pages 287–294, San Mateo, CA, 1992. Morgan Kaufmann.

[7] Y. Freund, H.S. Seung, E. Shamir, and N. Tishby. Information, prediction, and query by committee. In *Advances in Neural Information Processing Systems*, volume 5, San Mateo, California, 1993. Morgan Kaufmann.

Limits on Learning Machine Accuracy Imposed by Data Quality

Corinna Cortes, L. D. Jackel, and Wan-Ping Chiang
AT&T Bell Laboratories
Holmdel, NJ 07733

Abstract

Random errors and insufficiencies in databases limit the performance of any classifier trained from and applied to the database. In this paper we propose a method to estimate the limiting performance of classifiers imposed by the database. We demonstrate this technique on the task of predicting failure in telecommunication paths.

1 Introduction

Data collection for a classification or regression task is prone to random errors, e.g. inaccuracies in the measurements of the input or mis-labeling of the output. Missing or insufficient data are other sources that may complicate a learning task and hinder accurate performance of the trained machine. These insufficiencies of the data limit the performance of any learning machine or other statistical tool constructed from and applied to the data collection — no matter how complex the machine or how much data is used to train it.

In this paper we propose a method for estimating the limiting performance of learning machines imposed by the quality of the database used for the task. The method involves a series of learning experiments. The extracted result is, however, independent of the choice of learning machine used for these experiments since the estimated limiting performance expresses a characteristic of the data. The only requirements on the learning machines are that their capacity (VC-dimension) can be varied and can be made large, and that the learning machines with increasing capacity become capable of implementing *any* function.

We have applied the technique to data collected for the purpose of predicting failures in telecommunication channels of the AT&T network. We extracted information from one of AT&T's large databases that continuously logs performance parameters of the network. The character and amount of data comes to more material than humans can survey. The processing of the extracted information is therefore automated by learning machines.

We conjecture that the quality of the data imposes a limiting error rate on any learning machine of ~ 25%, so that even with an unlimited amount of data, and an arbitrarily complex learning machine, the performance for this task will not exceed ~ 75% correct. This conjecture is supported by experiments.

The relatively high noise-level of the data, which carries over to a poor performance of the trained classifier, is typical for many applications: the data collection was not designed for the task at hand and proved inadequate for constructing high performance classifiers.

2 Basic Concepts of Machine Learning

We can picture a learning machine as a device that takes an unknown input vector and produces an output value. More formally, it performs some mapping from an input space to an output space. The particular mapping it implements depends of the setting of the internal parameters of the learning machine. These parameters are adjusted during a learning phase so that the labels produced on the training set match, as well as possible, the labels provided. The number of patterns that the machine can match is loosely called the "capacity" of the machine. Generally, the capacity of a machine increases with the number of free parameters. After training is complete, the generalization ability of of the machine is estimated by its performance on a test set which the machine has never seen before.

The test and training error depend on both the the number of training examples l, the capacity h of the machine, and, of course, how well suited the machine is to implement the task at hand. Let us first discuss the typical behavior of the test and training error for a noise corrupted task as we vary h but keep the amount l of training data fixed. This scenario can, e.g., be obtained by increasing the number of hidden units in a neural network or increasing the number of codebook vectors in a Learning Vector Quantization algorithm [6]. Figure 1a) shows typical training and test error as a function of the capacity of the learning machine. For $h \ll l$ we have many fewer free parameters than training examples and the machine is over constrained. It does not have enough complexity to model the regularities of the training data, so both the training and test error are large (underfitting). As we increase h the machine can begin to fit the general trends in the data which carries over to the test set, so both error measures decline. Because the performance of the machine is optimized on only part of the full pattern space the test error will always be larger than the training error. As we continue to increase the capacity of the learning machine the error on the training set continues to decline, and eventually it reaches zero as we get enough free parameters to completely model the training set. The behavior of the error on the test set is different. Initially it decreases, but at some capacity, $h^\star$, it starts to rise. The rise occurs because the now ample resources of the training machine are applied to learning vagaries of the training

Figure 1: Errors as function of capacity and training set size. Figure 1a) shows characteristic plots of training and test error as a function of the learning machine capacity for fixed training set size. The test error reaches a minimum at $h = h^\star$ while the training error decreases as h increases. Figure 1b) shows the training and test errors at fixed h for varying l. The dotted line marks the asymptotic error E_∞ for infinite l. Figure 1c) shows the asymptotic error as a function of h. This error is limited from below by the intrinsic noise in the data.

set, which are not reproduced in the test set (overfitting). Notice how in Figure 1a) the optimal test error is achieved at a capacity $h^\star$ that is smaller than the capacity for which zero error is achieved on the training set. The learning machine with capacity $h^\star$ will typically commit errors on misclassified or outlying patterns of the training set.

We can alternatively discuss the error on the test and training set as a function of the training set size l for fixed capacity h of the learning machine. Typical behavior is sketched in Figure 1b). For small l we have enough free parameters to completely model the training set, so the training error is zero. Excess capacity is used by the learning machine to model details in the training set, leading to a large test error. As we increase the training set size l we train on more and more patterns so the test error declines. For some critical size of the training set, l_c, the machine can no longer model all the training patterns and the training error starts to rise. As we further increase l the irregularities of the individual training patterns smooth out and the parameters of the learning machine is more and more used to model the true underlying function. The test error declines, and asymptotically the training and test error reach the same error value E_∞. This error value is the limiting performance of the given learning machine to the task. In practice we never have the infinite amount of training data needed to achieve E_∞. However, recent theoretical calculations [8, 1, 2, 7, 5] and experimental results [3] have shown that we can estimate E_∞ by averaging the training and test errors for $l > l_c$. This means we can predict the optimal performance of a given machine.

For a given type of learning machine the value of the asymptotic error E_∞ of the machine depends on the quality of the data and the set of functions it can implement. The set of available functions increases with the capacity of the machine:

low capacity machines will typically exhibit a high asymptotic error due to a big difference between the true noise-free function of the patterns and the function implemented by the learning machine, but as we increase h this difference decreases. If the learning machine with increasing h becomes a *universal* machine capable of modeling *any* function the difference eventually reaches zero, so the asymptotic error E_∞ only measures the intrinsic noise level of the data. Once a capacity of the machine has been reached that matches the complexity of the true function no further improvement in E_∞ can be achieved. This is illustrated in Figure 1c). The intrinsic noise level of the data or the limiting performance of any learning machine may hence be estimated as the asymptotic value of E_∞ as obtained for asymptotically universal learning machines with increasing capacity applied to the task. This technique will be illustrated in the following section.

3 Experimental Results

In this section we estimate the limiting performance imposed by the data of any learning machine applied to the particular prediction task.

3.1 Task Description

To ensure the highest possible quality of service, the performance parameters of the AT&T network are constantly monitored. Due to the high complexity of the network this performance surveillance is mainly corrective: when certain measures exceed preset thresholds action is taken to maintain reliable, high quality service. These reorganizations can lead to short, minor impairments of the quality of the communication path. In contrast, the work reported here is preventive: our objective is to make use of the performance parameters to form predictions that are sufficiently accurate that preemptive repairs of the channels can be made during periods of low traffic.

In our study we have examined the characteristics of long-distance, 45 Mbits/s communication paths in the domestic AT&T network. The paths are specified from one city to another and may include different kinds of physical links to complete the paths. A path from New York City to Los Angeles might include both optical fiber and coaxial cable. To maintain high-quality service, particular links in a path may be switched out and replaced by other, redundant links.

There are two primary ways in which performance degradation is manifested in the path. First is the simple bit-error rate, the fraction of transmitted bits that are not correctly received at the termination of the path. Barring catastrophic failure (like a cable being cut), this error rate can be measured by examining the error-checking bits that are transmitted along with the data. The second instance of degradation, "framing error", is the failure of synchronization between the transmitter and receiver in a path. A framing error implies a high count of errored bits.

In order to better characterize the distribution of bit errors, several measures are historically used to quantify the path performance in a 15 minutes interval. These measures are:

Low-Rate The number of seconds with exactly 1 error.

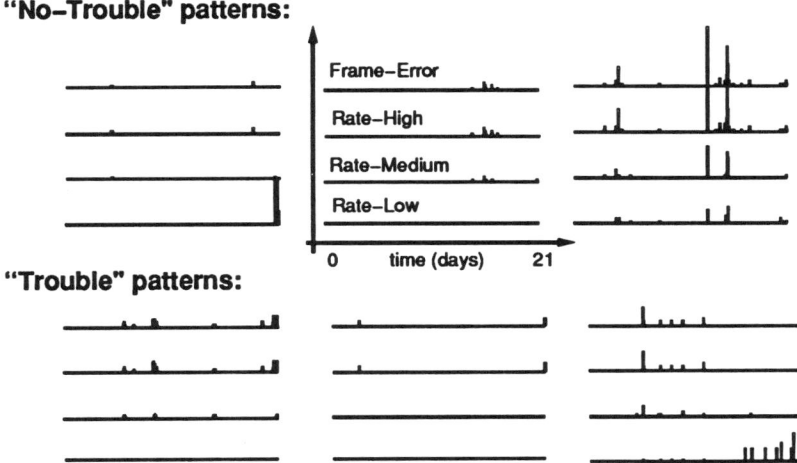

Figure 2: Errors as function of time. The 3 top patterns are members of the "No-Trouble" class. The 3 bottom ones are members of the "Trouble" class. Errors are here plotted as mean values over hours.

Medium-Rate The number of seconds with more than one but less than 45 errors.

High-Rate The number of seconds with 45 or more errors, corresponding to a bit error rate of at least 10^{-6}.

Frame-Error The number of seconds with a framing error. A second with a frame-error is always accompanied by a second of High-Rate error.

Although the number of seconds with the errors described above in principle could be as high as 900, any value greater than 255 is automatically clipped back to 255 so that each error measure value can be stored in 8 bits.

Daily data that include these measures are continuously logged in an AT&T database that we call Perf(ormance)Mon(itor). Since a channel is error free most of the time, an entry in the database is only made if its error measures for a 15 minute period exceed fixed low thresholds, e.g. 4 Low-Rate seconds, 1 Medium- or High-Rate second, or 1 Frame-Error. In our research we "mined" PerfMon to formulate a prediction strategy. We extracted examples of path histories 28 days long where the path at day 21 had at least 1 entry in the PerfMon database. We labeled the examples according to the error-measures over the next 7 days. If the channel exhibited a 15-minute period with at least 5 High-Rate seconds we labeled it as belonging to the class "Trouble". Otherwise we labeled it as member of "No-Trouble".

The length of the history- and future-windows are set somewhat arbitrarily. The history has to be long enough to capture the state of the path but short enough that our learning machine will run in a reasonable time. Also the longer the history the more likely the physical implementation of the path was modified so the error measures correspond to different media. Such error histories could in principle be eliminated from the extracted examples using the record of the repairs and changes of the network. The complexity of this database, however, hinders this filtering of examples. The future-window of 7 days was set as a design criterion by the network system engineers.

Examples of histories drawn from PerfMon are shown in Figure 2. Each group of traces in the figure includes plots of the 4 error measures previously described. The 3 groups at the top are examples that resulted in No-Trouble while the examples at the bottom resulted in Trouble. Notice how bursty and irregular the errors are, and how the overall level of Frame- and High-Rate errors for the Trouble class seems only slightly higher than for the No-Trouble class, indicating the difficulty of the classification task as defined from the database PerfMon. PerfMon constitutes, however, the only stored information about the state of a given channel in its entirety and thus all the knowledge on which one can base channel end-to-end predictions: it is impossible to install extra monitoring equipment to provide other than the 4 mentioned end-to-end error measures.

The above criteria for constructing examples and labels for 3 months of PerfMon data resulted in 16325 examples from about 900 different paths with 33.2% of the examples in the class Trouble. This means, that always guessing the label of the largest class, No-Trouble, would produce an error rate of about 33%.

3.2 Estimating Limiting Performance

The 16325 path examples were randomly divided into a training set of 14512 examples and a test set of 1813 examples. Care was taken to ensure that a path only contributes to one of the sets so the two sets were independent, and that the two sets had similar statistical properties.

Our input data has a time-resolution of 15 minutes. For the results reported here the 4 error measures of the patterns were subsampled to mean values over days yielding an input dimensionality of 4×21.

We performed two sets of independent experiments. In one experiment we used fully connected neural networks with one layer of hidden units. In the other we used LVQ learning machines with an increasing number of codebook vectors. Both choices of machine have two advantages: the capacity of the machine can easily be increased by adding more hidden units, and by increasing the number of hidden units or number of codebook vectors we can eventually model *any* mapping [4]. We first discuss the results with neural networks.

Baseline performance was obtained from a threshold classifier by averaging all the input signals and thresholding the result. The training data was used to adjust the single threshold parameter. With this classifier we obtained 32% error on the training set and 33% error on the test set. The small difference between the two error measures indicate statistically induced differences in the difficulty of the training and test sets. An analysis of the errors committed revealed that the performance of this classifier is almost identical to always guessing the label of the largest class "No-Trouble": close to 100% of the errors are false negative.

A linear classifier with about 200 weights (the network has two output units) obtained 28% error on the training set and 32% error on the test set.

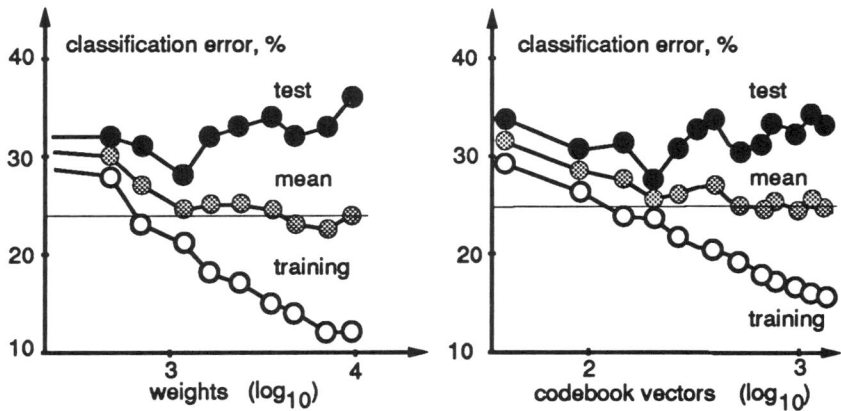

Figure 3: a) Measured classification errors for neural networks with increasing number of weights (capacity). The mean value between the test and training error estimates the performance of the given classifier trained with unlimited data. b) Measured classification errors for LVQ classifiers with increasing number of codebook vectors.

Further experiments exploited neural nets with one layer of respectively 3, 5, 7, 10, 15, 20, 30, and 40 hidden units. All our results are summarized in Figure 3a). This figure illustrates several points mentioned in the text above. As the complexity of the network increases, the training error decreases because the networks get more free parameters to memorize the data. Compare to Figure 1a). The test error also decreases at first, going through a minimum of 29% at the network with 5 hidden units. This network apparently has a capacity that best matches the amount and character of the available training data. For higher capacity the networks overfit the data at the expense of increased error on the test set.

Figure 3a) should also be compared to Figure 1c). In Figure 3a) we plotted approximate values of E_∞ for the various networks — the minimal error of the network to the given task. The values of E_∞ are estimated as the mean of the training and test errors. The value of E_∞ appears to flatten out around the network with 30 units, asymptotically reaching a value of 24% error.

An asymptotic E_∞-value of 25% was obtained from LVQ-experiments with increasing number of codebook vectors. These results are summarized in Figure 3b). We therefore conjecture that the intrinsic noise level of the task is about 25%, and this number is the limiting error rate imposed by the quality of the data on any learning machine applied to the task.

4 Conclusion

In this paper we have proposed a method for estimating the limits on performance imposed by the quality of the database on which a task is defined. The method involves a series of learning experiments. The extracted result is, however, independent of the choice of learning machine used for these experiments since the estimated limiting performance expresses a characteristic of the data. The only requirements on the learning machines are that their capacity can be varied and be made large, and that the machines with increasing capacity become capable of implementing *any* function. In this paper we have demonstrated the robustness of our method to the choice of classifiers: the result obtained with neural networks is in statistical agreement with the result obtained for LVQ classifiers.

Using the proposed method we have investigated how well prediction of upcoming trouble in a telecommunication path can be performed based on information extracted from a given database. The analysis has revealed a very high intrinsic noise level of the extracted information and demonstrated the inadequacy of the data to construct high performance classifiers. This study is typical for many applications where the data collection was not necessarily designed for the problem at hand.

Acknowledgments

We gratefully acknowledge Vladimir Vapnik who brought this application to the attention of the Holmdel authors. One of the authors (CC) would also like to thank Walter Dziama, Charlene Paul, Susan Blackwood, Eric Noel, and Harris Drucker for lengthy explanations and helpful discussions of the AT&T transport system.

References

[1] S. Bös, W. Kinzel, and M. Opper. The generalization ability of perceptrons with continuous output. *Physical Review E*, 47:1384–1391, 1993.

[2] Corinna Cortes. *Prediction of Generalization Ability in Learning Machines.* PhD thesis, University of Rochester, NY, 1993.

[3] Corinna Cortes, L. D. Jackel, Sara A. Solla, V. Vapnik, and John S. Denker. Learning curves: Asymptotic value and rate of convergence. In *Advances in Neural Information Processing Systems*, volume 6. Morgan Kaufman, 1994.

[4] G. Cybenko, K. Hornik, M. Stinchomb, and H. White. Multilayer feedforward neural networks are universal approximators. *Neural Networks*, 2:359–366, 1989.

[5] T. L. Fine. Statistical generalization and learning. Technical Report EE577, Cornell University, 1993.

[6] Teuvo Kohonen, György Barna, and Ronald Chrisley. Statistical pattern recognition with neural networks: Benchmarking studies. In *Proc. IEEE Int. Conf. on Neural Networks, IJCNN-88*, volume 1, pages I-61—I-68, 1988.

[7] N. Murata, S. Yoshizawa, and S. Amari. Learning curves, model selection, and complexity of neural networks. In *Advances in Neural Information Processing Systems*, volume 5, pages 607–614. Morgan Kaufman, 1992.

[8] H. S. Seung, H. Sompolinsky, and N. Tishby. Statistical mechanics of learning from examples. *Physical Review A*, 45:6056–6091, 1992.

Higher Order Statistical Decorrelation without Information Loss

Gustavo Deco
Siemens AG
Central Research
Otto-Hahn-Ring 6
81739 Munich
Germany

Wilfried Brauer
Technische Universität München
Institut für Informatik
Arcisstr. 21
80290 Munich
Germany

Abstract

A neural network learning paradigm based on information theory is proposed as a way to perform in an unsupervised fashion, redundancy reduction among the elements of the output layer without loss of information from the sensory input. The model developed performs nonlinear decorrelation up to higher orders of the cumulant tensors and results in probabilistically independent components of the output layer. This means that we don't need to assume Gaussian distribution neither at the input nor at the output. The theory presented is related to the unsupervised-learning theory of Barlow, which proposes redundancy reduction as the goal of cognition. When nonlinear units are used nonlinear principal component analysis is obtained. In this case nonlinear manifolds can be reduced to minimum dimension manifolds. If such units are used the network performs a generalized principal component analysis in the sense that non-Gaussian distributions can be linearly decorrelated and higher orders of the correlation tensors are also taken into account. The basic structure of the architecture involves a general transformation that is volume conserving and therefore the entropy, yielding a map without loss of information. Minimization of the mutual information among the output neurons eliminates the redundancy between the outputs and results in statistical decorrelation of the extracted features. This is known as factorial learning.

1 INTRODUCTION

One of the most important theories of feature extraction is the one proposed by Barlow (1989). Barlow describes the process of cognition as a preprocessing of the sensorial information performed by the nervous system in order to extract the statistically relevant and independent features of the inputs without loosing information. This means that the brain should statistically decorrelate the extracted information. As a learning strategy Barlow (1989) formulated the principle of redundancy reduction. This kind of learning is called factorial learning. Recently Atick and Redlich (1992) and Redlich (1993) concentrate on the original idea of Barlow yielding a very interesting formulation of early visual processing and factorial learning. Redlich (1993) reduces redundancy at the input by using a network structure which is a reversible cellular automaton and therefore guarantees the conservation of information in the transformation between input and output. Some nonlinear extensions of PCA for decorrelation of sensorial input signals were recently introduced. These follow very closely Barlow's original ideas of unsupervised learning. Redlich (1993) use similar information theoretic concepts and reversible cellular automata architectures in order to define how nonlinear decorrelation can be performed. The aim of our work is to formulate a neural network architecture and a novel learning paradigm that performs Barlow's unsupervised learning in the most general fashion. The basic idea is to define an architecture that assures perfect transmission without loss of information. Consequently the nonlinear transformation defined by the neural architecture is always bijective. The architecture performs a volume-conserving transformation (determinant of the Jacobian matrix is equal one). As a particular case we can derive the reversible cellular automata architecture proposed by Redlich (1993). The learning paradigm is defined so that the components of the output signal are statistically decorrelated. Due to the fact that the output distribution is not necessarily Gaussian, even if the input is Gaussian, we perform a cumulant expansion of the output distribution and find the rules that should be satisfied by the higher order correlation tensors in order to be decorrelated.

2 THEORETICAL FORMALISM

Let us consider an input vector $\vec{x}$ of dimensionality d with components distributed according to the probability distribution $P(\vec{x})$, which is not factorial, i.e. the components of $\vec{x}$ are correlated. The goal of Barlow's unsupervised learning rule is to find a transformation

$$\vec{y} = \vec{F}(\vec{x}) \tag{2.1}$$

such that the components of the output vector d-dimensional $\vec{y}$ are statistically decorrelated.

This means that the probability distributions of the components y_i are independent and therefore,

$$P(\vec{y}) = \prod_i^d P(y_i). \tag{2.2}$$

The objective of factorial learning is to find a neural network, which performs the transformation $\vec{F}(\ )$ such that the joint probability distribution $P(\vec{y})$ of the output signals is factorized as in eq. (2.2). In order to implement factorial learning, the information contained in the input should be transferred to the output neurons without loss but, the probability distribution of the output neurons should be statistically decorrelated. Let us now define these facts from the information theory perspective. The first aspect is to assure the entropy is conserved, i.e.

$$H(\vec{x}) = H(\vec{y}) \qquad (2.3)$$

where the symbol $H(\vec{a})$ denotes the entropy of $\vec{a}$ and $H(\vec{a}/\vec{b})$ the conditional entropy of $\vec{a}$ given $\vec{b}$. One way to achieve this goal is to construct an architecture that independently of its synaptic parameters satisfies always eq. (2.3). Thus the architecture will conserve information or entropy. The transmitted entropy satisfies

$$H(\vec{y}) \leq H(\vec{x}) + \int P(\vec{x}) \ln\left(\det\left(\frac{\partial \vec{F}}{\partial \vec{x}}\right)\right) d\vec{x} \qquad (2.4)$$

where equality holds only if $\vec{F}$ is bijective, i.e. reversible. Conservation of information and bijectivity is assured if the neural transformation conserves the volume, which mathematically can be expressed by the fact that the Jacobian of the transformation should have determinant unity. In section 3 we formulate an architecture that always conserves the entropy. Let us now concentrate on the main aspect of factorial learning, namely the decorrelation of the output components. Here the problem is to find a volume-conserving transformation that satisfies eq. (2.2). The major problem is that the distribution of the output signal will not necessarily be Gaussian. Therefore it is impossible to use the technique of minimizing the mutual information between the components of the output as done by Redlich (1993). The only way to decorrelate non-Gaussian distributions is to expand the distribution in higher orders of the correlation matrix and impose the independence condition of eq. (2.2). In order to achieve this we propose to use a cumulant expansion of the output distribution. Let us define the Fourier transform of the output distribution,

$$\phi(\vec{K}) = \int d\vec{y}\, e^{i(\vec{K}\cdot\vec{y})} P(\vec{y}); \; \phi(K_i) = \int dy_i\, e^{i(K_i \cdot y_i)} P(y_i) \qquad (2.5)$$

The cumulant expansion of a distribution is (Papoulis, 1991)

$$\phi(\vec{K}) = e^{\sum_{n=1}^{\infty} \frac{i^n}{n!} \sum_{i_1,i_2,\ldots,i_n} \aleph_{i_1,i_2,\ldots,i_n} K_{i_1} K_{i_2} \ldots K_{i_n}} \qquad \phi(K_i) = e^{\sum_{n=1}^{\infty} \frac{i^n}{n!} \aleph_i^{(n)} K_i^n} \qquad (2.6)$$

In the Fourier space the independence condition is given by (Papoulis, 1991)

$$\phi(\vec{K}) = \prod_i \phi(K_i) \qquad (2.7)$$

which is equivalent to

$$\ln(\phi(\vec{K})) = \ln\left(\prod_i \phi(K_i)\right) = \sum_i \ln(\phi(K_i)) \qquad (2.8)$$

Putting eq. (2.8) and the cumulant expansions of eq. (2.6) together, we obtain that in the case of independence the following equality is satisfied

$$\sum_{n=1}^{\infty} \frac{i^n}{n!} \sum_{i_1,i_2,\ldots,i_n} \aleph_{i_1,i_2,\ldots,i_n} K_{i_1} K_{i_2} \ldots K_{i_n} = \sum_{i=1}^{d} \sum_{n=1}^{\infty} \frac{i^n}{n!} \aleph_i^{(n)} K_i^n \qquad (2.9)$$

In both expansions we will only consider the first four cumulants. After an extra transformation

$$\vec{y}' = \vec{y} - \overline{(\vec{y})} \qquad (2.10)$$

to remove the bias $\overline{(\vec{y})}$, we can rewrite eq. (2.9) using the cumulants expression derived in the Papoulius (1991):

$$-\frac{1}{2}\sum_{i,j}K_iK_j\{C_{ij}-C_i^{(2)}\delta_{ij}\} - \frac{i}{6}\sum_{i,j,k}K_iK_jK_k\{C_{ijk}-C_i^{(3)}\delta_{ijk}\}$$
$$+\frac{1}{24}\sum_{i,j,k,l}K_iK_jK_kK_l\{(C_{ijkl}-3C_{ij}C_{kl})-(C_i^{(4)}-3(C_i^{(2)})^2)\delta_{ijkl}\} = 0 \quad (2.11)$$

Equation (2.11) should be satisfied for all values of $\vec{K}$. The multidimensional correlation tensors $C_{i...j}$ and the one-dimensional higher order moments $C_i^{(n)}$ are given by

$$C_{i...j} = \int d\vec{y}'\, P(\vec{y}')\, y'_i...y'_j\,; \quad C_i^{(n)} = \int dy'_i\, P(y'_i)\, (y'_i) \quad (2.12)$$

The $\delta_{i...j}$ denotes Kroenecker's delta. Due to the fact that eq. (2.11) should be satisfied for all $\vec{K}$, all coefficients in each summation of eq. (2.11) must be zero. This means that

$$C_{ij} = 0, \quad if(i \neq j) \quad (2.13)$$
$$C_{ijk} = 0, \quad if(i \neq j \vee i \neq k) \quad (2.14)$$
$$C_{ijkl} = 0, \quad if(\{i \neq j \vee i \neq k \vee i \neq l\} \wedge \neg L) \quad (2.15)$$
$$C_{iijj} - C_{ii}C_{jj} = 0, \quad if(i \neq j)\,. \quad (2.16)$$

In eq. (2.15) L is the logical expression

$$L = \{(i = j \wedge k = l \wedge j \neq k) \vee (i = k \wedge j = l \wedge i \neq j) \vee (i = l \wedge j = k \wedge i \neq j)\}, \quad (2.17)$$

which excludes the cases considered in eq. (2.16). The conditions of independence given by eqs. (2.13-2.16) can be achieved by minimization of the cost function

$$E = \alpha\sum_{i<j}C_{ij}^2 + \beta\sum_{i<j\leq k}C_{ijk}^2 + \gamma\sum_{i<j\leq k\leq l}C_{ijkl}^2 + \delta\sum_{i<j}(C_{iijj}-C_{ii}C_{jj})^2 \quad (2.18)$$

where $\alpha, \beta, \gamma, \delta$ are the inverse of the number of elements in each summation respectively.

In conclusion, minimizing the cost given by eq. (2.18) with a volume-conserving network, we achieve nonlinear decorrelation of non-Gaussian distributions. It is very easy to test wether a factorized probability distribution (eq. 2.2) satisfies the eqs. (2.13-2.16). As a particular case if only second order terms are used in the cumulant expansion, the learning rule reduces to eq. (2.13), which expresses nothing more than the diagonalization of the second order covariance matrix. In this case, by anti-transforming the cumulant expansion of the Fourier transform of the distribution, we obtain a Gaussian distribution. Diagonalization of the covariance matrix decorrelates statistically the components of the output only if we assume a Gaussian distribution of the outputs. In general the distribution of the output is not Gaussian and therefore higher orders of the cumulant expansion should be taken into account, yielding the learning rule conditions eqs. (2.13-2.16) (up to fourth order, generalization to higher orders is straightforward). In the case of Gaussian distribution, minimization of the sum of the variances at each output leads to statistically decorrelation. This fact has a nice information theoretic background namely the minimization of the mutual information between the output components. Statistical independence as expressed in eq. (2.2) is equivalent to (Atick and Redlich, 1992)

$$MH = \sum_j H(y_j) - H(\underset{\sim}{y}) = 0 \quad (2.19)$$

This means that in order to minimize the redundancy at the output we minimize the mutual information between the different components of the output vector. Due to the fact that the volume-conserving structure of the neural network conserves the entropy, the minimization of MH reduces to the minimization of $\sum_j H(y_j)$.

3 VOLUME-CONSERVING ARCHITECTURE AND LEARNING RULE

In this section we define a neural network architecture that is volume-conserving and therefore can be used for the implementation of the learning rules described in the last section. Figure 1.a shows the basic architecture of one layer. The dimensionality of input and output layer is the same and equal to d. A similar architecture was proposed by Redlich (1993b) using the theory of reversible cellular automata.

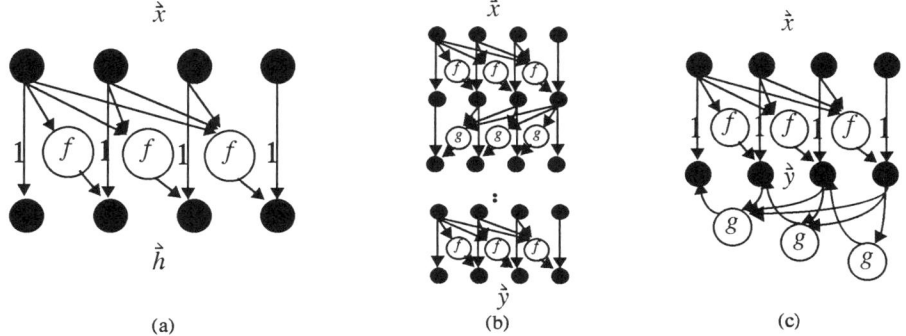

Figure 1: Volume-conserving Neural Architectures.

The analytical definition of the transformation defined by this architecture can be written as,

$$y_i = x_i + f_i(x_0, ..., x_j, \vec{\omega}_i), \qquad \text{with } j < i \qquad (3.1)$$

where $\vec{\omega}_i$ represents a set of parameters of the function f_i. Note that independently of the functions f_i the network is always volume-conserving. In particular f_i can be calculated by another neural network, by a sigmoid neuron, by polynomials (higher order neurons), etc. Due to the asymmetric dependence on the input variables and the direct connections with weights equal to 1 between corresponding components of input and output neurons, the Jacobian matrix of the transformation defined in eq. (3.1) is an upper triangular matrix with diagonal elements all equal to one, yielding a determinant equal to one. A network with inverted asymmetry also can be defined as

$$y_i = x_i + g_i(x_j, ..., x_d, \vec{\theta}_i), \qquad \text{with } i < j \qquad (3.2)$$

corresponding to a lower triangular Jacobian matrix with diagonal elements all equal to one, being therefore volume-conserving. The vectors $\vec{\theta}_i$ represent the parameters of functions g_i. In order to yield a general nonlinear transformation from inputs to outputs (without asymmetric dependences) it is possible to build a multilayer architecture like the one shown in Fig. 1.b, which involves mixed versions of networks described by eq. (3.1) and eq. (3.2), respectively. Due to the fact that successive application of volume-conserving transformation is also volume-conserving, the multilayer architecture is also volume-conserving. In the two-layer case (Fig. 1.c) the second layer can be interpreted as asymmetric lateral connections between the neurons of the first layer. However, in our case the feedforward connections between input layer and first layer are also asymmetric. As demonstrated in the last section, we minimize a cost function E to decorrelate nonlinearly correlated non-Gaussian inputs. Let us analyze for simplicity a two-layer architecture (Fig. 1.c) with the first layer given by eq. (3.1) and the second layer by eq. (3.2). Let us denote the output of the hidden layer by $\vec{h}$ and use it as input of eq. (3.2) with output $\vec{y}$. The extension to multilayer architectures is straightforward. The learning rule can be easily expressed by gradient descent method:

$$\vec{\theta}_i = \vec{\theta}_i - \eta \frac{\partial E}{\partial \vec{\theta}_i} \quad ; \quad \vec{\omega}_i = \vec{\omega}_i - \eta \frac{\partial E}{\partial \vec{\omega}_i} \tag{3.3}$$

In order to calculate the derivative of the cost functions we need

$$\frac{C_{i...j}}{\Theta} = \frac{1}{N} \sum_P \{ \frac{\partial}{\partial \Theta}(y_i - \bar{y}_i) \dots (y_j - \bar{y}_j) + (y_i - \bar{y}_i) \dots \frac{\partial}{\partial \Theta}(y_j - \bar{y}_j) \; ; \; \frac{\partial \bar{y}_i}{\partial \Theta} = \frac{1}{N} \sum_P \{ \frac{\partial}{\partial \Theta}(y_i) \} \tag{3.4}$$

where Θ represents the parameters $\vec{\theta}_i$ and $\vec{\omega}_i$. The sums in both equations extend over the N training patterns. The gradients of the different outputs are

$$\frac{\partial}{\partial \vec{\theta}_i} y_i = \frac{\partial}{\partial \vec{\theta}_i} g_i \; ; \; \frac{\partial}{\partial \vec{\omega}_i} y_k = (\frac{\partial}{\partial h_i} g_k)(\frac{\partial}{\partial \vec{\omega}_i} f_i) \delta_{i>k} + (\frac{\partial}{\partial \vec{\omega}_i} f_i) \tag{3.5}$$

where $\delta_{i>k}$ is equal to 1 if $i > k$ and 0 otherwise. In this paper we choose a polynomial form for the functions f and g. This model involves higher order neurons. In this case each function f_i or g_i is a product of polynomial functions of the inputs. The update equations are given by

$$h_i = \prod_{j=0}^{i-1} \left(\sum_{r=0}^{R} \omega_{ijr} x_j^r \right) \; ; \; y_i = \prod_{j=i+1}^{d} \left(\sum_{r=0}^{R} \theta_{ijr} h_j^r \right) \tag{3.6}$$

where R is the order of the polynomial used. In this case the two-layer architecture is a higher order network with a general volume-conserving structure. The derivatives involved in the learning rule are given by

$$\frac{\partial}{\partial \theta_{ijr}} y_k = \delta_{ki} \delta_{j>i} h_j^r \left(\frac{y_i}{\sum_{r=0}^{R} \theta_{ijr} h_j^r} \right) \; ;$$

$$\frac{\partial}{\partial \omega_{ijr}} y_k = \left(\left(\frac{y_k}{\sum_{r=0}^{R} \theta_{kir} h_i^r} \right) \left(\sum_{r=0}^{R} \theta_{kir} r h_i^{r-1} \right) \delta_{i>k} + \delta_{ik} \right) \delta_{j<i} x_j^r \left(\frac{h_i}{\sum_{r=0}^{R} \omega_{ijr} x_j^r} \right) \tag{3.7}$$

4 RESULTS AND SIMULATIONS

We will present herein two different experiments using the architecture defined in this paper. The input space in all experiments is two-dimensional in order to show graphically the results and effects of the presented model. The experiments aim at learning noisy non-linear polynomial and rational curves. Figure 2.a and 2.b plot the input and output space of the second experiment after training is finished, respectively. In this case the noisy logistic map was used to generate the input:

$$x_2 = 4x_1(1-x_1) + \upsilon \qquad (4.1)$$

where υ introduces 1% Gaussian noise. In this case a one-layer polynomial network with $R = 2$ was used. The learning constant was $\eta = 0.01$ and 20000 iterations of training were performed. The result of Fig. 2.b is remarkable. The volume-conserving network decorrelated the output space extracting the strong nonlinear correlation that generated the curve in the input space. This means that after training only one coordinate is important to describe the curve.

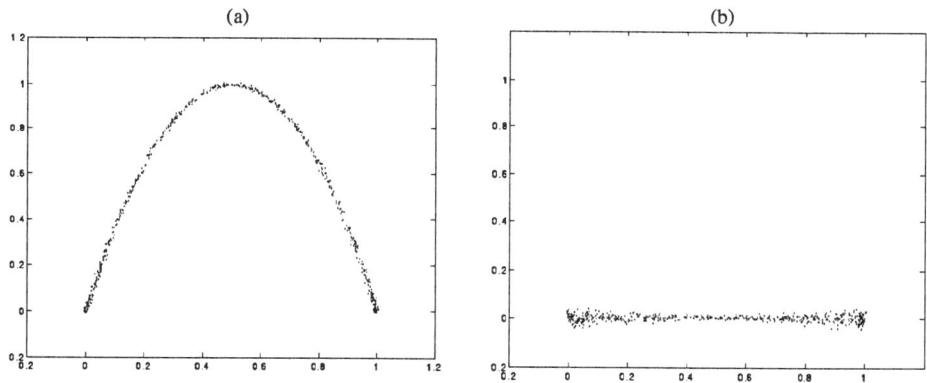

Figure 2: Input and Output space distribution after training with a one-layer polynomial volume-conserving network of order for the logistic map. (a) input space; (b) output space.

The whole information was compressed into the first coordinate of the output. This is the generalization of data compression normally performed by using linear PCA (also called Karhunen-Loewe transformation). The next experiment is similar, but in this case a two-layer network of order $R = 4$ was used. The input space is given by the rational function

$$x_2 = 0.2x_1 + \frac{x_1^3}{(1+x_1^2)} + \upsilon \qquad (4.2)$$

where x_1 and υ are as in the last case. The results are shown in Fig. 4.a (input space) and Fig. 4.b (output space). Fig. 4.c shows the evolution of the four summands of eq (2.18) during learning. It is important to remark that at the beginning the tensors of second and third order are equally important. During learning all summands are simultaneously minimized, resulting in a statistically decorrelated output. The training was performed during 20000 iterations and the learning constant was $\eta = 0.005$.

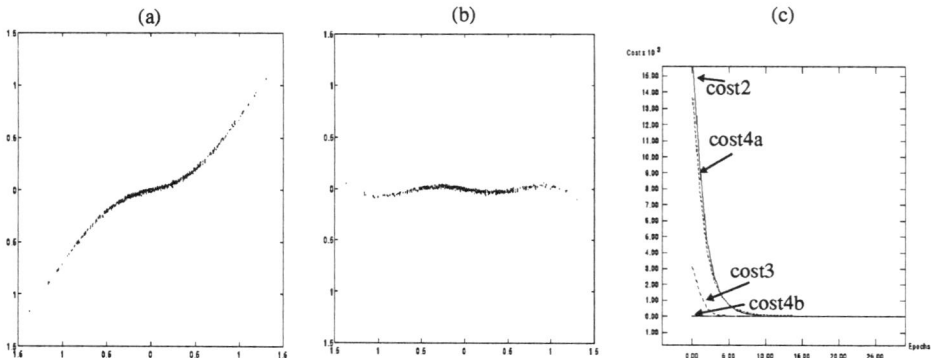

Figure 4: Input and Output space distribution after training with a two-layer polynomial volume-conserving network of order for the noisy curve of eq. (4.2). (a) input space; (b) output space (c) Development of the four summands of the cost function (eq. 2.18) during learning: (cost 2) first summand (second order correlation tensor); (cost 3) second summand (third correlation order tensor); (cost 4a) third summand (fourth order correlation tensor); (cost4b) fourth summand (fourth order correlation tensor).

5 CONCLUSIONS

We proposed a unsupervised neural paradigm, which is based on Information Theory. The algorithm performs redundancy reduction among the elements of the output layer without loosing information, as the data is sent through the network. The model developed performs a generalization of Barlow's unsupervised learning, which consists in nonlinear decorrelation up to higher orders of the cumulant tensors. After training the components of the output layer are statistically independent. Due to the use of higher order cumulant expansion arbitrary non-Gaussian distributions can be rigorously handled. When nonlinear units are used nonlinear principal component analysis is obtained. In this case nonlinear manifolds can be reduced to a minimum dimension manifolds. When linear units are used, the network performs a generalized principal component analysis in the sense that non-Gaussian distribution can be linearly decorrelated.This paper generalizes previous works on factorial learning in two ways: the architecture performs a general nonlinear transformation without loss of information and the decorrelation is performed without assuming Gaussian distributions.

References:

H. Barlow. (1989) Unsupervised Learning. *Neural Computation*, 1, 295-311.

A. Papoulis. (1991) *Probability, Random Variables, and Stochastic Processes.* 3. Edition, McGraw-Hill, New York.

A. N. Redlich. (1993) Supervised Factorial Learning. *Neural Computation*, 5, 750-766.

Hyperparameters, Evidence and Generalisation for an Unrealisable Rule

Glenn Marion and David Saad
glenny@ed.ac.uk, D.Saad@ed.ac.uk
Department of Physics, University of Edinburgh,
Edinburgh, EH9 3JZ, U.K.

Abstract

Using a statistical mechanical formalism we calculate the evidence, generalisation error and consistency measure for a linear perceptron trained and tested on a set of examples generated by a non linear teacher. The teacher is said to be unrealisable because the student can never model it without error. Our model allows us to interpolate between the known case of a linear teacher, and an unrealisable, nonlinear teacher. A comparison of the hyperparameters which maximise the evidence with those that optimise the performance measures reveals that, in the non-linear case, the evidence procedure is a misleading guide to optimising performance. Finally, we explore the extent to which the evidence procedure is unreliable and find that, despite being sub-optimal, in some circumstances it might be a useful method for fixing the hyperparameters.

1 INTRODUCTION

The analysis of supervised learning or learning from examples is a major field of research within neural networks. In general, we have a probabilistic[1] *teacher*, which maps an N dimensional input vector $\mathbf{x}$ to output $y_t(\mathbf{x})$ according to some distribution $P(y_t \mid \mathbf{x})$. We are supplied with a data set $\mathcal{D} = (\{y_t(\mathbf{x}^\mu), \mathbf{x}^\mu\} : \mu = 1..p)$ generated from $P(y_t \mid \mathbf{x})$ by independently sampling the input distribution, $P(\mathbf{x})$, p times. One attempts to optimise a model mapping (*a student*), parameterised by

---
[1]This accommodates teachers with deterministic output corrupted by noise.

some vector **w**, with respect to the underlying teacher. The training error $E_\mathbf{w}(\mathcal{D})$ is some measure of the difference between the student and the teacher outputs over the set $\mathcal{D}$. Simply minimising the training error leads to the problem of *over-fitting*. In order to make successful predictions out-with the set $\mathcal{D}$ it is essential to have some prior preference for particular rules. *Occams razor* is an expression of our preference for the simplest rules which account for the data. Clearly $E_\mathbf{w}(\mathcal{D})$ is an unsatisfactory performance measure since it is limited to the training examples. Very often we are interested in the students ability to model a random example drawn from $P(y_t \mid \mathbf{x})P(\mathbf{x})$, but not necessarily in the training set, one measure of this performance is the generalisation error. It is also desirable to predict, or estimate, the level of this error. The teacher is said to be an *unrealisable rule*, for the student in question, if the minimum generalisation error is non-zero.

One can consider the Supervised Learning Paradigm within the context of Bayesian Inference. In particular MacKay [MacKay 92(a)] advocates the *evidence procedure* as a 'principled' method which, in some situations, does seem to improve performance [Thodberg 93]. However, in others, as MacKay points out the evidence procedure can be misleading [MacKay 92(b)].

In this paper we do not seek to comment on the validity of of the evidence procedure as an approximation to Hierarchical Bayes (see for example [Wolpert and Strauss 94]). Rather, we ask which performance measures do we seek to optimise and under what conditions will the evidence procedure optimise them? Theoretical results have been obtained for a linear perceptron trained on data produced by a linear perceptron [Bruce and Saad 94]. They suggest that the evidence procedure is a useful guide to optimising the learning algorithm's performance.

In what follows we examine the evidence procedure for the case of a linear perceptron learning a non linear teacher. In the next section we review the Bayesian scheme and define the evidence and the relevant performance measures. In section 3 we introduce our student and teacher and discuss the calculation. Finally, in section 4 we examine the extent to which the evidence procedure optimises performance.

2 BAYESIAN FORMALISM

2.1 THE EVIDENCE

If we take $E_\mathbf{w}(\mathcal{D})$ to be the usual sum squared error and assume that our data is corrupted by Gaussian noise with variance $1/2\beta$ then the probability, or *likelihood*, of the data($\mathcal{D}$) being produced given the model **w** and β is $P(D \mid \beta, \mathbf{w}) \propto e^{-\beta E_\mathbf{w}(\mathcal{D})}$. In order to incorporate Occams Razor we also assume a prior distribution on the teacher rules, that is, we believe *a priori* in some rules more strongly than others. Specifically we believe that $P(\mathbf{w} \mid \gamma) \propto e^{-\gamma C(\mathbf{w})}$. Multiplying the likelihood by the prior we obtain the post training or student distribution[2] $P(\mathbf{w} \mid \mathcal{D}, \gamma, \beta) \propto e^{-\beta E_\mathbf{w}(\mathcal{D}) - \gamma C(\mathbf{w})}$. It is clear that the most probable model $\mathbf{w}^*$ is given by minimising the composite cost function $\beta E_\mathbf{w}(\mathcal{D}) + \gamma C(\mathbf{w})$ with respect to the weights (**w**). This formalises the trade off between fitting the data and minimising student complexity. In this sense the Bayesian viewpoint coincides with the usual *backprop* standpoint.

---

[2]Integrating this over β and γ gives us the posterior $P(\mathbf{w} \mid \mathcal{D})$.

In fact, it should be noted that stochastic minimisation can also give rise to the same post training distribution [Seung *et al* 92]. The parameters β and γ are known as the *hyperparameters*. Here we consider $C(\mathbf{w}) = \mathbf{w}^t\mathbf{w}$ in which case γ is termed the weight decay.

The evidence is the normalisation constant in the above expression for the post training distribution.

$$P(\mathcal{D} \mid \gamma, \beta) = \int \prod_j dw_j \, P(\mathcal{D} \mid \beta, \mathbf{w}) P(\mathbf{w} \mid \gamma)$$

That is, the probability of the data set ($\mathcal{D}$) given the hyperparameters. The **evidence procedure** fixes the hyperparameters to the values that maximise this probability.

2.2 THE PERFORMANCE MEASURES

Many performance measures have been introduced in the literature (See *e.g.*, [Krogh and Hertz 92] and [Seung *et al* 92]). Here, we consider the squared difference between the average (over the post training distribution) of the student output $\langle y_s(\mathbf{x}) \rangle_\mathbf{w}$ and that of the teacher, $y_t(\mathbf{x})$, averaged over all possible test questions and teacher outputs, $P(y_t, \mathbf{x})$ and finally over all possible sets of data, $\mathcal{D}$.

$$\epsilon_g = \langle (y_t(\mathbf{x}) - \langle y_s(\mathbf{x})\rangle_\mathbf{w})^2 \rangle_{P(\mathbf{x},y_t),\mathcal{D}}$$

This is equivalent to the generalisation error given by Krogh and Hertz.

Another factor we can consider is the variance of the output over the student distribution $\langle \{y_s(\mathbf{x}) - \langle y_s(\mathbf{x})\rangle_\mathbf{w}\}^2 \rangle_{\mathbf{w},P(\mathbf{x})}$. This gives us a measure of the confidence we should have in our post training distribution and could possibly be calculated if we could estimate the input distribution $P(\mathbf{x})$. Here we extend Bruce and Saad's definition [Bruce and Saad 94] of the consistency measure δ_c to include unrealisable rules by adding the asymptotic error $\epsilon_g^\infty = \lim_{p \to \infty} \epsilon_g$,

$$\delta_c = \langle \{y_s(\mathbf{x}) - \langle y_s(\mathbf{x})\rangle_\mathbf{w}\}^2 \rangle_{\mathbf{w},P(\mathbf{x}),\mathcal{D}} - \epsilon_g + \epsilon_g^\infty$$

We regard $\delta_c = 0$ as optimal since then the variance over our student distribution is an accurate prediction of the decaying part of the generalisation error.

We can consider both these performance measures as *objective* functions measuring the students ability to mimic the underlying teacher. Clearly, they can only be calculated in theory and perhaps, estimated in practice. In contrast, the evidence is only a function of our assumptions and the data and the evidence procedure is, therefore, a practical method of setting the hyperparameters.

3 THE MODEL

In our model the student is simply a linear perceptron. The output for an input vector $\mathbf{x}^\mu$ is given by $y_s^\mu = \mathbf{w}.\mathbf{x}^\mu/\sqrt{N}$. The examples, against which the student is trained and tested, are produced by sampling the input distribution, $P(\mathbf{x})$ and then generating outputs from the distribution,

$$P(y_t \mid \mathbf{x}) = \sum_{\Omega=1}^n \frac{P(y_t \mid \mathbf{x}, \Omega) P(\mathbf{x} \mid \Omega) P_\Omega^t}{\sum_{\Omega=1}^n P(\Omega) P(\mathbf{x} \mid \Omega)}$$

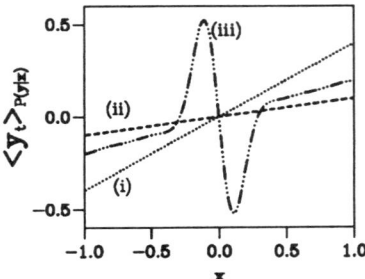

Figure 1: A 2-teacher in 1D : The average output $\langle y_t \rangle_{P(y|x)}$ (i) for $D_w = 0$, (ii) for $D_w > 0$ ($\sigma_{x_1} = \sigma_{x_2}$) and (iii) with $D_w > 0$ ($\sigma_{x_1} \neq \sigma_{x_2}$).

where $P(y_t \mid \mathbf{x}, \Omega) \propto \exp([y_t - \mathbf{w}^\Omega . \mathbf{x}]^2 / 2\sigma^2)$, $P(\mathbf{x} \mid \Omega)$ is $\mathrm{N}(\bar{a}_\Omega, \sigma^2_{x_\Omega})$ [3] and P^t_Ω is chosen such that $\sum_{\Omega=1}^{n} P^t_\Omega = 1$. Thus, each component in the sum is a linear perceptron, whose output is corrupted by Gaussian noise of variance σ^2, and we refer to this teacher as an n-teacher.

In what follows, for simplicity, we consider a two teacher ($n=2$) with $\bar{a}_\Omega = 0$. The parameter $D_w = \frac{1}{N} |\mathbf{w}^1 - \mathbf{w}^2|^2$ and the input distribution determine the form of the teacher. This is shown in Figure 1. which displays the average output of a 2-teacher with one dimensional input vector. For $\sigma_{x_1} = \sigma_{x_2}$, D_w controls the variance about a linear mean output, and for fixed $\sigma_{x_1} \neq \sigma_{x_2}$, D_w controls the nonlinearity of the teacher. In the latter case, in the large N limit the variance of $P(y_t \mid \mathbf{x})$ is zero.

We can now explicitly write the evidence and perform the integration over the student parameters (*over weights*). Taking the logarithm of the resulting expression leads to $\ln P(\mathcal{D} \mid \lambda, \beta) = -Nf(\mathcal{D})$ where the f is analogous to a free energy in statistical physics.

$$-f(\mathcal{D}) = \frac{1}{2} \ln \frac{\lambda}{\pi} + \frac{\alpha}{2} \ln \frac{\beta}{\pi} + \frac{1}{2N} \ln \det g + \frac{1}{2} \ln 2\pi + \frac{1}{N} \rho_j g_{jk} \rho_k - \Theta$$

and,

$$\rho_j = \{A^\Omega_{jk} w^\Omega_k + \frac{1}{\sqrt{N}} \eta^{\mu\Omega} x^{\mu\Omega}_j\}$$

$$\Theta = \frac{\beta}{N} \{A^\Omega_{jk} w^\Omega_j w^\Omega_k + \frac{2}{\sqrt{N}} \eta^{\mu\Omega} x^{\mu\Omega}_j w^\Omega_j + \eta^{\mu\Omega} \eta^{\mu\Omega}\}$$

$$g^{-1}_{jk} = \sum_{\Omega=1}^{n} A^\Omega_{jk} + \lambda \delta_{jk} \quad A^\Omega_{jk} = \frac{1}{N} x^{\mu\Omega}_j x^{\mu\Omega}_k \quad \lambda = \frac{\gamma}{\beta} \quad \alpha = \frac{p}{N}$$

Here we are using the convention that summations are implied where repeated indices occur.

---
[3] Where $\mathrm{N}(\bar{\mathbf{x}}, \sigma^2)$ denotes a normal distribution with mean $\bar{\mathbf{x}}$ and variance σ^2.

The performance measures for this model are

$$\epsilon_g = \langle \frac{\sigma_{\Omega x}^2}{N} P_\Omega^t \{w_j^\Omega w_j^\Omega - 2w_j^\Omega \langle w_j \rangle_w + \langle w_j \rangle_w^2 \} \rangle_\mathcal{D}$$

$$\delta_c = \frac{\sigma_{x\text{eff}}^2}{N\beta} \langle trg \rangle_\mathcal{D} - \epsilon_g + \epsilon_g^\infty$$

where, $\langle w_j \rangle_w = \rho_k g_{kj}$ and $\sigma_{x\text{eff}}^2 = P_\Omega^t \sigma_{x_\Omega}^2$

In order to pursue the calculation we consider the average of $f(\mathcal{D})$ over all possible data sets just as, earlier, we defined our performance measures as averages over all data sets. This is some what artificial as we would normally be able to calculate $f(\mathcal{D})$ and be interested in the generalisation error for our learning algorithm given a particular instance of the data. However, here we consider the thermodynamic limit (i.e., $N, p \to \infty$ s.t. $\alpha = p/N = const.$) in which, due to our sampling assumptions, the behaviours for typical examples of $\mathcal{D}$ coincide with that of the average. Details of the calculation will be published else where [Marion and Saad 95].

4 RESULTS AND DISCUSSION

We can now examine the evidence and the performance measures for our unlearnable problem. We note that in two limits we recover the learnable, linear teacher, case. Specifically if the probability of picking one of the component teachers is zero or if both component teacher vectors are aligned. In what follows we set $P_1^t = P_2^t$ and normalise the components of the teacher such that $|\mathbf{w}^\Omega| = 1$.

Firstly let us consider the performance measures. The asymptotic value of both ϵ_g and $|\delta_c|$ for large α is $P_1^t P_2^t \sigma_{x_1}^2 \sigma_{x_2}^2 D_w / \sigma_{x\text{eff}}^2$. This is the minimum generalisation error attainable and reflects the effective noise level due to the mismatch between student and teacher.

We note here that the generalisation error is a function of λ rather than β and γ independently. Figure 2a shows the generalisation error plotted against α. The addition of unlearnability ($Dw > 0$) has a similar effect to the addition of noise on the examples. The appearance of the *hump* can be easily understood; If there is no noise or λ is large enough then there is a steady reduction in ϵ_g. However, if this is not so then for small α the student learns this effective noise and the generalisation error increases with α. As the student gets more examples the effects of the noise begin to average out and the student starts to learn the rule. The point at which the generalisation error starts to decrease is influenced by the effective noise level and the prior constraint. Figure 2b shows the absolute value of the consistency measure v's α for non-optimal β. Again we see that unlearnability acts as an effective noise. For a few examples with λ small or with large effective noise the student distribution is narrowed until the δ_c is zero. However, the generalisation error is still increasing (as described above) and $|\delta_c|$ increases to a local maximum, it then asymptotically tends to ϵ_g. If there is no noise or λ is large enough then $|\delta_c|$ steadily reduces as the number of examples increases.

We now examine the evidence procedure. Firstly we define $\beta_{ev}(\gamma)$ and $\gamma_{ev}(\beta)$ to be the hyperparameters which maximise the evidence. The evidence procedure

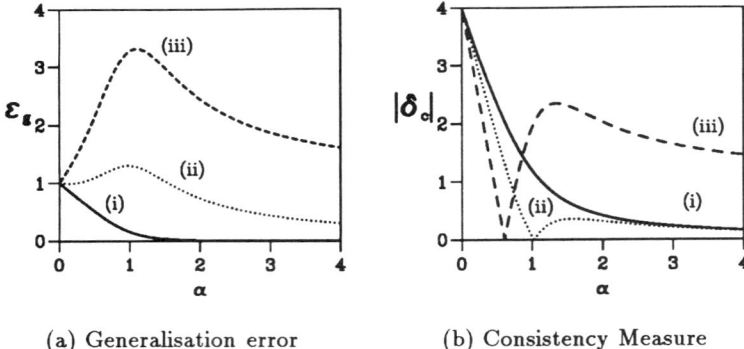

(a) Generalisation error (b) Consistency Measure

Figure 2: The performance measures: Graph a shows ϵ_g for finite lambda. a(i) and a(ii) are the learnable case with noise in the latter case. a(iii) shows that the effect of *adding* unlearnability is qualitatively the same as adding noise. Graph b. shows the modulus of the consistency error v's α. Curves b(i) and b(ii) are the learnable case without and with noise respectively. Curve b(iii) is an unlearnable case with the same noise level.

picks the point in hyperparameter space where these curves coincide. We denote the asymptotic values of $\beta_{ev}(\gamma)$ and $\gamma_{ev}(\beta)$ in the limit of large α by β_∞ and γ_∞ respectively.

In the linear case ($D_w = 0$) the evidence procedure assignments of the hyperparameters (for finite α) coincide with β_∞ and γ_∞ and also optimise ϵ_g and δ_c in agreement with [Bruce and Saad 94]. This is shown in Figure 3a where we plot the β which optimises the evidence (β_{ev}), the consistency measure (β_{δ_c}) and the generalisation error (β_{ϵ_g}) versus γ. The point at which the three curves coincide is the point in the β-γ plane identified by the evidence procedure. However, we note here that, if one of the hyperparameters is poorly determined then maximising the evidence with respect to the other is a misleading guide to optimising performance even in the linear case.

The results for an unrealisable rule in the linear regime ($D_w > 0$, $\sigma_{x_1} = \sigma_{x_2}$) are similar to the learnable case but with an increased noise due to the unlearnability. The evidence procedure still optimises performance.

In the non-linear regime ($D_w > 0$, $\sigma_{x_1} \neq \sigma_{x_2}$) the evidence procedure fails to minimise either performance measure. This is shown in Figure 3b where the evidence procedure point does not lie on $\beta_{\epsilon_g}(\gamma)$ or $\beta_{\delta_c}(\gamma)$. Indeed, its hyperparameter assignments do not coincide with β_∞ and γ_∞ but are α dependent.

How badly does the evidence procedure fail? We define the percentage degradation in generalisation performance as $\mathcal{K} = 100 * (\epsilon_g(\lambda_{ev}) - \epsilon_g^{opt})/\epsilon_g^{opt}$. Where λ_{ev} is the evidence procedure assignment and ϵ_g^{opt} is the optimal generalisation error with respect to λ. This is plotted in Figure 4a. We also define $\mathcal{K}_\delta = 100 * |\delta_c(\lambda_{ev})| / \epsilon_g(\lambda_{ev})$. This measures the error in using the variance of the

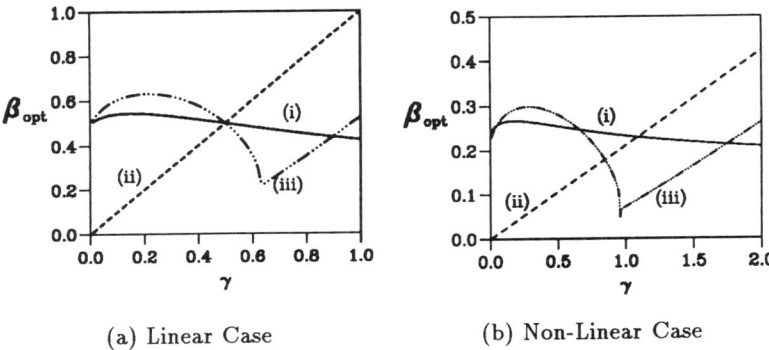

Figure 3: The evidence procedure:Optimal β v's γ. In both graphs for (i) the evidence(β_{ev}), (ii) the generalisation error (β_{ϵ_g}) and (iii) the consistency measure (β_{δ_c}). The point which the evidence procedure picks in the linear case is that where all three curves coincide, whereas in the non linear case it coincides only with β_{ev}.

post training distribution to estimate the generalisation error as a percentage of the generalisation error itself. Examples of this quantity are plotted in Figure 4b. There are three important points to note concerning κ and κ_δ. Firstly, the larger the deviation from a linear rule the greater is the error. Secondly, that it is the magnitude of the effective noise due to unlearnability relative to the real noise which determines this error. In other words, if the real noise is large enough to swamp the non-linearity of the rule then the evidence procedure will not be very misleading. Finally, the magnitude of the error for relatively large deviations from linearity is only a few percent and thus the evidence procedure might well be a reasonable, if not optimal, method for setting the hyperparameters. However, clearly it would be preferable to improve our student space to enable it to model the teacher.

5 CONCLUSION

We have examined the generalisation error, the consistency measure and the evidence procedure within a model which allows us to interpolate between a learnable and an unlearnable scenario. We have seen that the unlearnability acts like an effective noise on the examples. Furthermore, we have seen that for a linear student the evidence procedure breaks down, in that it fails to optimise performance, when the teacher output is non-linear. However, even for relatively large deviations of the teacher from linearity the evidence procedure is close to optimal.

Bayesian methods, such as the evidence procedure, are based on the assumption that the student or hypothesis space contains the teacher generating the data. In our case, in the non-linear regime, this is clearly not true and so it is perhaps not surprising that the evidence procedure is sub-optimal. Whether or not such a breakdown of the evidence procedure is a generic feature of a mismatch between the hypothesis space and the teacher is a matter for further study.

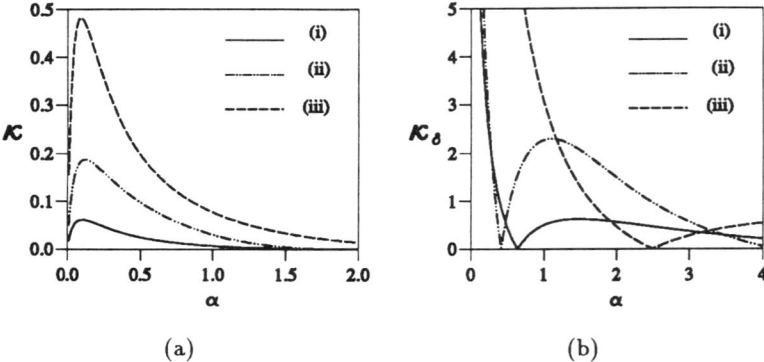

Figure 4: The relative degradation in performance compared to the optimal when using the evidence procedure to set the hyperparameters. Graph (a) shows the percentage degradation in generalisation performance $\mathcal{K}$. a(i) has $D_w = 1$ with the real noise level $\sigma = 1$. a(ii) has this noise level reduced to $\sigma = 0.1$ and a(iii) has increased non-linearity, $D_w = 3$, and $\sigma = 1$. Graph (b) shows the error made in predicting the generalisation error from the variance of the post training distribution as a percentage of the generalisation error itself, $\mathcal{K}_\delta$. b(i) and b(ii) have the same parameter values as a(i) and a(ii), whilst b(iii) has $D_w = 3$ and $\sigma = 0.1$

Acknowledgments

We are very grateful to Alastair Bruce and Peter Sollich for useful discussions. GM is supported by an E.P.S.R.C. studentship.

References

Bruce, A.D. and Saad, D. (1994) Statistical mechanics of hypothesis evaluation. *J. of Phys. A: Math. Gen.* **27**:3355-3363

Krogh, A. and Hertz, J. (1992) Generalisation in a linear perceptron in the presence of noise. *J. of Phys. A: Math. Gen.* **25**:1135-1147

MacKay, D.J.C. (1992a) Bayesian interpolation. *Neural Comp.* **4**:415-447

MacKay, D.J.C. (1992b) A practical Bayesian framework for backprop networks. *Neural Comp.* **4**:448-472

Marion, G. and Saad, D. (1995) A statistical mechanical analysis of a Bayesian inference scheme for an unrealisable rule. To appear in *J. of Phys. A: Math. Gen.*

Seung, H. S, Sompolinsky, H., Tishby, N. (1992) Statistical mechanics of learning from examples. *Phys. Rev. A*, **45**:6056-6091

Thodberg, H.H. (1994) Bayesian backprop in action:pruning, ensembles, error bars and application to spectroscopy. *Advances in Neural Information Processing Systems* **6**:208-215. Cowan *et al.*(Eds.), Morgan Kauffmann, San Mateo, CA

Wolpert, D. H and Strauss, C. E. M. (1994) What Bayes has to say about the evidence procedure. To appear in *Maximum entropy and Bayesian methods*. G. Heidbreder (Ed.), Kluwer.

Temporal Dynamics of Generalization in Neural Networks

Changfeng Wang
Department of Systems Engineering
University Of Pennsylvania
Philadelphia, PA 19104
fwang@pender.ee.upenn.edu

Santosh S. Venkatesh
Department of Electrical Engineering
University Of Pennsylvania
Philadelphia, PA 19104
venkatesh@ee.upenn.edu

Abstract

This paper presents a rigorous characterization of how a general nonlinear learning machine generalizes during the training process when it is trained on a random sample using a gradient descent algorithm based on reduction of training error. It is shown, in particular, that best generalization performance occurs, in general, before the global minimum of the training error is achieved. The different roles played by the complexity of the machine *class* and the complexity of the *specific* machine in the class during learning are also precisely demarcated.

1 INTRODUCTION

In learning machines such as neural networks, two major factors that affect the 'goodness of fit' of the examples are network size (complexity) and training time. These are also the major factors that affect the generalization performance of the network.

Many theoretical studies exploring the relation between generalization performance and machine complexity support the parsimony heuristics suggested by Occam's razor, to wit that amongst machines with similar training performance one should opt for the machine of least complexity. Multitudinous numerical experiments (cf. [5]) suggest, however, that machines of larger size than strictly necessary to explain the data can yield generalization performance similar to that of smaller machines (with similar empirical error) if learning is optimally stopped at a critical point before the global minimum of the training error is achieved. These results seem to fly in contradiction with a learning theoretic interpretation of Occam's razor.

In this paper, we ask the following question: How does the gradual reduction of training error affect the generalization error when a machine of given complexity is trained on a finite number of examples? Namely, we study the simultaneous effects of machine size and training time on the generalization error when a finite sample of examples is available.

Our major result is a rigorous characterization of how a given learning machine generalizes during the training process when it is trained using a learning algorithm based on minimization of the empirical error (or a modification of the empirical error). In particular, we are enabled to analytically determine conditions for the existence of a finite *optimal stopping time* in learning for achieving optimal generalization. We interpret the results in terms of a *time-dependent, effective machine size* which forms the link between generalization error and machine complexity *during* learning viewed as an evolving process in time.

Our major results are obtained by introducing new theoretical tools which allow us to obtain finer results than would otherwise be possible by direct applications of the uniform strong laws pioneered by Vapnik and Červonenkis (henceforth refered to as VC-theory). The different roles played by the complexity of the machine *class* and the complexity of the *specific* machine in the class during learning are also precisely demarcated in our results.

Since the generalization error is defined in terms of an abstract loss function, the results find wide applicability including but not limited to regression (square-error loss function) and density estimation (log-likelihood loss) problems.

2 THE LEARNING PROBLEM

We consider the problem of learning from examples a relation between two vectors x and y determined by a *fixed but unknown* probability distribution $P(x, y)$. This model includes, in particular, the input-output relation described by

$$y = g(x, \xi), \qquad (1)$$

where g is some *unknown* function of x and ξ, which are random vectors on the same probability space. The vector x can be viewed as the input to an unknown system, ξ a random noise term (possibly dependent on x), and y the system's output.

The hypothesis class from which the learning procedure selects a candidate function (hypothesis) approximating g is a parametric family of functions $\mathcal{H}_d = \{ f(x, \theta) : \theta \in \Theta_d \subseteq \Re^d \}$ indexed by a subset Θ_d of d-dimensional Euclidean space. For example, if $x \in \Re^m$ and y is a scalar, $\mathcal{H}_d$ can be the class of functions computed by a feedforward neural network with one hidden layer comprised of h neurons and activation function ψ, viz.,

$$f(x, \theta) = \psi \left(\sum_{i=1}^{h} \theta_i \psi \left(\sum_{j=1}^{m} \theta_{ij} x_j + \theta_{i0} \right) + \theta_0 \right).$$

In the above, $d = (m+2)h$ denotes the number of adjustable parameters.

The goal of learning within the hypothesis class $\mathcal{H}_d$ is to find the best approximation of the relation between x and y in $\mathcal{H}_d$ from a finite set of n examples $\mathcal{D}_n = \{(x_1, y_1), \ldots, (x_n, y_n)\}$ drawn by independent sampling from the distribution $P(x,y)$. A learning algorithm is simply a map which, for every sample $\mathcal{D}_n$ ($n \geq 1$), produces a hypothesis in $\mathcal{H}_d$.

In practical learning situations one first selects a network of fixed structure (a fixed hypothesis class $\mathcal{H}_d$), and then determines the "best" weight vector θ^* (or equivalently, the best function $f(x, \theta^*)$ in this class) using some training algorithm. The proximity of an approximation $f(x, \theta)$ to the target function $g(x, \xi)$ at each point x is measured by a *loss function* $q : (f(x, \theta), g(x, \xi)) \mapsto \Re^+$. For a given hypothesis class, the function $f(\cdot, \theta)$ is completely determined by the parameter vector θ. With g fixed, the loss function may be written, with a slight abuse of notation, as a map $q(x, y, \theta)$ from $\Re^m \times \Re \times \Theta$ into $\Re^+$. Examples of the forms of loss functions are the familiar square-law loss function $q(x, y, \theta) = \bigl(g(x, \xi) - f(x, \theta)\bigr)^2$ commonly used in regression and learning in neural networks, and the Kulback-Leibler distance (or relative entropy) $q(x, y, \theta) = \ln \frac{p(y|f(x,\theta))}{p(y|g(x,\xi))}$ for density estimation, where $p(y \mid i(x, \theta))$ denotes the conditional density function of y given $i(x, \theta)$.

The closeness of $f(\cdot, \theta)$ to $g(\cdot)$ is measured by the expected (ensemble) loss or error

$$\mathcal{E}(\theta, d) \triangleq \int q(x, y, \theta) P(dx, dy).$$

The optimal approximation $f(\cdot, \theta^*)$ is such that $\mathcal{E}(\theta^*, d) = \min_{\theta \in \Theta_d} \mathcal{E}(\theta, d)$. In similar fashion, we define the corresponding *empirical loss* (or *training error*) by

$$\mathcal{E}_n(\theta, d) = \int q(x, y, \theta) P_n(dx, dy) = \frac{1}{n} \sum_{i=1}^n q(x_i, y_i, \theta).$$

where P_n denotes the joint empirical distribution of input-output pairs (x, y). The global minimum of the empirical error over Θ_d is denoted by $\hat{\theta}$, namely, $\hat{\theta} = \arg\min_{\theta \in \Theta} \mathcal{E}_n(\theta, d)$. An iterative algorithm for minimizing $\mathcal{E}_n(\theta, d)$ (or a modification of it) over Θ_d generates at each epoch t a random vector $\theta_t : \mathcal{D}_n \to \Theta_d$. The quantity $\mathcal{E}(\theta_t, d) = \mathbf{E} \int q(x, \theta_t) P(dx, d\xi)$ is referred to as the *generalization error* of θ_t. We are interested in the properties of the process $\{\theta_t : t = 1, 2, \ldots\}$, and the time-evolution of the sequence $\{\mathcal{E}(\theta_t, d) : t = 1, 2, \ldots\}$.

Note that each θ_t is a functional of P_n. When $P = P_n$, learning reduces to an optimization problem. Deviations from optimality arise intrinsically as a consequence of the discrepancy between P_n and P. The central idea of this work is to analyze the consequence of the deviation $\Delta_n \triangleq P_n - P$ on the generalization error.

To simplify notation, we henceforth suppress d and write simply Θ, $\mathcal{E}(\theta)$ and $\mathcal{E}_n(\theta)$ instead of Θ_d, $\mathcal{E}(\theta, d)$, and $\mathcal{E}_n(\theta, d)$, respectively.

2.1 Regularity Conditions

We will be interested in the local behavior of learning algorithms. Consequently, we assume that Θ is a compact set, and θ^* is the unique global minimum of $\mathcal{E}(\theta)$ on Θ.

It can be argued that these assumptions are an idealization of one of the following situations:

- A global algorithm is used which is able to find the global minimum of $\mathcal{E}_n(\theta)$, and we are interested in the stage of training when θ_t has entered a region Θ where θ^* is the only global minimum of $\mathcal{E}(\theta)$;
- A local algorithm is used, and the algorithm has entered a region Θ which contains θ^* as the unique global minimum of $\mathcal{E}(\theta)$ or as a unique local minimum with which we are content.

In the sequel, we write $\partial/\partial\theta$ to denote the gradient operator with respect to the vector θ, and likewise write $\partial^2/\partial\theta^2$ to denote the matrix of operators $\left[\frac{\partial^2}{\partial\theta_i \partial\theta_j}\right]_{i,j=1}^{d}$.

In the rest of the development we assume the following *regularity conditions*:

A1. The loss function $q(x, y, \cdot)$ is twice continuously differential for all $\theta \in \Theta$ and for almost all (x, y);
A2. $P(x, y)$ has compact support;
A3. The optimal network θ^* is an interior point of Θ;
A4. The matrix $\Phi(\theta^*) = \frac{\partial^2}{\partial\theta^2}\mathcal{E}(\theta^*)$ is nonsingular.

These assumptions are typically satisfied in neural network applications. We will also assume that the learning algorithm converges to the global minimum of $\mathcal{E}_n(\theta)$ over Θ (note that $\hat{\theta}$ may not be a true *global* minimum, so the assumption applies to gradient descent algorithms which converge locally). It is easy to demonstrate that for each such algorithm, there exists an algorithm which decreases the empirical error monotonically at each step of iteration. Thus, without loss of generality, we also assume that all the algorithms we consider have this monotonicity property.

3 GENERALIZATION DYNAMICS

3.1 First Phase of Learning

The quality of learning based on the minimization of the empirical error depends on the value of the quantity $\sup_{\Theta} |\mathcal{E}_n(\theta) - \mathcal{E}(\theta)|$. Under the above assumptions, it is shown in [3] that

$$\mathcal{E}(\theta) = \mathcal{E}_n(\theta) + O_p\left(\frac{\ln n}{\sqrt{n}}\right) \quad \text{and} \quad \mathcal{E}(\hat{\theta}) = \mathcal{E}(\theta^*) + O\left(\frac{\ln n}{n}\right).$$

Therefore, for *any* iterative algorithm for minimizing $\mathcal{E}_n(\theta)$, in the initial phase of learning the reduction of training error is essentially equivalent to the reduction of generalization error. It can be further shown that this situation persists until the estimates θ_t enter an $n^{-\delta_n}$ neighborhood of $\hat{\theta}$, where $\delta_n \to 1/2$.

The basic tool we have used in arriving at this conclusion is the VC-method. The characterization of the precise generalization properties of the machine after θ_t enters an $n^{-\delta}$ neighborhood of the limiting solution needs a more precise language than can be provided by the VC-method, and is the main content of the rest of this work.

3.2 Learning by Gradient Descent

In the following, we focus on generalization properties when the machine is trained using the gradient descent algorithm (Backpropagation is a Gauss-Seidel implementation of this algorithm); in particular, the adaptation is governed by the recurrence

$$\theta_{t+1} = \theta_t - \epsilon \frac{\partial}{\partial \theta} \mathcal{E}_n(\theta_t) \qquad (t \geq 0), \tag{2}$$

where the positive quantity ϵ governs the rate of learning. Learning and generalization properties for other algorithms can be studied using similar techniques.

Replace $\mathcal{E}_n$ by $\mathcal{E}$ in (2) and let $\{\theta_t^*, t \geq 0\}$ denote the generated sequence of vectors. We can show (though we will not do so here) that the weight vector θ_t is asymptotically normally distributed with expectation θ_t^* and covariance matrix with all entries of order $O(\frac{1}{n})$. It is precisely the deviation of θ_t from θ_t^* caused by the perturbation of amount $\Delta_n = P_n - P$ to the true distribution P which results in interesting artifacts such as a finite optimal stopping time when the number of examples is finite.

3.3 The Main Equation of Generalization Dynamics

Under the regularity conditions mentioned in the last section, we can find the generalization error at each epoch of learning as an explicit function of the number of iterations, machine parameters, and the initial error. Denote by $\lambda_1 \geq \lambda_2 \geq \cdots \geq \lambda_d$ the eigenvalues of the matrix $\Phi(\theta^*)$ and suppose T is the orthogonal diagonalizing matrix for $\Phi(\theta^*)$, viz., $T'\phi(\theta^*)T = \text{diag}(\lambda_1, \ldots, \lambda_d)$. Set $\delta = (\delta_1, \ldots, \delta_d)' \triangleq T(\theta_0 - \theta^*)$ and for each i let ν_i denote the ith diagonal element of the $d \times d$ matrix $T'\mathbf{E}\{(\frac{\partial}{\partial \theta}q(x,\theta^*))(\frac{\partial}{\partial \theta}q(x,\theta^*))'\}T$. Also let $S(\theta, \rho)$ denote the open ball of radius ρ at θ.

MAIN THEOREM *Under Assumptions A1–A4, the generalization error of the machine trained according to (2) is governed by the following equation for all starting points $\theta_0 \in S(\theta^*, n^{-r})$ $(0 < r \leq \frac{1}{2})$, and uniformly for all $t \geq 0$:*

$$\mathcal{E}(\theta_t) = \mathcal{E}(\theta^*) + \frac{1}{2n} \sum_{i=1}^{d} \left\{ \frac{\nu_i}{\lambda_i} [1 - (1-\epsilon\lambda_i)^t]^2 + \delta_i^2 \lambda_i (1-\epsilon\lambda_i)^{2t} \right\} + O(n^{-3r}). \tag{3}$$

If $\theta_0 \notin S(\theta^*, n^{-\frac{1}{3}})$, then the generalization dynamics is governed by the following equation valid for all $r > 0$:

$$\mathcal{E}(\theta_t) = \mathcal{E}(\theta^*) + \frac{1}{2n} \sum_{i=1}^{d} \left\{ \frac{\nu_i}{\lambda_i} + C(t_1)(1-\epsilon\lambda_i)^t + C_i(t_1)(1-\epsilon\lambda_i)^{2t} \delta_i^2 \right\} + O(n^{-3r}), \tag{4}$$

where t_1 is the smallest t such that $\mathbf{E}\,|[I - \epsilon\Phi]^{t_1}| = An^{-r}$ for some $A > 0$, and $C(t_1)$, $C_i(t_1) \geq 0$ are constants depending on network parameters and t_1.

In the special case when the data is generated by the following additive noise model

$$y = g(x) + \xi, \tag{5}$$

with $\mathbf{E}\left[\xi|x\right] = 0$, and $\mathbf{E}\left[\xi^2|x\right] = \sigma^2 = constant$, if $g(x) = f(x, \theta^*)$ and the loss function $q(x, \theta)$ is given by the square-error loss function, the above equation reduces to the following form:

$$\mathcal{E}(\theta_t) = \mathcal{E}(\theta^*) + \frac{\sigma^2}{2n}\sum_{i=1}^{d}\left\{\left[1 - (1 - \epsilon\lambda_i)^t\right]^2 + \delta_i^2\lambda_i(1-\epsilon\lambda_i)^{2t}\right\} + O(n^{-3r}).$$

In particular, if $f(x, \theta)$ is linear in θ, we obtain our previous result [4] for linear machines. The result (3) is hence a substantive extension of the earlier result to very general settings. It is noted that the extension goes beyond nonlinearity and the original additive noise data generating model—we no longer require that the 'true' model be contained in the hypothesis class.

3.4 Effective Complexity

Write $c_i \triangleq \nu_i/\lambda_i$. The *effective complexity* of the nonlinear machine θ_t at t is defined to be

$$C(\theta^*, d, t) \triangleq \sum_{i=1}^{d} c_i\left(1 - (1-\epsilon\lambda_i)^t\right)^2.$$

Analysis shows that the term c_i indicates the level of sensitivity of output of the machine to the ith component of the normalized weight vector, θ; $C(\theta^*, d, t)$ denotes the degree to which the approximation power of the machine is invoked by the learning process at epoch t. Indeed, as $t \to \infty$, $C(\theta^*, d, t) \to C_d = \sum_{i=1}^{d} c_i$, which is the complexity of the limiting machine $\hat{\theta}$ which represents the maximal fitting of examples to the machine (i.e., minimized training error). For the additive noise data generating model (5) and square-error loss function, the effective complexity becomes,

$$C(\theta^*, d, t) = \sum_{i=1}^{d}\left(1 - (1-\epsilon\lambda_i)^t\right)^2.$$

The sum can be interpreted as the *effective number of parameters used at epoch t*. At the end of training, it becomes exactly the number of parameters of the machine.

Now write $\theta_t^* \triangleq \theta^* + (\theta_0 - \theta^*)(1 - \epsilon\lambda_i)^t$. With these definitions, (3) can be rewritten to give the following approximation error and complexity error decomposition of generalization error in the learning process:

$$\mathcal{E}(\theta_t) = \mathcal{E}(\theta_t^*) + \frac{C(\theta^*, d, t)}{2n} + O(n^{-3r}) \qquad (t \geq 0). \tag{6}$$

The first term on the right-hand-side, $\mathcal{E}(\theta_t^*)$, denotes the *approximation error at epoch t* and is the error incurred in using θ_t^* as an approximation of the 'truth.' Note that the approximation error depends on time t and the initial value θ_0, but not the examples. Clearly, it is the error one would obtain at epoch t in minimizing the function $\mathcal{E}(\theta)$ (as opposed to $\mathcal{E}_n(\theta)$) using the same learning algorithm and starting with the same step length ϵ and initial value θ_0. The second term on the right-hand-side is the *complexity error at epoch t*. This is the part of the generalization error at t due to the substitution of $\mathcal{E}_n(\theta)$ for $\mathcal{E}(\theta)$.

The overfitting phenomena in learning is often intuitively attributed to the 'fitting of noise.' We see that is only partly correct: it is in fact due to the increasing use of the capacity of the machine, that the complexity penalty becomes increasingly large, this being true even when the data is clean, i.e., when $\xi \equiv 0$! Therefore, we see that (6) gives an exact trade-off of the approximation error and complexity error in the learning process.

For the case of large initial error, we see from the main theorem that the complexity error is essentially the same as that at the end of training, when the initial error is reduced to about the same order as before. The reduction of the training error leads to monotone decrease in generalization error in this case.

3.5 Optimal Stopping Time

We can phrase the following succinct open problem in learning in neural networks: When should learning be ideally stopped? The question was answered for linear machines which is a special form of neural networks in [4]. This section extends the result to general nonlinear machines (including neural networks) in regular cases. For this purpose, we write the generalization error in the following form:

$$\mathcal{E}(\theta_t) = \mathcal{E}(\hat{\theta}) + \phi(t) + O(n^{-3r}).$$

where

$$\phi(t) \triangleq \frac{\sigma^2}{n} \sum_{i=1}^{d} \left\{ l_i(1 - \epsilon\lambda_i)^{2t} - d_i(1 - \epsilon\lambda_i)^t \right\},$$

and d_i and l_i are machine parameters. The time-evolution of generalization error during the learning process is completely determined by the function $\phi(t)$.

Define $t_{\min} \in \{\tau \geq 0 : \mathcal{E}(\theta_\tau) \leq \mathcal{E}(\theta_t) \text{ for all } t \geq 0\}$, that is $t_{\min}$ denotes an epoch at which the generalization error is minimized. The smallest such number will be referred to as the *optimal stopping time* of learning. In general we have $c_i > 0$ for all i. In this case, it is possible to determine that there is a finite optimal stopping time. More specifically, there exists two constants t_l and t_u which depend on the machine parameters such that $t_l \leq t_{\min} \leq t_u$. Furthermore, it can be shown that the function $\phi(t)$ decreases monotonically for $t \leq t_l$ and increases monotonically for all $t \geq t_u$. Finally, we can relate the generalization performance when learning is optimally stopped to the best achievable performance by means of the following inequality:

$$\mathcal{E}(\theta_{t_{\min}}) \leq \mathcal{E}(\theta^*) + \frac{(1-\kappa)C_d}{2n},$$

where $\kappa = O(n^0)$ is a constant depending on l_i and d_i's, and is in the interval $(0, \frac{1}{4}]$, and C_d denotes, as before, the limiting value of the effective machine complexity $C(\theta^*, d, t)$ as $t \to \infty$.

In the pathological case where there exists i such that $c_i = 0$, there may not exist a finite optimal stopping time. However, even in such cases, it can be shown that if $\ln(1 - \epsilon\lambda_1)/\ln(1 - \epsilon\lambda_d) < 2$, a finite optimal stopping time still exists.

4 CONCLUDING REMARKS

This paper describes some major results of our recent work on a rigorous characterization of the generalization process in neural network types of learning machines. In particular, we have shown that reduction of training error may not lead to improved generalization performance. Two major techniques involved are the uniform weak law (VC-theory) and differentiable statistical functionals, with the former delivering an initial estimate, and the latter giving finer results. The results shows that the complexity (e.g. VC-dimension) of a machine class does not suffice to describe the rôle of machine complexity in generalization during the learning process; the appropriate complexity notion required is a time-varying and algorithm-dependent concept of effective machine complexity.

Since results in this work contain parameters which are typically unknown, they cannot be used directly in practical situations. However, it is possible to frame criteria overcoming such difficulties. More details of the work described here and its extensions and applications can be found in [3]. The methodology adopted here is also readily adapted to study the dynamical effect of regularization on the learning process [3].

Acknowledgements

This research was supported in part by the Air Force Office of Scientific Research under grant F49620-93-1-0120.

References

[1] Kolmogorov, A. and V. Tihomirov (1961). ϵ-entropy and ϵ-capacity of sets in functional spaces. *Amer. Math. Soc. Trans. (Ser. 2)*, 17:277-364.

[2] Vapnik, V. (1982). *Estimation of Dependences Based on Empirical Data.* Springer-Verlag, New York.

[3] Wang, C. (1994). *A Theory of Generalization in Learning Machines.* Ph. D. Thesis, University of Pennsylvania.

[4] Wang, C., S. S. Venkatesh, and J. S. Judd (1993). Optimal stopping and effective machine size in learning. Proceedings of NIPS'93.

[5] Weigend, A. (1993). On overtraining and the effective number of hidden units. *Proceedings of the* 1993 *Connectionist Models Summer School.* 335-342. Ed. Mozer, M. C. et al. Hillsdale, NJ: Erlbaum Associates.

Stochastic Dynamics of Three–State Neural Networks

Toru Ohira
Sony Computer Science Laboratory
3-14-13 Higashi-gotanda,
Tokyo 141, Japan
ohira@csl.sony.co.jp

Jack D. Cowan
Depts. of Mathematics and Neurology
University of Chicago
Chicago, IL 60637
cowan@synapse.uchicago.edu

Abstract

We present here an analysis of the stochastic neurodynamics of a neural network composed of three–state neurons described by a master equation. An outer–product representation of the master equation is employed. In this representation, an extension of the analysis from two to three–state neurons is easily performed. We apply this formalism with approximation schemes to a simple three–state network and compare the results with Monte Carlo simulations.

1 INTRODUCTION

Studies of single neurons or networks under the influence of noise have been a continuing item in neural network modelling. In particular, the analogy with spin systems at finite temprature has produced many important results on networks of two–state neurons. However, studies of networks of three–state neurons have been rather limited (Meunier, Hansel and Verga, 1989). A master equation was introduced by Cowan (1991) to study stochastic neural networks. The equation uses the formalism of "second quantization" for classical many–body systems (Doi, 1976a; Grassberger and Scheunert, 1980), and was used to study networks of of two–state neurons (Ohira and Cowan, 1993, 1994). In this paper, we reformulate the master equation using an outer–product representation of operators and extend our previous analysis to networks of three–state neurons. A hierarchy of moment equations for such networks is derived and approximation schemes are used to obtain equa-

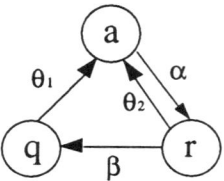

Figure 1: Transition rates for a three–state neuron.

tions for the macroscopic activities of model networks. We compare the behavior of the solutions of these equations with Monte Carlo simulations.

2 THE BASIC NEURAL MODEL

We first introduce the network described by the master equation. In this network (Cowan, 1991), neurons at each site, say the ith site, are assumed to cycle through three states: "quiescent", "activated" and "refractory", labelled 'q_i', 'a_i', and 'r_i' respectively. We consider four transitions: $q \to a$, $r \to a$, $a \to r$, and $r \to q$. Two of these, $q \to a$ and $r \to a$, are functions of the neural input current. We assume these are smoothly increasing functions of the input current and denoted them by θ_1, and θ_2. The other two transition rates, $a \to r$, and $r \to q$, are defined as constants α and β. The resulting stochastic transition scheme is shown in Figure 1. We assume that these transition rates depend only on the current state of the network and not on past states, and that all neural state transitions are asynchronous. This Markovian assumption is essential to the master equation description of this model.

We represent the state of each neuron by three–dimensional basis vectors using the Dirac notation $|a_i>$, $|r_i>$ and $|q_i>$. They correspond, in more standard vector notation, to:

$$|q_i> = \begin{pmatrix} 0 \\ 0 \\ 1 \end{pmatrix}_i, \quad |a_i> = \begin{pmatrix} 1 \\ 0 \\ 0 \end{pmatrix}_i, \quad |r_i> = \begin{pmatrix} 0 \\ 1 \\ 0 \end{pmatrix}_i \quad (1)$$

We define the inner product of these states as

$$<a_i|a_i> = <q_i|q_i> = <r_i|r_i> = 1, \quad (2)$$

$$<q_i|a_i> = <a_i|q_i> = <r_i|a_i> = <a_i|r_i> = <r_i|q_i> = <q_i|r_i> = 0. \quad (3)$$

Let the states (or configurations) of a network be represented by $\{|\Omega>\}$, the direct product space of each neuron in the network.

$$|\Omega> = |v_1>|v_2> \ldots |v_N>, \quad v_i = a_i, \ r_i, \text{or } q_i. \quad (4)$$

Let P[Ω, t] be the probability of finding the network in a particular state Ω at time t. We introduce the "neural state vector" for N neurons in a network as

$$|\Phi(t)> = \sum_{\{\Omega\}} P[\Omega, t] |\Omega>, \quad (5)$$

where the sum is taken over all possible network states.

With these definitions, we can write the master equation for a network with the transition rates shown in Figure 1, using the outer–product representations of operators (Sakurai, 1985). For example:

$$|a_i\rangle\langle q_i| = \begin{pmatrix} 0 & 0 & 1 \\ 0 & 0 & 0 \\ 0 & 0 & 0 \end{pmatrix}_i \tag{6}$$

The master equation then takes the form of an evolution equation:

$$-\frac{\partial}{\partial t}|\Phi(t)\rangle = L|\Phi(t)\rangle \tag{7}$$

with the network "Liouvillian" L given by:

$$L = \alpha \sum_{i=1}^{N}(|a_i\rangle\langle a_i| - |r_i\rangle\langle a_i|) + \sum_{i=1}^{N}(|r_i\rangle\langle r_i| - |a_i\rangle\langle r_i|)\theta_2(\frac{1}{\bar{n}}\sum_{j=1}^{N} w_{ij}|a_j\rangle\langle a_j|)$$

$$+\beta \sum_{i=1}^{N}(|r_i\rangle\langle r_i| - |q_i\rangle\langle r_i|) + \sum_{i=1}^{N}(|q_i\rangle\langle q_i| - |a_i\rangle\langle q_i|)\theta_1(\frac{1}{\bar{n}}\sum_{j=1}^{N} w_{ij}|a_j\rangle\langle a_j|). \tag{8}$$

where $\bar{n}$ is an average number of connections to each neuron, and w_{ij} is the "weight" from the jth to the ith neuron. Thus the weights are normalized with respect to the average number $\bar{n}$ of connections per neuron.

The master equation given here is the same as the one introduced by Cowan using Gell-Mann matrices (Cowan, 1991). However, we note that with the outer–product representation, we can extend the description from two to three–state neurons simply by including one more basis vector.

In analogy with the analysis of two–state neurons, we introduce the state vector:

$$\langle \vec{a}\ \vec{r}\ \vec{q}| = \prod_{i=1}^{N}(q_i\langle q_i| + r_i\langle r_i| + a_i\langle a_i|). \tag{9}$$

where the product is taken as a direct product, and a_i, r_i, and q_i are parameters. We also introduce the point moments $\ll a_i(t)\gg$, $\ll q_i(t)\gg$, and $\ll r_i(t)\gg$ as the probability that the ith neuron is active, quiescent, and refractory respectively, at time t. Similarly, we can define the multiple moment, for example, $\ll a_i q_j r_k \ldots (t)\gg$ as the probability that the ith neuron is active, the jth neuron is quiescent, the kth neuron is refractory and so on at time t. Then, it can be shown that they are given by:

$$\ll s_i s_j s_k \ldots (t)\gg = \langle \vec{a} = \vec{r} = \vec{q} = 1|s_i\rangle\langle s_i| \otimes |s_j\rangle\langle s_j| \otimes |s_k\rangle\langle s_k|\ldots |\Phi(t)\rangle,$$
$$s = a,\ r\ ,q \tag{10}$$

For example,

$$\ll r_i q_j a_k(t)\gg = \langle \vec{a} = \vec{r} = \vec{q} = 1|r_i\rangle\langle r_i| \otimes |q_j\rangle\langle q_j| \otimes |a_k\rangle\langle a_k|\Phi(t)\rangle \tag{11}$$

We note the following relations,

$$\ll a_i(t)\gg + \ll q_i(t)\gg + \ll r_i(t)\gg = 1 \tag{12}$$

and

$$\ll a_i^2(t)\gg = \ll a_i(t)\gg,\quad \ll r_i^2(t)\gg = \ll r_i(t)\gg,\quad \ll q_i^2(t)\gg = \ll q_i(t)\gg. \tag{13}$$

3 THE HIERARCHY OF MOMENT EQUATIONS

We can now obtain an equation of motion for the moments. As is typical in the case of many–body problems, we obtain an analogue of the BBGKY hierarchy of equations (Doi, 1976b). This can be done by using the definition of moments, the master equation, and the a-r-q state vector. We show the hierarchy up to the second order:

$$-\frac{\partial}{\partial t}\ll a_i\gg = \alpha\ll a_i\gg - \ll r_i\theta_2(\frac{1}{n}\sum_{j=1}^{N}w_{ij}a_j)\gg - \ll q_i\theta_1(\frac{1}{n}\sum_{j=1}^{N}w_{ij}a_j)\gg \quad (14)$$

$$-\frac{\partial}{\partial t}\ll r_i\gg = -\alpha\ll a_i\gg + \beta\ll r_i\gg + \ll r_i\theta_2(\frac{1}{n}\sum_{j=1}^{N}w_{ij}a_j)\gg \quad (15)$$

$$-\frac{\partial}{\partial t}\ll q_i\gg = -\beta\ll r_i\gg + \ll q_i\theta_1(\frac{1}{n}\sum_{j=1}^{N}w_{ij}a_j)\gg \quad (16)$$

$$-\frac{\partial}{\partial t}\ll a_ia_j\gg = 2\alpha\ll a_ia_j\gg - \ll r_ia_j\theta_2(\frac{1}{n}\sum_{k=1}^{N}w_{ik}a_k)\gg - \ll a_ir_j\theta_2(\frac{1}{n}\sum_{k=1}^{N}w_{jk}a_k)\gg$$
$$-\ll q_ia_j\theta_1(\frac{1}{n}\sum_{k=1}^{N}w_{ik}a_k)\gg - \ll a_iq_j\theta_1(\frac{1}{n}\sum_{k=1}^{N}w_{jk}a_k)\gg \quad (17)$$

$$-\frac{\partial}{\partial t}\ll r_ir_j\gg = -\alpha(\ll r_ia_j\gg + \ll a_ir_j\gg) + 2\beta\ll r_ir_j\gg$$
$$+\ll r_ir_j\theta_2(\frac{1}{n}\sum_{k=1}^{N}w_{ik}a_k)\gg + \ll r_ir_j\theta_2(\frac{1}{n}\sum_{k=1}^{N}w_{jk}a_k)\gg \quad (18)$$

$$-\frac{\partial}{\partial t}\ll a_ir_j\gg = -\alpha(\ll a_ia_j\gg - \ll a_ir_j\gg) + \beta\ll a_ir_j\gg + \ll a_ir_j\theta_2(\frac{1}{n}\sum_{k=1}^{N}w_{ik}a_k)\gg$$
$$-\ll r_ir_j\theta_2(\frac{1}{n}\sum_{k=1}^{N}w_{ik}a_k)\gg - \ll q_ir_j\theta_1(\frac{1}{n}\sum_{k=1}^{N}w_{ik}a_k)\gg \quad (19)$$

We note that since
$$\ll a_i\gg + \ll r_i\gg + \ll q_i\gg = 1, \quad (20)$$
one of the parameters can be eliminated. We also note that the equations are coupled into higher orders in this hierarchy. This leads to a need for approximation schemes which can terminate the hierarchy at an appropriate order.

In the following, we introduce first and the second moment level approximation schemes. For simplicity, we consider the special case in which θ_1 and θ_2 are linear and equal.

$$\theta_1(\frac{1}{n}\sum_{j=1}^{N}w_{ij}\ll a_j\gg) = \theta_2(\frac{1}{n}\sum_{j=1}^{N}w_{ij}\ll a_j\gg) = \frac{1}{n}\sum_{j=1}^{N}w_{ij}\ll a_j\gg \quad (21)$$

With the above simplication the first moment (mean field) approximation leads to:

$$-\frac{\partial}{\partial t}\ll a_i\gg = \alpha\ll a_i\gg - \overline{w_i}(\ll r_i\gg + \ll q_i\gg) \tag{22}$$

$$-\frac{\partial}{\partial t}\ll r_i\gg = -\alpha\ll a_i\gg + \beta\ll r_i\gg + \overline{w_i}\ll r_i\gg, \tag{23}$$

$$-\frac{\partial}{\partial t}\ll q_i\gg = -\beta\ll r_i\gg + \overline{w_i}\ll q_i\gg, \tag{24}$$

where

$$\overline{w_l} = \frac{1}{n}\sum_{k=1}^{N} w_{lk}\ll a_k\gg. \tag{25}$$

We also obtain the second moment approximation as:

$$-\frac{\partial}{\partial t}\ll a_i\gg = \alpha\ll a_i\gg - \frac{1}{n}\sum_{j=1}^{N} w_{ij}(\ll q_i a_j\gg + \ll r_i a_j\gg), \tag{26}$$

$$-\frac{\partial}{\partial t}\ll r_i\gg = -\alpha\ll a_i\gg + \beta\ll r_i\gg + \frac{1}{n}\sum_{j=1}^{N} w_{ij}\ll r_i a_j\gg, \tag{27}$$

$$-\frac{\partial}{\partial t}\ll q_i\gg = -\beta\ll r_i\gg + \frac{1}{n}\sum_{j=1}^{N} w_{ij}\ll q_i a_j\gg, \tag{28}$$

$$-\frac{\partial}{\partial t}\ll a_i a_j\gg = 2\alpha\ll a_i a_j\gg - \overline{w_{ij}}(\ll r_i a_j\gg + \ll q_i a_j\gg) \\ - \overline{w_{ji}}(\ll a_i r_j\gg + \ll a_i q_j\gg), \tag{29}$$

$$-\frac{\partial}{\partial t}\ll r_i r_j\gg = -\alpha(\ll r_i a_j\gg + \ll a_i r_j\gg) + 2\beta\ll r_i r_j\gg + 2\overline{w_{ij}}\ll r_i r_j\gg, \tag{30}$$

$$-\frac{\partial}{\partial t}\ll a_i r_j\gg = -\alpha(\ll a_i a_j\gg - \ll a_i r_j\gg) + \beta\ll a_i r_j\gg + \overline{w_{ji}}\ll a_i r_j\gg \\ - \overline{w_{ij}}(\ll r_i r_j\gg + \ll q_i r_j\gg), \tag{31}$$

where

$$\overline{w_{lm}} = \frac{1}{n}[\sum_{k=1,(k\neq m)}^{N} w_{lk}\ll a_k\gg + w_{lm}]. \tag{32}$$

We note that the first moment dynamics obtained via the first approximation differs from that obtained from the second moment approximation. In the next section, we briefly examine this difference by comparing these approximations with Monte Carlo simulations.

4 COMPARISON WITH SIMULATIONS

In this section, we compare first and second moment approximations with Monte Carlo simulation of a one dimensional ring of three–state neurons. This was studied in a previous publication (Ohira and Cowan, 1993) for two-state neurons. As shown there, each three-state neuron in the ring interacts with its two neighbors.

More precisely, the Liouville operator is

$$L = \alpha \sum_{i=1}^{N}(|a_i\rangle\langle a_i| - |r_i\rangle\langle a_i|) + \beta \sum_{i=1}^{N}(|r_i\rangle\langle r_i| - |q_i\rangle\langle r_i|) \quad (33)$$

$$+ \frac{1}{2}w_2 \sum_{i=1}^{N}(|r_i\rangle\langle r_i| - |a_i\rangle\langle r_i|)(|a_{i+1}\rangle\langle a_{i+1}| + |a_{i-1}\rangle\langle a_{i-1}|)$$

$$+ \frac{1}{2}w_1 \sum_{i=1}^{N}(|q_i\rangle\langle q_i| - |a_i\rangle\langle q_i|)(|a_{i+1}\rangle\langle a_{i+1}| + |a_{i-1}\rangle\langle a_{i-1}|)$$

We now define the dynamical variables of interest as follows:

$$\chi_a = \frac{1}{N}\sum_{i=1}^{N} \ll a_i \gg, \quad \chi_r = \frac{1}{N}\sum_{i=1}^{N} \ll r_i \gg, \quad \chi_q = \frac{1}{N}\sum_{i=1}^{N} \ll q_i \gg, \quad (34)$$

$$\eta_{aa} = \frac{1}{N}\sum_{i=1}^{N} \ll a_i a_{i+1} \gg, \quad \eta_{rr} = \frac{1}{N}\sum_{i=1}^{N} \ll r_i r_{i+1} \gg, \quad \eta_{ar} = \frac{1}{N}\sum_{i=1}^{N} \ll a_i r_{i+1} \gg. \quad (35)$$

Then, for this network, the first moment approximation is given by

$$\begin{aligned}
-\frac{\partial}{\partial t}\chi_a &= \alpha\chi - w_2\chi_a\chi_r - w_1\chi_q\chi_a, \\
-\frac{\partial}{\partial t}\chi_r &= -\alpha\chi - \beta\chi_r + w_2\chi_q\chi_a, \\
\chi_q &= 1 - \chi_a - \chi_r.
\end{aligned} \quad (36)$$

The second moment approximation is given by

$$\begin{aligned}
-\frac{\partial}{\partial t}\chi_a &= \alpha\chi - w_2\eta_{ar} - w_1(\chi_a - \eta_{ar} - \eta_{aa}), \\
-\frac{\partial}{\partial t}\chi_r &= -\alpha\chi - \beta\chi_r + w_2\eta_{ar}, \\
-\frac{\partial}{\partial t}\eta_{aa} &= 2\alpha\eta_{aa} - w_2\eta_{ar}(\chi_a + 1) - w_1(\chi_a + 1)(\chi_a - \eta_{ar} - \eta_{aa}), \\
-\frac{\partial}{\partial t}\eta_{ar} &= -\alpha(\eta_{aa} - \eta_{ar}) - \beta\eta_{ar} + \frac{1}{2}w_2\eta_{ar}(\chi_a + 1), \\
&\quad + \frac{1}{2}\eta_{rr}\chi_a + w_1\chi_a(\chi_r - \eta_{rr} - \eta_{ar}), \\
-\frac{\partial}{\partial t}\eta_{rr} &= -2\alpha\eta_{ar} - 2\beta\eta_{rr} + w_2\eta_{rr}\chi_a.
\end{aligned} \quad (37)$$

Monte Carlo simulations of a ring of 10000 neurons were performed and compared with the first and second moment approximation predictions. We fixed the following parameters:

$$\alpha = 1.0, \quad \beta = 0.2, \quad w_1 = 0.01 \cdot w_0, \quad w_2 = 0.6 \cdot w_0 \tag{38}$$

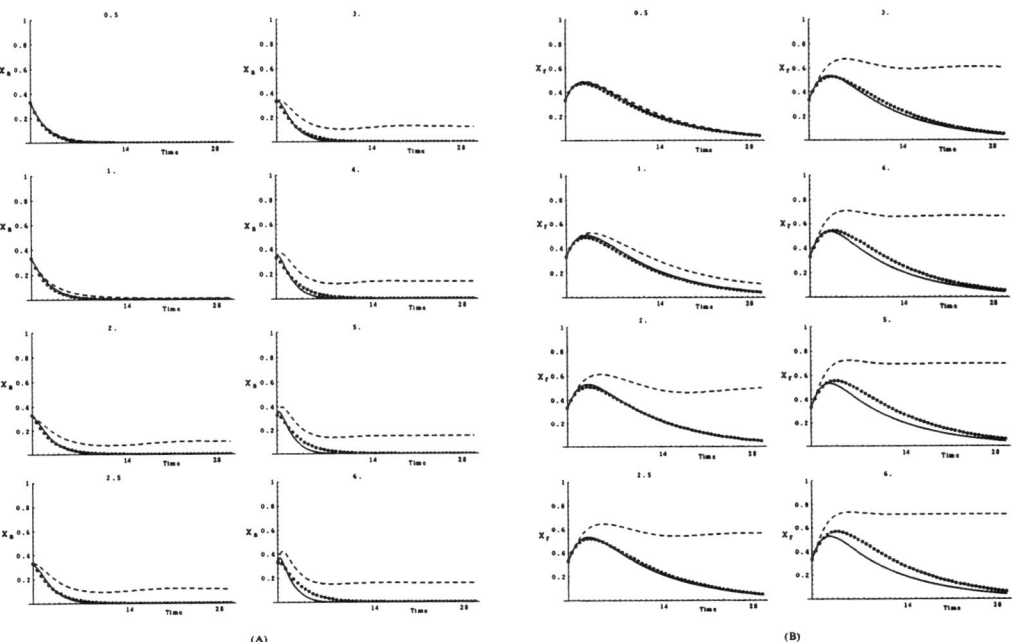

Figure 2: Comparison of Monte Carlo simulations (dots) with the first moment (dashed line) and the second moment (solid line) approximations for the three state case with the fraction of total active and refractory state variables χ_a (A) and χ_r (B). Each graph is labeled by the values of w_0/α.

We varied w_0 and sampled the numerical dynamics of these parameters. Some comparisons are shown in Figure 2 for the time dependence of the total number of active and refractory state variables. We clearly see the improvement of the second over the first moment level approximation. More simulations with different parameter ranges remain to be explored.

5 CONCLUSION

We have introduced here a neural network master equation using the outer-product representation. In this representation, the extension from two to three-state neurons is transparent. We have taken advantage of this natural extension to analyse three-state networks. Even though the calculations involved are more intricate, we have obtained results indicating that the second moment level approximation is significantly more accurate than the first moment level approximation. We also note that as in the two-state case, the first moment level approximation produces more activation than the simulation. Further analytical and theoretical investigations are needed to fully uncover the dynamics of three-state networks described by the master equation introduced above.

Acknowledgements

This work was supported in part by the Robert R. McCormick fellowship at the University of Chicago, and in part by grant No. N0014-89-J-1099 from the US Department of the Navy, Office of Naval Research.

References

Cowan JD (1991) Stochastic neurodynamics in Advances in Neural Information Processing Systems (D. S. Touretzky, R. P. Lippman, J. E. Moody, ed.), vol. 3, Morgan Kaufmann Publishers, San Mateo

Doi M (1976a) Second quantization representation for classical many-particle system. J. Phys. A: Math Gen. 9:1465–1477.

Doi M (1976b) Stochastic theory of diffusion-controlled reactions. J. Phys. A: Math. Gen. 9:1479.

Grassberger P, Scheunert M (1980) Fock-space methods for identical classical objects. Fortschritte der Physik 28:547

Meunier C, Hansel D, Verga A (1989) Information processing in three-state neural networks. J. Stat. Phys. 55:859

Ohira T, Cowan JD (1993) Master-equation approach to stochastic neurodynamics. Phys. Rev. E 48:2259

Ohira T, Cowan JD (1994) Feynman Diagrams for Stochastic Neurodynamics. In Proceedings of Fifth Australian Conference of Neural Networks, pp218-221

Sakurai JJ (1985) Modern Quantum Mechanics. Benjamin/Cummings, Menlo Park

Learning Stochastic Perceptrons Under k-Blocking Distributions

Mario Marchand
Ottawa-Carleton Institute for Physics
University of Ottawa
Ottawa, Ont., Canada K1N 6N5
mario@physics.uottawa.ca

Saeed Hadjifaradji
Ottawa-Carleton Institute for Physics
University of Ottawa
Ottawa, Ont., Canada K1N 6N5
saeed@physics.uottawa.ca

Abstract

We present a statistical method that PAC learns the class of stochastic perceptrons with arbitrary monotonic activation function and weights $w_i \in \{-1, 0, +1\}$ when the probability distribution that generates the input examples is member of a family that we call *k-blocking distributions*. Such distributions represent an important step beyond the case where each input variable is statistically independent since the 2k-blocking family contains all the Markov distributions of order k. By stochastic perceptron we mean a perceptron which, upon presentation of input vector **x**, outputs 1 with probability $f(\sum_i w_i x_i - \theta)$. Because the same algorithm works for any monotonic (nondecreasing or nonincreasing) activation function f on Boolean domain, it handles the well studied cases of sigmoïds and the "usual" radial basis functions.

1 INTRODUCTION

Within recent years, the field of computational learning theory has emerged to provide a rigorous framework for the design and analysis of learning algorithms. A central notion in this framework, known as the "Probably Approximatively Correct" (PAC) learning criterion (Valiant, 1984), has recently been extended (Hassler, 1992) to analyze the learnability of *probabilistic* concepts (Kearns and Schapire, 1994; Schapire, 1992). Such concepts, which are stochastic rules that give the probability that input example **x** is classified as being positive, are natural probabilistic extensions of the deterministic concepts originally studied by Valiant (1984).

Motivated by the stochastic nature of many "real-world" learning problems and by the indisputable fact that biological neurons are probabilistic devices, some preliminary studies about the PAC learnability of simple probabilistic neural concepts have been reported recently (Golea and Marchand, 1993; Golea and Marchand, 1994). However, the probabilistic behaviors considered in these studies are quite specific and clearly need to be extended. Indeed, only classification noise superimposed on a deterministic signum function was considered in Golea and Marchand (1993). The probabilistic network, analyzed in Golea and Marchand (1994), consists of a linear superposition of signum functions and is thus solvable as a (simple) case of linear regression. What is clearly needed is the extension to the non-linear cases of sigmoids and radial basis functions. Another criticism about Golea and Marchand (1993, 1994) is the fact that their learnability results was established only for distributions where each input variable is statistically independent from all the others (sometimes called product distributions). In fact, very few positive learning results for non-trivial p-concepts classes are known to hold for larger classes of distributions. Therefore, in an effort to find algorithms that will work in practice, we introduce in this paper a new family of distributions that we call *k-blocking*. As we will argue, this family has the dual advantage of avoiding malicious and unnatural distributions that are prone to render simple concept classes unlearnable (Lin and Vitter, 1991) and of being likely to contain several distributions found in practice.

Our main contribution is to present a simple statistical method that PAC learns (in polynomial time) the class of stochastic perceptrons with monotonic (but otherwise arbitrary) activation functions and weights $w_i \in \{-1, 0, +1\}$ when the input examples are generated according to any distribution member of the k-blocking family. Due to space constraints, only a sketch of the proofs is presented here.

2 DEFINITIONS

The instance (input) space, $\mathcal{I}^n$, is the Boolean domain $\{-1, +1\}^n$. The set of all input variables is denoted by X. Each input example $\mathbf{x}$ is generated according to some unknown distribution D on $\mathcal{I}^n$. We will often use $p_D(\mathbf{x})$, or simply $p(\mathbf{x})$, to denote the probability of observing the vector value $\mathbf{x}$ under distribution D. If U and V are two disjoint subsets of X, $\mathbf{x}_U$ and $\mathbf{x}_V$ will denote the restriction (or projection) of $\mathbf{x}$ over the variables of U and V respectively and $p_D(\mathbf{x}_U|\mathbf{x}_V)$ will denote the probability, under distribution D, of observing the vector value $\mathbf{x}_U$ (for the variables in U) given that the variables in V are set to the vector value $\mathbf{x}_V$.

Following Kearns and Schapire (1994), a *probabilistic concept* (p-concept) is a map $c : \mathcal{I}^n \to [0, 1]$ for which $c(\mathbf{x})$ represents the probability that example $\mathbf{x}$ is classified as positive. More precisely, upon presentation of input $\mathbf{x}$, an output of $\sigma = 1$ is generated (by an unknown target p-concept) with probability $c(\mathbf{x})$ and an output of $\sigma = 0$ is generated with probability $1 - c(\mathbf{x})$.

A *stochastic perceptron* is a p-concept parameterized by a vector of n weights w_i and a *activation function* $f(\cdot)$ such that, the probability that input example $\mathbf{x}$ is classified as positive is given by

$$\Pr(\sigma = 1 \,|\, \mathbf{x}) \;=\; f\left(\sum_{i=1}^{n} w_i x_i\right) \;. \tag{1}$$

We consider the case of a non-linear function $f(\cdot)$ since the linear case can be solved by a standard least square approximation like the one performed by Kearns in Schapire (1994) for linear sums of basis functions. We restrict ourselves to the case where $f(\cdot)$ is *monotonic i.e.* either nondecreasing or nonincreasing. But since any nonincreasing $f(\cdot)$ combined with a weight vector $\mathbf{w}$ can always be represented by a nondecreasing $f(\cdot)$ combined with a weight vector $-\mathbf{w}$, we can assume without loss of generality that the target stochastic perceptron has a nondecreasing $f(\cdot)$. Hence, we allow any sigmoïd-type of activation function (with arbitrary threshold). Also, since our instance space $\mathcal{I}^n$ is on a n-sphere, eq. 1 also include any nonincreasing radial basis function of the type $\phi(z^2)$ where $z = |\mathbf{x} - \mathbf{w}|$ and $\mathbf{w}$ is interpreted as the "center" of ϕ. The only significant restriction is on the weights where we allow only for $w_i \in \{-1, 0, +1\}$.

As usual, the goal of the learner is to return an *hypothesis* h which is a good approximation of the target p-concept c. But, in contrast with *decision rule learning* which attempts to "filter out" the noisy behavior by returning a deterministic hypothesis, the learner will attempt the harder (and more useful) task of modeling the target p-concept by returning a p-concept hypothesis. As a measure of error between the target and the hypothesis p-concepts we adopt the *variation distance* $d_v(\cdot,\cdot)$ defined as:

$$err(h,c) \;=\; d_v(h,c) \stackrel{\text{def}}{=} \sum_{\mathbf{x}} p_D(\mathbf{x}) \,|h(\mathbf{x}) - c(\mathbf{x})| \tag{2}$$

Where the summation is over all the 2^n possible values of $\mathbf{x}$. Hence, the same D is used for both training and testing. The following formulation of the PAC criterion (Valiant, 1984; Hassler, 1992) will be sufficient for our purpose.

Definition 1 *Algorithm A is said to PAC learn the class C of p-concepts by using the hypothesis class H (of p-concepts) under a family $\mathcal{D}$ of distributions on instance space $\mathcal{I}^n$, iff for any $c \in C$, any $D \in \mathcal{D}$, any $0 < \epsilon, \delta < 1$, algorithm A returns in a time polynomial in $(1/\epsilon, 1/\delta, n)$, an hypothesis $h \in H$ such that with probability at least $1 - \delta$, $err(h,c) < \epsilon$.*

3 K-BLOCKING DISTRIBUTIONS

To learn the class of stochastic perceptrons, the algorithm will try to discover each weight w_i that connects to input variable x_i by estimating how the probability of observing a positive output ($\sigma = 1$) is affected by "hard-wiring" variable x_i to some fixed value. This should clearly give some information about w_i when x_i is statistically independent from all the other variables as was the case for Golea and Marchand (1993) and Schapire (1992). However, if the input variables are correlated, then the process of fixing variable x_i will carry over neighboring variables which in turn will affect other variables until all the variables are perturbed (even in the simplest case of a first order Markov chain). The information about w_i will then be smeared by all the other weights. Therefore, to obtain information only on w_i, we need to break this "chain reaction" by fixing some other variables. The notion of *blocking sets* serves this purpose.

Loosely speaking, a set of variables is said to be a blocking set[1] for variable x_i if the distribution on all the remaining variables is unaffected by the setting of x_i whenever all the variables of the blocking set are set to a fixed value. More precisely, we have:

Definition 2 *Let B be a subset of X and let $U = X - (B \cup \{x_i\})$. Let $\mathbf{x}_B$ and $\mathbf{x}_U$ be the restriction of $\mathbf{x}$ on B and U respectively and let $\mathbf{b}$ be an assignment for $\mathbf{x}_B$. Then B is said to be a blocking set for variable x_i (with respect to D), iff:*

$$p_D(\mathbf{x}_U|\mathbf{x}_B = \mathbf{b}, x_i = +1) = p_D(\mathbf{x}_U|\mathbf{x}_B = \mathbf{b}, x_i = -1) \quad \text{for all } \mathbf{b} \text{ and } \mathbf{x}_U$$

In addition, if B is not anymore a blocking set when we remove anyone of its variables, we then say that B is a minimal *blocking set for variable x_i.*

We thus adopt the following definition for the k-blocking family.

Definition 3 *Distribution D on $\mathcal{I}^n$ is said to be k-blocking iff $|B_i| \leq k$ for $i = 1, 2 \cdots n$ when each B_i is a minimal blocking set for variable x_i.*

The k-blocking family is quite a large class of distributions. In fact we have the following property:

Property 1 *All Markov distributions of kth order are members of the 2k-blocking family.*

Proof: By kth order Markov distributions, we mean distributions which can be exactly written as a Chow(k) expansion (see Hoeffgen, 1993) for some permutation of the variables. We prove it here (by using standard techniques such as in Abend et. al, 1965) for first order Markov distributions, the generalization for $k > 1$ is straightforward. Recall that for Markov chain distributions we have: $p(x_j|x_{j-1}, \cdots x_1) = p(x_j|x_{j-1})$ for $1 < j \leq n$. Hence:

$$\begin{aligned} &p(x_1 \cdots x_{j-2}, x_{j+2} \cdots x_n | x_{j-1}, x_j, x_{j+1}) \\ &= p(x_1)p(x_2|x_1) \cdots p(x_j|x_{j-1})p(x_{j+1}|x_j) \cdots p(x_n|x_{n-1})/p(x_{j-1}, x_j, x_{j+1}) \\ &= p(x_1)p(x_2|x_1) \cdots p(x_{j-1}|x_{j-2})p(x_{j+2}|x_{j+1}) \cdots p(x_n|x_{n-1})/p(x_{j-1}) \\ &= p(x_1 \cdots x_{j-2}, x_{j+2} \cdots x_n | x_{j-1}, \overline{x_j}, x_{j+1}) \end{aligned}$$

where $\overline{x_j}$ denotes the negation of $\mathbf{x}_j$. Thus, we see that Markov chain distributions are a special case of 2-blocking distributions: the blocking set of each variable consisting only of the two first-neighbor variables. □.

The proposed algorithm for learning stochastic perceptrons needs to be provided with a blocking set (of at most k variables) for each input variable. Hoeffgen (1993) has recently proven that Chow(1) and Chow($k > 1$) expansions are efficiently learnable; the latter under some restricted conditions. We can thus use these algorithms

---

[1]The wording "blocking set" was also used by Hancock & Mansour (*Proc. of COLT'91*, 179–183, Morgan Kaufmann Publ.) to denote a property of the target concept. In contrast, our definition of blocking set denotes a property of the input distribution only.

to discover the blocking sets for such distributions. However, the efficient learnability of unrestricted Chow($k > 1$) expansions and larger classes of distributions, such as the k-blocking family, is still unknown. In fact, from the hardness results of Hoeffgen (1993), we can see that it is definitely very hard (perhaps NP-complete) to find the blocking sets if the learner has no information available other than the fact that the distribution is k-blocking. On the other hand, we can argue that the "natural" ordering of the variables present in many "real-world" situations is such that the blocking set of any given variable is among the neighboring variables. In vision for example, we expect that the setting of a pixel will directly affect only those located in it's neighborhood; the other pixels being affected only through this neighborhood. In such cases, the neighborhood of a variable "naturally" provides its blocking set.

4 LEARNING STOCHASTIC PERCEPTRONS

We first establish (the intuitive fact) that, without making much error, we can always consider that the target p-concept is defined only over the variables which are not almost always set to the same value.

Lemma 1 *Let V be a set of v variables x_i for which $\Pr(x_i = a_i) > 1 - \alpha$. Let c be a p-concept and let c' be the same p-concept as c except that the reading of each variable $x_i \in V$ is replaced by the reading of the constant value a_i. Then $err(c', c) < v \cdot \alpha$.*

Proof: Let $\mathbf{a}$ be the vector obtained from the concatenation of all a_is and let $\mathbf{x}_V$ be the vector obtained from $\mathbf{x}$ by keeping only the components x_i which are in V. Then $err(c', c) \leq \Pr(\mathbf{x}_V \neq \mathbf{a}) \leq \sum_{i \in V} \Pr(x_i \neq a_i)$. □

For a given set of blocking sets $\{B_i\}_{i=1}^n$, the algorithm will try to discover each weight w_i by estimating the *blocked influence* of x_i defined as:

$$\text{Binf}(x_i|\mathbf{b}_i) \stackrel{\text{def}}{=} \Pr(\sigma = 1|\mathbf{x}_{B_i} = \mathbf{b}_i, x_i = +1) - \Pr(\sigma = 1|\mathbf{x}_{B_i} = \mathbf{b}_i, x_i = -1)$$

where $\mathbf{x}_{B_i}$ denotes the restriction of $\mathbf{x}$ on the blocking set B_i for variable x_i and $\mathbf{b}_i$ is an assignment for $\mathbf{x}_{B_i}$. The following lemma ensures the learner that $\text{Binf}(x_i|\mathbf{b}_i)$ contains enough information about w_i.

Lemma 2 *Let the target p-concept be a stochastic perceptron on $\mathcal{I}^n$ having a nondecreasing activation function and weights taken from $\{-1, 0, +1\}$. Then, for any assignment $\mathbf{b}_i$ for the variables in the blocking set B_i of variable x_i, we have:*

$$\text{Binf}(x_i|\mathbf{b}_i) \begin{cases} \geq 0 & \text{if } w_i = +1 \\ = 0 & \text{if } w_i = 0 \\ \leq 0 & \text{if } w_i = -1 \end{cases} \tag{3}$$

Proof sketch: Let $U = X - (B_i \cup \{x_i\})$, $s = \sum_{j \in U} w_j x_j$ and $\zeta = \sum_{k \in B_i} w_k b_k$. Let $p(s)$ denote the probability of observing s (under D). Then $\text{Binf}(x_i|\mathbf{b}_i) = \sum_s p(s)\left[f(s + \zeta + w_i) - f(s + \zeta - w_i)\right]$; from which we find the desired result for a nondecreasing $f(\cdot)$. □

In principle, lemma 2 enables the learner to discover w_i from $\text{Binf}(x_i|\mathbf{b}_i)$. The learner, however, has only access to its *empirical estimate* $\widehat{\text{Binf}}(x_i|\mathbf{b}_i)$ from a finite sample. Hence, we will use Hoeffding's inequality (Hoeffding, 1963) to find the number of examples needed for a probability p to be close to its empirical estimate $\hat{p}$ with high probability.

Lemma 3 (Hoeffding, 1963) *Let $Y_1, \ldots, Y_m$ be a sequence of m independent Bernoulli trials, each succeeding with probability p. Let $\hat{p} = \sum_{i=1}^{m} Y_i/m$. Then:*

$$\Pr(|\hat{p} - p| > \epsilon) \leq 2\exp(-2m\epsilon^2)$$

Hence, by writing $\text{Binf}(x_i|\mathbf{b}_i)$ in terms of (unconditional) probabilities that can be estimated from *all* the training examples, we find from lemma 3 that the number $m_0(\epsilon, \delta, n)$ of examples needed to have $|\widehat{\text{Binf}}(x_i|\mathbf{b}_i) - \text{Binf}(x_i|\mathbf{b}_i)| < \epsilon$ with probability at least $1 - \delta$ is given by:

$$m_0(\epsilon, \delta, n) \geq \frac{1}{2}\left(\frac{8}{\kappa\epsilon}\right)^2 \ln\left(\frac{4}{\delta}\right)$$

where $\kappa = \alpha^{k+1}$ is the lowest permissible value for $p_D(\mathbf{b}_i, x_i)$ (see lemma 1). So, if the minimal nonzero value for $|\text{Binf}(x_i|\mathbf{b}_i)|$ is β, then the number of examples needed to find, with confidence at least $1 - \delta$, the exact value for w_i among $\{-1, 0, +1\}$ is such that we need to have: $\Pr(|\widehat{\text{Binf}}(x_i|\mathbf{b}_i) - \text{Binf}(x_i|\mathbf{b}_i)| < \beta/2) > 1 - \delta$. Thus, whenever β is of $\Omega(e^{-n})$, we will need of $O(e^{2n})$ examples to find (with prob $> 1-\delta$) the value for w_i. So, in order to be able to PAC learn from a polynomial sample, we must arrange ourselves so that we do not need to worry about such low values for $|\text{Binf}(x_i|\mathbf{b}_i)|$. We therefore consider the *maximum blocked influence* defined as:

$$\text{Binf}(x_i) \stackrel{\text{def}}{=} \text{Binf}(x_i|\mathbf{b}_i^*)$$

where $\mathbf{b}_i^*$ is the vector value for which $|\text{Binf}(x_i|\mathbf{b}_i)|$ is the largest. We now show that the learner can ignore all variables x_i for which $|\text{Binf}(x_i)|$ is too small (without making much error).

Lemma 4 *Let c be a stochastic perceptron with nondecreasing activation function $f(\cdot)$ and weights taken from $\{-1, 0, +1\}$. Let $V \subset X$ and let c_V be the same stochastic perceptron as c except that $w_i = 0$ for all $x_i \in V$ and its activation function is changed to $f(\cdot + \theta)$. Then, there always exists a value for θ such that:*

$$err(c_V, c) \leq \sum_{i \in V} |\text{Binf}(x_i)|$$

Proof sketch: By induction on $|V|$. To first verify the lemma for $V = \{x_1\}$, let $\mathbf{b}$ be a vector of values for the setting of all $x_i \in B_1$ and let $\mathbf{x}_U$ be a vector of values for the setting of all $x_j \in U = X - (B_1 \cup \{x_1\})$. Let $s = \sum_{j \in U} w_j x_j$ and $\zeta = \sum_{j \in B_1} w_j x_j$, then for $\theta = w_1$, we have:

$$err(c_V, c) = \sum_{\mathbf{x}_U}\sum_{\mathbf{b}} p_D(\mathbf{x}_U|\mathbf{b}) p_D(\mathbf{b}|x_1 = -1) p_D(x_1 = -1)$$
$$\times |f(s + \zeta + w_1) - f(s + \zeta - w_1)| \leq |\text{Binf}(x_1)|$$

We now assume that the lemma holds for $V = \{x_1, x_2 \cdots x_k\}$ and prove it for $W = V \cup \{x_{k+1}\}$. Let $S = \{x_{k+1}\}$ and let $f(\cdot + \theta_W)$, $f(\cdot + \theta_V)$ and $f(\cdot + \theta_S)$ denote respectively the activation function for c_W, c_V and c_S. By inspecting the expressions for $err(c_V, c)$ and $err(c_W, c_S)$, we can see that there always exist a value for $\theta_W \in \{\theta_V + w_{k+1}, \theta_V - w_{k+1}\}$ and $\theta_S \in \{w_{k+1}, -w_{k+1}\}$ such that $err(c_W, c_S) \leq err(c_V, c)$. And since $d_v(\cdot, \cdot)$ satisfies the triangle inequality, $err(c_W, c) \leq err(c_V, c) + |\text{Binf}(x_{k+1})|$. □

After discovering the weights, the hypothesis p-concept h returned by the learner will simply be the table look-up of the estimated probabilities of observing a positive classification given that $\sum_{i=1}^{n} w_i x_i = s$ for all s values that are observed with sufficient probability (the hypothesis can output any value for the values of s that are observed very rarely). We thus have the following learning algorithm for stochastic perceptrons.

Algorithm LearnSP$(n, \epsilon, \delta, \{B_i\}_{i=1}^n)$

1. Call $m = 128 \left(\frac{2n}{\epsilon}\right)^{2k+4} \ln\left(\frac{16n}{\delta}\right)$ training examples (where $k = max_i |B_i|$).

2. Compute $\hat{\Pr}(x_i = +1)$ for each variable x_i. Neglect x_i whenever we have $\hat{\Pr}(x_i = +1) < \epsilon/(4n)$ or $\hat{\Pr}(x_i = +1) > 1 - \epsilon/(4n)$.

3. For each variable x_i and for each of its blocking vector value $\mathbf{b}_i$, compute $\hat{\text{Binf}}(x_i|\mathbf{b}_i)$. Let $\mathbf{b}_i^*$ be the value of $\mathbf{b}_i$ for which $|\hat{\text{Binf}}(x_i|\mathbf{b}_i)|$ is the largest. Let $\hat{\text{Binf}}(x_i) = \hat{\text{Binf}}(x_i|\mathbf{b}_i^*)$.

4. For each variable x_i:
   (a) Let $w_i = +1$ whenever $\hat{\text{Binf}}(x_i) > \epsilon/(4n)$.
   (b) Let $w_i = -1$ whenever $\hat{\text{Binf}}(x_i) < \epsilon/(4n)$.
   (c) Otherwise let $w_i = 0$

5. Compute $\hat{\Pr}(\sum_{i=1}^{n} w_i x_i = s)$ for $s = -n, \ldots +n$.

6. Return the hypothesis p-concept h formed by the table look-up:
$$h(\mathbf{x}) = h'(s) = \hat{\Pr}\left(\sigma = 1 \middle| \sum_{i=1}^{n} w_i x_i = s\right)$$
for all s for which $\hat{\Pr}(\sum_{i=1}^{n} w_i x_i = s) > \epsilon/(8n+8)$. For the other s values, let $h'(s) = 0$ (or any other value).

Theorem 1 *Algorithm* **LearnSP** *PAC learns the class of stochastic perceptrons on $\mathcal{I}^n$ with monotonic activation functions and weights $w_i \in \{-1, 0, +1\}$ under any k-blocking distribution (when a blocking set for each variable is known). The number of examples required is $m = 128\left(\frac{2n}{\epsilon}\right)^{2k+4} \ln\left(\frac{16n}{\delta}\right)$ (and the time needed is $O(n \times m)$) for the returned hypothesis to make error at most ϵ with confidence at least $1 - \delta$.*

Proof sketch: From Hoeffding's inequality (lemma 3) we can show that this sample size is sufficient to ensure that:

- $\left|\hat{\Pr}(x_i = +1) - \Pr(x_i = +1)\right| < \epsilon/(4n)$ with confidence at least $1 - \delta/(4n)$
- $\left|\hat{\text{Binf}}(x_i) - \text{Binf}(x_i)\right| < \epsilon/(4n)$ with confidence at least $1 - \delta/(4n)$
- $\left|\hat{\Pr}(\sum_{i=1}^{n} w_i x_i = s) - \Pr(\sum_{i=1}^{n} w_i x_i = s)\right| < \epsilon^2/[64(n+1)]$ with confidence at least $1 - \delta/(4n+4)$
- $\left|\widehat{\Pr}\left(\sigma = 1 | \sum_{i=1}^{n} w_i x_i = s\right) - \Pr\left(\sigma = 1 | \sum_{i=1}^{n} w_i x_i = s\right)\right| < \epsilon/4$ with confidence at least $1 - \delta/4$

From this and from lemma 1, 2 and 4, it follows that returned hypothesis will make error at most ϵ with confidence at least $1 - \delta$. □.

Acknowledgments

We thank Mostefa Golea, Klaus-U. Hoeffgen and Stefan Poelt for useful comments and discussions about technical points. M. Marchand is supported by NSERC grant OGP0122405. Saeed Hadjifaradji is supported by the MCHE of Iran.

References

Abend K., Hartley T.J. & Kanal L.N. (1965) "Classification of Binary Random Patterns", *IEEE Trans. Inform. Theory* vol. IT-11, 538–544.

Golea, M. & Marchand M. (1993) "On Learning Perceptrons with Binary Weights", *Neural Computation* vol. 5, 765–782.

Golea, M. & Marchand M. (1994) "On Learning Simple Deterministic and Probabilistic Neural Concepts", in Shawe-Talor J., Anthony M. (eds.), *Computational Learning Theory: EuroCOLT'93*, Oxford University Press, pp. 47–60.

Haussler D. (1992) "Decision Theoritic Generalizations of the PAC Model for Neural Net and Other Learning Applications", *Information and Computation* vol. 100, 78–150.

Hoeffgen K.U. (1993) "On Learning and Robust Learning of Product Distributions", *Proceedings of the 6th ACM Conference on Computational Learning Theory*, ACM Press, 77–83.

Hoeffding W. (1963) "Probability inequalities for sums of bounded random variables", *Journal of the American Statistical Association*, vol. 58(301), 13–30.

Kearns M.J. and Schapire R.E. (1994) " Efficient Distribution-free Learning of Probabilistic Concepts", *Journal of Computer and System Sciences*, Vol. 48, pp. 464–497.

Lin J.H. & Vitter J.S. (1991) "Complexity Results on Learning by Neural Nets", *Machine Learning*, Vol. 6, 211–230.

Schapire R.E. (1992) *The Design and Analysis of Efficient Learning Algorithms*, Cambridge MA: MIT Press.

Valiant L.G. (1984) "A Theory of the Learnable", *Comm. ACM*, Vol. 27, 1134–1142.

Learning from queries for maximum information gain in imperfectly learnable problems

Peter Sollich   David Saad
Department of Physics, University of Edinburgh
Edinburgh EH9 3JZ, U.K.
P.Sollich@ed.ac.uk, D.Saad@ed.ac.uk

Abstract

In supervised learning, learning from queries rather than from random examples can improve generalization performance significantly. We study the performance of query learning for problems where the student cannot learn the teacher perfectly, which occur frequently in practice. As a prototypical scenario of this kind, we consider a linear perceptron student learning a binary perceptron teacher. Two kinds of queries for maximum information gain, *i.e.*, minimum entropy, are investigated: Minimum *student space* entropy (MSSE) queries, which are appropriate if the teacher space is unknown, and minimum *teacher space* entropy (MTSE) queries, which can be used if the teacher space is assumed to be known, but a student of a simpler form has deliberately been chosen. We find that for MSSE queries, the structure of the student space determines the efficacy of query learning, whereas MTSE queries lead to a higher generalization error than random examples, due to a lack of feedback about the progress of the student in the way queries are selected.

1 INTRODUCTION

In systems that learn from examples, the traditional approach has been to study generalization from random examples, where each example is an input-output pair with the input chosen randomly from some fixed distribution and the corresponding output provided by a teacher that one is trying to approximate. However, random examples contain less and less new information as learning proceeds. Therefore, generalization performance can be improved by learning from queries, *i.e.*, by choosing the input of each new training example such that it will be, together with its expected output, in some sense 'maximally useful'. The most widely used measure of 'usefulness' is the information gain, *i.e.*, the decrease in entropy of the post-training probability distributions in the parameter space of the student or the teacher. We shall call the resulting queries 'minimum (student or teacher space) entropy (MSSE/MTSE) queries'; their effect on generalization performance has recently been investigated for *perfectly learnable* problems, where student and teacher space are identical (Seung *et al.*, 1992, Freund *et al.*, 1993, Sollich, 1994), and was found to depend qualitatively on the structure of the teacher. For a linear perceptron, for example, one obtains a relative reduction in generalization error compared to learning from random examples which becomes insignificant as the number of training examples, p, tends to infinity. For a perceptron with binary output, on the other hand, minimum entropy queries result in a generalization error which decays exponentially as p increases, a marked improvement over the much slower algebraic decay with p in the case of random examples.

In practical situations, one almost always encounters *imperfectly learnable* problems, where the student can only approximate the teacher, but not learn it perfectly. Imperfectly learnable problems can arise for two reasons: Firstly, the teacher space (*i.e.*, the space of models generating the data) might be unknown. Because the teacher space entropy is then also unknown, MSSE (and not MTSE) queries have to be used for query learning. Secondly, the teacher space may be known, but a student of a simpler structure might have deliberately been chosen to facilitate or speed up training, for example. In this case, MTSE queries could be employed as an alternative to MSSE queries. The motivation for doing this would be strongest if, as in the learning scenario that we consider below, it is known from analyses of perfectly learnable problems that the structure of the teacher space allows more significant improvements in generalization performance from query learning than the structure of the student space.

With the above motivation in mind, we investigate in this paper the performance of both MSSE and MTSE queries for a prototypical imperfectly learnable problem, in which a linear perceptron student is trained on data generated by a binary perceptron teacher. Both student and teacher are specified by an N-dimensional weight vector with real components, and we will consider the thermodynamic limit $N \to \infty, p \to \infty, \alpha = p/N = $ const. In Section 2 below we calculate the generalization error for learning from random examples. In Sections 3 and 4 we compare the result to MSSE and MTSE queries. Throughout, we only outline the necessary calculations; for details, we refer the reader to a forthcoming publication. We conclude in Section 5 with a summary and brief discussion of our results.

2 LEARNING FROM RANDOM EXAMPLES

We denote students and teachers by $\mathcal{N}$ (for 'Neural network') and $\mathcal{V}$ (for 'element of the Version space', see Section 4), respectively, and their corresponding weight

vectors by $\mathbf{w}_\mathcal{N}$ and $\mathbf{w}_\mathcal{V}$. For an input vector $\mathbf{x}$, the outputs of a given student and teacher are
$$y_\mathcal{N} = \frac{1}{\sqrt{N}} \mathbf{x}^T \mathbf{w}_\mathcal{N}, \quad y_\mathcal{V} = \text{sgn}\left(\frac{1}{\sqrt{N}} \mathbf{x}^T \mathbf{w}_\mathcal{V}\right).$$
Assuming that inputs are drawn from a uniform distribution over the hypersphere $\mathbf{x}^2 = N$, and taking as our error measure the standard squared output difference $\frac{1}{2}(y_\mathcal{N} - y_\mathcal{V})^2$, the generalization error, *i.e.*, the average error between student $\mathcal{N}$ and teacher $\mathcal{V}$ when tested on random test inputs, is given by

$$\epsilon_g(\mathcal{N}, \mathcal{V}) = \frac{1}{2}\left[Q_\mathcal{N} + 1 - 2\frac{R}{\sqrt{Q_\mathcal{V}}}\left(\frac{2}{\pi}\right)^{1/2}\right], \tag{1}$$

where we have set $R = \frac{1}{N}\mathbf{w}_\mathcal{N}^T \mathbf{w}_\mathcal{V}, Q_\mathcal{N} = \frac{1}{N}\mathbf{w}_\mathcal{N}^2, Q_\mathcal{V} = \frac{1}{N}\mathbf{w}_\mathcal{V}^2$.

As our training algorithm we take stochastic gradient descent on the training error E_t, which for a training set $\Theta^{(p)} = \{(\mathbf{x}^\mu, y^\mu = y_\mathcal{V}(\mathbf{x}^\mu)), \mu = 1\ldots p\}$ is $E_t = \frac{1}{2}\sum_\mu (y^\mu - y_\mathcal{N}(\mathbf{x}^\mu))^2$. A weight decay term $\frac{1}{2}\lambda \mathbf{w}_\mathcal{N}^2$ is added for regularization, *i.e.*, to prevent overfitting. Stochastic gradient descent on the resulting energy function $E = E_t + \frac{1}{2}\lambda \mathbf{w}_\mathcal{N}^2$ yields a Gibbs post-training distribution of students, $P(\mathbf{w}_\mathcal{N}|\Theta^{(p)}) \propto \exp(-E/T)$, where the training temperature T measures the amount of stochasticity in the training algorithm. For the linear perceptron students considered here, this distribution is Gaussian, with covariance matrix $T\mathbf{M}_\mathcal{N}^{-1}$, where ($\mathbf{1}_N$ denotes the $N \times N$ identity matrix)

$$\mathbf{M}_\mathcal{N} = \lambda \mathbf{1}_N + \frac{1}{N}\sum_{\mu=1}^p \mathbf{x}^\mu (\mathbf{x}^\mu)^T.$$

Since the length of the teacher weight vector $\mathbf{w}_\mathcal{V}$ does not affect the teacher outputs, we assume a spherical prior on teacher space, $P(\mathbf{w}_\mathcal{V}) \propto \delta(\mathbf{w}_\mathcal{V}^2 - N)$, for which $Q_\mathcal{V} = 1$. Restricting attention to the limit of zero training temperature, it is straightforward to calculate from eq. (1) the average generalization error obtained by training on random examples

$$\epsilon_g - \epsilon_{g,\min} = \frac{1}{\pi}\left[\lambda_{\text{opt}} G + \lambda(\lambda_{\text{opt}} - \lambda)\frac{\partial G}{\partial \lambda}\right], \tag{2}$$

with the function $G = \langle \frac{1}{N}\text{tr}\, \mathbf{M}_\mathcal{N}^{-1}\rangle_{P(\{\mathbf{x}^\mu\})}$ given by (Krogh and Hertz, 1992)

$$G = \frac{1}{2\lambda}\left[1 - \alpha - \lambda + \sqrt{(1 - \alpha - \lambda)^2 + 4\lambda}\right]. \tag{3}$$

In eq. (2) we have explicitly subtracted the minimum achievable generalization error, $\epsilon_{g,\min} = \frac{1}{2}(1 - 2/\pi)$, which is nonzero since a linear perceptron cannot approximate a binary perceptron perfectly. At finite α, the generalization error is minimized when the weight decay is set to its optimal value $\lambda = \lambda_{\text{opt}} = \pi/2 - 1$. Note that since both G and $\partial G/\partial \lambda$ tend to zero as $\alpha \to \infty$, the generalization error for random examples approaches the minimum achievable generalization error in this limit.

3 MINIMUM STUDENT SPACE ENTROPY QUERIES

We now calculate the generalization performance resulting from MSSE queries. For the training algorithm introduced in the last section, the student space entropy (normalized by N) is given by

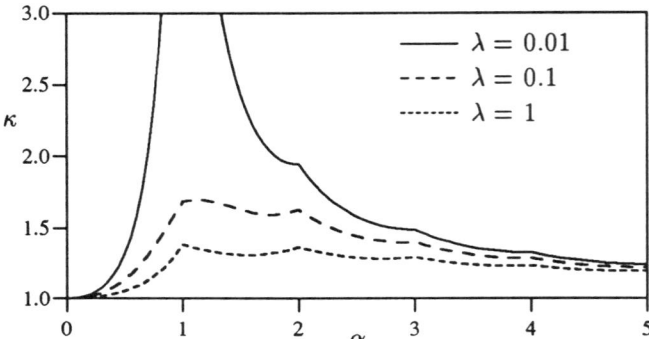

Figure 1: Relative improvement κ in generalization error due to MSSE queries, for weight decay $\lambda = 0.01, 0.1, 1$.

$$S_\mathcal{N} = -\frac{1}{2N} \ln \det \mathbf{M}_\mathcal{N},$$

where we have omitted an unimportant constant which depends on the training temperature only. This entropy is minimized by choosing each new query along the direction corresponding to the minimal eigenvalue of the existing $\mathbf{M}_\mathcal{N}$ (Sollich, 1994). The expression for the resulting average generalization error is given by eq. (2) with G replaced by its analogue for MSSE queries (Sollich, 1994)

$$G_Q = \frac{\Delta\alpha}{\lambda + [\alpha] + 1} + \frac{1 - \Delta\alpha}{\lambda + [\alpha]},$$

where $[\alpha]$ is the greatest integer less than or equal to α and $\Delta\alpha = \alpha - [\alpha]$. We define the improvement factor κ as the ratio of the generalization error (with the minimum achievable generalization error subtracted as in eq. (2)) for random examples to that for MSSE queries. Figure 1 shows $\kappa(\alpha)$ for several values of the weight decay λ. Comparing with existing results (Sollich, 1994), we find that κ is *exactly* the same as if our linear student were trying to approximate a linear teacher with additive noise of variance λ_{opt} on the outputs. For large α, one can show (Sollich, 1994) that $\kappa = 1 + 1/\alpha + O(1/\alpha^2)$ and hence the relative reduction in generalization error due to querying tends to zero as $\alpha \to \infty$. We investigate in the next section whether it is possible to improve generalization performance more significantly by using MTSE queries.

4 MINIMUM TEACHER SPACE ENTROPY QUERIES

We now consider the generalization performance achieved by MTSE queries. We remind readers that such queries could be used if the teacher space is known, but a student of a simpler functional form has deliberately chosen. The aim in using MTSE rather than MSSE queries would be to exploit the structure of the teacher space if this is known (for perfectly learnable problems) to make query learning very efficient compared to random examples.

For the case of noise free training data under consideration, the posterior probability distribution in teacher space given a certain training set is proportional to the prior distribution on the version space (the set of all teachers that could have produced the training set without error) and zero everywhere else. From this the (normalized) teacher space entropy can be derived to be, up to an additive constant,

$$S_\nu = \frac{1}{N} \ln V(p),$$

where the version space volume $V(p)$ is given by ($\Theta(z) = 1$ for $z > 0$ and 0 otherwise)

$$V(p) = \int d\mathbf{w}_\nu \, P(\mathbf{w}_\nu) \prod_{\mu=1}^{p} \Theta\left(\frac{1}{\sqrt{N}} y^\mu \mathbf{w}_\nu^T \mathbf{x}^\mu\right).$$

It can easily be verified that this entropy is minimized[1] by choosing queries $\mathbf{x}$ which 'bisect' the existing version space, *i.e.*, for which the hyperplane perpendicular to $\mathbf{x}$ splits the version space into two equal halves (Seung *et al.*, 1992, Freund *et al.*, 1993). Such queries lead to an exponentially shrinking version space, $V(p) = 2^{-p}$, and hence a linear decrease of the entropy, $S_\nu = -\alpha \ln 2$. We consider instead queries which achieve qualitatively the same effect, but permit a much simpler analysis of the resulting student performance. They are similar to those studied in the context of a learnable problem by Watkin and Rau (1992), and are defined as follows. The $(p+1)$th query is obtained by first picking a random teacher vector $\mathbf{w}_p$ from the version space defined by the existing p training examples, and then picking the new training input $\mathbf{x}_{p+1}$ from the distribution of random inputs but under the constraint that $\mathbf{x}_{p+1}^T \mathbf{w}_p = 0$.

For the calculation of the student performance, *i.e.*, the average generalization error, achieved by the approximate MTSE queries described above, we use an approximation based on the following observation. As the number of training examples, p, increases, the teacher vectors $\mathbf{w}_p$ from the version space will align themselves with the true teacher $\mathbf{w}_\nu^0$; their components along the direction of $\mathbf{w}_\nu^0$ will increase, whereas their components perpendicular to $\mathbf{w}_\nu^0$ will decrease, varying widely across the $N-1$ dimensional hyperplane perpendicular to $\mathbf{w}_\nu^0$. Following Watkin and Rau (1992), we therefore assume that the only significant effect of choosing queries $\mathbf{x}_{p+1}$ with $\mathbf{x}_{p+1}^T \mathbf{w}_p = 0$ is on the distribution of the component of $\mathbf{x}_{p+1}$ along $\mathbf{w}_\nu^0$. Writing this component as $x_{p+1}^0 = \mathbf{x}_{p+1}^T \mathbf{w}_\nu^0 / |\mathbf{w}_\nu^0|$, its probability distribution can readily be shown to be

$$P(x_{p+1}^0) \propto \exp\left(-\tfrac{1}{2}(x_{p+1}^0/s_p)^2\right), \tag{4}$$

where s_p is the sine of the angle between $\mathbf{w}_p$ and $\mathbf{w}_\nu^0$. For finite N, the value of s_p is dependent on the p previous training examples that define the existing version space and on the teacher vector $\mathbf{w}_p$ sampled randomly from this version space. In the thermodynamic limit, however, the variations of s_p become vanishingly small and we can thus replace s_p by its average value, which is a function of p alone. In the thermodynamic limit, this average value becomes a continuous function of $\alpha = p/N$, the number of training examples per weight, which we denote simply by $s(\alpha)$. The calculation can then be split into two parts: First, the function $s(\alpha)$ is obtained from a calculation of the teacher space entropy using the replica method, generalizing the results of Györgi and Tishby (1990). The average generalization

---

[1] More precisely, what is minimized is the value of the entropy after a new training example $(\mathbf{x}, y)$ is added, averaged over the distribution of the unknown new training output y given the new training input $\mathbf{x}$ and the existing training set; see Sollich (1994).

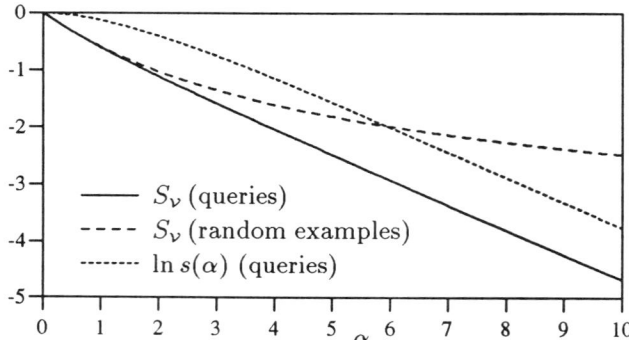

Figure 2: MTSE queries: Teacher space entropy, S_ν (with value for random examples plotted for comparison), and $\ln s$, the log of the sine of the angle between the true teacher and a random teacher from the version space.

error can then be calculated by using an extension of the response function method described in (Sollich, 1994b) or by another replica calculation (now in student space) as in (Dunmur and Wallace, 1993).

Figure 2 shows the effects of (approximate) MTSE queries in teacher space. For large α values, the teacher space entropy decreases linearly with α, with gradient $c \approx 0.44$, whereas the entropy for random examples, also shown for comparison, decreases much more slowly (asymptotically like $-\ln \alpha$, see (Györgi and Tishby, 1990)). The linear α-dependence of the entropy for queries corresponds to an average reduction of the version space volume with each new training example by a factor of $\exp(-c) \approx 0.64$, which is reasonably close to the factor $\frac{1}{2}$ for proper bisection of the version space. This justifies our choice of analysing approximate MTSE queries rather than true MTSE queries, since the former achieve qualitatively the same results as the latter.

Before discussing the student performance achieved by (approximate) MTSE queries, we note from figure 2 that $\ln s(\alpha)$ decreases linearly with α for large α, with the same gradient as the teacher space entropy. Hence $s(\alpha) \propto \exp(-c\alpha)$ for large α, and MTSE queries force the average teacher from the version space to approach the true teacher exponentially quickly. It can easily be shown that if we were learning with a binary perceptron student, $i.e.$, if the problem were perfectly learnable, then this would result in an exponentially decaying generalization error, $\epsilon_g \propto \exp(-c\alpha)$. MTSE queries would thus lead to a marked improvement in generalization performance over random examples (for which $\epsilon_g \propto 1/\alpha$, see (Györgi and Tishby, 1990)). It is this significant benefit (in teacher space) of query learning that provides the motivation for using MTSE queries in imperfectly learnable problems such as the one considered here.

The results plotted in Figure 3 for the average generalization error achieved by the linear perceptron student show, however, that MTSE queries do not have the desired effect. Far from translating the benefits in teacher space into improvements in generalization performance for the linear student, they actually lead to a deterioration of generalization performance, $i.e.$, a larger generalization error than that

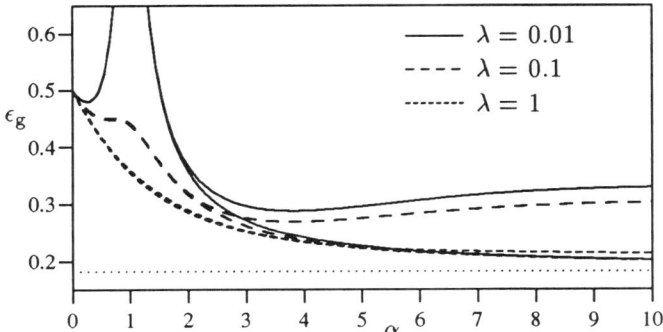

Figure 3: Generalization error for MTSE queries (higher curves of each pair) and random examples (lower curves), for weight decay $\lambda = 0.01, 0.1, 1$. The curves for random examples (which are virtually indistinguishable from one another already at $\alpha = 10$) converge to the minimum achievable generalization error $\epsilon_{g,\min}$ (dotted line) as $\alpha \to \infty$.

obtained for random examples. Worse still, they 'mislead' the student to such an extent that the minimum achievable generalization error is not reached even for an infinite number of training examples, $\alpha \to \infty$. How does this happen? It can be verified that the angle between the student and teacher weight vectors tends to zero for $\alpha \to \infty$ as expected, while $Q_\mathcal{N}$, the normalized squared length of the student weight vector, approaches

$$Q_\mathcal{N}(\alpha \to \infty) = \frac{2}{\pi} \left(\frac{\overline{s}}{\lambda + \overline{s^2}} \right)^2, \qquad (5)$$

where $\overline{s} = \int_0^\infty d\alpha\, s(\alpha)$, $\overline{s^2} = \int_0^\infty d\alpha\, s^2(\alpha)$. Unless the weight decay parameter λ happens to be equal to $\overline{s} - \overline{s^2}$, this is different from the optimal asymptotic value, which is $2/\pi$. This is the reason why in general the linear student does not reach the minimum possible generalization error even as $\alpha \to \infty$. The approach of $Q_\mathcal{N}$ to its non-optimal asymptotic value can cause an increase in the generalization error for large α and a corresponding minimum of the generalization error at some finite α, as can be seen in the plots for $\lambda = 0.01$ and 0.1 in Figure 3. For $\lambda = 0$, eq. (5) has the following intuitive interpretation: As α increases, the version space shrinks around the true teacher $\mathbf{w}_\nu^0$, and hence MTSE queries become 'more and more orthogonal' to $\mathbf{w}_\nu^0$. As a consequence, the distribution of training inputs along the direction of $\mathbf{w}_\nu^0$ is narrowed down progressively (compare eq. (4)). Trying to find a best fit to the teacher's binary output function over this narrower range of inputs, the linear student learns a function which is steeper than the best fit over the range of random inputs (which would give minimum generalization error). This corresponds to a suboptimally large length of the student weight vector in agreement with eq. (5): $Q_\mathcal{N}(\alpha \to \infty) > 2/\pi$ for $\lambda = 0$ because $\overline{s^2} < \overline{s}$.

Summarizing the results of this section, we have found that although MTSE queries are very beneficial in teacher space, they are entirely misleading for the linear student, to the extent that the student does not learn to approximate the teacher optimally even for an infinite number of training examples.

5 SUMMARY AND DISCUSSION

We have found in our study of an imperfectly learnable problem with a linear student and a binary teacher that queries for minimum student and teacher space entropy, respectively, have very different effects on generalization performance. Minimum student space entropy (MSSE) queries essentially have the same effect as for a linear student learning a noisy linear teacher, apart from a nonzero minimum value of the generalization error due to the unlearnability of the problem. Hence the structure of the student space is the dominating influence on the efficacy of query learning. Minimum teacher space entropy queries (MTSE), on the other hand, perform worse than random examples, leading to a higher generalization error even for an infinite number of training examples. With the benefit of hindsight, we note that this makes intuitive sense since the teacher space entropy, according to which MTSE queries are selected, contains no feedback about the progress of the student in learning the required generalization task, and thus MTSE queries cannot be guaranteed to have a positive effect.

Our results, then, are a mixture of good and bad news for query learning for maximum information gain in imperfectly learnable problems: The bad news is that MTSE queries, due to a lack of feedback information about student progress, are not enough to translate significant benefits in teacher space into similar improvements of student performance and may in fact yield worse performance than random examples. The good news is that for MSSE queries, we have found evidence that the structure of the student space is the key factor in determining the efficacy of query learning. If this result holds more generally, then statements about the benefits of query learning can be made on the basis of *how one is trying to learn* only, independently of *what one is trying to learn*—a result of great practical significance.

References

A P Dunmur and D J Wallace (1993). Learning and generalization in a linear perceptron stochastically trained with noisy data. *J. Phys. A*, 26:5767–5779.

Y Freund, H S Seung, E Shamir, and N Tishby (1993). Information, prediction, and query by committee. In S J Hanson, J D Cowan, and C Lee Giles, editors, *NIPS 5*, pages 483–490, San Mateo, CA, Morgan Kaufmann.

G Györgi and N Tishby (1990). Statistical theory of learning a rule. In W Theumann and R Köberle, editors, *Neural Networks and Spin Glasses*, pages 3–36. Singapore, World Scientific.

A Krogh and J A Hertz (1992). Generalization in a linear perceptron in the presence of noise. *J. Phys. A*, 25:1135–1147.

P Sollich (1994). Query construction, entropy, and generalization in neural network models. *Phys. Rev. E*, 49:4637–4651.

P Sollich (1994b). Finite-size effects in learning and generalization in linear perceptrons. *J. Phys. A*, 27:7771–7784.

H S Seung, M Opper, and H Sompolinsky (1992). Query by committee. In *Proceedings of COLT '92*, pages 287–294, New York, ACM.

T L H Watkin and A Rau (1992). Selecting examples for perceptrons. *J. Phys. A*, 25:113–121.

Bias, Variance and the Combination of Least Squares Estimators

Ronny Meir
Faculty of Electrical Engineering
Technion, Haifa 32000
Israel
rmeir@ee.technion.ac.il

Abstract

We consider the effect of combining several least squares estimators on the expected performance of a regression problem. Computing the exact bias and variance curves as a function of the sample size we are able to quantitatively compare the effect of the combination on the bias and variance separately, and thus on the expected error which is the sum of the two. Our exact calculations, demonstrate that the combination of estimators is particularly useful in the case where the data set is small and noisy and the function to be learned is unrealizable. For large data sets the single estimator produces superior results. Finally, we show that by splitting the data set into several independent parts and training each estimator on a different subset, the performance can in some cases be significantly improved.

Key words: Bias, Variance, Least Squares, Combination.

1 INTRODUCTION

Many of the problems related to supervised learning can be boiled down to the question of balancing bias and variance. While reducing bias can usually be accomplished quite easily by simply increasing the complexity of the class of models studied, this usually comes at the expense of increasing the variance in such a way that the overall expected error (which is the sum of the two) is often increased.

Thus, many efforts have been devoted to the issue of decreasing variance, while attempting to keep the concomitant increase in bias as small as possible. One of the methods which has become popular recently in the neural network community is variance reduction by combining estimators, although the idea has been around in the statistics and econometrics literature at least since the late sixties (see Granger 1989 for a review). Nevertheless, it seems that not much analytic work has been devoted to a detailed study of the effect of noise and an effectively *finite* sample size on the bias/variance balance. It is the explicit goal of this paper to study in detail a simple problem of linear regression, where the full bias/variance curve can be computed exactly for *any* effectively finite sample size and noise level. We believe that this simple and exactly solvable model can afford us insight into more complex non-linear problems, which are at the heart of much of the recent work in neural networks.

A further aspect of our work is related to the question of the partitioning of the data set between the various estimators. Thus, while most studies assume the each estimator is trained on the complete data set, it is possible to envisage a situation where the data set is broken up into several subsets, using each subset of data to form a different estimator. While such a scheme seems wasteful from the bias point of view, we will see that in fact it produces superior forecasts in some situations. This, perhaps suprising, result is due to a large decrease in variance resulting from the independence of the estimators, in the case where the data subsets are independent.

2 ON THE COMBINATION OF ESTIMATORS

The basic objective of regression is the following: given a finite training set, D, composed of n input/output pairs, $D = \{(\mathbf{x}_\mu, y_\mu)\}_{\mu=1}^n$, drawn according to an *unkown* distribution $P(\mathbf{x}, y)$, find a function ('estimator'), $f(\mathbf{x}; D)$, which 'best' approximates y. Using the popular mean-squared error criterion and taking expectations with respect to the data distribution one finds the well-known separation of the error into a bias and variance terms respectively (Geman et al. 1992)

$$\mathcal{E}(\mathbf{x}) = (E_D f(\mathbf{x}; D) - E[y|\mathbf{x}])^2 + E_D \left[f(\mathbf{x}; D) - E_D f(\mathbf{x}; D) \right]^2. \quad (1)$$

We consider a data source of the form $y = g(\mathbf{x}) + \eta$, where the 'target' function $g(\mathbf{x})$ is an unknown (and potentially non-linear) function and η is a Gaussian random variable with zero mean and variance σ^2. Clearly then $E[y|\mathbf{x}] = g(\mathbf{x})$.

In the usual scenario for parameter estimation one uses the complete data set, D, to form an estimator $f(\mathbf{x}; D)$. In this paper we consider the case where the data set D is broken up into K subsets (not necessarily disjoint), such that $D = \cap_{k=1}^K D^{(k)}$, and a separate estimator is found for each subset. The full estimator is then given by the linear combination (Granger 1989)

$$f(\mathbf{x}; D) = \sum_{k=1}^K b_k f_k(\mathbf{x}; D^{(k)}). \quad (2)$$

The optimal values of the parameters b_k can be easily obtained if the data distribution, $P(\mathbf{x}, y)$, is known, by simply minimizing the mean-squared error (Granger

1989). In the more typical case where this distribution is unkown, one may resort to other schemes such as least-squares fitting for the parameter vector $\mathbf{b} = \{b_1, \ldots, b_K\}$. The bias and variance of the combined estimator can be simply expressed in this case, and are given by

$$B(\mathbf{x}; g) = \left(\sum_{k=1}^{K} b_k \overline{f_k}(\mathbf{x}) - g(\mathbf{x})\right)^2 \quad ; \quad V(\mathbf{x}; g) = \sum_{k,k'} b_k b_{k'} \{\overline{f_k f_{k'}}(\mathbf{x}) - \overline{f_k}(\mathbf{x})\overline{f_{k'}}(\mathbf{x})\} \tag{3}$$

where the overbars denote an average with respect to the data. It is immediately apparent that the variance term is composed of two contributions. The first term, corresponding to $k = k'$, simply computes a weighted average of the single estimator variances, while the second term measures the average covariance between the different estimators. While the first term in the variance can be seen to decay as $1/K$ in the case where all the weights b_k are of the same order of magnitude, the second term is finite *unless* the covariances between estimators are very small. It would thus seem beneficial to attempt to make the estimators as weakly correlated as possible in order to decrease the variance. Observe that in the extreme case where the data sets are independent of each other, the second term in the variance vanishes identically. Note that the bias term depends only on single estimator properties and can thus be computed from the theory of the single estimator. As mentioned above, however, the second term in the variance expression explicitly depends on correlations between the different estimators, and thus requires the computation of quantities beyond those of single estimators.

3 THE SINGLE LINEAR ESTIMATOR

Before considering the case of a combination of estimators, we first review the case of a single *linear* estimator, given by $f(\mathbf{x}; D) = \hat{\mathbf{w}}^T \cdot \mathbf{x}$, where $\hat{\mathbf{w}}$ is estimated from the data set D. Following Bös et al. (1993) we further assume that the data arises through an equation of the form $y = g(\mathbf{x}) + \eta$ with $g = g(\mathbf{w}_0^T \cdot \mathbf{x})$. Looking back at equations (3) it is clear that the bias and variance are explicit functions of $\mathbf{x}$ and the weight vector $\mathbf{w}_0$. In order to remove the explicit dependence we compute in what follows expectations with respect to the probability distribution of $\mathbf{x}$ and $\mathbf{w}_0$, denoted respectively by $E_p[\cdot]$ and $E_0[\cdot]$. Thus, we define the averaged bias and variance by $B = E_0 E_p[B(\mathbf{x}; \mathbf{w}_0)]$ and $V = E_0 E_p[V(\mathbf{x}; \mathbf{w}_0)]$ and the expected error is then $\mathcal{E} = B + V$.

In this work we consider *least-squares* estimation which corresponds to minimizing the empirical error, $\mathcal{E}_{\text{emp}}(\mathbf{w}, D) = \|X\mathbf{w} - Y\|^2$, where X is the $n \times d$ data matrix, Y is the $n \times 1$ output vector and $\mathbf{w}$ is a $d \times 1$ weight vector. The components of the 'target' vector Y are given by $y_\mu = g(\mathbf{w}_0^T \cdot \mathbf{x}_\mu) + \eta_\mu$ where η_μ are i.i.d normal random variables with zero mean and variance σ^2. Note that while we take the estimator itself to be linear we allow the target function $g(\cdot)$ to be non-linear. This is meant to model the common situation where the model we are trying to fit is inadequate, since the correct model (even it exists) is usually unkown.

Thus, the least squares estimator is given by $\hat{\mathbf{w}} \in \arg\min_{\mathbf{w}} \mathcal{E}_{\text{emp}}(\mathbf{w}, D)$. Since in this case the error-function is quadratic it possesses either a unique global minimum or a degenerate manifold of minima, in the case where the Hessian matrix, $X^T X$, is singular.

The solution to the least squares problem is well known (see for example Scharf 1991), and will be briefly summarized. When the number of examples, n, is smaller than the input dimension, d, the problem is underdetermined and there are many solutions with *zero* empirical error. The solutions can be written out explicitly in the form

$$\hat{\mathbf{w}} = X^T(XX^T)^{-1}Y + (I - X^T(XX^T)^{-1}X) V \qquad (n < d), \qquad (4)$$

where V is an *arbitrary d*-dimensional vector. It should be noted that any vector $\mathbf{w}$ satisfying this equation (and thus any least-squares estimator) becomes singular as n approaches d from below, since the matrix XX^T becomes singular. The minimal norm solution, often referred to as the *Moore-Penrose* solution, is given in this case by the choice $V = 0$. It is common in the literature to neglect the study of the underdetermined regime since the solution is not unique in this case. We however will pay specific attention to this case, corresponding to the often prevalent situation where the amount of data is small, attempting to show that the combination of estimators approach can significantly improve the quality of predictors in this regime. Moreover, many important inverse problems in signal processing fall into this category (Scharf 1991).

In the overdetermined case, $n > d$ (assuming the matrix X to be of full rank), a zero error solution is possible only if the function $g(\cdot)$ is linear and there is no noise, namely $E[\eta^2] = 0$. In any other case, the problem becomes *unrealizable* and the minimum error is non-zero. In any event, in this regime the *unique* solution minimizing the empirical error is given by

$$\hat{\mathbf{w}} = (X^T X)^{-1} X^T Y \qquad (n > d). \qquad (5)$$

It is eay to see that this estimator is unbiased for linear $g(\cdot)$.

In order to compute the bias and variance for this model we use Eqs. (3) with $K = 1$ and $b_k = 1$. In order to actually compute the expectations with respect to $\mathbf{x}$ and the weight vector $\mathbf{w}_0$ we assume in what follows that the random vector $\mathbf{x}$ is distributed according to a multi-dimensional normal distributions of zero mean and covariance matrix $(1/d)I$. The vector $\mathbf{w}_0$ is similarly distributed with unit covariance matrix. The reason for the particular scaling chosen for the covariance matrices will become clear below. In the remainder of the paper we will be concerned with exact calculations in the so called *thermodynamic limit*: $n, d \to \infty$ and $\alpha = n/d$ finite. This limit is particularly useful in that the central limit theorem allows one to make precise statements about the behavior of the system, for an *effectively finite* sample size, α. We note in passing that in the thermodynamic limit, $d \to \infty$, we have $\sum_i x_i^2 \to 1$ with probability 1 and similarly for $(1/d) \sum_i w_{0i}^2$. Using these simple distributions we can, after some algerbra, directly compute the bias and variance. Denoting $R = E_0[\overline{\mathbf{w}}^T \cdot \mathbf{w}_0]$, $r = E_0 \|\overline{\mathbf{w}}\|^2$, $Q = E_0 \overline{\|\hat{\mathbf{w}}\|^2}$, one can show that the bias and variance are given by

$$B = r - 2\overline{ug}R + \overline{g^2} \quad ; \quad V = Q - r. \qquad (6)$$

In the above equations we have used $\overline{g^2} = \int Du g^2(u)$ and $\overline{ug} = \int Du\, ug(u)$ where the Gaussian measure Du is defined by $Du = (e^{-u^2/2}/\sqrt{2\pi})du$. We note in passing that the same result is obtained for any i.i.d variables, x_i, with zero mean and variance $1/d$. We thus note that a complete calculation of the expected bias and variance requires the explicit computation of the variables R, r and Q defined above. In principle, with the explicit expressions (4) and (5) at hand one may proceed to compute all the quantities relevant to the evaluation of the bias and variance. Unfortunately, it turns out that a direct computation of r, R and Q using these expressions is a rather difficult task in the theory of random matrices, keeping in mind the potential non-linearity of the function $g(\cdot)$. A way to solve the problem can be undertaken via a slightly indirect route, using tools from statistical physics. The variables R and Q above have been recently computed by Bös et al. (1993) using replicas and by Opper and Kinzel (1994) by a direct calculation. The variable r can be computed along similar lines resulting in the following expressions for the bias and variance (given for brevity for the Moore-Penrose solution):

$$\alpha < 1 : \quad B = \overline{g^2} - \alpha(2-\alpha)\overline{ug}^2 \quad , \quad V = \frac{\alpha}{1-\alpha}\left[\overline{g^2} + \sigma^2 - \alpha(2-\alpha)\overline{ug}^2\right]$$

$$\alpha > 1 : \quad B = \overline{g^2} - \overline{ug}^2 \quad , \quad V = \frac{1}{\alpha-1}\left[\overline{g^2} + \sigma^2 - \overline{ug}^2\right] \quad (7)$$

We see from this solution that for $\alpha > 1$ the bias is constant, while the variance is monotonically decreasing with the sample size α. For $\alpha < 1$, there are of course multiple solutions corresponding to different normalizations Q. It is easy to see, however, that the Moore-Penrose solution, gives rise to the smallest variance of all least-squares estimators (the bias is unaffected by the normalization of the solution). The expected (or generalization) error is given simply by $\mathcal{E} = B + V$, and is thus smallest for the Moore-Penrose solution. Note that this latter result is independent of whether the function $g(\cdot)$ is linear or not. We note in passing that in the simple case where the target function $g(\cdot)$ is *linear* and the data is noise-free ($\sigma^2 = 0$) one obtains the particularly simple result $\mathcal{E} = 1 - \alpha$ for $\alpha < 1$ and $\mathcal{E} = 0$ above $\alpha = 1$. Note however that in any other case the expected error is a non-linear function of the normalized sample size α.

4 COMBINING LINEAR ESTIMATORS

Having summarized the situation in the case of a single estimator, we proceed to the case of K linear estimators. In this case we assume that the complete data set, D, is broken up into K subsets $D^{(k)}$ of size $n_k = \alpha_k d$ each. In particular we consider two extreme situations: (i) The data sets are independent of each other, namely $D^{(k)} \cap D^{(k')} = \emptyset$ for all k, and (ii) $D^{(k)} = D$ for all k. We refer to the first situation as the non-overlapping case, while to the second case where all estimators are trained on the same data set as the fully-overlapping case. Denoting by $\hat{\mathbf{w}}^{(k)}$ the k'th least-squares estimator, based on training set $D^{(k)}$, we define the following quantities:

$$R^{(k)} = E_0\left[\overline{\hat{\mathbf{w}}^{(k)T}} \cdot \mathbf{w}_0\right] \ , \ r^{(k,k')} = E_0\left[\overline{\hat{\mathbf{w}}^{(k)T} \cdot \hat{\mathbf{w}}^{(k')}}\right] \ , \ \rho^{(k,k')} = E_0\left[\overline{\hat{\mathbf{w}}^{(k)T}} \cdot \overline{\hat{\mathbf{w}}^{(k')}}\right] . \quad (8)$$

Making use of Eqs. (3) and the probability distribution of $\mathbf{w}_0$ one then straighforwardly finds for the mixture estimator

$$B_K = \sum_{k,k'} b_k b_{k'} r^{(k,k')} - 2\overline{ug} \sum_k b_k R^{(k)} + \overline{g^2},$$

$$V_K = \sum_k b_k^2 \left[\rho^{(k,k)} - r^{(k,k)} \right] + \sum_{k \neq k'} b_k b_{k'} \left[\rho^{(k,k')} - r^{(k,k')} \right]. \qquad (9)$$

Now, the computation of the parameters $\rho^{(k,k)}$ and $R^{(k)}$ is identical to the case of a single estimator and can be directly read from the results of Bös et al. (1993) with the single modification of rescaling the sample size α to α_k. The only interaction between estimators arises from the terms $\rho^{(k,k')}$ and $r^{(k,k')}$ which couple two different estimators. Note however that $r^{(k,k')}$ is independent of the degree of overlap between the data sets $D^{(k)}$ since each estimator is averaged independently. In fact, a straighforward, if lengthy, calculation leads to the conclusion that in general $r^{(k,k')} = R^{(k)} R^{(k')}$. For the case where the data sets are independent of each other, namely $D^{(k)} \cap D^{(k')} = \emptyset$ it is obvious that $\rho^{(k,k')} = r^{(k,k')}$. One then finds $\rho^{(k,k')} = r^{(k,k')} = R^{(k)} R^{(k')}$ for independent data sets. In the case where the data sets are identical, $D^{(k)} = D$ for all k, the variable $\rho^{(k,k')}$ has been computed by Bös et al. (1993). At this point we proceed by discussing individually the two data generation scenarios described in section 1.

4.1 NON-OVERLAPPING DATA SETS

As shown above, since the data sets are independent of each other one has in this case $\rho^{(k,k')} = r^{(k,k')}$, implying that the second term in the expression for the variance in Eq. (9) vanishes. Specializing now to the case where the sizes of the data sets are equal, namely $\alpha_k = n_k/d = \alpha/K$ for all k, we expect the variables $R^{(k)}$ and $Q^{(k)}$ to be independent of the specific index k. In the particular case of a *uniform* mixture ($b_k = 1/K$ for all k) we obtain

$$B_K^{(u)} = R_K^2 - 2\overline{ug} R_K + \overline{g^2} \quad ; \quad V_K^{(u)} = (Q_K - R_K^2)/K, \qquad (10)$$

where the subscript K indicates that the values of the corresponding variables must be taken with respect to $\alpha_K = \alpha/K$. The specific values of the parameters R_K and Q_K can be found directly from the solution of Bös et al. (1993) by replacing α by α/K and dividing the variance term by a further K factor. Since the bias is a non-increasing function α it is always increased (or at best unchanged) by combining estimators from non-overlapping data subsets. It can also be seen from the above equation that as K increases the variance can be made arbitrarily small, albeit at the expense of increasing the bias. It can thus be expected that for any sample size α there is an optimal number of estimators minimizing the expected error, $\mathcal{E} = B + V$. In fact, for small α one may expand the equations for the bias and variance obtaining the expected error from which it is easy to see that the optimal value of K is given by $K^* = (\overline{g^2} + \sigma^2)/\overline{ug}^2$. As could be expected we see that the optimal value of K scales with the noise level σ^2, since the effect of combining multiple independent estimators is to reduce the effective noise variance by a factor of K. As the sample size α increases and outweighs the effect of the noise, we find that the bias increase due to the data partitioning dominates the decrease in variance and the combined estimator performs more and more poorly relative to the single estimator. Finally, for $\alpha > K$ we find the choice $K = 1$ always yields a lower expected error. Thus, while we have shown that for small sample sizes the effect of splitting the data set into independent subsets is helpful, this is no longer the case if the sample size is sufficiently large, in which case a single estimator based on the complete data set is superior. For $\alpha \to \infty$, however, one finds that all uniform mixtures converge (to leading order) at the same rate, namely $\mathcal{E}_K(\alpha) \approx \mathcal{E}_\infty + (\mathcal{E}_\infty + \sigma^2)/\alpha$, where $\mathcal{E}_\infty = \overline{g^2} - \overline{ug}^2$. For finite values of α, however, the value of K has a strong effect on the quality of the stimator.

4.2 FULLY OVERLAPPING DATA SETS

We focus now on the case where all estimators are formed from the same data set D, namely $D^{(k)} = D$ for all k. Since there is a unique solution to the least-squares estimation problem for $\alpha > 1$, all least-squares estimators coincide in this regime. Thus, we focus here on the case $\alpha < 1$, where multiple least-squares estimators coexist. We further assume that only mixtures of estimators of the same norm Q are allowed. We obtain for the uniform mixture

$$B_K^{(u)} = R^2 - 2\overline{ug}R + \overline{g^2} \quad ; \quad V_K^{(u)} = (Q - R^2) - (Q - q)(1 - \frac{1}{K}) \quad (\alpha < 1) \quad (11)$$

Clearly the expression for the bias in this case is identical to that obtained for the single estimator, since all estimators are based on the same data set and the bias term depends only on single estimator properties. The variance term, however, is modified due to the correlation between the estimators expressed through the variable $\rho^{(k,k')}$. Since the variance for the case of a single estimator is $Q - R^2$ and since $q \leq Q$ it is clear in this case that the variance is reduced while the bias remains unchanged. Thus we conclude that the mixture of estimators in this case indeed produces superior performance to that of the single estimator. However, it can be seen that in the case of the Moore-Penrose solution, corresponding to choosing the smallest possible norm Q, the expected error is minimal. We thus conclude that for $\alpha < 1$ the Moore-Penrose pseudo-inverse solution yields the lowest expected error, and this *cannot* be improved on by combining least-squares estimators obtained from the full data set D.

Recall that we have shown in the previous section that (for small and noisy data sets) combining estimators formed using non-overlapping data subsets produced results superior to those of any single estimator trained on the complete data set. An interesting conclusion of these results is that splitting the data set into non-overlapping subsets is a better strategy than training each estimator with the full data. As mentioned previously, the basic reason for this is the independence of the estimators formed in this fashion, which helps to reduce the variance term more drastically than in the case where the estimators are dependent (having been exposed to overlapping data sets).

5 CONCLUSIONS

In this paper we have studied the effect of combining different estimators on the performance of linear regression. In particular we have focused on the case of linear least-squares estimation, computing exactly the full bias and variance curves for the case where the input dimension is very large (the so called thermodynamic limit). While we have focused specifically on the case of linear estimators, it should not be hard to extend these results to simple non-linear functions of the form $f(\mathbf{w}^T \cdot \mathbf{x})$ (see section 2). The case of a combination of more complex estimators (such as multi-layered neural networks) is much more demanding, as even the case of a single such network is rather difficult to analyzes.

Several positive conclusions we can draw from our study are the following. First, the general claim that combining experts is always helpful is clearly fallacious. While we have shown that combining estimators is beneficial in some cases (such as small noisy data sets), this is not the case in general. Second, we have shown that in some situations (specifically unrealizable rules and small sample size) it is advantageous to split the data into several non-overlapping subsets. It turns out that in this case the decrease in variance resulting from the independence of the different estimators, is larger than the concomitant increase in bias. It would be interesting to try to generalize our results to the case where the data is split in a more efficient manner. Third, our results agree with the general notion that when attempting to learn an unrealizable function (whether due to noise or to a mismatch with the target function) the best option is to learn with errors.

Ultimately one would like to have a general theory for combining empirical estimators. Our work has shown that the effect of noise and finite sample size is expected to produce non-trivial effects which are impossible to observe when considering only the asymptotic limit.

Acknowledgements

The author thanks Manfred Opper for a very helpful conversation and the Ollendorff center of the Electrical Engineering department at the Technion for financial support.

References

S. Bös., W. Kinzel and M. Opper 1993, The generalization ability of perceptrons with continuous outputs, *Phys. Rev. A* 47:1384-1391.

S. Geman, E. Bienenstock and R. Dorsat 1992, Neural networks and the bias/variance dilemma, *Neural Computation* 4:1-58.

C.W.J. Granger 1989, Combining forecasts - twenty years later, *J. of Forecast.* 8:167-173.

M. Opper and W. Kinzel 1994, Statistical mechanics of generalization, in *Physics of Neural networks*, van Hemmen, J.S., E. Domany and K. Schulten eds., Springer-Verlag, Berlin.

L.L. Scharf, 1991 *Statistical Signal Processing: Detection, Estimation and Time Series Analysis*, Addison-Wesley, Massachusetts.

On-line Learning of Dichotomies

N. Barkai
Racah Institute of Physics
The Hebrew University
Jerusalem, Israel 91904
naama@fiz.huji.ac.il

H. S. Seung
AT&T Bell Laboratories
Murray Hill, NJ 07974
seung@physics.att.com

H. Sompolinsky
Racah Institute of Physics
The Hebrew University
Jerusalem, Israel 91904
and AT&T Bell Laboratories
haim@fiz.huji.ac.il

Abstract

The performance of on-line algorithms for learning dichotomies is studied. In on-line learning, the number of examples P is equivalent to the learning time, since each example is presented only once. The learning curve, or generalization error as a function of P, depends on the schedule at which the learning rate is lowered. For a target that is a perceptron rule, the learning curve of the perceptron algorithm can decrease as fast as P^{-1}, if the schedule is optimized. If the target is not realizable by a perceptron, the perceptron algorithm does not generally converge to the solution with lowest generalization error. For the case of unrealizability due to a simple output noise, we propose a new on-line algorithm for a perceptron yielding a learning curve that can approach the optimal generalization error as fast as $P^{-1/2}$. We then generalize the perceptron algorithm to any class of thresholded smooth functions learning a target from that class. For "well-behaved" input distributions, if this algorithm converges to the optimal solution, its learning curve can decrease as fast as P^{-1}.

1 Introduction

Much work on the theory of learning from examples has focused on *batch* learning, in which the learner is given all examples simultaneously, or is allowed to cycle through them repeatedly. In many situations, it is more natural to consider *on-line* learning paradigms, in which at each time step a new example is chosen. The examples are never recycled, and the learner is not allowed to simply store them (see e.g, Heskes, 1991; Hansen, 1993; Radons, 1993). Stochastic approximation theory (Kushner, 1978) provides a framework for understanding of the local convergence properties of on-line learning of *smooth* functions. This paper addresses the problem of on-line learning of *dichotomies*, for which no similarly complete theory yet exists.

We begin with on-line learning of perceptron rules. Since its introduction in the early 60's, the perceptron algorithm has been used as a simple model of learning a binary classification rule. The algorithm has been proven to converge in finite time and to yield a half plane separating any set of linearly separable examples. The perceptron algorithm, however, is not efficient in the sense of distribution-free PAC learning (Valiant, 1984), for one can construct input distributions that require an arbitrarily long convergence time. In a recent paper (Baum, 1990) Baum proved that the perceptron algorithm applied in an on-line mode, converges as $P^{-1/3}$ when learning a half space under a uniform input distribution, where P is the number of presented examples drawn at random. For on-line learning P is also the number of time steps. Baum also generalized his result to any "non-malicious" distribution. Kabashima has found the same power law for learning a two-layer parity machine with non-overlapping inputs, using an on-line least action algorithm (Kabashima, 1994).

If efficiency is measured only by the number of examples used (disregarding time), these particular on-line algorithms are much worse than batch algorithms. Any batch algorithm which is able to correctly classify a given set of P examples will converge as P^{-1} (Vapnik, 1982; Amari, 1992; Seung, 1992). In this paper, we construct on-line algorithms that can actually achieve the same power law as batch algorithms, demonstrating that the results of Baum and Kabashima do not reflect a fundamental limitation of on-line learning.

In Section 3, we study on-line algorithms for perceptron learning of a target rule that is not realizable by a perceptron. Here it is nontrivial to construct an algorithm that even converges to the optimal one, let alone to optimize the rate of convergence. For the special case of a target rule that is a perceptron corrupted by output noise this can be done. In Section 4, our results are generalized to dichotomies generated by thresholding smooth functions. In Section 5 we summarize the results.

2 On-line learning of a perceptron rule

We consider a half space rule generated by a normalized teacher perceptron $\mathbf{W}_0 \in R^N$, $\mathbf{W}_0 \cdot \mathbf{W}_0 = 1$ such that any vector $\mathbf{S} \in R^N$ is given a label $\sigma_0(\mathbf{S}) = \text{sgn}(\mathbf{W}_0 \cdot \mathbf{S})$. We study the case of a Gaussian input distribution centered at zero with a unit variance in each direction in space:

$$P(\mathbf{S}) = \prod_{i=1}^{N} \frac{1}{\sqrt{2\pi}} e^{-S_i^2/2} \qquad (1)$$

Averages over this input distribution will be written with angle brackets $\langle \rangle$. A student perceptron $\mathbf{W}$ is trained by an on-line perceptron algorithm. At each time step, an input $\mathbf{S} \in R^N$ is drawn at random, according to distribution Eq. (1) and the student's output $\sigma(\mathbf{S}) = \text{sgn}(\mathbf{W} \cdot \mathbf{S})$ is calculated. The student is then updated according to the perceptron rule:

$$\mathbf{W}' = \mathbf{W} + \frac{\eta}{N}\epsilon(\mathbf{S};\mathbf{W})\sigma_0(\mathbf{S})\mathbf{S} \qquad (2)$$

and is then normalized so that $\mathbf{W} \cdot \mathbf{W} = 1$ at all times. The factor $\epsilon(\mathbf{S};\mathbf{W})$ denotes the error of the student perceptron on the input $\mathbf{S}$: $\epsilon = 1$ if $\sigma(\mathbf{S})\sigma_0(\mathbf{S}) = 1$, and 0 otherwise. The *learning rate* η is the magnitude of change of the weights at each time step. It is scaled by N to ensure that the change in the overlap $R = \mathbf{W} \cdot \mathbf{W}_0$ is of order $1/N$. Thus, a change of $\mathcal{O}(1)$ occurs only after presentation of $P = \mathcal{O}(N)$ examples.

The performance of the student is measured by the generalization error, defined as the probability of disagreement between the student and the teacher on an arbitrary input $\epsilon_g = \langle \epsilon(\mathbf{S};\mathbf{W}) \rangle$. In the present case, ϵ_g is

$$\epsilon_g = \frac{\cos^{-1} R}{\pi}. \qquad (3)$$

Although for simplicity we analyze below the performance of the perceptron rule (2) only for large N, our results apply to finite N as well. Multiplying Eq. (2) by $\mathbf{W}_0$ after incorporation of the normalization operation and averaging with respect to the input distribution (1), yields the following differential equation for $R(\alpha)$ where $\alpha = P/N$,

$$\frac{dR}{d\alpha} = \eta \frac{1-R^2}{\sqrt{2\pi}} - \eta^2 \frac{R\cos^{-1} R}{2\pi}. \qquad (4)$$

Here terms of order $\sqrt{\eta/N}$ have been neglected.

The evolution of the overlap R, and thus of the generalization error, depends on the schedule at which the learning rate η decreases. We consider two cases, a constant η and a time-dependent η.

Constant learning rate: When η is held fixed, Eq. (4) has a stable fixed point at $R < 1$, and hence ϵ_g converges to an η-dependent nonzero value $\epsilon_\infty(\eta)$. For $\eta \ll 1$, $1 - R_\infty(\eta) \propto \eta^2$ and $\epsilon_g \propto \sqrt{1 - R}$ is therefore proportional to η,

$$\epsilon_\infty(\eta) = \eta/\sqrt{2\pi^3} \ . \tag{5}$$

The convergence to this value is exponential in α, $\epsilon_g(\alpha) - \epsilon_\infty(\eta) \sim \exp(-\eta\alpha/\sqrt{2\pi})$.

Time-dependent learning rate: Convergence to $\epsilon_g = 0$ can be achieved if η decreases slowly enough with α. We study the limiting behaviour of the system for η which is decreasing with time as $\eta = \left(\eta_0\sqrt{2\pi}\right)\alpha^{-z}$.

$z > 1$. In this case the rate is reduced too fast before a sufficient number of examples have been seen. This results in R which does not converge to 1 but instead to a smaller value that depends on its initial value.

$z < 1$. The system follows the change in η adiabatically. Hence, to first order in α^{-1}, $\epsilon_g(\alpha) = \epsilon_\infty(\eta(\alpha))$. Thus, ϵ_g converges to zero with an asymptotic rate $\epsilon_g(\alpha) \sim \alpha^{-z}$.

$z = 1$. The behaviour of the system depends on the prefactor η_0:

$$\begin{aligned}
\epsilon_g &\sim \left(\frac{1}{\pi}\frac{\eta_0^2}{\eta_0 - 1}\right)\frac{1}{\alpha} & \eta_0 > 1 \\
&\sim \frac{\sqrt{\log \alpha}}{\alpha} & \eta_0 = 1 \\
&\sim \frac{A}{\alpha^{\eta_0}} & \eta_0 < 1
\end{aligned} \tag{6}$$

where A depends on the initial condition. Thus the optimal asymptotic change of η is $2\sqrt{2\pi}/\alpha$, in which case the error will behave asymptotically as $\epsilon_g(\alpha) \sim 1.27/\alpha$. This is not far from the batch asymptotic (Seung, 1992) $\epsilon_g(\alpha) \sim 0.625/\alpha$. We have confirmed these results by numerical simulation of the algorithm Eq. (2). Figure 1 presents the results of the optimal learning schedule, i.e., $\eta = 2\sqrt{2\pi}/\alpha$. The numerical results are in excellent agreement with the prediction $\epsilon_g(\alpha) = 1.27/\alpha$ for the asymptotic behavior. Finally, we note that our analysis of the time-dependent case is similar to that of Kabashima and Shinomoto for a different on-line learning problem (Kabashima, 1993).

3 On-line learning of a perceptron with output noise

In the case discussed above, the task can be fully realized by a perceptron, i.e., there is a perceptron $\mathbf{W}$ such that $\epsilon_g = 0$. In more realistic situations a perceptron will only provide an approximation of the target function, so that the minimal value of ϵ_g is greater than zero. These cases are called *unrealizable tasks*. A drawback of the above on-line algorithm is that, for a general unrealizable task, it does not converge to the optimal perceptron, i.e., it does not approach the minimum of ϵ_g. To illustrate this fact we consider a perceptron rule corrupted by output noise. The label of an input $\mathbf{S}$ is $\sigma_0(\mathbf{S})$, where $\sigma_0(\mathbf{S}) = \text{sgn}(\mathbf{W}_0 \cdot \mathbf{S})$ with probability $1 - p$, and $-\text{sgn}(\mathbf{W}_0 \cdot \mathbf{S})$ with probability p. We assume $0 \leq p \leq 1/2$. For reasons which will become clear later, the input distribution is taken as a Gaussian centered at $\mathbf{U}$

$$P(\mathbf{S}) = \prod_{i=1}^{N} \frac{1}{\sqrt{2\pi}} e^{-(S_i - U_i)^2/2} \tag{7}$$

In this case ϵ_g is given by

$$\epsilon_g = p + \left(\int_{-\infty}^{-q} Dy H(\frac{-q_0 - Ry}{\sqrt{1-R^2}}) + \int_{-q}^{\infty} Dy H(\frac{q_0 + Ry}{\sqrt{1-R^2}})\right). \tag{8}$$

where $q_0 = \mathbf{U} \cdot \mathbf{W}_0$ denotes the overlap between the center of the distribution and the teacher perceptron, and $q = \mathbf{U} \cdot \mathbf{W}$ is the overlap between the center of the distribution and $\mathbf{W}$. The integrals in Eq. (8) are with respect to a Gaussian measure $Dy = \exp(-y^2/2)/\sqrt{2\pi}$ and $H(x) = \int_x^\infty Dy$. Note that the optimal perceptron is the teacher $\mathbf{W} = \mathbf{W}_0$ i.e., $R = 1, q = q_0$, which yields the minimal error $\epsilon_{min} = p$.

First, we consider training with the normalized perceptron rule (2). In this case, we obtain differential equations for two variables: R and q. Solving these equations we find that in general, $\mathbf{W}$ converges to a vector with a direction which is in the plane of $\mathbf{W}_0$ and $\mathbf{U}$ and is does not point in the direction of $\mathbf{W}_0$ even in the limit of $\eta \to 0$. Here we present the result for the limit of $\eta \to 0$ and small noise level, i.e., $p \ll 1$. In this case, we obtain for $\epsilon_\infty(\eta = 0)$

$$\epsilon_\infty(0) = p + p\frac{(1 - 2H(q_0))\sqrt{u^2 - q_0^2}}{1 + (u^2 - q_0^2)} + \mathcal{O}(p^2) \tag{9}$$

where $u = |\mathbf{U}|$ is the magnitude of the center of the input distribution. For $p = 0$, the only solution is $R = 1$ and $q = q_0$, in agreement with the previous results. For $p > 0$ the optimal solution is retrieved only in the following special cases: (i) the input distribution is isotropic, i.e., $q_0 = u = 0$; (ii) when $\mathbf{U}$ is parallel to $\mathbf{W}_0$, i.e., $u = q_0$; and (iii) when $\mathbf{U}$ is orthogonal to $\mathbf{W}_0$, i.e., $q_0 = 0$. This holds also for large value of p. In these special cases, the symmetry of the input distribution relative to the teacher vector, guarantees that the deviations from $\mathbf{W} = \mathbf{W}_0$ incurred by the inputs that come with the wrong label cancel each other on average. According to Eq. (9), for other directions of $\mathbf{U}$, ϵ_g is above the optimal value. Note that the additional term in ϵ_g is of the same order of magnitude ($\mathcal{O}(p)$) as the minimal error.

In the following we suggest a modified on-line algorithm for learning a perceptron rule with output noise. The student weights are changed according to

$$\mathbf{W}' = \mathbf{W} + \frac{\eta}{N}\epsilon(\mathbf{S}; \mathbf{W})\sigma_0(\mathbf{S})(\mathbf{S} - \mathbf{T}(\mathbf{S})) \tag{10}$$

followed by a normalization of $\mathbf{W}$. This algorithm differs from the perceptron algorithm in that the change in $\mathbf{W}$ is not proportional to the present input, but to a shifted vector. The shifting vector $\mathbf{T}(\mathbf{S})$, is determined by the requirement that the teacher $\mathbf{W}_0$ will be a fixed point of the algorithm in the limit of $\eta \to 0$. This is equivalent to the condition

$$\langle \epsilon_0(\mathbf{S})\sigma_0(\mathbf{S})(\mathbf{S} - \mathbf{T}(\mathbf{S}))\rangle = 0 \tag{11}$$

where $\epsilon_0(\mathbf{S})$ is the error function for $\mathbf{S}$ when $\mathbf{W} = \mathbf{W}_0$. This condition does not determine $\mathbf{T}$ uniquely. A simple choice is one for which $\mathbf{T}$ is independent of $\mathbf{S}$. This leads to

$$\mathbf{T} = \frac{\langle \text{sgn}(\mathbf{W}_0 \cdot \mathbf{S})\mathbf{S}\rangle}{\langle \text{sgn}(\mathbf{W}_0 \cdot \mathbf{S})\rangle} = \frac{\langle \sigma_0 \mathbf{S}\rangle}{\langle \sigma_0 \rangle} \tag{12}$$

where we used the fact that for any $\mathbf{S}$, $\epsilon_0(\mathbf{S})\sigma_0(\mathbf{S})$ equals $-\text{sgn}(\mathbf{W}_0 \cdot \mathbf{S})$ with probability p, and zero with probability $(1 - p)$. This uniform shift is possible only when $\langle \sigma_0 \rangle \neq 0$, namely when the average frequencies of $+1$ and -1 labels are not equal. If this is not the case, one has to choose nonuniform forms of $\mathbf{T}(\mathbf{S})$. Note that in general $\mathbf{T}$ has to be learned so that Eq. (10) has to be supplemented by appropriate equations for changing $\mathbf{T}$. In the case of Eq. (12), one can easily learn separately the numerator and denominator by running averages of $\sigma_0 \mathbf{S}$ and σ_0, respectively. We have studied analytically the above algorithm for the case of the Gaussian input distribution Eq. (7), in the limit of large N. The shifting vector is given by

$$\mathbf{T} = \mathbf{U} + \mathbf{W}_0\sqrt{\frac{2}{\pi}}\frac{\exp(-q_0^2/2)}{1 - 2H(q_0)} \tag{13}$$

The differential equations for the overlaps R and q in the neighborhood of the point $R = 1$ and $q = q_0$ are,

$$\frac{d\delta R}{d\alpha} = -\eta\sqrt{2/\pi}\exp(-q_0^2/2)\delta R + \frac{1}{2}\eta^2 p$$

$$\frac{d\delta q}{d\alpha} = -\eta\frac{\exp(-q_0^2/2)}{\sqrt{2\pi}}(\delta q + q_0\delta R) + \frac{1}{2}\eta^2 q_0 p \tag{14}$$

where $\delta R = 1 - R$ and $\delta q = q_0 - q$. In the limit $\eta \to 0$, $R = 1$ and $q = q_0$ is indeed a stable fixed point of the algorithm, so that the student converges to the optimal perceptron $\mathbf{W}_0$, and hence the generalization error converges to its minimal value $\epsilon_{min} = p$. Since, unlike Eq. (4), the coefficient of the η^2 term in Eq.

(14) is constant, $\delta R_\infty(\eta) \propto \eta$, for small fixed η, and not to η^2. Thus, in this case, the generalization error approaches, in the limit $\alpha \to \infty$, the value

$$\epsilon_\infty(\eta) = p + \sqrt{\eta p}\frac{\exp(-q_0^2/4)}{(2\pi^3)^{1/4}} \ . \tag{15}$$

For a time-dependent η, the convergence to the optimal weights depends on the choice of $\eta(n)$, as in the case of the noiseless perceptron rule. For $\eta = \left(\eta_0\sqrt{\pi/2}\exp(q_0^2/2)\right)\alpha^{-z}$, with $z \leq 1$, the error converges to p. For $z < 1$, to first order in $1/\alpha$, $\epsilon_g(\alpha) = \epsilon_\infty(\eta(\alpha))$, yielding

$$\epsilon_g(\alpha) - p \sim \alpha^{-z/2}. \tag{16}$$

When $z = 1$, the rate of convergence depends on the value of η_0.

$$\epsilon_g(\alpha) - p \sim \begin{cases} \alpha^{-1/2}, & \eta_0 > 1 \\ \alpha^{-\eta_0/2}, & \eta_0 < 1 \end{cases} \tag{17}$$

and logarithmic corrections to $\alpha^{-1/2}$ for $\eta_0 = 1$. Thus, the optimal rate of convergence is

$$\epsilon_g(\alpha) - p \approx \sqrt{\frac{2p}{\pi\alpha}} \tag{18}$$

which is achieved for $\eta_0 = 2$.

We have tested successfully this algorithm by simulations of learning a perceptron rule with output noise with several input distributions, including the Gaussian, of Eq. (7). Figure 2 presents the generalization error as a function of α for the Gaussian distribution, with $p = 0.2$, and we have chosen $\eta_0 = 2$. The error converges to the optimal value 0.2 as $\alpha^{-1/2}$ in agreement with the theory. For comparison the result of the usual perceptron algorithm is also presented. This algorithm converges to $\epsilon_g \approx 0.32$, clearly larger than the optimal value.

4 On-line learning of thresholded smooth functions

Our results for the realizable perceptron can be extended to a more general class of dichotomies, namely thresholded smooth functions. They are defined as dichotomies of the form

$$\sigma(\mathbf{S};\mathbf{W}) = \mathrm{sgn}(f(\mathbf{S};\mathbf{W})) \tag{19}$$

where f is a differentiable function of a set of parameters, denoted by $\mathbf{W}$, and $\mathbf{S}$ is the input vector. We consider here the case of a realizable task, where the examples are given with labels σ_0 corresponding to a target machine $\mathbf{W}_0$ which is in the $\mathbf{W}$ space. For this task we propose the following generalization of the perceptron rule (2)

$$\mathbf{W}' = \mathbf{W} + \eta\epsilon(\mathbf{S};\mathbf{W})\sigma_0(\mathbf{S})\nabla f(\mathbf{S};\mathbf{W}) \tag{20}$$

where ∇ denotes a gradient w.r.t. $\mathbf{W}$. Then, as we argue below, the vector $\mathbf{W}_0$ is a stable fixed point in the limit of $\eta \to 0$. Furthermore, for constant small η the residual error scales as $\epsilon_\infty \propto \eta$. For $\eta \sim \alpha^{-z}$, $z < 1$, $\epsilon_g(\alpha) \sim \epsilon_\infty(\eta(\alpha)) \sim \alpha^{-z}$.

To show this, let us consider for simplicity the one-dimensional case, $w' = w + \eta g(w,s)$, where

$$g(w,s) = \theta(-f(w,s)f(w_0,s))\,\mathrm{sgn}(f(w_0,s))\frac{\partial f}{\partial w} \ . \tag{21}$$

This equation can be converted into a Markov equation for the probability distribution, $P(w,n)$ (Van Kampen, 1981)

$$P(w, n+1) = \int dw' W(w'|w)P(w', n) \tag{22}$$

where $W(w|w') = <\delta(w' - w - \eta g(w,s))>$ is the transition rate from w to w'. In the limit of small fixed η, the equilibrium distribution, P_∞, can be shown to have the following scaling form,

$$P_\infty(w;\eta) = \frac{1}{\eta}F(\delta w/\eta) \tag{23}$$

where $\delta w = w - w_0$ and $F(x)$ obeys the following difference equation

$$\hat{L}F(x) \equiv \sum_{\sigma=\pm 1}\theta((f_0' + \sigma x)f_0')|(f_0' + \sigma x)|F(x + \sigma f_0') - |x|F(x) = 0 \qquad (24)$$

where f_0' is the value of the gradient $\partial f(w_0, s)/\partial w$ at the decision boundary of $f(w_0, s)$, namely at the point s obeying $f(w_0, s) = 0$. Note that since we are interested in normalizable solutions of Eq. (24), $F(x)$ has to vanish for for all $x > |f_0'|$. This result is valid provided the input distribution is smooth and nonvanishing near the decision boundary. Furthermore, $\partial f/\partial w$ at w_0 may not vanish on the decision boundary. Under the same conditions, it can be shown that the error is homogeneous in δw with degree 1, hence it should scale linearly with η, i.e., $\epsilon_\infty \propto \eta$. It should be noted that, unlike other on-line learning problems (Heskes, 1991; Hansen, 1993; Radons, 1993), the equilibrium distribution is our case is not Gaussian.

For a time-dependent η of the form $\eta = \eta_0 n^{-z}$, $z < 1$, $P(w, n)$ at long times is of the form

$$P(w, n) = \frac{1}{\eta(n)}\left(F(\delta w/\eta(n)) + \frac{G(\delta w/\eta(n))}{n^{1-z}}\right) \qquad (25)$$

where F is the stationary distribution, given by Eq. (24) and the coefficient of the correction, G, solves the inhomogeneous equation

$$zx\frac{dF}{dx} + zF(x) = \eta_0\hat{L}G(x) \qquad (26)$$

where the linear operator $\hat{L}$ is defined in Eq. (24). Thus, to leading order in inverse time, the system follows adiabatically the finite-η stationary distribution, yielding $\epsilon_g(n)$ which vanishes asymptotically as $\epsilon_g(n) \propto \eta(n) \sim n^{-z}$. The optimal schedule is obtained for $z = 1$. In this case, $P(w, n) = \eta^{-1}(n)F(\delta w/\eta(n))$ where $F(x)$ solves the homogeneous equation

$$zx\frac{dF}{dx} + zF(x) = \eta_0\hat{L}F(x) \qquad (27)$$

For sufficiently large η_0, this equation has a solution, implying that $\epsilon_g \propto n^{-1}$.

Similarly, the results of Section 3 can also be extended to the case of thresholded- smooth functions with a probability p of an error due to isotropic output noise. In this case, the optimal choice is again $\eta \propto n^{-1}$ yielding $\epsilon_g - p \approx \sqrt{\eta}$. It should be noted that for this case, the probability distribution for small η does reduce to a Gaussian distribution in $\delta w/\sqrt{\eta}$. Using a multidimensional Markov equation, it is straightforward to extend these results to higher dimensions. The small η limit yields equations similar to Eqs. (24-26), that involve integration over the decision boundary of $f(\mathbf{W}, \mathbf{S})$.

5 Summary and Discussion

We have found that the perceptron rule (2) with normalization can lead to a variety of learning curves, depending on the schedule at which the learning rate is decreased. The optimal schedule leads to an inverse power law learning curve, $\epsilon_g \sim \alpha^{-1}$. Baum's results (Baum, 1990) of a non-normalized perceptron with a constant learning rate can be viewed as a special case of the above analysis. In the non-normalized perceptron algorithm, the magnitude of the student's weights grow with α as $|\mathbf{W}| \sim \alpha^{1/3}$. The time evolution of the overlap R, and thus of the generalization error is governed by the effective learning rate $\eta_{\text{eff}} = \eta/|\mathbf{W}|$ leading via Eq. (6) to the result $\epsilon_g \sim \alpha^{-1/3}$. Similar results apply to the two-layer parity machine studied in (Kabashima, 1994).

Our analysis, leading to the equations of motion (4) and (14), was based on the limit of large N and P, such that $\alpha = P/N$ remains finite. We would like to stress however, that this limit is only necessary in deriving the full form of the learning curve, i.e., $R(\alpha)$ for all α. On the other hand, our results for the large P asymptote of the learning curve for small η are valid for finite N as well, as implied by the general treatment of the previous section.

Unrealizable perceptron rules present a more complicated problem. We have presented here a modified perceptron algorithm that converges to the optimal solution in the special case of an isotropic output noise.

In this case, the convergence to the optimal error is as $\alpha^{-1/2}$. This is the same power law as obtained in the standard sample complexity upper bounds (Vapnik, 1982) and in the approximate replica symmetric calculations (Seung, 1992) for batch learning of unrealizable rules. It should be stressed however, that the success of the modified algorithm in the case of an output noise depends on the fact that the errors made by the optimal solution are uncorrelated with the input. Thus, finding an on-line algorithm that can cope with other types of unrealizability remains an important problem.

The learning algorithms for the perceptron rule, without and with output noise, can be generalized to learning thresholded smooth functions, assuming certain reasonable properties of the input distribution are present, as shown in Section 4. The dependence of the learning curve on the learning rate schedule remains roughly the same as in the perceptron case. This implies that on-line learning of realizable dichotomies, with possible output noise, can achieve the same power laws in the number of examples that is typical of batch learning of such rules. Furthermore, the on-line formulation possesses the theoretical virtues of addressing time as well as sample complexity, so that the same power laws imply the polynomial relationship between the time and the achieved error level. The above conclusions assume that the equilibrium state at small learning rates is unique, which in general is not the case. The issue of overcoming local minima in on-line learning is a difficult problem (Heskes, 1992) Finally, the theoretical results for on-line learning has the important advantage of not requiring the use of the often problematic replica formalism.

Acknowledgements

We are grateful for helpful discussions with Y. Freund, M. Kearns, R. Schapire, and E. Shamir, and thank Y. Kabashima for bringing his paper to our attention. HS is partially supported by the Fund for Basic Research of the Israeli Academy of Arts and Sciences.

References

S. Amari, N. Fujita, and S. Shinomoto. Four types of learning curves. *Neural Comput.*, 4:605–618, 1992.

E. B. Baum. The perceptron algorithm is fast for nonmalicious distributions. *Neural Comput.*, 2:248–260, 1990.

H. J. Kushner and D. S. Clark. *Stochastic approximation methods for constrained and unconstrained systems.* Springer, Berlin, 1978.

L. K. Hansen, R. Pathria, and P. Salamon. Stochastic dynamics of supervised learning. *J. Phys.*, A26:63–71, 1993.

T. Heskes and B. Kappen. Learning processes in neural networks. *Phys. Rev.*, A44:2718–2762, 1991.

T. Heskes, E. T. P. Slijpen, and B. Kappen. Learning in neural networks with local minima. *Phys. Rev.*, A46:5221–5231, 1992.

Y. Kabashima. Perfect loss of generalization due to noise in $k = 2$ parity machines. *J. Phys.*, A27:1917–1927, 1994.

Y. Kabashima and S. Shinomoto. Incremental learning with and without queries in binary choice problems. In *Proc. of IJCNN*, 1993.

G. Radons. On stochastic dynamics of supervised learning. *J. Phys.*, A26:3455–3461, 1993.

H. S. Seung, H. Sompolinsky, and N. Tishby. Statistical mechanics of learning from examples. *Phys. Rev.*, A45:6056–6091, 1992.

L. G. Valiant. A theory of the learnable. *Commun. ACM*, 27:1134–1142, 1984.

N. G. Van Kampen. *Stochastic processes in physics and chemistry.* North holland 1981.

V. N. Vapnik. *Estimation of Dependences based on Empirical Data.* Springer-Verlag, New York, 1982.

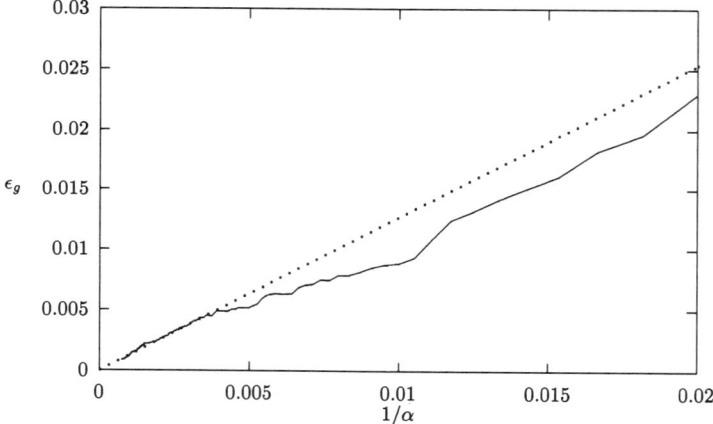

Figure 1: Asymptotic performance of a realizable perceptron. Simulation results for $\eta_0 = 2$ and $N = 50$ (solid curve) are compared with the theoretical prediction $\epsilon_g = 1.27/\alpha$ (dashed curve).

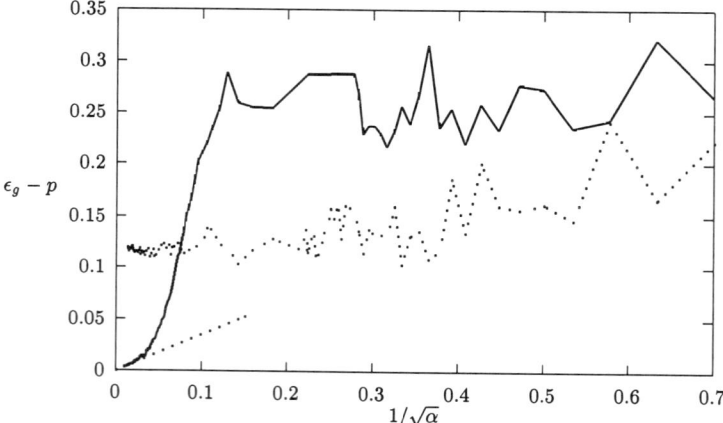

Figure 2: Simulation results for on-line learning of a perceptron with output noise. Here $\eta_0 = 2$, $p = 0.2$, $N = 250$, $u = 4$, and $q_0 = -1.95$. The regular perceptron learning (dashed curve) is compared with the modified algorithm (solid curve). The dashed line shows the theoretical prediction Eq. (18)

Dynamic Modelling of Chaotic Time Series with Neural Networks

Jose C. Principe, Jyh-Ming Kuo
Computational NeuroEngineering Laboratory
University of Florida, Gainesville, FL32611
principe@synapse.ee.ufl.edu

Abstract

This paper discusses the use of artificial neural networks for dynamic modelling of time series. We argue that multistep prediction is more appropriate to capture the dynamics of the underlying dynamical system, because it constrains the iterated model. We show how this method can be implemented by a recurrent ANN trained with trajectory learning. We also show how to select the trajectory length to train the iterated predictor for the case of chaotic time series. Experimental results corroborate the proposed method.

1.0 Introduction

The search for a model of an experimental time series has been an important problem in science. For a long time the linear model was almost exclusively used to describe the system that produced the time series [1], but recently nonlinear models have also been proposed to replace the linear ones [2]. Lapedes and Farber [3] showed how artificial neural networks (ANNs) can be used to identify the dynamics of the unknown system that produced the time series. He simply used a multilayer perceptron to predict the next point in state space, and trained this topology with backpropagation. This paper explores more complex neural topologies and training methods with the goal of improving the quality of the identification of the dynamical system, and to understand better the issues of dynamic modelling with neural networks which are far from being totally understood.

According to Takens' embedding theorem, a map $F: R^{2m+1} \to R^{2m+1}$ exists that transforms the current reconstructed state $\mathring{y}(t)$ to the next state $\mathring{y}(t+1)$, i.e.

$$\mathring{y}(t+1) = F(\mathring{y}(t)) \qquad (1)$$

or

$$\begin{bmatrix} x(t+1) \\ \ldots \\ x(t+1-2m) \end{bmatrix} = F\left(\begin{bmatrix} x(t) \\ \ldots \\ x(t-2m) \end{bmatrix}\right)$$

where m is the estimated dimension of the unknown dynamical system Φ. Note that the map contains several trivial (nonlinear) filters and a predictor. The predictive mapping $F^\perp: R^{2m+1} \to R$ can be expressed as

$$x(t+1) = F^\perp(\tilde{x}(t)) \tag{2}$$

where $\tilde{x}(t) = [x(t-2m)\ldots x(t-1)x(t)]^T$. This is actually the estimated nonlinear autoregressive model of the input time series. *The existence of this predictive model lays a theoretical basis for dynamic modelling in the sense that we can build from a vector time series a model to approximate the mapping $F^\perp$*. If the conditions of Takens embedding theorem are met, this mapping captures some of the properties of the unknown dynamical system Φ that produced the time series [7].

Presently one still does not have a capable theory to guarantee if the predictor has successfully identified the original model Φ. The simple point by point comparison between the original and predicted time series used as goodness of fit for non-chaotic time series breaks down for chaotic ones [5]. Two chaotic time series can be very different pointwise but be produced by the same dynamical system (two trajectories around the same attractor). The dynamic invariants (correlation dimension, Lyapunov exponents) measure global properties of the attractor, so they should be used as the rule to decide about the success of dynamic modelling. Hence, *a pragmatic approach in dynamic modelling is to seed the predictor with a point in state space, feed the output to its input as an autonomous system, and create a new time series*. If the dynamic invariants computed from this time series match the ones from the original time series, then we say that dynamic modelling was successful [5]. The long term behavior of the autonomous predictive model seems to be the key factor to find out if the predictor identified the original model. This is the distinguishing factor between prediction of chaotic time series and dynamic modelling. The former only addresses the instantaneous prediction error, while the latter is interested in long term behavior.

In order to use this theory, one needs to address the choices of predictor implementation. Due to the universal mapping characteristics of multilayer perceptrons (MLPs) and the existence of well established learning rules to adapt the MLP coefficients, this type of network appears as an appropriate choice [3]. However, one must realize that the MLP is a static mapper, and in dynamic modelling we are dealing with time varying signals, where the past of the signal contains vital information to describe the mapping. The design considerations to select the neural network topology are presented elsewhere [4]. We just would like to say that the MLP has to be enhanced with short term memory mechanisms, and that the *estimation of the correlation dimension should be used to set the size of the memory layer*. The main goal of the paper is to establish the methodology to efficiently train neural networks for dynamic modelling.

2. Iterated versus Single Step Prediction.

From eqn. 2 it seems that the resulting dynamic model F can be obtained through single step prediction. This has been the conventional way to handle dynamic modelling [2],[3]. The predictor is adapted by minimizing the error

$$E = \sum_{i=2m+1}^{L} dist(x(i+1) - \tilde{F}^{\perp}(\hat{x}(i)))\tag{3}$$

where L is the length of the time series, x(i) is the ith data sample, $\tilde{F}^{\perp}$ is the map developed by the predictor and *dist()* is a distance measure (normally the L2 norm). Notice that the training to obtain the mapping is done independently from sample to sample, i.e.

$$x(i+1) = \tilde{F}^{\perp}(\hat{x}(i)) + \delta_1$$
$$\ldots\ldots$$
$$x(i+j) = \tilde{F}^{\perp}(\hat{x}(i+j-1)) + \delta_j$$

where δ_j are the instantaneous prediction errors, which are minimized during training. Notice that the predictor is being optimized under the assumption that the previous point in state space is known without error.

The problem with this approach can be observed when we iterate the predictor as an autonomous system to generate the time series samples. If one wants to produce two samples in the future from sample i the predicted sample i+1 needs to be utilized to generate sample i+2. The predictor was not optimized to do this job, because during training the true i+1 sample was assumed known. As long as δ_1 is nonzero (as will be always the case for nontrivial problems), errors will accumulate rapidly. Single step prediction is more associated with extrapolation than with dynamic modelling, which requires the identification of the unique mapping that produces the time series.

When the autonomous system generates samples, past values are used as inputs to generate the following samples, which means that the training should constrain also the iterates of the predictive mapping. Putting it in a simple way, we should train the predictor in the same way we are going to use it for testing (i.e. as an autonomous system).

We propose multistep prediction (or trajectory learning) as the way to constrain the iterates of the mapping developed by the predictor. Let us define

$$E = \sum_{i=2m+1}^{k} dist(x(i+1) - \tilde{x}(i+1))\tag{4}$$

where k is the number of prediction steps (length of the trajectory) and $\tilde{x}(i+1)$ is an estimate of the predictive map

$$\tilde{x}(i+1) = \tilde{F}^{\perp}(\hat{x}(i-2m),\ldots,\hat{x}(i))\tag{5}$$

with

$$\hat{x}(i) = \begin{bmatrix} x(i) & 0 \le i \le 2m \\ \tilde{F}^\perp(x(i-2m-1),...,x(i-1)) & i > 2m \end{bmatrix}$$

Equation (5) states that $\tilde{x}(i)$ is the i-2m iterate of the predictive part of the map (for i>2m), i.e.

$$\tilde{x}(i+1) = (\tilde{F}^\perp(\tilde{F}^\perp(...\tilde{F}^\perp(\hat{x}(2m))))) = (\tilde{F}^\perp(\hat{x}(2m)))^{i-2m} \qquad (6)$$

Hence, minimizing the criterion expressed by equation (4) an optimal multistep predictor is obtained. The number of constraints that are imposed during learning is associated with k, the number of prediction steps, which corresponds to the number of iterations of the map. The more iterations, the less likely a sub-optimal solution is found, but note that the training time is being proportionally increased. In a chaotic time series there is a more important consideration that must be brought into the picture, the divergence of nearby trajectories, as we are going to see in a following section.

3. Multistep prediction with neural networks

Figure 1 shows the topology proposed in [4] to identify the nonlinear mapping. Notice that the proposed topology is a *recurrent neural network, with a global feedback loop*. This topology was selected to allow the training of the predictor in the same way as it will be used in testing, i.e. using the previous network outputs to predict the next point. This recurrent architecture should be trained with a mechanism that will constrain the iterates of the map as was discussed above. Single step prediction does not fit this requirement.

With multistep prediction, the model system can be trained in the same way as it is used in testing. We seed the dynamic net with a set of input samples, disconnect the input and feed back the predicted sample to the input for k steps. The mean square error between the predicted and true sample at each step is used as the cost function (equation (4)). If the network topology was feedforward, batch learning could be used to train the network, and static backpropagation applied to train the net. However, as a recurrent topology is utilized, a learning paradigm such as backpropagation through time (BPTT) or real time recurrent learning (RTRL) must be utilized [6]. The use of these training methods should not come as a surprise since we are in fact fitting a trajectory over time, so the gradients are time varying. This learning method is sometimes called "trajectory learning" in the recurrent learning literature [6]. A criterion to select the length of the trajectory k will be presented below.

The procedure described above must be repeated for several different segments of the time series. For each new training segment, 2m+1 samples of the original time series are used to seed the predictor. To ease the training we suggest that successive training sequences of length k overlap by q samples (q<k). For chaotic time series we also suggest that the error be weighted according to the largest Lyapunov exponent. Hence

the cost function becomes

$$E = \sum_{j=0}^{r} \sum_{i=2m+1}^{k} h(i) \cdot dist(x(i+jq+1) - \tilde{x}(i+jq+1)) \qquad (7)$$

where r is the number of training sequences, and

$$h(i) = (e^{\lambda_{max}\Delta t})^{-(i-2m-1)} \qquad (8)$$

In this equation λ_{max} is the largest Lyapunov exponent and Δt the sampling interval. With this weighting the errors for later iteration are given less credit, as they should since due to the divergence of trajectories a small error is magnified proportionally to the largest Lyapunov exponent [7].

4. Finding the length of the trajectory

From the point of view of dynamic modelling, each training sequences should preferably contain enough information to model the attractor. This means that each sequence should be no shorter than the orbital length around the attractor. We proposed to estimate the orbital length as the reciprocal of the median frequency of the spectrum of the time series [8]. Basically this quantity is the average time required for a point to return to the same neighborhood in the attractor.

The length of the trajectory is also equivalent to the number of constraints we impose on the iterative map describing the dynamical model. However, in a chaotic time series there is another fundamental limitation imposed on the trajectory length - the natural divergence of trajectories which is controlled by λ_{max}, the largest Lyapunov exponent. If the trajectory length is too long, then instabilities in the training can be expected. A full discussion of this topic is beyond the scope of this paper, and is presented elsewhere [8]. We just want to say that when λ_{max} is positive there is an uncertainty region around each predicted point that is a function of the number of prediction steps (due to cummulative error). If the trajectory length is too long the uncertainty regions from two neighboring trajectories will overlap, creating conflicting requirements for training (the model is requried to develop a map to follow both segments A and B- Figure 2).

It turns out that one can approximately find the number of iterations i_s that will guarantee no overlap of uncertainty regions [8]. The length of the principal axis of the uncertainty region around a signal trajectory at iteration i can be estimated as

$$\varepsilon_i = \varepsilon_0 e^{\lambda_{max} i \Delta t} \qquad (9)$$

where ε_0 is the initial separation. Now assuming that the two principal axis of nearby trajectories are colinear, we should choose the number of iterations i_s such that the distance d_i between trajectories is larger than the uncertainty region, i.e. $d_{i_s} \geq 2\varepsilon_{i_s}$.

The estimate of i_s should be averaged over a number of neighboring training sequences (~50 depending on the signal dynamics).

Hence, to apply this method three quantities must be estimated: the largest Lyapunov exponent, using one of the accepted algorithms. The initial separation can be estimated from the one-step predictor. And i_s by averaging local divergence. The computation time required to estimate these quantities is usually much less than setting by trial and error the length of the trajectory until a reasonable learning curve is achieved.

We also developed a method to train predictors for chaotic signals with large λ_{max}, but it will not be covered in this paper [8].

5. Results

We used this methodology to model the Mackey-Glass system (d=30, sampled at 1/6 Hz). A signal of 500 samples was obtained by 4th order Runge-Kutta integration and normalized between -1,1. The largest Lyapunov exponent for this signal is 0.0071 nats/sec. We selected a time delay neural network (TDNN) with topology 8-14-1. The output unit is linear, and the hidden layer has sigmoid nonlinearities. The number of taps in the delay line is 8.

We trained a one-step predictor and the multistep predictor with the methodology developed in this paper to compare results. The single step predictor was trained with static backpropagation with no momentum and step size of 0.001. Trained was stopped after 500 iterations. The final MSE was 0.000288. After training, the predictor was seeded with the first 8 points of the time series and iterated for 3,000 times. Figure 3a shows the corresponding output. Notice that the waveform produced by the model is much more regular that the Mackey-Glass signal, showing that some fine detail of the attractor has not been captured.

Next we trained the same TDNN with a global feedback loop (TDNNGF). The estimate of the i_s over the neighboring orbits provided an estimate of 14, and it is taken as the length of the trajectory. We displaced each training sequence by 3 samples (q=3 in eqn 7). BPTT was used to train the TDNNGF for 500 iterations over the same signal. The final MSE was 0.000648, higher than for the TDNN case. We could think that the resulting predictor was worse. The TDNNGF predictor was initialized with the same 8 samples of the time series and iterated for 3,000 times. Figure 3b shows the resulting waveform. It "looks" much closer to the original Mackey-Glass time series. We computed the average prediction error as a function of iteration for both predictors and also the theoretical rate of divergence of trajectories assuming an initial error ε_0 (Casdagli conjecture, which is the square of eqn 9) [7]. As can be seen in Figure 4 the TDNNGF is much closer to the theoretical limit, which means a much better model. We also computed the correlation dimension and the Lyapunov exponent estimated from the generated time series, and the figures obtained from TDNNGF are closer to the original time series.

Figure 5 shows the instability present in the training when the trajectory length is above the estimated value of 14. For this case the trajectory length is 20. As can be seen the MSE decreases but then fluctuates showing instability in the training.

6. Conclusions

This paper addresses dynamic modelling with artificial neural networks. We showed that the network topology should be recurrent such that the iterative map is constrained during learning. This is a necessity since dynamic modelling seeks to capture the long term behavior of the dynamical system. These models can also be used as a sample by sample predictors. Since the network topology is recurrent, backpropagation through time or real time recurrent learning should be used in training. In this paper we showed how to select the length of the trajectory to avoid instability during training.

A lot more work needs to be done to reliably capture dynamical properties of time series and encapsulate them in artificial models. But we believe that the careful analysis of the dynamic characteristics and the study of its impact on the predictive model performance is much more promising than guess work. According to this (and others) studies, modelling of chaotic time series of low λ_{max} seems a reality. We have extended some of this work for time series with larger λ_{max}, and successfully captured the dynamics of the Lorenz system [8]. But there, the parameters for learning have to be much more carefully selected, and some of the choices are still arbitrary. The main issue is that the trajectories diverge so rapidly that predictors have a hard time to capture information regarding the global system dynamics. It is interesting to study the limit of predictability of this type of approach for high dimensional and high λ_{max} chaos.

Predictor	Corr. Dim.	Lyapunov
MG30	2.70+/-0.05	0.0073+/-0.0001
TDNNGF	2.65+/-0.03	0.0074+/-0.0001
TDNN	1.60+/-0.10	0.0063+/-0.0001

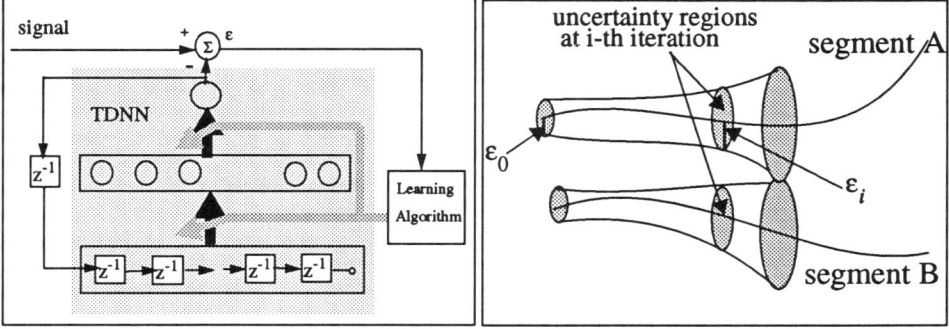

Figure 1. Proposed recurrent architecture (TDNNGF)   Figure 2. State space representation in training a model

7. Acknowledgments

This work was partially supported by NSF grant #ECS-9208789, and ONR #1494-94-1-0858.

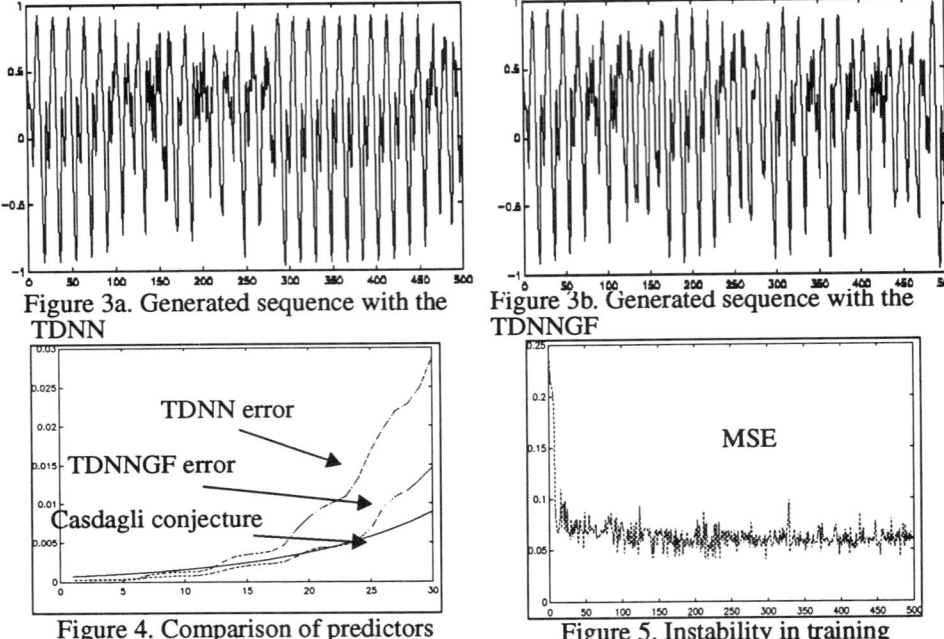

Figure 3a. Generated sequence with the TDNN

Figure 3b. Generated sequence with the TDNNGF

Figure 4. Comparison of predictors

Figure 5. Instability in training

8. References

[1] Box, G. E., and G. M. Jenkins, Time Series Analysis, Forecasting and Control, Holden Day, San Francisco, 1970.

[2] Weigend, A. S., B. A. Huberman, and D. E. Rumelhart, "Predicting the future: a connectionist approach," International Journal of Neural Systems, vol. 1, pp. 193-209, 1990.

[3] Lapedes, R., and R. Farber, "Nonlinear signal processing using neural networks: prediction and system modelling," Technical Report LA-UR87-2662, Los Alamos National Laboratory, Los Alamos, New Mexico, 1987.

[4] Kuo J-M., Principe J.C., "A systematic approach to chaotic time series modeling with neural networks", in IEEE Workshop on Neural Nets for Signal Processing, Ermioni, Greece, 1994.

[5] Principe, J. C., A. Rathie, and J. M. Kuo, "Prediction of chaotic time series with neural networks and the issue of dynamic modeling," International Journal of Biburcation and Chaos, vol. 2, no. 4, pp. 989-996, 1992.

[6] Hertz, J, A. Krogh, and R. G. Palmer, Introduction to the Theory of Neural Computation, Addison-Wesley, Redwood City, CA, 1991.

[7] Casdagli, M., "Nonlinear prediction of chaotic time series," Physica D 35, pp.335-356, 1989.

[8] Kuo, J.M., "Nonlinear Dynamic Modelling with Artificial neural networks", Ph.D. dissertation, University of FLorida, 1993.

A Rigorous Analysis Of Linsker-type Hebbian Learning

J. Feng
Mathematical Department
University of Rome "La Sapienza"
P. le A. Moro, 00185 Rome, Italy
feng@mat.uniroma1.it

H. Pan   V. P. Roychowdhury
School of Electrical Engineering
Purdue University
West Lafayette, IN 47907
hpan@ecn.purdue.edu
vwani@drum.ecn.purdue.edu

Abstract

We propose a novel rigorous approach for the analysis of Linsker's unsupervised Hebbian learning network. The behavior of this model is determined by the underlying nonlinear dynamics which are parameterized by a set of parameters originating from the Hebbian rule and the arbor density of the synapses. These parameters determine the presence or absence of a specific receptive field (also referred to as a 'connection pattern') as a saturated fixed point attractor of the model. In this paper, we perform a qualitative analysis of the underlying nonlinear dynamics over the parameter space, determine the effects of the system parameters on the emergence of various receptive fields, and predict precisely within which parameter regime the network will have the potential to develop a specially designated connection pattern. In particular, this approach exposes, for the first time, the crucial role played by the synaptic density functions, and provides a complete precise picture of the parameter space that defines the relationships among the different receptive fields. Our theoretical predictions are confirmed by numerical simulations.

1 Introduction

For the purpose of understanding the self-organization mechanism of primary visual system, Linsker has proposed a multilayered unsupervised Hebbian learning network with random uncorrelated inputs and localized arborization of synapses between adjacent layers (Linsker, 1986 & 1988). His simulations have shown that for appropriate parameter regimes, several structured connection patterns (e.g., centre-surround and oriented afferent receptive fields (aRFs)) occur progressively as the Hebbian evolution of the weights is carried out layer by layer. The behavior of Linsker's model is determined by the underlying nonlinear dynamics which are parameterized by a set of parameters originating from the Hebbian rule and the arbor density of the synapses. For a nonlinear system, usually, there *coexist* several attractors for the same set of system parameters. That is, for a given set of the parameters, the state space comprises several attractive basins, each corresponding to a steady state respectively. The initial condition determines which attractor will be eventually reached. At the same time, a nonlinear system could have a different group of coexisting attractors for a different set of system parameters. That is, one could make the presence or absence of a specific state as a fixed point attractor by varying the set of the parameters. For a development model like Linsker's network, what is expected to be observed is that the different aRFs could emerge under different sets of parameters but should be relatively not sensitive to the initial conditions. In other words, the dynamics should avoid the coexistence of several attractors in an appropriate way. The purpose of this paper is to gain more insights into the dynamical mechanism of this self-organization model by performing a rigorous analysis on its parameter space without any approximation. That is, our goal is to reveal the effects of the system parameters on the stability of aRFs, and to predict *precisely* within which parameter regime the network will have the potential to develop a specially designated aRF. The novel rigorous approach presented here applies not only to the Linsker-type Hebbian learning but also to other related self-organization models about neural development.

In Linsker's network, each cell in the present layer $\mathcal{M}$ receives synaptic inputs from a number of cells in the preceding layer $\mathcal{L}$. The density of these synaptic connections decreases monotonically with distance $r_\mathcal{L}$ from the point underlying the $\mathcal{M}$-cell's position. Since the synaptic weights change on a long time scale compared to the variation of random inputs, by averaging the Hebb rule over the ensemble of inputs in layer $\mathcal{L}$, the dynamical equation for the development of the synaptic strength $\omega_\tau(i)$ between a $\mathcal{M}$-cell and i-th $\mathcal{L}$-cell at time τ is

$$\omega_{\tau+1}(i) = f\{\omega_\tau(i) + k_1 + \sum_{j=1}^{N_\mathcal{L}}[Q_{ij}^\mathcal{L} + k_2]r(j)\omega_\tau(j)\} \tag{1}$$

where k_1, k_2 are system parameters which are particular combinations of the constants of the Hebb rule, $r(\cdot)$ is a non-negative normalized synaptic density function (SDF) [1], and $\sum_{i \in \mathcal{L}} r(i) = 1$, and $f(\cdot)$ is a limiter function defined by $f(x) = \omega_{max}$, if $x > \omega_{max}$; $= x$, if $|x| \leq \omega_{max}$; and $= -\omega_{max}$, if $x < -\omega_{max}$. The covariance

---

[1] The SDF is explicitly incorporated into the dynamics (1) which is equivalent to Linsker's formulation. A rigorous explanation for this equivalence is given in MacKay & Miller, 1990.

matrix $\{Q_{ij}\}$ of the layer $\mathcal{L}$ describes the correlation of activities of the i-th and the j-th $\mathcal{L}$-cells. Actually, the covariance matrix of each layer is determined by SDFs $r(\cdot)$ of all layers preceding the layer under consideration.

The idea of this paper is the following. It is well known that in general it is intractable to characterize the behavior of a nonlinear dynamics, since the nonlinearity is the cause of the coexistence of many attractors. And one has the difficulty in obtaining the complete characteristics of attractive basins in the state space. But usually for some cases, it is relatively easy to derive a necessary and sufficient condition to check whether a given state is a fixed point of the dynamics. In terms of this condition, the *whole* parameter regime for the emergence of a fixed point of the dynamics may be obtained in the parameter space. If we are further able to prove the stability of the fixed point, which implies that this fixed point is a steady state if the initial condition is in a nonempty vicinity in the state space, we can assert the occurrence of this fixed point attractor in that parameter regime. For Linsker's network, fortunately, the above idea can be carried out because of the specific form of the nonlinear function $f(\cdot)$. Due to space limitations, the rigorous proofs are in (Feng, Pan, & Roychowdhury, 1995).

2   The Set Of Saturated Fixed Point Attractors And The Criterion For The Division Of Parameter Regimes

In fact, Linsker's model is a system of first-order nonlinear difference equations, taking the form

$$\omega_{\tau+1}(i) = f[\omega_\tau(i) + h_i(\omega_\tau, k_1, k_2)], \qquad \omega_\tau = \{\omega_\tau(j), j=1,...,N_\mathcal{L}\}, \qquad (2)$$

where $h_i(\omega_\tau, k_1, k_2) = k_1 + \sum_{j=1}^{N_\mathcal{L}}[Q_{ij}^\mathcal{L} + k_2]r(j)\omega_\tau(j)$. And the aRFs observed in Linsker's simulation are the *saturated fixed point attractors* of this nonlinear system (2). Since the limiter function $f(\cdot)$ is defined on a hypercube $\Omega = [-\omega_{max}, \omega_{max}]^{N_\mathcal{L}}$ in weight state space within which the dynamics is dominated by the linear system $\omega_{\tau+1}(i) = \omega_\tau(i) + h_i(\omega_\tau, k_1, k_2)$, the short-time behaviors of evolution dynamics of connection patterns can be fully characterized in terms of the properties of eigenvectors and their eigenvalues. But this method of stability analysis will not be suitable for the long-time evolution of equation (1) or (2), provided the hypercube constraint is reached as the first largest component of ω reaches saturation. However, it is well-known that a *fixed point* or an *equilibrium state* of dynamics (2) satisfies

$$\omega_\tau(i) = f[\omega_\tau(i) + h_i(\omega_\tau, k_1, k_2)]. \qquad (3)$$

Because of the special form of the nonlinear function $f(\cdot)$, the fixed point equation (3) implies that $\exists \mathcal{T}$, such that for $\tau > \mathcal{T}$,

$$\mid \omega_\tau(i) + h_i(\omega_\tau, k_1, k_2) \mid \geq \omega_{max},$$

if $h_i(\omega, k_1, k_2) \neq 0$. So a saturated fixed point $\omega_\tau(i)$ must have the same sign as $h_i(\omega_\tau, k_1, k_2)$, i.e.

$$\omega_\tau(i) h_i(\omega_\tau, k_1, k_2) > 0.$$

By using the above idea, our Theorems 1 & 2 (proven in Feng, Pan, & Roychowdhury, 1995) state that the set of saturated fixed point attractors of the dynamics in

equation (1) is given by
$$\Omega_{FP} = \{\omega \mid \omega(i)h_i(\omega_\tau, k_1, k_2) > 0, \ 1 \leq i \leq N_{\mathcal{L}}\},$$
and $\omega \in \Omega_{FP}$ is stable, where the weight vector ω belongs to the set of all extreme points of the hypercube Ω (we assume $\omega_{max} = 1$ without loss of generality).

We next derive an explicit necessary and sufficient condition for the emergence of structured aRFs, i.e., we derive conditions to determine whether a given ω belongs to Ω_{FP}. Define $J^+(\omega) = \{i \mid \omega(i) = 1\}$ as the index set of cells at the preceding layer $\mathcal{L}$ with excitatory weight for a connection pattern ω, and $J^-(\omega) = \{i \mid \omega(i) = -1\}$ as the index set of $\mathcal{L}$-cells with inhibitory weight for ω. Note from the property of fixed point attractors that a connection pattern ω is an attractor of the dynamics (1) if and only if for $i \in J^+(\omega)$, we have

$$\omega(i)\{k_1 + \sum_j [Q^{\mathcal{L}}_{ij} + k_2]r(j)\omega(j)\} =$$
$$\omega(i)\{k_1 + \sum_{j \in J^+(\omega)}[Q^{\mathcal{L}}_{ij} + k_2]r(j)\omega(j) + \sum_{j \in J^-(\omega)}[Q^{\mathcal{L}}_{ij} + k_2]r(j)\omega(j)\} > 0.$$

By the definition of $J^+(\omega)$ and $J^-(\omega)$, we deduce from the above inequality that
$$k_1 + \sum_{j \in J^+(\omega)}[Q^{\mathcal{L}}_{ij} + k_2]r(j) - \sum_{j \in J^-(\omega)}[Q^{\mathcal{L}}_{ij} + k_2]r(j) > 0$$
namely
$$k_1 + k_2[\sum_{j \in J^+(\omega)} r(j) - \sum_{j \in J^-(\omega)} r(j)] > \sum_{j \in J^-(\omega)} Q^{\mathcal{L}}_{ij}r(j) - \sum_{j \in J^+(\omega)} Q^{\mathcal{L}}_{ij}r(j).$$

Inequality above is satisfied for all i in $J^+(\omega)$, and the left hand is independent of i. Hence,
$$k_1 + k_2[\sum_{j \in J^+(\omega)} r(j) - \sum_{j \in J^-(\omega)} r(j)] > \max_{i \in J^+(\omega)}[\sum_{j \in J^-(\omega)} Q^{\mathcal{L}}_{ij}r(j) - \sum_{j \in J^+(\omega)} Q^{\mathcal{L}}_{ij}r(j)].$$

On the other hand, for $i \in J^-(\omega)$, we can similarly deduce that
$$k_1 + k_2[\sum_{j \in J^+(\omega)} r(j) - \sum_{j \in J^-(\omega)} r(j)] < \min_{i \in J^-(\omega)}[\sum_{j \in J^-(\omega)} Q^{\mathcal{L}}_{ij}r(j) - \sum_{j \in J^+(\omega)} Q^{\mathcal{L}}_{ij}r(j)].$$

We introduce the *slope function*:
$$c(\omega) \stackrel{\text{def}}{=} \sum_{j \in J^+(\omega)} r(j) - \sum_{j \in J^-(\omega)} r(j)$$

which is the difference of sums of the SDF $r(\cdot)$ over $J^+(\omega)$ and $J^-(\omega)$, and two k_1-*intercept functions*:

$$d_1(\omega) \stackrel{\text{def}}{=} \begin{cases} \max_{i \in J^+(\omega)}(\sum_{j \in J^-(\omega)} Q^{\mathcal{L}}_{ij}r(j) - \sum_{j \in J^+(\omega)} Q^{\mathcal{L}}_{ij}r(j)), & \text{if } J^+(\omega) \neq \emptyset \\ -\infty, & \text{if } J^+(\omega) = \emptyset \end{cases}$$

and

$$d_2(\omega) \stackrel{\text{def}}{=} \begin{cases} \min_{i \in J^-(\omega)}(\sum_{j \in J^-(\omega)} Q^{\mathcal{L}}_{ij}r(j) - \sum_{j \in J^+(\omega)} Q^{\mathcal{L}}_{ij}r(j)), & \text{if } J^-(\omega) \neq \emptyset \\ \infty, & \text{if } J^-(\omega) = \emptyset \end{cases}$$

A Rigorous Analysis of Linsker-type Hebbian Learning

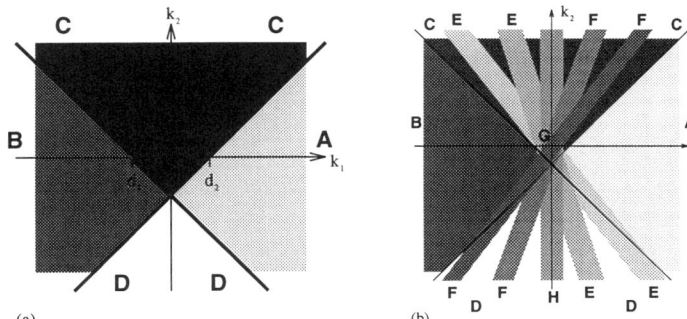

Figure 1: The parameter subspace of (k_1, k_2). (a) Parameter regime of (k_1, k_2) to ensure the emergence of all-excitatory (regime A) and all-inhibitory (regime B) connection patterns. The dark grey regime C is the coexistence regime for both all-excitatory and all-inhibitory connection patterns. And the regime D without texture are the regime that Linsker's simulation results are based on, in which both all-excitatory and all-inhibitory connection patterns are no longer an attractor. (b) The principal parameter regimes.

Now from our Theorem 3 in Feng, Pan, & Roychowdhury, 1995, for every layer of Linsker's network, the new rigorous criterion for the division of stable parameter regimes to ensure the development of various structured connection patterns is

$$d_2(\omega) > k_1 + c(\omega)k_2 > d_1(\omega).$$

That is, for a given SDF $r(\cdot)$, the parameter regime of (k_1, k_2) to ensure that ω is a stable attractor of dynamics (1) is a band between two parallel lines $k_1 + c(\omega)k_2 > d_1(\omega)$ and $k_1 + c(\omega)k_2 < d_2(\omega)$ (See regimes E and F in Fig.1(b)). It is noticed that as $d_1(\omega) > d_2(\omega)$, there is no regime of (k_1, k_2) for the occurrence of that aRF ω as an attractor of equation (1). Therefore, the existence of such a structured aRF ω as an attractor of equation (1) is determined by k_1-intercept functions $d_1(\cdot)$ and $d_2(\cdot)$, and therefore by the covariance matrix $Q^{\mathcal{L}}$ or SDFs $r(\cdot)$ of all preceding layers.

3 Parameter Regimes For aRFs Between Layers $\mathcal{B}$ And $\mathcal{C}$

Based on our general theorems applicable to all layers, we mainly focus on describing the stabilization process of synaptic development from the 2nd ($\mathcal{B}$) to the 3rd layer ($\mathcal{C}$) by considering the effect of the system parameters on the weight development. For the sake of convenience, we assume that the input at 1st layer ($\mathcal{A}$) is independent normal distribution with mean 0 and variance 1, and the connection strengths from layer $\mathcal{A}$ to $\mathcal{B}$ are all-excitatory same as in Linsker's simulations. The emergence of various aRFs between layer $\mathcal{B}$ and $\mathcal{C}$ have been previously studied in the literature, and in this paper we mention only the following new results made possible by our approach:

(1) For the cell in layer $\mathcal{C}$, the all-excitatory and the all-inhibitory connection patterns still have the largest stable regimes. Denote both SDFs from layer $\mathcal{A}$ to $\mathcal{B}$ and from $\mathcal{B}$ to $\mathcal{C}$ as $r^{\mathcal{AB}}(\cdot, \cdot)$ and $r^{\mathcal{BC}}(\cdot)$ respectively. The parameter plane of (k_1, k_2)

Table 1: **The Principal Parameter Regimes**

TYPE	PARAMETER REGIME	ATTRACTOR
Regime A	$k_1 + k_2 > d_1(+)$ (approx. $-k_1/k_2 < 1$)	All-excitatory aRF
Regime B	$k_1 - k_2 < d_2(-)$ (approx. $-k_1/k_2 > -1$)	All-inhibitory aRF
Regime C =A∩B	$k_1 + k_2 > d_1(+)$ and $k_1 - k_2 < d_2(-)$	All-excitatory and all-inhibitory aRFs coexist
Regime D =(A∪B)^c	$k_2 < d_1(+) = -d_2(-)$ and approx. $-1 < -k_1/k_2 < 1$	The structured aRFs may have separate parameter regimes
Regime E	$d_2(\omega) > k_1 + c(\omega)k_2 > d_1(\omega)$ where $c(\omega) > 0$	Any connection pattern in which the excitatory connections constitute the majority
Regime F	$d_2(\omega) > k_1 + c(\omega)k_2 > d_1(\omega)$ where $c(\omega) < 0$	Any connection pattern in which the inhibitory connections constitute the majority
Regime G =E∩F∩A∩B	$d_2(\omega^1) > k_1 + c(\omega^1)k_2 > d_1(\omega^1)$ ...... $d_2(\omega^\mu) > k_1 + c(\omega^\mu)k_2 > d_1(\omega^\mu)$	A small coexistence regime of many connection patterns around the origin point of the parameter plane of (k_1, k_2)

is divided into four regimes by

$$k_1 + k_2 > d_1(+) = -\min_{1 \leq i \leq N_B} \sum_{j=1}^{N_B} \sum_{l=1}^{N_A} r^{\mathcal{AB}}(i,l)r^{\mathcal{AB}}(j,l)r^{\mathcal{BC}}(j)$$

for all-excitatory pattern and

$$k_1 - k_2 < d_2(-) = \min_{1 \leq i \leq N_B} \sum_{j=1}^{N_B} \sum_{l=1}^{N_A} r^{\mathcal{AB}}(i,l)r^{\mathcal{AB}}(j,l)r^{\mathcal{BC}}(j) = -d_1(+)$$

for all-inhibitory pattern (See Fig.1(a)).

(2) The parameter with large and negative k_2 and approximately $-1 < -k_1/k_2 < 1$ is favorable for the emergence of various structured connection patterns (e.g., ON-center cells, OFF-center cells, bi-lobed cells, and oriented cells). This is because this regime (See regime D in Fig.1) is removed from the parameter regime where both all-excitatory and all-inhibitory aRFs are dominant, including the coexistence regime of many kind of attractors around the origin point (See regime G in Fig.1(b)). The above results provide a precise picture about the principal parameter regimes summarized in Table 1.

(3) The relative size of the radiuses of two SDFs $r^{\mathcal{AB}}(\cdot,\cdot)$ and $r^{\mathcal{BC}}(\cdot)$ plays a key role in the evolution of various structured aRFs from $\mathcal{B}$ to $\mathcal{C}$. A given SDF $r^{\mathcal{LM}}(i,j), i \in \mathcal{M}, j \in \mathcal{L}$ will be said to have a *range* $r_\mathcal{M}$ if $r^{\mathcal{LM}}(i,j)$ is 'sufficient small' for $||i-j|| \geq r_\mathcal{M}$. For a Gaussian SDF $r^{\mathcal{LM}}(j,k) \sim \exp(-||j-k||/r_\mathcal{M}^2)$, $j \in \mathcal{L}, k \in \mathcal{M}$, the range $r_\mathcal{M}$ is its standard deviation. We give the analytic prediction about the influence of the SDF's ranges $r_\mathcal{B}, r_\mathcal{C}$ on the dynamics by changing $r_\mathcal{B}$ from the smallest extreme to the largest one with respect to $r_\mathcal{C}$. For the smallest extreme of $r_\mathcal{B}$ (i.e. the

synaptic connections from $\mathcal{A}$ to $\mathcal{B}$ are concentrated enough, and those from layer $\mathcal{B}$ to $\mathcal{C}$ are fully feedforward connected), we proved that any kind of connection pattern has a stable parameter regime and emerge under certain parameters, because each synaptic connection within an aRF is developed independently. As $r_\mathcal{B}$ is changed from the smallest to the largest extreme, the development of synaptic connections between layer $\mathcal{B}$ and $\mathcal{C}$ will depend on each other stronger and stronger in the sense that most of connections have the same sign as their neighbors in an aRF. So for the largest extreme of $r_\mathcal{B}$ (i.e. the weights from layer $\mathcal{A}$ to $\mathcal{B}$ are fully feedforward but there is no constraint on the SDF $r^{\mathcal{BC}}(\cdot)$), any structured aRFs except for the all-excitatory and the all-inhibitory connection patterns will never arise at all, although there exist correlation in input activities (for a proof see Feng, Pan, & Roychowdhury, 1995). Therefore, without localized SDF, there would be no structured covariance matrix $\bar{Q} = \{[Q_{ij} + k_2]r(j)\}$ which embodies localized correlation in afferent activities. And without structured covariance matrix $\bar{Q}$, no structured aRFs would emerge.

(4) As another application of our analyses, we present several numerical results on the parameter regimes of $(k_1, k_2, r_\mathcal{B}, r_\mathcal{C})$ for the formation of various structured aRFs (Feng & Pan, 1993; Feng, Pan, & Roychowdhury, 1995) (where we assume that $r^{\mathcal{AB}}(i,j) \sim \exp(-||i-j||/r_\mathcal{B}^2)$, $i \in \mathcal{B}, j \in \mathcal{A}$, and $r^{\mathcal{BC}}(i) \sim \exp(-||i||/r_\mathcal{C}^2)$, $i \in \mathcal{B}$ as in (Linsker, 1986 & 1988)). For example, we show that various aRFs as attractors have different relative stability. For a fixed $r_\mathcal{C}$, the SDF's range $r_\mathcal{B}$ of the preceding layer as the third system parameter has various critical values for different attractors. That is, an attractor will no longer be stable if $r_\mathcal{B}$ exceeds its corresponding critical value (See Fig. 2). For circularly symmetric ON-center cells, those aRFs with large ON-center core (which have positive or small negative slope value $c(\omega) \approx -k_1/k_2$) always have a stable parameter regime. But for those ON-center cells with large negative slope value $c(\omega)$, their stable parameter regimes decrease in size with $c(\omega)$. Similarly, circularly symmetric OFF-center cells with large OFF-center core (which have negative or small positive slope value $c(\omega)$) will be more stable than those with large positive average of weights. But for non-circularly-symmetric patterns (e.g., bi-lobed cells and oriented cells), only those attractors with zero average synaptic strength might always have a stable parameter regime (See regime H in Fig.1(b)). If the third parameter $r_\mathcal{B}$ is large enough to exceed its critical values for other aRFs and k_2 is large and negative, then ON-center aRFs with positive $c(\omega)$ and OFF-center aRFs with negative $c(\omega)$ will be almost only attractors in regime D∩E and regime D∩F respectively. This conclusion makes it clear why we usually obtain ON-center aRFs in regime D∩E and OFF-center aRFs in regime D∩F much more easily than other patterns.

4 Concluding Remarks

One advantage of our rigorous approach to this kind of unsupervised Hebbian learning network is that, without approximation, it unifies the treatment of many diverse problems about dynamical mechanisms. It is important to notice that there is no assumption on the second item $h_i(\omega_\tau)$ on the right hand side of equation (1), and there is no restriction on the matrix Q. Our Theorems 1 and 2 provide the general framework for the description of the fixed point attractors for any difference equation of the type stated in (2) that uses a limiter function. Depending on the

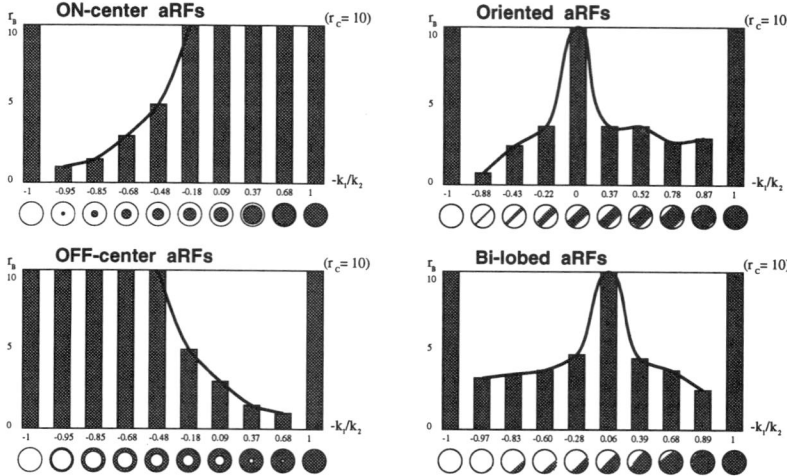

Figure 2: The critical values of the SDF's range r_B for different connection patterns.

structure of the second item, $h_i(\omega_\tau)$, it is not difficult to adapt our Theorem 3 to obtain the precise relationship among system parameters in other kind of models as long as $f(\cdot)$ is a limiter function. Since the functions in the necessary and sufficient condition are computable (like our slope and k_1-intercept functions), one is always able to check whether a designated fixed point is stable for a specific set of parameters.

Acknowledgements

The work of V. P. Roychowdhury and H. Pan was supported in part by the General Motors Faculty Fellowship and by the NSF Grant No. ECS-9308814. J. Feng was partially supported by Chinese National Key Project of Fundamental Research "Climbing Program" and CNR of Italy.

References

R. Linsker. (1986) From basic network principle to neural architecture (series). *Proc. Natl. Acad. Sci. USA* **83**: 7508-7512, 8390-8394, 8779-8783.

R. Linsker. (1988) Self-organization in a perceptual network. *Computer* **21**(3): 105-117.

D. MacKay, & K. Miller. (1990) Analysis of Linsker's application of Hebbian rules to linear networks. *Network* **1**: 257-297.

J. Feng, & H. Pan. (1993) Analysis of Linsker-type Hebbian learning: Rigorous results. *Proc. 1993 IEEE Int. Conf. on Neural Networks - San Francisco Vol. III*, 1516-1521. Piscataway, NJ: IEEE.

J. Feng, H. Pan, & V. P. Roychowdhury. (1995) Linsker-type Hebbian learning: A qualitative analysis on the parameter space. (submitted).

Sample Size Requirements For Feedforward Neural Networks

Michael J. Turmon
Cornell Univ. Electrical Engineering
Ithaca, NY 14853
mjt@ee.cornell.edu

Terrence L. Fine
Cornell Univ. Electrical Engineering
Ithaca, NY 14853
tlfine@ee.cornell.edu

Abstract

We estimate the number of training samples required to ensure that the performance of a neural network on its training data matches that obtained when fresh data is applied to the network. Existing estimates are higher by orders of magnitude than practice indicates. This work seeks to narrow the gap between theory and practice by transforming the problem into determining the distribution of the supremum of a random field in the space of weight vectors, which in turn is attacked by application of a recent technique called the Poisson clumping heuristic.

1 INTRODUCTION AND KNOWN RESULTS

We investigate the tradeoffs among *network complexity*, *training set size*, and *statistical performance* of feedforward neural networks so as to allow a reasoned choice of network architecture in the face of limited training data. Nets are functions $\eta(x; w)$, parameterized by their weight vector $w \in \mathcal{W} \subseteq R^d$, which take as input points $x \in R^k$. For classifiers, network output is restricted to $\{0, 1\}$ while for forecasting it may be any real number. The architecture of all nets under consideration is $\mathcal{N}$, whose complexity may be gauged by its Vapnik-Chervonenkis (VC) dimension v, the size of the largest set of inputs the architecture can classify in any desired way ('shatter'). Nets $\eta \in \mathcal{N}$ are chosen on the basis of a training set $\mathcal{T} = \{(x_i, y_i)\}_{i=1}^n$. These n samples are i.i.d. according to an *unknown* probability law P. Performance of a network is measured by the mean-squared error

$$\begin{aligned}\mathcal{E}(w) &= E(\eta(x;w) - y)^2 & (1)\\ &= P(\eta(x;w) \neq y) \quad \text{(for classifiers)} & (2)\end{aligned}$$

and a good (perhaps not unique) net in the architecture is $w^0 = \arg\min_{w \in \mathcal{W}} \mathcal{E}(w)$. To select a net using the training set we employ the empirical error

$$\nu_T(w) = \frac{1}{n} \sum_{i=1}^{n} (\eta(x_i; w) - y_i)^2 \qquad (3)$$

sustained by $\eta(\cdot; w)$ on the training set T. A good choice for a classifier is then $w^* = \arg\min_{w \in \mathcal{W}} \nu_T(w)$. In these terms, the issue raised in the first sentence of the section can be restated as, "How large must n be in order to ensure $\mathcal{E}(w^*) - \mathcal{E}(w^0) \leq \epsilon$ with high probability?"

For purposes of analysis we can avoid dealing directly with the stochastically chosen network w^* by noting

$$\mathcal{E}(w^*) - \mathcal{E}(w^0) \leq |\nu_T(w^*) - \mathcal{E}(w^*)| + |\nu_T(w^0) - \mathcal{E}(w^0)| \leq 2 \sup_{w \in \mathcal{W}} |\nu_T(w) - \mathcal{E}(w)|$$

A bound on the last quantity is also useful in its own right.

The best-known result is in (Vapnik, 1982), introduced to the neural network community by (Baum & Haussler, 1989):

$$P(\sup_{w \in \mathcal{W}} |\nu_T(w) - \mathcal{E}(w)| \geq \epsilon) \leq 6 \frac{(2n)^v}{v!} e^{-n\epsilon^2/2} \qquad (4)$$

This remarkable bound not only involves no unknown constant factors, but holds independent of the data distribution P. Analysis shows that sample sizes of about

$$n_c = (4v/\epsilon^2) \log 3/\epsilon \qquad (5)$$

are enough to force the bound below unity, after which it drops exponentially to zero. Taking $\epsilon = .1$, $v = 50$ yields $n_c = 68\,000$, which disagrees by orders of magnitude with the experience of practitioners who train such simple networks.

More recently, Talagrand (1994) has obtained the bound

$$P(\sup_{w \in \mathcal{W}} |\nu_T(w) - \mathcal{E}(w)| \geq \epsilon) \leq K_1 \left(\frac{K_2 n\epsilon^2}{v}\right)^v e^{-2n\epsilon^2}, \qquad (6)$$

yielding a sufficient condition of order v/ϵ^2, but the values of K_1 and K_2 are inaccessible so the result is of no practical use.

Formulations with finer resolution near $\mathcal{E}(w) = 0$ are used. Vapnik (1982) bounds $P(\sup_{w \in \mathcal{W}} |\nu_T(w) - \mathcal{E}(w)|/\mathcal{E}(w)^{1/2} \geq \epsilon)$—note $\mathcal{E}(w)^{1/2} \approx \text{Var}(\nu_T(w))^{1/2}$ when $\mathcal{E}(w) \approx 0$—while Blumer et al. (1989) and Anthony and Biggs (1992) work with $P(\sup_{w \in \mathcal{W}} |\nu_T(w) - \mathcal{E}(w)| 1_{\{0\}}(\nu_T(w)) \geq \epsilon)$. The latter obtain the sufficient condition

$$n_c = (5.8v/\epsilon) \log 12/\epsilon \qquad (7)$$

for nets, if any, having $\nu_T(w) = 0$. If one is guaranteed to do reasonably well on the training set, a smaller order of dependence results.

Results (Turmon & Fine, 1993) for perceptrons and P a Gaussian mixture imply that at least $v/280\epsilon^2$ samples are needed to force $\mathcal{E}(w^*) - \mathcal{E}(w^0) < 2\epsilon$ with high probability. (Here w^* is the best linear discriminant with weights estimated from the data.) Combining with Talagrand's result, we see that the general (not assuming small $\nu_T(w)$) functional dependence is v/ϵ^2.

2 APPLYING THE POISSON CLUMPING HEURISTIC

We adopt a new approach to the problem. For the moderately large values of n we anticipate, the central limit theorem informs us that $\sqrt{n}\,[\nu_T(w) - \mathcal{E}(w)]$ has nearly the distribution of a zero-mean Gaussian random variable. It is therefore reasonable[1] to suppose that

$$P(\sup_{w \in \mathcal{W}} |\nu_T(w) - \mathcal{E}(w)| \geq \epsilon) \simeq P(\sup_{w \in \mathcal{W}} |Z(w)| \geq \epsilon\sqrt{n}) \leq 2P(\sup_{w \in \mathcal{W}} Z(w) \geq \epsilon\sqrt{n})$$

where $Z(w)$ is a Gaussian process with mean zero and covariance

$$R(w,v) = EZ(w)Z(v) = Cov\big((y - \eta(x;w))^2, (y - \eta(x;v))^2\big) \quad .$$

The problem about extrema of the original empirical process is equivalent to one about extrema of a corresponding Gaussian process.

The Poisson clumping heuristic (PCH), introduced in the remarkable (Aldous, 1989), provides a general tool for estimating such exceedance probabilities. Consider the excursions above level $b\,(= \epsilon\sqrt{n} \gg 1)$ by a stochastic process $Z(w)$. At left below, the set $\{w : Z(w) \geq b\}$ is seen as a group of "clumps" scattered in weight space $\mathcal{W}$. The PCH says that, provided Z has no long-range dependence and the level b is large, the centers of the clumps fall according to the points of a Poisson process on $\mathcal{W}$, and the clump shapes are independent. The vertical arrows (below right) illustrate two clump centers (points of the Poisson process); the clumps are the bars centered about the arrows.

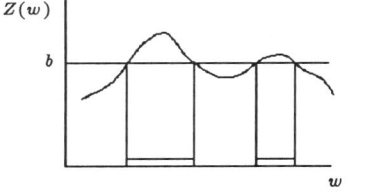
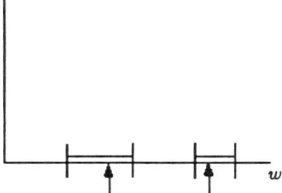

In fact, with $p_b(w) = P(Z(w) \geq b)$, $C_b(w)$ the size of a clump located at w, and $\lambda_b(w)$ the rate of occurrence of clump centers, the fundamental equation is

$$p_b(w) \simeq \lambda_b(w) E C_b(w). \tag{8}$$

The number of clumps in $\mathcal{W}$ is a Poisson random variable N_b with parameter $\int_{\mathcal{W}} \lambda_b(w)\,dw$. The probability of a clump is $P(N_b > 0) = 1 - \exp(-\int_{\mathcal{W}} \lambda_b(w)\,dw) \simeq \int_{\mathcal{W}} \lambda_b(w)\,dw$ where the approximation holds because our goal is to operate in a regime where this probability is near zero. Letting $\bar{\Phi}(b) = P(N(0,1) > b)$ and $\sigma^2(w) = R(w,w)$, we have $p_b(w) = \bar{\Phi}(b/\sigma(w))$. The fundamental equation becomes

$$P(\sup_{w \in \mathcal{W}} Z(w) \geq b) \simeq \int_{\mathcal{W}} \frac{\bar{\Phi}(b/\sigma(w))}{EC_b(w)}\,dw \quad . \tag{9}$$

It remains only to find the mean clump size $EC_b(w)$ in terms of the network architecture and the statistics of (x,y).

---

[1] See ch. 7 of (Pollard, 1984) for treatment of some technical details in this limit.

3 POISSON CLUMPING FOR SMOOTH PROCESSES

Assume $Z(w)$ has two mean-square derivatives in w. (If the network activation functions have two derivatives in w, for example, $Z(w)$ will have two almost sure derivatives.) Z then has a parabolic approximation about some w_0 via its gradient $G = \nabla Z(w)$ and Hessian matrix $\mathbf{H} = \nabla\nabla Z(w)$ at w_0. Provided $Z_0 \geq b$, that is that there is a clump at w_0, simple computations reveal

$$C_b(w_0) \simeq \kappa_d \frac{(2(Z_0 - b) - G^T \mathbf{H}^{-1} G)^{d/2}}{|\mathbf{H}|^{1/2}} \qquad (10)$$

where κ_d is the volume of the unit ball in R^d and $|\cdot|$ is the determinant. The mean clump size is the expectation of this conditioned on $Z(w_0) \geq b$.

The same argument used to show that $Z(w)$ is approximately normal shows that G and $\mathbf{H}$ are approximately normal too. In fact,

$$E[\mathbf{H}|Z(w_0) = z] = \frac{z}{\sigma^2(w_0)} \Lambda(w_0)$$
$$\Lambda(w_0) = -EZ(w_0)\mathbf{H} = -\nabla_w \nabla_w R(w_0, w)|_{w=w_0}$$

so that, since b (and hence z) is large, the second term in the numerator of (10) may be neglected. The expectation is then easily computed, resulting in

Lemma 1 (Smooth process clump size) *Let the network activation functions be twice continuously differentiable, and let $b \gg \sigma(w)$. Then*

$$EC_b(w) \simeq (2\pi)^{d/2} \left|\frac{\Lambda(w)}{\sigma^2(w)}\right|^{-1/2} \left(\frac{\sigma(w)}{b}\right)^d .$$

Substituting into (9) yields

$$P(\sup_{w \in \mathcal{W}} Z(w) \geq b) \simeq (2\pi)^{-\frac{d+1}{2}} \int_\mathcal{W} \left|\frac{\Lambda(w)}{\sigma^2(w)}\right|^{1/2} \left(\frac{b}{\sigma(w)}\right)^{d-1} e^{-b^2/2\sigma^2(w)} dw, \qquad (11)$$

where use of the asymptotic expansion $\bar{\Phi}(z) \simeq (z\sqrt{2\pi})^{-1} \exp(-z^2/2)$ is justified since $(\forall w) b \gg \sigma(w)$ is necessary to have the individual $P(Z(w) \geq b)$ low—let alone the supremum. To go farther, we need information about the variance $\sigma^2(w)$ of $(y - \eta(x; w))^2$. In general this must come from the problem at hand, but suppose for example the process has a unique variance maximum $\bar{\sigma}^2$ at $\bar{w}$. Then, since the level b is large, we can use Laplace's method to approximate the d-dimensional integral.

Laplace's method finds asymptotic expansions for integrals

$$\int_\mathcal{W} g(w) \exp(-f(w)^2/2) \, dw$$

when $f(w)$ is $\mathcal{C}^2$ with a unique positive minimum at w_0 in the interior of $\mathcal{W} \subseteq R^d$, and $g(w)$ is positive and continuous. Suppose $f(w_0) \gg 1$ so that the exponential factor is decreasing much faster than the slowly varying g. Expanding f to second order about w_0, substituting into the exponential, and performing the integral shows that

$$\int_\mathcal{W} g(w) \exp(-f(w)^2/2) \, dw \simeq (2\pi)^{d/2} |f(w_0) K|^{-1/2} g(w_0) \exp(-f(w_0)^2/2)$$

where $K = \nabla\nabla f(w)|_{w_0}$, the Hessian of f. See (Wong, 1989) for a proof. Applying this to (11) and using the asymptotic expansion for $\bar{\Phi}$ in reverse yields

Theorem 1 *Let the network activation functions be twice continuously differentiable. Let the variance have a unique maximum $\bar{\sigma}$ at $\bar{w}$ in the interior of $\mathcal{W}$ and the level $b \gg \bar{\sigma}$. Then the PCH estimate of exceedance probability is given by*

$$P(\sup_{w \in \mathcal{W}} Z(w) \geq b) \simeq \frac{|\Lambda(\bar{w})|^{1/2}}{|\Lambda(\bar{w}) - \Gamma(\bar{w})|^{1/2}} \bar{\Phi}(b/\bar{\sigma}) \qquad (12)$$

where $\Gamma(\bar{w}) = \nabla_w \nabla_v R(w,v)|_{w=v=\bar{w}}$. Furthermore, $\Lambda - \Gamma$ is positive-definite at $\bar{w}$; it is $-1/2$ the Hessian of $\sigma^2(w)$. The leading constant thus strictly exceeds unity.

The above probability is just $P(Z(\bar{w}) \geq b)$ multiplied by a factor accounting for the other networks in the supremum. Letting $b = \epsilon\sqrt{n}$ reveals

$$n_c = \frac{\bar{\sigma}^2 \log(|\Lambda(\bar{w})|/|\Lambda(\bar{w}) - \Gamma(\bar{w})|)}{\epsilon^2} \qquad (13)$$

samples force $P(\sup_w |\nu_T(w) - \mathcal{E}(w)| \geq \epsilon)$ below unity. If the variance maximum is not unique but occurs over a $\bar{d}$-dimensional set within $\mathcal{W}$, the sample size estimate becomes proportional to $\bar{\sigma}^2 \bar{d}/\epsilon^2$. With $\bar{d}$ playing the role of VC dimension v, this is similar to Vapnik's bound although we retain dependence on P and $\mathcal{N}$.

The above probability is determined by behavior near the maximum-variance point, which for example in classification is where $\mathcal{E}(w) = 1/2$. Such nets are uninteresting as classifiers, and certainly it is undesirable for them to dominate the entire probability. This problem is avoided by replacing $Z(w)$ with $Z(w)/\sigma(w)$, which additionally allows a finer resolution where $\mathcal{E}(w)$ nears zero. Indeed, for classification, if n is such that with high probability

$$\sup_{w \in \mathcal{W}} \frac{|\nu_T(w) - \mathcal{E}(w)|}{\sigma(w)} = \sup_{w \in \mathcal{W}} \frac{|\nu_T(w) - \mathcal{E}(w)|}{\sqrt{\mathcal{E}(w)(1 - \mathcal{E}(w))}} < \epsilon \quad , \qquad (14)$$

then $\nu_T(w^*) = 0 \Rightarrow \mathcal{E}(w^*) < \epsilon^2(1+\epsilon^2)^{-1} \simeq \epsilon^2 \ll \epsilon$. Near $\nu_T(w^*) = 0$, condition (14)/ is much more powerful than the corresponding unnormalized one. Sample size estimates using this setup give results having a functional form similar to (7).

4 ANOTHER MEANS OF COMPUTING CLUMP SIZE

Conditional on there being a clump center at w, the upper bound

$$C_b(w) \leq D_b(w) \equiv \int_{\mathcal{W}} 1_{[0,\infty)}(Z(w') - b)\, dw' \qquad (15)$$

is evidently valid: the volume of the clump at w is no larger than the total volume of all clumps. (The right hand side is indeed a function of w because we condition on occurrence of a clump center at w.) The bound is an overestimate when the number N_b of clumps exceeds one, but recall that we are in a regime where b (equivalently n) is large enough so that $P(N_b > 1)/P(N_b = 1) \simeq \int_{\mathcal{W}} \lambda_b(w)\, dw \ll 1$. Thus error in (15) due to this source is negligible. To compute its mean, we approximate

$$ED_b(w) = \int_{\mathcal{W}} P(Z(w') \geq b | w \text{ a clump center})\, dw'$$

$$\simeq \int_{\mathcal{W}} P(Z(w') \geq b | Z(w) \geq b) \, dw' \quad . \tag{16}$$

The point is that occurrence of a clump center at w_0 is a smaller class of events than merely $Z(w_0) \geq b$: the latter can arise from a clump center at a nearby $w \in \mathcal{W}$ capturing w_0. Since $Z(w)$ and $Z(w')$ are jointly normal, abbreviate $\sigma = \sigma(w)$, $\sigma' = \sigma(w')$, $\rho = \rho(w, w') = R(w, w')/(\sigma \sigma')$, and let

$$\zeta = \zeta(w, w') = (\sigma/\sigma') \frac{1 - \rho \sigma'/\sigma}{\sqrt{1 - \rho^2}} \tag{17}$$

$$= \left((1 - \rho)/(1 + \rho)\right)^{1/2} \quad \text{(constant variance case)} \quad . \tag{18}$$

Evaluating the conditional probabilities of (16) presents no problem, and we obtain

Lemma 2 (Clump size estimate) *For $b \gg \sigma$ the mean clump size is*

$$EC_b(w) \simeq ED_b(w) \simeq \int_{\mathcal{W}} \bar{\Phi}((b/\sigma)\zeta) \, dw' \quad . \tag{19}$$

Remark 1. This integral will be used in (9) to find

$$P(\sup_w Z(w) > b) \simeq \int_{\mathcal{W}} \frac{\bar{\Phi}(b/\sigma)}{\int_{\mathcal{W}} \bar{\Phi}((b/\sigma)\zeta) \, dw'} \, dw \quad . \tag{20}$$

Since b is large, the main contribution to the outer integral occurs for w near a variance maximum, i.e. for $\sigma'/\sigma \leq 1$. If the variance is constant then all $w \in \mathcal{W}$ contribute. In either case ζ is nonnegative. By lemma 1 we expect (19) to be, as a function of b, of the form (const $\sigma/b)^p$ for, say, $p = d$. In particular, we do not anticipate the exponentially small clump sizes resulting if $(\forall w')\zeta(w, w') \geq M \gg 0$. Therefore ζ should approach zero over some range of w', which happens only when $\rho \approx 1$, that is, for w' near w. The behavior of $\rho(w, w')$ for $w' \approx w$ is the key to finding the clump size.

Remark 2. There is a simple interpretation of the clump size; it represents the volume of $w' \in \mathcal{W}$ for which $Z(w')$ is highly correlated with $Z(w)$. The exceedance probability is a sum of the point exceedance probabilities (the numerator of (20)), each weighted according to how many other points are correlated with it. In effect, the space $\mathcal{W}$ is partitioned into regions that tend to "have exceedances together," with a large clump size $EC_b(w)$ indicating a large region. The overall probability can be viewed as a sum over all these regions of the corresponding point exceedance probability. This has a similarity to the Vapnik argument which lumps networks together according to their $n^v/v!$ possible actions on n items in the training set. In this sense the mean clump size is a fundamental quantity expressing the ability of an architecture to generalize.

5 EMPIRICAL ESTIMATES OF CLUMP SIZE

The clump size estimate of lemma 2 is useful in its own right if one has information about the covariance of Z. Other known techniques of finding $EC_b(w)$ exploit special features of the process at hand (e.g. smoothness or similarity to other well-studied processes); the above expression is valid for any covariance structure. In this section we show how one may *estimate* the clump size using the training set, and thus obtain probability approximations in the absence of analytical information about the unknown P and the potentially complex network architecture $\mathcal{N}$.

Here is a practical way to approximate the integral giving $ED_b(w)$. For $\gamma < 1$ define a set of significant w'

$$S_\gamma(w) = \{w' \in \mathcal{W} : \zeta(w, w') \leq \gamma\} \quad V_\gamma(w) = \text{vol}(S_\gamma(w)) \quad ; \quad (21)$$

then monotonicity of $\bar{\Phi}$ yields $ED_b(w) \geq \int_{S_\gamma} \bar{\Phi}((b/\sigma)\zeta)\, dw' \geq V_\gamma(w)\, \bar{\Phi}((b/\sigma)\gamma)$. This apparently crude lower bound for $\bar{\Phi}$ is accurate enough near the origin to give satisfactory results in the cases we have studied. For example, we can characterize the covariance $R(w, w')$ of the smooth process of lemma 1 and thus find its ζ function. The bound above is then easily calculated and differs by only small constant factors from the clump size in the lemma.

The lower bound for $ED_b(w)$ yields the upper bound

$$P(\sup_w Z(w) \geq b) \leq \int_{\mathcal{W}} \frac{\bar{\Phi}(b/\sigma)}{V_\gamma(w)\, \bar{\Phi}((b/\sigma)\gamma)}\, dw \quad . \quad (22)$$

We call $V_\gamma(w)$ the *correlation volume*, as it represents those weight vectors w' whose errors $Z(w')$ are highly correlated with $Z(w)$; one simple way to estimate the correlation volume is as follows. Select a weight w' and using the training set compute

$$(y_1 - \eta(x_1; w))^2, \ldots, (y_n - \eta(x_n; w))^2 \,\&\, (y_1 - \eta(x_1; w'))^2, \ldots, (y_n - \eta(x_n; w'))^2\,.$$

It is then easy to estimate σ^2, σ'^2, and ρ, and finally $\zeta(w, w')$, which is compared to the chosen γ to decide if $w' \in S_\gamma(w)$.

The difficulty is that for large d, $S_\gamma(w)$ is far smaller than any approximately-enclosing set. Simple Monte Carlo sampling and even importance sampling methods fail to estimate the volume of such high-dimensional convex bodies because so few hits occur in probing the space (Lovász, 1991). The simplest way to concentrate the search is to let $w' = w$ except in one coordinate and probe along each coordinate axis. The correlation volume is approximated as the product of the one-dimensional measurements.

Simulation studies of the above approach have been performed for a perceptron architecture in input uniform over $[-1, 1]^d$. The integral (22) is computed by Monte Carlo sampling, and based on a training set of size $100d$, $V_\gamma(w)$ is computed at each point via the above method. The result is that an estimated sample size of $5.4d/\epsilon^2$ is enough to ensure (14) with high probability. For nets, if any, having $\nu_T(w) = 0$, sample sizes larger than $5.4d/\epsilon$ will ensure reliable generalization, which compares favorably with (7).

6 SUMMARY AND CONCLUSIONS

To find realistic estimates of sample size we transform the original problem into one of finding the distribution of the supremum of a derived Gaussian random field, which is defined over the weight space of the network architecture. The latter problem is amenable to solution via the Poisson clumping heuristic. In terms of the PCH the question becomes one of estimating the mean clump size, that is, the typical volume of an excursion above a given level by the random field. In the "smooth" case we directly find the clump volume and obtain estimates of sample size that are (correctly) of order v/ϵ^2. The leading constant, while explicit, depends on properties of the architecture and the data—which has the advantage of being tailored to the given problem but the potential disadvantage of our having to compute them.

We also obtain a useful estimate for the clump size of a general process in terms of the correlation volume $V_\gamma(w)$. For normalized error, (22) becomes approximately

$$P\left(\sup_{w \in \mathcal{W}} \frac{\nu_T(w) - \mathcal{E}(w)}{\sigma(w)} \geq \epsilon\right) \approx E\left[\frac{\text{vol}(\mathcal{W})}{V_\gamma(w)}\right] e^{-(1-\gamma^2)n\epsilon^2/2}$$

where the expectation is taken with respect to a uniform distribution on $\mathcal{W}$. The probability of reliable generalization is roughly given by an exponentially decreasing factor (the exceedance probability for a single point) times a number representing degrees of freedom. The latter is the mean size of an equivalence class of "similarly-acting" networks. The parallel with the Vapnik approach, in which a worst-case exceedance probability is multiplied by a growth function bounding the number of classes of networks in $\mathcal{N}$ that can act differently on n pieces of data, is striking. In this fashion the correlation volume is an analog of the VC dimension, but one that depends on the interaction of the data and the architecture.

Lastly, we have proposed practical methods of estimating the correlation volume empirically from the training data. Initial simulation studies based on a perceptron with input uniform on a region in R^d show that these approximations can indeed yield informative estimates of sample complexity.

References

Aldous, D. 1989. *Probability Approximations via the Poisson Clumping Heuristic.* Springer.

Anthony, M., & Biggs, N. 1992. *Computational Learning Theory.* Cambridge Univ.

Baum, E., & Haussler, D. 1989. What size net gives valid generalization? *Pages 81-90 of:* Touretzky, D. S. (ed), *NIPS 1.*

Blumer, A., Ehrenfeucht, A., Haussler, D., & Warmuth, M. K. 1989. Learnability and the Vapnik-Chervonenkis dimension. *Jour. Assoc. Comp. Mach.*, **36**, 929-965.

Lovász, L. 1991. Geometric Algorithms and Algorithmic Geometry. *In: Proc. Internat. Congr. Mathematicians.* The Math. Soc. of Japan.

Pollard, D. 1984. *Convergence of Stochastic Processes.* Springer.

Talagrand, M. 1994. Sharper bounds for Gaussian and empirical processes. *Ann. Probab.*, **22**, 28-76.

Turmon, M. J., & Fine, T. L. 1993. Sample Size Requirements of Feedforward Neural Network Classifiers. *In: IEEE 1993 Intern. Sympos. Inform. Theory.*

Vapnik, V. 1982. *Estimation of Dependences Based on Empirical Data.* Springer.

Wong, R. 1989. *Asymptotic Approximations of Integrals.* Academic.

Asymptotics of Gradient-based Neural Network Training Algorithms

Sayandev Mukherjee
saymukh@ee.cornell.edu
School of Electrical Engineering
Cornell University
Ithaca, NY 14853

Terrence L. Fine
tlfine@ee.cornell.edu
School of Electrical Engineering
Cornell University
Ithaca, NY 14853

Abstract

We study the asymptotic properties of the sequence of iterates of weight-vector estimates obtained by training a multilayer feedforward neural network with a basic gradient-descent method using a fixed learning constant and no batch-processing. In the one-dimensional case, an exact analysis establishes the existence of a limiting distribution that is not Gaussian in general. For the general case and small learning constant, a linearization approximation permits the application of results from the theory of random matrices to again establish the existence of a limiting distribution. We study the first few moments of this distribution to compare and contrast the results of our analysis with those of techniques of stochastic approximation.

1 INTRODUCTION

The wide applicability of neural networks to problems in pattern classification and signal processing has been due to the development of efficient gradient-descent algorithms for the supervised training of multilayer feedforward neural networks with differentiable node functions. A basic version uses a fixed learning constant and updates all weights after each training input is presented (on-line mode) rather than after the entire training set has been presented (batch mode). The properties of this algorithm as exhibited by the sequence of iterates are not yet well-understood. There are at present two major approaches.

Stochastic approximation techniques (Bucklew,Kurtz,Sethares, 1993; Finnoff, 1993; Kuan,Hornik, 1991; White, 1989) study the limiting behavior of the stochastic process that is the piecewise-constant or piecewise-linear interpolation of the sequence of weight-vector iterates (assuming infinitely many i.i.d. training inputs) as the learning constant approaches zero. It can be shown (Bucklew,Kurtz,Sethares, 1993; Finnoff, 1993) that as the learning constant tends to zero, the fluctuation between the paths and their limit, suitably normalized, tends to a Gaussian diffusion process.

Leen and Moody (1993) and Orr and Leen (1993) have considered the Markov process formed by the sequence of iterates (again, assuming infinitely many i.i.d. training inputs) for a fixed nonzero learning constant. This approach has the merit of dealing with the nonzero learning constant case and of linking the study of the training algorithm with the well-developed literature on Markov processes.

In particular, it is possible to solve (Leen,Moody, 1993) for the asymptotic distribution of the sequence of weight-vector iterates from the Chapman-Kolmogorov equation after certain assumptions have been used to simplify it considerably. However, the assumptions are unrealistic: in particular, the assumption of detailed balance does not hold in more than one dimension. This approach also fails to establish the existence of a limiting distribution in the general case.

This paper follows the method of considering the sequence of weight-vector iterates as a discrete-time continuous state-space Markov process, when the learning constant is fixed and nonzero. We shall first seek to establish the existence of an asymptotic distribution, and then examine this distribution through its first few moments.

It can be proved (Mukherjee, 1994), using Foster's criteria (Tweedie, 1976) for the positive-recurrence of a Markov process, that when a single sigmoidal node with one parameter is trained using the iterative form of the basic gradient-descent training algorithm (without batch-processing), the sequence of iterates of the parameter has a limiting distribution which is in general non-Gaussian, thereby qualifying the oft-stated claims in the literature (see, for example, (Bucklew,Kurtz,Sethares, 1993; Finnoff, 1993; White, 1989)). However, this method proves to be intractable in the multiple parameter case.

2 THE GENERAL CASE AND LINEARIZATION IN $\underline{W}_n$

The general version of this problem for a neural network η with scalar output involves training η with the i.i.d. training sequence $\{(\underline{X}_n, Y_n)\}$, loss function $\mathcal{E}(\underline{x}, y, \underline{w}) = \frac{1}{2}[y - \eta(\underline{x}, \underline{w})]^2$ ($\underline{x} \in \mathbb{R}^d, y \in \mathbb{R}, \underline{w} \in \mathbb{R}^m$) and the gradient-descent updating equation for the estimates of the weight vector given by

$$\begin{aligned}\underline{W}_{n+1} &= \underline{W}_n - \mu \nabla_{\underline{w}} \mathcal{E}(\underline{x}, y, \underline{w})|_{(\underline{X}_{n+1}, Y_{n+1}, \underline{W}_n)} \\ &= \underline{W}_n + \mu[Y_{n+1} - \eta(\underline{W}_n, \underline{X}_{n+1})] \nabla_{\underline{w}} \eta(\underline{w}, \underline{x})|_{\underline{W}_n, \underline{X}_{n+1}}.\end{aligned}$$

As is customary in this kind of analysis, the training set is assumed infinite, so that $\{\underline{W}_n\}_{n=0}^{\infty}$ forms a homogeneous Markov process in discrete time. In our analysis, the training data is assumed to come from the model

$$Y = \eta(\underline{w}^0, \underline{X}) + Z,$$

where Z and $\underline{X}$ are independent, and Z has zero mean and variance σ^2. Hence, the unrestricted Bayes estimator of Y given $\underline{X}$, $\mathbb{E}(Y|\underline{X}) = \eta(\underline{w}^0, \underline{X})$, is in the class of neural network estimators, and $\underline{w}^0$ is the goal of training. For convenience, we define $\underline{\tilde{W}} = \underline{W} - \underline{w}^0$.

Assuming that μ is small and that after a while, successive iterates, with high probability, jitter about in a close neighborhood of the optimal value $\underline{w}^0$, we make the important assumption that

$$\underline{\tilde{W}}_n = O_{\mathbf{P}}(\mu^k) \qquad (1)$$

for some $0 < k < 1$ (see Section 4) [1]. Applying Taylor series expansions to η and $\nabla_{\underline{w}} \eta$ and neglecting all terms $O_{\mathbf{P}}(\mu^{1+2k})$ and higher, we obtain the following linearized form of the updating equation:

$$\underline{\tilde{W}}_{n+1} = \mathbf{A}_{n+1} \underline{\tilde{W}}_n + \underline{B}_{n+1}, \qquad (2)$$

where

$$\underline{B}_{n+1} = \mu Z_{n+1} \nabla_{\underline{w}} \eta(\underline{w}, \underline{x})|_{\underline{w}^0, \underline{X}_{n+1}},$$

$$\begin{aligned}
\mathbf{A}_{n+1} &= \mathsf{I}_m - \mu (\nabla_{\underline{w}} \eta(\underline{w}, \underline{x})|_{\underline{w}^0, \underline{X}_{n+1}})(\nabla_{\underline{w}} \eta(\underline{w}, \underline{x})|_{\underline{w}^0, \underline{X}_{n+1}})^T \\
&\quad + \mu Z_{n+1} \nabla_{\underline{w}} \nabla_{\underline{w}} \eta(\underline{w}, \underline{x})|_{\underline{w}^0, \underline{X}_{n+1}} \qquad (3) \\
&= \mathsf{I}_m - \mu (\mathbf{G}_{n+1} - Z_{n+1} \mathbf{J}_{n+1}), \qquad (4)
\end{aligned}$$

$$\mathbf{G}_{n+1} = (\nabla_{\underline{w}} \eta(\underline{w}, \underline{x})|_{\underline{w}^0, \underline{X}_{n+1}})(\nabla_{\underline{w}} \eta(\underline{w}, \underline{x})|_{\underline{w}^0, \underline{X}_{n+1}})^T$$

$$\mathbf{J}_{n+1} = (\nabla_{\underline{w}} \nabla_{\underline{w}} \eta(\underline{w}, \underline{x})|_{\underline{w}^0, \underline{X}_{n+1}})$$

do not depend on $\underline{W}_n$. The matrices $\{(\mathbf{A}_{n+1}, \underline{B}_{n+1})\}$ form an i.i.d. sequence, but $\mathbf{A}_{n+1}$ and $\underline{B}_{n+1}$ are dependent for each n. Hence the linearized $\underline{W}_n$ again forms a homogeneous Markov process in discrete time.

In what follows we analyze this process in the hope that its asymptotics agree with those of the original Markov process.

3 EXISTENCE OF A LIMITING DISTRIBUTION

Let $\mathbf{A}$, $\underline{B}$, $\mathbf{G}$, $\mathbf{J}$ denote random matrices with the common distributions of the i.i.d. sequences $\{\mathbf{A}_n\}$, $\{\underline{B}_n\}$, $\{\mathbf{G}_n\}$, and $\{\mathbf{J}_n\}$ respectively, and let $\mathbf{T}: \mathbb{R}^m \to \mathbb{R}^m$ be the random affine transformation

$$\underline{\tilde{w}} \mapsto \mathbf{A}\underline{\tilde{w}} + \underline{B}.$$

The following result establishes the existence of a limiting distribution of $\underline{W}_n$.

Lemma 1 (Berger Thm. V, p.162) *Suppose*

$$\mathbb{E}[\log^+ \|\mathbf{A}\| + \log^+ \|\underline{B}\|] < \infty; \qquad (5)$$

$$\mathbb{E} \log \|\mathbf{A}_n \mathbf{A}_{n-1} \cdots \mathbf{A}_1\| < 0 \text{ for some } n \qquad (6)$$

where

$$\log^+ x = \log x \vee 0.$$

Then the following conclusions hold:

---
[1] I.e., $(\forall \epsilon > 0)(\exists M_\epsilon)(\forall n) \mathbb{P}(\mu^{-k} \|\underline{\tilde{W}}_n\| \leq M_\epsilon) \geq 1 - \epsilon$.

1. *Unique stationary distribution:* There exists a unique random variable $\underline{\tilde{W}} \in \mathbb{R}^m$, upto distribution, that is stationary with respect to $\mathbf{T}$ (i.e., $\underline{\tilde{W}}$ is independent of $\mathbf{T}$, and $\mathbf{T}\underline{\tilde{W}}$ has the same distribution as $\underline{\tilde{W}}$).

2. *Asymptotic stationarity:* We have convergence in distribution:

$$\underline{\tilde{W}}_n \xrightarrow{\mathcal{D}} \underline{\tilde{W}}.$$

Our choice of norm is the operator norm for the matrix $\mathbf{A}$,

$$\|\mathbf{A}\| = \max |\lambda(\mathbf{A})|,$$

where $\{\lambda(\mathbf{A})\}$ are the eigenvalues of $\mathbf{A}$, and the Euclidean norm for the vector $\underline{B}$,

$$\|\underline{B}\| = \sqrt{\sum_{i=1}^{m} |B_i|^2}.$$

We first verify (5). From the inequality $\forall x \in \mathbb{R}$, $\log^+ x \le x^2$, it is easily seen that if η is a feedforward net where all activation functions are twice-continuously differentiable in the weights, all hidden-layer activation functions are bounded and have bounded derivatives up to order 2, and if the training sequence $(\underline{X}_n, Y_n)$ is i.i.d. with finite fourth moments, then (5) holds for the Euclidean norm for $\underline{B}$ and the Frobenius norm for $\mathbf{A}$, $\|\mathbf{A}\|^2 = \sum_{i=1}^{m} \sum_{j=1}^{m} |A_{ij}|^2$. Since

$$(\max |\lambda(\mathbf{A})|)^2 \le \sum |\lambda(\mathbf{A})|^2 \le \sum_{i=1}^{m} \sum_{j=1}^{m} |A_{ij}|^2, \tag{7}$$

we see that (5) also holds for the operator norm of $\mathbf{A}$.

Assumption (6) forces the product $\mathbf{A}_n \cdots \mathbf{A}_1$ to tend to $\mathbf{0}^{m \times m}$ almost surely (Berger, 1993, p.146) and therefore removes the dependence of the asymptotic distribution of $\{\underline{\tilde{W}}_n\}$ on that of the initial value $\underline{\tilde{W}}_0$. A sufficient condition for (6) is given by the following lemma.

Lemma 2 *Suppose $\mathbb{E}\mathbf{G}$ is positive definite (note that it is positive semidefinite by definition), and for all n, $\mathbb{E}\mathbf{A}^n < \infty$. Then (6) holds for sufficiently small, positive μ.*

Proof: By assumption, $\min \lambda(\mathbb{E}\mathbf{G}) = \delta > 0$ for some δ.

Let $\mathbf{H}_n = \frac{1}{n}\sum_{i=1}^{n}(\mathbf{G}_i - Z_i\mathbf{J}_i)$. By the Strong Law of Large Numbers applied to the i.i.d. random matrices $(\mathbf{G}_i - Z_i\mathbf{J}_i)$, we have $\mathbf{H}_n \to \mathbb{E}\mathbf{G}$ a.s., so

$$\min \lambda(\mathbf{H}_n) \to \min \lambda(\mathbb{E}\mathbf{G}) \text{ a.s.} \tag{8}$$

Applying (7) to $\min \lambda(\mathbf{H}_n)$, it is easily shown that the same conditions on η and the training sequence that are sufficient for (5) also give $\sup_n \mathbb{E}[\min \lambda(\mathbf{H}_n)]^2 < \infty$, which in turn implies that $\{\min \lambda(\mathbf{H}_n)\}$ are uniformly integrable. Together with (8), this implies (Loéve, 1977, p.165) that $\min \lambda(\mathbf{H}_n) \to \min \lambda(\mathbb{E}\mathbf{G})$ in L^1. Hence there exists some (nonrandom) N, say, such that $\mathbb{E}|\min\lambda(\mathbf{H}_N) - \min\lambda(\mathbb{E}\mathbf{G})| \leq \delta/2$. Since

$$|\mathbb{E}\min\lambda(\mathbf{H}_N) - \min\lambda(\mathbb{E}\mathbf{G})| \leq \mathbb{E}|\min\lambda(\mathbf{H}_N) - \min\lambda(\mathbb{E}\mathbf{G})| \leq \delta/2,$$

we therefore have

$$\mathbb{E}\left[\min\lambda\left(\frac{1}{N}\sum_{i=1}^{N}(\mathbf{G}_i - Z_i\mathbf{J}_i)\right)\right] \geq \min\lambda(\mathbb{E}\mathbf{G}) - \delta/2 = \delta - \delta/2 = \delta/2 > 0. \quad (9)$$

We shall prove that (6) holds for this N ($\geq m$) by showing that

$$\mathbb{E}\log\|\mathbf{A}_N\mathbf{A}_{N-1}\cdots\mathbf{A}_1\|^2 = 2\mathbb{E}\log\|\mathbf{A}_N\mathbf{A}_{N-1}\cdots\mathbf{A}_1\| < 0.$$

For our choice of norm, we therefore want $\mathbb{E}[\log(\max|\lambda(\mathbf{A}_N\cdots\mathbf{A}_1)|)^2] < 0$. From Jensen's inequality, it is sufficient to have $\log\mathbb{E}[\max|\lambda(\mathbf{A}_N\cdots\mathbf{A}_1)|]^2 < 0$, or equivalently,

$$\mathbb{E}[\max|\lambda(\mathbf{A}_N\cdots\mathbf{A}_1)|]^2 < 1. \quad (10)$$

Now, since N is fixed, we can choose μ small enough that

$$\mathbf{A}_N\cdots\mathbf{A}_1 = \mathbf{I}_m - \mu\sum_{i=1}^{N}(\mathbf{G}_i - Z_i\mathbf{J}_i) + O_\mathbf{P}(\mu^2).$$

Hence, $\lambda(\mathbf{A}_N\cdots\mathbf{A}_1) = 1 - \mu\lambda(\sum_{i=1}^{N}(\mathbf{G}_i - Z_i\mathbf{J}_i)) + O_\mathbf{P}(\mu^2)$, and N is fixed, so

$$|\lambda(\mathbf{A}_N\cdots\mathbf{A}_1)|^2 = 1 - 2\mu\lambda\left(\sum_{i=1}^{N}(\mathbf{G}_i - Z_i\mathbf{J}_i)\right) + O_\mathbf{P}(\mu^2),$$

giving

$$\max|\lambda(\mathbf{A}_N\cdots\mathbf{A}_1)|^2 \leq 1 - 2\mu\min\lambda\left(\sum_{i=1}^{N}(\mathbf{G}_i - Z_i\mathbf{J}_i)\right) + O_\mathbf{P}(\mu^2),$$

$$\mathbb{E}\max|\lambda(\mathbf{A}_N\cdots\mathbf{A}_1)|^2 \leq 1 - N\delta\mu + o(\mu), \quad (11)$$

where we use (9) and the observation that the structure of the last $O_\mathbf{P}(\mu^2)$ term is such that its expectation (guaranteed finite by the hypothesis $\mathbb{E}\mathbf{A}^N < \infty$) is $O(\mu^2)$, or $o(\mu)$, and we also restrict $\mu < 1/N\delta$ so that

$$1 - 2\mu\mathbb{E}\min\lambda\left(\sum_{i=1}^{N}(\mathbf{G}_i - Z_i\mathbf{J}_i)\right) > 0.$$

From (11), it is clear that (10) holds for all sufficiently small, positive μ ($\ll 1/N\delta$). Therefore (6) holds for $n = N$.

We can combine these two lemmas into the following theorem.

Theorem 1 *Let η be a feedforward net where all activation functions are twice-continuously differentiable in the weights, all hidden-layer activation functions are bounded and have bounded derivatives up to order 2, and let the training sequence $(\underline{X}_n, Y_n)$ be i.i.d. with finite moments. Further, assume that $\mathbb{E}\mathbf{G}$ is positive definite. Then, for all sufficiently small, positive μ the sequence of random vectors $\{\underline{\tilde{W}}_n\}_{n=1}^{\infty}$ obtained from the updating equation (2) has a unique limiting distribution.*

We circumvent the generally intractable problem of finding the limiting distribution by calculating and investigating the behavior of its moments.

4 MOMENTS OF THE LIMITING DISTRIBUTION

Let us assume that the mean and variance of the limiting distribution exist, and that $Z \sim \mathcal{N}(0, \sigma^2)$. From (2) and the form of $\mathbf{A}_{n+1}$ and $\underline{B}_{n+1}$, it is easy to show that $\mathbb{E}\tilde{W} = 0$, or $\mathbb{E}\underline{W} = \underline{w}^0$, so the optimal value $\underline{w}^0$ is the mean of the limiting distribution of the sequence of iterates $\{\underline{W}_n\}$. It can also be shown (Mukherjee, 1994) that $\mathbb{E}\underline{\tilde{W}}\underline{\tilde{W}}^T = (\mu\sigma^2/2)\mathsf{I}_m$, yielding $\underline{\tilde{W}} = O_\mathbf{P}(\sqrt{\mu})$. This is consistent with our assumption (1) with $k = 1/2$.

In the one-dimensional case ($d = m = 1$), we have $\mathbb{E}\tilde{W} = 0$ and $\mathbb{E}\tilde{W}^2 = \frac{1}{2}\mu\sigma^2$ if $\mathbb{E}[X_{n+1}\eta'(w^0 X_{n+1})]^2 \neq 0$. Using these results, the fact that $Z \sim \mathcal{N}(0, \sigma^2)$, $\mathbb{E}\tilde{W} = 0$, the independence of Z and X, and assuming that $\mathbb{E}X^8 < \infty$, it is not difficult to compute the expressions

$$\mathbb{E}\tilde{W}^3 = \frac{\mu^2 \sigma^4 \mathbb{E}[X^3 \eta'' \eta'(1 - \mu X^2 \eta'^2)]}{\mathbb{E}[X^2 \eta'^2 - \mu X^4(\eta'^4 + \sigma^2 \eta''^2) + \mu^2 X^6 \eta'^2(\eta'^4/3 + \sigma^2 \eta''^2)]},$$

and

$$\mathbb{E}\tilde{W}^4 = 3(\mathbb{E}\tilde{W}^2)^2 K_1(\mu) + \mathbb{E}\tilde{W}^3 K_2(\mu),$$

where

$$K_1(\mu) = \frac{\mathbb{E}[X^2 \eta'^2 (1 - \mu X^2 \eta'^2)^2 + \mu X^4 \eta'^4 + 3\mu^2 X^6 \eta''^2 \eta'^2]}{K(\mu)},$$

$$K_2(\mu) = \frac{18\mu^2 \sigma^2 \mathbb{E}[X^3 \eta'' \eta' (1 - \mu X^2 \eta'^2)^2 + \mu^4 \sigma^4 X^7 \eta''^3 \eta']}{K(\mu)},$$

$$K(\mu) = \mathbb{E}[X^2 \eta'^2 - \frac{3}{2}\mu X^4 (\eta'^4 + \sigma^2 \eta''^2 (1 - \mu X^2 \eta'^2)^2)$$
$$+ \mu^2 X^6 \eta'^6 - \frac{1}{4}\mu^3 X^8 (\eta'^8 + 3\sigma^4 \eta''^4)],$$

and η' and η'' are evaluated at the argument $w^0 X$ for η.

From the above expressions, it is seen that if $\eta(\cdot) = 1/[1 + e^{-(\cdot)}]$ and X has a symmetric distribution (say $\mathcal{N}(0, 1)$), then $\mathbb{E}\tilde{W}^3 \neq 0$ and $\mathbb{E}\tilde{W}^4 \neq 3(\mathbb{E}\tilde{W}^2)^2$, implying that $\tilde{W}$ is non-Gaussian in general. This result is consistent with that obtained by direct application of Foster's criterion (Mukherjee, 1994).

5 RECONCILING LINEARIZATION AND STOCHASTIC APPROXIMATION METHODS

The results of stochastic approximation analysis give a Gaussian distribution for $\tilde{W}$ in the limit as $\mu \to 0$ (Bucklew, Kurtz, Sethares, 1993; Finnoff, 1993). However, our results establish that the Gaussian distribution result is not valid for small nonzero μ in general. To reconcile these results, recall $\underline{\tilde{W}} = O_\mathbf{P}(\sqrt{\mu})$. Hence, if we consider only moments of the normalized quantity $\tilde{W}/\sqrt{\mu}$ (and neglect higher-order terms in $O_{\mathbf{P}}(\sqrt{\mu})$), we obtain $\mathbb{E}(\tilde{W}/\sqrt{\mu})^3 = 0$ and $\mathbb{E}(\tilde{W}/\sqrt{\mu})^4 = 3[\mathbb{E}(\tilde{W}/\sqrt{\mu})^2]^2$, which suggests that the normalized quantity $\tilde{W}/\sqrt{\mu}$ is Gaussian in the limit of vanishing μ, a conclusion also reached from stochastic approximation analysis.

In support of this theoretical indication that the conclusions of our analysis (based on linearization for small μ) might tally with those of stochastic approximation techniques for small values of μ, simulations were done on the simple one-dimensional training case of the previous section for 8 cases: $\mu = 0.1, 0.2, 0.3, 0.5$, and $\sigma^2 = 0.1, 0.5$ for each value of μ, with w^0 fixed at 3. For each of the 8 cases, either 5 or 10 runs were made, with lengths (for the given values of μ) of 810000, 500000, 300000, and 200000 respectively. Each run gave a pair of sequences $\{\tilde{W}_n\}$ obtained by starting off at $\tilde{W}_0 = 0$ and training the network independently twice. Each resulting sequence $\{\tilde{W}_n\}$ was then downsampled at a large enough rate that the true autocorrelation of the downsampled sequence was less than 0.05, followed by deleting the first 10% of the samples of this downsampled sequence, so as to remove any dependence on initial conditions that might persist. (Autocorrelation at lag unity for this Markov Chain was so high that when $\mu = 0.1$, a decimation rate of 9000 was required.) This was done to ensure that the elements of the resulting downsampled sequences could be assumed independent for the various hypothesis tests that were to follow.

(a) For each run of each case, the empirical distribution functions of the two downsampled sequences thus generated were compared by means of the Kolmogorov-Smirnov test (Bickel,Doksum, 1977) at level 0.95, with the null hypothesis being that both sequences had the same actual cumulative distribution function (assumed continuous). This test was passed with ease on all trials, thereby showing that a limiting distribution existed and was attained by such a training algorithm.

(b) For each run of each case, a skewness test and a kurtosis test (Bickel,Doksum, 1977) for normality were done at level 0.95 to test for normality. The sequences generated failed both tests for the (μ, σ) pair (0.1,0.1) and passed them both for the pairs (0.1,0.5), (0.3,0.1), (0.5,0.1), and (0.5,0.5). For the pair (0.2,0.5), the skewness test was passed and the kurtosis test failed, and for the pairs (0.2,0.1) and (0.3,0.5), the skewness test was failed and the kurtosis test passed.

(c) All trials cleared the Kolmogorov tests (Bickel,Doksum, 1977) for normality at level 0.95, both when the normal distribution was taken to have the sample mean and variance (computed on the downsampled sequence), and when the normal distribution function had the asymptotic values of mean (zero) and variance ($\mu\sigma^2/2$).

Hence we may conclude:

1. The limiting distribution of $\{W_n\}$ exists.
2. For small values of μ, the deviation from Gaussianness is so small that the Gaussian distribution may be taken as a good approximation to the limiting distribution.

In other words, though stochastic approximation analysis states that $\tilde{W}/\sqrt{\mu}$ is Gaussian only in the limit of vanishing μ, our simulation shows that this is a good approximation for small values of μ as well.

Acknowledgements

The research reported here was partially supported by NSF Grant SBR-9413001.

References

Berger, Marc A. *An Introduction to Probability and Stochastic Processes.* Springer-Verlag, New York, 1993.

Bickel, Peter, and Doksum, Kjell. *Mathematical Statistics: Basic Ideas and Selected Topics.* Holden-Day, San Francisco, 1977.

Bucklew, J.A., Kurtz, T.G., and Sethares, W.A. "Weak Convergence and Local Stability Properties of Fixed Step Size Recursive Algorithms," *IEEE Trans. Inform. Theory,* vol. 39, pp. 966-978, 1993.

Finnoff, W. "Diffusion Approximations for the Constant Learning Rate Backpropagation Algorithm and Resistence to Local Minima." In Giles, C.L., Hanson, S.J., and Cowan, J.D., editors, *Advances in Neural Information Processing Systems 5.* Morgan Kaufmann Publishers, San Mateo CA, 1993, p.459 ff.

Kuan, C-M, and Hornik, K. "Convergence of Learning Algorithms with Constant Learning Rates," *IEEE Trans. Neural Networks,* vol. 2, pp. 484-488, 1991.

Leen, T.K., and Moody, J.E. "Weight Space Probability Densities in Stochastic Learning: I. Dynamics and Equilibria," *Adv. in NIPS 5,* Morgan Kaufmann Publishers, San Mateo CA, 1993, p.451 ff.

Loéve, M. *Probability Theory I,* 4th ed. Springer-Verlag, New York, 1977.

Mukherjee, Sayandev. *Asymptotics of Gradient-based Neural Network Training Algorithms.* M.S. thesis, Cornell University, Ithaca, NY, 1994.

Orr, G.B., and Leen, T.K. "Probability densities in stochastic learning: II. Transients and Basin Hopping Times," *Adv. in NIPS 5,* Morgan Kaufmann Publishers, San Mateo CA, 1993, p.507 ff.

Rumelhart, D.E., Hinton, G.E., and Williams, R.J. "Learning interval representations by error propagation." In D.E. Rumelhart and J.L. McClelland, editors, *Parallel Distributed Processing,* Ch. 8, MIT Press, Cambridge MA, 1985.

Tweedie, R.L. "Criteria for Classifying General Markov Chains," *Adv. Appl. Prob.,* vol. 8, 737-771, 1976.

White, H. "Some Asymptotic Results for Learning in Single Hidden-Layer Feedforward Network Models," *J. Am. Stat. Assn.,* vol. 84, 1003-1013, 1989.

PART IV
REINFORCEMENT LEARNING

Reinforcement Learning Algorithm for Partially Observable Markov Decision Problems

Tommi Jaakkola
tommi@psyche.mit.edu

Satinder P. Singh
singh@psyche.mit.edu

Michael I. Jordan
jordan@psyche.mit.edu

Department of Brain and Cognitive Sciences, Bld. E10
Massachusetts Institute of Technology
Cambridge, MA 02139

Abstract

Increasing attention has been paid to reinforcement learning algorithms in recent years, partly due to successes in the theoretical analysis of their behavior in Markov environments. If the Markov assumption is removed, however, neither generally the algorithms nor the analyses continue to be usable. We propose and analyze a new learning algorithm to solve a certain class of non-Markov decision problems. Our algorithm applies to problems in which the environment is Markov, but the learner has restricted access to state information. The algorithm involves a Monte-Carlo policy evaluation combined with a policy improvement method that is similar to that of Markov decision problems and is guaranteed to converge to a local maximum. The algorithm operates in the space of stochastic policies, a space which can yield a policy that performs considerably better than any deterministic policy. Although the space of stochastic policies is continuous—even for a discrete action space—our algorithm is computationally tractable.

1 INTRODUCTION

Reinforcement learning provides a sound framework for credit assignment in unknown stochastic dynamic environments. For Markov environments a variety of different reinforcement learning algorithms have been devised to predict and control the environment (e.g., the TD(λ) algorithm of Sutton, 1988, and the Q-learning algorithm of Watkins, 1989). Ties to the theory of dynamic programming (DP) and the theory of stochastic approximation have been exploited, providing tools that have allowed these algorithms to be analyzed theoretically (Dayan, 1992; Tsitsiklis, 1994; Jaakkola, Jordan, & Singh, 1994; Watkins & Dayan, 1992).

Although current reinforcement learning algorithms are based on the assumption that the learning problem can be cast as Markov decision problem (MDP), many practical problems resist being treated as an MDP. Unfortunately, if the Markov assumption is removed examples can be found where current algorithms cease to perform well (Singh, Jaakkola, & Jordan, 1994). Moreover, the theoretical analyses rely heavily on the Markov assumption.

The non-Markov nature of the environment can arise in many ways. The most direct extension of MDP's is to deprive the learner of perfect information about the state of the environment. Much as in the case of Hidden Markov Models (HMM's), the underlying environment is assumed to be Markov, but the data do not appear to be Markovian to the learner. This extension not only allows for a tractable theoretical analysis, but is also appealing for practical purposes. The decision problems we consider here are of this type.

The analog of the HMM for control problems is the partially observable Markov decision process (POMDP; see e.g., Monahan, 1982). Unlike HMM's, however, there is no known computationally tractable procedure for POMDP's. The problem is that once the state estimates have been obtained, DP must be performed in the continuous space of probabilities of state occupancies, and this DP process is computationally infeasible except for small state spaces. In this paper we describe an alternative approach for POMDP's that avoids the state estimation problem and works directly in the space of (stochastic) control policies. (See Singh, et al., 1994, for additional material on stochastic policies.)

2 PARTIAL OBSERVABILITY

A Markov decision problem can be generalized to a POMDP by restricting the state information available to the learner. Accordingly, we define the learning problem as follows. There is an underlying MDP with states $\mathcal{S} = \{s_1, s_2, \ldots, s_N\}$ and transition probability $p^a_{ss'}$, the probability of jumping from state s to state s' when action a is taken in state s. For every state and every action a (random) reward is provided to the learner. In the POMDP setting, the learner is not allowed to observe the state directly but only via messages containing information about the state. At each time step t an observable message m_t is drawn from a finite set of messages according to an unknown probability distribution $P(m|s_t)$ [1]. We assume that the learner does

---

[1] For simplicity we assume that this distribution depends only on the current state. The analyses go through also with distributions dependent on the past states and actions

not possess any prior information about the underlying MDP beyond the number of messages and actions. The goal for the learner is to come up with a policy—a mapping from messages to actions—that gives the highest expected reward.

As discussed in Singh et al. (1994), stochastic policies can yield considerably higher expected rewards than deterministic policies in the case of POMDP's. To make this statement precise requires an appropriate technical definition of "expected reward," because in general it is impossible to find a policy, stochastic or not, that maximizes the expected reward for each observable message separately. We take the time-average reward as a measure of performance, that is, the total accrued reward per number of steps taken (Bertsekas, 1987; Schwartz, 1993). This approach requires the assumption that every state of the underlying controllable Markov chain is reachable.

In this paper we focus on a *direct* approach to solving the learning problem. Direct approaches are to be compared to *indirect* approaches, in which the learner first identifies the parameters of the underlying MDP, and then utilizes DP to obtain the policy. As we noted earlier, indirect approaches lead to computationally intractable algorithms. Our approach can be viewed as providing a generalization of the direct approach to MDP's to the case of POMDP's.

3   A MONTE-CARLO POLICY EVALUATION

Advantages of Monte-Carlo methods for policy evaluation in MDP's have been reviewed recently (Barto and Duff, 1994). Here we present a method for calculating the value of a stochastic policy that has the flavor of a Monte-Carlo algorithm. To motivate such an approach let us first consider a simple case where the average reward is known and generalize the well-defined MDP value function to the POMDP setting. In the Markov case the value function can be written as (cf. Bertsekas, 1987):

$$V(s) = \lim_{N \to \infty} \sum_{t=1}^{N} E\{R(s_t, u_t) - R | s_1 = s\} \tag{1}$$

where s_t and a_t refer to the state and the action taken at the tth step respectively. This form generalizes easily to the level of messages by taking an additional expectation:

$$V(m) = E\{V(s) | s \to m\} \tag{2}$$

where $s \to m$ refers to all the instances where m is observed in s and $E\{\cdot | s \to m\}$ is a Monte-Carlo expectation. This generalization yields a POMDP value function given by

$$V(m) = \sum_{s \in m} P(s|m) V(s) \tag{3}$$

in which $P(s|m)$ define the limit occupancy probabilities over the underlying states for each message m. As is seen in the next section value functions of this type can be used to refine the currently followed control policy to yield a higher average reward.

Let us now consider how the generalized value functions can be computed based on the observations. We propose a recursive Monte-Carlo algorithm to effectively compute the averages involved in the definition of the value function. In the simple case when the average payoff is known this algorithm is given by

$$\beta_t(m) = (1 - \frac{\chi_t(m)}{K_t(m)})\gamma_t \beta_{t-1}(m) + \frac{\chi_t(m)}{K_t(m)} \qquad (4)$$

$$V_t(m) = (1 - \frac{\chi_t(m)}{K_t(m)})V_{t-1}(m) + \beta_t(m)[R(s_t, a_t) - R] \qquad (5)$$

where $\chi_t(m)$ is the indicator function for message m, $K_t(m)$ is the number of times m has occurred, and γ_t is a discount factor converging to one in the limit. This algorithm can be viewed as recursive averaging of (discounted) sample sequences of different lengths each of which has been started at a different occurrence of message m. This can be seen by unfolding the recursion, yielding an explicit expression for $V_t(m)$. To this end, let t_k denote the time step corresponding to the kth occurrence of message m and for clarity let $R_t = R(s_t, u_t) - R$ for every t. Using these the recursion yields:

$$V_t(m) = \frac{1}{K_t(m)}[R_{t_1} + \Gamma_{1,1} R_{t_1+1} + \ldots + \Gamma_{1,t-t_1} R_t$$
$$\ldots$$
$$+ R_{t_k} + \Gamma_{k,1} R_{t_k+1} + \ldots + \Gamma_{k,t-t_k} R_t] \qquad (6)$$

where we have for simplicity used $\Gamma_{k,T}$ to indicate the discounting at the Tth step in the kth sequence. Comparing the above expression to equation 1 indicates that the discount factor has to converge to one in the limit since the averages in $V(s)$ or $V(m)$ involve no discounting.

To address the question of convergence of this algorithm let us first assume a constant discounting (that is, $\gamma_t = \gamma < 1$). In this case, the algorithm produces at best an approximation to the value function. For large $K(m)$ the convergence rate by which this approximate solution is found can be characterized in terms of the bias and variance. This gives $Bias\{V(m)\} \propto (1 - \bar{\gamma})^{-1}/K(m)$ and $Var\{V(m)\} \propto (1 - \bar{\gamma})^{-2}/K(m)$ where $\bar{\gamma} = E\{\gamma^{t_k - t_{k-1}}\}$ is the expected effective discounting between observations. Now, in order to find the correct value function we need an appropriate way of letting $\gamma_t \to 1$ in the limit. However, not all such schedules lead to convergent algorithms; setting $\gamma_t = 1$ for all t, for example, would not. By making use of the above bounds a feasible schedule guaranteeing a vanishing bias and variance can be found. For instance, since $\gamma > \bar{\gamma}$ we can choose $\gamma_{k(m)} = 1 - K(m)^{1/4}$. Much faster schedules are possible to obtain by estimating $\bar{\gamma}$.

Let us now revise the algorithm to take into account the fact that the learner in fact has no prior knowledge of the average reward. In this case the true average reward appearing in the above algorithm needs to be replaced with an incrementally updated estimate R_{t-1}. To improve the effect this changing estimate has on the values we transform the value function whenever the estimate is updated. This transformation is given by

$$C_t(m) = (1 - \frac{\chi_t(m)}{K_t(m)})C_{t-1}(m) + \beta_t(m) \qquad (7)$$

$$V_t(m) \to V_t(m) - C_t(m)(R_t - R_{t-1}) \qquad (8)$$

and, as a result, the new values are as if they had been computed using the current estimate of the average reward.

To carry these results to the control setting and assign a figure of merit to stochastic policies we need a quantity related to the actions for each observed message. As in the case of MDP's, this is readily achieved by replacing m in the algorithm just described by (m, a). In terms of equation 6, for example, this means that the sequences started from m are classified according to the actions taken when m is observed. The above analysis goes through when m is replaced by (m, a), yielding "Q-values" on the level of messages:

$$Q^\pi(m, a) = \sum_s P^\pi(s|m) Q^\pi(s, a) \tag{9}$$

In the next section we show how these values can be used to search efficiently for a better policy.

4 POLICY IMPROVEMENT THEOREM

Here we present a policy improvement theorem that enables the learner to search efficiently for a better policy in the continuous policy space using the "Q-values" $Q(m, a)$ described in the previous section. The theorem allows the policy refinement to be done in a way that is similar to policy improvement in a MDP setting.

Theorem 1 *Let the current stochastic policy $\pi(a|m)$ lead to Q-values $Q^\pi(m, a)$ on the level of messages. For any policy $\pi^1(a|m)$ define*

$$J^{\pi^1}(m) = \sum_a \pi^1(a|m)[Q^\pi(m, a) - V^\pi(m)]$$

The change in the average reward resulting from changing the current policy according to $\pi(a|m) \to (1-\epsilon)\pi(a|m) + \epsilon\pi^1(a|m)$ is given by

$$\Delta R^\pi = \epsilon \sum_m P^\pi(m) J^{\pi^1}(m) + O(\epsilon^2)$$

where $P^\pi(m)$ are the occupancy probabilities for messages associated with the current policy.

The proof is given in Appendix. In terms of policy improvement the theorem can be interpreted as follows. Choose the policy $\pi^1(a|m)$ such that

$$J^{\pi^1}(m) = \max_a [Q^\pi(m, a) - V^\pi(m)] \tag{10}$$

If now $J^{\pi^1}(m) > 0$ for some m then we can change the current policy towards π^1 and expect an increase in the average reward as shown by the theorem. The ϵ factor suggests local changes in the policy space and the policy can be refined until $\max_{\pi^1} J^{\pi^1}(m) = 0$ for all m which constitutes a local maximum for this policy improvement method. Note that the new direction $\pi^1(a|m)$ in the policy space can be chosen separately for each m.

5 THE ALGORITHM

Based on the theoretical analysis presented above we can construct an algorithm that performs well in a POMDP setting. The algorithm is composed of two parts: First,

$Q(m, a)$ values—analogous to the Q-values in MDP—are calculated via a Monte-Carlo approach. This is followed by a policy improvement step which is achieved by increasing the probability of taking the best action as defined by $Q(m, a)$. The new policy is guaranteed to yield a higher average reward (see Theorem 1) as long as for some m

$$\max_a [Q(m, a) - V(m)] > 0 \tag{11}$$

This condition being false constitutes a local maximum for the algorithm. Examples illustrating that this indeed is a local maximum can be found fairly easily.

In practice, it is not feasible to wait for the Monte-Carlo policy evaluation to converge but to try to improve the policy before the convergence. The policy can be refined concurrently with the Monte-Carlo method according to

$$\pi(a|m_n) \to \pi(a|m_n) + \epsilon[Q_n(m_n, a) - V_n(m_n)] \tag{12}$$

with normalization. Other asynchronous or synchronous on-online updating schemes can also be used. Note that if $Q_n(m, a) = Q(m, a)$ then this change would be statistically equivalent to that of the batch version with the concomitant guarantees of giving a higher average reward.

6 CONCLUSIONS

In this paper we have proposed and theoretically analyzed an algorithm that solves a reinforcement learning problem in a POMDP setting, where the learner has restricted access to the state of the environment. As the underlying MDP is not known the problem appears to the learner to have a non-Markov nature. The average reward was chosen as the figure of merit for the learning problem and stochastic policies were used to provide higher average rewards than can be achieved with deterministic policies. This extension from MDP's to POMDP's greatly increases the domain of potential applications of reinforcement learning methods.

The simplicity of the algorithm stems partly from a Monte-Carlo approach to obtaining action-dependent values for each message. These new "Q-values" were shown to give rise to a simple policy improvement result that enables the learner to gradually improve the policy in the continuous space of probabilistic policies.

The batch version of the algorithm was shown to converge to a local maximum. We also proposed an on-line version of the algorithm in which the policy is changed concurrently with the calculation of the "Q-values." The policy improvement of the on-line version resembles that of learning automata.

APPENDIX

Let us denote the policy after the change by π^ϵ. Assume first that we have access to $Q^\pi(s, a)$, the Q-values for the underlying MDP, and to $P^{\pi^\epsilon}(s|m)$, the occupancy probabilities after the policy refinement. Define

$$J(m, \pi^\epsilon, \pi^\epsilon, \pi) = \sum_a \pi^\epsilon(a|m) \sum_{s \in m} P^{\pi^\epsilon}(s|m)[Q^\pi(s, a) - V^\pi(s)] \tag{13}$$

where we have used the notation that the policies on the left hand side correspond to the policies on the right respectively. To show how the average reward depends on this quantity we need to make use of the following facts. The Q-values for the underlying MDP satisfy (Bellman's equation)

$$Q^\pi(s,a) = R(s,a) - R^\pi + \sum_{s'} p^a_{ss'} V^\pi(s') \qquad (14)$$

In addition, $\sum_a \pi(a|m) Q^\pi(s,a) = V^\pi(s)$, implying that $J(m, \pi^\epsilon, \pi^\epsilon, \pi^\epsilon) = 0$ (see eq. 13). These facts allow us to write

$$\begin{aligned}
J(m, \pi^\epsilon, \pi^\epsilon, \pi) &= J(m, \pi^\epsilon, \pi^\epsilon, \pi) - J(m, \pi^\epsilon, \pi^\epsilon, \pi^\epsilon) \\
&= \sum_a \pi^\epsilon(a|m) \sum_s P^{\pi^\epsilon}(s|m)[Q^\pi(s,a) - V^\pi(s) - Q^{\pi^\epsilon}(s,a) + V^{\pi^\epsilon}(s)] \\
&= R^{\pi^\epsilon} - R^\pi + \sum_s P^{\pi^\epsilon}(s|m) \sum_{s'} p^{\pi^\epsilon}_{ss'}[V^\pi(s') - V^{\pi^\epsilon}(s')] \\
&\quad - \sum_s P^{\pi^\epsilon}(s|m)[V^\pi(s) - V^{\pi^\epsilon}(s)] \qquad (15)
\end{aligned}$$

By weighting this result for each class by $P^{\pi^\epsilon}(m)$ and summing over the messages the probability weightings for the last two terms become equal and the terms cancel. This procedure gives us

$$R^{\pi^\epsilon} - R^\pi = \sum_m P^{\pi^\epsilon}(m) J(m, \pi^\epsilon, \pi^\epsilon, \pi) \qquad (16)$$

This result does not allow the learner to assess the effect of the policy refinement on the average reward since the $J()$ term contains information not available to the learner. However, making use of the fact that the policy has been changed only slightly this problem can be avoided.

As π^ϵ is a policy satisfying $\max_{ma} |\pi^\epsilon(a|m) - \pi(a|m)| \leq \epsilon$, it can then be shown that there exists a constant C such that the maximum change in $P(s|m)$, $P(s)$, $P(m)$ is bounded by $C\epsilon$. Using these bounds and indicating the difference between π^ϵ and π dependent quantities by Δ we get

$$\begin{aligned}
\sum_a [\pi(a|m) + \Delta\pi(a|m)] & \sum_s [P^\pi(s|m) + \Delta P^\pi(s|m)][Q^\pi(s,a) - V^\pi(s)] \\
&= \sum_a \Delta\pi(a|m) \sum_{s \in m} P^\pi(s|m)[Q^\pi(s,a) - V^\pi(s)] + \\
&\quad + \sum_a \Delta\pi(a|m) \sum_s \Delta P^\pi(s|m)[Q^\pi(s,a) - V^\pi(s)] \\
&= \epsilon \sum_a \pi^1(a|m) \sum_s P^\pi(s|m)[Q^\pi(s,a) - V^\pi(s)] + O(\epsilon^2) \qquad (17)
\end{aligned}$$

where the second equality follows from $\sum_a \pi(a|m)[Q^\pi(s,a) - V^\pi(s)] = 0$ and the third from the bounds stated earlier.

The equation characterizing the change in the average reward due to the policy change (eq. 16) can be now rewritten as follows:

$$R^{\pi^\epsilon} - R^\pi = \sum_m P^{\pi^\epsilon}(m) J(m, \pi^\epsilon, \pi, \pi) + O(\epsilon^2)$$

$$= \sum_m P^\pi(m) \sum_a \pi^\epsilon(a|m)[Q^\pi(m,a) - V^\pi(m)] + O(\epsilon^2) \qquad (18)$$

where the bounds (see above) have been used for $P^{\pi^\epsilon}(m) - P^\pi(m)$. This completes the proof. □

Acknowledgments

The authors thank Rich Sutton for pointing out errors at early stages of this work. This project was supported in part by a grant from the McDonnell-Pew Foundation, by a grant from ATR Human Information Processing Research Laboratories, by a grant from Siemens Corporation and by grant N00014-94-1-0777 from the Office of Naval Research. Michael I. Jordan is a NSF Presidential Young Investigator.

References

Barto, A., and Duff, M. (1994). Monte-Carlo matrix inversion and reinforcement learning. In *Advances of Neural Information Processing Systems 6*, San Mateo, CA, 1994. Morgan Kaufmann.

Bertsekas, D. P. (1987). *Dynamic Programming: Deterministic and Stochastic Models*. Englewood Cliffs, NJ: Prentice-Hall.

Dayan, P. (1992). The convergence of TD(λ) for general λ. *Machine Learning, 8*, 341-362.

Jaakkola, T., Jordan M. I., and Singh, S. P. (1994). On the convergence of stochastic iterative Dynamic Programming algorithms. *Neural Computation 6*, 1185-1201.

Monahan, G. (1982). A survey of partially observable Markov decision processes. *Management Science, 28*, 1-16.

Singh, S. P., Jaakkola, T., Jordan, M. I. (1994). Learning without state estimation in partially observable environments. In *Proceedings of the Eleventh Machine Learning Conference*.

Sutton, R. S. (1988). Learning to predict by the methods of temporal differences. *Machine Learning, 3*, 9-44.

Schwartz, A. (1993). A reinforcement learning method for maximizing undiscounted rewards. In *Proceedings of the Tenth Machine Learning Conference*.

Tsitsiklis J. N. (1994). Asynchronous stochastic approximation and Q-learning. *Machine Learning 16*, 185-202.

Watkins, C.J.C.H. (1989). *Learning from delayed rewards*. PhD Thesis, University of Cambridge, England.

Watkins, C.J.C.H, & Dayan, P. (1992). Q-learning. *Machine Learning, 8*, 279-292.

Advantage Updating Applied to a Differential Game

Mance E. Harmon
Wright Laboratory
WL/AAAT Bldg. 635 2185 Avionics Circle
Wright-Patterson Air Force Base, OH 45433-7301
harmonme@aa.wpafb.mil

Leemon C. Baird III*
Wright Laboratory
baird@cs.usafa.af.mil

A. Harry Klopf
Wright Laboratory
klopfah@aa.wpafb.mil

Category: Control, Navigation, and Planning
Keywords: Reinforcement Learning, Advantage Updating, Dynamic Programming, Differential Games

Abstract

An application of reinforcement learning to a linear-quadratic, differential game is presented. The reinforcement learning system uses a recently developed algorithm, the residual gradient form of advantage updating. The game is a Markov Decision Process (MDP) with continuous time, states, and actions, linear dynamics, and a quadratic cost function. The game consists of two players, a missile and a plane; the missile pursues the plane and the plane evades the missile. The reinforcement learning algorithm for optimal control is modified for differential games in order to find the minimax point, rather than the maximum. Simulation results are compared to the optimal solution, demonstrating that the simulated reinforcement learning system converges to the optimal answer. The performance of both the residual gradient and non-residual gradient forms of advantage updating and Q-learning are compared. The results show that advantage updating converges faster than Q-learning in all simulations. The results also show advantage updating converges regardless of the time step duration; Q-learning is unable to converge as the time step duration grows small.

* U.S.A.F. Academy, 2354 Fairchild Dr. Suite 6K41, USAFA, CO 80840-6234

1 ADVANTAGE UPDATING

The advantage updating algorithm (Baird, 1993) is a reinforcement learning algorithm in which two types of information are stored. For each state x, the value $V(x)$ is stored, representing an estimate of the total discounted return expected when starting in state x and performing optimal actions. For each state x and action u, the *advantage*, $A(x,u)$, is stored, representing an estimate of the degree to which the expected total discounted reinforcement is increased by performing action u rather than the action currently considered best. The optimal value function $V^*(x)$ represents the true value of each state. The optimal advantage function $A^*(x,u)$ will be zero if u is the optimal action (because u confers no advantage relative to itself) and $A^*(x,u)$ will be negative for any suboptimal u (because a suboptimal action has a negative advantage relative to the best action). The optimal advantage function A^* can be defined in terms of the optimal value function V^*:

$$A^*(x,u) = \frac{1}{\Delta t}\left[R_{\Delta t}(x,u) - V^*(x) + \gamma^{\Delta t} V^*(x')\right] \quad (1)$$

The definition of an advantage includes a $1/\Delta t$ term to ensure that, for small time step duration Δt, the advantages will not all go to zero.

Both the value function and the advantage function are needed during learning, but after convergence to optimality, the policy can be extracted from the advantage function alone. The optimal policy for state x is any u that maximizes $A^*(x,u)$. The notation

$$A_{\max}(x) = \max_u A(x,u) \quad (2)$$

defines $A_{\max}(x)$. If $A_{\max}$ converges to zero in every state, the advantage function is said to be *normalized*. Advantage updating has been shown to learn faster than Q-learning (Watkins, 1989), especially for continuous-time problems (Baird, 1993).

If advantage updating (Baird, 1993) is used to control a deterministic system, there are two equations that are the equivalent of the Bellman equation in value iteration (Bertsekas, 1987). These are a pair of two simultaneous equations (Baird, 1993):

$$A(x,u) - \max_{u'} A(x,u') = \left(R + \gamma^{\Delta t} V(x') - V(x)\right)\frac{1}{\Delta t} \quad (3)$$

$$\max_u A(x,u) = 0 \quad (4)$$

where a time step is of duration Δt, and performing action u in state x results in a reinforcement of R and a transition to state $x_{t+\Delta t}$. The optimal advantage and value functions will satisfy these equations. For a given A and V function, the *Bellman residual errors*, E, as used in Williams and Baird (1993) and defined here as equations (5) and (6).are the degrees to which the two equations are not satisfied:

$$E_1(x_t,u) = \left(R(x_t,u) + \gamma^{\Delta t} V(x_{t+\Delta t}) - V(x_t)\right)\frac{1}{\Delta t} - A(x_t,u) + \max_{u'} A(x_t,u') \quad (5)$$

$$E_2(x,u) = -\max_u A(x,u) \quad (6)$$

2 RESIDUAL GRADIENT ALGORITHMS

Dynamic programming algorithms can be guaranteed to converge to optimality when used with look-up tables, yet be completely unstable when combined with function-approximation systems (Baird & Harmon, In preparation). It is possible to derive an algorithm that has guaranteed convergence for a quadratic function approximation system (Bradtke, 1993), but that algorithm is specific to quadratic systems. One solution to this problem is to derive a learning algorithm to perform gradient descent on the mean squared Bellman residuals given in (5) and (6). This is called the *residual gradient* form of an algorithm.

There are two Bellman residuals, (5) and (6), so the residual gradient algorithm must perform gradient descent on the sum of the two squared Bellman residuals. It has been found to be useful to combine reinforcement learning algorithms with function approximation systems (Tesauro, 1990 & 1992). If function approximation systems are used for the advantage and value functions, and if the function approximation systems are parameterized by a set of adjustable weights, and if the system being controlled is deterministic, then, for incremental learning, a given weight W in the function-approximation system could be changed according to equation (7) on each time step:

$$\Delta W = -\frac{\alpha}{2} \frac{\partial [E_1^2(x_t, u_t) + E_2^2(x_t, u_t)]}{\partial W}$$

$$= -\alpha E_1(x_t, u_t) \frac{\partial E_1(x_t, u_t)}{\partial W} - \alpha E_2(x_t, u_t) \frac{\partial E_2(x_t, u_t)}{\partial W}$$

$$= -\alpha \left(\frac{1}{\Delta t}\left(R + \gamma^{\Delta t} V(x_{t+\Delta t}) - V(x_t)\right) - A(x_t, u_t) + \max_u A(x_t, u) \right)$$

$$\bullet \left(\frac{1}{\Delta t}\left(\gamma^{\Delta t} \frac{\partial V(x_{t+\Delta t})}{\partial W} - \frac{\partial V(x_t)}{\partial W} \right) - \frac{\partial A(x_t, u_t)}{\partial W} + \frac{\partial \max_u A(x_t, u)}{\partial W} \right) \quad (7)$$

$$- \alpha \max_u A(x_t, u) \frac{\partial \max_u A(x_t, u)}{\partial W}$$

As a simple, gradient-descent algorithm, equation (7) is guaranteed to converge to the correct answer for a deterministic system, in the same sense that backpropagation (Rumelhart, Hinton, Williams, 1986) is guaranteed to converge. However, if the system is nondeterministic, then it is necessary to independently generate two different possible "next states" $x_{t+\Delta t}$ for a given action u_t performed in a given state x_t. One $x_{t+\Delta t}$ must be used to evaluate $V(x_{t+\Delta t})$, and the other must be used to evaluate $\partial/\partial W \, V(x_{t+\Delta t})$.

This ensures that the weight change is an unbiased estimator of the true Bellman-residual gradient, but requires a system such as in Dyna (Sutton, 1990) to generate the second $x_{t+\Delta t}$. The differential game in this paper was deterministic, so this was not needed here.

3 THE SIMULATION

3.1 GAME DEFINITION

We employed a linear-quadratic, differential game (Isaacs, 1965) for comparing Q-learning to advantage updating, and for comparing the algorithms in their residual gradient forms. The game has two players, a missile and a plane, as in games described by Rajan, Prasad, and Rao (1980) and Millington (1991). The state **x** is a vector (x_m, x_p) composed of the state of the missile and the state of the plane, each of which are composed of the position and velocity of the player in two-dimensional space. The action **u** is a vector (u_m, u_p) composed of the action performed by the missile and the action performed by the plane, each of which are the acceleration of the player in two-dimensional space. The dynamics of the system are linear; the next state x_{t+1} is a linear function of the current state x_t and action u_t. The reinforcement function R is a quadratic function of the accelerations and the distance between the players.

$$R(x,u) = [\text{distance}^2 + (\text{missile acceleration})^2 - 2(\text{plane acceleration})^2]\Delta t \qquad (8)$$

$$R(\mathbf{x},\mathbf{u}) = \left[(\mathbf{x}_m - \mathbf{x}_p)^2 + \mathbf{u}_m^2 - 2\mathbf{u}_p^2\right]\Delta t \qquad (9)$$

In equation (9), squaring a vector is equivalent to taking the dot product of the vector with itself. The missile seeks to minimize the reinforcement, and the plane seeks to maximize reinforcement. The plane receives twice as much punishment for acceleration as does the missile, thus allowing the missile to accelerate twice as easily as the plane.

The value function V is a quadratic function of the state. In equation (10), $\mathbf{D}_m$ and $\mathbf{D}_p$ are weight matrices that change during learning.

$$V(\mathbf{x}) = \mathbf{x}_m^T \mathbf{D}_m \mathbf{x}_m + \mathbf{x}_p^T \mathbf{D}_p \mathbf{x}_p \qquad (10)$$

The advantage function A is a quadratic function of the state **x** and action **u**. The actions are accelerations of the missile and plane in two dimensions.

$$A(\mathbf{x},\mathbf{u}) = \mathbf{x}_m^T \mathbf{A}_m \mathbf{x}_m + \mathbf{x}_m^T \mathbf{B}_m \mathbf{C}_m \mathbf{u}_m + \mathbf{u}_m^T \mathbf{C}_m \mathbf{u}_m + \\ \mathbf{x}_p^T \mathbf{A}_p \mathbf{x}_p + \mathbf{x}_p^T \mathbf{B}_p \mathbf{C}_p \mathbf{u}_p + \mathbf{u}_p^T \mathbf{C}_p \mathbf{u}_p \qquad (11)$$

The matrices **A**, **B**, and **C** are the adjustable weights that change during learning. Equation (11) is the sum of two general quadratic functions. This would still be true if the second and fifth terms were **xBu** instead of **xBCu**. The latter form was used to simplify the calculation of the policy. Using the **xBu** form, the gradient is zero when $\mathbf{u} = -\mathbf{C}^{-1}\mathbf{B}\mathbf{x}/2$. Using the **xBCu** form, the gradient of $A(\mathbf{x},\mathbf{u})$ with respect to **u** is zero when $\mathbf{u} = -\mathbf{B}\mathbf{x}/2$, which avoids the need to invert a matrix while calculating the policy.

3.2 THE BELLMAN RESIDUAL AND UPDATE EQUATIONS

Equations (5) and (6) define the Bellman residuals when maximizing the total discounted reinforcement for an optimal control problem; equations (12) and (13) modify the algorithm to solve differential games rather than optimal control problems.

$$E_1(x_t,u_t) = \left(R(x_t,u_t) + \gamma^{\Delta t}V(x_{t+\Delta t}) - V(x_t)\right)\frac{1}{\Delta t} - A(x_t,u_t) + \text{minimax } A(x_t) \quad (12)$$

$$E_2(x_t,u_t) = -\text{minimax } A(x_t) \quad (13)$$

The resulting weight update equation is:

$$\Delta W = -\alpha\left(\left(R + \gamma^{\Delta t}V(x_{t+\Delta t}) - V(x_t)\right)\frac{1}{\Delta t} - A(x_t,u_t) + \text{minimax } A(x_t)\right)$$
$$\bullet\left(\left(\gamma^{\Delta t}\frac{\partial V(x_{t+\Delta t})}{\partial W} - \frac{\partial V(x_t)}{\partial W}\right)\frac{1}{\Delta t} - \frac{\partial A(x_t,u_t)}{\partial W} + \frac{\partial \text{minimax } A(x_t)}{\partial W}\right) \quad (14)$$
$$-\alpha\text{minimax } A(x_t)\frac{\partial \text{minimax } A(x_t)}{\partial W}$$

For Q-learning, the residual-gradient form of the weight update equation is:

$$\Delta W = -\alpha\left(R + \gamma^{\Delta t} \text{ minimax } Q(x_{t+\Delta t}) - Q(x_t,u_t)\right)$$
$$\bullet\left(\gamma^{\Delta t}\tfrac{\partial}{\partial W}\text{minimax } Q(x_{t+\Delta t}) - \tfrac{\partial}{\partial W}Q(x_t,u_t)\right) \quad (15)$$

4 RESULTS

4.1 RESIDUAL GRADIENT ADVANTAGE UPDATING RESULTS

The optimal weight matrices $\mathbf{A}^*$, $\mathbf{B}^*$, $\mathbf{C}^*$, and $\mathbf{D}^*$ were calculated numerically with *Mathematica* for comparison. The residual gradient form of advantage updating learned the correct policy weights, $\mathbf{B}$, to three significant digits after extensive training. Very interesting behavior was exhibited by the plane under certain initial conditions. The plane learned that in some cases it is better to turn toward the missile in the short term to increase the distance between the two in the long term. A tactic sometimes used by pilots. Figure 1 gives an example.

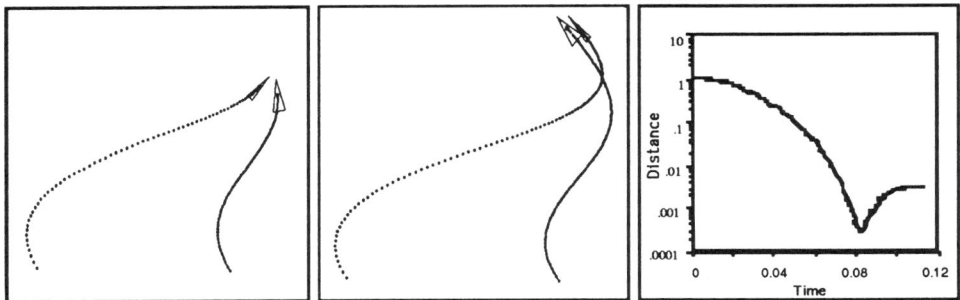

Figure 1: Simulation of a missile (dotted line) pursuing a plane (solid line), each having learned optimal behavior. The graph of distance vs. time show the effects of the plane's maneuver in turning toward the missile.

4.2 COMPARATIVE RESULTS

The error in the policy of a learning system was defined to be the sum of the squared errors in the **B** matrix weights. The optimal policy weights in this problem are the same for both advantage updating and Q-learning, so this metric can be used to compare results for both algorithms. Four different learning algorithms were compared: advantage updating, Q-learning, Residual Gradient advantage updating, and Residual Gradient Q-learning. Advantage updating in the non-residual-gradient form was unstable to the point that no meaningful results could be obtained, so simulation results cannot be given for it.

4.2.1 Experiment Set 1

The learning rates for both forms of Q-learning were optimized to one significant digit for each simulation. A single learning rate was used for residual-gradient advantage updating in all four simulations. It is possible that advantage updating would have performed better with different learning rates. For each algorithm, the error was calculated after learning for 40,000 iterations. The process was repeated 10 times using different random number seeds and the results were averaged. This experiment was performed for four different time step durations, 0.05, 0.005, 0.0005, and 0.00005. The non-residual-gradient form of Q-learning appeared to work better when the weights were initialized to small numbers. Therefore, the initial weights were chosen randomly between 0 and 1 for the residual-gradient forms of the algorithms, and between 0 and 10^{-8} for the non-residual-gradient form of Q-learning. For small time steps, nonresidual-gradient Q-learning performed so poorly that the error was lower for a learning rate of zero (no learning) than it was for a learning rate of 10^{-8}. Table 1 gives the learning rates used for each simulation, and figure 2 shows the resulting error after learning.

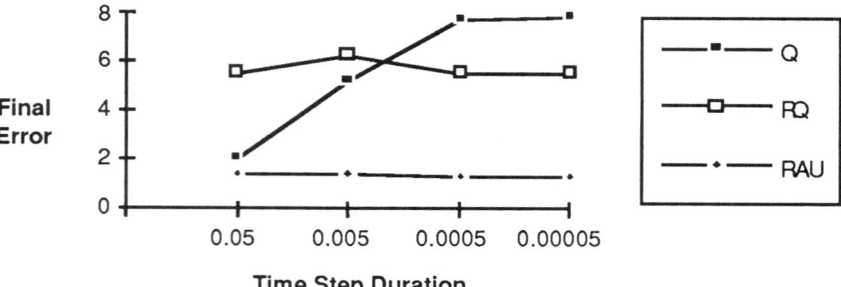

Figure 2: Error vs. time step size comparison for Q-Learning (Q), residual-gradient Q-Learning(RQ), and residual-gradient advantage updating(RAU) using rates optimal to one significant figure for both forms of Q-learning, and not optimized for advantage updating. The final error is the sum of squared errors in the **B** matrix weights after 40,000 time steps of learning. The final error for advantage updating was lower than both forms of Q-learning in every case. The errors increased for Q-learning as the time step size decreased.

	Time step duration, Δt			
	$5 \cdot 10^{-2}$	$5 \cdot 10^{-3}$	$5 \cdot 10^{-4}$	$5 \cdot 10^{-5}$
Q	0.02	0.06	0.2	0.4
RQ	0.08	0.09	0	0
RAU	0.005	0.005	0.005	0.005

Table 1: Learning rates used for each simulation. Learning rates are optimal to one significant figure for both forms of Q-learning, but are not necessarily optimal for advantage updating.

4.2.2 Experiment Set 2

Figure 3 shows a comparison of the three algorithms' ability to converge to the correct policy. The figure shows the total squared error in each algorithms' policy weights as a function of learning time. This simulation ran for a much longer period than the simulations in table 1 and figure 2. The learning rates used for this simulation were identical to the rates that were found to be optimal for the shorter run. The weights for the non-Residual gradient form of Q-learning grew without bound in all of the long experiments, even after the learning rate was reduced by an order of magnitude. Residual gradient advantage updating was able to learn the correct policy, while Q-learning was unable to learn a policy that was better than the initial, random weights.

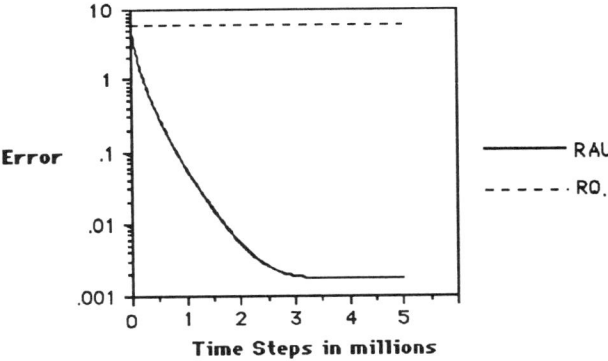

Figure 3

5 Conclusion

The experimental data shows residual-gradient advantage updating to be superior to the three other algorithms in all cases. As the time step grows small, Q-learning is unable to learn the correct policy. Future research will include the use of more general networks and implementation of the wire fitting algorithm proposed by Baird and Klopf (1994) to calculate the policy from a continuous choice of actions in more general networks.

Acknowledgments

This research was supported under Task 2312R1 by the Life and Environmental Sciences Directorate of the United States Air Force Office of Scientific Research.

References

Baird, L.C. (1993). *Advantage updating* Wright-Patterson Air Force Base, OH. (Wright Laboratory Technical Report WL-TR-93-1146, available from the Defense Technical information Center, Cameron Station, Alexandria, VA 22304-6145).

Baird, L.C., & Harmon, M. E. (In preparation). *Residual gradient algorithms* Wright-Patterson Air Force Base, OH. (Wright Laboratory Technical report).

Baird, L.C., & Klopf, A. H. (1993). *Reinforcement learning with high-dimensional, continuous actions* Wright-Patterson Air Force Base, OH. (Wright Laboratory technical report WL-TR-93-1147, available from the Defense Technical information Center, Cameron Station, Alexandria, VA 22304-6145).

Bertsekas, D. P. (1987). *Dynamic programming: Deterministic and stochastic models.* Englewood Cliffs, NJ: Prentice-Hall.

Bradtke, S. J. (1993). Reinforcement Learning Applied to Linear Quadratic Regulation. *Proceedings of the 5th annual Conference on Neural Information Processing Systems* .

Isaacs, Rufus (1965). *Differential games.* New York: John Wiley and Sons, Inc.

Millington, P. J. (1991). *Associative reinforcement learning for optimal control.* Unpublished master's thesis, Massachusetts Institute of Technology, Cambridge, MA.

Rajan, N., Prasad, U. R., and Rao, N. J. (1980). Pursuit-evasion of two aircraft in a horizontal plane. *Journal of Guidance and Control.* **3**(3), May-June, 261-267.

Rumelhart, D., Hinton, G., & Williams, R. (1986). Learning representations by backpropagating errors. *Nature.* **323**, 9 October, 533-536.

Sutton, R. S. (1990). Integrated architectures for learning, planning, and reacting based on approximating dynamic programming. *Proceedings of the Seventh International Conference on Machine Learning.*

Tesauro, G. (1990). Neurogammon: A neural-network backgammon program. *Proceedings of the International Joint Conference on Neural Networks,* **3**, (pp. 33-40). San Diego, CA.

Tesauro, G. (1992). Practical issues in temporal difference learning. *Machine Learning,* **8(3/4)**, 279-292.

Watkins, C. J. C. H. (1989). *Learning from delayed rewards.* Doctoral thesis, Cambridge University, Cambridge, England.

Reinforcement Learning with Soft State Aggregation

Satinder P. Singh
singh@psyche.mit.edu

Tommi Jaakkola
tommi@psyche.mit.edu

Michael I. Jordan
jordan@psyche.mit.edu

Dept. of Brain & Cognitive Sciences (E-10)
M.I.T.
Cambridge, MA 02139

Abstract

It is widely accepted that the use of more compact representations than lookup tables is crucial to scaling reinforcement learning (RL) algorithms to real-world problems. Unfortunately almost all of the theory of reinforcement learning assumes lookup table representations. In this paper we address the pressing issue of combining function approximation and RL, and present 1) a function approximator based on a simple extension to state aggregation (a commonly used form of compact representation), namely *soft* state aggregation, 2) a theory of convergence for RL with arbitrary, but fixed, soft state aggregation, 3) a novel intuitive understanding of the effect of state aggregation on online RL, and 4) a new heuristic *adaptive* state aggregation algorithm that finds improved compact representations by exploiting the non-discrete nature of soft state aggregation. Preliminary empirical results are also presented.

1 INTRODUCTION

The strong theory of convergence available for reinforcement learning algorithms (e.g., Dayan & Sejnowski, 1994; Watkins & Dayan, 1992; Jaakkola, Jordan & Singh, 1994; Tsitsiklis, 1994) makes them attractive as a basis for building learning control architectures to solve a wide variety of search, planning, and control problems. Unfortunately, almost all of the convergence results assume lookup table representations for value functions (see Sutton, 1988; Dayan, 1992; Bradtke, 1993; and Vanroy & Tsitsiklis, personal communication; for exceptions). It is widely accepted that the use of more compact representations than lookup tables is crucial to scaling RL algorithms to real-world problems.

In this paper we address the pressing issue of combining function approximation and RL, and present 1) a function approximator based on a simple extension to state aggregation (a commonly used form of compact representation, e.g., Moore, 1991), namely *soft* state aggregation, 2) a theory of convergence for RL with arbitrary, but fixed, soft state aggregation, 3) a novel intuitive understanding of the effect of state aggregation on online RL, and 4) a new heuristic *adaptive* state aggregation algorithm that finds improved compact representations by exploiting the non-discrete nature of soft state aggregations. Preliminary empirical results are also presented.

Problem Definition and Notation: We consider the problem of solving large Markovian decision processes (MDPs) using RL algorithms and compact function approximation. We use the following notation: $\mathcal{S}$ for state space, $\mathcal{A}$ for action space, $P^a(s, s')$ for transition probability, $R^a(s)$ for payoff, and γ for discount factor. The objective is to maximize the expected, infinite horizon, discounted sum of payoffs.

1.1 FUNCTION APPROXIMATION: SOFT STATE CLUSTERS

In this section we describe a new function approximator (FA) for RL. In section 3 we will analyze it theoretically and present convergence results. The FA maps the state space $\mathcal{S}$ into $M > 0$ aggregates or clusters from cluster space $\mathcal{X}$. Typically, $M << |\mathcal{S}|$. We allow *soft* clustering, where each state s belongs to cluster x with probability $P(x|s)$, called the clustering probabilities. This allows each state s to belong to several clusters. An interesting special case is that of the usual state aggregation where each state belongs only to one cluster. The theoretical model is that the agent can observe the underlying state but can only update a value function for the clusters. The value of a cluster *generalizes* to all states in proportion to the clustering probabilities. Throughout we use the symbols x and y to represent individual clusters and the symbols s and s' to represent individual states.

2 A GENERAL CONVERGENCE THEOREM

An online RL algorithm essentially sees a sequence of quadruples, $< s_t, a_t, s_{t+1}, r_t >$, representing a transition from current state s_t to next state s_{t+1} on current action a_t with an associated payoff r_t. We will first prove a general convergence theorem for Q-learning (Watkins & Dayan, 1992) applied to a sequence of quadruples that may or may not be generated by a Markov process (Bertsekas, 1987). This is required because the RL problem at the level of the clusters may be *non*-Markovian. Conceptually, the sequence of quadruples can be thought of as being produced by some process that is allowed to modify the sequence of quadruples produced by a Markov process, e.g., by mapping states to clusters. In Section 3 we will specialize the following theorem to provide specific results for our function approximator.

Consider any stochastic process that generates a sequence of random quadruples, $\Psi = \{< x_i, a_i, y_i, r_i >\}_i$, where $x_i, y_i \in Y$, $a_i \in A$, and r_i is a bounded real number. Note that x_{i+1} does not have to be equal to y_i. Let $|Y|$ and $|A|$ be finite, and define

indicator variables
$$\chi_i(x,a,y) = \begin{cases} 1 & \text{when } \Psi_i = <x,a,y,.> \text{ (for any } r) \\ 0 & \text{otherwise,} \end{cases}$$

and
$$\chi_i(x,a) = \begin{cases} 1 & \text{when } \Psi_i = <x,a,.,.> \text{ (for any } y, \text{ and any } r) \\ 0 & \text{otherwise.} \end{cases}$$

Define
$$P^a_{i,j}(x,y) = \frac{\sum_{k=i}^{j} \chi_k(x,a,y)}{\sum_{k=i}^{j} \chi_k(x,a)} \quad \text{and} \quad R^a_{i,j}(x) = \frac{\sum_{k=1}^{j} r_k \chi_k(x,a)}{\sum_{k=i}^{j} \chi_k(x,a)}$$

Theorem 1: If $\forall \epsilon > 0$, $\exists M_\epsilon < \infty$, such that for all $i \geq 0$, for all $x, y \in Y$, and for all $a \in A$, the following conditions characterize the infinite sequence Ψ: with probability $1 - \epsilon$,

$$|P^a_{i,i+M_\epsilon}(x,y) - \bar{P}^a(x,y)| < \epsilon \quad \text{and}$$
$$|R^a_{i,i+M_\epsilon}(x) - \bar{R}^a(x)| < \epsilon, \tag{1}$$

where for all x, a, and y, with probability one $P^a_{0,\infty}(x,y) = \bar{P}^a(x,y)$, and $R^a_{0,\infty}(x) = \bar{R}^a(x)$. Then, online Q-learning applied to such a sequence will converge with probability one to the solution of the following system of equations: $\forall x \in Y$, and $\forall a \in A$,

$$Q(x,a) = \bar{R}^a(x) + \gamma \sum_{y \in Y} \bar{P}^a(x,y) \max_{a' \in A} Q(y,a') \tag{2}$$

Proof: Consider the semi-batch version of Q-learning that collects the changes to the value function for M steps before making the change. By assumption, for any ϵ, making M_ϵ large enough will ensure that with probability $1 - \epsilon$, the sample quantities for the ith batch, $P^a_{i,i+M_\epsilon(i)}(x,y)$ and $R^a_{i,i+M_\epsilon(i)}(x)$ are within ϵ of the asymptotic quantities. In Appendix A we prove that the semi-batch version of Q-learning outlined above converges to the solution of Equation 2 with probability one. The semi-batch proof can be extended to online Q-learning by using the analysis developed in Theorem 3 of Jaakkola et al. (1994). In brief, it can be shown that the difference caused by the online updating vanishes in the limit thereby forcing semi-batch Q-learning and online Q-learning to be equal asymptotically. The use of the analysis in Theorem 3 from Jaakkola et al. (1994) requires that the learning rate parameters α are such that $\frac{\alpha_t(x)}{max_{t \in M_\epsilon(k)} \alpha_t(x)} \to 1$ uniformly w.p.1.; $M_\epsilon(k)$ is the kth batch of size M_ϵ. If $\alpha_t(x)$ is non-increasing in addition to satisfying the conventional Q-learning conditions, then it will also meet the above requirement. □

Theorem 1 provides the most general convergence result available for Q-learning (and TD(0)); it shows that for an arbitrary quadruple sequence satisfying the ergodicity conditions given in Equations 1, Q-learning will converge to the solution of *the* MDP constructed with the limiting probabilities ($P_{0,\infty}$) and payoffs ($R_{0,\infty}$). Theorem 1 combines and generalizes the results on hard state aggregation and value iteration presented in Vanroy & Tsitsiklis (personal communication), and on partially observable MDPs in Singh et al. (1994).

3 RL AND SOFT STATE AGGREGATION

In this section we apply Theorem 1 to provide convergence results for two cases: 1) using Q-learning and our FA to solve MDPs, and 2) using Sutton's (1988) TD(0) and our FA to determine the value function for a fixed policy. As is usual in online RL, we continue to assume that the transition probabilities and the payoff function of the MDP are unknown to the learning agent. Furthermore, being online such algorithms cannot sample states in arbitrary order. In this section, the clustering probabilities $P(x|s)$ are assumed to be fixed.

Case 1: Q-learning and Fixed Soft State Aggregation

Because of function approximation, the domain of the learned Q-value function is constrained to be $\mathcal{X} \times A$ ($\mathcal{X}$ is cluster space). This section develops a "Bellman equation" (e.g., Bertsekas, 1987) for Q-learning at the level of the cluster space. We assume that the agent follows a stationary stochastic policy π that assigns to each state a non-zero probability of executing every action in every state. Furthermore, we assume that the Markov chain under policy π is ergodic. Such a policy π is a *persistently exciting* policy. Under the above conditions $P^\pi(s|x) = \frac{P(x|s)P^\pi(s)}{\sum_{s'} P(x|s')P^\pi(s')}$, where for all s, $P^\pi(s)$ is the steady-state probability of being in state s.

Corollary 1: Q-learning with soft state aggregation applied to an MDP while following a persistently exciting policy π will converge with probability one to the solution of the following system of equations: $\forall (x, a) \in (\mathcal{X} \times A)$,

$$Q(x, a) = \sum_s P^\pi(s|x) \left[R^a(s) + \gamma \sum_y P^a(s, y) \max_{a'} Q(y, a') \right] \quad (3)$$

and $P^a(s, y) = \sum_{s'} P^a(s, s') P(y|s')$. The Q-value function for the state space can then be constructed via $Q(s, a) = \sum_x P(x|s) Q(x, a)$ for all (s, a).

Proof: It can be shown that the sequence of quadruples produced by following policy π and independently mapping the current state s to a cluster x with probability $P(x|s)$ satisfies the conditions of Theorem 1. Also, it can be shown that

$$\bar{P}^a(x, y) = \sum_s P^\pi(s|x) P^a(s, y), \text{ and } \bar{R}^a(x) = \sum_s P^\pi(s|x) R^a(s).$$

Note that the Q-values found by clustering are dependent on the sampling policy π, unlike the lookup table case.

Case 2: TD(0) and Fixed Soft State Aggregation

We present separate results for TD(0) because it forms the basis for policy-iteration-like methods for solving Markov control problems (e.g., Barto, Sutton & Anderson, 1983) — a fact that we will use in the next section to derive adaptive state aggregation methods. As before, because of function approximation, the domain of the learned value function is constrained to be the cluster space $\mathcal{X}$.

Corollary 2: TD(0) with soft state aggregation applied to an MDP while following a policy π will converge with probability one to the solution of the following system of equations: $\forall x \in \mathcal{X}$,

$$V(x) = \sum_s P^\pi(s|x) \left[R^\pi(s) + \gamma \sum_y P^\pi(s,y) V(y) \right] \quad (4)$$

where again as in Q-learning the value function for the state space can be constructed via $V(s) = \sum_x P(x|s) V(x)$ for all s.

Proof: Corollary 1 implies Corollary 2 because TD(0) is a special case of Q-learning for MDPs with a single (possibly randomized) action in each state. Equation 4 provides a "Bellman equation" for TD(0) at the level of the cluster space. □

4 ADAPTIVE STATE AGGREGATION

In previous sections we restricted attention to a function approximator that had a *fixed* compact representation. How might one adapt the compact representation online in order to get better approximations of value functions? This section presents a novel *heuristic* adaptive algorithm that improves the compact representation by finding good clustering probabilities given an a priori fixed number of clusters. Note that for arbitrary clustering, while Corollaries 1 and 2 show that RL will find solutions with zero Bellman error in cluster space, the associated Bellman error in the state space will *not* be zero in general. Good clustering is therefore naturally defined in terms of reducing the Bellman error for the states of the MDP.

Let the clustering probabilities be parametrized as follows $P(x|s;\theta) = \frac{e^{\theta(x,s)}}{\sum_{x'} e^{\theta(x',s)}}$, where $\theta(x,s)$ is the weight between state s and cluster x. Then the Bellman error at state s given parameter θ (a matrix) is,

$$J(s|\theta) = V(s|\theta) - \left[R^\pi(s) + \gamma \sum_{s'} P^\pi(s,s') V(s'|\theta) \right]$$

$$= \sum_x P(x|s;\theta) V(x|\theta) - \left[R^\pi(s) + \gamma \sum_{s'} P^\pi(s,s') \sum_x P(x|s';\theta) V(x|\theta) \right]$$

Adaptive State Aggregation (ASA) Algorithm:

    Step 1: Compute $V(x|\theta)$ for all $x \in \mathcal{X}$ using the TD(0) algorithm.
    Step 2: Let $\Delta \theta = -\alpha \frac{\partial J^2(\theta)}{\partial \theta}$. Go to step 1.

where Step 2 tries to minimize the Bellman error for the states by holding the cluster values fixed to those computed in Step 1. We have

$$\frac{\partial J^2(s|\theta)}{\partial \theta(y,s)} = 2 J(s|\theta) \left[P(y|s;\theta)(1 - \gamma P^\pi(s,s))(V(y|\theta) - V(s|\theta)) \right].$$

The Bellman error $J(s|\theta)$ cannot be computed directly because the transition probabilities $P(s,s')$ are unknown. However, it can be estimated by averaging the sample

Bellman error. $P(y|s;\theta)$ is known, and $(1 - \gamma P^\pi(s,s))$ is always positive, and independent of y, and can therefore be absorbed into the step-size α. The quantities $V(y|\theta)$ and $V(s|\theta)$ are available at the end of Step 1. In practice, Step 1 is only carried out partially before Step 2 is implemented. Partial evaluation works well because the changes in the clustering probabilities at Step 2 are small, and because the final $V(x|\theta)$ at the previous Step 1 is used to initialize the computation of $V(x|\theta)$ at the next Step 1.

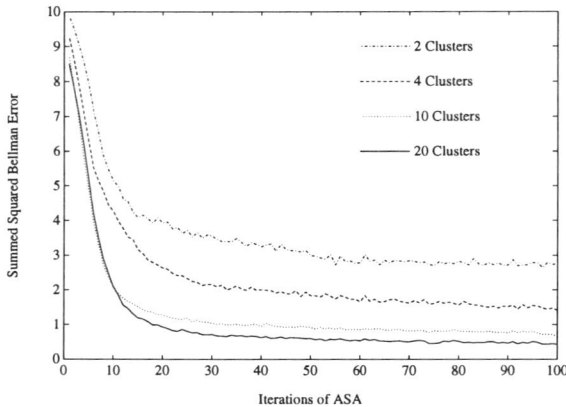

Figure 1: Adaptive State Clustering. See text for explanation.

Figure 1 presents preliminary empirical results for the ASA algorithm. It plots the squared Bellman error summed over the state space as a function of the number of iterations of the ASA algorithm with constant step-size α. It shows error curves for 2, 4, 10 and 20 clusters averaged over ten runs of randomly constructed 20 state Markov chains. Figure 4 shows that ASA is able to adapt the clustering probabilities to reduce the Bellman error in state space, and as expected the more clusters the smaller the asymptotic Bellman error. In future work we plan to test the policy iteration version of the adaptive soft aggregation algorithm on Markov control problems.

5 SUMMARY AND FUTURE WORK

Doing RL on aggregated states is potentially very advantageous because the value of each cluster generalizes across all states in proportion to the clustering probabilities. The same generalization is also potentially perilous because it can interfere with the contraction-based convergence of RL algorithms (see Yee, 1992; for a discussion). This paper resolves this debate for the case of soft state aggregation by defining a set of Bellman Equations (3 and 4) for the control and policy evaluation problems in the non-Markovian cluster space, and by proving that Q-learning and TD(0) solve them respectively with probability one. Theorem 1 presents a general convergence result that was applied to state aggregation in this paper, but is also a generalization of the results on hidden state presented in Singh *et al.* (1994), and may be applicable to other novel problems. It supports the intuitive picture that if a non-Markovian sequence of state transitions and payoffs is ergodic in the sense of Equation 1, then RL algorithms will converge w.p.1. to the solution of an MDP constructed with the limiting transition probabilities and payoffs.

We also presented a new algorithm, ASA, for adapting compact representations, that takes advantage of the soft state aggregation proposed here to do gradient descent in clustering probability space to minimize squared Bellman error in the state space. We demonstrated on simple examples that ASA is able to adapt the clustering probabilities to dramatically reduce the Bellman error in state space. In future work we plan to extend the convergence theory presented here to discretizations of continuous state MDPs, and to further test the ASA algorithms.

A Convergence of semi-batch Q-learning (Theorem 1)

Consider a semi-batch algorithm that collects the changes to the Q-value function for M steps before making the change to the Q-value function. Let

$$R_k^a(x) = \sum_{i=(k-1)M}^{kM} r_i \chi_i(x,a); \quad M_k(x,a) = \sum_{i=(k-1)M}^{kM} \chi_i(x,a)$$

and

$$M_k(x,a,y) = \sum_{i=(k-1)M}^{kM} \chi_i(x,a,y)$$

Then the Q-value of (x,a) after the kth batch is given by:

$$Q_{k+1}(x,a) = (1 - M_k(x,a)\alpha_k(x,a))Q_k(x,a)$$
$$+ M_k(x,a)\alpha_k(x,a)\left[\frac{R_k^a(x)}{M_k(x,a)} + \gamma \sum_{y \in Y} \frac{M_k(x,a,y)}{M_k(x,a)} \max_{a'} Q_k(y,a')\right]$$

Let $\bar{Q}$ be the solution to Equation 2. Define,

$$F_k(x,a) = \frac{R_k^a(x)}{M_k(x,a)} + \gamma \sum_{y \in Y} \frac{M_k(x,a,y)}{M_k(x,a)} \max_{a'} Q_k(y,a') - \bar{Q}(x,a),$$

then, if $V_k(x) = \max_a Q_k(x,a)$ and $\bar{V}(x) = \max_a \bar{Q}(x,a)$,

$$F_k(x,a) = \gamma \sum_y \frac{M_k(x,a,y)}{M_k(x,a)}[V_k(y) - \bar{V}(y)] + \left(\frac{R_k^a(x)}{M_k(x,a)} - R_{0,\infty}^a(x)\right)$$
$$+ \gamma \sum_y \left[\left(\frac{M_k(x,a,y)}{M_k(X,a)} - P_{0,\infty}^a(x,y)\right)\bar{V}(y)\right],$$

The quantity $F_k(x,a)$ can be bounded by
$\|F_k(x,a)\| \le \gamma \|V_k - \bar{V}\| + \|(\frac{R_k^a(x)}{M_k(x,a)} - R_{0,\infty}^a(x))\|$
$+\gamma \|\sum_y (\frac{M_k(x,a,y)}{M_k(x,a)} - P_{0,\infty}^a(x,y))\bar{V}(y)\| \le \gamma \|V_k - \bar{V}\| + C\epsilon_k^M$,
where ϵ_k^M is the larger of $|\frac{R_k^a(x)}{M_k(x,a)} - R_{0,\infty}^a(x)|$, and $\gamma|\sum_y (\frac{M_k(x,a,y)}{M_k(x,a)} - P_{0,\infty}^a(x,y))|$. By

assumption for any $\epsilon > 0$, $\exists M_\epsilon < \infty$ such that $\epsilon_k^{M_\epsilon} < \epsilon$ with probability $1 - \epsilon$. The variance of $F_k(x,a)$ can also be shown to be bounded because the variance of the sample probabilities is bounded (everything else is similar to standard Q-learning for MDPs). Therefore by Theorem 1 of Jaakkola *et al.* (1994), for any $\epsilon > 0$, with probability $(1 - \epsilon)$, $Q_k(x,a) \to Q_\infty(x,a)$, where $|Q_\infty(x,a) - \bar{Q}(x,a)| \leq C\epsilon$. Therefore, semi-batch Q-learning converges with probability one. □

Acknowledgements

This project was supported in part by a grant from the McDonnell-Pew Foundation, by a grant from ATR Human Information Processing Research Laboratories, and by a grant from Siemens Corporation. Michael I. Jordan is a NSF Presidential Young Investigator.

References

A. G. Barto, R. S. Sutton, & C. W. Anderson. (1983) Neuronlike elements that can solve difficult learning control problems. *IEEE SMC*, 13:835–846.

D. P. Bertsekas. (1987) *Dynamic Programming: Deterministic and Stochastic Models*, Prentice-Hall.

S. J. Bradtke. (1993) Reinforcement learning applied to linear quadratic regulation. In *Advances in Neural Information Processing Systems 5*, pages 295–302.

P. Dayan. (1992) The convergence of TD(λ) for general λ. *Machine Learning*, 8(3/4):341–362.

P. Dayan & T.J. Sejnowski. (1994) TD(λ) converges with probability 1. *Machine Learning*, 13(3).

T. Jaakkola, M. I. Jordan, & S. P. Singh. (1994) On the convergence of stochastic iterative dynamic programming algorithms. *Neural Computation*, 6(6):1185–1201.

A. W. Moore. (1991) Variable resolution dynamic programming: Efficiently learning action maps in multivariate real-valued state-spaces. In *Maching Learning: Proceedings of the Eighth International Workshop*, pages 333–337.

S. P. Singh, T. Jaakkola, & M. I. Jordan. (1994) Learning without state-estimation in partially observable markovian decision processes. In *Machine Learning: Proceedings of the Eleventh International Conference*, pages 284–292.

R. S. Sutton. (1988) Learning to predict by the methods of temporal differences. *Machine Learning*, 3:9–44.

J. Tsitsiklis. (1994) Asynchronous stochastic approximation and Q-learning. *Machine Learning*, 16(3):185–202.

B. Vanroy & J. Tsitsiklis. (personal communication)

C. J. C. H. Watkins & P. Dayan. (1992) Q-learning. *Machine Learning*, 8(3/4):279–292.

R. C. Yee. (1992) Abstraction in control learning. Technical Report COINS Technical Report 92-16, Department of Computer and Information Science, University of Massachusetts, Amherst, MA 01003. A dissertation proposal.

Generalization in Reinforcement Learning: Safely Approximating the Value Function

Justin A. Boyan and **Andrew W. Moore**
Computer Science Department
Carnegie Mellon University
Pittsburgh, PA 15213
jab@cs.cmu.edu, awm@cs.cmu.edu

Abstract

A straightforward approach to the curse of dimensionality in reinforcement learning and dynamic programming is to replace the lookup table with a generalizing function approximator such as a neural net. Although this has been successful in the domain of backgammon, there is no guarantee of convergence. In this paper, we show that the combination of dynamic programming and function approximation is not robust, and in even very benign cases, may produce an entirely wrong policy. We then introduce Grow-Support, a new algorithm which is safe from divergence yet can still reap the benefits of successful generalization.

1 INTRODUCTION

Reinforcement learning—the problem of getting an agent to learn to act from sparse, delayed rewards—has been advanced by techniques based on dynamic programming (DP). These algorithms compute a *value function* which gives, for each state, the minimum possible long-term cost commencing in that state. For the high-dimensional and continuous state spaces characteristic of real-world control tasks, a discrete representation of the value function is intractable; some form of generalization is required.

A natural way to incorporate generalization into DP is to use a function approximator, rather than a lookup table, to represent the value function. This approach, which dates back to uses of Legendre polynomials in DP [Bellman *et al.*, 1963], has recently worked well on several dynamic control problems [Mahadevan and Connell, 1990, Lin, 1993] and succeeded spectacularly on the game of backgammon [Tesauro, 1992, Boyan, 1992]. On the other hand, many sensible implementations have been less successful [Bradtke, 1993, Schraudolph *et al.*, 1994]. Indeed, given the well-established success on backgammon, the absence of similarly impressive results appearing for other games is perhaps an indication that using function approximation in reinforcement learning does not always work well.

In this paper, we demonstrate that the straightforward substitution of function approximators for lookup tables in DP is not robust and, even in very benign cases, may diverge, resulting in an entirely wrong control policy. We then present Grow-Support, a new algorithm designed to converge robustly. Grow-Support grows a collection of states over which function approximation is stable. One-step backups based on Bellman error are not used; instead, values are assigned by performing "rollouts"—explicit simulations with a greedy policy. We discuss potential computational advantages of this method and demonstrate its success on some example problems for which the conventional DP algorithm fails.

2 DISCRETE AND SMOOTH VALUE ITERATION

Many popular reinforcement learning algorithms, including Q-learning and TD(0), are based on the dynamic programming algorithm known as value iteration [Watkins, 1989, Sutton, 1988, Barto *et al.*, 1989], which for clarity we will call *discrete value iteration*. Discrete value iteration takes as input a complete model of the world as a Markov Decision Task, and computes the optimal value function J^*:

$$J^*(x) = \text{the minimum possible sum of future costs starting from } x$$

To assure that J^* is well-defined, we assume here that costs are nonnegative and that some absorbing goal state—with all future costs 0—is reachable from every state. For simplicity we also assume that state transitions are deterministic. Note that J^* and the world model together specify a "greedy" policy which is optimal for the domain:

$$\text{optimal action from state } x = \arg\min_{a \in A} \left(\text{COST}(x, a) + J^*(\text{NEXT-STATE}(x, a)) \right)$$

We now consider extending discrete value iteration to the continuous case: we replace the lookup table over all states with a function approximator trained over a sample of states. The *smooth value iteration* algorithm is given in the appendix. Convergence is no longer guaranteed; we instead recognize four possible classes of behavior:

good convergence The function approximator accurately represents the intermediate value functions at each iteration (that is, after m iterations, the value function correctly represents the cost of the cheapest m-step path), and successfully converges to the optimal J^* value function.

lucky convergence The function approximator does not accurately represent the intermediate value functions at each iteration; nevertheless, the algorithm manages to converge to a value function whose greedy policy is optimal.

bad convergence The algorithm converges, i.e. the target J-values for the N training points stop changing, but the resulting value function and policy are poor.

divergence Worst of all: small fitter errors may become magnified from one iteration to the next, resulting in a value function which never stops changing.

The hope is that the intermediate value functions will be smooth and we will achieve "good convergence." Unfortunately, our experiments have generated all four of these behaviors—and the divergent behavior occurs frequently, even for quite simple problems.

2.1 DIVERGENCE IN SMOOTH VALUE ITERATION

We have run simulations in a variety of domains—including a continuous gridworld, a car-on-the-hill problem with nonlinear dynamics, and tic-tac-toe versus a stochastic opponent—and using a variety of function approximators, including polynomial regression, backpropagation, and local weighted regression. In our experiments, none of these function approximators was immune from divergence.

The first set of results is from the **2-D continuous gridworld**, described in Figure 1. By quantizing the state space into a 100×100 grid, we can compute J^* with discrete value iteration, as shown in Figure 2. The optimal value function is exactly linear: $J^*(x,y) = 20 - 10x - 10y$.

Since J^* is linear, one would hope smooth value iteration could converge to it with a function approximator as simple as linear or quadratic regression. However, the intermediate value functions of Figure 2 are not smooth and cannot be fit accurately by a low-order polynomial. Using linear regression on a sample of 256 randomly-chosen states, smooth value iteration took over 500 iterations before "luckily" converging to optimal. Quadratic regression, though it always produces a smaller fit error than linear regression, did not converge (Figure 3). The quadratic function, in trying to both be flat in the middle of state space and bend down toward 0 at the goal corner, must compensate by underestimating the values at the corner opposite the goal. These underestimates then enlarge on each iteration, as the one-step DP lookaheads erroneously indicate that points can lower their expected cost-to-go by stepping farther away from the goal. The resulting policy is anti-optimal.

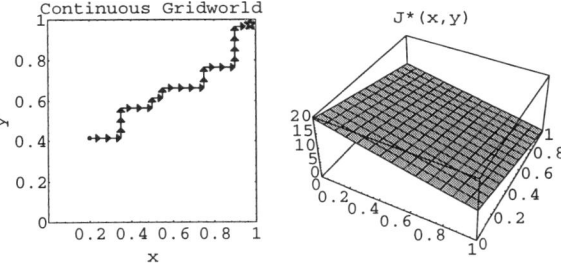

Figure 1: In the continuous gridworld domain, the state is a point $(x,y) \in [0,1]^2$. There are four actions corresponding to short steps (length 0.05, cost 0.5) in each compass direction, and the goal region is the upper right-hand corner. $J^*(x,y)$ is linear.

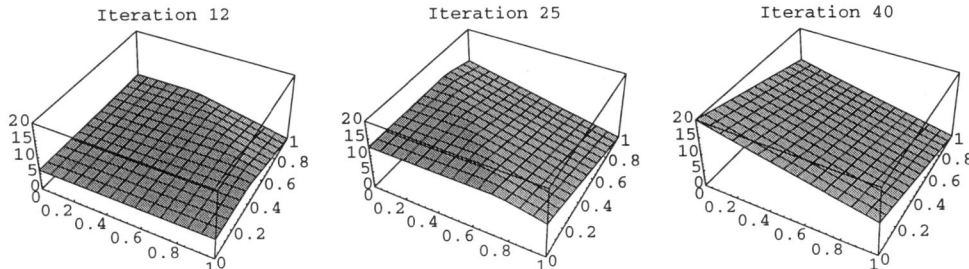

Figure 2: Computation of J^* by discrete value iteration

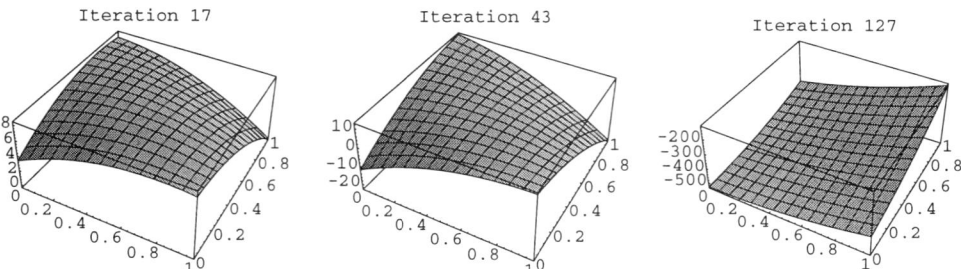

Figure 3: Divergence of smooth value iteration with quadratic regression (note z-axis).

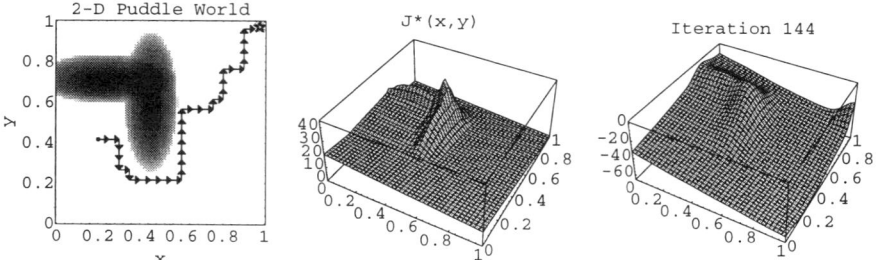

Figure 4: The 2-D continuous gridworld with puddles, its optimal value function, and a diverging approximation of the value function by Local Weighted Regression (note z-axis).

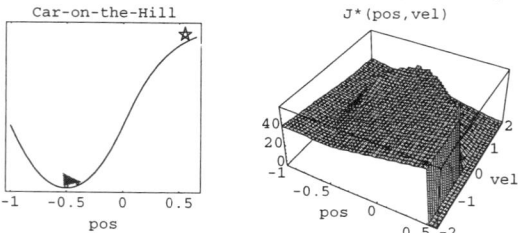

Figure 5: The car-on-the-hill domain. When the velocity is below a threshold, the car must reverse up the left hill to gain enough speed to reach the goal, so J^* is discontinuous.

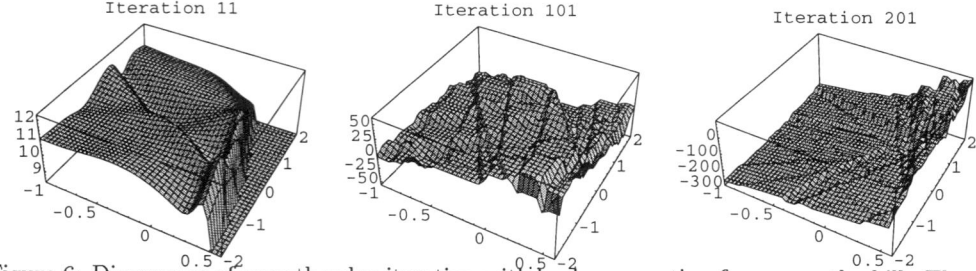

Figure 6: Divergence of smooth value iteration with backpropagation for car-on-the-hill. The neural net, a 2-layer MLP with 80 hidden units, was trained for 2000 epochs per iteration.

It may seem as though the divergence of smooth value iteration shown above can be attributed to the global nature of polynomial regression. In fact, when the domain is made slightly less trivial, the same types of instabilities appear with even a highly

Table 1: Summary of convergence results: Smooth value iteration

Domain	Linear	Quadratic	LWR	Backprop
2-D gridworld	lucky	diverge	good	lucky
2-D puddle world	—	—	diverge	diverge
Car-on-the-hill	—	—	good	diverge

local memory-based function approximator such as local weighted regression (LWR) [Cleveland and Delvin, 1988]. Figure 4 shows the continuous gridworld augmented to include two oval "puddles" through which it is costly to step. Although LWR can fit the corresponding J^* function nearly perfectly, smooth value iteration with LWR nonetheless reliably diverges. On another two-dimensional domain, the car-on-the-hill (Figure 5), smooth value iteration with LWR did converge, but a neural net trained by backpropagation did not (see Figure 6). Table 1 summarizes our results.

In light of such experiments, we conclude that the straightforward combination of DP and function approximation is not robust. A general-purpose learning method will require either using a function approximator constrained to be robust during DP [Yee, 1992], or an algorithm which explicitly prevents divergence even in the face of imperfect function approximation, such as the Grow-Support algorithm we present in Section 3.

2.2 RELATED WORK

Theoretically, it is not surprising that inserting a smoothing process into a recursive DP procedure can lead to trouble. In [Thrun and Schwartz, 1993] one case is analyzed with the assumption that errors due to function approximation bias are independently distributed. Another area of theoretical analysis concerns inadequately approximated J^* functions. In [Singh and Yee, 1994] and [Williams, 1993] bounds are derived for the maximum reduction in optimality that can be produced by a given error in function approximation. If a basis function approximator is used, then the reduction can be large [Sabes, 1993]. These results assume generalization from a dataset containing true optimal values; the true reinforcement learning scenario is even harder because each iteration of DP requires its own function approximation.

3 THE GROW-SUPPORT ALGORITHM

The Grow-Support algorithm is designed to construct the optimal value function with a generalizing function approximator while being robust and stable. It recognizes that function approximators cannot always be relied upon to fit the intermediate value functions produced by DP. Instead, it assumes only that the function approximator can represent the final J^* function accurately. The specific principles of Grow-Support are these:

1. We maintain a "support" set of states whose final J^* values have been computed, starting with goal states, and growing this set out from the goal. The fitter is trained only on these values, which we assume it is capable of fitting.

2. Instead of propagating values by one-step DP backups, we use simulations with the current greedy policy, called "rollouts". They explicitly verify the achievability of a state's cost-to-go estimate before adding that state to the

support. In a rollout, the J values are derived from costs of actual paths to the goal, not from the values of the previous iteration's function approximation. This prevents divergence.

3. We take maximum advantage of generalization. Each iteration, we add to the support set any sample state which can, by executing a single action, reach a state that passes the rollout test. In a discrete environment, this would cause the support set to expand in one-step concentric "shells" back from the goal. But in our continuous case, the function approximator may be able to extrapolate correctly well beyond the support region—and when this happens, we can add many points to the support set at once. This leads to the very desirable behavior that the support set grows in big jumps in regions where the value function is smooth.

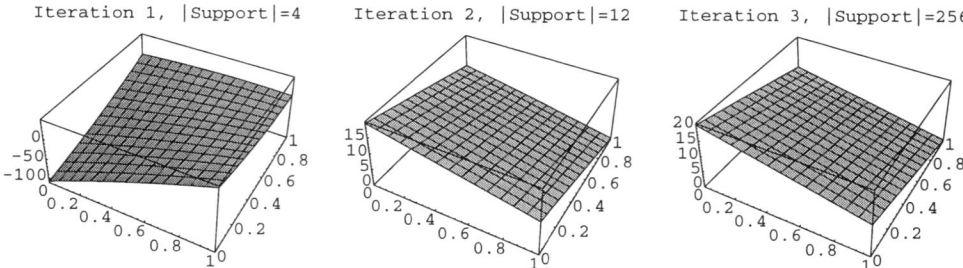

Figure 7: Grow-Support with quadratic regression on the gridworld. (Compare Figure 3.)

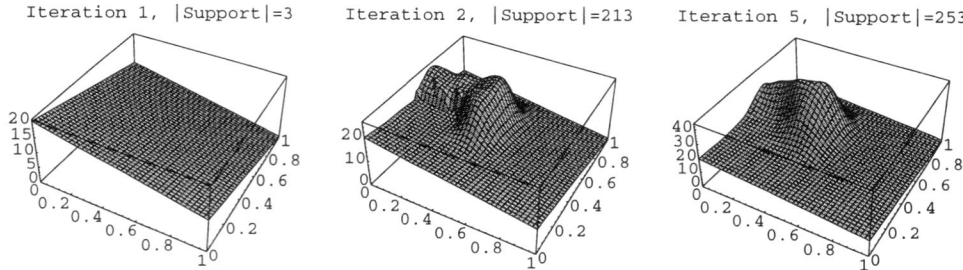

Figure 8: Grow-Support with LWR on the two-puddle gridworld. (Compare Figure 4.)

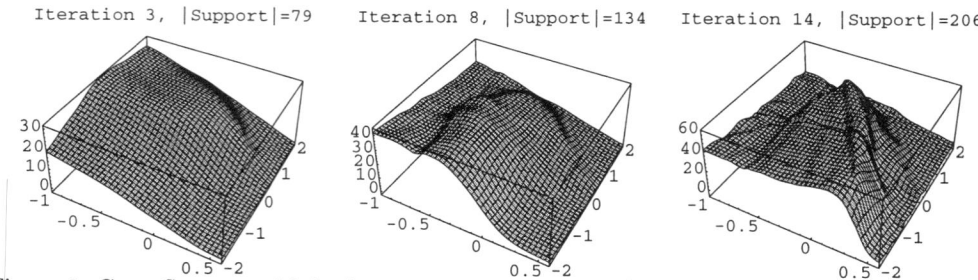

Figure 9: Grow-Support with backprop on car-on-the-hill. (Compare Figure 6.)

The algorithm, again restricted to the deterministic case for simplicity, is outlined in the appendix. In Figures 7–9, we illustrate its convergence on the same combinations of domain and function approximator which caused smooth value iteration to diverge. In Figure 8, all but three points are added to the support within only five iterations, and the resulting greedy policy is optimal. In Figure 9, after 14 iterations, the algorithm terminates. Although 50 states near the discontinuity were not added to the support set, the resulting policy is optimal within the support set. Grow-support converged to a near-optimal policy for all the problems and fitters in Table 1.

The Grow-Support algorithm is more robust than value iteration. Empirically, it was also seen to be no more computationally expensive (and often much cheaper) despite the overhead of performing rollouts. Reasons for this are (1) the rollout test is not expensive; (2) once a state has been added to the support, its value is fixed and it needs no more computation; and most importantly, (3) the aggressive exploitation of generalization enables the algorithm to converge in very few iterations. However, with a nondeterministic problem, where multiple rollouts are required to assess the accuracy of a prediction, Grow-Support would become more expensive.

It is easy to prove that Grow-Support will always terminate after a finite number of iterations. If the function approximator is inadequate for representing the J^* function, Grow-Support may terminate before adding all sample states to the support set. When this happens, we then know exactly which of the sample states are having trouble and which have been learned. This suggests potential schemes for adaptively adding sample states to the support in problematic regions. Investigation of these ideas is in progress.

In conclusion, we have demonstrated that dynamic programming methods may diverge when their tables are replaced by generalizing function approximators. Our Grow-Support algorithm uses rollouts, rather than one-step backups, to assign training values and to keep inaccurate states out of the training set. We believe these principles will contribute substantially to producing practical, robust, reinforcement learning.

Acknowledgements

We thank Scott Fahlman, Geoff Gordon, Mary Lee, Michael Littman and Marc Ringuette for their suggestions, and the NDSEG fellowship and NSF Grant IRI-9214873 for their support.

APPENDIX: ALGORITHMS

Smooth Value Iteration($X, G, A,$ NEXT-STATE, COST, FITJ):
  Given: • a finite collection of states $\hat{X} = \{x_1, x_2, \ldots x_N\}$ sampled from the
           continuous state space $X \subset \Re^n$, and goal region $G \subset X$
         • a finite set of allowable actions A
         • a deterministic transition function NEXT-STATE : $X \times A \to X$
         • the 1-step cost function COST : $X \times A \to \Re$
         • a smoothing function approximator FITJ

iter := 0
$j^{(0)}[i] := 0 \quad \forall i = 1 \ldots N$
repeat
    Train FITJ$^{(\text{iter})}$ to approximate the training set: $\left\{ \begin{array}{c} x_1 \mapsto j^{(\text{iter})}[1] \\ \vdots \\ x_N \mapsto j^{(\text{iter})}[N] \end{array} \right\}$
    iter := iter + 1;
    for $i := 1 \ldots N$ do
        $j^{(\text{iter})}[i] := \left\{ \begin{array}{ll} 0 & \text{if } x_i \in G \\ \min_{a \in A} \left(\text{COST}(x_i, a) + \text{FITJ}^{(\text{iter}-1)}(\text{NEXT-STATE}(x_i, a)) \right) & \text{otherwise} \end{array} \right.$
until j array stops changing

subroutine **RolloutCost**(x, J):
   Starting from state x, follow the greedy policy defined by value function J until
   either reaching the goal, or exceeding a total path cost of $J(x) + \epsilon$. Then return:
   $\longrightarrow$ the actual total cost of the path, if goal is reached from x with cost $\leq J(x) + \epsilon$;
   $\longrightarrow \infty$, if goal is not reached in cost $J(x) + \epsilon$.

Grow-Support$(X, G, A, \text{NEXT-STATE}, \text{COST}, \text{FITJ})$:
   Given: • exactly the same inputs as Smooth Value Iteration.
   SUPPORT $:= \{(x_i \mapsto 0) \mid x_i \in G\}$
   repeat
      Train FITJ to approximate the training set SUPPORT
      for each $x_i \notin$ SUPPORT do
         $c := \min_{a \in A} [\text{COST}(x_i, a) + \textbf{RolloutCost}(\text{NEXT-STATE}(x_i, a), \text{FITJ})]$
         if $c < \infty$ then
            add $(x_i \mapsto c)$ to the training set SUPPORT
   until SUPPORT stops growing or includes all sample points.

References

[Barto et al., 1989] A. Barto, R. Sutton, and C. Watkins. Learning and sequential decision making. Technical Report COINS 89-95, Univ. of Massachusetts, 1989.

[Bellman et al., 1963] R. Bellman, R. Kalaba, and B. Kotkin. Polynomial approximation—a new computational technique in dynamic programming: Allocation processes. *Mathematics of Computation*, 17, 1963.

[Boyan, 1992] J. A. Boyan. Modular neural networks for learning context-dependent game strategies. Master's thesis, Cambridge University, 1992.

[Bradtke, 1993] S. J. Bradtke. Reinforcement learning applied to linear quadratic regulation. In S. J. Hanson, J. Cowan, and C. L. Giles, editors, *NIPS-5*. Morgan Kaufmann, 1993.

[Cleveland and Delvin, 1988] W. S. Cleveland and S. J. Delvin. Locally weighted regression: An approach to regression analysis by local fitting. *JASA*, 83(403):596–610, September 1988.

[Lin, 1993] L.-J. Lin. *Reinforcement Learning for Robots Using Neural Networks*. PhD thesis, Carnegie Mellon University, 1993.

[Mahadevan and Connell, 1990] S. Mahadevan and J. Connell. Automatic programming of behavior-based robots using reinforcement learning. Technical report, IBM T. J. Watson Research Center, NY 10598, 1990.

[Sabes, 1993] P. Sabes. Approximating Q-values with basis function representations. In *Proceedings of the Fourth Connectionist Models Summer School*, 1993.

[Schraudolph et al., 1994] N. Schraudolph, P. Dayan, and T. Sejnowski. Using TD(λ) to learn an evaluation function for the game of Go. In J. D. Cowan, G. Tesauro, and J. Alspector, editors, *NIPS-6*. Morgan Kaufmann, 1994.

[Singh and Yee, 1994] S. P. Singh and R. Yee. An upper bound on the loss from approximate optimal-value functions. *Machine Learning*, 1994. Technical Note (to appear).

[Sutton, 1988] R. Sutton. Learning to predict by the methods of temporal differences. *Machine Learning*, 3, 1988.

[Tesauro, 1992] G. Tesauro. Practical issues in temporal difference learning. *Machine Learning*, 8(3/4), May 1992.

[Thrun and Schwartz, 1993] S. Thrun and A. Schwartz. Issues in using function approximation for reinforcement learning. In *Proceedings of the Fourth Connectionist Models Summer School*, 1993.

[Watkins, 1989] C. Watkins. *Learning from Delayed Rewards*. PhD thesis, Cambridge University, 1989.

[Williams, 1993] R. Williams. Tight performance bounds on greedy policies based on imperfect value functions. Technical Report NU-CCS-93-13, Northeastern University, 1993.

[Yee, 1992] R. Yee. Abstraction in control learning. Technical Report COINS 92-16, Univ. of Massachusetts, 1992.

Instance-Based State Identification for Reinforcement Learning

R. Andrew McCallum
Department of Computer Science
University of Rochester
Rochester, NY 14627-0226
mccallum@cs.rochester.edu

Abstract

This paper presents *instance-based state identification*, an approach to reinforcement learning and hidden state that builds disambiguating amounts of short-term memory on-line, and also learns with an order of magnitude fewer training steps than several previous approaches. Inspired by a key similarity between learning with hidden state and learning in continuous geometrical spaces, this approach uses instance-based (or "memory-based") learning, a method that has worked well in continuous spaces.

1 BACKGROUND AND RELATED WORK

When a robot's next course of action depends on information that is hidden from the sensors because of problems such as occlusion, restricted range, bounded field of view and limited attention, the robot suffers from hidden state. More formally, we say a reinforcement learning agent suffers from the *hidden state problem* if the agent's state representation is non-Markovian with respect to actions and utility.

The hidden state problem arises as a case of *perceptual aliasing*: the mapping between states of the world and sensations of the agent is not one-to-one [Whitehead, 1992]. If the agent's perceptual system produces the same outputs for two world states in which different actions are required, and if the agent's state representation consists only of its percepts, then the agent will fail to choose correct actions. Note that even if an agent's state representation includes some internal state beyond its immediate percepts, the agent can still suffer from hidden state if it does not keep *enough* internal state to uncover the non-Markovian-ness of its environment.

One solution to the hidden state problem is simply to avoid passing through the aliased states. This is the approach taken in Whitehead's *Lion* algorithm [Whitehead, 1992]. Whenever the agent finds a state that delivers inconsistent reward, it sets that state's utility so low that the policy will never visit it again. The success of this algorithm depends on a deterministic world and on the existence of a path to the goal that consists of only unaliased states.

Other solutions do not avoid aliased states, but do as best they can given a non-Markovian state representation [Littman, 1994; Singh *et al.*, 1994; Jaakkola *et al.*, 1995]. They involve either learning deterministic policies that execute incorrect actions in some aliased states, or learning stochastic policies with action choice probabilities matching the proportions of the different underlying aliased world states. These approaches do not depend on a path of unaliased states, but they have other limitations: when faced with many aliased states, a stochastic policy degenerates into random walk; when faced with potentially harmful results from incorrect actions, deterministically incorrect or probabilistically incorrect action choice may prove too dangerous; and when faced with performance-critical tasks, inefficiency that is proportional to the amount of aliasing may be unacceptable.

The most robust solution to the hidden state problem is to augment the agent's state representation on-line so as to disambiguate the aliased states. *State identification* techniques uncover the hidden state information—that is, they make the agent's internal state space Markovian. This transformation from an *imperfect state information model* to a *perfect state information model* has been formalized in the decision and control literature, and involves adding previous percepts and actions to the definition of agent internal state [Bertsekas and Shreve, 1978]. By augmenting the agent's perception with history information—short-term memory of past percepts, actions and rewards—the agent can distinguish perceptually aliased states, and can then reliably choose correct actions from them.

Predefined, fixed memory representations such as order n Markov models (also known as constant-sized perception windows, linear traces or tapped-delay lines) are often undesirable. When the length of the window is more than needed, they exponentially increase the number of internal states for which a policy must be stored and learned; when the length of the memory is less than needed, the agent reverts to the disadvantages of undistinguished hidden state. Even if the agent designer understands the task well enough to know its maximal memory requirements, the agent is at a disadvantage with constant-sized windows because, for most tasks, different amounts of memory are needed at different steps of the task.

The on-line memory creation approach has been adopted in several reinforcement learning algorithms. The Perceptual Distinctions Approach [Chrisman, 1992] and Utile Distinction Memory [McCallum, 1993] are both based on splitting states of a finite state machine by doing off-line analysis of statistics gathered over many steps. Recurrent-Q [Lin, 1993] is based on training recurrent neural networks. Indexed Memory [Teller, 1994] uses genetic programming to evolve agents that use load and store instructions on a register bank. A chief disadvantage of all these techniques is that they require a very large number of steps for training.

2 INSTANCE-BASED STATE IDENTIFICATION

This paper advocates an alternate solution to the hidden state problem we term *instance-based state identification*. The approach was inspired by the successes of instance-based (also called "memory-based") methods for learning in continuous perception spaces, (*i.e.* [Atkeson, 1992; Moore, 1992]).

The application of instance-based learning to short-term memory for hidden state is driven by the important insight that learning in continuous spaces and learning with hidden state have a crucial feature in common: they both begin learning without knowing the final granularity of the agent's state space. The former learns which regions of continuous input space can be represented uniformly and which areas must be finely divided among many states. The later learns which percepts can be represented uniformly because they uniquely identify a course of action without the need for memory, and which percepts must be divided among many states each with their own detailed history to distinguish them from other perceptually aliased world states. The first approach works with a continuous geometrical input space, the second works with a percept-action-reward "sequence" space, (or "history" space). Large continuous regions correspond to less-specified, small memories; small continuous regions correspond to more-specified, large memories.

Furthermore, learning in continuous spaces and sequence spaces both have a lot to gain from instance-based methods. In situations where the state space granularity is unknown, it is especially useful to memorize the raw previous experiences. If the agent tries to fit experience to its current, flawed state space granularity, it is bound to lose information by attributing experience to the wrong states. Experience attributed to the wrong state turns to garbage and is wasted. When faced with an evolving state space, keeping raw previous experience is the path of least commitment, and thus the most cautious about losing information.

3 NEAREST SEQUENCE MEMORY

There are many possible instance-based techniques to choose from, but we wanted to keep the first application simple. With that in mind, this initial algorithm is based on k-nearest neighbor. We call it *Nearest Sequence Memory*, (NSM). It bears emphasizing that this algorithm is the most straightforward, simple, almost naive combination of instance-based methods and history sequences that one could think of; there are still more sophisticated instance-based methods to try. The surprising result is that such a simple technique works as well as it does.

Any application of k-nearest neighbor consists of three parts: 1) recording each experience, 2) using some distance metric to find neighbors of the current query point, and 3) extracting output values from those neighbors. We apply these three parts to action-percept-reward sequences and reinforcement learning by Q-learning [Watkins, 1989] as follows:

1. For each step the agent makes in the world, it records the action, percept and reward by adding a new state to a single, long chain of states. Thus, each state in the chain contains a snapshot of immediate experience; and all the experiences are laid out in a time-connected history chain.

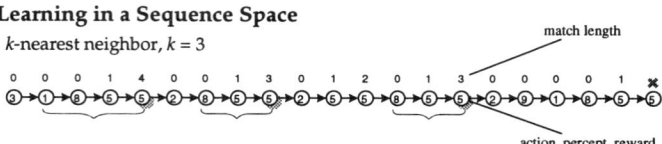

Learning in a Geometric Space
k-nearest neighbor, k = 3

Learning in a Sequence Space
k-nearest neighbor, k = 3

Figure 1: A continuous space compared with a sequence space. In each case, the "query point" is indicated with a gray cross, and the three nearest neighbors are indicated with gray shadows. In a geometric space, the neighborhood metric is defined by Euclidean distance. In a sequence space, the neighborhood metric is determined by sequence match length—the number of preceding states that match the states preceding the query point.

2. When the agent is about to choose an action, it finds states considered to be similar by looking in its state chain for states with histories similar to the current situation. The longer a state's string of previous experiences matches the agent's most recent experiences, the more likely the state represents where the agent is now.

3. Using the states, the agent obtains Q-values by averaging together the expected future reward values associated with the k nearest states for each action. The agent then chooses the action with the highest Q-value. The regular Q-learning update rule is used to update the k states that voted for the chosen action.

Choosing to represent short-term memory as a linear trace is a simple, well-established technique. Nearest Sequence Memory uses a linear trace to represent memory, but it differs from the *fixed-sized* window approaches because it provides a variable memory-length—like k-nearest neighbor, NSM can represent varying resolution in different regions of state space.

4 DETAILS OF THE ALGORITHM

A more complete description of Nearest Sequence Memory, its performance and its possible improvements can be found in [McCallum, 1995].

The interaction between the agent and its environment is described by actions, percepts and rewards. There is a finite set of possible actions, $\mathcal{A} = \{a_1, a_2, ..., a_m\}$, a finite set of possible percepts, $\mathcal{O} = \{o_1, o_2, ..., o_n\}$, and scalar range of possible rewards, $\mathcal{R} = [x, y], x, y \in \Re$. At each time step, t, the agent executes an action, $a_t \in \mathcal{A}$, then as a result receives a new percept, $o_t \in \mathcal{O}$, and a reward, $r_t \in \mathcal{R}$. The agent records its raw experience at time t in a "state" data point, s_t. Also associated with s_t is a slot to hold a single expected future discounted reward value, denoted $q(s_t)$. This value is associated with a_t and no other action.

1. Find the k nearest neighbor (most similar) states for each possible future action. The state currently at the end of the chain is the "query point" from which we measure all the distances. The neighborhood metric is defined by the number of preceding experience records that match the experience records preceding the "query point" state. (Here higher values of $n(s_i, s_j)$ indicate that s_i and s_j are closer neighbors.)

$$n(s_i, s_j) = \begin{cases} 1 + n(s_{i-1}, s_{j-1}), & \text{if } (a_{i-1} = a_{j-1}) \wedge (o_{i-1} = o_{j-1}) \wedge (r_{i-1} = r_{j-1}) \\ 0, & \text{otherwise} \end{cases} \quad (1)$$

Considering each of the possible future actions in turn, we find the k nearest neighbors and give them a vote, $v(s_i)$.

$$v(s_i) = \begin{cases} 1, & \text{if } n(s_t, s_i) \text{ is among the } k \max_{\forall s_j | a_j = a_i} n(s_t, s_j)\text{'s} \\ 0, & \text{otherwise} \end{cases} \quad (2)$$

2. Determine the Q-value for each action by averaging individual the q-values from the k voting states for that action.

$$Q_t(a_i) = \sum_{\forall s_j | a_j = a_i} (v(s_i)/k) \, q(s_j) \quad (3)$$

3. Select an action by maximum Q-value, or by random exploration. According to an exploration probability, e, either let a_{t+1} be randomly chosen from $\mathcal{A}$, or

$$a_{t+1} = \operatorname{argmax}_a Q_t(a) \quad (4)$$

4. Execute the action chosen in step 3, and record the resulting experience. Do this by creating a new "state" representing the current state of the environment, and storing the action-percept-reward triple associated with it:

Increment the time counter: $t \leftarrow t + 1$. Create s_t; record in it a_t, o_t, r_t.

The agent can limit its storage and computational load by limiting the number of instances it maintains to N (where N is some reasonably large number). Once the agent accumulates N instances, it can discard the oldest instance each time it adds a new one. This also provides a way to handle a changing environment.

5. Update the q-values by vote. Perform the dynamic programming step using the standard Q-learning rule to update those states that voted for the chosen action. Note that this actually involves performing steps 1 and 2 to get the next Q-values needed for calculating the utility of the agent's current state, U_t. (Here β is the learning rate.)

$$U_t = \max_a Q_t(a) \quad (5)$$

$$(\forall s_i | a_i = a_{t-1}) \, q(s_i) \leftarrow (1 - \beta v(s_i)) q(s_i) + \beta v(s_i)(r_i + \gamma U_t) \quad (6)$$

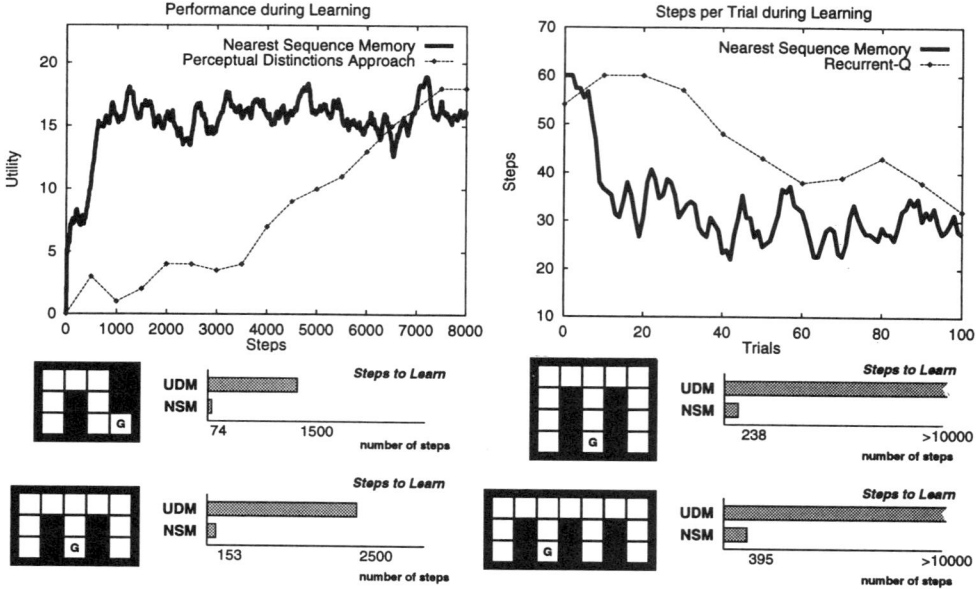

Figure 2: Comparing Nearest Sequence Memory with three other algorithms: Perceptual Distinction Approach, Recurrent-Q and Utile Distinction Memory. In each case, NSM learns with roughly an order of magnitude fewer steps.

5 EXPERIMENTAL RESULTS

The performance of NSM is compared to three other algorithms using the tasks chosen by the other algorithms' designers. In each case, NSM learns the task with roughly an order of magnitude fewer steps. Although NSM learns good policies quickly, it does not always learn optimal policies. In section 6 we will discuss why the policies are not always optimal and how NSM could be improved.

The Perceptual Distinctions Approach [Chrisman, 1992] was demonstrated in a space ship docking application with hidden state. The task was made difficult by noisy sensors and actions. Some of the sensors returned incorrect values 30% of the time. Various actions failed 70, 30 or 20% of the time, and when they failed, resulted in random states. NSM used $\beta = 0.2$, $\gamma = 0.9$, $k = 8$, and $N = 1000$. PDA takes almost 8000 steps to learn the task. NSM learns a good policy in less than 1000 steps, although the policy is not quite optimal.

Utile Distinction Memory [McCallum, 1993] was demonstrated on several local perception mazes. Unlike most reinforcement learning maze domains, the agent perceives only four bits indicating whether there is a barrier to the immediately adjacent north, east, south and west. NSM used $\beta = 0.9$, $\gamma = 0.9$, $k = 4$, and $N = 1000$. In two of the mazes, NSM learns the task in only about 1/20th the time required by UDM; in the other two, NSM learns mazes that UDM did not solve at all.

Recurrent-Q [Lin, 1993] was demonstrated on a robot 2-cup retrieval task. The environment is deterministic, but the task is made difficult by two nested levels of hidden state and by providing no reward until the task is completely finished. NSM used $\beta = 0.9$, $\gamma = 0.9$, $k = 4$, and $N = 1000$. NSM learns good performance in about 15 trials, Recurrent-Q takes about 100 trials to reach equivalent performance.

6 DISCUSSION

Nearest Sequence Memory offers much improved on-line performance and fewer training steps than its predecessors. Why is the improvement so dramatic? I believe the chief reason lies with the inherent advantage of instance-based methods, as described in section 2: the key idea behind Instance-Based State Identification is the recognition that recording raw experience is particularly advantageous when the agent is learning a policy over a changing state space granularity, as is the case when the agent is building short-term memory for disambiguating hidden state.

If, instead of using an instance-based technique, the agent simply averages new experiences into its current, flawed state space model, the experiences will be applied to the wrong states, and cannot be reused when the agent reconfigures its state space. Furthermore, and perhaps even more detrimentally, incoming data is always interpreted in the context of the flawed state space, always biased in an inappropriate way—not simply recorded, kept uncommitted and open to easy reinterpretation in light of future data.

The experimental results in this paper bode well for instance-based state identification. Nearest Sequence Memory is simple—if such a simplistic implementation works as well as it does, more sophisticated approaches may work even better. Here are some ideas for improvement:

The agent should use a more sophisticated neighborhood distance metric than exact string match length. A new metric could account for distances between different percepts instead of considering only exact matches. A new metric could also handle continuous-valued inputs.

Nearest Sequence Memory demonstrably solves tasks that involve noisy sensation and action, but it could perhaps handle noise even better if it used some technique for explicitly separating noise from structure. K-nearest neighbor does not explicitly discriminate between structure and noise. If the current query point has neighbors with wildly varying output values, there is no way to know if the variations are due to noise, (in which case they should all be averaged), or due to fine-grained structure of the underlying function (in which case only the few closest should be averaged). Because NSM is built on k-nearest neighbor, it suffers from the same inability to methodically separate history differences that are significant for predicting reward and history differences that are not. I believe this is the single most important reason that NSM sometimes did not find optimal policies.

Work in progress addresses the structure/noise issue by combining instance-based state identification with the structure/noise separation method from Utile Distinction Memory [McCallum, 1993]. The algorithm, called *Utile Suffix Memory*, uses a tree-structured representation, and is related to work with Ron, Singer and Tishby's Prediction Suffix Trees, Moore's Parti-game, Chapman and Kaelbling's

G-algorithm, and Moore's Variable Resolution Dynamic Programming. See [McCallum, 1994] for more details as well as references to this related work.

Acknowledgments

This work has benefited from discussions with many colleagues, including: Dana Ballard, Andrew Moore, Jeff Schneider, and Jonas Karlsson. This material is based upon work supported by NSF under Grant no. IRI-8903582 and by NIH/PHS under Grant no. 1 R24 RR06853-02.

References

[Atkeson, 1992] Christopher G. Atkeson. Memory-based approaches to approximating continuous functions. In M. Casdagli and S. Eubank, editors, *Nonlinear Modeling and Forecasting*, pages 503–521. Addison Wesley, 1992.

[Bertsekas and Shreve, 1978] Dimitri. P. Bertsekas and Steven E. Shreve. *Stochastic Optimal Control*. Academic Press, 1978.

[Chrisman, 1992] Lonnie Chrisman. Reinforcement learning with perceptual aliasing: The perceptual distinctions approach. In *Tenth Nat'l Conf. on AI*, 1992.

[Jaakkola et al., 1995] Tommi Jaakkola, Satinder Pal Singh, and Michael I. Jordan. Reinforcement learning algorithm for partially observable markov decision problems. In *Advances of Neural Information Processing Systems 7*. Morgan Kaufmann, 1995.

[Lin, 1993] Long-Ji Lin. *Reinforcement Learning for Robots Using Neural Networks*. PhD thesis, Carnegie Mellon, School of Computer Science, January 1993.

[Littman, 1994] Michael Littman. Memoryless policies: Theoretical limitations and practical results. In *Proceedings of the Third International Conference on Simulation of Adaptive Behavior: From Animals to Animats*, 1994.

[McCallum, 1993] R. Andrew McCallum. Overcoming incomplete perception with utile distinction memory. In *The Proceedings of the Tenth International Machine Learning Conference*. Morgan Kaufmann Publishers, Inc., 1993.

[McCallum, 1994] R. Andrew McCallum. Utile suffix memory for reinforcement learning with hidden state. TR 549, U. of Rochester, Computer Science, 1994.

[McCallum, 1995] R. Andrew McCallum. Hidden state and reinforcement learning with instance-based state identification. *IEEE Trans. on Systems, Man, and Cybernetics*, 1995. (In press) [Earlier version available as U. of Rochester TR 502].

[Moore, 1992] Andrew Moore. *Efficient Memory-based Learning for Robot Control*. PhD thesis, University of Cambridge, November 1992.

[Singh et al., 1994] Satinder Pal Singh, Tommi Jaakkola, and Michael I. Jordan. Model-free reinforcement learning for non-markovian decision problems. In *The Proceedings of the Eleventh International Machine Learning Conference*, 1994.

[Teller, 1994] Astro Teller. The evolution of mental models. In Kim Kinnear, editor, *Advances in Genetic Programming*, chapter 9. MIT Press, 1994.

[Watkins, 1989] Chris Watkins. *Learning from delayed rewards*. PhD thesis, Cambridge University, 1989.

[Whitehead, 1992] Steven Whitehead. *Reinforcement Learning for the Adaptive Control of Perception and Action*. PhD thesis, Department of Computer Science, University of Rochester, 1992.

Finding Structure in Reinforcement Learning

Sebastian Thrun
University of Bonn
Department of Computer Science III
Römerstr. 164, D-53117 Bonn, Germany
E-mail: thrun@carbon.informatik.uni-bonn.de

Anton Schwartz
Dept. of Computer Science
Stanford University
Stanford, CA 94305
Email: schwartz@cs.stanford.edu

Abstract

Reinforcement learning addresses the problem of learning to select actions in order to maximize one's performance in unknown environments. To scale reinforcement learning to complex real-world tasks, such as typically studied in AI, one must ultimately be able to discover the structure in the world, in order to abstract away the myriad of details and to operate in more tractable problem spaces.

This paper presents the SKILLS algorithm. SKILLS discovers skills, which are partially defined action policies that arise in the context of multiple, related tasks. Skills collapse whole action sequences into single operators. They are learned by minimizing the compactness of action policies, using a description length argument on their representation. Empirical results in simple grid navigation tasks illustrate the successful discovery of structure in reinforcement learning.

1 Introduction

Reinforcement learning comprises a family of incremental planning algorithms that construct reactive controllers through real-world experimentation. A key scaling problem of reinforcement learning, as is generally the case with unstructured planning algorithms, is that in large real-world domains there might be an enormous number of decisions to be made, and pay-off may be sparse and delayed. Hence, instead of learning all single fine-grain actions all at the same time, one could conceivably learn much faster if one abstracted away the myriad of micro-decisions, and focused instead on a small set of important decisions. But this immediately raises the problem of how to recognize the important, and how to distinguish it from the unimportant.

This paper presents the SKILLS algorithm. SKILLS finds partially defined action policies, called skills, that occur in more than one task. Skills, once found, constitute parts of solutions to multiple reinforcement learning problems. In order to find maximally useful skills, a description length argument is employed. Skills reduce the number of bytes required to describe action policies. This is because instead of having to describe a complete action policy for each task separately, as is the case in plain reinforcement learning, skills constrain multiple task to pick the same actions, and thus reduce the total number of actions required for representing action policies. However, using skills comes at a price. In general, one cannot constrain actions to be the same in multiple tasks without ultimately suffering a loss in performance. Hence, in order to find maximally useful skills that infer a minimum loss in performance, the SKILLS algorithm minimizes a function of the form

$$E = \text{PERFORMANCE LOSS} + \eta \cdot \text{DESCRIPTION LENGTH}. \tag{1}$$

This equation summarizes the rationale of the SKILLS approach. The reminder of this paper gives more precise definitions and learning rules for the terms *"PERFORMANCE LOSS"* and *"DESCRIPTION LENGTH,"* using the vocabulary of reinforcement learning. In addition, experimental results empirically illustrate the successful discovery of skills in simple grid navigation domains.

2 Reinforcement Learning

Reinforcement learning addresses the problem of learning, through experimentation, to act so as to maximize one's pay-off in an unknown environment. Throughout this paper we will assume that the environment of the learner is a *partially controllable Markov chain* [1]. At any instant in time the learner can observe the state of the environment, denoted by $s \in S$, and apply an action, $a \in A$. Actions change the state of the environment, and also produce a scalar pay-off value, denoted by $r_{s,a} \in \Re$. Reinforcement learning seeks to identify an *action policy*, $\pi : S \longrightarrow A$, *i.e.*, a mapping from states $s \in S$ to actions $a \in A$ that, if actions are selected accordingly, maximizes the *expected discounted sum of future pay-off*

$$R = E\left[\sum_{t=t_0}^{\infty} \gamma^{t-t_0} r_t\right]. \tag{2}$$

Here γ (with $0 \leq \gamma \leq 1$) is a *discount factor* that favors pay-offs reaped sooner in time, and r_t refers to the expected pay-off at time t. In general, pay-off might be delayed. Therefore, in order to learn an optimal π, one has to solve a *temporal credit assignment problem* [11].

To date, the single most widely used algorithm for learning from delayed pay-off is Q-Learning [14]. Q-Learning solves the problem of learning π by learning a *value function*, denoted by $Q : S \times A \longrightarrow \Re$. Q maps states $s \in S$ and actions $a \in A$ to scalar values. After learning, $Q(s, a)$ ranks actions according to their goodness: The larger the expected cumulative pay-off for picking action a at state s, the larger the value $Q(s, a)$. Hence Q, once learned, allows to maximize R by picking actions greedily with respect to Q:

$$\pi(s) = \underset{\hat{a} \in A}{\text{argmax}}\, Q(s, \hat{a})$$

The value function Q is learned on-line through experimentation. Initially, all values $Q(s, a)$ are set to zero. Suppose during learning the learner executes action a at state s, which leads to a new state s' and the immediate pay-off $r_{s,a}$. Q-Learning uses this state transition to update $Q(s, a)$:

$$Q(s, a) \longleftarrow (1 - \alpha) \cdot Q(s, a) + \alpha \cdot \left(r_{s,a} + \gamma \cdot V(s')\right) \tag{3}$$
$$\text{with}\quad V(s') = \max_{\hat{a}} Q(s', \hat{a})$$

The scalar α ($0<\alpha\leq 1$) is the *learning rate*, which is typically set to a small value that is decayed over time. Notice that if $Q(s, a)$ is represented by a lookup-table, as will be the case throughout this paper, the Q-Learning rule (3) has been shown[1] to converge to a value function $Q^{\text{opt}}(s, a)$ which measures the future discounted pay-off one can expect to receive upon applying action a in state s, and acting optimally thereafter [5, 14]. The greedy policy $\pi(s) = \text{argmax}_{\hat{a}}\, Q^{\text{opt}}(s, \hat{a})$ maximizes R.

---

[1] under certain conditions concerning the exploration scheme, the environment and the learning rate

3 Skills

Suppose the learner faces a whole collection of related tasks, denoted by B, with identical states S and actions A. Suppose each task $b \in B$ is characterized by its individual payoff function, denoted by $r_b(s, a)$. Different tasks may also face different state transition probabilities. Consequently, each task requires a task-specific value function, denoted by $Q_b(s, a)$, which induces a task-specific action policy, denoted by π_b. Obviously, plain Q-Learning, as described in the previous section, can be employed to learn these individual action policies. Such an approach, however, cannot discover the structure which might inherently exist in the tasks.

In order to identify commonalities between different tasks, the SKILLS algorithm allows a learner to acquire *skills*. A skill, denoted by k, represents an action policy, very much like π_b. There are two crucial differences, however. Firstly, skills are only locally defined, on a subset S_k of all states S. S_k is called the *domain of skill k*. Secondly, skills are not specific to individual tasks. Instead, they apply to entire sets of tasks, in which they replace the task-specific, local action policies.

Let K denote the set of all skills. In general, some skills may be appropriate for some tasks, but not for others. Hence, we define a vector of *usage values* $u_{k,b}$ (with $0 \leq u_{k,b} \leq 1$ for all $k \in K$ and all $b \in B$). Policies in the SKILLS algorithm are stochastic, and usages $u_{k,b}$ determine how frequently skill k is used in task b. At first glance, $u_{k,b}$ might be interpreted as a probability for using skill k when performing task b, and one might always want to use skill k in task b if $u_{k,b} = 1$, and never use skill k if $u_{k,b} = 0$.[2] However, skills might overlap, *i.e.*, there might be states s which occurs in several skill domains, and the usages might add to a value greater than 1. Therefore, usages are normalized, and actions are drawn probabilistically according to the normalized distribution:

$$P_b(k|s) = \frac{u_{b,k}^2 \cdot m_k(s)}{\sum_{k' \in K} u_{b,k'} \cdot m_{k'}(s)} \quad \text{(with } \tfrac{0}{0} = 0\text{)} \tag{4}$$

Here $P_b(k|s)$ denotes the *probability* for using skill k at state s, if the learner faces task b. The indicator function $m_k(s)$ is the *membership function* for skill domains, which is 1 if $s \in S_k$ and 0 otherwise. The probabilistic action selection rule (4) makes it necessary to redefine the value $V_b(s)$ of a state s. If no skill dictates the action to be taken, actions will be drawn according to the Q_b-optimal policy

$$\pi_b^*(s) = \underset{\hat{a} \in A}{\operatorname{argmax}} \, Q_b(s, \hat{a}) \,,$$

as is the case in plain Q-Learning. The probability for this to happen is

$$P_b^*(s) = 1 - \sum_{k \in K} P_b(k|s) \,.$$

Hence, the *value* of a state is the weighted sum

$$V_b(s) = P_b^*(s) \cdot V_b^*(s) + \sum_{k \in K} P_b(k|s) \cdot Q_b(s, \pi_k(s)) \tag{5}$$

$$\text{with } V_b^*(s) = Q_b(s, \pi_b^*(s)) = \max_{\hat{a} \in A} Q_b(s, \hat{a})$$

Why should a learner use skills, and what are the consequences? Skills reduce the freedom to select actions, since multiple policies have to commit to identical actions. Obviously, such

---

[2]This is exactly the action selection mechanism in the SKILLS algorithm if only *one* skill is applicable at any given state s.

a constraint will generally result in a *loss in performance*. This loss is obtained by comparing the actual value of each state s, $V_b(s)$, and the value if no skill is used, $V_b^*(s)$:

$$LOSS = \sum_{s \in S} \underbrace{\sum_{b \in B} V_b^*(s) - V_b(s)}_{= LOSS(s)} \tag{6}$$

If actions prescribed by the skills are close to optimal, *i.e.*, if $V_b^*(s) \approx V_b(s)(\forall s \in S)$, the loss will be small. If skill actions are poor, however, the loss can be large.

Counter-balancing this loss is the fact that skills give a more compact representation of the learner's policies. More specifically, assume (without loss of generality) actions can be represented by a single byte, and consider the total number of bytes it takes to represent the policies of all tasks $b \in B$. In the absence of skills, representing all individual policies requires $|B| \cdot |S|$ bytes, one byte for each state in S and each task in B. If skills are used across multiple tasks, the description length is reduced by the amount of overlap between different tasks. More specifically, the total description length required for the specification of all policies is expressed by the following term:

$$DL = \sum_{s \in S} \sum_{b \in B} P_b^*(s) + \sum_{k \in K} |S_k| = \sum_{s \in S} \underbrace{\left(\sum_{b \in B} P_b^*(s) + \sum_{k \in K} m_k(s) \right)}_{= DL(s)} \tag{7}$$

If all probabilities are binary, *i.e.*, $P_b(k|s)$ and $P_b^*(s) \in \{0, 1\}$, DL measures precisely the number of bytes needed to represent all skill actions, plus the number of bytes needed to represent task-specific policy actions where no skill is used. Eq. (7) generalizes this measure smoothly to stochastic policies. Notice that the number of skills $|K|$ is assumed to be constant and thus plays no part in the description length DL.

Obviously, minimizing $LOSS$ maximizes the pay-off, and minimizing DL maximizes the compactness of the representation of the learner's policies. In the SKILLS approach, one seeks to minimize both (*cf.* Eq. (1))

$$E = LOSS + \eta DL = \sum_{s \in S} LOSS(s) + \eta DL(s). \tag{8}$$

$\eta > 0$ is a gain parameter that trades off both target functions. E-optimal policies make heavily use of large skills, yet result in a minimum loss in performance. Notice that the state space may be partitioned completely by skills, and solutions to the individual tasks can be uniquely described by the skills and its usages. If such a complete partitioning does not exist, however, tasks may instead rely to some extent on task-specific, local policies.

4 Derivation of the Learning Algorithm

Each skill k is characterized by three types of adjustable variables: *skill actions* $\pi_k(s)$, the *skill domain* S_k, and *skill usages* $u_{b,k}$, one for each task $b \in B$. In this section we will give update rules that perform hill-climbing in E for each of these variables. As in Q-Learning these rules apply only at the currently visited state (henceforth denoted by s). Both learning action policies (*cf.* Eq. (3)) and learning skills is fully interleaved.

Actions. Determining skill actions is straightforward, since what action is prescribed by a skill exclusively affects the performance loss, but does not play any part in the description length. Hence, the action policy $\pi_k(s)$ minimizes $LOSS(s)$ (*cf.* Eqs. (5) and (6)):

$$\pi_k(s) = \operatorname*{argmax}_{\hat{a} \in A} \sum_{b \in B} P_b(k|s) \cdot Q_b(s, \hat{a}) \tag{9}$$

Domains. Initially, each skill domain S_k contains only a single state that is chosen at random. S_k is changed incrementally by minimizing $E(s)$ for states s which are visited during learning. More specifically, for each skill k, it is evaluated whether or not to include s in S_k by considering $E(s) = LOSS(s) + \eta DL(s)$.

$$s \in S_k, \quad \text{if and only if} \quad E(s)|_{s \in S_k} < E(s)|_{s \notin S_k} \quad \text{(otherwise } s \notin S_k) \tag{10}$$

If the domain of a skill k vanishes completely, *i.e.*, if $S_k = \emptyset$, it is re-initialized by a randomly selected state. In addition all usage values $\{u_{b,k} | b \in B\}$ are initialized randomly. This mechanism ensures that skills, once overturned by other skills, will not get lost forever.

Usages. Unlike skill domains, which are discrete quantities, usages are real-valued numbers. Initially, they are chosen at random in $[0, 1]$. Usages are optimized by stochastic gradient descent in E. According to Eq. (8), the derivative of $E(s)$ is the sum of $\frac{\partial LOSS(s)}{\partial u_{b,k}}$ and $\frac{\partial DL(s)}{\partial u_{b,k}}$. The first term is governed by

$$\frac{\partial LOSS(s)}{\partial u_{b,k}} = -\frac{\partial V_b(s)}{\partial u_{b,k}} = -\frac{\partial P_b^*(s)}{\partial u_{b,k}} \cdot Q_b(\pi_b^*(s), s) - \sum_{j \in K} \frac{\partial P_b(j|s)}{\partial u_{b,k}} \cdot Q_b(s, \pi_j(s))$$

with $\frac{\partial P_b(j|s)}{\partial u_{b,k}} = m_j(s) \cdot \left(\frac{2\delta_{kj} u_{b,j}}{\sum_{k' \in K} m_{k'}(s) u_{b,k'}} - \frac{u_{b,j}^2 m_k(s)}{\left(\sum_{k' \in K} m_{k'}(s) u_{b,k'}\right)^2} \right) \tag{11}$

and $\frac{\partial P_b^*(s)}{\partial u_{b,j}} = -\sum_{j \in K} \frac{\partial P_b(j|s)}{\partial u_{b,j}}. \tag{12}$

Here δ_{kj} denotes the Kronecker delta function, which is 1 if $k = j$ and 0 otherwise. The second term is given by

$$\frac{\partial DL(s)}{\partial u_{b,k}} = \frac{\partial P_b^*(s)}{\partial u_{k,b}}, \tag{13}$$

which can be further transformed using Eqs. (12) and (11). In order to minimize E, usages are incrementally refined in the opposite direction of the gradients:

$$u_{k,b} \longleftarrow u_{k,b} - \beta \cdot \left(\frac{\partial V(s)}{\partial u_{k,b}} + \eta \frac{\partial DL(s)}{\partial u_{k,b}} \right) \tag{14}$$

Here $\beta > 0$ is a small learning rate. This completes the derivation of the SKILLS algorithm. After each action execution, Q-Learning is employed to update the Q-function. SKILLS also re-calculates, for any applicable skill, the skill policy according to Eq. (9), and adjusts skill domains and usage values based upon Eqs. (10) and (14).

5 Experimental Results

The SKILLS algorithm was applied to discover skills in a simple, discrete grid-navigation domain, depicted in Fig. 1. At each state, the agent can move to one of at most eight adjacent grid cells. With a 10% chance the agent is carried to a random neighboring state, regardless of the commanded action. Each corner defines a starting state for one out of four task, with the corresponding goal state being in the opposite corner. The pay-off (costs) for executing actions is -1, except for the goal state, which is an absorbing state with zero pay-off. In a first experiment, we supplied the agent with two skills $K = \{k_1, k_2\}$. All four tasks were trained in a time-shared manner, with time slices being 2,000 steps long. We used the following parameter settings: $\eta = 1.2$, $\gamma = 1$, $\alpha = 0.1$, and $\beta = 0.001$.

After 30 000 training steps for each task, the SKILLS algorithm has successfully discovered the two skills shown in Figure 1. One of these skills leads the agent to the right door, and

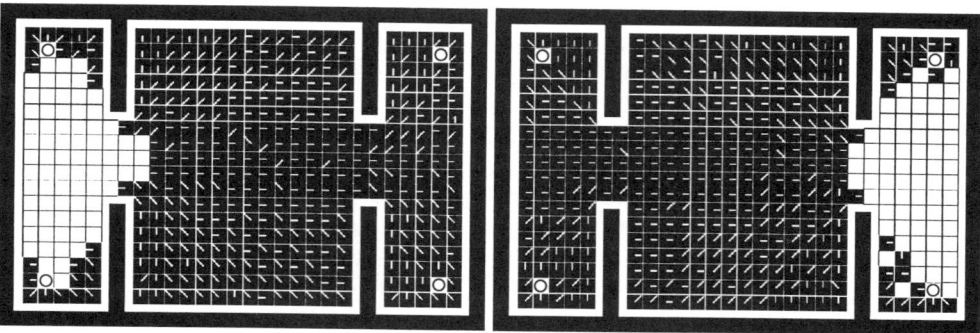

Figure 1: Simple 3-room environment. Start and goal states are marked by circles. The diagrams also shows two skills (black states), which lead to the doors connecting the rooms.

the second to the left. Each skill is employed by two tasks. By forcing two tasks to adopt a single policy in the region of the skill, they both have to sacrifice performance, but the loss in performance is considerably small. Beyond the door, however, optimal actions point into opposite directions. There, forcing both tasks to select actions according to the same policy would result in a significant performance loss, which would clearly outweigh the savings in description length. The solution shown in Fig. 1 is (approximately) the global minimum of E, given that only two skills are available. It is easy to be seen that these skills establish helpful building blocks for many navigation tasks.

When using more than two skills, E can be minimized further. We repeated the experiment using six skills, which can partition the state space in a more efficient way. Two of the resulting skills were similar to the skills shown in Fig. 1, but they were defined only between the doors. The other four skills were policies for moving out of a corner, one for each corner. Each of the latter four skills can be used in three tasks (unlike two tasks for passing through the middle room), resulting in an improved description length when compared to the two-skill solution shown in Fig. 1.

We also applied skill learning to a more complex grid world, using 25 skills for a total of 20 tasks. The environment, along with one of the skills, is depicted in Fig. 2. Different tasks were defined by different starting positions, goal positions and door configurations which could be open or closed. The training time was typically an order of magnitude slower than in the previous task, and skills were less stable over time. However, Fig. 2 illustrates that modular skills could be discovered even in such complex a domain.

6 Discussion

This paper presents the SKILLS algorithm. SKILLS learns skills, which are partial policies that are defined on a subset of all states. Skills are used in as many tasks as possible, while affecting the performance in these tasks as little as possible. They are discovered by minimizing a combined measure, which takes a task performance and a description length argument into account.

While our empirical findings in simple grid world domains are encouraging, there are several open questions that warrant future research.

Learning speed. In our experiments we found that the time required for finding useful skills is up to an order of magnitude larger than the time it takes to find close-to-optimal policies.

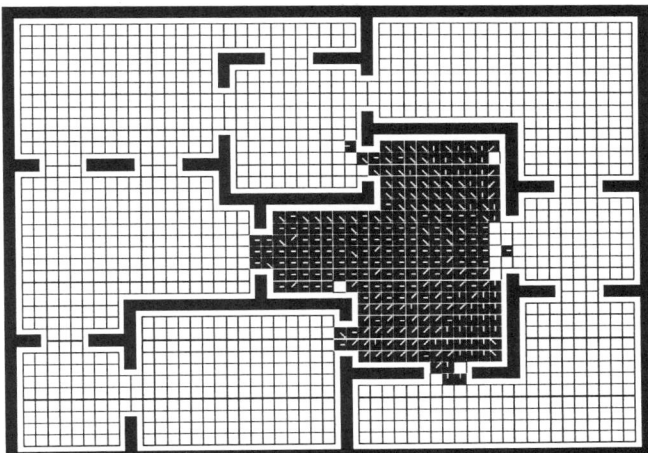

Figure 2: Skill found in a more complex grid navigation task.

Similar findings are reported in [9]. This is because discovering skills is much harder than learning control. Initially, nothing is know about the structure of the state space, and unless reasonably accurate Q-tables are available, SKILLS cannot discover meaningful skills. Faster methods for learning skills, which might precede the development of optimal value functions, are clearly desirable.

Transfer. We conjecture that skills can be helpful when one wants to learn new, related tasks. This is because if tasks are related, as is the case in many natural learning environments, skills allow to transfer knowledge from previously learned tasks to new tasks. In particular, if the learner faces tasks with increasing complexity, as proposed by Singh [10], learning skills could conceivable reduce the learning time in complex tasks, and hence scale reinforcement learning techniques to more complex tasks.

Using function approximators. In this paper, performance loss and description length has been defined based on table look-up representations of Q. Recently, various researchers have applied reinforcement learning in combination with generalizing function approximators, such as nearest neighbor methods or artificial neural networks (*e.g.*, [2, 4, 12, 13]). In order to apply the SKILLS algorithm together with generalizing function approximators, the notions of skill domains and description length have to be modified. For example, the membership function m_k, which defines the domain of a skill, could be represented by a function approximator which allows to derive gradients in the description length.

Generalization in state space. In the current form, SKILLS exclusively discovers skills that are used across multiple tasks. However, skills might be useful under multiple circumstances even in single tasks. For example, the (generalized) skill of climbing a staircase may be useful several times in one and the same task. SKILLS, in its current form, cannot represent such skills.

The key to learning such generalized skills is generalization. Currently, skills generalize exclusively over tasks, since they can be applied to entire sets of tasks. However, they cannot generalize over states. One could imagine an extension to the SKILLS algorithm, in which skills are free to pick what to generalize over. For example, they could chose to ignore certain state information (like the color of the staircase). It remains to be seen if effective learning mechanisms can be designed for learning such generalized skills.

Abstractions and action hierarchies. In recent years, several researchers have recognized the importance of structuring reinforcement learning in order to build abstractions and action hierarchies. Different approaches differ in the origin of the abstraction, and the way it is incorporated into learning. For example, abstractions have been built upon previously learned, simpler tasks [9, 10], previously learned low-level behaviors [7], subgoals, which are either known in advance [15] or determined at random [6], or based on a pyramid of different levels of perceptual resolution, which produces a whole spectrum of problem solving capabilities [3]. For all these approaches, drastically improved problem solving capabilities have been reported, which are far beyond that of plain, unstructured reinforcement learning. This paper exclusively focuses on how to discover the structure inherent in a family of related tasks. Using skills to form abstractions and learning in the resulting abstract problem spaces is beyond the scope of this paper. The experimental findings indicate, however, that skills are powerful candidates for operators on a more abstract level, because they collapse whole action sequences into single entities.

References

[1] A. G. Barto, S. J. Bradtke, and S. P. Singh. Learning to act using real-time dynamic programming. *Artificial Intelligence*, to appear.

[2] J. A. Boyan. Generalization in reinforcement learning: Safely approximating the value function. Same volume.

[3] P. Dayan and G. E. Hinton. Feudal reinforcement learning. In J. E. Moody, S. J. Hanson, and R. P. Lippmann, editors, *Advances in Neural Information Processing Systems 5*, 1993. Morgan Kaufmann.

[4] V. Gullapalli, J. A. Franklin, and Hamid B. Acquiring robot skills via reinforcement learning. *IEEE Control Systems*, 272(1708), 1994.

[5] T. Jaakkola, M. I. Jordan, and S. P. Singh. On the convergence of stochastic iterative dynamic programming algorithms. Technical Report 9307, Department of Brain and Cognitive Sciences, MIT, July 1993.

[6] L. P. Kaelbling. Hierarchical learning in stochastic domains: Preliminary results. In Paul E. Utgoff, editor, *Proceedings of the Tenth International Conference on Machine Learning*, 1993. Morgan Kaufmann.

[7] L.-J. Lin. *Self-supervised Learning by Reinforcement and Artificial Neural Networks*. PhD thesis, Carnegie Mellon University, School of Computer Science, 1992.

[8] M. Ring. Two methods for hierarchy learning in reinforcement environments. In *From Animals to Animates 2: Proceedings of the Second International Conference on Simulation of Adaptive Behavior*. MIT Press, 1993.

[9] S. P. Singh. Reinforcement learning with a hierarchy of abstract models. In *Proceeding of the Tenth National Conference on Artificial Intelligence AAAI-92*, 1992. AAAI Press/The MIT Press.

[10] S. P. Singh. Transfer of learning by composing solutions for elemental sequential tasks. *Machine Learning*, 8, 1992.

[11] R. S. Sutton. *Temporal Credit Assignment in Reinforcement Learning*. PhD thesis, Department of Computer and Information Science, University of Massachusetts, 1984.

[12] G. J. Tesauro. Practical issues in temporal difference learning. *Machine Learning*, 8, 1992.

[13] S. Thrun and A. Schwartz. Issues in using function approximation for reinforcement learning. In M. Mozer, Pa. Smolensky, D. Touretzky, J. Elman, and A. Weigend, editors, *Proceedings of the 1993 Connectionist Models Summer School*, 1993. Erlbaum Associates.

[14] C. J. C. H. Watkins. *Learning from Delayed Rewards*. PhD thesis, King's College, Cambridge, England, 1989.

[15] S. Whitehead, J. Karlsson, and J. Tenenberg. Learning multiple goal behavior via task decomposition and dynamic policy merging. In J. H. Connell and S. Mahadevan, editors, *Robot Learning*. Kluwer Academic Publisher, 1993.

Reinforcement Learning Methods for Continuous-Time Markov Decision Problems

Steven J. Bradtke
Computer Science Department
University of Massachusetts
Amherst, MA 01003
bradtke@cs.umass.edu

Michael O. Duff
Computer Science Department
University of Massachusetts
Amherst, MA 01003
duff@cs.umass.edu

Abstract

Semi-Markov Decision Problems are continuous time generalizations of discrete time Markov Decision Problems. A number of reinforcement learning algorithms have been developed recently for the solution of Markov Decision Problems, based on the ideas of asynchronous dynamic programming and stochastic approximation. Among these are TD(λ), Q-learning, and Real-time Dynamic Programming. After reviewing semi-Markov Decision Problems and Bellman's optimality equation in that context, we propose algorithms similar to those named above, adapted to the solution of semi-Markov Decision Problems. We demonstrate these algorithms by applying them to the problem of determining the optimal control for a simple queueing system. We conclude with a discussion of circumstances under which these algorithms may be usefully applied.

1 Introduction

A number of reinforcement learning algorithms based on the ideas of asynchronous dynamic programming and stochastic approximation have been developed recently for the solution of Markov Decision Problems. Among these are Sutton's TD(λ) [10], Watkins' Q-learning [12], and Real-time Dynamic Programming (RTDP) [1,

3]. These learning alogorithms are widely used, but their domain of application has been limited to processes modeled by discrete-time Markov Decision Problems (MDP's).

This paper derives analogous algorithms for semi-Markov Decision Problems (SMDP's) — extending the domain of applicability to continuous time. This effort was originally motivated by the desire to apply reinforcement learning methods to problems of adaptive control of queueing systems, and to the problem of adaptive routing in computer networks in particular. We apply the new algorithms to the well-known problem of routing to two heterogeneous servers [7]. We conclude with a discussion of circumstances under which these algorithms may be usefully applied.

2 Semi-Markov Decision Problems

A semi-Markov process is a continuous time dynamic system consisting of a countable state set, $\mathcal{X}$, and a finite action set, $\mathcal{A}$. Suppose that the system is originally observed to be in state $x \in \mathcal{X}$, and that action $a \in \mathcal{A}$ is applied. A semi-Markov process [9] then evolves as follows:

- The next state, y, is chosen according to the transition probabilities $P_{xy}(a)$
- A reward rate $\rho(x, a)$ is defined until the next transition occurs
- Conditional on the event that the next state is y, the time until the transition from x to y occurs has probability distribution $F_{xy}(\cdot|a)$

One form of the SMDP is to find a policy the minimizes the expected infinite horizon discounted cost, the "value" for each state:

$$\mathcal{E}\left\{\int_0^\infty e^{-\beta t}\rho(x(t),a(t))dt\right\},$$

where $x(t)$ and $a(t)$ denote, respectively, the state and action at time t.

For a fixed policy π, the value of a given state x must satisfy

$$V_\pi(x) = \sum_{y\in\mathcal{X}} P_{xy}(\pi(x)) \int_0^\infty \int_0^t e^{-\beta s}\rho(x,\pi(x))ds dF_{xy}(t|\pi(x)) + \\ \sum_{y\in\mathcal{X}} P_{xy}(\pi(x)) \int_0^\infty e^{-\beta t}V_\pi(y)dF_{xy}(t|\pi(x)). \quad (1)$$

Defining

$$R(x,y,a) = \int_0^\infty \int_0^t e^{-\beta s}\rho(x,\pi(x))ds dF_{xy}(t|\pi(x)),$$

the expected reward that will be received on transition from state x to state y on action a, and

$$\gamma(x,y,a) = \int_0^\infty e^{-\beta t}dF_{xy}(t|\pi(x)),$$

the expected discount factor to be applied to the value of state y on transition from state x on action a, it is clear that equation (1) is nearly identical to the value-function equation for discrete time Markov reward processes,

$$V_\pi(x) = R(x, \pi(x)) + \gamma \sum_{y \in \mathcal{X}} P_{xy}(\pi(x)) V_\pi(y), \qquad (2)$$

where $R(x, a) = \sum_{y \in \mathcal{X}} P_{xy}(a) R(x, y, a)$. If transition times are identically one for an SMDP, then a standard discrete-time MDP results.

Similarly, while the value function associated with an *optimal* policy for an MDP satisfies the Bellman optimality equation

$$V^*(x) = \max_{a \in \mathcal{A}} \left\{ R(x, a) + \gamma \sum_{y \in \mathcal{X}} P_{xy}(a) V^*(y) \right\}, \qquad (3)$$

the optimal value function for an SMDP satisfies the following version of the Bellman optimality equation:

$$V^*(x) = \max_{a \in \mathcal{A}} \left\{ \sum_{y \in \mathcal{X}} P_{xy}(a) \int_0^\infty \int_0^t e^{-\beta s} \rho(x,a) ds dF_{xy}(t|a) + \sum_{y \in \mathcal{X}} P_{xy}(a) \int_0^\infty e^{-\beta t} V^*(y) dF_{xy}(t|a) \right\}. \qquad (4)$$

3 Temporal Difference learning for SMDP's

Sutton's TD(0) [10] is a stochastic approximation method for finding solutions to the system of equations (2). Having observed a transition from state x to state y with sample reward $r(x, y, \pi(x))$, TD(0) updates the value function estimate $V^{(k)}(x)$ in the direction of the sample value $r(x, y, \pi(x)) + \gamma V^{(k)}(y)$. The TD(0) update rule for MDP's is

$$V^{(k+1)}(x) = V^{(k)}(x) + \alpha_k [r(x, y, \pi(x)) + \gamma V^{(k)}(y) - V^{(k)}(x)], \qquad (5)$$

where α_k is the learning rate. The sequence of value-function estimates generated by the TD(0) proceedure will converge to the true solution, V_π, with probability one [5, 8, 11] under the appropriate conditions on the α_k and on the definition of the MDP.

The TD(0) learning rule for SMDP's, intended to solve the system of equations (1) given a sequence of sampled state transitions, is:

$$V^{(k+1)}(x) = V^{(k)}(x) + \alpha_k \left[\frac{1 - e^{-\beta \tau}}{\beta} r(x, y, \pi(x)) + e^{-\beta \tau} V^{(k)}(y) - V^{(k)}(x) \right], \qquad (6)$$

where the sampled transition time from state x to state y was τ time units, $\frac{1-e^{-\beta \tau}}{\beta} r(x, y, \pi(x))$ is the sample reward received in τ time units, and $e^{-\beta \tau}$ is the sample discount on the value of the next state given a transition time of τ time units. The TD(λ) learning rule for SMDP's is straightforward to define from here.

4 Q-learning for SMDP's

Denardo [6] and Watkins [12] define Q_π, the Q-function corresponding to the policy π, as

$$Q_\pi(x,a) = R(x,a) + \gamma \sum_{y \in \mathcal{X}} P_{xy}(a) V_\pi(y) \tag{7}$$

Notice that a can be *any* action. It is not necesarily the action $\pi(x)$ that would be chosen by policy π. The function Q^* corresponds to the optimal policy. $Q_\pi(x,a)$ represents the total discounted return that can be expected if any action is taken from state x, and policy π is followed thereafter. Equation (7) can be rewritten as

$$Q_\pi(x,a) = R(x,a) + \gamma \sum_{y \in \mathcal{X}} P_{xy}(a) Q_\pi(y, \pi(y)), \tag{8}$$

and Q^* satisfies the Bellman-style optimality equation

$$Q^*(x,a) = R(x,a) + \gamma \sum_{y \in \mathcal{X}} P_{xy}(a) \max_{a' \in \mathcal{A}} Q^*(y,a'), \tag{9}$$

Q-learning, first described by Watkins [12], uses stochastic approximation to iteratively refine an estimate for the function Q^*. The Q-learning rule is very similar to TD(0). Upon a sampled transition from state x to state y upon selection of a, with sampled reward $r(x,y,a)$, the Q-function estimate is updated according to

$$Q^{(k+1)}(x,a) = Q^{(k)}(x,a) + \alpha_k \left[r(x,y,a) + \gamma \max_{a'} Q^{(k)}(y,a') - Q^{(k)}(x,a) \right]. \tag{10}$$

Q-functions may also be defined for SMDP's. The optimal Q-function for an SMDP satisfies the equation

$$\begin{aligned} Q^*(x,a) &= \sum_{y \in \mathcal{X}} P_{xy}(a) \int_0^\infty \int_0^t e^{-\beta s} \rho(x,a) ds dF_{xy}(t|a) + \\ &\quad \sum_{y \in \mathcal{X}} P_{xy}(a) \int_0^\infty e^{-\beta t} \max_{a' \in \mathcal{A}} Q^*(y,a') dF_{xy}(t|a). \end{aligned} \tag{11}$$

This leads to the following Q-learning rule for SMDP's:

$$Q^{(k+1)}(x,a) = Q^{(k)}(x,a) + \alpha_k \left[\frac{1 - e^{-\beta \tau}}{\beta} r(x,y,a) + e^{-\beta \tau} \max_{a'} Q^{(k)}(y,a') - Q^{(k)}(x,a) \right] \tag{12}$$

5 RTDP and Adaptive RTDP for SMDP's

The TD(0) and Q-learning algorithms are model-free, and rely upon stochastic approximation for asymptotic convergence to the desired function (V_π and Q^*, respectively). Convergence is typically rather slow. Real-Time Dynamic Programming (RTDP) and Adaptive RTDP [1, 3] use a system model to speed convergence.

RTDP assumes that a system model is known *a priori*; Adaptive RTDP builds a model as it interacts with the system. As discussed by Barto *et al.* [1], these asynchronous DP algorithms can have computational advantages over traditional DP algorithms even when a system model is given.

Inspecting equation (4), we see that the model needed by RTDP in the SMDP domain consists of three parts:

1. the state transition probabilities $P_{xy}(a)$,

2. the expected reward on transition from state x to state y using action a, $R(x, y, a)$, and

3. the expected discount factor to be applied to the value of the next state on transition from state x to state y using action a, $\gamma(x, y, a)$.

If the process dynamics are governed by a continuous time Markov chain, then the model needed by RTDP can be analytically derived through *uniformization* [2]. In general, however, the model can be very difficult to analytically derive. In these cases Adaptive RTDP can be used to incrementally build a system model through direct interaction with the system. One version of the Adaptive RTDP algorithm for SMDP's is described in Figure 1.

```
1   Set k = 0, and set x_0 to some start state.
2   Initialize P̂, R̂, and γ̂.
3   repeat forever {
4       For all actions a, compute
```
$$Q^{(k)}(x_k, a) = \sum_{y \in \mathcal{X}} \hat{P}_{x_k y}(a) \left[\hat{R}(x_k, y, a) + \hat{\gamma}(x_k, y, a) V^{(k)}(y) \right]$$
```
5       Perform the update V^(k+1)(x_k) = min_{a∈A} Q^(k)(x_k, a)
6       Select an action, a_k.
7       Perform a_k and observe the transition to x_{k+1} after τ time units. Update
```
$\hat{P}$. Use the sample reward $\frac{1-e^{-\beta\tau}}{\beta}r(x_k, x_{k+1}, a_k)$ and the sample discount factor $e^{-\beta\tau}$ to update $\hat{R}$ and $\hat{\gamma}$.
```
8       k = k + 1
9   }
```

Figure 1: Adaptive RTDP for SMDP's. $\hat{P}$, $\hat{R}$, and $\hat{\gamma}$ are the estimates maintained by Adaptive RTDP of P, R, and γ.

Notice that the action selection procedure (line 6) is left unspecified. Unlike RTDP, Adaptive RTDP can not always choose the greedy action. This is because it only has an *estimate* of the system model on which to base its decisions, and the estimate could initially be quite inaccurate. Adaptive RTDP needs to explore, to choose actions that do not currently appear to be optimal, in order to ensure that the estimated model converges to the true model over time.

6 Experiment: Routing to two heterogeneous servers

Consider the queueing system shown in Figure 2. Arrivals are assumed to be Poisson with rate λ. Upon arrival, a customer must be routed to one of the two queues, whose servers have service times that are exponentially distributed with parameters μ_1 and μ_2 respectively. The goal is compute a policy that minimizes the objective function:

$$\mathcal{E}\left\{\int_0^\infty e^{-\beta t}[c_1 n_1(t) + c_2 n_2(t)]dt\right\},$$

where c_1 and c_2 are scalar cost factors, and $n_1(t)$ and $n_2(t)$ denote the number of customers in the respective queues at time t. The pair $(n_1(t), n_2(t))$ is the state of the system at time t; the state space for this problem is countably infinite. There are two actions available at every state: if an arrival occurs, route it to queue 1 or route it to queue 2.

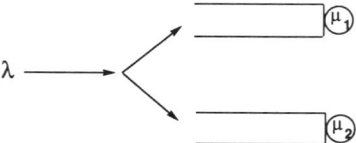

Figure 2: Routing to two queueing systems.

It is known for this problem (and many like it [7]), that the optimal policy is a *threshold* policy; i.e., the set of states S_1 for which it is optimal to route to the first queue is characterized by a monotonically nondecreasing threshold function F via $S_1 = \{(n_1, n_2)|n_1 \leq F(n_2)\}$. For the case where $c_1 = c_2 = 1$ and $\mu_1 = \mu_2$, the policy is simply to join the shortest queue, and the theshold function is a line slicing diagonally through the state space.

We applied the SMDP version of Q-learning to this problem in an attempt to find the optimal policy for some subset of the state space. The system parameters were set to $\lambda = \mu_1 = \mu_2 = 1$, $\beta = 0.1$, and $c_1 = c_2 = 1$. We used a feedforward neural network trained using backpropagation as a function approximator.

Q-learning must take exploratory actions in order to adequately sample all of the available state transitions. At each decision time k, we selected the action a_k to be applied to state x_k via the Boltzmann distribution

$$Pr\{a_k = a\} = \frac{e^{-Q^{(k)}(x_k, a)/T_k}}{\sum_{a' \in \mathcal{A}} e^{-Q^{(k)}(x_k, a')/T_k}},$$

where T_k is the "computational temperature." The temperature is initialized to a relatively high value, resulting in a uniform distribution for prospective actions. T_k is gradually lowered as computation proceeds, raising the probability of selecting actions with lower (and for this application, better) Q-values. In the limit, the action that is greedy with respect to the Q-function estimate is selected. The temperature and the learning rate α_k are decreased over time using a "search then converge" method [4].

Figure 3 shows the results obtained by Q-learning for this problem. Each square denotes a state visited, with $n_1(t)$ running along the x-axis, and $n_2(t)$ along the y-axis. The color of each square represents the probability of choosing action 1 (route arrivals to queue 1). Black represents probability 1, white represents probability 0. An optimal policy would be black above the diagonal, white below the diagonal, and could have arbitrary colors along the diagonal.

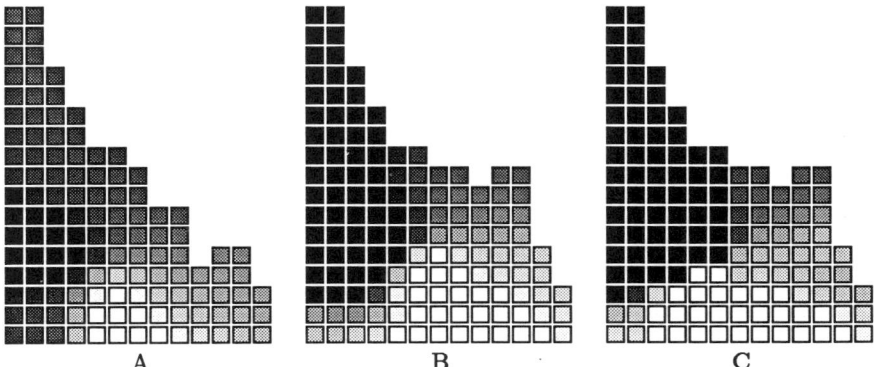

Figure 3: Results of the Q-learning experiment. Panel A represents the policy after 50,000 total updates, Panel B represents the policy after 100,000 total updates, and Panel C represents the policy after 150,000 total updates.

One unsatisfactory feature of the algorithm's performance is that convergence is rather slow, though the schedules governing the decrease of Boltzmann temperature T_k and learning rate α_k involve design parameters whose tweakings may result in faster convergence. If it is known that the optimal policies are of theshold type, or that some other structural property holds, then it may be of extreme practical utility to make use of this fact by constraining the value-functions in some way or perhaps by representing them as a combination of appropriate basis vectors that implicity realize or enforce the given structural property.

7 Discussion

In this paper we have proposed extending the applicability of well-known reinforcement learning methods developed for discrete-time MDP's to the continuous time domain. We derived semi-Markov versions of TD(0), Q-learning, RTDP, and Adaptive RTDP in a straightforward way from their discrete-time analogues. While we have not given any convergence proofs for these new algorithms, such proofs should not be difficult to obtain if we limit ourselves to problems with finite state spaces. (Proof of convergence for these new algorithms is complicated by the fact that, in general, the state spaces involved are infinite; convergence proofs for traditional reinforcement learning methods assume the state space is finite.) Ongoing work is directed toward applying these techniques to more complicated systems, examining distributed control issues, and investigating methods for incorporating prior knowledge (such as structured function approximators).

Acknowledgements

Thanks to Professor Andrew Barto, Bob Crites, and to the members of the Adaptive Networks Laboratory. This work was supported by the National Science Foundation under Grant ECS-9214866 to Professor Barto.

References

[1] A. G. Barto, S. J. Bradtke, and S. P. Singh. Learning to act using real-time dynamic programming. *Artificial Intelligence*. Accepted.

[2] D. P. Bertsekas. *Dynamic Programming: Deterministic and Stochastic Models*. Prentice Hall, Englewood Cliffs, NJ, 1987.

[3] S. J. Bradtke. *Incremental Dynamic Programming for On-line Adaptive Optimal Control*. PhD thesis, University of Massachusetts, 1994.

[4] C. Darken, J. Chang, and J. Moody. Learning rate schedules for faster stochastic gradient search. In *Neural Networks for Signal Processing 2 — Proceedings of the 1992 IEEE Workshop*. IEEE Press, 1992.

[5] P. Dayan and T. J. Sejnowski. Td(λ): Convergence with probability 1. *Machine Learning*, 1994.

[6] E. V. Denardo. Contraction mappings in the theory underlying dynamic programming. *SIAM Review*, 9(2):165–177, April 1967.

[7] B. Hajek. Optimal control of two interacting service stations. *IEEE-TAC*, 29:491–499, 1984.

[8] T. Jaakkola, M. I. Jordan, and S. P. Singh. On the convergence of stochastic iterative dynamic programming algorithms. *Neural Computation*, 1994.

[9] S. M. Ross. *Applied Probability Models with Optimization Applications*. Holden-Day, San Francisco, 1970.

[10] R. S. Sutton. Learning to predict by the method of temporal differences. *Machine Learning*, 3:9–44, 1988.

[11] J. N. Tsitsiklis. Asynchronous stochastic approximation and Q-learning. Technical Report LIDS-P-2172, Laboratory for Information and Decision Systems, MIT, Cambridge, MA, 1993.

[12] C. J. C. H. Watkins. *Learning from Delayed Rewards*. PhD thesis, Cambridge University, Cambridge, England, 1989.

An Actor/Critic Algorithm that is Equivalent to Q-Learning

Robert H. Crites
Computer Science Department
University of Massachusetts
Amherst, MA 01003
crites@cs.umass.edu

Andrew G. Barto
Computer Science Department
University of Massachusetts
Amherst, MA 01003
barto@cs.umass.edu

Abstract

We prove the convergence of an actor/critic algorithm that is equivalent to Q-learning by construction. Its equivalence is achieved by encoding Q-values within the policy and value function of the actor and critic. The resultant actor/critic algorithm is novel in two ways: it updates the critic only when the most probable action is executed from any given state, and it rewards the actor using criteria that depend on the relative probability of the action that was executed.

1 INTRODUCTION

In actor/critic learning systems, the actor implements a stochastic policy that maps states to action probability vectors, and the critic attempts to estimate the value of each state in order to provide more useful reinforcement feedback to the actor. The result is two interacting adaptive processes: the actor adapts to the critic, while the critic adapts to the actor.

The foundations of actor/critic learning systems date back at least to Samuel's checker program in the late 1950s (Samuel,1963). Examples of actor/critic systems include Barto, Sutton, & Anderson's (1983) ASE/ACE architecture and Sutton's (1990) Dyna-PI architecture. Sutton (1988) notes that the *critic* in these systems performs temporal credit assignment using what he calls *temporal difference* (TD) methods. Barto, Sutton, & Watkins (1990) note a relationship between actor/critic architectures and a dynamic programming (DP) algorithm known as *policy iteration*.

Although DP is a collection of general methods for solving Markov decision processes (MDPs), these algorithms are computationally infeasible for problems with very large state sets. Indeed, classical DP algorithms require multiple complete sweeps of the entire state set. However, progress has been made recently in developing asynchronous, incremental versions of DP that can be run online concurrently with control (Watkins, 1989; Barto et al, 1993). Most of the theoretical results for incremental DP have been for algorithms based on a DP algorithm known as *value iteration*. Examples include Watkins' (1989) Q-learning algorithm (motivated by a desire for on-line learning), and Bertsekas & Tsitsiklis' (1989) results on asynchronous DP (motivated by a desire for parallel implementations). Convergence proofs for incremental algorithms based on *policy iteration* (such as actor/critic algorithms) have been slower in coming.

Williams & Baird (1993) provide a valuable analysis of the convergence of certain actor/critic learning systems that use deterministic policies. They assume that a model of the MDP (including all the transition probabilities and expected rewards) is available, allowing the use of operations that look ahead to all possible next states. When a model is not available for the evaluation of alternative actions, one must resort to other methods for exploration, such as the use of stochastic policies. We prove convergence for an actor/critic algorithm that uses stochastic policies and does not require a model of the MDP.

The key idea behind our proof is to construct an actor/critic algorithm that is equivalent to Q-learning. It achieves this equivalence by encoding Q-values within the policy and value function of the actor and critic. By illustrating the way Q-learning appears as an actor/critic algorithm, the construction sheds light on two significant differences between Q-learning and traditional actor/critic algorithms. Traditionally, the critic attempts to provide feedback to the actor by estimating V^π, the value function corresponding to the current policy π. In our construction, instead of estimating V^π, the critic directly estimates the optimal value function V^*. In practice, this means that the value function estimate $\hat{V}$ is updated only when the *most probable* action is executed from any given state. In addition, our actor is provided with more discriminating feedback, based not only on the TD error, but also on the relative probability of the action that was executed. By adding these modifications, we can show that this algorithm behaves exactly like Q-learning constrained by a particular exploration strategy. Since a number of proofs of the convergence of Q-learning already exist (Tsitsiklis, 1994; Jaakkola et al, 1993; Watkins & Dayan, 1992), the fact that this algorithm behaves exactly like Q-learning implies that it too converges to the optimal value function with probability one.

2 MARKOV DECISION PROCESSES

Actor/critic and Q-learning algorithms are usually studied within the Markov decision process framework. In a finite MDP, at each discrete time step, an agent observes the state x from a finite set X, and selects an action a from a finite set A_x by using a stochastic policy π that assigns a probability to each action in A_x. The agent receives a reward with expected value $R(x, a)$, and the state at the next time step is y with probability $p^a(x, y)$. For any policy π and $x \in X$, let $V^\pi(x)$ denote the *expected infinite-horizon discounted return* from x given that the agent uses policy π. Letting r_t denote the reward at time t, this is defined as:

$$V^\pi(x) = E_\pi\left[\sum_{t=0}^\infty \gamma^t r_t | x_0 = x\right], \tag{1}$$

where x_0 is the initial state, $0 \leq \gamma < 1$ is a factor used to discount future rewards, and E_π is the expectation assuming the agent always uses policy π. It is usual to call $V^\pi(x)$ the *value* of x under π. The function V^π is the *value function* corresponding to π. The objective is to find an optimal policy, i.e., a policy, π^*, that maximizes the value of each state x defined by (1). The unique *optimal value function*, V^*, is the value function corresponding to any optimal policy. Additional details on this and other types of MDPs can be found in many references.

3 ACTOR/CRITIC ALGORITHMS

A generic actor/critic algorithm is as follows:

1. Initialize the stochastic policy and the value function estimate.

2. From the current state x, execute action a randomly according to the current policy. Note the next state y, the reward r, and the TD error

   $$\varepsilon = [r + \gamma \hat{V}(y)] - \hat{V}(x),$$

   where $0 \leq \gamma < 1$ is the discount factor.

3. Update the actor by adjusting the action probabilities for state x using the TD error. If $\varepsilon > 0$, action a performed relatively well and its probability should be increased. If $\varepsilon < 0$, action a performed relatively poorly and its probability should be decreased.

4. Update the critic by adjusting the estimated value of state x using the TD error:

   $$\hat{V}(x) \leftarrow \hat{V}(x) + \alpha\, \varepsilon$$

   where α is the learning rate.

5. $x \leftarrow y$. Go to step 2.

There are a variety of implementations of this generic algorithm in the literature. They differ in the exact details of how the policy is stored and updated. Barto et al (1990) and Lin (1993) store the action probabilities indirectly using parameters $w(x, a)$ that need not be positive, and need not sum to one. Increasing (or decreasing) the probability of action a in state x is accomplished by increasing (or decreasing) the value of the parameter $w(x, a)$. Sutton (1990) modifies the generic algorithm so that these parameters can be interpreted as action value estimates. He redefines ε in step 2 as follows:

$$\varepsilon = [r + \gamma \hat{V}(y)] - w(x, a).$$

For this reason, the Dyna-PI architecture (Sutton, 1990) and the modified actor/critic algorithm we present below both reward less probable actions more readily because of their lower estimated values.

Barto et al (1990) select actions by adding exponentially distributed random numbers to each parameter $w(x, a)$ for the current state, and then executing the action with the maximum sum. Sutton (1990) and Lin (1993) convert the parameters $w(x, a)$ into action probabilities using the Boltzmann distribution, where given a temperature T, the probability of selecting action i in state x is

$$\frac{e^{w(x,i)/T}}{\sum_{a \in A_x} e^{w(x,a)/T}}.$$

In spite of the empirical success of these algorithms, their convergence has never been proven.

4 Q-LEARNING

Rather than learning the values of states, the Q-learning algorithm learns the values of state/action pairs. $Q(x, a)$ is the expected discounted return obtained by performing action a in state x and performing optimally thereafter. Once the Q function has been learned, an optimal action in state x is any action that maximizes $Q(x, \cdot)$. Whenever an action a is executed from state x, the Q-value estimate for that state/action pair is updated as follows:

$$\hat{Q}(x, a) \leftarrow \hat{Q}(x, a) + \alpha_{xa}(n) \left[r + \gamma \max_{b \in A_y} \hat{Q}(y, b) - \hat{Q}(x, a) \right],$$

where $\alpha_{xa}(n)$ is the non-negative learning rate used the nth time action a is executed from state x. Q-Learning does not specify an exploration mechanism, but requires that all actions be tried infinitely often from all states. In actor/critic learning systems, exploration is fully determined by the action probabilities of the actor.

5 A MODIFIED ACTOR/CRITIC ALGORITHM

For each value $v \in \Re$, the modified actor/critic algorithm presented below uses an invertible function, H_v, that assigns a real number to each action probability ratio:

$$H_v : (0, \infty) \to \Re.$$

Each H_v must be a continuous, strictly increasing function such that $H_v(1) = v$, and

$$H_{H_v(z_2)}\left(\frac{z_1}{z_2}\right) = H_v(z_1) \text{ for all } z_1, z_2 > 0.$$

One example of such a class of functions is $H_v(z) = T \ln(z) + v$, $v \in \Re$, for some positive T. This class of functions corresponds to Boltzmann exploration in Q-learning. Thus, a kind of simulated annealing can be accomplished in the modified actor/critic algorithm (as is often done in Q-learning) by gradually lowering the "temperature" T and appropriately renormalizing the action probabilities. It is also possible to restrict the range of H_v if bounds on the possible values for a given MDP are known *a priori*.

For a state x, let p_a be the probability of action a, let p_{max} be the probability of the most probable action, a_{max}, and let $z_a = \frac{p_a}{p_{max}}$.

The modified actor/critic algorithm is as follows:

1. Initialize the stochastic policy and the value function estimate.
2. From the current state x, execute an action randomly according to the current policy. Call it action i. Note the next state y and the immediate reward r, and let
$$\varepsilon = [r + \gamma \hat{V}(y)] - H_{\hat{V}(x)}(z_i).$$
3. Increase the probability of action i if $\varepsilon > 0$, and decrease its probability if $\varepsilon < 0$. The precise probability update is as follows. First calculate
$$z_i^* = H_{\hat{V}(x)}^{-1}[H_{\hat{V}(x)}(z_i) + \alpha_{xi}(n)\,\varepsilon].$$
Then determine the new action probabilities by dividing by normalization factor $N = z_i^* + \sum_{j \neq i} z_j$, as follows:
$$p_i \leftarrow \tfrac{z_i^*}{N}, \quad \text{and} \quad p_j \leftarrow \tfrac{z_j}{N}, \ j \neq i.$$
4. Update $\hat{V}(x)$ only if $i = a_{max}$. Since the action probabilities are updated after every action, the most probable action may be different before and after the update. If $i = a_{max}$ both before *and* after step 3 above, then update the value function estimate as follows:
$$\hat{V}(x) \leftarrow \hat{V}(x) + \alpha_{xi}(n)\,\varepsilon$$
Otherwise, if $i = a_{max}$ before *or* after step 3:
$$\hat{V}(x) \leftarrow H_{\hat{V}(x)}(Np_k),$$
where action k is the most probable action after step 3.
5. $x \leftarrow y$. Go to step 2.

6 CONVERGENCE OF THE MODIFIED ALGORITHM

Theorem: *The modified actor/critic algorithm given above converges to the optimal value function V^* with probability one if:*

1. *The state and action sets are finite.*
2. $\sum_{n=0}^{\infty} \alpha_{xa}(n) = \infty$ and $\sum_{n=0}^{\infty} \alpha_{xa}^2(n) < \infty$.

Space does not permit us to supply the complete proof, which follows this outline:

1. The modified actor/critic algorithm behaves exactly the same as a Q-learning algorithm constrained by a particular exploration strategy.
2. Q-learning converges to V^* with probability one, given the conditions above (Tsitsiklis, 1993; Jaakkola et al, 1993; Watkins & Dayan, 1992).
3. Therefore, the modified actor/critic algorithm also converges to V^* with probability one.

The commutative diagram below illustrates how the modified actor/critic algorithm behaves exactly like Q-learning constrained by a particular exploration strategy. The function H recovers Q-values from the policy π and value function $\hat{V}$. H^{-1} recovers $(\pi, \hat{V})$ from the Q-values, thus determining an exploration strategy. Given the ability to move back and forth between $(\pi, \hat{V})$ and $\hat{Q}$, we can determine how to change $(\pi, \hat{V})$ by converting to $\hat{Q}$, determining updated Q-values, and then converting back to obtain an updated $(\pi, \hat{V})$. The modified actor/critic algorithm simply collapses this process into one step, bypassing the explicit use of Q-values.

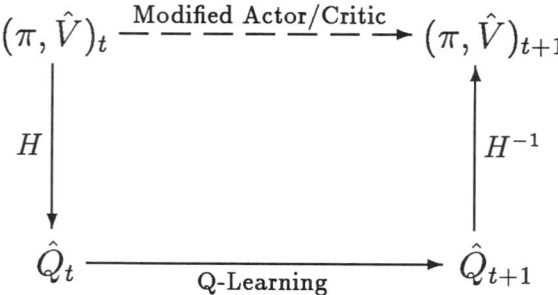

Following the diagram above, $(\pi, \hat{V})$ can be converted to Q-values as follows:

$$\hat{Q}(x,a) = H_{\hat{V}(x)}(z_a).$$

Going the other direction, Q-values can be converted to $(\pi, \hat{V})$ as follows:

$$\hat{V}(x) = max_{a \in A_x} \hat{Q}(x,a) \quad \text{and} \quad p_a = \frac{H^{-1}_{\hat{V}(x)}[\hat{Q}(x,a)]}{\sum_{b \in A_x} H^{-1}_{\hat{V}(x)}[\hat{Q}(x,b)]}.$$

The only Q-value that should change at time t is the one corresponding to the state/action pair that was visited at time t; call it $\hat{Q}(x,i)$. In order to prove the convergence theorem, we must verify that after an iteration of the modified actor/critic algorithm, its encoded Q-values match the values produced by Q-learning:

$$\hat{Q}_{t+1}(x,a) = \hat{Q}_t(x,i) + \alpha_{xi}(n) [r + \gamma \max_{b \in A_y} \hat{Q}_t(y,b) - \hat{Q}_t(x,i)], \quad a = i. \quad (2)$$

$$\hat{Q}_{t+1}(x,a) = \hat{Q}_t(x,a), \quad a \neq i. \quad (3)$$

In verifying this, it is necessary to consider the four cases where $\hat{Q}(x,i)$ is, or is not, the maximum Q-value for state x at times t and $t+1$. Only enough space exists to present a detailed verification of one case.

Case 1: $\hat{Q}_t(x,i) = max \, \hat{Q}_t(x,\cdot)$ and $\hat{Q}_{t+1}(x,i) = max \, \hat{Q}_{t+1}(x,\cdot)$.

In this case, $p_i(t) = p_{max}(t)$ and $p_i(t+1) = p_{max}(t+1)$, since $H_{\hat{V}_t(x)}$ and $H_{\hat{V}_{t+1}(x)}$ are strictly increasing. Therefore $z_i(t) = 1$ and $z_i(t+1) = 1$. Therefore, $\hat{V}_t(x) = H_{\hat{V}_t(x)}[1] = H_{\hat{V}_t(x)}[z_i(t)] = \hat{Q}_t(x,i)$, and

$$\begin{aligned}
\hat{Q}_{t+1}(x,i) &= H_{\hat{V}_{t+1}(x)}[z_i(t+1)] \\
&= H_{\hat{V}_{t+1}(x)}[1] \\
&= \hat{V}_{t+1}(x) \\
&= \hat{V}_t(x) + \alpha_{xi}(n)\,\varepsilon \\
&= \hat{Q}_t(x,i) + \alpha_{xi}(n)\,[r + \gamma \max_{b \in A_y} \hat{Q}_t(y,b) - \hat{Q}_t(x,i)].
\end{aligned}$$

This establishes (2). To show that (3) holds, we have that

$$\begin{aligned}
\hat{V}_{t+1}(x) &= \hat{V}_t(x) + \alpha_{xi}(n)\,\varepsilon \\
&= \hat{Q}_t(x,i) + \alpha_{xi}(n)\,\varepsilon \\
&= H_{\hat{V}_t(x)}[z_i(t)] + \alpha_{xi}(n)\,\varepsilon \\
&= H_{\hat{V}_t(x)}[H^{-1}_{\hat{V}_t(x)}[H_{\hat{V}_t(x)}[z_i(t)] + \alpha_{xi}(n)\,\varepsilon]] \\
&= H_{\hat{V}_t(x)}[z_i^\star(t)] \qquad (4)
\end{aligned}$$

and

$$\begin{aligned}
\hat{Q}_{t+1}(x,a) &= H_{\hat{V}_{t+1}(x)}[z_a(t+1)] \\
&= H_{\hat{V}_{t+1}(x)}[\frac{p_a(t+1)}{p_{max}(t+1)}] \\
&= H_{\hat{V}_{t+1}(x)}[\frac{z_a(t)/N}{z_i^\star(t)/N}] \quad \text{if } a \neq i \\
&= H_{\hat{V}_{t+1}(x)}[\frac{z_a(t)}{z_i^\star(t)}] \\
&= H_{H_{\hat{V}_t(x)}[z_i^\star(t)]}[\frac{z_a(t)}{z_i^\star(t)}] \quad \text{by (4)} \\
&= H_{\hat{V}_t(x)}[z_a(t)] \quad \text{by a property of } H \\
&= \hat{Q}_t(x,a).
\end{aligned}$$

The other cases can be shown similarly.

7 CONCLUSIONS

We have presented an actor/critic algorithm that is equivalent to Q-learning constrained by a particular exploration strategy. Like Q-learning, it estimates V^* directly without a model of the underlying decision process. It uses exactly the same amount of storage as Q-learning: one location for every state/action pair. (For each state, $|A| - 1$ locations are needed to store the action probabilities, since they must sum to one. The remaining location can be used to store the value of that state.) One advantage of Q-learning is that its exploration is uncoupled from its value function estimates. In the modified actor/critic algorithm, the exploration strategy is more constrained.

It is still an open question whether other actor/critic algorithms are guaranteed to converge. One way to approach this question would be to investigate further the relationship between the modified actor/critic algorithm described here and the actor/critic algorithms that have been employed by others.

Acknowledgements

We thank Vijay Gullapalli and Rich Sutton for helpful discussions. This research was supported by Air Force Office of Scientific Research grant F49620-93-1-0269.

References

A. G. Barto, S. J. Bradtke & S. P. Singh. (1993) Learning to act using real-time dynamic programming. *Artificial Intelligence*, Accepted.

A. G. Barto, R. S. Sutton & C. W. Anderson. (1983) Neuronlike adaptive elements that can solve difficult learning control problems. *IEEE Transactions on Systems, Man, and Cybernetics* **13**:835-846.

A. G. Barto, R. S. Sutton & C. J. C. H. Watkins. (1990) Learning and sequential decision making. In M. Gabriel & J. Moore, editors, *Learning and Computational Neuroscience: Foundations of Adaptive Networks*. MIT Press, Cambridge, MA.

D. P. Bertsekas & J. N. Tsitsiklis. (1989) *Parallel and Distributed Computation: Numerical Methods*. Prentice-Hall, Englewood Cliffs, NJ.

T. Jaakkola, M. I. Jordan & S. P. Singh. (1993) On the convergence of stochastic iterative dynamic programming algorithms. MIT Computational Cognitive Science Technical Report 9307.

L. Lin. (1993) *Reinforcement Learning for Robots Using Neural Networks*. PhD Thesis, Carnegie Mellon University, Pittsburgh, PA.

A. L. Samuel. (1963) Some studies in machine learning using the game of checkers. In E. Feigenbaum & J. Feldman, editors, *Computers and Thought*. McGraw-Hill, New York, NY.

R. S. Sutton. (1988) Learning to predict by the methods of temporal differences. *Machine Learning* **3**:9-44.

R. S. Sutton. (1990) Integrated architectures for learning, planning, and reacting based on approximating dynamic programming. In *Proceedings of the Seventh International Conference on Machine Learning*.

J. N. Tsitsiklis. (1994) Asynchronous stochastic approximation and Q-learning. *Machine Learning* **16**:185-202.

C. J. C. H. Watkins. (1989) *Learning from Delayed Rewards*. PhD thesis, Cambridge University.

C. J. C. H. Watkins & P. Dayan. (1992) Q-learning. *Machine Learning* **8**:279-292.

R. J. Williams & L. C. Baird. (1993) Analysis of some incremental variants of policy iteration: first steps toward understanding actor-critic learning systems. Technical Report NU-CCS-93-11. Northeastern University College of Computer Science.

PART V
ALGORITHMS AND ARCHITECTURES

FINANCIAL APPLICATIONS OF LEARNING FROM HINTS

Yaser S. Abu-Mostafa
California Institute of Technology
and
NeuroDollars, Inc.
e-mail: yaser@caltech.edu

Abstract

The basic paradigm for learning in neural networks is 'learning from examples' where a training set of input-output examples is used to teach the network the target function. Learning from hints is a generalization of learning from examples where additional information about the target function can be incorporated in the same learning process. Such information can come from common sense rules or special expertise. In financial market applications where the training data is very noisy, the use of such hints can have a decisive advantage. We demonstrate the use of hints in foreign-exchange trading of the U.S. Dollar versus the British Pound, the German Mark, the Japanese Yen, and the Swiss Franc, over a period of 32 months. We explain the general method of learning from hints and how it can be applied to other markets. The learning model for this method is not restricted to neural networks.

1 INTRODUCTION

When a neural network learns its target function from examples (training data), it knows nothing about the function except what it sees in the data. In financial market applications, it is typical to have limited amount of relevant training data, with high noise levels in the data. The information content of such data is modest, and while the learning process can try to make the most of what it has, it cannot create new information on its own. This poses a fundamental limitation on the learning approach, not only for neural networks, but for all other models as well. It is not uncommon to see simple rules such as the moving average outperforming an elaborate learning-from-examples system.

Learning from hints (Abu-Mostafa, 1990, 1993) is a value-added feature to learning from examples that boosts the information content in the data. The method allows us to use prior knowledge about the target function, that comes from common sense or expertise, along with the training data in the *same* learning process. Different types of hints that may be available in a given application can be used simultaneously. In this paper, we give experimental evidence of the impact of hints on learning performance, and explain the method in some detail to enable the readers to try their own hints in different markets.

Even simple hints can result in significant improvement in the learning performance. Figure 1 shows the learning performance for foreign exchange (FX) trading with and without the symmetry hint (see section 3), using only the closing price history. The plots are the Annualized Percentage Returns (cumulative daily, unleveraged, transaction cost included), for a sliding one-year test window in the period from April 1988 to November 1990, averaged over the four major FX markets with more than 150 runs per currency. The error bar in the upper left corner is 3 standard deviations long (based on 253 trading days, assuming independence between different runs). The plots establish a statistically significant differential in performance due to the use of hints. This differential holds for all four currencies.

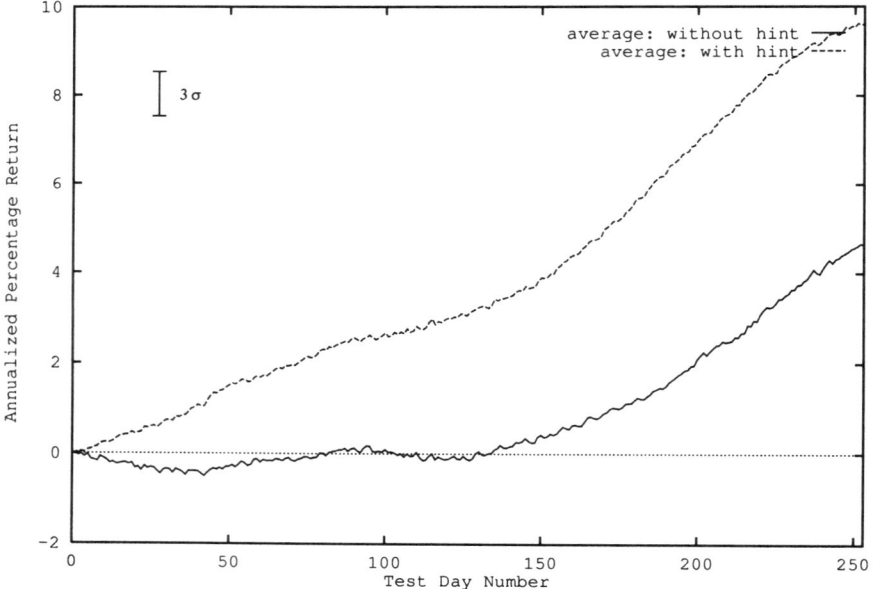

Figure 1: Learning performance with and without hint

Since the goal of hints is to add information to the training data, the differential in performance is likely to be less dramatic if we start out with more informative training data. Similarly, an additional hint may not have a pronounced effect if we have already used a few hints in the same application. There is a saturation in performance in any market that reflects how well the future can be forecast from the past. (Believers in the Efficient Market Hypothesis consider this saturation to be at zero performance). Hints will not make us forecast a market better than whatever that saturation level may be. They will, however, enable us to approach that level *through learning*.

This paper is organized as follows. Section 2 characterizes the notion of very noisy data by defining the '50% performance range'. We argue that the need for extra information in financial market applications is more pronounced than in other pattern recognition applications. In section 3, we discuss our method for learning from hints. We give examples of different types of hints, and explain how to represent hints to the learning process. Section 4 gives result details on the use of the symmetry hint in the four major FX markets. Section 5 provides experimental evidence that it is indeed the information content of the hint, rather than the incidental regularization effect, that results in the performance differential that we observe.

2 FINANCIAL DATA

This section provides a characterization of very noisy data that applies to the financial markets. For a broad treatment of neural-network applications to the financial markets, the reader is referred to (Abu-Mostafa et al, 1994).

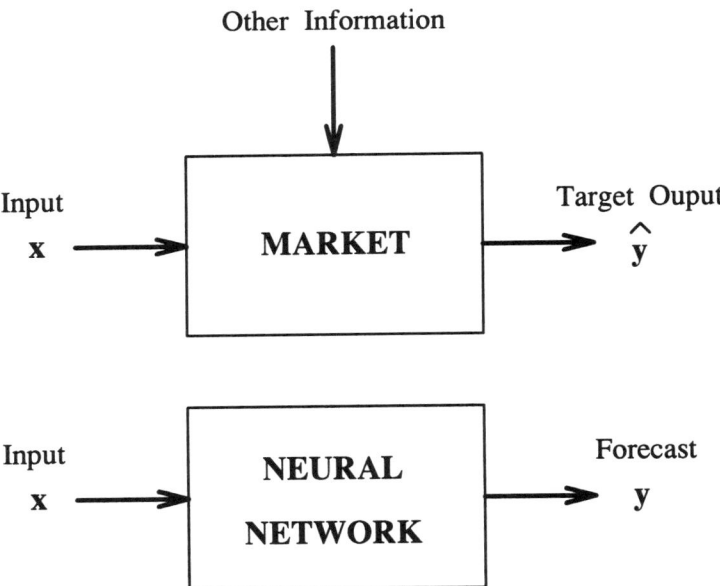

Figure 2: Illustration of the nature of noise in financial markets

Consider the market as a system that takes in a lot of information (fundamentals, news events, rumors, who bought what when, etc.) and produces an output $\hat{y}$ (say up/down price movement for simplicity). A model, e.g., a neural network, attempts to simulate the market (figure 2), but it takes an input x which is only a small subset of the information. The 'other information' cannot be modeled and plays the role of noise as far as x is concerned. The network cannot determine the target output $\hat{y}$ based on x alone, so it approximates it with its output y. It is typical that this approximation will be correct only slightly more than half the time.

What makes us consider x 'very noisy' is that y and $\hat{y}$ agree only $\frac{1}{2} + \epsilon$ of the time (50% performance range). This is in contrast to the typical pattern recognition application, such as optical character recognition, where y and $\hat{y}$ agree $1 - \epsilon$ of the time (100% performance range). It is not the poor performance *per se* that poses a problem in the 50% range, but rather the additional difficulty of learning in this range. Here is why.

In the 50% range, a performance of $\frac{1}{2} + \epsilon$ is good, while a performance of $\frac{1}{2} - \epsilon$ is disastrous. During learning, we need to distinguish between good and bad hypotheses based on a limited set of N examples. The problem with the 50% range is that the number of bad hypotheses that look good on N points is huge. This is in contrast to the 100% range where a good performance is as high as $1 - \epsilon$. The number of bad hypotheses that look good here is limited. Therefore, one can have much more confidence in a hypothesis that was learned in the 100% range than one learned in the 50% range. It is not uncommon to see a random trading policy making good money for a few weeks, but it is very unlikely that a random character recognition system will read a paragraph correctly.

Of course this problem would diminish if we used a very large set of examples, because the law of large numbers would make it less and less likely that y and $\hat{y}$ can agree $\frac{1}{2} + \epsilon$ of the time just by 'coincidence'. However, financial data has the other problem of non-stationarity. Because of the continuous evolution in the markets, old data may represent patterns of behavior that no longer hold. Thus, the relevant data for training purposes is limited to fairly recent times. Put together, noise and non-stationarity mean that the training data will not contain enough information for the network to learn the function. More information is needed, and hints can be the means of providing it.

3 HINTS

In this section, we give examples of different types of hints and discuss how to represent them to the learning process. We describe a simple way to use hints that allows the reader to try the method with minimal effort. For a more detailed treatment, please see (Abu-Mostafa, 1993).

As far as our method is concerned, a hint is any property that the target function is known to have. For instance, consider the symmetry hint in FX markets as it applies to the U.S. Dollar versus the German Mark (figure 3). This simple hint asserts that if a pattern in the price history implies a certain move in the market, then this implication holds whether you are looking at the market from the U.S. Dollar viewpoint or the German Mark viewpoint. Formally, in terms of normalized prices, the hint translates to invariance under inversion of these prices.

Is the symmetry hint valid? The ultimate test for this is how the learning performance is affected by the introduction of the hint. The formulation of hints is an art.

We use our experience, common sense, and analysis of the market to come up with a list of what we believe to be valid properties of this market. We then represent these hints in a canonical form as we will see shortly, and proceed to incorporate them in the learning process. The improvement in performance will only be as good as the hints we put in.

Figure 3: Illustration of the symmetry hint in FX markets

The canonical representation of hints is a more systematic task. The first step in representing a hint is to choose a way of generating 'virtual examples' of the hint. For illustration, suppose that the hint asserts that the target function $\hat{y}$ is an odd function of the input. An example of this hint would have the form $\hat{y}(-x) = -\hat{y}(x)$ for a particular input x. One can generate as many virtual examples as needed by picking different inputs.

After a hint is represented by virtual examples, it is ready to be incorporated in the learning process along with the examples of the target function itself. Notice that an example of the function is learned by minimizing an error measure, say $(y(x) - \hat{y}(x))^2$, as a way of ultimately enforcing the condition $y(x) = \hat{y}(x)$. In the same way, a virtual example of the oddness hint can be learned by minimizing $(y(x) + y(-x))^2$ as a way of ultimately enforcing the condition $y(-x) = -y(x)$. This involves inputting both x and $-x$ to the network and minimizing the difference between the two outputs. It is easy to show that this can be done using backpropagation (Rumelhart et al, 1986) twice.

The generation of a virtual example of the hint does not require knowing the value of the target function; neither $\hat{y}(x)$ nor $\hat{y}(-x)$ is needed to compute the error for the oddness hint. In fact, x and $-x$ can be artificial inputs. The fact that we do not need the value of the target function is crucial, since it was the limited resource of examples for which we know the value of the target function that got us interested in hints in the first place. On the other hand, for some hints, we can take the examples of the target function that we have, and employ the hint to duplicate these examples. For instance, an example $\hat{y}(x) = 1$ can be used to infer a second example $\hat{y}(-x) = -1$ using the oddness hint. Representing the hint by duplicate examples is an easy way to try simple hints using the same software that we use for learning from examples.

Let us illustrate how to represent two common types of hints. Perhaps the most common type is *the invariance hint*. This hint asserts that $\hat{y}(x) = \hat{y}(x')$ for certain pairs x, x'. For instance, "$\hat{y}$ is shift-invariant" is formalized by the pairs x, x' that are shifted versions of each other. To represent the invariance hint, an invariant pair (x, x') is picked as a virtual example. The error associated with this example is $(y(x) - y(x'))^2$. Another related type of hint is *the monotonicity hint*. The hint asserts for certain pairs x, x' that $\hat{y}(x) \leq \hat{y}(x')$. For instance, "$\hat{y}$ is monotonically nondecreasing in x" is formalized by the pairs x, x' such that $x < x'$. One application where the monotonicity hint occurs is the extension of personal credit. If person A is identical to person B except that A makes less money than B, then the approved credit line for A cannot exceed that of B. To represent the monotonicity hint, a monotonic pair (x, x') is picked as a virtual example. The error associated with this example is given by $(y(x) - y(x'))^2$ if $y(x) > y(x')$ and zero if $y(x) \leq y(x')$.

4 FX TRADING

We applied the symmetry hint in the four FX markets of the U.S. Dollar versus the British Pound, the German Mark, the Japanese Yen, and the Swiss Franc. In each case, only the closing prices for the preceding 21 days were used for inputs. The objective (fitness) function we chose was the total return on the training set, and we used simple filtering methods on the inputs and outputs of the networks. In each run, the training set consisted of 500 days, and the test was done on the following 253 days.

All four currencies show an improved performance when the symmetry hint is used. Roughly speaking, we are in the market half the time, each trade takes 4 days, the hit rate is close to 50%, and the A.P.R. without hint is 5% and with hint is 10% (the returns are annualized, unleveraged, and include the transaction cost; spread and average slippage). Notice that having the return as the objective function resulted in a fairly good return with a modest hit rate.

5 CROSS CHECKS

In this final section, we report more experimental results aimed at validating our claim that the information content of the hint is the reason behind the improved performance. Why is this debatable? A hint plays an incidental role as a constraint on the neural network during learning, since it restricts the solutions the network may settle in. Because overfitting is a common problem in learning from examples, any restriction may improve the out-of-sample performance by reducing overfitting (Akaike, 1969, Moody, 1992). This is the idea behind regularization.

To isolate the informative role from the regularizing role of the symmetry hint, we ran two experiments. In the first experiment, we used an uninformative hint, or 'noise' hint, which provides a random target output for the same inputs used in the examples of the symmetry hint. Figure 4 contrasts the performance of the noise hint with that of the real symmetry hint, averaged over the four currencies. Notice that the performance with the noise hint is close to that without any hint (figure 1), which is consistent with the notion of uninformative hint. The regularization effect seems to be negligible.

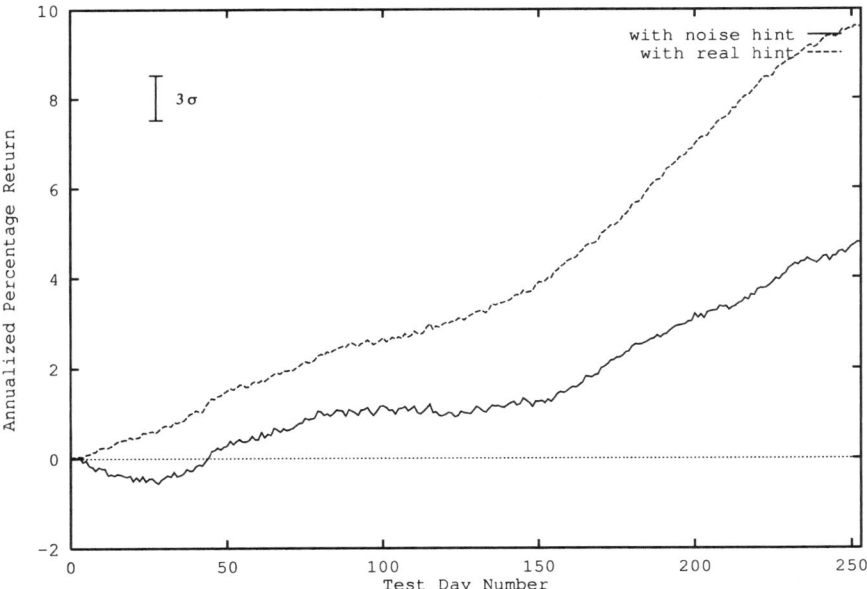

Figure 4: Performance of the real hint versus a noise hint

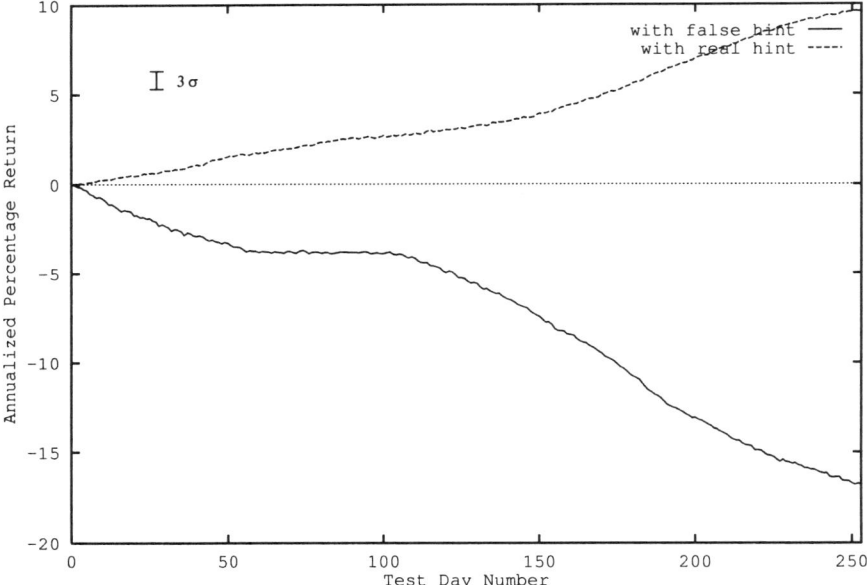

Figure 5: Performance of the real hint versus a false hint

In the second experiment, we used a harmful hint, or 'false' hint, in place of the symmetry hint. The hint takes the same examples used in the symmetry hint and asserts antisymmetry instead. Figure 5 contrasts the performance of the false hint with that of the real symmetry hint. As we see, the false hint had a detrimental effect on the performance. This is consistent with the hypothesis that the symmetry hint is valid, since its negation results in worse performance than no hint at all. Notice that the transaction cost is taken into consideration in all of these plots, which works as a negative bias and amplifies the losses of bad trading policies.

CONCLUSION

We have explained learning from hints, a systematic method for combining rules and data in the same learning process, and reported experimental results of a statistically significant improvement in performance in the four major FX markets that resulted from using a simple symmetry hint. We have described different types of hints and simple ways of using them in learning, to enable the readers to try their own hints in different markets.

Acknowledgements

I would like to acknowledge Dr. Amir Atiya for his valuable input. I am grateful to Dr. Ayman Abu-Mostafa for his expert remarks.

References

Abu-Mostafa, Y. S. (1990), Learning from hints in neural networks, *Journal of Complexity* **6**, pp. 192-198.

Abu-Mostafa, Y. S. (1993), A method for learning from hints, *Advances in Neural Information Processing Systems* **5**, S. Hanson et al (eds), pp. 73-80, Morgan-Kaufmann.

Abu-Mostafa, Y. S. et al (eds) (1994), *Proceedings of Neural Networks in the Capital Markets*, Pasadena, California, November 1994.

Akaike, H. (1969), Fitting autoregressive models for prediction, *Ann. Inst. Stat. Math.* **21**, pp. 243-247.

Moody, J. (1992), The effective number of parameters: An analysis of generalization and regularization in nonlinear learning systems, in *Advances in Neural Information Processing Systems* **4**, J. Moody et al (eds), pp. 847-854, Morgan Kaufmann.

Rumelhart, D. E., Hinton, G. E., and Williams, R. J. (1986), Learning internal representations by error propagation, *Parallel Distributed Processing* **1**, D. Rumelhart et al, pp. 318-362, MIT Press.

Weigend, A., Rumelhart, D., and Huberman, B. (1991), Generalization by weight elimination with application to forecasting, in *Advances in Neural Information Processing Systems* **3**, R. Lippmann et al (eds), pp. 875-882, Morgan Kaufmann.

Combining Estimators Using Non-Constant Weighting Functions

Volker Tresp* and Michiaki Taniguchi
Siemens AG, Central Research
Otto-Hahn-Ring 6
81730 München, Germany

Abstract

This paper discusses the linearly weighted combination of estimators in which the weighting functions are dependent on the input. We show that the weighting functions can be derived either by evaluating the input dependent variance of each estimator or by estimating how likely it is that a given estimator has seen data in the region of the input space close to the input pattern. The latter solution is closely related to the mixture of experts approach and we show how learning rules for the mixture of experts can be derived from the theory about learning with missing features. The presented approaches are modular since the weighting functions can easily be modified (no retraining) if more estimators are added. Furthermore, it is easy to incorporate estimators which were not derived from data such as expert systems or algorithms.

1 Introduction

Instead of modeling the global dependency between input $x \in \Re^D$ and output $y \in \Re$ using a single estimator, it is often very useful to decompose a complex mapping

---

*At the time of the research for this paper, a visiting researcher at the Center for Biological and Computational Learning, MIT. Volker.Tresp@zfe.siemens.de

into simpler mappings in the form[1]

$$\hat{y}(x) = \frac{1}{n(x)} \sum_{i=1}^{M} h_i(x) NN_i(x) = \sum_{i=1}^{M} g_i(x) NN_i(x) \qquad (1)$$

$$n(x) = \sum_{i=1}^{M} h_i(x) \quad h_i(x) >= 0 \quad g_i(x) = \frac{h_i(x)}{n(x)}.$$

The weighting functions $h_i(x)$ act as soft switches for the modules $NN_i(x)$. In the mixture of experts (Jacobs et al., 1991) the decomposition is learned in an unsupervised manner driven by the training data and the main goal is a system which learns quickly. In other cases, the individual modules are trained individually and then combined using Equation 1. We can distinguish two motivations: first, in the work on averaging estimators (Perrone, 1993, Meir, 1994, Breiman, 1992) the modules are trained using identical data and the weighting functions are constant and, in the simplest case, all equal to one. The goal is to achieve improved estimates by averaging the errors of the individual modules. Second, a decomposition as described in Equation 1 might represent some "natural" decomposition of the problem leading to more efficient representation and training (Hampshire and Waibel, 1989). A good example is a decomposition into analysis and action. $h_i(x)$ might be the probability of disease i given the symptoms x, the latter consisting of a few dozen variables. The amount of medication the patient should take given disease i on the other hand — represented by the output of module $NN_i(x)$ — might only depend on a few inputs such as weight, gender and age.[2] Similarly, we might consider $h_i(x)$ as the IF-part of the rule, evaluating the weight of the rule given x, and as $NN_i(x)$ the conclusion or action which should be taken under rule i (compare Tresp, Hollatz and Ahmad, 1993). Equation 1 might also be the basis for biological models considering for example the role of neural modulators in the brain. Nowlan and Sejnowsky (1994) recently presented a biologically motivated filter selection model for visual motion in which modules provide estimates of the direction and amount of motion and weighting functions select the most reliable module.

In this paper we describe novel ways of designing the weighting functions. Intuitively, the weighting functions should represent the competence or the certainty of a module, given the available information x. One possible measure is related to the number of training data that a module has seen in the neighborhood of x. Therefore, $\hat{P}(x|i)$, which is an estimate of the distribution of the input data which were used to train module i is an obvious candidate as weighting function. Alternatively, the certainty a module assigns to its own prediction, represented by the inverse of the variance $1/var(NN_i(x))$ is a plausible candidate for a weighting function. Both approaches seem to be the flip-sides of the same coin, and indeed, we can show that both approaches are extremes of a unified approach.

---

[1] The *hat* stands for an estimates value.
[2] Note, that we include the case that the weighting functions and the modules might explicitly only depend on different subsets of x.

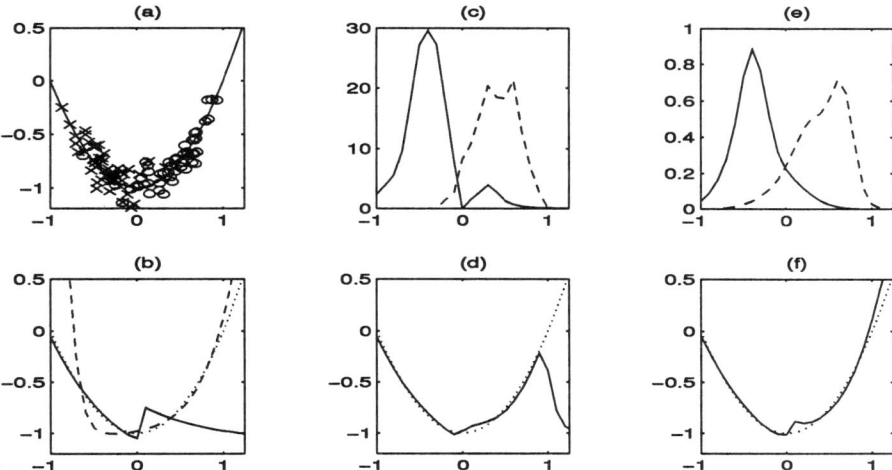

Figure 1: (a): Two data sets (1:*, 2:o) and the underlying function (continuous). (b) The approximations of the two neural networks trained on the data sets (continuous: 1, dashed: 2). Note, that the approximation of a network is only reliable in the regions of the input space in which it has "seen" data. (c) The weighting functions for variance-based weighting. (d) The approximation using variance-based weighting (continuous). The approximation is excellent, except to the very right. (e) The weighting functions for density-based weighting (Gaussian mixtures approximation). (f) The approximation using density-based weighting (continuous). In particular to the right, the extrapolation is better than in (d).

2 Variance-based Weighting

Here, we assume that the different modules $NN_i(x)$ were trained with different data sets $\{(x_k^i, y_k^i)\}_{k=1}^{K_i}$ but that they model identical input-output relationships (see Figure 1 a,b). To give a concrete example, this would correspond to the case that we trained two handwritten digit classifiers using different data sets and we want to use both for classifying new data.

If the errors of the individual modules are uncorrelated and unbiased,[3] the combined estimator is also unbiased and has the smallest variance if we select the weighting functions inversely proportional the the variance of the modules

$$h_i(x) = \frac{1}{var(NN_i(x))}. \qquad (2)$$

This can be shown using $var(\sum_{i=1}^{M} g_i(x) NN_i(x)) = \sum_{i=1}^{M} g_i^2(x) var(NN_i(x))$ and using Lagrange multiplier to enforce the constraint that $\sum_i g_i(x) = 1$. Intuitively,

---

[3]The errors are uncorrelated since the modules were trained with different data; correlation and bias are discussed in Section 8.1.

Equation 2 says that a module which is uncertain about its own prediction should also obtain a smaller weight. We estimate the variance from the training data as

$$var(NN_i(x)) \approx \frac{\partial NN_i(x)}{\partial w}^T H_i^{-1} \frac{\partial NN_i(x)}{\partial w}.$$

H_i is the Hessian, which can be approximated as (σ^2 is the output-noise variance, Tibshirani, 1994)

$$H_i \approx \frac{1}{\sigma^2} \sum_{k=1}^{K_i} \frac{\partial NN_i(x_k^i)}{\partial w} \frac{\partial NN_i(x_k^i)}{\partial w}^T.$$

3 Density-based Weighting

In particular if the different modules were trained with data sets from different regions of the input space, it might be a reasonable assumption that the different modules represent different input-output relationships. In terms of our example, this corresponds to the problem, that we have two handwritten digit classifiers, one trained with American data and one with European data. If the classifiers are used in an international setting, confusions are possible, since, for example, an American seven might be confused with a European one. Formally, we introduce an additional variable which is equal to zero if the writer is American and is equal to one if the writer is European. During recall, we don't know the state of that variable and we are formally faced with the problem of estimation with missing inputs. From previous work (Ahmad and Tresp, 1993) we know that we have to integrate over the unknown input weighted by the conditional probability of the unknown input given the known variables. In this case, this translates into Equation 1, where the weighting function is

$$h_i(x) = P(i|x) = \frac{P(i,x)}{P(x)} \propto P(x|i)P(i).$$

In our example, $P(i|x)$ would estimate the probability that the writer is American or European given the data.

Depending on the problem $P(i|x)$ might be estimated in different ways. If x represents continuous variables, we use a mixture of Gaussians model

$$\hat{P}(x|i) = \sum_j P^{ij} G(x; c^{ij}, \Sigma^{ij}) \quad \hat{P}(i) = \frac{K_i}{\sum_i K_i} \quad (3)$$

where $G(x; c^{ij}, \Sigma^{ij})$ is our notation for a normal density centered at c^{ij} and with covariance Σ^{ij}.

Note that we have obtained a mixture of experts network with $\hat{P}(i|x)$ as gating network. A novel feature of our approach is that we maintain an estimate of the input data distribution (Equation 3), which is not modeled in the original mixture of experts network. This is advantageous if we have training data which are not assigned to a module (in the mixture of experts, no data are assigned) which corresponds to training with missing inputs (the missing input is the missing assignment), for which the solution is known (Tresp et al., 1994). If we use Gaussian mixtures to approximate $P(x|i)$, we can use generalized EM learning rules for adaptation. The adaptation of the parameters in the "gating network" which models $P(x|i)$ is therefore somewhat simpler than in the original mixture of experts learning rules (see Section 8.2).

4 Unified Approach

In reality, the modules will often represent different mappings, but these mappings are not completely independent. Let's assume that we have an excellent American handwritten digit classifier but our European handwritten digit classifier is still very poor, since we only had few training data. We might want to take into account the results of the American classifier, even if we know that the writer was European. Mathematically, we can introduce a coupling between the modules. Let's assume that the prediction of the i-th module $NN_i(x) = f_i(x) + \epsilon_i$ is a noisy version of the true underlying relationship $f_i(x)$ and that ϵ_i is independent Gaussian noise with variance $var(NN_i(x))$. Furthermore, we assume that the true underlying functions are coupled through a prior distribution (for simplicity we only assume two modules)

$$P(f_1(x), f_2(x)) \propto \exp(-\frac{1}{2var_c}(f_1(x) - f_2(x))^2).$$

We obtain as best estimates

$$\hat{f}_1(x) = \frac{1}{K(x)}[(var(NN_2(x)) + var_c)\, NN_1(x) + var(NN_1(x))\, NN_2(x)]$$

$$\hat{f}_2(x) = \frac{1}{K(x)}[var(NN_2(x))\, NN_1(x) + (var(NN_1(x)) + var_c)\, NN_2(x)]$$

where

$$K(x) = var(NN_1(x)) + var(NN_2(x)) + var_c.$$

We use density-based weighting to combine the two estimates: $\hat{y}(x) = P(1|x)\hat{f}_1(x) + P(2|x)\hat{f}_2(x)$. Note, that if $var_c \to \infty$ (no coupling) we obtain the density-based solution and for $var_c \to 0$ (the mappings are forced to be identical) we obtain the variance-based solution. A generalization to more complex couplings can be found in Section 8.2.1.

5 Experiments

We tested our approaches using the Boston housing data set (13 inputs, one continuous output). The training data set consisted of 170 samples which were divided into 20 groups using k-means clustering. The clusters were then divided randomly into two groups and two multi-layer perceptrons (MLP) were trained using those two data sets. Table 1 shows that the performances of the individual networks are pretty bad which indicates that both networks have only acquired local knowledge with only limited extrapolation capability. Variance-based weighting gives considerably better performance, although density-based weighting and the unified approach are both slightly better. Considering the assumptions, variance-based weighting should be superior since the underlying mappings are identical. One problem might be that we assumed that the modules are unbiased which might not be true in regions were a given module has seen no data.

Table 1: Generalization errors

NN_1	NN_2	variance-based	density-based	unified
0.6948	1.188	0.4821	0.4472	0.4235

6 Error-based Weighting

In most learning tasks only one data set is given and the task is to obtain optimal predictions. Perrone (1994) has shown that simply averaging the estimates of a small number (i. e. 10) of neural network estimators trained on the same training data set often gives better performance than the best estimator out of this ensemble. Alternatively, bootstrap samples of the original data set can be used for training (Breimann, personal communication). Instead of averaging, we propose that Equation 1, where

$$h_i(x) = \frac{1}{var(NN_i(x)) + Res(NN_i(x))}$$

might give superior results (error-based weighting). $Res(NN_i(x))$ stands for an estimate of the input dependent residual squared error at x. As a simple approximation, $Res(NN_i(x))$ can be estimated by training a neural network with the residual squared errors of NN_i. Error-based weighting should be superior to simple averaging in particular if the estimators in the pool have different complexity. A more complex system would obtain larger weights in regions where the mapping is complex, since an estimator which is locally too simple has a large residual error, whereas in regions, where the mapping is simple, both estimators have sufficient complexity, but the simpler one has less variance. In our experiments we only tried networks with the same complexity. Preliminary results indicate that variance-based weighting and error-based weighting are sometimes superior to simple averaging. The main reason seems to be that the local overfitting of a network is reflected in a large variance near that location in input space. The overfitting estimator therefore obtains a small weight in that region (compare the overfitting of network 1 in Figure 1b near $x = 0$ and the small weight of network 1 close to $x = 0$ in Figure 1c).

7 Conclusions

We have presented modular ways for combining estimators. The weighting functions of each module can be determined independently of the other modules such that additional modules can be added without retraining of the previous system. This can be a useful feature in the context of the problem of *catastrophic forgetting*: additional data can be used to train an additional module and the knowledge in the remaining modules is preserved. Also note that estimators which are not derived from data can be easily included if it is possible to estimate the input dependent certainty or competence of that estimator.

Acknowledgements: Valuable discussions with David Cohn, Michael Duff and Cesare Alippi are greatfully acknowledged. The first author would like to thank the Center for Biological and Computational Learning (MIT) for providing and excellent research environment during the summer of 1994.

8 Appendix

8.1 Variance-based Weighting: Correlated Errors and Bias

We maintain that $\sum_i g_i(x) = 1$. In general (i.e. the modules have seen the same data, or partially the same data), we cannot assume that the errors in the individual modules are independent. Let the $M \times M$ matrix $\Omega(x)$ be the covariance between the predictions of the modules $NN_i(x)$. With $h(x) = (h_1(x)....h_M(x))^T$, the optimal weighting vector becomes

$$h(x) = \Omega^{-1}(x)\, u \quad n(x) = u'\, \Omega^{-1}(x)\, u$$

where u is the M-dimensional unit vector.

If the individual modules are biased ($bias_i(x) = E_D(NN_i(x)) - E_{y|x}(y|x)$),[4] we form the $M \times M$ matrix $B(x)$, with $B_{ij}(x) = bias_i(x) bias_j(x)$, and the minimum variance solution is found for

$$h(x) = (\Omega(x) + B(x))^{-1}\, u \quad n(x) = u'\, (\Omega(x) + B(x))^{-1}\, u.$$

8.2 Density-based Weighting: GEM-learning

Let's assume a training pattern (x_k, y_k) which is not associated with a particular module. If w^i is a parameter in network NN_i the error gradient becomes

$$\frac{\partial error_k}{\partial w^i} = -(y_k - NN_i(x_k))\, \hat{P}(i|x_k, y_k) \frac{\partial NN_i(x_k)}{\partial w^i}.$$

This equation can be derived from the solution to the problem of training with missing features (here: the true i is unknown, see Tresp, Ahmad and Neuneier, 1994). This corresponds also to the M-step in a generalized EM algorithm, where the E-step calculates

$$\hat{P}(i|x_k, y_k) = \frac{\hat{P}(y_k|x_k, i)\hat{P}(x_k|i)\hat{P}(i)}{\sum_i \hat{P}(y_k|x_k, i)\hat{P}(x_k|i)\hat{P}(i)} \quad \hat{P}(y_k|x_k, i) = G(y_k; NN_i(x_k), \sigma^2).$$

---

[4] E stands for the expected value; the expectation E_D is taken with respect to all data sets of the same size.

using the current parameters. The M-step in the "gating network" $\hat{P}(x|i)$ is particularly simple using the well known EM-rules for Gaussian mixtures. Note, that $\hat{P}$(module = i, mixture component : $j|x_k, y_k$) needs to be calculated.

8.2.1 Unified Approach: Correlated Errors and General Coupling

Let's form the vectors $NN(x) = (NN_1(x),...NN_M(x))^T$ and $f(x) = (f_1(x),...,f_M(x))^T$. In a more general case, the prior coupling between the underlying functions is described by
$$P(f(x)) = G(f(x); g(x), \Sigma_g(x))$$
where $g(x) = (g_1(x),...,g_M(x))^T$. Furthermore, in a more general case, the estimates are not independent,
$$P(NN(x)|f(x)) = G(NN(x); f(x), \Sigma_N(x)).$$

The minimum variance solution is now
$$\hat{f}(x) = (\Sigma_N^{-1}(x) + \Sigma_g^{-1}(x))^{-1}(\Sigma_N^{-1}NN(x) + \Sigma_g^{-1}g(x)).$$

The equations in Section 4 are special cases with $M = 2$, $g(x) = 0$, $\Sigma_g^{-1}(x) = 1/var_c \times (1,-1)(1,-1)^T$, $\Sigma_N(x) = I\ (var(NN_1(x)), var(NN_2(x)))^T$ (I is the 2D-unit matrix).

References

Ahmad, S. and Tresp, V. (1993). Some Solutions to the Missing Feature Problem in Vision. In S. J. Hanson, J. D. Cowan and C. L. Giles, (Eds.), *Advances in Neural Information Processing Systems 5*. San Mateo, CA: Morgan Kaufmann.

Breiman, L. (1992). Stacked Regression. Dept. of Statistics, Berkeley, TR No. 367.

Hampshire, J. and Waibel, A. (1989). The meta-pi network: Building Distributed Knowledge Representations for Robust Pattern Recognition. TR CMU-CS-89-166, CMU, PA.

Jacobs, R. A., Jordan, M. I., Nowlan, S. J. and Hinton, J. E. (1991). Adaptive Mixtures of Local Experts. *Neural Computation*, Vol. 3, pp. 79-87.

Meir, R. (1994). Bias, Variance and the Combination of Estimators: The Case of Linear Least Squares. TR: Dept. of Electrical Engineering, Technion, Haifa.

Nowlan, S. J and Sejnowski, T. J. (1994). Filter Selection Model for Motion Segmentation and Velocity Integration. *J. Opt. Soc. Am. A*, Vol. 11, No. 12, pp. 1-24.

Perrone, M. P. (1993). *Improving Regression Estimates: Averaging Methods for Variance Reduction with Extensions to General Convex Measure Optimization*. PhD thesis. Brown University.

Tibshirani, R. (1994). A Comparison of Some Error Estimates for Neural Network Models. TR Department of Statistics, University of Toronto.

Tresp, V., Ahmad, S. and Neuneier, R. (1994). Training Neural Networks with Deficient Data. In: Cowan, J. D., Tesauro, G., and Alspector, J., eds., *Advances in Neural Information Processing Systems 6*, San Mateo, CA, Morgan Kaufman.

Tresp, V., Hollatz J. and Ahmad, S. (1993). Network Structuring and Training Using Rule-based Knowledge. In S. J. Hanson, J. D. Cowan and C. L. Giles, (Eds.), *Advances in Neural Information Processing Systems 5*, San Mateo, CA: Morgan Kaufmann.

An Input Output HMM Architecture

Yoshua Bengio[*]
Dept. Informatique et Recherche
Opérationnelle
Université de Montréal, Qc H3C-3J7
bengioy@IRO.UMontreal.CA

Paolo Frasconi
Dipartimento di Sistemi e Informatica
Università di Firenze (Italy)
paolo@mcculloch.ing.unifi.it

Abstract

We introduce a recurrent architecture having a modular structure and we formulate a training procedure based on the EM algorithm. The resulting model has similarities to hidden Markov models, but supports recurrent networks processing style and allows to exploit the supervised learning paradigm while using maximum likelihood estimation.

1 INTRODUCTION

Learning problems involving sequentially structured data cannot be effectively dealt with static models such as feedforward networks. Recurrent networks allow to model complex dynamical systems and can store and retrieve contextual information in a flexible way. Up until the present time, research efforts of supervised learning for recurrent networks have almost exclusively focused on error minimization by gradient descent methods. Although effective for learning short term memories, practical difficulties have been reported in training recurrent neural networks to perform tasks in which the temporal contingencies present in the input/output sequences span long intervals (Bengio et al., 1994; Mozer, 1992).

Previous work on alternative training algorithms (Bengio et al., 1994) could suggest that the root of the problem lies in the essentially *discrete* nature of the process of storing information for an indefinite amount of time. Thus, a potential solution is to propagate, backward in time, targets in a discrete state space rather than differential error information. Extending previous work (Bengio & Frasconi, 1994a), in this paper we propose a statistical approach to target propagation, based on the EM algorithm. We consider a parametric dynamical system with discrete states and we introduce a modular architecture, with subnetworks associated to discrete states. The architecture can be interpreted as a statistical model and can be trained by the EM or generalized EM (GEM) algorithms (Dempster et al., 1977), considering the internal state trajectories as missing data. In this way learning is decoupled into

---

[*]also, AT&T Bell Labs, Holmdel, NJ 07733

a temporal credit assignment subproblem and a static learning subproblem that consists of fitting parameters to the next-state and output mappings defined by the estimated trajectories. In order to iteratively tune parameters with the EM or GEM algorithms, the system propagates forward and backward a discrete distribution over the n states, resulting in a procedure similar to the Baum-Welch algorithm used to train standard hidden Markov models (HMMs) (Levinson et al., 1983). HMMs however adjust their parameters using unsupervised learning, whereas we use EM in a supervised fashion. Furthermore, the model presented here could be called *Input/Output HMM*, or IOHMM, because it can be used to learn to map input sequences to output sequences (unlike standard HMMs, which learn the output sequence distribution). This model can also be seen as a recurrent version of the Mixture of Experts architecture (Jacobs et al., 1991), related to the model already proposed in (Cacciatore and Nowlan, 1994). Experiments on artificial tasks (Bengio & Frasconi, 1994a) have shown that EM recurrent learning can deal with long term dependencies more effectively than backpropagation through time and other alternative algorithms. However, the model used in (Bengio & Frasconi, 1994a) has very limited representational capabilities and can only map an input sequence to a final discrete state. In the present paper we describe an extended architecture that allows to fully exploit both input and output portions of the data, as required by the supervised learning paradigm. In this way, general sequence processing tasks, such as production, classification, or prediction, can be dealt with.

2 THE PROPOSED ARCHITECTURE

We consider a discrete state dynamical system based on the following state space description:
$$\begin{aligned} x_t &= f(x_{t-1}, u_t) \\ y_t &= g(x_t, u_t) \end{aligned} \quad (1)$$
where $u_t \in R^m$ is the input vector at time t, $y_t \in R^r$ is the output vector, and $x_t \in \{1, 2, \ldots, n\}$ is a discrete state. These equations define a generalized Mealy finite state machine, in which inputs and outputs may take on continuous values. In this paper, we consider a *probabilistic* version of these dynamics, where the current inputs and the current state distribution are used to estimate the state distribution and the output distribution for the next time step. Admissible state transitions will be specified by a directed graph $\mathcal{G}$ whose vertices correspond to the model's states and the set of successors for state j is $\mathcal{S}_j$.

The system defined by equations (1) can be modeled by the recurrent architecture depicted in Figure 1(a). The architecture is composed by a set of *state networks* $\mathcal{N}_j, j = 1 \ldots n$ and a set of *output networks* $\mathcal{O}_j, j = 1 \ldots n$. Each one of the state and output networks is uniquely associated to one of the states, and all networks share the same input u_t. Each state network $\mathcal{N}_j$ has the task of predicting the next state distribution, based on the current input and given that $x_{t-1} = j$. Similarly, each output network $\mathcal{O}_j$ predicts the output of the system, given the current state and input. All the subnetworks are assumed to be static and they are defined by means of smooth mappings $N_j(u_t; \theta_j)$ and $O_j(u_t; \vartheta_j)$, where θ_j and ϑ_j are vectors of adjustable parameters (e.g., connection weights). The ranges of the functions $N_j()$ may be constrained in order to account for the underlying transition graph $\mathcal{G}$. Each output $\varphi_{ij,t}$ of the state subnetwork $\mathcal{N}_j$ (at time t) is associated to one of the successors i of state j. Thus the last layer of $\mathcal{N}_j$ has as many units as the cardinality of $\mathcal{S}_j$. For convenience of notation, we suppose that $\varphi_{ij,t}$ are defined for each $i, j = 1, \ldots, n$ and we impose the condition $\varphi_{ij,t} = 0$ for each i not belonging to $\mathcal{S}_j$. The *softmax* function is used in the last layer: $\varphi_{ij,t} = e^{a_{ij,t}} / \sum_{\ell \in \mathcal{S}_j} e^{a_{\ell j,t}}$, $j = 1, \ldots, n$, $i \in \mathcal{S}_j$ where $a_{ij,t}$ are intermediate variables that can be thought of as the

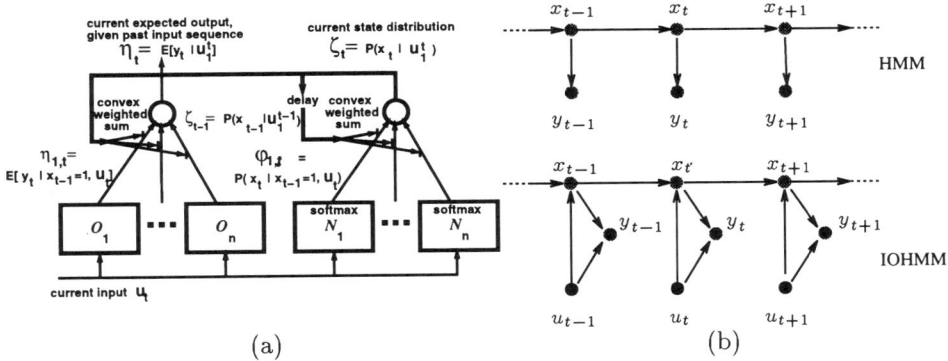

Figure 1: (a): The proposed IOHMM architecture. (b): Bottom: Bayesian network expressing conditional dependencies for an IOHMM; top: Bayesian network for a standard HMM

activations of the output units of subnetwork $\mathcal{N}_j$. In this way $\sum_{i=1}^{n} \varphi_{ij,t} = 1 \ \forall j, t$. The vector $\zeta_t \in \mathbf{R}^n$ represents the internal state of the model and it is computed as a linear combination of the outputs of the state networks, gated by the previously computed internal state:

$$\zeta_t = \sum_{j=1}^{n} \zeta_{j,t-1} \varphi_{j,t} \qquad (2)$$

where $\varphi_{j,t} = [\varphi_{1j,t}, \ldots, \varphi_{nj,t}]'$. Output networks compete to predict the global output of the system $\eta_t \in \mathbf{R}^r$:

$$\eta_t = \sum_{j=1}^{n} \zeta_{jt} \eta_{jt} \qquad (3)$$

where $\eta_{jt} \in \mathbf{R}^r$ is the output of subnetwork $\mathcal{O}_j$. At this level, we do not need to further specify the internal architecture of the state and output subnetworks. Depending on the task, the designer may decide whether to include hidden layers and what activation rule to use for the hidden units.

This connectionist architecture can be also interpreted as a probability model. Let us assume a multinomial distribution for the state variable x_t and let us consider ζ_t, the main variable of the temporal recurrence (2). If we initialize the vector ζ_0 to positive numbers summing to 1, it can be interpreted as a vector of initial state probabilities. In general, we obtain relation $\zeta_{it} = \mathrm{P}(x_t = i \mid \boldsymbol{u}_1^t)$, having denoted with $\boldsymbol{u}_1^t$ the subsequence of inputs from time 1 to t, inclusively. Equation (2) then has the following probabilistic interpretation:

$$P(x_t = i \mid \boldsymbol{u}_1^t) = \sum_{j=1}^{n} P(x_t = i \mid x_{t-1} = j, \boldsymbol{u}_t) P(x_{t-1} = j \mid \boldsymbol{u}_1^{t-1}) \qquad (4)$$

i.e., the subnetworks $\mathcal{N}_j$ compute transition probabilities conditioned on the input sequence u_t:

$$\varphi_{ij,t} = \mathrm{P}(x_t = i \mid x_{t-1} = j, \boldsymbol{u}_t) \qquad (5)$$

As in neural networks trained to minimize the output squared error, the output η_t of this architecture can be interpreted as an expected "position parameter" for the probability distribution of the output y_t. However, in addition to being conditional on an input u_t, this expectation is also conditional on the state x_t, i.e.

$\eta_t = E[\boldsymbol{y}_t \mid x_t, \boldsymbol{u}_t]$. The actual form of the output density, denoted $f_Y(\boldsymbol{y}_t; \boldsymbol{\eta}_t)$, will be chosen according to the task. For example a multinomial distribution is suitable for sequence classification, or for symbolic mutually exclusive outputs. Instead, a Gaussian distribution is adequate for producing continuous outputs. In the first case we use a softmax function at the output of subnetworks $\mathcal{O}_j$; in the second case we use linear output units for the subnetworks $\mathcal{O}_j$.

In order to reduce the amount of computation, we introduce an independency model among the variables involved in the probabilistic interpretation of the architecture. We shall use a Bayesian network to characterize the probabilistic dependencies among these variables. Specifically, we suppose that the directed acyclic graph $\mathcal{G}$ depicted at the bottom of Figure 1b is a Bayesian network for the dependency model associated to the variables $\boldsymbol{u}_1^T, x_1^T, \boldsymbol{y}_1^T$. One of the most evident consequences of this independency model is that only the previous state and the current input are relevant to determine the next-state. This one-step memory property is analogue to the Markov assumption in hidden Markov models (HMM). In fact, the Bayesian network for HMMs can be obtained by simply removing the $\boldsymbol{u}_t$ nodes and arcs from them (see top of Figure 1b).

3 A SUPERVISED LEARNING ALGORITHM

The learning algorithm for the proposed architecture is derived from the maximum likelihood principle. The training data are a set of P pairs of input/output sequences (of length T_p): $\mathcal{D} = \{(\boldsymbol{u}_1^{T_p}(p), \boldsymbol{y}_1^{T_p}(p)); p = 1 \ldots P\}$. Let $\boldsymbol{\Theta}$ denote the vector of parameters obtained by collecting all the parameters $\boldsymbol{\theta}_j$ and $\boldsymbol{\vartheta}_i$ of the architecture. The likelihood function is then given by

$$L(\boldsymbol{\Theta}; \mathcal{D}) = \prod_{p=1}^{P} \mathrm{P}(\boldsymbol{y}_1^{T_p}(p) \mid \boldsymbol{u}_1^{T_p}(p); \boldsymbol{\Theta}). \tag{6}$$

The output values (used here as targets) may also be specified intermittently. For example, in sequence classification tasks, one may only be interested in the output $\boldsymbol{y}_T$ at the end of each sequence. The modification of the likelihood to account for intermittent targets is straightforward. According to the maximum likelihood principle, the optimal parameters are obtained by maximizing (6). In order to apply EM to our case we begin by noting that the state variables x_t are not observed. Knowledge of the model's state trajectories would allow one to decompose the temporal learning problem into $2n$ static learning subproblems. Indeed, if x_t were known, the probabilities ζ_{it} would be either 0 or 1 and it would be possible to train each subnetwork separately, without taking into account any temporal dependency. This observation allows to link EM learning to the target propagation approach discussed in the introduction. Note that if we used a Viterbi-like approximation (i.e., considering only the most likely path), we would indeed have $2n$ static learning problems at each epoch. In order to we derive the learning equations, let us define the *complete data* as $\mathcal{D}_c = \{(\boldsymbol{u}_1^{T_p}(p), \boldsymbol{y}_1^{T_p}(p), x_1^{T_p}(p)); p = 1 \ldots P\}$. The corresponding complete data log-likelihood is

$$l_c(\boldsymbol{\Theta}; \mathcal{D}_c) = \sum_{p=1}^{P} \log \mathrm{P}(\boldsymbol{y}_1^{T_p}(p), \boldsymbol{z}_1^{T_p}(p) \mid \boldsymbol{u}_1^{T_p}(p); \boldsymbol{\Theta}). \tag{7}$$

Since $l_c(\boldsymbol{\Theta}; \mathcal{D}_c)$ depends on the hidden state variables it cannot be maximized directly. The MLE optimization is then solved by introducing the auxiliary function $Q(\boldsymbol{\Theta}; \hat{\boldsymbol{\Theta}})$ and iterating the following two steps for $k = 1, 2, \ldots$:

Estimation: Compute $Q(\boldsymbol{\Theta}; \hat{\boldsymbol{\Theta}}) = E[l_c(\boldsymbol{\Theta}; \mathcal{D}_c) \mid \mathcal{D}, \hat{\boldsymbol{\Theta}}]$
Maximization: Update the parameters as $\hat{\boldsymbol{\Theta}} \leftarrow \arg\max_{\boldsymbol{\Theta}} Q(\boldsymbol{\Theta}; \hat{\boldsymbol{\Theta}})$ (8)

The expectation of (7) can be expressed as

$$Q(\boldsymbol{\Theta};\hat{\boldsymbol{\Theta}}) = \sum_{p=1}^{P}\sum_{t=1}^{T_p}\sum_{i=1}^{N} \hat{\zeta}_{it} \log \mathrm{P}(\boldsymbol{y}_t \mid x_t = i, \boldsymbol{u}_t; \boldsymbol{\Theta}) + \sum_{j=1}^{N} \hat{h}_{ij,t} \log \varphi_{ij,t} \qquad (9)$$

where $h_{ij,t} = E[z_{it}z_{j,t-1} \mid \boldsymbol{u}_1^T, \boldsymbol{y}_1^T; \boldsymbol{\Theta}]$, denoting z_{it} for an indicator variable $= 1$ if $x_t = i$ and 0 otherwise. The hat in $\hat{\zeta}_{it}$ and $\hat{h}_{ij,t}$ means that these variables are computed using the "old" parameters $\hat{\boldsymbol{\Theta}}$. In order to compute $h_{ij,t}$ we introduce the forward probabilities $\alpha_{it} = \mathrm{P}(\boldsymbol{y}_1^t, x_t = i; \boldsymbol{u}_1^t)$ and the backward probabilities $\beta_{it} = \mathrm{P}(\boldsymbol{y}_t^T \mid x_t = i, \boldsymbol{u}_t^T)$, that are updated as follows:

$$\begin{aligned}\beta_{it} &= f_Y(\boldsymbol{y}_t; \boldsymbol{\eta}_{it}) \sum_{\ell} \varphi_{\ell i}(\boldsymbol{u}_{t+1})\beta_{\ell,t+1} \\ \alpha_{it} &= f_Y(\boldsymbol{y}_t; \boldsymbol{\eta}_{it}) \sum_{\ell} \varphi_{i\ell}(\boldsymbol{u}_t)\alpha_{\ell,t-1}.\end{aligned} \qquad (10)$$

$$h_{ij,t} = \frac{\beta_{it}\alpha_{j,t-1}\varphi_{ij}(\boldsymbol{u}_t)}{\sum_i \alpha_{iT}} \qquad (11)$$

Each iteration of the EM algorithm requires to maximize $Q(\boldsymbol{\Theta};\hat{\boldsymbol{\Theta}})$. We first consider a simplified case, in which the inputs are quantized (i.e., belonging to a finite alphabet $\{\sigma_1,\ldots,\sigma_K\}$) and the subnetworks behave like lookup tables addressed by the input symbols σ_t, i.e. we interpret each parameter as $w_{ijk} = \mathrm{P}(x_t = i \mid x_{t-1} = j, \sigma_t = k)$. For simplicity, we restrict the analysis to classification tasks and we suppose that targets are specified as desired final states for each sequence. Furthermore, no output subnetworks are used in this particular application of the algorithm. In this case we obtain the reestimation formulae:

$$w_{ijk} = \frac{\sum_{p=1}^{P}\sum_{t:\sigma_t=k} \frac{\hat{\beta}_{it}\hat{\zeta}_{j,t-1}}{\hat{\zeta}_{x_T^\star,T}}}{\sum_{i\in\mathcal{S}_j}\sum_{p=1}^{P}\sum_{t:\sigma_t=k} \frac{\hat{\beta}_{it}\hat{\zeta}_{j,t-1}}{\hat{\zeta}_{x_T^\star,T}}} \qquad (12)$$

In general, however, if the subnetworks have hidden sigmoidal units, or use a softmax function to constrain their outputs to sum to one, the maximum of Q cannot be found analytically. In these cases we can resort to a GEM algorithm, that simply produces an increase in Q, for example by gradient ascent. In this case, the derivatives of Q with respect to the parameters can be easily computed as follows. Let θ_{jk} be a generic weight in the state subnetwork $\mathcal{N}_j$. From equation (9):

$$\frac{\partial Q(\boldsymbol{\Theta};\hat{\boldsymbol{\Theta}})}{\partial \theta_{jk}} = \sum_p \sum_t \sum_i \hat{h}_{ij,t} \frac{1}{\varphi_{ij,t}} \frac{\partial \varphi_{ij,t}}{\partial \theta_{jk}} \qquad (13)$$

where the partial derivatives $\frac{\partial \varphi_{ij,t}}{\partial \theta_{jk}}$ can be computed using backpropagation. Similarly, denoting with ϑ_{ik} a generic weight of the output subnetwork $\mathcal{O}_i$, we have:

$$\frac{\partial Q(\boldsymbol{\Theta};\hat{\boldsymbol{\Theta}})}{\partial \vartheta_{ik}} = \sum_p \sum_t \sum_\ell \hat{\zeta}_{i,t} \frac{\partial}{\partial \eta_{i\ell,t}} \log f_Y(\boldsymbol{y}_y; \boldsymbol{\eta}_{it}) \frac{\partial \eta_{i\ell,t}}{\partial \vartheta_{ik}} \qquad (14)$$

where $\frac{\partial \eta_{i\ell,t}}{\partial \vartheta_{ik}}$ are also computed using backpropagation. Intuitively, the parameters are updated as if the estimation step of EM had provided targets for the outputs of the $2n$ subnetworks, for each time t. Although GEM algorithms are also guaranteed to find a local maximum of the likelihood, their convergence may be significantly slower compared to EM. In several experiments we noticed that convergence can be accelerated with stochastic gradient ascent.

4 COMPARISONS

It appears natural to find similarities between the recurrent architecture described so far and standard HMMs (Levinson et al., 1983). The architecture proposed in this paper differs from standard HMMs in two respects: computing style and learning. With IOHMMs, sequences are processed similarly to recurrent networks, e.g., an input sequence can be synchronously transformed into an output sequence. This computing style is real-time and predictions of the outputs are available as the input sequence is being processed. This architecture thus allows one to implement all three fundamental sequence processing tasks: *production, prediction*, and *classification*. Finally, transition probabilities in standard HMMs are fixed, i.e. states form a *homogeneous* Markov chain. In IOHMMs, transition probabilities are conditional on the input and thus depend on time, resulting in an *inhomogeneous* Markov chain. Consequently, the *dynamics* of the system (specified by the transition probabilities) are not fixed but are *adapted* in time depending on the input sequence.

The other fundamental difference is in the learning procedure. While interesting for their capabilities of modeling sequential phenomena, a major weakness of standard HMMs is their poor discrimination power due to unsupervised learning. An approach that has been found useful to improve discrimination in HMMs is based on maximum mutual information (MMI) training. It has been pointed out that supervised learning and discriminant learning criteria like MMI are actually strictly related (Bridle, 1989). Although the parameter adjusting procedure we have defined is based on MLE, $\boldsymbol{y}_1^T$ is used as *desired output* in response to the input $\boldsymbol{u}_1^T$, resulting in discriminant supervised learning. Finally, it is worth mentioning that a number of hybrid approaches have been proposed to integrate connectionist approaches into the HMM framework. For example in (Bengio et al., 1992) the observations used by the HMM are generated by a feedforward neural network. In (Bourlard and Wellekens, 1990) a feedforward network is used to estimate state probabilities, conditional to the acoustic sequence. A common feature of these algorithms and the one proposed in this paper is that neural networks are used to extract temporally local information whereas a Markovian system integrates long-term constraints.

We can also establish a link between IOHMMs and adaptive mixtures of experts (ME) (Jacobs et al., 1991). Recently, Cacciatore & Nowlan (1994) have proposed a recurrent extension to the ME architecture, called *mixture of controllers* (MC), in which the gating network has feedback connections, thus allowing to take temporal context into account. Our IOHMM architecture can be interpreted as a special case of the MC architecture, in which the set of state subnetworks play the role of a gating network having a modular structure and second order connections.

5 REGULAR GRAMMAR INFERENCE

In this section we describe an application of our architecture to the problem of grammatical inference. In this task the learner is presented a set of labeled strings and is requested to infer a set of rules that define a formal language. It can be considered as a prototype for more complex language processing problems. However, even in the "simplest" case, i.e. regular grammars, the task can be proved to be NP-complete (Angluin and Smith, 1983). We report experimental results on a set of regular grammars introduced by Tomita (1982) and afterwards used by other researchers to measure the accuracy of inference methods based on recurrent networks (Giles et al., 1992; Pollack, 1991; Watrous and Kuhn, 1992).

We used a scalar output with supervision on the final output y_T that was modeled as a Bernoulli variable $f_Y(y_T; \eta_T) = \eta_T^{y_T}(1 - \eta_T)^{1-y_T}$, with $y_T = 0$ if the string is rejected and $y_T = 1$ if it is accepted. In this application we did not apply

Table 1: Summary of experimental results on the seven Tomita's grammars.

Grammar	Sizes		Convergence	Accuracies			
	$n^\star$	FSA min		Average	Worst	Best	W&K Best
1	2	2	.600	1.000	1.000	1.000	1.000
2	8	3	.800	.965	.834	1.000	1.000
3	7	5	.150	.867	.775	1.000	.783
4	4	4	.100	1.000	1.000	1.000	.609
5	4	4	.100	1.000	1.000	1.000	.668
6	3	3	.350	1.000	1.000	1.000	.462
7	3	5	.450	.856	.815	1.000	.557

external inputs to the output networks. This corresponds to modeling a Moore finite state machine. Given the absence of prior knowledge about plausible state paths, we used an *ergodic* transition graph (i.e., fully connected).In the experiments we measured convergence and generalization performance using different sizes for the recurrent architecture. For each setting we ran 20 trials with different seeds for the initial weights. We considered a trial successful if the trained network was able to correctly label all the training strings. The model size was chosen using a cross-validation criterion based on performance on 20 randomly generated strings of length $T \leq 12$. For comparison, in Table 1 we also report for each grammar the number of states of the minimal recognizing FSA (Tomita, 1982). We tested the trained networks on a corpus of $2^{13} - 1$ binary strings of length $T \leq 12$. The final results are summarized in Table 1. The column "Convergence" reports the fraction of trials that succeeded to separate the training set. The next three columns report averages and order statistics (worst and best trial) of the fraction of correctly classified strings, measured on the successful trials. For each grammar these results refer to the model size $n^\star$ selected by cross-validation. Generalization was always perfect on grammars 1,4,5 and 6. For each grammar, the best trial also attained perfect generalization. These results compare very favorably to those obtained with second-order networks trained by gradient descent, when using the learning sets proposed by Tomita. For comparison, in the last column of Table 1 we reproduce the results reported by Watrous & Kuhn (1992) in the best of five trials. In most of the successful trials the model learned an actual FSA behavior with transition probabilities asymptotically converging either to 0 or to 1. This renders trivial the extraction of the corresponding FSA. Indeed, for grammars 1,4,5, and 6, we found that the trained networks behave exactly like the minimal recognizing FSA.

A potential training problem is the presence of local maxima in the likelihood function. For example, the number of converged trials for grammars 3, 4, and 5 is quite small and the difficulty of discovering the optimal solution might become a serious restriction for tasks involving a large number of states. In other experiments (Bengio & Frasconi, 1994a), we noticed that restricting the connectivity of the transition graph can significantly help to remove problems of convergence. Of course, this approach can be effectively exploited only if some prior knowledge about the state space is available. For example, applications of HMMs to speech recognition always rely on structured topologies.

6 CONCLUSIONS

There are still a number of open questions. In particular, the effectiveness of the model on tasks involving large or very large state spaces needs to be carefully evaluated. In (Bengio & Frasconi 1994b) we show that learning long term dependencies in these models becomes more difficult as we increase the connectivity of the state transition graph. However, because transition probabilities of IOHMMs change at each t, they deal better with this problem of long-term dependencies than standard HMMs. Another interesting aspect to be investigated is the capability of the model to successfully perform tasks of sequence production or prediction. For example, interesting tasks that could also be approached are those related to time series modeling and motor control learning.

References

Angluin, D. and Smith, C. (1983). Inductive inference: Theory and methods. *Computing Surveys*, 15(3):237–269.

Bengio, Y. and Frasconi, P. (1994a). Credit assignment through time: Alternatives to backpropagation. In Cowan, J., Tesauro, G., and Alspector, J., editors, *Advances in Neural Information Processing Systems 6*. Morgan Kaufmann.

Bengio, Y. and Frasconi, P. (1994b). An EM Approach to Learning Sequential Behavior. Tech. Rep. RT-DSI/11-94, University of Florence.

Bengio, Y., De Mori, R., Flammia, G., and Kompe, R. (1992). Global optimization of a neural network-hidden markov model hybrid. *IEEE Transactions on Neural Networks*, 3(2):252–259.

Bengio, Y., Simard, P., and Frasconi, P. (1994). Learning long-term dependencies with gradient descent is difficult. *IEEE Trans. Neural Networks*, 5(2).

Bourlard, H. and Wellekens, C. (1990). Links between hidden markov models and multilayer perceptrons. *IEEE Trans. Pattern An. Mach. Intell.*, 12:1167–1178.

Bridle, J. S. (1989). Training stochastic model recognition algorithms as networks can lead to maximum mutual information estimation of parameters. In D.S.Touretzky, ed., *NIPS2*, pages 211–217. Morgan Kaufmann.

Cacciatore, T. W. and Nowlan, S. J. (1994). Mixtures of controllers for jump linear and non-linear plants. In Cowan, J. et. al., editors, *Advances in Neural Information Processing Systems 6*, San Mateo, CA. Morgan Kaufmann.

Dempster, A. P., Laird, N. M., and Rubin, D. B. (1977). Maximum-likelihood from incomplete data via the EM algorithm. *J. Royal Stat. Soc. B*, 39:1–38.

Giles, C. L., Miller, C. B., Chen, D., Sun, G. Z., Chen, H. H., and Lee, Y. C. (1992). Learning and extracting finite state automata with second-order recurrent neural networks. *Neural Computation*, 4(3):393–405.

Jacobs, R. A., Jordan, M. I., Nowlan, S. J., and Hinton, G. E. (1991). Adaptive mixture of local experts. *Neural Computation*, 3:79–87.

Levinson, S. E., Rabiner, L. R., and Sondhi, M. M. (1983). An introduction to the application of the theory of probabilistic functions of a markov process to automatic speech recognition. *Bell System Technical Journal*, 64(4):1035–1074.

Mozer, M. C. (1992). The induction of multiscale temporal structure. In Moody, J. et. al., eds, *NIPS 4* pages 275–282. Morgan Kaufmann.

Pollack, J. B. (1991). The induction of dynamical recognizers. *Machine Learning*, 7(2):196–227.

Tomita, M. (1982). Dynamic construction of finite-state automata from examples using hill-climbing. *Proc. 4th Cog. Science Conf.*, pp. 105–108, Ann Arbor MI.

Watrous, R. L. and Kuhn, G. M. (1992). Induction of finite-state languages using second-order recurrent networks. *Neural Computation*, 4(3):406–414.

Boltzmann Chains and Hidden Markov Models

Lawrence K. Saul and Michael I. Jordan
lksaul@psyche.mit.edu, jordan@psyche.mit.edu
Center for Biological and Computational Learning
Massachusetts Institute of Technology
79 Amherst Street, E10-243
Cambridge, MA 02139

Abstract

We propose a statistical mechanical framework for the modeling of discrete time series. Maximum likelihood estimation is done via Boltzmann learning in one-dimensional networks with tied weights. We call these networks Boltzmann chains and show that they contain hidden Markov models (HMMs) as a special case. Our framework also motivates new architectures that address particular shortcomings of HMMs. We look at two such architectures: parallel chains that model feature sets with disparate time scales, and looped networks that model long-term dependencies between hidden states. For these networks, we show how to implement the Boltzmann learning rule exactly, in polynomial time, without resort to simulated or mean-field annealing. The necessary computations are done by exact decimation procedures from statistical mechanics.

1 INTRODUCTION AND SUMMARY

Statistical models of discrete time series have a wide range of applications, most notably to problems in speech recognition (Juang & Rabiner, 1991) and molecular biology (Baldi, Chauvin, Hunkapiller, & McClure, 1992). A common problem in these fields is to find a probabilistic model, and a set of model parameters, that account for sequences of observed data. Hidden Markov models (HMMs) have been particularly successful at modeling discrete time series. One reason for this is the powerful learning rule (Baum, 1972), a special case of the Expectation-Maximization (EM) procedure for maximum likelihood estimation (Dempster, Laird, & Rubin, 1977).

In this work, we develop a statistical mechanical framework for the modeling of discrete time series. The framework enables us to relate HMMs to a large family of exactly solvable models in statistical mechanics. The connection to statistical mechanics was first noticed by Sourlas (1989), who studied spin glass models of error-correcting codes. We view the estimation procedure for HMMs as a special (and particularly tractable) case of the Boltzmann learning rule (Ackley, Hinton, & Sejnowski, 1985; Byrne, 1992).

The rest of this paper is organized as follows. In Section 2, we review the modeling problem for discrete time series and establish the connection between HMMs and Boltzmann machines. In Section 3, we show how to quickly determine whether or not a particular Boltzmann machine is tractable, and if so, how to efficiently compute the correlations in the Boltzmann learning rule. Finally, in Section 4, we look at two architectures that address particular weaknesses of HMMs: the modelling of disparate time scales and long-term dependencies.

2 MODELING DISCRETE TIME SERIES

A discrete time series is a sequence of symbols $\{j_\ell\}_{\ell=1}^L$ in which each symbol belongs to a finite countable set, i.e. $j_\ell \in \{1, 2, \ldots, m\}$. Given one long sequence, or perhaps many shorter ones, the modeling task is to characterize the probability distribution from which the time series are generated.

2.1 HIDDEN MARKOV MODELS

A first-order Hidden Markov Model (HMM) is characterized by a set of n hidden states, an alphabet of m symbols, a transmission matrix $a_{ii'}$, an emission matrix b_{ij}, and a prior distribution π_i over the initial hidden state. The sequence of states $\{i_\ell\}_{\ell=1}^L$ and symbols $\{j_\ell\}_{\ell=1}^L$ is modeled to occur with probability

$$P(\{i_\ell, j_\ell\}) = \pi_{i_1} a_{i_1 i_2} a_{i_2 i_3} \ldots a_{i_{L-1} i_L} b_{i_1 j_1} b_{i_2 j_2} \ldots b_{i_L j_L}. \tag{1}$$

The modeling problem is to find the parameter values $(a_{ii'}, b_{ij}, \pi_i)$ that maximize the likelihood of observed sequences of training data. We will elaborate on the learning rule in section 2.3, but first let us make the connection to a well-known family of stochastic neural networks, namely Boltzmann machines.

2.2 BOLTZMANN MACHINES

Consider a Boltzmann machine with m-state visible units, n-state hidden units, tied weights, and the linear architecture shown in Figure 1. This example represents the simplest possible Boltzmann "chain", one that is essentially equivalent to a first-order HMM unfolded in time (MacKay, 1994). The transition weights $A_{ii'}$ connect adjacent hidden units, while the emission weights B_{ij} connect each hidden unit to

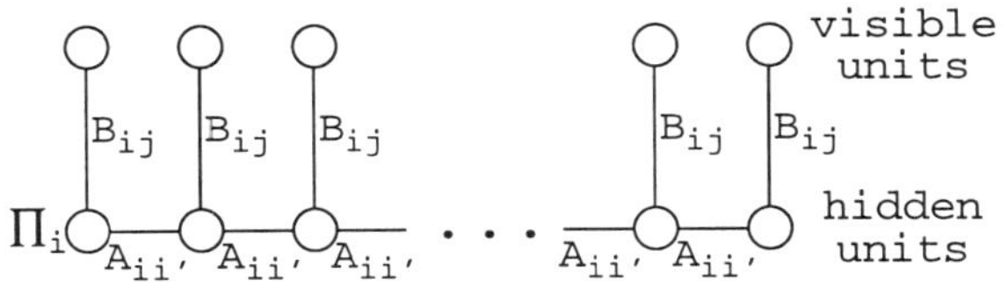

Figure 1: Boltzmann chain with n-state hidden units, m-state visible units, transition weights $A_{ii'}$, emission weights B_{ij}, and boundary weights Π_i.

its visible counterpart. In addition, boundary weights Π_i model an extra bias on the first hidden unit. Each configuration of units represents a state of energy

$$\mathcal{H}[\{i_\ell, j_\ell\}] = -\Pi_{i_1} - \sum_{\ell=1}^{L-1} A_{i_\ell i_{\ell+1}} - \sum_{\ell=1}^{L} B_{i_\ell j_\ell}, \qquad (2)$$

where $\{i_\ell\}_{\ell=1}^{L}$ ($\{j_\ell\}_{\ell=1}^{L}$) is the sequence of states over the hidden (visible) units. The probability to find the network in a particular configuration is given by

$$P(\{i_\ell, j_\ell\}) = \frac{1}{Z} e^{-\beta \mathcal{H}}, \qquad (3)$$

where $\beta = 1/T$ is the inverse temperature, and the partition function

$$Z = \sum_{\{i_\ell, j_\ell\}} e^{-\beta \mathcal{H}} \qquad (4)$$

is the sum over states that normalizes the Boltzmann distribution, eq. (3).

Comparing this to the HMM distribution, eq. (1), it is clear that any first-order HMM can be represented by the Boltzmann chain of figure 1, provided we take[1]

$$A_{ii'} = T \ln a_{ii'}, \quad B_{ij} = T \ln b_{ij}, \quad \Pi_i = T \ln \pi_i. \qquad (5)$$

Later, in Section 4, we will consider more complicated chains whose architectures address particular shortcomings of HMMs. For now, however, let us continue to develop the example of figure 1, making explicit the connection to HMMs.

2.3 LEARNING RULES

In the framework of Boltzmann learning (Williams & Hinton, 1990), the data for our problem consist of sequences of states over the visible units; the goal is to find the weights $(A_{ii'}, B_{ij}, \Pi_i)$ that maximize the likelihood of the observed data. The likelihood of a sequence $\{j_\ell\}$ is given by the ratio

$$P(\{j_\ell\}) = \frac{P(\{i_\ell, j_\ell\})}{P(\{i_\ell\}|\{j_\ell\})} = \frac{e^{-\beta \mathcal{H}}/Z}{e^{-\beta \mathcal{H}}/Z_c} = \frac{Z_c}{Z}, \qquad (6)$$

---

[1] Note, however, that the reverse statement—that for any set of parameters, this Boltzmann chain can be represented as an HMM—is *not* true. The weights in the Boltzmann chain represent arbitrary energies between $\pm\infty$, whereas the HMM parameters represent probabilities that are constrained to obey sum rules, such as $\sum_{i'} a_{ii'} = 1$. The Boltzmann chain of figure 1 therefore has slightly more degrees of freedom than a first-order HMM. An interpretation of these extra degrees of freedom is given by MacKay (1994).

where Z_c is the clamped partition function

$$Z_c = \sum_{\{i_\ell\}} e^{-\beta \mathcal{H}}. \qquad (7)$$

Note that the sum in Z_c is only over the hidden states in the network, while the visible states are clamped to the observed values $\{j_\ell\}$.

The Boltzmann learning rule adjusts the weights of the network by gradient-ascent on the log-likelihood. For the example of figure 1, this leads to weight updates

$$\Delta A_{ii'} = \eta\beta \sum_{\ell=1}^{L-1} \left[\langle \delta_{ii_\ell} \delta_{i'i_{\ell+1}} \rangle_c - \langle \delta_{ii_\ell} \delta_{i'i_{\ell+1}} \rangle \right], \qquad (8)$$

$$\Delta B_{ij} = \eta\beta \sum_{\ell=1}^{L} \left[\langle \delta_{ii_\ell} \delta_{jj_\ell} \rangle_c - \langle \delta_{ii_\ell} \delta_{jj_\ell} \rangle \right], \qquad (9)$$

$$\Delta \Pi_i = \eta\beta \left[\langle \delta_{ii_1} \rangle_c - \langle \delta_{ii_1} \rangle \right], \qquad (10)$$

where δ_{ij} stands for the Kronecker delta function, η is a learning rate, and $\langle \cdot \rangle$ and $\langle \cdot \rangle_c$ denote expectations over the free and clamped Boltzmann distributions.

The Boltzmann learning rule may also be derived as an Expectation–Maximization (EM) algorithm. The EM procedure is an alternating two-step method for maximum likelihood estimation in probability models with hidden and observed variables. For Boltzmann machines in general, neither the E-step nor the M-step can be done exactly; one must estimate the necessary statistics by Monte Carlo simulation (Ackley et al., 1985) or mean-field theory (Peterson & Anderson, 1987). In certain special cases (e.g. trees and chains), however, the necessary statistics can be computed to perform an exact E-step (as shown below). While the M-step in these Boltzmann machines cannot be done exactly, the weight updates can be approximated by gradient descent. This leads to learning rules in the form of eqs. (8–10).

HMMs may be viewed as a special case of Boltzmann chains for which both the E-step *and* the M-step are analytically tractable. In this case, the maximization in the M-step is performed subject to the constraints $\sum_i e^{\beta \Pi_i} = 1$, $\sum_{i'} e^{\beta A_{ii'}} = 1$, and $\sum_j e^{\beta B_{ij}} = 1$. These constraints imply $Z = 1$ and lead to closed-form equations for the weight updates in HMMs.

3 EXACT METHODS FOR BOLTZMANN LEARNING

The key technique to compute partition functions and correlations in Boltzmann chains is known as decimation. The idea behind decimation[2] is the following. Consider three units connected in series, as shown in Figure 2a. Though not directly connected, the end units have an effective interaction that is mediated by the middle one. In fact, the two weights in series exert the same influence as a single *effective* weight, given by

$$e^{\beta A_{ii''}} = \sum_{i'} e^{\beta A^{(1)}_{ii'} + \beta A^{(2)}_{i'i''} + \beta B_{i'}}. \qquad (11)$$

---

[2] A related method, the transfer matrix, is described by Stolorz (1994).

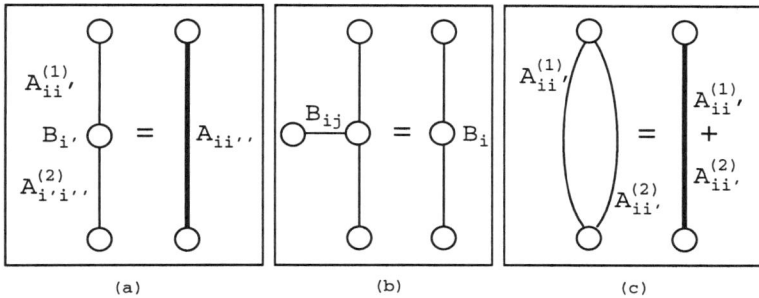

Figure 2: Decimation, pruning, and joining in Boltzmann machines.

Replacing the weights in this way amounts to integrating out, or decimating, the degree of freedom represented by the middle unit. An analogous rule may be derived for the situation shown in Figure 2b. Summing over the degrees of freedom of the dangling unit generates an effective bias on its parent, given by

$$e^{\beta B_i} = \sum_j e^{\beta B_{ij}}. \qquad (12)$$

We call this the pruning rule. Another type of equivalence is shown in Figure 2c. The two weights in parallel have the same effect as the sum total weight

$$A_{ii'} = A_{ii'}^{(1)} + A_{ii'}^{(2)}. \qquad (13)$$

We call this the joining rule. It holds trivially for biases as well as weights.

The rules for decimating, pruning, and joining have simple analogs in other types of networks (e.g. the law for combining resistors in electric circuits), and the strategy for exploiting them is a familiar one. Starting with a complicated network, we iterate the rules until we have a simple network whose properties are easily computed. A network is tractable for Boltzmann learning if it can be reduced to any pair of connected units. In this case, we may use the rules to compute all the correlations required for Boltzmann learning. Clearly, the rules do not make all networks tractable; certain networks (e.g. trees and chains), however, lend themselves naturally to these types of operations.

4 DESIGNER NETS

The rules in section 3 can be used to quickly assess whether or not a network is tractable for Boltzmann learning. Conversely, they can be used to design networks that are computationally tractable. This section looks at two networks designed to address particular shortcomings of HMMs.

4.1 PARALLEL CHAINS AND DISPARATE TIME SCALES

An important problem in speech recognition (Juang et al., 1991) is how to "combine feature sets with fundamentally different time scales." Spectral parameters, such

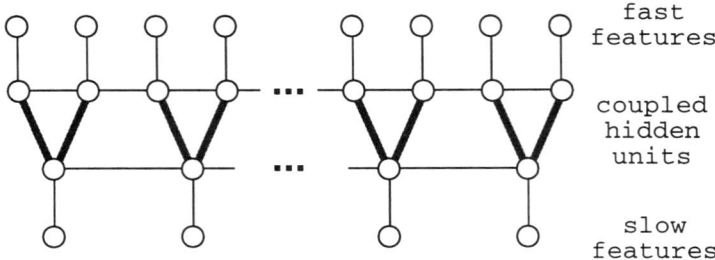

Figure 3: Coupled parallel chains for features with different time scales.

as the cepstrum and delta-cepstrum, vary on a time scale of 10 msec; on the other hand, prosodic parameters, such as the signal energy and pitch, vary on a time scale of 100 msec. A model that takes into account this disparity should avoid two things. The first is redundancy—in particular, the rather lame solution of oversampling the nonspectral features. The second is overfitting. How might this arise? Suppose we have trained two separate HMMs on sequences of spectral and prosodic features, knowing that the different features "may not warrant a single, unified Markov chain" (Juang et al., 1991). To exploit the correlation between feature sets, we must now couple the two HMMs. A naive solution is to form the Cartesian product of their hidden state spaces and resume training. Unfortunately, this results in an explosion in the number of parameters that must be fit from the training data. The likely consequences are overfitting and poor generalization.

Figure 3 shows a network for modeling feature sets with disparate time scales—in this case, a 2:1 disparity. Two parallel Boltzmann chains are coupled by weights that connect their hidden units. Like the transition and emission weights within each chain, the coupling weights are tied across the length of the network. Note that coupling the time scales in this way introduces far fewer parameters than forming the Cartesian product of the hidden state spaces. Moreover, the network is tractable by the rules of section 3. Suppose, for example, that we wish to compute the correlation between two neighboring hidden units in the middle of the network. This is done by first pruning all the visible units, then repeatedly decimating hidden units from both ends of the network.

Figure 4 shows typical results on a simple benchmark problem, with data generated by an artificially constructed HMM. We tested the parallel chains model on 10 training sets, with varying levels of built-in correlation between features. A two-step method was used to train the parallel chains. First, we set the coupling weights to zero and trained each chain by a separate Baum-Welch procedure. Then, after learning in this phase was complete, we lifted the zero constraints and resumed training with the full Boltzmann learning rule. The percent gain in this second phase was directly related to the degree of correlation built into the training data, suggesting that the coupling weights were indeed capturing the correlation between feature sets. We also compared the performance of this Boltzmann machine versus that of a simple Cartesian-product HMM trained by an additional Baum-Welch procedure. While in both cases the second phase of learning led to reduced training error, the Cartesian product HMMs were decidedly more prone to overfitting.

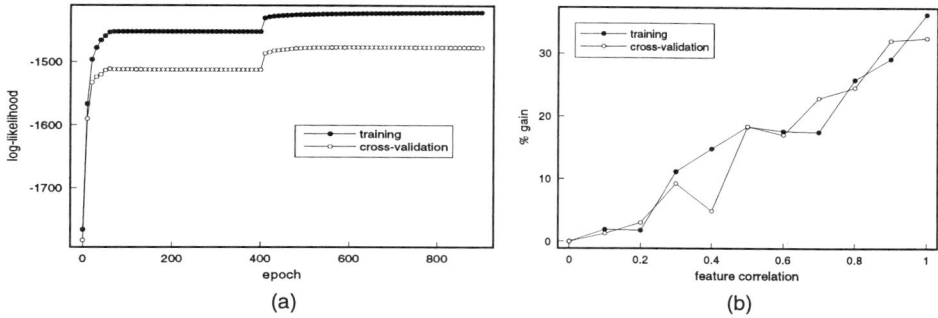

Figure 4: (a) Log-likelihood versus epoch for parallel chains with 4-state hidden units, 6-state visible units, and 100 hidden–visible unit pairs (per chain). The second jump in log-likelihood occurred at the onset of Boltzmann learning (see text). (b) Percent gain in log-likelihood versus built-in correlation between feature sets.

4.2 LOOPS AND LONG-TERM DEPENDENCIES

Another shortcoming of first-order HMMs is that they cannot exhibit long-term dependencies between the hidden states (Juang et al., 1991). Higher-order and duration-based HMMs have been used in this regard with varying degrees of success. The rules of section 3 suggest another approach—namely, designing tractable networks with limited long-range connectivity. As an example, Figure 5a shows a Boltzmann chain with an internal loop and a long-range connection between the first and last hidden units. These extra features could be used to enforce known periodicities in the time series. Though tractable for Boltzmann learning, the loops in this network do not fit naturally into the framework of HMMs. Figure 5b shows learning curves for a toy problem, with data generated by another looped network.

Carefully chosen loops and long-range connections provide additional flexibility in the design of probabilistic models for time series. Can networks with these extra features capture the long-term dependencies exhibited by real data? This remains an important issue for future research.

Acknowledgements

We thank G. Hinton, D. MacKay, P. Stolorz, and C. Williams for useful discussions. This work was funded by ATR Human Information Processing Laboratories, Siemens Corporate Research, and NSF grant CDA-9404932.

References

D. H. Ackley, G. E. Hinton, and T. J. Sejnowski. (1985) A Learning Algorithm for Boltzmann Machines. *Cog. Sci.* **9**: 147–160.

P. Baldi, Y. Chauvin, T. Hunkapiller, and M. A. McClure. (1992) *Proc. Nat. Acad. Sci. (USA)* **91**: 1059-1063.

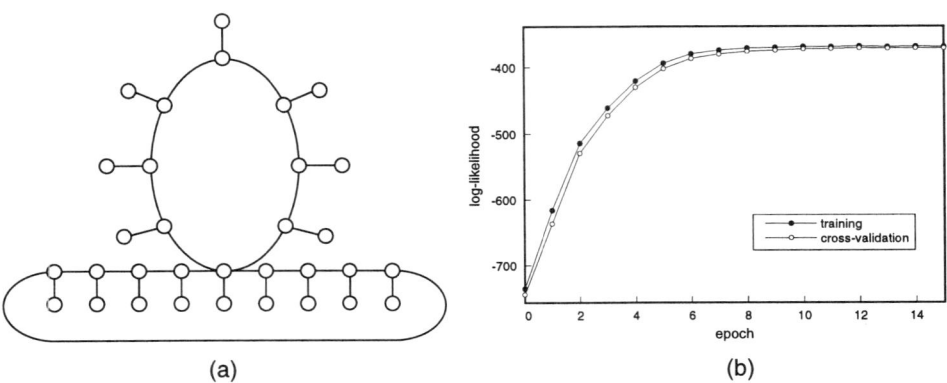

Figure 5: (a) Looped network. (b) Log-likelihood versus epoch for a looped network with 4-state hidden units, 6-state visible units, and 100 hidden–visible unit pairs.

L. Baum. (1972) An Inequality and Associated Maximization Technique in Statistical Estimation of Probabilistic Functions of Markov Processes, *Inequalities* **3**:1–8.

Byrne, W. (1992) Alternating Minimization and Boltzmann Machine Learning. *IEEE Trans. Neural Networks* **3**:612–620.

A. P. Dempster, N. M. Laird, and D. B. Rubin. (1977) Maximum Likelihood from Incomplete Data via the EM Algorithm. *J. Roy. Statist. Soc. B*, **39**:1–38.

C. Itzykson and J. Drouffe. (1991) *Statistical Field Theory*, Cambridge: Cambridge University Press.

B. H. Juang and L. R. Rabiner. (1991) Hidden Markov Models for Speech Recognition, *Technometrics* **33**: 251–272.

D. J. MacKay. (1994) Equivalence of Boltzmann Chains and Hidden Markov Models, submitted to *Neural Comp.*

C. Peterson and J. R. Anderson. (1987) A Mean Field Theory Learning Algorithm for Neural Networks, *Complex Systems* **1**:995–1019.

L. Saul and M. Jordan. (1994) Learning in Boltzmann Trees. *Neural Comp.* **6**: 1174–1184.

N. Sourlas. (1989) Spin Glass Models as Error Correcting Codes. *Nature* **339**: 693–695.

P. Stolorz. (1994) Links Between Dynamic Programming and Statistical Physics for Heterogeneous Systems, JPL/Caltech preprint.

C. Williams and G. E. Hinton. (1990) Mean Field Networks That Learn To Discriminate Temporally Distorted Strings. *Proc. Connectionist Models Summer School*: 18–22.

Bayesian Query Construction for Neural Network Models

Gerhard Paass **Jörg Kindermann**
German National Research Center for Computer Science (GMD)
D-53757 Sankt Augustin, Germany
paass@gmd.de   kindermann@gmd.de

Abstract

If data collection is costly, there is much to be gained by actively selecting particularly informative data points in a sequential way. In a Bayesian decision-theoretic framework we develop a query selection criterion which explicitly takes into account the intended use of the model predictions. By Markov Chain Monte Carlo methods the necessary quantities can be approximated to a desired precision. As the number of data points grows, the model complexity is modified by a Bayesian model selection strategy. The properties of two versions of the criterion are demonstrated in numerical experiments.

1 INTRODUCTION

In this paper we consider the situation where data collection is costly, as when for example, real measurements or technical experiments have to be performed. In this situation the approach of query learning ('active data selection', 'sequential experimental design', etc.) has a potential benefit. Depending on the previously seen examples, a new input value ('query') is selected in a systematic way and the corresponding output is obtained. The motivation for query learning is that random examples often contain redundant information, and the concentration on non-redundant examples must necessarily improve generalization performance.

We use a Bayesian decision-theoretic framework to derive a criterion for query construction. The criterion reflects the intended use of the predictions by an appropriate loss function. We limit our analysis to the selection of the next data point, given a set of data already sampled. The proposed procedure derives the expected loss for candidate inputs and selects a query with minimal expected loss.

There are several published surveys of query construction methods [Ford et al. 89, Plutowski White 93, Sollich 94]. Most current approaches, e.g. [Cohn 94], rely on the information matrix of parameters. Then however, all parameters receive equal attention regardless of their influence on the intended use of the model [Pronzato Walter 92]. In addition, the estimates are valid only asymptotically. Bayesian approaches have been advocated by [Berger 80], and applied to neural networks [MacKay 92]. In [Sollich Saad 95] their relation to maximum information gain is discussed. In this paper we show that by using Markov Chain Monte Carlo methods it is possible to determine all quantities necessary for the selection of a query. This approach is valid in small sample situations, and the procedure's precision can be increased with additional computational effort. With the square loss function, the criterion is reduced to a variant of the familiar integrated mean square error [Plutowski White 93].

In the next section we develop the query selection criterion from a decision-theoretic point of view. In the third section we show how the criterion can be calculated using Markov Chain Monte Carlo methods and we discuss a strategy for model selection. In the last section, the results of two experiments with MLPs are described.

2 A DECISION-THEORETIC FRAMEWORK

Assume we have an input vector x and a scalar output y distributed as $y \sim p(y \mid x, w)$ where w is a vector of parameters. The conditional expected value is a deterministic function $f(x, w) := E(y \mid x, w)$ where $y = f(x, w) + \epsilon$ and ϵ is a zero mean error term. Suppose we have iteratively collected observations $D_{(n)} := ((\tilde{x}_1, \tilde{y}_1), \ldots, (\tilde{x}_n, \tilde{y}_n))$. We get the Bayesian posterior $p(w \mid D_{(n)}) = p(D_{(n)} \mid w) p(w) / \int p(D_{(n)} \mid w) p(w) \, dw$ and the predictive distribution $p(y \mid x, D_{(n)}) = \int p(y \mid x, w) p(w \mid D_{(n)}) \, dw$ if $p(w)$ is the prior distribution.

We consider the situation where, based on some data x, we have to perform an action α whose result depends on the unknown output y. Some decisions may have more severe effects than others. The loss function $L(y, \alpha) \in [0, \infty)$ measures the loss if y is the true value and we have taken the action $\alpha \in \mathcal{A}$. In this paper we consider real-valued actions, e.g. setting the temperature α in a chemical process. We have to select an $\alpha \in \mathcal{A}$ only knowing the input x. According to the *Bayes Principle* [Berger 80, p.14] we should follow a decision rule $d : x \rightarrow \alpha$ such that the average risk $\int R(w, d) p(w \mid D_{(n)}) \, dw$ is minimal, where the risk is defined as $R(w, d) := \int L(y, d(x)) p(y \mid x, w) p(x) \, dy \, dx$. Here $p(x)$ is the distribution of future inputs, which is assumed to be known.

For the *square loss* function $L(y, \alpha) = (y - \alpha)^2$, the conditional expectation $d(x) := E(y \mid x, D_{(n)})$ is the optimal decision rule. In a control problem the loss may be larger at specific critical points. This can be addressed with a *weighted square loss* function $L(y, \alpha) := h(y)(y - \alpha)^2$, where $h(y) \geq 0$ [Berger 80, p.111]. The expected loss for an action is $\int (y - \alpha)^2 h(y) p(y \mid x, D_{(n)}) \, dy$. Replacing the predictive density $p(y \mid x, D_{(n)})$ with the weighted predictive density

$\tilde{p}(y \mid x, D_{(n)}) := h(y) p(y \mid x, D_{(n)})/G(x)$, where $G(x) := \int h(y) p(y \mid x, D_{(n)}) dy$, we get the optimal decision rule $d(x) := \int y \tilde{p}(y \mid x, D_{(n)}) dy$ and the average loss $G(x) \int (y - E(y \mid x, D_{(n)}))^2 \tilde{p}(y \mid x, D_{(n)}) dy$ for a given input x. With these modifications, all later derivations for the square loss function may be applied to the weighted square loss.

The aim of query sampling is the selection of a new observation $\check{x}$ in such a way that the average risk will be maximally reduced. Together with its still unknown y-value, $\check{x}$ defines a new observation $(\check{x}, \check{y})$ and new data $D_{(n)} \cup (\check{x}, \check{y})$. To determine this risk for some given $\check{x}$ we have to perform the following conceptual steps for a candidate query $\check{x}$:

1. *Future Data:* Construct the possible sets of 'future' observations $D_{(n)} \cup (\check{x}, \check{y})$, where $\check{y} \sim p(y \mid \check{x}, D_{(n)})$.

2. *Future posterior:* Determine a 'future' posterior distribution of parameters $p(w \mid D_{(n)} \cup (\check{x}, \check{y}))$ that depends on $\check{y}$ in the same way as though it had actually been observed.

3. *Future Loss:* Assuming $d^*_{\check{y},\check{x}}(x)$ is the optimal decision rule for given values of $\check{x}$, $\check{y}$, and x, compute the resulting loss as

$$\bar{r}^*_{\check{y},\check{x}}(x) := \int L(y, d^*_{\check{y},\check{x}}(x)) p(y \mid x, w) p(w \mid D_{(n)} \cup (\check{x}, \check{y})) dy \, dw \quad (1)$$

4. *Averaging:* Integrate this quantity over the future trial inputs x distributed as $p(x)$ and the different possible future outputs $\check{y}$, yielding
$\bar{r}^*_{\check{x}} := \int \bar{r}^*_{\check{y},\check{x}}(x) p(x) p(\check{y} \mid \check{x}, D_{(n)}) dx \, d\check{y}$.

This procedure is repeated until an $\check{x}$ with minimal average risk is found. Since local optima are typical, a global optimization method is required. Subsequently we then try to determine whether the current model is still adequate or whether we have to increase its complexity (e.g. by adding more hidden units).

3 COMPUTATIONAL PROCEDURE

Let us assume that the real data $D_{(n)}$ was generated according to a regression model $y = f(x, w) + \epsilon$ with i.i.d. Gaussian noise $\epsilon \sim N(0, \sigma^2(w))$. For example $f(x, w)$ may be a multilayer perceptron or a radial basis function network. Since the error terms are independent, the posterior density is $p(w \mid D_{(n)}) \propto p(w) \prod_{i=1}^{n} p(\tilde{y}_i \mid \tilde{x}_i, w)$ even in the case of query sampling [Ford et al. 89].

As the analytic derivation of the posterior is infeasible except in trivial cases, we have to use approximations. One approach is to employ a normal approximation [MacKay 92], but this is unreliable if the number of observations is small compared to the number of parameters. We use Markov Chain Monte Carlo procedures [Paaß 91, Neal 93] to generate a sample $W_{(B)} := \{w_1, \ldots w_B\}$ of parameters distributed according to $p(w \mid D_{(n)})$. If the number of sampling steps approaches infinity, the distribution of the simulated w_b approximates the posterior arbitrarily well.

To take into account the range of future $\check{y}$-values, we create a set of them by simulation. For each $w_b \in W_{(B)}$ a number of $\check{y} \sim p(y \mid \check{x}, w_b)$ is generated. Let

$\check{Y}_{(\check{x},R)} := \{\check{y}_1, \ldots, \check{y}_R\}$ be the resulting set. Instead of performing a new Markov Monte Carlo run to generate a new sample according to $p(w \mid D_{(n)} \cup (\check{x}, \check{y}))$, we use the old set $W_{(B)}$ of parameters and reweight them (importance sampling). In this way we may approximate integrals of some function $g(w)$ with respect to $p(w \mid D_{(n)} \cup (\check{x}, \check{y}))$ [Kalos Whitlock 86, p.92]:

$$\int g(w)\, p(w \mid D_{(n)} \cup (\check{x},\check{y}))\, dw \;\approx\; \frac{\sum_{b=1}^{B} g(w_b)\, p(\check{y} \mid \check{x}, w_b)}{\sum_{b=1}^{B} p(\check{y} \mid \check{x}, w_b)} \qquad (2)$$

The approximation error approaches zero as the size of $W_{(B)}$ increases.

3.1 APPROXIMATION OF FUTURE LOSS

Consider the future loss $\bar{r}^*_{\check{y},\check{x}}(x)$ given new observation $(\check{x}, \check{y})$ and trial input x_t. In the case of the square loss function, (1) can be transformed to

$$\bar{r}^*_{\check{y},\check{x}}(x_t) \;=\; \int [f(x_t, w) - E(y \mid x_t, D_{(n)} \cup (\check{x},\check{y}))]^2\, p(w \mid D_{(n)} \cup (\check{x},\check{y}))\, dw \qquad (3)$$
$$+ \int \sigma^2(w)\, p(w \mid D_{(n)} \cup (\check{x},\check{y}))\, dw$$

where $\sigma^2(w) := \operatorname{Var}(y \mid x, w)$ is independent of x. Assume a set $X_T = \{x_1, \ldots, x_T\}$ is given, which is representative of trial inputs for the distribution $p(x)$. Define $S(\check{x}, \check{y}) := \sum_{b=1}^{B} p(\check{y} \mid \check{x}, w_b)$ for $\check{y} \in \check{Y}_{(\check{x},R)}$. Then from equations (2) and (3) we get $\hat{E}(y \mid x_t, D_{(n)} \cup (\check{x},\check{y})) := 1/S(\check{x},\check{y}) \sum_{b=1}^{B} f(x_t, w_b)\, p(\check{y} \mid \check{x}, w_b)$ and

$$\bar{r}^*_{\check{y},\check{x}}(x_t) \;\approx\; \frac{1}{S(\check{x},\check{y})} \sum_{b=1}^{B} \sigma^2(w_b)\, p(\check{y} \mid \check{x}, w_b) \qquad (4)$$
$$+ \frac{1}{S(\check{x},\check{y})} \sum_{b=1}^{B} [f(x_t, w_b) - \hat{E}(y \mid x_t, D_{(n)} \cup (\check{x},\check{y}))]^2\, p(\check{y} \mid \check{x}, w_b)$$

The final value of $\bar{r}^*_{\check{x}}$ is obtained by averaging over the different $\check{y} \in \check{Y}_{(\check{x},R)}$ and different trial inputs $x_t \in X_T$. To reduce the variance, the trial inputs x_t should be selected by importance sampling (2) to concentrate them on regions with high current loss (see (5) below). To facilitate the search for an $\check{x}$ with minimal $\bar{r}^*_{\check{x}}$ we reduce the extent of random fluctuations of the $\check{y}$ values. Let $(v_1, \ldots, v_R)$ be a vector of random numbers $v_r \sim N(0,1)$, and let j_r be randomly selected from $\{1, \ldots, B\}$. Then for each $\check{x}$ the possible observations $\check{y}_r \in \check{Y}_{(\check{x},R)}$ are defined as $\check{y}_r := f(\check{x}, w_{j_r}) + v_r \sigma^2(w_{j_r})$. In this way the difference between neighboring inputs is not affected by noise, and search procedures can exploit gradients.

3.2 CURRENT LOSS

As a proxy for the future loss, we may use the current loss at $\check{x}$,

$$r_{curr}(\check{x}) = p(\check{x}) \int L(y, d^*(\check{x}))\, p(y \mid \check{x}, D_{(n)})\, dy \qquad (5)$$

where $p(\check{x})$ weights the inputs according to their relevance. For the square loss function the average loss at $\check{x}$ is the conditional variance $\text{Var}(y \mid \check{x}, D_{(n)})$. We get

$$r_{curr}(\check{x}) = p(\check{x}) \int (f(\check{x}, w) - E(y \mid \check{x}, D_{(n)}))^2 \, p(w \mid D_{(n)}) \, dw \qquad (6)$$
$$+ p(\check{x}) \int \sigma^2(w) \, p(w \mid D_{(n)}) \, dw$$

If $\hat{E}(y \mid \check{x}, D_{(n)}) := \frac{1}{B}\sum_{b=1}^{B} f(\check{x}, w_b)$ and the sample $W_{(B)} := \{w_1, \ldots, w_B\}$ is representative of $p(w \mid D_{(n)})$ we can approximate the current loss with

$$r_{curr}(\check{x}) \approx \frac{p(\check{x})}{B} \sum_{b=1}^{B} (f(\check{x}, w_b) - \hat{E}(y \mid \check{x}, D_{(n)}))^2 + \frac{p(\check{x})}{B} \sum_{b=1}^{B} \sigma^2(w_b) \qquad (7)$$

If the input distribution $p(x)$ is uniform, the second term is independent of $\check{x}$.

3.3 COMPLEXITY REGULARIZATION

Neural network models can represent arbitrary mappings between finite-dimensional spaces if the number of hidden units is sufficiently large [Hornik Stinchcombe 89]. As the number of observations grows, more and more hidden units are necessary to catch the details of the mapping. Therefore we use a sequential procedure to increase the capacity of our networks during query learning. White and Wooldridge call this approach the "method of sieves" and provide some asymptotic results on its consistency [White Wooldridge 91]. Gelfand and Dey compare Bayesian approaches for model selection and prove that, in the case of nested models M_1 and M_2, model choice by the ratio of popular Bayes factors $p(D_{(n)} \mid M_i) := \int p(D_{(n)} \mid w, M_i) \, p(w \mid M_i) \, dw$ will *always* choose the full model regardless of the data as $n \to \infty$ [Gelfand Dey 94]. They show that the *pseudo-Bayes factor*, a Bayesian variant of crossvalidation, is not affected by this paradox

$$\lambda(M_1, M_2) := \prod_{j=1}^{n} p(\tilde{y}_j \mid \tilde{x}_j, D_{(n,j)}, M_1) / \prod_{j=1}^{n} p(\tilde{y}_j \mid \tilde{x}_j, D_{(n,j)}, M_2) \qquad (8)$$

Here $D_{(n,j)} := D_{(n)} \setminus (\tilde{x}_j, \tilde{y}_j)$. As the difference between $p(w \mid D_{(n)})$ and $p(w \mid D_{(n,j)})$ is usually small, we use the full posterior as the importance function (2) and get

$$p(\tilde{y}_j \mid \tilde{x}_j, D_{(n,j)}, M_i) = \int p(\tilde{y}_j \mid \tilde{x}_j, w, M_i) \, p(w \mid D_{(n,j)}, M_i) \, dw$$
$$\approx B / \left(\sum_{b=1}^{B} 1/p(\tilde{y}_j \mid \tilde{x}_j, w_b, M_i) \right) \qquad (9)$$

4 NUMERICAL DEMONSTRATION

In a first experiment we tested the approach for a small a 1-2-1 MLP target function with Gaussian noise $N(0, 0.05^2)$. We assumed the square loss function and a uniform input distribution $p(x)$ over $[-5, 5]$. Using the "true" architecture for the approximating model we started with a single randomly generated observation. We

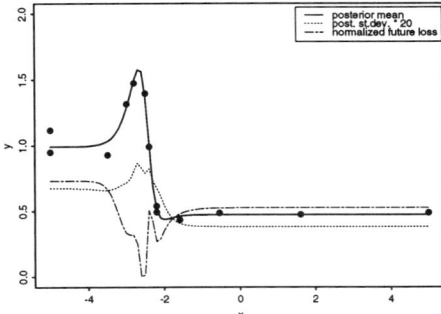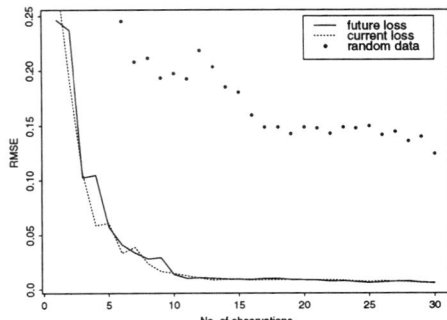

Figure 1: Future loss exploration: predicted posterior mean, future loss and current loss for 12 observations (left), and root mean square error of prediction (right).

estimated the future loss by (4) for 100 different inputs and selected the input with smallest future loss as the next query. $B = 50$ parameter vectors were generated requiring 200,000 Metropolis steps. Simultaneously we approximated the current loss criterion by (7). The left side of figure 1 shows the typical relation of both measures. In most situations the future loss is low in the same regions where the current loss (posterior standard deviation of mean prediction) is high. The queries are concentrated in areas of high variation and the estimated posterior mean approximates the target function quite well.

In the right part of figure 1 the RMSE of prediction averaged over 12 independent experiments is shown. After a few observations the RMSE drops sharply. In our example there is no marked difference between the prediction errors resulting from the future loss and the current loss criterion (also averaged over 12 experiments). Considering the substantial computing effort this favors the current loss criterion. The dots indicate the RMSE for randomly generated data (averaged over 8 experiments) using the same Bayesian prediction procedure. Because only few data points were located in the critical region of high variation the RMSE is much larger.

In the second experiment, a 2-3-1 MLP defined the target function $f(x, w_0)$, to which Gaussian noise of standard deviation 0.05 was added. $f(x, w_0)$ is shown in the left part of figure 2. We used five MLPs with 2-6 hidden units as candidate models $M_1, \ldots, M_5$ and generated $B = 45$ samples $W_{(B)}$ of the posterior $p(w \mid D_{(n)}, M_i)$, where $D_{(n)}$ is the current data. We started with 30,000 Metropolis steps for small values of n and increased this to 90,000 Metropolis steps for larger values of n. For a network with 6 hidden units and $n = 50$ observations, 10,000 Metropolis steps took about 30 seconds on a Sparc10 workstation. Next, we used equation (9) to compare the different models, and then used the optimal model to calculate the current loss (7) on a regular grid of $41 \times 41 = 1681$ query points $\check{x}$. Here we assumed the square loss function and a uniform input distribution $p(x)$ over $[-5, 5] \times [-5, 5]$. We selected the query point with maximal current loss and determined the final query point with a hillclimbing algorithm. In this way we were rather sure to get close to the true global optimum.

The main result of the experiment is summarized in the right part of figure 2. It

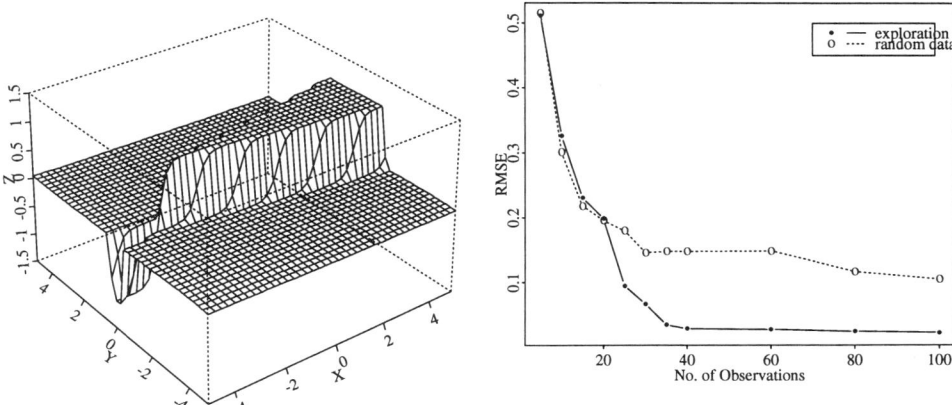

Figure 2: Current loss exploration: MLP target function and root mean square error.

shows - averaged over 3 experiments - the root mean square error between the true mean value and the posterior mean $E(y \mid x)$ on the grid of 1681 inputs in relation to the sample size. Three phases of the exploration can be distinguished (see figure 3). In the beginning a search is performed with many queries on the border of the input area. After about 20 observations the algorithm knows enough detail about the true function to concentrate on the relevant parts of the input space. This leads to a marked reduction of the mean square error. After 40 observations the systematic part of the true function has been captured nearly perfectly. In the last phase of the experiment the algorithm merely reduces the uncertainty caused by the random noise. In contrast, the data generated randomly does not have sufficient information on the details of $f(x, w)$, and therefore the error only gradually decreases. Because of space constraints we cannot report experiments with radial basis functions which led to similar results.

Acknowledgements

This work is part of the joint project 'REFLEX' of the German Fed. Department of Science and Technology (BMFT), grant number 01 IN 111A/4. We would like to thank Alexander Linden, Mark Ring, and Frank Weber for many fruitful discussions.

References

[Berger 80] Berger, J. (1980): *Statistical Decision Theory, Foundations, Concepts, and Methods*. Springer Verlag, New York.

[Cohn 94] Cohn, D. (1994): Neural Network Exploration Using Optimal Experimental Design. In J. Cowan et al. (eds.): *NIPS 5*. Morgan Kaufmann, San Mateo.

[Ford et al. 89] Ford, I., Titterington, D.M., Kitsos, C.P. (1989): Recent Advances in Nonlinear Design. *Technometrics*, **31**, p.49-60.

[Gelfand Dey 94] Gelfand, A.E., Dey, D.K. (1994): Bayesian Model Choice: Asymptotics and Exact Calculations. *J. Royal Statistical Society B*, **56**, pp.501-514.

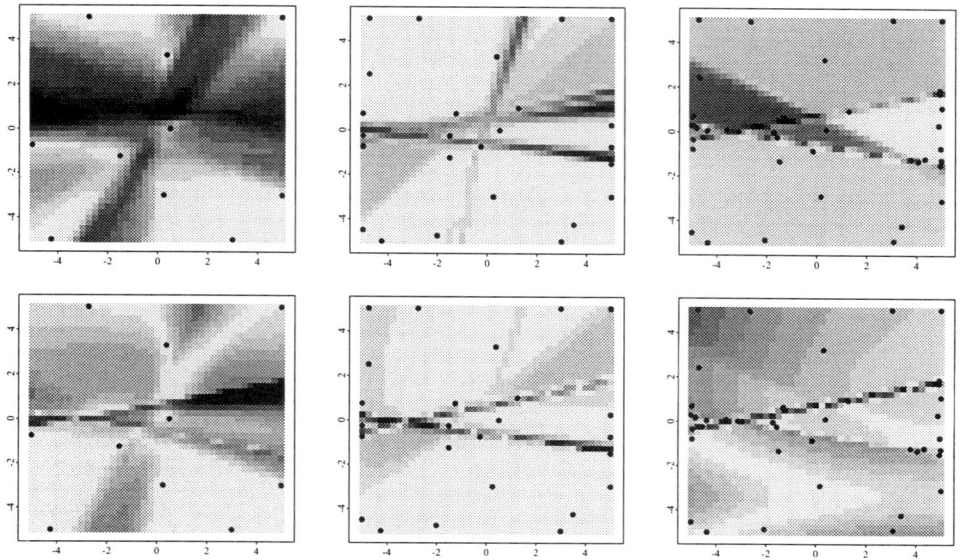

Figure 3: Squareroot of current loss (upper row) and absolute deviation from true function (lower row) for 10, 25, and 40 observations (which are indicated by dots).

[Hornik Stinchcombe 89] Hornik, K., Stinchcombe, M. (1989): Multilayer Feedforward Networks are Universal Approximators. *Neural Networks* **2**, p.359-366.

[Kalos Whitlock 86] Kalos, M.H., Whitlock, P.A. (1986): *Monte Carlo Methods*, Wiley, New York.

[MacKay 92] MacKay, D. (1992): Information-Based Objective Functions for Active Data Selection. *Neural Computation* **4**, p.590-604.

[Neal 93] Neal, R.M. (1993): *Probabilistic Inference using Markov Chain Monte Carlo Methods.* Tech. Report CRG-TR-93-1, Dep. of Computer Science, Univ. of Toronto.

[Paaß 91] Paaß, G. (1991): Second Order Probabilities for Uncertain and Conflicting Evidence. In: P.P. Bonissone et al. (eds.) *Uncertainty in Artificial Intelligence 6.* Elsevier, Amsterdam, pp. 447-456.

[Plutowski White 93] Plutowski, M., White, H. (1993): Selecting Concise Training Sets from Clean Data. *IEEE Tr. on Neural Networks*, **4**, p.305-318.

[Pronzato Walter 92] Pronzato, L., Walter, E. (1992): Nonsequential Bayesian Experimental Design for Response Optimization. In V. Fedorov, W.G. Müller, I.N. Vuchkov (eds.): *Model Oriented Data-Analysis.* Physica Verlag, Heidelberg, p. 89-102.

[Sollich 94] Sollich, P. (1994): Query Construction, Entropy and Generalization in Neural Network Models. To appear in Physical Review E.

[Sollich Saad 95] Sollich, P., Saad, D. (1995): Learning from Queries for Maximum Information Gain in Unlearnable Problems. This volume.

[White Wooldridge 91] White, H., Wooldridge, J. (1991): Some Results for Sieve Estimation with Dependent Observations. In W. Barnett et al. (eds.) : *Nonparametric and Semiparametric Methods in Econometrics and Statistics,* New York, Cambridge Univ. Press.

Using a Saliency Map for Active Spatial Selective Attention: Implementation & Initial Results

Shumeet Baluja
baluja@cs.cmu.edu
School of Computer Science
Carnegie Mellon University
Pittsburgh, PA 15213

Dean A. Pomerleau
pomerleau@cs.cmu.edu
School of Computer Science
Carnegie Mellon University
Pittsburgh, PA 15213

Abstract

In many vision based tasks, the ability to focus attention on the important portions of a scene is crucial for good performance on the tasks. In this paper we present a simple method of achieving spatial selective attention through the use of a saliency map. The saliency map indicates which regions of the input retina are important for performing the task. The saliency map is created through predictive auto-encoding. The performance of this method is demonstrated on two simple tasks which have multiple very strong distracting features in the input retina. Architectural extensions and application directions for this model are presented.

1 MOTIVATION

Many real world tasks have the property that only a small fraction of the available input is important at any particular time. On some tasks this extra input can easily be ignored. Nonetheless, often the similarity between the important input features and the irrelevant features is great enough to interfere with task performance. Two examples of this phenomena are the famous "cocktail party effect", otherwise known as speech recognition in a noisy environment, and image processing of a cluttered scene. In both cases, the extraneous information in the input signal can be easily confused with the important features, making the task much more difficult.

The concrete real world task which motivates this work is vision-based road following. In this domain, the goal is to control a robot vehicle by analyzing the scene ahead, and choosing a direction to travel based on the location of important features like lane marking and road edges. This is a difficult task, since the scene ahead is often cluttered with extraneous features such as other vehicle, pedestrians, trees, guardrails, crosswalks, road signs and many other objects that can appear on or around a roadway. [1] While we have had significant success on the road following task using simple feed-forward neural networks to transform images of the road ahead into steering commands for the vehicle [Pomerleau, 1993b], these methods fail when presented with cluttered environments like those encoun-

---

1. For the general task of autonomous navigation, these extra features are extremely important, but for restricted task of road following, which is the focus of this paper, these features are merely distractions. Although we are addressing the more general task using the techniques described here in combination with other methods, a description of these efforts is beyond the scope of this paper.

tered when driving in heavy traffic, or on city streets.

The obvious solution to this difficulty is to focus the attention of the processing system on only the relevant features by masking out the "noise". Because of the high degree of similarity between the relevant features and the noise, this filtering is often extremely difficult. Simultaneously learning to perform a task like road following and filtering out clutter in a scene is doubly difficult because of a chicken-and-egg problem. It is hard to learn which features to attend to before knowing how to perform the task, and it is hard to learn how to perform the task before knowing which features to attend to.

This paper describes a technique designed to solve this problem. It involves deriving a "saliency map" of the image from a neural network's internal representation which highlights regions of the scene considered to be important. This saliency map is used as feedback to focus the attention of the network's processing on subsequent images. This technique overcomes the chicken-and-egg problem by simultaneously learning to identify which aspects of the scene are important, and how to use them to perform a task.

2 THE SALIENCY MAP

A saliency map is designed to indicate which portions of the image are important for completing the required task. The trained network should be able to accomplish two goals with the presentation of each image. The first is to perform the given task using the inputs and the saliency map derived from the previous image, and the second is to predict the salient portions of the next image.

2.1 Implementation

The creation of the saliency map is similar to the technique of *Input Reconstruction Reliability Estimation* (IRRE) by [Pomerleau, 1993]. IRRE attempts to predict the reliability of a network's output. The prediction is made by reconstructing the input image from linear transformations of the activations in the hidden layer, and comparing it with the actual image. IRRE works on the premise that the greater the similarity between the input image and the reconstructed input image, the more the internal representation has captured the important input features, and therefore the more reliable the network's response.

A similar method to IRRE can be used to create a saliency map. The saliency map should be determined by the important features in the current image for the task to be performed. Because compressed representations of the important features in the current image are represented in the activations of the hidden units, the saliency map is derived from these, as shown in Figure 1. It should be noted that the hidden units, from which the saliency map is derived, do not necessarily contain information similar to principal components (as is achieved through auto-encoder networks), as the relevant task may only require information on a small portion of the image. In the simple architecture depicted in Figure 1, the internal representation must contain information which can be transformed by a single layer of adjustable weights into a saliency map for the next image. If such a transformation is not possible, separate hidden layers, with input from the task-specific internal representations could be employed to create the saliency map.

The saliency map is trained by using the next image, of a time-sequential data set, as the target image for the prediction, and applying standard error backpropagation on the differences between the next image and the predicted next image. The weights from the hidden

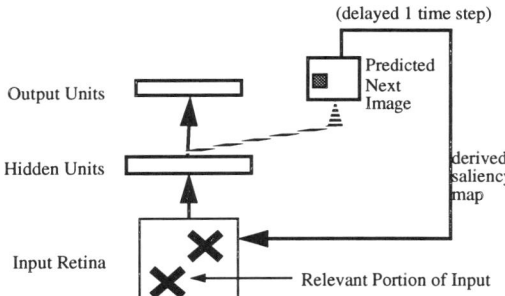

Figure 1: A simple architecture for using a saliency map. The dashed line represents "chilled connections", i.e. errors from these connections do not propagate back further to impact the activations of the hidden units. This architecture assumes that the target task contains information which will help determine the salient portions of the next frame.

units to the saliency map are adjusted using standard backpropagation, but the error terms are not propagated to the weights from the inputs to the hidden units. This ensures that the hidden representation developed by the network is determined only by the target task, and not by the task of prediction.

In the implementation used here, the feedback is to the input layer. The saliency map is created to either be the same size as the input layer, or is scaled to the same size, so that it can influence the representation in a straight-forward manner. The saliency map's values are scaled between 0.0 and 1.0, where 1.0 represents the areas in which the prediction matched the next image exactly. The value of 1.0 does not alter the activation of the input unit, a value of 0.0 turns off the activation. The exact construction of the saliency map is described in the next section, with the description of the experiments. The entire network is trained by standard backpropagation; in the experiments presented, no modifications to the standard training algorithm were needed to account for the feedback connections.

The training process for prediction is complicated by the potential presence of noise in the next image. The saliency map cannot "reconstruct" the noise in the next image, because it can only construct the portions of the next image which can be derived from the activation of the hidden units, which are task-specific. *Therefore, the noise in the next image will not be constructed, and thereby will be de-emphasized in the next time step by the saliency map.* The saliency map serves as a filter, which channels the processing to the important portions of the scene [Mozer, 1988]. One of the key differences between the filtering employed in this study, and that used in other focus of attention systems, is that this filtering is based on expectations from multiple frames, rather than on the retinal activations from a single frame. An alternative neural model of visual attention which was explored by [Olshausen et al., 1992] achieved focus of attention in single frames by using control neurons to dynamically modify synaptic strengths.

The saliency map may be used in two ways. It can either be used to highlight portions of the input retina or, when the hidden layer is connected in a retinal fashion using weight sharing, as in [LeCun et al., 1990], it can be used to highlight important spatial locations within the hidden layer itself. The difference is between highlighting individual pixels from which the features are developed or highlighting developed features. Discussion of the psychological evidence for both of these types of highlighting (in single-frame retinal activation based context), is given in [Pashler and Badgio, 1985].

This network architecture shares several characteristics with a Jordan-style recurrent network [Jordan, 1986], in which the output from the network is used to influence the processing of subsequent input patterns in a temporal sequence. One important distinction is that the feedback in this architecture is spatially constrained. The saliency map represents the importance of local patches of the input, and can influence only the network's processing of corresponding regions of the input. The second distinction is that the outputs are not general task outputs, rather they are specially constructed to predict the next image. The third distinction is in the form of this influence. Instead of treating the feedback as additional input units, which contribute to the weighted sum for the network's hidden units, this architecture uses the saliency map as a gating mechanism, suppressing or emphasizing the processing of various regions of the layer to which it is fed-back. In some respects, the influence of the saliency map is comparable to the gating network in the mixture of experts architecture [Jacobs et al., 1991]. Instead of gating between the outputs of multiple expert networks, in this architecture the saliency map is used to gate the activations of the input units within the same network.

3 THE EXPERIMENTS

In order to study the feasibility of the saliency map without introducing other extraneous factors, we have conducted experiments with two simple tasks described below. Extensions of these ideas to larger problems are discussed in sections 4 & 5. The first experiment is representative of a typical machine vision task, in which the relevant features move very little in consecutive frames. With the method used here, the relevant features are automatically determined and tracked. However, if the relevant features were known *a priori*, a more traditional vision feature tracker which begins the search for features within the vicinity of the location of the features in the previous frame, could also perform well. The second task is one in which the feature of interest moves in a discontinuous manner. A traditional feature tracker without exact knowledge the feature's transition rules would be unable to track this feature, in the presence of the noise introduced. The transition rules of the feature of interest are learned automatically through the use of the saliency map.

In the first task, there is a slightly tilted vertical line of high activation in a 30x32 input unit grid. The width of the line is approximately 9 units, with the activation decaying with distance from the center of the line. The rest of the image does not have any activation. The task is to center a gaussian of activation around the center of the x-intercept of the line, 5 pixels above the top of the image. The output layer contains 50 units. In consecutive images, the line can have a small translational move and/or a small rotational move. Sample training examples are given in Figure 2. This task can be easily learned in the presence of no noise. The task is made much harder when lines, which have the same visual appearance as the real line (in everything except for location and tilt) randomly appear in the image. In this case, it is vital that the network is able to distinguish between the real line and noise line by using information gathered from previous image(s).

In the second task, a cross ("+") of size 5x5 appears in a 20x20 grid. There are 16 positions in which the cross can appear, as shown in Figure 2c. The locations in which the cross appears is set according to the transition rules shown in Figure 2c. The object of this problem is to reproduce the cross in a smaller 10x10 grid, with the edges of the cross extended to the edges of the grid, as shown in Figure 2b. The task is complicated by the presence of randomly appearing noise. The noise is in the form of another cross which appears exactly similar to the cross of interest. Again, in this task, it is vital for the network to be able to distinguish between the real cross, and crosses which appear as noise. As in the first task, this is only possible with knowledge of the previous image(s).

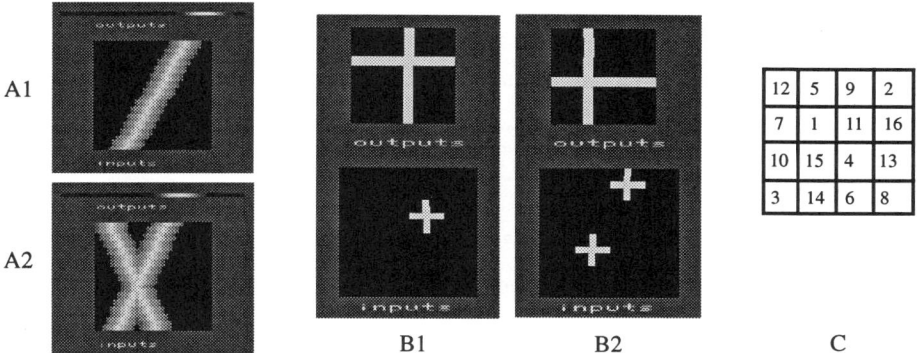

Figure 2: (A) The first task, image (A1) with no distractions, image (A2) with one distracting feature. (B) The second task, image (B1) with no distractions, image (B2) with two distractions. (C) Transition rules for the second task.

3.1 Results

The two problems described above were attempted with networks trained both with and without noise. Each of the training sessions were also tested with and without the saliency map. Each type of network was trained for the same number of pattern presentations with the same training examples. The results are shown in Table 1. The results reported in Table I represent the error accrued over 10,000 testing examples. For task 1, errors are reported in terms of the absolute difference between the peak's of the Gaussians produced in the output layer, summed for all of the testing examples (the max error per image is 49). In task 2, the errors are the sum of the absolute difference between the network's output and the target output, summed across all of the outputs and all of the testing examples.

When noise was added to the examples, it was added in the following manner (for both training and testing sets): In task 1, '1 noise' guarantees a noise element, similarly, '2 noise' guarantees two noise elements. However, in task 2, '1 noise' means that there is a 50% chance of a noise element occurring in the image, '2 noise' means that there is a 50% chance of another noise element occurring, independently of the appearance of the first noise element. The positions of the noise elements are determined randomly.

The best performance, in task 1, came from the cases in which there was no noise in testing or training, and no saliency map was used. This is expected, as this task is not difficult when no noise is present. Surprisingly, in task 2, the best case was found with the saliency map, when training *with* noise and testing without noise. This performed even better than training without noise. Investigation into this result is currently underway.

In task 1, when training and testing without noise, the saliency map can hurt performance. If the predictions made by the saliency map are not correct, the inputs appear slightly distorted; therefore, the task to be learned by the network becomes more difficult. Nevertheless, the benefit of using a saliency map is apparent when the test set contains noise.

In task 2, the network without the saliency map, trained with noise, and tested without noise cannot perform well; the performance further suffers when noise is introduced into the testing set. The noise in the training prevents accurate learning. This is not the case when the saliency map is used (Table 1, task 2). When the training set contains noise, the network with the saliency map works better when tested with and without noise.

Table 1: Summed Error of 10,000 Testing Examples

Training Set	Testing Set					
	Task 1			Task 2		
	0 Noise	1 Noise	2 Noise	0 Noise	1 Noise	2 Noise
0 Noise (Saliency)	12672	60926	82282	7174	94333	178883
0 Noise (No Saliency)	10241	91812	103605	7104	133496	216884
1 Noise (Saliency)	18696	26178	52668	4843	10427	94422
1 Noise (No Saliency)	14336	80668	97433	31673	150078	227650

When the noise increased beyond the level of training, to 2 noise elements per image, the performances of networks trained both with and without the saliency map declined. It is suspected that training the networks with increased noise will improve performance in the network trained with the saliency map. Nonetheless, due to the amount of noise compared to the small size of the input layer, improvements in results may not be dramatic.

In Figure 3, a typical test run of the second task is shown. In the figure, the inputs, the predicted and actual outputs, and the predicted and actual saliency maps, are shown. The actual saliency map is just a smaller version of the unfiltered next input image. The input size is 20x20, the outputs are 10x10, and the saliency map is 10x10. The saliency map is scaled to 20x20 when it is applied to the next inputs. Note that in the inputs to the network, one cross appears much brighter than the other; this is due to the suppression of the distracting cross by the saliency map. The particular use of the saliency map which is employed in this study, proceeded as follows: the difference between the saliency map (derived from input image$_i$) and the input image$_{i+1}$ was calculated. This difference image was scaled to the range of 0.0 to 1.0. Each pixel was then passed through a sigmoid; alternatively, a hard-step function could have been used. This is the saliency map. The saliency map was multiplied by input image$_{i+1}$; this was used as the input into the network. If the sigmoid is not used, features, such as incomplete crosses, sometimes appear in the input image. This happens because different portions of the cross may have slightly different saliency values associated with them -due to errors in prediction coupled with the scaling of the saliency map. Although the sigmoid helps to alleviate the problem, it does not eliminate it. This explains why training with no noise with a saliency map sometimes does not perform as well as training without a saliency map.

4 ALTERNATIVE IMPLEMENTATIONS

An alternative method of implementing the saliency map is with standard additive connections. However, these connection types have several drawbacks in comparison with the multiplicative ones use in this study. First, the additive connections can drastically change the meaning of the hidden unit's activation by changing the sign of the activation. The saliency map is designed to indicate which regions are important for accomplishing the task based upon the features in the hidden representations; as little alteration of the important features as possible is desired. Second, if the saliency map is incorrect, and suggests an area of which is not actually important, the additive connections will cause 'ghost' images to appear. These are activations which are caused *only* by the influence of the addi-

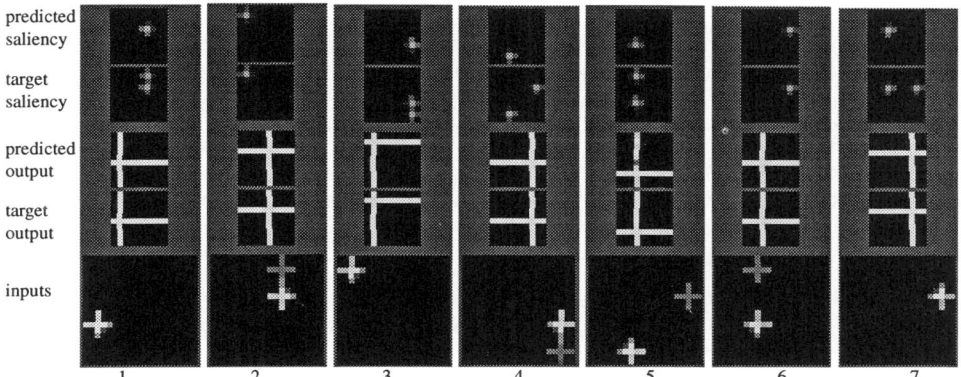

Figure 3: A typical sequence of inputs and outputs in the second task. Note that when two crosses are in the inputs, one is much brighter than the other. The "noise" cross is de-emphasized.

tive saliency map. The multiplicative saliency map, as is implemented here, does not have either of these problems.

A second alternative, which is more closely related to a standard recurrent network [Jordan, 1986], is to use the saliency map as extra inputs into the network. The extra inputs serve to indicate the regions which are expected to be important. Rather than hand-coding the method to represent the importance of the regions to the network, as was done in this study, the network learns to use the extra inputs when necessary. Further, the saliency map serves as the predicted next input. This is especially useful when the features of interest may have momentarily been partially obscured or have entirely disappeared from the image. This implementation is currently being explored by the authors for use in a autonomous road lane-tracking system in which the lane markers are not always present in the input image.

5 CONCLUSIONS & FUTURE DIRECTIONS

These experiments have demonstrated that an artificial neural network can learn to both identify the portions of a visual scene which are important, and to use these important features to perform a task. The selective attention architecture we have develop uses two simple mechanisms, predictive auto-encoding to form a saliency map, and a constrained form of feedback to allow this saliency map to focus processing in the subsequent image.

There are at least four broad directions in which this research should be extended. The first is, as described here, related to using the saliency map as a method for automatically actively focusing attention to important portions of the scene. Because of the spatial dependence of the task described in this paper, with the appropriate transformations, the output units could be directly fed back to the input layer to indicate saliency. Although this does not weaken the result, in terms of the benefit of using a saliency map, future work should also focus on problems which do not have this property to determine how easily a saliency map can be constructed. Will the use of weight sharing be enough to develop the necessary spatially oriented feature detectors? Harder problems are those with target tasks which does not explicitly contain spatial saliency information.

An implementation problem which needs to be resolved is in networks which contain more than a single hidden layer: from which layer should the saliency map be constructed? The trade-off is that at the higher layers, the information contained is more task specific. However, the higher layers may effectively extract the information required to perform the task, without maintaining the information required for saliency map creation. The opposite case is true in the lower layers; these may contain all of the information required, but may not provide enough discrimination to narrow the focus effectively.

The third area for research is an alternative use for the saliency map. ANNs have often been criticized for their uninterpretability, and lack of mechanism to explain performance. The saliency map provides a method for understanding, at a high level, what portions of the inputs the ANN finds the most important.

Finally, the fourth direction for research is the incorporation of higher level, or symbolic knowledge. The saliency map provides a very intuitive and direct method for focusing the network's attention to specific portions of the image. The saliency map may prove to be a useful mechanism to allow other processes, including human users, to simply "point at" the portion of the image to which the network should be paying attention.

The next step in our research is to test the effectiveness of this technique on the main task of interest, autonomous road following. Fortunately, the first demonstration task employed in this paper shares several characteristics with road following. Both tasks require the network to track features which move over time in a cluttered image. Both tasks also require the network to produce an output that depends on the positions of the important features in the image. Because of these shared characteristics, we believe that similar performance improvements should be possible in the autonomous driving domain.

Acknowledgments

Shumeet Baluja is supported by a National Science Foundation Graduate Fellowship. Support has come from "Perception for Outdoor Navigation" (contract number DACA76-89-C-0014, monitored by the US Army Topographic Engineering Center) and "Unmanned Ground Vehicle System" (contract number DAAE07-90-C-R059, monitored by TACOM). Support has also come from the National Highway Traffic Safety Administration under contract number DTNH22-93-C-07023. The views and conclusions contained in this document are those of the authors and should not be interpreted as representing official policies, either expressed or implied, of the National Science Foundation, ARPA, or the U.S. Government.

References

Cottrell, G.W. & Munro, P. (1988) Principal Component Analysis of Images via back-propagation. *Proc Soc. of Photo-Optical Instr. Eng.*, Cambridge, MA.

Jordan, M.I., (1989). Serial Order: A Parallel, Distributed Processing Approach. In *Advances in Connectionist Theory: Speech*, eds. J.L. Elman and D.E. Rumerlhart. Hillsdale: Erlbaum.

Jacobs, R.A., Jordan, M.I., Nowlan, S.J. & Hinton, G.E. (1991). Adaptive Mixtures of Local Experts. *Neural Computation*, 3:1.

LeCun, Y., Boser, B., Denker, J.S., Henderson, D. Howard, R.E., Hummand W., and Jackel, L.D. (1989) Back-propagation Applied to Handwritten Zip Code Recognition. Neural Computation 1, 541-551. MIT, 1989.

Mozer, M.C. (1988) A Connectionist Model of Selective Attention in Visual Perception. Technical Report, University of Toronto, CRG-TR-88-4.

Pashler, H. & Badgio, P. (1985). Visual Attention and Stimulus Identification. Journal of Experimental Psychology: Human Perception and Performance, 11 105-121.

Pomerleau, D.A. (1993) Input Reconstruction Reliability Estimation. In Giles, C.L. Hanson, S.J. and Cowan, J.D. (eds). *Advances in Neural Information Processing Systems 5*, CA: Morgan Kaufmann Publishers.

Pomerleau, D.A. (1993b) *Neural Network Perception for Mobile Robot Guidance*, Kluwer Academic Publishing.

Olshausen, B., Anderson, C., & Van Essen, D. (1992) A Neural Model of Visual Attention and Invariant Pattern Recognition. California Institute of Technology, CNS Program, memo-18.

Multidimensional Scaling and Data Clustering

Thomas Hofmann & Joachim Buhmann
Rheinische Friedrich–Wilhelms–Universität
Institut für Informatik III, Römerstraße 164
D-53117 Bonn, Germany
email:{th,jb}@cs.uni-bonn.de

Abstract

Visualizing and structuring pairwise dissimilarity data are difficult combinatorial optimization problems known as *multidimensional scaling* or *pairwise data clustering*. Algorithms for embedding dissimilarity data set in a Euclidian space, for clustering these data and for actively selecting data to support the clustering process are discussed in the maximum entropy framework. Active data selection provides a strategy to discover structure in a data set efficiently with partially unknown data.

1 Introduction

Grouping experimental data into compact clusters arises as a data analysis problem in psychology, linguistics, genetics and other experimental sciences. The data which are supposed to be clustered are either given by an explicit coordinate representation (*central* clustering) or, in the *non-metric* case, they are characterized by dissimilarity values for pairs of data points (*pairwise* clustering). In this paper we study algorithms **(i)** for embedding non-metric data in a D-dimensional Euclidean space, **(ii)** for simultaneous clustering and embedding of non–metric data, and **(iii)** for active data selection to determine a particular cluster structure with minimal number of data queries. All algorithms are derived from the maximum entropy principle (Hertz *et al.*, 1991) which guarantees robust statistics (Tikochinsky *et al.*, 1984).

The data are given by a real–valued, symmetric proximity matrix $\mathbf{D} \in \mathbf{R}^{N \times N}$, $\mathcal{D}_{kl}$ being the pairwise dissimilarity between the data points k, l. Apart from the symmetry constraint we make no further assumptions about the dissimilarities, i.e., we do not require $\mathbf{D}$ being a metric. The numbers $\mathcal{D}_{kl}$ quite often violate the triangular inequality and the dissimilarity of a datum to itself could be finite.

2 Statistical Mechanics of Multidimensional Scaling

Embedding dissimilarity data in a D-dimensional Euclidian space is a non-convex optimization problem which typically exhibits a large number of local minima. Stochastic search methods like simulated annealing or its deterministic variants have been very successfully applied to such problems. The question in multidimensional scaling is to find coordinates $\{\mathbf{x}_i\}_{i=1}^N$ in a D-dimensional Euclidian space with minimal embedding costs

$$\mathcal{H}^{\mathrm{MDS}} = \frac{1}{2N} \sum_{i,k=1}^N \left[|\mathbf{x}_i - \mathbf{x}_k|^2 - \mathcal{D}_{ik}\right]^2. \tag{1}$$

Without loss of generality we shift the center of mass in the origin ($\sum_{k=1}^N \mathbf{x}_k = 0$).

In the maximum entropy framework the coordinates $\{\mathbf{x}_i\}$ are regarded as random variables which are distributed according to the Gibbs distribution $P(\{\mathbf{x}_i\}) = \exp(-\beta(\mathcal{H}^{\mathrm{MDS}} - \mathcal{F}))$. The inverse temperature $\beta = 1/T$ controls the expected embedding costs $\langle \mathcal{H}^{\mathrm{MDS}} \rangle$ (expectation values are denoted by $\langle . \rangle$). To calculate the free energy $\mathcal{F}$ for $\mathcal{H}^{\mathrm{MDS}}$ we approximate the coupling term $2\sum_{i,k=1}^N \mathcal{D}_{ik} \mathbf{x}_i \mathbf{x}_k / N \approx \sum_{i=1}^N \mathbf{x}_i \mathbf{h}_i$ with the mean fields $\mathbf{h}_i = 4\sum_{k=1}^N \mathcal{D}_{ik} \langle \mathbf{x}_k \rangle / N$. Standard techniques to evaluate the free energy $\mathcal{F}$ yield the equations

$$\mathcal{Z}(\mathcal{H}^{\mathrm{MDS}}) \sim \int_{-\imath\infty}^{\imath\infty} d\hat{\mathbf{y}} \int_{-\infty}^{\infty} \prod_{d,d'=1}^D d\mathcal{R}_{d,d'} \exp(-\beta N \mathcal{F}), \tag{2}$$

$$\mathcal{F}(\mathcal{H}^{\mathrm{MDS}}) = 2 \sum_{d,d'=1}^D \mathcal{R}_{dd'}^2 - \frac{1}{\beta N} \sum_{i=1}^N \ln \int_{-\infty}^{\infty} d\mathbf{x}_i \exp(-\beta f(\mathbf{x}_i)), \tag{3}$$

$$f(\mathbf{x}_i) = |\mathbf{x}_i|^4 - \frac{2}{N}|\mathbf{x}_i|^2 \sum_{k=1}^N \mathcal{D}_{ik} + 4\mathbf{x}_i^T \mathcal{R} \mathbf{x}_i + \mathbf{x}_i^T (\mathbf{h}_i - 4\hat{\mathbf{y}}). \tag{4}$$

The integral in Eq. (2) is dominated by the absolute minimum of $\mathcal{F}$ in the limit $N \to \infty$. Therefore, we calculate the saddle point equations

$$\mathcal{R} = \frac{1}{N} \sum_{i=1}^N \left(\langle \mathbf{x}_i \mathbf{x}_i^T \rangle + \frac{1}{2}\langle|\mathbf{x}_i|^2\rangle \mathcal{I}\right) \quad \text{and} \quad 0 = \frac{1}{N} \sum_{i=1}^N \langle \mathbf{x}_i \rangle \tag{5}$$

$$\langle \mathbf{x}_i \rangle = \frac{\int \mathbf{x}_i \exp(-\beta f(\mathbf{x}_i)) d\mathbf{x}_i}{\int \exp(-\beta f(\mathbf{x}_i)) d\mathbf{x}_i}. \tag{6}$$

Equation (6) has been derived by differentiating $\mathcal{F}$ with respect to $\mathbf{h}_i$. $\mathcal{I}$ denotes the $D \times D$ unit matrix. In the low temperature limit $\beta \to \infty$ the integral in (3) is dominated by the minimum of $f(\mathbf{x}_i)$. Therefore, a new estimate of $\langle \mathbf{x}_i \rangle$ is calculated minimizing f with respect to $\mathbf{x}_i$. Since all explicit dependencies between the $\mathbf{x}_i$ have been eliminated, this minimization can be performed independently for all i, $1 \leq i \leq N$.

In the spirit of the EM algorithm for Gaussian mixture models we suggest the following algorithm to calculate a meanfield approximation for the multidimensional scaling problem.

```
initialize ⟨xᵢ⟩⁽⁰⁾ randomly; t = 0.
while ∑ᵢ₌₁ᴺ |⟨xᵢ⟩⁽ᵗ⁾ - ⟨xᵢ⟩⁽ᵗ⁻¹⁾| > ε
    E-step: estimate ⟨xᵢ⟩⁽ᵗ⁺¹⁾ as a function of ⟨xᵢ⟩⁽ᵗ⁾, ℛ⁽ᵗ⁾, ŷ⁽ᵗ⁾, hᵢ⁽ᵗ⁾
    M-step: calculate ℛ⁽ᵗ⁾, hᵢ⁽ᵗ⁾ and determine ŷ⁽ᵗ⁾ such
            that the centroid condition is satisfied.
```

This algorithm was used to determine the embedding of protein dissimilarity data as shown in Fig. 1d. The phenomenon that the data clusters are arranged in a circular fashion is explained by the lack of small dissimilarity values. The solution in Fig. 1d is about a factor of two better than the embedding found by a classical MDS program (Gower, 1966). This program determines a $(N-1)$- space where the ranking of the dissimilarities is preserved and uses principle component analysis to project this tentative embedding down to two dimensions. Extensions to other MDS cost functions are currently under investigation.

3 Multidimensional Scaling and Pairwise Clustering

Embedding data in a Euclidian space precedes quite often a visual inspection by the data analyst to discover structure and to group data into clusters. The question arises how both problems, the embedding problem and the clustering problem, can be solved simultaneously. The second algorithm addresses the problem to embed a data set in a Euclidian space such that the clustering structure is approximated as faithfully as possible in the maximum entropy sense by the clustering solution in this embedding space. The coordinates in the embedding space are the free parameters for this optimization problem.

Clustering of non-metric dissimilarity data, also called pairwise clustering (Buhmann, Hofmann, 1994a), is a combinatorial optimization problem which depends on Boolean assignments $M_{i\nu} \in \{0,1\}$ of datum i to cluster ν. The cost function for pairwise clustering with K clusters is

$$\mathcal{E}_K^{pc}(\mathbf{M}) = \sum_{\nu=1}^{K} \frac{1}{2p_\nu N} \sum_{k=1}^{N} \sum_{l=1}^{N} M_{k\nu} M_{l\nu} \mathcal{D}_{kl} \quad \text{with} \quad p_\nu = \frac{1}{N} \sum_{k=1}^{N} M_{k\nu}. \tag{7}$$

In the meanfield approach we approximate the Gibbs distribution $P(\mathcal{E}_K^{pc})$ corresponding to the original cost function by a family of approximating distributions. The distribution which represents most accurately the statistics of the original problem is determined by the minimum of the Kullback–Leibler divergence to the original Gibbs distribution. In the pairwise clustering case we introduce potentials $\{\mathcal{E}_{k\nu}\}$ for the effective interactions, which define a set of cost functions with non-interacting assignments.

$$\mathcal{E}_K^0(\mathbf{M}, \{\mathcal{E}_{k\nu}\}) = \sum_{\nu=1}^{K} \sum_{k=1}^{N} M_{k\nu} \mathcal{E}_{k\nu}. \tag{8}$$

The optimal potentials derived from this minimization procedure are

$$\{\mathcal{E}_{k\nu}^*\} = \arg\min_{\{\mathcal{E}_{k\nu}\}} \mathcal{D}_{\text{KL}}\left(P^0(\mathcal{E}_K^0) \| P(\mathcal{E}_K^{pc})\right), \tag{9}$$

where $P^0(\mathcal{E}_K^0)$ is the Gibbs distribution corresponding to $\mathcal{E}_K^0$, and $\mathcal{D}_{\text{KL}}(\cdot\|\cdot)$ is the KL–divergence. This method is equivalent to minimizing an upper bound on the free energy (Buhmann, Hofmann, 1994b),

$$\mathcal{F}(\mathcal{E}_K^{pc}) \leq \mathcal{F}_0(\mathcal{E}_K^0) + \langle \mathcal{V}_K \rangle_0, \quad \text{with} \quad \mathcal{V}_K = \mathcal{E}_K^{pc} - \mathcal{E}_K^0, \tag{10}$$

$\langle . \rangle_0$ denoting the average over all configurations of the cost function without interactions.

Correlations between assignment variables are statistically independent for $P^0(\mathcal{E}_K^0)$, i.e., $\langle M_{k\nu} M_{l\nu}\rangle_0 = \langle M_{k\nu}\rangle_0 \langle M_{l\nu}\rangle_0$. The averaged potential $\mathcal{V}_K$, therefore, amounts to

$$\langle \mathcal{V}_K \rangle = \sum_{\nu=1}^{K} \sum_{k,l=1}^{N} \langle M_{k\nu}\rangle \langle M_{l\nu}\rangle \frac{1}{2p_\nu N} \mathcal{D}_{kl} - \sum_{\nu=1}^{K} \sum_{k=1}^{N} \langle M_{k\nu}\rangle \mathcal{E}_{k\nu}, \tag{11}$$

the subscript of averages being omitted for conciseness. The expected assignment variables are

$$\langle M_{i\nu} \rangle = \frac{\exp(-\beta \mathcal{E}_{i\nu})}{\sum_{\mu=1}^{K} \exp(-\beta \mathcal{E}_{i\mu})}. \tag{12}$$

Minimizing the upper bound yields

$$\frac{\partial}{\partial \mathcal{E}_{i\alpha}} \left[\mathcal{F}_0(\mathcal{E}_K^0) + \langle \mathcal{V}_K \rangle \right] = -\sum_{\nu=1}^{K} \frac{\partial \langle M_{i\nu} \rangle}{\partial \mathcal{E}_{i\alpha}} \left(\mathcal{E}_{i\nu} - \mathcal{E}_{i\nu}^* \right) = 0. \tag{13}$$

The "optimal" potentials

$$\mathcal{E}_{i\nu}^* = \frac{1}{p_\nu N} \sum_{k=1}^{N} \langle M_{k\nu} \rangle \left(\mathcal{D}_{ik} - \frac{1}{2 p_\nu N} \sum_{l=1}^{N} \langle M_{l\nu} \rangle \mathcal{D}_{kl} \right) \tag{14}$$

depend on the given distance matrix, the averaged assignment variables and the cluster probabilities. They are optimal in the sense, that if we set

$$\mathcal{E}_{i\nu} = \mathcal{E}_{i\nu}^* + c_i \tag{15}$$

the $N*K$ stationarity conditions (13) are fulfilled for every $i \in \{1,...,N\}, \nu \in \{1,...,K\}$. A simultaneous solution of Eq. (15) with (12) constitutes a necessary condition for a minimum of the upper bound for the free energy $\mathcal{F}$.

The connection between the clustering and the multidimensional scaling problem is established, if we restrict the potentials $\mathcal{E}_{i\nu}$ to be of the form $|\mathbf{x}_i - \mathbf{y}_\nu|^2$ with the centroids $\mathbf{y}_\nu = \sum_{k=1}^{N} M_{k\nu} \mathbf{x}_\nu / \sum_{k=1}^{N} M_{k\nu}$. We consider the coordinates $\mathbf{x}_i$ as the variational parameters. The additional constraints restrict the family of approximating distributions, defined by $\mathcal{E}_K^0$ to a subset. Using the chain rule we can calculate the derivatives of the upper bound (10), resulting in the exact stationary conditions for $\mathbf{x}_i$,

$$\sum_{\alpha,\nu=1}^{K} \langle M_{i\alpha} \rangle \langle M_{j\alpha} \rangle \left(\Delta \mathcal{E}_{i\alpha} - \Delta \mathcal{E}_{i\nu} \right) \mathbf{y}_\alpha = \sum_{j=1}^{N} \sum_{\alpha,\nu=1}^{K} \frac{\langle M_{j\alpha} \rangle \langle M_{j\nu} \rangle}{N p_\alpha} \times$$

$$\left(\Delta \mathcal{E}_{i\alpha} - \Delta \mathcal{E}_{i\nu} \right) \left[\langle M_{i\alpha} \rangle I + \sum_{k=1}^{N} \left((\mathbf{x}_k - \mathbf{y}_\alpha) \frac{\partial \langle M_{k\alpha} \rangle}{\partial \mathbf{x}_i}^T \right) \right] (\mathbf{x}_j - \mathbf{y}_\alpha), \tag{16}$$

where $\Delta \mathcal{E}_{i\alpha} = \mathcal{E}_{i\alpha} - \mathcal{E}_{i\alpha}^*$. The derivatives $\partial \langle M_{k\alpha} \rangle / \partial \mathbf{x}_i$ can be exactly calculated, since they are given as the solutions of an linear equation system with $N \times K$ unknowns for every $\mathbf{x}_i$. To reduce the computational complexity an approximation can be derived under the assumption $\partial \mathbf{y}_\alpha / \partial \mathbf{x}_i \approx 0$. In this case the right hand side of (16) can be set to zero in a first order approximation yielding an explicit formula for $\mathbf{x}_i$,

$$\mathcal{K}_i \mathbf{x}_i \approx \frac{1}{2} \sum_{\nu=1}^{K} \langle M_{i\nu} \rangle \left(\|\mathbf{y}_\nu\|^2 - \mathcal{E}_{i\nu}^* \right) \left(\mathbf{y}_\nu - \sum_{\alpha=1}^{K} \langle M_{i\alpha} \rangle \mathbf{y}_\alpha \right), \tag{17}$$

with the covariance matrix $\mathcal{K}_i = \left(\langle \mathbf{y}\mathbf{y}^T \rangle_i - \langle \mathbf{y} \rangle_i \langle \mathbf{y} \rangle_i^T \right)$ and $\langle \mathbf{y} \rangle_i = \sum_{\nu=1}^{K} \langle M_{i\nu} \rangle \mathbf{y}_\nu$.
The derived system of transcendental equations given by (12), (17) and the centroid condition explicitly reflects the dependencies between the clustering procedure and the Euclidian representation. Solving these equations simultaneously leads to an efficient algorithm which

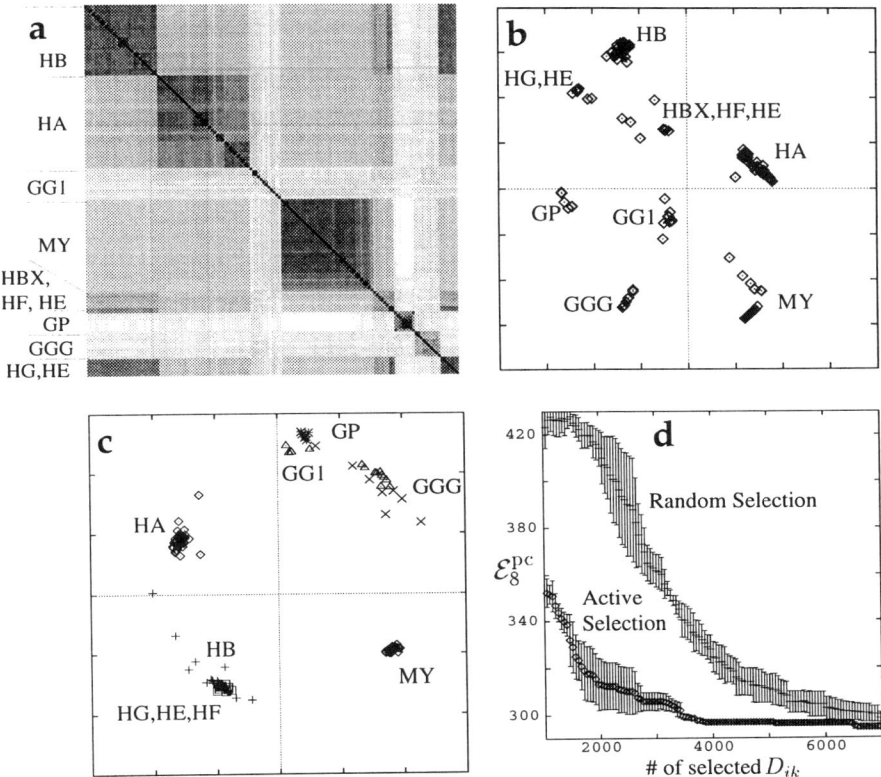

Figure 1: Similarity matrix of 145 protein sequences of the globin family (a): dark gray levels correspond to high similarity values; (b): clustering with embedding in two dimensions; (c): multidimensional scaling solution for 2-dimensional embedding; (d): quality of clustering solution with random and active data selection of $\mathcal{D}_{ik}$ values. $\mathcal{E}_8^{pc}$ has been calculated on the basis of the complete set of $\mathcal{D}_{ik}$ values.

interleaves the multidimensional scaling process and the clustering process and which avoids an artificial separation into two uncorrelated processes. The described algorithm for simultaneous Euclidian embedding and data clustering can be used for dimensionality reduction, e.g., high dimensional data can be projected to a low dimensional subspace in a nonlinear fashion which resembles local principle component analysis (Buhmann, Hofmann, 1994b).

Figure (1) shows the clustering result for a real–world data set of 145 protein sequences. The similarity values between pairs of sequences are determined by a sequence alignment program which takes biochemical and structural information into account. The sequences belong to different protein families like hemoglobin, myoglobin and other globins; they are abbreviated with the displayed capital letters. The gray level visualization of the dissimilarity matrix with dark values for similar protein sequences shows the formation of distinct "squares" along the main diagonal. These squares correspond to the discovered partition after clustering. The embedding in two dimensions shows inter–cluster distances which are in consistent agreement with the similarity values of the data. In three and four dimensions the error between the given dissimilarities and the constructed distances is further reduced. The results are in good agreement with the biological classification.

4 Active Data Selection for Data Clustering

Active data selection is an important issue for the analysis of data which are characterized by pairwise dissimilarity values. The size of the distance matrix grows like the square of the number of data 'points'. Such a $\mathcal{O}(N^2)$ scaling renders the data acquisition process expensive. It is, therefore, desirable to couple the data analysis process to the data acquisition process, i.e., to actively query the supposedly most relevant dissimilarity values. Before addressing active data selection questions for data clustering we have to discuss the problem how to modify the algorithm in the case of incomplete data.

If we want to avoid any assumptions about statistical dependencies, it is impossible to infer unknown values and we have to work directly with the partial dissimilarity matrix. Since the data enters only in the (re-)calculation of the potentials in (14), it is straightforward to appropriately modify these equations. All sums are restricted to terms with known dissimilarities and the normalization factors are adjusted accordingly.

Alternatively we can try to explicitly estimate the unknown dissimilarity values based on a statistical model. For this purpose we propose two models, relying on a known group structure of the data. The first model (I) assumes that all dissimilarities between a point i and points j belonging to a group G_μ are i.i.d. random variables with the probability density $p_{i\mu}$ parameterized by $\theta_{i\mu}$. In this scheme a subset of the known dissimilarities of i and j to other points k are used as samples for the estimation of $\mathcal{D}_{ij}$. The selection of the specific subset is determined by the clustering structure. In the second model (II) we assume that the dissimilarities between groups G_ν, G_μ are i.i.d. random variables with density $p_{\nu\mu}$ parameterized by $\theta_{\nu\mu}$. The parameters $\theta_{\nu\mu}$ are estimated on the basis of all known dissimilarities $\{\mathcal{D}_{ij} \in \mathcal{D}\}$ between points from G_ν and G_μ.

The assignments of points to clusters are not known a priori and have to be determined in the light of the (given and estimated) data. The data selection strategy becomes self-consistent if we interpret the mean fields $\langle M_{i\nu}\rangle$ of the clustering solution as posterior probabilities for the binary assignment variables. Combined with a maximum likelihood estimation for the unknown parameters given the posteriors, we arrive at an EM–like iteration scheme with the E–step replaced by the clustering algorithm.

The precise form of the M–Step depends on the parametric form of the densities $p_{i\mu}$ or $p_{\nu\mu}$, respectively. In the case of Gaussian distributions the M–Step is described by the following estimation equations for the location parameters

$$\bar{m}_{i\mu}^{(t)} = \frac{\sum_{\mathcal{D}_{ij}\in\mathcal{D}}\langle M_{j\mu}\rangle \mathcal{D}_{ij}}{\sum_{\mathcal{D}_{ij}\in\mathcal{D}}\langle M_{j\mu}\rangle} \quad \text{(I)}, \qquad \bar{m}_{\nu\mu}^{(t)} = \frac{\sum_{\mathcal{D}_{ij}\in\mathcal{D}}\pi_{\nu\mu}^{ij}\mathcal{D}_{ij}}{\sum_{\mathcal{D}_{ij}\in\mathcal{D}}\pi_{\nu\mu}^{ij}} \quad \text{(II)}, \qquad (18)$$

with $\pi_{\nu\mu}^{ij} = \frac{1}{1+\delta_{\nu\mu}}\left(\langle M_{i\nu}\rangle\langle M_{j\mu}\rangle + \langle M_{i\mu}\rangle\langle M_{j\nu}\rangle\right)$. Corresponding expressions are derived for the standard deviations $\bar{\sigma}_{i\nu}^{(t)}$ or $\bar{\sigma}_{\nu\mu}^{(t)}$, respectively. In the case of non–normal distributions the empirical mean might still be a good estimator of the location parameter, though not necessarily a maximum likelihood estimator. The missing dissimilarities are estimated by the following statistics, derived from the empirical means.

$$\bar{D}_{ij}^{(t)} = \sum_{\nu,\mu=1}^{K}\langle M_{i\nu}\rangle\langle M_{j\mu}\rangle\frac{N_{i\mu}\bar{m}_{i\mu}^{(t)} + N_{j\nu}\bar{m}_{j\nu}^{(t)}}{N_{i\mu}+N_{j\nu}} \quad \text{(I)}, \qquad \bar{D}_{ij}^{(t)} = \sum_{\nu\leq\mu}\pi_{\nu\mu}^{ij}\bar{m}_{\nu\mu}^{(t)} \quad \text{(II)}, \qquad (19)$$

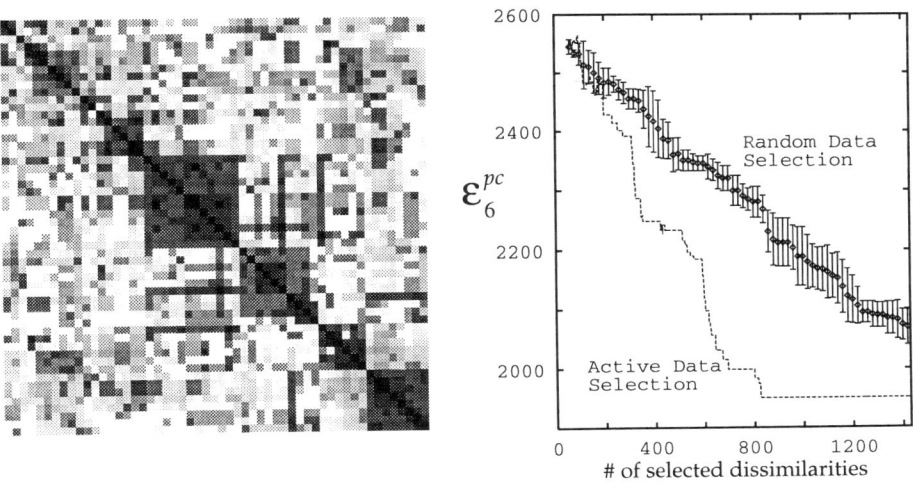

Figure 2: Similarity matrix of 54 word fragments generated by a dynamic programming algorithm. The clustering costs in the experiment with active data selection requires only half as much data as a random selection strategy.

with $N_{i\nu} = \sum_{\mathcal{D}_{ik} \in \mathcal{D}} \langle M_{k\nu} \rangle$. For model (I) we have used a pooled estimator to exploit the data symmetry. The iteration scheme finally leads to estimates $\bar{\theta}_{i\mu}$ or $\bar{\theta}_{\nu\mu}$ respectively for the parameters and $\bar{D}_{ij}$ for all unknown dissimilarities.

Criterion for Active Data Selection: We will use the expected reduction in the variance of the free energy $\mathcal{F}_0$ as a score, which should be maximized by the selection criterion. $\mathcal{F}_0$ is given by $\mathcal{F}_0(D) = -\frac{1}{\beta}\sum_{i=1}^{N} \log \sum_{\nu=1}^{K} \exp(-\beta \mathcal{E}_{i\nu}(D))$. If we query a new dissimilarity $\mathcal{D}_{ij}$ the expected reduction of the variance of the free energy is approximated by

$$\Delta_{ij} = 2 \left[\frac{\partial \mathcal{F}_0}{\partial \mathcal{D}_{ij}}\right]^2 \mathbf{V}\left[\mathcal{D}_{ij} - \bar{D}_{ij}\right] \quad (20)$$

The partial derivatives can be calculated exactly by solving a system of linear equations with $N \times K$ unknowns. Alternatively a first order approximation in $\epsilon_\nu = \mathcal{O}(1/Np_\nu)$ yields

$$\frac{\partial \mathcal{F}_0}{\partial \mathcal{D}_{ij}} \approx 2\sum_{\nu=1}^{K} \frac{\langle M_{i\nu}\rangle \langle M_{j\nu}\rangle}{Np_\nu} + O\left(\sum_{\nu=1}^{K} \epsilon_\nu^2\right). \quad (21)$$

This expression defines a relevance measure of $\mathcal{D}_{ij}$ for the clustering problem since a $\mathcal{D}_{ij}$ value contributes to the clustering costs only if the data i and j belong to the same cluster. Equation (21) summarizes the mean–field contributions $\partial \mathcal{F}_0/\partial \mathcal{D}_{ij} \approx \partial \langle H \rangle_0/\partial \mathcal{D}_{ij}$.

To derive the final form of our scoring function we have to calculate an approximation of the variance in Eq. (20) which measures the expected squared error for replacing the true value $\mathcal{D}_{ij}$ with our estimate $\bar{D}_{ij}$. Since we assumed statistical independence the variances are additive $\mathbf{V}\left[\mathcal{D}_{ij} - \bar{D}_{ij}\right] = \mathbf{V}\left[\mathcal{D}_{ij}\right] + \mathbf{V}\left[\bar{D}_{ij}\right]$. The total population variance is a sum of inner- and inter-cluster variances, that can be approximated by the empirical means and by the empirical variances instead of the unknown parameters of $p_{i\nu}$ or $p_{\nu\mu}$. The sampling variance of the statistics $\bar{D}_{ij}$ is estimated under the assumption, that the empirical means $\bar{m}_{i\nu}$

or $\bar{m}_{\nu\mu}$ respectively are uncorrelated. This holds in the hard clustering limit. We arrive at the following final expression for the variances of model (II)

$$\mathbf{V}\left[\mathcal{D}_{ij}-\bar{D}_{ij}\right] \approx \sum_{\nu \leq \mu} \pi_{\nu\mu}^{ij}\left[(\bar{D}_{ij}-\bar{m}_{\nu\mu})^2+\left(1+\frac{\pi_{\nu\mu}^{ij}}{\sum_{\mathcal{D}_{kl}\in\mathcal{D}}\pi_{\nu\mu}^{kl}}\bar{\sigma}_{\nu\mu}^2\right)\right] \quad (22)$$

For model (I) a slightly more complicated formula can be derived. Inserting the estimated variances into Eq. (20) leads to the final expression for our scoring function.

To demonstrate the efficiency of the proposed selection strategy, we have compared the clustering costs achieved by active data selection with the clustering costs resulting from randomly queried data. Assignments int the case of active selection are calculated with statistical model (I). Figure 1d demonstrates that the clustering costs decrease significantly faster when the selection criterion (20) is implemented. The structure of the clustering solution has been completely inferred with about 3300 selected $\mathcal{D}_{ik}$ values. The random strategy requires about 6500 queries for the same quality. Analogous comparison results for linguistic data are summarized in Fig. 2. Note the inconsistencies in this data set reflected by small $\mathcal{D}_{ik}$ values outside the cluster blocks (dark pixels) or by the large $\mathcal{D}_{ik}$ values (white pixels) inside a block.

Conclusion: Data analysis of dissimilarity data is a challenging problem in molecular biology, linguistics, psychology and, in general, in pattern recognition. We have presented three strategies to visualize data structures and to inquire the data structure by an efficient data selection procedure. The respective algorithms are derived in the maximum entropy framework for maximal robustness of cluster estimation and data embedding. Active data selection has been shown to require only half as much data for estimating a clustering solution of fixed quality compared to a random selection strategy. We expect the proposed selection strategy to facilitate maintenance of genome and protein data bases and to yield more robust data prototypes for efficient search and data base mining.

Acknowledgement: It is a pleasure to thank M. Vingron and D. Bavelier for providing the protein data and the linguistic data, respectively. We are also grateful to A. Polzer and H.J. Warneboldt for implementing the MDS algorithm. This work was partially supported by the Ministry of Science and Research of the state Nordrhein-Westfalen.

References

Buhmann, J., Hofmann, T. (1994a). Central and Pairwise Data Clustering by Competitive Neural Networks. *Pages 104–111 of: Advances in Neural Information Processing Systems 6*. Morgan Kaufmann Publishers.

Buhmann, J., Hofmann, T. (1994b). A Maximum Entropy Approach to Pairwise Data Clustering. *Pages 207–212 of: Proceedings of the International Conference on Pattern Recognition, Hebrew University, Jerusalem*, vol. II. IEEE Computer Society Press.

Gower, J. C. (1966). Some distance properties of latent root and vector methods used in multivariate analysis. *Biometrika*, **53**, 325–328.

Hertz, J., Krogh, A., Palmer, R. G. (1991). *Introduction to the Theory of Neural Computation*. New York: Addison Wesley.

Tikochinsky, Y., Tishby, N.Z., Levine, R. D. (1984). Alternative Approach to Maximum–Entropy Inference. *Physical Review A*, **30**, 2638–2644.

A Non-linear Information Maximisation Algorithm that Performs Blind Separation.

Anthony J. Bell
tony@salk.edu

Terrence J. Sejnowski
terry@salk.edu

Computational Neurobiology Laboratory
The Salk Institute
10010 N. Torrey Pines Road
La Jolla, California 92037-1099

and
Department of Biology
University of California at San Diego
La Jolla CA 92093

Abstract

A new learning algorithm is derived which performs online stochastic gradient ascent in the mutual information between outputs and inputs of a network. In the absence of *a priori* knowledge about the 'signal' and 'noise' components of the input, propagation of information depends on calibrating network non-linearities to the detailed higher-order moments of the input density functions. By incidentally minimising mutual information between outputs, as well as maximising their individual entropies, the network 'factorises' the input into independent components. As an example application, we have achieved near-perfect separation of ten digitally mixed speech signals. Our simulations lead us to believe that our network performs better at blind separation than the Herault-Jutten network, reflecting the fact that it is derived rigorously from the mutual information objective.

1 Introduction

Unsupervised learning algorithms based on information theoretic principles have tended to focus on linear decorrelation (Barlow & Földiák 1989) or maximisation of signal-to-noise ratios assuming Gaussian sources (Linsker 1992). With the exception of (Becker 1992), there has been little attempt to use non-linearity in networks to achieve something a linear network could not.

Non-linear networks, however, are capable of computing more general statistics than those second-order ones involved in decorrelation, and as a consequence they are capable of dealing with signals (and noises) which have detailed higher-order structure. The success of the 'H-J' networks at blind separation (Jutten & Herault 1991) suggests that it should be possible to separate statistically independent components, by using learning rules which make use of moments of all orders.

This paper takes a principled approach to this problem, by starting with the question of how to maximise the information passed on in non-linear feed-forward network. Starting with an analysis of a single unit, the approach is extended to a network mapping N inputs to N outputs. In the process, it will be shown that, under certain fairly weak conditions, the $N \to N$ network forms a minimally redundant encoding of the inputs, and that it therefore performs Independent Component Analysis (ICA).

2 Information maximisation

The information that output Y contains about input X is defined as:

$$I(Y, X) = H(Y) - H(Y|X) \tag{1}$$

where $H(Y)$ is the entropy (information) in the output, while $H(Y|X)$ is whatever information the output has which didn't come from the input. In the case that we have no noise (or rather, we don't know what is noise and what is signal in the input), the mapping between X and Y is deterministic and $H(Y|X)$ has its lowest possible value of $-\infty$. Despite this, we may still differentiate eq.1 as follows (see [5]):

$$\frac{\partial}{\partial w} I(Y, X) = \frac{\partial}{\partial w} H(Y) \tag{2}$$

Thus in the noiseless case, the mutual information can be maximised by maximising the entropy alone.

2.1 One input, one output.

Consider an input variable, x, passed through a transforming function, $g(x)$, to produce an output variable, y, as in Fig.2.1(a). In the case that $g(x)$ is monotonically increasing or decreasing (ie: has a unique inverse), the probability density function (pdf) of the output $f_y(y)$ can be written as a function of the pdf of the input $f_x(x)$, (Papoulis, eq. 5-5):

$$f_y(y) = \frac{f_x(x)}{\partial y / \partial x} \tag{3}$$

The entropy of the output, $H(y)$, is given by:

$$H(y) = -E\left[\ln f_y(y)\right] = -\int_{-\infty}^{\infty} f_y(y) \ln f_y(y) dy \qquad (4)$$

where $E[.]$ denotes expected value. Substituting eq.3 into eq.4 gives

$$H(y) = E\left[\ln \frac{\partial y}{\partial x}\right] - E\left[\ln f_x(x)\right] \qquad (5)$$

The second term on the right may be considered to be unaffected by alterations in a parameter, w, determining $g(x)$. Therefore in order to maximise the entropy of y by changing w, we need only concentrate on maximising the first term, which is the average log of how the input affects the output. This can be done by considering the 'training set' of x's to approximate the density $f_x(x)$, and deriving an 'online', stochastic gradient descent learning rule:

$$\Delta w \propto \frac{\partial H}{\partial w} = \frac{\partial}{\partial w}\left(\ln \frac{\partial y}{\partial x}\right) = \left(\frac{\partial y}{\partial x}\right)^{-1} \frac{\partial}{\partial w}\left(\frac{\partial y}{\partial x}\right) \qquad (6)$$

In the case of the logistic transfer function $y = (1 + e^{-u})^{-1}$, $u = wx + w_0$ in which the input is multiplied by a weight w and added to a bias-weight w_0, the terms above evaluate as:

$$\frac{\partial y}{\partial x} = wy(1-y) \qquad (7)$$

$$\frac{\partial}{\partial w}\left(\frac{\partial y}{\partial x}\right) = y(1-y)(1 + wx(1-2y)) \qquad (8)$$

Dividing eq.8 by eq.7 gives the learning rule for the logistic function, as calculated from the general rule of eq.6:

$$\Delta w \propto \frac{1}{w} + x(1-2y) \qquad (9)$$

Similar reasoning leads to the rule for the bias-weight:

$$\Delta w_0 \propto 1 - 2y \qquad (10)$$

The effect of these two rules can be seen in Fig. 1a. For example, if the input pdf $f_x(x)$ was gaussian, then the Δw_0-rule would centre the steepest part of the sigmoid curve on the peak of $f_x(x)$, matching input density to output slope, in a manner suggested intuitively by eq.3. The Δw-rule would then scale the slope of the sigmoid curve to match the variance of $f_x(x)$. For example, narrow pdfs would lead to sharply-sloping sigmoids. The Δw-rule is basically *anti-Hebbian*[1], with an *anti-decay* term. The anti-Hebbian term keeps y away from one uninformative situation: that of y being saturated to 0 or 1. But anti-Hebbian rules alone make weights go to zero, so the anti-decay term $(1/w)$ keeps y away from the other uninformative situation: when w is so small that y stays around 0.5. The effect of these two balanced forces is to produce an output pdf $f_y(y)$ which is close to the flat unit distribution, which is the maximum entropy distribution for a variable

---
[1] If $y = \tanh(wx + w_0)$ then $\Delta w \propto \frac{1}{w} - 2xy$

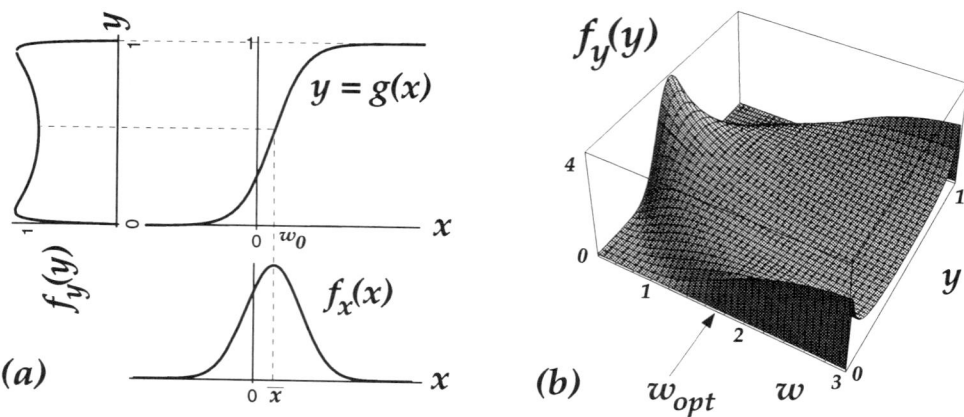

Figure 1: (a) Optimal information flow in sigmoidal neurons (Schraudolph et al 1992). Input x having density function $f_x(x)$, in this case a gaussian, is passed through a non-linear function $g(x)$. The information in the resulting density, $f_y(y)$ depends on matching the mean and variance of x to the threshold and slope of $g(x)$. In (b) $f_y(y)$ is plotted for different values of the weight w. The optimal weight, w_{opt} transmits most information.

bounded between 0 and 1. Fig. 1b illustrates a family of these distributions, with the highest entropy one occuring at w_{opt}.

A rule which maximises information for one input and one output may be suggestive for structures such as synapses and photoreceptors which must position the gain of their non-linearity at a level appropriate to the average value and size of the input fluctuations. However, to see the advantages of this approach in artificial neural networks, we now analyse the case of multi-dimensional inputs and outputs.

2.2 N inputs, N outputs.

Consider a network with an input vector $\mathbf{x}$, a weight matrix $\mathbf{W}$ and a monotonically transformed output vector $\mathbf{y} = g(\mathbf{Wx} + \mathbf{w}_0)$. Analogously to eq.3, the multivariate probability density function of $\mathbf{y}$ can be written (Papoulis, eq. 6-63):

$$f_\mathbf{y}(\mathbf{y}) = \frac{f_\mathbf{x}(\mathbf{x})}{|J|} \qquad (11)$$

where $|J|$ is the absolute value of the Jacobian of the transformation. The Jacobian is the determinant of the matrix of partial derivatives:

$$J = \det \begin{bmatrix} \frac{\partial y_1}{\partial x_1} & \cdots & \frac{\partial y_1}{\partial x_n} \\ \vdots & & \vdots \\ \frac{\partial y_n}{\partial x_1} & \cdots & \frac{\partial y_n}{\partial x_n} \end{bmatrix} \qquad (12)$$

The derivation proceeds as in the previous section except instead of maximising $\ln(\partial y/\partial x)$, now we maximise $\ln |J|$. For sigmoidal units, $\mathbf{y} = (\mathbf{1} + e^{-\mathbf{u}})^{-1}, \mathbf{u} =$

$\mathbf{Wx} + \mathbf{w}_0$, the resulting learning rules are familiar in form:

$$\Delta \mathbf{W} \propto \left[\mathbf{W}^T\right]^{-1} + \mathbf{x}(\mathbf{1} - 2\mathbf{y})^T \qquad (13)$$

$$\Delta \mathbf{w}_0 \propto \mathbf{1} - 2\mathbf{y} \qquad (14)$$

except that now $\mathbf{x}$, $\mathbf{y}$, $\mathbf{w}_0$ and $\mathbf{1}$ are vectors ($\mathbf{1}$ is a vector of ones), $\mathbf{W}$ is a matrix, and the anti-Hebbian term has become an outer product. The anti-decay term has generalised to the inverse of the transpose of the weight matrix. For an individual weight, w_{ij}, this rule amounts to:

$$\Delta w_{ij} \propto \frac{\text{cof } w_{ij}}{\det \mathbf{W}} + x_j(1 - 2y_i) \qquad (15)$$

where cof w_{ij}, the *cofactor* of w_{ij}, is $(-1)^{i+j}$ times the determinant of the matrix obtained by removing the ith row and the jth column from $\mathbf{W}$.

This rule is the same as the one for the single unit mapping, except that instead of $w = 0$ being an unstable point of the dynamics, now any degenerate weight matrix is unstable, since $\det \mathbf{W} = 0$ if $\mathbf{W}$ is degenerate. This fact enables different output units, y_i, to learn to represent different components in the input. When the weight vectors entering two output units become too similar, $\det \mathbf{W}$ becomes small and the natural dynamic of learning causes these weight vectors to diverge. This effect is mediated by the numerator, cof w_{ij}. When this cofactor becomes small, it indicates that there is a degeneracy in the weight matrix of the *rest* of the layer (ie: those weights not associated with input x_j or output y_i). In this case, any degeneracy in $\mathbf{W}$ has less to do with the specific weight w_{ij} that we are adjusting.

3 Finding independent components — blind separation

Maximising the information contained in a layer of units involves maximising the entropy of the individual units while minimising the mutual information (the *redundancy*) between them. Considering two units:

$$H(y_1, y_2) = H(y_1) + H(y_2) - I(y_1, y_2) \qquad (16)$$

For $I(y_1, y_2)$ to be zero, y_1 and y_2 must be statistically independent of each other, so that $f_{y_1 y_2}(y_1, y_2) = f_{y_1}(y_1) f_{y_2}(y_2)$. Achieving such a representation is variously called factorial code learning, redundancy reduction (Barlow 1961, Atick 1992), or independent component analysis (ICA), and in the general case of continuously valued variables of arbitrary distributions, no learning algorithm has been shown to converge to such a representation.

Our method *will* converge to a minimum redundancy, factorial representation as long as the individual entropy terms in eq.16 do not override the redundancy term, making an $I(y_1, y_2) = 0$ solution sub-optimal. One way to ensure this cannot occur is if we have *a priori* knowledge of the general form of the pdfs of the independent components. Then we can tailor our choice of node-function to be optimal for transmitting information about these components. For example, unit distributions require piecewise linear node-functions for highest $H(y)$, while the more common gaussian forms require roughly sigmoidal curves. Once we have chosen our node-functions appropriately, we can be sure that an output node y cannot have higher

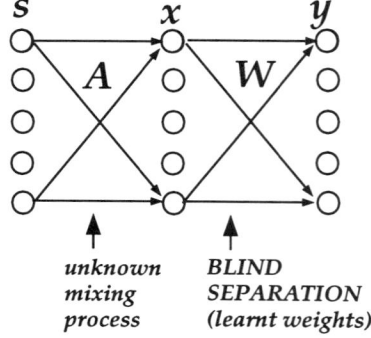

$$\begin{bmatrix} \boxed{-4.09} & 0.13 & 0.09 & -0.07 & -0.01 \\ 0.07 & \boxed{-2.92} & 0.00 & 0.02 & -0.06 \\ 0.02 & -0.02 & -0.06 & -0.08 & \boxed{-2.20} \\ 0.02 & 0.03 & 0.00 & \boxed{1.97} & 0.02 \\ -0.07 & 0.14 & \boxed{-3.50} & -0.01 & 0.04 \end{bmatrix}$$

Figure 2: (a) In blind separation, sources, **s**, have been linearly scrambled by a matrix, **A**, to form the inputs to the network, **x**. We must recover the sources at our output **y**, by somehow inverting the mapping **A** with our weight matrix **W**. The problem: we know nothing about **A** or the sources. (b) A successful 'unscrambling' occurs when **WA** is a 'permutation' matrix. This one resulted from separating five speech signals with our algorithm.

entropy by representing some combination of independent components than by representing just one. When this condition is satisfied for all output units, the residual goal, of minimising the mutual information between the outputs, will dominate the learning. See [5] for further discussion of this.

With this caveat in mind, we turn to the problem of *blind separation*, (Jutten & Herault 1991), illustrated in Fig.2. A set of sources, $s_1, \ldots, s_N$, (different people speaking, music, noise etc) are presumed to be mixed approximately linearly so that all we receive is N superpositions of them, $x_1, \ldots, x_N$, which are input to our single-layer information maximisation network. Providing the mixing matrix, **A**, is non-singular then the original sources can be recovered if our weight matrix, **W**, is such that **WA** is a 'permutation' matrix containing only one high value in each row and column.

Unfortunately we know nothing about the sources or the mixing matrix. However, if the sources are statistically independent and non-gaussian, then the information in the output nodes will be maximised when each output transmits one independent component only. This problem cannot be solved in general by linear decorrelation techniques such as those of (Barlow & Földiák 1989) since second-order statistics can only produce symmetrical decorrelation matrices.

We have tested the algorithm in eq.13 and eq.14 on digitally mixed speech signals, and it reliably converges to separate the individual sources. In one example, five separately-recorded speech signals from three individuals were sampled at 8kHz. Three-second segments from each were linearly mixed using a matrix of random values between 0.2 and 4. Each resulting mixture formed an incomprehensible babble. Time points were generated at random, and for each, the corresponding five mixed values were entered into the network, and weights were altered according to eq.13 and eq.14. After on the order of 500,000 points were presented, the network had converged so that **WA** was the matrix shown in Fig.2b. As can be seen from the permutation structure of this matrix, on average, 95% of each output unit is dedicated to one source only, with each unit carrying a different source. Any residual interference from the four other sources was inaudible.

We have not yet performed any systematic studies on rates of convergence or existence of local minima. However the algorithm has converged to separate N independent components in all our tests (for $2 \leq N \leq 10$). In contrast, we have not been able to obtain convergence of the H-J network on our data set for $N > 2$.

Finally, the kind of linear static mixing we have been using is not equivalent to what would be picked up by N microphones positioned around a room. However, (Platt & Faggin 1992) in their work on the H-J net, discuss extensions for dealing with time-delays and non-static filtering, which may also be applicable to our methods.

4 Discussion

The problem of Independent Component Analysis (ICA) has become popular recently in the signal processing community, partly as a result of the success of the H-J network. The H-J network is identical to the linear decorrelation network of (Barlow & Földiák 1989) except for non-linearities in the anti-Hebb rule which normally performs only decorrelation. These non-linearities are chosen somewhat arbitrarily in the hope that their polynomial expansions will yield higher-order cross-cumulants useful in converging to independence (Comon et al, 1991). The H-J algorithm lacks an objective function, but these insights have led (Comon 1994) to propose minimising mutual information between outputs (see also Becker 1992). Since mutual information cannot be expressed as a simple function of the variables concerned, Comon expands it as a function of cumulants of increasing order.

In this paper, we have shown that mutual information, and through it, ICA, can be tackled directly (in the sense of eq.16) through a stochastic gradient approach. Sigmoidal units, being bounded, are limited in their 'channel capacity'. Weights transmitting information try, by following eq.13, to project their inputs to where they can make a lot of difference to the output, as measured by the log of the Jacobian of the transformation. In the process, each set of statistically 'dependent' information is channelled to the same output unit.

The non-linearity is crucial. If the network were just linear, the weight matrix would grow without bound since the learning rule would be:

$$\Delta \mathbf{W} \propto [\mathbf{W}^T]^{-1} \qquad (17)$$

This reflects the fact that the information in the outputs grows with their variance. The non-linearity also supplies the higher-order cross-moments necessary to maximise the infinite-order expansion of the information. For example, when $\mathbf{y} = \tanh(\mathbf{u})$, the learning rule has the form $\Delta \mathbf{W} \propto [\mathbf{W}^T]^{-1} - 2\mathbf{y}\mathbf{x}^T$, from which we can write that the weights stabilise (or $\langle \Delta \mathbf{W} \rangle = 0$) when $\mathbf{I} = 2\langle \tanh(\mathbf{u})\mathbf{u}^T \rangle$. Since tanh is an odd function, its series expansion is of the form $\tanh(u) = \sum_j b_j u^{2p+1}$, the b_j being coefficients, and thus this convergence criterion amounts to the condition $\sum_{i,j} b_{ijp} \langle u_i^{2p+1} u_j \rangle = 0$ for all output unit pairs $i \neq j$, for $p = 0, 1, 2, 3 \ldots$, and for the coefficients b_{ijp} coming from the Taylor series expansion of the tanh function.

These and other issues are covered more completely in a forthcoming paper (Bell & Sejnowski 1995). Applications to blind deconvolution (removing the effects of unknown causal filtering) are also described, and the limitations of the approach are discussed.

Acknowledgements

We are much indebted to Nici Schraudolph, who not only supplied the original idea in Fig.1 and shared his unpublished calculations [13], but also provided detailed criticism at every stage of the work. Much constructive advice also came from Paul Viola and Alexandre Pouget.

References

[1] Atick J.J. 1992. Could information theory provide an ecological theory of sensory processing, *Network* 3, 213-251

[2] Barlow H.B. 1961. Possible principles underlying the transformation of sensory messages, in *Sensory Communication*, Rosenblith W.A. (ed), MIT press

[3] Barlow H.B. & Földiák P. 1989. Adaptation and decorrelation in the cortex, in Durbin R. et al (eds) *The Computing Neuron*, Addison-Wesley

[4] Becker S. 1992. An information-theoretic unsupervised learning algorithm for neural networks, *Ph.D. thesis*, Dept. of Comp. Sci., Univ. of Toronto

[5] Bell A.J. & Sejnowski T.J. 1995. An information-maximisation approach to blind separation and blind deconvolution, *Neural Computation*, in press

[6] Comon P., Jutten C. & Herault J. 1991. Blind separation of sources, part II: problems statement, *Signal processing*, 24, 11-21

[7] Comon P. 1994. Independent component analysis, a new concept? *Signal processing*, 36, 287-314

[8] Hopfield J.J. 1991. Olfactory computation and object perception, *Proc. Natl. Acad. Sci. USA*, vol. 88, pp.6462-6466

[9] Jutten C. & Herault J. 1991. Blind separation of sources, part I: an adaptive algorithm based on neuromimetic architecture, *Signal processing*, 24, 1-10

[10] Linsker R. 1992. Local synaptic learning rules suffice to maximise mutual information in a linear network, *Neural Computation*, 4, 691-702

[11] Papoulis A. 1984. *Probability, random variables and stochastic processes, 2nd edition*, McGraw-Hill, New York

[12] Platt J.C. & Faggin F. 1992. Networks for the separation of sources that are superimposed and delayed, in Moody J.E et al (eds) *Adv. Neur. Inf. Proc. Sys. 4*, Morgan-Kaufmann

[13] Schraudolph N.N., Hart W.E. & Belew R.K. 1992. Optimal information flow in sigmoidal neurons, *unpublished manuscript*

Plasticity-Mediated Competitive Learning

Nicol N. Schraudolph
nici@salk.edu

Terrence J. Sejnowski
terry@salk.edu

Computational Neurobiology Laboratory
The Salk Institute for Biological Studies
San Diego, CA 92186-5800

and

Computer Science & Engineering Department
University of California, San Diego
La Jolla, CA 92093-0114

Abstract

Differentiation between the nodes of a competitive learning network is conventionally achieved through competition on the basis of neural activity. Simple inhibitory mechanisms are limited to sparse representations, while decorrelation and factorization schemes that support distributed representations are computationally unattractive. By letting neural *plasticity* mediate the competitive interaction instead, we obtain diffuse, nonadaptive alternatives for fully distributed representations. We use this technique to simplify and improve our binary information gain optimization algorithm for feature extraction (Schraudolph and Sejnowski, 1993); the same approach could be used to improve other learning algorithms.

1 INTRODUCTION

Unsupervised neural networks frequently employ sets of nodes or subnetworks with identical architecture and objective function. Some form of competitive interaction is then needed for these nodes to differentiate and efficiently complement each other in their task.

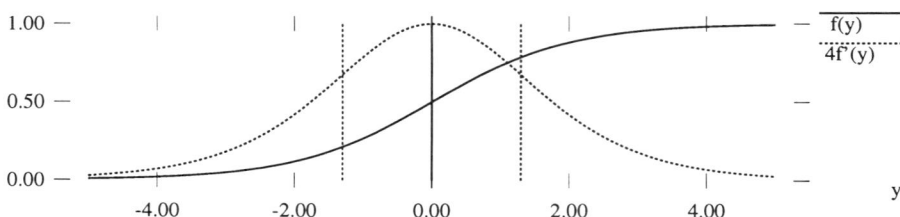

Figure 1: Activity f and plasticity f' of a logistic node as a function of its net input y. Vertical lines indicate those values of y whose pre-images in input space are depicted in Figure 2.

Inhibition is the simplest competitive mechanism: the most active nodes suppress the ability of their peers to learn, either directly or by depressing their activity. Since inhibition can be implemented by diffuse, nonadaptive mechanisms, it is an attractive solution from both neurobiological and computational points of view. However, inhibition can only form either localized (unary) or sparse distributed representations, in which each output has only one state with significant information content.

For fully distributed representations, schemes to decorrelate (Barlow and Földiák, 1989; Leen, 1991) and even factorize (Schmidhuber, 1992; Bell and Sejnowski, 1995) node activities do exist. Unfortunately these require specific, weighted lateral connections whose adaptation is computationally expensive and may interfere with feedforward learning. While they certainly have their place as competitive learning algorithms, the capability of biological neurons to implement them seems questionable.

In this paper, we suggest an alternative approach: we extend the advantages of simple inhibition to distributed representations by decoupling the competition from the activation vector. In particular, we use neural *plasticity* — the derivative of a logistic activation function — as a medium for competition.

Plasticity is low for both high and low activation values but high for intermediate ones (Figure 1); distributed patterns of activity may therefore have localized plasticity. If competition is controlled by plasticity then, simple competitive mechanisms will constrain us to localized plasticity but allow representations with distributed activity.

The next section reintroduces the binary information gain optimization (BINGO) algorithm for a single node; we then discuss how plasticity-mediated competition improves upon the decorrelation mechanism used in our original extension to multiple nodes. Finally, we establish a close relationship between the plasticity and the entropy of a logistic node that provides an intuitive interpretation of plasticity-mediated competitive learning in this context.

2 BINARY INFORMATION GAIN OPTIMIZATION

In (Schraudolph and Sejnowski, 1993), we proposed an unsupervised learning rule that uses logistic nodes to seek out binary features in its input. The output

$$z = f(y), \text{ where } f(y) = \frac{1}{1 + e^{-y}} \text{ and } y = \vec{w} \cdot \vec{x} \qquad (1)$$

of each node is interpreted stochastically as the probability that a given feature is present. We then search for informative directions in weight space by maximizing the information gained about an unknown binary feature through observation of z. This *binary information gain* is given by

$$\Delta H(z) = H(\hat{z}) - H(z), \qquad (2)$$

where $H(z)$ is the entropy of a binary random variable with probability z, and $\hat{z}$ is a prediction of z based on prior knowledge. Gradient ascent in this objective results in the learning rule

$$\Delta \vec{w} \propto f'(y) \cdot (y - \hat{y}) \cdot \vec{x}, \qquad (3)$$

where $\hat{y}$ is a prediction of y. In the simplest case, $\hat{y}$ is an empirical average $\langle y \rangle$ of past activity, computed either over batches of input data or by means of an exponential trace; this amounts to a nonlinear version of the *covariance rule* (Sejnowski, 1977).

Using just the average as prediction introduces a strong preference for splitting the data into two equal-sized clusters. While such a bias is appropriate in the initial phase of learning, it fails to take the nonlinear nature of f into account. In order to discount data in the saturated regions of the logistic function appropriately, we weigh the average by the node's plasticity $f'(y)$:

$$\hat{y} = \frac{\langle y \cdot f'(y) \rangle}{\langle f'(y) \rangle + \varepsilon}, \qquad (4)$$

where ε is a very small positive constant introduced to ensure numerical stability for large values of y. Now the bias for splitting the data evenly is gradually relaxed as the network's weights grow and data begins to fall into saturated regions of f.

3 PLASTICITY-MEDIATED COMPETITION

For multiple nodes the original BINGO algorithm used a decorrelating predictor as the competitive mechanism:

$$\widehat{\vec{y}} = \vec{y} + (\boldsymbol{Q}_{\vec{y}} - 2\boldsymbol{I})(\vec{y} - \langle \vec{y} \rangle), \qquad (5)$$

where $\boldsymbol{Q}_{\vec{y}}$ is the autocorrelation matrix of $\vec{y}$, and $\boldsymbol{I}$ the identity matrix. Note that $\boldsymbol{Q}_{\vec{y}}$ is computationally expensive to maintain; in connectionist implementations it

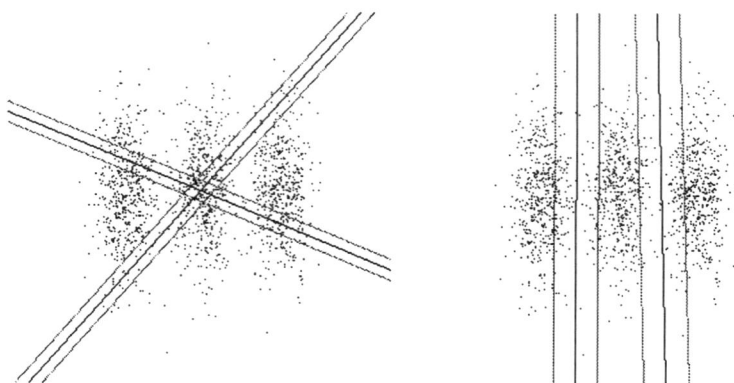

Figure 2: The "three cigars" problem. Each plot shows the pre-image of zero net input, superimposed on a scatter plot of the data set, in input space. The two flanking lines delineate the "plastic region" where the logistic is not saturated, providing an indication of weight vector size. Left, two-node BINGO network using decorrelation (Equations 3 & 5) fails to separate the three data clusters. Right, same network using plasticity-mediated competition (Equations 4 & 6) succeeds.

---

is often approximated by lateral anti-Hebbian connections whose adaptation must occur on a faster time scale than that of the feedforward weights (Equation 3) for reasons of stability (Leen, 1991). In practice this means that learning is slowed significantly.

In addition, decorrelation can be inappropriate when nonlinear objectives are optimized — in our case, two prominent binary features may well be correlated. Consider the "three cigars" problem illustrated in Figure 2: the decorrelating predictor (left) forces the two nodes into a near-orthogonal arrangement, interfering with their ability to detect the parallel gaps separating the data clusters.

For our purposes, decorrelation is thus too strong a constraint on the discriminants: all we require is that the discovered features be distinct. We achieve this by reverting to the simple predictor of Equation 4 while adding a global, plasticity-mediated excitation[1] factor to the weight update:

$$\Delta \vec{w}_i \propto f'(y_i) \cdot (y_i - \hat{y}_i) \cdot \vec{x} \cdot \sum_j f'(y_j) \qquad (6)$$

As Figure 2 (right) illustrates, this arrangement solves the "three cigars" problem. In the high-dimensional environment of hand-written digit recognition, this algorithm discovers a set of distributed binary features that preserve most of the information needed to classify the digits, even though the network was never given any class labels (Figure 3).

---

[1] The interaction is excitatory rather than inhibitory since a node's plasticity is *inversely* correlated with the magnitude of its net input.

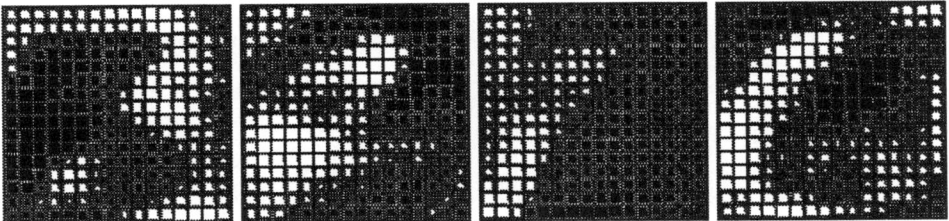

Figure 3: Weights found by a four-node network running the improved BINGO algorithm (Equations 4 & 6) on a set of 1200 handwritten digits due to (Guyon et al., 1989). Although the network is unsupervised, its four-bit output conveys most of the information necessary to classify the digits.

4 PLASTICITY AND BINARY ENTROPY

It is possible to establish a relationship between the plasticity f' of a logistic node and its entropy that provides an intuitive account of plasticity-mediated competition as applied to BINGO. Consider the binary entropy

$$H(z) = -z \log z - (1-z) \log(1-z) \tag{7}$$

A well-known quadratic approximation is

$$\tilde{H}(z) = 8e^{-1} z(1-z) \approx H(z) \tag{8}$$

Now observe that the plasticity of a logistic node

$$f'(y) = \frac{\partial}{\partial y} \frac{1}{1+e^{-y}} = \ldots = z(1-z) \tag{9}$$

is in fact proportional to $\tilde{H}(z)$ — that is, a logistic node's plasticity is in effect a convenient quadratic approximation to its binary output entropy. The overall entropy in a layer of such nodes equals the sum of individual entropies less their redundancy:

$$H(\vec{z}) = \sum_j H(z_j) - R(\vec{z}) \tag{10}$$

The plasticity-mediated excitation factor in Equation 6

$$\sum_j f'(y_j) \propto \sum_j \tilde{H}(z_j), \tag{11}$$

is thus proportional to an approximate upper bound on the entropy of the layer, which in turn indicates how much more information remains to be gained by learning from a particular input. In the context of BINGO, plasticity-mediated competition thus scales weight changes according to a measure of the network's ignorance: the less it is able to identify a given input in terms of its set of binary features, the more it tries to learn doing so.

5 CONCLUSION

By using the derivative of a logistic activation function as a medium for competitive interaction, we were able to obtain differentiated, fully distributed representations without resorting to computationally expensive decorrelation schemes. We have demonstrated this plasticity-mediated competition approach on the BINGO feature extraction algorithm, which is significantly improved by it. A close relationship between the plasticity of a logistic node and its binary output entropy provides an intuitive interpretation of this unusual form of competition.

Our general approach of using a nonmonotonic function of activity — rather than activity itself — to control competitive interactions may prove valuable in other learning schemes, in particular those that seek distributed rather than local representations.

Acknowledgements

We thank Rich Zemel and Paul Viola for stimulating discussions, and the McDonnell-Pew Center for Cognitive Neuroscience in San Diego for financial support.

References

Barlow, H. B. and Földiák, P. (1989). Adaptation and decorrelation in the cortex. In Durbin, R. M., Miall, C., and Mitchison, G. J., editors, *The Computing Neuron*, chapter 4, pages 54–72. Addison-Wesley, Wokingham.

Bell, A. J. and Sejnowski, T. J. (1995). A non-linear information maximisation algorithm that performs blind separation. In *Advances in Neural Information Processing Systems*, volume 7, Denver 1994.

Guyon, I., Poujaud, I., Personnaz, L., Dreyfus, G., Denker, J., and Le Cun, Y. (1989). Comparing different neural network architectures for classifying handwritten digits. In *Proceedings of the International Joint Conference on Neural Networks*, volume II, pages 127–132. IEEE.

Leen, T. K. (1991). Dynamics of learning in linear feature-discovery networks. *Network*, 2:85–105.

Schmidhuber, J. (1992). Learning factorial codes by predictability minimization. *Neural Computation*, 4(6):863–879.

Schraudolph, N. N. and Sejnowski, T. J. (1993). Unsupervised discrimination of clustered data via optimization of binary information gain. In Hanson, S. J., Cowan, J. D., and Giles, C. L., editors, *Advances in Neural Information Processing Systems*, volume 5, pages 499–506, Denver 1992. Morgan Kaufmann, San Mateo.

Sejnowski, T. J. (1977). Storing covariance with nonlinearly interacting neurons. *Journal of Mathematical Biology*, 4:303–321.

Phase-Space Learning

Fu-Sheng Tsung
Chung Tai Ch'an Temple
56, Yuon-fon Road, Yi-hsin Li, Pu-li
Nan-tou County, Taiwan 545
Republic of China

Garrison W. Cottrell*
Institute for Neural Computation
Computer Science & Engineering
University of California, San Diego
La Jolla, California 92093

Abstract

Existing recurrent net learning algorithms are inadequate. We introduce the conceptual framework of viewing recurrent training as matching vector fields of dynamical systems in phase space. Phase-space reconstruction techniques make the hidden states explicit, reducing temporal learning to a feed–forward problem. In short, we propose viewing *iterated prediction* [LF88] as the best way of training recurrent networks on deterministic signals. Using this framework, we can train multiple trajectories, insure their stability, and *design* arbitrary dynamical systems.

1 INTRODUCTION

Existing general-purpose recurrent algorithms are capable of rich dynamical behavior. Unfortunately, straightforward applications of these algorithms to training fully–recurrent networks on complex temporal tasks have had much less success than their feedforward counterparts. For example, to train a recurrent network to oscillate like a sine wave (the "hydrogen atom" of recurrent learning), existing techniques such as Real Time Recurrent Learning (RTRL) [WZ89] perform sub-optimally. Williams & Zipser trained a two-unit network with RTRL, with one teacher signal. One unit of the resulting network showed a distorted waveform, the other only half the desired amplitude. [Pea89] needed four hidden units. However, our work demonstrates that a two-unit recurrent network with no hidden units can learn the sine wave very well [Tsu94]. Existing methods also have several other

---
*Correspondence should be addressed to the second author: gary@cs.ucsd.edu

limitations. For example, networks often fail to converge even though a solution is known to exist; teacher forcing is usually necessary to learn periodic signals; it is not clear how to train multiple trajectories at once, or how to insure that the trained trajectory is stable (an *attractor*).

In this paper, we briefly analyze the algorithms to discover why they have such difficulties, and propose a general solution to the problem. Our solution is based on the simple idea of using the techniques of time series prediction as a methodology for recurrent network training.

First, by way of introducing the appropriate concepts, consider a system of coupled autonomous[1] first order network equations:

$$\begin{aligned} dx_1/dt &= F_1(x_1(t), x_2(t), \cdots, x_n(t)) \\ dx_2/dt &= F_2(x_1(t), x_2(t), \cdots, x_n(t)) \\ &\vdots \\ dx_n/dt &= F_n(x_1(t), x_2(t), \cdots, x_n(t)) \end{aligned}$$

or, in vector notation,

$$X(t) = F(X) \quad \text{where} \quad X(t) = (x_1(t), x_2(t), \cdots, x_n(t))$$

The **phase space** is the space of the dependent variables (X), it does not include t, while the **state space** incorporates t. The evolution of a trajectory $X(t)$ traces out a phase curve, or *orbit*, in the n-dimensional phase space of X. For low dimensional systems (2- or 3-D), it is easy to visualize the limit sets in the phase space: a fixed point and a limit cycle become a single point and a closed orbit (closed curve), respectively. In the state space they become an infinite straight line and a spiral. $F(X)$ defines the **vector field** of X, because it associates a vector with each point in the phase space of X whose direction and magnitude determines the movement of that point in the next instant of time (by definition, the tangent vector).

2 ANALYSIS OF CURRENT APPROACHES

To get a better understanding of why recurrent algorithms have not been very effective, we look at what happens during training with two popular recurrent learning techniques: RTRL and back propagation through time (BPTT). With each, we illustrate a different problem, although the problems apply equally to each technique.

RTRL is a forward-gradient algorithm that keeps a matrix of partial derivatives of the network activation values with respect to every weight. To train a periodic trajectory, it is necessary to *teacher-force* the visible units [WZ89], i.e., on every iteration, after the gradient has been calculated, the activations of the visible units are replaced by the teacher. To see why, consider learning a pair of sine waves offset by 90°. In phase space, this becomes a circle (Figure 1a). Initially the network

---

[1] Autonomous means the right hand side of a differential equation does not explicitly reference t, e.g. $dx/dt = 2x$ is autonomous, even though x is a function of t, but $dx/dt = 2x+t$ is not. Continuous neural networks without inputs are autonomous. A nonautonomous system can always be turned into an autonomous system in a higher dimension.

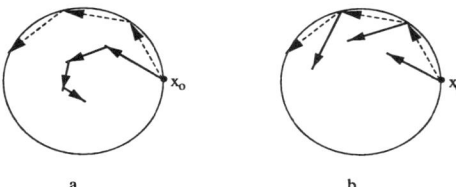

a b

Figure 1: Learning a pair of sine waves with RTRL learning. (a) without teacher forcing, the network dynamics (solid arrows) take it far from where the teacher (dotted arrows) assumes it is, so the gradient is incorrect. (b) With teacher forcing, the network's visible units are returned to the trajectory.

(thick arrows) is at position X_0 and has arbitrary dynamics. After a few iterations, it wanders far away from where the teacher (dashed arrows) assumes it to be. The teacher then provides an incorrect next target from the network's current position. Teacher-forcing (Figure 1b), resets the network back on the circle, where the teacher again provides useful information.

However, if the network has hidden units, then the phase space of the visible units is just a projection of the actual phase space of the network, and the teaching signal gives no information as to where the hidden units should be in this higher-dimensional phase space. Hence the hidden unit states, unaltered by teacher forcing, may be entirely unrelated to what they should be. This leads to the *moving targets* problem. During training, every time the visible units re–visit a point, the hidden unit activations will differ, Thus the mapping changes during learning. (See [Pin88, WZ89] for other discussions of teacher forcing.)

With BPTT, the network is unrolled in time (Figure 2). This unrolling reveals another problem: Suppose in the teaching signal, the visible units' next state is a non-linearly separable function of their current state. Then hidden units are needed *between* the visible unit layers, but there are no intermediate hidden units in the unrolled network. The network must thus take *two time steps* to get to the hidden units and back. One can deal with this by giving the teaching signal *every other iteration*, but clearly, this is not optimal (consider that the hidden units must "bide their time" on the alternate steps).[2]

The trajectories trained by RTRL and BPTT tend to be stable in simulations of simple tasks [Pea89, TCS90], but this stability is paradoxical. Using teacher forcing, the networks are trained to go from a point on the trajectory, to a point within the ball defined by the error criterion ϵ (see Figure 4 (a)). However, after learning, the networks behave such that from a place near the trajectory, they head for the trajectory (Figure 4 (b)). Hence the paradox. Possible reasons are: 1) the hidden unit moving targets provide training *off* the desired trajectory, so that *if* the training is successful, the desired trajectory is stable; 2) we would never consider the training successful if the network "learns" an unstable trajectory; 3) the stable dynamics in typical situations have simpler equations than the unstable dynamics [Nak93]. To create an unstable periodic trajectory would imply the existence of stable regions both inside and outside the unstable trajectory; dynamically this is

---

[2] At NIPS, 0 delay connections to the hidden units were suggested, which is essentially part of the solution given here.

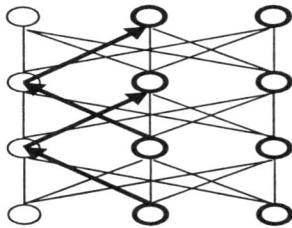
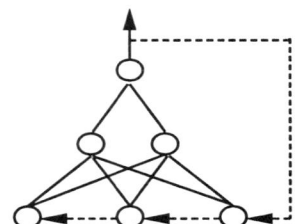

Figure 2: A nonlinearly separable mapping must be computed by the hidden units (the leftmost unit here) every other time step.

Figure 3: The network used for iterated prediction training. Dashed connections are used after learning.

a
b

Figure 4: The paradox of attractor learning with teacher forcing. (a) During learning, the network learns to move from the trajectory to a point near the trajectory. (b) After learning, the network moves from nearby points towards the trajectory.

more complicated than a simple periodic attractor. In dynamically complex tasks, a stable trajectory may no longer be the simplest solution, and stability could be a problem.

In summary, we have pointed out several problems in the RTRL (forward-gradient) and BPTT (backward-gradient) classes of training algorithms:

1. Teacher forcing with hidden units is at best an approximation, and leads to the moving targets problem.

2. Hidden units are not placed properly for some tasks.

3. Stability is paradoxical.

3 PHASE-SPACE LEARNING

The inspiration for our approach is prediction training [LF88], which at first appears similar to BPTT, but is subtly different. In the standard scheme, a feedforward network is given a time window, a set of previous points on the trajectory to be learned, as inputs. The output is the next point on the trajectory. Then, the inputs are shifted left and the network is trained on the next point (see Figure 3). Once the network has learned, it can be treated as recurrent by iterating on its own predictions.

The prediction network differs from BPTT in two important ways. First, the visible units encode a selected temporal history of the trajectory (the time window). The point of this *delay space embedding* is to reconstruct the phase space of the underlying system. [Tak81] has shown that this can always be done for a deterministic system. Note that in the reconstructed phase space, the mapping from one

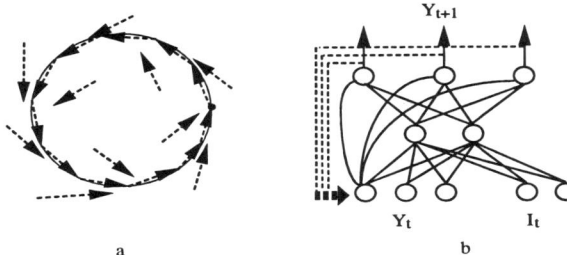

Figure 5: Phase-space learning. (a) The training set is a sample of the vector field. (b) Phase-space learning network. Dashed connections are used after learning.

point to the next (based on the vector field) is deterministic. *Hence what originally appeared to be a recurrent network problem can be converted into an entirely feed forward problem.* Essentially, the delay-space reconstruction makes hidden states visible, and recurrent hidden units unnecessary. Crucially, dynamicists have developed excellent reconstruction algorithms that not only automate the choices of delay and embedding dimension but also filter out noise or get a good reconstruction despite noise [FS91, Dav92, KBA92]. On the other hand, we clearly cannot deal with non-deterministic systems by this method.

The second difference from BPTT is that the hidden units are *between* the visible units, allowing the network to produce nonlinearly separable transformations of the visible units in a single iteration. In the recurrent network produced by iterated prediction, the sandwiched hidden units can be considered "fast" units with delays on the input/output links summing to 1.

Since we are now learning a mapping in phase space, stability is easily ensured by adding additional training examples that converge towards the desired orbit.[3] We can also explicitly *control* convergence speed by the size and direction of the vectors.

Thus, *phase-space learning* (Figure 5) consists of: (1) embedding the temporal signal to recover its phase space structure, (2) generating local approximations of the vector field near the desired trajectory, and (3) functional approximation of the vector field with a feedforward network. Existing methods developed for these three problems can be directly and independently applied to solve the problem. Since feedforward networks are universal approximators [HSW89], we are assured that at least locally, the trajectory can be represented. The trajectory is recovered from the iterated output of the pre-embedded portion of the visible units. Additionally, we may also extend the phase-space learning framework to also include inputs that affect the output of the system (see [Tsu94] for details).[4]

In this framework, training multiple attractors is just training orbits in different parts of the phase space, so they simply add more patterns to the training set. In fact, we can now create *designer dynamical systems* possessing the properties we want, e.g., with combinations of fixed point, periodic, or chaotic attractors.

---

[3] The common practice of adding noise to the input in prediction training is just a simple minded way of adding convergence information.

[4] Principe & Kuo(this volume) show that for chaotic attractors, it is better to treat this as a recurrent net and train using the predictions.

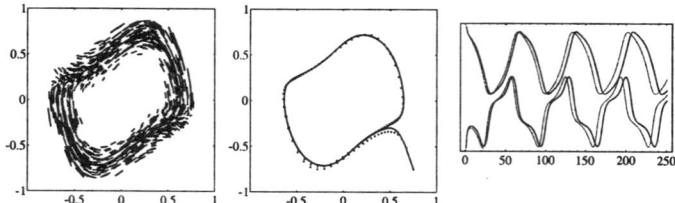

Figure 6: Learning the van der Pol oscillator. (a) the training set. (b) Phase space plot of network (solid curve) and teacher (dots). (c) State space plot.

As an example, to store any number of arbitrary periodic attractors $z_i(t)$ with periods T_i in a single recurrent network, create two new coordinates for each $z_i(t)$, $(x_i(t), y_i(t)) = (sin(\frac{2\pi}{T_i}t), cos(\frac{2\pi}{T_i}t))$, where (x_i, y_i) and (x_j, y_j) are disjoint circles for $i \neq j$. Then (x_i, y_i, z_i) is a valid embedding of all the periodic attractors in phase space, and the network can be trained. In essence, the first two dimensions form "clocks" for their associated trajectories.

4 SIMULATION RESULTS

In this section we illustrate the method by learning the van der Pol oscillator (a much more difficult problem than learning sine waves), learning four separate periodic attractors, and learning an attractor inside the basin of another attractor.

4.1 LEARNING THE VAN DER POL OSCILLATOR

The van der Pol equation is defined by:

$$\dot{x} = y \qquad \dot{y} = -\alpha(x^2 - b)y - \omega^2 x$$

We used the values 0.7, 1, 1 for the parameters α, b, and ω, for which there is a global periodic attractor (Figure 6). We used a step size of 0.1, which discretizes the trajectory into 70 points. The network therefore has two visible units. We used two hidden layers with 20 units each, so that the unrolled, feedforward network has a 2-20-20-2 architecture. We generated 1500 training pairs using the vector field near the attractor. The learning rate was 0.01, scaled by the fan-in, momentum was 0.75, we trained for 15000 epochs. The order of the training pairs was randomized. The attractor learned by the network is shown in (Figure 6 (b)). Comparison of the temporal trajectories is shown in Figure 6 (c); there is a slight frequency difference. The average MSE is 0.000136. Results from a network with two layers of 5 hidden units each with 500 data pairs were similar (MSE=0.00034).

4.2 LEARNING MULTIPLE PERIODIC ATTRACTORS

[Hop82] showed how to store multiple fixed-point attractors in a recurrent net. [Bai91] can store periodic and chaotic attractors by inverting the normal forms of these attractors into higher order recurrent networks. However, traditional recurrent training offers no obvious method of training multiple attractors. [DY89] were able

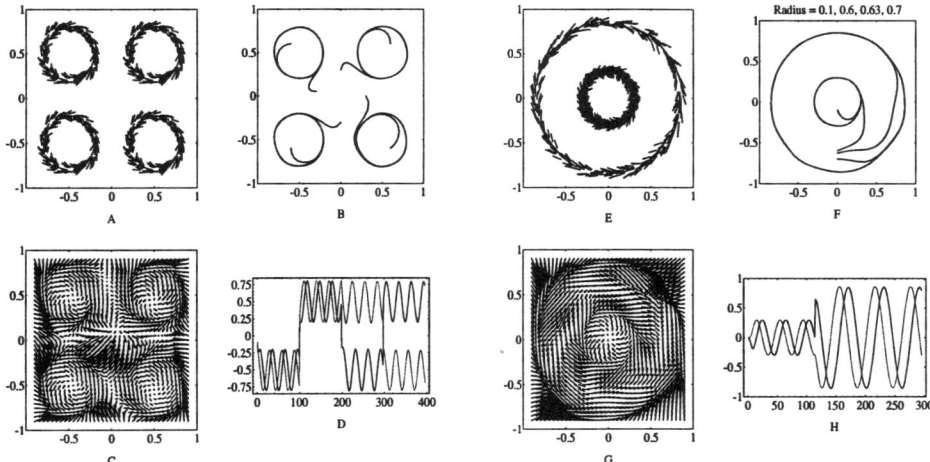

Figure 7: Learning multiple attractors. In each case, a 2-20-20-2 network using conjugate gradient is used. Learning 4 attractors: (A) Training set. (B) Eight trajectories of the trained network. (C) Induced vector field of the network. There are five unstable fixed points. (D) State space behavior as the network is "bumped" between attractors. Learning 2 attractors, one inside the other: (E) Training set. (F) Four trajectories of the trained network. (G) Induced vector field of the network. There is an unstable limit cycle between the two stable ones. (H) State space behavior with a "bump".

to store two limit cycles by starting with fixed points stored in a Hopfield net, and training each fixed point locally to become a periodic attractor. Our approach has no difficulty with multiple attractors. Figure 7 (A-D) shows the result of training four coexisting periodic attractors, one in each quadrant of the two-dimensional phase space. The network will remain in one of the attractor basins until an external force pushes it into another attractor basin. Figure 7 (E-H) shows a network with two periodic attractors, this time one inside the other. This vector field possess an unstable limit cycle between the two stable limit cycles. This is a more difficult task, requiring 40 hidden units, whereas 20 suffice for the previous task (not shown).

5 SUMMARY

We have presented a phase space view of the learning process in recurrent nets. This perspective has helped us to understand and overcome some of the problems of using traditional recurrent methods for learning periodic and chaotic attractors. Our method can learn multiple trajectories, explicitly insure their stability, and avoid overfitting; in short, we provide a practical approach to learning complicated temporal behaviors. The phase-space framework essentially breaks the problem into three sub-problems: (1) Embedding a temporal signal to recover its phase space structure, (2) generating local approximations of the vector field near the desired trajectory, and (3) functional approximation in feedforward networks. We have demonstrated that using this method, networks can learn complex oscillations and multiple periodic attractors.

Acknowledgements

This work was supported by NIH grant R01 MH46899-01A3. Thanks for comments from Steve Biafore, Kenji Doya, Peter Rowat, Bill Hart, and especially Dave DeMers for his timely assistance with simulations.

References

[Bai91] W. Baird and F. Eeckman. Cam storage of analog patterns and continuous sequences with $3n^2$ weights. In R.P. Lippmann, J.E. Moody, and D.S. Touretzky, editors, *Advances in Neural Information Processing Systems*, volume 3, pages 91–97, 1991. Morgan Kaufmann, San Mateo.

[Dav92] M. Davies. Noise reduction by gradient descent. *International Journal of Bifurcation and Chaos*, 3:113–118, 1992.

[DY89] K. Doya and S. Yoshizawa. Memorizing oscillatory patterns in the analog neuron network. In *IJCNN*, Washington D.C., 1989. IEEE.

[FS91] J.D. Farmer and J.J. Sidorowich. Optimal shadowing and noise reduction. *Physica D*, 47:373–392, 1991.

[Hop82] J.J. Hopfield. Neural networks and physical systems with emergent collective computational abilities. *Proceedings of the National Academy of Sciences, USA*, 79, 1982.

[HSW89] K. Hornik, M. Stinchcombe, and H. White. Multilayer feedforward networks are universal approximators. *Neural Networks*, 2:359–366, 1989.

[KBA92] M.B. Kennel, R. Brown, and H. Abarbanel. Determining embedding dimension for phase-space reconstruction using a geometrical construction. *Physical Review A*, 45:3403–3411, 1992.

[LF88] A. Lapedes and R. Farber. How neural nets work. In D.Z. Anderson, editor, *Neural Information Processing Systems*, pages 442–456, Denver 1987, 1988. American Institute of Physics, New York.

[Nak93] Hiroyuki Nakajima. A paradox in learning trajectories in neural networks. Working paper, Dept. of EE II, Kyoto U., Kyoto, JAPAN, 1993.

[Pea89] B.A. Pearlmutter. Learning state space trajectories in recurrent neural networks. *Neural Computation*, 1:263–269, 1989.

[Pin88] F.J. Pineda. Dynamics and architecture for neural computation. *Journal of Complexity*, 4:216–245, 1988.

[Tak81] F. Takens. Detecting strange attractors in turbulence. In D.A. Rand and L.-S. Young, editors, *Dynamical Systems and Turbulence*, volume 898 of *Lecture Notes in Mathematics*, pages 366–381, Warwick 1980, 1981. Springer-Verlag, Berlin.

[TCS90] F-S. Tsung, G. W. Cottrell, and A. I. Selverston. Some experiments on learning stable network oscillations. In *IJCNN*, San Diego, 1990. IEEE.

[Tsu94] F-S. Tsung. *Modelling Dynamical Systems with Recurrent Neural Networks*. PhD thesis, University of California, San Diego, 1994.

[WZ89] R.J. Williams and D. Zipser. A learning algorithm for continually running fully recurrent neural networks. *Neural Computation*, 1:270–280, 1989.

Learning Local Error Bars
for Nonlinear Regression

David A. Nix
Department of Computer Science
and Institute of Cognitive Science
University of Colorado
Boulder, CO 80309-0430
dnix@cs.colorado.edu

Andreas S. Weigend
Department of Computer Science
and Institute of Cognitive Science
University of Colorado
Boulder, CO 80309-0430
andreas@cs.colorado.edu [*]

Abstract

We present a new method for obtaining local error bars for nonlinear regression, i.e., estimates of the confidence in predicted values that depend on the input. We approach this problem by applying a maximum-likelihood framework to an assumed distribution of errors. We demonstrate our method first on computer-generated data with locally varying, normally distributed target noise. We then apply it to laser data from the *Santa Fe Time Series Competition* where the underlying system noise is known quantization error and the error bars give local estimates of model misspecification. In both cases, the method also provides a weighted-regression effect that improves generalization performance.

1 Learning Local Error Bars Using a Maximum Likelihood Framework: Motivation, Concept, and Mechanics

Feed-forward artificial neural networks used for nonlinear regression can be interpreted as predicting the mean of the target distribution as a function of (conditioned on) the input pattern (e.g., Buntine & Weigend, 1991; Bishop, 1994), typically using one linear output unit per output variable. If parameterized, this conditional target distribution (CTD) may also be

---

[*] http://www.cs.colorado.edu/~andreas/Home.html.
This paper is available with figures in colors as ftp://ftp.cs.colorado.edu/pub/Time-Series/MyPapers/nix.weigend_nips7.ps.Z .

viewed as an error model (Rumelhart *et al.*, 1995). Here, we present a simple method that provides higher-order information about the CTD than simply the mean. Such additional information could come from attempting to estimate the entire CTD with connectionist methods (e.g., "Mixture Density Networks," Bishop, 1994; "fractional binning, "Srivastava & Weigend, 1994) or with non-connectionist methods such as a Monte Carlo on a hidden Markov model (Fraser & Dimitriadis, 1994). While non-parametric estimates of the shape of a CTD require large quantities of data, our less data-hungry method (Weigend & Nix, 1994) assumes a specific parameterized form of the CTD (e.g., Gaussian) and gives us the value of the error bar (e.g., the width of the Gaussian) by finding those parameters which maximize the likelihood that the target data was generated by a particular network model. In this paper we derive the specific update rules for the Gaussian case. We would like to emphasize, however, that any parameterized unimodal distribution can be used for the CTD in the method presented here.[1]

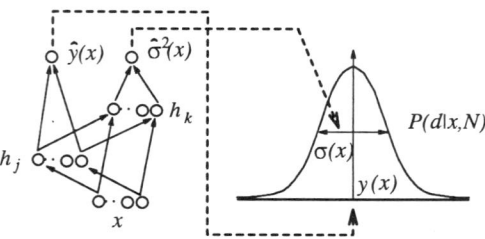

Figure 1: Architecture of the network for estimating error bars using an auxiliary output unit. All weight layers have full connectivity. This architecture allows the conditional variance $\hat{\sigma}^2$-unit access to both information in the input pattern itself and in the hidden unit representation formed while learning the conditional mean, $\hat{y}(\mathbf{x})$.

We model the desired observed target value d as $d(\mathbf{x}) = y(\mathbf{x}) + n(\mathbf{x})$, where $y(\mathbf{x})$ is the underlying function we wish to approximate and $n(\mathbf{x})$ is noise drawn from the assumed CTD. Just as the conditional mean of this CTD, $y(\mathbf{x})$, is a function of the input, the variance σ^2 of the CTD, the noise level, may also vary as a function of the input $\mathbf{x}$ (noise heterogeneity). Therefore, not only do we want the network to learn a function $\hat{y}(\mathbf{x})$ that estimates the conditional mean $y(\mathbf{x})$ of the CTD, but we also want it to learn a function $\hat{\sigma}^2(\mathbf{x})$ that estimates the conditional variance $\sigma^2(\mathbf{x})$. We simply add an auxiliary output unit, the $\hat{\sigma}^2$-unit, to compute our estimate of $\sigma^2(\mathbf{x})$. Since $\sigma^2(\mathbf{x})$ must be positive, we choose an exponential activation function to naturally impose this bound: $\hat{\sigma}^2(\mathbf{x}) = \exp\left[\sum_k w_{\hat{\sigma}^2 k} h_k(\mathbf{x}) + \beta\right]$, where β is the offset (or "bias"), and $w_{\hat{\sigma}^2 k}$ is the weight between hidden unit k and the $\hat{\sigma}^2$-unit. The particular connectivity of our architecture (Figure 1), in which the $\hat{\sigma}^2$-unit has a hidden layer of its own that receives connections from both the $\hat{y}$-unit's hidden layer and the input pattern itself, allows great flexibility in learning $\hat{\sigma}^2(\mathbf{x})$. In contrast, if the $\hat{\sigma}^2$-unit has no hidden layer of its own, the $\hat{\sigma}^2$-unit is constrained to approximate $\sigma^2(\mathbf{x})$ using only the exponential of a linear combination of basis functions (hidden units) already tailored to represent $\hat{y}(\mathbf{x})$ (since learning the conditional variance $\hat{\sigma}^2(\mathbf{x})$ before learning the conditional mean $\hat{y}(\mathbf{x})$ is troublesome at best). Such limited connectivity can be too constraining on the functional forms for $\hat{\sigma}^2(\mathbf{x})$ and, in our experience,

---

[1]The case of a single Gaussian to represent a unimodal distribution can also been generalized to a mixture of several Gaussians that allows the modeling of multimodal distributions (Bishop, 1994).

produce inferior results. This is a significant difference compared to Bishop's (1994) Gaussian mixture approach in which all output units are directly connected to one set of hidden units. The other extreme would be not to share any hidden units at all, i.e., to employ two completely separate sets of hidden units, one to the $\hat{y}(\mathbf{x})$-unit, the other one to the $\hat{\sigma}^2(\mathbf{x})$-unit. This is the right thing to do if there is indeed no overlap in the mapping from the inputs to y and from the inputs to σ^2. The two examples discussed in this paper are between these two extremes; this justifies the mixed architecture we use. Further discussion on shared vs. separate hidden units for the second example of the laser data is given by Kazlas & Weigend (1995, this volume).

For one of our network outputs, the $\hat{y}$-unit, the target is easily available—it is simply given by d. But what is the target for the $\hat{\sigma}^2$-unit? By maximizing the likelihood of our network model $\mathcal{N}$ given the data, $P(\mathcal{N}|\mathbf{x}, d)$, a target is "invented" as follows. Applying Bayes' rule and assuming statistical independence of the errors, we equivalently do gradient descent in the negative log likelihood of the targets d given the inputs and the network model, summed over all patterns i (see Rumelhart et al., 1995): $C = -\sum_i \ln P(d_i|\mathbf{x}_i, \mathcal{N})$. Traditionally, the resulting form of this cost function involves only the estimate $\hat{y}(\mathbf{x}_i)$ of the conditional mean; the variance of the CTD is assumed to be constant for all $\mathbf{x}_i$, and the constant terms drop out after differentiation. In contrast, we allow the conditional variance to depend on $\mathbf{x}$ and explicitly keep these terms in C, approximating the conditional variance for $\mathbf{x}_i$ by $\hat{\sigma}^2(\mathbf{x}_i)$. Given any network architecture and any parametric form for the CTD (i.e., any error model), the appropriate weight-update equations for gradient decent learning can be straightforwardly derived.

Assuming normally distributed errors around $y(\mathbf{x})$ corresponds to a CTD density function of $P(d_i|\mathbf{x}_i) = [2\pi\sigma^2(\mathbf{x}_i)]^{-1/2} \exp\left\{-\frac{[d_i - y(\mathbf{X}_i)]^2}{2\sigma^2(\mathbf{X}_i)}\right\}$. Using the network output $\hat{y}(\mathbf{x}_i) \approx y(\mathbf{x}_i)$ to estimate the conditional mean and using the auxiliary output $\hat{\sigma}^2(\mathbf{x}_i) \approx \sigma^2(\mathbf{x}_i)$ to estimate the conditional variance, we obtain the monotonically related negative log likelihood, $-\ln P(d_i|\mathbf{x}_i, \mathcal{N}) = \frac{1}{2}\ln 2\pi\hat{\sigma}^2(\mathbf{x}_i) + \frac{[d_i - \hat{y}(\mathbf{X}_i)]^2}{2\hat{\sigma}^2(\mathbf{X}_i)}$. Summation over all patterns gives the total cost:

$$C = \frac{1}{2}\sum_i \left\{ \frac{[d_i - y(\mathbf{x}_i)]^2}{\hat{\sigma}^2(\mathbf{x}_i)} + \ln \hat{\sigma}^2(\mathbf{x}_i) + \ln 2\pi \right\} \quad (1)$$

To write explicit weight-update equations, we must specify the network unit transfer functions. Here we choose a linear activation function for the $\hat{y}$-unit, tanh functions for the hidden units, and an exponential function for the $\hat{\sigma}^2$-unit. We can then take derivatives of the cost C with respect to the network weights. To update weights connected to the $\hat{y}$ and $\hat{\sigma}^2$-units we have:

$$\Delta w_{\hat{y}j} = \eta \frac{1}{\hat{\sigma}^2(\mathbf{x}_i)}[d_i - \hat{y}(\mathbf{x}_i)]\, h_j(\mathbf{x}_i) \quad (2)$$

$$\Delta w_{\hat{\sigma}^2 k} = \eta \frac{1}{2\hat{\sigma}^2(\mathbf{x}_i)} \left\{[d_i - \hat{y}(\mathbf{x}_i)]^2 - \hat{\sigma}^2(\mathbf{x}_i)\right\} h_k(\mathbf{x}_i) \quad (3)$$

where η is the learning rate. For weights not connected to the output, the weight-update equations are derived using the chain rule in the same way as in standard backpropagation. Note that Eq. (3) is equivalent to training a separate function-approximation network for $\hat{\sigma}^2(\mathbf{x})$ where the targets are the squared errors $[d_i - y(\mathbf{x}_i)]^2$. Note also that if $\hat{\sigma}^2(\mathbf{x}_i)$ is constant, Eqs. (1)–(2) reduce to their familiar forms for standard backpropagation with a sum-squared error cost function.

The $1/\hat{\sigma}^2(\mathbf{x})$ term in Eqs. (2)–(3) can be interpreted as a form of "weighted regression," increasing the effective learning rate in low-noise regions and reducing it in high-noise regions. As a result, the network emphasizes obtaining small errors on those patterns where it can (low $\hat{\sigma}^2$); it discounts learning patterns for which the expected error is going to be large anyway (large $\hat{\sigma}^2$). This weighted-regression term can itself be highly beneficial where outliers (i.e., samples from high-noise regions) would ordinarily pull network resources away from fitting low-noise regions which would otherwise be well approximated.

For simplicity, we use simple gradient descent learning for training. Other nonlinear minimization techniques could be applied, however, but only if the following problem is avoided. If the weighted-regression term described above is allowed a significant influence *early* in learning, local minima frequently result. This is because input patterns for which low errors are initially obtained are interpreted as "low noise" in Eqs. (2)–(3) and overemphasized in learning. Conversely, patterns for which large errors are initially obtained (because significant learning of $\hat{y}$ has not yet taken place) are erroneously discounted as being in "high-noise" regions and little subsequent learning takes place for these patterns, leading to highly-suboptimal solutions. This problem can be avoided if we separate training into the following three phases:

Phase I (Initial estimate of the conditional mean): Randomly split the available data into equal halves, sets $\mathcal{A}$ and $\mathcal{B}$. Assuming $\sigma^2(\mathbf{x})$ is constant, learn the estimate of the conditional mean $\hat{y}(\mathbf{x})$ using set $\mathcal{A}$ as the training set. This corresponds to "traditional" training using gradient descent on a simple squared-error cost function, i.e., Eqs. (1)–(2) *without* the $1/\hat{\sigma}^2(\mathbf{x})$ terms. To reduce overfitting, training is considered complete at the minimum of the squared error on the cross-validation set $\mathcal{B}$, monitored at the end of each complete pass through the training data.

Phase II (Initial estimate of the conditional variance): Attach a layer of hidden units connected to both the inputs and the hidden units of the network from Phase I (see Figure 1). Freeze the weights trained in Phase I, and train the $\hat{\sigma}^2$-unit to predict the *squared errors* (see Eq. (3)), again using simple gradient descent as in Phase I. The training set for this phase is set $\mathcal{B}$, with set $\mathcal{A}$ used for cross-validation. If set $\mathcal{A}$ were used as the training set in this phase as well, any overfitting in Phase I could result in seriously underestimating $\sigma^2(\mathbf{x})$. To avoid this risk, we interchange the data sets. The initial value for the offset β of the $\hat{\sigma}^2$-unit is the natural logarithm of the mean squared error (from Phase I) of set $\mathcal{B}$. Phase II stops when the squared error on set $\mathcal{A}$ levels off or starts to increase.

Phase III (Weighted regression): Re-split the available data into two new halves, $\mathcal{A}'$ and $\mathcal{B}'$. Unfreeze all weights and train all network parameters to minimize the full cost function C on set $\mathcal{A}'$. Training is considered complete when C has reached its minimum on set $\mathcal{B}'$.

2 Examples

Example #1: To demonstrate this method, we construct a one-dimensional example problem where $y(x)$ and $\sigma^2(x)$ are known. We take the equation $y(x) = \sin(\omega_\alpha x) \sin(\omega_\beta x)$ with $\omega_\alpha = 3$ and $\omega_\beta = 5$. We then generate (x, d) pairs by picking x uniformly from the interval $[0, \pi/2]$ and obtaining the corresponding target d by adding normally distributed noise $n(x) = N[0, \sigma^2(x)]$ to the underlying $y(x)$, where $\sigma^2(x) = 0.02 + 0.25 \times [1 - \sin(\omega_\beta x)]^2$.

Table 1: Results for Example #1. E_{NMS} denotes the mean squared error divided by the overall variance of the target; "Mean cost" represents the cost function (Eq. (1)) averaged over all patterns. Row 4 lists these values for the ideal model (true $y(x)$ and $\sigma^2(x)$) given the data generated. Row 5 gives the correlation coefficient between the network's predictions for the standard error (i.e., the square root of the $\hat{\sigma}^2$-unit's activation) and the actually occurring L1 residual errors, $|d(x_i) - \hat{y}(x_i)|$. Row 6 gives the correlation between the true $\sigma(x)$ and these residual errors. Rows 7–9 give the percentage of residuals smaller than one and two standard deviations for the obtained and ideal models as well as for an exact Gaussian.

row		Training ($N = 10^3$)		Evaluation ($N = 10^5$)	
		E_{NMS}	Mean cost	E_{NMS}	Mean cost
1	Phase I	0.576	0.853	0.593	0.882
2	Phase II	0.576	0.542	0.593	0.566
3	Phase III	0.552	0.440	0.570	0.462
4	$n(x)$ (exact additive noise)	0.545	0.430	0.563	0.441
		ρ		ρ	
5	$\rho(\hat{\sigma}(x),$ residual errors)	0.564		0.548	
6	$\rho(\sigma(x),$ residual errors)	0.602		0.584	
		1 std	2 std	1 std	2 std
7	% of errors $< \hat{\sigma}(x); 2\hat{\sigma}(x)$	64.8	95.4	67.0	94.6
8	% of errors $< \sigma(x); 2\sigma(x)$	66.6	96.0	68.4	95.4
9	(exact Gaussian)	68.3	95.4	68.3	95.4

We generate 1000 patterns for training and an additional 10^5 patterns for post-training evaluation.

Training follows exactly the three phases described above with the following details:[2] Phase I uses a network with one hidden layer of 10 tanh units and $\eta = 10^{-2}$. For Phase II we add an auxiliary layer of 10 tanh hidden units connected to the $\hat{\sigma}^2$-unit (see Figure 1) and use the same η. Finally, in Phase III the composite network is trained with $\eta = 10^{-4}$.

At the end of Phase I (Figure 2a), the only available estimate of $\sigma^2(x)$ is the *global* root-mean-squared error on the available data, and the model misspecification is roughly uniform over x—a typical solution were we training with only the traditional squared-error cost function. The corresponding error measures are listed in Table 1. At the end of Phase II, however, we have obtained an initial estimate of $\sigma^2(x)$ (since the weights to the $\hat{y}$-unit are frozen during this phase, no modification of $\hat{y}$ is made). Finally, at the end of Phase III, we have better estimates of both $y(x)$ and $\sigma^2(x)$. First we note that the correlations between the predicted errors and actual errors listed in Table 1 underscore the near-optimal prediction of local errors. We also see that these errors correspond, as expected, to the assumed Gaussian error model. Second, we note that not only has the value of the cost function dropped from Phase II to Phase III, but *the generalization error has also dropped*, indicating an improved estimate of $y(x)$. By comparing Phases I and III we see that the quality of $\hat{y}(x)$ has improved significantly in the low-noise regions (roughly $x < 0.6$) at a minor sacrifice of accuracy in the high-noise region.

Example #2: We now apply our method to a set of observed data, the 1000-point laser

---

[2] Further details: all inputs are scaled to zero mean and unit variance. All initial weights feeding into hidden units are drawn from a uniform distribution between $-1/i$ and $1/i$ where i is the number of incoming connections. All initial weights feeding into $\hat{y}$ or $\hat{\sigma}^2$ are drawn from a uniform distribution between $-s/i$ and s/i where s is the standard deviation of the (overall) target distribution. No momentum is used, and all weight updates are averaged over the forward passes of 20 patterns.

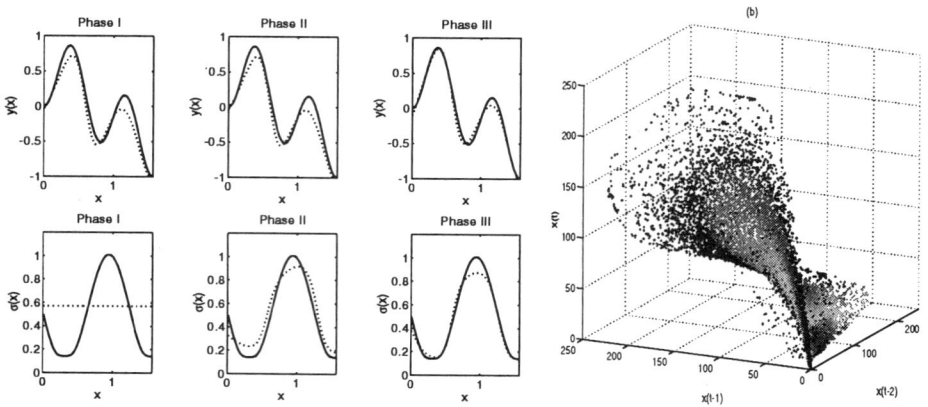

Figure 2: (a) Example #1: Results after each phase of training. The top row gives the true $y(x)$ (solid line) and network estimate $\hat{y}(x)$ (dotted line); the bottom row gives the true $\sigma^2(x)$ (solid line) and network estimate $\hat{\sigma}^2(x)$ (dotted line). (b) Example #2: state-space embedding of laser data (evaluation set) using linear grey-scaling of 0.50 (lightest) $< \hat{\sigma}(\mathbf{x}_t) <$ 6.92 (darkest). See text for details.

intensity series from the Santa Fe competition.[3] Since our method is based on the network's *observed* errors, the predicted error $\hat{\sigma}^2(\mathbf{x})$ actually represents the sum of the underlying system noise, characterized by $\sigma^2(\mathbf{x})$, and the model misspecification. Here, since we know the system noise is roughly uniform 8-bit sampling resolution quantization error, we can apply our method to evaluate the local quality of the manifold approximation.[4]

The prediction task is easier if we have more points that lie on the manifold, thus better constraining its shape. In the competition, Sauer (1994) upsampled the 1000 available data points with an FFT method by a factor of 32. This does not change the effective sampling rate, but it "fills in" more points, more precisely defining the manifold. We use the same upsampling trick (without filtered embedding), and obtain 31200 full $(\mathbf{x}, d)$ patterns for learning. We apply the three-phase approach described above for the simple network of Figure 1 with 25 inputs (corresponding to 25 past values), 12 hidden units feeding the $\hat{y}$-unit, and a liberal 30 hidden units feeding the $\hat{\sigma}^2$-unit (since we are uncertain as to the complexity of $\sigma^2(\mathbf{x})$ for this dataset). We use $\eta = 10^{-7}$ for Phase I and $\eta = 10^{-10}$ for Phases II and III. Since we know the quantization error is ± 0.5, error estimates less than this are meaningless. Therefore, we enforce a minimum value of $\sigma^2(\mathbf{x}) = 0.25$ (the quantization error squared) on the squared errors in Phases II and III.

---

[3]The data set and several predictions and characterizations are described in the volume edited by Weigend & Gershenfeld (1994). The data is available by anonymous ftp at ftp.cs.colorado.edu in /pub/Time-Series/SantaFe as A.dat. See also http://www.cs.colorado.edu/Time-Series/TSWelcome.html for further analyses of this and other time series data sets.

[4]When we make a single-step prediction where the manifold approximation is poor, we have little confidence making iterated predictions based on that predicted value. However, if we know we are in a low-error region, we can have increased confidence in iterated predictions that involve our current prediction.

Table 2: Results for Example #2 (See Table 1 caption for definitions).

row		Training	($N = 975$)	Evaluation	($N = 23,950$)
		E_{NMS}	Mean cost	E_{NMS}	Mean cost
1	Phase I	0.00125	1.941	0.0156	7.213
2	Phase II	0.00125	1.939	0.0156	5.628
3	Phase III	0.00132	1.725	0.0139	5.564
		ρ		ρ	
4	$\rho(\hat{\sigma}(x)$, residual errors)	0.557		0.366	
		1 std	2 std	1 std	2 std
5	% of errors $< \hat{\sigma}(x); 2\hat{\sigma}(x)$	69.4	94.9	63.1	88.0
6	(exact Gaussian)	68.3	95.4	68.3	95.4

Results are given in Table 2 for patterns generated from the available 1000 points and 24,000 additional points used for evaluation. Even though we have used a Gaussian error model, we know the distribution of errors is not Gaussian. This is reflected in rows 5 and 6, where the training data is modeled as having a Gaussian CTD but the evaluation values become considerably distorted from an exact Gaussian. Again, however, not only do we obtain significant predictability of the errors, but the method *also reduces the squared-error measure obtained in Phase I*. We can use the estimated error to characterize the quality of the manifold approximation on 24,000 post-training evaluation points, as illustrated in Figure 2b. The manifold approximation is poorer (darker) for higher predicted values of x_t and for values nearer the edge of the manifold. Note the dark-grey (high-error) vertical streak leaving the origin and dark points to its left which represent patterns involving sudden changes in oscillation intensity.

3 Discussion

Since we are in effect approximating two functions simultaneously, we can apply many of the existing variations for improving function approximation designed for networks learning only $\hat{y}(\mathbf{x})$. For example, when using limited amounts of data, especially if it is noisy, the particular split of data into training and cross-validation sets we use introduces significant variation in the resulting $\hat{y}(\mathbf{x})$ due to overfitting, as demonstrated on financial data by Weigend & LeBaron (1994). If we want to estimate local error bars, not only must we fear overfitting $\hat{y}(\mathbf{x})$, but we must also be concerned with overfitting $\hat{\sigma}^2(\mathbf{x})$. If the standard method of stopping at the minimum of an appropriate cross-validation set does not suffice for a given problem, it is straightforward to employ the usual anti-overfitting weaponry (smooth $\hat{\sigma}^2$ as a function of $\mathbf{x}$, pruning, weight-elimination, etc.). Furthermore, we can bootstrap over our available dataset and create multiple composite networks, averaging their predictions for both $\hat{y}(\mathbf{x})$ and $\hat{\sigma}^2(\mathbf{x})$. Additionally, to incorporate prior information in a Bayesian framework as a form of regularization, Wolpert (personal communication, 1994) suggests finding the maximum *a posteriori* (instead of maximum-likelihood) conditional mean and variance using the same interpretation of the network outputs.

In summary, we start with the maximum-likelihood principle and arrive at error estimates that vary with location in the input space. These local error estimates incorporate both underlying system noise and model misspecification. We have provided a computer-generated example to demonstrate the ease with which accurate error bars can be learned. We have also provided an example with real-world data in which the underlying system noise is small, uniform quantization error to demonstrate how the method can be used to characterize the local quality of the regression model. A significant feature of this method is its weighted-regression effect, which complicates learning by introducing local minima but can be potentially beneficial in constructing a more robust model with improved generalization abilities. In the framework presented, for any problem we must assume a specific parameterized CTD then add one auxiliary output unit for each higher moment of the CTD we wish to estimate locally. Here we have demonstrated the Gaussian case with a location parameter (conditional mean) and a scale parameter (local error bar) for a scalar output variable. The extension to multiple output variables is clear and allows a full covariance matrix to be used for weighted regression, including the cross-correlation between multiple targets.

Acknowledgments

This work is supported by the National Science Foundation under Grant No. RIA ECS-9309786 and by a Graduate Fellowship from the Office of Naval Research. We would like to thank Chris Bishop, Wray Buntine, Don Hush, Steve Nowlan, Barak Pearlmutter, Dave Rumelhart, and Dave Wolpert for helpful discussions.

References

C. Bishop. (1994) "Mixture Density Networks." Neural Computing Research Group Report NCRG/4288, Department of Computer Science, Aston University, Birmingham, UK.

W.L. Buntine and A.S. Weigend. (1991) "Bayesian Backpropagation." *Complex Systems*, 5: 603–643.

A.M. Fraser and A. Dimitriadis. (1994) "Forecasting Probability Densities Using Hidden Markov Models with Mixed States." In *Time Series Prediction: Forecasting the Future and Understanding the Past*, A.S. Weigend and N.A. Gershenfeld, eds., Addison-Wesley, pp. 265–282.

P.T. Kazlas and A.S. Weigend. (1995) "Direct Multi-Step Time Series Prediction Using TD(λ)." In *Advances in Neural Information Processing Systems 7 (NIPS*94, this volume)*. San Francisco, CA: Morgan Kaufmann.

D.E. Rumelhart, R. Durbin, R. Golden, and Y. Chauvin. (1995) "Backpropagation: The Basic Theory." In *Backpropagation: Theory, Architectures and Applications*, Y. Chauvin and D.E. Rumelhart, eds., Lawrence Erlbaum, pp. 1–34.

T. Sauer. (1994) "Time Series Prediction by Using Delay Coordinate Embedding." In *Time Series Prediction: Forecasting the Future and Understanding the Past*, A.S. Weigend and N.A. Gershenfeld, eds., Addison-Wesley, pp. 175-193.

A.N. Srivastava and A.S. Weigend. (1994) "Computing the Probability Density in Connectionist Regression." In *Proceedings of the IEEE International Conference on Neural Networks (IEEE–ICNN'94), Orlando, FL*, p. 3786–3789. IEEE-Press.

A.S. Weigend and N.A. Gershenfeld, eds. (1994) *Time Series Prediction: Forecasting the Future and Understanding the Past*. Addison-Wesley.

A.S. Weigend and B. LeBaron. (1994) "Evaluating Neural Network Predictors by Bootstrapping." In *Proceedings of the International Conference on Neural Information Processing (ICONIP'94), Seoul, Korea*, pp. 1207–1212.

A.S. Weigend and D.A. Nix. (1994) "Predictions with Confidence Intervals (Local Error Bars)." In *Proceedings of the International Conference on Neural Information Processing (ICONIP'94), Seoul, Korea*, p. 847–852.

Dynamic Cell Structures

Jörg Bruske and Gerald Sommer
Department of Cognitive Systems
Christian Albrechts University at Kiel
24105 Kiel - Germany

Abstract

Dynamic Cell Structures (DCS) represent a family of artificial neural architectures suited both for **unsupervised** and **supervised** learning. They belong to the recently [Martinetz94] introduced class of **Topology Representing Networks** (TRN) which build **perfectly topology preserving feature maps**. DCS employ a modified **Kohonen learning rule** in conjunction with **competitive Hebbian learning**. The Kohonen type learning rule serves to adjust the synaptic weight vectors while Hebbian learning establishes a dynamic **lateral connection structure** between the units reflecting the topology of the feature manifold. In case of supervised learning, i.e. function approximation, each neural unit implements a **Radial Basis Function**, and an additional layer of linear output units adjusts according to a **delta-rule**. DCS is the first RBF-based approximation scheme attempting to concurrently learn and utilize a perfectly topology preserving map for improved performance.
Simulations on a selection of CMU-Benchmarks indicate that the DCS idea applied to the **Growing Cell Structure** algorithm [Fritzke93] leads to an efficient and elegant algorithm that can beat conventional models on similar tasks.

1 Introduction

The quest for smallest topology preserving maps motivated the introduction of growing feature maps like Fritzke's Growing Cell Structures (**GCS**). In **GCS**, see [Fritzke93] for details, one starts with a k-dimensional simplex of $N = k+1$ neural units and $(k + 1) \cdot k/2$ lateral connections (edges). Growing of the network is performed such that after insertion of a new unit the network consists solely of k dimensional simplices again. Thus, like Kohonen's SOM, **GCS** can only learn a **perfectly topology preserving feature map**[1] if k meets the actual dimension of the feature manifold. Assuming that the lateral connections do reflect the actual topology the connections serve to define a neighborhood for a Kohonen like adaptation of the synaptic vectors w_i and guide the insertion of new units. Insertion happens incrementally and does not necessitate a retraining of the network. The principle is to insert new neurons in such a way that the expected value of a certain local error measure, which Fritzke calls the **resource**, becomes equal for all neurons. For instance, the number of times a neuron wins the competition, the sum of distances to stimuli for which the neuron wins or the sum of errors in the neuron's output can all serve as a resource and dramatically change the behavior of **GCS**. Using different error measures and guiding insertion by the lateral connections contributes much to the success of **GCS**.

The principle of DCS is to avoid any restriction of the topology of the network (lateral connection scheme between the neural units) but to concurrently learn and utilize a **perfectly topology preserving map**. This is achieved by adapting the lateral connection structure according to a **competitive Hebbian learning rule**[2]:

$$C_{ij}(t+1) = \begin{cases} max\{y_i \cdot y_j, C_{ij}(t)\} &: y_i \cdot y_j \geq y_k \cdot y_l \ \forall (1 \leq k, l \leq N) \\ 0 &: C_{ij}(t) < \theta \quad \text{""} \\ \alpha C_{ij}(t) &: \text{otherwise,} \quad \text{""} \end{cases} \quad (1)$$

where α, $0 < \alpha < 1$ is a forgetting constant, θ, $0 < \theta < 1$ serves as a threshold for deleting lateral connections, and $y_i = R(\|v - w_i\|)$ is the activation of the i-th unit with w_i as the centre of its receptive field on presentation of stimulus v. $R(.)$ can be any positive continuously monotonically decreasing function. For batch learning with a training set T of fixed size $|T|$, $\alpha = {}^{|T|}\!\!\sqrt{\theta}$ is a good choice.

Since the isomorphic representation of the topology of the feature manifold M in the lateral connection structure is central to performance, in many situations a **DCS** algorithm may be the right choice. These situations are characterized by missing **a priori** knowledge of the topology of the feature manifold M or a topology of M which cannot be readily mapped to the existing models. Of course, if such a priori knowledge is available then models like **GCS** or Kohonen's **SOM** allowing to incorporate such knowledge have an advantage, especially if training data are sparse.

Note that **DCS** algorithms can also aid in cluster analysis: In a perfectly topology preserving map clusters which are bounded by regions of $P(v) = 0$ can be identified simply by a connected component analysis. However, without prior knowledge about the feature manifold M it is in principal impossible to check for perfect topology preservation of S. Noise in the input data may render perfect topology learning even more difficult. So what can perfect topology learning be used for? The answer is simply that for every set S of reference vectors perfect topology learning yields maximum topology preservation[3] with respect to this set. And connected components with respect to the lateral connection structure C may well serve as an initialization for postprocessing by hierarchical cluster algorithms.

---

1. We use the term "perfectly topology preserving feature map" in accordance with its rigorous definition in [Martinetz93].
2. In his very recent and recommendable article [Martinetz94] the term Topology Representing Network (TRN) is coined for any network employing competitive Hebbian learning for topology learning.
3. if topology preservation is measured by the topographic function as defined in [Villmann94].

The first neural algorithm attempting to learn **perfectly topology preserving feature maps** is the **Neural Gas** algorithm of T. Martinetz [Martinetz92]. However, unlike **DCS** the **Neural Gas** does not further exploit this information: In every step the **Neural Gas** computes the k nearest neighbors to a given stimulus and, in the supervised case, employs all of them for function approximation. **DCS** avoids this computational burden by utilizing the lateral connection structure (topology) learned so far, and it restricts interpolation between activated units to the submanifold of the current stimulus.

Applying the principle of **DCS** to Fritzke's **GCS** yields our **DCS-GCS** algorithm. This algorithm sticks very closely to the basic structure of its ancestor **GCS** except the predefined k-dimensional simplex connection structure being replaced by perfect topology learning. Besides the conceptual advantage of perfect topology learning, **DCS-GCS** does decrease overhead (Fritzke has to handle quite sophisticated data structures in order to maintain the k-dimensional simplex structure after insertion/ deletion of units) and can be readily implemented on any serial computer.

2 Unsupervised DCS-GCS

The unsupervised DCS-GCS algorithm starts with initializing the network (graph) to two neural units (vertices) n_1 and n_2. Their weight vectors w_1, w_1 (centres of receptive fields) are set to points $v_1, v_2 \in M$ which are drawn from M according to P(v). They are connected by a lateral connection of weight $C_{12} = C_{21} = 1$. Note that lateral connections in **DCS** are always bidirectional and have symmetric weights.

Now the algorithm enters its outer loop which is repeated until some stopping criterium is fulfilled. This stopping criterium could for instance be a test whether the quantization error has already dropped below a predefined accuracy.

The inner loop is repeated for λ times. In off-line learning λ can be set to the number examples in the training set T. In this case, the inner loop just represents an epoch of training.

Within the inner loop, the algorithm first draws an input stimulus $v \in M$ from M according to P(v) and then proceeds to calculate the two neural units which weight vectors are first and second closest to v.

In the next step, the lateral connections between the neural units are modified according to eq. (1), the **competitive Hebbian learning rule**. As has already been mentioned, in off-line learning it is a good idea to set $\alpha = \lambda/\theta$.

Now the weight vectors w_i of the best matching unit and its neighbors are adjusted in a **Kohonen** like fashion:

$$\Delta w_{bmu} = \varepsilon_B (v - w_{bmu}) \text{ and } \Delta w_j = \varepsilon_{Nh} (v - w_j), \qquad (2)$$

where the neighborhood $Nh(j)$ of a unit j is defined by $Nh(j) = \{i \mid (C_{ji} \neq 0, 1 \leq i \leq N)\}$.

The inner loop ends with updating the **resource** value of the best matching unit. The resource of a neuron is a local error measure attached to each neural unit. As has been pointed out, one can choose alternative update functions corresponding to different error measures. For our experiments (section 2.1 and section 3.1) we used the accumulated squared distance to the stimulus, i.e. $\Delta \tau_{bmu} = \|v - w_{bmu}\|^2$.

The outer loop now proceeds by adding a new neural unit r to the network. This unit is located in-between the unit l with largest resource value and its neighbor n with second largest resource value:[4]

The exact location of its centre of receptive field w_r is calculated according to the ratio of the resource values τ_l, τ_n, and the resource values of units n and l are redistributed among r, n and l:

$$\gamma = \tau_n / (\tau_n + \tau_l), \; \Delta\tau_l = \frac{1}{2}(1-\gamma)\tau_l \text{ and } \Delta\tau_n = \frac{1}{2}\gamma\tau_n \qquad (3)$$

$$w_r = w_l + \gamma(w_n - w_l), \; \tau_r = \Delta\tau_n + \Delta\tau_l, \; \tau_l = \tau_l - \Delta\tau_l \text{ and } \tau_n = \tau_n - \Delta\tau_n. \qquad (4)$$

This gives an estimate of the resource values if the new unit had been in the network right from the start. Finally the lateral connections are changed,

$$C_{rl} = C_{lr} = 1, \; C_{rn} = C_{rn} = 1 \text{ and } C_{nl} = C_{ln} = 0, \qquad (5)$$

connecting unit r to unit l and disconnecting n and l.

This heuristic guided by the lateral connection structure and the resource values promises insertion of new units at good initial positions. It is responsible for the better performance of **DCS-GCS** and **GCS** compared to algorithms which do not exploit the neighborhood relation between existing units.

The outer loop closes by decrementing the resource values of all units, $\tau_i(t+1) = \beta\tau_i(t)$, $1 \le i \le N$, where $0 < \beta < 1$ is a constant. This last step just avoids overflow of the resource variables. For off-line learning, $\beta = 0$ is the natural choice.

2.1 Unsupervised DCS simulation results

Let us first turn to our simulation on artificial data. The training set T contains 2000 examples randomly drawn from a feature manifold M consisting of three squares, two of them connected by a line. The development of our unsupervised **DCS-GCS** network is depicted in Figure 1, with the initial situation of only two units shown in the upper left. Examples are represented by small dots, the centres of receptive fields by small circles and the lateral connections by lines connecting the circles. From left to right the network is examined after 0, 9 and 31 epochs of training (i.e. after insertion of 2, 11 and 33 neural units).

After 31 epochs the network has built a perfectly topology preserving map of M, the lateral connection structure nicely reflecting the shape of M: Where M is 2-dimensional the lateral connection structure is 2-dimensional, and it is 1-dimensional where M is 1-dimensional. Note, that a connected component analysis could recognize that the upper right square is separated from the rest of M. The accumulated squared distance to stimuli served as the resource.

The quantization error $E_q = \frac{1}{n}\sum_{v \in T}\|v - w_{bmu(v)}\|^2$ dropped from 100% (3 units) to 3% (33 units).

The second simulation deals with the two-spirals benchmark. Data were obtained by running the program "two-spirals" (provided by CMU) with parameters 5 (density) and 6.5 (spiral radius) resulting in a training set T of 962 examples. The data represent two distinct spirals in the x-y-plane. Unsupervised **DCS-GCS** at work is shown in Figure 2, after insertion of 80, 154 and, finally, 196 units. With 196 units a perfectly topology preserving map of M has emerged, and the two spirals are clearly separated. Note that the algorithm has learned the separation in a totally unsupervised manner, i.e. not using the labels of the data

---

4. Fritzke inserts new units at a slightly different location, using not the neighbor with second largest resource but the most distant neighbor.

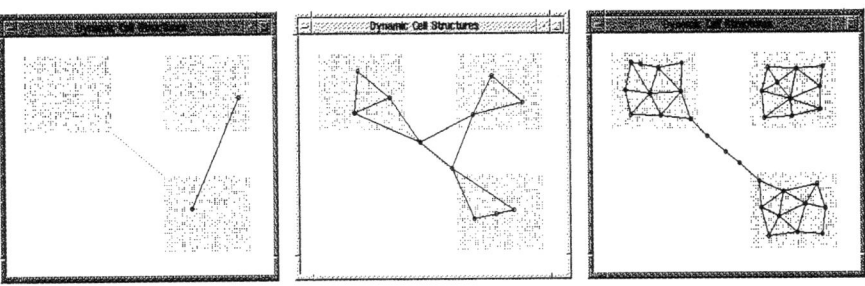

Figure 1: Unsupervised DCS-GCS on artificial data

points (which are provided by CMU for supervised learning). Again, the accumulated squared distance to stimuli served as the resource.

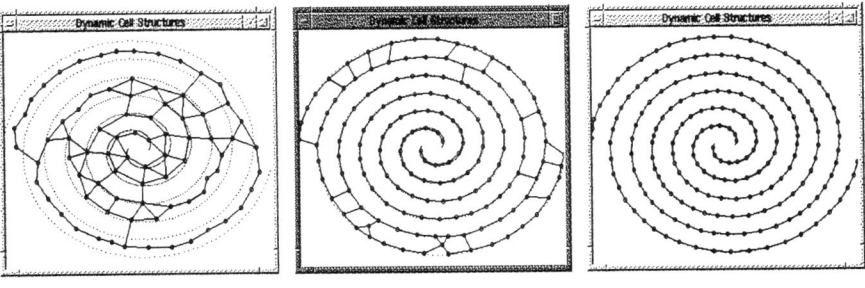

Figure 2: Unsupervised learning of two spirals

3 Supervised DCS-GCS

In supervised **DCS-GCS** examples consist not only of an input vector v but also include an additional teaching output vector u.

The supervised algorithm actually does work very similar to its unsupervised version except

- when a neural unit n_i is inserted an output vector o_i will be attached to it with $o_i = u$.
- the output y of the network is calculated as a weighted sum of the best matching unit's output vector o_{bmu} and the output vectors of its neighbors $o_i, i \in Nh(bmu)$,

$$y = (\sum_{i \in \{bmu \cup Nh(bmu)\}} a_i o_i) , \qquad (6)$$

where $a_i = 1/(\sigma \|v - w_i\|^2 + 1)$ is the activation of neuron i on stimulus v, $\sigma, \sigma > 0$, representing the size of the receptive fields. In our simulations, the size of receptive fields have been equal for all units.

- adaption of output vectors by the delta-rule: A simple delta-rule is employed to adjust the output vectors of the best matching unit and its neighbors.

Most important, the approximation (classification) error can be used for resource updating. This leads to insertion of new units in regions where the approximation error is worst, thus promising to outperform dynamic algorithms which do not employ such a criterion for insertion. In our simulations we used the accumulated squared distance of calculated and teaching output, $\Delta \tau_{bmu} = \|y - u\|^2$.

3.1 Supervised DCS-GCS simulation results

We applied our supervised **DCS-GCS** algorithm to three CMU benchmarks, the supervised two-spiral problem, the speaker independent vowel recognition problem and the sonar mine/ rock separation problem.[5]

The two spirals benchmark contains 194 examples, each consisting of an input vector $v \in \Re^2$ and a binary label indicating to which spiral the point belongs. The spirals can not be linearly separated. The task is to train the examples until the learning system can produce the correct output for all of them and to record the time.

The decision regions learned by supervised **DCS-GCS** are depicted in Figure 3 after 110 and 135 epochs of training, where the classification error on the training set has dropped to 0%. Black indicates assignment to the fist, white assignment to the second spiral. The network and the examples are overlaid.

Figure 3: Supervised learning of two spirals

Results reported by others are 20000 epochs of Backprop for a MLP by Lang and Witbrok [Lang89], 10000 epochs of Cross Entropy Backprop and 1700 epochs of Cascade-Correlation by Fahlman and Lebiere [Fahlman90] and 180 epochs of **GCS** training by Fritzke [Fritzke93].

---

5. For details of simulation, parameters and additional statistics for all of the reported experiments the reader is refered to [Bruske94] which is also available via *ftp.informatik.uni-kiel.de* in directory *pub/kiel/publications/TechnicalReports/Ps.Z/* as *1994tr03.ps.Z*

The data for the speaker independent recognition of 11 vowels comprises a training set of 582 examples and a test set of 462 examples, see [Robinson89].

We obtained 65% correctly classified test samples with only 108 neural units in the **DCS-GCS** network. This is superior to conventional models (including single and multi layer perceptron, Kanerva Model, Radial Basis Functions, Gaussian Node Network, Square Node Network and Nearest Neighbor) for which figures well below 57% have been reported by Robinson. It also qualitatively compares to GCS (jumps above the 60% margin), for which Fritzke reports best classification results of 61%(158 units) up to 67% (154 units) for a 3-dim **GCS**. On the other hand, our best **DCS-GCS** used much fewer units. Note that **DCS-GCS** did not rely on a pre-specified connection structure (but learned it!).

Our last simulation concerns a data set used by Gorman and Sejnowski in their study of classification of sonar data, [Gorman88]. The training and the test set contain 104 examples each.

Gorman and Sejnowski report their best results of 90.4% correctly classified test examples for a standard BP network with 12 hidden units and 82.7% for a nearest neighbor classifier. Supervised **DCS-GCS** reached a peak classification rate of 95% after only 88 epochs of training.

4 Conclusion

We have introduced the idea of RBF networks which concurrently learn and utilize perfectly topology preserving feature maps for adaptation and interpolation. This family of ANNs, which we termed Dynamic Cell Structures, offers conceptual advantage compared to classical Kohonen type SOMs since the emerging lateral connection structure maximally preserves topology. We have discussed the DCS-GCS algorithm as an instance of DCS. Compared to its ancestor GCS of Fritzke, this algorithm elegantly avoids computational overhead for handling sophisticated data structures. If connection updates (eq.(1)) are restricted to the best matching unit and its neighbors, DCS has linear (serial) time complexity[6] and thus may also be considered as an improvement of Martinetz's Neural Gas idea[7]. Space complexity of DCS is $O(N^2)$ in general and can be shown to become linear if the feature manifold M is two dimensional. The simulations on CMU-Benchmarks indicate that DCS indeed has practical relevance for classification and approximation.

Thus encouraged, we look forward to apply DCS at various sites in our active computer vision project, including image compression by dynamic vector quantization, sensorimotor maps for the oculomotor system and hand-eye coordination, cartography and associative memories. A recent application can be found in [Bruske95] where a DCS network attempts to learn a continous approximation of the Q-function in a reinforcement learning problem.

---

6. Here we refer to the serial time a DCS algorithm needs to process a single stimulus (including response calculation and adaptation).
7. The serial time complexity of the Neural Gas is $\Omega(N)$, approaching $O(N\log N)$ for $k \to N$, k the number of nearest neighbors.

References

[Bruske94] J. Bruske and G. Sommer, *Dynamic Cell Structures: Radial Basis Function Networks with Perfect Topology Preservation*, Inst. f. Inf. u. Prakt. Math, CAU zu Kiel, Technical Report 9403.

[Bruske95] J. Bruske, I. Ahrns and G. Sommer, *Heuristic Q-Learning*, submitted to ECML 95.

[Fahlman90] S.E. Fahlman, C.Lebiere, *The Cascade-Correlation Learning Architecture*, Advances in Neural Information processing systems 2, Morgan Kaufman, San Mateo, pp.524-534.

[Fahlman93] S.E. Fahlman, *CMU Benchmark Collection for Neural Net Learning Algorithms*, Carnegie Mellon Univ., School of Computer Science, machine-readable data repository, Pittsburgh.

[Fritzke92] B. Fritzke, *Growing Cell Structures - a self organizing network in k dimensions*, Artificial Neural Networks 2, I.Aleksander & J.Taylor eds., North-Holland, Amsterdam, 1992.

[Fritzke93] B. Fritzke, *Growing Cell Structures - a self organizing network for unsupervised and supervised training*, ICSI Berkeley, Technical Report, tr-93-026.

[Gorman88] R.B. Gorman and T.J. Sejnowski, *Analysis of Hidden Units in a Layered Network Trained to Classify Sonar Targets*, Neural Networks, Vol.1, pp. 75-89

[Lang89] K.J. Lang & M.J. Witbrock, *Learning to tell two spirals apart*, Proc. of the 1988 Connectionist Models Summer School, Morgan Kaufmann, pp.52-59.

[Martinetz92] Thomas Martinetz, *Selbstorganisierende neuronale Netzwerke zur Bewegungssteuerung*, Dissertation, DIFKI-Verlag, 1992.

[Martinetz93] Thomas Martinetz, *Competitive Hebbian Learning Rule Forms Perfectly Topology Preserving Maps*, Proc. of the ICANN 93, p.426-438, 1993.

[Martinetz94] Thomas Martinetz and Klaus Schulten, *Topology Representing Networks*, Neural Networks, No. 7, Vol. 3, pp. 505-522, 1994.

[Moody89] J.Moody, C.J. Darken, *Fast Learning in Networks of Locally-Tuned Processing Units*, Neural Computation Vol.1 Num.2, Summer 1989.

[Robinson89] A.J. Robinson, *Dynamic Error Propagation Networks*, Cambridge Univ., Ph.D. thesis, Cambridge.

[Villmann94] T. Villmann and R. Der and T. Martinetz, *A Novel Approach to Measure the Topology Preservation of Feature Maps*, Proc. of the ICANN 94, 1994.

Extracting Rules from Artificial Neural Networks with Distributed Representations

Sebastian Thrun
University of Bonn
Department of Computer Science III
Römerstr. 164, D-53117 Bonn, Germany
E-mail: thrun@carbon.informatik.uni-bonn.de

Abstract

Although artificial neural networks have been applied in a variety of real-world scenarios with remarkable success, they have often been criticized for exhibiting a low degree of human comprehensibility. Techniques that compile compact sets of symbolic rules out of artificial neural networks offer a promising perspective to overcome this obvious deficiency of neural network representations.

This paper presents an approach to the extraction of *if-then* rules from artificial neural networks. Its key mechanism is *validity interval analysis*, which is a generic tool for extracting symbolic knowledge by propagating rule-like knowledge through Backpropagation-style neural networks. Empirical studies in a robot arm domain illustrate the appropriateness of the proposed method for extracting rules from networks with real-valued and distributed representations.

1 Introduction

In the last few years artificial neural networks have been applied successfully to a variety of real-world problems. For example, neural networks have been successfully applied in the area of speech generation [12] and recognition [18], vision and robotics [8], handwritten character recognition [5], medical diagnostics [11], and game playing [13]. While in these and other approaches neural networks have frequently found to outperform more traditional approaches, one of their major shortcomings is their low degree of human comprehensibility.

In recent years, a variety of approaches for compiling rules out of networks have been proposed. Most approaches [1, 3, 4, 6, 7, 16, 17] compile networks into sets of rules with equivalent structure: Each processing unit is mapped into a separate rule–or a small set of rules–, and the ingoing weights are interpreted as preconditions to this rule. Sparse connectivity facilitates this type rule extraction, and so do binary activation values. In order to enforce such properties, which is a necessary prerequisite for these techniques to work effectively, some approaches rely on specialized training procedures, network initializations and/or architectures.

While such a methodology is intriguing, as it draws a clear one-to-one correspondence between neural inference and rule-based inference, it is not universally applicable to arbitrary Backpropagation-style neural networks. This is because artificial neural networks might not meet the strong representational and structural requirements necessary for these techniques to work successfully. When the internal representation of the network is distributed in nature, individual hidden units typically do not represent clear, logical entities. One might argue that networks, if one is interested in extracting rules, should be constructed appropriately. But this would outrule most existing network implementations, as such considerations have barely played a role. In addition, such an argument would suppress the development of distributed, non-discrete internal representations, which have often be attributed for the generalization properties of neural networks. It is this more general class of networks that is at stake in this paper.

This paper presents a rule extraction method which finds rules by analyzing networks as a whole. The rules are of the type *"if x then y,"* where both x and y are described by a linear set of constraints. The engine for proving the correspondence of rule and network classification is VI-Analysis. Rules extracted by VI-Analysis can be proven to exactly describe the network.

2 Validity-Interval Analysis

Validity Interval Analysis (in short: VI-Analysis) is a generic tool for analyzing the input-output behavior of Backpropagation-style neural networks. In short, they key idea of VI-Analysis is to attach *intervals* to the activation range of each unit (or a subset of all units, like input and output units only), such that the network's activations *must* lie within these intervals. These intervals are called *validity intervals*. VI-Analysis checks whether such a set of intervals is *consistent*, i.e., whether there exists a set of network activations inside the validity intervals. It does this by iteratively refining the validity intervals, excluding activations that are provably inconsistent with other intervals. In what follows we will present the general VI-Analysis algorithm, which can be found in more detail elsewhere [14].

Let n denote the total number of units in the network, and let x_i denote the *(output) activation* of unit i ($i = 1, \ldots, n$). If unit i is an input unit, its activation value will simply be the external input value. If not, i.e., if i refers to a hidden or an output unit, let $P(i)$ denote the set of units that are connected to unit i through a link. The activation x_i is computed in two steps:

$$x_i = \sigma_i(net_i) \quad \text{with} \quad net_i = \sum_{k \in P(i)} w_{ik} x_k + \theta_i$$

The auxiliary variable net_i is the *net-input* of unit i, and w_{ik} and θ_i are the *weights* and *biases*, respectively. σ_i denotes the transfer function (squashing function), which usually is given by

$$\sigma_i(net_i) = \frac{1}{1 + e^{-net_i}} \quad \text{with} \quad \sigma_i^{-1}(x_i) = -\ln\left(\frac{1}{x_i} - 1\right)$$

Validity intervals for activation values x_i are denoted by $[a_i, b_i]$. If necessary, validity intervals are projected into the net-input space of unit i, where they will be denoted by $[a'_i, b'_i]$. Let $\mathcal{I}$ be a set of validity intervals for (a subset of) all units. An activation vector $(x_1, \ldots, x_n)$ is said to be *admissible* with respect to $\mathcal{I}$, if all activations lie in $\mathcal{I}$. A set of intervals $\mathcal{I}$ is *consistent*, if there exists an admissible activation vector. Otherwise $\mathcal{I}$ is *inconsistent*.

Assume an initial set of intervals, denoted by $\mathcal{I}$, is given (in the next section we will present a procedure for generating initial intervals). VI-Analysis refines $\mathcal{I}$ iteratively using linear

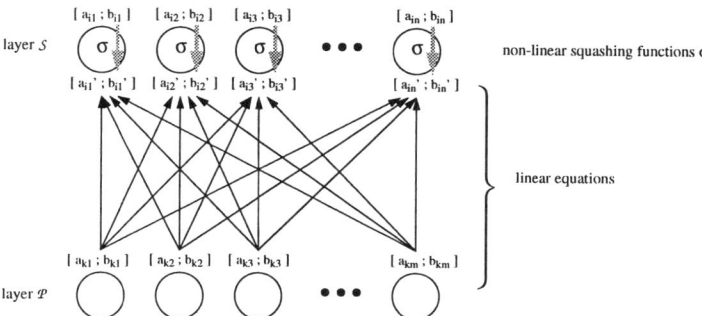

Figure 1: **VI-Analysis in a single weight layer.** Units in layer $\mathcal{P}$ are connected to the units in layer $\mathcal{S}$. A validity interval $[a_j, b_j]$ is assigned to each unit $j \in \mathcal{P} \cup \mathcal{S}$. By projecting the validity intervals for all $i \in \mathcal{S}$, intervals $[a'_i, b'_i]$ for the net-inputs net_i are created. These, plus the validity intervals for all units $k \in \mathcal{P}$, form a set of linear constraints on the activations x_k in layer $\mathcal{P}$. Linear programming is now employed to refine all interval bounds one-by-one.

programming [9], so that those activation values which are inconsistent with other intervals are excluded. In order to simplify the presentation, let us assume without loss of generality (a) that the network is layered and fully connected between two adjacent layers[1], and (b) that there is an interval $[a_i, b_i] \subseteq [0, 1]$ in $\mathcal{I}$ for every unit in $\mathcal{P}$ and $\mathcal{S}$.[2] Consider a single weight layer, connecting a layer of preceding units, denoted by $\mathcal{P}$, to a layer of succeeding units, denoted by $\mathcal{S}$ (cf. Fig. 1). In order to make linear programming techniques applicable, the non-linearity of the transfer function must be eliminated. This is achieved by projecting $[a_i, b_i]$ back to the corresponding net-input intervals[3] $[a'_i, b'_i] = \sigma^{-1}([a_i, b_i]) \in \bar{\Re}^2$ for all $i \in \mathcal{S}$. The resulting validity intervals in $\mathcal{P}$ and $\mathcal{S}$ form the following set of linear constraints on the activation values in $\mathcal{P}$:

$$\begin{array}{rl}
\forall k \in \mathcal{P}: & x_k \geq a_k \quad \text{and} \quad x_k \leq b_k \\
\forall i \in \mathcal{S}: & \sum_{k \in \mathcal{P}} w_{ik} x_k + \theta_i \geq a'_i \quad [\text{by substituting } net_i = \sum_{k \in \mathcal{P}} w_{ik} x_k + \theta_i] \\
& \sum_{k \in \mathcal{P}} w_{ik} x_k + \theta_i \leq b'_i \quad [\text{by substituting } net_i = \sum_{k \in \mathcal{P}} w_{ik} x_k + \theta_i]
\end{array} \quad (1)$$

Notice that all these constraints are linear in the activation values x_k ($k \in \mathcal{P}$). Linear programming allows to maximize or minimize arbitrary linear combinations of the variables x_j while not violating a set of linear constraints [9]. Hence, linear programming can be applied to refine lower and upper bounds for validity intervals one-by-one.

In VI-Analysis, constraints are propagated in two phases:

1. **Forward phase.** To refine the bounds a_i and b_i for units $i \in \mathcal{S}$, new bounds $\hat{a}_i$ and $\hat{b}_i$ are

---

[1] This assumption simplifies the description of VI-Analysis, although VI-Analysis can also be applied to arbitrary non-layered, partially connected network architectures, as well as recurrent networks not examined here.

[2] The canonical interval $[0, 1]$ corresponds to the state of maximum ignorance about the activation of a unit, and hence is the default interval if no more specific interval is known.

[3] Here $\bar{\Re}$ denotes the set of real numbers extended by $\pm \infty$. Notice that this projection assumes that the transfer function is monotonic.

derived:
$$\hat{a}_i = \sigma(\hat{a}'_i) \quad \text{with} \quad \hat{a}'_i = \min net_i = \min \sum_{k \in \mathcal{P}} w_{ik} x_k + \theta_i$$
$$\hat{b}_i = \sigma(\hat{b}'_i) \quad \text{with} \quad \hat{b}'_i = \max net_i = \max \sum_{k \in \mathcal{P}} w_{ik} x_k + \theta_i$$

If $\hat{a}_i > a_i$, a tighter lower bound is found and a_i is updated by $\hat{a}_i$. Likewise, b_i is set to $\hat{b}_i$ if $\hat{b}_i < b_i$. Notice that the min/max operator is computed within the bounds imposed by Eq. 1, using the Simplex algorithm (linear programming) [9].

2. **Backward phase.** In the backward phase the bounds a_k and b_k of all units $k \in \mathcal{P}$ are refined.
$$\hat{a}_k = \min x_k \quad \text{and} \quad \hat{b}_k = \max x_k$$
As in the forward phase, a_k is updated by $\hat{a}_k$ if $\hat{a}_k > a_k$, and b_k is updated by $\hat{b}_k$ if $\hat{b}_k < b_k$.

If the network has multiple weight layers, this process is applied to all weight layers one-by-one. Repetitive refinement results in the propagation of interval constraints through multiple layers in both directions. The convergence of VI-Analysis follows from the fact that the update rule that intervals are changed monotonically, since they can only shrink or stay the same.

Recall that the "input" of VI-Analysis is a set of intervals $\mathcal{I} \subseteq [0,1]^n$ that constrain the activations of the network. VI-Analysis generates a refined set of intervals, $\mathcal{I}' \subseteq \mathcal{I}$, so that all admissible activation values in the original intervals $\mathcal{I}$ are also in the refined intervals $\mathcal{I}'$. In other words, the difference between the original set of intervals and the refined set of intervals $\mathcal{I} - \mathcal{I}'$ is inconsistent.

In summary, VI-Analysis analyzes intervals $\mathcal{I}$ in order to detect inconsistencies. If $\mathcal{I}$ is found to be inconsistent, there is *provably* no admissible activation vector in $\mathcal{I}$. Detecting inconsistencies is the driving mechanism for the verification and extraction of rules presented in turn.

3 Rule Extraction

The rules considered in this paper are propositional *if-then rules*. Although VI-Analysis is able to prove rules expressed by arbitrary linear constraints [14], for the sake of simplicity we will consider only rules where the precondition is given by a set of intervals for the individual input values, and the output is a single target category. Rules of this type can be written as:

If input $\in$ some hypercube $\mathcal{I}$ then class is C (or short: $\mathcal{I} \longrightarrow C$)
for some target class C.

The compliance of a rule with the network can be verified through VI-Analysis. Assume, without loss of generality, the network has a single output unit, and input patterns are classified as members of class C if and only if the output activation, x_{out}, is larger than a threshold c (see [14] for networks with multiple output units). A rule conjecture $\mathcal{I} \longrightarrow C$ is then verified by showing that there is no input vector $\vec{x} \in \mathcal{I}$ that falls into the opposite class, $\neg C$. This is done by including the (negated) condition $x_{\text{out}} \in [0,c]$ into the set of intervals: $\mathcal{I}_{\text{neg}} = \mathcal{I} + \{x_{\text{out}} \in [0,c]\}$. If the rule is correct, x_{out} will never be in $[0,c]$. Hence, if VI-Analysis finds an inconsistency in $\mathcal{I}_{\text{neg}}$, the rule $\mathcal{I} \longrightarrow \neg C$ is proven to be incorrect, and thus the original rule $\mathcal{I} \longrightarrow C$ holds true for the network at hand. This illustrates how rules are *verified* using VI-Analysis.

It remains to be shown how such conjectures can be generated in a systematic way. Two major classes of approaches can be distinguished, *specific-to-general* and *general-to-specific*.

Figure 2: **Robot Arm.** (a) Front view of two arm configurations. (b) Two-dimensional side view. The grey area indicates the workspace, which partially intersects with the table.

1. **Specific-to-general.** A generic way to generate rules, which forms the basis for the experimental results reported in the next section, is to start with rather specific rules which are easy to verify, and gradually generalize those rules by enlarging the corresponding validity intervals. Imagine one has a training instance that, without loss of generality, falls into a class C. The input vector of the training instance already forms a (degenerate) set of validity intervals $\mathcal{I}$. VI-Analysis will, applied to $\mathcal{I}$, trivially confirm the membership in C, and hence the single-point rule $\mathcal{I} \longrightarrow C$. Starting with $\mathcal{I}$, a sequence of more general rule preconditions $\mathcal{I} \subset \mathcal{I}_1 \subset \mathcal{I}_2 \subset \ldots$ can be obtained by enlarging the precondition of the rule (i.e., the input intervals $\mathcal{I}$) by small amounts, and using VI-Analysis to verify if the new rule is still a member of its class. In this way randomly generated instances can be used as "seeds" for rules, which are then generalized via VI-Analysis.

2. **General-to-specific.** An alternative way to extract rules, which has been studied in more detail elsewhere [14], works from general to specific. General-to-specific rule search maintains a list of non-proven conjectures, R. R is initialized with the most general rules (like *"everything is in C"* and *"nothing is in C"*). VI-Analysis is then applied to prove rules in R. If it successfully confirms a rule, the rule and its complement is removed from R. If not, the rule is removed, too, but instead new rules are added to R. These new rules form a specialized version of the old rule, so that their disjunct is exactly the old rule. For example, new rules can be generated by splitting the hypercube spanned by the old rule into disjoint regions, one for each new rule. Then, the new set R is checked with VI-Analysis. The whole procedure continues till R is empty and the whole input domain is described by rules. In discrete domains, such a strategy amounts to searching directed acyclic graphs in breadth-first manner.

Obviously, there is a variety of alternative techniques to generate meaningful rule hypotheses. For example, one might employ a symbolic learning technique such as decision tree learning [10] to the same training data that was used for training the network. The rules, which are a result of the symbolic approach, constitute hypotheses that can be checked using VI-Analysis.

4 Empirical Results

In this section we will be interested in extracting rules in a real-valued robot arm domain. We trained a neural network to model the forward kinematics function of a 5 degree-of-freedom robot arm. The arm, a Mitsubishi RV-M1, is depicted in Fig. 2. Its kinematic function determines the position of the tip of the manipulator in (x, y, z) workspace coordinates and

coverage	average (per rule)	cumulative
first 10 rules	9.79%	30.2%
first 100 rules	2.59%	47.8%
first 1 000 rules	1.20%	61.6%
first 10 000 rules	0.335 %	84.4%

Table 1: Rule coverage in the robot arm domain. These numbers include rules for both concepts, *SAFE* and *UNSAFE*.

---

the angle of the manipulator h to the table based on the angles of the five joints. As can be seen in Fig. 2, the workspace intersects with the table on which the arm is mounted. Hence, some configurations of the joints are safe, namely those for which $z \geq 0$, while others can physically not be reached without a collision that would damage the robot (unsafe). When operating the robot arm one has to be able to tell safe from unsafe. Henceforth, we are interested in a set of rules that describes the subspace of safe and unsafe joint configurations.

A total of 8 192 training examples was used for training the network (four input, five hidden and four output units), resulting in a considerably accurate model of the kinematics of the robot arm. Notice that the network operates in a continuous space. Obviously, compiling the network into logical rules node-by-node, as frequently done in other approaches to rule extraction, is difficult due to the real-valued and distributed nature of the internal representation. Instead, we applied VI-Analysis using a specific-to-general mechanism as described above. More specifically, we incrementally constructed a collection of rules that gradually covered the workspace of the robot arm. Rules were generated whenever a (random) joint configuration was not covered by a previously generated rule. Table 1 shows average results that characterize the extraction of rules. Initially, each rule covers a rather large fraction of the 5-dimensional joint configuration space. As few as 11 rules, on average, suffice to cover more than 50% (by volume) of the whole input space. However, these 50% are the easy half. As the domain gets increasingly covered by rules, gradually more specific rules are generated in regions closer to the class boundary. After extracting 10,000 rules, only 84.4% of the input space is covered. Since the decision boundary between the two classes is highly non-linear, finitely many rules will never cover the input space completely.

How general are the rules extracted by VI-Analysis? Generally speaking, for joint configurations close to the class boundary, *i.e.*, where the tip of the manipulator is close to the table, we observed that the extracted rules were rather specific. If instead the initial configuration was closer to the center of a class, VI-Analysis was observed to produce more general rules that had a larger coverage in the workspace. Here VI-Analysis managed to extract surprisingly general rules. For example, the configuration $\vec{\alpha} = (30°, 80°, 20°, 60°, -20°)$, which is depicted in Fig. 3, yields the rule

if $\alpha_2 \leq 90.5°$ *and* $\alpha_3 \leq 27.3°$ *then* SAFE.

Notice that out of 10 initial constraints, 8 were successfully removed by VI-Analysis. The rule lacks both bounds on α_1, α_4 and α_5 and the lower bounds on α_2 and α_3. Fig. 3a shows the front view of the initial arm configuration and the generalized rule (grey area). Fig. 3b shows a side view of the arm, along with a slice of the rule (the base joint α_1 is kept fixed). Notice that this very rule covers 17.1% of the configuration space (by volume). Such general rules were frequently found in the robot arm domain.

This concludes the brief description of the experimental results. Not mentioned here are results with different size networks, and results obtained for the MONK's benchmark problems. For example, in the MONK's problems [15], VI-Analysis successfully extracted compact target

Figure 3: **A single rule, extracted from the network.** (a) Front view. (b) Two-dimensional side view. The grey area indicates safe positions for the tip of the manipulator.

concepts using the originally published weight sets. These results can be found in [14].

5 Discussion

In this paper we have presented a mechanism for the extraction of rules from Backpropagation-style neural networks. There are several limitations of the current approach that warrant future research. **(a) Speed.** While the one-to-one compilation of networks into rules is fast, rule extraction via VI-Analysis requires multiple runs of linear programming, each of which can be computationally expensive [9]. Searching the rule space without domain-specific search heuristics can thus be a most time-consuming undertaking. In all our experiments, however, we observed reasonably fast convergence of the VI-Algorithm, and we successfully managed to extract rules from larger networks in reasonable amounts of time. Recently, Craven and Shavlik proposed a more efficient search method which can be applied in conjunction with VI-Analysis [2]. **(b) Language.** Currently VI-Analysis is limited to the extraction of if-then rules with linear preconditions. While in [14] it has been shown how to generalize VI-Analysis to rules expressed by arbitrary linear constraints, a more powerful rule language is clearly desirable. **(c) Linear optimization.** Linear programming analyzes multiple weight layers independently, resulting in an overly careful refinement of intervals. This effect can prevent from detecting correct rules. If linear programming is replaced by a non-linear optimization method that considers multiple weight layers simultaneously, more powerful rules can be generated. On the other hand, efficient non-linear optimization techniques might find rules which do not describe the network accurately. Moreover, it is generally questionable whether there will ever exist techniques for mapping arbitrary networks accurately into compact rule sets. Neural networks are their own best description, and symbolic rules might not be appropriate for describing the input-output behavior of a complex neural network.

A key feature of of the approach presented in this paper is the particular way rules are extracted. Unlike other approaches to the extraction of rules, this mechanism does not compile networks into structurally equivalent set of rules. Instead it analyzes the input output relation of networks as a whole. As a consequence, rules can be extracted from unstructured networks with distributed and real-valued internal representations. In addition, the extracted rules describe the neural network accurately, regardless of the size of the network. This makes VI-Analysis a promising candidate for scaling rule extraction techniques to deep networks, in which approximate rule extraction methods can suffer from cumulative errors. We conjecture that such properties are important if meaningful rules are to be extracted in today's and tomorrow's successful Backpropagation applications.

Acknowledgment

The author wishes to express his gratitude to Marc Craven, Tom Dietterich, Clayton McMillan, Tom Mitchell and Jude Shavlik for their invaluable feedback that has influenced this research.

References

[1] M. W. Craven and J. W. Shavlik. Learning symbolic rules using artificial neural networks. In Paul E. Utgoff, editor, *Proceedings of the Tenth International Conference on Machine Learning*, 1993. Morgan Kaufmann.

[2] M. W. Craven and J. W. Shavlik. Using sampling and queries to extract rules from trained neural networks. In *Proceedings of the Eleventh International Conference on Machine Learning*, 1994. Morgan Kaufmann.

[3] L.-M. Fu. Integration of neural heuristics into knowledge-based inference. *Connection Science*, 1(3):325–339, 1989.

[4] C. L. Giles and C. W. Omlin. Rule refinement with recurrent neural networks. In *Proceedings of the IEEE International Conference on Neural Network*, 1993. IEEE Neural Network Council.

[5] Y. LeCun, B. Boser, J. S. Denker, D. Henderson, R. E. Howard, W. Hubbard, and L. D. Jackel. Backpropagation applied to handwritten zip code recognition. *Neural Computation*, 1:541–551, 1990.

[6] J. J. Mahoney and R. J. Mooney. Combining neural and symbolic learning to revise probabilistic rule bases. In J. E. Moody, S. J. Hanson, and R. P. Lippmann, editors, *Advances in Neural Information Processing Systems 5*, 1993. Morgan Kaufmann.

[7] C. McMillan, M. C. Mozer, and P. Smolensky. Rule induction through integrated symbolic and subsymbolic processing. In J. E. Moody, S. J. Hanson, and R. P. Lippmann, editors, *Advances in Neural Information Processing Systems 4*, 1992. Morgan Kaufmann.

[8] D. A. Pomerleau. ALVINN: an autonomous land vehicle in a neural network. Technical Report CMU-CS-89-107, Computer Science Dept. Carnegie Mellon University, Pittsburgh PA, 1989.

[9] W. H. Press. *Numerical recipes in C : the art of scientific computing*. Cambridge University Press, Cambridge [Cambridgeshire], New York, 1988.

[10] J. R. Quinlan. Induction of decision trees. *Machine Learning*, 1:81–106, 1986.

[11] J. Rennie. Cancer catcher: Neural net catches errors that slip through pap tests. *Scientific American*, 262, May 1990.

[12] T. J. Sejnowski and C. R. Rosenberg. Nettalk: A parallel network that learns to read aloud. Technical Report JHU/EECS-86/01, Johns Hopkins University, 1986.

[13] G. J. Tesauro. Practical issues in temporal difference learning. *Machine Learning*, 8, 1992.

[14] S. Thrun. Extracting provably correct rules from artificial neural networks. Technical Report IAI-TR-93-5, University of Bonn, Institut für Informatik III, D-53117 Bonn, May 1993.

[15] S. Thrun, J. Bala, E. Bloedorn, I. Bratko, B. Cestnik, J. Cheng, K. De Jong, S. Džeroski, D. Fisher, S. E. Fahlman, R. Hamann, K. Kaufman, S. Keller, I. Kononenko, J. Kreuziger, R. S. Michalski, T.M. Mitchell, P. Pachowicz, Y. Reich, H. Vafaie, W. Van de Welde, W. Wenzel, J. Wnek, and J. Zhang. The MONK's problems - a performance comparison of different learning algorithms. Technical Report CMU-CS-91-197, Carnegie Mellon University, Pittsburgh, PA, December 1991.

[16] G. Towell and J. W. Shavlik. Interpretation of artificial neural networks: Mapping knowledge-based neural networks into rules. In J. E. Moody, S. J. Hanson, and R. P. Lippmann, editors, *Advances in Neural Information Processing Systems 4*, 1992. Morgan Kaufmann.

[17] V. Tresp and J. Hollatz. Network structuring and training using rule-based knowledge. In J. E. Moody, S. J. Hanson, and R. P. Lippmann, editors, *Advances in Neural Information Processing Systems 5*, 1993. Morgan Kaufmann.

[18] A. H. Waibel. Modular construction of time-delay neural networks for speech recognition. *Neural Computation*, 1:39–46, 1989.

Capacity and Information Efficiency of a Brain-like Associative Net

Bruce Graham and David Willshaw
Centre for Cognitive Science, University of Edinburgh
2 Buccleuch Place, Edinburgh, EH8 9LW, UK
Email: bruce@cns.ed.ac.uk & david@cns.ed.ac.uk

Abstract

We have determined the capacity and information efficiency of an associative net configured in a brain-like way with partial connectivity and noisy input cues. Recall theory was used to calculate the capacity when pattern recall is achieved using a *winners-take-all* strategy. Transforming the *dendritic sum* according to *input activity* and *unit usage* can greatly increase the capacity of the associative net under these conditions. For moderately sparse patterns, maximum information efficiency is achieved with very low connectivity levels ($\leq 10\%$). This corresponds to the level of connectivity commonly seen in the brain and invites speculation that the brain is connected in the most information efficient way.

1 INTRODUCTION

Standard network associative memories become more plausible as models of associative memory in the brain if they incorporate (1) partial connectivity, (2) sparse activity and (3) recall from noisy cues. In this paper we consider the capacity of a binary associative net (Willshaw, Buneman, & Longuet-Higgins, 1969; Willshaw, 1971; Buckingham, 1991) containing these features. While the associative net is a very simple model of associative memory, its behaviour as a storage device is not trivial and yet it is tractable to theoretical analysis. We are able to calculate the capacity of the net in different configurations and with different pattern recall strategies. Here we consider the capacity as a function of connectivity level when *winners-take-all recall* is used.

The associative net is an heteroassociative memory in which pairs of binary patterns are stored by altering the connection weights between input and output units via a Hebbian learning rule. After pattern storage, an output pattern is recalled by presenting a previously stored input pattern on the input units. Which output units become active during recall is determined by applying a threshold of activation to measurements that each output unit makes of the input cue pattern. The most commonly used measurement is the weighted sum of the inputs, or *dendritic sum*. Amongst the simpler thresholding strategies is the *winners-take-all (WTA)* approach, which chooses the required number of output units with the highest dendritic sums to be active. This works well when the net is fully connected (each input unit is connected to every output unit), and input cues are noise-free. However, recall performance deteriorates rapidly if the net is partially connected (each input unit is connected to only some of the output units) and cues are noisy.

Marr (1971) recognised that when an associative net is only partially connected, another useful measurement for threshold setting is the total *input activity* (sum of the inputs, regardless of the connection weights). The ratio of the dendritic sum to the input activity can be a better discriminator of which output units should be active than the dendritic sum alone. Buckingham and Willshaw (1993) showed that differences in *unit usage* (the number of patterns in which an output unit is active during storage) causes variations in the dendritic sums that makes accurate recall difficult when the input cues are noisy. They incorporated both input activity and unit usage measurements into a recall strategy that minimised the number of errors in the output pattern by setting the activity threshold on a unit by unit basis. This is a rather more complex threshold setting strategy than a simple winners-take-all.

We have previously demonstrated via computer simulations (Graham & Willshaw, 1994) that the *WTA* threshold strategy can achieve the same recall performance as this minimisation approach if the dendritic sums are transformed by certain functions of the input activity and unit usage before a threshold is applied. Here we calculate the capacity of the associative net when *WTA* recall is used with three different functions of the dendritic sums: (1) pure dendritic sums, (2) modified by input activity and (3) modified by input activity and unit usage. The results show that up to four times the capacity can be obtained by transforming the dendritic sums by a function of both input activity and unit usage. This increase in capacity was obtained without a loss of information efficiency. For the moderately sparse patterns used, *WTA* recall is most information efficient at low levels of connectivity ($\leq 10\%$), as is the minimisation approach to threshold setting (Buckingham, 1991). This connectivity range is similar to that commonly seen in the brain.

2 NOTATION AND OPERATION

The associative net consists of N_B binary output units each connected to a proportion Z of the N_A binary input units. Pairs of binary patterns are stored in the net. Input and output patterns contain M_A and M_B active units, respectively (activity level $\alpha = M/N \ll 1$). All connection weights start at zero. On presentation to the net of a pattern pair for storage, the connection weight between an active input unit and an active output unit is set to 1. During recall an input cue pattern is presented on the input units. The input cue is a noisy version of a previously stored input pattern in which a fraction, s, of the M_A active units do not come from the stored pattern. A thresholding strategy is applied to the output units to determine which of them should be active. Those that should be active in response to the input cue will be called *high* units, and those that should be inactive will be called *low* units. We consider *winners-take-all (WTA)* thresholding strategies that choose to be active the M_B output units with the highest values of three functions of the dendritic sum, d, the input activity, a, and the unit usage, r. These functions are listed in Table 1. The *normalised* strategy deals with partial connectivity. The *transformed* strategy reduces variations in the dendritic sums due to differences in unit usage. This function minimises the variance of the *low* unit dendritic sums with respect to the unit usage (Graham & Willshaw, 1994).

Table 1: WTA Strategies

WTA Strategy	Function
Basic	d
Normalised	$d' = d/a$
Transformed	$d^* = 1 - (1 - d/a)^{1/r}$

3 RECALL THEORY

The capacity of the associative net is defined to be the number of pattern pairs that can be stored before there is one bit in error in a recalled output pattern. This cannot be calculated analytically for the net configuration under study. However, it can be determined numerically for the *WTA* recall strategy by calculating the recall response for different numbers of stored patterns, R, until the minimum value of R is found for which a recall error occurs. The *WTA* recall response can be calculated theoretically using expressions for the distributions of the dendritic sums of *low* and *high* output units. The probability that the dendritic sum of a *low* or *high* output unit should have a particular value x is, respectively (Buckingham & Willshaw, 1993; Buckingham, 1991)

$$P(d_l = x) = \sum_{r=1}^{R} \binom{R}{r} \alpha_B^r (1-\alpha_B)^{R-r} \binom{M_A}{x} (Z\rho[r])^x (1-Z\rho[r])^{M_A-x} \quad (1)$$

$$P(d_h = x) = \sum_{r=0}^{R-1} \binom{R}{r} \alpha_B^r (1-\alpha_B)^{R-r} \binom{M_A}{x} (Z\mu[r+1])^x (1 - Z\mu[r+1])^{M_A-x} \quad (2)$$

where $\rho[r]$ and $\mu[r]$ are the probabilities that an arbitrarily selected active input is on a connection with weight 1. For a *low* unit, $\rho[r] = 1 - (1 - \alpha_A)^r$. For a *high* unit a good approximation for μ is $\mu[r+1] \simeq g + s\rho[r] = 1 - s(1 - \alpha_A)^r$ where g and s are the probabilities that a particular active input in the cue pattern is *genuine* (belongs to the stored pattern) or *spurious*, respectively ($g + s = 1$) (Buckingham & Willshaw, 1993). The *basic WTA* response is calculated using these distributions by finding the threshold, T, that gives

$$(N_B - M_B)P(d_l \geq T) + M_B P(d_h \geq T) = M_B \quad (3)$$

The number of false positive and false negative errors of the response is given by

$$E = (N_B - M_B)P(d_l \geq T) + M_B(1 - P(d_h \geq T)) \quad (4)$$

The actual distributions of the *normalised* dendritic sums are the distributions of d/a. For the purposes of calculating the *normalised WTA* response, it is possible to use the *basic* distributions for the situation where every unit has the mean input activity, $a_m = M_A Z$. In this case the *low* and *high* unit distributions are approximately

$$P(d'_l = x) = \sum_{r=1}^{R} \binom{R}{r} \alpha_B^r (1-\alpha_B)^{R-r} \binom{a_m}{x} (\rho[r])^x (1 - \rho[r])^{a_m - x} \quad (5)$$

$$P(d'_h = x) = \sum_{r=0}^{R-1} \binom{R}{r} \alpha_B^r (1-\alpha_B)^{R-r} \binom{a_m}{x} (\mu[r+1])^x (1 - \mu[r+1])^{a_m - x} \quad (6)$$

Due to the nonlinear transformation used, it is not possible to calculate the *transformed* distributions as simple sums of binomials, so the following approach is used to generate the *transformed WTA* response. For a given *transformed* threshold, T^*, and for each possible value of unit usage, r, an equivalent *normalised* threshold is calculated via

$$T'[r] = a_m(1 - (1 - T^*)^r) \quad (7)$$

The *transformed* cumulative probabilities can then be calculated from the *normalised* distributions:

$$P(d_l^* \geq T^*) = \sum_{r=1}^{R} \binom{R}{r} \alpha_B^r (1-\alpha_B)^{R-r} P(d'_l \geq T'[r]) \quad (8)$$

$$P(d_h^* \geq T^*) = \sum_{r=0}^{R-1} \binom{R}{r} \alpha_B^r (1-\alpha_B)^{R-r} P(d'_h \geq T'[r+1]) \quad (9)$$

The *normalised* and *transformed* WTA responses are calculated in the same manner as the *basic* response, using the appropriate probability distributions.

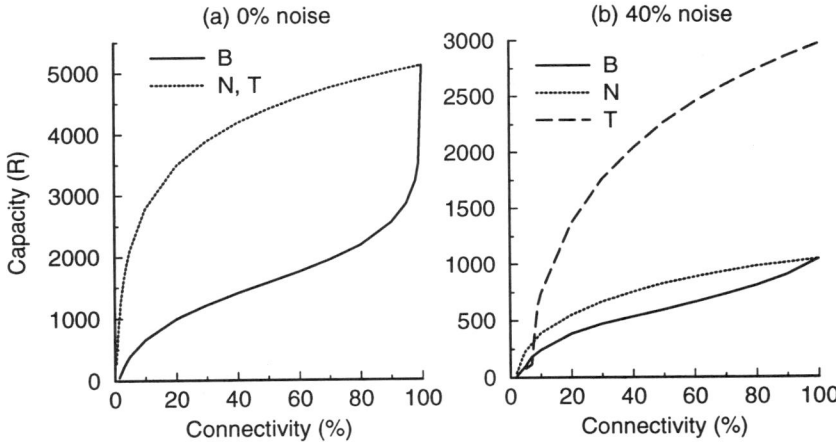

Figure 1: Capacity Versus Connectivity

4 RESULTS

Extensive simulations were previously carried out of *WTA* recall from a large associative net with the following specifications (Graham & Willshaw, 1994): $N_A = 48000$, $M_A = 1440$, $N_B = 6144$, $M_B = 180$. Agreement between the simulations and the theoretical recall described above is extremely good, indicating that the approximations used in the theory are valid. Here we use the theoretical recall to calculate capacity results for this large associative net that are not easily obtained via simulations. All the results shown have been generated using the theory described in the previous section.

Figure 1 shows the capacity as a function of connectivity for the different *WTA* strategies when there is no noise in the input cue, or 40% noise in the cue (legend: B = *basic WTA*, N = *normalised WTA*, T = *transformed WTA*; for clarity, individual data points are omitted). With no noise in the cue the *normalised* and *transformed* methods perform identically, so only the *normalised* results are shown. Figure 1(a) highlights the effectiveness of normalising the dendritic sums against input activity when the net is partially connected. Figure 1(b) shows the effect of noise on capacity. The capacity of each recall strategy at a given connectivity level is much reduced compared to the noise-free case. However, for connectivities greater than 10% the capacity of the *transformed WTA* is now much greater than either the *normalised* or *basic WTA*.

The relative capacities of the different strategies are shown in Figure 2 (legend: N/B = ratio of *normalised* to *basic* capacity, T/B = ratio of *transformed* to *basic*, T/N = ratio of *transformed* to *normalised*). In the noise-free case (Figure 2(a)), at low levels of connectivity the relative capacity is distorted because the *basic* capacity drops to near zero, so that even low *normalised* capacities are relatively very large. For most connectivity levels (10-90%) the *normalised WTA* provides 2-4 times the capacity of the *basic WTA*. In the noisy case (Figure 2(b)), the *normalised* capacity is only up to 1.5 times the *basic* capacity over this range of connectivities. The *transformed WTA*, however, provides 3 to nearly 4 times the *basic* capacity and 2.5 to nearly 3 times the *normalised* capacity for connectivities greater than 10%.

The capacities can be interpreted in information theoretic terms by considering the information efficiency of the net. This is the ratio of the amount of information that can be retrieved from the net to the number of bits of storage available and is given by $\eta_o = R_o I_o / Z N_A N_B$, where R_o is the capacity, I_o is the amount of information contained in an output pattern and $Z N_A N_B$ is the number of weights, or bits of storage required (Willshaw et al., 1969; Buckingham & Willshaw, 1992). Information efficiency as a function of connectivity is shown in Figure 3. There is a distinct peak in information efficiency for each of the recall strategies at some low level of connectivity. The peak information efficiencies and the efficiencies at full connectivity are summarised in Table 2. The greatest contrast between full and partial connectivity is seen with the *normalised WTA* and noise-free cues. At 1% connectivity the *normalised WTA* is nearly 14 times more efficient than at full connectivity. In absolute terms, however, the *normalised* capacity is only 694 at 1% connectivity, compared with 5122 at full connectivity. The peak efficiency of 53% obtained by the *normalised WTA* is approaching the theoretically approximate maximum of 69% for a fully connected net (Willshaw et al., 1969).

5 DISCUSSION

Previous simulations (Graham & Willshaw, 1994) have shown that, when the input cues are noisy, the recall performance of the *winners-take-all* thresholding strategy applied to the partially connected associative net is greatly improved if the dendritic sums of the output units are transformed by functions of input activity and unit usage. We have confirmed and extended these results here by calculating the theoretical capacity of the associative net as a function of connectivity.

For the moderately sparse patterns used, all of the recall strategies are most information efficient at very low levels of connectivity ($\leq 10\%$). However, the optimum connectivity level is dependent on the pattern coding rate. Extending the analysis of Willshaw et al. (1969) to a partially connected net using *normalised WTA* recall yields that maximum information efficiency is obtained when $ZM_A = \log_2(N_B)$. So for input coding rates higher than $\log_2(N_B)$, a partially connected net is most information efficient. For the input coding rate used here, this relationship gives an optimum connectivity level of 0.87%, very close to the 1% obtained from the recall theory.

Comparing the peak efficiencies across the different strategies for the noisy cue case, the *normalised WTA* is about twice as efficient as the *basic WTA*, while the *transformed WTA* is three times as efficient. This comparison does not include the

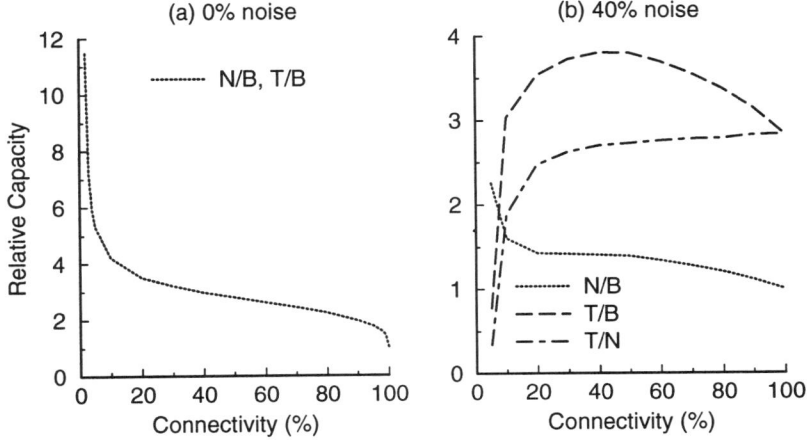

Figure 2: Relative Capacity Versus Connectivity

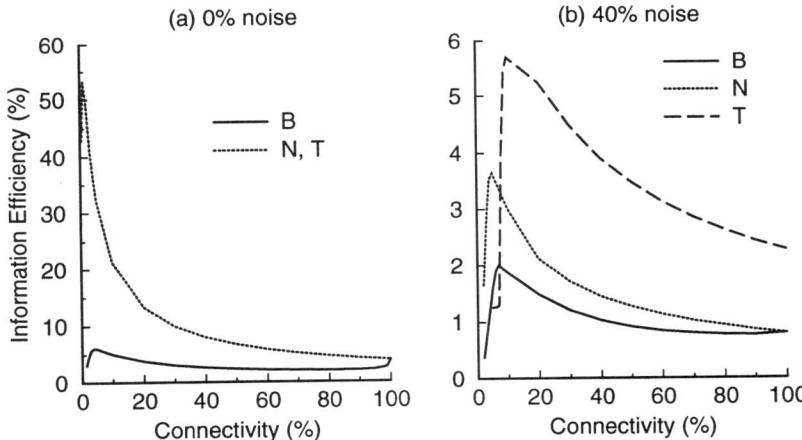

Figure 3: Information Efficiency Versus Connectivity

Table 2: Information Efficiency

WTA Strategy	0% Noise			40% Noise		
	η_o at Peak (%)	Z at Peak (%)	η_o at $Z=1$ (%)	η_o at Peak (%)	Z at Peak (%)	η_o at $Z=1$ (%)
Basic	6.1	4	3.9	2.0	7	0.8
Normalised	53.3	1	3.9	3.6	5	0.8
Transformed	53.3	1	3.9	5.7	10	2.3

cost of storing input activity and unit usage information. If one bit of storage per connection is required for the input activity, and another bit for the unit usage, then the information efficiency of the *normalised WTA* is halved, and the information efficiency of the *transformed WTA* is reduced by two thirds. This results in all the strategies having about the same peak efficiency. However, the absolute capacities of the different strategies at their peak efficiencies are 183, 237 and 741 for the *basic*, *normalised* and *transformed WTA*, respectively. So, at the same level of efficiency, the *transformed WTA* delivers four times the capacity of the *basic WTA*.

In conclusion, numerical calculations of the capacity of the associative net show that it is most information efficient at a very low level of connectivity when moderately sparse patterns are stored. Including input activity and unit usage information into the recall calculations results in a four-fold increase in storage capacity without loss of efficiency.

Acknowledgements

To the Medical Research Council for financial support under Programme Grant PG 9119632

References

Buckingham, J., & Willshaw, D. (1992). Performance characteristics of the associative net. *Network, 3*, 407–414.

Buckingham, J., & Willshaw, D. (1993). On setting unit thresholds in an incompletely connected associative net. *Network, 4*, 441–459.

Buckingham, J. (1991). *Delicate nets, faint recollections: a study of partially connected associative network memories*. Ph.D. thesis, University of Edinburgh.

Graham, B., & Willshaw, D. (1994). Improving recall from an associative memory. *Biol. Cybern.*, in press.

Marr, D. (1971). Simple memory: a theory for archicortex. *Phil. Trans. Roy. Soc. Lond. B, 262*, 23–81.

Shepherd, G. (Ed.). (1990). *The Synaptic Organization of the Brain* (Third edition). Oxford University Press, New York, Oxford.

Willshaw, D. (1971). *Models of distributed associative memory*. Ph.D. thesis, University of Edinburgh.

Willshaw, D., Buneman, O., & Longuet-Higgins, H. (1969). Non-holographic associative memory. *Nature, 222*, 960–962.

Boosting the Performance of RBF Networks with Dynamic Decay Adjustment

Michael R. Berthold
Forschungszentrum Informatik
Gruppe ACID (Prof. D. Schmid)
Haid–und–Neu–Strasse 10—14
76131 Karlsruhe, Germany
eMail: berthold@fzi.de

Jay Diamond
Intel Corporation
2200 Mission College Blvd.
Santa Clara, CA, USA
95052 MS:SC9-15
eMail: jdiamond@mipos3.intel.com

Abstract

Radial Basis Function (RBF) Networks, also known as networks of locally–tuned processing units (see [6]) are well known for their ease of use. Most algorithms used to train these types of networks, however, require a fixed architecture, in which the number of units in the hidden layer must be determined before training starts. The RCE training algorithm, introduced by Reilly, Cooper and Elbaum (see [8]), and its probabilistic extension, the P–RCE algorithm, take advantage of a growing structure in which hidden units are only introduced when necessary. The nature of these algorithms allows training to reach stability much faster than is the case for gradient–descent based methods. Unfortunately P–RCE networks do not adjust the standard deviation of their prototypes individually, using only one global value for this parameter.

This paper introduces the Dynamic Decay Adjustment (DDA) algorithm which utilizes the constructive nature of the P–RCE algorithm together with independent adaptation of each prototype's decay factor. In addition, this radial adjustment is class dependent and distinguishes between different neighbours. It is shown that networks trained with the presented algorithm perform substantially better than common RBF networks.

1 Introduction

Moody and Darken proposed Networks with locally–tuned processing units, which are also known as *Radial Basis Functions* (RBFs, see [6]). Networks of this type have a single layer of units with a selective response for some range of the input variables. Each unit has an overall response function, possibly a Gaussian:

$$R_i(\vec{x}) = exp(-\frac{||\vec{x} - \vec{r}_i||^2}{\sigma_i^2}) \tag{1}$$

Here $\vec{x}$ is the input to the network, $\vec{r}_i$ denotes the center of the i-th RBF and σ_i determines its standard deviation. The second layer computes the output function for each class as follows:

$$f(\vec{x}) = \sum_{i=1}^{m} A_i * R_i(\vec{x}) \tag{2}$$

with m indicating the number of RBFs and A_i being the weight for each RBF. Moody and Darken propose a hybrid training, a combination of unsupervised clustering for the centers and radii of the RBFs and supervised training of the weights. Unfortunately their algorithm requires a fixed network topology, which means that the number of RBFs must be determined in advance. The same problem applies to the Generalized Radial Basis Functions (GRBF), proposed in [12]. Here a gradient descent technique is used to implement a supervised training of the center locations, which has the disadvantage of long training times.

In contrast RCE (*Restricted Coulomb Energy*) Networks construct their architecture dynamically during training (see [7] for an overview). This algorithm was inspired by systems of charged particles in a three–dimensional space and is analogous to the Liapunov equation:

$$\xi = -\frac{1}{L} \sum_{i=1}^{m} \frac{Q_i}{||\vec{x} - \vec{r}_i||_2^L} \tag{3}$$

where ξ is the electrostatic potential induced by fixed particles with charges $-Q_i$ and locations $\vec{r}_i$. One variation of this type of networks is the so called P–RCE network, which attempts to classify data using a probabilistic distribution derived from the training set. The underlying training algorithm for P–RCE is identical to RCE training with gaussian activation functions used in the forward pass to resemble a Probabilistic Neural Network (PNN [10]). PNNs are not suitable for large databases because they commit one new prototype for each training pattern they encounter, effectively becoming a referential memory scheme. In contrast, the P–RCE algorithm introduces a new prototype only when necessary. This occurs when the prototype of a conflicting class misclassifies the new pattern during the training phase. The probabilistic extension is modelled by incrementing the a–priori rate of occurrence for prototypes of the same class as the input vector, therefore weights are only connecting RBFs and an output node of the same class. The recall phase of the P–RCE network is similar to RBFs, except that it uses one global radius for all prototypes and scales each gaussian by the a-priori rate of occurrence:

$$act_c(\vec{x}) = \sum_{i=1}^{m_c} A_i^c * exp(-\frac{||\vec{x} - \vec{r}_i^c||^2}{R^2}) \tag{4}$$

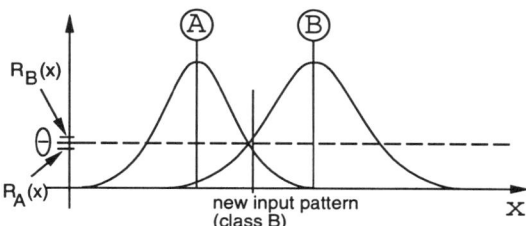

Figure 1: This picture shows how a new pattern results in a slightly higher activity for a prototype of the right class than for the conflicting prototype. Using only one threshold, no new prototype would be introduced in this case.

where c denotes the class for which the activation is computed, m_c is the number of prototypes for class c, and R is the constant radius of the gaussian activation functions. The global radius of this method and the inability to recognize areas of conflict, leads to confusion in some areas of the feature space, and therefore non–optimal recognition performance.

The Dynamic Decay Adjustment (DDA) algorithm presented in this paper was developed to solve the inherent problems associated with these methods. The constructive part of the P–RCE algorithm is used to build a network with an appropriate number of RBF units, for which the decay factor is computed based on information about neighbours. This technique increases the recognition accuracy in areas of conflict.

The following sections explain the algorithm, compare it with others, and examine some simulation results.

2 The Algorithm

Since the P–RCE training algorithm already uses an independent *area of influence* for each RBF, it is relatively straightforward to extract an individual radius. This results, however, in the problem illustrated in figure 1. The new pattern $\vec{p}$ of class B is properly covered by the right prototype of the same class. However, the left prototype of conflicting class A results in almost the same activation and this leads to a very low confidence when the network must classify the pattern $\vec{p}$.

To solve this dilemma, two different radii, or thresholds[1] are introduced: a so–called *positive threshold* (θ^+), which must be overtaken by an activation of a prototype of the same class so that no new prototype is added, and a *negative threshold* (θ^-), which is the upper limit for the activation of conflicting classes. Figure 2 shows an example in which the new pattern correctly results in activations above the positive threshold for the correct class B and below the negative threshold for conflicting class A. This results in better classification–confidence in areas where training

---

[1] The conversion from the threshold to the radius is straightforward as long as the activation function is invertible.

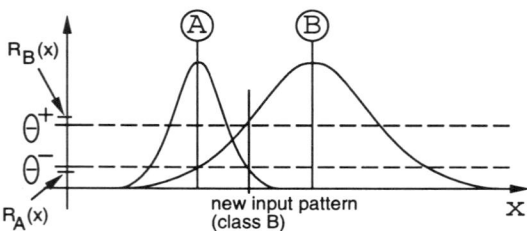

Figure 2: The proposed algorithm distinguishes between prototypes of correct and conflicting classes and uses different thresholds. Here the level of confidence is higher for the correct classification of the new pattern.

patterns did not result in new prototypes. The network is required to hold the following two equations for every pattern $\vec{x}$ of class c from the training data:

$$\exists i : R_i^c(\vec{x}) \geq \theta^+ \tag{5}$$

$$\forall k \neq c, 1 \leq j \leq m_k : R_j^k(\vec{x}) < \theta^- \tag{6}$$

The algorithm to construct a classifier can be extracted partly from the RCE algorithm. The following pseudo code shows what the training for one new pattern $\vec{x}$ of class c looks like:

// reset weights:
FORALL prototypes p_i^k **DO**
   $A_i^k = 0.0$
ENDFOR
// train one complete epoch
FORALL training pattern $(\vec{x}, c)$ **DO**:
   IF $\exists p_i^c : R_i^c(\vec{x}) \geq \theta^+$ **THEN**
      $A_i^c + = 1.0$
   ELSE
      // "commit": introduce new prototype
      add new prototype $p_{m_c+1}^c$ with:
      $\vec{r}_{m_c+1}^c = \vec{x}$
      $\sigma_{m_c+1}^c = \max_{k \neq c \wedge 1 \leq j \leq m_k} \{\sigma : R_{m_c+1}^c(\vec{r}_j^k) < \theta^-\}$
      $A_{m_c+1}^c = 1.0$
      $m_c + = 1$
   ENDIF
   // "shrink": adjust conflicting prototypes
   FORALL $k \neq c, 1 \leq j \leq m_k$ **DO**
      $\sigma_j^k = \max\{\sigma : R_j^k(\vec{x}) < \theta^-\}$
ENDFOR

First, all weights are set to zero because otherwise they would accumulate duplicate information about training patterns. Next all training patterns are presented to the

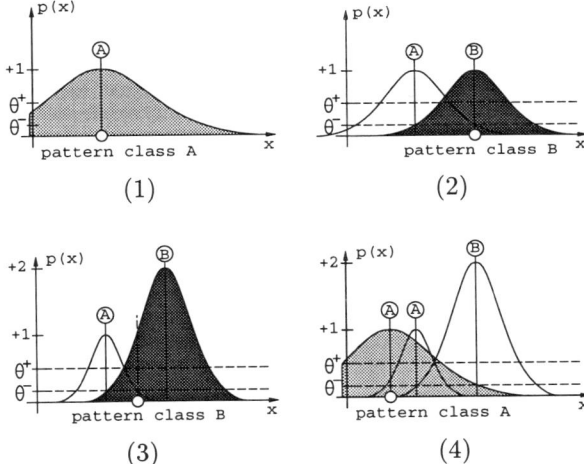

Figure 3: An example of the DDA–algorithm: (1) a pattern of class A is encountered and a new RBF is created; (2) a training pattern of class B leads to a new prototype for class B and shrinks the radius of the existing RBF of class A; (3) another pattern of class B is classified correctly and shrinks again the prototype of class A; (4) a new pattern of class A introduces another prototype of that class.

network. If the new pattern is classified correctly, the weight of the closest prototype is increased; otherwise a new protoype is introduced with the new pattern defining its center. The last step of the algorithm shrinks all prototypes of conflicting classes if their activations are too high for this specific pattern.

Running this algorithm over the training data until no further changes are required ensures that equations (5) and (6) hold.

The choice of the two new parameters, θ^+ and θ^- are not as critical as it would initially appear[2]. For all of the experiments reported, the settings $\theta^+ = 0.4$ and $\theta^- = 0.1$ were used, and no major correlations of the results to these values were noted. Note that when choosing $\theta^+ = \theta^-$ one ends up with an algorithm having the problem mentioned in figure 1.

Figure 3 shows an example that illustrates the first few training steps of the DDA–algorithm.

3 Results

Several well-known databases were chosen to evaluate this algorithm (some can be found in the CMU Neural Network Benchmark Databases (see [13])). The DDA–

---

[2]Theoretically one would expect the dimensionality of the input–space to play a major role for the choice of those parameters

algorithm was compared against PNN, RCE and P–RCE as well as a classic Multi Layer Perceptron which was trained using a modified Backpropagation algorithm (Rprop, see [9]). The number of hidden nodes of the MLP was optimized manually. In addition an RBF–network with a fixed number of hidden nodes was trained using unsupervised clustering for the center positions and a gradient descent to determine the weights (see [6] for more details). The number of hidden nodes was again optimized manually.

- Vowel Recognition: Speaker independent recognition of the eleven steady state vowels of *British* English using a specified training set of Linear Predictive Coding (LPC) derived log area ratios (see [3]) resulting in 10 inputs and 11 classes to distinguish. The training set consisted of 528 tokens, with 462 different tokens used to test the network.

algorithm	performance	#units	#epochs
Nearest Neighbour	56%	—	1
MLP (RPROP)	57%	5	~200
PNN	61%	528	—
RBF	59%	70	~100
RCE	27%	125	3
P–RCE	59%	125	3
DDA–RBF	**65%**	204	4

- Sonar Database: Discriminate between sonar signals bounced off a metal cylinder and those bounced off a roughly cylindrical rock (see [4] for more details). The data has 60 continuous inputs and is separated into two classes. For training and testing 104 samples each were used.

algorithm	performance	#units	#epochs
MLP (RPROP)	90.4%	50	~250
PNN	91.3%	104	—
RBF	90.7%	80	~150
RCE	77.9%	68	3
P–RCE	90.4%	68	3
DDA–RBF	**93.3%**	68	3

- Two Spirals: This well–known problem is often used to demonstrate the generalization capability of a network (see [5]). The required task involves discriminating between two intertwined spirals. For this paper the spirals were changed slightly to make the problem more demanding. The original spirals radius declines linearly and can be correctly classified by RBF networks with one global radius. To demonstrate the ability of the DDA–algorithm to adjust the radii of each RBF individually, a quadratic decline was chosen for the radius of both spirals (see figure 4). The training set consisted of 194 points, and the spirals made three complete revolutions. Figure 4 shows both the results of an RBF Network trained with the DDA technique and the same problem solved with a Multi-Layer Perceptron (2–20–20–1) trained using a modified Error Back Propagation algorithm (Rprop, see [9]). Note that in both cases all training points are classified correctly.

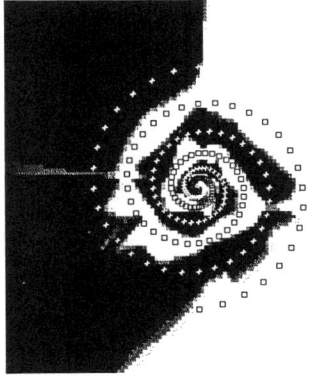 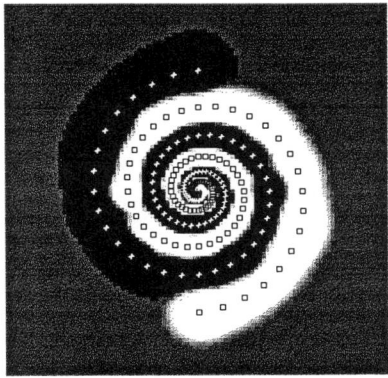

Figure 4: The (quadratic) "two spirals problem" solved by a MLP (left) using Error Back Propagation (after 40000 epochs) and an RBF network (right) trained with the proposed DDA–algorithm (after 4 epochs). Note that all training patterns (indicated by squares vs. crosses) are classified correctly.

In addition to these tasks, the BDG–database was used to compare the DDA algorithm to other approaches. This database was used by Waibel et al (see [11]) to introduce the Time Delay Neural Network (TDNN). Previously it has been shown that RBF networks perform equivalently (when using a similar architecture, [1], [2]) with the DDA technique used for training of the RBF units. The BDG task involves distinguishing the three stop consonants "B", "D" and "G". While 783 training sets were used, 749 data sets were used for testing. Each of these contains 15 frames of melscale coefficients, computed from a 10kHz, 12bit converted signal. The final frame frequency was 100Hz.

algorithm	performance	#epochs
TDNN	98.5%	~50
TDRBF (P–RCE)	85.2%	5
TDRBF (DDA)	**98.3%**	6

4 Conclusions

It has been shown that Radial Basis Function Networks can boost their performance by using the dynamic decay adjustment technique. The algorithm necessary to construct RBF networks based on the RCE method was described and a method to distinguish between conflicting and matching prototypes at the training phase was proposed. An increase in performance was noted, especially in areas of conflict, where standard (P–)RCE did not commit new prototypes.

Four different datasets were used to show the performance of the proposed DDA–algorithm. In three of the cases, RBF networks trained with dynamic decay adjustment outperformed known RBF training methods and MLPs. For the fourth task, the BDG–recognition dataset, the TDRBF was able to reach the same level of performance as a TDNN.

In addition, the new algorithm trains very quickly. Fewer than 6 epochs were sufficient to reach stability for all problems presented.

Acknowledgements

Thanks go to our supervisors Prof. D. Schmid and Mark Holler for their support and the opportunity to work on this project.

References

[1] M. R. Berthold: "A Time Delay Radial Basis Function Network for Phoneme Recognition" in Proc. of the IEEE International Conference on Neural Networks, 7, p.4470–4473, 1994.

[2] M. R. Berthold: "The TDRBF: A Shift Invariant Radial Basis Function Network" in Proc. of the Irish Neural Network Conference, p.7–12, 1994.

[3] D. Deterding: "Speaker Normalization for Automatic Speech Recognition", PhD Thesis, University of Cambridge, 1989.

[4] R. Gorman, T. Sejnowski: "Analysis of Hidden Units in a Layered Network Trained to Classify Sonar Targets" in Neural Networks 1, pp.75.

[5] K. Lang, M. Witbrock: "Learning to Tell Two Spirals Apart", in Proc. of Connectionist Models Summer School, 1988.

[6] J. Moody, C.J. Darken: "Fast Learning in Networks of Locally–Tuned Processing Units" in Neural Computation 1, p.281–294, 1989.

[7] M.J. Hudak: "RCE Classifiers: Theory and Practice" in Cybernetics and Systems 23, p.483–515, 1992.

[8] D.L. Reilly, L.N. Cooper, C. Elbaum: "A Neural Model for Category Learning" in Biol. Cybernet. 45, p.35–41, 1982.

[9] M. Riedmiller, H. Braun: "A Direct Adaptive Method for Faster Backpropagation Learning: The Rprop Algorithm" in Proc. of the IEEE International Conference on Neural Networks, 1, p.586–591, 1993.

[10] D.F. Specht: "Probabilistic Neural Networks" in Neural Networks 3, p.109–118, 1990.

[11] A. Waibel, T. Hanazawa, G. Hinton, K. Shikano, K. Lang: "Phoneme Recognition Using Time–Delay Neural Networks" in IEEE Trans. in Acoustics, Speech and Signal Processing Vol. 37, No. 3, 1989.

[12] D. Wettschereck, T. Dietterich: "Improving the Performance of Radial Basis Function Networks by Learning Center Locations" in Advances in Neural Information Processing Systems 4, p.1133–1140, 1991.

[13] S. Fahlman, M. White: "The Carnegie Mellon University Collection of Neural Net Benchmarks" from ftp.cs.cmu.edu in /afs/cs/project/connect/bench.

SIMPLIFYING NEURAL NETS BY DISCOVERING FLAT MINIMA

Sepp Hochreiter* Jürgen Schmidhuber[†]
Fakultät für Informatik, H2
Technische Universität München
80290 München, Germany

Abstract

We present a new algorithm for finding low complexity networks with high generalization capability. The algorithm searches for large connected regions of so-called "flat" minima of the error function. In the weight-space environment of a "flat" minimum, the error remains approximately constant. Using an MDL-based argument, flat minima can be shown to correspond to low expected overfitting. Although our algorithm requires the computation of second order derivatives, it has backprop's order of complexity. Experiments with feedforward and recurrent nets are described. In an application to stock market prediction, the method outperforms conventional backprop, weight decay, and "optimal brain surgeon".

1 INTRODUCTION

Previous algorithms for finding low complexity networks with high generalization capability are based on significant prior assumptions. They can be broadly classified as follows: *(1) Assumptions about the prior weight distribution.* Hinton and van Camp [3] and Williams [17] assume that pushing the posterior distribution (after learning) close to the prior leads to "good" generalization. Weight decay can be derived e.g. from Gaussian priors. Nowlan and Hinton [10] assume that networks with many similar weights generated by Gaussian mixtures are "better" a priori. MacKay's priors [6] are implicit in additional penalty terms, which embody the

---

*hochreit@informatik.tu-muenchen.de
[†]schmidhu@informatik.tu-muenchen.de

assumptions made. *(2) Prior assumptions about how theoretical results on early stopping and network complexity carry over to practical applications.* Examples are methods based on validation sets (see [8]), Vapnik's "structural risk minimization" [1] [14], and the methods of Holden [5] and Wang et al. [15]. Our approach requires less prior assumptions than most other approaches (see appendix A.1).

Basic idea of flat minima search. Our algorithm finds a large region in weight space with the property that each weight vector from that region has *similar* small error. Such regions are called "flat minima". To get an intuitive feeling for why "flat" minima are interesting, consider this (see also Wolpert [18]): a "sharp" minimum corresponds to weights which have to be specified with high precision. A "flat" minimum corresponds to weights many of which can be given with low precision. In the terminology of the theory of minimum description length (MDL), fewer bits of information are required to pick a "flat" minimum (corresponding to a "simple" or low complexity-network). The MDL principle suggests that low network complexity corresponds to high generalization performance (see e.g. [4, 13]). Unlike Hinton and van Camp's method [3] (see appendix A.3), our approach does not depend on explicitly choosing a "good" prior.

Our algorithm finds "flat" minima by searching for weights that minimize both training error and weight precision. This requires the computation of the Hessian. However, by using Pearlmutter's and Møller's efficient second order method [11, 7], we obtain the same order of complexity as with conventional backprop. *Automatically, the method effectively reduces numbers of units, weigths, and input lines, as well as the sensitivity of outputs with respect to remaining weights and units.* Excellent experimental generalization results will be reported in section 4.

2 TASK / ARCHITECTURE / BOXES

Generalization task. The task is to approximate an unknown relation $\bar{D} \subset X \times Z$ between a set of inputs $X \subset R^N$ and a set of outputs $Z \subset R^K$. $\bar{D}$ is taken to be a function. A relation D is obtained from $\bar{D}$ by adding noise to the outputs. All training information is given by a finite relation $D_0 \subset D$. D_0 is called the *training set*. The pth element of D_0 is denoted by an input/target pair (x_p, d_p).

Architecture. For simplicity, we will focus on a standard feedforward net (but in the experiments, we will use recurrent nets as well). The net has N input units, K output units, W weights, and differentiable activation functions. It maps input vectors $x_p \in R^N$ to output vectors $o_p \in R^K$. The weight from unit j to i is denoted by w_{ij}. The W-dimensional weight vector is denoted by w.

Training error. Mean squared error $E_q(w, D_0) := \frac{1}{|D_0|} \sum_{(x_p, d_p) \in D_0} \| d_p - o_p \|^2$ is used, where $\| \cdot \|$ denotes the Euclidian norm, and $|\cdot|$ denotes the cardinality of a set. To define regions in weight space with the property that each weight vector from that region has "*similar* small error", we introduce the tolerable error E_{tol}, a positive constant. "Small" error is defined as being smaller than E_{tol}. $E_q(w, D_0) > E_{tol}$ implies "underfitting".

Boxes. Each weight w satisfying $E_q(w, D_0) \leq E_{tol}$ defines an "acceptable minimum". **We are interested in large regions of connected acceptable minima.**

Such regions are called flat minima. They are associated with low expected generalization error (see [4]). To simplify the algorithm for finding large connected regions (see below), we do not consider maximal connected regions but focus on so-called *"boxes"* within regions: for each acceptable minimum w, its *box* M_w in weight space is a W-dimensional hypercuboid with center w. For simplicity, each edge of the box is taken to be parallel to one weight axis. Half the length of the box edge in direction of the axis corresponding to weight w_{ij} is denoted by Δw_{ij}, which is the maximal (positive) value such that for all i, j, all positive $\kappa_{ij} \leq \Delta w_{ij}$ can be added to or subtracted from the corresponding component of w simultaneously without violating $E_q(., D_0) \leq E_{tol}$ (Δw_{ij} gives the precision of w_{ij}). M_w's *box volume* is defined by $\Delta w := 2^W \prod_{i,j} \Delta w_{ij}$.

3 THE ALGORITHM

The algorithm is designed to find a w defining a box M_w with maximal box volume Δw. This is equivalent to finding a box M_w with minimal $\tilde{B}(w, D_0) := -\log(\Delta w / 2^W) = \sum_{i,j} -\log \Delta w_{ij}$. Note the relationship to MDL ($\tilde{B}$ is the number of bits required to describe the weights). In appendix A.2, we derive the following algorithm. It minimizes $E(w, D_0) = E_q(w, D_0) + \lambda B(w, D_0)$, where

$$B = \frac{1}{2}\left(-W\log\epsilon + \sum_{i,j}\log\sum_k(\frac{\partial o^k}{\partial w_{ij}})^2 + W\log\sum_k\left(\sum_{i,j}\frac{|\frac{\partial o^k}{\partial w_{ij}}|}{\sqrt{\sum_k(\frac{\partial o^k}{\partial w_{ij}})^2}}\right)^2\right). \quad (1)$$

Here o^k is the activation of the kth output unit, ϵ is a constant, and λ is a positive variable ensuring either $E_q(w, D_0) \leq E_{tol}$, or ensuring an expected decrease of $E_q(., D_0)$ during learning (see [16] for adjusting λ).

$E(w, D_0)$ is minimized by gradient descent. To minimize $B(w, D_0)$, we compute

$$\frac{\partial B(w, D_0)}{\partial w_{uv}} = \sum_{k,i,j} \frac{\partial B(w, D_0)}{\partial(\frac{\partial o^k}{\partial w_{ij}})} \frac{\partial^2 o^k}{\partial w_{ij} \partial w_{uv}} \text{ for all } u, v. \quad (2)$$

It can be shown (see [4]) that by using Pearlmutter's and Møller's efficient second order method [11, 7], the gradient of $B(w, D_0)$ can be computed in $O(W)$ time (see details in [4]). **Therefore, our algorithm has the same order of complexity as standard backprop.**

4 EXPERIMENTAL RESULTS (see [4] for details)

EXPERIMENT 1 – noisy classification. The first experiment is taken from Pearlmutter and Rosenfeld [12]. The task is to decide whether the x-coordinate of a point in 2-dimensional space exceeds zero (class 1) or does not (class 2). Noisy training examples are generated as follows: data points are obtained from a Gaussian with zero mean and stdev 1.0, bounded in the interval $[-3.0, 3.0]$. The data points are misclassified with a probability of 0.05. Final input data is obtained by adding a zero mean Gaussian with stdev 0.15 to the data points. In a test with 2,000,000 data points, it was found that the procedure above leads to 9.27 per cent

	Backprop		New approach			Backprop		New approach	
	MSE	dto	MSE	dto		MSE	dto	MSE	dto
1	0.220	1.35	0.193	0.00	6	0.219	1.24	0.187	0.04
2	0.223	1.16	0.189	0.09	7	0.215	1.14	0.187	0.07
3	0.222	1.37	0.186	0.13	8	0.214	1.10	0.185	0.01
4	0.213	1.18	0.181	0.01	9	0.218	1.21	0.190	0.09
5	0.222	1.24	0.195	0.25	10	0.214	1.21	0.188	0.07

Table 1: *10 comparisons of conventional backprop (BP) and our new method (FMS). The second row (labeled "MSE") shows mean squared error on the test set. The third row ("dto") shows the difference between the fraction (in per cent) of misclassifications and the optimal fraction (9.27). The remaining rows provide the analoguous information for the new approach, which clearly outperforms backprop.*

misclassified data. *No* method will misclassify less than 9.27 per cent, due to the inherent noise in the data. The training set is based on 200 fixed data points. The test set is based on 120,000 data points.

Results. 10 conventional backprop (BP) nets were tested against 10 equally initialized networks based on our new method ("flat minima search", FMS). *After 1,000 epochs, the weights of our nets essentially stopped changing (automatic "early stopping"), while backprop kept changing weights to learn the outliers in the data set and overfit.* In the end, our approach left a single hidden unit h with a maximal weight of 30.0 or -30.0 from the x-axis input. Unlike with backprop, the other hidden units were effectively pruned away (outputs near zero). So was the y-axis input (zero weight to h). It can be shown that this corresponds to an "optimal" net with minimal numbers of units and weights. Table 1 illustrates the superior performance of our approach.

EXPERIMENT 2 – recurrent nets. The method works for continually running fully recurrent nets as well. At every time step, a recurrent net with sigmoid activations in $[0,1]$ sees an input vector from a stream of randomly chosen input vectors from the set $\{(0,0),(0,1),(1,0),(1,1)\}$. The task is to switch on the first output unit whenever an input $(1,0)$ had occurred two time steps ago, and to switch on the second output unit without delay in response to any input $(0,1)$. The task can be solved by a single hidden unit.

Results. With conventional recurrent net algorithms, after training, both hidden units were used to store the input vector. Not so with our new approach. We trained 20 networks. All of them learned perfect solutions. Like with weight decay, most weights to the output decayed to zero. But *unlike* with weight decay, **strong inhibitory** connections (-30.0) switched off one of the hidden units, effectively pruning it away.

EXPERIMENT 3 – stock market prediction. We predict the DAX (German stock market index) based on fundamental (experiments 3.1 and 3.2) and technical (experiment 3.3) indicators. We use strictly layered feedforward nets with sigmoid units active in [-1,1], and the following performance measures:

Confidence: output $o > \alpha \rightarrow$ positive tendency, $o < -\alpha \rightarrow$ negative tendency.
Performance: Sum of confidently, incorrectly predicted DAX changes is subtracted

from sum of confidently, correctly predicted ones. The result is divided by the sum of absolute changes.

EXPERIMENT 3.1: Fundamental inputs: (a) German interest rate ("*Umlaufsrendite*"), (b) industrial production divided by money supply, (c) business sentiments ("*IFO Geschäftsklimaindex*"). 24 training examples, 68 test examples, quarterly prediction, confidence: $\alpha = 0.0/0.6/0.9$, architecture: (3-8-1).

EXPERIMENT 3.2: Fundamental inputs: (a), (b), (c) as in exp. 3.1, (d) dividend rate, (e) foreign orders in manufacturing industry. 228 training examples, 100 test examples, monthly prediction, confidence: $\alpha = 0.0/0.6/0.8$, architecture: (5-8-1).

EXPERIMENT 3.3: Technical inputs: (a) 8 most recent DAX-changes, (b) DAX, (c) change of 24-week relative strength index ("RSI"), (d) difference of "5 week statistic", (e) "MACD" (difference of exponentially weighted 6 week and 24 week DAX). 320 training examples, 100 test examples, weekly predictions, confidence: $\alpha = 0.0/0.2/0.4$, architecture: (12-9-1).

The following methods are tested: (1) Conventional backprop (BP), (2) optimal brain surgeon (OBS [2]), (3) weight decay (WD [16]), (4) flat minima search (FMS).

Results. Our method clearly outperforms the other methods. FMS is up to 63 per cent better than the best competitor (see [4] for details).

APPENDIX – THEORETICAL JUSTIFICATION

A.1. OVERFITTING ERROR

In analogy to [15] and [1], we decompose the generalization error into an "overfitting" error and an "underfitting" error. There is no significant underfitting error (corresponding to Vapnik's empirical risk) if $E_q(w, D_0) \leq E_{tol}$. Some thought is required, however, to define the "overfitting" error. We do this in a novel way. Since we do not know the relation D, we cannot know $p(\alpha \mid D)$, the "optimal" posterior weight distribution we would obtain by training the net on D ($\rightarrow$ "sure thing hypothesis"). But, for theoretical purposes, suppose we *did* know $p(\alpha \mid D)$. Then we could use $p(\alpha \mid D)$ to initialize weights before learning the training set D_0. Using the Kullback-Leibler distance, we measure the information (due to noise) conveyed by D_0, but not by D. In conjunction with the initialization above, this provides the conceptual setting for defining an overfitting error measure. But, the initialization does not really matter, because it does not heavily influence the posterior (see [4]).

The overfitting error is the Kullback-Leibler distance of the posteriors:
$E_o(D, D_0) = \int p(\alpha \mid D_0) \log \left(p(\alpha \mid D_0)/p(\alpha \mid D) \right) d\alpha$. $E_o(D, D_0)$ is the expectation of $\log \left(p(\alpha \mid D_0)/p(\alpha \mid D) \right)$ (the expected difference of the minimal description of α with respect to D and D_0, after learning D_0). Now we measure the **expected overfitting error relative to** M_w (see section 2) by computing the expectation of $\log \left(p(\alpha \mid D_0)/p(\alpha \mid D) \right)$ in the range M_w:

$$E_{ro}(w) = \beta \left(\int_{M_w} p_{M_w}(\alpha \mid D_0) E_q(\alpha, D) d\alpha - \bar{E}_q(D_0, M_w) \right) . \qquad (3)$$

Here $p_{M_w}(\alpha \mid D_0) := p(\alpha \mid D_0)/\int_{M_w} p(\tilde{\alpha} \mid D_0) d\tilde{\alpha}$ is the posterior of D_0 scaled to obtain a distribution within M_w, and $\bar{E}_q(D_0, M_w) := \int_{M_w} p_{M_w}(\alpha \mid D_0) E_q(\alpha, D_0) d\alpha$ is the mean error in M_w with respect to D_0.

Clearly, we would like to pick w such that $E_{ro}(w)$ is minimized. Towards this purpose, we need two additional *prior assumptions*, which are actually implicit in most previous approaches (which make additional stronger assumptions, see section 1):
(1) "Closeness assumption": Every minimum of $E_q(., D_0)$ is "close" to a maximum of $p(\alpha|D)$ (see formal definition in [4]). Intuitively, "closeness" ensures that D_0 can indeed tell us something about D, such that training on D_0 may indeed reduce the error on D. *(2) "Flatness assumption"*: The peaks of $p(\alpha|D)$'s maxima are not sharp. This MDL-like assumption holds if not *all* weights have to be known exactly to model D. It ensures that there are regions with low error on D.

A.2. HOW TO FLATTEN THE NETWORK OUTPUT

To find nets with flat outputs, two conditions will be defined to specify $B(w, D_0)$ (see section 3). The first condition ensures flatness. The second condition enforces "equal flatness" in all weight space directions. In both cases, linear approximations will be made (to be justified in [4]). We are looking for weights (causing tolerable error) that can be perturbed without causing significant output changes. Perturbing the weights w by δw (with components δw_{ij}), we obtain $ED(w, \delta w) := \sum_k (o^k(w + \delta w) - o^k(w))^2$, where $o^k(w)$ expresses o^k's dependence on w (in what follows, however, w often will be suppressed for convenience). Linear approximation (justified in [4]) gives us **"Flatness Condition 1"**:

$$ED(w, \delta w) \approx \sum_k (\sum_{i,j} \frac{\partial o^k}{\partial w_{ij}} \delta w_{ij})^2 \leq \sum_k (\sum_{i,j} |\frac{\partial o^k}{\partial w_{ij}}||\delta w_{ij}|)^2 \leq \epsilon , \qquad (4)$$

where $\epsilon > 0$ defines tolerable output changes within a box and is small enough to allow for linear approximation (it does not appear in $B(w, D_0)$'s gradient, see section 3).

Many M_w satisfy flatness condition 1. To select a particular, very flat M_w, the following **"Flatness Condition 2"** uses up degrees of freedom left by (4):

$$\forall i, j, u, v : (\delta w_{ij})^2 \sum_k (\frac{\partial o^k}{\partial w_{ij}})^2 = (\delta w_{uv})^2 \sum_k (\frac{\partial o^k}{\partial w_{uv}})^2 . \qquad (5)$$

Flatness Condition 2 enforces equal "directed errors" $ED_{ij}(w, \delta w_{ij}) = \sum_k (o^k(w_{ij} + \delta w_{ij}) - o^k(w_{ij}))^2 \approx \sum_k (\frac{\partial o^k}{\partial w_{ij}} \delta w_{ij})^2$, where $o^k(w_{ij})$ has the obvious meaning. *It can be shown (see [4]) that with given box volume, we* **need** *flatness condition 2 to minimize the expected description length of the box center.* Flatness condition 2 influences the algorithm as follows: (1) The algorithm prefers to increase the δw_{ij}'s of weights which currently are not important to generate the target output. (2) The algorithm enforces equal sensitivity of all output units with respect to the weights. Hence, the algorithm tends to group hidden units according to their relevance for groups of output units. Flatness condition 2 is essential: flatness condition 1 by itself corresponds to nothing more but first order derivative reduction (ordinary sensitivity reduction, e.g. [9]). Linear approximation is justified by the choice of ϵ in equation (4).

We first solve equation (5) for $|\delta w_{ij}| = |\delta w_{uv}| \left(\sqrt{\sum_k \left(\frac{\partial o^k}{\partial w_{uv}}\right)^2} / \sqrt{\sum_k \left(\frac{\partial o^k}{\partial w_{ij}}\right)^2} \right)$

(fixing u, v for all i, j). Then we insert $|\delta w_{ij}|$ into equation (4) (replacing the second "$\leq$" in (4) by "="). This gives us an equation for the $|\delta w_{ij}|$ (which depend on w, but this is notationally suppressed):

$$|\delta w_{ij}| = \sqrt{\epsilon} / \left(\sqrt{\sum_k (\frac{\partial o^k}{\partial w_{ij}})^2} \sqrt{\sum_k \left(\sum_{i,j} \frac{|\frac{\partial o^k}{\partial w_{ij}}|}{\sqrt{\sum_k (\frac{\partial o^k}{\partial w_{ij}})^2}} \right)^2} \right). \qquad (6)$$

The $|\delta w_{ij}|$ approximate the Δw_{ij} from section 2. Thus, $\tilde{B}(w, D_0)$ (see section 3) can be approximated by $B(w, D_0) := \sum_{i,j} -\log |\delta w_{ij}|$. This immediately leads to the algorithm given by equation (1).

How can this approximation be justified? **The learning process itself enforces its validity (see justification in [4])**. Initially, the conditions above are valid only in a very small environment of an "initial" acceptable minimum. But during search for new acceptable minima with more associated box volume, the corresponding environments are enlarged, which implies that the absolute values of the entries in the Hessian decrease. It can be shown (see [4]) that the algorithm tends to suppress the following values: (1) unit activations, (2) first order activation derivatives, (3) the sum of all contributions of an arbitary unit activation to the net output. Since weights, inputs, activation functions, and their first and second order derivatives are bounded, it can be shown (see [4]) that the entries in the Hessian decrease where the corresponding $|\delta w_{ij}|$ increase.

A.3. RELATION TO HINTON AND VAN CAMP

Hinton and van Camp [3] minimize the sum of two terms: the first is conventional error plus variance, the other is the distance $\int p(\alpha \mid D_0) \log (p(\alpha \mid D_0)/p(\alpha)) \, d\alpha$ between posterior $p(\alpha \mid D_0)$ and prior $p(\alpha)$. The problem is to choose a "good" prior. In contrast to their approach, our approach does not require a "good" prior given in advance. Furthermore, Hinton and van Camp have to compute variances of weights and units, which (in general) *cannot* be done using linear approximation. Intuitively speaking, their weight variances are related to our Δw_{ij}. Our approach, however, *does* justify linear approximation.

References

[1] I. Guyon, V. Vapnik, B. Boser, L. Bottou, and S. A. Solla. Structural risk minimization for character recognition. In J. E. Moody, S. J. Hanson, and R. P. Lippman, editors, *Advances in Neural Information Processing Systems 4*, pages 471–479. San Mateo, CA: Morgan Kaufmann, 1992.

[2] B. Hassibi and D. G. Stork. Second order derivatives for network pruning: Optimal brain surgeon. In J. D. Cowan S. J. Hanson and C. L. Giles, editors, *Advances in Neural Information Processing Systems 5*, pages 164–171. San Mateo, CA: Morgan Kaufmann, 1993.

[3] G. E. Hinton and D. van Camp. Keeping neural networks simple. In *Proceedings of the International Conference on Artificial Neural Networks, Amsterdam*, pages 11–18. Springer, 1993.

[4] S. Hochreiter and J. Schmidhuber. Flat minima search for discovering simple nets. Technical Report FKI-200-94, Fakultät für Informatik, Technische Universität München, 1994.

[5] S. B. Holden. *On the Theory of Generalization and Self-Structuring in Linearly Weighted Connectionist Networks*. PhD thesis, Cambridge University, Engineering Department, 1994.

[6] D. J. C. MacKay. A practical Bayesian framework for backprop networks. *Neural Computation*, 4:448–472, 1992.

[7] M. F. Møller. Exact calculation of the product of the Hessian matrix of feed-forward network error functions and a vector in O(N) time. Technical Report PB-432, Computer Science Department, Aarhus University, Denmark, 1993.

[8] J. E. Moody and J. Utans. Architecture selection strategies for neural networks: Application to corporate bond rating prediction. In A. N. Refenes, editor, *Neural Networks in the Capital Markets*. John Wiley & Sons, 1994.

[9] A. F. Murray and P. J. Edwards. Synaptic weight noise during MLP learning enhances fault-tolerance, generalisation and learning trajectory. In J. D. Cowan S. J. Hanson and C. L. Giles, editors, *Advances in Neural Information Processing Systems 5*, pages 491–498. San Mateo, CA: Morgan Kaufmann, 1993.

[10] S. J. Nowlan and G. E. Hinton. Simplifying neural networks by soft weight sharing. *Neural Computation*, 4:173–193, 1992.

[11] B. A. Pearlmutter. Fast exact multiplication by the Hessian. *Neural Computation*, 1994.

[12] B. A. Pearlmutter and R. Rosenfeld. Chaitin-Kolmogorov complexity and generalization in neural networks. In R. P. Lippmann, J. E. Moody, and D. S. Touretzky, editors, *Advances in Neural Information Processing Systems 3*, pages 925–931. San Mateo, CA: Morgan Kaufmann, 1991.

[13] J. H. Schmidhuber. Discovering problem solutions with low Kolmogorov complexity and high generalization capability. Technical Report FKI-194-94, Fakultät für Informatik, Technische Universität München, 1994.

[14] V. Vapnik. Principles of risk minimization for learning theory. In J. E. Moody, S. J. Hanson, and R. P. Lippman, editors, *Advances in Neural Information Processing Systems 4*, pages 831–838. San Mateo, CA: Morgan Kaufmann, 1992.

[15] C. Wang, S. S. Venkatesh, and J. S. Judd. Optimal stopping and effective machine complexity in learning. In J. D. Cowan, G. Tesauro, and J. Alspector, editors, *Advances in Neural Information Processing Systems 6*, pages 303–310. Morgan Kaufmann, San Mateo, CA, 1994.

[16] A. S. Weigend, D. E. Rumelhart, and B. A. Huberman. Generalization by weight-elimination with application to forecasting. In R. P. Lippmann, J. E. Moody, and D. S. Touretzky, editors, *Advances in Neural Information Processing Systems 3*, pages 875–882. San Mateo, CA: Morgan Kaufmann, 1991.

[17] P. M. Williams. Bayesian regularisation and pruning using a Laplace prior. Technical report, School of Cognitive and Computing Sciences, University of Sussex, Falmer, Brighton, 1994.

[18] D. H. Wolpert. Bayesian backpropagation over i-o functions rather than weights. In J. D. Cowan, G. Tesauro, and J. Alspector, editors, *Advances in Neural Information Processing Systems 6*, pages 200–207. San Mateo, CA: Morgan Kaufmann, 1994.

Learning with Product Units

Laurens R. Leerink
Australian Gilt Securities LTD
37-49 Pitt Street
NSW 2000, Australia
laurens@sedal.su.oz.au

C. Lee Giles
NEC Research Institute
4 Independence Way
Princeton, NJ 08540, USA
giles@research.nj.nec.com

Bill G. Horne
NEC Research Institute
4 Independence Way
Princeton, NJ 08540, USA
horne@research.nj.nec.com

Marwan A. Jabri
Department of Electrical Engineering
The University of Sydney
NSW 2006, Australia
marwan@sedal.su.oz.au

Abstract

Product units provide a method of automatically learning the higher-order input combinations required for efficient learning in neural networks. However, we show that problems are encountered when using backpropagation to train networks containing these units. This paper examines these problems, and proposes some atypical heuristics to improve learning. Using these heuristics a constructive method is introduced which solves well-researched problems with significantly less neurons than previously reported. Secondly, product units are implemented as candidate units in the Cascade Correlation (Fahlman & Lebiere, 1990) system. This resulted in smaller networks which trained faster than when using sigmoidal or Gaussian units.

1 Introduction

It is well-known that supplementing the inputs to a neural network with higher-order combinations of the inputs both increases the capacity of the network (Cover, 1965) and the the ability to learn geometrically invariant properties (Giles & Maxwell,

1987). However, there is a combinatorial explosion of higher order terms as the number of inputs to the network increases. Yet in order to implement a certain logical function, in most cases only a few of these higher order terms are required (Redding et al., 1993).

The product units (PUs) introduced by (Durbin & Rumelhart, 1989) attempt to make use of this fact. These networks have the advantage that, given an appropriate training algorithm, the units can automatically learn the higher order terms that are required to implement a specific logical function.

In these networks the hidden layer units compute the weighted product of the inputs, that is

$$\prod_{i=1}^{N} x_i^{w_i} \quad \text{instead of} \quad \sum_{i=1}^{N} x_i w_i \qquad (1)$$

as in standard networks. An additional advantage of PUs is the increased information capacity of these units compared to standard summation networks. It is approximately $3N$ (Durbin & Rumelhart, 1989), compared to $2N$ for a single threshold logic function (Cover, 1965), where N is the number of inputs to the unit.

The larger capacity means that the same functions can be implemented by networks containing less units. This is important for certain applications such as speech recognition where the data bandwidth is high or if realtime implementations are desired.

When PUs are used to process Boolean inputs, best performance is obtained (Durbin & Rumelhart, 1989) by using inputs of $\{+1, -1\}$. If the imaginary component is ignored, with these inputs, the activation function is equivalent to a cosine summation function with $\{-1, +1\}$ inputs mapped $\{1, 0\}$ (Durbin & Rumelhart, 1989). In the remainder of this paper the terms *product unit (PU)* and *cos(ine) unit* will be used interchangeably as all the problems examined have Boolean inputs.

2 Learning with Product Units

As the basic mechanism of a PU is multiplicative instead of additive, one would expect that standard neural network training methods and procedures cannot be directly applied when training these networks. This is indeed the case. If a neural network simulation environment is available the basic functionality of a PU can be obtained by simply adding the *cos* function $cos(\pi * input)$ to the existing list of transfer functions. This assumes that Boolean mappings are being implemented and the appropriate $\{-1, +1\} \rightarrow \{1, 0\}$ mapping has been performed on the input vectors. However, if we then attempt to train a network on on the parity-6 problem shown in (Durbin & Rumelhart, 1989), it is found that the standard backpropagation (BP) algorithm simply does not work. We have found two main reasons for this.

The first is weight initialization. A typical first step in the backpropagation procedure is to initialize all weights to small random values. The main reason for this is to use the dynamic range of the sigmoid function and it's derivative. However, the dynamic range of a PU is unlimited. Initializing the weights to small random values results in an input to the unit where the derivative is small. So apart from choosing small weights centered around $n\pi$ with $n = \pm 1, \pm 2, \ldots$ this is the worst possible choice. In our simulations weights were initialized randomly in the range $[-2, 2]$. In fact, learning seems insensitive to the size of the weights, as long as they are large enough.

The second problem is local minima. Previous reports have mentioned this problem, (Lapedes & Farber, 1987) commented that "using *sin*'s often leads to numerical problems, and nonglobal minima, whereas sigmoids seemed to avoid such problems". This comment summarizes our experience of training with PUs. For small problems (less than 3 inputs) backpropagation provides satisfactory training. However, when the number of inputs are increased beyond this number, even with the weight initialization in the correct range, training usually ends up in a local minima.

3 Training Algorithms

With these aspects in mind, the following training algorithms were evaluated: online and batch versions of Backpropagation (BP), Simulated Annealing (SA), a Random Search Algorithm (RSA) and combinations of these algorithms.

BP was used as a benchmark and for use in combination with the other algorithms. The Delta-Bar-Delta learning rate adaptation rule (Jacobs, 1988) was used along with the batch version of BP to accelerate convergence, with the parameters were set to $\theta = 0.35, \kappa = 0.05$ and $\phi = 0.90$. RSA is a global search method (i.e. the whole weight space is explored during training). Weights are randomly chosen from a predefined distribution, and replaced if this results in an error decrease. SA (Kirkpatrick et al., 1983) is a standard optimization method. The operation of SA is similar to RSA, with the difference that with a decreasing probability solutions are accepted which increase the training error. The combination of algorithms were chosen (BP & SA, BP & RSA) to combine the benefits of global and local search. Used in this manner, BP is used to find the local minima. If the training error at the minima is sufficiently low, training is terminated. Otherwise, the global method initializes the weights to another position in weight space from which local training can continue.

The BP-RSA combination requires further explanation. Several BP-(R)SA combinations were evaluated, but best performance was obtained using a fixed number of iterations of BP (in this case 120) along with one initial iteration of RSA. In this manner BP is used to move to the local minima, and if the training error is still above the desired level the RSA algorithm generates a new set of random weights from which BP can start again.

The algorithms were evaluated on two problems, the parity problem and learning all logical functions of 2 and 3 inputs. The infamous parity problem is (for the product unit at least) an appropriate task. As illustrated by (Durbin & Rumelhart, 1989), this problem can be solved by one product unit. The question is whether the training algorithms can find a solution. The target values are $\{-1, +1\}$, and the output is taken to be correct if it has the correct sign. The simulation results are shown in Table 1. It should be noted that one epoch of both SA and RSA involves relaxing the network across the training set for every weight, so in computational terms their $\overline{n}_{epoch}$ values should be multiplied by a factor of $(N+1)$.

Parity N	Online BP		Batch BP		SA		RSA	
	n_{conv}	$\overline{n}_{epoch}$	n_{conv}	$\overline{n}_{epoch}$	n_{conv}	$\overline{n}_{epoch}$	n_{conv}	$\overline{n}_{epoch}$
6	10	30.4	7	34	10	12.6	10	15.2
8	8	101.3	2	700	10	52.8	10	45.4
10	6	203.3	0	-	10	99.9	10	74.1

Table 1: The parity N problem: The table shows n_{conv} the number of runs out of 10 that have converged and $\overline{n}_{epoch}$, the average number of training epochs required when training converged.

For the parity problem it is clear that local learning alone does not provide good convergence. For this problem, global search algorithms have the following advantages: (1) The search space is bounded (all weights are restricted to $[-2, +2]$) (2) The dimension of search space is low (maximum of 11 weights for the problems examined). (3) The fraction of the weight space which satisfies the parity problem relative to the total bounded weight space is high.

In a second set of simulations, one product unit was trained to calculate all $2^{(2^N)}$ logical functions of the N input variables. Unfortunately, this is only practical for $N \in \{2,3\}$. For $N = 2$ there are only 16 functions, and a product unit has no problem learning all these functions rapidly with all four training algorithms. In comparison a single summation unit can learn 14 (not the XOR & XNOR functions). For $N=3$, a product unit is able to implement 208 of the 256 functions, while a single summation unit could only implement 104. The simulation results are displayed in Table 2.

Online BP		Batch BP		SA		RSA		BP-RSA	
$\overline{n}_{logic}$	$\overline{n}_{epoch}$	$\overline{n}_{logic}$	$\overline{n}_{epoch}$	$\overline{n}_{logic}$	$\overline{n}_{epoch}$	$\overline{n}_{logic}$	$\overline{n}_{epoch}$	$\overline{n}_{logic}$	$\overline{n}_{epoch}$
147.3	42.6	189.2	20.5	196.1	43.8	167.4	60.2	208	44.3

Table 2: Learning all logical functions of 3 inputs: The rows display $\overline{n}_{logic}$, the average number of logical functions implemented by a product unit and $\overline{n}_{epoch}$, the number of epochs required for convergence. Ten simulations were performed for each of the 256 logical functions, each for a maximum of 1,000 iterations.

4 Constructive Learning with Product Units

Selecting the optimal network architecture for a specific application is a nontrivial and time-consuming task, and several algorithms have been proposed to automate this process. These include pruning methods and growing algorithms. In this section a simple method is proposed for adding PUs to the hidden layer of a three layer network. The output layer contains a single sigmoidal unit.

Several constructive algorithms proceed by freezing a subset of the weights and limiting training to the newly added units. As mentioned earlier, for PUs a global

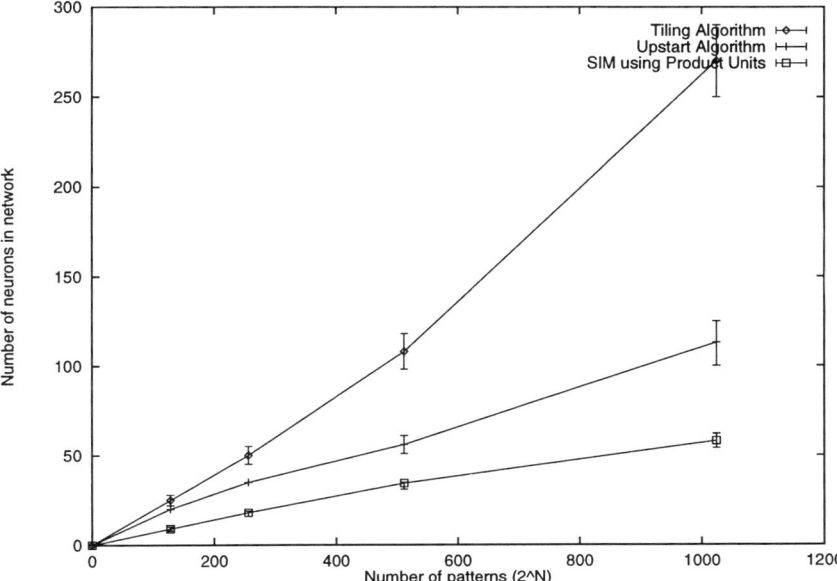

Figure 1: The number of units required for learning the random mapping problems by the 'Tiling', 'Upstart' and SIM algorithms.

search is required to solve the local-minima problems. Freezing a subset of the weights restricts the new solution to an affine subset of the existing weight space, often resulting in non-minimal networks (Ash, 1989). For this reason a simple incremental method (SIM) was implemented which retains the global search for all weights during the whole training process. The method used in our simulations is as follows:

- Train a network using the BP-RSA combination on a network with a specified minimum number of hidden PUs.
- If there is no convergence within a specified number of epochs, add a PU to the network. Reinitialize weights and continue training with the BP-RSA combination.
- Repeat process until a solution is found or the network has grown a predetermined maximum size.

The method of (Ash, 1989) was also evaluated, where neurons with small weights were added to a network according to certain criteria. The SIM performed better, possibly because of the global search performed by the RSA step.

The 'Upstart' (Frean, 1990) and 'Tiling' (Mézard & Nadal, 1989) constructive algorithms were chosen as benchmarks. A constructive PU network was trained on two problems described in these papers, namely the parity problem and the random mapping problem. In (Frean, 1990) it was reported that the Upstart algorithm required N units for all parity N problems, and 1,000 training epochs were sufficient for all values of N except $N = 10$, which required 10,000. As seen earlier, one PU is able to perform any parity function, and SIM required an an average of 74.1 iterations for $N = 6, 8, 10$.

The random mapping problem is defined by assigning each of the 2^N patterns its target $\{-1, +1\}$ with 50% probability. This is a difficult problem, due to the absence of correlations and structure in the input. As in (Frean, 1990; Mézard & Nadal, 1989) the average of 25 runs were performed, each on a different training set. The number of units required by SIM is plotted in Figure 1. The values for the Tiling and Upstart algorithms are approximate and were obtained through inspection from a similar graph in (Frean, 1990).

5 Using Cosine Candidate Units in Cascade Correlation

Initially we wanted to compare the performance of SIM with the well-known 'cascade-correlation' (CC) algorithm of (Fahlman & Lebiere, 1990). However, the network architectures differ and a direct comparison between the number of units in the respective architectures does not reflect the efficiency of the algorithms. Instead, it was decided to integrate PUs into the CC system as candidate units.

For these simulations a public domain version of CC was used (White, 1993) which supports four different candidate types; the asymmetric sigmoid, symmetric sigmoid, variable sigmoid and gaussian units. Facilities exist for either constructing homogeneous networks by selecting one unit type, or training with a pool of different units allowing the construction of hybrid networks. It was thus relatively simple to add PU candidate units to the system. Table 3 displays the results when CC was trained on the random logic problem using three types of homogeneous candidate units.

N	CC Sigmoid		CC Gauss		CC PU	
	$\overline{n}_{units}$	$\overline{n}_{epochs}$	$\overline{n}_{units}$	$\overline{n}_{epochs}$	$\overline{n}_{units}$	$\overline{n}_{epochs}$
7	6.6	924.5	6.7	642.6	5.7	493.8
8	12.1	1630.9	11.5	1128.2	9.9	833.8
9	20.5	2738.3	18.4	1831.1	16.4	1481.8
10	32.9	4410.9	30.2	2967.6	26.6	2590.8

Table 3: Learning random logic functions of N inputs: The table shows $\overline{n}_{units}$, the average number of units required and $\overline{n}_{epochs}$, the average number of training epochs required for convergence of CC using sigmoidal, Gaussian and PU candidate units. Figures are based on 25 simulations.

In a separate experiment the performance of hybrid networks were re-evaluated on the same random logic problem. To enable a fair competition between candidate units of different types, the simulations were run with 40 candidate units, 8 of each type. The simulations were evaluated on 25 trails for each of the random mapping problems (7,8,9 and 10 inputs, a total of 1920 input vectors). In total 1460 hidden units were allocated, and in *all cases* PU candidate units were chosen above units of the 4 other types during the competitive stage. During this comparison all parameters were set to default values, i.e. the weights of the PU candidate units were random numbers initialized in the range of $[-1, +1]$. As discussed earlier, this puts the PUs at a slight disadvantage as their optimum range is $[-2, +2]$.

6 Discussion

The BP-RSA combination is in effect equivalent to the 'local optimization with random restarts' process discussed by (Karmarkar & Karp, 1982), where the local optimization is this case is performed by the BP algorithm. They reported that for certain problems where the error surface was 'exceedingly mountainous', multiple random-start local optimization outperformed more sophisticated methods. We hypothesize that adding PUs to a network makes the error surface sufficiently mountainous so that a global search is required.

As expected, the higher separating capacity of the PU enables the construction of networks with less neurons than those produced by the Tiling and Upstart algorithms. The fact that SIM works this well is mainly a result of the error surface; the surface is so irregular that even training a network of fixed architecture is best done by reinitializing the weights if convergence does not occur within certain bounds. This again is in accordance with the results of (Karmarkar & Karp, 1982) discussed above.

When used in CC we hypothesize that there are three main reasons for the choice of PUs above any of the other types during the competitive learning phase. Firstly, the higher capacity (in a information capacity sense) of the PUs allows a better correlation with the error signal. Secondly, having N competing candidate units is equivalent to selecting the best of N random restarts, and performs the required global search. Thirdly, although the error surface of networks with PUs contains more local minima than when using standard transfer functions, the surface is locally smooth. This allows effective use of higher-order error derivatives, resulting in fast convergence by the quickprop algorithm.

In (Dawson & Schopflocher, 1992) it was shown that networks with Gaussian units train faster and require less units than networks with standard sigmoidal units. This is supported by our results shown in Table 3. However, for the problem examined, PUs outperform Gaussian units by approximately the same margin as Gaussian units outperform sigmoidal units. It should also be noted that these problems where not chosen for their suitability for PUs. In fact, if the problems are symmetric/regular the difference in performance is expected to increase.

7 Conclusion

Of the learning algorithms examined BP provides the fastest training, but is prone to nonglobal minima. On the other hand, global search methods are impractical for larger networks. For the problems examined, a combination of local and global search methods were found to perform best. Given a network containing PUs, there are some atypical heuristics that can be used: (a) correct weight initialization (b) reinitialization of the weights if convergence is not rapidly reached. In addition, the representational power of PUs have enabled us to solve standard problems using significantly smaller networks than previously reported, using a very simple constructive method. When implemented in the CC architecture, for the problems examined PUs resulted in smaller networks which trained faster than other units. When included in a pool of competing candidate units, simulations showed that in all cases PU candidate units were preferred over candidate units of the other four types.

References

Ash, T. (1989). Dynamic node creation in backpropagation networks. *Connection Science*, *1*(4), 365–375.

Cover, T. (1965). Geometrical and statistical properties of systems of linear inequalities with applications in pattern recognition. *IEEE Transactions on Electronic Computers*, *14*, 326–334.

Dawson, M. & Schopflocher, D. (1992). Modifying the generalized delta rule to train networks of nonmonotonic processors for pattern classification. *Connection Science*, *4*, 19–31.

Durbin, R. & Rumelhart, D. (1989). Product units: A computationally powerful and biologically plausible extension to backpropagation networks. *Neural Computation*, *1*, 133–142.

Fahlman, S. & Lebiere, C. (1990). The cascade-correlation learning architecture. In Touretzky, D. (Ed.), *Advances in Neural Information Processing Systems*, volume 2, (pp. 524–532)., San Mateo. (Denver 1989), Morgan Kaufmann.

Frean, M. (1990). The upstart algorithm: A method for constructing and training feedforward neural networks. *Neural Computation*, *2*, 198–209.

Giles, C. & Maxwell, T. (1987). Learning, invariance, and generalization in high-order neural networks. *Applied Optics*, *26*(23), 4972–4978.

Jacobs, R. (1988). Increased rates of convergence through learning rate adaptation. *Neural Networks*, *1*, 295–307.

Karmarkar, N. & Karp, R. (1982). The differencing method of set partitioning. Technical Report UCB/CSD 82/113, Computer Science Division, University of California, Berkeley, California.

Kirkpatrick, S., Jr., C. G., , & Vecchi, M. (1983). Optimization by simulated annealing. *Science*, *220*. Reprinted in (?).

Lapedes, A. & Farber, R. (1987). Nonlinear signal processing using neural networks: Prediction and system modelling. Technical Report LA–UR–87–2662, Los Alamos National Laboratory, Los Alamos, NM.

Mézard, M. & Nadal, J.-P. (1989). Learning in feedforward layered networks: The tiling algorithm. *Journal of Physics A*, *22*, 2191–2204.

Redding, N., Kowalczyk, A., & Downs, T. (1993). A constructive higher order network algorithm that is polynomial-time. *Neural Networks*, *6*, 997.

White, M. (1993). A public domain C implementation of the Cascade Correlation algorithm. Department of Computer Science, Carnegie Mellon University, Pittsburgh, PA.

Deterministic Annealing Variant of the EM Algorithm

Naonori Ueda   **Ryohei Nakano**
ueda@cslab.kecl.ntt.jp   nakano@cslab.kecl.ntt.jp
NTT Communication Science Laboratories
Hikaridai, Seika-cho, Soraku-gun,
Kyoto 619-02 Japan

Abstract

We present a deterministic annealing variant of the EM algorithm for maximum likelihood parameter estimation problems. In our approach, the EM process is reformulated as the problem of minimizing the thermodynamic free energy by using the *principle of maximum entropy* and *statistical mechanics analogy*. Unlike simulated annealing approaches, this minimization is *deterministically* performed. Moreover, the derived algorithm, unlike the conventional EM algorithm, can obtain better estimates free of the initial parameter values.

1 INTRODUCTION

The Expectation-Maximization (EM) algorithm (Dempster, Laird & Rubin, 1977) is an iterative statistical technique for computing maximum likelihood parameter estimates from incomplete data. It has generally been employed to a wide variety of parameter estimation problems. Recently, the EM algorithm has also been successfully employed as the learning algorithm of the hierarchical mixture of experts (Jordan & Jacobs, 1993). In addition, it has been found to have some relationship to the learning of the Boltzmann machines (Byrne, 1992).

This algorithm has attractive features such as reliable global convergence, low cost per iteration, economy of storage, and ease of programming, but it is not free from problems in practice. The serious practical problem associated with the algorithm is the local maxima problem. This problem makes the performance dependent on the initial parameter value. Indeed, the EM algorithm should be performed from as wide a choice of starting values as possible according to some ad hoc criterion.

To overcome this problem, we adopt the principle of statistical mechanics. Namely, by using the principle of maximum entropy, the thermodynamic free energy is defined as an effective cost function that depends on the *temperature*. The maximization of *log-likelihood* is done by minimizing the cost function. Unlike simulated annealing (Geman & Geman, 1984) where stochastic search is performed on the given energy surface, this cost function is *deterministically* optimized at each temperature.

Such deterministic annealing (DA) approach has been successfully adopted for vector quantization or clustering problems (Rose et al., 1992; Buhmann et al., 1993; Wong, 1993). Recently, Yuile et al.(Yuile, Stolorz, & Utans, 1994) have shown that the EM algorithm can be used in conjunction with the DA. In our previous paper, independent of Yuile's work, we presented a new EM algorithm with DA for mixture density estimation problems (Ueda & Nakano, 1994). The aim of this paper is to generalize our earlier work and to derive a DA variant of the general EM algorithm. Since the EM algorithm can be used not only for the mixture estimation problems but also for other parameter estimation problems, this generalization is expected to be of value in practice.

2 GENERAL THEORY OF THE EM ALGORITHM

Suppose that a measure space $\mathcal{Y}$ of "unobservable data" exists corresponding to a measure space $\mathcal{X}$ of "observable data". An observable data sample $\boldsymbol{x}(\in \mathcal{X})$ with density $p(\boldsymbol{x}; \boldsymbol{\Theta})$ is called incomplete and $(\boldsymbol{x}, \boldsymbol{y})$ with joint density $p(\boldsymbol{x}, \boldsymbol{y}; \boldsymbol{\Theta})$ is called complete, where $\boldsymbol{y}$ is an unobservable data sample [1] corresponding to $\boldsymbol{x}$. Note that $\boldsymbol{x} \in \mathcal{R}^n$ and $\boldsymbol{y} \in \mathcal{R}^m$. $\boldsymbol{\Theta}$ is parameter of the density distribution to be estimated.

Given incomplete data samples $\boldsymbol{X} = \{\boldsymbol{x}_k | k = 1, \cdots, N\}$, the goal of the EM algorithm is to compute the maximum-likelihood estimate of $\boldsymbol{\Theta}$ that maximizes the following log-likelihood function:

$$L(\boldsymbol{\Theta}; \boldsymbol{X}) = \sum_{k=1}^{N} \log p(\boldsymbol{x}_k; \boldsymbol{\Theta}), \quad (1)$$

by using the following complete data log-likelihood function:

$$L_c(\boldsymbol{\Theta}; \boldsymbol{X}) = \sum_{k=1}^{N} \log p(\boldsymbol{x}_k, \boldsymbol{y}_k; \boldsymbol{\Theta}). \quad (2)$$

In the EM algorithm, the parameter $\boldsymbol{\Theta}$ is iteratively estimated. Suppose that $\boldsymbol{\Theta}^{(t)}$ denotes the current estimate of $\boldsymbol{\Theta}$ after the tth iteration of the algorithm. Then $\boldsymbol{\Theta}^{(t+1)}$ at the next iteration is determined by the following two steps:

---

[1] In such unsupervised learning as mixture problems, y reduces to an integer value ($y \in \{1, 2, \ldots, C\}$, where C is the number of components), indicating the component from which a data sample x originates.

E-step: Compute the Q-function defined by the conditional expectation of the complete data log-likelihood given $\boldsymbol{X}$ and $\boldsymbol{\Theta}^{(t)}$:

$$Q(\boldsymbol{\Theta};\boldsymbol{\Theta}^{(t)}) \stackrel{\text{def}}{=} E\{L_c(\boldsymbol{\Theta};\boldsymbol{X})|\boldsymbol{X},\boldsymbol{\Theta}^{(t)}\}. \tag{3}$$

M-step: Set $\boldsymbol{\Theta}^{(t+1)}$ equal to $\boldsymbol{\Theta}$ which maximizes $Q(\boldsymbol{\Theta},\boldsymbol{\Theta}^{(t)})$.

It has theoretically been shown that an iterative procedure for maximizing Q over $\boldsymbol{\Theta}$ will cause the likelihood L to monotonically increase, e.g., $L(\boldsymbol{\Theta}^{(t+1)}) \geq L(\boldsymbol{\Theta}^{(t)})$. Eventually, $L(\boldsymbol{\Theta}^{(t)})$ converges to a local maximum. The EM algorithm is especially useful when the maximization of the Q-function can be more easily performed than that of L.

By substituting Eq. 2 into Eq. 3, we have

$$\begin{aligned}Q(\boldsymbol{\Theta};\boldsymbol{\Theta}^{(t)}) &= \sum_{k=1}^{N}\int\cdots\int\{\log p(\boldsymbol{x}_k,\boldsymbol{y}_k;\boldsymbol{\Theta})\}\prod_{j=1}^{N}p(\boldsymbol{y}_j|\boldsymbol{x}_j;\boldsymbol{\Theta}^{(t)})d\boldsymbol{y}_1\cdots d\boldsymbol{y}_N \\ &= \sum_{k=1}^{N}\int\{\log p(\boldsymbol{x}_k,\boldsymbol{y}_k;\boldsymbol{\Theta})\}p(\boldsymbol{y}_k|\boldsymbol{x}_k;\boldsymbol{\Theta}^{(t)})d\boldsymbol{y}_k.\end{aligned} \tag{4}$$

$\boldsymbol{\Theta}$ that maximizes $Q(\boldsymbol{\Theta};\boldsymbol{\Theta}^{(t)})$ should satisfy $\partial Q/\partial \boldsymbol{\Theta} = 0$, or equivalently,

$$\sum_{k=1}^{N}\int\{\frac{\partial}{\partial\boldsymbol{\Theta}}\log p(\boldsymbol{x}_k,\boldsymbol{y}_k;\boldsymbol{\Theta})\}p(\boldsymbol{y}_k|\boldsymbol{x}_k;\boldsymbol{\Theta}^{(t)})d\boldsymbol{y}_k = 0. \tag{5}$$

Here, $p(\boldsymbol{y}_k|\boldsymbol{x}_k,\boldsymbol{\Theta}^{(t)})$ denotes the posterior and can be computed by the following Bayes rule:

$$p(\boldsymbol{y}_k|\boldsymbol{x}_k;\boldsymbol{\Theta}^{(t)}) = \frac{p(\boldsymbol{x}_k,\boldsymbol{y}_k;\boldsymbol{\Theta}^{(t)})}{\int p(\boldsymbol{x}_k,\boldsymbol{y}_k;\boldsymbol{\Theta}^{(t)})d\boldsymbol{y}_k}. \tag{6}$$

It can be interpreted that the missing information is estimated by using the posterior. However, because the reliability of the posterior highly depends on the parameter $\boldsymbol{\Theta}^{(t)}$, the performance of the EM algorithm is sensitive to an initial parameter value $\boldsymbol{\Theta}^{(0)}$. This has often caused the algorithm to become trapped by some local maxima. In the next section, we will derive a new variant of the EM algorithm as an attempt at global maximization of the Q-function in the EM process.

3 DETERMINISTIC ANNEALING APPROACH

3.1 DERIVATION OF PARAMETERIZED POSTERIOR

Instead of the posterior given in Eq. 6, we introduce another posterior $f(\boldsymbol{y}_k|\boldsymbol{x}_k)$. The function form of f will be specified later. Using $f(\boldsymbol{y}_k|\boldsymbol{x}_k)$, we consider a new function instead of Q, say E, defined as:

$$E \stackrel{\text{def}}{=} \sum_{k=1}^{N}\int\{-\log p(\boldsymbol{x}_k,\boldsymbol{y}_k;\boldsymbol{\Theta})\}f(\boldsymbol{y}_k|\boldsymbol{x}_k)d\boldsymbol{y}_k. \tag{7}$$

(Note: E is always nonnegative.) One can easily see that $(-E)$ is also the conditional expectation of the complete data log-likelihood but it differs from Q in that the expectation is taken with respect to $f(\boldsymbol{y}_k|\boldsymbol{x}_k)$ instead of the posterior given by Eq. 6. In other words, if $f(\boldsymbol{y}_k|\boldsymbol{x}_k) = p(\boldsymbol{y}_k|\boldsymbol{x}_k;\boldsymbol{\Theta}^{(t)})$, then $E \equiv -Q$.

Since we do not have *a priori* knowledge about $f(\boldsymbol{y}_k|\boldsymbol{x}_k)$, we apply the *principle of maximum entropy* to specify it. That is, by maximizing the entropy given by:

$$H = -\sum_{k=1}^{N} \int \{\log f(\boldsymbol{y}_k|\boldsymbol{x}_k)\} f(\boldsymbol{y}_k|\boldsymbol{x}_k) d\boldsymbol{y}_k, \tag{8}$$

with respect to f, under the constraints of Eq. 7 and $\int f d\boldsymbol{y}_k = 1$, we can obtain the following Gibbs distribution:

$$f(\boldsymbol{y}_k|\boldsymbol{x}_k) = \frac{1}{Z_{\boldsymbol{x}_k}} \exp\{-\beta(-\log p(\boldsymbol{x}_k,\boldsymbol{y}_k;\boldsymbol{\Theta}))\}, \tag{9}$$

where $Z_{\boldsymbol{x}_k} = \int \exp\{-\beta(-\log p(\boldsymbol{x}_k,\boldsymbol{y}_k;\boldsymbol{\Theta}))\} d\boldsymbol{y}_k$, and is called the *partition function*. The parameter β is the Lagrange multiplier determined by the value E. From an analogy of the *annealing*, $1/\beta$ corresponds to the *"temperature"*.

By simplifying Eq. 9, we obtain a new posterior parameterized by β,

$$f(\boldsymbol{y}_k|\boldsymbol{x}_k) = \frac{p(\boldsymbol{x}_k,\boldsymbol{y}_k;\boldsymbol{\Theta})^{\beta}}{\int p(\boldsymbol{x}_k,\boldsymbol{y}_k;\boldsymbol{\Theta})^{\beta} d\boldsymbol{y}_k}. \tag{10}$$

Clearly, when $\beta = 1$, $f(\boldsymbol{y}_k|\boldsymbol{x}_k)$ reduces to the original posterior given in Eq. 6. The effect of β will be explained later.

Since $\boldsymbol{x}_1,\ldots,\boldsymbol{x}_N$ are identically and independently distributed observations, the partition function $Z_\beta(\boldsymbol{\Theta})$ for $\boldsymbol{X}$ becomes $\prod_k Z_{\boldsymbol{x}_k}$. Therefore,

$$Z_\beta(\boldsymbol{\Theta}) = \prod_{k=1}^{N} \int p(\boldsymbol{y}_k,\boldsymbol{y}_k;\boldsymbol{\Theta})^{\beta} d\boldsymbol{y}_k. \tag{11}$$

Once the partition function is obtained explicitly, using statistical mechanics analogy, we can define the *free energy* as an effective cost function that depends on the temperature:

$$F_\beta(\boldsymbol{\Theta}) \stackrel{\text{def}}{=} -\frac{1}{\beta} \log Z_\beta(\boldsymbol{\Theta})$$

$$= -\frac{1}{\beta} \sum_{k=1}^{N} \log \int p(\boldsymbol{x}_k,\boldsymbol{y}_k;\boldsymbol{\Theta})^{\beta} d\boldsymbol{y}_k. \tag{12}$$

At equilibrium, it is well known that a thermodynamic system settles into a configuration that minimizes its free energy. Hence, $\boldsymbol{\Theta}$ should satisfy $\partial F_\beta(\boldsymbol{\Theta})/\partial \boldsymbol{\Theta} = 0$. It follows that

$$\sum_{k=1}^{N} \int \{\frac{\partial}{\partial \boldsymbol{\Theta}} \log p(\boldsymbol{x}_k,\boldsymbol{y}_k;\boldsymbol{\Theta})\} f(\boldsymbol{y}_k|\boldsymbol{x}_k) d\boldsymbol{y}_k = 0. \tag{13}$$

Interestingly, we have arrived at the same equation as the result of the maximization of the Q-function, except that the posterior $p(\boldsymbol{y}_k|\boldsymbol{x}_k;\boldsymbol{\Theta}^{(t)})$ in Eq. 5 is replaced by $f(\boldsymbol{y}_k|\boldsymbol{x}_k)$.

3.2 ANNEALING VARIANT OF THE EM ALGORITHM

Let $Q_\beta(\Theta;\Theta^{(t)})$ be the expectation of the complete data log-likelihood by the parameterized posterior $f(y_k|x_k)$. Then, the following deterministic annealing variant of the EM algorithm can be naturally derived to maximize $-F_\beta(\Theta)$.

[Annealing EM (AEM) algorithm]
1. Set $\beta \leftarrow \beta_{min} (0 < \beta_{min} \ll 1)$.
2. *Arbitrarily* choose an initial estimate $\Theta^{(0)}$. Set $t \leftarrow 0$.
3. Iterate the following two steps until convergence[2]:
   E-step: Compute

$$Q_\beta(\Theta;\Theta^{(t)}) = \sum_{k=1}^{N} \int \{\log p(x_k,y_k;\Theta)\} \frac{p(x_k,y_k;\Theta^{(t)})^\beta}{\int p(x_k,y_k;\Theta^{(t)})^\beta dy_k} dy_k. \qquad (14)$$

   M-step: Set $\Theta^{(t+1)}$ equal to Θ which maximizes $Q_\beta(\Theta;\Theta^{(t)})$.
4. Increase β.
5. If $\beta < \beta_{max}$, set $t \leftarrow t+1$, and repeat from step 3; otherwise stop.

One can see that in the proposed algorithm, an outer loop is added to the original EM algorithm for the annealing process. An important distinction to keep in mind is that unlike simulated annealing, the optimization in step 3 is *deterministically* performed at each β. Now let's consider the effect of the posterior parameterization of Eq. 10. The annealing process begins at small β (high temperature). Clearly, at this time, since $f(y_k|x_k)$ becomes uniform, $-F_\beta(\Theta)$ has only one global maximum. Hence, the maximum can be easily found. Then by gradually increasing β, the influence of each x_k is gradually localized. At $\beta > 0$, function Q_β will have several local maxima. However, at each step, it can be assumed that the new global maximum is close to the previous one. Hence, by this assumption, the algorithm can track the global maximum at each β while increasing β. Clearly, when $\beta = 1$ the parameterized posterior coincides with the original one. Moreover, noting that $-F_1(\Theta) \equiv L(\Theta)$, β_{max} ought be one.

4 Demonstration

To visualize how the proposed algorithm works, we consider a simple one-dimensional, two-component normal mixture problem. The mixture is given by $p(x;m_1,m_2) = 0.3\frac{1}{\sqrt{2\pi}}\exp\{-\frac{1}{2}(x-m_1)^2\} + 0.7\frac{1}{\sqrt{2\pi}}\exp\{-\frac{1}{2}(x-m_2)^2\}$. In this case, $\Theta = (m_1,m_2)$, $y_k \in \{1,2\}$, and therefore, the joint density $p(x,1;m_1,m_2) = 0.3\frac{1}{\sqrt{2\pi}}\exp\{-\frac{1}{2}(x-m_1)^2\}$, while $p(x,2;m_1,m_2) = 0.7\frac{1}{\sqrt{2\pi}}\exp\{-\frac{1}{2}(x-m_2)^2\}$.

One hundred samples in total were generated from this mixture with $m_1 = -2$ and $m_2 = 2$. Figure 1 shows contour plots of the $-F_\beta(m_1,m_2)/N$ surface. It is interesting to see how $F_\beta(m_1,m_2)$ varies with β. One can see that a finer and truer structure emerges by increasing β. Note that as explained before, when $\beta = 1$,

---

[2] When the sequence converges to a saddle point (e.g., when the Hessian matrix of $-F_\beta(\Theta)$ has at least one positive eigen value), a local line search in the direction of the eigen vector corresponding to the largest eigen value should be performed to escape the solution from the saddle point.

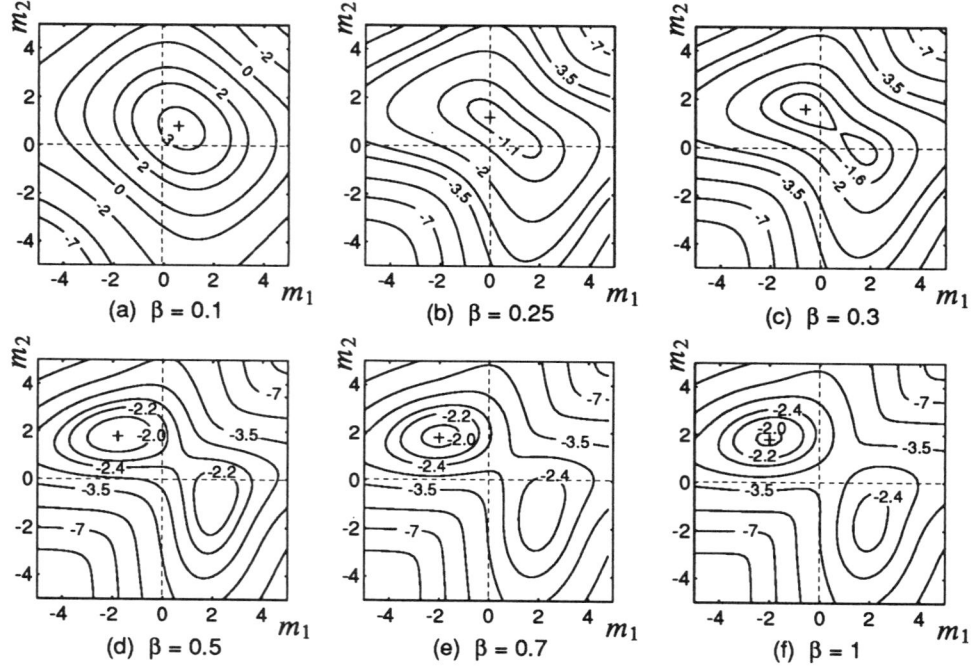

Figure 1: Contour plots of $-F_\beta(m_1, m_2)/N$ surface.
("+" denotes a global maximum at each β.)

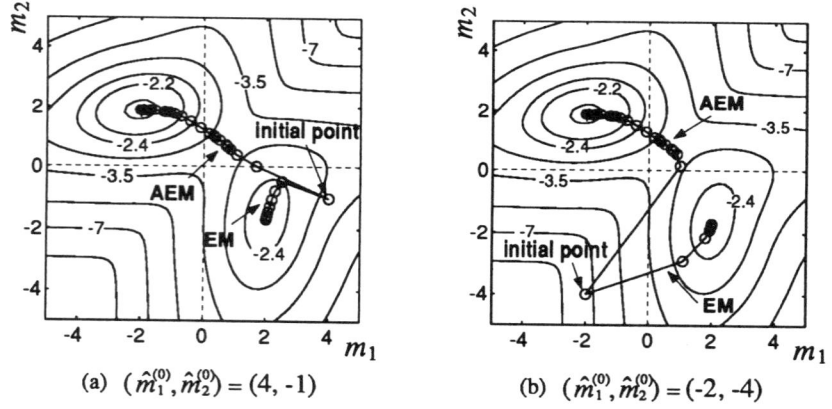

(a) $(\hat{m}_1^{(0)}, \hat{m}_2^{(0)}) = (4, -1)$

(b) $(\hat{m}_1^{(0)}, \hat{m}_2^{(0)}) = (-2, -4)$

Figure 2: Trajectories for EM and AEM procedures.

$-F_1(m_1, m_2) \equiv L(m_1, m_2)$. The maximum of $-F_1$ (or L) occurs at $\hat{m}_1 = -2.0$ and $\hat{m}_2 = 1.9$. As initial points, $(\hat{m}_1^{(0)}, \hat{m}_2^{(0)}) = (4, -1), (-2, -4)$ were tested. Note that these points are close to a local maximum. Figure 2 shows how both algorithms converge from these starting points[3].

The original EM algorithm converges to $(\hat{m}_1^{(12)}, \hat{m}_2^{(12)}) = (2.002, -1.687)$ (Figure 2(a)) and to $(\hat{m}_1^{(19)}, \hat{m}_2^{(19)}) = (1.999, -1.696)$ (Figure 2(b)). In contrast, the proposed AEM algorithm converges to $(\hat{m}_1^{(43)}, \hat{m}_2^{(43)}) = (-2.022, 1.879)$ (Figure 2(a)) and $(\hat{m}_1^{(43)}, \hat{m}_2^{(43)}) = (-2.022, 1.879)$ (Figure 2(b)). Since these starting points are close to the local maximum point, the original EM algorithm becomes trapped by the local maximum point, while the proposed algorithm successfully converges to the global maximum in both cases.

5 Discussion

A new view of the EM algorithm has recently been presented (Hathaway, 1986; Neal & Hinton, 1993). This view states that the EM steps can be regarded as a grouped version of the method of *coordinate ascent* of the following objective function:

$$J \stackrel{\text{def}}{=} \sum_{k}^{N} E_{p(\boldsymbol{y}_k)}\{\log p(\boldsymbol{x}_k, \boldsymbol{y}_k; \boldsymbol{\Theta})\} - \sum_{k}^{N} E_{p(\boldsymbol{y}_k)}\{\log p(\boldsymbol{y}_k)\} \qquad (15)$$

over $p(\boldsymbol{y}_k)$ and $\boldsymbol{\Theta}$. That is, the E-step corresponds to the maximization of J with respect to $p(\boldsymbol{y}_k)$ with fixed $\boldsymbol{\Theta}$, while the M-step corresponds to that of J with respect to $\boldsymbol{\Theta}$ with fixed $p(\boldsymbol{y}_k)$. Neal & Hinton mentioned that apart from the sign change, J is analogous to the "free energy" well known in statistical physics.

It is worth mentioning another interpretation of the derived parameterized posterior; i.e., it plays a central role in the AEM algorithm. Taking the logarithm on both sides of Eq. 10, we have

$$-\frac{1}{\beta} \log \int p(\boldsymbol{x}_k, \boldsymbol{y}_k; \boldsymbol{\Theta})^{\beta} d\boldsymbol{y}_k = -\log p(\boldsymbol{x}_k, \boldsymbol{y}_k; \boldsymbol{\Theta}) + \frac{1}{\beta} \log f(\boldsymbol{y}_k|\boldsymbol{x}_k). \qquad (16)$$

Moreover, taking the conditional expectation[4] given $\boldsymbol{x}_k$, summing over k, and using Eq. 12, we have

$$F_{\beta}(\boldsymbol{\Theta}) = \sum_{k=1}^{N} E_{f(\boldsymbol{y}_k|\boldsymbol{x}_k)}\{-\log p(\boldsymbol{x}_k, \boldsymbol{y}_k; \boldsymbol{\Theta})\} + \frac{1}{\beta} \sum_{k=1}^{N} E_{f(\boldsymbol{y}_k|\boldsymbol{x}_k)}\{\log f(\boldsymbol{y}_k|\boldsymbol{x}_k)\}. \qquad (17)$$

From Eqs. 7 and 8, Eq. 17 can be rewritten as $F_{\beta}(\boldsymbol{\Theta}) = E - \frac{1}{\beta}H$. Noting that $1/\beta$ corresponds to the "temperature", one can see that this expression exactly agrees with the *free energy*, while Eq. 15 is completely without the "temperature". In other words, $F_{\beta}(\boldsymbol{\Theta})$ can be interpreted as an annealing variant of $-J$. Clearly, when $\beta = 1$, $F_{\beta}(\boldsymbol{\Theta}) \equiv -J$.

---

[3] Although the AEM procedure was actually performed for successive β ($\beta_{new} \leftarrow \beta \times 1.4$), the results are superimposed on $-F_1(m_1, m_2)/N$ surface for convenience.

[4] Since the LHS of Eq. 16 is independent of $\boldsymbol{y}_k$, it does not change after expectation.

The proposed algorithm is also applicable to the learning of the (Generalized) Radial Basis Function (RBF, GRBF) networks. Indeed, Nowlan (Nowlan, 1990), for instance, proposes a maximum likelihood competitive learning algorithm for the RBF networks. In his study, *"soft competition"* and *"hard competition"* are experimentally compared and it is shown that the soft competition can give better performance. In our algorithm, on the other hand, the soft model exactly corresponds to the case $\beta = 1$, while the hard model corresponds to the case $\beta \to \infty$. Consequently, both models can be regarded as special cases in our algorithm.

Acknowledgements

We would like to thank Dr. Tsukasa Kawaoka, NTT CS labs, for his encouragement.

References

J. Buhmann & H. Kuhnel. (1993) Complexity optimized data clustering by competitive neural networks. *Neural Computation*, **5**:75–88.

W. Byrne. (1992) Alternating minimization and Boltzmann machine learning. *IEEE Trans. Neural Networks*, **3**:612-620.

A. P. Dempster, N. M. Laird & D. B. Rubin. (1977) Maximum-likelihood from incomplete data via the EM algorithm. *J. Royal Statist. Soc. Ser. B (methodological)*, **39**:1-38.

S. Geman & D. Geman. (1984) Stochastic relaxation, Gibbs distribution and the Baysian restortion in images. *IEEE Trans. Pattern Anal. Machine Intell.*, **6**,6:721-741.

R. J. Hathaway. (1986) Another interpretation of the EM algorithm for mixture distributions. *Statistics & Probability Letters*, 4: 53-56.

M. I. Jordan & R. A. Jacob. (1993) Hierarchical mixtures of experts and the EM algorithm. MIT Dept. of Brain and Cognitive Science preprint.

R. M. Neal & G. E. Hinton. (1993) A new view of the EM algorithm that justifies incremental and other variants. submitted to *Biometrika*.

S. J. Nowlan. (1990) Maximum likelihood competitve learning. in D. S. Touretzky et al. eds., *Advances in Neural Information Systems* 2, Morgan Kaufmann. 574-582.

K. Rose, E. Gurewitz & G. C. Fox. (1992) Vector quantization by deterministic annealing. *IEEE Trans. Information Theory*, **38**,4:1249-1257.

N. Ueda & R. Nakano. (1994) Mixture density estimation via EM algorithm with deterministic annealing. in proc. *IEEE Neural Networks for Signal Processing*, 69-77.

Y. Wong. (1993) Clustering data by melting. *Neural Computation*, **5**:89-104.

A. L. Yuille, P. Stolorz & J. Utans. (1994) Statistical physics, mixtures of distributions, and the EM algorithm. *Neural Computation*, **6**:334-340.

Diffusion of Credit in Markovian Models

Yoshua Bengio[*]
Dept. I.R.O., Université de Montréal,
Montreal, Qc, Canada H3C-3J7
bengioy@IRO.UMontreal.CA

Paolo Frasconi
Dipartimento di Sistemi e Informatica
Universitá di Firenze, Italy
paolo@mcculloch.ing.unifi.it

Abstract

This paper studies the problem of diffusion in Markovian models, such as hidden Markov models (HMMs) and how it makes very difficult the task of learning of long-term dependencies in sequences. Using results from Markov chain theory, we show that the problem of diffusion is reduced if the transition probabilities approach 0 or 1. Under this condition, standard HMMs have very limited modeling capabilities, but input/output HMMs can still perform interesting computations.

1 Introduction

This paper presents an important new element in our research on the problem of learning long-term dependencies in sequences. In our previous work [4] we found theoretical reasons for the difficulty in training **recurrent networks** (or more generally parametric non-linear dynamical systems) to learn long-term dependencies. The main result stated that either long-term storing or gradient propagation would be harmed, depending on whether the norm of the Jacobian of the state to state function was greater or less than 1. In this paper we consider a special case in which the norm of the Jacobian of the state to state function is constrained to be exactly 1 because this matrix is a **stochastic** matrix.

We consider both homogeneous and non-homogeneous Markovian models. Let n be the number of states and A_t be the transition matrices (constant in the homogeneous case): $A_{ij}(\boldsymbol{u}_t) = P(q_t = j \mid q_{t-1} = i, \boldsymbol{u}_t; \boldsymbol{\Theta})$ where $\boldsymbol{u}_t$ is an external input (constant in the homogeneous case) and $\boldsymbol{\Theta}$ is a vector of parameters. In the homogeneous case (e.g., standard HMMs), such models can learn the distribution of output sequences by associating an output distribution to each state. In

---

[*]also, AT&T Bell Labs, Holmdel, NJ 07733

the non-homogeneous case, transition and output distributions are conditional on
the input sequences, allowing to model relationships between input and output sequences (e.g. to do sequence regression or classification as with recurrent networks).
We thus called **Input/Output HMM** (IOHMM) this kind of non-homogeneous
HMM. In [3, 2] we proposed a connectionist implementation of IOHMMs. In both
cases, training requires propagating forward probabilities and backward probabilities, taking products with the transition probability matrix or its transpose. This
paper studies in which conditions these **products of matrices** might gradually
converge to lower rank, thus harming storage and learning of **long-term context**.
However, we find in this paper that IOHMMs can better deal with this problem
than homogeneous HMMs.

2 Mathematical Preliminaries

2.1 Definitions

A matrix A is said to be *non-negative*, written $A \geq 0$, if $A_{ij} \geq 0$ $\forall i,j$. Positive
matrices are defined similarly. A non-negative square matrix $A \in \mathbf{R}^{n \times n}$ is called
row stochastic (or simply *stochastic* in this paper) if $\sum_{j=1}^{n} A_{ij} = 1$ $\forall i = 1 \ldots n$.
A non-negative matrix is said to be *row [column] allowable* if every row [column]
sum is positive. An *allowable* matrix is both row and column allowable. A non-negative matrix can be associated to the directed transition graph $\mathcal{G}$ that constrains
the Markov chain. An *incidence matrix* $\tilde{A}$ corresponding to a given non-negative
matrix A replaces all positive entries of A by 1. The incidence matrix of $\tilde{A}$ is a
connectivity matrix corresponding to the graph $\mathcal{G}$ (assumed to be connected here).
Some algebraic properties of A are described in terms of the *topology* of $\mathcal{G}$.

Definition 1 *(Irreducible Matrix) A non-negative $n \times n$ matrix A is said to be
irreducible if for every pair i,j of indices, $\exists\ m = m(i,j)$ positive integer s.t.
$(A^m)_{ij} > 0$.*

A matrix A is irreducible if and only if the associated graph is strongly connected
(i.e., there exists a path between any pair of states i,j). If $\exists k$ s.t. $(A^k)_{ii} > 0$, $d(i)$
is called the *period* of index i if it is the greatest common divisor (g.c.d.) of those k
for which $(A^k)_{ii} > 0$. In an irreducible matrix all the indices have the same period
d, which is called the *period* of the matrix. The period of a matrix is the g.c.d. of
the lengths of all cycles in the associated transition graph.

Definition 2 *(Primitive matrix) A non-negative matrix A is said to be primitive
if there exists a positive integer k s.t. $A^k > 0$.*

An irreducible matrix is either periodic or primitive (i.e. of period 1). A primitive
stochastic matrix is necessarily allowable.

2.2 The Perron-Frobenius Theorem

Theorem 1 (See [6], Theorem 1.1.) *Suppose A is an $n \times n$ non-negative primitive matrix. Then there exists an eigenvalue r such that:*

1. *r is real and positive;*
2. *with r can be associated strictly positive left and right eigenvectors;*
3. *$r > |\lambda|$ for any eigenvalue $\lambda \neq r$;*
4. *the eigenvectors associated with r are unique to constant multiples.*
5. *If $0 \leq B \leq A$ and β is an eigenvalue of B, then $|\beta| \leq r$. Moreover, $|\beta| = r$ implies $B = A$.*

6. *r is simple root of the characteristic equation of A.*

A simple consequence of the theorem for stochastic matrices is the following:

Corollary 1 *Suppose A is a primitive stochastic matrix. Then its largest eigenvalue is 1 and there is only one corresponding right eigenvector, which is* $\mathbf{1} = [1, 1 \cdots 1]'$. *Furthermore, all other eigenvalues* < 1.

Proof. $A\mathbf{1} = \mathbf{1}$ by definition of stochastic matrices. This eigenvector is unique and all other eigenvalues < 1 by the Perron-Frobenius Theorem.

If A is stochastic but periodic with period d, then A has d eigenvalues of module 1 which are the d complex roots of 1.

3 Learning Long-Term Dependencies with HMMs

In this section we analyze the case of a primitive transition matrix as well as the general case with a canonical re-ordering of the matrix indices. We discuss how ergodicity coefficients can be used to measure the difficulty in learning long-term dependencies. Finally, we find that in order to avoid all diffusion, the transitions should be deterministic (0 or 1 probability).

3.1 Training Standard HMMs

Theorem 2 (See [6], Theorem 4.2.) *If A is a primitive stochastic matrix, then as $t \to \infty$, $A^t \to \mathbf{1}v'$ where v' is the unique stationary distribution of the Markov chain. The rate of approach is geometric.*

Thus if A is primitive, then $\lim_{t\to\infty} A^t$ converges to a matrix whose eigenvalues are all 0 except for $\lambda = 1$ (with eigenvector $\mathbf{1}$), i.e. the rank of this product converges to 1, i.e. its rows are equal. A consequence of theorem 2 is that it is very difficult to train ordinary hidden Markov models, with a primitive transition matrix, to model long-term dependencies in observed sequences. The reason is that the distribution over the states at time $t > t_0$ becomes gradually independent of the distribution over the states at time t_0 as t increases. It means that states at time t_0 become equally responsible for increasing the likelihood of an output at time t. This corresponds in the backward phase of the EM algorithm for training HMMs to a *diffusion of credit* over all the states. In practice we train HMMs with finite sequences. However, training will become more and more numerically ill-conditioned as one considers longer term dependencies. Consider two events e_0 (occurring at t_0) and e_t (occurring at t), and suppose there are also "interesting" events occurring in between. Let us consider the overall influence of states at times $\tau < t$ upon the likelihood of the outputs at time t. Because of the phenomenon of diffusion of credit, and because gradients are added together, the influence of intervening events (especially those occurring shortly before t) will be much stronger than the influence of e_0. Furthermore, this problem gets **geometrically** worse as t increases. Clearly a positive matrix is primitive. Thus in order to learn long-term dependencies, we would like to have many zeros in the matrix of transition probabilities. Unfortunately, this generally supposes **prior knowledge** of an appropriate connectivity graph.

3.2 Coefficients of ergodicity

To study products of non-negative matrices and the loss of information about initial state in Markov chains (particularly in the non-homogeneous case), we introduce the projective distance between vectors x and y:

$$d(x', y') = \max_{i,j} \ln(\frac{x_i y_j}{x_j y_i}).$$

Clearly, some *contraction* takes place when $d(x'A, y'A) \leq d(x', y')$.

Definition 3 *Birkhoff's contraction coefficient $\tau_B(A)$, for a non-negative column-allowable matrix A, is defined in terms of the projective distance:*

$$\tau_B(A) = \sup_{x,y>0; x\neq \lambda y} \frac{d(x'A, y'A)}{d(x', y')}.$$

Dobrushin's coefficient $\tau_1(A)$, for a stochastic matrix A, is defined as follows:

$$\tau_1(A) = \frac{1}{2} \sup_{i,j} \sum_k |a_{ik} - a_{jk}|.$$

Both are *proper ergodicity coefficients*: $0 \leq \tau(A) \leq 1$ and $\tau(A) = 0$ if and only if A has identical rows. Furthermore, $\tau(A_1 A_2) \leq \tau(A_1)\tau(A_2)$ (see [6]).

3.3 Products of Stochastic Matrices

Let $A^{(1,t)} = A_1 A_2 \cdots A_{t-1} A_t$ denote a *forward product* of stochastic matrices $A_1, A_2, \cdots A_t$. From the properties of τ_B and τ_1, if $\tau(A_t) < 1, t > 0$ then $\lim_{t \to \infty} \tau(A^{(1,t)}) = 0$, i.e. $A^{(1,t)}$ has rank 1 and identical rows. Weak **ergodicity** is then defined in terms of a proper ergodic coefficient τ such as τ_B and τ_1:

Definition 4 *(Weak Ergodicity) The products of stochastic matrices $A^{(p,r)}$ are weakly ergodic if and only if for all $t_0 \geq 0$ as $t \to \infty$, $\tau(A^{(t_0,t)}) \to 0$.*

Theorem 3 (See [6], Lemma 3.3 and 3.4.) *Let $A^{(1,t)}$ a forward product of non-negative and allowable matrices, then the products $A^{(1,t)}$ are weakly ergodic if and only if the following conditions both hold:*
1. $\exists t_0$ s.t. $A^{(t_0,t)} > 0 \; \forall t \geq t_0$
2. $\frac{A^{(t_0,t)}_{i,k}}{A^{(t_0,t)}_{j,k}} \to W_{ij}(t) > 0$ as $t \to \infty$, *i.e. rows of $A^{(t_0,t)}$ tend to proportionality.*

For stochastic matrices, row-proportionality is equivalent to row-equality since rows sum to 1. $\lim_{t \to \infty} A^{(t_0,t)}$ does not need to exist in order to have weak ergodicity.

3.4 Canonical Decomposition and Periodic Graphs

Any non-negative matrix A can be rewritten by relabeling its indices in the following *canonical decomposition* [6], with diagonal blocks B_i, C_i and Q:

$$A = \begin{pmatrix} B_1 & 0 & \cdots & 0 & \cdots & 0 \\ 0 & B_2 & \cdots & 0 & \cdots & 0 \\ \cdots & \cdots & \cdots & \cdots & \cdots & \cdots \\ 0 & \cdots & C_{s+1} & 0 & \cdots & 0 \\ \cdots & \cdots & \cdots & \cdots & \cdots & \cdots \\ 0 & 0 & \cdots & \cdots & C_r & 0 \\ L_1 & L_2 & \cdots & \cdots & L_r & Q \end{pmatrix} \quad (1)$$

where B_i and C_i are irreducible, B_i are primitive and C_i are periodic. Define the corresponding sets of states as S_{B_i}, S_{C_i}, S_Q. Q might be reducible, but the groups of states in S_Q leak into the B or C blocks, i.e., S_Q represents the transient part of the state space. This decomposition is illustrated in Figure 1a. For homogeneous and non-homogeneous Markov models (with constant incidence matrix $\tilde{A}_t = \tilde{A}_0$), because $P(q_t \in S_Q | q_{t-1} \in S_Q) < 1$, $\lim_{t \to \infty} P(q_t \in S_Q | q_0 \in S_Q) = 0$. Furthermore, because the B_i are primitive, we can apply Theorem 1, and starting from a state in S_{B_i}, all information about an initial state at t_0 is gradually lost.

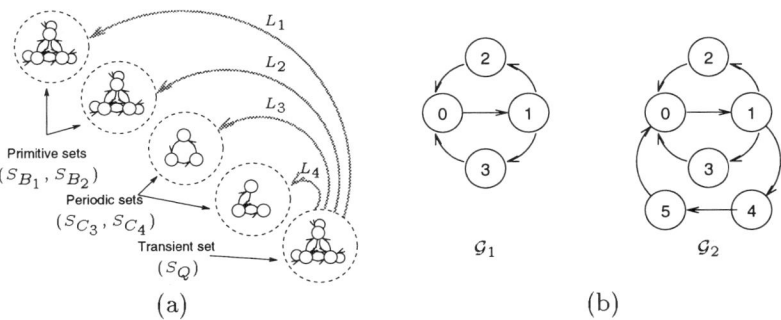

Figure 1: (a): Transition graph corresponding to the canonical decomposition. (b): Periodic graph $\mathcal{G}_1$ becomes primitive (period 1) $\mathcal{G}_2$ when adding loop with states 4,5.

A more difficult case is the one of $(A^{(t_0,t)})_{jk}$ with initial state $j \in S_{C_i}$. Let d_i be the period of the ith periodic block C_i. It can be shown [6] that taking d products of periodic matrices with the same incidence matrix and period d yields a block-diagonal matrix whose d blocks are primitive. Thus $C^{(t_0,t)}$ retains information about the initial **block** in which q_t was. However, for every such block of size > 1, information will be gradually lost about the exact identity of the state *within* that block. This is best demonstrated through a simple example. Consider the incidence matrix represented by the graph $\mathcal{G}_1$ of Figure 1b. It has period 3 and the only non-deterministic transition is from state 1, which can yield into either one of two loops. When many stochastic matrices with this graph are multiplied together, information about *the loop* in which the initial state was is gradually lost (i.e. if the initial state was 2 or 3, this information is gradually lost). What is retained is the *phase* information, i.e. in which block ($\{0\}$, $\{1\}$, or $\{2,3\}$) of a cyclic chain was the initial state. This suggests that it will be easy to learn about the type of outputs associated to each block of a cyclic chain, but it will be hard to learn anything else. Suppose now that the sequences to be modeled are slightly more complicated, requiring an extra loop *of period 4* instead of 3, as in Figure 1b. In that case A is primitive: all information about the initial state will be gradually lost.

3.5 Learning Long-Term Dependencies: a Discrete Problem?

We might wonder if, starting from a positive stochastic matrix, the learning algorithm could **learn** the topology, i.e. replace some transition probabilities by zeroes. Let us consider the update rule for transition probabilities in the EM algorithm:

$$A_{ij} \leftarrow \frac{A_{ij} \frac{\partial L}{\partial A_{ij}}}{\sum_j A_{ij} \frac{\partial L}{\partial A_{ij}}}. \tag{2}$$

Starting from $A_{ij} > 0$ we could obtain a new $A_{ij} = 0$ only if $\frac{\partial L}{\partial A_{ij}} = 0$, i.e. on a local maximum of the likelihood L. Thus the EM training algorithm will not *exactly* obtain zero probabilities. Transition probabilities might however *approach* 0.

It is also interesting to ask in which conditions we are guaranteed that there will **not be any diffusion** (of influence in the forward phase, and credit in the backward phase of training). It requires that some of the eigenvalues other than $\lambda_1 = 1$ have a norm that is also 1. This can be achieved with periodic matrices C (of period

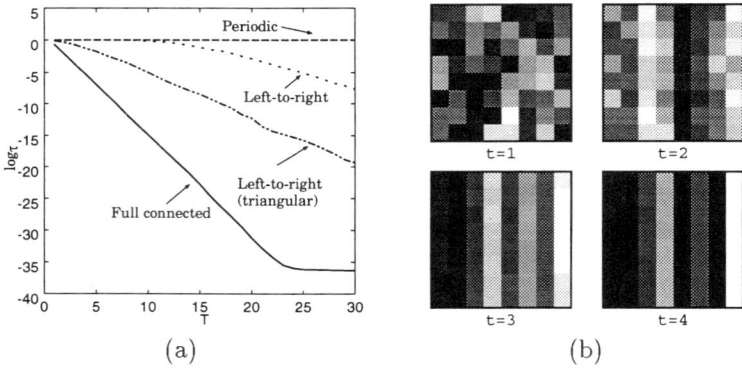

Figure 2: (a) Convergence of Dobrushin's coefficient (see Definition 3. (b) Evolution of products $A^{(1,t)}$ for fully connected graph. Matrix elements are visualized with gray levels.

d), which have d eigenvalues that are the d roots of 1 on the complex unit circle. To avoid any loss of information also requires that $C^d = I$ be the identity, since any diagonal block of C^d with size more than 1 will yield to a loss of information (because of diffusion in primitive matrices). This can be generalized to reducible matrices whose canonical form is composed of periodic blocks C_i with $C_i^d = I$.

The condition we are describing actually corresponds to a matrix with only 1's and 0's. If $\tilde{A}_t$ is fixed, it would mean that the Markov chain is also homogeneous. It appears that many interesting computations can not be achieved with such constraints (i.e. only allowing one or more cycles of the same period and a purely deterministic and homogeneous Markov chain). Furthermore, if the parameters of the system are the transition probabilities themselves (as in ordinary HMMs), such solutions correspond to a subset of the **corners of the 0-1 hypercube** in parameter space. Away from those solutions, learning is mostly influenced by *short term* dependencies, because of diffusion of credit. Furthermore, as seen in equation 2, algorithms like EM will tend to stay near a corner once it is approached. This suggests that *discrete optimization* algorithms, rather continuous local algorithms, may be more appropriate to explore the (legal) corners of this hypercube.

4 Experiments

4.1 Diffusion: Numerical Simulations

Firstly, we wanted to measure how (and if) different kinds of products of stochastic matrices converged, for example to a matrix of equal rows. We ran 4 simulations, each with an 8 states non-homogeneous Markov chain but with different constraints on the transition graph: 1) $\mathcal{G}$ fully connected; 2) $\mathcal{G}$ is a left-to-right model (i.e. $\tilde{A}$ is upper triangular); 3) $\mathcal{G}$ is left-to-right but only one-state skips are allowed (i.e. $\tilde{A}$ is upper bidiagonal); 4) A_t are periodic with period 4. Results shown in Figure 2 confirm the convergence towards zero of the ergodicity coefficient[1], at a rate that depends on the graph topology. In Figure 2, we represent visually the convergence of fully connected matrices, in only 4 time steps, towards equal columns.

---
[1] except for the experiments with periodic matrices, as expected

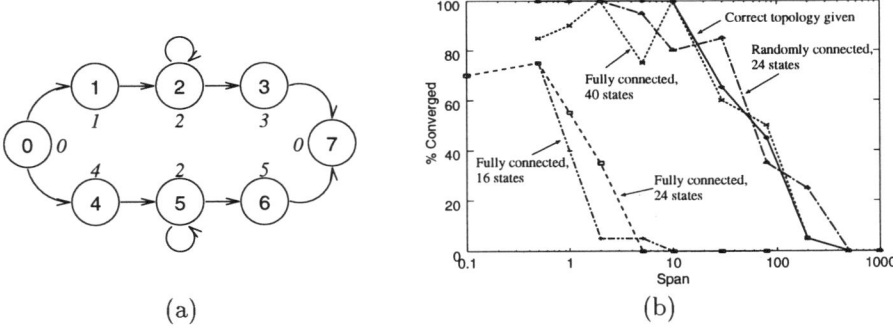

Figure 3: (a): Generating HMM. Numbers out of state circles denote output symbols. (b): Percentage of convergence to a good solution (over 20 trials) for various series of experiments as the span of dependencies is increased.

4.2 Training Experiments

To evaluate how diffusion impairs training, a set of controlled experiments were performed, in which the training sequences were generated by a simple homogeneous HMM with long-term dependencies, depicted in Figure 3a. Two branches generate similar sequences except for the first and last symbol. The extent of the long-term context is controlled by the self transition probabilities of states 2 and 5, $\lambda = P(q_t = 2|q_{t-1} - 2) = P(q_t = 5|q_{t-1} = 5)$. Span or "half-life" is $\log(.5)/\log(\lambda)$, i.e. $\lambda^{\text{span}} = .5)$. Following [4], data was generated for various span of long-term dependencies (0.1 to 1000).

For each series of experiments, varying the span, 20 different training trials were run per span value, with 100 training sequences[2]. Training was stopped either after a maximum number of epochs (200), of after the likelihood did not improve significantly, i.e., $(L(t) - L(t-1))/|L(t)| < 10^{-5}$, where $L(t)$ is the logarithm of the likelihood of the training set at epoch t.

If the HMM is fully connected (except for the final absorbing state) and has just the right number of states, trials *almost never converge* to a good solution (1 in 160 did). Increasing the number of states and randomly putting zeroes helps. The randomly connected HMMs had 3 times more states than the generating HMM and random connections were created with 20% probability. Figure 3b shows the average number of converged trials for these different types of HMM topology. A trial is considered successful when it yields a likelihood almost as good or better than the likelihood of the generating HMM on the same data. In all cases the number of successful trials rapidly drops to zero beyond some value of span.

5 Conclusion and Future Work

In previous work on recurrent networks we had found that **propagating credit** over the long term was incompatible with **storing** information for the long term. For Markovian models, we found that when the transition probabilities are close to 1 and 0, information can be stored for the long term AND credit can be prop-

---

[2]it appeared sufficient since the likelihood of the generating HMM did not improve much when trained on this data

agated over the long term. However, like for recurrent networks, this makes the problem of learning long-term dependencies look more like a *discrete* optimization problem. Thus it appears difficult for local learning algorithm such as EM to learn optimal transition probabilities near 1 or 0, i.e. to learn the topology, while taking into account long-term dependencies. The arguments presented are essentially an application of established mathematical results on Markov chains to the problem of learning long term dependencies in homogeneous and non-homogeneous HMMs. These arguments were also supported by experiments on artificial data, studying the phenomenon of diffusion of credit and the corresponding difficulty in training HMMs to learn long-term dependencies.

IOHMMs [1] introduce a reparameterization of the problem: instead of directly learning the transition probabilities, we learn parameters of a function of an input sequence. Even with a fully connected topology, transition probabilities computed at each time step might be very close to 0 and 1. Because of the non-stationarity, more interesting computations can emerge than the simple cycles studied above. For example in [3] we found IOHMMs effective in *grammar inference* tasks. In [1] comparative experiments were performed with a preliminary version of IOHMMs and other algorithms such as recurrent networks, on artificial data on which the span of long-term dependencies was controlled. IOHMMs were found much better than the other algorithms at learning these tasks.

Based on the analysis presented here, we are also exploring another approach to learning long-term dependencies that consists in building a **hierarchical** representation of the state. This can be achieved by introducing several sub-state variables whose Cartesian product corresponds to the system state. Each of these sub-state variables can operate at a different time scale, thus allowing credit to propagate over long temporal spans for some of these variables. Another interesting issue to be investigated is whether techniques of symbolic **prior knowledge** injection (such as in [5]) can be exploited to choose good topologies. One advantage, compared to traditional neural network approaches, is that the model has an underlying finite state structure and is thus well suited to inject discrete transition rules.

Acknowledgments

We would like to thank Léon Bottou for his many useful comments and suggestions, and the NSERC and FCAR Canadian funding agencies for support.

References

[1] Y. Bengio and P. Frasconi. Credit assignment through time: Alternatives to backpropagation. In J. D. Cowan, et al., eds., *Advances in Neural Information Processing Systems 6*. Morgan Kaufmann, 1994.

[2] Y. Bengio and P. Frasconi. An Input Output HMM Architecture. In this volume: J. D. Cowan, et al., eds., *Advances in Neural Information Processing Systems 7*. Morgan Kaufmann, 1994.

[3] Y. Bengio and P. Frasconi. An EM approach to learning sequential behavior. Technical Report RT-DSI-11/94, University of Florence, 1994.

[4] Y. Bengio, P. Simard, and P. Frasconi. Learning long-term dependencies with gradient descent is difficult. *IEEE Trans. Neural Networks*, 5(2):157–166, 1994.

[5] P. Frasconi, M. Gori, M. Maggini, and G. Soda. Unified integration of explicit rules and learning by example in recurrent networks. *IEEE Trans. on Knowledge and Data Engineering*, 7(1), 1995.

[6] E. Seneta. *Nonnegative Matrices and Markov Chains*. Springer, New York, 1981.

Factorial Learning by Clustering Features

Joshua B. Tenenbaum and Emanuel V. Todorov
Department of Brain and Cognitive Sciences
Massachusetts Institute of Technology
Cambridge, MA 02139
{jbt,emo}@psyche.mit.edu

Abstract

We introduce a novel algorithm for factorial learning, motivated by segmentation problems in computational vision, in which the underlying factors correspond to clusters of highly correlated input features. The algorithm derives from a new kind of competitive clustering model, in which the cluster generators compete to explain each feature of the data set and cooperate to explain each input example, rather than competing for examples and cooperating on features, as in traditional clustering algorithms. A natural extension of the algorithm recovers hierarchical models of data generated from multiple unknown categories, each with a different, multiple causal structure. Several simulations demonstrate the power of this approach.

1 INTRODUCTION

Unsupervised learning is the search for structure in data. Most unsupervised learning systems can be viewed as trying to invert a particular generative model of the data in order to recover the underlying causal structure of their world. Different learning algorithms are then primarily distinguished by the different generative models they embody, that is, the different kinds of structure they look for.

Factorial learning, the subject of this paper, tries to find a set of independent causes that cooperate to produce the input examples. We focus on *strong* factorial learning, where the goal is to recover the actual degrees of freedom responsible for generating the observed data, as opposed to the more general *weak* approach, where the goal

Figure 1: A simple factorial learning problem. The learner observes an articulated hand in various configurations, with each example specified by the positions of 16 tracked features (shown as black dots). The learner might recover four underlying factors, corresponding to the positions of the fingers, each of which claims responsiblity for four features of the data set.

is merely to recover some factorial model that explains the data efficiently. Strong factorial learning makes a claim about the nature of the world, while weak factorial learning only makes a claim about the nature of the learner's representations (although the two are clearly related). Standard subspace algorithms, such as principal component analysis, fit a linear, factorial model to the input data, but can only recover the true causal structure in very limited situations, such as when the data are generated by a linear combination of independent factors with significantly different variances (as in signal-from-noise separation).

Recent work in factorial learning suggests that the general problem of recovering the true, multiple causal structure of an arbitrary, real-world data set is very difficult, and that specific approaches must be tailored to specific, but hopefully common, classes of problems (Foldiak, 1990; Saund, 1995; Dayan and Zemel, 1995). Our own interest in multiple cause learning was motivated by segmentation problems in computational vision, in which the underlying factors correspond ideally to disjoint clusters of highly correlated input features. Examples include the segmentation of articulated objects into functionally independent parts, or the segmentation of multiple-object motion sequences into tracks of individual objects. These problems, as well as many other problems of pattern recognition and analysis, share a common set of constraints which makes factorial learning both appropriate and tractable. Specifically, while each observed example depends on some combination of several factors, any one input feature always depends on only one such factor (see Figure 1). Then the generative model decomposes into independent sets of functionally grouped input features, or *functional parts* (Tenenbaum, 1994).

In this paper, we propose a learning algorithm that extracts these functional parts. The key simplifying assumption, which we call the *membership constraint*, states that each feature belongs to at most one functional part, and that this membership is constant over the set of training examples. The membership constraint allows us to treat the factorial learning problem as a novel kind of clustering problem. The cluster generators now compete to explain each feature of the data set and cooperate to explain each input example, rather than competing for examples and cooperating on features, as in traditional clustering systems such as K-means or mixture models. The following sections discuss the details of the feature clustering algorithm for extracting functional parts, a simple but illustrative example, and extensions. In particular, we demonstrate a natural way to relax the strict membership constraint and thus learn hierarchical models of data generated from multiple unknown categories, each with a different multiple causal structure.

2 THE FEATURE CLUSTERING ALGORITHM

Our algorithm for extracting functional parts derives from a statistical mechanics formulation of the soft clustering problem (inspired by Rose, Gurewitz, and Fox, 1990; Hinton and Zemel, 1994). We take as input a data set $\{x_j^{(i)}\}$, with I examples of J real-valued features. The best K-cluster representation of these J features is given by an optimal set of cluster parameters, $\{\theta_k\}$, and an optimal set of assignments, $\{p_{jk}\}$. The assignment p_{jk} specifies the probability of assigning feature j to cluster k, and depends directly on $E_{jk} = \sum_i (x_j^{(i)} - f_{jk}^{(i)})^2$, the total squared difference (over the I training examples) between the observed feature values $x_j^{(i)}$ and cluster k's predictions $f_{jk}^{(i)}$. The parameters θ_k define cluster k's generative model, and thus determine the predictions $f_{jk}^{(i)}(\theta_k)$.

If we limit functional parts to clusters of *linearly* correlated features, then the appropriate generative model has $f_{jk}^{(i)} = w_{jk} y_k^{(i)} + u_j$, with cluster parameters $\theta_k = \{y_k^{(i)}, w_{jk}, u_j\}$ to be estimated. That is, for each example i, part k predicts the value of input feature j as a linear function of some part-specific factor $y_k^{(i)}$ (such as finger position in Figure 1). For the purposes of this paper, we assume zero-mean features and ignore the u_j terms. Then $E_{jk} = \sum_i (x_j^{(i)} - w_{jk} y_k^{(i)})^2$.

The optimal cluster parameters and assignments can now be found by maximizing the complete log likelihood of the data given the K-cluster representation, or equivalently, in the framework of statistical mechanics, by minimizing the free energy

$$F = E - \frac{1}{\beta} H = \sum_j \sum_k p_{jk} (E_{jk} + \frac{1}{\beta} \log p_{jk}) \qquad (1)$$

subject to the membership constraints, $\sum_k p_{jk} = 1, (\forall j)$. Minimizing the energy,

$$E = \sum_j \sum_k p_{jk} E_{jk}, \qquad (2)$$

reduces the expected reconstruction error, leading to more accurate representations. Maximizing the entropy,

$$H = -\sum_j \sum_k p_{jk} \log p_{jk}, \qquad (3)$$

distributes responsibility for each feature across many parts, thus decreasing the independence of the parts and leading to simpler representations (with fewer degrees of freedom). In line with Occam's Razor, minimizing the energy-entropy tradeoff finds the representation that, at a particular temperature $1/\beta$, best satisfies the conflicting requirements of low error and low complexity.

We minimize the free energy with a generalized EM procedure (Neal and Hinton, 1994), setting derivatives to zero and iterating the resulting update equations:

$$p_{jk} = \frac{e^{-\beta E_{jk}}}{\sum_k e^{-\beta E_{jk}}} \qquad (4)$$

$$y_k^{(i)} = \sum_j p_{jk} w_{jk} x_j^{(i)} \qquad (5)$$

$$w_{jk} = \sum_i x_j^{(i)} y_k^{(i)}. \qquad (6)$$

This update procedure assumes a normalization step $y_k^{(i)} = y_k^{(i)}/(\sum_{i'}(y_k^{(i')})^2)^{1/2}$ in each iteration, because without some additional constraint on the magnitudes of $y_k^{(i)}$ (or w_{jk}), inverting the generative model $f_{jk}^{(i)} = w_{jk}y_k^{(i)}$ is an ill-posed problem.

This algorithm maps naturally onto a simple network architecture. The hidden unit activities, representing the part-specific factors $y_k^{(i)}$, are computed from the observations $x_j^{(i)}$ via bottom-up weights $p_{jk}w_{jk}$, normalized, and multiplied by top-down weights w_{jk} to generate the network's predictions $f_{jk}^{(i)}$. The weights adapt according to a hybrid learning rule, with w_{jk} determined by a Hebb rule (as in subspace learning algorithms), and p_{jk} determined by a competitive, softmax function of the reconstruction error E_{jk} (as in soft mixture models).

3 LEARNING A HIERARCHY OF PARTS

The following simulation illustrates the algorithm's behavior on a simple, part segmentation task. The training data consist of 60 examples with 16 features each, representing the horizontal positions of 16 points on an articulated hand in various configurations (as in Figure 1). The data for this example were generated by a hierarchical, random process that produced a low correlation between all 16 features, a moderate correlation between the four features on each finger, and a high correlation between the two features on each joint (two joints per finger). To fully explain this data set, the algorithm should be able to find a corresponding hierarchy of increasingly complex functional part representations.

To evaluate the network's representation of this data set, we inspect the learned weights $p_{jk}w_{jk}$, which give the total contribution of feature j to part k in (5). In Figure 2, these weights are plotted for several different values of β, with gray boxes indicating zero weights, white indicating strong positive weights, and black indicating strong negative weights. The network was configured with $K = 16$ part units, to ensure that all potential parts could be found. When fewer than K distinct parts are found, some of the cluster units have identical parameters (appearing as identical columns in Figure 2). These results were generated by deterministic annealing, starting with $\beta \ll 1$, and perturbing the weights slightly each time β was increased, in order to break symmetries.

Figure 2 shows that the number of distinct parts found increases with β, as more accurate (and more complex) representations become favored. In (4), we see that β controls the number of distinct parts via the strength of the competition for features. At $\beta = 0$, every part takes equal responsibility for every feature. Without competition, there can be no diversity, and thus only one distinct part is discovered at low β, corresponding to the whole hand (Figure 2a). As β increases, the competition for features gets stiffer, and parts split into their component subparts. The network finds first four distinct parts (with four features each), corresponding to individual fingers (Figure 2c), and then eight distinct parts (with two features each), corresponding to individual joints (Figure 2d). Figure 2b shows an intermediate representation, with something between one and four parts. Four distinct columns are visible, but they do not cleanly segregate the features.

Figure 3 plots the decrease in mean reconstruction error (expressed by the energy E)

Factorial Learning by Clustering Features

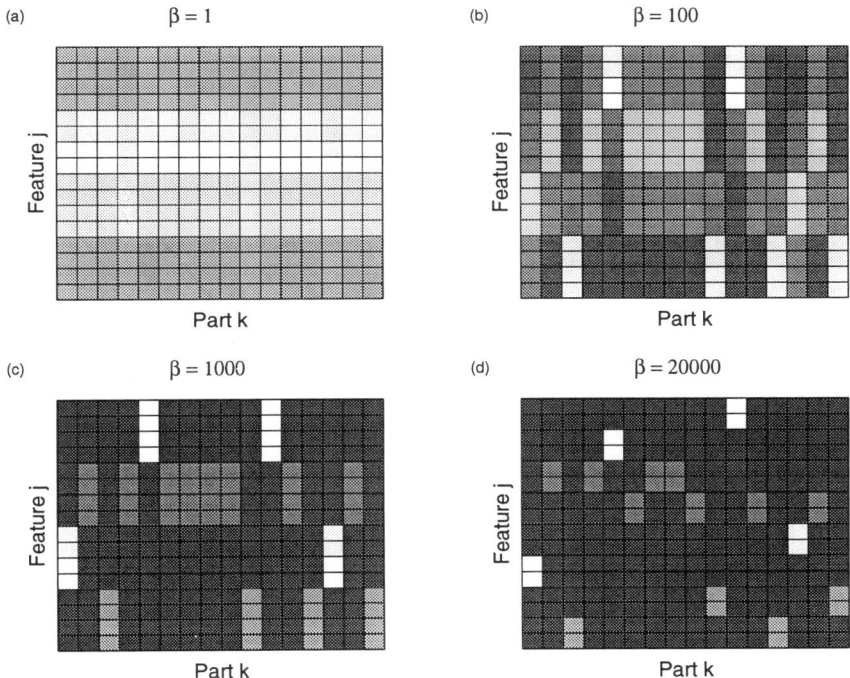

Figure 2: A hierarchy of functional part representations, parameterized by β.

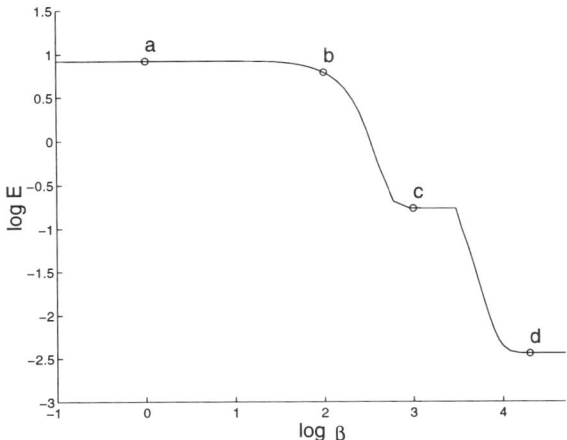

Figure 3: A phase diagram distinguishes true parts (a, c, d) from spurious ones (b).

as β increases and more distinct parts emerge. Notice that within the three stable phases corresponding to good part decompositions (Figures 2a, 2c, 2d), E remains practically constant over wide variations in β. In contrast, E varies rapidly at the boundaries between phases, where spurious part structure appears (Figure 2b). In general, good representations should lie at stable points of this phase diagram, where the error-complexity tradeoff is robust. Thus the actual number of parts in a particular data set, as well as their hierarchical structure, need not be known in advance, but can be inferred from the dynamics of learning.

4 LEARNING MULTIPLE CATEGORIES

Until this point, we have assumed that each feature belongs to at most one part over the entire set of training examples, and tried to find the single K-part model that best explains the data as a whole. But the notion that a single model must explain the whole data set is quite restrictive. The data may contain several categories of examples, each characterized by a different pattern of feature correlations, and then we would like to learn a *set* of models, each capturing the distinctive part structure of one such category. Again we are motivated by human vision, which easily recognizes many categories of motion defined by high-level patterns of coordinated part movement, such as hand gestures and facial expressions.

If we know which examples belong to which categories, learning multiple models is no harder than learning one, as in the previous section. A separate model can be fit to each category m of training examples, and the weights $p_{jk}^m w_{jk}^m$ are frozen to produce a set of category templates. However, if the category identities are unknown, we face a novel kind of hierarchical learning task. We must simultaneously discover the optimal clustering of examples into categories, as well as the optimal clustering of features into parts *within* each category. We can formalize this hierarchical clustering problem as minimizing a familiar free energy,

$$F = \sum_i \sum_m g^{im}(T^{im} + \frac{1}{\alpha}\log g^{im}), \qquad (7)$$

in which g^{im} specifies the probability of assigning example i to category m, and T^{im} is the associated cost. This cost is itself the free energy of the mth K-part model on the ith example,

$$T^{im} = \sum_j \sum_k p_{jk}^m (E_{jk}^{im} + \frac{1}{\beta}\log p_{jk}^m), \qquad (8)$$

in which p_{jk}^m specifies the probability of assigning feature j to part k within category m, and $E_{jk}^{im} = (x_j^i - w_{jk}^m y_k^{im})^2$ is the usual reconstruction error from Section 2.

This algorithm was tested on a data set of 256 hand configurations with 20 features each (similar to those in Figure 1), in which each example expresses one of four possible "gestures", i.e. patterns of feature correlation. As Table 1 indicates, the five features on each finger are highly correlated across the entire data set, while variable correlations between the four fingers distinguish the gesture categories. Note that a single model with four parts explains the full variance of the data just as well as the actual four-category generating process. However, most of the data

Table 1: The 20 features are grouped into either 2, 3, or 4 functional parts.

Examples	No. of parts	Part composition			
1 - 64	2	1————10	11————————20		
65 - 127	3	1————10	11—15	16—20	
128 - 192	3	1—5	6—10	11————————20	
193 - 256	4	1—5	6—10	11—15	16—20

can also be explained by one of several simpler models, making the learner's task a challenging balancing act between accuracy and simplicity.

Figure 4 shows a typical representation learned for this data set. The algorithm was configured with $M = 8$ category models (each with $K = 8$ parts), but only four distinct categories of examples are found after annealing on α (holding β constant), and their weights $p_{jk}^m w_{jk}^m$ are depicted in Figure 4a. Each category faithfully captures one of the actual generating categories in Table 1, with the correct number and composition of functional parts. Figure 4b depicts the responsibility g^{im} that each learned category m takes for each feature i. Notice the inevitable effect of a bias towards simpler representations. Many examples are misassigned relative to Table 1, when categories with fewer degrees of freedom than their true generating categories can explain them almost as accurately.

5 CONCLUSIONS AND FUTURE DIRECTIONS

The notion that many data sets are best explained in terms of functionally independent clusters of correlated features resonates with similar proposals of Foldiak (1990), Saund (1995), Hinton and Zemel (1994), and Dayan and Zemel (1995). Our approach is unique in actually formulating the learning task as a clustering problem and explicitly extracting the functional parts of the data. Factorial learning by clustering features has three principal advantages. First, the free energy cost function for clustering yields a natural complexity scale-space of functional part representations, parameterized by β. Second, the generalized EM learning algorithm is simple and quick, and maps easily onto a network architecture. Third, by nesting free energies, we can seamlessly compose objective functions for quite complex, hierarchical unsupervised learning problems, such as the multiple category, multiple part mixture problem of Section 4.

The primary limitation of our approach is that when the generative model we assume does not in fact apply to the data, the algorithm may fail to recover any meaningful structure. In ongoing work, we are pursuing a more flexible generative model that allows the underlying causes to compete directly for arbitrary feature-example pairs ij, rather than limiting competition only to features j, as in Section 2, or only to examples i, as in conventional mixture models, or segregating competition for examples and features into hierarchical stages, as in Section 4. Because this introduces many more degrees of freedom, robust learning will require additional constraints, such as temporal continuity of examples or spatial continuity of features.

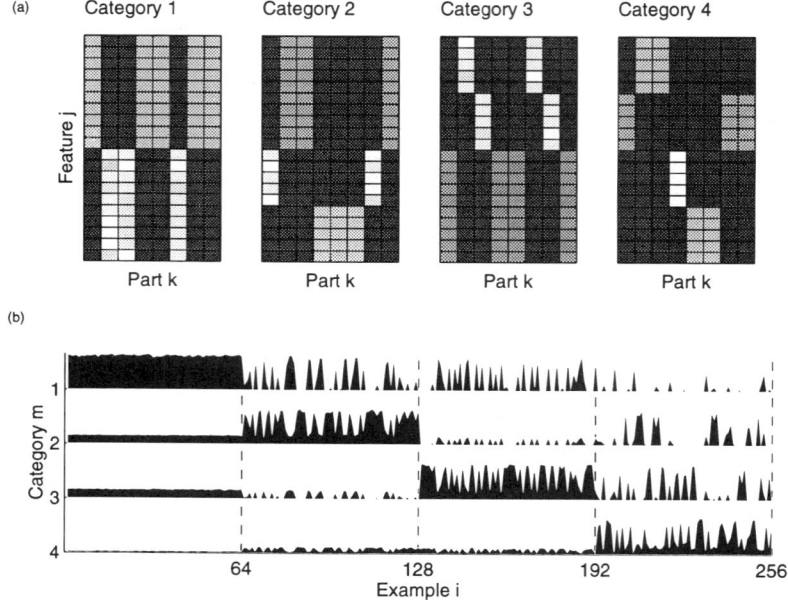

Figure 4: Learning multiple categories, each with a different part structure.

Acknowledgements

Both authors are Howard Hughes Medical Institute Predoctoral Fellows. We thank Whitman Richards, Yair Weiss, and Stephen Gilbert for helpful discussions.

References

Dayan, P. and Zemel, R. S. (1995). Competition and multiple cause models. *Neural Computation*, in press.

Foldiak, P. (1990). Forming sparse representations by local anti-hebbian learning. *Biological Cybernetics* **64**, 165-170.

Hinton, G. E. and Zemel, R. S. (1994). Autoencoders, minimum description length and Helmholtz free energy. In J. D. Cowan, G. Tesauro, & J. Alspector (eds.), *Advances in Neural Information Processing Systems 6*. San Mateo, CA: Morgan Kaufmann, 3-10.

Neal, R. M., and Hinton, G. E. (1994). A new view of the EM algorithm that justifies incremental and other variants.

Rose, K., Gurewitz, F., and Fox, G. (1990). Statistical mechanics and phase transitions in clustering. *Physical Review Letters* **65**, 945-948.

Saund, E. (1995). A multiple cause mixture model for unsupervised learning. *Neural Computation* **7**, 51-71.

Tenenbaum, J. (1994). Functional parts. In A. Ram & K. Eiselt (eds.), *Proceedings of the Sixteenth Annual Conference of the Cognitive Science Society*. Hillsdale, NJ: Lawrence Erlbaum, 864-869.

Interior Point Implementations of Alternating Minimization Training

Michael Lemmon
Dept. of Electrical Engineering
University of Notre Dame
Notre Dame, IN 46556
lemmon@maddog.ee.nd.edu

Peter T. Szymanski
Dept. of Electrical Engineering
University of Notre Dame
Notre Dame, IN 46556
pszymans@maddog.ee.nd.edu

Abstract

This paper presents an alternating minimization (AM) algorithm used in the training of radial basis function and linear regressor networks. The algorithm is a modification of a small-step interior point method used in solving primal linear programs. The algorithm has a convergence rate of $O(\sqrt{n}L)$ iterations where n is a measure of the network size and L is a measure of the resulting solution's accuracy. Two results are presented that specify how aggressively the two steps of the AM may be pursued to ensure convergence of each step of the alternating minimization.

1 Introduction

In recent years, considerable research has investigated the use of alternating minimization (AM) techniques in the supervised training of radial basis function networks. AM techniques were first introduced in soft-competitive learning algorithms[1]. This training procedure was later shown to be closely related to Expectation-Maximization algorithms used by the statistical estimation community[2]. Alternating minimizations search for optimal network weights by breaking the search into two distinct minimization problems. A given network performance functional is extremalized first with respect to one set of network weights and then with respect to the remaining weights. These learning procedures have found applications in the training of local expert systems [3], and in Boltzmann machine training [4]. More recently, convergence rates have been derived by viewing the AM method as a variable metric algorithm [5].

This paper examines AM as a perturbed linear programming (LP) problem. Recent advances in the application of barrier function methods to LP problems have resulted in the development of "path following" or "interior point" (IP) algorithms [6]. These algorithms are characterized by a fast convergence rate that scales in a sublinear manner with problem size. This paper shows how a *small-step* IP algorithm for solving a primal LP problem can be modified into an AM training procedure. The principal results of the paper are bounds on how aggressively the legs of the alternating minimization can be pursued so that the AM algorithm maintains the sublinear convergence rate characteristic of its LP counterpart and so that both legs converge to an optimal solution.

2 Problem Statement

Consider a function approximation problem where a stochastic approximator learns a mapping $f : \mathbb{R}^N \to \mathbb{R}$. The approximator computes a *predicted output*, $\hat{y} \in \mathbb{R}$, given the input $\mathbf{z} \in \mathbb{R}^N$. The prediction is computed using a finite set of M regressors. The mth regressor is characterized by the pair $(\theta_m, \omega_m) \in \mathbb{R}^N \times \mathbb{R}^N$ ($m = 1, \ldots, M$). The output of the mth regressor, $\hat{y}_m \in \mathbb{R}$, in response to an input, $\mathbf{z} \in \mathbb{R}^N$ is given by the linear function

$$\hat{y}_m = \theta_m^T \mathbf{z}. \tag{1}$$

The mth regressor ($m = 1, \ldots, M$) has an associated radial basis function (RBF) with parameter vector $\omega_m \in \mathbb{R}^N$. The mth RBF weights the contribution of the mth output in computing $\hat{y}$ and is defined as a normal probability density function

$$Q(m|\mathbf{z}) = k_m \exp(-\sigma^{-2} ||\omega_m - \mathbf{z}||^2) \tag{2}$$

where k_m is a normalizing constant. The set of all weights or *gating probabilities* is denoted by Q. The parameterization of the mth regressor is $\Theta_m = \langle \theta_m^T, \omega_m^T \rangle^T \in \mathbb{R}^{2N}$ ($m = 1, \ldots, M$) and the parameterization of the set of M linear regressors is

$$\Theta = \langle \Theta_1^T, \ldots, \Theta_M^T \rangle^T. \tag{3}$$

The preceding stochastic approximator can be viewed as a neural network. The network consists of $M+1$ neurons. M of the neurons are *agent neurons* while the other neuron is referred to as a *gating neuron*. The mth agent neuron is parameterized by θ_m, the first element of the pair $\Theta_m = \langle \theta_m^T, \omega_m^T \rangle^T$ ($m = 1, \ldots, M$). The agent neurons receive as input, the vector $\mathbf{z} \in \mathbb{R}^N$. The output of the mth agent neuron in response to an input $\mathbf{z}$ is $\hat{y}_m = \theta_m^T \mathbf{z}$ ($m = 1, \ldots, M$). The gating neuron is parameterized by the conditional gating probabilities, Q. The gating probabilities are defined by the set of vectors, $\bar{\omega} = \{\omega_1, \ldots, \omega_M\}$. The gating neuron receives the agent neurons' outputs and the vector $\mathbf{z}$ as its input. The gating neuron computes the network's output, $\hat{y}$, as a hard (4) or soft (5) choice

$$\hat{y} = \hat{y}_m; \quad m = \arg \max_{m=1,\ldots,M} Q(m|\mathbf{z}) \tag{4}$$

$$\hat{y} = \frac{\sum_{m=1}^{M} Q(m|\mathbf{z}) \hat{y}_m}{\sum_{m=1}^{M} Q(m|\mathbf{z})}. \tag{5}$$

The network will be said to be "optimal" with respect to a training set $\mathcal{T} = \{(\mathbf{z}_i, y_i) : y_i = f(\mathbf{z}_i), i = 1, \ldots, R\}$ if a mean square error criterion is minimized. Define the square output error of the mth agent neuron to be $e_m(\mathbf{z}_i) = (y_i - \theta_m^T \mathbf{z}_i)^2$ and the square weighting or *classifier* error of the mth RBF to be $c_m(\mathbf{z}_i) = ||\omega_m - \mathbf{z}_i||^2$. Let the combined square approximation error of the mth neuron be $d_m(\mathbf{z}_i) = \kappa_e e_m(\mathbf{z}_i) + \kappa_c c_m(\mathbf{z}_i)$ and let the average square approximation error of the network be

$$\bar{d}(Q, \Theta, \mathcal{T}) = \sum_{m=1}^{M} \sum_{i=1}^{R} p(\mathbf{z}_i) Q(m|\mathbf{z}_i) d_m(\mathbf{z}_i). \tag{6}$$

Minimizing (6) corresponds to minimizing both the output error in the M linear regressors and the classifier error in assigning inputs to the M regressors. Since $\mathcal{T}$ is a discrete set and the Q are gating probabilities, the minimization of $\bar{d}(Q, \Theta, \mathcal{T})$ is constrained so that Q is a valid conditional probability mass function over the training set, $\mathcal{T}$.

Network training can therefore be viewed as a constrained optimization problem. In particular, this optimization problem can be expressed in a form very similar to conventional LP problems. The following notational conventions are adopted to highlight this connection. Let $\mathbf{x} \in \mathbb{R}^{MR}$ be the gating neuron's weight vector where

$$\mathbf{x} = \langle Q(1|\mathbf{z}_1), \ldots, Q(1|\mathbf{z}_R), Q(2|\mathbf{z}_1), \ldots, Q(m|\mathbf{z}_i), \ldots \rangle^T. \tag{7}$$

Let $\Theta_m = \langle \theta_m^T, \omega_m^T \rangle^T \in \mathbb{R}^{2N}$ denote the parameter vectors associated with the mth regressor and define the cost vector conditioned on $\Theta = \langle \Theta_1^T, \ldots, \Theta_M^T \rangle^T$ as

$$\mathbf{c}(\Theta) = \langle p(\mathbf{z}_1) d_1(\mathbf{z}_1), \ldots, p(\mathbf{z}_R) d_1(\mathbf{z}_R), p(\mathbf{z}_2) d_2(\mathbf{z}_2), \ldots, p(\mathbf{z}_i) d_m(\mathbf{z}_i), \ldots \rangle^T \tag{8}$$

With this notation, the network training problem can be stated as follows,

$$\begin{array}{ll} \text{minimize} & \mathbf{c}^T(\Theta)\mathbf{x} \\ \text{with respect to} & \mathbf{x}, \Theta \\ \text{subject to} & A\mathbf{x} = \mathbf{b}, \mathbf{x} \geq 0 \end{array} \tag{9}$$

where $\mathbf{b} = (1, \cdots, 1)^T \in \mathbb{R}^R$, $A = [I_{R \times R} \cdots I_{R \times R}] \in \mathbb{R}^{R \times MR}$, and $\mathbf{x} \geq 0$ implies $x_i \geq 0$ for $i = 1, \ldots, MR$.

One approach for solving this problem is to break up the optimization into two steps. The first step involves minimizing the above cost functional with respect to $\mathbf{x}$ assuming a fixed Θ. This is the Q-update of the algorithm. The second leg of the algorithm minimizes the functional with respect to Θ assuming fixed $\mathbf{x}$. This leg is called the Θ-update. Because the proposed optimization alternates between two different subsets of weights, this training procedure is often referred to as *alternating minimization*. Note that the Q-update is an LP problem while the Θ-update is a quadratic programming problem. Consequently, the AM training procedure can be viewed as a perturbed LP problem.

3 Proposed Training Algorithm

The preceding section noted that network training can be viewed as a perturbed LP problem. This observation is significant for there exist very efficient LP solvers based on barrier function methods used in non-linear optimization. Recent advances in path following or interior point (IP) methods have developed LP solvers which exhibit convergence rates which scale in a sublinear way with problem size [6]. This section introduces a modification of a small-step primal IP algorithm that can be used for neural network training. The proposed modification is later shown to preserve the computational efficiency enjoyed by its LP counterpart.

To see how such a modification might arise, we first need to examine path following LP solvers. Consider the following LP problem.

$$\begin{array}{ll} \text{minimize} & \mathbf{c}^T \mathbf{x} \\ \text{with respect to} & \mathbf{x} \in \mathbb{R}^n \\ \text{subject to} & A\mathbf{x} = \mathbf{b}, \mathbf{x} \geq 0 \end{array} \quad (10)$$

This problem can be solved by solving a sequence of augmented optimization problems arising from the primal parameterization of the LP problem.

$$\begin{array}{ll} \text{minimize} & \alpha^{(k)} \mathbf{c}^T \mathbf{x}^{(k)} - \sum_i \log x_i^{(k)} \\ \text{with respect to} & \mathbf{x}^{(k)} \in \mathbb{R}^n \\ \text{subject to} & A\mathbf{x}^{(k)} = \mathbf{b}, \mathbf{x}^{(k)} \geq 0 \end{array} \quad (11)$$

where $\alpha^{(k)} \geq 0$ ($k = 1, \cdots, K$) is a finite length, monotone increasing sequence of real numbers. $\mathbf{x}^*(\alpha^{(k)})$ denotes the solution for the kth optimization problem in the sequence and is referred to as a *central point*. The locus of all points, $\mathbf{x}^*(\alpha^{(k)})$ where $\alpha^{(k)} \geq 0$ is called the *central path*. The augmented problem takes the original LP cost function and adds a logarithmic barrier which keeps the central point away from the boundaries of the feasible set. As α increases, the effect of the barrier is decreased, thereby allowing the kth central point to approach the LP problem's solution in a controlled manner.

Path following (IP) methods solve the LP problem by approximately solving the sequence of augmented problems shown in (11). The parameter sequence, $\alpha^{(0)}, \alpha^{(1)}, \cdots, \alpha^{(K)}$, is chosen to be a monotone increasing sequence so that the central points, $\mathbf{x}^*(\alpha^{(k)})$, of each augmented optimization approach the LP solution in a monotone manner. It has been shown that for specific choices of the α sequence, that the sequence of approximate central points will converge to an ϵ-neighborhood of the LP solution after a finite number of iterations. For primal IP algorithms, the required condition is that successive approximations of the central points lie within the region of quadratic convergence for a scaling steepest descent (SSD) algorithm [6]. In particular, it has been shown that if the kth approximating solution is sufficiently close to the kth central point and if $\alpha^{(k+1)} = \alpha^{(k)}(1 + \nu/\sqrt{n})$ where $\nu \leq 0.1$ controls the distance between successive central points, then the "closeness" to the $(k+1)^{st}$ central point is guaranteed and the resulting algorithm will converge in $O(\sqrt{n}L)$ iterations where $L = n + p + 1$ specifies the size of the LP problem and p is the total number of bits used to represent the data in A, $\mathbf{b}$, and $\mathbf{c}$. If the algorithm takes small steps, then it is guaranteed to converge efficiently.

The preceding discussion reveals that a key component to a path following method's computational efficiency lies in controlling the iteration so that successive central points lie within the SSD algorithm's region of quadratic convergence. If we are to successfully extend such methods to (9), then this "closeness" of successive solutions must be preserved by the Θ-update of the algorithm. Due to the quadratic nature of the Θ-update, this minimization can be done exactly using a single Newton-Raphson iteration. Let Θ^* denote Θ-update's minimizer. If we update Θ to Θ^*, it is quite possible that the cost vector, $\mathbf{c}(\Theta)$, will be rotated in such a way that the current solution, $\mathbf{x}^{(k)}$, no longer lies in the region of quadratic convergence. Therefore, if we are to preserve the IP method's computational efficiency it will be necessary to be less "aggressive" in the Θ-update. In particular, this paper proposes the following convex combination as the Θ-update

$$\Theta_m^{(k+1)} = (1 - \gamma^{(k)})\Theta_m^{(k)} + \gamma^{(k)}\Theta_m^{(k+1),*} \qquad (12)$$

where $\Theta_m^{(k)}$ is the mth parameter vector at time k and $0 < \gamma^{(k)} < 1$ controls the size of the update. This will ensure convergence of the Q-update.

Convergence of the AM algorithm also requires convergence of the Θ-update. For the Θ-update to converge, $\gamma^{(k)}$ in (12) must go to unity as k increases. Convergence of $\gamma^{(k)}$ to unity requires that the sequence $||\Theta_m^{(k+1),*} - \Theta_m^{(k)}||$ be monotone decreasing. As the Θ-update minimizer, $\Theta^{(k+1),*}$, depends upon the current weights, $Q^{(k)}(m|\mathbf{z})$, large changes to Q can prevent the sequence from being monotone decreasing. Thus, it is necessary to also be less "aggressive" in the Q-update. An appropriate bound on ν is the proposed solution to guarantee convergence of the Θ-update.

Algorithm 1 (Proposed Training Algorithm)

Initialize
    $k = 0$.
    Choose $x_i^{(k)}$, $\Theta_m^{(k)}$, and $\alpha^{(k)}$ for $i = 1, \cdots, (MR)$, and for $m = 1, \cdots, M$.
repeat
    $\alpha^{(k+1)} = \alpha^{(k)}(1 + \nu/\sqrt{n})$, where $\nu \leq 0.1$.
    Q-update:
        $\mathbf{x}_0 = \mathbf{x}^{(k)}$
        for $i = 0, \cdots, P-1$
            $\mathbf{x}_{i+1} = ScalingSteepestDescent(\mathbf{x}_i^{(k+1)}, \alpha^{(k+1)}, \Theta^{(k)})$
        $\mathbf{x}^{(k+1)} = \mathbf{x}_P$
    Θ-update: For $m = 1, \ldots, M$
$$\Theta_m^{(k+1)} = (1 - \gamma^{(k)})\Theta_m^{(k)} + \gamma^{(k)}\Theta_m^{(k+1),*}$$
    $k = k + 1$
until$(\Delta < \epsilon)$

---

4 Theoretical Results

This section provides bounds on the parameter, $\gamma^{(k)}$, controlling the AM algorithm's Θ-update so that successive $\mathbf{x}^{(k)}$ vector solutions lie within the SSD algorithm's region of quadratic convergence and on ν controlling the Q-update so that successive central points are not too far apart, thus allowing convergence of the Θ-update.

Theorem 1 *Let $\Theta_m^{(k)}$ and $\Theta_m^{(k),*}$ be the current and minimizing parameter vectors at time k. Let $\mathbf{c}^{(k)} = \mathbf{c}(\Theta^{(k)})$ and $\mathbf{c}^{(k),*} = \mathbf{c}(\Theta^{(k),*})$. Let $\delta(\mathbf{x}, \alpha, \Theta) =$*

$\|P_{AX}X\left(\alpha \mathbf{c}(\Theta) - \mathbf{x}^{-1}\right)\|$ be the step size of the SSD update where $P_A = I - A^T(AA^T)^{-1}A$ and $X = \text{diag}(x_1, \ldots, x_n)$. Assume that $\delta(\mathbf{x}^{(k+1)}, \alpha^{(k+1)}, \Theta^{(k)}) = \delta_1 < 0.5$ and let $\Theta_m^{(k+1)} = (1 - \gamma^{(k)})\Theta_m^{(k)} + \gamma^{(k)}\Theta_m^{(k+1),*}$. If $\gamma^{(k)}$ is chosen as

$$\gamma^{(k)} \leq \frac{\delta_2 - \delta_1}{n(1 + \nu/\sqrt{n})\|\mathbf{c}^{(k+1),*} - \mathbf{c}^{(k)}\|} \quad (13)$$

where $\delta_1 < \delta_2 = 0.5$, then $\delta(\mathbf{x}^{(k+1)}, \alpha^{(k+1)}, \Theta^{(k+1)}) \leq \delta_2 = 0.5$.

Proof: The proof must show that the choice of $\gamma^{(k)}$ maintains the nearness of $\mathbf{x}^{(k+1)}$ to the central path after the Θ-update. Let $\mathbf{h}(\mathbf{x}, \alpha, \Theta) = P_{AX}X\left(\alpha \mathbf{c}(\Theta) - \mathbf{x}^{-1}\right)$, $\mathbf{h}_1 = \mathbf{h}(\mathbf{x}^{(k+1)}, \alpha^{(k+1)}, \Theta^{(k)})$ and $\mathbf{h}_2 = \mathbf{h}(\mathbf{x}^{(k+1)}, \alpha^{(k+1)}, \Theta^{(k+1)})$. Using the triangle inequality produces

$$\|\mathbf{h}_2\| \leq \|\mathbf{h}_2 - \mathbf{h}_1\| + \|\mathbf{h}_1\|.$$

$\|\mathbf{h}_1\| = \delta_1$ by assumption, so

$$\|\mathbf{h}_2\| \leq \|\alpha^{(k+1)}P_{AX}X(\mathbf{c}^{(k+1)} - \mathbf{c}^{(k)})\| + \delta_1.$$

Using the convexity of the cost vectors produces $(\mathbf{c}^{(k+1)} - \mathbf{c}^{(k)}) \leq (1 - \gamma^{(k)})\mathbf{c}^{(k)} + \gamma^{(k)}\mathbf{c}^{(k+1),*} - \mathbf{c}^{(k)}$ resulting in

$$\|\mathbf{h}_2\| \leq \|\alpha^{(k+1)}\gamma^{(k)}P_{AX}X(\mathbf{c}^{(k+1),*} - \mathbf{c}^{(k)})\| + \delta_1.$$

Using the fact that $\|P_{AX}X\| \leq \Delta = n/\alpha^{(k)}$ (Δ is the *duality gap*),

$$\begin{aligned}\|\mathbf{h}_2\| &\leq \gamma^{(k)}\alpha^{(k+1)}\|P_{AX}X\|\,\|\mathbf{c}^{(k+1),*} - \mathbf{c}^{(k)}\| + \delta_1. \\ &\leq \gamma^{(k)}n(1 + \nu/\sqrt{n})\|\mathbf{c}^{(k+1),*} - \mathbf{c}^{(k)}\| + \delta_1.\end{aligned}$$

Plugging in the value of $\gamma^{(k)}$ from (13) and simplifying produces the desired result $\|\mathbf{h}_2\| \leq \delta_2 \leq 0.5$, guaranteeing that $\mathbf{x}^{(k+1)}$ remains close to $\mathbf{x}^{(k+1),*}$ after the Θ-update. $\square$

Theorem 1 shows that the non-linear optimization can be embedded within the steps of the path following algorithm without it taking solutions too far from successive central points. The following two results, found in [7], provide a bound on ν to guarantee convergence of the Θ-update. The bound on ν forces successive central points to be close and ensures convergence of the Θ-update.

Proposition 1 *Let* $B = \sum_{\mathbf{z}} p_{\mathbf{z}} Q(m|\mathbf{z})\mathbf{z}\mathbf{z}^T$, $E = \sum_{\mathbf{z}} p_{\mathbf{z}} \Delta Q(m|\mathbf{z})\mathbf{z}\mathbf{z}^T$, $\mathbf{w} = \sum_{\mathbf{z}} p_{\mathbf{z}} Q(m|\mathbf{z})y(\mathbf{z})\mathbf{z}$, *and* $\Delta \mathbf{w} = \sum_{\mathbf{z}} p_{\mathbf{z}} \Delta Q(m|\mathbf{z})y(\mathbf{z})\mathbf{z}$, *where* $Q(m|\mathbf{z}) = Q^{(k)}(m|\mathbf{z})$ *and* $\Delta Q(m|\mathbf{z}) = Q^{(k+1)}(m|\mathbf{z}) - Q^{((k)}m|\mathbf{z})$. *Assume that* $|y(\mathbf{z})| \leq Y$, $\|\mathbf{z}\| \leq \zeta$, *and that* B *is of full rank for all valid* Q's. *Finally, let* $\mu_{max} = \sup_Q \|B^{-1}\|$. *Then,*

$$\|\Theta_m^{(k+1),*} - \Theta_m^{(k),*}\| \leq 2(\nu^2 + 2\nu)K \quad (14)$$

where $K = \mu_{max}Y\zeta\left(1 + \frac{\zeta^2 \mu_{max}}{1-r}\right)$ *and* $r = \|B^{-1}\|\,\|E\| < 1$.

Theorem 2 *Assume that* $\|\mathbf{z}\| \leq \zeta$, $|y(\mathbf{z})| \leq Y$, $\|\Theta_m\| \leq \Theta_{max}$, *and that* $B = \sum_{\mathbf{z}} p_{\mathbf{z}} Q(m|\mathbf{z})\mathbf{z}\mathbf{z}^T$ *is of full rank for all valid* Q's *and that* $\|B^{-1}\|\,\|E\| = r < 1$. *If*

$$\begin{aligned}\nu \leq \min\{&0.1, \\ &-1 + \sqrt{1 + r/(2\zeta^2 \mu_{max})}, \\ &-1 + \sqrt{1 + \gamma_{min}\epsilon_\Theta/(2K)}\}\end{aligned} \quad (15)$$

where $K = \mu_{max} Y \zeta (1 + \zeta^2 \mu_{max}/(1-r))$, $\gamma_{min} = (\delta_2 - \delta_1)/(n(1 + 0.1/\sqrt{n}) ||\mathbf{c}^{(1),*} - \mathbf{c}^{(0)}||)$ and ϵ_Θ is the largest $||\Theta_m^{(k+1),*} - \Theta_m^{(k)}||$ such that $\gamma^{(k)} = 1$, then the Θ-update will converge with $||\Theta_m^{(k+1),*} - \Theta_m^{(k)}|| \to 0$ and $\gamma^{(k)} \to 1$ as k increases.

The preceding results guarantee the convergence of the component minimizations separately. Convergence of the total algorithm relies on the simultaneous convergence of both steps. This is currently being addressed using contraction mapping concepts and stability results from nonlinear stability analysis [8].

The convergence rate of the algorithm is established using the LP problem's duality gap. The duality gap is the difference between the current solutions for the primal and dual formulations of the LP problem. Path following algorithms allow the duality gap to be expressed as follows

$$\Delta(\alpha^{(k)}) = \frac{n + 0.5\sqrt{n}}{\alpha^{(k)}}. \qquad (16)$$

and thus provide a convenient stopping criterion for the algorithm. Note that $\alpha^{(k)} = \alpha^{(0)}/\beta^k$ where $\beta \leq (1+\nu/\sqrt{n})$. This implies that $\Delta^{(k)} = \beta^k \Delta^{(0)} \leq \beta^k 2^L$. If k is chosen so that $\beta^k 2^L \leq 2^{-L}$, then $\Delta^{(k)} \leq 2^{-L}$ which implies that $k \geq 2L/\log(1/\beta)$. Inserting our choice of β one finds that $k \geq (2\sqrt{n}L/\nu) + 2L$. The preceding argument establishes that the proposed convergence rate of $O(\sqrt{n}L)$ iterations. In other words, the procedure's training time scales in a *sublinear* manner with network size.

5 Simulation Example

Simulations were run on a time series prediction task to test the proposed algorithm. The training set is $\mathcal{T} = \{(\mathbf{z}_i, y_i) : y_i = y(iT), \mathbf{z}_i = \langle y_{i-1}, y_{i-2}, \ldots, y_{i-N} \rangle^T \in \mathbb{R}^N\}$ for $i = 0, 1, \ldots, 100$, $N = 4$, and $T = 0.04$ where the time series is defined as

$$y(t) = \sin(\pi t) - \sin(2\pi t) + \sin(3\pi t) - \sin(\pi t/2) \qquad (17)$$

The results describe the convergence of the algorithm. These experiments consisted of 100 randomly chosen samples with $N = 4$ and a number of agent neurons ranging from $M = 4$ to 20. This corresponds to an LP problem dimension of $n = 404$ to 2020. The stopping criteria for the tests was to run until the solution was within $\epsilon = 10^{-3}$ of a local minimum. The number of iterations and floating point operations (FLOPS) for the AM algorithm to converge are shown in Figures 1(a) and 1(b) with AM results denoted by "o" and the theoretical rates by a solid line. The algorithm exhibits approximately $O(\sqrt{n}L)$ iterations to converge as predicted. The computational cost, however is $O(n^2 L)$ FLOPS which is better than the predicted $O(n^{3.5}L)$. The difference is due to the use of sparse matrix techniques which reduce the number of computations. The resulting AM algorithm then has the complexity of a *matrix multiplication* instead of a matrix inversion. The use of the algorithm resulted in networks having mean square errors on the order of 10^{-3}.

6 Discussion

This paper has presented an AM algorithm which can be proven to converge in $O(\sqrt{n}L)$ iterations. The work has established a means by which IP methods can be

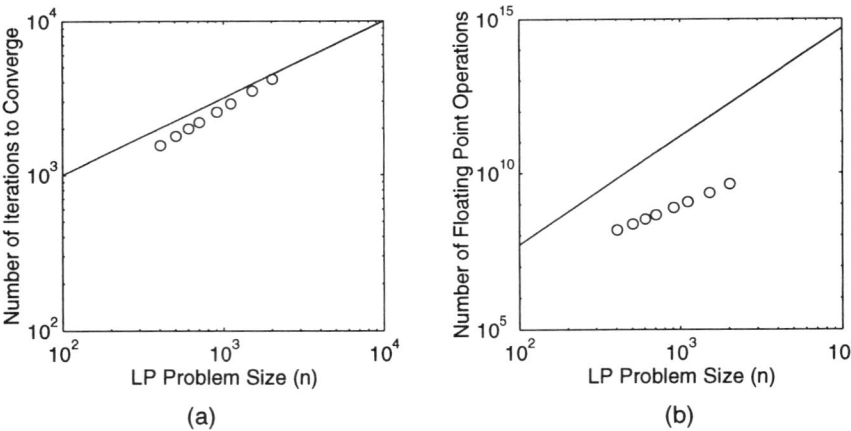

Figure 1: Convergence rates as a function of n

applied to NN training in a way which preserves the computational efficiency of IP solvers. The AM algorithm can be used to solve off-line problems such as codebook generation and parameter identification in colony control applications. The method is currently being used to solve hybrid control problems of the type in [9]. Areas of future research concern the study of large-step IP methods and extensions of AM training to other EM algorithms.

References

[1] S. Nowlan, "Maximum likelihood competitive learning," in *Advances in Neural Information Processing Systems 2*, pp. 574–582, San Mateo, California: Morgan Kaufmann Publishers, Inc., 1990.

[2] M. Jordan and R. Jacobs, "Hierarchical mixtures of experts and the EM algorithm," Tech. Rep. 9301, MIT Computational Cognitive Science, Apr. 1993.

[3] R. Jacobs, M. Jordan, S. Nowlan, and G. Hinton, "Adaptive mixtures of local experts," *Neural Computation*, vol. 3, pp. 79–87, 1991.

[4] W. Byrne, "Alternating minimization and Boltzmann machine learning," *IEEE Transactions on Neural Networks*, vol. 3, pp. 612–620, July 1992.

[5] M. Jordan and L. Xu, "Convergence results for the EM approach to mixtures of experts architectures," Tech. Rep. 9303, MIT Computational Cognitive Science, Sept. 1993.

[6] C. Gonzaga, "Path-following methods for linear programming," *SIAM Review*, vol. 34, pp. 167–224, June 1992.

[7] P. Szymanski and M. Lemmon, "A modified interior point method for supervisory controller design," in *Proceedings of the 33rd IEEE Conference on Decision and Control*, pp. 1381–1386, Dec. 1994.

[8] M. Vidyasagar, *Nonlinear Systems Analysis*. Englewood Cliffs, New Jersey: Prentice-Hall, Inc., 1993.

[9] M. Lemmon, J. Stiver, and P. Antsaklis, "Event identification and intelligent hybrid control," in *Hybrid Systems* (R. L. Grossman, A. Nerode, A. P. Ravn, and H. Rischel, eds.), vol. 736 of *Lecture Notes in Computer Science*, pp. 265–296, Springer-Verlag, 1993.

SARDNET: A Self-Organizing Feature Map for Sequences

Daniel L. James and Risto Miikkulainen
Department of Computer Sciences
The University of Texas at Austin
Austin, TX 78712
`dljames,risto@cs.utexas.edu`

Abstract

A self-organizing neural network for sequence classification called SARDNET is described and analyzed experimentally. SARDNET extends the Kohonen Feature Map architecture with activation retention and decay in order to create unique distributed response patterns for different sequences. SARDNET yields extremely dense yet descriptive representations of sequential input in very few training iterations. The network has proven successful on mapping arbitrary sequences of binary and real numbers, as well as phonemic representations of English words. Potential applications include isolated spoken word recognition and cognitive science models of sequence processing.

1 INTRODUCTION

While neural networks have proved a good tool for processing static patterns, classifying sequential information has remained a challenging task. The problem involves recognizing patterns in a time series of vectors, which requires forming a good internal representation for the sequences. Several researchers have proposed extending the self-organizing feature map (Kohonen 1989, 1990), a highly successful static pattern classification method, to sequential information (Kangas 1991; Samarabandu and Jakubowicz 1990; Scholtes 1991). Below, three of the most recent of these networks are briefly described. The remainder of the paper focuses on a new architecture designed to overcome the shortcomings of these approaches.

Recently, Chappel and Taylor (1993) proposed the Temporal Kohonen Map (TKM) architecture for classifying sequences. The TKM keeps track of the activation history of each node by updating a value called leaky integrator potential, inspired by the membrane potential in biological neural systems. The activity of a node depends both on the current input vector and the previous input vectors, represented by the node's potential. A given sequence is processed by mapping one vector at a time, and the last winning node serves to represent the entire sequence. This way, there needs to be a separate node for every possible sequence, which is a disadvantage when the number of sequences to be classified is large. The TKM also suffers from loss of context. Which node wins depends almost entirely upon the most recent input vectors. For example, the string **baaaa** would most likely map to the same node as **aaaaa**, making the approach applicable only to short sequences.

The SOFM-S network proposed by van Harmelen (1993) extends TKM such that the activity of each map node depends on the current input vector and the past activation of all map nodes. The SOFM-S is an improvement of TKM in that contextual information is not lost as quickly, but it still uses a single node to represent a sequence.

The TRACE feature map (Zandhuis 1992) has two feature map layers. The first layer is a topological map of the individual input vectors, and is used to generate a trace (i.e. path) of the input sequence on the map. The second layer then maps the trace pattern to a single node. In TRACE, the sequences are represented by distributed patterns on the first layer, potentially allowing for larger capacity, but it is difficult to encode sequences where the same vectors repeat, such as **baaaa**. All a-vectors would be mapped on the same unit in the first layer, and any number of a-vectors would be indistinguishable.

The architecture described in this paper, SARDNET (Sequential Activation Retention and Decay NETwork), also uses a subset of map nodes to represent the sequence of vectors. Such a distributed approach allows a large number of representations be "packed" into a small map—like sardines. In the following sections, we will examine how SARDNET differs from conventional self-organizing maps and how it can be used to represent and classify a large number of complex sequences.

2 THE SARDNET ARCHITECTURE

Input to SARDNET consists of a sequence of n-dimensional vectors $\mathbf{S} = \mathbf{V}_1, \mathbf{V}_2, \mathbf{V}_3, ..., \mathbf{V}_l$ (figure 1). The components of each vector are real values in the interval $[0, 1]$. For example, each vector might represent a sample of a speech signal in n different frequencies, and the entire sequence might constitute a spoken word. The SARDNET input layer consists of n nodes, one for each component in the input vector, and their values are denoted as $\mathbf{A} = (a_1, a_2, a_3, ..., a_n)$. The map consists of $m \times m$ nodes with activation o_{jk}, $1 \leq j, k \leq m$. Each node has an n-dimensional input weight vector $\mathbf{W}_{jk}$, which determines the node's response to the input activation.

In a conventional feature map network as well as in SARDNET, each input vector is mapped on a particular unit on the map, called the winner or the maximally responding unit. In SARDNET, however, once a node wins an input, it is made

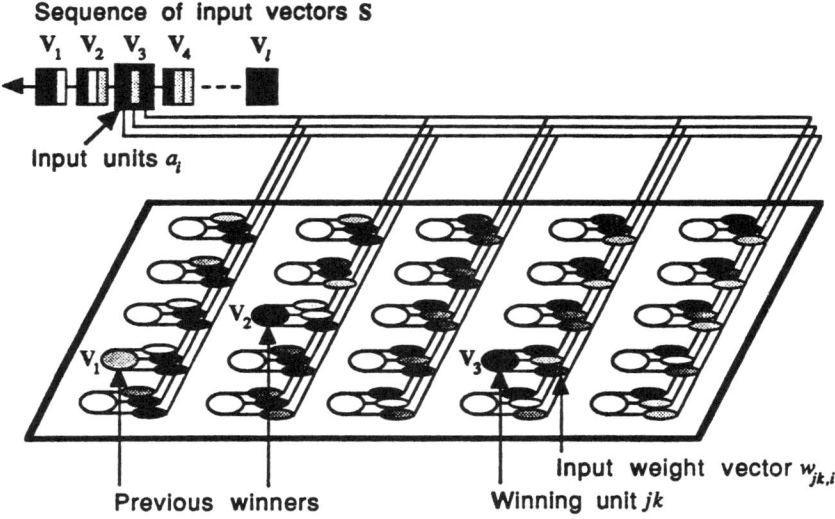

Figure 1: **The SARDNET architecture.** A sequence of input vectors activates units on the map one at a time. The past winners are excluded from further competition, and their activation is decayed gradually to indicate position in the sequence.

INITIALIZATION: Clear all map nodes to zero.
MAIN LOOP: While not end of sequence 1. Find unactivated weight vector that best matches the input. 2. Assign 1.0 activation to that unit. 3. Adjust weight vectors of the nodes in the neighborhood. 4. Exclude the winning unit from subsequent competition. 5. Decrement activation values for all other active nodes.
RESULT: Sequence representation = activated nodes ordered by activation values

Table 1: **The SARDNET training algorithm.**

uneligible to respond to the subsequent inputs in the sequence. This way a different map node is allocated for every vector in the sequence. As more vectors come in, the activation of the previous winners decays. In other words, each sequence of length l is represented by l active nodes on the map, with their activity indicating the order in which they were activated. The algorithm is summarized in table 1.

Assume the maximum length of the sequences we wish to classify is l, and each input vector component can take on p possible values. Since there are p^n possible input vectors, lp^n map nodes are needed to represent all possible vectors in all possible positions in the sequence, and a distributed pattern over the lp^n nodes can be used to represent all p^{nl} different sequences. This approach offers a significant advantage over methods in which p^{nl} nodes would be required for p^{nl} sequences.

The specific computations of the SARDNET algorithm are as follows: The winning node (j, k) in each iteration is determined by the Euclidean distance D_{jk} of the input vector **A** and the node's weight vector $\mathbf{W}_{jk}$:

$$D_{jk} = \sum_{i=0}^{n}(w_{jk,i} - a_i)^2. \qquad (1)$$

The unit with the smallest distance is selected as the winner and activated with 1.0. The weights of this node and all nodes in its neighborhood are changed according to the standard feature map adaptation rule:

$$\Delta w_{jk} = \alpha(w_{jk,i} - a_i), \qquad (2)$$

where α denotes the learning rate. As usual, the neighborhood starts out large and is gradually decreased as the map becomes more ordered. As the last step in processing an input vector, the activation η_{jk} of all active units in the map are decayed proportional to the decay parameter d:

$$\eta_{jk}(t+1) = d\eta_{jk}(t), \qquad 0 < d < 1. \qquad (3)$$

As in the standard feature map, as the weight vectors adapt, input vectors gradually become encoded in the weight vectors of the winning units. Because weights are changed in local neighborhoods, neighboring weight vectors are forced to become as similar as possible, and eventually the network forms a topological layout of the input vector space. In SARDNET, however, if an input vector occurs multiple times in the same input sequence, it will be represented multiple times on the map as well. In other words, the map representation expands those areas of the input space that are visited most often during an input sequence.

3 EXPERIMENTS

SARDNET has proven successful in learning and recognizing arbitrary sequences of binary and real numbers, as well as sequences of phonemic representations for English words. This section presents experiments on mapping three-syllable words. This data was selected because it shows how SARDNET can be applied to complex input derived from a real-world task.

3.1 INPUT DATA

The phonemic word representations were obtained from the CELEX database of the Max Planck Institute for Psycholinguistics and converted into International Phonetic Alphabet (IPA)-compliant representation, which better describes similarities among the phonemes. The words vary from five to twelve phonemes in length. Each phoneme is represented by five values: place, manner, sound, chromacity and sonority. For example, the consonant p is represented by a single vector (bilabial, stop, unvoiced, nil, nil), or in terms of real numbers, (.125, .167, .750, 0, 0). The diphthong sound ai as in "buy", is represented by the two vectors (nil, vowel, voiced, front, low) and (nil, vowel, voiced, front-center, hi-mid), or in real numbers, (0, 1, .25, .2, 1) and (0, 1, .25, .4, .286).

There are a total of 43 phonemes in this data set, including 23 consonants and 20 vowels. To represent all phonemic sequences of length 12, TKM and SOFM-S would

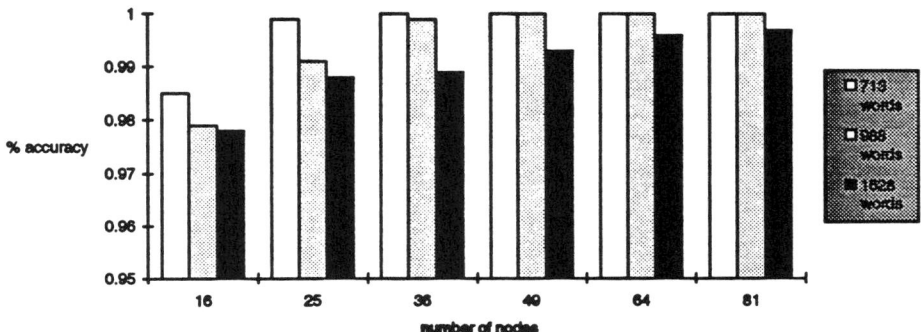

Figure 2: **Accuracy of SARDNET for different map and data set sizes.** The accuracy is measured as a percentage of unique representations out of all word sequences.

need to have $45^{12} \approx 6.9^{19}$ map nodes, whereas SARDNET would need only 45 x 12 = 540 nodes. Of course, only a very small subset of the possible sequences actually occur in the data. Three data sets consisting of 713, 988, and 1628 words were used in the experiments. If the maximum number of occurrences of phoneme i in any single sequence is c_i, then the number of nodes SARDNET needs is $C = \sum_{i=0}^{N} c_i$, where N is the number of phonemes. This number of nodes will allow SARDNET to map each phoneme in each sequence to a unit with an exact representation of that phoneme in its weights. Calculated this way, SARDNET should scale up very well with the number of words: it would need 81 nodes for representing the 713 word set, 84 for the 988 set and 88 for the 1628 set.

3.2 DENSENESS AND ACCURACY

A series of experiments with the above three data sets and maps of 16 to 81 nodes were run to see how accurately SARDNET can represent the sequences. Self-organization was quite fast: each simulation took only about 10 epochs, with $\alpha = 0.45$ and the neighborhood radius decreasing gradually from 5-1 to zero. Figure 2 shows the percentage of unique representations for each data set and map size.

SARDNET shows remarkable representational power: accuracy for all sets is better than 97.7%, and SARDNET manages to pack 1592 unique representations even on the smallest 16-node map. Even when there are not enough units to represent each phoneme in each sequence exactly, the map is sometimes able to "reuse" units to represent multiple similar phonemes. For example, assume units with exact representations for the phonemes **a** and **b** exist somewhere on the map, and the input data does not contain pairs of sequences such as **aba–abb**, in which it is crucial to distinguished the second **a** from the second **b**. In this case, the second occurrence of both phonemes could be represented by the same unit with a weight vector that is the average of **a** and **b**. This is exactly what the map is doing: it is finding the most descriptive representation of the data, given the available resources.

Note that it would be possible to determine the needed $C = \sum_{i=0}^{N} c_i$ phoneme representation vectors directly from the input data set, and without any learning or a map structure at all, establish distributed representations on these vectors with the SARDNET algorithm. However, feature map learning is necessary if the number of available representation vectors is less than C. The topological organization of the map allows finding a good set of reusable vectors that can stand for different phonemes in different sequences, making the representation more efficient.

3.3 REPRESENTING SIMILARITY

Not only are the representations densely packed on the map, they are also descriptive in the sense that similar sequences have similar representations. Figure 3 shows the final activation patterns on the 36-unit, 713-word map for six example words. The first two words, "misplacement" and "displacement," sound very similar, and are represented by very similar patterns on the map. Because there is only one **m** in "displacement", it is mapped on the same unit as the initial **m** of "misplacement." Note that the two **m**s are mapped next to each other, indicating that the map is indeed topological, and small changes in the input cause only small changes in the map representation. Note also how the units in this small map are reused to represent several different phonemes in different contexts.

The other examples in figure 3 display different types of similarities with "misplacement". The third word, "miscarried", also begins with "mis", and shares that subpart of the representation exactly. Similarly, "repayment" shares a similar tail and "pessimist" the subsequence "mis" in a different part or the word. Because they appear in a different context, these subsequences are mapped on slightly different units, but still very close to their positions with "misplacement." The last word, "burundi" sounds very different, as its representation on the map indicates.

Such descriptive representations are important when the map has to represent information that is incomplete or corrupted with noise. Small changes in the input sequence cause small changes in the pattern, and the sequence can still be recognized. This property should turn out extremely important in real-world applications of SARDNET, as well as in cognitive science models where confusing similar patterns with each other is often plausible behavior.

4 DISCUSSION AND FUTURE RESEARCH

Because the sequence representations on the map are distributed, the number of possible sequences that can be represented in m units is exponential in m, instead of linear as in most previous sequential feature map architectures. This denseness together with the tendency to map similar sequences to similar representations should turn out useful in real-world applications, which often require scale-up to large and noisy data sets. For example, SARDNET could form the core of an isolated word recognition system. The word input would be encoded in duration-normalized sequences of sound samples such as a string of phonemes, or perhaps representations of salient transitions in the speech signal. It might also be possible to modify SARDNET to form a more continuous trajectory on the map so that SARDNET itself would take care of variability in word duration. For example, a

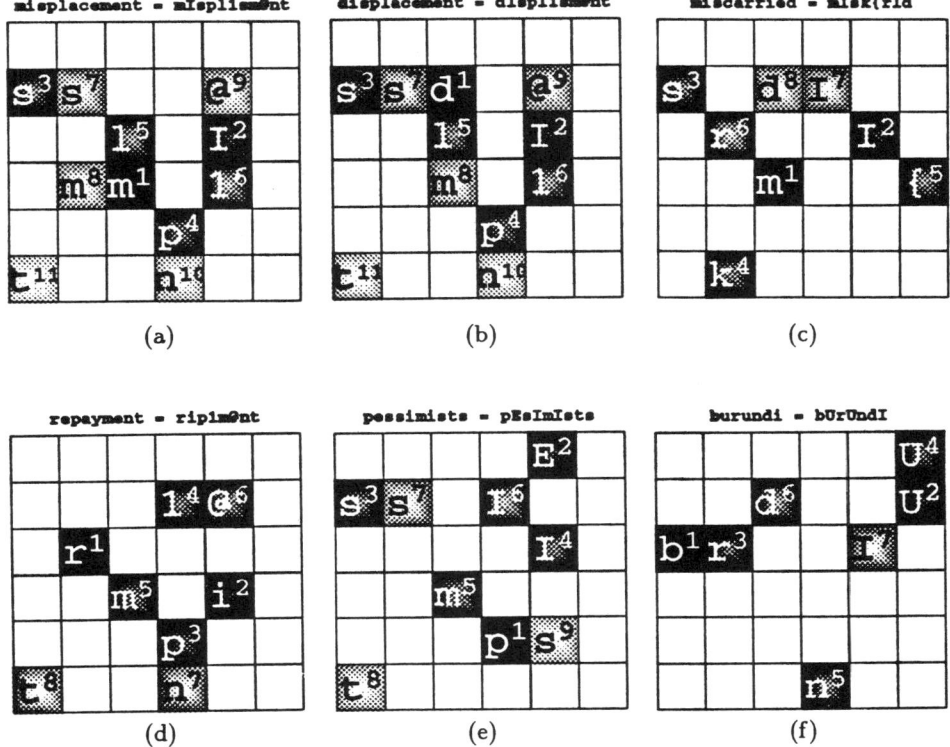

Figure 3: **Example map representations.**

sequence of redundant inputs could be reduced to a single node if all these inputs fall within the same neighborhood.

Even though the sequence representations are dense, they are also descriptive. Category memberships are measured not by labels of the maximally responding units, but by the differences in the response patterns themselves. This sort of distributed representation should be useful in cognitive systems where sequential input must be mapped to an internal static representation for later retrieval and manipulation. Similarity-based reasoning on sequences should be easy to implement, and the sequence can be easily recreated from the activity pattern on the map.

Given part of a sequence, SARDNET may also be modified to predict the rest of the sequence. This can be done by adding lateral connections between the nodes in the map layer. The lateral connections between successive winners would be strengthened during training. Thus, given part of a sequence, one could follow the strongest lateral connections to complete the sequence.

5 CONCLUSION

SARDNET is a novel feature map architecture for classifying sequences of input vectors. Each sequence is mapped on a distributed representation on the map, making it possible to pack a remarkable large number of category representations on a small feature map. The representations are not only dense, they also represent the similarities of the sequences, which should turn out useful in cognitive science as well as real-world applications of the architecture.

Acknowledgments

Thanks to Jon Hilbert for converting CELEX data into the International Phonetic Alphabet format used in the experiments. This research was supported in part by the National Science Foundation under grant #IRI-9309273.

References

Chappel, G. J., and Taylor, J. G. (1993). The temporal Kohonen map. *Neural Networks*, 6:441-445.

Kangas, J. (1991). Time-dependent self-organizing maps for speech recognition. In *Proceedings of the International Conference on Artificial Neural Networks* (Espoo, Finland), 1591-1594. Amsterdam; New York: North-Holland.

Kohonen, T. (1989). *Self-Organization and Associative Memory*. Berlin; Heidelberg; New York: Springer. Third edition.

Kohonen, T. (1990). The self-organizing map. *Proceedings of the IEEE*, 78:1464-1480.

Samarabandu, J. K., and Jakubowicz, O. G. (1990). Principles of sequential feature maps in multi-level problems. In *Proceedings of the International Joint Conference on Neural Networks* (Washington, DC), vol. II, 683-686. Hillsdale, NJ: Erlbaum.

Scholtes, J. C. (1991). Recurrent Kohonen self-organization in natural language processing. In *Proceedings of the International Conference on Artificial Neural Networks* (Espoo, Finland), 1751-1754. Amsterdam; New York: North-Holland.

van Harmelen, H. (1993). Time dependent self-organizing feature map for speech recognition. Master's thesis, University of Twente, Enschede, the Netherlands.

Zandhuis, J. A. (1992). Storing sequential data in self-organizing feature maps. Internal Report MPI-NL-TG-4/92, Max-Planck-Institute für Psycholinguistik, Nijmegen, the Netherlands.

Convergence Properties of the K-Means Algorithms

Léon Bottou
Neuristique,
28 rue des Petites Ecuries,
75010 Paris, France
leon@neuristique.fr

Yoshua Bengio[*]
Dept. I.R.O.
Université de Montréal
Montreal, Qc H3C-3J7, Canada
bengioy@iro.umontreal.ca

Abstract

This paper studies the convergence properties of the well known K-Means clustering algorithm. The K-Means algorithm can be described either as a gradient descent algorithm or by slightly extending the mathematics of the EM algorithm to this hard threshold case. We show that the K-Means algorithm actually minimizes the quantization error using the very fast Newton algorithm.

1 INTRODUCTION

K-Means is a popular clustering algorithm used in many applications, including the initialization of more computationally expensive algorithms (Gaussian mixtures, Radial Basis Functions, Learning Vector Quantization and some Hidden Markov Models). The practice of this initialization procedure often gives the frustrating feeling that K-Means performs most of the task in a small fraction of the overall time. This motivated us to better understand this convergence speed.

A second reason lies in the traditional debate between hard threshold (e.g. K-Means, Viterbi Training) and soft threshold (e.g. Gaussian Mixtures, Baum Welch) algorithms (Nowlan, 1991). Soft threshold algorithms are often preferred because they have an elegant probabilistic framework and a general optimization algorithm named EM (expectation-maximization) (Dempster, Laird and Rubin, 1977). In the case of a gaussian mixture, the EM algorithm has recently been shown to *approximate* the Newton optimization algorithm (Xu and Jordan, 1994). We prove in this

---

[*]also, AT&T Bell Labs, Holmdel, NJ 07733

paper that the corresponding hard threshold algorithm, K-Means, minimizes the quantization error using *exactly* the Newton algorithm.

In the next section, we derive the K-Means algorithm as a gradient descent procedure. Section 3 extends the mathematics of the EM algorithm to the case of K-Means. This second derivation of K-Means provides us with proper values for the learning rates. In section 4 we show that this choice of learning rates optimally rescales the parameter space using Newton's method. Finally, in section 5 we present and discuss a few experimental results comparing various versions of the K-Means algorithm. The 5 clustering algorithms presented here were chosen for a good coverage of the algorithms related to K-Means, but this paper does not have the ambition of presenting a literature survey on the subject.

2 K-MEANS AS A GRADIENT DESCENT

Given a set of P examples (x_i), the K-Means algorithm computes k prototypes $w = (w_k)$ which minimize the *quantization error*, i.e., the average distance between each pattern and the closest prototype:

$$E(w) \stackrel{\text{def}}{=} \sum_i L(x_i, w) \stackrel{\text{def}}{=} \sum_i \frac{1}{2} \min_k (x_i - w_k)^2 \qquad (1)$$

Writing $s_i(w)$ for the subscript of the closest prototype to example x_i, we have

$$E(w) = \sum_i \frac{1}{2}(x_i - w_{s_i(w)})^2 \qquad (2)$$

2.1 GRADIENT DESCENT ALGORITHM

We can then derive a *gradient descent* algorithm for the quantization error: $\Delta w = -\epsilon_t \frac{\partial E(w)}{\partial w}$. This leads to the following *batch update* equation (updating prototypes after presenting all the examples):

$$\Delta w_k = \sum_i \begin{cases} \epsilon_t (x_i - w_k) & \text{if } k = s_i(w) \\ 0 & \text{otherwise.} \end{cases} \qquad (3)$$

We can also derive a corresponding *online* algorithm which updates the prototypes after the presentation of each pattern x_i:

$$\Delta w = -\epsilon_t \frac{\partial L(x_i, w)}{\partial w}, \quad \text{i.e.,}$$

$$\Delta w_k = \begin{cases} \epsilon_t (x_i - w_k) & \text{if } k = s_i(w) \\ 0 & \text{otherwise.} \end{cases} \qquad (4)$$

The proper value of the learning rate ϵ_t remain to be specified in both batch and online algorithms. Convergence proofs for both algorithms (Bottou, 1991) exist for decreasing values of the learning rates satisfying the conditions $\sum \epsilon_t = \infty$ and $\sum \epsilon_t^2 < \infty$. Following (Kohonen, 1989), we could choose $\epsilon_t = \epsilon_0/t$. We prove however in this paper that there exist a much better choice of learning rates.

3 K-MEANS AS AN EM STYLE ALGORITHM

3.1 EM STYLE ALGORITHM

The following derivation of K-Means is similar to the derivation of (MacQueen, 1967). We insist however on the identity between this derivation and the mathematics of EM (Liporace, 1976) (Dempster, Laird and Rubin, 1977).

Although K-Means does not fit in a probabilistic framework, this similarity holds for a very deep reason: The semi-ring of probabilies $(\Re^+, +, \times)$ and the idempotent semi-ring of hard-threshold scores $(\Re, \mathrm{Min}, +)$ share the most significant algebraic properties (Bacceli, Cohen and Olsder, 1992). This assertion completely describes the similarities and the potential differences between soft-threshold and hard-threshold algorithms. A complete discussion however stands outside the scope of this paper.

The principle of EM is to introduce additional "hidden" variables whose knowledge would make the optimization problem easier. Since these hidden variables are unknown, we maximize an auxiliary function which averages over the values of the hidden variables given the values of the parameters at the previous iteration. In our case, the hidden variables are the assignments $s_i(w)$ of the patterns to the prototypes. Instead of considering the expected value over the distribution on these hidden variables, we just consider the values of the hidden variables that minimize the cost, given the previous values of the parameters:

$$Q(w', w) \stackrel{\text{def}}{=} \sum_i \frac{1}{2}(x_i - w'_{s_i(w)})^2$$

The next step consists then in finding a new set of prototypes w' which minimizes $Q(w', w)$ where w is the previous set of prototypes. We can analytically compute the explicit solution of this minimization problem. Solving the equation $\partial Q(w', w)/\partial w'_k = 0$ yields:

$$w'_k = \frac{1}{N_k} \sum_{i\,:\,k=s_i(w)} x_i \qquad (5)$$

where N_k is the number of examples assigned to prototype w_k. The algorithm consists in repeatedly replacing w by w' using update equation (6) until convergence. Since $s_i(w')$ is by definition the best assignment of patterns x_i to the prototypes w'_k, we have the following inequality:

$$E(w') - Q(w', w) = \frac{1}{2}\sum_i (x_i - w'_{s_i(w')})^2 - (x_i - w'_{s_i(w)})^2 \leq 0$$

Using this result, the identity $E(w) = Q(w, w)$ and the definition of w', we can derive the following inequality:

$$\begin{aligned} E(w') - E(w) &= E(w') - Q(w', w) + Q(w', w) - Q(w, w) \\ &\leq Q(w', w) - Q(w, w) \ \leq \ 0 \end{aligned}$$

Each iteration of the algorithm thus decreases the otherwise positive quantization error E (equation 1) until the error reaches a fixed point where condition $w^{*\prime} = w^*$ is verified (unicity of the minimum of $Q(\bullet, w^*)$). Since the assignment functions $s_i(w)$ are discrete, there is an open neighborhood of w^* on which the assignments are constant. According to their definition, functions $E(\bullet)$ and $Q(\bullet, w^*)$ are equal on this neighborhood. Being the minimum of function $Q(\bullet, w^*)$, the fixed point w^* of this algorithm is also a local minimum of the quantization error E. □

3.2 BATCH K-MEANS

The above algorithm (5) can be rewritten in a form similar to that of the batch gradient descent algorithm (3).

$$\Delta w_k = w'_k - w_k = \sum_i \begin{cases} \frac{1}{N_k}(x_i - w_k) & \text{if } k = s(x_i, w) \\ 0 & \text{otherwise.} \end{cases} \quad (6)$$

This algorithm is thus equivalent to a batch gradient descent with a specific, prototype dependent, learning rate $\frac{1}{N_k}$.

3.3 ONLINE K-MEANS

The online version of our EM style update equation (5) is based on the computation of the mean μ_t of the examples $x_1, \cdots, x_t$ with the following recursive formula:

$$\mu_{t+1} = \frac{1}{t+1}(t\,\mu_t + x_{t+1}) = \mu_t + \frac{1}{t+1}(x_{t+1} - \mu_t)$$

Let us introduce new variables n_k which count the number of examples so far assigned to prototype w_k. We can then rewrite (5) as an online update applied after the presentation of each pattern x_i:

$$\begin{aligned} \Delta n_k &= \begin{cases} 1 & \text{if } k = s(x_i, w) \\ 0 & \text{otherwise.} \end{cases} \\ \Delta w_k &= \begin{cases} \frac{1}{n_k}(x_i - w_k) & \text{if } k = s(x_i, w) \\ 0 & \text{otherwise.} \end{cases} \end{aligned} \quad (7)$$

This algorithm is equivalent to an online gradient descent (4) with a specific, prototype dependent, learning rate $\frac{1}{n_k}$. Unlike in the batch case, the pattern assignments $s(x_i, w)$ are thus changing after each pattern presentation. Before applying this algorithm, we must of course set n_k to zero and w_k to some initial value. Various methods have been proposed including initializing w_k with the first k patterns.

3.4 CONVERGENCE

General convergence proofs for the batch and online gradient descent (Bottou, 1991; Driancourt, 1994) directly apply for all four algorithms. Although the derivatives are undefined on a few points, these theorems prove that the algorithms almost surely converge to a local minimum because the local variations of the loss function are conveniently bounded (semi-differentiability). Unlike previous results, the above convergence proofs allow for non-linearity, non-differentiability (on a few points) (Bottou, 1991), and replacing learning rates by a positive definite matrix (Driancourt, 1994).

4 K-MEANS AS A NEWTON OPTIMIZATION

We prove in this section that Batch K-Means (6) applies the Newton algorithm.

4.1 THE HESSIAN OF K-MEANS

Let us compute the Hessian H of the K-Means cost function (2). This matrix contains the second derivatives of the cost $E(w)$ with respect to each pair of parameters. Since $E(w)$ is a sum of terms $L(x_i, w)$, we can decompose H as the sum of matrices H_i for each term of the cost function:

$$L(x_i, w) = \min_k \frac{1}{2}(x_i - w_k)^2.$$

Furthermore, the H_i can be decomposed in blocks corresponding to each pair of prototypes. Since $L(x_i, w)$ depends only on the closest prototype to pattern x_i, all these blocks are zero except block $(s_i(w), s_i(w))$ which is the identity matrix. Summing the partial Hessian matrices H_i thus gives a diagonal matrix whose diagonal elements are the counts of examples N_k assigned to each prototype.

$$H = \begin{pmatrix} N_1 I & 0 & \cdots & 0 \\ 0 & N_2 I & \cdots & 0 \\ \vdots & \vdots & & \vdots \\ 0 & 0 & \cdots & N_K I \end{pmatrix}$$

We can thus write the Newton update of the parameters as follows:

$$\Delta w = -H^{-1} \frac{\partial E(w)}{\partial w}$$

which can be exactly rewritten as the batch EM style algorithm (6) presented earlier:

$$\Delta w_k = \sum_i \begin{cases} \frac{1}{N_k}(x_i - w_k) & \text{if } k = s(x_i, w) \\ 0 & \text{otherwise.} \end{cases} \quad (8)$$

4.2 CONVERGENCE SPEED

When optimizing a quadratic function, Newton's algorithm requires only one step. In the case of a non quadratic function, Newton's algorithm is superlinear if we can bound the variations of the second derivatives. Standard theorems that bound this variation using the third derivative are not useful for K-Means because the gradient of the cost function is discontinuous. We could notice that the variations of the second derivatives are however nicely bounded and derive similar proofs for K-Means.

For the sake of brevity however, we are just giving here an intuitive argument: we can make the cost function indefinitely differentiable by rounding up the angles around the non differentiable points. We can even restrict this cost function change to an arbitrary small region of the space. The iterations of K-Means will avoid this region with a probability arbitrarily close to 1. In practice, we obtain thus a superlinear convergence.

Batch K-Means thus searches for the optimal prototypes at Newton speed. Once it comes close enough to the optimal prototypes (i.e. the pattern assignment is optimal and the cost function becomes quadratic), K-Means jumps to the optimum and terminates.

Online K-Means benefits of these optimal learning rates because they remove the usual conditioning problems of the optimization. However, the stochastic noise induced by the online procedure limits the final convergence of the algorithm. Final convergence speed is thus essentially determined by the schedule of the learning rates.

Online K-Means also benefits from the redundancies of the training set. It converges significantly faster than batch K-Means during the first training epochs (Darken

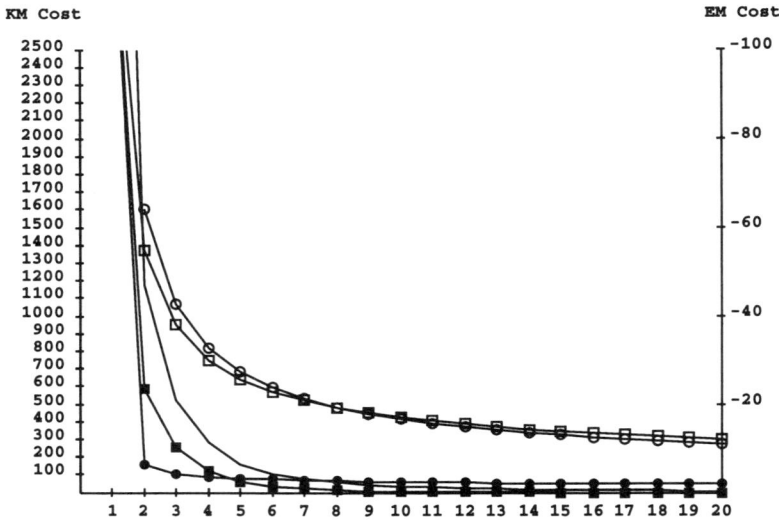

Figure 1: $E_t - E_\infty$ versus t. black circles: online K-Means; black squares: batch K-Means; empty circles: online gradient; empty squares: batch gradient; no mark: EM+Gaussian mixture

and Moody, 1991). After going through the first few patterns (depending of the amount of redundancy), online K-Means indeed improves the prototypes as much as a complete batch K-Means epoch. Other researchers have compared batch and online algorithms for neural networks, with similar conclusions (Bengio, 1991).

5 EXPERIMENTS

Experiments have been carried out with Fisher's iris data set, which is composed of 150 points in a four dimensional space representing physical measurements on various species of iris flowers. Codebooks of six prototypes have been computed using both batch and online K-Means with the proper learning rates (6) and (7). These results are compared with those obtained using both gradient descent algorithms (3) and (4) using learning rate $\epsilon_t = 0.03/t$ that we have found optimal. Results are also compared with likelihood maximization with the EM algorithm, applied to a mixture of six Gaussians, with fixed and uniform mixture weights, and fixed unit variance. Inputs were scaled down empirically so that the average cluster variance was around unity. Thus only the cluster positions were learned, as for the K-Means algorithms.

Each run of an algorithm consists in (a) selecting a random initial set of prototypes, (b) running the algorithm during 20 epochs and recording the error measure E_t after each epoch, (c) running the batch K-Means algorithm[1] during 40 more epochs in order to locate the local minimum E_∞ corresponding to the current initialization of the algorithm. For the four K-Means algorithms, E_t is the quantization error (equation 1). For the Gaussian mixture trained with EM, the cost E_t is the negative

---

[1]except for the case of the mixture of Gaussians, in which the EM algorithm was applied

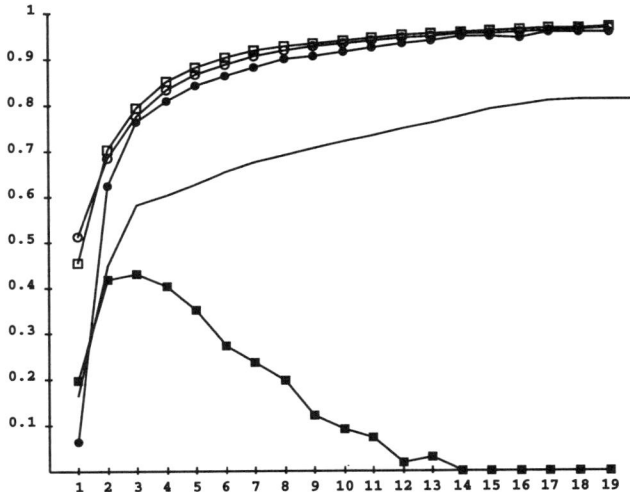

Figure 2: $\frac{E_{t+1}-E_\infty}{E_t-E_\infty}$ versus t. black circles: online K-Means; black squares: batch K-Means; empty circles: online gradient; empty squares: batch gradient; no mark: EM+Gaussian mixture

logarithm of the likelihood of the data given the model.

Twenty trials were run for each algorithm. Using more than twenty runs did not improve the standard deviation of the averaged measures because various initializations lead to very different local minima. The value E_∞ of the quantization error on the local minima ranges between 3300 and 5800. This variability is caused by the different initializations and not by the different algorithms. The average values of E_∞ for each algorithm indeed fall in a very small range (4050 to 4080).

Figure 1 shows the average value of the residual error $E_t - E_\infty$ during the first 20 epochs. Online K-Means (black circles) outperforms all other algorithms during the first five epochs and stabilizes on a level related to the stochastic noise of the online procedure. Batch K-Means (black squares) initially converges more slowly but outperforms all other methods after 5 epochs. All 20 runs converged before the 15th epoch. Both gradients algorithms display poor convergence because they do not benefit of the Newton effect. Again, the online version (white circles) starts faster then the batch version (white square) but is outperformed in the long run. The negative logarithm of the Gaussian mixture is shown on the curve with no point marks, and the scale is displayed on the right of Figure 1.

Figure 2 show the final convergence properties of all five algorithms. The evolutions of the ratio $(E_{t+1} - E_\infty)/(E_t - E_\infty)$ characterize the relative improvement of the residual error after each iteration. All algorithms exhibit the same behavior after a few epochs except batch K-Means (black squares). The fast convergence of this ratio to zero demonstrates the final convergence of batch K-Means. The EM algorithm displays a better behavior than all the other algorithms except batch K-Means. Clearly, however, its relative improvement ratio doesn't display the fast convergence behavior of batch K-Means.

The online K-Means curve crosses the batch K-Means curve during the second epoch, suggesting that it is better to run the online algorithm (7) during one epoch and then switch to the batch algorithm (6).

6 CONCLUSION

We have shown with theoretical arguments and simple experiments that a well implemented K-Means algorithm minimizes the quantization error using Newton's algorithm. The EM style derivation of K-Means shows that the mathematics of EM are valid well outside the framework of probabilistic models. Moreover the provable convergence properties of the hard threshold K-Means algorithm are superior to those of the EM algorithm for an equivalent soft threshold mixture of Gaussians. Extending these results to other hard threshold algorithms (e.g. Viterbi Training) is an interesting open question.

References

Bacceli, F., Cohen, G., and Olsder, G. J. (1992). *Synchronization and Linearity.* Wiley.

Bengio, Y. (1991). *Artificial Neural Networks and their Application to Sequence Recognition.* PhD thesis, McGill University, (Computer Science), Montreal, Qc., Canada.

Bottou, L. (1991). *Une approche théorique de l'apprentissage connexioniste; applications à la reconnaissance de la parole.* PhD thesis, Université de Paris XI.

Darken, C. and Moody, J. (1991). Note on learning rate schedules for stochastic optimization. In Lippman, R. P., Moody, R., and Touretzky, D. S., editors, *Advances in Neural Information Processing Systems 3*, pages 832–838, Denver, CO. Morgan Kaufmann, Palo Alto.

Dempster, A. P., Laird, N. M., and Rubin, D. B. (1977). Maximum-likelihood from incomplete data via the EM algorithm. *Journal of Royal Statistical Society B*, 39:1–38.

Driancourt, X. (1994). *Optimisation par descente de gradient stochastique ....* PhD thesis, Université de Paris XI, 91405 Orsay cedex, France.

Kohonen, T. (1989). *Self-Organization and Associative Memory.* Springer-Verlag, Berlin, 3 edition.

Liporace, L. A. (1976). PTAH on continuous multivariate functions of Markov chains. Technical Report 80193, Institute for Defense Analysis, Communication Research Department.

MacQueen, J. (1967). Some methods for classification and analysis of multivariate observations. In *Proceedings of the Fifth Berkeley Symposium on Mathematics, Statistics and Probability, Vol. 1*, pages 281–296.

Nowlan, S. J. (1991). *Soft Competitive Adaptation: Neural Network Learning Algorithms based on Fitting Statistical Mixtures.* CMU-CS-91-126, School of Computer Science, Carnegie Mellon University, Pittsburgh, PA.

Xu, L. and Jordan, M. (1994). Theoretical and experimental studies of convergence properties of the em algorithm for unsupervised learning based on finite mixtures. Presented at the Neural Networks for Computing Conference.

Active Learning for Function Approximation

Kah Kay Sung
(sung@ai.mit.edu)
Massachusetts Institute of Technology
Artificial Intelligence Laboratory
545 Technology Square
Cambridge, MA 02139

Partha Niyogi
(pn@ai.mit.edu)
Massachusetts Institute of Technology
Artificial Intelligence Laboratory
545 Technology Square
Cambridge, MA 02139

Abstract

We develop a principled strategy to sample a function optimally for function approximation tasks within a Bayesian framework. Using ideas from optimal experiment design, we introduce an objective function (incorporating both bias and variance) to measure the degree of approximation, and the potential utility of the data points towards optimizing this objective. We show how the general strategy can be used to derive precise algorithms to select data for two cases: learning unit step functions and polynomial functions. In particular, we investigate whether such active algorithms can learn the target with fewer examples. We obtain theoretical and empirical results to suggest that this is the case.

1 INTRODUCTION AND MOTIVATION

Learning from examples is a common supervised learning paradigm that hypothesizes a target concept given a stream of training examples that describes the concept. In function approximation, *example-based learning* can be formulated as synthesizing an approximation function for data sampled from an unknown target function (Poggio and Girosi, 1990).

Active learning describes a class of example-based learning paradigms that seeks out new training examples from specific regions of the input space, instead of passively accepting examples from some data generating source. By judiciously selecting examples instead of allowing for possible random sampling, *active learning* techniques can conceivably have faster learning rates and better approximation results than passive learning methods.

This paper presents a Bayesian formulation for *active learning* within the function approximation framework. Specifically, here is the problem we want to address: Let $D_n = \{(x_i, y_i) | i = 1, \ldots, n\}$ be a set of n data points sampled from an unknown target function g, possibly in the presence of noise. Given an approximation function concept class, $\mathcal{F}$, where each $f \in \mathcal{F}$ has prior probability $\mathcal{P}_{\mathcal{F}}[f]$, one can use regularization techniques to approximate g from D_n (in the Bayes optimal sense) by means of a function $\hat{g} \in \mathcal{F}$. We want a strategy to determine at what input location one should sample the next data point, (x_{N+1}, y_{N+1}), in order to obtain the "best" possible Bayes optimal approximation of the unknown target function g with our concept class $\mathcal{F}$.

The data sampling problem consists of two parts:

1) Defining what we mean by the "best" possible Bayes optimal approximation of an unknown target function. In this paper, we propose an optimality criterion for evaluating the "goodness" of a solution with respect to an *unknown* target function.

2) Formalizing precisely the task of determining where in input space to sample the next data point. We express the above mentioned optimality criterion as a cost function to be minimized, and the task of choosing the next sample as one of minimizing the cost function with respect to the input space location of the next sample point.

Earlier work (Cohn, 1991; MacKay, 1992) have tried to use similar optimal experiment design (Fedorov, 1972) techniques to collect data that would provide maximum information about the target function. Our work differs from theirs in several respects. First, we use a different, and perhaps more general, optimality criterion for evaluating solutions to an unknown target function, based on a measure of function uncertainty that incorporates both bias and variance components of the total *output* generalization error. In contrast, MacKay and Cohn use only variance components in model parameter space. Second, we address the important sample complexity question, i.e., does the active strategy require fewer examples to learn the target to the same degree of uncertainty? Our results are stated in PAC-style (Valiant, 1984). After completion of this work, we learnt that Sollich (1994) had also recently developed a similar formulation to ours. His analysis is conducted in a statistical physics framework.

The rest of the paper is organized as follows: Section 2, develops our active sampling paradigm. In Sections 3 and 4, we consider two classes of functions for which active strategies are obtained, and investigate their performance both theoretically and empirically.

2 THE MATHEMATICAL FRAMEWORK

In order to optimally select examples for a learning task, one should first have a clear notion of what an "ideal" learning goal is for the task. We can then measure an example's utility in terms of how well the example helps the learner achieve the goal, and devise an active sampling strategy that selects examples with maximum potential utility. In this section, we propose one such learning goal — to find an approximation function $\hat{g} \in \mathcal{F}$ that "best" estimates the *unknown* target function g. We then derive an example utility cost function for the goal and finally present a general procedure for selecting examples.

2.1 EVALUATING A SOLUTION TO AN UNKNOWN TARGET — THE EXPECTED INTEGRATED SQUARED DIFFERENCE

Let g be the target function that we want to estimate by means of an approximation function $\hat{g} \in \mathcal{F}$. If the target function g were known, then one natural measure of how well (or badly) $\hat{g}$ approximates g would be the *Integrated Squared Difference* (ISD) of the two functions:

$$\delta(\hat{g}, g) = \int_{x_{lo}}^{x_{hi}} (g(x) - \hat{g}(x))^2 dx. \qquad (1)$$

In most function approximation tasks, the target g is unknown, so we clearly cannot express the quality of a learning result, $\hat{g}$, in terms of g. We can, however, obtain an *expected* integrated squared difference (EISD) between the *unknown* target, g, and its estimate, $\hat{g}$, by treating the unknown target g as a random variable from the approximation function concept class $\mathcal{F}$. Taking into account the n data points, D_n, seen so far, we have the following a-posteriori likelihood for g: $P(g|D_n) \propto \mathcal{P}_{\mathcal{F}}[g]P(D_n|g)$. The *expected* integrated squared difference (EISD) between an unknown target, g, and its estimate, $\hat{g}$, given D_n, is thus:

$$E_{\mathcal{F}}[\delta(\hat{g}, g)|D_n] = \int_{g \in \mathcal{F}} P(g|D_n)\delta(\hat{g}, g)dg = \int_{g \in \mathcal{F}} \mathcal{P}_{\mathcal{F}}[g]P(D_n|g)\delta(\hat{g}, g)dg. \qquad (2)$$

2.2 SELECTING THE NEXT SAMPLE LOCATION

We can now express our learning goal as minimizing the *expected integrated squared difference* (EISD) between the unknown target g and its estimate $\hat{g}$. A reasonable sampling strategy would be to choose the next example from the input location that minimizes the EISD between g and the new estimate $\hat{g}_{n+1}$. How does one predict the new EISD that results from sampling the next data point at location x_{n+1}?

Suppose we also know the target output value (possibly noisy), y_{n+1}, at x_{n+1}. The EISD between g and its new estimate $\hat{g}_{n+1}$ would then be $E_{\mathcal{F}}[\delta(\hat{g}_{n+1}, g)|D_n \cup (x_{n+1}, y_{n+1})]$, where $\hat{g}_{n+1}$ can be recovered from $D_n \cup (x_{n+1}, y_{n+1})$ via regularization. In reality, we do not know y_{n+1}, but we can derive for it the following conditional probability distribution:

$$P(y_{n+1}|x_{n+1}, D_n) \propto \int_{f \in \mathcal{F}} P(D_n \cup (x_{n+1}, y_{n+1})|f)\mathcal{P}_{\mathcal{F}}[f]df. \qquad (3)$$

This leads to the following *expected* value for the new EISD, if we sample our next data point at x_{n+1}:

$$\mathcal{U}(\hat{g}_{n+1}|D_n, x_{n+1}) = \int_{-\infty}^{\infty} P(y_{n+1}|x_{n+1}, D_n)E_{\mathcal{F}}[\delta(\hat{g}_{n+1}, g)|D_n \cup (x_{n+1}, y_{n+1})]dy_{n+1}. \qquad (4)$$

Clearly, the optimal input location to sample next is the location that minimizes the cost function in Equation 4 (henceforth referred to as the *total output uncertainty*), i.e.,

$$\hat{x}_{n+1} = \arg\min_{x_{n+1}} \mathcal{U}(\hat{g}_{n+1}|D_n, x_{n+1}). \qquad (5)$$

2.3 SUMMARY OF ACTIVE LEARNING PROCEDURE

We summarize the key steps involved in finding the optimal next sample location:

1) Compute $P(g|D_n)$. This is the a-posteriori likelihood of the different functions g given D_n, the n data points seen so far.

2) Fix a new point x_{n+1} to sample.

3) Assume a value y_{n+1} for this x_{n+1}. One can compute $P(g|D_n \cup (x_{n+1}, y_{n+1}))$ and hence the *expected* integrated squared difference between the target and its new estimate. This is given by $E_{\mathcal{F}}[\delta(\hat{g}_{n+1}, g)|D_n \cup (x_{n+1}, y_{n+1})]$. See also Equation 2.

4) At the given x_{n+1}, y_{n+1} has a probability distribution given by Equation 3. Averaging over all y_{n+1}'s, we obtain the *total output uncertainty* for x_{n+1}, given by $\mathcal{U}(\hat{g}_{n+1}|D_n, x_{n+1})$ in Equation 4.

5) Sample at the input location that minimizes the *total output uncertainty* cost function.

3 EXAMPLE 1: UNIT STEP FUNCTIONS

To demonstrate the usefulness of the above procedure, let us first consider the following simple class of indicator functions parameterized by a single parameter a which takes values in $[0, 1]$. Thus

$$\mathcal{F} = \{1_{[a,1]} | 0 \le a \le 1\}$$

We obtain a prior $P(g = 1_{[a,1]})$ by assuming that a has an a-priori uniform distribution on $[0, 1]$. Assume that data, $D_n = \{(x_i; y_i); i = 1, ..n\}$ consistent with some unknown target function $1_{[a_t, 1]}$ (which the learner is to approximate) has been obtained. We are interested in choosing a point $x \in [0, 1]$ to sample which will provide us with maximal information. Following the general procedure outlined above we go through the following steps.

For ease of notation, let x_R be the right most point belonging to D_n whose y value is 0, i.e., $x_R = \max_{i=1,..n}\{x_i | y_i = 0\}$. Similarly let $x_L = \min_{i=1,..n}\{x_i | y_i = 1\}$ and let $x_L - x_R = w$.

1) We first need to get $P(g|D_n)$. It is easy to show that

$$P(g = 1_{[a,1]}|D_n) = \frac{1}{w} \text{ if } a \in [x_R, x_L]; 0 \text{ otherwise}$$

2) Suppose we sample next at a particular $x \in [0, 1]$, we would obtain y with the distribution

$$P(y = 0|D_n, x) = \frac{(x_L - x)}{x_L - x_R} = \frac{(x_L - x)}{w} \text{ if } x \in [x_R, x_L]; 1 \text{ if } x \le x_R; 0 \text{ otherwise}$$

For a particular y, the new data set would be $D_{n+1} = D_n \cup (x, y)$ and the corresponding EISD can be easily obtained using the distribution $P(g|D_{n+1})$. Averaging this over $P(y|D_n, x)$ as in step 4 of the general procedure, we obtain

$$\mathcal{U}(\hat{g}_{n+1}|D_n, x) = \begin{cases} w^2/12 & \text{if } x \le x_R \text{ or } x \ge x_L \\ (1/12w)((x_L - x)^3 + (x - x_R)^3) & \text{otherwise} \end{cases}$$

Clearly the point which minimizes the expected *total output uncertainty* is the midpoint of x_L and x_R.
$$\hat{x}_{n+1} = \arg \min_{x \in [0,1]} \mathcal{U}(g|D_n, x) = (x_L + x_R)/2$$

Thus applying the general procedure to this special case reduces to a binary search learning algorithm which queries the midpoint of x_R and x_L. An interesting question at this stage is whether such a strategy provably reduces the sample complexity; and if so, by how much. It is possible to prove the following theorem which shows that for a certain pre-decided *total output uncertainty* value, the active learning algorithm takes fewer examples to learn the target to the same degree of *total output uncertainty* than a random drawing of examples according to a uniform distribution.

Theorem 1 *Suppose we want to collect examples so that we are guaranteed with high probability (i.e. probability $> 1 - \delta$) that the* total output uncertainty *is less than ϵ. Then a passive learner would require at least $\frac{1}{\sqrt{(48\epsilon)}} \ln(1/\delta)$ examples while the active strategy described earlier would require at most $(1/2) \ln(1/12\epsilon)$ examples.*

4 EXAMPLE 2: THE CASE OF POLYNOMIALS

In this section we turn our attention to a class of univariate polynomials (from $[-5, 5]$ to $\Re$) of maximum degree K, i.e.,
$$\mathcal{F} = \{g(a_0, \ldots, a_K) = \sum_{i=0}^{K} a_i x^i\}$$

As before, the prior on $\mathcal{F}$ is obtained here by assuming a prior on the parameters; in particular we assume that $\mathbf{a} = (a_0, a_1, \ldots, a_K)$ has a multivariate normal distribution $N(0, \mathcal{S})$. For simplicity, it is assumed that the parameters are independent, i.e., $\mathcal{S}$ is a diagonal matrix with $\mathcal{S}_{i,i} = \sigma_i^2$. In this example we also incorporate noise (distributed normally according to $N(0, \sigma^2)$). As before, there is a target $g_t \in G$ which the learner is to approximate on the basis of data. Suppose the learner is in possession of a data set $D_n = \{(x_i, y_i = g_t(x_i) + \eta); i = 1 \ldots n\}$ and is to receive another data point. The two options are 1) to sample the function at a point x according to a uniform distribution on the domain $[-5, 5]$ (passive learning) and 2) follow our principled active learning strategy to select the next point to be sampled.

4.1 ACTIVE STRATEGY

Here we derive an exact expression for $\hat{x}_{n+1}$ (the next query point) by applying the general procedure described earlier. Going through the steps as before,

1) It is possible to show that $P(g(\mathbf{a})|D_n) = P(\mathbf{a}|D_n)$ is again a multivariate normal distribution $N(\mu, \Sigma_n)$ where $\mu = \sum_{i=1}^{N} y_i \mathbf{x_i}$, $\mathbf{x_i} = (1, x_i, x_i^2, \ldots, x_i^K)^T$ and
$$\Sigma_n^{-1} = \mathcal{S}^{-1} + \frac{1}{2\sigma^2} \sum_{i=1}^{n} (\mathbf{x_i} \mathbf{x_i}^T)$$

2) Computation of the *total output uncertainty* $\mathcal{U}(\hat{g}_{n+1}|D_n, x)$ requires several steps. Taking advantage of the Gaussian distribution on both the parameters $\mathbf{a}$ and the noise, we obtain (see Niyogi and Sung, 1995 for details):
$$\mathcal{U}(g|D_n, x) = |\Sigma_{n+1} \mathbf{A}|$$

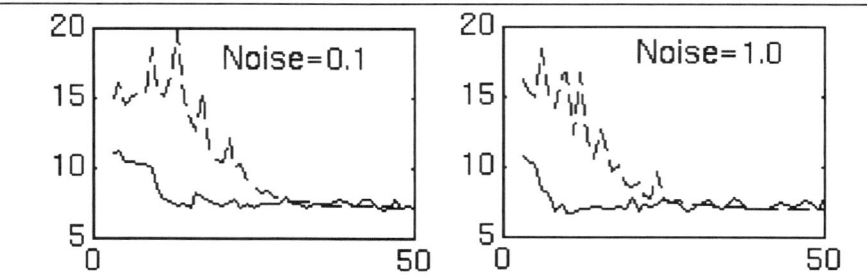

Figure 1: Comparing active and passive learning average error rates at different sample noise levels. The two graphs above plot log error rates against number of samples. See text for detailed explanation. The solid and dashed curves are the active and passive learning error rates respectively.

where **A** is a matrix of numbers whose i,j element is $\int_{-5}^{5} t^{(i+j-2)}dt$. Σ_{n+1} has the same form as Σ_n and depends on the previous data, the priors, noise and x_{n+1}. When minimized over x_{n+1}, we get $\hat{x}_{n+1}$ as the maximum utility location where the active learner should next sample the unknown target function.

4.2 SIMULATIONS

We have performed several simulations to compare the performance of the active strategy developed in the previous section to that of a passive learner (who receives examples according to a uniform random distribution on the domain $[-5,5]$). The following issues have been investigated.

1) Average error rate as a function of the number of examples: Is it indeed the case that the active strategy has superior error performance for the same number of examples? To investigate this we generated 1000 test target polynomial functions (of maximum degree 9) according to the following Gaussian prior on the parameters: for each a_i, $P(a_i) = N(0, 0.9^i)$. For each target polynomial, we collected data according to the active strategy as well as the passive (random) strategy for varying number of data points. Figure 1 shows the average error rate (i.e., the integrated squared difference between the actual target function and its estimate, averaged over the 1000 different target polynomials) as a function of the number of data points. Notice that the active strategy has a lower error rate than the passive for the same number of examples and is particularly true for small number of data. The active strategy uses the same priors that generate the test target functions. We show results of the same simulation performed at two noise levels (noise standard deviation 0.1 and 1.0). In both cases the active strategy outperforms the passive learner indicating robustness in the face of noise.

2) Incorrect priors: How sensitive is the active learner to possible differences between its prior assumptions on the class $\mathcal{F}$ and the true priors? We repeated the function learning task of the earlier case with the test targets generated in the same way as before. The active learner assumes a slightly different Gaussian prior and polynomial degree from the target ($\text{Std}(a_i) = 0.7^i$ and $K = 7$ for the active learner versus $\text{Std}(a_i) = 0.8^i$ and $K = 8$ for the target). Despite its inaccurate priors, the

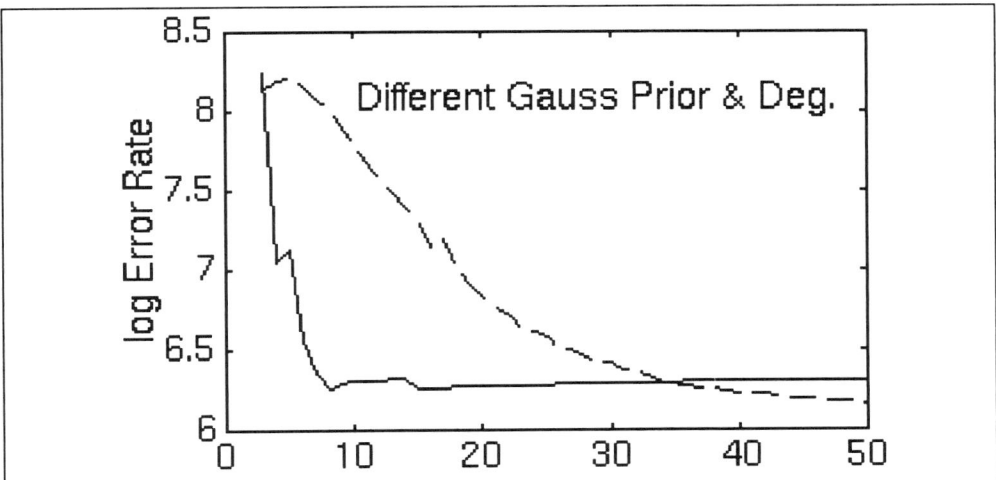

Figure 2: Active learning results with different Gaussian priors for coefficients, and a lower a priori polynomial degree K. See text for detailed explanation. The solid and dashed curves are the active and passive learning error rates respectively.

active learner outperforms the passive case.

3) The distribution of points: How does the active learner choose to sample the domain for maximally reducing uncertainty? There are a few sampling trends which are noteworthy here. First, the learner does not simply sample the domain on a uniform grid. Instead it chooses to cluster its samples typically around $K+1$ locations for concept classes with maximum degree K as borne out by simulations where K varies from 5 to 9. One possible explanation for this is it takes only $K+1$ points to determine the target in the absence of noise. Second, as the noise increases, although the number of clusters remains fixed, they tend to be distributed away from the origin. It seems that for higher noise levels, there is less pressure to fit the data closely; consequently the prior assumption of lower order polynomials dominates. For such lower order polynomials, it is profitable to sample away from the origin as it reduces the variance of the resulting fit. (Note the case of linear regression).

Remarks
1) Notice that because the class of polynomials is linear in its model parameters, **a**, the new sample location ($\hat{x}_{n+1}$) does not depend on the y values actually observed but only on the x values sampled. Thus if the learner is to collect n data points, it can pre-compute the n points at which to sample from the start. In this sense the active algorithm is not really adaptive. This behavior has also been observed by MacKay (1992) and Sollich (1994).
2) Needless to say, the general framework from optimal design can be used for any function class within a Bayesian framework. We are currently investigating the possibility of developing active strategies for Radial Basis Function networks. While it is possible to compute exact expressions for $\hat{x}_{n+1}$ for such RBF networks with fixed centers, for the case of moving centers, one has to resort to numerical minimization. For lack of space we do not include those results in this paper.

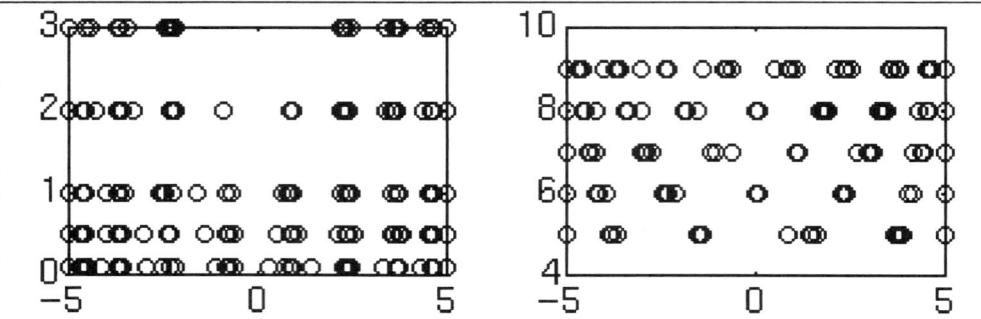

Figure 3: Distribution of active learning sample points as a function of (i) noise strength and (ii) a-priori polynomial degree. The horizontal axis of both graphs represents the input space [-5,5]. Each circle indicates a sample location. The **Left** graph shows the distribution of sample locations (on x axis) for different noise level (indicated on y-axis). The **Right** graph shows the distribution of sample locations (on x-axis) for different assumptions on the maximum polynomial degree K (indicated on y-axis).

5 CONCLUSIONS

We have developed a Bayesian framework for active learning using ideas from optimal experiment design. Our focus has been to investigate the possibility of improved sample complexity using such active learning schemes. For a simple case of unit step functions, we are able to derive a binary search algorithm from a completely different standpoint. Such an algorithm then provably requires fewer examples for the same error rate. We then show how to derive specific algorithms for the case of polynomials and carry out extensive simulations to compare their performance against the benchmark of a passive learner with encouraging results. This is an application of the optimal design paradigm to function learning and seems to bear promise for the design of more efficient learning algorithms.

References

D. Cohn. (1991) A Local Approach to Optimal Queries. In D. Touretzky (ed.), *Proc. of 1990 Connectionist Summer School*, San Mateo, CA, 1991. Morgan Kaufmann Publishers.

V. Fedorov. (1972) *Theory of Optimal Experiments*. Academic Press, New York, 1972.

D. MacKay. (1992) *Bayesian Methods for Adaptive Models*. PhD thesis, CalTech, 1992.

P. Niyogi and K. Sung. (1995) Active Learning for Function Approximation: Paradigms from Optimal Experiment Design. Tech Report AIM-1483, AI Lab., MIT, In Preparation.

M. Plutowski and H. White. (1991) Active Selection of Training Examples for Network Learning in Noiseless Environments. Tech Report CS91-180, Dept. of Computer Science and Engineering, University of California, San Diego, 1991.

T. Poggio and F. Girosi. (1990) Regularization Algorithms for Learning that are Equivalent to Multilayer Networks. *Science*, 247:978-982, 1990.

P. Sollich. (1994) Query Construction, Entropy, Generalization in Neural Network Models. *Physical Review E*, 49:4637-4651, 1994.

L. Valiant. (1984) A Theory of Learnable. *Proc. of the 1984 STOC*, p436-445, 1984.

Analysis of Unstandardized Contributions in Cross Connected Networks

Thomas R. Shultz
shultz@psych.mcgill.ca

Yuriko Oshima-Takane
yuriko@psych.mcgill.ca

Yoshio Takane
takane@psych.mcgill.ca

Department of Psychology
McGill University
Montréal, Québec, Canada H3A 1B1

Abstract

Understanding knowledge representations in neural nets has been a difficult problem. Principal components analysis (PCA) of contributions (products of sending activations and connection weights) has yielded valuable insights into knowledge representations, but much of this work has focused on the correlation matrix of contributions. The present work shows that analyzing the variance-covariance matrix of contributions yields more valid insights by taking account of weights.

1 INTRODUCTION

The knowledge representations learned by neural networks are usually difficult to understand because of the non-linear properties of these nets and the fact that knowledge is often distributed across many units. Standard network analysis techniques, based on a network's connection weights or on its hidden unit activations, have been limited. Weight diagrams are typically complex and weights vary across multiple networks trained on the same problem. Analysis of activation patterns on hidden units is limited to nets with a single layer of hidden units without cross connections.

Cross connections are direct connections that bypass intervening hidden unit layers. They increase learning speed in static networks by focusing on linear relations (Lang & Witbrock, 1988) and are a standard feature of generative algorithms such as cascade-correlation (Fahlman & Lebiere, 1990). Because such cross connections do so much of the work, analyses that are restricted to hidden unit activations furnish only a partial picture of the network's knowledge.

Contribution analysis has been shown to be a useful technique for multi-layer, cross connected nets. Sanger (1989) defined a contribution as the product of an output weight, the activation of a sending unit, and the sign of the output target for that input. Such contributions are potentially more informative than either weights alone or hidden unit activations alone since they take account of both weight and sending activation. Shultz and Elman (1994) used PCA to reduce the dimensionality of such contributions in several different types of cascade-correlation nets. Shultz and Oshima-Takane (1994) demonstrated that PCA of unscaled contributions produced even better insights into cascade-correlation solutions than did comparable analyses of contributions scaled by the sign of output targets. Sanger (1989) had recommended scaling contributions by the signs of output targets in order to determine whether the contributions helped or hindered the network's solution. But since the signs of output targets are only available to networks during error correction learning, it is more natural to use unscaled contributions in analyzing knowledge representations.

There is an issue in PCA about whether to use the correlation matrix or the variance-covariance matrix. The correlation matrix contains 1s in the diagonal and Pearson correlation coefficients between contributions off the diagonal. This has the effect of standardizing the variables (contributions) so that each has a mean of 0 and standard deviation of 1. Effectively, this ensures that the PCA of a correlation matrix exploits variation in input activation patterns but ignores variation in connection weights (because variation in connection weights is eliminated as the contributions are standardized).

Here, we report on work that investigates whether more useful insights into network knowledge structures can be revealed by PCA of unstandardized contributions. To do this, we apply PCA to the variance-covariance matrix of contributions. The variance-covariance matrix has contribution variances along the diagonal and covariances between contributions off the diagonal. Taking explicit account of the variation in connection weights in this way may produce a more valid picture of the network's knowledge.

We use some of the same networks and problems employed in our earlier work (Shultz & Elman, 1994; Shultz & Oshima-Takane, 1994) to facilitate comparison of results. The problems include continuous XOR, arithmetic comparisons involving addition and multiplication, and distinguishing between two interlocking spirals. All of the nets were generated with the cascade-correlation algorithm (Fahlman & Lebiere, 1990).

Cascade-correlation begins as a perceptron and recruits hidden units into the network as it needs them in order to reduce error. The recruited hidden unit is the one whose activations correlate best with the network's current error. Recruited units are installed in a cascade, each on a separate layer and receiving input from the input units and from any previously existing hidden units. We used the default values for all cascade-correlation parameters.

The goal of understanding knowledge representations learned by networks ought to be useful in a variety of contexts. One such context is cognitive modeling, where the ability of nets to merely simulate psychological phenomena is not sufficient (McCloskey, 1991). In addition, it is important to determine whether the network representations bear any systematic relation to the representations employed by human subjects.

2 PCA OF CONTRIBUTIONS

Sanger's (1989) original contribution analysis began with a three-dimensional array of contributions (output unit x hidden unit x input pattern). In contrast, we start with a two-dimensional output weight x input pattern array of contributions. This is more efficient than the slicing technique used by Sanger to focus on particular output or hidden units and still allows identification of the roles of specific contributions (Shultz & Elman, 1994; Shultz & Oshima-Takane, 1994).

We subject the variance-covariance matrix of contributions to PCA in order to identify the main dimensions of variation in the contributions (Jolliffe, 1986). A component is a line of best fit to a set of data points in multi-dimensional space. The goal of PCA is to summarize a multivariate data set with a relatively small number of components by capitalizing on covariance among the variables (in this case, contributions).

We use the scree test (Cattell, 1966) to determine how many components are useful to include in the analysis. Varimax rotation is applied to improve the interpretability of the solution. Component scores are plotted to identify the function of each component.

3 APPLICATION TO CONTINUOUS XOR

The classical binary XOR problem does not have enough training patterns to make contribution analysis worthwhile. However, we constructed a continuous version of the XOR problem by dividing the input space into four quadrants. Starting from 0.1, input values were incremented in steps of 0.1, producing 100 x, y input pairs that can be partitioned into four quadrants of the input space. Quadrant a had values of x less than

0.55 combined with values of y above 0.55. Quadrant b had values of x and y greater than 0.55. Quadrant c had values of x and y less than 0.55. Quadrant d had values of x greater than 0.55 combined with values of y below 0.55. Similar to binary XOR, problems from quadrants a and d had a positive output target (0.5) for the net, whereas problems from quadrants b and c had a negative output target (-0.5). There was a single output unit with a sigmoid activation.

Three cascade-correlation nets were trained on continuous XOR. Each of these nets generated a unique solution, recruiting five or six hidden units and taking from 541 to 765 epochs to learn to correctly classify all of the input patterns. Generalization to test patterns not in the training set was excellent. PCA of unscaled, unstandardized contributions yielded three components. A plot of rotated component scores for the 100 training patterns of net 1 is shown in Figure 1. The component scores are labeled according to their respective quadrant in the input space. Three components are required to account for 96.0% of the variance in the contributions.

Figure 1 shows that component 1, with 44.3% of the variance in contributions, has the role of distinguishing those quadrants with a positive output target (a and d) from those with a negative output target (b and c). This is indicated by the fact that the black shapes are at the top of the component space cube in Figure 1 and the white shapes are at the bottom. Components 2 and 3 represent variation along the x and y input dimensions, respectively. Component 2 accounted for 26.1% of the variance in contributions, and component 3 accounted for 25.6% of the variance in contributions. Input pairs from quadrants b and d (square shapes) are concentrated on the negative end of component 2, whereas input pairs from quadrants a and c (circle shapes) are concentrated on the positive end of component 2. Similarly, input pairs from quadrants a and b cluster on the negative end of component 3, and input pairs from quadrants c and d cluster on the positive end of component 3. Although the network was not explicitly trained to represent the x and y input dimensions, it did so as an incidental feature of its learning the distinction between quadrants a and d vs. quadrants b and c. Similar results were obtained from the other two nets learning the continuous XOR problem.

In contrast, PCA of the correlation matrix from these nets had yielded a somewhat less clear picture with the third component separating quadrants a and d from quadrants b and c, and the first two components representing variation along the x and y input dimensions (Shultz & Oshima-Takane, 1994). PCA of the correlation matrix of scaled contributions had performed even worse, with plots of component scores indicating interactive separation of the four quadrants, but with no clear roles for the individual components (Shultz & Elman, 1994).

Standardized, rotated component loadings for net 1 are plotted in Figure 2. Such plots can be examined to determine the role played by each contribution in the network. For example, hidden units 2, 3, and 4 all play a major role in the job done by component 1, distinguishing positive from negative outputs.

4 APPLICATION TO COMPARATIVE ARITHMETIC

Arithmetic comparison requires a net to conclude whether a sum or a product of two integers is greater than, less than, or equal to a comparison integer. Several psychological simulations have used neural nets to make additive and multiplicative comparisons and this has enhanced interest in this type of problem (McClelland, 1989; Shultz, Schmidt, Buckingham, & Mareschal, in press).

The first input unit coded the type of arithmetic operation to be performed: 0 for addition and 1 for multiplication. Three additional linear input units encoded the integers. Two of these input units each coded a randomly selected integer in the range of 0 to 9, inclusive; another input unit coded a randomly selected comparison integer. For addition problems, comparison integers ranged from 0 to 19, inclusive; for multiplication, comparison integers ranged from 0 to 82, inclusive. Two sigmoid output units coded the results of the comparison operation. Target outputs of 0.5, -0.5 represented a *greater than* result, targets of -0.5, 0.5 represented *less than*, and targets of 0.5, 0.5 represented *equal to*.

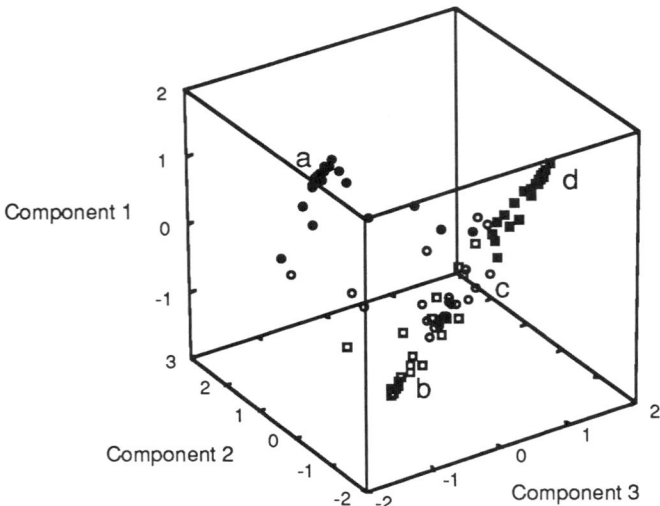

Figure 1. Rotated component scores for a continuous XOR net. Component scores for the x, y input pairs in quadrant a are labeled with black circles, those from quadrant b with white squares, those from quadrant c with white circles, and those from quadrant d with black squares. The network's task is to distinguish pairs from quadrants a and d (the black shapes) from pairs from quadrants b and c (the white shapes). Some of the white shapes appear black because they are so densely packed, but all of the truly black shapes are relatively high in the cube.

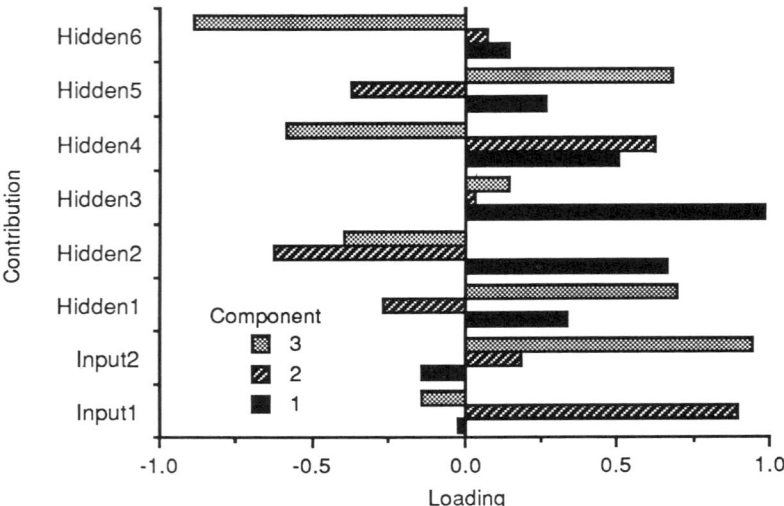

Figure 2. Standardized, rotated component loadings for a continuous XOR net. Rotated loadings were standardized by dividing them by the standard deviation of the respective contribution scores.

The training patterns had 100 addition and 100 multiplication problems, randomly selected, with the restriction that 45 of each had correct answers of *greater than*, 45 of each had correct answers of *less than*, and 10 of each had correct answers of *equal to*. These constraints were designed to reduce the natural skew of comparative values in the high direction on multiplication problems.

We ran three nets for 1000 epochs each, at which point they were very close to mastering the training patterns. Either seven or eight hidden units were recruited along the way. Generalization to previously unseen test problems was very accurate. Four components were sufficient to account for most the variance in unstandardized contributions, 88.9% in the case of net 1.

Figure 3 displays the rotated component scores for the first two components of net 1. Component 1, accounting for 51.1% of the variance, separated problems with *greater than* answers from problems with *less than* answers, and located problems with *equal to* answers in the middle, at least for addition problems. Component 2, with 20.2% of the variance, clearly separated multiplication from addition. Contributions from the first input unit were strongly associated with component 2. Similar results obtained for the other two nets.

Components 3 and 4, with 10.6% and 7.0% of the variance, were sensitive to variation in the second and third inputs, respectively. This is supported by an examination of the mean input values of the 20 most extreme component scores on these two components. Recall that the second and third inputs coded the two integers to be added or multiplied. The negative end of component 3 had a mean second input value of 8.25; the positive end of this component had a mean second input value of 0.55. Component 4 had mean third input value of 2.00 on the negative end and 7.55 on the positive end.

In contrast, PCA of the correlation matrix for these nets had yielded a far more clouded picture, with the largest components focusing on input variation and lesser components doing bits and pieces of the separation of answer types and operations in an interactive manner (Shultz & Oshima-Takane, 1994). Problems with *equal to* answers were not isolated by any of the components. PCA of scaled contributions had produced three components that interactively separated the three answer types and operations, but failed to represent variation in input integers (Shultz & Elman, 1994). Essentially similar advantages for using the variance-covariance matrix were found for nets learning either addition alone or multiplication alone.

5 APPLICATION TO THE TWO-SPIRALS PROBLEM

The two-spirals problem requires a particularly difficult discrimination and a large number of hidden units. The input space is defined by two interlocking spirals that wrap around their origin three times. There are two sets of 97 real-valued x, y pairs, with each set representing one of the spirals, and a single sigmoid output unit coded for the identity of the spiral. Our three nets took between 1313 and 1723 epochs to master the distinction, and recruited from 12 to 16 hidden units. All three nets generalized well to previously unseen input pairs on the paths of the two spirals.

PCA of the variance-covariance matrix for net 1 revealed that six components accounted for a total of 97.9% of the variance in contributions. The second and fourth of these components together distinguished one spiral from the other, with 20.7% and 9.8% of the variance respectively. Rotated component scores for these two components are plotted in Figure 4. A diagonal line drawn on Figure 4 from coordinates -2, 2 to 2, -2 indicates that 11 points from each spiral were misclassified by components 2 and 4. This is only 11.3% of the data points in the training patterns. The fact that the net learned all of the training patterns implies that these exceptions were picked up by other components.

Components 1 and 6, with 40.7% and 6.4% of the variance, were sensitive to variation in the x and y inputs, respectively. Again, this was confirmed by the mean input values of the 20 most extreme component scores on these two components. On component 1, the negative end had a mean x value of 3.55 and the positive end had a mean y value of -3.55.

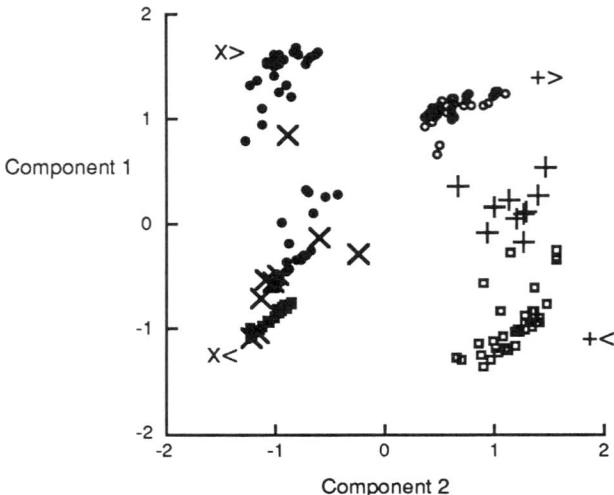

Figure 3. Rotated component scores for an arithmetic comparison net. *Greater than* problems are symbolized by circles, *less than* problems by squares, addition by white shapes, and multiplication by black shapes. For *equal to* problems only, addition is represented by + and multiplication by X. Although some densely packed white shapes may appear black, they have no overlap with truly black shapes. All of the black squares are concentrated around coordinates -1, -1.

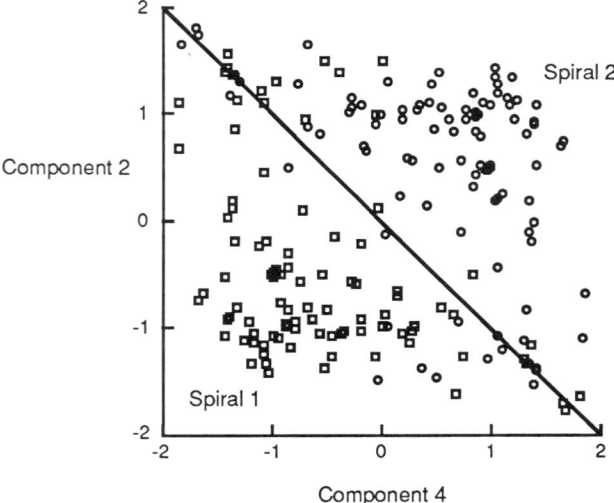

Figure 4. Rotated component scores for a two-spirals net. Squares represent data points from spiral 1, and circles represent data points from spiral 2.

On component 6, the negative end had a mean x value of 2.75 and the positive end had a mean y value of -2.75. The skew-symmetry of these means is indicative of the perfectly symmetrical representations that cascade-correlation nets achieve on this highly symmetrical problem. Every data point on every component has a mirror image negative with the opposite signed component score on that same component. This $-x, -y$ mirror image point is always on the other spiral. Other components concentrated on particular regions of the spirals. The other two nets yielded essentially similar results.

These results can be contrasted with our previous analyses of the two-spirals problem, none of which succeeded in showing a clear separation of the two spirals. PCAs based on scaled (Shultz & Elman, 1994) or unscaled (Shultz & Oshima-Takane, 1994) correlation matrices showed extensive symmetries but never a distinction between one spiral and another.[1] Thus, although it was clear that the nets had encoded the problem's inherent symmetries, it was still unclear from previous work how the nets used this or other information to distinguish points on one spiral from points on the other spiral.

6 DISCUSSION

On each of these problems, there was considerable variation among network solutions, as revealed, for example, by variation in numbers of hidden units recruited and signs and sizes of connection weights. In spite of such variation, the present technique of applying PCA to the variance-covariance matrix of contributions yielded results that are sufficiently abstract to characterize different nets learning the same problem. The knowledge representations produced by this analysis clearly identify the essential information that the net is being trained to utilize as well as more incidental features of the training patterns such as the nature of the input space.

This research strengthens earlier conclusions that PCA of network contributions is a useful technique for understanding network performance (Sanger, 1989), including relatively intractable multi-level cross connected nets (Shultz & Elman, 1994; Shultz & Oshima-Takane, 1994). However, the current study underscores the point that there are several ways to prepare a contribution matrix for PCA, not all of which yield equally valid or useful results. Rather than starting with a three dimensional matrix of output unit x hidden unit x input pattern and focusing on either one output unit at a time or one hidden unit at a time (Sanger, 1989), it is preferable to collapse contributions into a two dimensional matrix of output weight x input pattern. The latter is not only more efficient, but yields more valid results that characterize the network as a whole, rather than small parts of the network.

Also, rather than scaling contributions by the sign of the output target (Sanger, 1989), it is better to use unscaled contributions. Unscaled contributions are not only more realistic, since the network has no knowledge of output targets during its feed-forward phase, but also produce clearer interpretations of the net's knowledge representations (Shultz & Oshima-Takane, 1994). The latter claim is particularly true in terms of sensitivity to input dimensions and to operational distinctions between adding and multiplying. Plots of component scores based on unscaled contributions are typically not as dense as those based on scaled contributions but are more revealing of the network's knowledge.

Finally, rather than applying PCA to the correlation matrix of contributions, it makes more sense to apply it to the variance-covariance matrix. As noted in the introduction, using the correlation matrix effectively standardizes the contributions to have identical means and variances, thus obscuring the role of network connection weights. The present results indicate much clearer knowledge representations when the variance-covariance matrix is used since connection weight information is explicitly retained. Matrix differences were especially marked on the more difficult problems, such as two-spirals, where the only PCAs to reveal how nets distinguished the spirals were those based on

---

[1]Results from unscaled contributions on the two-spirals problem were not actually presented in Shultz & Oshima-Takane (1994) since they were not very clear.

variance-covariance matrices. But the relative advantages of using the variance-covariance matrix were evident on the easier problems too.

There has been recent rapid progress in the study of the knowledge representations learned by neural nets. Feed-forward nets can be viewed as function approximators for relating inputs to outputs. Analysis of their knowledge representations should reveal how inputs are encoded and transformed to produce the correct outputs. PCA of network contributions sheds light on how these function approximations are done. Components emerging from PCA are orthonormalized ingredients of the transformations of inputs that produce the correct outputs. Thus, PCA helps to identify the nature of the required transformations.

Further progress might be expected from combining PCA with other matrix decomposition techniques. Constrained PCA uses external information to decompose multivariate data matrices before applying PCA (Takane & Shibayama, 1991).

Analysis techniques emerging from this research will be useful in understanding and applying neural net research. Component loadings, for example, could be used to predict the results of lesioning experiments with neural nets. Once the role of a hidden unit has been identified by virtue of its association with a particular component, then one could predict that lesioning this unit would impair the function served by the component.

Acknowledgments

This research was supported by the Natural Sciences and Engineering Research Council of Canada.

References

Cattell, R. B. (1966). The scree test for the number of factors. *Multivariate Behavioral Research*, 1, 245-276.

Fahlman, S. E., & Lebiere, C. (1990.) The Cascade-Correlation learning architecture. In D. Touretzky (Ed.), *Advances in neural information processing systems 2*, (pp. 524-532). Mountain View, CA: Morgan Kaufmann.

Jolliffe, I. T. (1986). *Principal component analysis*. Berlin: Springer Verlag.

Lang, K. J., & Witbrock, M. J. (1988). Learning to tell two spirals apart. In D. Touretzky, G. Hinton, & T. Sejnowski (Eds.), *Proceedings of the Connectionist Models Summer School*, (pp. 52-59). Mountain View, CA: Morgan Kaufmann.

McClelland, J. L. (1989). Parallel distributed processing: Implications for cognition and development. In Morris, R. G. M. (Ed.), *Parallel distributed processing: Implications for psychology and neurobiology*, pp. 8-45. Oxford University Press.

McCloskey, M. (1991). Networks and theories: The place of connectionism in cognitive science. *Psychological Science*, 2, 387-395.

Sanger, D. (1989). Contribution analysis: A technique for assigning responsibilities to hidden units in connectionist networks. *Connection Science*, 1, 115-138.

Shultz, T. R., & Elman, J. L. (1994). Analyzing cross connected networks. In J. D. Cowan, G. Tesauro, & J. Alspector (Eds.), *Advances in Neural Information Processing Systems 6*. San Francisco, CA: Morgan Kaufmann.

Shultz, T. R., & Oshima-Takane, Y. (1994). Analysis of unscaled contributions in cross connected networks. In *Proceedings of the World Congress on Neural Networks* (Vol. 3, pp. 690-695). Hillsdale, NJ: Lawrence Erlbaum.

Shultz, T. R., Schmidt, W. C., Buckingham, D., & Mareschal, D. (In press). Modeling cognitive development with a generative connectionist algorithm. In G. Halford & T. Simon (Eds.), *Developing cognitive competence: New approaches to process modeling*. Hillsdale, NJ: Erlbaum.

Takane, Y., & Shibayama, T. (1991). Principal component analysis with external information on both subjects and variables. *Psychometrika*, 56, 97-120.

Template-Based Algorithms for Connectionist Rule Extraction

Jay A. Alexander and Michael C. Mozer
Department of Computer Science and
Institute for Cognitive Science
University of Colorado
Boulder, CO 80309–0430

Abstract

Casting neural network weights in symbolic terms is crucial for interpreting and explaining the behavior of a network. Additionally, in some domains, a symbolic description may lead to more robust generalization. We present a principled approach to symbolic rule extraction based on the notion of *weight templates*, parameterized regions of weight space corresponding to specific symbolic expressions. With an appropriate choice of representation, we show how template parameters may be efficiently identified and instantiated to yield the optimal match to a unit's actual weights. Depending on the requirements of the application domain, our method can accommodate arbitrary disjunctions and conjunctions with $O(k)$ complexity, simple n-of-m expressions with $O(k^2)$ complexity, or a more general class of recursive n-of-m expressions with $O(k^3)$ complexity, where k is the number of inputs to a unit. Our method of rule extraction offers several benefits over alternative approaches in the literature, and simulation results on a variety of problems demonstrate its effectiveness.

1 INTRODUCTION

The problem of understanding why a trained neural network makes a given decision has a long history in the field of connectionist modeling. One promising approach to this problem is to convert each unit's weights and/or activities from continuous numerical quantities into discrete, symbolic descriptions [2, 4, 8]. This type of reformulation, or *rule extraction*, can both explain network behavior and facilitate transfer of learning. Additionally, in intrinsically symbolic domains, there is evidence that a symbolic description can lead to more robust generalization [4].

We are interested in extracting symbolic rules on a unit-by-unit basis from connectionist nets that employ the conventional inner product activation and sigmoidal output functions. The basic language of description for our rules is that of *n-of-m* expressions. An *n-of-m* expression consists of a list of *m* subexpressions and a value *n* such that $1 \le n \le m$. The overall expression is true when at least *n* of the *m* subexpressions are true. An example of an *n*-of-*m* expression stated using logical variables is the majority voter function $X = 2\ of\ (A, B, C)$. *N*-of-*m* expressions are interesting because they are able to model behaviors intermediate to standard Boolean OR ($n = 1$) and AND ($n = m$) functions. These intermediate behaviors reflect a limited form of two-level Boolean logic. (To see why this is true, note that the expression for X above is equivalent to $AB + BC + AC$.) In a later section we describe even more general behaviors that can be represented using recursive forms of these expressions. *N*-of-*m* expressions fit well with the activation behavior of sigmoidal units, and they are quite amenable to human comprehension.

To extract an *n*-of-*m* rule from a unit's weights, we follow a three-step process. First we generate a minimal set of candidate templates, where each template is parameterized to represent a given *n*-of-*m* expression. Next we instantiate each template's parameters with optimal values. Finally we choose the symbolic expression whose instantiated template is nearest to the actual weights. Details on each of these steps are given below.

2 TEMPLATE-BASED RULE EXTRACTION

2.1 Background

Following McMillan [4], we define a *weight template* as a parameterized region of weight space corresponding to a specific symbolic function. To see how weight templates can be used to represent symbolic functions, consider the weight vector for a sigmoidal unit with four inputs and a bias:

$$w\ =\ w_1\ \ w_2\ \ w_3\ \ w_4\ \ b$$

Now consider the following two template vectors:

$$t_1\ =\ -p\ \ \ p\ \ \ 0\ \ \ -p\ \ \ 1.5p$$
$$t_2\ =\ \ p\ \ -p\ \ \ p\ \ \ \ p\ \ -0.5p$$

These templates are parameterized by the variable *p*. Given a large positive value of *p* (say 5.0) and an input vector I (whose components are approximately 0 and 1), t_1 describes the symbolic expression $1\ of\ (\bar{I}_1, I_2, \bar{I}_4)$, while t_2 describes the symbolic expression $2\ of\ (I_1, \bar{I}_2, I_3, I_4)$. A general description for *n*-of-*m* templates of this form is the following:

1. *M* of the weight values are set to $\pm p$, $p > 0$; all others are set to 0.
   (+*p* is used for normal subexpressions, –*p* for negated subexpressions)

2. The bias value is set to $(0.5 + m_{neg} - n)p$, where m_{neg} represents the number of negated subexpressions.

When the inputs are Boolean with values –1 and +1, the form of the templates is the same, except the template bias takes the value $(1 + m - 2n)p$. This seemingly trivial difference turns out to have a significant effect on the efficiency of the extraction process.

2.2 Basic extraction algorithm

Generating candidate templates

Given a sigmoidal unit with k inputs plus a bias, the total number of n-of-m expressions that unit may compute is an exponential function of k:

$$T = \sum_{m=1}^{k} \sum_{n=1}^{m} 2^m \binom{k}{m} = \sum_{m=1}^{k} \frac{2^m k!}{(k-m)!(m-1)!} = 2k3^{k-1}$$

For example, $T_{k=10}$ is 393,660, while $T_{k=20}$ is over 46 *billion*. Fortunately we can apply knowledge of the unit's actual weights to explore this search space without generating a template for each possible n-of-m expression. Alexander [1] proves that when the $-1/+1$ input representation is used, we need consider at most one template for each possible choice of n and m. For a given choice of n and m, a template is indicated when $sign(1 + m - 2n) = sign(b)$. A required template is formed by setting the template weights corresponding to the m highest absolute value actual weights to sp, where s represents the sign of the corresponding actual weight. The template bias is set to $(1 + m - 2n)p$. This reduces the number of templates required to a polynomial function of k:

$$T_{n\text{-of-}m} = \sum_{m=1}^{k} \sum_{n=1}^{\lfloor \frac{m+1}{2} \rfloor} 1 = \left\lfloor \frac{1}{4}k^2 + \frac{1}{2}k + \frac{1}{4} \right\rfloor$$

Values for $T_{k=10}$ and $T_{k=20}$ are now 30 and 110, respectively, making for a very efficient pruning of the search space. When 0/1 inputs are used, this simple procedure does not suffice and many more templates must be generated. For this reason, in the remainder of this paper we focus on the $-1/+1$ case and assume the use of symmetric sigmoid functions.

Instantiating template parameters

Instantiating a weight template t requires finding a value for p such that the Euclidean distance $d = \|t - w\|^2$ is minimized. Letting $u_i = 1$ if template weight t_i is nonzero, $u_i = 0$ otherwise, the value of p that minimizes this distance for any $-1/+1$ template is given by:

$$p^* = \frac{\sum_{i=1}^{k} |w_i| u_i + (1 + m - 2n) b}{m + (1 + m - 2n)^2}$$

Finding the nearest template and checking extraction validity

Once each template is instantiated with its value of p^*, the distance between the template and the actual weight vector is calculated, and the minimal distance template is selected as the basis for rule extraction. Having found the nearest template t^*, we can use its values as part of a rudimentary check on extraction validity. For example, we can define the *extraction error* as $100\% \times \|t^* - w\|^2 / \|w\|^2$ to measure how well the nearest symbolic rule fits the actual weights. We can also examine the value of p^* used in t^*. Small values of p^* translate into activation levels in the linear regime of the sigmoid functions, compromising the assumption of Boolean outputs propagating to subsequent inputs.

2.3 Extending expressiveness

While the n-of-m expressions treated thus far are fairly powerful, there is an interesting class of symbolic behaviors that cannot be captured by simple n-of-m expressions. The simplest example of this type of behavior may be seen in the single hidden unit version of *xor* described in [6]. In this 2–1–1 network the hidden unit H learns the expression $AND(\bar{I}_1, \bar{I}_2)$, while the output unit (which connects to the two inputs as well as to the hidden unit) learns the expression $AND[OR(\bar{I}_1, \bar{I}_2), \bar{H}]$. This latter expression may be viewed as a nested or recursive form of n-of-m expression, one where some of the m subexpressions may themselves be n-of-m expressions. The following two forms of recursive n-of-m expressions are linearly separable and are thus computable by a single sigmoidal unit:

$$OR\ [\ C_{n\text{-of-}m},\ C_{OR}\ ]$$
$$AND\ [\ C_{n\text{-of-}m},\ C_{AND}\ ]$$

where $C_{n\text{-of-}m}$ is a nested n-of-m expression ($1 \le n \le m$)
C_{OR} is a nested OR expression ($n = 1$)
C_{AND} is a nested AND expression ($n = m$)

These expressions may be seen to generalize simple n-of-m expressions in the same way that simple n-of-m expressions generalize basic disjunctions and conjunctions.[1] We term the above forms *augmented* n-of-m expressions because they extend simple n-of-m expressions with additional disjuncts or conjuncts. Templates for these expressions (under the –1/+1 input representation) may be efficiently generated and instantiated using a procedure similar to that described for simple n-of-m expressions. When augmented expressions are included in the search, the total number of templates required becomes:

$$T_{augmented} = \left\lfloor \frac{1}{6}k^3 - \frac{1}{4}k^2 + \frac{5}{6}k + \frac{1}{4} \right\rfloor$$

This figure is $O(k)$ worse than for simple n-of-m expressions, but it is still polynomial in k and is quite manageable for many problems. (Values for $T_{k=10}$ and $T_{k=20}$ are 150 and 1250, respectively.) A more detailed treatment of augmented n-of-m expressions is given in [1].

3 RELATED WORK

Here we briefly consider two alternative systems for connectionist rule extraction. Many other methods have been developed; a recent summary and categorization appears in [2].

3.1 McMillan

McMillan described the *projection* of actual weights to simple weight templates in [4]. McMillan's parameter selection and instantiation procedures are inefficient compared to those described here, though they yield equivalent results for the classes of templates he used. McMillan treated only expressions with $m \le 2$ and no negated subexpressions.

---

[1] In fact the nesting may continue beyond one level. Thus sigmoidal units can compute expressions like $OR[AND(C_{n\text{-of-}m}, C_{AND}), C_{OR}]$. We have not yet experimented with extensions of this sort.

3.2 Towell and Shavlik

Towell and Shavlik [8] use a domain theory to initialize a connectionist network, train the network on a set of labeled examples, and then extract rules that describe the network's behavior. To perform rule extraction, Towell and Shavlik first group weights using an iterative clustering algorithm. After applying additional training, they typically check each training pattern against each weight group and eliminate groups that do not affect the classification of any pattern. Finally, they scan remaining groups and attempt to express a rule in purely symbolic n-of-m form. However, in many cases the extracted rules take the form of a linear inequality involving multiple numeric quantities. For example, the following rule was extracted from part of a network trained on the promoter recognition task [5] from molecular biology:

```
Minus35 = -10 < + 5.0 * nt(@-37 '--T-G--A')
               + 3.1 * nt(@-37 '---GT---')
               + 1.9 * nt(@-37 '----C-CT')
               + 1.5 * nt(@-37 '---C--A-')
               - 1.5 * nt(@-37 '------GC')
               - 1.9 * nt(@-37 '--CAW---')
               - 3.1 * nt(@-37 '--A----C')

where nt() returns the number of true subexpressions,
@-37 locates the subexpressions on the DNA strand,
and "-" indicates a don't-care subexpression.
```

Towell and Shavlik's method can be expected to give more accurate results than our approach, but at a cost. Their method is very compute intensive and relies substantially on access to a fixed set of training patterns. Additionally, it is not clear that their rules are completely symbolic. While numeric expressions were convenient for the domains they studied, in applications where one is interested in more abstract descriptions, such expressions may be viewed as providing too much detail, and may be difficult for people to interpret and reason about. Sometimes one wants to determine the nearest symbolic interpretation of unit behavior rather than a precise mathematical description. Our method offers a simpler paradigm for doing this. Given these differences, we conclude that both methods have their place in rule extraction tool kits.

4 SIMULATIONS

4.1 Simple logic problems

We used a group of simple logic problems to verify that our extraction algorithms could produce a correct set of rules for networks trained on the complete pattern space of each function. Table 1 summarizes the results.[2] The *rule-plus-exception* problem is defined as $f = AB + \overline{A}\,\overline{B}\,\overline{C}\,\overline{D}$; *xor-1* is the 2–1–1 version of *xor* described in Section 2.3; and *xor-2* is a strictly layered (2–2–1) version of *xor* [6]. The *negation* problem is also described in [6]; in this problem one of the four inputs controls whether the other inputs appear normally or negated at the outputs. (As with *xor-1*, the network for *negation* makes use of direct input/output connections.) In addition to the perfect classification performance of the rules, the large values of p^* and small values of extraction error (as defined in Section 2.2) provide evidence that the extraction process is very accurate.

Problem	Network Topology	Hidden Unit Penalty Term	Average p^*		Extraction Error		Patterns Correctly Classified by Rules
			Hidden Unit(s)	Output Unit(s)	Hidden Unit(s)	Output Unit(s)	
rule-plus-exception	4–2–1	–	2.72	6.15	0.8 %	1.3 %	100.0 %
xor-1	2–1–1	–	5.68	4.40	0.1 %	0.1 %	100.0 %
xor-2	2–2–1	–	4.34	5.68	0.4 %	1.0 %	100.0 %
negation	4–3–4	activation	5.40	5.17	0.2 %	2.2 %	100.0 %

Table 1: Simulation summary for simple logic problems

Symbolic solutions for these problems often come in forms different from the canonical form of the function. For example, the following rules for the *rule-plus-exception* problem show a level of negation within the network:

```
H₁  =   OR (A, B, C, D)
H₂  =   AND (A, B)
O   =   OR (H̄₁, H₂)
```

Example results on *xor-1* show the expected use of an augmented *n*-of-*m* expression:

```
H   =   OR (I₁, Ī₂)
O   =   OR [AND(I₁, Ī₂), H̄]
```

4.2 The MONK's problems

We tested generalization performance using the MONK's problems [5, 7], a set of three problems used to compare a variety of symbolic and connectionist learning algorithms. A summary of these tests appears in Table 2. Our performance was equal to or better than all of the systems tested in [7] for the *monks-1* and *monks-2* problems. Moreover, the rules extracted by our algorithm were very concise and easy to understand, in contrast to those produced by several of the symbolic systems. (The two connectionist systems reported in [7] were opaque, i.e., no rules were extracted.) As an example, consider the following output for the *monks-2* problem:

```
H₁  =  2 of (head_shape round, body_shape round, is_smiling yes,
             holding sword, jacket_color red, has_tie yes)
H₂  =  3 of (head_shape round, body_shape round, is_smiling yes,
             holding sword, jacket_color red, has_tie not no)
O   =  AND (H₁, H̄₂)
```

The target concept for this problem is *exactly 2 of the attributes have their first value*. These rules demonstrate an elegant use of *n*-of-*m* expressions to describe the idea of "exactly 2" as "at least 2 but not 3". The *monks-3* problem is difficult due to (intentional) training set noise, but our results are comparable to the other systems tested in [7].

---

[2] All results in this paper are for networks trained using batch-mode back propagation on the cross-entropy error function. Training was stopped when outputs were within 0.05 of their target values for each pattern or a fixed number of epochs (typically 1000) was reached. Where indicated, a penalty term for non-Boolean hidden activations or hidden weight decay was added to the main error function. For the breast cancer problem shown in Table 4.3, hidden rules were extracted first and the output units were retrained briefly before extracting their rules. Results for the problems in Table 4.3 used leave-one-out testing or 10-fold cross-validation (with 10 different initial orderings) as indicated. All results are averages over 10 replications with different initial weights.

Problem	Network Topology	Hidden Unit Penalty Term	Training Set			Test Set		
			# of Patterns	Perf. of Network	Perf. of Rules	# of Patterns	Perf. of Network	Perf. of Rules
monks-1	17–3–1	decay	124	100.0 %	100.0 %	432	100.0 %	100.0 %
monks-2	17–2–1	decay	169	100.0 %	100.0 %	432	100.0 %	100.0 %
monks-3	17–0–1	–	122	93.4 %	93.4 %	432	97.2 %	97.2 %

Table 2: Simulation summary for the MONK's problems

4.3 UCI repository problems

The final set of simulations addresses extraction performance on three real-world databases from the UCI repository [5]. Table 3 shows that good results were achieved. For the *promoters* task, we achieved generalization performance of nearly 88%, compared to 93-96% reported by Towell and Shavlik [8]. However, our results are impressive when viewed in light of the simplicity and comprehensibility of the extracted output. While Towell and Shavlik's results for this task included 5 rules like the one shown in Section 3.2, our single rule is quite simple:

```
promoter   =  5 of (@-45 'AA-------TTGA-A-----T------T-----AAA----C')
```

Results for the *house-votes-84* and *breast-cancer-wisc* problems are especially noteworthy since the generalization performance of the rules is virtually identical to that of the raw networks. This indicates that the rules are capturing a significant portion of the computation being performed by the networks. The following rule was the one most frequently extracted for the *house-votes-84* problem, where the task is to predict party affiliation:

```
Democrat   =  OR [ 5 of (V₃, V̄₇, V₉, V̄₁₀, V₁₁, V̄₁₂), V̄₄ ]
   where V₃   =  voted for adoption-of-the-budget-resolution bill
         V₄   =  voted for physician-fee-freeze bill
         V₇   =  voted for anti-satellite-test-ban bill
         V₉   =  voted for mx-missile bill
         V₁₀  =  voted for immigration bill
         V₁₁  =  voted for synfuels-corporation-cutback bill
         V₁₂  =  voted for education-spending bill
```

Shown below is a typical rule set extracted for the *breast-cancer-wisc* problem. Here the goal is to diagnose a tumor as benign or malignant based on nine clinical attributes.

```
Malignant  =  AND (H₁, H₂)
         H₁ =  4 of (thickness > 3, size > 1, adhesion > 1, epithelial > 5,
                     nuclei > 3, chromatin > 1, normal > 2, mitoses > 1)
         H₂ =  3 of (thickness > 6, size > 1, shape > 1, epithelial > 1,
                     nuclei > 8, normal > 9)
         H₃ =  not used
```

As suggested by the rules, we used a thermometer (cumulative) coding of the nominally valued attributes so that less-than or greater-than subexpressions could be efficiently represented in the hidden weights. Such a representation is often useful in diagnosis tasks. We also limited the hidden weights to positive values due to the nature of the attributes.

Problem	Network Topology	Training Set			Test Set		
		# of Patterns	Perf. of Network	Perf. of Rules	# of Patterns	Perf. of Network	Perf. of Rules
promoters	228–0–1	105	100.0 %	95.9 %	1	94.2 %	87.6 %
house-votes-84	16–0–1	387	97.3 %	96.2 %	43	95.7 %	95.9 %
breast-cancer-wisc	81–3–1	630	98.5 %	96.3 %	70	95.8 %	95.2 %

Table 3: Simulation summary for UCI repository problems

Taken as a whole our simulation results are encouraging, and we are conducting further research on rule extraction for more complex tasks.

5 CONCLUSION

We have described a general approach for extracting various types of n-of-m symbolic rules from trained networks of sigmoidal units, assuming approximately Boolean activation behavior. While other methods for interpretation of this sort exist, ours represents a valuable price/performance point, offering easily-understood rules and good extraction performance with computational complexity that scales well with the expressiveness desired. The basic principles behind our approach may be flexibly applied to a wide variety of problems.

References

[1] Alexander, J. A. (1994). *Template-based procedures for neural network interpretation*. MS Thesis. Department of Computer Science, University of Colorado, Boulder, CO.

[2] Andrews, R., Diederich, J., and Tickle, A. B. (1995). *A survey and critique of techniques for extracting rules from trained artificial neural networks*. To appear in Fu, L. M. (Ed.), Knowledge-Based Systems, Special Issue on Knowledge-Based Neural Networks.

[3] Mangasarian, O. L. and Wolberg, W. H. (1990). *Cancer diagnosis via linear programming*. SIAM News 23:5, pages 1 & 18.

[4] McMillan, C. (1992). *Rule induction in a neural network through integrated symbolic and subsymbolic processing*. PhD Thesis. Department of Computer Science, University of Colorado, Boulder, CO.

[5] Murphy, P. M. and Aha, D. W. (1994). *UCI repository of machine learning databases*. [Machine-readable data repository]. Irvine, CA: University of California, Department of Information and Computer Science. Monks data courtesy of Sebastian Thrun, promoters data courtesy of M. Noordewier and J. Shavlik, congressional voting data courtesy of Jeff Schlimmer, breast cancer data courtesy of Dr. William H. Wolberg (see also [3] above).

[6] Rumelhart, D. E., Hinton, G. E., and Williams, R. J. (1986). Learning internal representations by error propagation. In Rumelhart, D. E., McClelland, J. L., and the PDP Research Group, *Parallel Distributed Processing: Explorations in the Microstructure of Cognition. Volume 1: Foundations*, pages 318-362. Cambridge, MA: MIT Press.

[7] Thrun, S. B., and 23 other authors (1991). *The MONK's problems - A performance comparison of different learning algorithms*. Technical Report CS-CMU-91-197. Carnegie Mellon University, Pittsburgh, PA.

[8] Towell, G. and Shavlik, J. W. (1992). Interpretation of artificial neural networks: Mapping knowledge-based neural networks into rules. In Moody, J. E., Hanson, S. J., and Lippmann, R. P. (Eds.), *Advances in Neural Information Processing Systems*, 4:977-984. San Mateo, CA: Morgan Kaufmann.

Factorial Learning and the *EM* Algorithm

Zoubin Ghahramani
zoubin@psyche.mit.edu

Department of Brain & Cognitive Sciences
Massachusetts Institute of Technology
Cambridge, MA 02139

Abstract

Many real world learning problems are best characterized by an interaction of multiple independent causes or factors. Discovering such causal structure from the data is the focus of this paper. Based on Zemel and Hinton's cooperative vector quantizer (CVQ) architecture, an unsupervised learning algorithm is derived from the Expectation–Maximization (EM) framework. Due to the combinatorial nature of the data generation process, the exact E-step is computationally intractable. Two alternative methods for computing the E-step are proposed: Gibbs sampling and mean-field approximation, and some promising empirical results are presented.

1 Introduction

Many unsupervised learning problems fall under the rubric of *factorial learning*—that is, the goal of the learning algorithm is to discover multiple independent causes, or factors, that can well characterize the observed data (Barlow, 1989; Redlich, 1993; Hinton and Zemel, 1994; Saund, 1995). Such learning problems often arise naturally in response to the actual process by which the data have been generated. For instance, images may be generated by combining multiple objects, or varying colors, locations, and poses, with different light sources. Similarly, speech signals may result from an interaction of factors such as the tongue position, lip aperture, glottal state, communication line, and background noises. The goal of factorial learning is to invert this data generation process, discovering a representation that will both parsimoniously describe the data and reflect its underlying causes.

A recent approach to factorial learning uses the Minimum Description Length (MDL) principle (Rissanen, 1989) to extract a compact representation of the input (Zemel, 1993; Hinton and Zemel, 1994). This has resulted in a learning architecture called Cooperative Vector Quantization (CVQ), in which a set of vector quantizers cooperates to reproduce the input. Within each vector quantizer a competitive learning mechanism operates to select an appropriate vector code to describe the input. The CVQ is related to algorithms based on mixture models, such as soft competitive clustering, mixtures of experts (Jordan and Jacobs, 1994), and hidden Markov models (Baum et al., 1970), in that each vector quantizer in the CVQ is itself a mixture model. However, it generalizes this notion by allowing the mixture models to cooperate in describing features in the data set, thereby creating a distributed representations of the mixture components. The learning algorithm for the CVQ uses MDL to derive a cost function composed of a reconstruction cost (e.g. sum squared error), representation cost (negative entropy of the vector code), and model complexity (description length of the network weights), which is minimized by gradient descent.

In this paper we first formulate the factorial learning problem in the framework of statistical physics (section 2). Through this formalism, we derive a novel learning algorithm for the CVQ based on the Expectation–Maximization (EM) algorithm (Dempster et al., 1977) (section 3). The exact EM algorithm is intractable for this and related factorial learning problems—however, a tractable mean-field approximation can be derived. Empirical results on Gibbs sampling and the mean-field approximation are presented in section 4.

2 Statistical Physics Formulation

The CVQ architecture, shown in Figure 1, is composed of hidden and observable units, where the observable units, $\mathbf{y}$, are real-valued, and the hidden units are discrete and organized into vectors $\mathbf{s}_i$, $i = 1, \ldots, d$. The network models a data generation process which is assumed to proceed in two stages. First, a factor is independently sampled from each hidden unit vector, $\mathbf{s}_i$, according to its prior probability density, $\boldsymbol{\pi}_i$. Within each vector the factors are mutually exclusive, i.e. if $s_{ij} = 1$ for some j, then $s_{ik} = 0$, $\forall k \neq j$. The observable is then generated from a Gaussian distribution with mean $\sum_{i=1}^{d} W_i \mathbf{s}_i$.

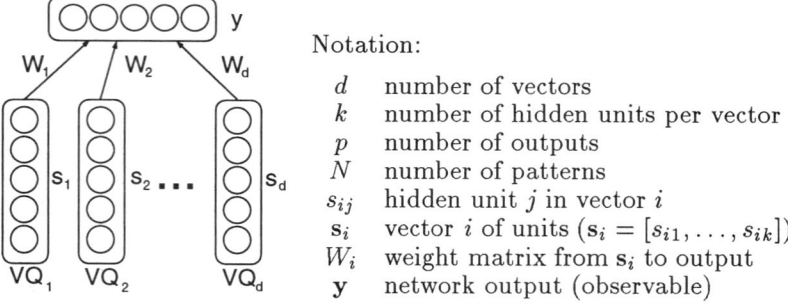

Notation:
d number of vectors
k number of hidden units per vector
p number of outputs
N number of patterns
s_{ij} hidden unit j in vector i
$\mathbf{s}_i$ vector i of units ($\mathbf{s}_i = [s_{i1}, \ldots, s_{ik}]$)
W_i weight matrix from $\mathbf{s}_i$ to output
$\mathbf{y}$ network output (observable)

Figure 1. The factorial learning architecture.

Defining the energy of a particular configuration of hidden states and outputs as

$$\mathcal{H}(\mathbf{s}, \mathbf{y}) = \frac{1}{2}\|\mathbf{y} - \sum_{i=1}^{d} W_i \mathbf{s}_i\|^2 - \sum_{i=1}^{d}\sum_{j=1}^{k} s_{ij} \log \pi_{ij}, \qquad (1)$$

the Boltzmann distribution

$$p(\mathbf{s},\mathbf{y}) = \frac{1}{Z_{free}} \exp\{-\mathcal{H}(\mathbf{s},\mathbf{y})\}, \qquad (2)$$

exactly recovers the probability model for the CVQ. The causes or factors are represented in the multinomial variables $\mathbf{s}_i$ and the observable in the multivariate Gaussian $\mathbf{y}$. The unclamped partition function, Z_{free}, can be evaluated by summing and integrating over all the possible configurations of the system to obtain

$$Z_{free} = \sum_s \int_y \exp\{-\mathcal{H}(\mathbf{s},\mathbf{y})\} dy = (2\pi)^{p/2}, \qquad (3)$$

which is constant, independent of the weights. This constant partition function results in desirable properties, such as the lack of a Boltzmann machine-like sleep phase (Neal, 1992), which we will exploit in the learning algorithm.

The system described by equation (1)[1] can be thought of as a special form of the Boltzmann machine (Ackley et al., 1985). Expanding out the quadratic term we see that there are pairwise interaction terms between every unit. The evaluation of the partition function (3) tells us that when $\mathbf{y}$ is unclamped the quadratic term can be integrated out and therefore all $\mathbf{s}_i$ are independent. However, when $\mathbf{y}$ is clamped all the $\mathbf{s}_i$ become dependent.

3 The EM Algorithm

Given a set of observable vectors, the goal of the unsupervised learning algorithm is to find weight matrices such that the network is most likely to have generated the data. If the hidden causes for each observable where known, then the weight matrices could be easily estimated. However, the hidden causes cannot be inferred unless these weight matrices are known. This chicken-and-egg problem can be solved by iterating between computing the expectation of the hidden causes given the current weights and maximizing the likelihood of the weights given these expected causes—the two steps forming the basis of the Expectation–Maximization (EM) algorithm (Dempster et al., 1977).

Formally, from (2) we obtain the expected log likelihood of the parameters ϕ':

$$Q(\phi,\phi') = \langle -\mathcal{H}(\mathbf{s},\mathbf{y}) - \log Z_{free} \rangle_{c,\phi} \qquad (4)$$

where ϕ denotes the current parameters, $\phi = \{W_i\}_{i=1}^d$, and $\langle \cdot \rangle_{c,\phi}$ denotes expectation given ϕ and the clamped observables. The E-step of EM consists of computing this expected log likelihood. As the only random variables are the hidden causes, this simplifies to computing the $\langle \mathbf{s}_i \rangle_c$ and $\langle \mathbf{s}_i \mathbf{s}_j^T \rangle_c$ terms appearing in the quadratic expansion of $\mathcal{H}$. Once these terms have been computed, the M-step consists of maximizing Q with respect to the parameters. Setting the derivatives to zero we obtain a linear system,

$$\frac{\partial Q}{\partial W_j} = \mathbf{y}\langle \mathbf{s}_j \rangle_c^T - \sum_{i=1}^d W_i \langle \mathbf{s}_i \mathbf{s}_j^T \rangle_c = 0,$$

---

[1] For the remainder of the paper we will ignore the second term in (1), thereby assuming equal priors on the hidden states. Relaxing this assumption and estimating priors from the data is straightforward.

which can be solved via the normal equations,

$$\widehat{W}_{(d \times k \times p)} = \left[\sum_N \langle \mathbf{ss}^T \rangle \langle \mathbf{ss}^T \rangle \right]^{-1}_{(d \times k)^2} \left[\sum_N \langle \mathbf{ss}^T \rangle \langle \mathbf{s} \rangle \mathbf{y}^T \right]_{(d \times k \times p)}$$

where $\mathbf{s}$ is the vector of concatenated $\mathbf{s}_i$ and the subscripts denote matrix size.

For models in which the observable is a monotonic differentiable function of $\sum_i W_i \mathbf{s}_i$, i.e. generalized linear models, least squares estimates of the weights for the M-step can be obtained iteratively by the method of scoring (McCullagh and Nelder, 1989).

3.1 E-step: Exact

The difficulty arises in the E-step of the algorithm. The expectation of hidden unit j in vector i given pattern $\mathbf{y}$ is:

$$\langle s_{ij} \rangle_c = P(s_{ij} = 1 | \mathbf{y}; W) \propto P(\mathbf{y} | s_{ij} = 1; W) \pi_{ij}$$

$$\propto \sum_{j_1=1}^{k} \cdots \sum_{j_h \neq i=1}^{k} \cdots \sum_{j_d=1}^{k} P(\mathbf{y} | s_{ij} = 1, s_{1j_1} = 1, \ldots, s_{dj_d} = 1; W) \pi_{ij}$$

To compute this expectation it is necessary to sum over all possible configurations of the other hidden units. If each vector quantizer has k hidden units, each expectation has time complexity of $\mathcal{O}(k^{d-1})$, i.e. $\mathcal{O}(Nk^d)$ for a full E-step. The exponential time is due inherently to the cooperative nature of the model—the setting of one vector only determines the observable if all the other vectors are fixed.

3.2 E-step: Gibbs sampling

Rather than summing over all possible hidden unit patterns to compute the exact expectations, a natural approach is to approximate them through a Monte Carlo method. As with Boltzmann machines, the CVQ architecture lends itself well to Gibbs sampling (Geman and Geman, 1984). Starting from a clamped observable $\mathbf{y}$ and a random setting of the hidden units $\{\mathbf{s}_j\}$, the setting of each vector is updated in turn stochastically according to its conditional distribution $\mathbf{s}_i \sim p(\mathbf{s}_i | \mathbf{y}, \{\mathbf{s}_j\}_{j \neq i}; W)$. Each conditional distribution calculation requires k forward passes through the network, one for each possible state of the vector being updated, and k Gaussian distance calculations between the resulting predicted and clamped observables. If all the probabilities are bounded away from zero this process is guaranteed to converge to the equilibrium distribution of the hidden units given the observable. The first and second-order statistics, for $\langle \mathbf{s}_i \rangle_c$ and $\langle \mathbf{s}_i \mathbf{s}_j^T \rangle_c$ respectively, can be collected using the s_{ij}'s visited and $p(\mathbf{s}_i | \mathbf{y}, \{\mathbf{s}_j\}_{j \neq i}; W)$ calculated during this sampling process. These estimated expectations are then used in the E-step.

3.3 E-step: Mean-field approximation

Although Gibbs sampling is generally much more efficient than exact calculations, it too can be computationally demanding. A more promising approach is to approximate the intractable system with a tractable mean-field approximation (Parisi, 1988), and perform the E-step calculation on this approximation. We can write the negative log likelihood minimized by the original system as a difference between the clamped and unclamped free energies:

$$\begin{aligned}\text{Cost} &= -\log p(\mathbf{y}|W) = -\log \sum_{\mathbf{s}} p(\mathbf{y},\mathbf{s}|W) \\ &= -\log \sum_{\mathbf{s}} \exp\{-\mathcal{H}(\mathbf{y},\mathbf{s})\} + \log \sum_{\mathbf{s}} \int_{\mathbf{y}} \exp\{-\mathcal{H}(\mathbf{y},\mathbf{s})\} d\mathbf{y} \\ &= F_{cl} - F_{free}\end{aligned}$$

The mean-field approximation allows us to replace each free energy in this cost with an upper bound approximation $\text{Cost}^{MF} = F_{cl}^{MF} - F_{free}^{MF}$. Unfortunately, a difference of two upper bounds is not generally an upper bound, and therefore minimizing Cost^{MF} in, for example, mean-field Boltzmann machines does not guarantee that we are minimizing an upper bound on Cost. However, for the factorial learning architectures described in this paper we have the property that F_{free} is constant, and therefore the mean-field approximation of the cost is an upper bound on the exact cost.

The mean-field approximation can be obtained by approximating the probability density given by (1) and (2) by a completely factorized probability density:

$$\tilde{p}(\mathbf{s},\mathbf{y}) = \frac{1}{(2\pi)^{p/2}} \exp\{-\frac{1}{2}\|\mathbf{y}-\boldsymbol{\mu}\|^2\} \prod_{i,j} m_{ij}^{s_{ij}}$$

In this approximation all units are independent: the observables are Gaussian distributed with mean $\boldsymbol{\mu}$ and each hidden unit is binomially distributed with mean m_{ij}. To obtain the mean-field approximation we solve for the mean values that minimize the Kullback-Leibler divergence $\mathcal{KL}(p,\tilde{p}) \equiv E_{\tilde{p}}[\log \tilde{p}] - E_{\tilde{p}}[\log p]$.

Noting that: $E_{\tilde{p}}[s_{ij}] = m_{ij}$, $E_{\tilde{p}}[s_{ij}^2] = m_{ij}$, $E_{\tilde{p}}[s_{ij}s_{kl}] = m_{ij}m_{kl}$, and $E_{\tilde{p}}[s_{ij}s_{ik}] = 0$, we obtain the mean-field fixed point equations

$$\mathbf{m}_i = \text{softmax}\left(W_i^T(\mathbf{y}-\hat{\mathbf{y}}) + W_i^T W_i(\mathbf{m}_i - 1/2)\right), \tag{5}$$

where $\hat{\mathbf{y}} \equiv \sum_i W_i \mathbf{m}_i$. The softmax function is the exponential normalized over the k hidden units in each $\mathbf{m}_i$ vector. The first term inside the softmax has an intuitive interpretation as the projection of the error in the observable onto the weights of the hidden unit vector i. The more a hidden unit can reduce this error, the higher its mean. The second term arises from the fact that $E_{\tilde{p}}[s_{ij}^2] = m_{ij}$ and not $E_{\tilde{p}}[s_{ij}^2] = m_{ij}^2$. The means obtained by iterating equation (5) are used in the E-step by substituting $\mathbf{m}_i$ for $\langle \mathbf{s}_i \rangle_c$ and $\mathbf{m}_i \mathbf{m}_j^T$ for $\langle \mathbf{s}_i \mathbf{s}_j^T \rangle_c$.

4 Empirical Results

Two methods, Gibbs sampling and mean-field, have been provided for computing the E-step of the factorial learning algorithm. There is a key empirical question that needs to be answered to determine the efficiency and accuracy of each method. For Gibbs sampling it is important to know how many samples will provide robust estimates of the expectations required for the E-step. It is well known that for stochastic Boltzmann machines the number of samples needed to obtain good estimates of the gradients is generally large and renders the learning algorithm prohibitively slow. Will this architecture suffer from the same problem? For mean-field it is important to know the loss incurred by approximating the true likelihood. We explore these questions by presenting empirical results on two small unsupervised learning problems.

The first benchmark problem consists of a data set of 4×4 greyscale images generated by a combination of two factors: one producing a single horizontal line and the other, a vertical line (Figure 2a; cf. Zemel, 1993). Using a network with 2 vectors of 4 hidden units each, both the Gibbs sampling and mean-field EM algorithms converge on a solution after about a dozen steps (Figure 2b). The solutions found resemble the generative model of the data (Figure 2c & d).

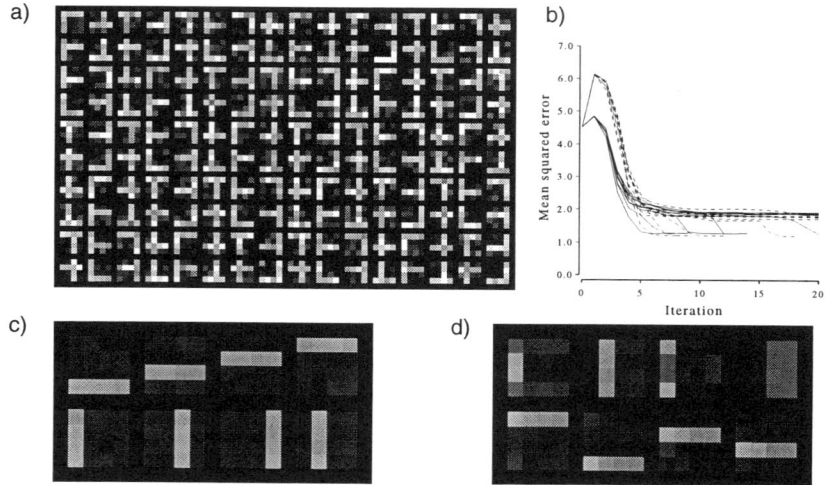

Figure 2. Lines Problem. a) Complete data set of 160 patterns. b) Learning curves for Gibbs (solid) and mean-field (dashed) forms of the algorithm. c) A sample output weight matrix after learning (MSE=1.20). The top vector of hidden units has come to represent horizontal lines, and the bottom, vertical lines. d) Another typical output weight matrix (MSE=1.78).

The second problem consists of a data set of 6×6 images generated by a combination of three shapes—a cross, a diagonal line, and an empty square—each of which can appear in one of 16 locations (Figure 3a). The data set of 300 out of 4096 possible images was presented to a network with the architecture shown in Figure 3b. After 30 steps of EM, each consisting of 5 Gibbs samples of each hidden unit, the network reconstructed a representation that approximated the three underlying causes of the data—dedicating one vector mostly to diagonal lines, one to hollow squares, and one to crosses (Figure 3c).

To assess how many Gibbs samples are required to obtain accurate estimates of the expectations for the E-step we repeated the lines problem varying the number of samples. Clearly, as the number of samples becomes large the Gibbs E-step becomes exact. Therefore we expect performance to asymptote at the performance of the exact E-step. The results indicate that, for this problem, 3 samples are sufficient to achieve ceiling performance (Figure 4). Surprisingly, a single iteration of the

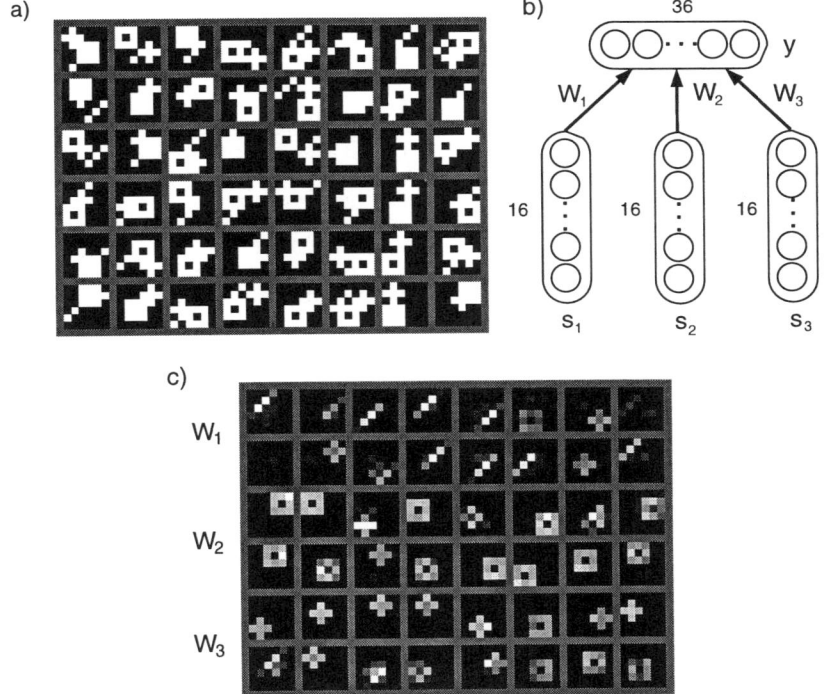

Figure 3. Shapes Problem. a) Sample images from the data set. b) Learning architecture used. c) Output weight matrix after learning.

mean-field equations also performs quite well.

5 Discussion

The factorial learning problem for cooperative vector quantizers has been formulated in the EM framework, and two learning algorithms, based on Gibbs sampling and mean-field approximation, have been derived. Unlike the Boltzmann machine, Gibbs sampling for this architecture seems to require very few samples for adequate performance. This may be due to the fact that, whereas the Boltzmann machine relies on *differences* of noisy estimates for its weight changes, due to the constant partition function the factorial learning algorithm does not. The mean-field approximation also seems to perform quite well on all problems tested to date. This may also be a consequence of the constant partition function which guarantees that the mean-field cost is an upper bound on the exact cost.

The framework can be extended to hidden Markov models (HMMs), showing that simple HMMs are a special case of dynamical CVQs, with the general case corresponding to parallel, factorial HMMs. The two principal advantages of such architectures are (1) unlike the traditional HMM, the state space can be represented as a combination of features, and (2) time series generated by multiple sources can be modeled. Simulation results on the Gibbs and mean-field EM algorithms for factorial HMMs are also promising (Ghahramani, 1995).

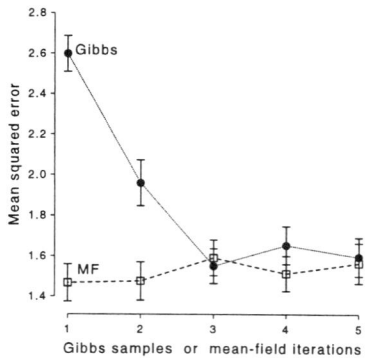

Figure 4. Comparison of the Gibbs and mean-field EM algorithms for the lines data. Each data point shows the mean squared training error averaged over 10 runs of 20 EM steps, with standard error bars. For the Gibbs curve the abscissa is the number of samples per vector of hidden units; for the mean-field curve it is the number of iterations of equation (5).

Acknowledgements

The author wishes to thank Lawrence Saul and Michael Jordan for invaluable discussions. This project was supported in part by a grant from the McDonnell-Pew Foundation, by a grant from ATR Human Information Processing Research Laboratories, by a grant from Siemens Corporation, and by grant N00014-94-1-0777 from the Office of Naval Research.

References

Ackley, D., Hinton, G., and Sejnowski, T. (1985). A learning algorithm for Boltzmann machines. *Cognitive Science*, 9:147-169.

Barlow, H. (1989). Unsupervised learning. *Neural Computation*, 1:295-311.

Baum, L., Petrie, T., Soules, G., and Weiss, N. (1970). A maximization technique occurring in the statistical analysis of probabilistic functions of Markov chains. *The Annals of Mathematical Statistics*, 41:164-171.

Dempster, A., Laird, N., and Rubin, D. (1977). Maximum likelihood from incomplete data via the EM algorithm. *J. Royal Statistical Society Series B*, 39:1-38.

Geman, S. and Geman, D. (1984). Stochastic relaxation, Gibbs distributions, and the Bayesian restoration of images. *IEEE Transactions on Pattern Analysis and Machine Intelligence*, 6:721-741.

Ghahramani, Z. (1995). Factorial learning and the *EM* algorithm. *MIT Computational Cognitive Science TR 9501*.

Hinton, G. and Zemel, R. (1994). Autoencoders, minimum description length, and Helmholtz free energy. In Cowan, J., Tesauro, G., and Alspector, J., editors, *Advances in Neural Information Processing Systems 6*. Morgan Kaufmanm Publishers, San Francisco, CA.

Jordan, M. and Jacobs, R. (1994). Hierarchical mixtures of experts and the EM algorithm. *Neural Computation*, 6:181-214.

McCullagh, P. and Nelder, J. (1989). *Generalized Linear Models*. Chapman & Hall, London.

Neal, R. (1992). Connectionist learning of belief networks. *Artificial Intelligence*, 56:71-113.

Parisi, G. (1988). *Statistical Field Theory*. Addison-Wesley, Redwood City, CA.

Redlich, A. (1993). Supervised factorial learning. *Neural Computation*, 5:750-766.

Rissanen, J. (1989). *Stochastic Complexity in Statistical Inquiry*. World Scientific, Singapore.

Saund, E. (1995). A multiple cause mixture model for unsupervised learning. *Neural Computation*, 7(1):51-71.

Zemel, R. (1993). *A minimum description length framework for unsupervised learning.* Ph.D. Thesis, Dept. of Computer Science, University of Toronto, Toronto, Canada.

A Growing Neural Gas Network Learns Topologies

Bernd Fritzke
Institut für Neuroinformatik
Ruhr-Universität Bochum
D-44780 Bochum
Germany

Abstract

An incremental network model is introduced which is able to learn the important topological relations in a given set of input vectors by means of a simple Hebb-like learning rule. In contrast to previous approaches like the "neural gas" method of Martinetz and Schulten (1991, 1994), this model has no parameters which change over time and is able to continue learning, adding units and connections, until a performance criterion has been met. Applications of the model include vector quantization, clustering, and interpolation.

1 INTRODUCTION

In unsupervised learning settings only input data is available but no information on the desired output. What can the goal of learning be in this situation?

One possible objective is *dimensionality reduction:* finding a low-dimensional subspace of the input vector space containing most or all of the input data. Linear subspaces with this property can be computed directly by principal component analysis or iteratively with a number of network models (Sanger, 1989; Oja, 1982). The Kohonen feature map (Kohonen, 1982) and the "growing cell structures" (Fritzke, 1994b) allow projection onto non-linear, discretely sampled subspaces of a dimensionality which has to be chosen *a priori*. Depending on the relation between inherent data dimensionality and dimensionality of the target space, some information on the topological arrangement of the input data may be lost in the process.

This is not astonishing since a reversible mapping from high-dimensional data to lower-dimensional spaces (or structures) does not exist in general.

Asking how structures must look like to allow reversible mappings directly leads to another possible objective of unsupervised learning which can be described as *topology learning*: Given some high-dimensional data distribution $P(\xi)$, find a topological structure which closely reflects the topology of the data distribution. An elegant method to construct such structures is "competitive Hebbian learning" (CHL) (Martinetz, 1993). CHL requires the use of some vector quantization method. Martinetz and Schulten propose the "neural gas" (NG) method for this purpose (Martinetz and Schulten, 1991).

We will briefly introduce and discuss the approach of Martinetz and Schulten. Then we propose a new network model which also makes use of CHL. In contrast to the above-mentioned CHL/NG combination, this model is incremental and has only constant parameters. This leads to a number of advantages over the previous approach.

2 COMPETITIVE HEBBIAN LEARNING AND NEURAL GAS

CHL (Martinetz, 1993) assumes a number of centers in $\mathbf{R}^n$ and successively inserts topological connections among them by evaluating input signals drawn from a data distribution $P(\xi)$. The principle of this method is:

> For each input signal x connect the two closest centers (measured by Euclidean distance) by an edge.

The resulting graph is a subgraph of the Delaunay triangulation (fig. 1a) corresponding to the set of centers. This subgraph (fig. 1b), which is called the "induced Delaunay triangulation", is limited to those areas of the input space $\mathbf{R}^n$ where $P(\xi) > 0$. The "induced Delaunay triangulation" has been shown to optimally preserve topology in a very general sense (Martinetz, 1993).

Only centers lying on the input data submanifold or in its vicinity actually develop any edges. The others are useless for the purpose of topology learning and are often called *dead units*. To make use of all centers they have to be placed in those regions of $\mathbf{R}^n$ where $P(\xi)$ differs from zero. This could be done by any vector quantization (VQ) procedure. Martinetz and Schulten have proposed a particular kind of VQ method, the mentioned NG method (Martinetz and Schulten, 1991). The main principle of NG is the following:

> For each input signal x adapt the k nearest centers whereby k is decreasing from a large initial to a small final value.

A large initial value of k causes adaptation (movement towards the input signal) of a large fraction of the centers. Then k (the adaptation range) is decreased until finally only the nearest center for each input signal is adapted. The adaptation strength underlies a similar decay schedule. To realize the parameter decay one has to define the total number of adaptation steps for the NG method in advance.

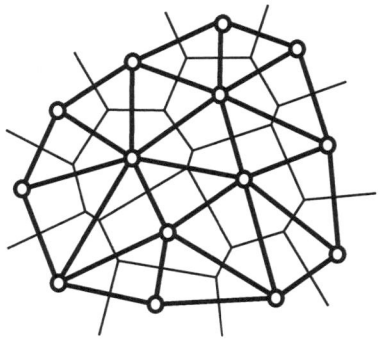 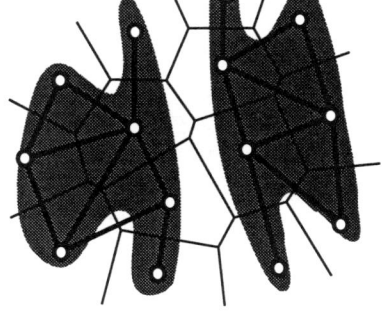

a) Delaunay triangulation   b) induced Delaunay triangulation

Figure 1: Two ways of defining closeness among a set of points. a) The *Delaunay triangulation* (thick lines) connects points having neighboring *Voronoi polygons* (thin lines). Basically this reduces to points having small Euclidean distance w.r.t. the given set of points. b) The *induced Delaunay triangulation* (thick lines) is obtained by masking the original Delaunay triangulation with a data distribution $P(\xi)$ (shaded). Two centers are only connected if the common border of their Voronoi polygons lies at least partially in a region where $P(\xi) > 0$ (closely adapted from Martinetz and Schulten, 1994)

For a given data distribution one could now first run the NG algorithm to distribute a certain number of centers and then use CHL to generate the topology. It is, however, also possible to apply both techniques concurrently (Martinetz and Schulten, 1991). In this case a method for removing obsolete edges is required since the motion of the centers may make edges invalid which have been generated earlier. Martinetz and Schulten use an *edge aging* scheme for this purpose. One should note that the CHL algorithm does not influence the outcome of the NG method in any way since the adaptations in NG are based only on distance in input space and not on the network topology. On the other hand NG does influence the topology generated by CHL since it moves the centers around.

The combination of NG and CHL described above is an effective method for topology learning. A problem in practical applications, however, may be to determine *a priori* a suitable number of centers. Depending on the complexity of the data distribution which one wants to model, very different numbers of centers may be appropriate. The nature of the NG algorithm requires a decision in advance and, if the result is not satisfying, one or several new simulations have to be performed from scratch. In the following we propose a method which overcomes this problem and offers a number of other advantages through a flexible scheme for center insertion.

3 THE GROWING NEURAL GAS ALGORITHM

In the following we consider networks consisting of

- a set A of units (or nodes). Each unit $c \in A$ has an associated *reference vector* $w_c \in \mathbf{R}^n$. The reference vectors can be regarded as positions in input space of the corresponding units.
- a set N of connections (or edges) among pairs of units. These connections are not weighted. Their sole purpose is the definition of topological structure.

Moreover, there is a (possibly infinite) number of n-dimensional input signals obeying some unknown probability density function $P(\xi)$.

The main idea of the method is to successively add new units to an initially small network by evaluating local statistical measures gathered during previous adaptation steps. This is the same approach as used in the "growing cell structures" model (Fritzke, 1994b) which, however, has a topology with a fixed dimensionality (e.g., two or three).

In the approach described here, the network topology is generated incrementally by CHL and has a dimensionality which depends on the input data and may vary locally. The complete algorithm for our model which we call "growing neural gas" is given by the following:

0. Start with two units a and b at random positions w_a and w_b in $\mathbf{R}^n$.
1. Generate an input signal ξ according to $P(\xi)$.
2. Find the nearest unit s_1 and the second-nearest unit s_2.
3. Increment the age of all edges emanating from s_1.
4. Add the squared distance between the input signal and the nearest unit in input space to a local counter variable:

$$\Delta \text{error}(s_1) = \|w_{s_1} - \xi\|^2$$

5. Move s_1 and its direct topological neighbors[1] towards ξ by fractions ϵ_b and ϵ_n, respectively, of the total distance:

$$\begin{aligned} \Delta w_{s_1} &= \epsilon_b(\xi - w_{s_1}) \\ \Delta w_n &= \epsilon_n(\xi - w_n) \text{ for all direct neighbors } n \text{ of } s_1 \end{aligned}$$

6. If s_1 and s_2 are connected by an edge, set the age of this edge to zero. If such an edge does not exist, create it.[2]
7. Remove edges with an age larger than a_{max}. If this results in points having no emanating edges, remove them as well.

---

[1] Throughout this paper the term *neighbors* denotes units which are topological neighbors in the graph (as opposed to units within a small Euclidean distance of each other in input space).

[2] This step is Hebbian in its spirit since correlated activity is used to decide upon insertions.

8. If the number of input signals generated so far is an integer multiple of a parameter λ, insert a new unit as follows:
   - Determine the unit q with the maximum accumulated error.
   - Insert a new unit r halfway between q and its neighbor f with the largest error variable:
   $$w_r = 0.5\,(w_q + w_f).$$
   - Insert edges connecting the new unit r with units q and f, and remove the original edge between q and f.
   - Decrease the error variables of q and f by multiplying them with a constant α. Initialize the error variable of r with the new value of the error variable of q.
9. Decrease all error variables by multiplying them with a constant d.
10. If a stopping criterion (e.g., net size or some performance measure) is not yet fulfilled go to step 1.

How does the described method work? The adaptation steps towards the input signals (5.) lead to a general movement of all units towards those areas of the input space where signals come from ($P(\xi) > 0$). The insertion of edges (6.) between the nearest and the second-nearest unit with respect to an input signal generates a single connection of the "induced Delaunay triangulation" (see fig. 1b) *with respect to the current position of all units*.

The removal of edges (7.) is necessary to get rid of those edges which are no longer part of the "induced Delaunay triangulation" because their ending points have moved. This is achieved by *local* edge aging (3.) around the nearest unit combined with age re-setting of those edges (6.) which already exist between nearest and second-nearest units.

With insertion and removal of edges the model tries to construct and then track the "induced Delaunay triangulation" which is a slowly moving target due to the adaptation of the reference vectors.

The accumulation of squared distances (4.) during the adaptation helps to identify units lying in areas of the input space where the mapping from signals to units causes much error. To reduce this error, new units are inserted in such regions.

4 SIMULATION RESULTS

We will now give some simulation results to demonstrate the general behavior of our model. The probability distribution in fig. 2 has been proposed by Martinetz and Schulten (1991) to demonstrate the non-incremental "neural gas" model. It can be seen that our model quickly learns the important topological relations in this rather complicated distribution by forming structures of different dimensionalities.

The second example (fig. 3) illustrates the differences between the proposed model and the original NG network. Although the final topology is rather similar for both models, intermediate stages are quite different. Both models are able to identify the clusters in the given distribution. Only the "growing neural gas" model, however,

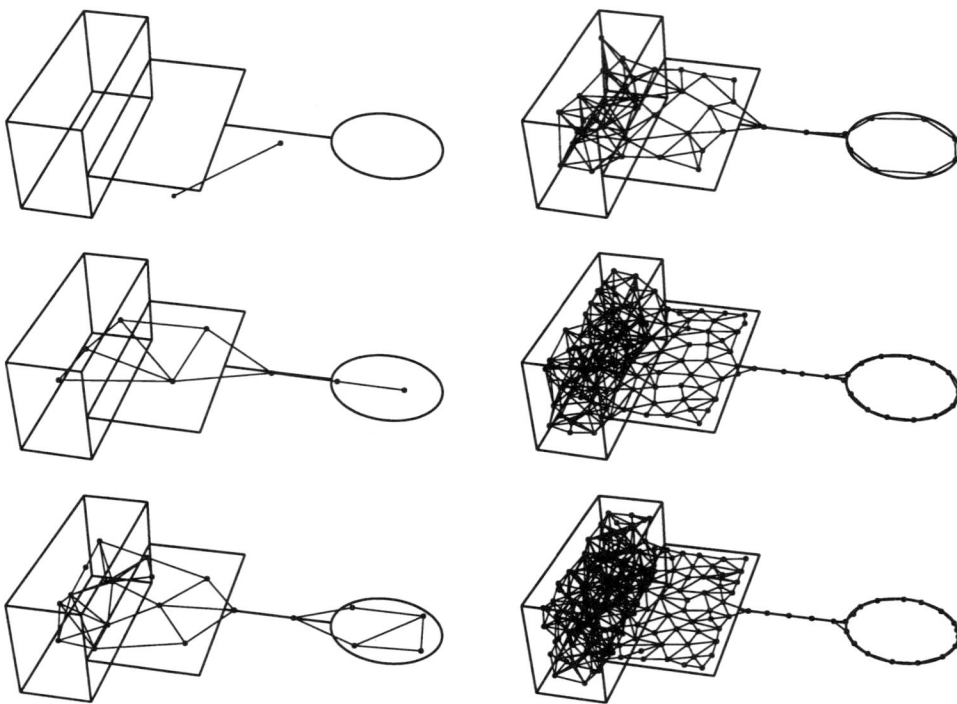

Figure 2: The "growing neural gas" network adapts to a signal distribution which has different dimensionalities in different areas of the input space. Shown are the initial network consisting of two randomly placed units and the networks after 600, 1800, 5000, 15000 and 20000 input signals have been applied. The last network shown is not the necessarily the "final" one since the growth process could in principle be continued indefinitely. The parameters for this simulation were: $\lambda = 100$, $\epsilon_b = 0.2$, $\epsilon_n = 0.006$, $\alpha = 0.5$, $a_{max} = 50$, $d = 0.995$.

could continue to grow to discover still smaller clusters (which are not present in this particular example, though).

5 DISCUSSION

The "growing neural gas" network presented here is able to make explicit the important topological relations in a given distribution $P(\xi)$ of input signals. An advantage over the NG method of Martinetz and Schulten is the incremental character of the model which eliminates the need to pre-specify a network size. Instead, the growth process can be continued until a user-defined performance criterion or network size is met. All parameters are constant over time in contrast to other models which heavily rely on decaying parameters (such as the NG method or the Kohonen feature map).

It should be noted that the topology generated by CHL is not an optional feature

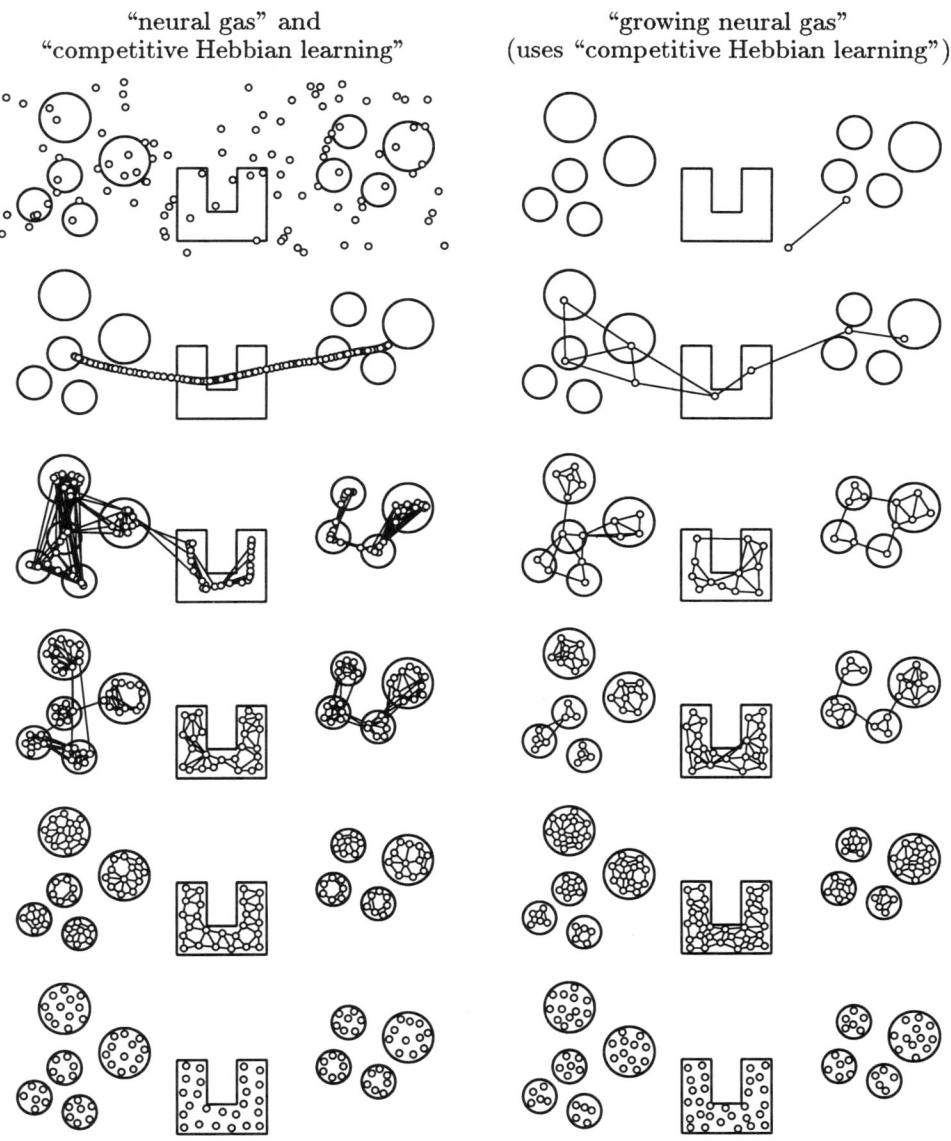

Figure 3: The NG/CHL network of Martinetz and Schulten (1991) and the author's "growing neural gas" model adapt to a clustered probability distribution. Shown are the respective initial states (top row) and a number of intermediate stages. Both the number of units in the NG model and the *final* number of units in the "growing neural gas" model are 100. The bottom row shows the distribution of centers after 10000 adaptation steps (the edges are as in the previous row but not shown). The center distribution is rather similar for both models although the intermediate stages differ significantly.

of our method (as it is for the NG model) but an essential component since it is used to direct the (completely local) adaptation as well as insertion of centers. It is probably the proper initialization of new units by interpolation from existing ones which makes it possible to have only constant parameters and local adaptations.

Possible applications of our model are clustering (as shown) and vector quantization. The network should perform particularly well in situations where the neighborhood information (in the edges) is used to implement interpolation schemes between neighboring units. By using the error occuring in early phases it can be determined where to insert new units to generate a topological look-up table of different density and different dimensionality in particular areas of the input data space.

Another promising direction of research is the combination with supervised learning. This has been done earlier with the "growing cell structures" (Fritzke, 1994c) and recently also with the "growing neural gas" described in this paper (Fritzke, 1994a). A crucial property for this kind of application is the possibility to choose an arbitrary insertion criterion. This is a feature not present, e.g., in the original "growing neural gas". The first results of this new supervised network model, an incremental radial basis function network, are very promising and we are further investigating this currently.

References

Fritzke, B. (1994a). Fast learning with incremental rbf networks. *Neural Processing Letters*, 1(1):2–5.

Fritzke, B. (1994b). Growing cell structures – a self-organizing network for unsupervised and supervised learning. *Neural Networks*, 7(9):1441–1460.

Fritzke, B. (1994c). Supervised learning with growing cell structures. In Cowan, J., Tesauro, G., and Alspector, J., editors, *Advances in Neural Information Processing Systems 6*, pages 255–262. Morgan Kaufmann Publishers, San Mateo, CA.

Kohonen, T. (1982). Self-organized formation of topologically correct feature maps. *Biological Cybernetics*, 43:59–69.

Martinetz, T. M. (1993). Competitive Hebbian learning rule forms perfectly topology preserving maps. In *ICANN'93: International Conference on Artificial Neural Networks*, pages 427–434, Amsterdam. Springer.

Martinetz, T. M. and Schulten, K. J. (1991). A "neural-gas" network learns topologies. In Kohonen, T., Mäkisara, K., Simula, O., and Kangas, J., editors, *Artificial Neural Networks*, pages 397–402. North-Holland, Amsterdam.

Martinetz, T. M. and Schulten, K. J. (1994). Topology representing networks. *Neural Networks*, 7(3):507–522.

Oja, E. (1982). A simplified neuron model as a principal component analyzer. *Journal of Mathematical Biology*, 15:267–273.

Sanger, T. D. (1989). An optimality principle for unsupervised learning. In Touretzky, D. S., editor, *Advances in Neural Information Processing Systems 1*, pages 11–19. Morgan Kaufmann, San Mateo, CA.

An Alternative Model for Mixtures of Experts

Lei Xu
Dept. of Computer Science, The Chinese University of Hong Kong
Shatin, Hong Kong, Email lxu@cs.cuhk.hk

Michael I. Jordan
Dept. of Brain and Cognitive Sciences
MIT
Cambridge, MA 02139

Geoffrey E. Hinton
Dept. of Computer Science
University of Toronto
Toronto, M5S 1A4, Canada

Abstract

We propose an alternative model for mixtures of experts which uses a different parametric form for the gating network. The modified model is trained by the EM algorithm. In comparison with earlier models—trained by either EM or gradient ascent—there is no need to select a learning stepsize. We report simulation experiments which show that the new architecture yields faster convergence. We also apply the new model to two problem domains: piecewise nonlinear function approximation and the combination of multiple previously trained classifiers.

1 INTRODUCTION

For the *mixtures of experts* architecture (Jacobs, Jordan, Nowlan & Hinton, 1991), the EM algorithm decouples the learning process in a manner that fits well with the modular structure and yields a considerably improved rate of convergence (Jordan & Jacobs, 1994). The favorable properties of EM have also been shown by theoretical analyses (Jordan & Xu, in press; Xu & Jordan, 1994).

It is difficult to apply EM to some parts of the mixtures of experts architecture because of the nonlinearity of *softmax* gating network. This makes the maximization with respect to the parameters in gating network nonlinear and analytically unsolvable even for the simplest generalized linear case. Jordan and Jacobs (1994) suggested a double-loop approach in which an inner loop of iteratively-reweighted least squares (IRLS) is used to perform the nonlinear optimization. However, this requires extra computation and the stepsize must be chosen carefully to guarantee the convergence of the inner loop.

We propose an alternative model for mixtures of experts which uses a different parametric form for the gating network. This form is chosen so that the maximization with respect to the parameters of the gating network can be handled analytically. Thus, a single-loop EM can be used, and no learning stepsize is required to guarantee convergence. We report simulation experiments which show that the new architecture yields faster convergence. We also apply the model to two problem domains. One is a piecewise nonlinear function approximation problem with smooth blending of pieces specified by polynomial, trigonometric, or other prespecified basis functions. The other is to combine classifiers developed previously—a general problem with a variety of applications (Xu, et al., 1991, 1992). Xu and Jordan (1993) proposed to solve the problem by using the mixtures of experts architecture and suggested an algorithm for bypassing the difficulty caused by the softmax gating networks. Here, we show that the algorithm of Xu and Jordan (1993) can be regarded as a special case of the single-loop EM given in this paper and that the single-loop EM also provides a further improvement.

2 MIXTURES OF EXPERTS AND EM LEARNING

The *mixtures of experts* model is based on the following conditional mixture:

$$P(y|x,\Theta) = \sum_{j=1}^{K} g_j(x,\nu) P(y|x,\theta_j),$$

$$P(y|x,\theta_j) = \frac{1}{(2\pi)^{n/2}|\Gamma_j|^{1/2}} \exp\{-\frac{1}{2}[y - f_j(x,w_j)]^T \Gamma_j^{-1}[y - f_j(x,w_j)]\} \quad (1)$$

where $x \in R^n$, and Θ consists of $\nu, \{\theta_j\}_1^K$, and θ_j consists of $\{w_j\}_1^K, \{\Gamma_j\}_1^K$. The vector $f_j(x, w_j)$ is the output of the j-th expert net. The scalar $g_j(x,\nu), j = 1, \cdots, K$ is given by the *softmax* function:

$$g_j(x,\nu) = e^{\beta_j(x,\nu)} / \sum_i e^{\beta_i(x,\nu)}. \quad (2)$$

In this equation, $\beta_j(x,\nu), j = 1, \cdots, K$ are the outputs of the *gating network*.

The parameter Θ is estimated by Maximum Likelihood (ML), where the log likelihood is given by $L = \sum_t \ln P(y^{(t)}|x^{(t)}, \Theta)$. The ML estimate can be found iteratively using the EM algorithm as follows. Given the current estimate $\Theta^{(k)}$, each iteration consists of two steps.

(1) E-step. For each pair $\{x^{(t)}, y^{(t)}\}$, compute $h_j^{(k)}(y^{(t)}|x^{(t)}) = P(j|x^{(t)}, y^{(t)})$, and then form a set of objective functions:

$$Q_j^e(\theta_j) = \sum_t h_j^{(k)}(y^{(t)}|x^{(t)}) \ln P(y^{(t)}|x^{(t)}, \theta_j), \ j = 1, \cdots, K;$$

$$Q^g(\nu) = \sum_t \sum_j h_j^{(k)}(y^{(t)}|x^{(t)}) \ln g_j^{(k)}(x^{(t)}, \nu^{(k)}). \qquad (3)$$

(2). M-step. Find a new estimate $\Theta^{(k+1)} = \{\{\theta_j^{(k+1)}\}_{j=1}^K, \nu^{(k+1)}\}$ with:

$$\theta_j^{(k+1)} = \arg\max_{\theta_j} Q_j^e(\theta_j), j = 1, \cdots, K; \quad \nu^{(k+1)} = \arg\max_{\nu} Q^g(\nu). \qquad (4)$$

In certain cases, for example when $f_j(x, w_j)$ is linear in the parameters w_j, $\max_{\theta_j} Q_j^e(\theta_j)$ can be solved by solving $\partial Q_j^e/\partial \theta_j = 0$. When $f_j(x, w_j)$ is nonlinear with respect to w_j, however, the maximization cannot be performed analytically. Moreover, due to the nonlinearity of *softmax*, $\max_{\nu} Q^g(\nu)$ cannot be solved analytically in any case. There are two possibilities for attacking these nonlinear optimization problems. One is to use a conventional iterative optimization technique (e.g., gradient ascent) to perform one or more inner-loop iterations. The other is to simply find a new estimate such that $Q_j^e(\theta_j^{(k+1)}) \geq Q_j^e(\theta_j^{(k)})$, $Q^g(\nu^{(k+1)}) \geq Q^g(\nu^{(k)})$. Usually, the algorithms that perform a full maximization during the M step are referred as "EM" algorithms, and algorithms that simply increase the Q function during the M step as "GEM" algorithms. In this paper we will further distinguish between EM algorithms requiring and not requiring an iterative inner loop by designating them as *double-loop EM* and *single-loop EM* respectively.

Jordan and Jacobs (1994) considered the case of linear $\beta_j(x, \nu) = \nu_j^T[x, 1]$ with $\nu = [\nu_1, \cdots, \nu_K]$ and semi-linear $f_j(w_j^T[x, 1])$ with nonlinear $f_j(.)$. They proposed a double-loop EM algorithm by using the IRLS method to implement the inner-loop iteration. For more general nonlinear $\beta_j(x, \nu)$ and $f_j(x, \theta_j)$, Jordan and Xu (in press) showed that an extended IRLS can be used for this inner loop. It can be shown that IRLS and the extension are equivalent to solving eq. (3) by the so-called *Fisher Scoring* method.

3 A NEW GATING NET AND A SINGLE-LOOP EM

To sidestep the need for a nonlinear optimization routine in the inner loop of the EM algorithm, we propose the following modified gating network:

$$\begin{aligned} g_j(x, \nu) &= \alpha_j P(x|\nu_j)/\sum_i \alpha_i P(x|\nu_i), \quad \sum_j \alpha_j = 1, \alpha_j \geq 0, \\ P(x|\nu_j) &= a_j(\nu_j)^{-1} b_j(x) \exp\{c_j(\nu_j)^T t_j(x)\} \end{aligned} \qquad (5)$$

where $\nu = \{\alpha_j, \nu_j, j = 1, \cdots, K\}$, $t_j(x)$ is a vector of sufficient statistics, and the $P(x|\nu_j)$'s are density functions from the exponential family. The most common example is the Gaussian:

$$P(x|\nu_j) = \frac{1}{(2\pi)^{n/2}|\Sigma_j|^{1/2}} \exp\{-\frac{1}{2}(x - m_j)^T \Sigma_j^{-1}(x - m_j)\}, \qquad (6)$$

In eq. (5), $g_j(x, \nu)$ is actually the posterior probability $P(j|x)$ that x is assigned to the partition corresponding to the j-th expert net, obtained from Bayes' rule:

$$g_j(x, \nu) = P(j|x) = \alpha_j P(x|\nu_j)/P(x, \nu), \quad P(x, \nu) = \sum_i \alpha_i P(x|\nu_i). \qquad (7)$$

Inserting this $g_j(x,\nu)$ into the model eq. (1), we get

$$P(y|x,\Theta) = \sum_j \frac{\alpha_j P(x|\nu_j)}{P(x,\nu)} P(y|x,\theta_j). \tag{8}$$

If we do ML estimation directly on this $P(y|x,\Theta)$ and derive an EM algorithm, we again find that the maximization $\max_\nu Q^g(\nu)$ cannot be solved analytically. To avoid this difficulty, we rewrite eq. (8) as:

$$P(y,x) = P(y|x,\Theta)P(x,\nu) = \sum_j \alpha_j P(x|\nu_j) P(y|x,\theta_j). \tag{9}$$

This suggests an asymmetrical representation for the joint density. We accordingly perform ML estimation based on $L' = \sum_t \ln P(y^{(t)}, x^{(t)})$ to determine the parameters $\alpha_j, \nu_j, \theta_j$ of the gating net and the expert nets. This can be done by the following EM algorithm:

(1) E-step. Compute

$$h_j^{(k)}(y^{(t)}|x^{(t)}) = \frac{\alpha_j^{(k)} P(x^{(t)}|\nu_j^{(k)}) P(y^{(t)}|x^{(t)}, \theta_j^{(k)})}{\sum_i \alpha_i^{(k)} P(x^{(t)}|\nu_i^{(k)}) P(y^{(t)}|x^{(t)}, \theta_j^{(k)})}; \tag{10}$$

Then let $Q_j^e(\theta_j), j = 1, \cdots, K$ be the same as given in eq. (3), and decompose $Q^g(\nu)$ further into

$$\begin{aligned}
Q_j^g(\nu_j) &= \sum_t h_j^{(k)}(y^{(t)}|x^{(t)}) \ln P(x^{(t)}|\nu_j), \quad j = 1, \cdots, K; \\
Q^\alpha &= \sum_t \sum_j h_j^{(k)}(y^{(t)}|x^{(t)}) \ln \alpha_j, \quad \text{with } \alpha = \{\alpha_1, \cdots, \alpha_K\}.
\end{aligned} \tag{11}$$

(2). M-step. Find a new estimate for $j = 1, \cdots, K$

$$\begin{aligned}
\theta_j^{(k+1)} &= \arg\max_{\theta_j} Q_j^e(\theta_j), \quad \nu_j^{(k+1)} = \arg\max_{\nu_j} Q_j^g(\nu_j), \\
\alpha^{(k+1)} &= \arg\max_\alpha Q^\alpha, \ s.t. \ \sum_j \alpha_j = 1.
\end{aligned} \tag{12}$$

The maximization for the expert nets is the same as in eq. (4). However, for the gating net the maximization now becomes analytically solvable as long as $P(x|\nu_j)$ is from the exponential family. That is, we have:

$$\nu_j^{(k+1)} = \frac{\sum_t h_j^{(k)}(y^{(t)}|x^{(t)}) t_j(x^{(t)})}{\sum_t h_j^{(k)}(y^{(t)}|x^{(t)})}, \quad \alpha_j^{(k+1)} = \frac{1}{N} \sum_t h_j^{(k)}(y^{(t)}|x^{(t)}). \tag{13}$$

In particular, when $P(x|\nu_j)$ is a Gaussian density, the update becomes:

$$\begin{aligned}
m_j^{(k+1)} &= \frac{1}{\sum_t h_j^{(k)}(y^{(t)}|x^{(t)})} \sum_t h_j^{(k)}(y^{(t)}|x^{(t)}) x^{(t)}, \\
\Sigma_j^{(k+1)} &= \frac{1}{\sum_t h_j^{(k)}(y^{(t)}|x^{(t)})} \sum_t h_j^{(k)}(y^{(t)}|x^{(t)}) [x^{(t)} - m_j^{(k+1)}][x^{(t)} - m_j^{(k+1)}]^T.
\end{aligned} \tag{14}$$

Two issues deserve to be emphasized further:

(1) The gating nets eq. (2) and eq. (5) become identical when $\beta_j(x,\nu) = \ln \alpha_j + \ln b_j(x) + c_j(\nu_j)^T t_j(x) - \ln a_j(\nu_j)$. In other words, the gating net in eq. (5) explicitly uses this function family instead of the function family defined by a multilayer feedforward network.

(2) It follows from eq. (9) that $\max \ln P(y, x|\Theta) = \max [\ln P(y|x, \Theta) + \ln P(x|\nu)]$. So, the solution given by eqs. (10) through (14) is actually different from the one given by the original eqs. (3) and (4). The former tries to model both the mapping from x to y and the input x, while the latter only models the mapping from x and y. In fact, here we learn the parameters of the gating net and the expert nets via an asymmetrical representation eq. (9) of the joint density $P(y, x)$ which includes $P(y|x)$ implicitly. However, in the testing phase, the total output still follows eq. (8).

4 PIECEWISE NONLINEAR APPROXIMATION

The simple form $f_j(x, w_j) = w_j^T[x, 1]$ is not the only case to which single-loop EM applies. Whenever $f_j(x, w_j)$ can be written in a form linear in the parameters:

$$f_j(x, w_j) = \sum_i w_{i,j} \phi_{i,j}(x) + w_{0,j} = w_j^T [\phi_j(x), 1], \tag{15}$$

where $\phi_{i,j}(x)$ are prespecified basis functions, $\max_{\theta_j} Q_j^e(\theta_j), j = 1, \cdots, K$ in eq. (3) is still a weighted least squares problem that can be solved analytically. One useful special case is when $\phi_{i,j}(x)$ are canonical polynomial terms $x_1^{r_1} \cdots x_d^{r_d}$, $r_i \geq 0$. In this case, the mixture of experts model implements piecewise polynomial approximations. Another case is that $\phi_{i,j}(x)$ is $\prod_i \sin_i^r(j\pi x_1) \cos_i^r(j\pi x_1), r_i \geq 0$, in which case the mixture of experts implements piecewise trigonometric approximations.

5 COMBINING MULTIPLE CLASSIFIERS

Given pattern classes $C_i, i = 1, \cdots, M$, we consider classifiers e_j that for each input x produce an output $P_j(y|x)$:

$$P_j(y|x) = [p_j(1|x), \cdots, p_j(M|x)], \quad p_j(i|x) \geq 0, \quad \sum_i p_j(i|x) = 1. \tag{16}$$

The problem of *Combining Multiple Classifiers (CMC)* is to combine these $P_j(y|x)$'s to give a combined estimate of $P(y|x)$. Xu and Jordan (1993) proposed to solve CMC problems by regarding the problem as a special example of the mixture density problem eq. (1) with the $P_j(y|x)$'s known and only the gating net $g_j(x, \nu)$ to be learned. In Xu and Jordan (1993), one problem encountered was also the nonlinearity of *softmax* gating networks, and an algorithm was proposed to avoid the difficulty.

Actually, the single-loop EM given by eq. (10) and eq. (13) can be directly used to solve the CMC problem. In particular, when $P(x|\nu_j)$ is Gaussian, eq. (13) becomes eq. (14). Assuming that $\alpha_1 = \cdots = \alpha_K$ in eq. (7), eq. (10) becomes

$h_j^{(k)}(y^{(t)}|x^{(t)}) = P(x^{(t)}|\nu_j^{(k)})P(y^{(t)}|x^{(t)})/\sum_i P(x^{(t)}|\nu_i^{(k)})P(y^{(t)}|x^{(t)})$. If we divide both the numerator and denominator by $\sum_i P(x^{(t)}|\nu_i^{(k)})$, we get $h_j^{(k)}(y^{(t)}|x^{(t)}) = g_j(x,\nu)P(y^{(t)}|x^{(t)})/\sum_i g_j(x,\nu)P(y^{(t)}|x^{(t)})$. Comparing this equation with eq. (7a) in Xu and Jordan (1993), we can see that the two equations are actually the same. Despite the different notation, $\alpha_j(\mathbf{x})$ and $P_j(\vec{y}^{(t)}|\mathbf{x}^{(t)})$ in Xu and Jordan (1993) are the same as $g_j(x,\nu)$ and $P(y^{(t)}|x^{(t)})$ in Section 3. So the algorithm of Xu and Jordan (1993) is a special case of the single-loop EM given in Section 3.

6 SIMULATION RESULTS

We compare the performance of the EM algorithm presented earlier with the model of mixtures of experts presented by Jordan and Jacobs (1994). As shown in Fig. 1(a), we consider a mixture of experts model with $K = 2$. For the expert nets, each $P(y|x,\theta_j)$ is Gaussian given by eq. (1) with linear $f_j(x,w_j) = w_j^T[x,1]$. For the new gating net, each $P(x,\nu_j)$ in eq. (5) is Gaussian given by eq. (6). For the old gating net eq. (2), $\beta_1(x,\nu) = 0$ and $\beta_2(x,\nu) = \nu^T[x,1]$. The learning speeds of the two are significantly different. The new algorithm takes k=15 iterations for the log-likelihood to converge to the value of -1271.8. These iterations require about $1,351,383$ MATLAB *flops*. For the old algorithm, we use the IRLS algorithm given in Jordan and Jacobs (1994) for the inner loop iteration. In experiments, we found that it usually took a large number of iterations for the inner loop to converge. To save computations, we limit the maximum number of iterations by $\tau_{max} = 10$. We found that this saved computation without obviously influencing the overall performance. From Fig. 1(b), we see that the outer loop converges in about 16 iterations. Each inner loop takes 290498 *flops* and the entire process requires $5,312,695$ *flops*. So, we see that the new algorithm yields a speedup of about $4,648,608/1,441,475 = 3.9$. Moreover, no external adjustment is needed to ensure the convergence of the new algorithm. But for the old one the direct use of IRLS can make the inner loop diverge and we need to appropriately rescale the updating stepsize of IRLS.

Figs. 2(a) and (b) show the results of a simulation of a piecewise polynomial approximation problem utilizing the approach described in Section 4. We consider a mixture of experts model with $K = 2$. For expert nets, each $P(y|x,\theta_j)$ is Gaussian given by eq. (1) with $f_j(x,w_j) = w_{3,j}x^3 + w_{2,j}x^2 + w_{1,j}x + w_{0,j}$. In the new gating net eq. (5), each $P(x,\nu_j)$ is again Gaussian given by eq. (6). We see that the higher order nonlinear regression has been fit quite well.

For multiple classifier combination, the problem and data are the same as in Xu and Jordan (1993). Table 1 shows the classification results. *Com-old* and *Com-new* denote the method given in in Xu and Jordan (1993) and in Section 5 respectively. We see that both improve the classification rate of each individual network considerably and that $Com - new$ improves on $Com - old$.

	Classifer e_1	Classifer e_1	$Com - old$	$Com - new$
Training set	89.9%	93.3%	98.6%	99.4%
Testing set	89.2%	92.7%	98.0%	99.0%

Table 1 A comparison of the correct classification rates

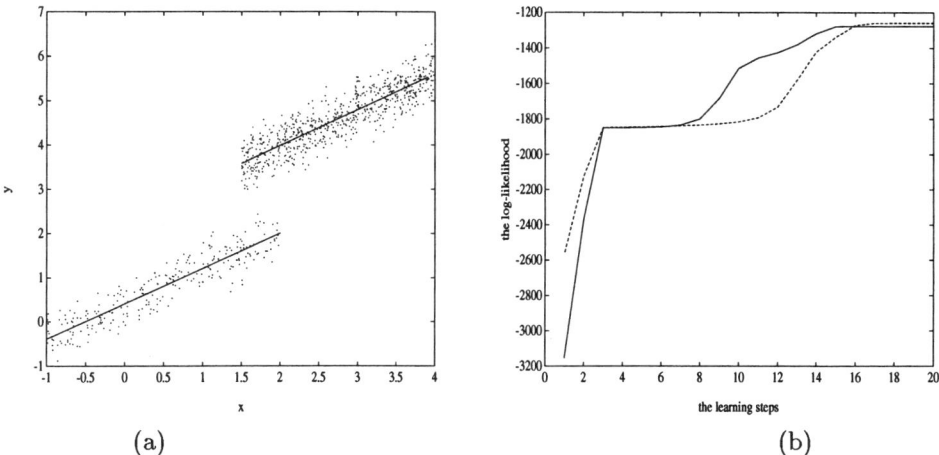

Figure 1: (a) 1000 samples from $y = a_1 x + a_2 + \varepsilon, a_1 = 0.8, a_2 = 0.4, x \in [-1, 1.5]$ with prior $\alpha_1 = 0.25$ and $y = a'_1 x + a'_2 + \varepsilon, a'_1 = 0.8, a'_2 =' 2.4, x \in [1, 4]$ with prior $\alpha_2 = 0.75$, where x is uniform random variable and z is from Gaussian $N(0, 0.3)$. The two lines through the clouds are the estimated models of two expert nets. The fits obtained by the two learning algorithms are almost the same. (b) The evolution of the log-likelihood. The solid line is for the modified learning algorithm. The dotted line is for the original learning algorithm (the outer loop iteration).

7 REMARKS

Recently, Ghahramani and Jordan (1994) proposed solving function approximation problems by using a mixture of Gaussians to estimate the joint density of the input and output (see also Specht, 1991; Tresp, et al., 1994). In the special case of linear $f_j(x, w_j) = w_j^T[x, 1]$ and Gaussian $P(x|\nu_j)$ with equal priors, the method given in Section 3 provides the same result as Ghahramani and Jordan (1994) although the parameterizations of the two methods are different. However, the method of this paper also applies to nonlinear $f_j(x, w_j) = w_j^T[\phi_j(x), 1]$ for piecewise nonlinear approximation or more generally $f_j(x, w_j)$ that is nonlinear with respect to w_j, and applies to cases in which $P(y, x|\nu_j, \theta_j)$ is not Gaussian, as well as the case of combining multiple classifiers. Furthermore, the methods proposed in Sections 3 and 4 can also be extended to the hierarchical mixture of experts architecture (Jacobs & Jordan, 1994) so that single-loop EM can be used to facilitate its training.

References

Ghahramani, Z., & Jordan, M.I. (1994). Function approximation via density estimation using the EM approach. In Cowan, J.D., Tesauro, G., and Alspector, J., (Eds.), *Advances in NIPS 6*. San Mateo, CA: Morgan Kaufmann.

Jacobs, R.A., Jordan, M.I., Nowlan, S.J., & Hinton, G.E. (1991). Adaptive mixtures of local experts. *Neural Computation, 3*, 79-87.

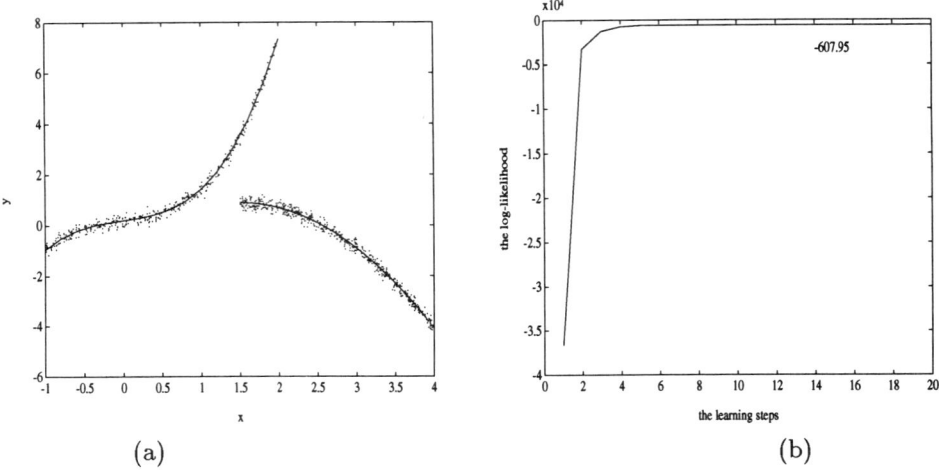

(a)   (b)

Figure 2: Piecewise 3rd polynomial approximation. (a) 1000 samples from $y = a_1x^3 + a_3x + a_4 + \varepsilon$, $x \in [-1, 1.5]$ with prior $\alpha_1 = 0.4$ and $y = a'_2x^2 + a'_3x^2 + a'_4 + \varepsilon$, $x \in [1, 4]$ with prior $\alpha_2 = 0.6$, where x is uniform random variable and z is from Gaussian $N(0, 0.15)$. The two curves through the clouds are the estimated models of two expert nets. (b) The evolution of the log-likelihood.

Jordan, M.I., & Jacobs, R.A. (1994). Hierarchical mixtures of experts and the EM algorithm. *Neural Computation, 6*, 181-214.

Jordan, M.I., & Xu, L. (in press). Convergence results for the EM approach to mixtures-of-experts architectures. *Neural Networks*.

Specht, D. (1991). A general regression neural network. *IEEE Trans. Neural Networks, 2*, 568-576.

Tresp, V., Ahmad, S., and Neuneier, R. (1994). Training neural networks with deficient data. In Cowan, J.D., Tesauro, G., & Alspector, J., (Eds.), *Advances in NIPS 6*, San Mateo, CA: Morgan Kaufmann.

Xu, L., Krzyzak A., & Suen, C.Y. (1991). Associative switch for combining multiple classifiers. *Proc. of 1991 IJCNN*, Vol. I. Seattle, 43-48.

Xu, L., Krzyzak A., & Suen, C.Y. (1992). Several methods for combining multiple classifiers and their applications in handwritten character recognition. *IEEE Trans. on SMC*, Vol. SMC-22, 418-435.

Xu, L., & Jordan, M.I. (1993). EM Learning on a generalized finite mixture model for combining multiple classifiers. *Proceedings of World Congress on Neural Networks*, Vol. IV. Portland, OR, 227-230.

Xu, L., & Jordan, M.I. (1994). On convergence properties of the EM algorithm for Gaussian mixtures. Submitted to *Neural Computation*.

Estimating Conditional Probability Densities for Periodic Variables

Chris M Bishop and Claire Legleye
Neural Computing Research Group
Department of Computer Science and Applied Mathematics
Aston University
Birmingham, B4 7ET, U.K.
c.m.bishop@aston.ac.uk

Abstract

Most of the common techniques for estimating conditional probability densities are inappropriate for applications involving periodic variables. In this paper we introduce three novel techniques for tackling such problems, and investigate their performance using synthetic data. We then apply these techniques to the problem of extracting the distribution of wind vector directions from radar scatterometer data gathered by a remote-sensing satellite.

1 INTRODUCTION

Many applications of neural networks can be formulated in terms of a multi-variate non-linear mapping from an input vector $\mathbf{x}$ to a target vector $\mathbf{t}$. A conventional neural network approach, based on least squares for example, leads to a network mapping which approximates the regression of $\mathbf{t}$ on $\mathbf{x}$. A more complete description of the data can be obtained by estimating the conditional probability density of $\mathbf{t}$, conditioned on $\mathbf{x}$, which we write as $p(\mathbf{t}|\mathbf{x})$. Various techniques exist for modelling such densities when the target variables live in a Euclidean space. However, a number of potential applications involve angle-like output variables which are periodic on some finite interval (usually chosen to be $(0, 2\pi)$). For example, in Section 3 we consider the problem of determining the wind direction (a periodic quantity) from radar scatterometer data obtained from remote sensing measurements. Most of the existing techniques for conditional density estimation cannot be applied in such cases.

A common technique for *unconditional* density estimation is based on mixture models of the form

$$p(\mathbf{t}) = \sum_{i=1}^{m} \alpha_i \phi_i(\mathbf{t}) \qquad (1)$$

where α_i are called mixing coefficients, and the kernel functions $\phi_i(\mathbf{t})$ are frequently chosen to be Gaussians. Such models can be used as the basis of techniques for *conditional* density estimation by allowing the mixing coefficients, and any parameters governing the kernel functions, to be general functions of the input vector $\mathbf{x}$. This can be achieved by relating these quantities to the outputs of a neural network which takes $\mathbf{x}$ as input, as shown in Figure 1. Such an approach forms the basis of

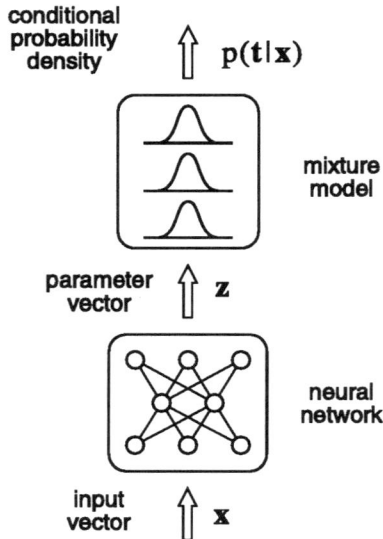

Figure 1: A general framework for conditional density estimation is obtained by using a feed-forward neural network whose outputs determine the parameters in a mixture density model. The mixture model then represents the conditional probability density of the target variables, conditioned on the input vector to the network.

the 'mixture of experts' model (Jacobs *et al.*, 1991) and has also been considered by a number of other authors (White, 1992; Bishop, 1994; Lui, 1994). In this paper we introduce three techniques for estimating conditional densities of *periodic* variables, based on extensions of the above formalism for Euclidean variables.

2 DENSITY ESTIMATION FOR PERIODIC VARIABLES

In this section we consider three alternative approaches to estimating the conditional density $p(\theta|\mathbf{x})$ of a periodic variable θ, conditioned on an input vector $\mathbf{x}$. They are based respectively on a transformation to an extended domain representation, the use of adaptive circular normal kernel functions, and the use of fixed circular normal kernels.

2.1 TRANSFORMATION TO AN EXTENDED VARIABLE DOMAIN

The first technique which we consider involves finding a transformation from the periodic variable $\theta \in (0, 2\pi)$ to a Euclidean variable $\chi \in (-\infty, \infty)$, such that standard techniques for conditional density estimation can be applied in χ-space. In particular, we seek a conditional density function $\widetilde{p}(\chi|\mathbf{x})$ which is to be modelled using a conventional Gaussian mixture approach as described in Section 1. Consider the transformation

$$p(\theta|\mathbf{x}) = \sum_{L=-\infty}^{\infty} \widetilde{p}(\theta + L2\pi|\mathbf{x}) \qquad (2)$$

Then it is clear by construction that the density model on the left hand side satisfies the periodicity requirement $p(\theta + 2\pi|\mathbf{x}) = p(\theta|\mathbf{x})$. Furthermore, if the density function $\widetilde{p}(\chi|\mathbf{x})$ is normalized, then we have

$$\begin{aligned}
\int_0^{2\pi} p(\theta|\mathbf{x})\,d\theta &= \sum_{L=-\infty}^{\infty} \int_0^{2\pi} \widetilde{p}(\theta + L2\pi|\mathbf{x})\,d\theta \\
&= \sum_{L=-\infty}^{\infty} \int_{L2\pi}^{(L+1)2\pi} \widetilde{p}(\chi|\mathbf{x})\,d\chi \\
&= \int_{-\infty}^{\infty} \widetilde{p}(\chi|\mathbf{x})\,d\chi = 1
\end{aligned} \qquad (3)$$

and so the corresponding periodic density $p(\theta|\mathbf{x})$ will also be normalized. We now model the density function $\widetilde{p}(\chi|\mathbf{x})$ using a mixture of Gaussians of the form

$$\widetilde{p}(\chi|\mathbf{x}) = \sum_{i=1}^{m} \alpha_i(\mathbf{x})\phi_i(\chi|\mathbf{x}) \qquad (4)$$

where the kernel functions are given by

$$\phi_i(\chi|\mathbf{x}) = \frac{1}{(2\pi)^{1/2}\sigma_i(\mathbf{x})} \exp\left(-\frac{\{\chi - \chi_i(\mathbf{x})\}^2}{2\sigma_i^2(\mathbf{x})}\right) \qquad (5)$$

and the parameters $\alpha_i(\mathbf{x})$, $\sigma_i(\mathbf{x})$ and $\chi_i(\mathbf{x})$ are determined by the outputs of a feed-forward network. In particular, the mixing coefficients $\alpha_i(\mathbf{x})$ are governed by a 'softmax' activation function to ensure that they lie in the range $(0, 1)$ and sum to unity; the width parameters $\sigma_i(\mathbf{x})$ are given by the exponentials of the corresponding network outputs to ensure their positivity; and the basis function centres $\chi_i(\mathbf{x})$ are given directly by network output variables.

The network is trained by maximizing the likelihood function, evaluated for set of training data, with respect to the weights and biases in the network. For a training set consisting of N input vectors $\mathbf{x}^n$ and corresponding targets θ^n, the likelihood is given by

$$\mathcal{L} = \prod_{n=1}^{N} p(\theta^n|\mathbf{x}^n)p(\mathbf{x}^n) \qquad (6)$$

where $p(\mathbf{x})$ is the unconditional density of the input data. Rather than work with $\mathcal{L}$ directly, it is convenient instead to minimize an error function given by the negative log of the likelihood. Making use of (2) we can write this in the form

$$E = -\ln \mathcal{L} \simeq -\sum_n \ln \sum_L \widetilde{p}(\theta^n + L2\pi|\mathbf{x}^n) \qquad (7)$$

where we have dropped the term arising from $p(\mathbf{x})$ since it is independent of the network weights. This expression is very similar to the one which arises if we perform density estimation on the real axis, except for the extra summation over L, which means that the data point θ^n recurs at intervals of 2π along the χ-axis. This is not equivalent simply to replicating the data, however, since the summation over L occurs inside the logarithm, rather than outside as with the summation over data points n.

In a practical implementation, it is necessary to restrict the summation over L. For the results presented in the next section, this summation was taken over 7 complete periods of 2π spanning the range $(-7\pi, 7\pi)$. Since the Gaussians have exponentially decaying tails, this represents an extremely good approximation in almost all cases, provided we take care in initializing the network weights so that the Gaussian kernels lie in the central few periods. Derivatives of E with respect to the network weights can be computed using the rules of calculus, to give a modified form of back-propagation. These derivatives can then be used with standard optimization techniques to find a minimum of the error function. (The results presented in the next section were obtained using the BFGS quasi-Newton algorithm).

2.2 MIXTURES OF CIRCULAR NORMAL DENSITIES

The second approach which we introduce is also based on a mixture of kernel functions of the form (1), but in this case the kernel functions themselves are periodic, thereby ensuring that the overall density function will be periodic. To motivate this approach, consider the problem of modelling the distribution of a velocity vector $\mathbf{v}$ in two dimensions (this arises, for example, in the application considered in Section 3). Since $\mathbf{v}$ lives in a Euclidean plane, we can model the density function $p(\mathbf{v})$ using a mixture of conventional spherical Gaussian kernels, where each kernel has

the form
$$\phi(v_x, v_y) = \frac{1}{2\pi\sigma^2} \exp\left(-\frac{\{v_x - \mu_x\}^2}{2\sigma^2} - \frac{\{v_y - \mu_y\}^2}{2\sigma^2}\right) \quad (8)$$

where (v_x, v_y) are the Cartesian components of $\mathbf{v}$, and (μ_x, μ_y) are the components of the center $\boldsymbol{\mu}$ of the kernel. From this we can extract the conditional distribution of the polar angle θ of the vector $\mathbf{v}$, given a value for $v = \|\mathbf{v}\|$. This is easily done with the transformation $v_x = v\cos\theta$, $v_y = v\sin\theta$, and defining θ_0 to be the polar angle of $\boldsymbol{\mu}$, so that $\mu_x = \mu\cos\theta_0$ and $\mu_y = \mu\sin\theta_0$, where $\mu = \|\boldsymbol{\mu}\|$. This leads to a distribution which can be written in the form

$$\phi(\theta) = \frac{1}{2\pi I_0(\lambda)} \exp\left\{\lambda \cos(\theta - \theta_0)\right\} \quad (9)$$

where the normalization coefficient has been expressed in terms of the zeroth order modified Bessel function of the first kind, $I_0(\lambda)$. The distribution (9) is known as a *circular normal* or *von Mises* distribution (Mardia, 1972). The parameter λ (which depends on v in our derivation) is analogous to the (inverse) variance parameter in a conventional normal distribution. Since (9) is periodic, we can construct a general representation for the conditional density of a periodic variable by considering a mixture of circular normal kernels, with parameters given by the outputs of a neural network. The weights of the network can again be determined by maximizing the likelihood function defined over a set of training data.

2.3 FIXED KERNELS

The third approach introduced here is again based on a mixture model in which the kernel functions are periodic, but where the kernel parameters (specifying their width and location) are fixed. The only adaptive parameters are the mixing coefficients, which are again determined by the outputs of a feed-forward network having a softmax final-layer activation function. Here we consider a set of equally-spaced circular normal kernels in which the width parameters are chosen to give a moderate degree of overlap between the kernels so that the resulting representation for the density function will be reasonably smooth. Again, a maximum likelihood formalism is employed to train the network. Clearly a major drawback of fixed-kernel methods is that the number of kernels must grow exponentially with the dimensionality of the output space. For a single output variable, however, they can be regarded as practical techniques.

3 RESULTS

In order to test and compare the methods introduced above, we first consider a simple problem involving synthetic data, for which the true underlying distribution function is known. This data set is intended to mimic the central properties of the real data to be discussed in the next section. It has a single input variable x and an output variable θ which lies in the range $(0, 2\pi)$. The distribution of θ is governed by a mixture of two triangular functions whose parameters (locations and widths) are functions of x. Here we present preliminary results from the application of the method introduced in section 2.1 (involving the transformation to Euclidean space) to this data. Figure 2 shows a plot of the reconstructed conditional density in both the extended χ variable, and in the reconstructed polar variable θ, for a particular value of the input variable x.

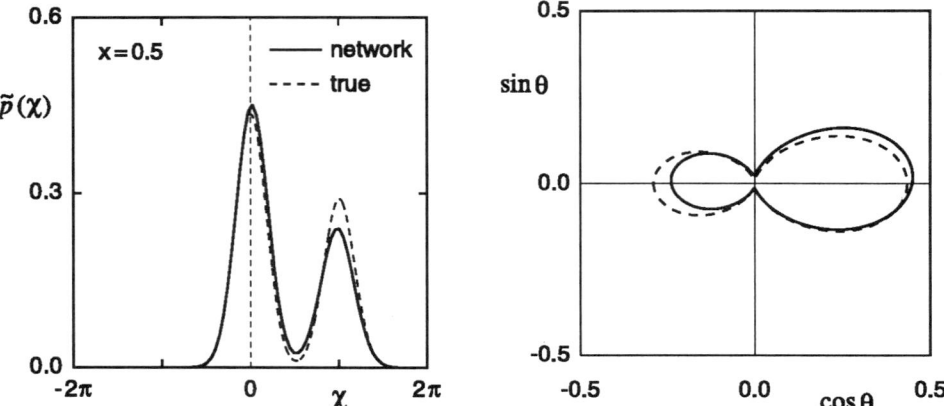

Figure 2: The left hand plot shows the predicted density (solid curve) together with the true density (dashed curve) in the extended χ space. The right hand plot shows the corresponding densities in the periodic θ space. In both cases the input variable is fixed at $x = 0.5$.

One of the original motivations for developing the techniques described in this paper was to provide an effective, principled approach to the analysis of radar scatterometer data from satellites such as the European Remote Sensing Satellite ERS-1. This satellite is equipped with three C-band radar antennae which measure the total backscattered power (called σ_0) along three directions relative to the satellite track, as shown in Figure 3. When the satellite passes over the ocean, the strengths of the backscattered signals are related to the surface ripples of the water (on length-scales of a few cm.) which in turn are determined by the low level winds. Extraction of the wind speed and direction from the radar signals represents an inverse problem which is typically multi-valued. For example, a wind direction of θ_1 will give rise to similar radar signals to a wind direction of $\theta_1 + \pi$. Often, there are additional such 'aliases' at other angles. A conventional neural network approach to this problem, based on least-squares, would predict wind directions which were given by conditional averages of the target data. Since the average of several valid wind directions is typically not itself a valid direction, such an approach would clearly fail. Here we aim to extract the complete distribution of wind directions (as a function of the three σ_0 values and on the angle of incidence of the radar beam) and hence avoid

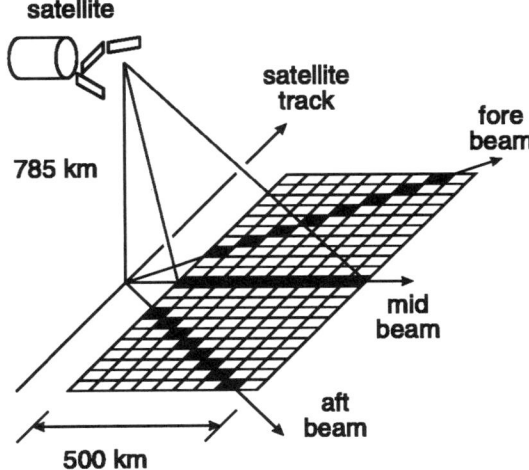

Figure 3: Schematic illustration of the ERS-1 satellite showing the footprints of the three radar scatterometers.

such difficulties. This approach also provides the most complete information for the next stage of processing (not considered here) which is to 'de-alias' the wind directions to extract the most probable overall wind field.

A large data set of ERS-1 measurements, spanning a wide range of meteorological conditions, has been assembled by the European Space Agency in collaboration with the UK Meteorological Office. Labelling of the data set was performed using wind vectors from the Meteorological Office Numerical Weather Prediction code. An example of the results from the fixed-kernel method of Section 2.3 are presented in Figure 4. This clearly shows the existence of a primary alias at an angle of π relative to the principal direction, as well as secondary aliases at $\pm\pi/2$.

Acknowledgements

We are grateful to the European Space Agency and the UK Meteorological Office for making available the ERS-1 data. We would also like to thank Iain Strachan and Ian Kirk of AEA Technology for a number of useful discussions relating to the interpretation of this data.

References

Bishop C M (1994). Mixture density networks. Neural Computing Research Group Report, NCRG/4288, Department of Computer Science, Aston University, Birmingham, U.K.

Jacobs R A, Jordan M I, Nowlan S J and Hinton G E (1991). Adaptive mixtures

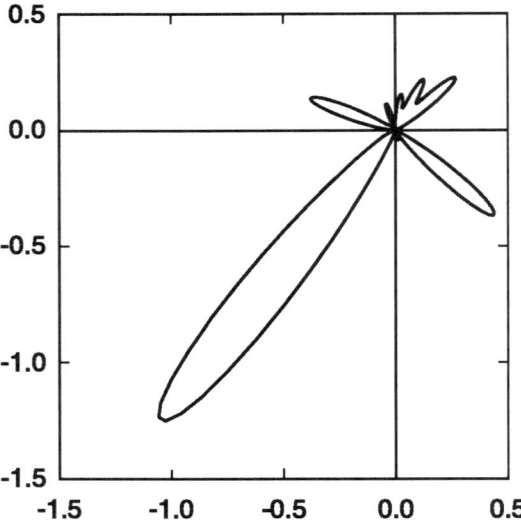

Figure 4: An example of the results obtained with the fixed-kernel method applied to data from the ERS-1 satellite. As well as the primary wind direction, there are aliases at π and $\pm\pi/2$.

of local experts. *Neural Computation*, **3** 79–87.

Lui Y (1994) Robust parameter estimation and model selection for neural network regression. *Advances in Neural Information Processing Systems* **6** Morgan Kaufmann, 192–199..

Mardia K V (1972). *Statistics of Directional Data*. Academic Press, London.

White H (1992). Parametric statistical estimation with artificial neural networks. University of California, San Diego, Technical Report.

Effects of Noise on Convergence and Generalization in Recurrent Networks

Kam Jim   Bill G. Horne   C. Lee Giles*

NEC Research Institute, Inc., 4 Independence Way, Princeton, NJ 08540
{kamjim,horne,giles}@research.nj.nec.com

*Also with
UMIACS, University of Maryland, College Park, MD 20742

Abstract

We introduce and study methods of inserting *synaptic noise* into dynamically-driven recurrent neural networks and show that applying a controlled amount of noise during training may improve convergence and generalization. In addition, we analyze the effects of each noise parameter (additive vs. multiplicative, cumulative vs. non-cumulative, per time step vs. per string) and predict that best overall performance can be achieved by injecting additive noise at each time step. Extensive simulations on learning the dual parity grammar from temporal strings substantiate these predictions.

1 INTRODUCTION

There has been much research in applying noise to neural networks to improve network performance. It has been shown that using noisy hidden nodes during training can result in error-correcting codes which increase the tolerance of feedforward nets to unreliable nodes (Judd and Munro, 1992). Also, randomly disabling hidden nodes during the training phase increases the tolerance of MLP's to node failures (Séquin and Clay, 1990). Bishop showed that training with noisy data is equivalent to Tikhonov Regularization and suggested directly minimizing the regularized error function as a practical alternative (Bishop, 1994). Hanson developed a stochastic version of the delta rule which adapt weight means and standard deviations instead of clean weight values (Hanson, 1990). (Mpitsos and Burton, 1992) demonstrated faster learning rates by adding noise to the weight updates and adapting the magnitude of such noise to the output error. Most relevant to this paper, *synaptic noise* has been applied to MLP's during training to improve fault tolerance and training quality. (Murray and Edwards, 1993)

In this paper, we extend these results by introducing several methods of inserting synaptic noise into recurrent networks, and demonstrate that these methods can improve both convergence and generalization. Previous work on improving these two performance measures have focused on ways of simplifying the network and methods of searching the coarse regions of state space before the fine regions. Our work shows that synaptic noise can improve convergence by searching for *promising regions* of state space, and enhance generalization by enforcing *saturated* states.

2 NOISE INJECTION IN RECURRENT NETWORKS

In this paper, we inject noise into a High Order recurrent network (Giles et al., 1992) consisting of N recurrent state neurons S_j, L non-recurrent input neurons I_k, and $N^2 L$ weights W_{ijk}. (For justification of its use see Section 4.) The recurrent network operation is defined by the state process $S_i^{t+1} = g(\sum_{j,k} W_{ijk} S_j^t I_k^t)$, where $g(\cdot)$ is a sigmoid discriminant function. During training, an error function is computed as $E_p = \frac{1}{2}\epsilon_p^2$, where $\epsilon_p = S_O^T - d_p$, S_O^T is the output neuron, and d_p is the target output value for pattern p.

Synaptic noise has been simulated on Multi-Layered-Perceptrons by inserting noise to the weights of each layer during training (Murray et al., 1993). Applying this method to recurrent networks is not straightforward because effectively the same weights are propagated forward in time. This can be seen by recalling the BPTT representation of *unrolling* a recurrent network in time into T layers with identical weights, where T is the length of the input string. In Tables 2 and 3, we introduce the noise injection steps for eight recurrent network noise models representing all combinations of the following noise parameters: additive vs. multiplicative, cumulative vs. non-cumulative, per time step vs. per string. As their name imply, additive and multiplicative noise add or multiply the weights by a small noise term. In cumulative noise, the injected noise is accumulated, while in non-cumulative noise the noise from the current step is removed before more noise is injected on the next step. Per time step and per string noise refer to when the noise is inserted: either at each time step or only once for each training string respectively. Table 1 illustrates noise accumulation examples for all additive models (the multiplicative case is analogous).

3 ANALYSIS ON THE EFFECTS OF SYNAPTIC NOISE

The effects of each noise model is analyzed by taking the Taylor expansion on the error function around the noise-free weight set. By truncating this expansion to second and lower order terms, we can interpret the effect of noise as a set of regularization terms applied to the error function. From these terms predictions can be made about the effects on generalization and convergence. A similar analysis was performed on MLP's to demonstrate the effects of synaptic noise on fault tolerance and training quality (Murray et. al., 1993). Tables 2 and 3 list the noise injection step and the resulting first and second order Taylor expansion terms for all noise models. These results are derived by assuming the noise to be zero-mean white with variance σ^2 and uncorrelated in time.

3.1 Predictions on Generalization

One common cause of bad generalization in recurrent networks is the presence of unsaturated state representations. Typically, a network cannot revisit the exact same point in state space, but tends to wander away from its learned state representation. One approach to alleviate this problem is to encourage state nodes to operate in the saturated regions of the sigmoid. The first order error expansion terms of most noise models considered are capable of encouraging the network to achieve saturated states. This can be shown by applying the chain rule to the partial derivative in the first order expansion terms:

$$\frac{\partial S_O^T}{\partial W_{t,ijk}} = \frac{\partial S_O^T}{\partial \Theta_O^T} \sum_l \left[\left(\frac{\partial \Theta_O^T}{\partial S_l^{T-1}} \frac{\partial S_l^{T-1}}{\partial \Theta_l^{T-1}} \right) \cdots \sum_n \left(\frac{\partial \Theta_m^{t+1}}{\partial S_n^t} \frac{\partial S_n^t}{\partial W_{t,ijk}} \right) \right], \quad (1)$$

where Θ_i^t is the net input to state node i at time step t. The partial derivatives $\frac{\partial S}{\partial \Theta}$ favor internal representations such that the effects of perturbations to the net inputs Θ_i^t are minimized.

Multiplicative noise implements a form of weight decay because the error expansion terms include the weight products $W_{t,ijk}^2$ or $W_{t,ijk}W_{u,ijk}$. Although weight decay has been shown to improve generalization on feedforward networks (Krogh and Hertz, 1992) we hypothesize this may not be the case for recurrent networks that are learning to solve FSA problems. Large weights are necessary to saturate the state nodes to the upper and lower limits of the sigmoid discriminant function. Therefore, we predict additive noise will allow better generalization because of its absence of weight decay.

Noise models whose first order error term contain the expression $\frac{\partial S_O^T}{\partial W_{t,ijk}} \frac{\partial S_O^T}{\partial W_{u,lmn}}$ will favor saturated states for those partials whose sign correspond to the sign of a majority of the partials. It will favor unsaturated states, operating in the linear region of the sigmoid, for partials whose sign is the minority. Such *sign-dependent enforcement* is not optimal.

The error terms for cumulative per time step noises sum a product with the expression $v \frac{\partial S_O^T}{\partial W_{t,ijk}} \frac{\partial S_O^T}{\partial W_{u,lmn}}$, where $v = min(t+1, u+1)$. The effect of cumulative noise increases more rapidly because of v and thus optimal generalization and detrimental noise effects will occur at lower amplitudes than non-cumulative noise.

For cumulative per string noise models, the products $(t+1)(u+1)$ and $\Psi_{t,ijk}\Psi_{u,lmn}$ in the expansion terms rapidly overwhelm the raw error term. Generalization improvement is not expected for these models.

We also reason that all generalization enhancements will be valid only for a range of noise values, above which noise overwhelms the raw error information.

3.2 Predictions on Convergence

Synaptic noise can improve convergence by favoring *promising* weights in the beginning stages of training. This can be demonstrated by examining the second order error expansion term for non-cumulative, multiplicative, per time step noise:

$$\frac{1}{2}\epsilon_p \sigma^2 \sum_{t=0}^{T-1} \sum_{ijk} (W_{t,ijk})^2 \left(\frac{\partial^2 S_O^T}{\partial (W_{t,ijk})^2} \right).$$

When ϵ_p is negative, solutions with a negative second order state-weight partial derivative will be de-stabilized. In other words, when the output S_O^T is too small the network will favor updating in a direction such that the first order partial derivative is increasing. A corresponding relationship can be observed for the case when ϵ_p is positive. Thus the second order term of the error function will allow a higher raw error ϵ_p to be favored if such an update will place the weights in a more promising area, i.e. a region where weight changes are likely to move S_O^T in a direction to reduce the raw error. The *anticipatory effect* of this term is more important in the beginning stages of training where ϵ_p is large, and will become insignificant in the finishing stages of training as ϵ_p approaches zero.

Similar to arguments in Section 3.1, the absence of weight decay will make the learning task easier and improve convergence.

From this discussion it can be inferred that additive per time step noise models should yield the best generalization and convergence performance because of their sign-independent favoring of saturated states and the absence of weight decay. Furthermore, convergence and generalization performance is more *sensitive* to cumulative noise, i.e. optimal performance and detrimental effects will occur at lower amplitudes than in non-cumulative noise.

4 SIMULATION RESULTS

In order to perform many experiments in a reasonable amount of computation time, we attempt to learn the simple "hidden-state" dual parity automata from sample strings encoded as temporal sequences. (Dual parity is a 4-state automata that recognizes binary strings containing an even number of ones and zeroes.) We choose a second-order recurrent network since such networks have demonstrated good performance on such problems (Giles et. al., 1992). Thus our experiments consist of 500 simulations for each data point and achieve useful (90%) confidence levels. Experiments are performed with both 3 and 4 state networks, both of which are adequate to learn the automata. The learning rate and momentum are set to 0.5, and the weights are initialized to random values between [-1.0, 1.0]. The data consists of 8191 strings of lengths 0 to 12. The networks are trained on a subset of the training set, called the *working set*, which gradually increases in size until the entire training set is classified correctly. Strings from the working set are presented in *alphabetical order*. The training set consists of the first 1023 strings of lengths 0 to 9, while the initial working set consists of 31 strings of lengths 0 to 4. During testing no noise is added to the weights of the network.

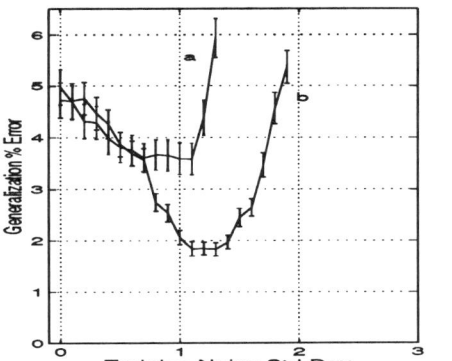 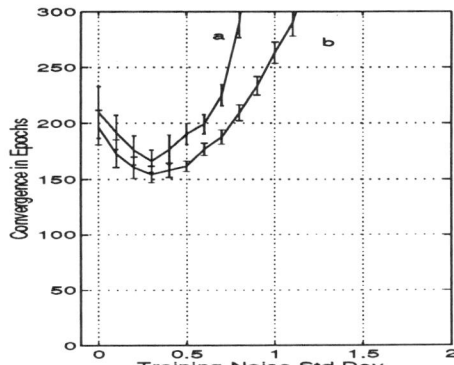

Figure 1: Best Convergence/Generalization for Additive and Multiplicative Noises. (a) multiplicative non-cumulative per time step; (b) additive cumulative per time step.

4.1 Convergence and Generalization Performance

Simulated performance closely mirror our predictions. Improvements were observed for all noise models except for cumulative per string noises which failed to converge for all runs. Generalization improvement was more emphasized on networks with 4 states, while convergence enhancement was more noticeable on 3-state networks. The simulations show the following results:

- Additive noise is better tolerated than multiplicative noise, and achieves better convergence and generalization (Figure 1).

- Cumulative noise achieves optimal generalization and convergence at lower amplitudes than non-cumulative noise. Cumulative noise also has a narrower range of beneficial noise, which is defined as the range of noise amplitudes which yields better performance than that of a noiseless network (Figure 2a illustrates this for generalization).

- Per time step noise achieves better convergence/generalization and has a wider range of beneficial values than per string noise (Figure 2b).

Overall, the best performance is obtained by applying cumulative and non-cumulative additive noise at each time step. These results closely match the predictions of section 3.1. The only exceptions are that all multiplicative noise models seem to yield equivalent performance. This discrepancy between prediction and simulation may be due to the detrimental effects of weight decay in multiplicative noise, which can conflict with the advantages of cumulative and per time step noise.

4.2 The Payoff Picture: Generalization vs. Convergence

Generalization vs. Convergence results are plotted in Figure 3. Increasing noise amplitudes proceed from the left end-point of each curve to the right end-point.

Table 1: Examples: Additive Noise Accumulation. Δ_i is the noise at time step t_i

NOISE MODEL	TIME STEPS			
	t_1	t_2	t_3	...
per time step non-cumulative	$W + \Delta_1$	$W + \Delta_2$	$W + \Delta_3$	...
per time step cumulative	$W + \Delta_1$	$W + \Delta_1 + \Delta_2$	$W + \Delta_1 + \Delta_2 + \Delta_3$	...
per sequence non-cumulative	$W + \Delta_1$	$W + \Delta_1$	$W + \Delta_1$	...
per sequence cumulative	$W + \Delta_1$	$W + 2\Delta_1$	$W + 3\Delta_1$	...

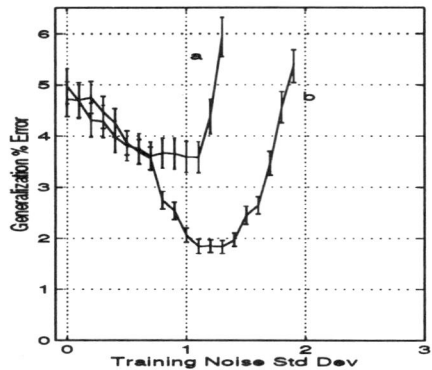
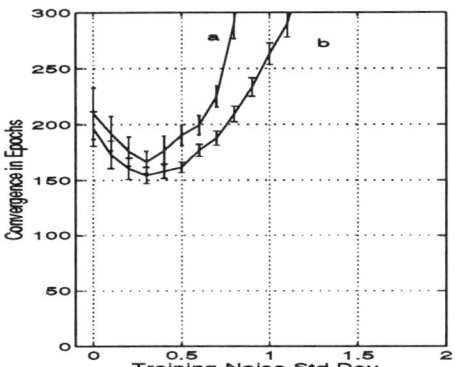

Figure 2: (I) Best Generalization for Cumulative and Non-Cumulative Noises: a) cumulative additive per time step; b) non-cumulative additive per time step. (II) Best Generalization for Per Time Step and Per String Noises: a) non-cumulative per string additive; b) non-cumulative per time step additive.

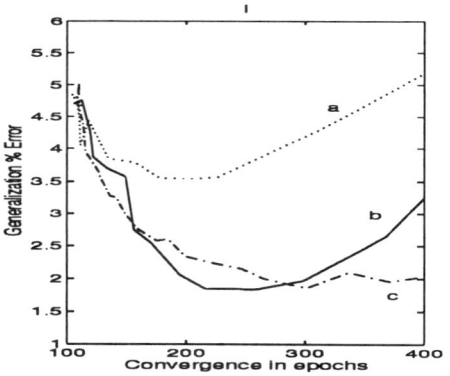
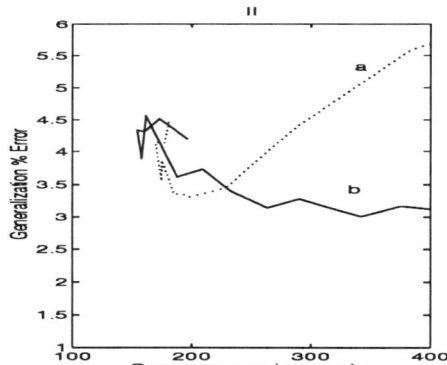

Figure 3: Payoff: Mean Generalization vs. Convergence for 4-state (I) and 3-state(II) recurrent network. (Ia) *Worst 4-state* – non-cumulative multiplicative per string; (Ib, Ic) *Best 4-state* – cumulative and non-cumulative additive per time step, respectively; (IIa) *Worst 3-state* – non-cumulative multiplicative per string ; (IIb) *Best 3-state* – cumulative additive per time step.

Table 2: Noise injection step and error expansion terms for *per time step* noise models. $v = min(t+1, u+1)$. W^* is the noise-free weight set.

	NON-CUMULATIVE	
	Additive	Multiplicative
Noise step	$W_{t,ijk} = W^*_{ijk} + \Delta_{t,ijk}$	$W_{t,ijk} = W^*_{ijk} + W^*_{ijk}\Delta_{t,ijk}$
1st order	$\frac{1}{2}\sigma^2 \sum_{t=0}^{T-1}\sum_{ijk} \left(\frac{\partial S^T_O}{\partial W_{t,ijk}}\right)^2$	$\frac{1}{2}\sigma^2 \sum_{t=0}^{T-1}\sum_{ijk} \left[W_{t,ijk}\frac{\partial S^T_O}{\partial W_{t,ijk}}\right]^2$
2nd order	$\frac{1}{2}\epsilon_p\sigma^2 \sum_{t=0}^{T-1}\sum_{ijk} \frac{\partial^2 S^T_O}{\partial (W_{t,ijk})^2}$	$\frac{1}{2}\epsilon_p\sigma^2 \sum_{t=0}^{T-1}\sum_{ijk} \left[(W_{t,ijk})^2 \frac{\partial^2 S^T_O}{\partial (W_{t,ijk})^2}\right]$
	CUMULATIVE	
	Additive	Multiplicative
Noise step	$W_{t,ijk} = W^*_{ijk} + \sum_{\tau=0}^{t}\Delta_{\tau,ijk}$	$W_{t,ijk} = W^*_{ijk} \prod_{\tau=0}^{t}(1 + \Delta_{\tau,ijk})$
1st order	$\frac{1}{2}\sigma^2 \sum_{t,u=0}^{T-1}\sum_{ijk} v \frac{\partial S^T_O}{\partial W_{t,ijk}}\frac{\partial S^T_O}{\partial W_{u,ijk}}$	$\frac{1}{2}\sigma^2 \sum_{t,u=0}^{T-1}\sum_{ijk} v W_{t,ijk} W_{u,ijk} \frac{\partial S^T_O}{\partial W_{t,ijk}}\frac{\partial S^T_O}{\partial W_{u,ijk}}$
2nd order	$\frac{1}{2}\epsilon_p\sigma^2 \sum_{t,u=0}^{T-1}\sum_{ijk} v \frac{\partial^2 S^T_O}{\partial W_{t,ijk}\partial W_{u,ijk}}$	$\frac{1}{2}\epsilon_p\sigma^2 \sum_{t,u=0}^{T-1}\sum_{ijk} v W_{t,ijk} W_{u,ijk} \frac{\partial^2 S^T_O}{\partial W_{t,ijk}\partial W_{u,ijk}}$

Table 3: Noise injection step and error expansion terms for *per string* case. $\Psi_{t,ijk} = W_{t,ijk} \sum_{\tau=0}^{t} c_{t,\tau}(\Delta_{ijk})^{\tau+1}$, $w = t+1$, $x = u+1$. W^* is the noise-free weight set.

	NON-CUMULATIVE	
	Additive	Multiplicative
Noise step	$W_{t,ijk} = W^*_{ijk} + \Delta_{ijk}$	$W_{t,ijk} = W^*_{ijk} + W^*_{ijk}\Delta_{ijk}$
1st order	$\frac{1}{2}\sigma^2 \sum_{t,u=0}^{T-1}\sum_{ijk} \frac{\partial S^T_O}{\partial W_{t,ijk}}\frac{\partial S^T_O}{\partial W_{u,ijk}}$	$\frac{1}{2}\sigma^2 \sum_{t,u=0}^{T-1}\sum_{ijk} W_{t,ijk} W_{u,ijk} \frac{\partial S^T_O}{\partial W_{t,ijk}}\frac{\partial S^T_O}{\partial W_{u,ijk}}$
2nd order	$\frac{1}{2}\epsilon_p\sigma^2 \sum_{t,u=0}^{T-1}\sum_{ijk} \frac{\partial^2 S^T_O}{\partial W_{t,ijk}\partial W_{u,ijk}}$	$\frac{1}{2}\epsilon_p\sigma^2 \sum_{t,u=0}^{T-1}\sum_{ijk} W_{t,ijk} W_{u,ijk} \frac{\partial^2 S^T_O}{\partial W_{t,ijk} W_{u,ijk}}$
	CUMULATIVE	
	Additive	Multiplicative
Noise step	$W_{t,ijk} = W^*_{ijk} + (t+1)\Delta_{ijk}$	$W_{t,ijk} = W^*_{ijk}(1+\Delta_{ijk})^t$ $= W^*_{ijk} + \sum_{\tau=0}^{t} c_{t,\tau}(\Delta_{ijk})^{\tau+1}$
1st order	$\frac{1}{2}\sigma^2 \sum_{t,u=0}^{T-1}\sum_{ijk} wx \frac{\partial S^T_O}{\partial W_{t,ijk}}\frac{\partial S^T_O}{\partial W_{u,ijk}}$	$\frac{1}{2}\sum_{t,u=0}^{T-1}\sum_{ijk,lmn} \Psi_{t,ijk}\Psi_{u,lmn} \frac{\partial S^T_O}{\partial W_{t,ijk}}\frac{\partial S^T_O}{\partial W_{u,lmn}}$ $+2\epsilon_p^2 \sum_{t=0}^{T-1}\sum_{ijk} \Psi_{t,ijk} \frac{\partial S^T_O}{\partial W_{t,ijk}}$
2nd order	$\frac{1}{2}\epsilon_p\sigma^2 \sum_{t,u=0}^{T-1}\sum_{ijk} wx \frac{\partial^2 S^T_O}{\partial W_{t,ijk}\partial W_{u,ijk}}$	$\frac{1}{2}\epsilon_p \sum_{t,u=0}^{T-1}\sum_{ijk,lmn} \Psi_{t,ijk}\Psi_{u,lmn} \frac{\partial^2 S^T_O}{\partial w_{t,ijk}\partial W_{u,lmn}}$

These plots illustrate the cases where both convergence and generalization are improved. In figure 3II the curves clearly curl down and to the left for lower noise amplitudes before rising to the right at higher noise amplitudes. These lower regions are important because they represent noise values where generalization and convergence improve simultaneously and do not trade off.

5 CONCLUSIONS

We have presented several methods of injecting synaptic noise to recurrent neural networks. We summarized the results of an analysis of these methods and empirically tested them on learning the dual parity automaton from strings encoded as temporal sequences. (For a complete discussion of results, see (Jim, Giles, and Horne, 1994)). Results show that most of these methods can improve generalization and convergence *simultaneously* – most other methods previously discussed in literature cast convergence as a cost for improved generalization performance.

References

[1] Chris M. Bishop. Training with noise is equivalent to Tikhonov Regularization. *Neural Computation*, 1994. To appear.

[2] Robert M. Burton, Jr. and George J. Mpitsos. Event-dependent control of noise enhances learning in neural networks. *Neural Networks*, 5:627–637, 1992.

[3] C.L. Giles, C.B. Miller, D. Chen, H.H. Chen, G.Z. Sun, and Y.C. Lee. Learning and extracting finite state automata with second-order recurrent neural networks. *Neural Computation*, 4(3):393–405, 1992.

[4] Stephen José Hanson. A stochastic version of the delta rule. *Physica D.*, 42:265–272, 1990.

[5] Kam Jim, C.L. Giles, and B.G. Horne. Synaptic noise in dynamically-driven recurrent neural networks: Convergence and generalization. Technical Report UMIACS-TR-94-89 and CS-TR-3322, Institute for Advanced Computer Studies, University of Maryland, College Park, MD, 1994.

[6] Stephen Judd and Paul W. Munro. Nets with unreliable hidden nodes learn error-correcting codes. In S.J Hanson, J.D. Cowan, and C.L. Giles, editors, *Advances in Neural Information Processing Systems 5*, pages 89–96, San Mateo, CA, 1993. Morgan Kaufmann Publishers.

[7] Anders Krogh and John A. Hertz. A simple weight decay can improve generalization. In J.E. Moody, S.J. Hanson, and R.P. Lippmann, editors, *Advances in Neural Information Processing Systems 4*, pages 450–957, San Mateo, CA, 1992. Morgan Kaufmann Publishers.

[8] Alan F. Murray and Peter J. Edwards. Synaptic weight noise during multilayer perceptron training: Fault tolerance and training improvements. *IEEE Trans. on Neural Networks*, 4(4):722–725, 1993.

[9] Carlo H. Séquin and Reed D. Clay. Fault tolerance in artificial neural networks. In *Proc. of IJCNN*, volume I, pages I-703–708, 1990.

Learning Many Related Tasks at the Same Time With Backpropagation

Rich Caruana
School of Computer Science
Carnegie Mellon University
Pittsburgh, PA 15213
caruana@cs.cmu.edu

Abstract

Hinton [6] proposed that generalization in artificial neural nets should improve if nets learn to represent the domain's underlying regularities. Abu-Mustafa's *hints* work [1] shows that the *outputs* of a backprop net can be used as *inputs* through which domain-specific information can be given to the net. We extend these ideas by showing that a backprop net learning many related tasks at the same time can use these tasks as inductive bias for each other and thus learn better. We identify five mechanisms by which multitask backprop improves generalization and give empirical evidence that multitask backprop generalizes better in real domains.

1 INTRODUCTION

You and I rarely learn things one at a time, yet we often ask our programs to—it *must* be easier to learn things one at a time than to learn many things at once. Maybe not. The things you and I learn are related in many ways. They are processed by the same sensory apparatus, controlled by the same physical laws, derived from the same culture, ... Perhaps it is the *similarity* between the things we learn that helps us learn so well. What happens when a net learns many related functions at the same time? Will the extra information in the teaching signal of the related tasks help it learn better?

Section 2 describes five mechanisms that improve generalization in backprop nets trained simultaneously on related tasks. Section 3 presents empirical results from a road-following domain and an object-recognition domain where backprop with multiple tasks improves generalization 10–40%. Section 4 briefly discusses when and how to use multitask backprop. Section 5 cites related work and Section 6 outlines directions for future work.

2 MECHANISMS OF MULTITASK BACKPROP

We identified five mechanisms that improve generalization in backprop nets trained simultaneously on multiple related tasks. The mechanisms all derive from the summing of error gradient terms at the hidden layer from the different tasks. Each exploits a different relationship between the tasks.

2.1 Data Amplification

Data amplification is an *effective* increase in sample size due to extra information in the training signal of related tasks. There are two types of data amplification.

2.1.1 Statistical Data Amplification

Statistical amplification, occurs when there is noise in the training signals. Consider two tasks, T and T', with independent noise added to their training signals, that both benefit from computing a feature F of the inputs. A net learning both T and T' can, if it recognizes that the two tasks share F, use the two training signals to learn F better by averaging F through the noise. The simplest case is when $T = T'$, i.e., when the two outputs are independently corrupted versions of the same signal.

2.1.2 Blocking Data Amplification

The 2nd form of data amplification occurs even if there is no noise. Consider two tasks, T and T', that use a common feature F computable from the inputs, but each uses F for different training patterns. A simple example is $T = A\ OR\ F$ and $T' = NOT(A)\ OR\ F$. T uses F when $A = 0$ and provides no information about F when $A = 1$. Conversely, T' provides information about F only when $A = 1$. A net learning just T gets information about F only on training patterns for which $A = 0$, but is *blocked* when $A = 1$. But a net learning both T and T' at the same time gets information about F on every training pattern; it is never blocked. *It does not see more training patterns, it gets more information for each pattern.* If the net learning both tasks recognizes the tasks share F, it will see a larger sample of F. Experiments with blocked functions like T and T' (where F is a hard but learnable function of the inputs such as parity) indicate backprop does learn common subfeatures better due to the larger effective sample size.

2.2 Attribute Selection

Consider two tasks, T and T', that use a common subfeature F. Suppose there are many inputs to the net, but F is a function of only a few of the inputs. A net learning T will, if there is limited training data and/or significant noise, have difficulty distinguishing inputs relevant to F from those irrelevant to it. A net learning both T and T', however, will better select the attributes relevant to F because data amplification provides better training signals for F and that allows it to better determine which inputs to use to compute F. (Note: data amplification occurs even when there is no attribute selection problem. Attribute selection is a consequence of data amplification that makes data amplification work better when a selection problem exists.) We detect attribute selection by looking for connections to relevant inputs that grow stronger compared to connections for irrelevant inputs when multiple tasks are trained on the net.

2.3 Eavesdropping

Consider a feature F, useful to tasks, T and T', that is easy to learn when learning T, but difficult to learn when learning T' because T' uses F in a more complex way. A net learning T will learn F, but a net learning just T' may not. If the net learning T' also learns T, T' can *eavesdrop* on the hidden layer learned for T (e.g., F) and thus learn better. Moreover, once the connection is made between T' and the evolving representation for F, the extra information from T' about F will help the net learn F better via the other mechanisms. The simplest case of eavesdropping is when $T = F$. Abu-Mostafa calls these *catalytic hints*[1]. In this case the net is being told explicitly to learn a feature F that is useful to the main task. Eavesdropping sometimes causes non-monotonic generalization curves for the tasks that eavesdrop on other tasks. This happens when the eavesdropper begins to overtrain, but then finds something useful learned by another task, and begins to perform better as it starts using this new information.

2.4 Representation Bias

Because nets are initialized with random weights, backprop is a stochastic search procedure; multiple runs rarely yield identical nets. Consider the set of all nets (for fixed architecture) learnable by backprop for task T. Some of these generalize better than others because they better "represent" the domain's regularities. Consider one such regularity, F, learned differently by the different nets. Now consider the set of all nets learnable by backprop for another task T' that also learns regularity F. If T and T' are both trained on one net and the net recognizes the tasks share F, search will be biased towards representations of F near the intersection of what would be learned for T or T' alone. We conjecture that representations of F near this intersection often better capture the true regularity of F because they satisfy more than one task from the domain.

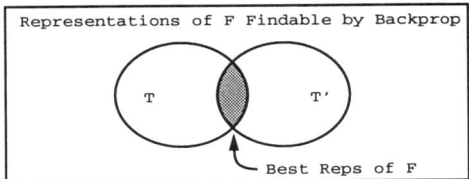

A form of representation bias that is easier to experiment with occurs when the representations for F sampled by the two tasks are different minima. Suppose there are two minima, A and B, a net can find for task T. Suppose a net learning task T' also has two minima, A and C. Both share the minima at A (i.e., both would perform well if the net entered that region of weight space), but do not overlap at B and C. We ran two experiments. In the first, we selected the minima so that nets trained on T alone are equally likely to find A or B, and nets trained on T' alone are equally likely to find A or C. Nets trained on both T and T' usually fall into A for both tasks.[1] *Tasks prefer hidden layer representations that other tasks prefer.*

In the second experiment we selected the minima so that T has a strong preference

---

[1] In these experiments the nets have sufficient capacity to find independent minima for the tasks. They are not forced to share the hidden layer representations. But because the initial weights are random, they do initially share the hidden layer and will separate the tasks (i.e., use independent chunks of the hidden layer for each task) only if learning causes them to.

for B over A: a net trained on T always falls into B. T', however, still has no preference between A or C. When both T and T' are trained on one net, T falls into B as expected: the bias from T' is unable to pull it to A. Surprisingly, T' usually falls into C, the minima it does not share with T! T creates a "tide" in the hidden layer representation towards B that flows away from A. T' has no preference for A or C, but is subject to the tide created by T. Thus T' usually falls into C; it would have to fight the tide from T to fall into A. *Tasks prefer NOT to use hidden layer representations that other tasks prefer NOT to use.*

2.5 How the Mechanisms are Related

The "tide" mentioned while discussing representation bias results from the aggregation of error gradients from multiple tasks at the hidden layer. It is what makes the five mechanisms tick. It biases the search trajectory towards better performing regions of weight space. Because the mechanisms arise from the same underlying cause, it easy for them to act in concert. Their combined effect can be substantial.

Although the mechanisms all derive from gradient summing, they are not the same. Each emphasizes a different relationship between tasks and has different effects on what is learned. Changes in architecture, representation, and the learning procedure affect the mechanisms in different ways. One particularly noteworthy difference between the mechanisms is that if there are minima, representation bias affects learning even with infinite sample size. The other mechanisms work only with finite sample size: data amplification (and thus attribute selection) and eavesdropping are beneficial only when the sample size is too small for the training signal for one task to provide enough information to the net for it to learn good models.

3 EMPIRICAL RESULTS

Experiments on carefully crafted test problems verify that each of the mechanisms can work.[2] These experiments, however, do not indicate how effective multitask backprop is on real problems: tweaking the test problems alters the size of the effects. Rather than present results for contrived problems, we present a more convincing demonstration of multitask backprop by testing it on two realistic domains.

3.1 1D-ALVINN

1D-ALVINN uses a road image simulator developed by Pomerleau. It was modified to generate 1-D road images comprised of a single 32-pixel horizontal scan line instead of the original 2-D 30x32-pixel image. This was done to speed learning to allow thorough experimentation. 1D-ALVINN retains much of the complexity of the original 2-D domain—the complexity lost is road curvature and that due to the smaller input (960 pixels vs. 32 pixels). The principle task in 1D-ALVINN is to predict steering direction. Eight additional tasks were used for multitask backprop:

- whether the road is one or two lanes
- location of left edge of road
- location of road center
- intensity of region bordering road
- location of centerline (2-lane roads only)
- location of right edge of road
- intensity of road surface
- intensity of centerline (2-lane roads only)

---

[2]We have yet to determine how to directly test the hypothesis that representations for F in the intersection of T and T' perform better. Testing this requires interpreting representations learned for *real* tasks; experiments on test problems demonstrate only that search is biased towards the intersection, not that the intersection is the right place to be.

Table 1 shows the performance of single and multitask backprop (STB and MTB, respectively) on 1D-ALVINN using nets with one hidden layer. The MTB net has 32 inputs, 16 hidden units, and 9 outputs. The 36 STB nets have 32 inputs, 2, 4, 8 or 16 hidden units, and 1 output. A similar experiment using nets with 2 hidden layers containing 2, 4, 8, 16, or 32 hidden units per layer for STB and 32 hidden units per layer for MTB yielded comparable results. The size of the MTB nets is not optimized in either experiment.

Table 1: Performance of STB and MTB with One Hidden Layer on 1D-ALVINN

TASK	ROOT-MEAN SQUARED ERROR ON TEST SET						
	Single Task Backprop				MTB	% Change	% Change
	2HU	4HU	8HU	16HU	16HU	Best STB	Mean STB
1 or 2 Lanes	.201	.209	.207	*.178*	.156	14.1	27.4
Left Edge	*.069*	.071	.073	.073	.062	11.3	15.3
Right Edge	.076	.062	.058	*.056*	.051	9.8	23.5
Line Center	.153	*.152*	.152	.152	.151	0.7	0.8
Road Center	.038	*.037*	.039	.042	.034	8.8	14.7
Road Greylevel	*.054*	.055	.055	.054	.038	42.1	43.4
Edge Greylevel	*.037*	.038	.039	.038	.038	-2.6	0.0
Line Greylevel	.054	.054	*.054*	.054	.054	0.0	0.0
Steering	.093	*.069*	.087	.072	.058	19.0	38.4

The entries under the STB and MTB headings are the peak generalization error for nets of the specified size. The italicized STB entries are the STB runs that yielded best performance. The last two columns compare STB and MTB. The first is the percent difference between MTB and the best STB run. Positive percentages indicate MTB performs better. This test is biased towards STB because it compares a single run of MTB on an unoptimized net size with several independent runs of STB that use different random seeds and are able to find near-optimal net size. The last column is the percent difference between MTB and the average STB. Note that on the important steering task, MTB outperforms STB 20-40%.

3.2 1D-DOORS

To test multitask backprop on a real problem, we created an object recognition domain similar in some respects to 1D-ALVINN. In 1D-DOORS the main tasks are to locate doorknobs and recognize door types (single or double) in images of doors collected with a robot-mounted camera. Figure 1 shows several door images. As with 1D-ALVINN, the problem was simplified by using horizontal stripes from image, one for the green channel and one for the blue channel. Each stripe is 30 pixels wide (accomplished by applying Gaussian smoothing to the original 150 pixel wide image) and occurs at the vertical location of the doorknob. 10 tasks were used:

- horizontal location of doorknob
- horizontal location of doorway center
- horizontal location of left door jamb
- width of left door jamb
- horizontal location of left edge of door
- single or double door
- width of doorway
- horizontal location of right door jamb
- width of right door jamb
- horizontal location of right edge of door

The difficulty of 1D-DOORS precludes running as exhaustive a set of experiments as with 1D-ALVINN: runs were done only for the two most important and difficult tasks: doorknob location and door type. STB was tested on nets using 6, 24, and 96 hidden units. MTB was tested on a net with 120 hidden units. The results

Figure 1: Sample Doors from the 1D-DOORS Domain

are in Table 2. STB generalizes 35–45% worse than MTB on these tasks. Less thorough experiments on the other eight tasks suggest MTB probably always yields performance equal to or better than STB.

Table 2: Performance of STB and MTB on 1D-DOORS.

TASK	Single Task Backprop			MTB	Change MTB
	6HU	24HU	96HU	120HU	to Best STB
Doorknob Loc	.085	.082	*.081*	.062	+33.9 %
Door Type	.129	*.086*	.096	.059	+45.8 %

4 DISCUSSION

In our experience, multitask backprop usually generalizes better than single task backprop. The few cases where STB has been better is on simpler tasks, and there the difference between MTB and STB was small. Multitask backprop appears to provide the most benefit on hard tasks. MTB also usually learns in fewer epochs than STB. When all tasks must be learned, MTB is computationally more efficient than training single nets. When few tasks are important, however, STB is usually more efficient (but also less accurate).

Tasks do not always learn at the same rate. It is important to watch the training curve of each MTB task individually and stop training each task when its performance peaks. The easiest way to do this to take a snapshot of the net when performance peaks on a task of interest. MTB does not mean one net should be used to predict all tasks, only that all tasks should be trained on one net so they may benefit each other. *Do not treat tasks as one task just because they are being trained on one net!* Balancing tasks (e.g., using different learning rates for different outputs) sometimes helps tasks learn at similar rates, thus maximizing the potential benefits of MTB. Also, because the training curves for MTB are often more complex due to interactions between tasks (MTB curves are frequently multimodal), it is important to train MTB nets until all tasks appear to be overtraining. Restricting the capacity of MTB nets to force sharing or prevent overtraining usually hurts performance instead of helping it. MTB does not depend on restricted net capacity.

We *created* the extra tasks in 1D-ALVINN and 1D-DOORS specifically because we thought they would improve performance on the important tasks. Multitask backprop can be used in other ways. Often the world gives us related tasks to learn. For example, the Calendar Apprentice System (CAP)[4] learns to predict the *Location*, *Time_Of_Day*, *Day_Of_Week*, and *Duration* of the meetings it schedules. These tasks are functions of the same data, share many common features, and would be easy to learn together. Sometimes the world gives us related tasks in mysterious ways. For example, in a medical domain we are examining where the goal is to predict illness severity, half of the lab tests are cheap and routinely measured before admitting a patient (e.g., blood pressure, pulse, age). The rest are expensive tests requiring hospitalization. Users tell us it would be useful to predict if the severity of the illness warrants admission (and further testing) using just the pre-admission tests. Rather than ignore the most diagnostically useful information in the database, we use the expensive tests as additional tasks the net must learn. They are not very predictable from the simple pre-admission tests, but providing them to the net as outputs helps it learn illness severity better. Multitask backprop is one way of providing to a net information that at run time would only be available in the future. The training signals are needed only for the training set because they are outputs—not inputs—to the net.

5 RELATED WORK

Training nets with many outputs is not new; NETtalk [9] used one net to learn phonemes and stress. This approach was natural for NETtalk where the goal was to control a synthesizer that needed both phoneme and stress commands at the same time. No analysis, however, was made of the advantages of using one net for all the tasks[3], and the different outputs were not treated as independent tasks. For example, the NETtalk stress task overtrains badly long before the phoneme task is learned well, but NETtalk did not use different snapshots of the net for different tasks. NETtalk also made no attempt to balance tasks so that they would learn at a similar rate, or to add new tasks that might improve learning but which would not be useful for controlling the synthesizer.

Work has been done on serial transfer between nets [8]. Improved learning speed was reported, but not improved generalization. The key difficulties with serial transfer are that it is difficult to scale to many tasks, it is hard to prevent catastrophic interference from erasing what was learned previously, the learning sequence must be defined manually, and serial learning precludes mutual benefit between tasks. This work is most similar to catalytic hints [1][10] where extra tasks correspond to important learnable features of a main task. This work extends hints by showing that tasks can be related in more diverse ways, by expanding the class of mechanisms responsible for multitask backprop, by showing that capacity restriction is not an important mechanism for multitask backprop [2], and by demonstrating that creating many new related tasks may be an efficient way of providing domain-specific inductive bias to backprop nets.

6 FUTURE WORK

We used *vanilla* backprop to show the benefit of training many related tasks on one net. Additional techniques may enhance the effects. Regularization and incremental net growing procedures might improve performance by promoting sharing without restricting capacity. New techniques may also be necessary to enhance the benefit of multitask backprop. Automatic balancing of task learning rates would make MTB easier to use. It would also be valuable to know when the different MTB mechanisms are working—they might be useful in different kinds of domains and might benefit from different regularization or balancing techniques. Finally, although MTB usually seems to help and rarely hurts, the only way to know it

---

[3] See [5] for evidence that NETtalk is harder to learn using separate nets.

helps is to try it. It would be better to have a predictive theory of how tasks should relate to benefit MTB, particularly if new tasks are to be created only to provide a multitask benefit for the other important tasks in the domain.

7 SUMMARY

Five mechanisms that improve generalization performance on nets trained on multiple related tasks at the same time have been identified. These mechanisms work without restricting net capacity or otherwise reducing the net's VC-dimension. Instead, they exploit backprop's ability to combine the error terms for related tasks into an aggregate gradient that points towards better underlying representations. Multitask backprop was tested on a simulated domain, 1D-ALVINN, and on a real domain, 1D-DOORS. It improved generalization performance on hard tasks in these domains 20–40% compared with the best performance that could be obtained from multiple trials of single task backprop.

Acknowledgements

Thanks to Tom Mitchell, Herb Simon, Dean Pomerleau, Tom Dietterich, Andrew Moore, Dave Touretzky, Scott Fahlman, Sebastian Thrun, Ken Lang, and David Zabowski for suggestions that have helped shape this work. This research is sponsored in part by the Advanced Research Projects Agency (ARPA) under grant no. F33615-93-1-1330.

References

[1] Y.S. Abu-Mostafa, "Learning From Hints in Neural Networks," *Journal of Complexity* **6**:2, pp. 192–198, 1989.

[2] Y.S. Abu-Mostafa, "Hints and the VC Dimension," *Neural Computation,* **5**:2, 1993.

[3] R. Caruana, "Multitask Connectionist Learning," *Proceedings of the 1993 Connectionist Models Summer School,* pp. 372–379, 1993.

[4] L. Dent, J. Boticario, J. McDermott, T. Mitchell, and D. Zabowski, "A Personal Learning Apprentice," *Proceedings of 1992 National Conference on Artificial Intelligence,* 1992.

[5] T.G. Dietterich, H. Hild, and G. Bakiri, "A Comparative Study of ID3 and Backpropagation for English Text-to-speech Mapping," *Proceedings of the Seventh International Conference on Artificial Intelligence,* pp. 24–31, 1990.

[6] G.E. Hinton, "Learning Distributed Representations of Concepts," *Proceedings of the Eight International Conference of The Cognitive Science Society,* pp. 1–12, 1986.

[7] D.A. Pomerleau, "Neural Network Perception for Mobile Robot Guidance," Carnegie Mellon University: *CMU-CS-92-115,* 1992.

[8] L.Y. Pratt, J. Mostow, and C.A. Kamm, "Direct Transfer of Learned Information Among Neural Networks," *Proceedings of AAAI-91,* 1991.

[9] T.J. Sejnowski and C.R. Rosenberg, "NETtalk: A Parallel Network that Learns to Read Aloud," John Hopkins: *JHU/EECS-86/01,* 1986.

[10] S.C. Suddarth and A.D.C. Holden, "Symbolic-neural Systems and the Use of Hints for Developing Complex Systems," *International Journal of Max-Machine Studies* **35**:3, pp. 291–311, 1991.

A Rapid Graph-based Method for Arbitrary Transformation-Invariant Pattern Classification

Alessandro Sperduti
Dipartimento di Informatica
Università di Pisa
Corso Italia 40
56125 Pisa, ITALY
perso@di.unipi.it

David G. Stork
Machine Learning and Perception Group
Ricoh California Research Center
2882 Sand Hill Road #115
Menlo Park, CA USA 94025-7022
stork@crc.ricoh.com

Abstract

We present a graph-based method for rapid, accurate search through prototypes for transformation-invariant pattern classification. Our method has in theory the same recognition accuracy as other recent methods based on "tangent distance" [Simard et al., 1994], since it uses the same categorization rule. Nevertheless ours is significantly faster during classification because far fewer tangent distances need be computed. Crucial to the success of our system are 1) a novel graph architecture in which transformation constraints and geometric relationships among prototypes are encoded during learning, and 2) an improved graph search criterion, used during classification. These architectural insights are applicable to a wide range of problem domains. Here we demonstrate that on a handwriting recognition task, a basic implementation of our system requires less than half the computation of the Euclidean sorting method.

1 INTRODUCTION

In recent years, the crucial issue of incorporating invariances into networks for pattern recognition has received increased attention, most especially due to the work of

Simard and his colleagues. To a regular hierachical backpropagation network Simard et al. [1992] added a Jacobian network, which insured that directional derivatives were also learned. Such derivatives represented directions in feature space corresponding to the invariances of interest, such as rotation, translation, scaling and even line thinning. On small training sets for a function approximation problem, this hybrid network showed performance superior to that of a highly tuned backpropagation network taken alone; however there was negligible improvement on large sets. In order to find a simpler method applicable to real-world problems, Simard, Le Cun & Denker [1993] later used a variation of the nearest neighbor algorithm, one incorporating "tangent distance" (T-distance or D_T) as the classification metric — the smallest Euclidean distance between patterns after the optimal transformation. In this way, state-of-the-art accuracy was achieved on an isolated handwritten character task, though at quite high computational complexity, owing to the inefficient search and large number of Euclidean and tangent distances that had to be calculated.

Whereas Simard, Hastie & Saeckinger [1994] have recently sought to reduce this complexity by means of pre-clustering stored prototypes, we here take a different approach, one in which a (graph) data structure formed during learning contains information about transformations and geometrical relations among prototypes. Nevertheless, it should be noted that our method can be applied to a reduced (clustered) training set such as they formed, yielding yet faster recognition. Simard [1994] recently introduced a hierarchical structure of successively lower resolution patterns, which speeds search only if a minority of patterns are classified more accurately by using the tangent metric than by other metrics. In contrast, our method shows significant improvement even if the majority or all of the patterns are most accurately classified using the tangent distance.

Other methods seeking fast invariant classification include Wilensky and Manukian's scheme [1994]. While quite rapid during recall, it is more properly considered *distortion* (rather than coherent transformation) invariant. Moreover, some transformations such as line thinning cannot be naturally incorporated into their scheme. Finally, it appears as if their scheme scales poorly (compared to tangent metric methods) as the number of invariances is increased.

It seems somewhat futile to try to improve significantly upon the recognition *accuracy* of the tangent metric approach — for databases such as NIST isolated handwritten characters, Simard et al. [1993] reported accuracies matching that of *humans*! Nevertheless, there remains much that can be done to increase the computational efficiency during recall. This is the problem we address.

2 TRANSFORMATION INVARIANCE

In broad overview, during learning our method constructs a labelled graph data structure in which each node represents a stored prototype (labelled by its category) as given by a training set, linked by arcs representing the T-distance between them. Search through this graph (for classification) takes advantage of the graph structure and an improved search criterion. To understand the underlying computations, we must first consider tangent space.

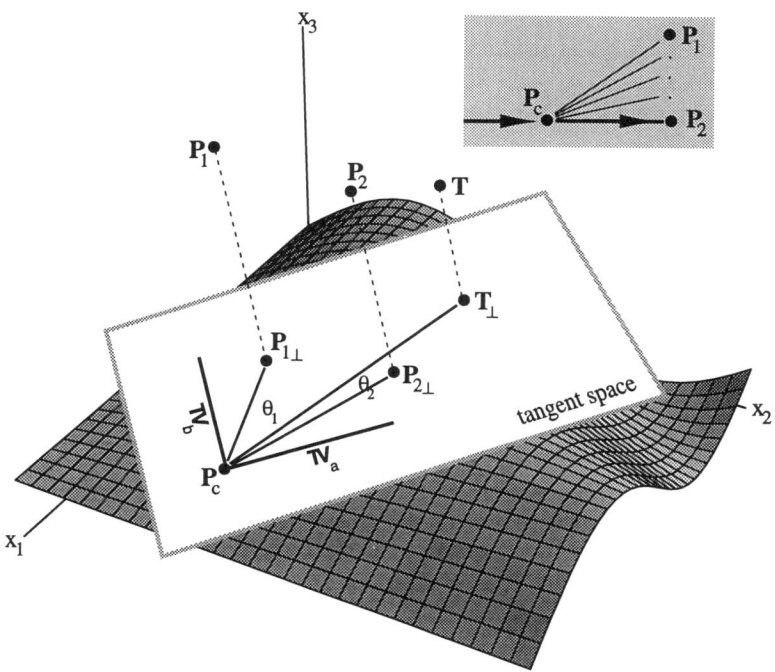

Figure 1: Geometry of tangent space. Here, a three-dimensional feature space contains the "current" prototype, $\mathbf{P}_c$, and the subspace consisting of all patterns obtainable by performing continuous transformations of it (shaded). Two candidate prototypes and a test pattern, $\mathbf{T}$, as well as their projections onto the T-space of $\mathbf{P}_c$ are shown. The insert (above) shows the progression of search through the corresponding portion of the recognition graph. The goal is to rapidly find the prototype closest to $\mathbf{T}$ (in the T-distance sense), and our algorithm (guided by the minimum angle θ_j in the tangent space) finds that $\mathbf{P}_2$ is so closer to $\mathbf{T}$ than are either $\mathbf{P}_1$ or $\mathbf{P}_c$ (see text).

Figure 1 illustrates geometry of tangent space and the relationships among the fundamental entities in our trained system. A labelled ("current") trained pattern is represented by $\mathbf{P}_c$, and the (shaded) surface corresponds to patterns arising under continuous transformations of $\mathbf{P}_c$. Such transformations might include rotation, translation, scaling, line thinning, etc. Following Simard et al. [1993], we approximate this surface in the vicinity of $\mathbf{P}_c$ by a subspace — the tangent space or T-space of $\mathbf{P}_c$ — which is spanned by "tangent" vectors, whose directions are determined by infinitesimally transforming the prototype $\mathbf{P}_c$. The figure shows an ortho-normal basis $\{\mathsf{TV}_a, \mathsf{TV}_b\}$, which helps to speed search during classification, as we shall see. A test pattern $\mathbf{T}$ and two other (candidate) prototypes as well as their projections onto the T-space of $\mathbf{P}_c$ are shown.

3 THE ALGORITHMS

Our overall approach includes constructing a graph (during learning), and searching it (for classification). The graph is constructed by the following algorithm:

Graph construction

Initialize $N = $ # patterns; $k = $ # nearest neighbors; $t = $ # invariant transformations

Begin Loop For each prototype $\mathbf{P}_i$ ($i = 1 \to N$)

- Compute a t-dimensional orthonormal basis for the T-space of $\mathbf{P}_i$
- Compute ("one-sided") T-distance of each of the $N - 1$ prototypes $\mathbf{P}_j$ ($j \neq i$) using $\mathbf{P}_i$'s T-space
- Represent $\mathbf{P}_{j\perp}$ (the projection of $\mathbf{P}_j$ onto the T-space of $\mathbf{P}_i$) in the tangent orthonormal frame of $\mathbf{P}_i$
- Connect $\mathbf{P}_i$ to each of its k T-nearest neighbors, storing their associated normalized projections $\mathbf{P}_{j\perp}^*$

End Loop

During classification, our algorithm permits rapid search through prototypes. Thus in Figure 1, starting at $\mathbf{P}_c$ we seek to find another prototype (here, $\mathbf{P}_2$) that is closer to the test point $\mathbf{T}$. After $\mathbf{P}_2$ is so chosen, *it* becomes the current pattern, and the search is extended using *its* T-space. Graph search ends when the closest prototype to $\mathbf{T}$ is found (i.e., closest in a T-distance sense).

We let D_T^c denote the current minimum tangent distance. Our search algorithm is:

Graph search

Input Test pattern $\mathbf{T}$

Initialize
- Choose initial candidate prototype, $\mathbf{P}_o$
- Set $\mathbf{P}_c \leftarrow \mathbf{P}_o$
- Set $D_T^c \leftarrow D_T(\mathbf{P}_c, \mathbf{T})$, i.e., the T-distance of $\mathbf{T}$ from $\mathbf{P}_c$

Do
- For each prototype $\mathbf{P}_j$ connected to $\mathbf{P}_c$ compute $cos(\theta_j) = \frac{T_\perp \cdot P_{j\perp}^*}{|T_\perp|}$
- Sort these prototypes by increasing values of θ_j and put them into a candidate list
- Pick $\mathbf{P}_j$ from the top of the candidate list
- In T-space of $\mathbf{P}_j$, compute $D_T(\mathbf{P}_j, \mathbf{T})$
  If $D_T(\mathbf{P}_j, \mathbf{T}) < D_T^c$ then $\mathbf{P}_c \leftarrow \mathbf{P}_j$ and $D_T^c \leftarrow D_T(\mathbf{P}_j, \mathbf{T})$
  otherwise mark $\mathbf{P}_j$ as a "failure" (F), and pick next prototype from the candidate list

Until Candidate list empty

Return D_T^c or the category label of the optimum prototype found

---

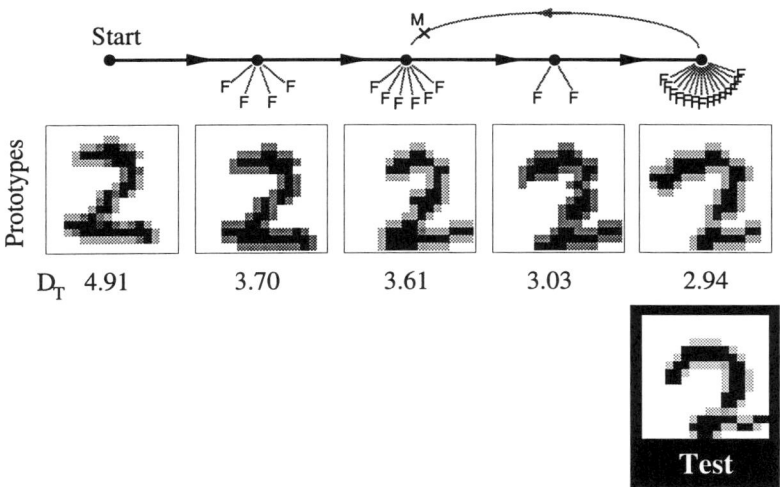

Figure 2: The search through the "2" category graph for the T-nearest stored prototype to the test pattern is shown ($N = 720$ and $k = 15$ nearest neighbors). The number of T-distance calculations is equal to the number of nodes visited plus the number of failures (marked F); i.e., in the case shown $5 + 26 = 31$. The backward search step attempt is thwarted because the middle node has already been visited (marked M). Notice in the prototypes how the search is first a downward shift, then a counter-clockwise rotation — a mere four steps through the graph.

Figure 2 illustrates search through a network of "2" prototypes. Note how the T-distance of the test pattern decreases, and that with only four steps through the graph the optimal prototype is found.

There are several ways in which our search technique can be incorporated into a classifier. One is to store all prototypes, regardless of class, in a single large graph and perform the search; the test pattern is classified by the label of the optimal prototype found. Another, is to employ *separate* graphs, one for each category, and search through them (possibly in parallel); the test is classified by the minimum T-distance prototype found. The choice of method depends upon the hardware limitations, performance speed requirements, etc. Figure 3 illustrates such a search through a "2" category graph for the closest prototype to a test pattern "5." We report below results using a single graph per category, however.

3.1 Computational complexity

If a graph contains N prototypes with k pointers (arcs) each, and if the patterns are of dimension m, then the storage requirement is $O(N((t+1) \cdot m^2 + kt))$. The time complexity of training depends upon details of ortho-normalization, sorting, etc., and is of little interest anyway. Construction is more than an order of magnitude faster than neural network training on similar problems; for instance construction of a graph for $N = 720$ prototypes and $k = 100$ nearest neighbors takes less than

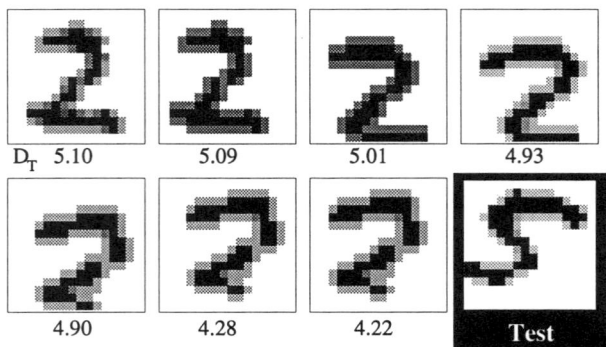

Figure 3: The search through a "2" category graph given a "5" test pattern. Note how the search first tries to find a prototype that matches the upper arc of the "5," and then one possessing skew or rotation. For this test pattern, the minimum T-distance found for the "5" category (3.62) is smaller than the one found for the "2" category shown here (4.22), and indeed for any other category. Thus the test pattern is correctly classified as a "5."

20 minutes on a Sparc 10.

The crucial quantity of interest is the time complexity for search. This is, of course, problem related, and depends upon the number of categories, transformation and prototypes and their statistical properties (see next Section). Worst case analyses (e.g., it is theoretically conceivable that nearly all prototypes must be visited) are irrelevant to practice.

We used a slightly non-obvious search criterion at each step, the function $cos(\theta_j)$, as shown in Figure 1. Not only could this criterion be calculated very efficiently in our orthonormal basis (by using simple inner products), but it actually led to a slightly more accurate search than Euclidean distance in the T-space — perhaps the most natural choice of criterion. The angle θ_j seems to guide the "flow" of the search along transformation directions toward the test point.

4 Simulations and results

We explored the search capabilities of our system on the binary handwritten digit database of Guyon, et al. [1991]. We needed to scale all patterns by a linear factor (0.833) to insure that rotated versions did not go outside the 16 × 16 pixel grid. As required in all T-space methods, the patterns must be continuous valued (i.e., here grayscale); this was achieved by convolution with a spatially symmetric Gaussian having $\sigma = .55$ pixels. We had 720 training examples in each of ten digit categories; the test set consisted of 1320 test patterns formed by transforming independent prototypes in all meaningful combinations of the $t = 6$ transformations (four spatial directions and two rotation senses).

We compared the Euclidean sorting method of Simard et al. [1993] to our graph

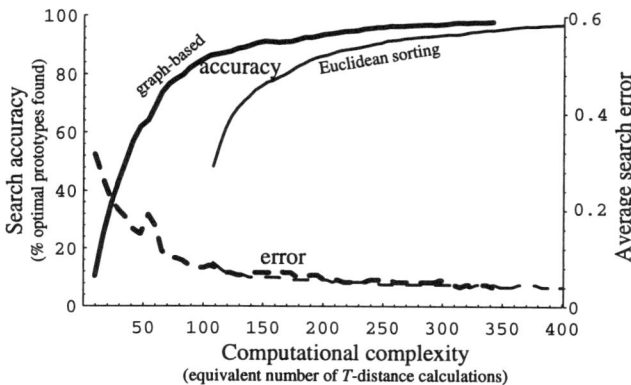

Figure 4: Comparison of graph-based (heavy lines) and standard Euclidean sorting searches (thin lines). Search accuracy is the percentage of optimal prototypes found on the full test set of 1320 patterns in a single category (solid lines). The average search error is the per pattern difference between the global optimum T-distance and the one actually found, averaged over the non-optimal prototypes found through the search (dashed lines). Note especially that for the same computational complexity, our method has the same average error, but that this average is taken over a much smaller number of (non-optimal) prototypes. For a given criterion search accuracy, our method requires significantly less computation. For instance, if 90% of the prototypes must be found for a requisite categorization accuracy (a typical value for asymptotically high recognition accuracy), our graph-based method requires less than half the computation of the Euclidean sorting method.

based method using the same data and transformations, over the full range of relevant computational complexities. Figure 4 summarizes our results. For our method, the computational complexity is adjusted by the number of neighbors inspected, k. For their Euclidean sorting method, it is adjusted by the percentage of Euclidean nearest neighbors that were then inspected for T-distance. We were quite careful to employ as many computational tricks and shortcuts on *both* methods we could think of. Our results reflect fairly on the full computational complexity, which was dominated by tangent and Euclidean distance calculations.

We note parenthetically that many of the recognition errors for both methods could be explained by the fact that we did not include the transformation of line thinning (solely because we lacked the preprocessing capabilities); the overall accuracy of both methods will increase when this invariance is also included.

5 CONCLUSIONS AND FUTURE WORK

We have demonstrated a graph-based method using tangent distance that permits search through prototypes significantly faster than the most popular current approach. Although not shown above, ours is also superior to other tree-based methods, such as k-d-trees, which are less accurate. Since our primary concern was reducing the computational complexity of search (while matching Simard et al.'s accuracy), we have not optimized over preprocessing steps, such as the Gaussian kernel width or transformation set. We note again that our method can be applied to reduced training sets, for instance ones pruned by the method of Simard, Hastie & Saeckinger [1994]. Simard's [1994] recent method — in which *low-resolution* versions of training patterns are organized into a hierarchical data structure so as to reduce the number of multiply-accumulates required during search — is in some sense "orthogonal" to ours. Our graph-based method will work with his low-resolution images too, and thus these two methods can be unified into a hybrid system.

Perhaps most importantly, our work suggests a number of research avenues. We used just a single ("central") prototype $\mathbf{P}_o$ to start search; presumably having several candidate starting points would be faster. Our general method may admit gradient descent learning of parameters of the search criterion. For instance, we can imagine scaling the different tangent basis vectors according to their relevance in guiding correct searches as determined using a validation set. Finally, our approach may admit elegant parallel implementations for real-world applications.

Acknowledgements

This work was begun during a visit by Dr. Sperduti to Ricoh CRC. We thank I. Guyon for the use of her database of handwritten digits and Dr. K. V. Prasad for assistance in image processing.

References

I. Guyon, P. Albrecht, Y. Le Cun, J. Denker & W. Hubbard. (1991) "Comparing different neural network architectures for classifying handwritten digits," *Proc. of the Inter. Joint Conference on Neural Networks*, vol. II, pp. 127-132, IEEE Press.

P. Simard. (1994) "Efficient computation of complex distance metrics using hierarchical filtering," in J. D. Cowan, G. Tesauro and J. Alspector (eds.) *Advances in Neural Information Processing Systems-6* Morgan Kaufmann pp. 168-175.

P. Simard, B. Victorrio, Y. Le Cun & J. Denker. (1992) "Tangent Prop — A formalism for specifying selected invariances in an adaptive network," in J. E. Moody, S. J. Hanson and R. P. Lippmann (eds.) *Advances in Neural Information Processing Systems-4* Morgan Kaufmann pp. 895-903.

P. Y. Simard, Y. Le Cun & J. Denker. (1993) "Efficient Pattern Recognition Using a New Transformation Distance," in S. J. Hanson, J. D. Cowan and C. L. Giles (eds.) *Advances in Neural Information Processing Systems-5* Morgan Kaufmann pp. 50-58.

P. Y. Simard, T. Hastie & E. Saeckinger. (1994) "Learning Prototype Models for Tangent Distance," *Neural Networks for Computing* Snowbird, UT (April, 1994).

G. D. Wilensky & N. Manukian. (1994) "Nearest Neighbor Networks: New Neural Architectures for Distortion-Insensitive Image Recognition," *Neural Networks for Computing* Snowbird, UT (April, 1994).

Recurrent Networks: Second Order Properties and Pruning

Morten With Pedersen and Lars Kai Hansen
CONNECT, Electronics Institute
Technical University of Denmark B349
DK-2800 Lyngby, DENMARK
emails: with,lkhansen@ei.dtu.dk

Abstract

Second order properties of cost functions for recurrent networks are investigated. We analyze a layered fully recurrent architecture, the virtue of this architecture is that it features the conventional feedforward architecture as a special case. A detailed description of recursive computation of the *full Hessian* of the network cost function is provided. We discuss the possibility of invoking simplifying approximations of the Hessian and show how weight decays *iron* the cost function and thereby greatly assist training. We present tentative pruning results, using Hassibi et al.'s *Optimal Brain Surgeon*, demonstrating that recurrent networks can construct an efficient internal memory.

1 LEARNING IN RECURRENT NETWORKS

Time series processing is an important application area for neural networks and numerous architectures have been suggested, see e.g. (Weigend and Gershenfeld, 94). The most general structure is a fully recurrent network and it may be adapted using *Real Time Recurrent Learning* (RTRL) suggested by (Williams and Zipser, 89). By invoking a recurrent network, the *length* of the network memory can be adapted to the given time series, while it is fixed for the conventional lag-space net (Weigend et al., 90). In forecasting, however, feedforward architectures remain the most popular structures; only few applications are reported based on the Williams&Zipser approach. The main difficulties experienced using RTRL are slow convergence and lack of generalization. Analogous problems in feedforward nets are solved using second order methods for training and pruning (LeCun et al., 90; Hassibi et al., 92; Svarer et al., 93). Also, regularization by weight decay significantly improves training and generalization. In this work we initiate the investigation of second order properties for RTRL; a detailed calculation scheme for the cost function Hessian is presented, the importance of weight decay is demonstrated, and preliminary pruning results using Hassibi et al.'s Optimal Brain Surgeon (OBS) are presented. We find that the recurrent network discards the available lag space and constructs its own efficient internal memory.

1.1 REAL TIME RECURRENT LEARNING

The fully connected feedback nets studied by Williams&Zipser operate like a state machine, computing the outputs from the internal units according to a state vector $z(t)$ containing *previous* external inputs and internal unit outputs. Let $\mathbf{x}(t)$ denote a vector containing the external inputs to the net at time t, and let $\mathbf{y}(t)$ denote a vector containing the outputs of the units in the net. We now arrange the indices on $\mathbf{x}$ and $\mathbf{y}$ so that the elements of $\mathbf{z}(t)$ can be defined as

$$z_k(t) = \begin{cases} x_k(t) &, k \in I \\ y_k(t) &, k \in U \end{cases}$$

where I denotes the set of indices for which z_k is an input, and U denotes the set of indices for which z_k is the output of a unit in the net. Thresholds are implemented using an input permanently clamped to unity. The k'th unit in the net is now updated according to

$$y_k(t+1) = f_k[s_k(t)] = f_k\left[\sum_{j \in I} w_{kj} x_j(t) + \sum_{j \in U} w_{kj} y_j(t)\right] = f_k\left[\sum_{j \in I \cup U} w_{kj} z_j(t)\right]$$

where w_{kj} denotes the weight to unit k from input/unit j and $f_k(\cdot)$ is the activation function of the k'th unit.

When used for time series prediction, the input vector (excluding threshold) is usually defined as $\mathbf{x}(t) = [x(t), \ldots, x(t-L+1)]$ where L denotes the dimension of the *lag space*. One of the units in the net is designated to be the output unit y_o, and its activating function f_o is often chosen to be linear in order to allow for arbitrary dynamical range. The prediction of $x(t+1)$ is $\hat{x}(t+1) = f_o[s_o(t)]$. Also, if the first prediction is at $t = 1$, the first example is presented at $t = 0$ and we set $\mathbf{y}(0) = \mathbf{0}$. We analyse here a modification of the standard Williams&Zipser construction that is appropriate for forecasting purposes. The studied architecture is *layered*. Firstly, we remove the external inputs from the linear output unit in order to prevent the network from getting trapped in a linear mode. The output then reads

$$\hat{x}(t+1) = y_o(t+1) = \sum_{j \in U} w_{oj} y_j(t) + w_{\text{thres},o} \quad (1)$$

Since $\mathbf{y}(0) = \mathbf{0}$ we obtain a first prediction yielding $\hat{x}(1) = w_{\text{thres},o}$ which is likely to be a poor prediction, and thereby introducing a significant error that is fed back into the network and used in future predictions. Secondly, when pruning a fully recurrent feedback net we would like the net to be able to reduce to a simple two-layer feedforward net if necessary. Note that this is *not* possible with the conventional Williams&Zipser update rule, since it doesn't include a layered feedforward net as a special case. In a layered feedforward net the output unit is disconnected from the external inputs; in this case, cf. (1) we see that $\hat{x}(t+1)$ is based on the internal 'hidden' unit outputs $y_k(t)$ which are calculated on the basis of $\mathbf{z}(t-1)$ and thereby $\mathbf{x}(t-1)$. Hence, besides the startup problems, we also get a two-step ahead predictor using the standard architecture.

In order to avoid the problems with the conventional Williams&Zipser update scheme we use a layered updating scheme inspired by traditional feedforward nets, in which we distinguish between hidden layer units and the output unit. At time t, the hidden units work from the input vector $\mathbf{z}^h(t)$

$$z_k^h(t) = \begin{cases} x_k(t-1) &, k \in I \\ y_k^h(t-1) &, k \in U \\ y^o(t-1) &, k = O \end{cases}$$

where I denotes the input indices, U denotes the hidden layer units and O the output unit. Further, we use superscripts h and o to distinguish between hidden unit and output units. The activation of the hidden units is calculated according to

$$y_k^h(t) = f_k^h[s_k^h(t)] = f_k^h\left[\sum_{j \in I \cup U \cup O} w_{kj} z_j^h(t)\right] , \quad k \in U \qquad (2)$$

The hidden unit outputs are forwarded to the output unit, which then sees the input vector $\mathbf{z}_k^o(t)$

$$z_k^o(t) = \begin{cases} y_k^h(t) &, k \in U \\ y^o(t-1) &, k = O \end{cases}$$

and is updated according to

$$y^o(t) = f^o[s^o(t)] = f^o\left[\sum_{j \in U \cup O} w_{oj} z_j^o(t)\right] \qquad (3)$$

The cost function is defined as $C = E + \mathbf{w}^T \mathbf{R} \mathbf{w}$. $\mathbf{R}$ is a regularization matrix, $\mathbf{w}$ is the concatenated set of parameters, and the sum of squared errors is

$$E = \frac{1}{2}\sum_{t=1}^{T}[e(t)]^2 , \quad e(t) = x(t) - y^o(t), \qquad (4)$$

where T is the size of the training set series. RTRL is based on gradient descent in the cost function, here we investigate accelerated training using Newton methods. For that we need to compute first and second derivatives of the cost function. The essential difficulty is to determine derivatives of the sum of squared errors:

$$\frac{\partial E}{\partial w_{ij}} = -\sum_{t=1}^{T} e(t)\frac{\partial y^o(t)}{\partial w_{ij}} \qquad (5)$$

The derivative of the output unit is computed as

$$\frac{\partial y^o(t)}{\partial w_{ij}} = \frac{\partial f^o[s^o(t)]}{\partial s^o(t)} \cdot \frac{\partial s^o(t)}{\partial w_{ij}} \quad (6)$$

where

$$\frac{\partial s^o(t)}{\partial w_{ij}} = \delta_{oi} z_j^o(t) + \sum_{j' \in U} w_{oj'} \frac{\partial y_{j'}^h(t)}{\partial w_{ij}} + w_{oo} \frac{\partial y^o(t-1)}{\partial w_{ij}} \quad (7)$$

where δ_{jk} is the Kronecker delta. This expression contains the derivative of the hidden units

$$\frac{\partial y_k^h(t)}{\partial w_{ij}} = \frac{\partial f_k^h[s_k^h(t)]}{\partial s_k^h(t)} \cdot \frac{\partial s_k^h(t)}{\partial w_{ij}} \quad , \quad k \in U \quad (8)$$

where

$$\frac{\partial s_k^h(t)}{\partial w_{ij}} = \delta_{ki} z_j^h(t) + \sum_{j' \in U} w_{kj'} \frac{\partial y_{j'}^h(t-1)}{\partial w_{ij}} + w_{ko} \frac{\partial y^o(t-1)}{\partial w_{ij}} \quad (9)$$

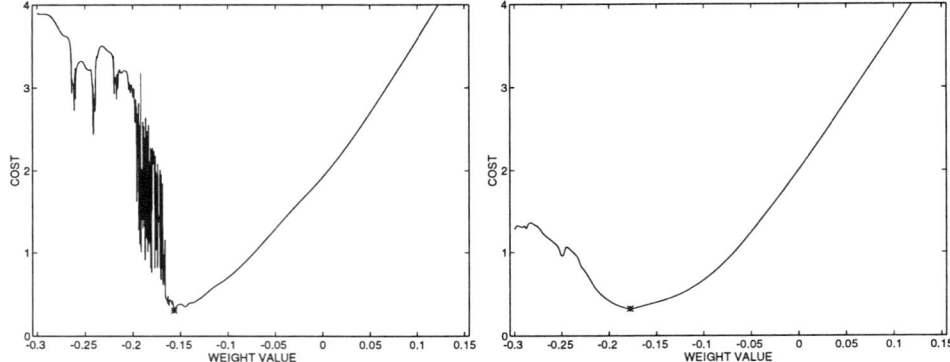

Figure 1: Cost function dependence of a weight connecting two hidden units for the sunspot benchmark series. Left panel: Cost function with small weight decay, the (local) optimum chosen is marked by an asterix. Right panel: The same slice through the cost function but here retrained with higher weight decay.

The complexity of the training problem for the recurrent net using RTRL is demonstrated in figure 1. The important role of weight decay (we have used a simple weight decay $\mathbf{R} = \alpha \mathbf{1}$) in controlling the complexity of the cost function is evident in the right panel of figure 1. The example studied is the sunspot benchmark problem (see e.g. (Weigend et al., 90) for a definition). First, we trained a network with the small weight decay and recorded the left panel result. Secondly, the network was retrained with increased weight decay and the particular weight connecting two hidden units was varied to produce the right panel result. In both cases all other weights remained fixed at their optimal values for the given weight decay. In addition to the complexity visible in these one-parameter slices of the cost function, the cost function is highly anisotropic in weight space and consequently the network Hessian is ill-conditioned. Hence, gradient descent is hampered by slow convergence.

2 SECOND ORDER PROPERTIES OF THE COST FUNCTION

To improve training by use of Newton methods and for use in OBS-pruning we compute the second derivative of the error functional:

$$\frac{\partial^2 E}{\partial w_{ij} \partial w_{pq}} = -\sum_{t=1}^{T} \left[e(t) \frac{\partial^2 y^o(t)}{\partial w_{ij} \partial w_{pq}} - \frac{\partial y^o(t)}{\partial w_{ij}} \cdot \frac{\partial y^o(t)}{\partial w_{pq}} \right] \quad (10)$$

The second derivative of the output is

$$\frac{\partial^2 y^o(t)}{\partial w_{ij} \partial w_{pq}} = \frac{\partial^2 f^o[s^o(t)]}{\partial s^o(t)^2} \cdot \frac{\partial s^o(t)}{\partial w_{ij}} \cdot \frac{\partial s^o(t)}{\partial w_{pq}} + \frac{\partial f^o[s^o(t)]}{\partial s^o(t)} \cdot \frac{\partial^2 s^o(t)}{\partial w_{ij} \partial w_{pq}} \quad (11)$$

with

$$\frac{\partial^2 s^o(t)}{\partial w_{ij} \partial w_{pq}} = \delta_{oi} \frac{\partial z_j^o(t)}{\partial w_{pq}} + \sum_{j' \in U} w_{oj'} \frac{\partial^2 y_{j'}^h(t)}{\partial w_{ij} \partial w_{pq}} + w_{oo} \frac{\partial^2 y^o(t-1)}{\partial w_{ij} \partial w_{pq}} + \delta_{op} \frac{\partial z_q^o(t)}{\partial w_{ij}} \quad (12)$$

This expression contains the second derivative of the hidden unit outputs

$$\frac{\partial^2 y_k^h(t)}{\partial w_{ij} \partial w_{pq}} = \frac{\partial^2 f_k^h[s_k^h(t)]}{\partial s_k^h(t)^2} \cdot \frac{\partial s_k^h(t)}{\partial w_{ij}} \cdot \frac{\partial s_k^h(t)}{\partial w_{pq}} + \frac{\partial f_k^h[s_k^h(t)]}{\partial s_k^h(t)} \cdot \frac{\partial^2 s_k^h(t)}{\partial w_{ij} \partial w_{pq}} \quad (13)$$

with

$$\frac{\partial^2 s_k^h(t)}{\partial w_{ij} \partial w_{pq}} = \delta_{ki} \frac{\partial z_j^h(t)}{\partial w_{pq}} + \sum_{j' \in U} w_{kj'} \frac{\partial^2 y_{j'}^h(t-1)}{\partial w_{ij} \partial w_{pq}} + w_{ko} \frac{\partial^2 y^o(t-1)}{\partial w_{ij} \partial w_{pq}} + \delta_{kp} \frac{\partial z_q^h(t)}{\partial w_{ij}} \quad (14)$$

Recursion in the five index quantity (14) imposes a significant computational burden; in fact the first term of the Hessian in (10), involving the second derivative, is often neglected for computational convenience (LeCun et al., 90). Here we start by analyzing the significance of this term during training. We train a layered architecture to predict the sunspot benchmark problem. In figure 2 the ratio between the largest eigenvalue of the second derivative term in (10) and the largest eigenvalue of the full Hessian is shown. The ratio is presented for two different magnitudes of weight decay. In line with our observations above the second order properties of the "ironed" cost function are manageable, and we can simplify the Hessian calculation by neglecting the second derivative term in (10), i.e., apply the Gauss-Newton approximation.

3 PRUNING BY THE OPTIMAL BRAIN SURGEON

Pruning of recurrent networks has been pursued by (Giles and Omlin, 94) using a heuristic pruning technique, and significant improvement in generalization for a sequence recognition problem was demonstrated. Two pruning schemes are based on systematic estimation of weight *saliency*: the Optimal Brain Damage (OBD) scheme of (LeCun et al., 90) and OBS by (Hassibi et al., 93). OBD is based on the diagonal approximation of the Hessian and is very robust for forecasting (Svarer et al., 93). If an estimate of the full Hessian is available OBS can be used

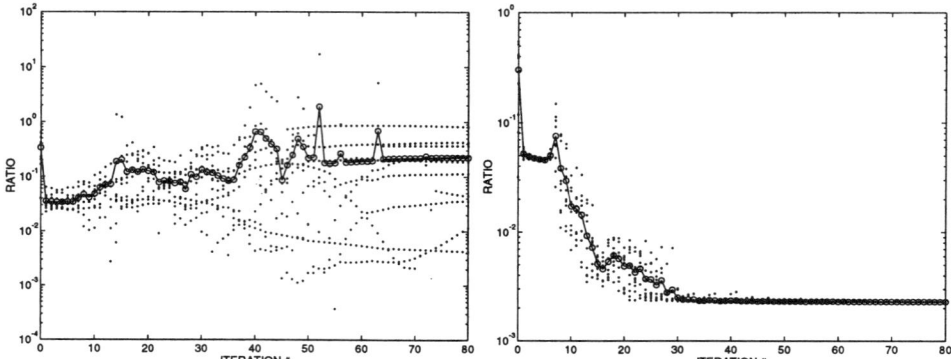

Figure 2: Ratio between the largest magnitude eigenvalue of the second derivative term of the Hessian (c.f. equation (10)) and the largest magnitude eigenvalue of the complete Hessian as they appeared during ten training sessions. The connected circles represent the average ratio. Left panel: Training with small weight decay. Right panel: Training with a high weight decay.

for estimation of saliencies incorporating *linear* retraining. In (Hansen and With Pedersen, 94) OBS was generalized to incorporate weight decays; we use these modifications in our experiments. Note that OBS in its standard form only allows for one weight to be eliminated at a time. The result of a pruning session is a nested family of networks. In order to select the optimal network within the family it was suggested in (Svarer et al., 93.) to use the estimated test error. In particular we use Akaike's Final Prediction Error (Akaike, 69) to estimate the network test error $\widehat{E}_{\text{test}} = ((T + N)/(T - N)) \cdot 2E/T$ [1], and N is the number of parameters in the network. In figure 3 we show the results of such a pruning session on the sunspot data starting from a (4-4-1) network architecture. The recurrent network was trained using a *damped* Gauss-Newton scheme. Note that the training error increases as weights are eliminated, while the test error and the estimated test error both pass through shallow minima showing that generalization is slightly improved by pruning. In fact, by retraining the optimal architecture with reduced weight decay both training and test errors are decreased in line with the observations in (Svarer et al., 93). It is interesting to observe that the network, though starting with access to a lag-space of four delay units, has lost three of the delayed inputs; hence, rely solely on its internal memory, as seen in the right panel of figure 3. To further illustrate the memory properties of the optimal network, we show in figure 4 the network response to a unit impulse. It is interesting that the response of the network extends for approximately 12 time steps corresponding to the "period" of the sunspot series.

---

[1] The use of Akaike's estimate is not well justified for a feedback net, test error estimates for feedback models is a topic of current research.

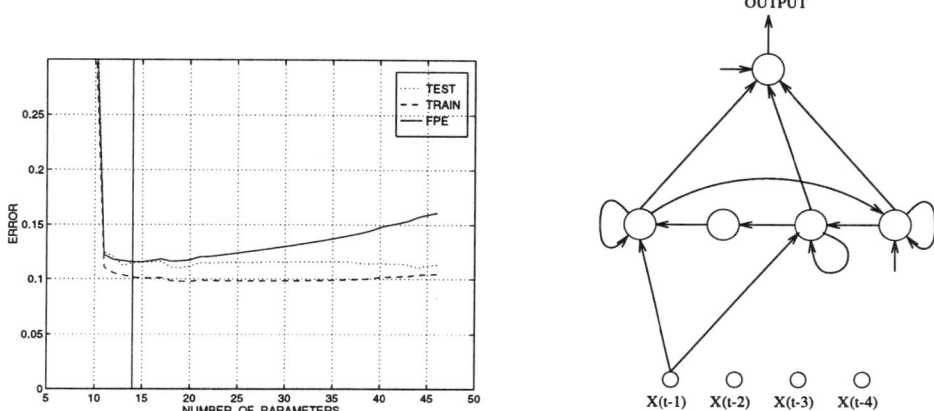

Figure 3: Left panel: OBS pruning of a (4-4-1) recurrent network trained on sunspot benchmark. Development of training error, test error, and Akaike estimated test error (FPE). Right panel: Architecture of the FPE-optimal network. Note that the network discards the available lag space and solely predicts from internal memory.

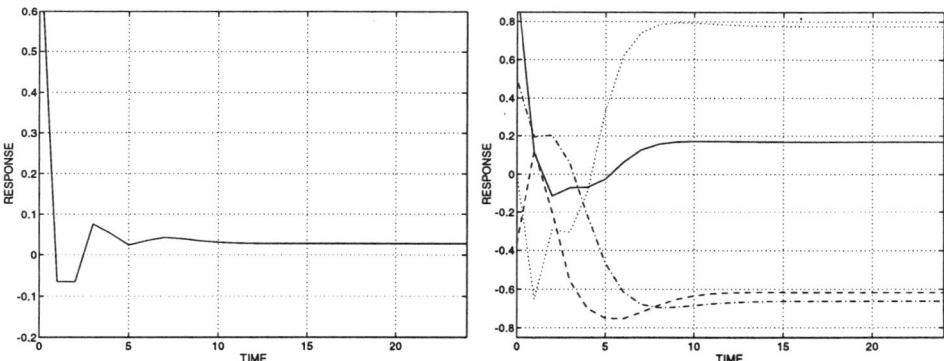

Figure 4: Left panel: Output of the pruned network after a unit impulse input at $t = 0$. The internal memory is about 12 time units long which is, in fact, roughly the period of the sunspot series. Right panel: Activity of the four hidden units in the pruned network after a unit impulse at time $t = 0$.

4 CONCLUSION

A layered recurrent architecture, which has a feedforward net as a special case, has been investigated. A scheme for recursive estimation of the Hessian of the fully recurrent neural net is devised. It's been shown that weight decay plays a decisive role when adapting recurrent networks. Further, it is shown that the second order information may be used to train and prune a recurrent network and in this process the network may discard the available lag space. The network builds an efficient internal memory extending beyond the lag space that was originally available.

Acknowledgments

We thank Jan Larsen, Sara Solla, and Claus Svarer for useful discussions, and Lee Giles for providing us with a preprint of (Giles and Omlin, 94). We thank the anonymous reviewers for valuable comments on the manuscript. This research is supported by the Danish Natural Science and Technical Research Councils through the Computational Neural Network Center (CONNECT).

References

H. Akaike: *Fitting Autoregressive Models for Prediction.* Ann. Inst. Stat. Mat. **21**, 243-247, (1969).

Y. Le Cun, J.S. Denker, and S.A. Solla: *Optimal Brain Damage.* In Advances in Neural Information Processing Systems 2, (Ed. D.S. Touretzsky) Morgan Kaufmann, 598-605, (1990).

C.L. Giles and C.W. Omlin: *Pruning of Recurrent Neural Networks for Improved Generalization Performance.* IEEE Transactions on Neural Networks, to appear. Preprint NEC Research Institute (1994).

L.K. Hansen and M. With Pedersen: *Controlled Growth of Cascade Correlation Nets*, International Conference on Artificial Neural Networks ICANN'94 Sorrento. (Eds. M. Marinaro and P.G. Morasso) Springer, 797-801, (1994).

B. Hassibi, D. G. Stork, and G. J. Wolff, *Optimal Brain Surgeon and General Network Pruning*, in Proceedings of the 1993 IEEE International Conference on Neural Networks, San Francisco (Eds. E.H. Ruspini et al.) IEEE, 293-299 (1993).

C. Svarer, L.K. Hansen, and J. Larsen: *On Design and Evaluation of Tapped Delay Line Networks*, In Proceedings of the 1993 IEEE International Conference on Neural Networks, San Francisco, (Eds. E.H. Ruspini et al.) 46-51, (1993).

A.S. Weigend, B.A. Huberman, and D.E. Rumelhart: *Predicting the future: A Connectionist Approach.* Int. J. of Neural Systems **3**, 193-209 (1990).

A.S. Weigend and N.A. Gershenfeld, Eds.: *Times Series Prediction: Forecasting the Future and Understanding the Past.* Redwood City, CA: Addison-Wesley (1994).

R.J. Williams and D. Zipser: *A Learning Algorithm for Continually Running Fully Recurrent Neural Networks*, Neural Computation **1**, 270-280, (1989).

Classifying with Gaussian Mixtures and Clusters

Nanda Kambhatla and Todd K. Leen
Department of Computer Science and Engineering
Oregon Graduate Institute of Science & Technology
P.O. Box 91000 Portland, OR 97291-1000
nanda@cse.ogi.edu, tleen@cse.ogi.edu

Abstract

In this paper, we derive classifiers which are *winner-take-all (WTA)* approximations to a Bayes classifier with Gaussian mixtures for class conditional densities. The derived classifiers include clustering based algorithms like LVQ and k-Means. We propose a *constrained rank Gaussian mixtures* model and derive a WTA algorithm for it. Our experiments with two speech classification tasks indicate that the constrained rank model and the WTA approximations improve the performance over the unconstrained models.

1 Introduction

A classifier assigns vectors from $\mathcal{R}^n$ (n dimensional feature space) to one of K classes, partitioning the feature space into a set of K disjoint regions. A *Bayesian* classifier builds the partition based on a model of the class conditional probability densities of the inputs (the partition is optimal for the given model).

In this paper, we assume that the class conditional densities are modeled by mixtures of Gaussians. Based on Nowlan's work relating Gaussian mixtures and clustering (Nowlan 1991), we derive *winner-take-all (WTA)* algorithms which approximate a Gaussian mixtures Bayes classifier. We also show the relationship of these algorithms to non-Bayesian cluster-based techniques like LVQ and k-Means.

The main problem with using Gaussian mixtures (or WTA algorithms thereof) is the explosion in the number of parameters with the input dimensionality. We propose a constrained rank Gaussian mixtures model for classification. Constraining the rank of the Gaussians reduces the effective number of model parameters thereby regularizing the model. We present the model and derive a WTA algorithm for it. Finally, we compare the performance of the different mixture models discussed in this paper for two speech classification tasks.

2 Gaussian Mixture Bayes (GMB) classifiers

Let x denote the feature vector ($x \in \mathcal{R}^n$), and $\{\Omega^I, I = 1, \ldots, K\}$ denote the classes. Class priors are denoted $p(\Omega^I)$ and the class-conditional densities are denoted $p(x \mid \Omega^I)$. The discriminant function for the Bayes classifier is

$$\delta^I(x) = p(\Omega^I) \ p(x \mid \Omega^I) . \tag{1}$$

An input feature vector x is assigned to class I if $\delta^I(x) > \delta^J(x) \ \forall J \neq I$. Given the class conditional densities, this choice minimizes the classification error rate (Duda and Hart 1973).

We model each class conditional density by a mixture composed of Q^I component Gaussians. The Bayes discriminant function (see Figure 1) becomes

$$\hat{\delta}^I(x) = p(\Omega^I) \sum_{j=1}^{Q^I} \frac{\alpha_j^I}{(2\pi)^{n/2}\sqrt{|\Sigma_j^I|}} \exp\left[-\frac{1}{2}(x - \mu_j^I)^T \Sigma_j^{I^{-1}} (x - \mu_j^I)\right] , \tag{2}$$

where μ_j^I and Σ_j^I are the mean and the covariance matrix of the jth mixture component for Ω^I.

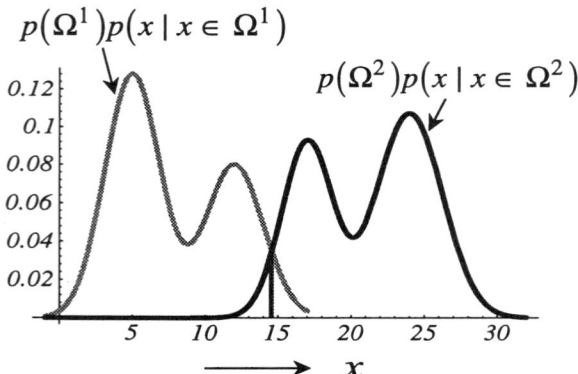

Fig. 1: Figure showing the decision rule of a GMB classifier for a two class problem with one input feature. The horizontal axis represents the feature and the vertical axis represents the Bayes discriminant functions. In this example, the class conditional densities are modelled as a mixture of two Gaussians and equal priors are assumed.

To implement the Gaussian mixture Bayes classifier (GMB) we first separate the training data into the different classes. We then use the EM algorithm (Dempster *et al* 1977, Nowlan 1991) to determine the parameters for the Gaussian mixture density for each class.

3 Winner-take-all approximations to GMB classifiers

In this section, we derive winner-take-all (WTA) approximations to GMB classifiers. We also show the relationship of these algorithms to non-Bayesian cluster-based techniques like LVQ and k-Means.

3.1 The WTA model for GMB

The WTA assumptions (relating hard clustering to Gaussian mixtures; see (Nowlan 1991)) are:

- $p(x \mid \Omega^I)$ are mixtures of Gaussians as in (2).
- The summation in (2) is dominated by the largest term. This is "equivalent to assigning all of the responsibility for an observation to the Gaussian with the highest probability of generating that observation" (Nowlan 1991).

To draw the relation between GMB and cluster-based classifiers, we further assume that:

- The mixing proportions (α_j^I) are equal for a given class.
- The number of mixture components Q^I is proportional to $p(\Omega^I)$.

Applying all the above assumptions to (2), taking logs and discarding the terms that are identical for each class, we get the discriminant function

$$\hat{\gamma}^I(x) = - \min_{j=1}^{Q^I} \left[\frac{1}{2}\log(|\Sigma_j^I|) + \frac{1}{2}(x - \mu_j^I)^T \Sigma_j^{I-1}(x - \mu_j^I) \right]. \quad (3)$$

The discriminant function (3) suggests an algorithm that approximates the Bayes classifier. We segregate the feature vectors by class and then train a separate vector quantizer (VQ) for each class. We then compute the means μ_j^I and the covariance matrices Σ_j^I for each Voronoi cell of each quantizer, and use (3) for classifying new patterns. We call this algorithm **VQ-Covariance**. Note that this algorithm *does not* do a maximum likelihood estimation of its parameters based on the probability model used to derive (3). The probability model is only used to classify patterns.

3.2 The relation to LVQ and k-Means

Further assume that for each class, the mixture components are spherically symmetric with covariance matrix $\Sigma_j^I = \sigma^2 I$, with σ^2 identical for all classes. We obtain the discriminant function,

$$\hat{\gamma}^I(x) = - \min_{j=1}^{Q^I} \| x - \mu_j^I \|^2. \quad (4)$$

This is exactly the discriminant function used by the learning vector quantizer (LVQ; Kohonen 1989) algorithm. Though LVQ employs a discriminatory training procedure (i.e it directly learns the class boundaries and does not *explicitly* build a separate model for each class), the implicit model of the class conditional densities used by LVQ corresponds to a GMB model under all the assumptions listed above. This is also the implicit model underlying any classifier which makes its classification decision based on the Euclidean distance measure between a feature vector and a set of prototype vectors (e.g. a k-Means clustering followed by classification based on (4)).

4 Constrained rank GMB classifiers

In the preceding sections, we have presented a GMB classifier and some WTA approximations to GMB. Mixture models such as GMB generally have too many parameters for small data sets. In this section, we propose a way of regularizing the mixture densities and derive a WTA classifier for the regularized model.

4.1 The constrained rank model

In section 2, we assumed that the class conditional densities of the feature vectors x are mixtures of Gaussians

$$
\begin{aligned}
p(x \mid \Omega^I) &= \sum_{j=1}^{Q^I} \frac{\alpha_j^I}{(2\pi)^{n/2}\sqrt{|\Sigma_j^I|}} \exp\left[-\frac{1}{2}(x-\mu_j^I)^T \Sigma_j^{I^{-1}}(x-\mu_j^I)\right] \\
&= \sum_{j=1}^{Q^I} \frac{\alpha_j^I}{(2\pi)^{n/2}\sqrt{\prod_{i=1}^n \lambda_{ji}^I}} \exp\left[-\frac{1}{2}(x-\mu_j^I)^T \left(\sum_{i=1}^n \frac{e_{ji}^I e_{ji}^{I\,T}}{\lambda_{ji}^I}\right)(x-\mu_j^I)\right]
\end{aligned}
\tag{5}
$$

where μ_j^I and Σ_j^I are the means and covariance matrices for the jth component Gaussian. e_{ji}^I and λ_{ji}^I are the orthonormal eigenvectors and eigenvalues of Σ_j^I (ordered such that $\lambda_{j1}^I \geq \ldots \geq \lambda_{jn}^I$). In (5), we have written the Mahalanobis distance in terms of the eigenvectors.

For a particular data point x, the Mahalanobis distance is very sensitive to changes in the squared projections onto the *trailing* eigen-directions, since the variances are very small in these directions. This is a potential problem with small data sets. When there are insufficient data points to estimate all the parameters of the mixture density accurately, the trailing eigen-directions and their associated eigenvalues are likely to be poorly estimated. Using the Mahalanobis distance in (5) can lead to erroneous results in such cases.

We propose a method for regularizing Gaussian mixture classifiers based on the above ideas. We assume that the trailing $n - m$ eigen-directions of each Gaussian component are inaccurate due to overfitting to the training set. We rewrite the class conditional densities (5) retaining only the leading m ($0 < m \leq n$) eigen-directions in the determinants and the Mahalanobis distances

$$p(x\,|\,\Omega^I) = \sum_{j=1}^{Q^I} \frac{\alpha_j^I}{(2\pi)^{m/2}\sqrt{\prod_{i=1}^m \lambda_{ji}^I}} \exp\left[-\frac{1}{2}(x-\mu_j^I)^T \left(\sum_{i=1}^m \frac{e_{ji}^I {e_{ji}^I}^T}{\lambda_{ji}^I}\right)(x-\mu_j^I)\right]. \tag{6}$$

We choose the value of m (the reduced rank) by cross-validation over a separate validation set. Thus, our model can be considered to be regularizing or constraining the class conditional mixture densities.

If we apply the above model and derive the Bayes discriminant functions (1), we get,

$$\hat{\delta}^I(x) = p(\Omega^I) \sum_{j=1}^{Q^I} \frac{\alpha_j^I}{(2\pi)^{m/2}\sqrt{\prod_{i=1}^m \lambda_{ji}^I}} \exp\left[-\frac{1}{2}(x-\mu_j^I)^T \left(\sum_{i=1}^m \frac{e_{ji}^I {e_{ji}^I}^T}{\lambda_{ji}^I}\right)(x-\mu_j^I)\right]. \tag{7}$$

We can implement a constrained rank Gaussian mixture Bayes (GMB-Reduced) classifier based on (7) using the EM algorithm to determine the parameters of the mixture density for each class. We segregate the data into different classes and use the EM algorithm to determine the parameters of the full mixture density (5). We then use (7) to classify patterns.

4.2 A constrained rank WTA algorithm

We now derive a winner-take-all (WTA) approximation for the constrained rank mixture model described above. We assume (similar to section 3.1) that

- $p(x\,|\,\Omega^I)$ are constrained mixtures of Gaussians as in (6).
- The summation in (6) is dominated by the largest term (the *WTA* assumption).
- The mixing proportions (α_j^I) are equal for a given class and the number of components Q^I is proportional to $p(\Omega^I)$.

Applying these assumptions to (7), taking logs and discarding the terms that are identical for each class, we get the discriminant function

$$\hat{\gamma}^I(x) = -\min_{j=1}^{Q^I} \left[\frac{1}{2}\sum_{i=1}^m \log(\lambda_{ji}^I) + \frac{1}{2}(x-\mu_j^I)^T \left(\sum_{i=1}^m \frac{e_{ji}^I {e_{ji}^I}^T}{\lambda_{ji}^I}\right)(x-\mu_j^I)\right]. \tag{8}$$

It is interesting to compare (8) with (3). Our model postulates that the trailing $n-m$ eigen-directions of each Gaussian represent overfitting to noise in the training set. The discriminant functions reflect this; (8) retains only those terms of (3) which are in the leading m eigen-directions of each Gaussian.

We can generate an algorithm based on (8) that approximates the reduced rank Bayes classifier. We separate the data based on classes and train a separate vector quantizer (VQ) for each class. We then compute the means μ_j^I, the covariance matrices Σ_j^I for each Voronoi cell of each quantizer and the orthonormal eigenvectors

Table 1: The **test set** classification accuracies for the TIMIT vowels data for different algorithms.

ALGORITHM	ACCURACY
MLP (40 nodes in hidden layer)	46.8%
GMB (1 component; full)	41.4%
GMB (1 component; diagonal)	46.3%
GMB-Reduced (1 component; 13-D)	51.2%
VQ-Covariance (1 component)	41.4%
VQ-Covariance-Reduced (1 component; 13-D)	51.2%
LVQ (48 cells)	41.4%

$e_j^I i$ and eigenvalues λ_j^I for each covariance matrix Σ_j^I. We use (8) for classifying new patterns. Notice that the algorithm described above is a reduced rank version of VQ-Covariance (described in section 3.1). We call this algorithm **VQ-Covariance-Reduced**.

5 Experimental Results

In this section we compare the different mixture models and a multi layer perceptron (MLP) for two speech phoneme classification tasks. The measure used is the classification accuracy.

5.1 TIMIT data

The first task is the classification of 12 monothongal vowels from the TIMIT database (Fisher and Doddington 1986). Each feature vector consists of the lowest 32 DFT coefficients, time-averaged over the central third of the vowel. We partitioned the data into a training set (1200 vectors), a validation set (408 vectors) for model selection, and a test set (408 vectors). The training set contained 100 examples of each class. The values of the free parameters for the algorithms (the number of component densities, number of hidden nodes for the MLP etc.) were selected by maximizing the performance on the validation set.

Table 1 shows the results obtained with different algorithms. The constrained rank models (GMB-Reduced and VQ-Covariance-Reduced[1]) perform much better than all the unconstrained ones and even beat a MLP for this task. This data set consists of very few data points per class, and hence is particularly susceptible to overfitting by algorithms with a large number of parameters (like GMB). It is not surprising that constraining the number of model parameters is a big win for this task.

---

[1]Note that since the best validation set performance is obtained with only one component for each mixture density, the WTA algorithms are identical to the GMB algorithms (for these results).

Table 2: The **test set** classification accuracies for the CENSUS data for different algorithms.

ALGORITHM	ACCURACY
MLP (80 nodes in hidden layer)	88.2%
GMB (1 component; full)	77.2%
GMB (8 components; diagonal)	70.9%
GMB-Reduced (2 components; 35-D)	82.5%
VQ-Covariance (3 components)	77.5%
VQ-Covariance-Reduced (4 components; 38-D)	84.2%
LVQ (55 cells)	67.3%

5.2 CENSUS data

The next task we experimented with was the classification of 9 vowels (found in the utterances of the days of the week). The data was drawn from the CENSUS speech corpus (Cole et al 1994). Each feature vector was 70 dimensional (perceptual linear prediction (PLP) coefficients (Hermansky 1990) over the vowel and surrounding context). We partitioned the data into a training set (8997 vectors), a validation set (1362 vectors) for model selection, and a test set (1638 vectors). The training set had close to a 1000 vectors per class. The values of the free parameters for the different algorithms were selected by maximizing the validation set performance.

Table 2 gives a summary of the classification accuracies obtained using the different algorithms. This data set has a lot more data points per class than the TIMIT data set. The best accuracy is obtained by a MLP, though the constrained rank mixture models still greatly outperform the unconstrained ones.

6 Discussion

We have derived WTA approximations to GMB classifiers and shown their relation to LVQ and k-Means algorithms. The main problem with Gaussian mixture models is the explosion in the number of model parameters with input dimensionality, resulting in poor generalization performance. We propose *constrained rank* Gaussian mixture models for classification. This approach ignores some directions (*"noise"*) locally in the input space, and thus reduces the effective number of model parameters. This can be considered as a way of regularizing the mixture models. Our results with speech vowel classification indicate that this approach works better than using full mixture models, especially when the data set size is small.

The WTA algorithms proposed in this paper do not perform a maximum likelihood estimation of their parameters. The probability model is only used to classify data. We can potentially improve the performance of these algorithms by doing maximum likelihood training with respect to the models presented here.

Acknowledgments

This work was supported by grants from the Air Force Office of Scientific Research (F49620-93-1-0253), Electric Power Research Institute (RP8015-2) and the Office of Naval Research (N00014-91-J-1482). We would like to thank Joachim Utans, OGI for several useful discussions and Zoubin Ghahramani, MIT for providing MATLAB code for the EM algorithm. We also thank our colleagues in the Center for Spoken Language Understanding at OGI for providing speech data.

References

R.A. Cole, D.G. Novick, D. Burnett, B. Hansen, S. Sutton, M. Fanty. (1994) Towards Automatic Collection of the U.S. Census. *Proceedings of the International Conference on Acoustics, Speech and Signal Processing 1994.*

A.P. Dempster, N.M. Laird, and D.B. Rubin. (1977) Maximum Likelihood from Incomplete Data via the EM Algorithm. *J. Royal Statistical Society Series B*, vol. 39, pp. 1-38.

R.O. Duda and P.E. Hart. (1973) Pattern Classification and Scene Analysis. John Wiley and Sons Inc.

W.M Fisher and G.R Doddington. (1986) The DARPA speech recognition database: specification and status. In *Proceedings of the DARPA Speech Recognition Workshop*, p93-99, Palo Alto CA.

H. Hermansky. (1990) Perceptual Linear Predictive (PLP) analysis of speech. *J. Acoust. Soc. Am.*, 87(4):1738-1752.

T. Kohonen. (1989) Self-Organization and Associative Memory (3rd edition). Berlin: Springer-Verlag.

S.J. Nowlan. (1991) Soft Competitive Adaptation: Neural Network Learning Algorithms based on Fitting Statistical Mixtures. CMU-CS-91-126 PhD thesis, School of Computer Science, Carnegie Mellon University.

Efficient Methods for Dealing with Missing Data in Supervised Learning

Volker Tresp[*]
Siemens AG
Central Research
Otto-Hahn-Ring 6
81730 München
Germany

Ralph Neuneier
Siemens AG
Central Research
Otto-Hahn-Ring 6
81730 München
Germany

Subutai Ahmad
Interval Research Corporation
1801-C Page Mill Rd.
Palo Alto, CA 94304

Abstract

We present efficient algorithms for dealing with the problem of missing inputs (incomplete feature vectors) during training and recall. Our approach is based on the approximation of the input data distribution using Parzen windows. For recall, we obtain closed form solutions for arbitrary feedforward networks. For training, we show how the backpropagation step for an incomplete pattern can be approximated by a weighted averaged backpropagation step. The complexity of the solutions for training and recall is independent of the number of missing features. We verify our theoretical results using one classification and one regression problem.

1 Introduction

The problem of missing data (incomplete feature vectors) is of great practical and theoretical interest. In many applications it is important to know how to react if the available information is incomplete, if sensors fail or if sources of information become

---

[*] At the time of the research for this paper, a visiting researcher at the Center for Biological and Computational Learning, MIT. E-mail: Volker.Tresp@zfe.siemens.de

unavailable. As an example, when a sensor fails in a production process, it might not be necessary to stop everything if sufficient information is implicitly contained in the remaining sensor data. Furthermore, in economic forecasting, one might want to continue to use a predictor even when an input variable becomes meaningless (for example, due to political changes in a country). As we have elaborated in earlier papers, heuristics such as the substitution of the mean for an unknown feature can lead to solutions that are far from optimal (Ahmad and Tresp, 1993, Tresp, Ahmad, and Neuneier, 1994). Biological systems must deal continuously with the problem of unknown uncertain features and they are certainly extremely good at it. From a biological point of view it is therefore interesting which solutions to this problem can be derived from theory and if these solutions are in any way related to the way that biology deals with this problem (compare Brunelli and Poggio, 1991). Finally, having efficient methods for dealing with missing features allows a novel pruning strategy: if the quality of the prediction is not affected if an input is pruned, we can remove it and use our solutions for prediction with missing inputs or retrain the model without that input (Tresp, Hollatz and Ahmad, 1995).

In Ahmad and Tresp (1993) and in Tresp, Ahmad and Neuneier (1994) equations for training and recall were derived using a probabilistic setting (compare also Buntine and Weigend, 1991, Ghahramani and Jordan, 1994). For general feedforward neural networks the solution was in the form of an integral which has to be approximated using numerical integration techniques. The computational complexity of these solutions grows exponentially with the number of missing features. In these two publications, we could only obtain efficient algorithms for networks of normalized Gaussian basis functions. It is of great practical interest to find efficient ways of dealing with missing inputs for general feedforward neural networks which are more commonly used in applications. In this paper we describe an efficient approximation for the problem of missing information that is applicable to a large class of learning algorithms, including feedforward networks. The main results are Equation 2 (recall) and Equation 3 (training). One major advantage of the proposed solution is that the complexity does not increase with an increasing number of missing inputs. The solutions can easily be generalized to the problem of uncertain (noisy) inputs.

2 Missing Information During Recall

2.1 Theory

We assume that a neural network $NN(x)$ has been trained to predict $E(y|x)$, the expectation of $y \in \Re$ given $x \in \Re^D$. During recall we would like to know the network's prediction based on an incomplete input vector $x = (x^c, x^u)$ where x^c denotes the known inputs and x^u the unknown inputs. The optimal prediction given the known features can be written as (Ahmad and Tresp, 1993)

$$E(y|x^c) = \int E(y|x^c, x^u) P(x^u|x^c) \, dx^u \approx \frac{1}{P(x^c)} \int NN(x^c, x^u) P(x^c, x^u) \, dx^u.$$

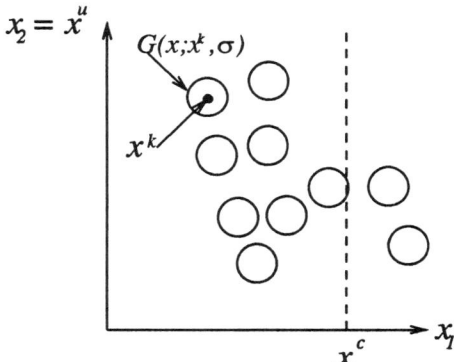

Figure 1: The circles indicate 10 Gaussians approximating the input density distribution. $x^c = x_1$ indicates the known input, $x_2 = x^u$ is unknown.

Similarly, for a network trained to estimate class probabilities, $NN_i(x) \approx P(class_i|x)$, simply substitute $P(class_i|x^c)$ for $E(y|x^c)$ and $NN_i(x^c, x^u)$ for $NN(x^c, x^u)$ in the last equation.

The integrals in the last equations can be problematic. In the worst case they have to be approximated numerically (Tresp, Ahmad and Neuneier, 1994) which is costly, since the computation is exponential in the number of missing inputs. For networks of normalized Gaussians, there exist closed form solutions to the integrals (Ahmad and Tresp, 1993). The following section shows how to efficiently approximate the integral for a large class of algorithms.

2.2 An Efficient Approximation

Parzen windows are commonly used to approximate densities. Given N training data $\{(x^k, y^k)|k = 1, ..., N\}$, we can approximate

$$P(x) \approx \frac{1}{N} \sum_{k=1}^{N} G(x; x^k, \sigma) \qquad (1)$$

where

$$G(x; x^k, \sigma) = \frac{1}{(2\pi\sigma^2)^{D/2}} \exp(-\frac{1}{2\sigma^2}||x - x^k||^2)$$

is a multidimensional properly normalized Gaussian centered at data x^k with variance σ^2. It has been shown (Duda and Hart (1973)) that Parzen windows approximate densities for $N \to \infty$ arbitrarily well, if σ is appropriately scaled.

Using Parzen windows we may write

$$E(y|x^c) \approx \frac{1}{\sum_{k=1}^{N} G(x^c; x^{c,k}, \sigma)} \sum_{k=1}^{N} [\int NN(x^c, x^u) \, G(x^c, x^u; x^k, \sigma) \, dx^u]$$

where we have used the fact that

$$P(x^c) \approx \frac{1}{N} \sum_{k=1}^{N} G(x^c; x^{c,k}, \sigma)$$

and where $G(x^c; x^{c,k}, \sigma)$ is a Gaussian projected onto the known input dimensions (by simply leaving out the unknown dimensions in the exponent and in the normalization, see Ahmad and Tresp, 1993). $x^{c,k}$ are the components of the training data corresponding to the known input (compare Figure 1).

Now, if we assume that the network prediction is approximately constant over the "width" of the Gaussians, σ, we can approximate

$$\int NN(x^c, x^u) \, G(x^c, x^u; x^k, \sigma) \, dx^u \approx NN(x^c, x^{u,k}) \, G(x^c; x^{c,k}, \sigma)$$

where $NN(x^c, x^{u,k})$ is the network prediction which we obtain if we substituted the corresponding components of the training data for the unknown inputs.

With this approximation,

$$E(y|x^c) \approx \frac{\sum_{k=1}^{N} \alpha_k \, G(x^c; x^{c,k}, \sigma)}{\sum_{k=1}^{N} G(x^c; x^{c,k}, \sigma)}, \quad \alpha_k = NN(x^c, x^{u,k}). \tag{2}$$

Interestingly, we have obtained a network of normalized Gaussians which are centered at the known components of the data points. The "output weights" $NN(x^c, x^{u,k})$ consist of the neural network predictions where for the unknown input the corresponding components of the training data points have been substituted. Note, that we have obtained an approximation which has the same structure as the solution for normalized Gaussian basis functions (Ahmad and Tresp, 1994).

In many applications it might be easy to select a reasonable value for σ using prior knowledge but there are also two simple ways to obtain a good estimate for σ using leave-one-out methods. The first method consists of removing the $k-th$ pattern from the training data and calculating $\tilde{P}(x^k) \approx \frac{1}{N-1} \sum_{l=1, l \neq k}^{N} G(x^k; x^l, \sigma)$. Then select the σ for which the log likelihood $\sum_k \log \tilde{P}(x^k)$ is maximum. The second method consists of treating an input of the $k-th$ training pattern as missing and then testing how well our algorithm (Equation 2) can predict the target. Select the σ which gives the best performance. In this way it would even be possible to select input-dimension-specific widths σ_i leading to "elliptical", axis-parallel Gaussians (Ahmad and Tresp, 1993).

Note that the complexity of the solution is independent of the number of missing inputs! In contrast, the complexity of the solution for feedforward networks suggested in Tresp, Ahmad and Neuneier (1994) grows exponentially with the number of missing inputs. Although similar in character to the solution for normalized RBFs, here we have no restrictions on the network architecture which allows us to choose the network most appropriate for the application.

If the amount of training data is large, one can use the following approximations:

- Select only the K nearest data points. The distance is determined based on the known inputs. K can probably be reasonably small (< 10). In the extreme case, $K = 1$ and we obtain a nearest-neighbor solution. Efficient tree-based algorithms exist for computing the K-nearest neighbors.

- Use Gaussian mixtures instead of Parzen windows to estimate the input data distribution. Use the centers and variances of the components in Equation 2.

- Use a clustering algorithm and use the cluster centers instead of the data points in Equation 2.

Note that the solution which substitutes the components of the training data closest to the input seems biologically plausible.

2.3 Experimental Results

We tested our algorithm using the same data as in Ahmad and Tresp, 1993. The task was to recognize a hand gesture based on its 2D projection. As input, the classifier is given the 2D polar coordinates of the five finger tip positions relative to the 2D center of mass of the hand (the input space is therefore 10-D). A multi-layer perceptron was trained on 4368 examples (624 poses for each gesture) and tested on a similar independent test set. The inputs were normalized to a variance of one and σ was set to 0.1. (For a complete description of the task see (Ahmad and Tresp, 1993).) As in (Ahmad & Tresp, 1993) we defined a correct classification as one in which the correct class was either classified as the most probable or the second most probable. Figure 2 shows experimental results. On the horizontal axis, the number of randomly chosen missing inputs is shown. The continuous line shows the performance using Equation 2 where we used only the 10 nearest neighbors in the approximation. Even with 5 missing inputs we obtain a score of over 90 % which is slightly better than the solution we obtained in Ahmad and Tresp (1993) for normalized RBFs. We expect our new solution to perform very well in general since we can always choose the best network for prediction and are not restricted in the architecture. As a benchmark we also included the case where the mean of the missing input was substituted. With 5 missing inputs, the performance is less than 60 %.

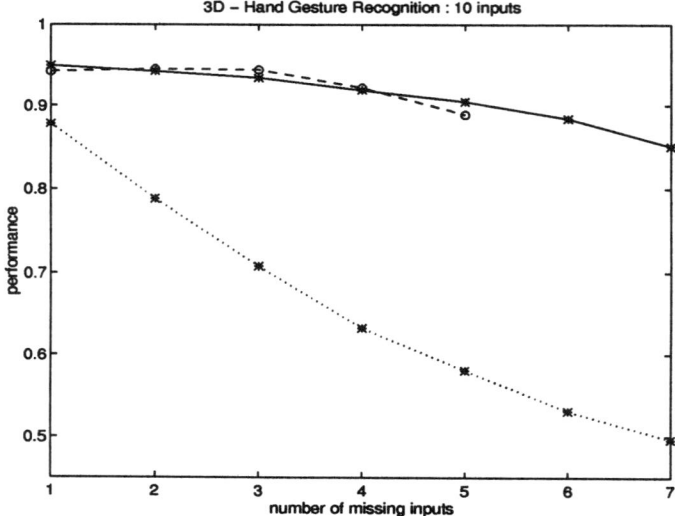

Figure 2: Experimental results using a generalization data set. The continuous line indicates the performance using our proposed method. The dotted lines indicate the performance if the mean of the missing input variable is substituted. As a comparison, we included the results obtained in Ahmad and Tresp (1993) using the closed-form solution for RBF-networks (dashed).

3 Training (Backpropagation)

For a complete pattern (x^k, y^k), the weight update of a backpropagation step for weight w_j is

$$\Delta w_j \propto (y^k - NN_w(x^k)) \frac{\partial NN_w(x^k)}{\partial w_j}.$$

Using the approximation of Equation 1, we obtain for an incomplete data point (compare Tresp, Ahmad and Neuneier, 1994)

$$\Delta w_j \propto \frac{\sum_{l \in compl} \alpha_l \ G(y^k; NN_w(x^{c,k}, x^{u,l}), \sigma_y) \ G(x^{c,k}; x^{c,l}, \sigma)}{\sum_{l \in compl} G(y^k; NN_w(x^{c,k}, x^{u,l}), \sigma_y) \ G(x^{c,k}; x^{c,l}, \sigma)}. \quad (3)$$

Here, $l \in compl$ indicates the sum over complete patterns in the training set, and σ_y is the standard deviation of the output noise. Note that the gradient is a network of normalized Gaussian basis functions where the "output-weight" is now

$$\alpha_l = (y^k - NN_w(x^{c,k} x^{u,l})) \frac{\partial NN_w(x^{c,k} x^{u,l})}{\partial w_j}$$

The derivation of the last equation can be found in the Appendix. Figure 3 shows experimental results.

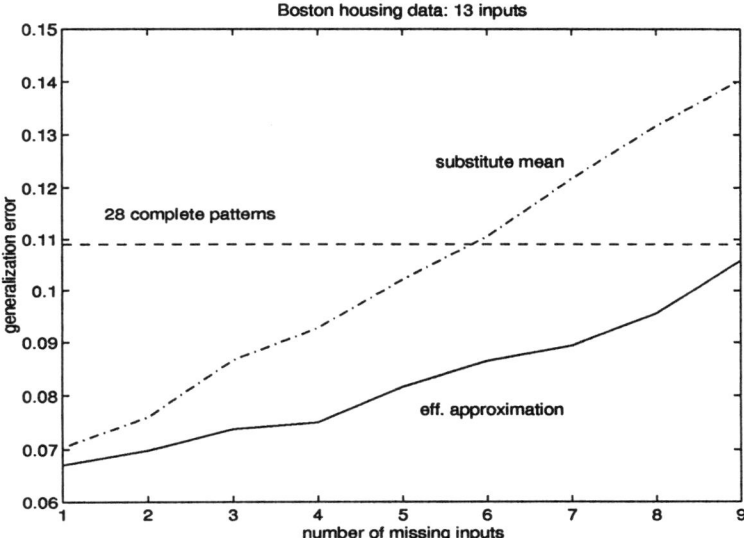

Figure 3: In the experiment, we used the Boston housing data set, which consists of 506 samples. The task is to predict the housing price from 13 variables which were thought to influence the housing price in a neighborhood. The network (multi-layer perceptron) was trained with 28 complete patterns plus an additional 225 incomplete samples. The horizontal axis indicates how many inputs were missing in these 225 samples. The vertical axis shows the generalization performance. The continuous line indicates the performance of our approach and the dash-dotted line indicates the performance, if the mean is substituted for a missing variable. The dashed line indicates the performance of a network only trained with the 28 complete patterns.

4 Conclusions

We have obtained efficient and robust solutions for the problem of recall and training with missing data. Experimental results verified our method. All of our results can easily be generalized to the case of noisy inputs.

Acknowledgement

Valuable discussions with Hans-Georg Zimmermann, Tomaso Poggio, Michael Jordan and Zoubin Ghahramani are greatfully acknowledged. The first author would like to thank the Center for Biological and Computational Learning (MIT) for providing and excellent research environment during the summer of 1994.

5 Appendix

Assuming the standard signal-plus-Gaussian-noise model we obtain for a complete sample
$$P(x^k, y^k | \{w_i\}) = G(y^k; NN_w(x^k), \sigma_y) \, P(x^k)$$
where $\{w_i\}$ is the set of weights in the network. For an incomplete sample
$$P(x^{c,k}, y^k | \{w_i\}) = \frac{1}{P(x^{c,k}, y^k)} \int G(y^k; NN_w(x^{c,k}, x^u), \sigma_y) \, P(x^{c,k}, x^u) \, dx^u.$$
Using the same approximation as in Section 2.2,
$$P(x^{c,k}, y^k | \{w_i\}) \approx \sum_{l \in compl} G(y^k; NN_w(x^{c,k}, x^{u,l}), \sigma_y) \, G(x^{c,k}; x^{c,l}, \sigma)$$
where l sums over all complete samples. As before, we substitute for the missing components the ones from the complete training data. The log-likelihood $\mathcal{L}$ (a function of the network weights $\{w_i\}$) can be calculated as (x^k can be either complete or incomplete) $\mathcal{L} = \sum_{k=1}^{N} \log P(x^k, y^k | \{w_i\})$. The maximum likelihood solution consists of finding weights $\{w_i\}$ which maximize the log-likelihood. Using the approximation of Equation 1, we obtain for an incomplete sample as gradient Equation 3 (compare Tresp, Ahmad and Neuneier, 1994).

References

Ahmad, S. and Tresp, V. (1993). Some Solutions to the Missing Feature Problem in Vision. In S. J. Hanson, J. D. Cowan and C. L. Giles, (Eds.), *Advances in Neural Information Processing Systems 5,* San Mateo, CA: Morgan Kaufmann.

Brunelli, R. and Poggio, T. (1991). *HyperBF Networks for Real Object Recognition.* IJCAI.

Buntine, W. L. and Weigend, A. S. (1991). Bayesian Back-Propagation. *Complex systems,* Vol. 5, pp. 605-643.

Duda, R. O. and Hart, P. E. (1973). *Pattern Classification and Scene Analysis.* John Wiley and Sons, New York.

Ghahramani, Z. and Jordan, M. I. (1994). Supervised Learning from Incomplete Data via an EM approach. In: Cowan, J. D., Tesauro, G., and Alspector, J., eds., *Advances in Neural Information Processing Systems 6,* San Mateo, CA, Morgan Kaufman.

Tresp, V., Ahmad, S. and Neuneier, R. (1994). Training Neural Networks with Deficient Data. In: Cowan, J. D., Tesauro, G., and Alspector, J., eds., *Advances in Neural Information Processing Systems 6,* San Mateo, CA, Morgan Kaufman.

Tresp, V., Hollatz, J. and Ahmad, S. (1995). Representing Probabilistic Rules with Networks of Gaussian Basis Functions. Accepted for publication in *Machine Learning.*

An experimental comparison of recurrent neural networks

Bill G. Horne and C. Lee Giles[*]
NEC Research Institute
4 Independence Way
Princeton, NJ 08540
{horne,giles}@research.nj.nec.com

Abstract

Many different discrete–time recurrent neural network architectures have been proposed. However, there has been virtually no effort to compare these architectures experimentally. In this paper we review and categorize many of these architectures and compare how they perform on various classes of simple problems including grammatical inference and nonlinear system identification.

1 Introduction

In the past few years several recurrent neural network architectures have emerged. In this paper we categorize various discrete–time recurrent neural network architectures, and perform a quantitative comparison of these architectures on two problems: grammatical inference and nonlinear system identification.

2 RNN Architectures

We broadly divide these networks into two groups depending on whether or not the states of the network are guaranteed to be observable. A network with observable states has the property that the states of the system can always be determined from observations of the input and output alone. The archetypical model in this class

---

[*]Also with UMIACS, University of Maryland, College Park, MD 20742

Table 1: Terms that are weighted in various single layer network architectures. u_i represents the ith input at the current time step, z_i represents the value of the jth node at the previous time step.

Architecture	bias	u_i	z_i	$u_i u_j$	$z_i u_j$	$z_i z_j$
First order	x	x	x			
High order					x	
Bilinear		x	x		x	
Quadratic	x	x	x	x	x	x

was proposed by Narendra and Parthasarathy [9]. In their most general model, the output of the network is computed by a multilayer perceptron (MLP) whose inputs are a window of past inputs and outputs, as shown in Figure 1a. A special case of this network is the Time Delay Neural Network (TDNN), which is simply a tapped delay line (TDL) followed by an MLP [7]. This network is not recurrent since there is no feedback; however, the TDL does provide a simple form of dynamics that gives the network the ability model a limited class of nonlinear dynamic systems. A variation on the TDNN, called the Gamma network, has been proposed in which the TDL is replaced by a set of cascaded filters [2]. Specifically, if the output of one of the filters is denoted $x_j(k)$, and the output of filter i connects to the input of filter j, the output of filter j is given by,

$$x_j(k+1) = \mu x_i(k) + (1-\mu)x_j(k).$$

In this paper we only consider the case where μ is fixed, although better results can be obtained if it is adaptive.

Networks that have hidden dynamics have states which are not directly accessible to observation. In fact, it may be impossible to determine the states of a system from observations of it's inputs and outputs alone. We divide networks with hidden dynamics into three classes: single layer networks, multilayer networks, and networks with local feedback.

Single layer networks are perhaps the most popular of the recurrent neural network models. In a single layer network, every node depends on the previous output of all of the other nodes. The function performed by each node distinguishes the types of recurrent networks in this class. In each of the networks, nodes can be characterized as a nonlinear function of a weighted sum of inputs, previous node outputs, or products of these values. A bias term may also be included. In this paper we consider first–order networks, high–order networks [5], bilinear networks, and Quadratic networks[12]. The terms that are weighted in each of these networks are summarized in Table 1.

Multilayer networks consist of a feedforward network coupled with a finite set of delays as shown in Figure 1b. One network in this class is an architecture proposed by Robinson and Fallside [11], in which the feedforward network is an MLP. Another popular networks that fits into this class is Elman's Simple Recurrent Network (SRN) [3]. An Elman network can be thought of as a single layer network with an extra layer of nodes that compute the output function, as shown in Figure 1c.

In locally recurrent networks the feedback is provided locally within each individual

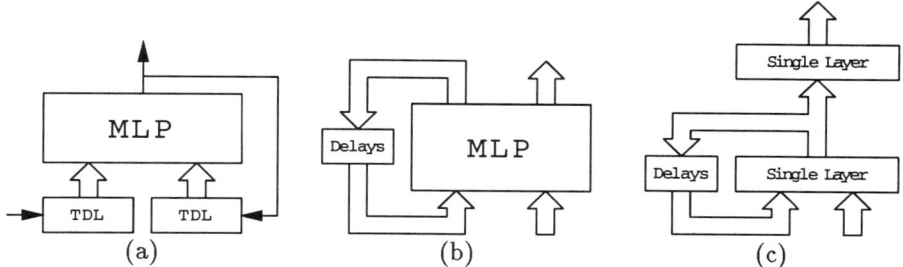

Figure 1: Network architectures: (a) Narendra and Parthasarathy's Recurrent Neural Network, (b) Multilayer network and (c) an Elman network.

node, but the nodes are connected together in a feed forward architecture. Specifically, we consider nodes that have local output feedback in which each node weights a window of its own past outputs and windows of node outputs from previous layers. Networks with local recurrence have been proposed in [1, 4, 10].

3 Experimental Results

3.1 Experimental methodology

In order to make the comparison as fair as possible we have adopted the following methodology.

- **Resources.** We shall perform two fundamental comparisons. One in which the number of weights is roughly the same for all networks, another in which the number of states is equivalent. In either case, we shall make these numbers large enough that most of the networks can achieve interesting performance levels.

  Number of weights. For static networks it is well known that the generalization performance is related to the number of weights in the network. Although this theory has never been extended to recurrent neural networks, it seems reasonable that a similar result might apply. Therefore, in some experiments we shall try to keep the number of weights approximately equal across all networks.

  Number of states. It can be argued that for dynamic problems the size of the state space is a more relevant measure for comparison than the number of weights. Therefore, in some experiments we shall keep the number of states equal across all networks.

- **Vanilla learning.** Several heuristics have been proposed to help speed learning and improve generalization of gradient descent learning algorithms. However, such heuristics may favor certain architectures. In order to avoid these issues, we have chosen simple gradient descent learning algorithms.

- **Number of simulations.** Due to random initial conditions, the recurrent neural network solutions can vary widely. Thus, to try to achieve a statistically significant estimation of the generalization of these networks, a large number of experiments were run.

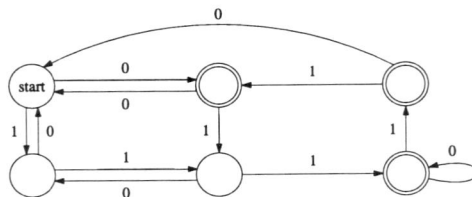

Figure 2: A randomly generated six state finite state machine.

3.2 Finite state machines

We chose two finite state machine (FSM) problems for a comparison of the ability of the various recurrent networks to perform grammatical inference. The first problem is to learn the minimal, randomly generated six state machine shown in Figure 2. The second problem is to infer a sixty–four state finite memory machine [6] described by the logic function

$$y(k) = \bar{u}(k-3)\bar{u}(k) + \bar{u}(k-3)y(k-3) + u(k)u(k-3)\bar{y}(k-3)$$

where $u(k)$ and $y(k)$ represent the input and output respectively at time k and $\bar{x}$ represents the complement of x.

Two experiments were run. In the first experiment all of the networks were designed such that the number of weights was less than, but as close to 60 as possible. In the second experiment, each network was restricted to six state variables, and if possible, the networks were designed to have approximately 75 weights. Several alternative architectures were tried when it was possible to configure the architecture differently and yield the same number of weights, but those used gave the best results.

A complete set of 254 strings consisting of all strings of length one through seven is sufficient to uniquely identify both of these FSMs. For each simulation, we randomly partitioned the data into a training and testing set consisting of 127 strings each. The strings were ordered lexographically in the training set.

For each architecture 100 runs were performed on each problem. The on–line Back Propagation Through Time (BPTT) algorithm was used to train the networks. Vanilla learning was used with a learning rate of 0.5. Training was stopped at 1000 epochs. The weights of all networks were initialized to random values uniformly distributed in the range $[-0.1, 0.1]$. All states were initialize to zeros at the beginning of each string except for the High Order net in which one state was arbitrarily initialized to a value of 1.

Table 2 summarizes the statistics for each experiment. From these results we draw the following conclusions.

- The bilinear and high–order networks do best on the small randomly generated machine, but poorly on the finite memory machine. Thus, it would appear that there is benefit to having second order terms in the network, at least for small finite state machine problems.
- Narendra and Parthasarathy's model and the network with local recurrence do far better than the other networks on the problem of inferring the finite memory

Table 2: Percentage classification error on the FSM experiment for (a) networks with approximately the same number of weights, (b) networks with the same number of state variables. %P = The percentage of trials in which the training set was learned perfectly, #W = the number of weights, and #S = the number of states.

FSM	Architecture[†]	training error mean	(std)	testing error mean	(std)	% P	# W	#S
RND	N & P	2.8	(4.4)	16.9	(8.6)	22	56	8
	TDNN	12.5	(2.1)	33.8	(4.1)	0	56	8
	Gamma	19.6	(2.4)	24.8	(3.2)	0	56	8
	First Order	12.9	(6.9)	26.5	(9.0)	0	48	6
	High Order	0.8	(1.5)	6.2	(6.1)	60	50	5
	Bilinear	1.3	(2.7)	5.7	(6.1)	46	55	5
	Quadratic	12.9	(13.4)	17.7	(14.1)	12	45	3
	Multilayer	19.4	(13.6)	23.4	(13.5)	6	54	4
	Elman	3.5	(5.5)	12.7	(9.1)	27	55	6
	Local	2.8	(1.5)	26.7	(7.6)	4	60	20
FMM	N & P	0.0	(0.2)	0.1	(1.1)	99	56	8
	TDNN	6.9	(2.1)	15.8	(3.2)	0	56	8
	Gamma	7.7	(2.2)	15.7	(3.3)	0	56	8
	First Order	4.8	(3.0)	16.0	(6.5)	1	48	6
	High Order	5.3	(4.0)	26.0	(5.1)	1	50	5
	Bilinear	9.5	(10.4)	25.8	(7.0)	0	55	5
	Quadratic	32.5	(10.8)	40.5	(7.3)	0	45	3
	Multilayer	36.7	(11.9)	43.5	(8.5)	0	54	4
	Elman	12.0	(12.5)	24.9	(7.9)	5	55	6
	Local	0.1	(0.3)	1.0	(3.0)	97	60	20

(a)

FSM	Architecture[††]	training error mean	(std)	testing error mean	(std)	% P	# W	#S
RND	N & P	4.6	(8.4)	14.1	(11.3)	38	73	6
	TDNN	11.7	(2.0)	34.3	(3.9)	0	73	6
	Gamma	19.0	(2.4)	25.2	(3.1)	0	74	6
	First Order	12.9	(6.9)	26.5	(9.0)	0	48	6
	High Order	0.3	(0.5)	4.6	(5.1)	79	74	6
	Bilinear	0.6	(0.9)	4.4	(4.6)	55	78	6
	Quadratic	0.2	(0.5)	3.2	(2.6)	83	216	6
	Multilayer	15.4	(14.1)	19.9	(14.4)	16	76	6
	Elman	3.5	(5.5)	12.7	(9.1)	27	55	6
	Local	13.9	(4.5)	20.2	(5.7)	0	26	6
FMM	N & P	0.1	(0.8)	0.3	(1.4)	97	73	6
	TDNN	6.8	(1.7)	16.2	(2.9)	0	73	6
	Gamma	9.0	(2.9)	14.9	(2.8)	0	73	6
	First Order	4.8	(3.0)	16.0	(6.5)	1	48	6
	High Order	1.2	(1.7)	25.1	(5.1)	31	74	6
	Bilinear	2.6	(4.2)	20.3	(7.2)	21	78	6
	Quadratic	12.6	(17.3)	26.1	(12.8)	13	216	6
	Multilayer	38.1	(12.6)	42.8	(9.2)	0	76	6
	Elman	12.8	(14.8)	27.6	(10.7)	8	55	6
	Local	15.3	(3.8)	22.2	(4.9)	0	26	6

(b)

[†]The TDNN and Gamma network both had 8 input taps and 4 hidden layer nodes. For the Gamma network, $\mu = 0.3$ (RND) and $\mu = 0.7$ (FMM). Narendra and Parthasarathy's network had 4 input and output taps and 5 hidden layer nodes. The High–order network used a "one–hot" encoding of the input values [5]. The multilayer network had 4 hidden and output layer nodes. The locally recurrent net had 4 hidden layer nodes with 5 input and 3 output taps, and one output node with 3 input and output taps.

[††]The TDNN, Gamma network, and Narendra and Parthasarathy's network all had 8 hidden layer nodes. For the Gamma network, $\mu = 0.3$ (RND) and $\mu = 0.7$ (FMM). The High–order network again used a "one–hot" encoding of the input values. The multilayer network had 5 hidden and 6 output layer nodes. The locally recurrent net had 3 hidden layer nodes and one output layer node, all with only one input and output tap.

machine when the number of states is not constrained. It is not surprising that the former network did so well since the sequential machine implementation of a finite memory machine is similar to this architecture [6]. However, the result for the locally recurrent network was unexpected.

- All of the recurrent networks do better than the TDNN on the small random machine. However, on the finite memory machine the TDNN does surprisingly well, perhaps because its structure is similiar to Narendra and Parthasarathy's network which was well suited for this problem.
- Gradient–based learning algorithms are not adequate for many of these architectures. In many cases a network is capable of representing a solution to a problem that the algorithm was not able to find. This seems particularly true for the Multilayer network.
- Not surprisingly, an increase in the number of weights typically leads to overtraining. Although, the quadratic network, which has 216 weights, can consistently find solutions for the random machine that generalize well even though there are only 127 training samples.
- Although the performance on the training set is not always a good indicator of generalization performance on the testing set, we find that if a network is able to frequently find perfect solutions for the training data, then it also does well on the testing data.

3.3 Nonlinear system identification

In this problem, we train the network to learn the dynamics of the following set of equations proposed in [8]

$$x_1(k+1) = \frac{x_1(k) + 2x_2(k)}{1 + x_2^2(k)} + u(k)$$

$$x_2(k+1) = \frac{x_1(k)x_2(k)}{1 + x_2^2(k)} + u(k)$$

$$y(k) = x_1(k) + x_2(k)$$

based on observations of $u(k)$ and $y(k)$ alone.

The same networks that were used for the finite state machine problems were used here, except that the output node was changed to be linear instead of sigmoidal to allow the network to have an appropriate dynamic range. We found that this caused some stability problems in the quadratic and locally recurrent networks. For the fixed number of weights comparison, we added an extra node to the quadratic network, and dropped any second order terms involving the fed back output. This gave a network with 64 weights and 4 states. For the fixed state comparison, dropping the second order terms gave a network with 174 weights. The locally recurrent network presented stability problems only for the fixed number of weights comparison. Here, we used a network that had 6 hidden layer nodes and one output node with 2 taps on the inputs and outputs each, giving a network with 57 weights and 16 states. In the Gamma network a value of $\mu = 0.8$ gave the best results.

The networks were trained with 100 uniform random noise sequences of length 50. Each experiment used a different randomly generated training set. The noise was

Table 3: Normalized mean squared error on a sinusoidal test signal for the nonlinear system identification experiment.

Architecture	Fixed # weights	Fixed # states
N & P	0.101	0.067
TDNN	0.160	0.165
Gamma	0.157	0.151
First Order	0.105	0.105
High Order	1.034	1.050
Bilinear	0.118	0.111
Quadratic	0.108	0.096
Multilayer	0.096	0.084
Elman	0.115	0.115
Local	0.117	0.123

uniformly distributed in the range $[-2.0, 2.0]$, and each sequence started with an initial value of $x_1(0) = x_2(0) = 0$. The networks were tested on the response to a sine wave of frequency 0.04 radians/second. This is an interesting test signal because it is fundamentally different than the training data.

Fifty runs were performed for each network. BPTT was used for 500 epochs with a learning rate of 0.002. The weights of all networks were initialized to random values uniformly distributed in the range $[-0.1, 0.1]$.

Table 3 shows the normalized mean squared error averaged over the 50 runs on the testing set. From these results we draw the following conclusions.

- The high order network could not seem to match the dynamic range of its output to the target, as a result it performed much worse than the other networks. It is clear that there is benefit to adding first order terms since the bilinear network performed so much better.
- Aside from the high order network, all of the other recurrent networks performed better than the TDNN, although in most cases not significantly better.
- The multilayer network performed exceptionally well on this problem, unlike the finite state machine experiments. We speculate that the existence of target output at every point along the sequence (unlike the finite state machine problems) is important for the multilayer network to be successful.
- Narendra and Parthasarathy's architecture did exceptionally well, even though it is not clear that its structure is well matched to the problem.

4 Conclusions

We have reviewed many discrete-time recurrent neural network architectures and compared them on two different problem domains, although we make no claim that any of these results will necessarily extend to other problems.

Narendra and Parthasarathy's model performed exceptionally well on the problems we explored. In general, single layer networks did fairly well, however it is important to include terms besides simple state/input products for nonlinear system identification. All of the recurrent networks usually did better than the TDNN except on the finite memory machine problem. In these experiments, the use of averaging filters as a substitute for taps in the TDNN did not seem to offer any distinct advantages in performance, although better results might be obtained if the value of μ is adapted.

We found that the relative comparison of the networks did not significantly change whether or not the number of weights or states were held constant. In fact, holding one of these values constant meant that in some networks the other value varied wildly, yet there appeared to be little correlation with generalization.

Finally, it is interesting to note that though some are much better than others, many of these networks are capable of providing adequate solutions to two seemingly disparate problems.

Acknowledgements

We would like to thank Leon Personnaz and Isabelle Rivals for suggesting we perform the experiments with a fixed number of states.

References

[1] A.D. Back and A.C. Tsoi. FIR and IIR synapses, a new neural network architecture for time series modeling. *Neural Computation*, 3(3):375–385, 1991.

[2] B. de Vries and J.C. Principe. The gamma model: A new neural model for temporal processing. *Neural Networks*, 5:565–576, 1992.

[3] J.L. Elman. Finding structure in time. *Cognitive Science*, 14:179–211, 1990.

[4] P. Frasconi, M. Gori, and G. Soda. Local feedback multilayered networks. *Neural Computation*, 4:120–130, 1992.

[5] C.L. Giles, C.B. Miller, et al. Learning and extracting finite state automata with second–order recurrent neural networks. *Neural Computation*, 4:393–405, 1992.

[6] Z. Kohavi. *Switching and finite automata theory*. McGraw–Hill, NY, 1978.

[7] K.J. Lang, A.H. Waibel, and G.E. Hinton. A time–delay neural network architecture for isolated word recognition. *Neural Networks*, 3:23–44, 1990.

[8] K.S. Narendra. Adaptive control of dynamical systems using neural networks. In *Handbook of Intelligent Control*, pages 141–183. Van Nostrand Reinhold, NY, 1992.

[9] K.S. Narendra and K. Parthasarathy. Identification and control of dynamical systems using neural networks. *IEEE Trans. on Neural Networks*, 1:4–27, 1990.

[10] P. Poddar and K.P. Unnikrishnan. Non–linear prediction of speech signals using memory neuron networks. In *Proc. 1991 IEEE Work. Neural Networks for Sig. Proc.*, pages 1–10. IEEE Press, 1991.

[11] A.J. Robinson and F. Fallside. Static and dynamic error propagation networks with application to speech coding. In *NIPS*, pages 632–641, NY, 1988. AIP.

[12] R.L. Watrous and G.M. Kuhn. Induction of finite–state automata using second–order recurrent networks. In *NIPS4*, pages 309–316, 1992.

Active Learning with Statistical Models

David A. Cohn, Zoubin Ghahramani, and Michael I. Jordan
cohn@psyche.mit.edu, zoubin@psyche.mit.edu, jordan@psyche.mit.edu
Department of Brain and Cognitive Sciences
Massachusetts Institute of Technology
Cambridge, MA 02139

Abstract

For many types of learners one can compute the statistically "optimal" way to select data. We review how these techniques have been used with feedforward neural networks [MacKay, 1992; Cohn, 1994]. We then show how the same principles may be used to select data for two alternative, statistically-based learning architectures: mixtures of Gaussians and locally weighted regression. While the techniques for neural networks are expensive and approximate, the techniques for mixtures of Gaussians and locally weighted regression are both efficient and accurate.

1 ACTIVE LEARNING – BACKGROUND

An *active* learning problem is one where the learner has the ability or need to influence or select its own training data. Many problems of great practical interest allow active learning, and many even require it.

We consider the problem of actively learning a mapping $X \to Y$ based on a set of training examples $\{(x_i, y_i)\}_{i=1}^{m}$, where $x_i \in X$ and $y_i \in Y$. The learner is allowed to iteratively select new inputs $\tilde{x}$ (possibly from a constrained set), observe the resulting output $\tilde{y}$, and incorporate the new examples $(\tilde{x}, \tilde{y})$ into its training set.

The primary question of active learning is how to choose which $\tilde{x}$ to try next. There are many heuristics for choosing $\tilde{x}$ based on intuition, including choosing places where we don't have data, where we perform poorly [Linden and Weber, 1993], where we have low confidence [Thrun and Möller, 1992], where we expect it to change our model [Cohn et al, 1990], and where we previously found data that resulted in learning [Schmidhuber and Storck, 1993].

In this paper we consider how one may select $\tilde{x}$ "optimally" from a statistical viewpoint. We first review how the statistical approach can be applied to neural networks, as described in MacKay [1992] and Cohn [1994]. We then consider two alternative, statistically-based learning architectures: mixtures of Gaussians and locally weighted regression. While optimal data selection for a neural network is computationally expensive and approximate, we find that optimal data selection for the two statistical models is efficient and accurate.

2 ACTIVE LEARNING – A STATISTICAL APPROACH

We denote the learner's output given input x as $\hat{y}(x)$. The mean squared error of this output can be expressed as the sum of the learner's bias and variance. The variance $\sigma_{\hat{y}}^2(x)$ indicates the learner's uncertainty in its estimate at x.[1] Our goal will be to select a new example $\tilde{x}$ such that when the resulting example $(\tilde{x}, \tilde{y})$ is added to the training set, the integrated variance IV is minimized:

$$IV = \int \sigma_{\hat{y}}^2 P(x) dx. \quad (1)$$

Here, $P(x)$ is the (known) distribution over X. In practice, we will compute a Monte Carlo approximation of this integral, evaluating $\sigma_{\hat{y}}^2$ at a number of random points drawn according to $P(x)$.

Selecting $\tilde{x}$ so as to minimize IV requires computing $\tilde{\sigma}_{\hat{y}}^2$, the new variance at x given $(\tilde{x}, \tilde{y})$. Until we actually commit to an $\tilde{x}$, we do not know what corresponding $\tilde{y}$ we will see, so the minimization cannot be performed deterministically.[2] Many learning architectures, however, provide an estimate of $P(\tilde{y}|\tilde{x})$ based on current data, so we can use this estimate to compute the *expectation* of $\tilde{\sigma}_{\hat{y}}^2$. Selecting $\tilde{x}$ to minimize the expected integrated variance provides a solid statistical basis for choosing new examples.

2.1 EXAMPLE: ACTIVE LEARNING WITH A NEURAL NETWORK

In this section we review the use of techniques from Optimal Experiment Design (OED) to minimize the estimated variance of a neural network [Fedorov, 1972; MacKay, 1992; Cohn, 1994]. We will assume we have been given a learner $\hat{y} = f_{\hat{w}}()$, a training set $\{(x_i, y_i)\}_{i=1}^{m}$ and a parameter vector $\hat{w}$ that maximizes a likelihood measure. One such measure is the minimum sum squared residual

$$S^2 = \frac{1}{m} \sum_{i=1}^{m} (y_i - \hat{y}(x_i))^2.$$

---

[1] Unless explicitly denoted, $\hat{y}$ and $\sigma_{\hat{y}}^2$ are functions of x. For simplicity, we present our results in the univariate setting. All results in the paper extend easily to the multivariate case.

[2] This contrasts with related work by Plutowski and White [1993], which is concerned with filtering an existing data set.

The estimated output variance of the network is

$$\sigma_{\hat{y}}^2 \approx S^2 \left(\frac{\partial \hat{y}(x)}{\partial w}\right)^T \left(\frac{\partial^2 S^2}{\partial w^2}\right)^{-1} \left(\frac{\partial \hat{y}(x)}{\partial w}\right)$$

The standard OED approach assumes normality and local linearity. These assumptions allow replacing the distribution $P(\tilde{y}|\tilde{x})$ by its estimated mean $\hat{y}(\tilde{x})$ and variance S^2. The expected value of the new variance, $\tilde{\sigma}_{\hat{y}}^2$, is then:

$$\langle \tilde{\sigma}_{\hat{y}}^2 \rangle \approx \sigma_{\hat{y}}^2 - \frac{\sigma_{\hat{y}}^2(x,\tilde{x})}{S^2 + \sigma_{\hat{y}}^2(\tilde{x})}, \text{ [MacKay, 1992].} \quad (2)$$

where we define

$$\sigma_{\hat{y}}(x,\tilde{x}) \equiv S^2 \left(\frac{\partial \hat{y}(x)}{\partial w}\right)^T \left(\frac{\partial^2 S^2}{\partial w^2}\right)^{-1} \left(\frac{\partial \hat{y}(\tilde{x})}{\partial w}\right).$$

For empirical results on the predictive power of Equation 2, see Cohn [1994].

The advantages of minimizing this criterion are that it is grounded in statistics, and is optimal given the assumptions. Furthermore, the criterion is continuous and differentiable. As such, it is applicable in continuous domains with continuous action spaces, and allows hillclimbing to find the "best" $\tilde{x}$.

For neural networks, however, this approach has many disadvantages. The criterion relies on simplifications and strong assumptions which hold only approximately. Computing the variance estimate requires inversion of a $|w| \times |w|$ matrix for each new example, and incorporating new examples into the network requires expensive retraining. Paass and Kindermann [1995] discuss an approach which addresses some of these problems.

3 MIXTURES OF GAUSSIANS

The mixture of Gaussians model is gaining popularity among machine learning practitioners [Nowlan, 1991; Specht, 1991; Ghahramani and Jordan, 1994]. It assumes that the data is produced by a mixture of N Gaussians g_i, for $i = 1, ..., N$. We can use the EM algorithm [Dempster et al, 1977] to find the best fit to the data, after which the conditional expectations of the mixture can be used for function approximation.

For each Gaussian g_i we will denote the estimated input/output means as $\mu_{x,i}$ and $\mu_{y,i}$ and estimated covariances as $\sigma_{x,i}^2$, $\sigma_{y,i}^2$ and $\sigma_{xy,i}$. The conditional variance of y given x may then be written

$$\sigma_{y|x,i}^2 = \sigma_{y,i}^2 - \frac{\sigma_{xy,i}^2}{\sigma_{x,i}^2}.$$

We will denote as n_i the (possibly fractional) number of training examples for which g_i takes responsibility:

$$n_i = \sum_{j=1}^{m} \frac{P(x_j, y_j|i)}{\sum_{k=1}^{N} P(x_j, y_j|k)}.$$

For an input x, each g_i has conditional expectation $\hat{y}_i$ and variance $\sigma^2_{\hat{y},i}$:

$$\hat{y}_i = \mu_{y,i} + \frac{\sigma_{xy,i}}{\sigma^2_{x,i}}(x - \mu_{x,i}), \qquad \sigma^2_{\hat{y},i} = \frac{\sigma^2_{y|x,i}}{n_i}\left(1 + \frac{(x-\mu_{x,i})^2}{\sigma^2_{x,i}}\right).$$

These expectations and variances are mixed according to the prior probability that g_i has of being responsible for x:

$$h_i \equiv h_i(x) = \frac{P(x|i)}{\sum_{j=1}^N P(x|j)}.$$

For input x then, the conditional expectation $\hat{y}$ of the resulting mixture and its variance may be written:

$$\hat{y} = \sum_{i=1}^N h_i\, \hat{y}_i, \qquad \sigma^2_{\hat{y}} = \sum_{i=1}^N \frac{h_i^2 \sigma^2_{y|x,i}}{n_i}\left(1 + \frac{(x-\mu_{x,i})^2}{\sigma^2_{x,i}}\right).$$

In contrast to the variance estimate computed for a neural network, here $\sigma^2_{\hat{y}}$ can be computed efficiently with no approximations.

3.1 ACTIVE LEARNING WITH A MIXTURE OF GAUSSIANS

We want to select $\tilde{x}$ to minimize $\left\langle \tilde{\sigma}^2_{\hat{y}} \right\rangle$. With a mixture of Gaussians, the model's estimated distribution of $\tilde{y}$ given $\tilde{x}$ is explicit:

$$P(\tilde{y}|\tilde{x}) = \sum_{i=1}^N \tilde{h}_i P(\tilde{y}|\tilde{x}, i) = \sum_{i=1}^N \tilde{h}_i N(\hat{y}_i(\tilde{x}), \sigma^2_{y|x,i}(\tilde{x})),$$

where $\tilde{h}_i \equiv h_i(\tilde{x})$. Given this, calculation of $\left\langle \tilde{\sigma}^2_{\hat{y}} \right\rangle$ is straightforward: we model the change in each g_i separately, calculating its expected variance given a new point sampled from $P(\tilde{y}|\tilde{x}, i)$ and weight this change by $\tilde{h}_i$. The new expectations combine to form the learner's new expected variance

$$\left\langle \tilde{\sigma}^2_{\hat{y}} \right\rangle = \sum_{i=1}^N \frac{\tilde{h}_i^2 \left\langle \tilde{\sigma}^2_{y|x,i} \right\rangle}{n_i + \tilde{h}_i}\left(1 + \frac{(x-\tilde{\mu}_{x,i})^2}{\tilde{\sigma}^2_{x,i}}\right) \qquad (3)$$

where the expectation can be computed exactly in closed form:

$$\left\langle \tilde{\sigma}^2_{y|x,i} \right\rangle = \left\langle \tilde{\sigma}^2_{y,i} \right\rangle - \frac{\left\langle \tilde{\sigma}^2_{xy,i} \right\rangle}{\tilde{\sigma}^2_{x,i}}, \qquad \left\langle \tilde{\sigma}^2_{y,i} \right\rangle = \frac{n\sigma^2_{y,i} + \tilde{h}_i \sigma^2_{y,i}(\tilde{x})}{n+\tilde{h}_i} + \frac{n\tilde{h}_i(\hat{y}_i(\tilde{x})-\mu_{y,i})^2}{(n+\tilde{h}_i)^2},$$

$$\tilde{\mu}_{x,i} = \frac{n_i \mu_{x,i} + \tilde{h}_i \tilde{x}}{n_i + \tilde{h}_i}, \qquad \left\langle \tilde{\sigma}_{xy,i} \right\rangle = \frac{n\sigma_{xy,i}}{n+\tilde{h}_i} + \frac{n\tilde{h}_i(\tilde{x}-\mu_{x,i})(\hat{y}_i(\tilde{x})-\mu_{y,i})}{(n+\tilde{h}_i)^2},$$

$$\tilde{\sigma}^2_{x,i} = \frac{n\sigma^2_{x,i}}{n+\tilde{h}_i} + \frac{n\tilde{h}_i(\tilde{x}-\mu_{x,i})^2}{(n+\tilde{h}_i)^2}, \qquad \left\langle \tilde{\sigma}^2_{xy,i} \right\rangle = \left\langle \tilde{\sigma}_{xy,i} \right\rangle^2 + \frac{n^2 \tilde{h}_i^2 \sigma^2_{y,i}(\tilde{x})(\tilde{x}-\mu_{x,i})^2}{(n+\tilde{h}_i)^4}.$$

4 LOCALLY WEIGHTED REGRESSION

We consider here two forms of locally weighted regression (LWR): kernel regression and the LOESS model [Cleveland et al, 1988]. Kernel regression computes $\hat{y}$ as an average of the y_i in the data set, weighted by a kernel centered at x. The LOESS model performs a linear regression on points in the data set, weighted by a kernel centered at x. The kernel shape is a design parameter: the original LOESS model uses a "tricubic" kernel; in our experiments we use the more common Gaussian

$$h_i(x) \equiv h(x - x_i) = \exp(-k(x - x_i)^2),$$

where k is a smoothing constant. For brevity, we will drop the argument x for $h_i(x)$, and define $n = \sum_i h_i$. We can then write the estimated means and covariances as:

$$\mu_x = \frac{\sum_i h_i x_i}{n}, \quad \sigma_x^2 = \frac{\sum_i h_i (x_i - x)^2}{n}, \quad \sigma_{xy} = \frac{\sum_i h_i (x_i - x)(y_i - \mu_y)}{n}$$

$$\mu_y = \frac{\sum_i h_i y_i}{n}, \quad \sigma_y^2 = \frac{\sum_i h_i (y_i - \mu_y)^2}{n}, \quad \sigma_{y|x}^2 = \sigma_y^2 - \frac{\sigma_{xy}^2}{\sigma_x^2}.$$

We use them to express the conditional expectations and their estimated variances:

$$\text{kernel:} \quad \hat{y} = \mu_y, \quad \sigma_{\hat{y}}^2 = \frac{\sigma_y^2}{n} \quad (4)$$

$$\text{LOESS:} \quad \hat{y} = \mu_y + \frac{\sigma_{xy}}{\sigma_x^2}(x - \mu_x), \quad \sigma_{\hat{y}}^2 = \frac{\sigma_{y|x}^2}{n}\left(1 + \frac{(x - \mu_x)^2}{\sigma_x^2}\right) \quad (5)$$

4.1 ACTIVE LEARNING WITH LOCALLY WEIGHTED REGRESSION

Again we want to select $\tilde{x}$ to minimize $\langle \tilde{\sigma}_{\hat{y}}^2 \rangle$. With LWR, the model's estimated distribution of $\tilde{y}$ given $\tilde{x}$ is explicit:

$$P(\tilde{y}|\tilde{x}) = N(\hat{y}(\tilde{x}), \sigma_{y|x}^2(\tilde{x}))$$

The estimate of $\langle \tilde{\sigma}_{\hat{y}}^2 \rangle$ is also explicit. Defining $\tilde{h}$ as the weight assigned to $\tilde{x}$ by the kernel, the learner's expected new variance is

$$\text{kernel:} \quad \langle \tilde{\sigma}_{\hat{y}}^2 \rangle = \frac{\langle \tilde{\sigma}_y^2 \rangle}{n + \tilde{h}} \qquad \text{LOESS:} \quad \langle \tilde{\sigma}_{\hat{y}}^2 \rangle = \frac{\langle \tilde{\sigma}_{y|x}^2 \rangle}{n + \tilde{h}}\left(1 + \frac{(x - \tilde{\mu}_x)^2}{\tilde{\sigma}_x^2}\right) \quad (6)$$

where the expectation can be computed exactly in closed form:

$$\langle \tilde{\sigma}_{y|x}^2 \rangle = \langle \tilde{\sigma}_y^2 \rangle - \frac{\langle \tilde{\sigma}_{xy}^2 \rangle}{\tilde{\sigma}_x^2}, \quad \langle \tilde{\sigma}_y^2 \rangle = \frac{n\sigma_y^2 + \tilde{h}\sigma_y^2(\tilde{x})}{n + \tilde{h}} + \frac{n\tilde{h}(\hat{y}(\tilde{x}) - \mu_y)^2}{(n + \tilde{h})^2},$$

$$\tilde{\mu}_x = \frac{n\mu_x + \tilde{h}\tilde{x}}{n + \tilde{h}}, \quad \langle \tilde{\sigma}_{xy} \rangle = \frac{n\sigma_{xy}}{n + \tilde{h}} + \frac{n\tilde{h}(\tilde{x} - \mu_x)(\hat{y}(\tilde{x}) - \mu_y)}{(n + \tilde{h})^2},$$

$$\tilde{\sigma}_x^2 = \frac{n\sigma_x^2}{n + \tilde{h}} + \frac{n\tilde{h}(\tilde{x} - \mu_x)^2}{(n + \tilde{h})^2}, \quad \langle \tilde{\sigma}_{xy}^2 \rangle = \langle \tilde{\sigma}_{xy} \rangle^2 + \frac{n^2\tilde{h}^2\sigma_y^2(\tilde{x})(\tilde{x} - \mu_x)^2}{(n + \tilde{h})^4}.$$

5 EXPERIMENTAL RESULTS

Below we describe two sets of experiments demonstrating the predictive power of the query selection criteria in this paper. In the first set, learners were trained on data from a noisy sine wave. The criteria described in this paper were applied to predict how a new training example selected at point $\tilde{x}$ would decrease the learner's variance. These predictions, along with the actual changes in variance when the training points were queried and added, are plotted in Figure 1.

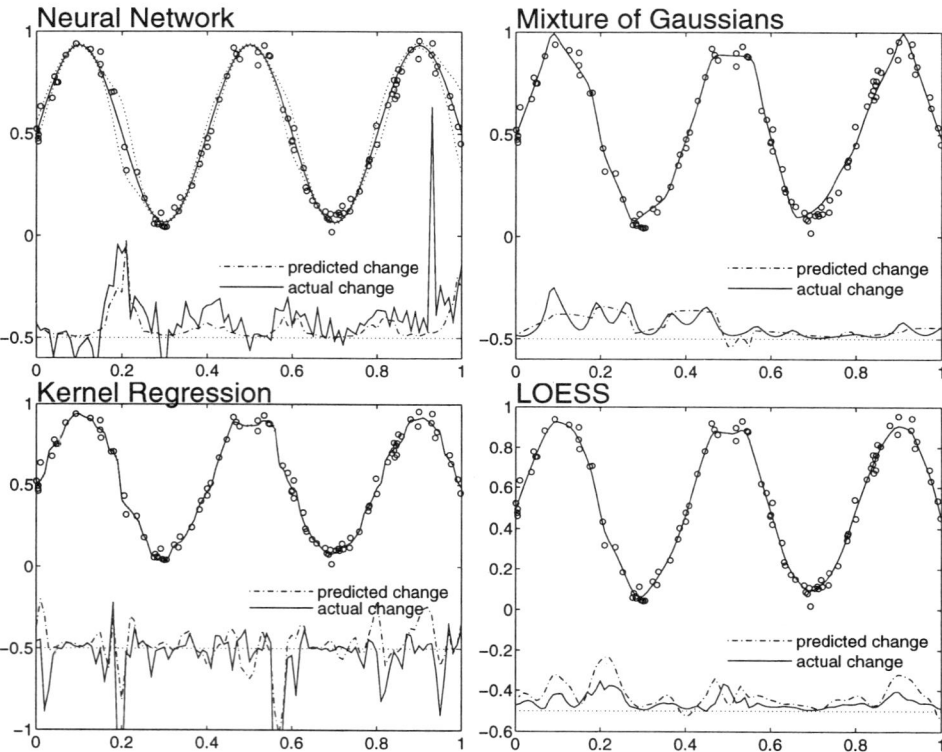

Figure 1: The upper portion of each plot indicates each learner's fit to noisy sinusoidal data. The lower portion of each plot indicates predicted and actual changes in the learner's average estimated variance when $\tilde{x}$ is queried and added to the training set, for $\tilde{x} \in [0, 1]$. Changes are not plotted to scale with learners' fits.

In the second set of experiments, we applied the techniques of this paper to learning the kinematics of a two-joint planar arm (Figure 2; see Cohn [1994] for details). Below, we illustrate the problem using the LOESS algorithm.

An example of the correlation between predicted and actual changes in variance on this problem is plotted in Figure 2. Figure 3 demonstrates that this correlation may be exploited to guide sequential query selection. We compared a LOESS learner which selected each new query so as to minimize expected variance with LOESS learners which selected queries according to various heuristics. The variance-minimizing learner significantly outperforms the heuristics in terms of both variance and MSE.

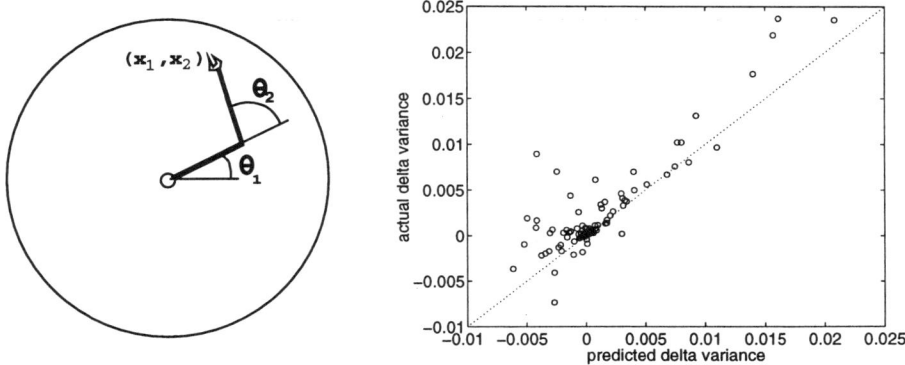

Figure 2: (left) The arm kinematics problem. (right) Predicted vs. actual changes in model variance for LOESS on the arm kinematics problem. 100 candidate points are shown for a model trained with 50 initial random examples. Note that most of the potential queries produce very little improvement, and that the algorithm successfully identifies those few that will help most.

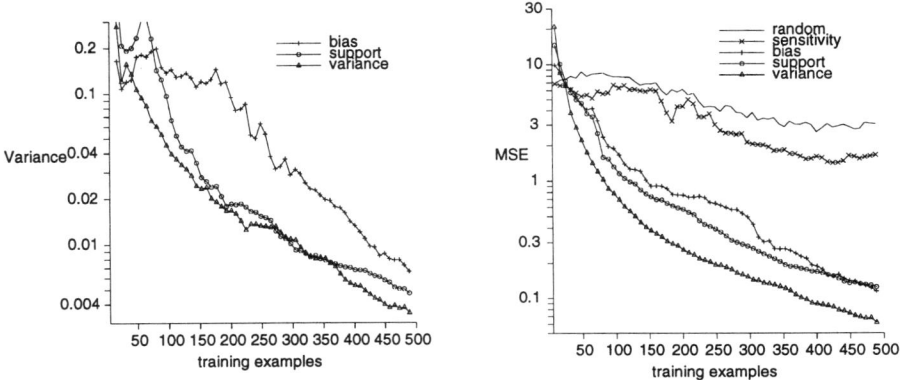

Figure 3: Variance and MSE for a LOESS learner selecting queries according to the variance-minimizing criterion discussed in this paper and according to several heuristics. "Sensitivity" queries where output is most sensitive to new data, "Bias" queries according to a bias-minimizing criterion, "Support" queries where the model has the least data support. The variance of "Random" and "Sensitivity" are off the scale. Curves are medians over 15 runs with non-Gaussian noise.

6 SUMMARY

Mixtures of Gaussians and locally weighted regression are two statistical models that offer elegant representations and efficient learning algorithms. In this paper we have shown that they also offer the opportunity to perform active learning in an efficient and statistically correct manner. The criteria derived here can be computed cheaply and, for problems tested, demonstrate good predictive power.

Acknowledgements

This work was funded by NSF grant CDA-9309300, the McDonnell-Pew Foundation, ATR Human Information Processing Laboratories and Siemens Corporate Research. We thank Stefan Schaal for helpful discussions about locally weighted regression.

References

W. Cleveland, S. Devlin, and E. Grosse. (1988) Regression by local fitting. *Journal of Econometrics* **37**:87–114.

D. Cohn, L. Atlas and R. Ladner. (1990) Training Connectionist Networks with Queries and Selective Sampling. In D. Touretzky, ed., *Advances in Neural Information Processing Systems 2*, Morgan Kaufmann.

D. Cohn. (1994) Neural network exploration using optimal experiment design. In J. Cowan et al., eds., *Advances in Neural Information Processing Systems 6*. Morgan Kaufmann.

A. Dempster, N. Laird and D. Rubin. (1977) Maximum likelihood from incomplete data via the EM algorithm. *J. Royal Statistical Society Series B*, **39**:1–38.

V. Fedorov. (1972) *Theory of Optimal Experiments*. Academic Press, New York.

Z. Ghahramani and M. Jordan. (1994) Supervised learning from incomplete data via an EM approach. In J. Cowan et al., eds., *Advances in Neural Information Processing Systems 6*. Morgan Kaufmann.

A. Linden and F. Weber. (1993) Implementing inner drive by competence reflection. In H. Roitblat et al., eds., *Proc. 2nd Int. Conf. on Simulation of Adaptive Behavior*, MIT Press, Cambridge.

D. MacKay. (1992) Information-based objective functions for active data selection, *Neural Computation* **4**(4): 590–604.

S. Nowlan. (1991) Soft Competitive Adaptation: Neural Network Learning Algorithms based on Fitting Statistical Mixtures. CMU-CS-91-126, School of Computer Science, Carnegie Mellon University, Pittsburgh, PA.

Paass, G., and Kindermann, J. (1995). Bayesian Query Construction for Neural Network Models. *In this volume*.

M. Plutowski and H. White (1993). Selecting concise training sets from clean data. *IEEE Transactions on Neural Networks*, 4, 305–318.

S. Schaal and C. Atkeson. (1994) Robot Juggling: An Implementation of Memory-based Learning. *Control Systems Magazine*, **14**(1):57–71.

J. Schmidhuber and J. Storck. (1993) Reinforcement driven information acquisition in nondeterministic environments. Tech. Report, Fakultät für Informatik, Technische Universität München.

D. Specht. (1991) A general regression neural network. *IEEE Trans. Neural Networks*, 2(6):568–576.

S. Thrun and K. Möller. (1992) Active exploration in dynamic environments. In J. Moody et al., editors, *Advances in Neural Information Processing Systems 4*. Morgan Kaufmann.

Learning with Preknowledge: Clustering with Point and Graph Matching Distance Measures

Steven Gold[1], **Anand Rangarajan**[1] and **Eric Mjolsness**[2]
Department of Computer Science
Yale University
New Haven, CT 06520-8285

Abstract

Prior constraints are imposed upon a learning problem in the form of distance measures. Prototypical 2-D point sets and graphs are learned by clustering with point matching and graph matching distance measures. The point matching distance measure is approx. invariant under affine transformations - translation, rotation, scale and shear - and permutations. It operates between noisy images with missing and spurious points. The graph matching distance measure operates on weighted graphs and is invariant under permutations. Learning is formulated as an optimization problem. Large objectives so formulated ($\sim$ million variables) are efficiently minimized using a combination of optimization techniques - algebraic transformations, iterative projective scaling, clocked objectives, and deterministic annealing.

1 Introduction

While few biologists today would subscribe to Locke's description of the nascent mind as a tabula rasa, the nature of the inherent constraints - Kant's preknowl-

---

[1] E-mail address of authors: lastname-firstname@cs.yale.edu
[2] Department of Computer Science and Engineering, University of California at San Diego (UCSD), La Jolla, CA 92093-0114. E-mail: emj@cs.ucsd.edu

edge - that helps organize our perceptions remains much in doubt. Recently, the importance of such preknowledge for learning has been convincingly argued from a statistical framework [Geman et al., 1992]. Researchers have proposed that our brains may incorporate preknowledge in the form of distance measures [Shepard, 1989]. The neural network community has begun to explore this idea via tangent distance [Simard et al., 1993], model learning [Williams et al., 1993] and point matching distances [Gold et al., 1994]. However, only the point matching distances have been invariant under permutations. Here we extend that work by enhancing both the scope and function of those distance measures, significantly expanding the problem domains where learning may take place.

We learn objects consisting of noisy 2-D point-sets or noisy weighted graphs by clustering with point matching and graph matching distance measures. The point matching measure is approx. invariant under permutations and affine transformations (separately decomposed into translation, rotation, scale and shear) and operates on point-sets with missing or spurious points. The graph matching measure is invariant under permutations. These distance measures and others like them may be constructed using Bayesian inference on a probabilistic model of the visual domain. Such models introduce a carefully designed bias into our learning, which reduces its generality outside the problem domain but increases its ability to generalize within the problem domain. (From a statistical viewpoint, outside the problem domain it increases bias while within the problem domain it decreases variance). The resulting distance measures are similar to some of those hypothesized for cognition.

The distance measures and learning problem (clustering) are formulated as objective functions. Fast minimization of these objectives is achieved by a combination of optimization techniques - algebraic transformations, iterative projective scaling, clocked objectives, and deterministic annealing. Combining these techniques significantly increases the size of problems which may be solved with recurrent network architectures [Rangarajan et al., 1994]. Even on single-cpu workstations non-linear objectives with a million variables can routinely be minimized. With these methods we learn prototypical examples of 2-D points set and graphs from randomly generated experimental data.

2 Distance Measures in Unsupervised Learning

2.1 An Affine Invariant Point Matching Distance Measure

The first distance measure quantifies the degree of dissimilarity between two unlabeled 2-D point images, irrespective of bounded affine transformations, i.e. differences in position, orientation, scale and shear. The two images may have different numbers of points. The measure is calculated with an objective that can be used to find correspondence and pose for unlabeled feature matching in vision. Given two sets of points $\{X_j\}$ and $\{Y_k\}$, one can minimize the following objective to find the affine transformation and permutation which best maps Y onto X:

$$E_{pm}(m,t,A) = \sum_{j=1}^{J}\sum_{k=1}^{K} m_{jk}\|X_j - t - A \cdot Y_k\|^2 + g(A) - \alpha \sum_{j=1}^{J}\sum_{k=1}^{K} m_{jk}$$

with constraints: $\forall j \sum_{k=1}^{K} m_{jk} \leq 1$, $\forall k \sum_{j=1}^{J} m_{jk} \leq 1$, $\forall jk\ m_{jk} \geq 0$.

A is decomposed into scale, rotation, vertical shear and oblique shear components. $g(A)$ regularizes our affine transformation - bounding the scale and shear components. m is a fuzzy correspondence matrix which matches points in one image with corresponding points in the other image. The inequality constraint on m allows for null matches - that is a given point in one image may match to no corresponding point in the other image. The α term biases the objective towards matches.

Then given two sets of points $\{X_j\}$ and $\{Y_k\}$ the distance between them is defined as:

$$D(\{X_j\}, \{Y_k\}) = \min_{m,t,A}(E_{pm}(m, t, A) \mid \text{constraints on } m)$$

This measure is an example of a more general image distance measure derived in [Mjolsness, 1992]:

$$d(x, y) = \min_T d(x, T(y)) \in [0, \infty)$$

where T is a set of transformation parameters introduced by a visual grammar.

Using slack variables, and following the treatment in [Peterson and Söderberg, 1989; Yuille and Kosowsky, 1994] we employ Lagrange multipliers and an $x \log x$ barrier function to enforce the constraints with the following objective:

$$E_{pm}(m,t,A) = \sum_{j=1}^{J}\sum_{k=1}^{K} m_{jk}\|X_j - t - A \cdot Y_k\|^2 + g(A) - \alpha \sum_{j=1}^{J}\sum_{k=1}^{K} m_{jk}$$
$$+ \frac{1}{\beta}\sum_{j=1}^{J+1}\sum_{k=1}^{K+1} m_{jk}(\log m_{jk} - 1) + \sum_{j=1}^{J}\mu_j(\sum_{k=1}^{K+1} m_{jk} - 1) + \sum_{k=1}^{K}\nu_k(\sum_{j=1}^{J+1} m_{jk} - 1) \quad (1)$$

In this objective we are looking for a saddle point. (1) is minimized with respect to m, t, and A which are the correspondence matrix, translation, and affine transform, and is maximized with respect to μ and ν, the Lagrange multipliers that enforce the row and column constraints for m.

The above can be used to define many different distance measures, since given the decomposition of A it is trivial to construct measures which are invariant only under some subset of the transformations (such as rotation and translation). The regularization and α terms may also be individually adjusted in an appropriate fashion for a specific problem domain.

2.2 Weighted Graph Matching Distance Measures

The following distance measure quantifies the degree of dissimilarity between two unlabeled weighted graphs. Given two graphs, represented by adjacency matrices G_{ab} and g_{ij}, one can minimize the objective below to find the permutation which best maps G onto g:

$$E_{gm}(m) = \sum_{a=1}^{A}\sum_{i=1}^{I}(\sum_{b=1}^{B} G_{ab}m_{bi} - \sum_{j=1}^{J} m_{aj}g_{ji})^2$$

with constraints: $\forall a \sum_{i=1}^{I} m_{ai} = 1$, $\forall i \sum_{a=1}^{A} m_{ai} = 1$, $\forall ai \ m_{ai} \geq 0$. These constraints are enforced in the same fashion as in (1). An algebraic fixed-point transformation and self-amplification term further transform the objective to:

$$E_{gm}(m) = \sum_{a=1}^{A}\sum_{i=1}^{I}(\mu_{ai}(\sum_{b=1}^{B} G_{ab}m_{bi} - \sum_{j=1}^{J} m_{aj}g_{ji}) - \frac{1}{2}\mu_{ai}^2 - \gamma\sigma_{ai}m_{ai} + \frac{\gamma}{2}\sigma_{ai}^2)$$

$$+\frac{1}{\beta}\sum_{a=1}^{A}\sum_{i=1}^{I} m_{ai}(\log m_{ai} - 1) + \sum_{a=1}^{A} \kappa_a(\sum_{i=1}^{I} m_{ai} - 1) + \sum_{i=1}^{I} \lambda_i(\sum_{a=1}^{A} m_{ai} - 1) \quad (2)$$

In this objective we are also looking for a saddle point.

A second, functionally equivalent, graph matching objective is also used in the clustering problem:

$$E_{gm'}(m) = \sum_{a=1}^{A}\sum_{b=1}^{B}\sum_{i=1}^{I}\sum_{j=1}^{J} m_{ai}m_{bj}(G_{ab} - g_{ji})^2 \quad (3)$$

with constraints: $\forall a \sum_{i=1}^{I} m_{ai} = 1$, $\forall i \sum_{a=1}^{A} m_{ai} = 1$, $\forall ai \ m_{ai} \geq 0$.

2.3 The Clustering Objective

The learning problem is formulated as follows: Given a set of I objects, $\{X_i\}$ find a set of A cluster centers $\{Y_a\}$ and match variables $\{M_{ia}\}$ defined as

$$M_{ia} = \begin{cases} 1 & \text{if } X_i \text{ is in } Y_a\text{'s cluster} \\ 0 & \text{otherwise,} \end{cases}$$

such that each object is in only one cluster, and the total distance of all the objects from their respective cluster centers is minimized. To find $\{Y_a\}$ and $\{M_{ia}\}$ minimize the cost function,

$$E_{cluster}(Y, M) = \sum_{i=1}^{I}\sum_{a=1}^{A} M_{ia}D(X_i, Y_a)$$

with the constraint that $\forall i \sum_a M_{ia} = 1$, $\forall ai \ M_{ai} \geq 0$. $D(X_i, Y_a)$, the distance function, is a measure of dissimilarity between two objects.

The constraints on M are enforced in a manner similar to that described for the distance measure, except that now only the rows of the matrix M need to add to one, instead of both the rows and the columns.

$$E_{cluster}(Y, M) = \sum_{i=1}^{I}\sum_{a=1}^{A} M_{ia}D(X_i, Y_a) + \frac{1}{\beta}\sum_{i=1}^{I}\sum_{a=1}^{A} M_{ia}(\log M_{ia} - 1)$$

$$+ \sum_{i=1}^{I} \lambda_i(\sum_{a=1}^{A} M_{ia} - 1) \quad (4)$$

Here, the objects are point-sets or weighted graphs. If point-sets the distance measure $D(X_i, Y_a)$ is replaced by (1), if graphs it is replaced by (2) or (3).

Therefore, given a set of objects, X, we construct $E_{cluster}$ and upon finding the appropriate saddle point of that objective, we will have Y, their cluster centers, and M, their cluster memberships.

3 The Algorithm

The algorithm to minimize the clustering objectives consists of two loops - an inner loop to minimize the distance measure objective [either (1) or (2)] and an outer loop to minimize the clustering objective (4). Using coordinate descent in the outer loop results in dynamics similar to the EM algorithm [Jordan and Jacobs, 1994] for clustering. All variables occurring in the distance measure objective are held fixed during this phase. The inner loop uses coordinate ascent/descent which results in repeated row and column projections for m. The minimization of m, and the distance measure variables [either t, A of (1) or μ, σ of (2)], occurs in an incremental fashion, that is their values are saved after each inner loop call from within the outer loop and are then used as initial values for the next call to the inner loop. This tracking of the values of the distance measure variables in the inner loop is essential to the efficiency of the algorithm since it greatly speeds up each inner loop optimization. Most coordinate ascent/descent phases are computed analytically, further speeding up the algorithm. Some local minima are avoided, by deterministic annealing in both the outer and inner loops. The multi-phase dynamics maybe described as a clocked objective. Let $\{D\}$ be the set of distance measure variables excluding m. The algorithm is as follows:

Initialize $\{D\}$ to the equivalent of an identity transform, Y to random values
Begin Outer Loop
  Begin Inner Loop
    Initialize $\{D\}$ with previous values
    Find m, $\{D\}$ for each ia pair :
      Find m by softmax, projecting across j, then k, iteratively
      Find $\{D\}$ by coordinate descent
  End Inner Loop
  Find M,Y using fixed values of m, $\{D\}$, determined in inner loop:
    Find M by softmax, across i
    Find Y by coordinate descent
  Increase β_M, β_m
End Outer Loop

When analytic solutions are computed for Y the outer loop takes a form similar to fuzzy ISODATA clustering, with annealing on the fuzziness parameter.

4 Methods and Experimental Results

Four series of experiments were ran with randomly generated data to evaluate the learning algorithms. Point sets were clustered in the first three experiments and weighted graphs were clustered in the fourth. In each experiment a set of object models were randomly generated. Then from each object model a set of object instances were created by transforming the object model according to the problem domain assumed for that experiment. For example, an object represented by points in two dimensional space was translated, rotated, scaled, sheared, and permuted to form a new point set. A object represented by a weighted graph was permuted. Noise was added to further distort the object. Parts of the object were deleted and spurious features (points) were added. In this manner, from a set of object models, a larger number of object instances were created. Then with no knowledge of the original objects models or cluster memberships, we clustered the object instances using the algorithms described above.

The results were evaluated by comparing the object prototypes (cluster centers) formed by each experimental run to the object models used to generate the object instances for that experiment. The distance measures used in the clustering were used for this comparison, i.e. to calculate the distance between the learned prototype and the original object. Note that this distance measure also incorporates the transformations used to create the object instances. The mean and standard deviations of these distances were plotted (Figure 1) over hundreds of experiments, varying the object instance generation noise. The straight line appearing on each graph displays the effect of the noise only. It is the expected object model-object prototype distance if no transformations were applied, no features were deleted or added, and the cluster memberships of the object instances were known. It serves as an absolute lower bound on our learning algorithm. The noise was increased in each series of experiments until the curve flattened - that is the object instances became so distorted by noise that no information about the original objects could be recovered by the algorithm.

In the first series of experiments (Figure 1a), point set objects were translated, rotated, scaled, and permuted. Initial object models were created by selecting points with a uniform distribution within a unit square. The transformations to create the object instance were selected with a uniform distribution within the following bounds; translation: $\pm.5$, rotation: $\pm 27°$, $\log(scale)$: $\pm \log(.5)$. 100 object instances were generated from 10 object models. All objects contained 20 points.The standard deviation of the Gaussian noise was varied by .02 from .02 to .16. 15 experiments were run at each noise level. The data point at each error bar represents 150 distances (15 experiments times 10 model-prototype distances for each experiment).

In the second and third series of experiments (Figures 1b and 1c), point set objects were translated, rotated, scaled, sheared (obliquely and vertically), and permuted. Each object point had a 10% probability of being deleted and a 5% probability of generating a spurious point. The point sets and transformations were randomly generated as in the first experiment, except for these bounds; $\log(scale)$: $\pm \log(.7)$, $\log(verticalshear)$: $\pm \log(.7)$, and $\log(obliqueshear)$: $\pm \log(.7)$. In experiment 2, 64 object instances and 4 object models of 15 points each were used. In experiment 3, 256 object instances and 8 object models of 20 points each were used. Noise levels like experiment 1 were used, with 20 experiments run at each noise level in experiment 2 and 10 experiments run at each noise level in experiment 3.

In experiment 4 (Figure 1d), object models were represented by fully connected weighted graphs. The link weights in the initial object models were selected with a uniform distribution between 0 and 1. The objects were then randomly permuted

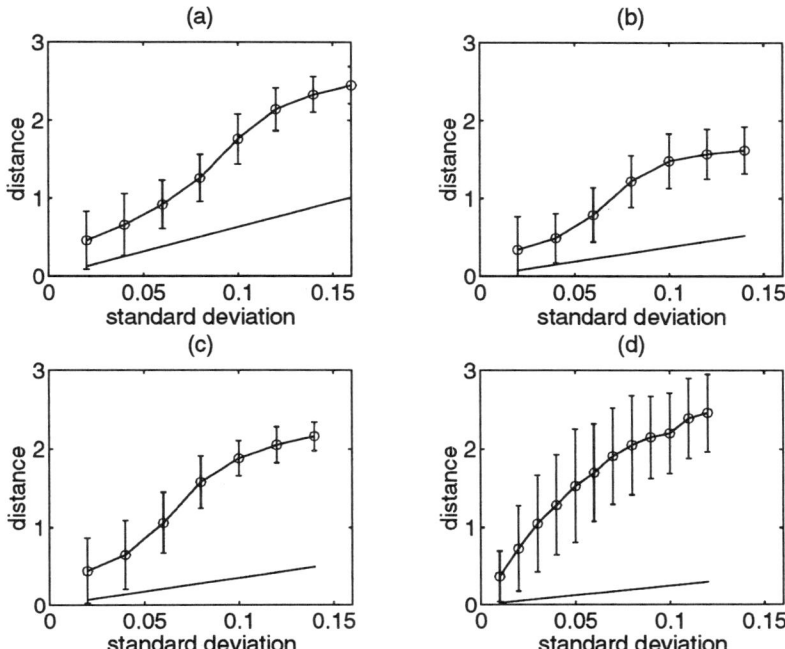

Figure 1: (a): 10 clusters, 100 point sets, 20 points each, scale ,rotation, translation, 120 experiments (b): 4 clusters, 64 point sets, 15 points each, affine, 10 % deleted, 5 % spurious, 140 experiments (c): 8 clusters, 256 point sets, 20 points each, affine, 10 % deleted, 5 % spurious, 70 experiments (d): 4 clusters, 64 graphs, 10 nodes each, 360 experiments

to form the object instance and uniform noise was added to the link weights. 64 object instances were generated from 4 object models consisting of 10 node graphs with 100 links. The standard deviation of the noise was varied by .01 from .01 to .12. 30 experiments where run at each noise level.

In most experiments at low noise levels ($\leq$ .06 for point sets, $\leq$ .03 for graphs), the object prototypes learned were very similar to the object models. Even at higher noise levels object prototypes similar to the object models are formed, though less consistently. Results from about 700 experiments are plotted. The objective for experiment 3 contained close to one million variables and converged in about 4 hours on an SGI Indigo workstation. The convergence times of the objectives of experiments 1, 2 and 4 were 120, 10 and 10 minutes respectively.

5 Conclusions

It has long been argued by many, that learning in complex domains typically associated with human intelligence requires some type of prior structure or knowledge. We have begun to develop a set of tools that will allow the incorporation of prior structure within learning. Our models incorporate many features needed in complex domains like vision - noise, missing and spurious features, non-rigid transformations. They can learn objects with inherent structure, like graphs. Many experiments have been run on experimentally generated data sets. Several directions for future research hold promise. One might be the learning of OCR data [Gold et al., 1995]. Second a supervised learning stage could be added to our algorithms. Finally the power of the distance measures can be enhanced to operate on attributed relational graphs with deleted nodes and links [Gold and Rangarajan, 1995].

Acknowledgements

ONR/DARPA: N00014-92-J-4048, AFOSR: F49620-92-J-0465 and Yale CTAN.

References

S. Geman, E. Bienenstock, and R. Doursat. (1992) Neural networks and the bias/variance dilemma. *Neural Computation* **4**:1-58.

S. Gold, E. Mjolsness and A. Rangarajan. (1994) Clustering with a domain-specific distance measure. In J. Cowan *et al.*, (eds.), *NIPS 6*. Morgan Kaufmann.

S. Gold, C. P. Lu, A. Rangarajan, S. Pappu and E. Mjolsness. (1995) New algorithms for 2D and 3D point matching: pose estimation and correspondence. In G. Tesauro *et al.*, (eds.), *NIPS 7*. San Francisco, CA: Morgan Kaufmann.

S. Gold and A. Rangarajan (1995) A graduated assignment algorithm for graph matching. YALEU/DCS/TR-1062, Yale Univ., CS Dept.

M. I. Jordan and R. A. Jacobs. (1994) Hierarchical mixtures of experts and the EM algorithm. *Neural Computation*, **6**:181-214.

E. Mjolsness. Visual grammars and their neural networks. (1992) *SPIE Conference on the Science of Artificial Neural Networks*, **1710**:63-85.

C. Peterson and B. Söderberg. A new method for mapping optimization problems onto neural networks. (1989) *International Journal of Neural Systems*, **1**(1):3-22.

A. Rangarajan, S. Gold and E. Mjolsness. (1994) A novel optimizing network architecture with applications. YALEU/DCS/TR-1036, Yale Univ., CS Dept.

R. Shepard. (1989). Internal representation of universal regularities: A challenge for connectionism. In L. Nadel *et al.*, (eds.), *Neural Connections, Mental Computation*. Cambridge, MA, London, England: Bradford/MIT Press.

P. Simard, Y. Le Cun, and J. Denker. (1993) Efficient pattern recognition using a transformation distance. In S. Hanson *et al.*, (eds.), *NIPS 5*. San Mateo, CA: Morgan Kaufmann.

C. Williams, R. Zemel, and M. Mozer. (1993) Unsupervised learning of object models. AAAI Tech. Rep. FSS-93-04, Univ. of Toronto, CS Dept.

A. L. Yuille and J.J. Kosowsky. (1994). Statistical physics algorithms that converge. *Neural Computation*, **6**:341-356.

Direct Multi-Step Time Series Prediction Using TD(λ)

Peter T. Kazlas
Department of Electrical
and Computer Engineering
University of Colorado
Boulder, CO 80309-0425
pkazlas@colorado.edu

Andreas S. Weigend
Department of Computer Science
and Institute of Cognitive Science
University of Colorado
Boulder, CO 80309-0430
andreas@cs.colorado.edu [*]

Abstract

This paper explores the application of Temporal Difference (TD) learning (Sutton, 1988) to forecasting the behavior of dynamical systems with real-valued outputs (as opposed to game-like situations). The performance of TD learning in comparison to standard supervised learning depends on the amount of noise present in the data. In this paper, we use a deterministic chaotic time series from a low-noise laser. For the task of direct five-step ahead predictions, our experiments show that standard supervised learning is better than TD learning. The TD algorithm can be viewed as linking adjacent predictions. A similar effect can be obtained by sharing the internal representation in the network. We thus compare two architectures for both paradigms: the first architecture ("separate hidden units") consists of individual networks for each of the five direct multi-step prediction tasks; the second ("shared hidden units") has a single (larger) hidden layer that finds a representation from which all five predictions for the next five steps are generated. For this data set we do not find any significant difference between the two architectures.

---

[*]http://www.cs.colorado.edu/~andreas/Home.html.
This paper is available with figures in colors as ftp://ftp.cs.colorado.edu/pub/Time-Series/MyPapers/kazlas.weigend_nips7.ps.Z .

1 Introduction

The *Santa Fe Time Series Prediction and Analysis Competition* (Weigend & Gershenfeld, 1994) saw a relatively large number of different nonlinear techniques applied to the prediction of a few time series. One of the results was that some neural networks did very well (but incidentally some other neural networks also did very poorly). All neural networks were trained with standard supervised learning where the network is trained based on differences between the predicted and observed values of the series. The differences only concerned the architecture; a good example was the time delay neural network architecture, also called finite impulse response network.

Standard supervised learning (SL), on the one hand, views time series prediction essentially as nonlinear regression; the fact that we are dealing with a time series is basically ignored. Temporal difference (TD) learning, on the other hand, takes a different approach: it adjusts the parameters based on differences between successive predictions in time (Sutton, 1988). TD learning has been shown to be very successful in the context of games such as backgammon (Tesauro, 1992). This paper investigates whether the TD paradigm can also be applied to the somewhat different task of time series prediction.

This paper is organized as follows: after briefly reviewing TD learning, Section 2 focuses on the application of TD learning to multi-step prediction of time series, and contrasts it to supervised learning (see Figure 1). Section 3 then describes the architectures and cost function as well as the data set used in the experiments. Section 4 presents the results, and Section 5 summarizes the paper.

2 TD learning for nonlinear, direct multi-step predictors

The key idea behind TD learning is that errors (used for gradient descent) are based on predictions that are adjacent in time. This is in contrast to the traditional SL approach where the errors are based on the difference between the prediction and the observed value. The general expression for the TD weight update rule (linear case), TD(λ), is given by (Sutton, 88)

$$\Delta w_t = \eta \left(\hat{y}_{t+1} - \hat{y}_t \right) \sum_{k=1}^{t} \lambda^{t-k} \nabla_w \hat{y}_k \qquad (1)$$

where η is the learning rate; $\hat{y}_{t+1}$ and $\hat{y}_t$ are two adjacent predictions of the *equivalent* target; λ is the recency weight with $0 \leq \lambda \leq 1$; and $\nabla_w \hat{y}_k$ is the gradient of the prediction at time k with respect to the weights of the network.

In Equation (1), we use the present weights to calculate the predictions $\hat{y}_t$ and $\hat{y}_{t+1}$ and we use the past weights to calculate the past gradients. In our experiments, since $\hat{y}_t$ is an output of a nonlinear connectionist network, we form $\hat{y}_t$ by propagating it through a multilayer network with hidden units and we backpropagate weight changes by applying the chain rule to the gradient $\nabla_w \hat{y}_k$ with respect to the hidden layer activation function. Several variants of TD(λ) exist: TD(0) only forms gradients based on the present pair of predictions $(\hat{y}_t, \hat{y}_{t+1})$; TD(1) continually adds gradients with no weighting of recency; and in the general case, TD(λ) weights the kth past gradient by a recency weight of λ^k. As will be shown in the subsequent section, in our example, TD(λ) tends to lead to the best results for λ around 0.3 (the optimal value of λ cannot be determined by first principles).

In multi-step prediction, we *directly* predict the value of a time series n time steps into the future (y_{t+n} denotes the observed value at $t+n$), given a set of m past values at time t denoted by the observation vector $\mathbf{x}_t : (y_t, y_{t-1}, \ldots y_{t-m-1})$. To cast the multi-step prediction problem into the TD framework, we first form an overlapping sequence of predictions as described by Sutton (1988): For an n-step ahead prediction problem, we form n successive predictions of the same target y_{t+n}: $\hat{y}_t^n, \hat{y}_{t+1}^{n-1}, \ldots \hat{y}_{t+n-1}^1$ ($\hat{y}_t^\delta$ is the prediction at time t for the time series δ steps ahead). At each time step, we form two sets of predictions $\hat{y}_t^\delta$ and $\hat{y}_{t+1}^{\delta-1}$ based on the observation pair $(\mathbf{x}_t, \mathbf{x}_{t+1})$. The corresponding weight update at time t involves the temporal difference of the these equivalent predictions:

$$\Delta w_t^\delta = \eta \, (\hat{y}_{t+1}^{\delta-1} - \hat{y}_t^\delta) \sum_{k=1}^{t} \lambda^{t-k} \nabla_w \hat{y}_k^\delta \qquad (2)$$

Equation (2) shows that the TD algorithm reduces to the SL algorithm for single-step predictions, since there is no temporal structure revealed in time (i.e. the actual value is available with the first observation pair $(\mathbf{x}_t, \mathbf{x}_{t+1})$ at time t, and therefore $\hat{y}_{t+1}^0 = y_{t+1}$). However, for a multi-step prediction problem, temporal structure exists in the revelation of the observation vectors. on-line, the

To differentiate the two algorithms, Figure 1 depicts the backpropagation of errors using SL and TD learning algorithms. In SL, errors are generated by the squared difference between predicted and target values: network training simply tries to minimize the error function based on *structural* difference between the predicted ($\hat{y}_t^k$, or simply $\hat{y}_k$) and target values (y_k), see (Figure 1(a)). In (Figure 1(b)), TD learning minimizes a different error function—the difference between successive predictions $\hat{y}_k(t)$ and $\hat{y}_{k-1}(t+1)$. Note, in the case of a noiseless time series, we do not expect to see a difference in performance between SL and TD learning, as the actual values of the time series are accurate descriptors of the system's output. In the case of a noisy time series, we conjecture that TD learning provides a better teaching signal than simply using the noisy observable. In this paper, we begin by comparing the performance of SL and TD learning on a low noise deterministic time series.

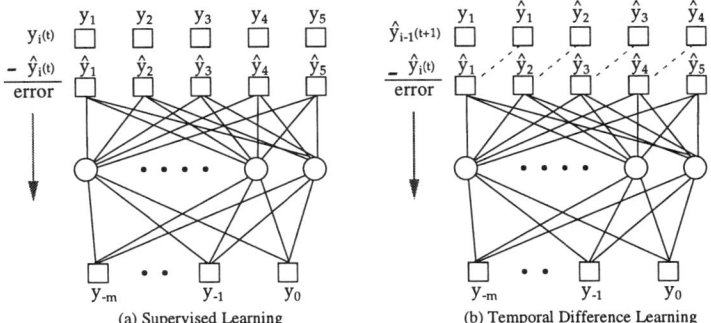

Figure 1: Backpropagation for Supervised and Temporal Difference learning.

3 Architecture and Data

The multi-step prediction problem we chose is to *directly* predict the next five values of a time series given the past five values. In comparing the two algorithms, we examine two architectures and compare their performance on a real-world dataset.

Architecture. Two network architectures were chosen to compare the SL and TD algorithms in the multi-step prediction task.

- **Separate hidden units.** The first architecture consists of five separate prediction networks, each forming a single prediction $\hat{y}_i$ for the ith step-ahead prediction of the series. The five outputs correspond to the predictions $\hat{y}_1$ through $\hat{y}_5$. Each network has five input units (corresponding to the past five values of the time series), 10 hidden units (arbitrarily chosen) and a single linear output for each task.

- **Shared hidden units.** The second architecture is a single network with five outputs corresponding to the five predictions ($\hat{y}_1 \ldots \hat{y}_5$). The network has the same five inputs, but has 20 tanh hidden units.

Cost Function. We train on sum squared error, weighting all five predictions equally. In the supervised learning case, the predictions are compared to the actual values, while in the TD case, errors are calculated based on successive predictions:

$$E_{TD}(t) = \sum_{k=1}^{5} (\hat{y}_{k-1}(t+1) - \hat{y}_k(t))^2 \tag{3}$$

Search. In network training, we use batch updates, i.e., update weights after each pass through the training data. Network training continues until the error on the cross-validation set stagnates or begins to increase. For networks trained by TD learning, λ, the recency weight, ranges from $0 \leq \lambda \leq 0.5$.

Data. We use the laser data from the *Santa Fe Competition*.[1] The data are intensity measurements of a NH_3 laser in a chaotic state, exhibiting Lorenz-like dynamics. We use the 1,000 competition data points for training, but also 1,000 further points for cross-validation of our model and 2,000 further points for testing. We depart from the competition rules in order to get higher statistical significance.

4 Results

Learning curves. We begin our analysis by plotting the squared error normalized by the variance for each of the five output units ($\hat{y}_1 - \hat{y}_5$) as a function of training time for both

---

[1] The data set and several predictions and characterizations are described in the volume edited by Weigend and Gershenfeld (1994). The data is available by anonymous ftp at **ftp.cs.colorado.edu** in **/pub/Time-Series/SantaFe** as **A.dat**. See also **http://www.cs.colorado.edu/Time-Series/TSWelcome.html** for further analyses of this and other time series data sets.

learning algorithms in Figure 2.[2] In the SL case, although the sum of the five curves monotonically decreases, they individually can fall and rise again. This plot shows the trade-offs in multi-task learning. For example, $\hat{y}_3$ is learned early and then levels off, because $\hat{y}_5$ is being learned. In the TD learning case, the five curves are ordered in the order that we would expect with the error associated with $\hat{y}_1$ always smaller than $\hat{y}_2$ and so on. This is expected, since the ith prediction $\hat{y}_i$ is driven by the prediction $\hat{y}_{i-1}$ projected one step into the future. We also note that the $\hat{y}_1$ curve is similar for both paradigms, since the error is driven by the same observed value y_1.

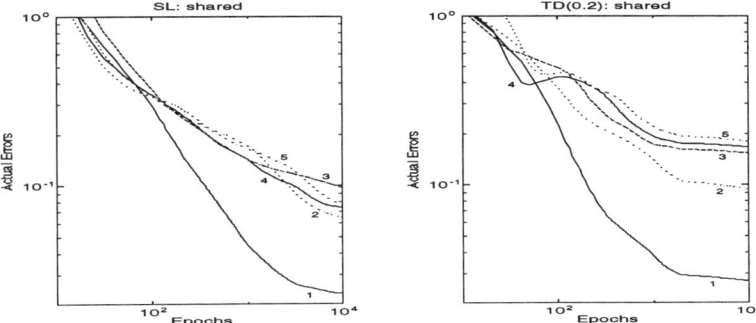

Figure 2: E_{NMS} for each output versus training epochs (training set) for both supervised and TD learning. Typical runs are shown and both architectures exhibit the same behavior. Learning rates were varied during training to accelerate learning. In the TD(0.2) case, the leveling of the error curves at 2,000 epochs is due to a decrease in learning rate.

Performance metric. We compare the performances with the normalized mean square error,

$$E_{NMS} = \frac{\sum_{k=1}^{N}(y_k - \hat{y}_k)^2}{\sum_{k=1}^{N}(y_k - \text{mean})^2} \quad (4)$$

where N is the number of samples; y_k and $\hat{y}_k$ are the actual and predicted values.

Comparison between SL and TD learning on five-step prediction. The longer the lead time for the forecast, the larger the expected difference in performance between TD and SL. We thus focus on five-step predictions where the difference between SL and TD is most pronounced from the set we considered ($\hat{y}_1$-$\hat{y}_5$). Figure 3 shows the individual performances of several runs for the task of direct five-step predictions. We vary the architecture (left side is shared hidden units, right side is separate hidden units), and we vary in each sub-plot the training (SL, TD(0), TD(0.2), TD(0.3), TD(0.5)). There is no large difference within TD for different values of λ. However, there is a significant difference between SL and TD: SL is better than TD. This result depends crucially on the fact that the data have very low noise (the main source of noise is just the quantization error of the 8-bit analog to digital converter).

---

[2]The normalized mean square errors E_{NMS} do not start with 1.0 as it would have been the case for very small initial weights; we ran the experiments (for no particular reason) with rather large initial weights, drawn from a uniform distribution between -1 and +1.

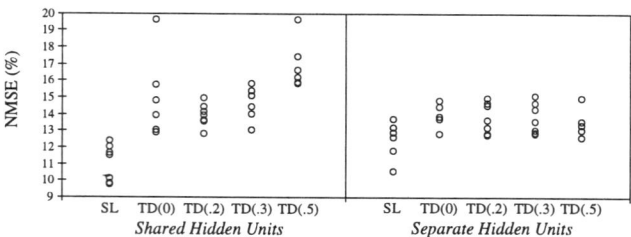

Figure 3: E_{NMS} for the direct five-step prediction $\hat{y}_5$ for both architectures (test set).

Performance comparison between single task and multi-task SL learning. Still for the task of five-step ahead prediction, we wanted to investigate whether predicting several tasks versus predicting a single task is beneficial. Comparing the SL column between the left and the right side of Figure 3 shows no significant difference. To eliminate the hypotheses that the performance was limited by the available number of hidden units, we also ran networks with only a single output unit for the one task of $\hat{y}_5$ and allocated up to 50 hidden units. The performance still remains the same. Thus, the fact that additional tasks *did not hurt* the performance indicates that the networks had sufficient resources. The fact that additional tasks *did not help* the performance indicates that there is only little noise in the data. This is different in high-noise problems, e.g., Weigend, Huberman and Rumelhart (1992) used multi-task predictions for currency exchange rates. See also Breiman and Friedman (1994), Caruana (1994), and Nix and Weigend (1995) for further discussions on multi-task learning.

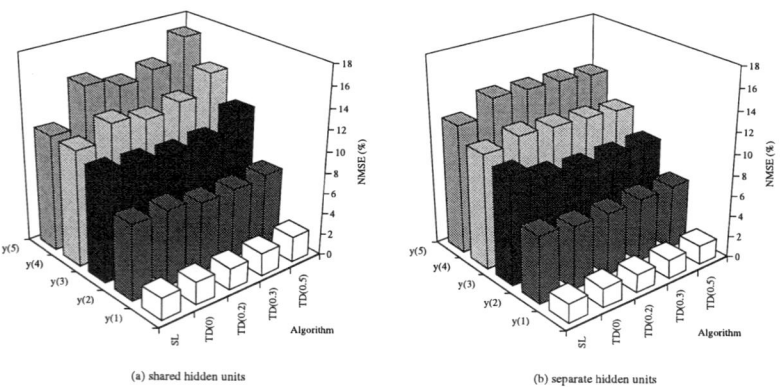

(a) shared hidden units   (b) separate hidden units

Figure 4: Summary of test set performance for SL and TD(λ) for both architectures.

SL vs. TD learning. Figure 4 and Table 1 summarize the performance of all the networks. As stated earlier, networks trained by SL outperformed networks trained by TD(λ) for $\hat{y}_5$. For earlier predictions $\hat{y}_1 - \hat{y}_4$, no significant performance discrepancies exist for either architecture or learning algorithm. Note, for $\hat{y}_1$, the results for the TD(0) and SL networks are equivalent for the separate hidden unit network, since the error function was equivalent for both algorithms. Among the networks trained by TD learning, the TD(0.3) and TD(0.5) networks exhibit the best average performance.

Prediction	SL	TD(0)	TD(0.2)	TD(0.3)	TD(0.5)	$\pm \sigma$
Shared:						
$\hat{y}_1$	2.1	2.1	2.0	2.1	2.3	0.13
$\hat{y}_2$	7.0	7.1	6.6	6.7	7.0	0.63
$\hat{y}_3$	10.2	10.0	9.8	10.0	11.8	0.83
$\hat{y}_4$	10.9	12.4	11.8	12.5	14.4	0.91
$\hat{y}_5$	11.0	14.8	13.9	14.6	16.8	1.30
Separate:						
$\hat{y}_1$	1.8	1.8	1.7	1.7	1.7	0.05
$\hat{y}_2$	6.2	5.8	5.8	6.0	6.1	0.25
$\hat{y}_3$	10.2	9.0	8.7	8.8	8.9	0.72
$\hat{y}_4$	10.8	11.5	11.3	11.2	11.0	0.57
$\hat{y}_5$	12.2	13.9	13.8	13.7	13.4	0.85

Table 1: Summary of test set performance for SL and TD(λ) (E_{NMS} is given in percent and σ is the empirical standard deviation averaged over each row).

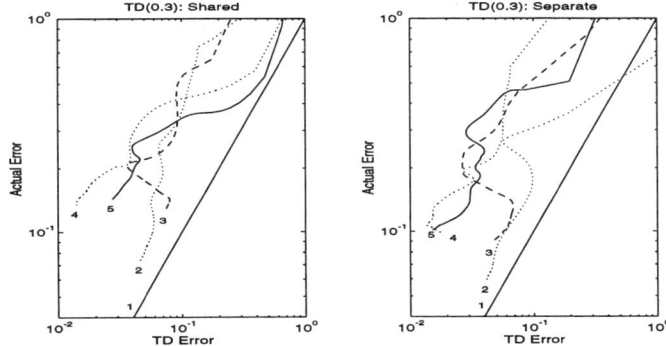

Figure 5: TD errors versus actual errors for both architectures ($\lambda = 0.3$)

Actual versus Temporal Difference errors. Since the temporal difference learning rule is based on the error between neighboring predictions in time, the following question may arise: How do the actual errors (between the predicted and observed values) vary with respect to the TD errors (between adjacent predictions of the same target) during training? Figure 5 plots the actual errors versus TD errors for λ=0.3 for both architectures. For both architectures, the TD errors are smaller than the actual errors. From Figure 5, in both architectures, nearer prediction errors influence further predictions. For noisier data sets, the curves in Figure 5, we expect, will take on an upward slope at the end of training, signaling that overfitting has begun.

5 Conclusions

We explored the application of Temporal Difference (TD) learning to forecasting real-valued time series, as opposed to game-like situations. After relating TD learning to supervised learning (SL) from a general perspective, we compare and analyze the performance of both paradigms on a specific data set, the deterministic chaotic laser data used in the Santa Fe Competition. For this low-noise time series data we find

- Within each paradigm, the learning curves (for the individual outputs) do not depend on the specific architecture of shared or separate hidden units.
- Across the two paradigms, the learning curves in SL show a larger error trade-off amongst the individual outputs than in TD learning.
- For the longest lead time considered (five-step ahead predictions), the difference between SL and TD is most pronounced: SL outperforms TD.
- Within SL, giving the network additional tasks (such as not only predicting the five-step ahead forecast but also the intermediate steps and using shared hidden units) did not change the performance compared to a single output with separate hidden units.
- The best choice of the recency weight λ appears to be in the range of $0.2 \leq \lambda \leq 0.5$.
- Plotting the TD error versus the actual error is a useful new diagnostic, particularly on out-of-sample data for noisy problems.

The performance of TD learning in comparison to SL depends on the amount of noise present in the data. For the low noise time series used in this paper, there is no advantage in using TD learning over SL. At present, we are comparing the two paradigms on noisy real-world data where overfitting is a serious challenge.

Acknowledgments

We thank Richard Sutton for his suggestions concerning the implementation. Andreas Weigend acknowledges support from the National Science Foundation, Research Initiation Grant No. RIA ECS-9309786.

References

L. Breiman and J.H. Friedman (1994) "A New Look at Multiple Outputs." Abstract, Neural Networks for Computing, Snowbird, UT, April 1994

R.A. Caruana (1994) "Multitask Connectionist Learning." In *Proceedings of the 1993 Connectionist Models Summer School*, edited by M. C. Mozer, P. Smolensky, D. S. Touretzky, J. L. Elman, and A. S. Weigend, p. 372-379. Hillsdale, NJ: Erlbaum Associates.

D.A. Nix and A.S. Weigend (1995) "Learning Local Error Bars for Nonlinear Regression." In *Advances in Neural Information Processing Systems 7 (NIPS*94, this volume)*. San Francisco, CA: Morgan Kaufmann.

R.S. Sutton (1988) "Learning to Predict by the Methods of Temporal Differences." *Machine Learning* **3**: 9-44.

G. Tesauro (1992) "Practical Issues in Temporal Difference learning." *Machine Learning* **8**: 257-277.

A.S. Weigend & N.A. Gershenfeld, eds. (1994) *Time Series Prediction: Forecasting the Future and Understanding the Past*. Reading, MA: Addison-Wesley.

A.S. Weigend, B.A. Huberman, and D.E. Rumelhart (1992) "Predicting Sunspots and Exchange Rates with Connectionist Networks." In *Nonlinear Modeling and Forecasting*, edited by M. Casdagli, and S. Eubank, p. 395-432. Redwood City, CA: Addison-Wesley.

PART VI
IMPLEMENTATIONS

ICEG Morphology Classification using an Analogue VLSI Neural Network

Richard Coggins, Marwan Jabri, Barry Flower and Stephen Pickard
Systems Engineering and Design Automation Laboratory
Department of Electrical Engineering J03,
University of Sydney, 2006, Australia.
Email: richardc@sedal.su.oz.au

Abstract

An analogue VLSI neural network has been designed and tested to perform cardiac morphology classification tasks. Analogue techniques were chosen to meet the strict power and area requirements of an Implantable Cardioverter Defibrillator (ICD) system. The robustness of the neural network architecture reduces the impact of noise, drift and offsets inherent in analogue approaches. The network is a 10:6:3 multi-layer perceptron with on chip digital weight storage, a bucket brigade input to feed the Intracardiac Electrogram (ICEG) to the network and has a winner take all circuit at the output. The network was trained in loop and included a commercial ICD in the signal processing path. The system has successfully distinguished arrhythmia for different patients with better than 90% true positive and true negative detections for dangerous rhythms which cannot be detected by present ICDs. The chip was implemented in $1.2um$ CMOS and consumes less than 200nW maximum average power in an area of $2.2 \times 2.2mm^2$.

1 INTRODUCTION

To the present time, most ICDs have used timing information from ventricular leads only to classify rhythms which has meant some dangerous rhythms can not be distinguished from safe ones, limiting the use of the device. Even two lead

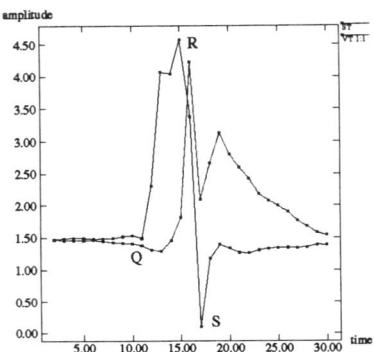

Figure 1: The Morphology of ST and VT retrograde 1:1.

atrial/ventricular systems fail to distinguish some rhythms when timing information alone is used [Leong and Jabri, 1992]. A case in point is the separation of Sinus Tachycardia (ST) from Ventricular Tachycardia with 1:1 retrograde conduction. ST is a safe arrhythmia which may occur during vigorous exercise and is characterised by a heart rate of approximately 120 beats/minute. VT retrograde 1:1 also occurs at the same low rate but can be a potentially fatal condition. False negative detections can cause serious heart muscle injury while false positive detections deplete the batteries, cause patient suffering and may lead to costly transplantation of the device. Figure 1 shows however, the way in which the morphology changes on the ventricular lead for these rhythms. Note, that the morphology change is predominantly in the "QRS complex" where the letters QRS are the conventional labels for the different points in the conduction cycle during which the heart is actually pumping blood.

For a number of years, researchers have studied template matching schemes in order to try and detect such morphology changes. However, techniques such as correlation waveform analysis [Lin et. al., 1988], though quite successful are too computationally intensive to meet power requirements. In this paper, we demonstrate that an analogue VLSI neural network can detect such morphology changes while still meeting the strict power and area requirements of an implantable system. The advantages of an analogue approach are born out when one considers that an energy efficient analogue to digital converter such as [Kusumoto et. al., 1993] uses 1.5nJ per conversion implying 375nW power consumption for analogue to digital conversion of the ICEG alone. Hence, the integration of a bucket brigade device and analogue neural network provides a very efficient way of interfacing to the analogue domain. Further, since the network is trained in loop with the ICD in real time, the effects of device offsets, noise, QRS detection jitter and signal distortion in the analogue circuits are largely alleviated.

The next section discusses the chip circuit designs. Section 3 describes the method

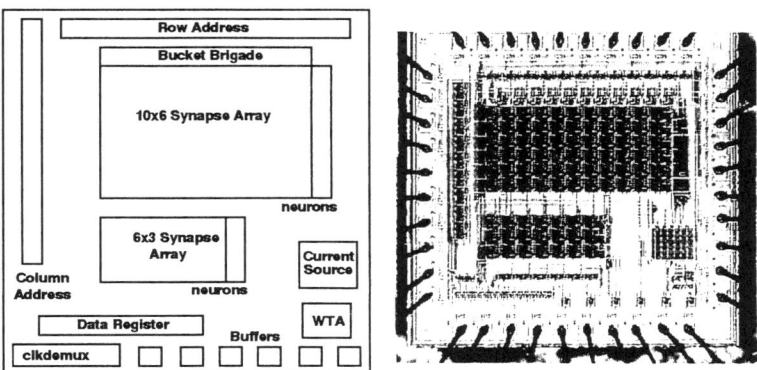

Figure 2: Floor Plan and Photomicrograph of the chip

used to train the network for the morphology classification task. Section 4 describes the classifier performance on seven patients with arrhythmia which can not be distinguished using the heart rate only. Section 5 summarises the results, remaining problems and future directions for the work.

2 ARCHITECTURE

The neural network chip consists of a 10:6:3 multilayer perceptron, an input bucket brigade device (BBD) and a winner take all (WTA) circuit at the output. A floor plan and photomicrograph of the chip appears in figure 2. The BBD samples the incoming ICEG at a rate of 250Hz. For three class problems, the winner take all circuit converts the winning class to a digital signal. For the two class problem considered in this paper, a simple thresholding function suffices. The following subsections briefly describe the functional elements of the chip. The circuit diagrams for the chip building blocks appear in figure 3.

2.1 BUCKET BRIGADE DEVICE

One stage of the bucket brigade circuit is shown in figure 3. The BBD uses a two phase clock to shift charge from cell to cell and is based on a design by Leong [Leong, 1992]. The BBD operates by transferring charge deficits from S to D in each of the cells. PHI1 and PHI2 are two phase non-overlapping clocks. The cell is buffered from the synapse array to maintain high charge transfer efficiency. A sample and hold facility is provided to store the input on the gates of the synapses. The BBD clocks are generated off chip and are controlled by the QRS complex detector in the ICD.

2.2 SYNAPSE

This synapse has been used on a number of neural network chips previously. e.g. [Coggins et. al., 1994]. The synapse has five bits plus sign weight storage which

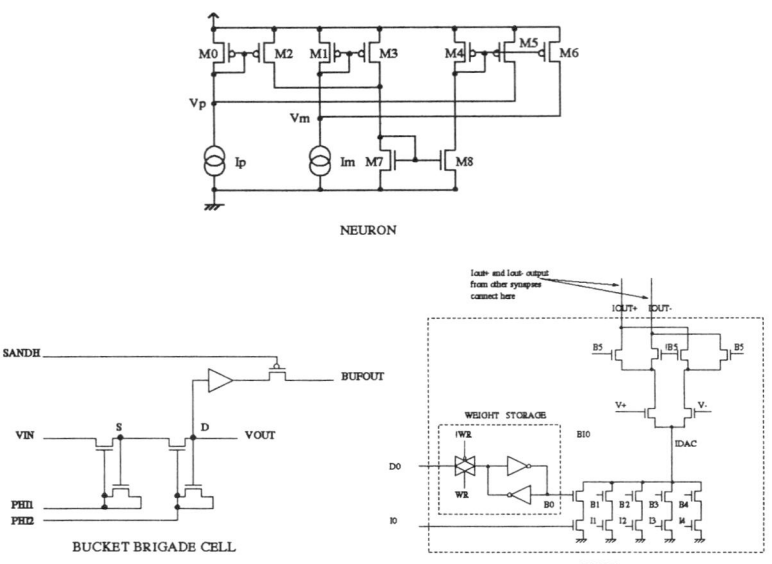

Figure 3: Neuron, Bucket Brigade and Synapse Circuit Diagrams.

sets the bias to a differential pair which performs the multiplication. The bias references for the weights are derived from a weighted current source in the corner of the chip. A four quadrant multiplication is achieved by the four switches at the top of the differential pair.

2.3 NEURON

Due to the low power requirements, the bias currents of the synapse arrays are of the order of hundreds of nano amps, hence the neurons must provide an effective resistance of many mega ohms to feed the next synapse layer while also providing gain control. Without special high resistance polysilicon, simple resistive neurons use prohibitive area. However, for larger networks with fan-in much greater than ten, an additional problem of common mode cancellation is encountered. That is, as the fan-in increases, a larger common mode range is required or a cancellation scheme using common mode feedback is needed.

The neuron of figure 3 implements such a cancellation scheme. The mirrors M0/M2 and M1/M3 divide the input current and facilitate the sum at the drain of M7. M7/M8 mirrors the sum so that it may be split into two equal currents by the mirrors formed by M4, M5 and M6 which are then subtracted from the input currents. Thus, the differential voltage $V_p - V_m$ is a function of the transistor transconductances, the common mode input current and the feedback factor. The gain of the neuron can be controlled by varying the width to length ratio of the mirror transistors M0 and M1. The implementation in this case allows seven gain combinations, using a three bit RAM cell to store the gain.

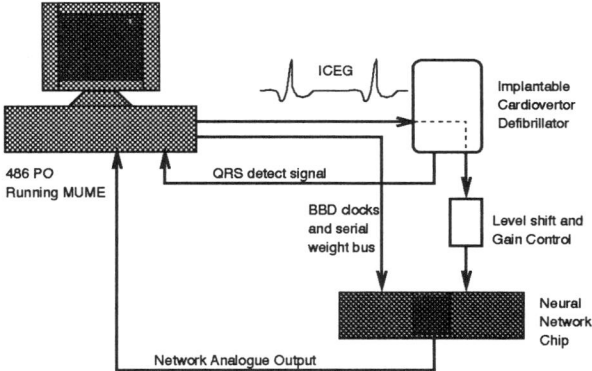

Figure 4: Block Diagram of the Training and Testing System.

The importance of a common mode cancellation scheme for large networks can be seen when compared to the straight forward approach of resistive or switched capacitor neurons. This may be illustrated by considering the energy usage of the two approaches. Firstly, we need to define the required gain of the neuron as a function of its fan-in. If we assume that useful inputs to the network are mostly sparse, i.e. with a small fraction of non-zero values, then the gain is largely independent of the fan-in, yet the common mode signal increases linearly with fan-in. For the case of a neuron which does not cancel the common mode, the power supply voltage must be increased to accommodate the common mode signal, thus leading to a quadratic increase in energy use with fan-in. A common mode cancelling neuron on the other hand, suffers only a linear increase in energy use with fan-in since extra voltage range is not required and the increased energy use arises only due to the linear increase in common mode current.

3 TRAINING SYSTEM

The system used to train and test the neural network is shown in figure 4. Control of training and testing takes place on the PC. The PC uses a PC-LAB card to provide analogue and digital I/O. The PC plays the ICEG signal to the input of the commercial ICD in real time. Note, that the PC is only required for initially training the network and in this case as a source of the heart signal. The commercial ICD performs the function of QRS complex detection using analogue circuits. The QRS complex detection signal is then used to freeze the BBD clocks of the chip, so that a classification can take place.

When training, a number of examples of the arrhythmia to be classified are selected from a single patient data base recorded during an electrophysiological study and previously classified by a cardiologist. Since most of the morphological information is in the QRS complex, only these segments of the data are repeatedly presented to

Patient	% Training Attempts Converged				Average Iterations
	Run 1		Run 2		
	H = 3	H = 6	H = 3	H = 6	
1	80	10	60	60	62
2	80	100	0	10	86
3	0	0	0	10	101
4	60	10	40	40	77
5	100	80	0	60	44
6	100	40	60	60	46
7	80	100	40	100	17

Table 1: Training Performance of the system on seven patients.

the network. The weights are adjusted according to the training algorithm running on the PC using the analogue outputs of the network to reduce the output error. The PC writes weights to the chip via the digital I/Os of the PC-LAB card and the serial weight bus of network. The software package implementing the training and testing, called MUME [Jabri et. al., 1992], provides a suite of training algorithms and control options. Online training was used due to its success in training small networks and because the presentation of the QRS complexes to the network was the slowest part of the training procedure. The algorithm used for weight updates in this paper was summed weight node perturbation [Flower and Jabri, 1993].

The system was trained on seven different patients separately all of whom had VT with 1: 1 retrograde conduction. Note, that patient independent training has been tried but with mixed results [Tinker, 1992]. Table 1 summarises the training statistics for the seven patients. For each patient and each architecture, five training runs were performed starting from a different random initial weight set. Each of the patients was trained with eight of each class of arrhythmia. The network architecture used was 10:H:1, where H is the number of hidden layer neurons and the unused neurons being disabled by setting their input weights to zero. Two sets of data were collected denoted Run 1 and Run 2. Run 1 corresponded to output target values of $\pm 0.6V$ within margin $0.45V$ and Run 2 to output target values of $\pm 0.2V$ within margin $0.05V$. A training attempt was considered to have converged when the training set was correctly classified within two hundred training iterations. Once the morphologies to be distinguished have been learned for a given patient, the remainder of the patient data base is played back in a continuous stream and the outputs of the classifier at each QRS complex are logged and may be compared to the classifications of a cardiologist. The resulting generalisation performance is discussed in the next section.

4 MORPHOLOGY CLASSIFIER GENERALISATION PERFORMANCE

Table 2 summarises the generalisation performance of the system on the seven patients for the training attempts which converged. Most of the patients show a correct classification rate better than 90% for at least one architecture on one of the

Patient	No. of Complexes		% Correct Classifications Run 1			
			H = 3		H = 6	
	ST	VT	ST	VT	ST	VT
1	440	61	89±10	89±3	58±0	99±0
2	94	57	99±1	99±1	100±0	99±1
3	67	146	-	-	-	-
4	166	65	66±44	76±37	99±1	50±3
5	61	96	82±1	75±13	94±6	89±9
6	61	99	84±8	97±1	90±5	99±1
7	28	80	98±5	97±3	99±1	99±1
			% Correct Classifications Run 2			
1	440	61	88±2	99±1	86±14	99±1
2	94	57	-	-	94±6	94±3
3	67	146	84±2	99±1	-	-
4	166	65	76±18	59±2	87±7	100±0
5	61	96	88±2	49±5	84±1	82±5
6	61	99	92±6	90±10	99±1	99±1
7	28	80	94±3	99±0	94±3	92±3

Table 2: Generalisation Performance of the system on seven patients.

runs, whereas, a timing based classifier can not separate these arrhythmia at all. For each convergent weight set the network classified the test set five times. Thus, the "% Correct" columns denote the mean and standard deviation of the classifier performance with respect to both training and testing variations. By duty cycling the bias to the network and buffers, the chip dissipates less than 200nW power for a nominal heart rate of 120 beats/minute during generalisation.

5 DISCUSSION

Referring to table 1 we see that the patient 3 data was relatively difficult to train. However, for the one occasion when training converged generalisation performance was quite acceptable. Inspection of this patients data showed that typically, the morphologies of the two rhythms were very similar. The choice of output targets, margins and architecture appear to be patient dependent and possibly interacting factors. Although larger margins make training easier for some patients they appear to also introduce more variability in generalisation performance. This may be due to the non-linearity of the neuron circuit. Further experiments are required to optimise the architecture for a given patient and to clarify the effect of varying targets, margins and neuron gain. Penalty terms could also be added to the error function to minimise the possibility of missed detections of the dangerous rhythm.

The relatively slow rate of the heart results in the best power consumption being obtained by duty cycling the bias currents to the synapses and the buffers. Hence, the bias settling time of the weighted current source is the limiting factor for reducing power consumption further for this design. By modifying the connection of the current source to the synapses using a bypassing technique to reduce transients in the weighted currents, still lower power consumption could be achieved.

6 CONCLUSION

The successful classification of a difficult cardiac arrhythmia problem has been demonstrated using an analogue VLSI neural network approach. Furthermore, the chip developed has shown very low power consumption of less than 200nW, meeting the requirements of an implantable system. The chip has performed well, with over 90% classification performance for most patients studied and has proved to be robust when the real world influence of analogue QRS detection jitter is introduced by a commercial implantable cardioverter defibrillator placed in the signal path to the classifier.

Acknowledgements

The authors acknowledge the funding for the work in this paper provided under Australian Generic Technology Grant Agreement No. 16029 and thank Dr. Phillip Leong of the University of Sydney and Dr. Peter Nickolls of Telectronics Pacing Systems Ltd., Australia for their helpful suggestions and advice.

References

[Castro et. al., 1993] H.A. Castro, S.M. Tam, M.A. Holler, "Implementation and Performance of an analogue Nonvolatile Neural Network," *Analogue Integrated Circuits and Signal Processing*, vol. 4(2), pp. 97-113, September 1993.

[Lin et. al., 1988] D. Lin, L.A. Dicarlo, and J.M. Jenkins, "Identification of Ventricular Tachycardia using Intracavitary Electrograms: analysis of time and frequency domain patterns," *Pacing & Clinical Electrophysiology*, pp. 1592–1606, November 1988.

[Leong, 1992] P.H.W. Leong, Arrhythmia Classification Using Low Power VLSI, PhD Thesis, University of Sydney, Appendix B, 1992.

[Kusumoto et. al., 1993] K. Kusumoto et. al., "A 10bit 20Mhz 30mW Pipelined Interpolating ADC," *ISSCC, Digest of Technical Papers*, pp. 62-63, 1993.

[Leong and Jabri, 1992] P.H.W. Leong and M. Jabri, "MATIC - An Intracardiac Tachycardia Classification System", *Pacing & Clinical Electrophysiology*, September 1992.

[Coggins et. al., 1994] R.J. Coggins and M.A. Jabri, "WATTLE: A Trainable Gain Analogue VLSI Neural Network", *NIPS6*, Morgan Kauffmann Publishers, 1994.

[Jabri et. al., 1992] M.A. Jabri, E.A. Tinker and L. Leerink, "MUME- A Multi-Net-Multi-Architecture Neural Simulation Environment", Neural Network Simulation Environments, Kluwer Academic Publications, January, 1994.

[Flower and Jabri, 1993] B. Flower and M. Jabri, "Summed Weight Neuron Perturbation: an O(N) improvement over Weight Perturbation," *NIPS5*, Morgan Kauffmann Publishers, pp. 212-219, 1993.

[Tinker, 1992] E.A. Tinker, "The SPASM Algorithm for Ventricular Lead Timing and Morphology Classification," SEDAL ICEG-RPT-016-92, Department of Electrical Engineering, University of Sydney, 1992.

A Silicon Axon

Bradley A. Minch, Paul Hasler, Chris Diorio, Carver Mead

Physics of Computation Laboratory
California Institute of Technology
Pasadena, CA 91125

bminch, paul, chris, carver@pcmp.caltech.edu

Abstract

We present a silicon model of an axon which shows promise as a building block for pulse-based neural computations involving correlations of pulses across both space and time. The circuit shares a number of features with its biological counterpart including an excitation threshold, a brief refractory period after pulse completion, pulse amplitude restoration, and pulse width restoration. We provide a simple explanation of circuit operation and present data from a chip fabricated in a standard $2\mu m$ CMOS process through the MOS Implementation Service (MOSIS). We emphasize the necessity of the restoration of the width of the pulse in time for stable propagation in axons.

1 INTRODUCTION

It is well known that axons are neural processes specialized for transmitting information over relatively long distances in the nervous system. Impulsive electrical disturbances known as *action potentials* are normally initiated near the cell body of a neuron when the voltage across the cell membrane crosses a threshold. These pulses are then propagated with a fairly stereotypical shape at a more or less constant velocity down the length of the axon. Consequently, axons excel at precisely preserving the relative timing of threshold crossing events but do not preserve any of the initial signal shape. Information, then, is presumably encoded in the relative timing of action potentials.

The biophysical mechanisms underlying the initiation and propagation of action potentials in axons have been well studied since the seminal work of Hodgkin and Huxley on the giant axon of *Loligo*. (Hodgkin & Huxley, 1952) Briefly, when the voltage across a small patch of the cell membrane increases to a certain level, a population of ion channels permeable to sodium opens, allowing an influx of sodium ions, which, in turn, causes the membrane voltage to increase further and a pulse to be initiated. This population of channels rapidly inactivates, preventing the passage of additional ions. Another population of channels permeable to potassium opens after a brief delay causing an efflux of potassium ions, restoring the membrane to a more negative potential and terminating the pulse. This cycle of ion migration is coupled to neighboring sections of the axon, causing the action potential to propagate. The sodium channels remain inactivated for a brief interval of time during which the affected patch of membrane will not be able to support another action potential. This period of time is known as the refractory period. The axon circuit which we present in this paper does not attempt to model the detailed dynamics of the various populations of ion channels, although such detailed neuromimes are both possible (Lewis, 1968; Mahowald & Douglas, 1991) and useful for learning about natural neural systems. Nonetheless, it shares a number of important features with its biological counterpart including having a threshold for excitation and a refractory period.

It is well accepted that the amplitude of the action potential must be restored as it propagates. It is not as universally understood is that the *width* of the action potential must be restored *in time* if it is to propagate over any appreciable distance. Otherwise, the pulse would smear out in time resulting in a loss of precise timing information, or it would shrink down to nothing and cease to propagate altogether. In biological axons, restoration of the pulse width is accomplished through the dynamics of sodium channel inactivation and potassium channel activation. In our silicon model, the pulse width is restored through feedback from the successive stage. This feedback provides an inactivation which is similar to that of the sodium channels in biological axons and is also the underlying cause of refractoriness in our circuit.

In the following section we provide a simple description of how the circuit behaves. Following this, data from a chip fabricated in a standard $2\mu m$ CMOS process through MOSIS are presented and discussed.

2 THE SILICON AXON CIRCUIT

An axon circuit which is to be used as a building block in large-scale computational systems should be made as simple and low-power as possible, since it would be replicated many times in any such system. Each stage of the axon circuit described below consists of five transistors and two small capacitors, making the axon circuit very compact. The axon circuit uses the delay through a stage to time the signal which is fed back to restore the pulse width, thus avoiding the need for an additional delay circuit for each section. Additonally, the circuit operates with low power; during typical operation (a pulse of width $2ms$ travelling at $10^3 stages/s$), pulse propagation costs about $4pJ/stage$ of energy. Under these circumstances, the circuit consumes about $2nW/stage$ of static power.

A Silicon Axon

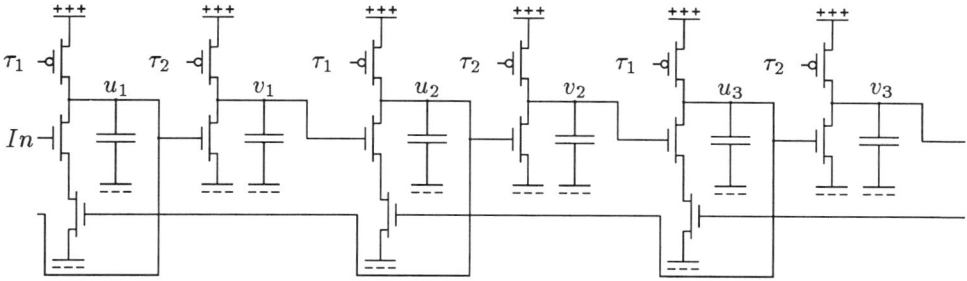

Figure 1: Three sections of the axon circuit.

Three stages of the axon circuit are depicted in Figure 1. A single stage consists of two capacitors and what would be considered a pseudo-nMOS NAND gate and a pseudo-nMOS inverter in digital logic design. These simple circuits are characterized by a *threshold voltage* for switching and a *slew rate* for recharging. Consider the inverter circuit. If the input is held low for a sufficiently long time, the pull-up transistor will have charged the output voltage almost completely to the positive rail. If the input voltage is ramped up toward the positive rail, the current in the pull-down transistor will increase rapidly. At some input voltage level, the current in the pull-down transistor will equal the saturation current of the pull-up transistor; this voltage is known as the threshold. The output voltage will begin to discharge at a rapidly increasing rate as the input voltage is increased further. After a very short time, the output will have discharged almost all the way to the negative rail. Now, if the input were decreased rapidly, the output voltage would ramp linearly in time (slew) up toward the positive rail at a rate set by the saturation current in the pull-up transistor and the capacitor on the output node. The NAND gate is similar except *both* inputs must be (roughly speaking) above the threshold in order for the output to go low. If *either* input goes low, the output will charge toward the positive rail. Note also that if one input of the NAND gate is held high, the circuit behaves exactly as an inverter.

The axon circuit is formed by cascading multiple copies of this simple five transistor circuit in series. Let the voltage on the first capacitor of the nth stage be denoted by u_n and the voltage on the second capacitor by v_n. Note that there is feedback from u_{n+1} to the lower input of the NAND gate of the nth stage. Under quiescent conditions, the input to the first stage is low (at the negative rail), the u nodes of all stages are high (at the positive rail), and all of the v nodes are held low (at the negative rail). The feedback signal to the final stage in the line would be tied to the positive rail. The level of the bias voltages τ_1 and τ_2 determine whether or not a narrow pulse fed into the input of the first stage will propagate and, if so, the width and velocity with which it does.

In order to obtain a semi-quantitative understanding of how the axon circuit behaves, we will first consider the dynamics of a cascade of simple inverters (three sections of which are depicted in Figure 2) and then consider the addition of feedback. Under most circumstances, discharges will occur on a much faster time scale than the recharges, so we make the simplifying assumption that when the input of an inverter reaches the threshold voltage, the output discharges instantaneously. Additionally, we assume that saturated transistors behave as ideal current sources (i.e., we neglect the Early effect) so that the recharges are linear ramps in time.

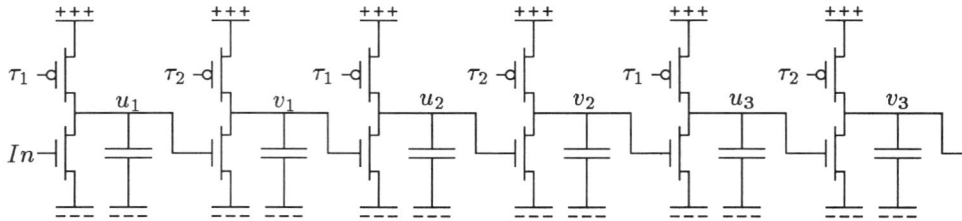

Figure 2: A cascade of pseudo-nMOS inverters.

Let I_1 and I_2 be the saturation currents in the pull-up transistors with bias voltages τ_1 and τ_2, respectively. Let Θ_1 and Θ_2 be the threshold voltages of the first and second inverters in a single stage, respectively. Also, let $\dot{u} = I_1/C$ and $\dot{v} = I_2/C$ be the slew rates for the u and v nodes, respectively. Let $\Delta_1 = \Theta_1/\dot{v}$ and $\Delta_2 = \Theta_2/\dot{u}$ be the time required for u_n to charge from the negative rail up to Θ_1 and for v_n to charge from the negative rail up to Θ_2, respectively. Finally, let v_n^* denote the peak value attained by the v signal of the nth stage.

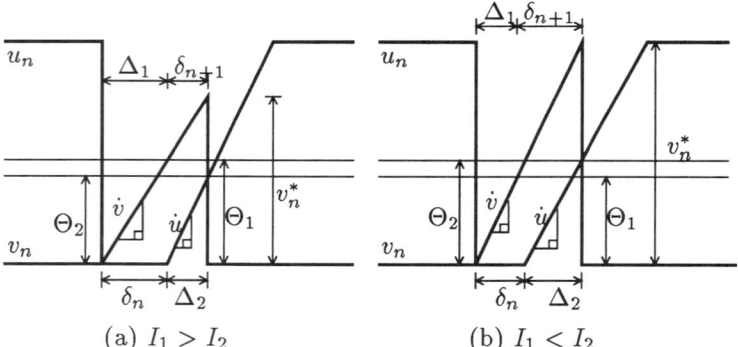

Figure 3: Geometry of the idealized u_n and v_n signals under the bias conditions (a) $I_1 > I_2$ and (b) $I_1 < I_2$.

Consider what would happen if v_{n-1} exceeded Θ_1 for a time δ_n. In this case, u_n would be held low for δ_n and then released. Meanwhile, v_n would ramp up to $\dot{v}\delta_n$. Then, u_n would begin to charge toward the positive rail while v_n continues to charge. This continues for a time Δ_2 at which point u_n will have reached Θ_2 causing

v_n to be discharged to the negative rail. Now, u_{n+1} is held low while v_n exceeds Θ_1 this interval of time is precisely δ_{n+1}. Figures 3a and 3b depict the geometry of the u_n and v_n signals in this scenario under the bias conditions $I_1 > I_2$ and $I_1 < I_2$, respectively. Simple Euclidean geometry implies that the evolution of δ_n will be governed by the first-order difference equation

$$\delta_{n+1} = \delta_n + (\Delta_2 - \Delta_1)$$

which is trivially solved by

$$\delta_n = \delta_1 + (n-1)(\Delta_2 - \Delta_1).$$

Thus, the quantity $\Delta_2 - \Delta_1$ determines what happens to the width of the pulse as it propagates. In the event that $\Delta_2 < \Delta_1$, the pulse will shrink down to nothing from its initial width. If $\Delta_2 > \Delta_1$, the pulse width will grow without bound from its initial width. The pulse width is preserved only if $\Delta_2 = \Delta_1$. This last case, however, is unrealistic. There will always be component mismatches (with both systematic and random parts), which will cause the width of the pulse to grow and shrink as it propagates down the line, perhaps cancelling on average. Any systematic offsets will cause the pulse to shrink to nothing or to grow without bound as it propagates. In any event, information about the detailed timing of the initial pulse will have been completely lost.

Now, consider the action of the feedback in the axon circuit (Figure 1). If u_n were to be held low for a time longer than Δ_1 (i.e., the time it takes v_n to charge up to Θ_1), u_{n+1} would come back and release u_n, regardless of the state of the input. Thus, the feedback enforces the condition $\delta_n \leq \Delta_1$. If $I_1 > I_2$ (i.e., $\Delta_2 < \Delta_1$), a pulse whose initial width is larger than Δ_1 will be clipped to Δ_1 and then shrink down to nothing and disappear. In the event that $I_1 < I_2$ (i.e., $\Delta_2 > \Delta_1$), a pulse whose initial duration is too small will grow up until its width is limited by the feedback. The axon circuit normally operates under the latter bias condition. The dynamics of the simple inverter chain cause a pulse which is to narrow to grow and the feedback loop serves to limit the pulse width; thus, the width of the pulse is restored in time. The feedback is also the source of the refractoriness in the axon; that is, until u_{n+1} charges up to (roughly) Θ_1, v_{n-1} can have no effect on u_n.

3 EXPERIMENTAL DATA

In this section, data from a twenty-five stage axon will be shown. The chip was fabricated in a standard $2\mu m$ p-well (Orbit) CMOS process through MOSIS.

Uniform Axon

A full space-time picture of pulse (taken at the v nodes of the circuit) propagation down a uniform axon is depicted on the left in Figure 4. The graph on the right in Figure 4 shows the same data from a different perspective. The lower sloped curve represents the time of the initial rapid discharge of the u node at each successive stage–this time marks the leading edge of the pulse taken at the v node of that stage.

The upper sloped curve marks the time of the final rapid discharge of the v node of each stage–this time is the end of the pulse taken at the v node of that stage. The propagation velocity of the pulse is given (in units of *stages/s*) by the reciprocal of the slope of the lower inclined curve. The third curve is the difference of the other two and represents the pulse width as a function of position along the axon. The graph on the left of Figure 5 shows propagation velocity as a function of the τ_2 bias voltage–so long as the pulse propagates, the velocity is nearly independent of τ_1. Two orders of magnitude of velocity are shown in the plot; these are especially well matched to the time scales of motion in auditory and visual sensory data. The circuit is tunable over a much wider range of velocities (from about one stage per second to well in excess of $10^4 stages/s$). The graph on the right of Figure 5 shows pulse width as a function of τ_1 for various values of τ_2–the pulse width is mainly determined by τ_1 with τ_2 setting a lower limit.

Tapered Axon

In biological axons, the propagation velocity of an action potential is related to the diameter of the axon–the bigger the diameter, the greater the velocity. If the axon were tapered, the velocity of the action potential would change as it propagated. If the bias transistors in the axon circuit are operated in their subthreshold region, the effect of an exponentially tapered axon can be simulated by applying a small voltage difference to the ends of each of the τ_1 and τ_2 bias lines. (Lyon & Mead, 1989) These narrow wires are made with a relatively resistive layer (polysilicon); hence, putting a voltage difference across the ends will linearly interpolate the bias voltages for each stage along the line. In subthreshold, the bias currents are exponentially related to the bias voltages. Since the pulse width and velocity are related to the bias currents, we expect that a pulse will either speed up and get narrower or slow down and get wider (depending on the sign of the applied voltage) exponentially as a function of position along the line. The graph on the left of Figure 6 depicts the boundaries of a pulse as it propagates along of the axon circuit for a positive (*'s) and negative (x's) voltage difference applied to the τ lines. The graph on the right of Figure 6 shows the corresponding pulse width for each applied voltage difference. Note that in each case, the width changes by more than an order of magnitude, but the pulse maintains its integrity. That is, the pulse does not disappear nor does it split into multiple pulses–this behavior would not be possible if the pulse width were not restored in time.

4 CONCLUSIONS

In this paper we have presented a low-power, compact axon circuit, explained its operation, and presented data from a working chip fabricated through MOSIS. The circuit shares a number of features with its biological counterpart including an excitation threshold, a brief refractory period after pulse completion, pulse amplitude restoration, and pulse width restoration. It is tunable over orders of magnitude in pulse propagation velocity–including those well matched to the time scales of auditory and visual signals–and shows promise for use in synthetic neural systems which perform computations by correlating events which occur over both space and time such as those presented in (Horiuchi *et al*, 1991) and (Lazzaro & Mead, 1989).

Acknowledgements

This material is based upon work supported in part under a National Science Foundation Graduate Research Fellowship, the Office of Naval Research, DARPA, and the Beckman Foundation.

References

A. L. Hodgkin and A. K. Huxley, (1952). A Quantitative Description of Membrane Current and its Application to Conduction and Excitation in Nerve. *Journal of Physiology*, 117:6, 500-544.

T. Horiuchi, J. Lazzaro, A. Moore, and C. Koch, (1991). A Delay-Line Based Motion Detection Chip. *Advances in Neural Information Processing Systems 3*. San Mateo, CA: Morgan Kaufmann Publishers, Inc. 406-412.

J. Lazzaro and C. Mead, (1989). A Silicon Model of Auditory Localization. *Neural Computation*, 1:1, 47-57.

R. Lyon and C. Mead, (1989). Electronic Cochlea. *Analog VLSI and Neural Systems*. Reading, MA: Addison-Wesley Publishing Company, Inc. 279-302.

E. R. Lewis, (1968). Using Electronic Circuits to Model Simple Neuroelectric Interactions. *Proceedings of the IEEE*, 56:6, 931-949.

M. Mahowald and R. Douglas, (1991). A Silicon Neuron. *Nature*, 354:19, 515-518.

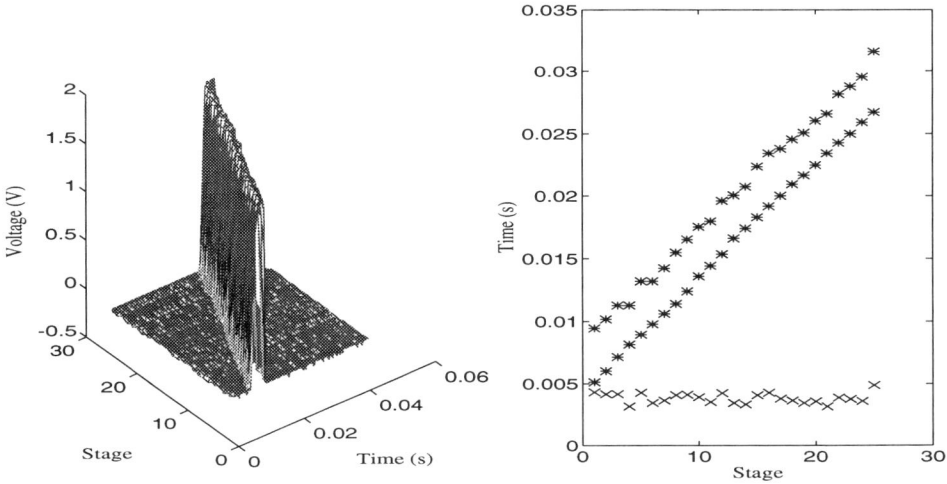

Figure 4: Pulse propagation along a uniform axon. (*Left*) Perspective view. (*Right*) Overhead view. *: pulse boundaries, x: pulse width. $\tau_1 = 0.720V$, $\tau_2 = 0.780V$. $Velocity = 1,100 stages/s$, $Width = 3.8ms$

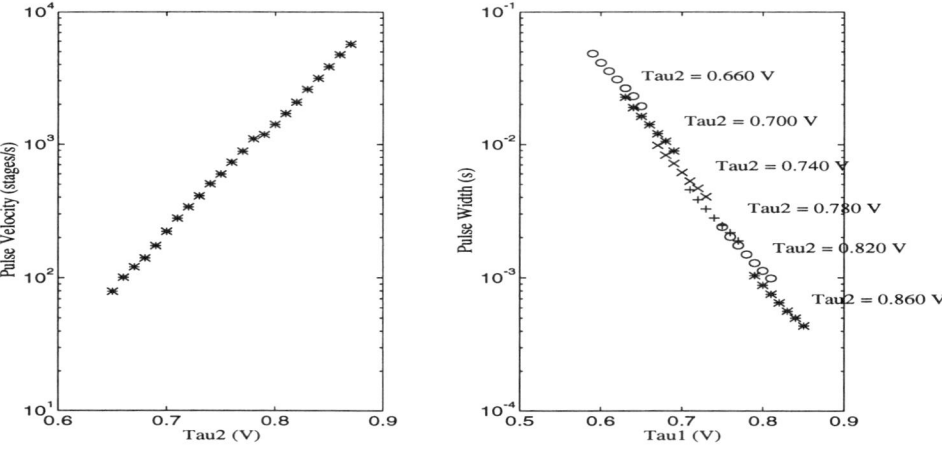

Figure 5: Uniform axon. (*Left*) Pulse velocity as a function of τ_2. (*Right*) Pulse width as a function of τ_1 for various values of τ_2.

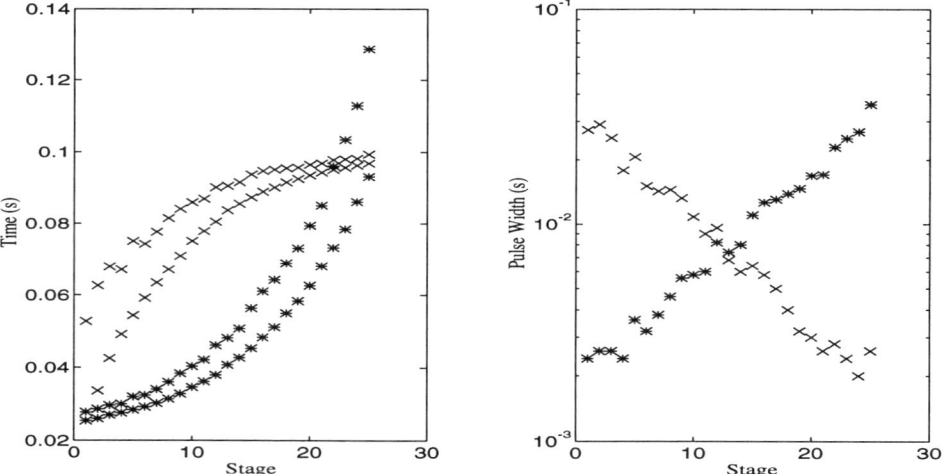

Figure 6: (*Left*) Pulse propagation along a tapered axon. (*Right*) Pulse width as a function of position along a tapered axon. *: $\tau_1^{left} = 0.770V$, $\tau_1^{right} = 0.600V$, $\tau_2^{left} = 0.820V$, $\tau_2^{right} = 0.650$. x: $\tau_1^{left} = 0.600V$, $\tau_1^{right} = 0.770V$, $\tau_2^{left} = 0.650V$, $\tau_2^{right} = 0.820V$.

The Ni1000: High Speed Parallel VLSI for Implementing Multilayer Perceptrons

Michael P. Perrone
Thomas J. Watson Research Center
P.O. Box 704
Yorktown Heights, NY 10598
mpp@watson.ibm.com

Leon N Cooper
Institute for Brain and Neural Systems
Brown University
Providence, Ri 02912
lnc@cns.brown.edu

Abstract

In this paper we present a new version of the standard multilayer perceptron (MLP) algorithm for the state-of-the-art in neural network VLSI implementations: the Intel Ni1000. This new version of the MLP uses a fundamental property of high dimensional spaces which allows the l_2-norm to be accurately approximated by the l_1-norm. This approach enables the standard MLP to utilize the parallel architecture of the Ni1000 to achieve on the order of 40000, 256-dimensional classifications per second.

1 The Intel Ni1000 VLSI Chip

The Nestor/Intel radial basis function neural chip (Ni1000) contains the equivalent of 1024 256-dimensional artificial digital neurons and can perform at least 40000 classifications per second [Sullivan, 1993]. To attain this great speed, the Ni1000 was designed to calculate "city block" distances (i.e. the l_1-norm) and thus to avoid the large number of multiplication units that would be required to calculate Euclidean dot products in parallel. Each neuron calculates the city block distance between its stored weights and the current input:

$$\text{neuron activity} = \sum_i |w_i - x_i| \qquad (1)$$

where w_i is the neuron's stored weight for the ith input and x_i is the ith input. Thus the Ni1000 is ideally suited to perform both the RCE [Reilly et al., 1982] and

PRCE [Scofield et al., 1987] algorithms or any of the other commonly used radial basis function (RBF) algorithms. However, dot products are central in the calculations performed by most neural network algorithms (e.g. MLP, Cascade Correlation, etc.). Furthermore, for high dimensional data, the dot product becomes the computation bottleneck (i.e. most of the network's time is spent calculating dot products). If the dot product can not be performed in parallel there will be little advantage using the Ni1000 for such algorithms. In this paper, we address this problem by showing that we can extend the Ni1000 to many of the standard neural network algorithms by representing the Euclidean dot product as a function of Euclidean norms and by then using a city block norm approximation to the Euclidean norm. Section 2, introduces the approximate dot product; Section 3 describes the City Block MLP which uses the approximate dot product; and Section 4 presents experiments which demonstrate that the City Block MLP performs well on the NIST OCR data and on human face recognition data.

2 Approximate Dot Product

Consider the following approximation [Perrone, 1993]:

$$||\vec{z}|| \approx \frac{1}{\sqrt{n}} |\vec{z}| \qquad (2)$$

where $\vec{z}$ is some n-dimensional vector, $||\cdot||$ is the Euclidean length (i.e. the l_2-norm) and $|\cdot|$ is the City Block length (i.e. the l_1-norm). This approximation is motivated by the fact that in high dimensional spaces it is accurate for a majority of the points in the space. In Figure 1, we suggest an intuitive interpretation of why this approximation is reasonable. It is clear from Figure 1 that the approximation is reasonable for about 20% of the points on the arc in 2 dimensions.[1] As the dimensionality of the data space increases, the tangent region in Figure 1 expands asymptotically to fill the entire space and thus the approximation becomes more valid. Below we examine how accurate this approximation is and how we can use it with the Ni1000, particularly in the MLP context. Given a set of vectors, V, all with equal city block length, we measure the accuracy of the approximation by the ratio of the variance of the Euclidean lengths in V to the squared mean Euclidean lengths in V. If the ratio is low, then the approximation is good and all we must do is scale the city block length to the mean Euclidean length to get a good fit.[2] In particular, it can be shown that assuming all the vectors of the space are equally likely, the following equation holds [Perrone, 1993]:

$$\sigma_n^2 < \left(\frac{2n}{\alpha_n^2(n+1)} - 1 \right) \mu_{\text{lower}}^2, \qquad (3)$$

where n is the dimension of the space; μ_n is the average Euclidean length of the set of vectors with fixed city block length S; σ_n^2 is the variance about the average Euclidean length; μ_{lower} is the lower bound for μ_n and is given by $\mu_{\text{lower}} \equiv \alpha_n S/\sqrt{n}$;

---
[1] In fact, approximately 20% of the points are within 1% of each other and 40% of the points are within 5% of each other.
[2] Note that in Equation 2 we scale by $1/\sqrt{n}$. For high dimensional spaces this is a good approximation to the ratio of the mean Euclidean length to the City Block length.

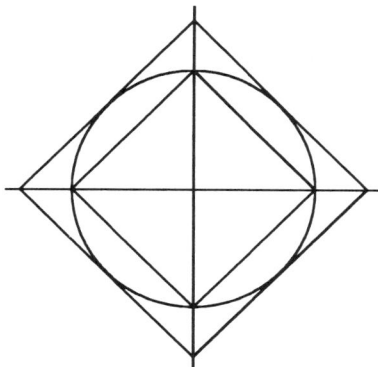

Figure 1: Two dimensional interpretation of the city block approximation. The circle corresponds to all of the vectors with the same Euclidean length. The inner square corresponds to all of the vectors with city block length equal the Euclidean length of the vectors in the circle. The outer square (tangent to the circle) corresponds to the set of vectors over which we will be making our approximation. In order to scale the outer square to the inner square, we multiple by $1/\sqrt{n}$ where n is the dimensionality of the space. The outer square approximates the circle in the regions near the tangent points. In high dimensional spaces, these tangent regions approximate a large portion of the total hypersphere and thus the city block distance is a good approximation along most of the hypersphere.

and α_n is defined by

$$\alpha_n \equiv \frac{n-1}{n+1}\sqrt{1+\frac{en}{2\pi(n-1)}}\left(\frac{n}{2}\right)^{\frac{1}{2n-2}}+\frac{2}{n+1}. \qquad (4)$$

From this equation we see that the ratio of σ_n^2 to μ_{lower}^2 in the large n limit is bounded above by 0.4. This bound is not very tight due to the complexity of the calculations required; however Figure 3 suggests that a much tighter bound must exist. A better bound exists if we are willing to add a minor constraint to our high dimensional space [Perrone, 1993]. In the case in which each dimension of the vector is constrained such that the entire vector cannot lie along a single axis,[3] we can show that

$$\sigma_n^2 \approx \frac{2(n-1)}{(n+1)^2}\left(\sqrt{\frac{n}{S}}-1\right)^2\frac{\mu_{\text{lower}}^2}{\alpha_n^2}, \qquad (5)$$

where S is the city block length of the vector in question. Thus in this case, the ratio of σ_n^2 to μ_{lower}^2 decreases at least as fast as $1/n$ since n/S will be some fixed constant independent of n.[4] This dependency on n and S is shown in Figure 2. This result suggests that the approximation will be very accurate for many real-world pattern

---

[3] For example, when the axes are constrained to be in the range $[0, 1]$ and the city block length of the vector is greater than 1. Note that this is true for the majority of the points in a n dimensional unit hypercube.

[4] Thus the accuracy improves as S increases towards its maximum value.

recognition tasks such as speech and high resolution image recognition which can typically have thousand or even tens of thousands of dimensions.

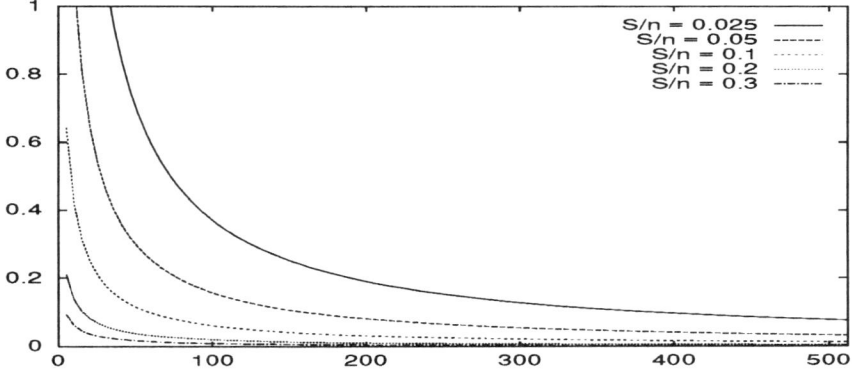

Figure 2: Plot of $\sigma_n/\mu_{\text{lower}}$ vs. n for constrained vectors with varying values of S/n. As S grows the ratio shrinks and consequently, accuracy improves. If we assume that all of the vectors are uniformly distributed in an n-dimensional unit hypercube, it is easy to show that the average city block length is $n/2$ and the variance of the city block length is $n/12$. Since S/n will generally be within one standard deviation of the mean, we find that typically $0.2 < S/n < 0.8$. We can use the same analysis on binary valued vectors to derive similar results.

We explore this phenomenon further by considering the following Monte Carlo simulation. We sampled 200000 points from a uniform distribution over an n-dimensional cube. The Euclidean distance of each of these points to a fixed corner of the cube was calculated and all the lengths were normalized by the largest possible length, $\sqrt{n}$. Histograms of the resulting lengths are shown in Figure 3 for four different values of n. Note that as the dimension increases the variance about the mean drops. From Figure 3 we see that for as few as 100 dimensions, the standard deviation is approximately 5% of the mean length.

3 The City Block MLP

In this section we describe how the approximation explained in Section 2 can be used by the Ni1000 to implement MLPs in parallel. Consider the following formula for the dot product

$$\vec{x} \cdot \vec{y} = \frac{1}{4}(\|\vec{x}+\vec{y}\|^2 - \|\vec{x}-\vec{y}\|^2) \qquad (6)$$

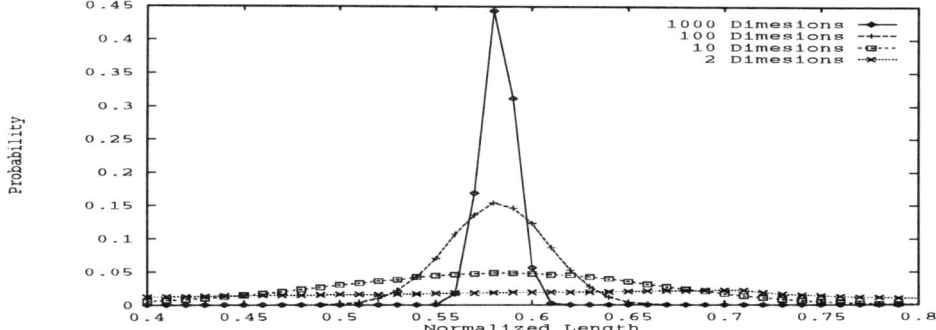

Figure 3: Probability distributions for randomly draw lengths. Note that as the dimension increases the variance about the mean length drops.

where $||\cdot||$ is the Euclidean length (i.e. l_2-norm).[5] Using Equation 2, we can approximation Equation 6 by

$$\vec{x} \cdot \vec{y} \approx \frac{1}{4n}(|\vec{x}+\vec{y}|^2 - |\vec{x}-\vec{y}|^2) \qquad (7)$$

where n is the dimension of the vectors and $|\cdot|$ is the city block length. The advantage to the approximation in Equation 7 is that it can be implemented in parallel on the Ni1000 while still behaving like a dot product. Thus we can use this approximation to implement MLP's on an Ni1000. The standard functional form for MLP's is given by [Rumelhart et al., 1986]

$$f_k(x;\alpha,\beta) = \sigma\big(\alpha_{0k} + \sum_{j=1}^{N} \alpha_{jk}\sigma(\beta_{0j} + \sum_{i=1}^{d} \beta_{ij}x_i)\big) \qquad (8)$$

were σ is a fixed ridge function chosen to be $\sigma(x) = (1+e^{-x})^{-1}$; N is the number of hidden units; k is the class label; d is the dimensionality of the data space; and α and β are adjustable parameters. The alternative which we propose, the City Block MLP, is given by [Perrone, 1993]

$$g_k(x;\alpha,\beta) = \sigma\big(\alpha_{0k} + \sum_{j=1}^{N} \alpha_{jk}\sigma(\beta_{0j} + \frac{1}{4n}(\sum_{i=1}^{d}|\beta_{ij}+x_i|)^2 - \frac{1}{4n}(\sum_{i=1}^{d}|\beta_{ij}-x_i|)^2)\big) \qquad (9)$$

---

[5] Note also that depending on the information available to us, we could use either

$$\vec{x} \cdot \vec{y} = \frac{1}{2}(||\vec{x}+\vec{y}||^2 - ||\vec{x}||^2 - ||\vec{y}||^2)$$

or

$$\vec{x} \cdot \vec{y} = \frac{1}{2}(||\vec{x}||^2 + ||\vec{y}||^2 - ||\vec{x}-\vec{y}||^2).$$

DATA SET	HIDDEN UNITS	STANDARD % CORRECT	CITYBLOCK % CORRECT	ENSEMBLE CITYBLOCK
Faces	12	94.6±1.4	92.2±1.9	96.3
Numbers	10	98.4±0.17	97.3±0.26	98.3
Lowercase	20	88.9±0.31	84.0±0.48	88.6
Uppercase	20	90.5±0.39	85.6±0.89	90.7

Table 1: Comparison of MLPs classification performance with and with out the city block approximation to the dot product. The final column shows the effect of function space averaging.

where the two city block calculation would be performed by neurons on the Ni1000 chip.[6] The City Block MLP learns in the standard way by minimizing the mean square error (MSE),

$$\text{MSE} = \sum_{ik} \bigl(g_k(x_i; \alpha, \beta) - t_{ki}\bigr)^2 \qquad (10)$$

where t_{ki} is the value of the data at x_i for a class k. The MSE is minimized using the backpropagation stochastic gradient descent learning rule [Werbos, 1974]: For a fixed stepsize η and each k, randomly choose a data point x_i and change γ by the amount

$$\Delta \gamma = -\eta \frac{\partial (\text{MSE}_i)}{\partial \gamma}, \qquad (11)$$

where γ is either α or β and MSE_i is the contribution to the MSE of the ith data point. Note that although we have motivated the City Block MLP above as an approximation to the standard MLP, the City Block MLP can also be thought of as special case of radial basis function network.

4 Experimental Results

This section describes experiments using the City Block MLP on a 120-dimensional representation of the NIST Handwritten Optical Character Recognition database and on a 2294-dimensional grayscale human face image database. The results indicate that the performance of networks using the approximation is as good as networks using the exact dot product [Perrone, 1993].

In order to test the performance of the City Block MLP, we simulated the behavior of the Ni1000 on a SPARC station in serial. We used the approximation only on the first layer of weights (i.e. those connecting the inputs to the hidden units) where the dimensionality is highest and the approximation is most accurate. The approximation was not used in the second layer of weights (i.e. those connecting the hidden units to the output units were calculated in serial) since the number of hidden units was low and therefore do not correspond to a major computational bottleneck. It should be noted that for a 2 layer MLP in which the number of hidden units and output units are much lower than the input dimensionality, the

---

[6] The dot product between the hidden and the output layers may also be approximated in the same way but it is not shown here. In fact, the Ni1000 could be used to perform all of the functions required by the network.

DATA SET	HIDDEN UNITS	STANDARD FOM	CITYBLOCK FOM	ENSEMBLE CITYBLOCK
Numbers	10	92.1±0.57	87.4±0.83	92.5
Lowercase	20	59.7±1.7	44.4±2.0	62.7
Uppercase	20	60.0±1.8	44.6±4.5	66.4

Table 2: Comparison of MLPs FOM. The FOM is defined as the 100 minus the number rejected minus 10 time the number incorrect.

majority of the computation is in the calculation of the dot products in the first weight layer. So even using the approximation only in the first layer will significantly accelerate the calculation. Also, the Ni1000 on-chip math coprocessor can perform a low-dimensional, second layer dot product while the high-dimensional, first layer dot product is being approximated in parallel by the city block units. In practice, if the number of hidden units is large, the approximation to the dot product may also be used in the second weight layer. In the simulations, the networks used the approximation when calculating the dot product only in the feedforward phase of the algorithm. For the feedbackward phase (i.e. the error backpropagation phase), the algorithm was identical to the original backward propagation algorithm. In other words the approximation was used to calculate the network activity but the stochastic gradient term was calculated as if the network activity was generated with the real dot product. This simplification does not slow the calculation because all the terms needed for the backpropagation phase are calculated in the forward propagation phase In addition, it allows us to avoid altering the backpropagation algorithm to incorporate the derivative of the city block approximation. We are currently working on simulations which use city block calculations in both the forward and backward passes. Since these simulations will use the correct derivative for the functional form of the City Block MLP, we expect that they will have better performance. In practice, the price we pay for making the approximation is reduced performance. We can avoid this problem by increasing the number of hidden units and thereby allow more flexibility in the network. This increase in size will not significantly slow the algorithm since the hidden unit activities are calculated in parallel. In Table 1 and Table 2, we compare the performance of a standard MLP without the city block approximation to a MLP using the city block approximation to calculate network activity. In all cases, a population of 10 neural networks were trained from random initial weight configurations and the means and standard deviations were listed. The number of hidden units was chosen to give a reasonable size network while at the same time reasonably quick training. Training was halted by cross-validating on an independent hold-out set. From these results, one can see that the relative performances with and with out the approximation are similar although the City Block is slightly lower. We also perform ensemble averaging [Perrone, 1993, Perrone and Cooper, 1993] to further improve the performance of the approximate networks. These results are given in the last column of the table. From these data we see that by combining the city block approximation with the averaging method, we can generate networks which have comparable and sometimes better performance than the standard MLPs. In addition, because the Ni1000 is running in parallel, there is minimal additional computational overhead for using the averaging.[7]

5 Discussion

We have described a new radial basis function network architecture which can be used in high dimensional spaces to approximate the learning characteristics of a standard MLP without using dot products. The absence of dot products allows us to implement this new architecture efficiently in parallel on an Ni1000; thus enabling us to take advantage of the Ni1000's extremely fast classification rates. We have also presented experimental results on real-world data which indicate that these high classifications rates can be achieved while maintaining or improving classification accuracy. These results illustrate that it is possible to use the inherent high dimensionality of real-world problems to our advantage.

References

[Perrone, 1993] Perrone, M. P. (1993). *Improving Regression Estimation: Averaging Methods for Variance Reduction with Extensions to General Convex Measure Optimization.* PhD thesis, Brown University, Institute for Brain and Neural Systems; Dr. Leon N Cooper, Thesis Supervisor.

[Perrone and Cooper, 1993] Perrone, M. P. and Cooper, L. N. (1993). When networks disagree: Ensemble method for neural networks. In Mammone, R. J., editor, *Artificial Neural Networks for Speech and Vision.* Chapman-Hall. Chapter 10.

[Reilly et al., 1982] Reilly, D. L., Cooper, L. N., and Elbaum, C. (1982). A neural model for category learning. *Biological Cybernetics,* 45:35–41.

[Rumelhart et al., 1986] Rumelhart, D. E., McClelland, J. L., and the PDP Research Group (1986). *Parallel Distributed Processing, Volume 1: Foundations.* MIT Press.

[Scofield et al., 1987] Scofield, C. L., Reilly, D. L., Elbaum, C., and Cooper, L. N. (1987). Pattern class degeneracy in an unrestricted storage density memory. In Anderson, D. Z., editor, *Neural Information Processing Systems.* American Institute of Physics.

[Sullivan, 1993] Sullivan, M. (1993). Intel and Nestor deliver second-generation neural network chip to DARPA: Companies launch beta site program. *Intel Corporation News Release.* Feb. 12.

[Werbos, 1974] Werbos, P. (1974). *Beyond Regression: New Tools for Prediction and Analysis in the Behavioral Sciences.* PhD thesis, Harvard University.

---

[7] The averaging can also be applied to the standard MLPs with a corresponding improvement in performance. However, for serial machines averaging slows calculations by a factor equal to the number of averaging nets.

A Real Time Clustering CMOS Neural Engine

T. Serrano-Gotarredona, B. Linares-Barranco, and J. L. Huertas

Dept. of Analog Design, National Microelectronics Center (CNM), Ed. CICA, Av. Reina Mercedes s/n, 41012 Sevilla, SPAIN. Phone: (34)-5-4239923, Fax: (34)-5-4624506, E-mail: `bernabe@cnm.us.es`

Abstract

We describe an analog VLSI implementation of the ART1 algorithm (Carpenter, 1987). A prototype chip has been fabricated in a standard low cost 1.5μm double-metal single-poly CMOS process. It has a die area of $1 cm^2$ and is mounted in a 120-pins PGA package. The chip realizes a modified version of the original ART1 architecture. Such modification has been shown to preserve all computational properties of the original algorithm (Serrano, 1994a), while being more appropriate for VLSI realizations. The chip implements an ART1 network with 100 *F1* nodes and 18 *F2* nodes. It can therefore cluster 100 binary pixels input patterns into up to 18 different categories. Modular expansibility of the system is possible by assembling an *N×M* array of chips without any extra interfacing circuitry, resulting in an *F1* layer with 100×*N* nodes, and an *F2* layer with 18×*M* nodes. Pattern classification is performed in less than 1.8μs, which means an equivalent computing power of 2.2×10^9 connections and connection-updates per second. Although internally the chip is analog in nature, it interfaces to the outside world through digital signals, thus having a true asynchrounous digital behavior. Experimental chip test results are available, which have been obtained through test equipments for digital chips.

1 INTRODUCTION

The original ART1 algorithm (Carpenter, 1987) proposed in 1987 is a massively parallel architecture for a self-organizing neural binary-pattern recognition machine. In response to arbitrary orderings of arbitrarily many and complex binary input patterns, ART1 is

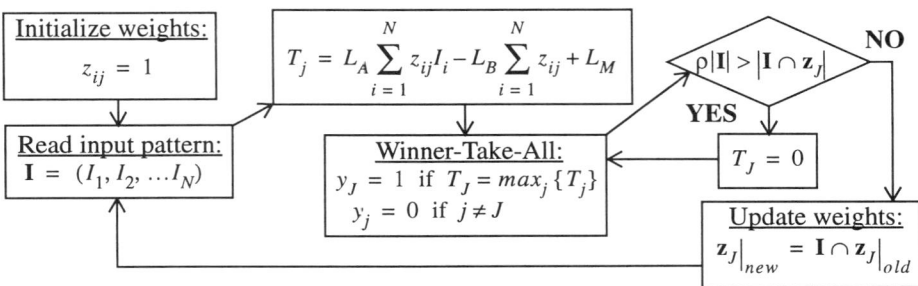

Fig. 1: Modified *Fast Learning* or *Type-3* ART1 implementation algorithm

capable of learning, in an unsupervised way, stable recognition codes. The ART1 architecture is described by a set of Short Term Memory (STM) and another set of Long Term Memory (LTM) time domain nonlinear differential equations. It is valid to assume that the STM equations settle much faster (instantaneously) than the LTM equations, so that the STM differential equations can be substituted by nonlinear algebraic equations that describe the steady-state of the STM differential equations. Furthermore, in the fast-learning mode (Carpenter, 1987), the LTM differential equations are as well substituted by their corresponding steady-state nonlinear algebraic equations. This way, the ART1 architecture can be behaviorally modelled by the sequential application of nonlinear algebraic equations. Three different levels of ART1 implementations (both in software and in hardware) can therefore be distinguished:

Type-1: Full Model Implementation: both STM and LTM time-domain differential equations are realized. This implementation is the most expensive (both in software and in hardware), and requires a large amount of computational power.

Type-2: STM steady-state Implementation: only the LTM time-domain differential equations are implemented. The STM behavior is governed by nonlinear algebraic equations. This implementation requires less resources than the previous one. However, a proper sequencing of STM events has to be introduced artificially, which is architecturally implicit in the *Type-1* implementation.

Type-3: Fast Learning Implementation: STM and LTM is implemented with algebraic equations. This implementation is computationally the less expensive one. In this case an artificial sequencing of STM and LTM events has to be done.

The implementation presented in this paper realizes a modified version of the original ART1 *Type-3* algorithm, more suitable for VLSI implementations. Such modified ART1 system has been shown to preserve all computational properties of the original ART1 architecture (Serrano, 1994a). The flow diagram that describes the modified ART1 architecture is shown in Fig. 1. Note that there is only one binary-valued weight template (z_{ij}), instead of the two weight templates (one binary-valued and the other real-valued) of the original ART1. For a more detailed discussion of the modified ART1 algorithm refer to (Serrano, 1994a, 1994b).

In the next Section we will provide an analog current-mode based circuit that implements in hardware the flow diagram of Fig. 1. Note that, although internally this circuit is analog in nature, from its input and output signals point of view it is a true asynchronous digital circuit, easy to interface with any conventional digital machine. Finally, in Section 3 we will provide experimental results measured from the chip using a digital data acquisition test equipment.

2 CIRCUIT DESCRIPTION

The ART1 chip reported in this paper has an *F1* layer with 100 neurons and an *F2* layer with 18 neurons. This means that it can handle binary input patterns of 100 pixels each, and cluster them into up to 18 different categories, according to a digitally adjustable vigilance parameter ρ. The circuit architecture of the chip is shown in Fig. 2(a). It consists of an array of 18×100 synapses, a 1×100 array of "vigilance synapses", a unity gain 18-outputs current mirror, an adjustable gain 18-outputs current mirror (with $\rho=0.0, 0.1, \ldots 0.9$)[1], 18 current-comparator-controlled switches and an 18-input-currents Winner-Take-All (WTA) (Serrano, 1994b). The inputs to the circuit are the 100 binary digital input voltages I_i, and the outputs of the circuit are the 18 digital output voltages y_j. External control signals allow to change parameters ρ, L_A, L_B, and L_M. Also, extra circuitry has been added for reading the internal weights z_{ij} while the system is learning.

Each row of synapses generates two currents,

$$T_j = L_A \sum_{i=1}^{100} z_{ij} I_i - L_B \sum_{i=1}^{100} z_{ij} + L_M$$
$$V_j = L_A \sum_{i=1}^{100} z_{ij} I_i \qquad (1)$$

while the row of the "vigilance synapses" generates the current

$$V_\rho = L_A \sum_{i=1}^{100} I_i \qquad (2)$$

Each of the current comparators compares the current V_j versus ρV_ρ, and allows current T_j to reach the WTA only if $\rho V_\rho \leq V_j$. This way competition and vigilance occur simultaneously and in parallel, speeding up significantly the search process.

Fig. 2(b) shows the content of a synapse in the 18×100 array. It consists of three current sources with switches, two digital AND gates and a flip-flop. Each synapse receives two input voltages I_i and y_j, and two global control voltages ϕ_l (to enable/disable learning) and *reset* (to initialize all weights z_{ij} to '1'). Each synapse generates two currents $L_A I_i z_{ij} - L_B z_{ij}$ and $L_A I_i z_{ij}$, which will be summed up for all the synapses in the same row to generate the currents T_j and V_j. If learning is enabled ($\phi_l = 1$) the value of z_{ij} will change to $I_i z_{ij}$ if $y_j = 1$. The "vigilance synapses" consist each of a current-source of value L_A with a switch controlled by the input voltage I_i. The current comparators are those proposed in (Domínguez-Castro, 1992), the WTA used is reported in (Lazzaro, 1989), and the digitally adjustable current mirror is based on (Loh, 1989), while its continuous gain fine tuning mechanism has been taken from (Adams, 1991).

---

1. An additional pin of the chip can fine-tune ρ between 0.9 and 1.0.

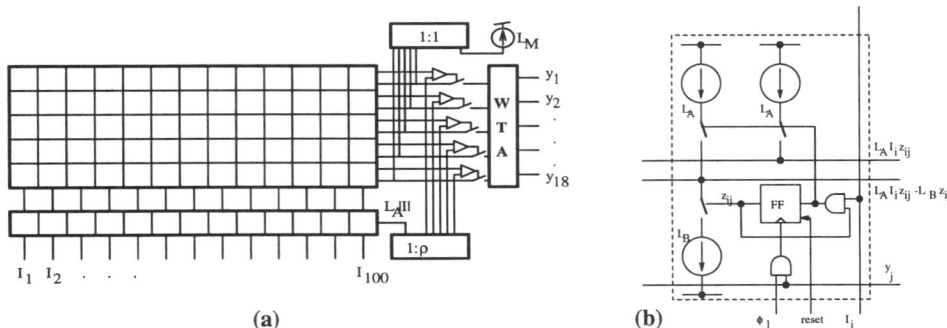

Fig. 2: (a) System Diagram of Current-Mode ART1 Chip, (b) Circuit Diagram of Synapse

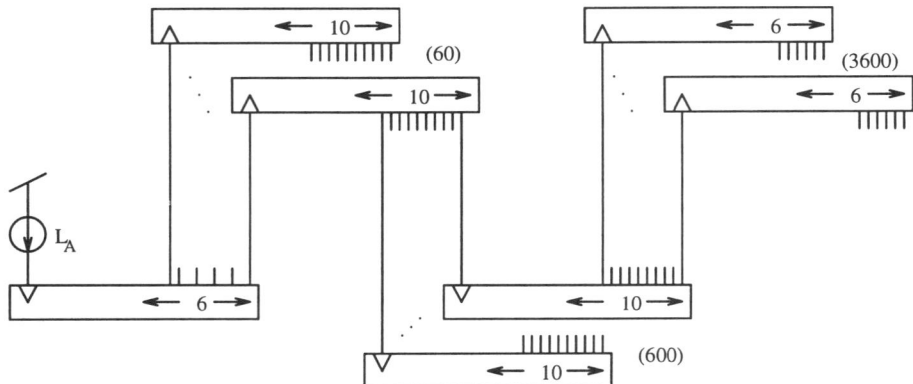

Fig. 3: Tree based current-mirror scheme for matched current sources

The circuit has been designed in such a way that the WTA operates with a precision around 1.5% (~6 bits). This means that all L_A and L_B current sources have to match within an error of less than that. From a circuit implementation point of view this is not easy to achieve, since there are 5500 current sources spread over a die area of $1cm^2$. Typical mismatch between reasonable size MOS transistors inside such an area extension can be expected to be above 10% (Pelgrom, 1989). To overcome this problem we implemented a tree-based current mirror scheme as is shown in Fig. 3. Starting from a unique current reference, and using high-precision 10(or less)-outputs current mirrors (each yielding a precision around 0.2%), only up to four cascades are needed. This way, the current mismatch attained at the synapse current sources was around 1% for currents between $L_{A/B} = 5\mu A$ and $L_{A/B} = 10\mu A$. This is shown in Fig. 4, where the measured dc output current-error (in %) versus input current of the tree based configuration for 18 of the 3600 L_A synapse sources is depicted.

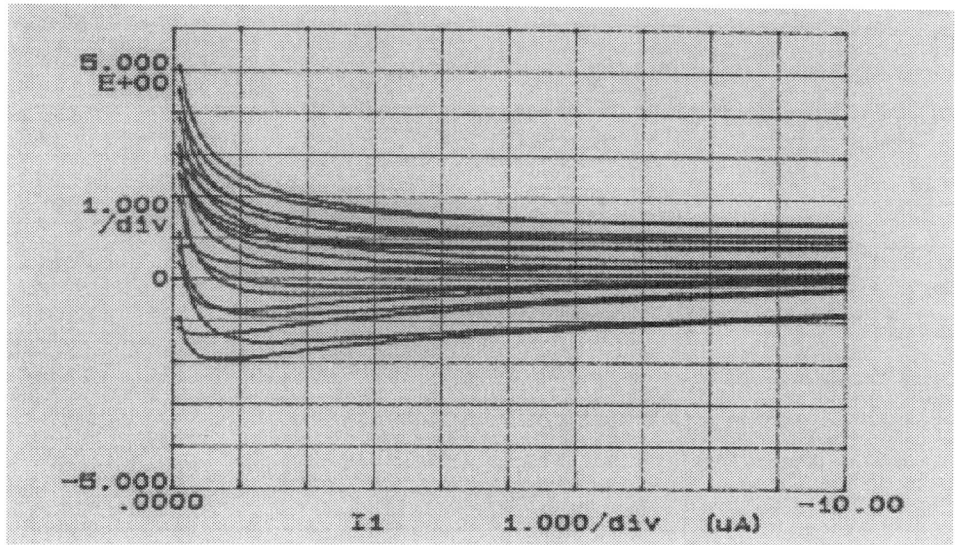

Fig. 4: Measured current mirror cascade missmatch (1%/div) for L_A for currents below 10µA

3 EXPERIMENTAL RESULTS

Fig. 5 shows a microphotograph of a prototype chip fabricated in a standard digital double-metal, single-poly 1.5µm low cost CMOS process. The chip die area is $1cm^2$, and it is mounted in a 120-pins PGA package. Fig. 6 shows a typical training sequence accomplished by the chip and obtained experimentally using a test equipment for digital chips. The only task performed by the test equipment was to provide the input data patterns **I** (first column in Fig. 6), detect which of the output nodes became '1' (pattern with a vertical bar to its right), and extract the learned weights. Each 10×10 square in Fig. 6 represents either a 100-pixels input vector **I**, or one row of 100-pixels synaptic weights $\mathbf{z}_j \equiv (z_{1j}, z_{2j}, ... z_{100j})$. Each row of squares in Fig. 6 represents the input pattern (first square) and the 18 vectors $\mathbf{z}_j$ after learning has been performed for this input pattern. The sequence shown in Fig. 6 has been obtained for $\rho = 0.7$, $L_A = 10\mu A$, $L_B = 9.5\mu A$, and $L_M = 950\mu A$. Only two iterations of input patterns presentations were necessary, in this case, for the system to learn and self-organize in response to these 18 input patterns.

The last row in Fig. 6 shows the final learned templates. Fig. 7 shows final learned templates for different values of ρ. The numbers below each square indicate the input patterns that have been clustered into each $\mathbf{z}_j$ category.

Delay time measurements have been performed for the feedforward action of the chip (establishment of currents T_j, V_j, and V_ρ, and their competitions until the WTA settles), and for the updating of weights. The feedforward delay is pattern and bias currents (L_A, L_B, L_M) dependent, but has been measured to be always below 1.6µs. The learning time is constant and is around $180ns$. Therefore, throughput time is less than 1.8µs. A digital neuroprocessor able to perform a connections/s, b connection-updates/s, and with a dedicated WTA section with a c seconds delay, must satisfy

Fig. 5: Microphotograph of ART1 chip

$$\frac{3700}{a} + \frac{100}{b} + c = 1.8 \mu s \tag{3}$$

to meet the performance of our prototype chip. If $a = b$ and $c = 100ns$, the equivalent speed would be $a = b = 2.2 \times 10^9$ connections and connection-updates per second.

4 CONCLUSIONS

A high speed analog current-mode categorizer chip has been built using a standard low cost digital CMOS process. The high performance of the chip is achieved thanks to a simplification of the original ART1 algorithm. The simplifications introduced are such that all the original computational properties are preserved. Experimental chip test results are provided.

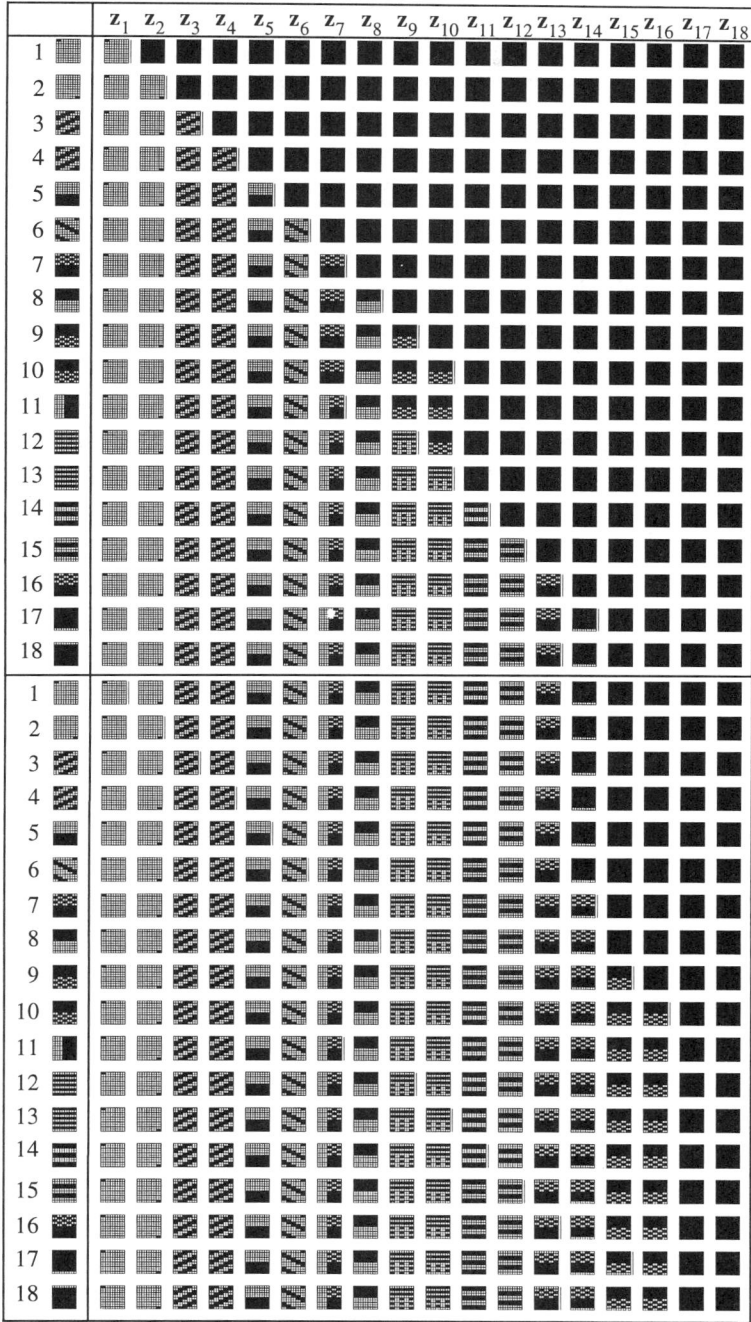

Fig. 6: Test sequence obtained experimentally for $\rho=0.7$, $L_A=10\mu A$, $L_B=9.5\mu A$, and $L_M=950\mu A$

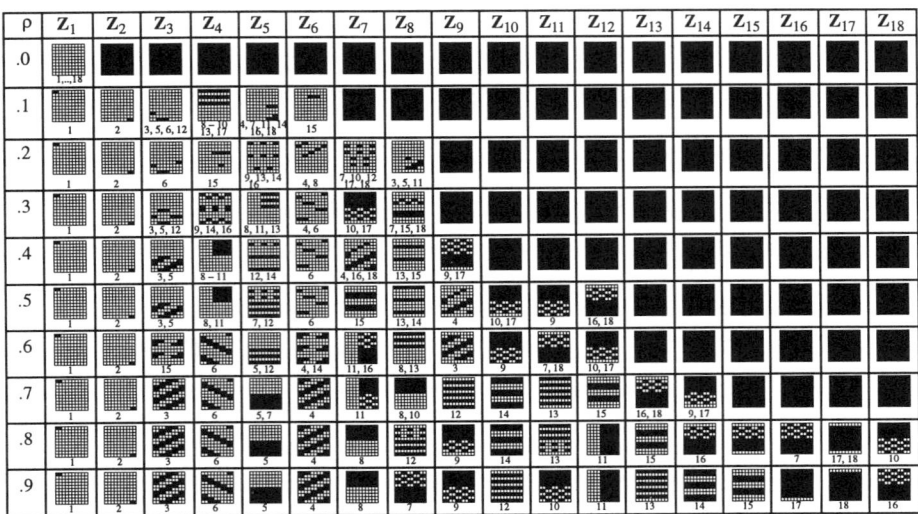

Fig. 7: Categorization of the input patterns for $L_A=3.2\mu A$, $L_B=3.0\mu A$, $L_M=400\mu A$, and different values of ρ

References

W. J. Adams and J. Ramímez-Angulo. (1991) "Extended Transconductance Adjustment/Linearisation Technique," *Electronics Letters,* vol. 27, No. 10, pp. 842-844, May 1991.

G. A. Carpenter and S. Grossberg. (1987) "A Massively Parallel Architecture for a Self-Organizing Neural Pattern Recognition Machine," *Computer Vision, Graphics, and Image Processing*, vol. 37, pp. 54-115, 1987.

R. Domínguez-Castro, A. Rodríguez-Vázquez, F. Medeiro, and J. L. Huertas. (1992) "High Resolution CMOS Current Comparators," *Proc. of the 1992 European Solid-State Circuits Conference (ESSCIRC'92),* pp. 242-245, 1992.

J. Lazzaro, R. Ryckebusch, M. A. Mahowald, and C. Mead. (1989) "Winner-Take-All Networks of O(n) Complexity," in *Advances in Neural Information Processing Systems*, vol. 1, D. S. Touretzky (Ed.), Los Altos, CA: Morgan Kaufmann, 1989, pp. 703-711.

K. Loh, D. L. Hiser, W. J. Adams, and R. L. Geiger. (1989) "A Robust Digitally Programmable and Reconfigurable Monolithic Filter Structure," *Proc. of the 1989 Int. Symp. on Circuits and Systems (ISCAS'89),* Portland, Oregon, vol. 1, pp. 110-113, 1989.

M. J. Pelgrom, A. C. J. Duinmaijer, and A. P. G. Welbers. (1989) "Matching Properties of MOS Transistors," *IEEE Journal of Solid-State Circuits,* vol. 24, No. 5, pp. 1433-1440, October 1989.

T. Serrano-Gotarredona and B. Linares-Barranco. (1994a) "A Modified ART1 Algorithm more suitable for VLSI Implementations," submitted for publication (journal paper).

T. Serrano-Gotarredona and B. Linares-Barranco. (1994b) "A Real-Time Clustering Microchip Neural Engine," submitted for publication (journal paper).

Pulsestream Synapses with Non-Volatile Analogue Amorphous-Silicon Memories.

A.J. Holmes, A.F. Murray, S. Churcher and J. Hajto
Department of Electrical Engineering
University of Edinburgh
Edinburgh, EH9 3JL

M. J. Rose
Dept. of Applied Physics and Electronics,
Dundee University
Dundee DD1 4HN

Abstract

A novel two-terminal device, consisting of a thin 1000Å layer of p^+ a-Si:H sandwiched between Vanadium and Chromium electrodes, exhibits a non-volatile, analogue memory action. This device stores synaptic weights in an ANN chip, replacing the capacitor previously used for dynamic weight storage. Two different synapse designs are discussed and results are presented.

1 INTRODUCTION

Analogue hardware implementations of neural networks have hitherto been hampered by the lack of a straightforward (local) analogue memory capability. The ideal storage mechanism would be compact, non-volatile, easily reprogrammable, and would not interfere with the normal silicon chip fabrication process.

Techniques which have been used to date include resistors (these are not generally reprogrammable, and suffer from being large and difficult to fabricate with any accuracy), dynamic capacitive storage [4] (this is compact, reprogrammable and simple, but implies an increase in system complexity, arising from off-chip refresh circuitry),

EEPROM ("floating gate") memory [5] (which is compact, reprogrammable, and non-volatile, but is slow, and cannot be reprogrammed in situ), and local digital storage (which is non-volatile, easily programmable and simple, but consumes area horribly).

Amorphous silicon has been used for synaptic weight storage [1, 2], but only as either a high-resistance fixed weight medium or a binary memory.

In this paper, we demonstrate that novel amorphous silicon memory devices can be incorporated into standard CMOS synapse circuits, to provide an analogue weight storage mechanism which is compact, non-volatile, easily reprogrammable, and simple to implement.

2   a-Si:H MEMORY DEVICES

The a-Si:H analogue memory device [3] comprises a 1000Å thick layer of amorphous silicon (p^+ a-Si:H) sandwiched between Vanadium and Chromium electrodes.

The a-Si device takes the form of a two-terminal, programmable resistor. It is an "add-on" to a conventional CMOS process, and does not demand that the normal CMOS fabrication cycle be disrupted. The a-Si device sits on top of the completed chip circuitry, making contact with the CMOS arithmetic elements via holes cut in the protective passivation layer, as shown in Figure 1.

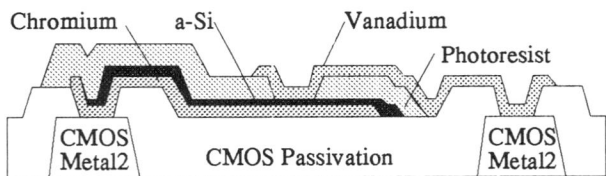

Figure 1: The construction of a-Si:H Devices on a CMOS chip

After fabrication a number of electronic procedures must be performed in order to program the device to a given resistance state.

Programming, and Pre-Programming Procedures

Before the a-Si device is usable, the following steps must be carried out:

- Forming: This is a once-only process, applied to the a-Si device in its "virgin" state, where it has a resistance of several MΩ. A series of 300ns pulses, increasing in amplitude from 5v to 14v, is applied to the device electrodes. This creates a vertical conducting channel or filament whose approximate resistance is 1KΩ. This filament can then be programmed to a value in the range 1KΩ to 1MΩ. The details of the physical mechanisms are not yet fully established, but it is clear that conduction occurs through a narrow (sub-micron) conducting channel.

- Write: To decrease the device's resistance, negative "Write", pulses are applied.

- Erase: To increase the device's resistance, positive "Erase", pulses are applied.

- Usage: Pulses below 0.5v do not change the device resistance. The resistance can therefore be utilised as a weight storage medium using a voltage of less than 0.5v without causing reprogramming.

Programming pulses, which range between 2v and 5v, are typically 120ns in duration. Programming is therefore much faster than for other EEPROM (floating gate) devices used in the same context, which use a series of $100\mu s$ pulses to set the threshold voltage [5].

The following sections describe synapse circuits using the a-Si:H devices. These synapses use the reprogrammable a-Si:H resistor in the place of a storage capacitor or EEPROM cell. These new synapses were implemented on a chip referred to as ASiTEST2, consisting of five main test blocks, each comprising of four synapses connected to a single neuron.

3 The EPSILON based synapse

The first synapse to be designed used the a-Si:H resistor as a direct replacement for the storage capacitor used in the EPSILON [4] synapse.

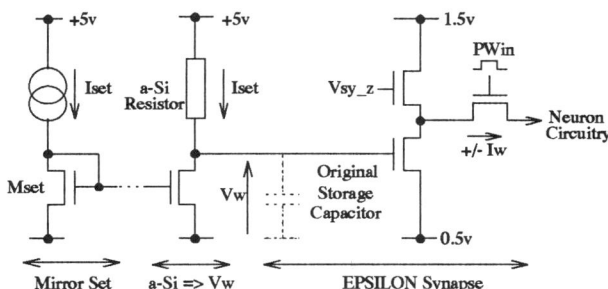

Figure 2: The EPSILON Synapse with a-Si:H weight storage

In the original EPSILON chip the weight voltage was stored as a voltage on a capacitor. In this new synapse design, shown in Figure 2, the a-Si:H resistance is set such that the voltage drop produced by Iset is equivalent to the original weight voltage, Vw, that was stored dynamically on the capacitor.

A new, simpler, synapse, which can be operated from a single +5v supply, was also be included on the ASiTEST2 chip.

4 The MkII synapse

The circuit is shown in Figure 3. The a-Si:H memory is used to store a current, Iasi. This current is subtracted from a zero current, Isy_z, to give a weight current , +/-Iw, which adds or subtracts charge from the activity capacitor, Cact, thus implementing excitation or inhibition respectively.

For the circuit to function correctly we must limit the voltage on the activity capacitor to the range [1.5v,3.5v], to ensure that the transistors mirroring Isy_z and Iasi remain in saturation. As Figure 3 shows, there are few reference signals and the circuit operates from a single +5v power supply rail, in sharp contrast to many earlier analogue neural circuits, including our own.

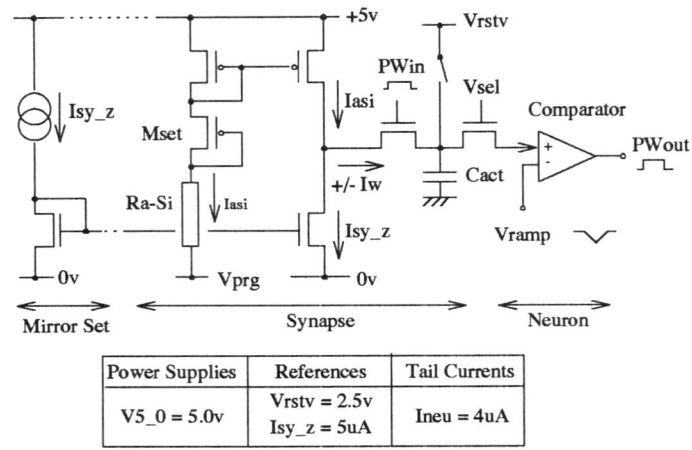

Power Supplies	References	Tail Currents
V5_0 = 5.0v	Vrstv = 2.5v Isy_z = 5uA	Ineu = 4uA

Figure 3: The MkII synapse

On first inspection the main drawback of this design would appear to be a reliance on the accuracy with which the zero current Isy_z is mirrored across an entire chip. The variation in this current means that two cells with the same synapse resistance could produce widely differing values of Iw. However, during programming we do not use the resistance of the a-Si:H device as a target value. We monitor the **voltage on Cact** for a given PWin signal, increasing or decreasing the resistance of the a-Si:H device until the desired **voltage level** is achieved.

Example: To set a weight to be the maximum positive value, we adjust the a-Si resistance until a PWin signal of 5us, the maximum input signal, gives a voltage of 3.5v on the integration capacitor.

We are able to set the synapse weight using the whole integration range of [1.5v,3.5v] by only closing Vsel for the desired synapse during programming. In normal operating mode all four Vsel switches will be closed so that the integration charge is summed over all four local capacitors.

4.1 Example - Stability Test

As an example of the use of integration voltage as means of monitoring the resistance of a particular synapse we have included a stability test. This was carried out on one of the test chips which contained the MkII synapse.

The four synapses on the test chip were programmed to give different levels of activation. The chip was then powered up for 30mins each day during a 7-day period, and the activation levels for each synapse were measured three times.

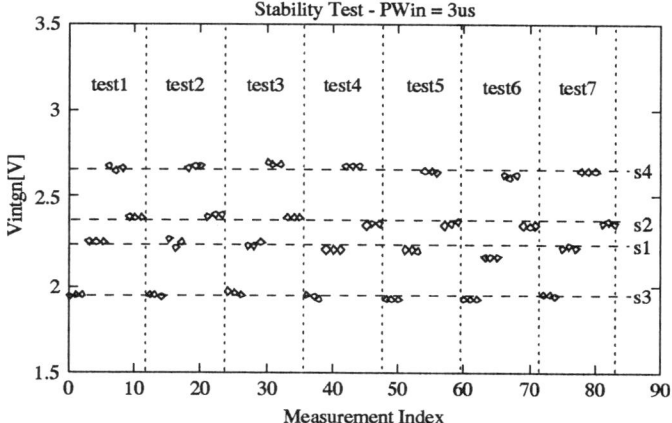

Figure 4: ASiTEST2- Stability Test

As figure 4 shows, the memories remain in the same resistance state (i.e retain their programmed weight value) over the whole 7-day period. Separate experiments on isolated devices indicate much longer hold times - of the order of months at least.

5 ASiTEST3

Recently we have received our latest, overtly neural, a-Si:H based test chip. This contains an 8x8 array of the MkII synapses.

The circuit board for this device has been constructed and partially tested while the ASiTEST3 chips are awaiting the deposition of the a-Si:H layers. We have been able to use an ASiTEST2 chip containing two of the MkII synapse test blocks i.e. 8 synapses and 2 neurons to exercise much of the board's functionality.

The test board contains a simple state machine which has four different states:

- State 0: Load Input Pulsewidths into SRAM from PC.
- State 1: Apply Input Pulsewidth signals to chip1.
- State 2: Use Vramp to generate threshold function for chip1. The resulting Pulsewidth outputs are used as the inputs to chip2, as well as being stored

in SRAM.
- State 3: Use Vramp to generate threshold function for chip2. Read resulting Pulsewidth Outputs into SRAM.
- State 0: Read Output Pulsewidths from SRAM into PC.

The results obtained during a typical test cycle are shown in Figure 5.

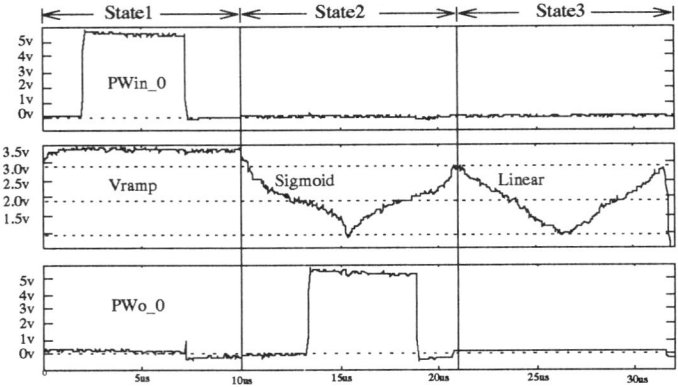

Figure 5: ASiTEST3 Board Scope Waveforms

As this figure shows different ramp signals, corresponding to different threshold functions, can be applied to chip1 and chip2 neurons.

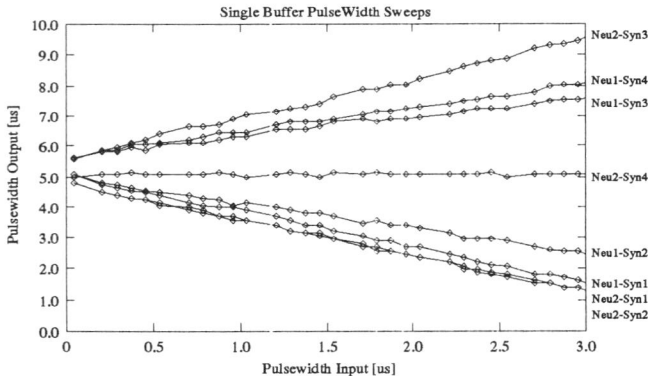

Figure 6: ASiTEST3 Board - MkII Synapse Characteristic

While the signals shown in Figure 5 appear noisy the multiplier characteristic that the chip produces is still admirably linear, as shown in Figure 6. In this experiment all eight synapses on a test chip were programmed into different resistance states and PWin was swept from 0 to 3us.

6 Conclusions

We have demonstrated the use of novel a-Si:H analogue memory devices as a means of storing synaptic weights in a Pulsewidth ANN. We have also demonstrated the operation of an interface board which allows two 8x8 ANN chips, operating as a two layer network, to be controlled by a simple PC interface card.

This technology is most suitable for small networks in, for example, remote control and other embedded-system applications where cost and power considerations favour a single all-inclusive ANN chip with non-volatile, but programmable weights.

Another possible application of this technology is in large networks constructed using Thin Film Technology(TFT). If TFT's were used in place of the CMOS transistors then the area constraint imposed by crystalline silicon would be removed, allowing truly massively parallel networks to be integrated.

In summary - the a-Si:H analogue memory devices described in this paper provide a route to an analogue, non-volatile and fast synaptic weight storage medium. At the present time neither the programming nor storage mechanisms are fully understood making it difficult to compare this new device with more established technologies such as the ubiquitous Floating-Gate EEPROM technique. Current research is focused on firstly, improving the yield on the a-Si:H device which is unacceptably low at present, a demerit that we attribute to imperfections in the a-Si fabrication process and secondly, improving understanding of the device physics and hence the programming and storage mechanisms.

Acknowledgements

This research has been jointly funded by BT, and EPSRC (formerly SERC), the Engineering and Physical Sciences Research Council.

References

[1] W. Hubbard et al.(1986) Electronic Neural Networks *AIP Conference Proceedings - Snowbird 1986* :227-234

[2] H.P. Graf (1986) VLSI Implementation of a NN memory with several hundreds of neurons *AIP Conference Proceedings - Snowbird 1986* :182-187.

[3] M.J. Rose et al (1989) Amorphous Silicon Analogue Memory Devices *Journal of Non-Crystalline Solids* **1**(115):168-170

[4] A.Hamilton et al. (1992) Integrated Pulse-Stream Neural Networks - Results, Issues and Pointers *IEEE Transactions on N.N.s* **3**(3):385-393

[5] M.Holler, S.Tam, H.Castro and R.Benson (1989) An Electrically Trainable ANN with 10240 Floating Gate Synapses. *Int Conf on N.N.s Proc* :191-196

[6] A.F.Murray and A.V.W.Smith.(1987) Asynchronous Arithmetic for VLSI Neural Systems. *Electronics Letters* **23**(12):642-643

[7] A.J. Holmes et al. (1993) Use of a-Si:H Memory Devices for Non-volatile Weight Storage in ANNs. *Proc ICAS 15* :817-820

A Lagrangian Formulation For Optical Backpropagation Training In Kerr-Type Optical Networks

James E. Steck
Mechanical Engineering
Wichita State University
Wichita, KS 67260-0035

Steven R. Skinner
Electrical Engineering
Wichita State University
Wichita, KS 67260-0044

Alvaro A. Cruz-Cabrara
Electrical Engineering
Wichita State University
Wichita, KS 67260-0044

Elizabeth C. Behrman
Physics Department
Wichita State University
Wichita, KS 67260-0032

Abstract

A training method based on a form of *continuous* spatially distributed optical error back-propagation is presented for an *all optical network* composed of *nondiscrete* neurons and weighted interconnections. The all optical network is feed-forward and is composed of thin layers of a Kerr-type self focusing/defocusing nonlinear optical material. The training method is derived from a Lagrangian formulation of the constrained minimization of the network error at the output. This leads to a formulation that describes training as a calculation of the distributed error of the optical signal at the output which is then reflected back through the device to assign a spatially distributed error to the internal layers. This error is then used to modify the internal weighting values. Results from several computer simulations of the training are presented, and a simple optical table demonstration of the network is discussed.

1 KERR TYPE MATERIALS

Kerr-type optical networks utilize thin layers of Kerr-type nonlinear materials, in which the index of refraction can vary within the material and depends on the amount of light striking the material at a given location. The material index of refraction can be described by: $n(x)=n_0+n_2I(x)$, where n_0 is the linear index of refraction, n_2 is the nonlinear coefficient, and $I(x)$ is the irradiance of a applied optical field as a function of position x across the material layer (Armstrong, 1962). This means that a beam of light (a signal beam carrying information perhaps) passing through a layer of Kerr-type material can be steered or controlled by another beam of light which applies a spatially varying pattern of intensity onto the Kerr-type material. Steering of light with a glass lens (having constance index of refraction) is done by varying the thickness of the lens (the amount of material present) as a function of position. Thus the Kerr effect can be **loosely** thought of as a glass lens whose geometry and therefore focusing ability could be dynamically controlled as a function of position across the lens. Steering in the Kerr material is accomplished by a gradient or change in the material index of refraction which is created by a gradient in applied light intensity. This is illustrated by the simple experiment in Figure 1 where a small weak probe beam is steered away from a straight path by the intensity gradient of a more powerful pump beam.

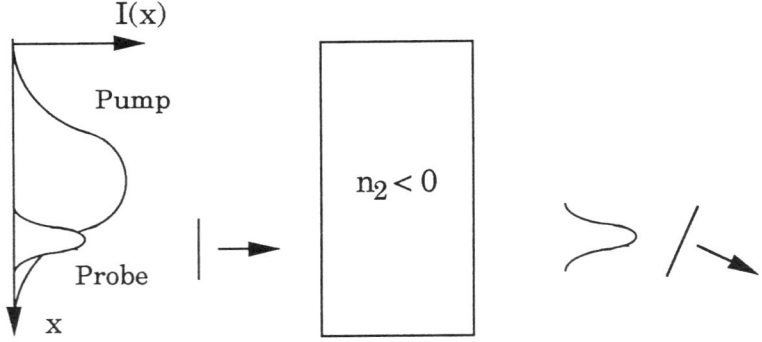

Figure 1: Light Steering In Kerr Materials

2 OPTICAL NETWORKS USING KERR MATERIALS

The Kerr optical network, shown in Figure 2, is made up of thin layers of the Kerr-type nonlinear medium separated by thick layers of a linear medium (free space) (Skinner, 1995). The signal beam to be processed propagates optically in a direction z perpendicular to the layers, from an input layer through several alternating linear and nonlinear layers to an output layer. The Kerr material layers perform the nonlinear processing and the linear layers serve as connection layers. The input ($I(x)$) and the weights ($W_1(x), W_2(x) ... W_n(x)$) are irradiance fields applied to the Kerr type layers, as functions of lateral position x, thus varying the refractive index profile of the nonlinear medium. Basically, the applied weight irradiences steer the signal beam via the Kerr effect discussed above to produce the correct output. The advantage of this type of optical network is that both neuron processing and weighted connections are achieved by uniform layers of the Kerr material. The all optical nature eliminates the need to physically construct neurons and connections on an individual basis.

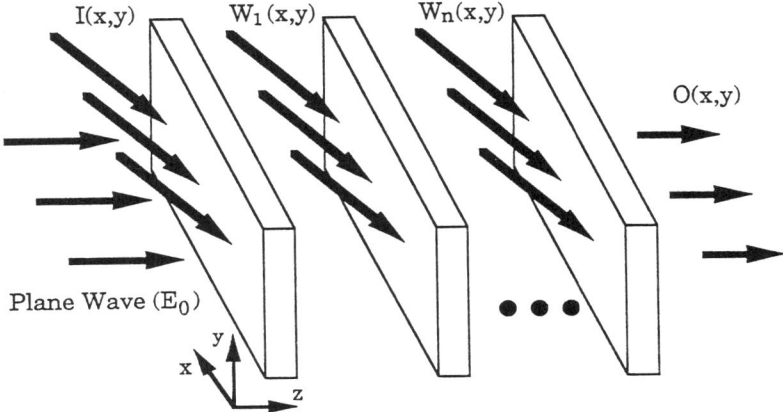

Figure 2: Kerr Optical Neural Network Architecture

If $E_i(\alpha)$ is the light entering the ith nonlinear layer at lateral position α, then the effect of the nonlinear layer is given by

$$F_i(\alpha) = E_i(\alpha) \, e^{-jk_0 \Delta NL_i n_2 (|W_i(\alpha)|^2 + |E_i(\alpha)|^2)} \tag{1}$$

where $W_i(\alpha)$ is the applied weight field. Transmission of light at lateral location α at the beginning of the ith linear layer to location β just before the $i+1^{th}$ nonlinear layer is given by

$$E_{i+1}(\beta) = \frac{jC_i}{\pi} \int_{\Omega_i} F_i(\alpha) \, e^{jC_i(\beta - \alpha)^2} d\alpha \quad \text{where} \quad C_i = \frac{k_0}{2 \Delta L_i} \tag{2}$$

3 OPTICAL BACK-PROPAGATION TRAINING

Traditional feed-forward artificial neural networks composed of a *finite* number of *discrete* neurons and weighted connections can be trained by many techniques. Some of the most successful techniques are based upon the well known training method called back-propagation which results from minimizing the network output error, with respect to the network weights by a gradient descent algorithm. The optical network is trained using a form of *continuous* optical back-propagation which is developed for a *nondiscrete* network. Gradient descent is applied to minimize the error over the entire output region of the optical network. This error is a continuous distribution of error calculated over the output region.

Optical back-propagation is a specific technique by which this error distribution is **optically** propagated backward through the linear and nonlinear optical layers to produce error signals by which the light applied to the nonlinear layers is modified. Recall that this applied light W_i controls what serves as connection "weights" in the optical network. Optical back-propagation minimizes the error L_o over an output region Ω_o, a subdomain of the final or n^{th} layer of the network,

$$L_0 = \frac{1}{2\gamma^2}[I_0 - D]^2 \quad \text{where} \quad I_0 = \gamma \int_{\Omega_o} O(\alpha) O^*(\alpha) d\alpha \tag{3}$$

subject to the constraint that the propagated light, $E_i(\alpha)$, satisfies the equations of forward propagation (1) and (2). $O(\beta) = E_{n+1}(\beta)$ and is the network output, γ is a scaling factor on the output intensity. L_0 then is the squared error between the desired output value D and the average intensity I_0 of the output distribution $O(\beta)$.

This constrained minimization problem is posed in a Lagrange formulation similar to the work of (le Cunn, 1988) for conventional feedforward networks and (Pineda, 1987) for conventional recurrent networks; the difference being that for the optical network of this paper the Electric field E and the Lagrange multiplier are complex and also continuous in the spatial variable thus requiring the Lagrangian below. A Lagrangian is defined as;

$$L = L_0 + \sum_{i=1}^{n} \int_{\Omega_i} \lambda_{i+}^*(\alpha) [E_{i+1}(\alpha) - \int_{\Omega_i} F_i(\beta) \frac{jC_i}{\pi} e^{-jC_i(\beta-\alpha)^2} d\beta] d\alpha$$
$$+ \sum_{i=1}^{n} \int_{\Omega_i} \lambda_{i+}(\alpha) [E_{i+1}(\alpha) - \int_{\Omega_i} F_i(\beta) \frac{jC_i}{\pi} e^{-jC_i(\beta-\alpha)^2} d\beta]^* d\alpha \tag{4}$$

Taking the variation of L with respect to E_i, the Lagrange multipliers λ_i, and using gradient descent to minimize L with respect to the applied weight fields W_i gives a set of equations that amount to calculating the error at the output and propagating the error optically backwards through the network. The pertinent results are given below. The distributed assignment of error on the output field is calculated by

$$\lambda_{n+1}(\beta) = \frac{1}{\gamma} O^*(\beta) [D - I_0] \tag{5}$$

This error is then propagated back through the nth or final *linear* optical layer by the equation

$$\delta_n(\beta) = \frac{jC_n}{\pi} \int_{\Omega_o} \lambda_{n+1}(\alpha) \, e^{-jC_n(\beta-\alpha)^2} d\alpha \tag{6}$$

which is used to update the "weight" light applied to the nth nonlinear layer. Optical back-propagation, through the ith *nonlinear* layer (giving $\lambda_i(\beta)$) followed by the *linear* layer (giving $\delta_{i-1}(\beta)$) is performed according to the equations

$$\lambda_i(\beta) = \delta_i(\beta) \; e^{j k_0 \Delta NL_i n_2 (|W_i(\beta)|^2 + |E_i(\beta)|^2)}$$
$$+ \; k_0 \Delta NL_i n_2 E_i^*(\beta) \; 2 \; IM[\; \delta_i(\beta) \; E_i(\beta) \; e^{j k_0 \Delta NL_i n_2 (|W_i(\beta)|^2 + |E_i(\beta)|^2)}\;] \tag{7}$$

$$\delta_{i-1}(\beta) = \frac{jC_{i-1}}{\pi} \int_{Q_i} \lambda_i(\alpha) \; e^{-\mathcal{L}_{i-1}(\beta - \alpha)^2} d\alpha$$

This gives the error signal $\delta_{i-1}(\beta)$ used to update the "weight" light distribution $W_{i-1}(\beta)$ applied to the i-1 nonlinear layer. The "weights" are updated based upon these errors according to the gradient descent rule

$$W_i^{new}(\beta) = W_i^{old}(\beta)$$
$$+ \eta_i(\beta) k_0 \Delta NL_i n_2 W_i^{old}(\beta) \; 2 \; IM [\; E_i(\beta) \; \delta_i(\beta) \; e^{-k_0 \Delta NL_i n_2 (|W_i^{old}(\beta)|^2 + |E_i(\beta)|^2)}\;] \tag{8}$$

where $\eta_i(\beta)$ is a learning rate which can be, but usually is not a function of layer number i and spatial position β. Figure 3 shows the optical network (thick linear layers and thin nonlinear layers) with the uniform plane wave E_0, the input signal distribution I, forward propagation signals $E_1 \; E_2 \; ... \; E_n$, the weighting light distributions at the nonlinear layers $W_1 \; W_2 \; ... \; W_n$. Also shown are the error signal λ_{n+1} at the output and the back-propagated error signals $\delta_n \; ... \; \delta_2 \; \delta_1$ for updating the nonlinear layers. Common nonlinear materials exist for which the material constants are such that the second term in the first of Equations 7 becomes small. Ignoring this second term gives an approximate form of optical back-propagation which amounts to **calculating the error at the output of the network and then reversing its direction to optically propagate this error backward through the device**. This can be easily seen by comparing Equations 6 and 7 (with the second term dropped) for optical back-propagation of the output error λ_n with Equations 1 and 2 for the forward propagation of the signal E_i. This means that the optical back-propagation training calculations potentially can be implemented in the same physical device as the forward network calculations. Equation (8) then becomes;

$$W_i^{new}(\beta) = W_i^{old}(\beta)$$
$$+ (2\eta_i(\beta) k_0 \Delta NL_i n_2) \; W_i^{old}(\beta) \; [\; (E_i(\beta) \; \lambda_i(\beta)) - (E_i(\beta) \; \lambda_i(\beta))^* \;] \tag{9}$$

which **may** be able to be implemented optically.

4   SIMULATION RESULTS

To prove feasibility, the network was then trained and tested on several benchmark classification problems, two of which are discussed here. More details on these and other simulations of the optical network can be found in (Skinner, 1995). In the first (Using Nworks, 1991), iris species were classified into one of three categories: Setosa, Versicolor or Virginica. Classification was based upon length and width of the sepals and petals. The network consisted of an input self-defocusing layer with an applied irradiance field which was divided into 4 separate Gaussian distributed input regions 25 microns in width followed by a linear layer. This pattern is repeated for 4 more groups composed of a nonlinear layer (with applied weights) followed by a linear layer. The final linear layer has three separate output regions 10 microns wide for binary classification as to species. The nonlinear layers were all 20 microns thick with $n_2 = -.05$ and the linear layers were 100 microns thick. The wavelength of applied light was 1 micron and the width of the network was 512 microns discretized into 512 pixels. This network was trained on a set of 50 training pairs to produce correct classification of all 50 training pairs. The network was then used to classify 50 additional pairs of test data which were not used in the training phase. The network classified 46 of these correctly for a 92% accuracy level which is comparable to a standard feedforward network with discrete sigmoidal neurons.

In the second problem, we tested the performance of the network on a set of data from a dolphin sonar discrimination experiment (Roitblat, 1991). In this study a dolphin was presented with one of three different types of objects (a tube, a sphere, and a cone), allowed to echolocate, and rewarded for choosing the correct one from a comparison array. The Fourier transforms of his click echoes, in the form of average amplitudes in each of 30 frequency bins, were then used as inputs for a neural network. Nine nonlinear layers were used along with 30 input regions and 3

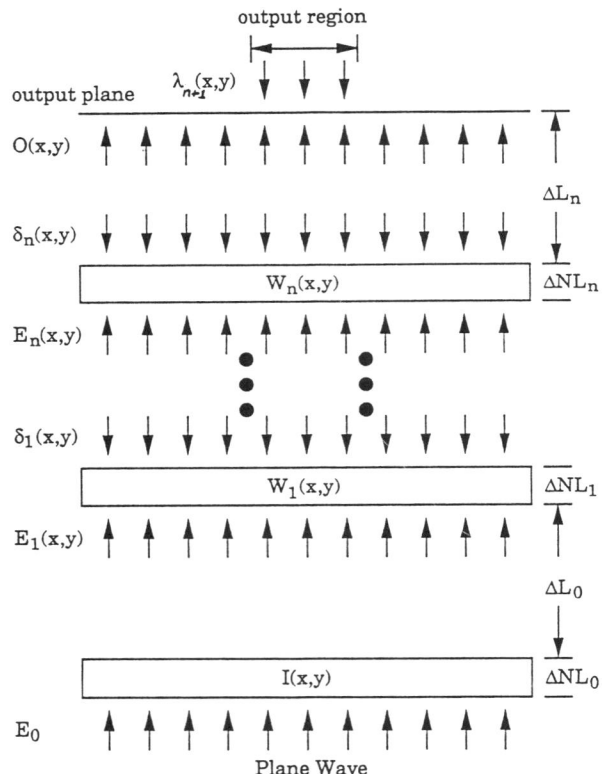

Figure 3: Optical Network Forward Data and Backward Error Data Flow

output regions, the remainder of the network physical parameters were the same as above for the iris classification. Half the data (13 sets of clicks) was used to train the network, with the other half of the data (14 sets) used to test the training. After training, classification of the test data set was 100% correct.

5 EXPERIMENTAL RESULTS

As a proof of the concept, the optical neural network was constructed in the laboratory to be trained to perform various logic functions. Two thermal self-defocusing layers were used, one for the input and the other for a single layer of weighting. The nonlinear coefficient of the index of refraction (n_2) was measured to be -3×10^{-4} cm^2/W. The nonlinear layers had a thickness (ΔNL_0 and ΔNL_1) of 630µm and were separated by a distance (ΔL_0) of 15cm. The output region was 100µm wide and placed 15cm (ΔL_1) behind the weighting layer. The experiment used HeNe laser light to provide the input plane wave and the input and weighting irradiances. The spatial profiles of the input and weighting layers were realized by imaging a LCD spatial light modulator onto the respective nonlinear layers. The inputs were two bright or dark regions on a Gaussian input beam producing the intensity profile:

$$I(x) = I_0 \, e^{-(x/K_0)^2} [1 + Q_0 rect((x+x_0)/K_1)][1 + Q_1 rect((x-x_0)/K_1)]$$

where $I_0 = 12.5$ mW/cm^2, $K_0 = 900$µm, $x_0 = 600$µm, $K_1 = 400$µm, and Q_0 and Q_1 are the logic inputs taking on a value of zero or one. The weight profile $W_1(x) = I_0 \exp[-(x/K_0)^2][1+w_1(x)]$ where $w_1(x)$ can range from zero to one and is found through training using an algorithm which probed the weighting mask in order update the training weights. Table 1 shows the experimental results for three different logic gates. Given is the normalized output before and after training. The network was trained to recognize a logic zero for a normalized output ≤ 0.9 and a logic one or a normalized output ≥ 1.1. An output value greater than 1 is considered a logic one and an output value less than one is a logic zero. RME is the root mean error.

6 CONCLUSIONS

Work is in progress to improve the logic gate results by increasing the power of propagating signal beam as well as both the input and weighting beams. This will effectively increase the nonlinear processing capability of the network since a higher power produces more nonlinear effect. Also, more power will allow expansion of all of the beams thereby increasing the effective resolution of the thermal materials. Thisreduces the effect of heat transfer within the material which tends to wash out or diffuse benificial steep gradients in temperature which are what produce the gradients in the index of refraction. In addition, the use of photorefractive crystals for optical weight storage shows promise for being able to optically phase conjugate and backpropagate the output errror as well as implement the weight update rule for all optical network training. This appears to be simpler than optical networks using volume hologram weight storage because the Kerr network requires only planar hologram storage.

	Inputs	0 0	0 1	1 0	1 1	RME
NOR	Start	1.001	.802	.698	.807	7.3%
	Finish	1.110	.884	.772	.896	0
	Change	.109	.082	.074	.089	-7.3%
	Output	1	0	0	0	
AND	Start	.998	1.092	1.148	1.440	16.4%
	Finish	.757	.855	.894	1.124	0
	Change	-.241	-.237	-.254	-.316	-16.4%
	Output	0	0	0	1	
XNOR	Start	.998	.880	.893	.994	7.3%
	Finish	1.084	.933	.928	1.073	2.7%
	Change	.086	.053	.035	.079	-4.6%
	Output	1	0	0	1	

Table 1: Preliminary Experimental Logic Gate Results

References

Armstrong, J.A., Bloembergen, N., Ducuing, J., and Pershan, P.S., (1962) "Interactions Between Light Waves in a Nonlinear Dielectric", *Physical Review*, Vol. 127, pp. 1918-1939.

le Cun, Yann, (1988) "A Theoretical Framework for Back-Propagation", Proceedings of the 1988 Connectionist Models Summer School, Morgan Kaufmann, pp. 21-28.

Pineda, F.J., (1987) "Generalization of backpropagation to recurrent and higher order neural networks", Proceedings of IEEE Conference on Neural information Processing Systems, November 1987, IEEE Press.

Roitblat., Moore, Nachtigall, and Penner, (1991) "Natural dolphin echo recognition using an integrator gateway network," in *Advances in Neural Processing Systems 3* Morgan Kaufmann, San Mateo, CA, 273-281.

Skinner, S.R., Steck, J.E., Behrman, E.C., (1995) "An Optical Neural Network Using Kerr Type Nonlinear Materials", To Appear in *Applied Optics*.

"Using Nworks, (1991) *An Extended Tutorial for NeuralWorks Professional II/Plus and NeuralWorks Explorer*, NeuralWare, Inc. Pittsburgh, PA, pg. UN-18.

A Charge-Based CMOS Parallel Analog Vector Quantizer

Gert Cauwenberghs
Johns Hopkins University
ECE Department
3400 N. Charles St.
Baltimore, MD 21218-2686
gert@jhunix.hcf.jhu.edu

Volnei Pedroni
California Institute of Technology
EE Department
Mail Code 128-95
Pasadena, CA 91125
pedroni@romeo.caltech.edu

Abstract

We present an analog VLSI chip for parallel analog vector quantization. The MOSIS 2.0 μm double-poly CMOS Tiny chip contains an array of 16×16 charge-based distance estimation cells, implementing a mean absolute difference (MAD) metric operating on a 16-input analog vector field and 16 analog template vectors. The distance cell including dynamic template storage measures 60×78 μm^2. Additionally, the chip features a winner-take-all (WTA) output circuit of linear complexity, with global positive feedback for fast and decisive settling of a single winner output. Experimental results on the complete 16×16 VQ system demonstrate correct operation with 34 dB analog input dynamic range and 3 μsec cycle time at 0.7 mW power dissipation.

1 Introduction

Vector quantization (VQ) [1] is a common ingredient in signal processing, for applications of pattern recognition and data compression in vision, speech and beyond. Certain neural network models for pattern recognition, such as Kohonen feature map classifiers [2], are closely related to VQ as well. The implementation of VQ, in its basic form, involves a search among a set of vector templates for the one which best matches the input vector, whereby the degree of matching is quantified by a given vector distance metric. Efficient hardware implementation requires a parallel search over the template set and a fast selection and encoding of the "winning" template. The chip presented here implements a parallel synchronous analog vector quantizer with 16 analog input vector components and 16 dynamically stored analog template vectors, producing a 4-bit digital output word encoding the winning template upon presentation of an input vector. The architecture is fully scalable as in previous implementations of analog vector quantizers, *e.g.* [3,4,5,6], and can be readily expanded toward a larger number of vector components and template vectors without structural modification of the layout. Distinct features of the present implementation include a linear winner-take-all (WTA) structure with globalized positive feedback for fast selection of the winning template, and a mean absolute difference (MAD) metric for the distance estimations, both realized with a minimum amount of circuitry. Using a linear charge-based circuit topology for MAD distance accumulation, a wide voltage range for the analog inputs and templates is achieved at relatively low energy consumption per computation cycle.

2 System Architecture

The core of the VQ consists of a 16×16 2-D array of distance estimation cells, configured to interconnect columns and rows according to the vector input components and template outputs. Each cell computes in parallel the absolute difference distance between one component x_j of the input vector $\mathbf{x}$ and the corresponding component $y^i{}_j$ of one of the template vectors $\mathbf{y}^i$,

$$d(x_j, y^i{}_j) = |x_j - y^i{}_j| , \quad i, j = 1 \ldots 16 . \tag{1}$$

The mean absolute difference (MAD) distance between input and template vectors is accumulated along rows

$$\hat{d}(\mathbf{x}, \mathbf{y}^i) = \frac{1}{16} \sum_{j=1}^{16} |x_j - y^i{}_j| , \quad i = 1 \ldots 16 \tag{2}$$

and presented to the WTA, which selects the single winner

$$k^{\text{WTA}} = \arg\min_i \hat{d}(\mathbf{x}, \mathbf{y}^i) . \tag{3}$$

Additional parts are included in the architecture for binary encoding of the winning output, and for address selection to write and refresh the template vectors.

3 VLSI Circuit Implementation

The circuit implementation of the major components of the VQ, for MAD distance estimation and WTA selection, is described below. Both MAD distance and WTA cells operate in clocked synchronous mode using a precharge/evaluate scheme in the voltage domain. The approach followed here offers a wide analog voltage range of inputs and templates at low power weak-inversion MOS operation, and a fast and decisive settling of the winning output using a single communication line for global positive feedback. The output encoding and address decoding circuitry are implemented using standard CMOS logic.

A Charge-Based CMOS Parallel Analog Vector Quantizer

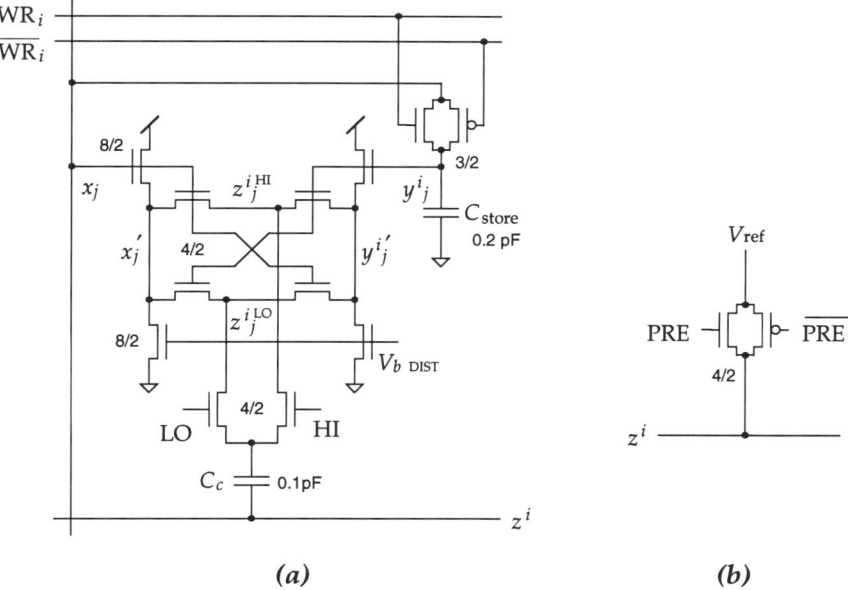

Figure 1: Schematic of distance estimation circuitry. *(a)* Absolute distance cell. *(b)* Output precharge circuitry.

3.1 Distance Estimation Cell

The schematic of the distance estimation cell, replicated along rows and columns of the VQ array, is shown in Figure 1 (a). The cell contains two source followers, which buffer the input voltage x_j and the template voltage $y^i{}_j$. The template voltage is stored dynamically onto C_{store}, written or refreshed by activating WR_i while the $y^i{}_j$ value is presented on the x_j input line. The WR_i and $\overline{\text{WR}_i}$ signal levels along rows of the VQ array are driven by the address decoder, which selects a single template vector $\mathbf{y}^i$ to be written to with data presented at the input $\mathbf{x}$ when WR is active.

Additional lateral transistors connect symmetrically to the source follower outputs $x_j{}'$ and $y^i{}_j{}'$. By means of resistive division, the lateral transistors construct the maximum and minimum of $x_j{}'$ and $y^i{}_j{}'$ on $z^i{}_j{}^{\text{HI}}$ and $z^i{}_j{}^{\text{LO}}$, respectively. In particular, when x_j is much larger than $y^i{}_j$, the voltage $z^i{}_j{}^{\text{HI}}$ approaches $x_j{}'$ and the voltage $z^i{}_j{}^{\text{LO}}$ approaches $y^i{}_j{}'$. By symmetry, the complementary argument holds in case x_j is much smaller than $y^i{}_j$. Therefore, the differential component of $z^i{}_j{}^{\text{HI}}$ and $z^i{}_j{}^{\text{LO}}$ approximately represents the absolute difference value of x_j and $y^i{}_j$:

$$\begin{aligned} z^i{}_j{}^{\text{HI}} - z^i{}_j{}^{\text{LO}} &\approx \max(x_j{}', y^i{}_j{}') - \min(x_j{}', y^i{}_j{}') \\ &= |x_j{}' - y^i{}_j{}'| \approx \kappa \, |x_j - y^i{}_j| , \end{aligned} \qquad (4)$$

with κ the MOS back gate effect coefficient [7].

The mean absolute difference (MAD) distances (2) are obtained by accumulating contributions (4) along rows of cells through capacitive coupling, using the well known technique of correlated double sampling. To this purpose, a coupling capacitor C_c is provided in every cell, coupling its differential output to the corresponding output row line. In the precharge phase, the maximum values $z^i{}_j{}^{HI}$ are coupled to the output by activating HI, and the output lines are preset to reference voltage V_{ref} by activating PRE, Figure 1 (b). In the evaluate phase, PRE is de-activated, and the minimum values $z^i{}_j{}^{LO}$ are coupled to the output by activating LO. From (4), the resulting voltage outputs on the floating row lines are given by

$$z^i = V_{ref} - \frac{1}{16}\sum_{j=1}^{16}(z^i{}_j{}^{HI} - z^i{}_j{}^{LO}) \qquad (5)$$

$$\approx V_{ref} - \kappa \frac{1}{16}\sum_{j=1}^{16}|x_j - y^i{}_j|.$$

The last term in (5) corresponds directly to the distance measure $\hat{d}(\mathbf{x}, \mathbf{y}^i)$ in (2). Notice that the negative sign in (5) could be reversed by interchanging clocks HI and LO, if needed. Since the subsequent WTA stage searches for maximum z^i, the inverted distance metric is in the form needed for VQ.

Characteristics of the MAD distance estimation (5), measured directly on the VQ array with uniform inputs x_j and templates $y^i{}_j$, are shown in Figure 2. The magnified view in Figure 2 (b) clearly illustrates the effective smoothing of the absolute difference function (4) near the origin, $x_j \approx y^i{}_j$. The smoothing is caused by the shift in x_j' and $y^i{}_j{}'$ due to the conductance of the lateral coupling transistors connected to the source follower outputs in Figure 1 (a), and extends over a voltage range comparable to the thermal voltage kT/q depending on the relative geometry of the transistors and current bias level of the source followers. The observed width of the flat region in Figure 2 spans roughly 60 mV, and shows little variation for bias current settings below 0.5 μA. Tuning of the bias current allows to balance speed and power dissipation requirements, since the output response is slew-rate limited by the source followers.

3.2 Winner-Take-All Circuitry

The circuit implementation of the winner-take-all (WTA) function combines the compact sizing and modularity of a linear architecture as in [4,8,9] with positive feedback for fast and decisive output settling independent of signal levels, as in [6,3]. Typical positive feedback structures for WTA operation use a logarithmic tree [6] or a fully interconnected network [3], with implementation complexities of order $O(n \log n)$ and $O(n^2)$ respectively, n being the number of WTA inputs. The present implementation features an $O(n)$ complexity in a linear structure by means of globalized positive feedback, communicated over a single line.

The schematic of the WTA cell, receiving the input z^i and constructing the digital output d_i through global competition communicated over the COMM line, is shown in Figure 3. The global COMM line is source connected to input transistor Mi and positive feedback transistor Mf, and receives a constant bias current $I_{b\ (WTA)}$ from Mb1. Locally, the WTA operation is governed by the dynamics of d_i' on (parasitic) capacitor C_p. A high pulse

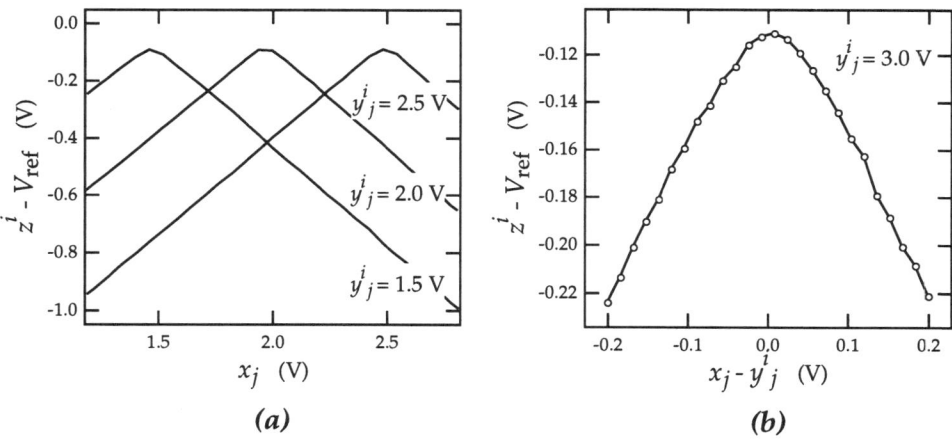

Figure 2: Distance estimation characteristics, (a) for various values of $y^i{}_j$; (b) magnified view.

on RST, resetting d_i' to zero, marks the beginning of the WTA cycle. With Mf initially inactive, the total bias current $n\, I_{b\,(\text{WTA})}$ through COMM is divided over all competing WTA cells, according to the relative z^i voltage levels, and each cell fraction is locally mirrored by the Mm1-Mm2 pair onto d_i', charging C_p. The cell with the highest z^i input voltage receives the largest fraction of bias current, and charges C_p at the highest rate. The winning output is determined by the first d_i' reaching the threshold to turn on the corresponding Mf feedback transistor, say $i = k$. This threshold voltage is given by the source voltage on COMM, common for all cells. The positive feedback of the state d_k' through Mf, which eventually claims the entire fraction of the bias current, enhances and latches the winning output level d_k' to the positive supply and shuts off the remaining losing outputs d_i' to zero, $i \neq k$. The additional circuitry at the output stage of the cell serves to buffer the binary d_i' value at the d_i output terminal.

No more than one winner can practically co-exist at equilibrium, by nature of the combined positive feedback and global renormalization in the WTA competition. Moreover, the output settling times of the winner and losers are fairly independent of the input signal levels, and are given mainly by the bias current level $I_{b\,(\text{WTA})}$ and the parasitic capacitance C_p. Tests conducted on a separate 16-element WTA array, identical to the one used on the VQ chip, have demonstrated single-winner WTA operation with response time below 0.5 μsec at less than 2 μW power dissipation per cell.

4 Functionality Test

To characterize the performance of the entire VQ system under typical real-time conditions, the chip was presented a periodic sequence of 16 distinct input vectors $\mathbf{x}(i)$, stored and refreshed dynamically in the 16 template locations $\mathbf{y}^i$ by circularly incrementing the template address and activating WR at the beginning of every cycle. The test vectors rep-

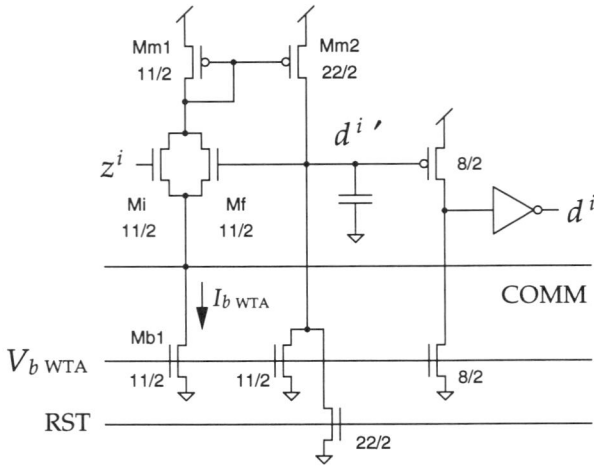

Figure 3: Circuit schematic of winner-take-all cell.

resent a single triangular pattern rotated over the 16 component indices with single index increments in sequence. The fundamental component $x_0(i)$ is illustrated on the top trace of the scope plot in Figure 4. The other components are uniformly displaced in time over one period, by a number of cycles equal to the index, $x_j(i) = x_0(i-j) \bmod 16$. Figure 4 also displays the VQ output waveforms in response to the triangular input sequence, with the desired parabolic profile for the analog distance output z^0 and the expected alternating bit pattern of the WTA least significant output bit.[1] The triangle test performed correctly at speeds limited by the instrumentation equipment, and the dissipated power on the chip measures 0.7 mW at 3 μsec cycle time[2] and 5 V supply voltage.

An estimate for the dynamic range of analog input and template voltages was obtained directly by observing the smallest and largest absolute voltage difference still resolved correctly by the VQ output, uniformly over all components. By tuning the voltage range of the triangular test vectors, the recorded minimum and maximum voltage amplitudes for 5 V supply voltage are $V_{\min} = 87.5$ mV and $V_{\max} = 4$ V, respectively. The estimated analog dynamic range $V_{\max}/V_{\min}$ is thus 45.7, or roughly 34 dB, per cell. The value obtained for $V_{\min}$ indicates that the dynamic range is limited mainly by the smoothing of the absolute distance measure characteristic (1) near the origin in Figure 2 (b). We notice that a similar limitation of dynamic range applies to other distance metrics with vanishing slope near the origin as well, the popular mean square error (MSE) formulation in particular. The MSE metric is frequently adopted in VQ implementations using strong inversion MOS circuitry, and offers a dynamic range typically worse than obtained here regardless of implementation accuracy, due to the relatively wide flat region of the MSE distance function near the origin.

---

[1]The voltages on the scope plot are inverted as a consequence of the chip test setup.
[2]including template write operations

A Charge-Based CMOS Parallel Analog Vector Quantizer

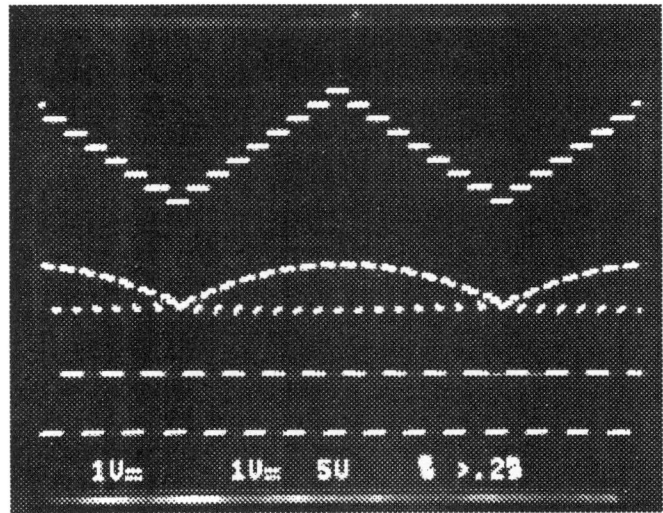

Figure 4: Scope plot of VQ waveforms. Top: Analog input x_0. Center: Analog distance output z^0. Bottom: Least significant bit of encoded output.

Table 1: Features of the VQ chip

Technology	2 µm p-well double-poly CMOS
Supply voltage	+ 5 V
Power dissipation	
VQ chip	0.7 mW (3 µsec cycle time)
Dynamic range	
inputs, templates	34 dB
Area	
VQ chip	2.2 mm X 2.25 mm
distance cell	60 µm X 78 µm
WTA cell	76 µm X 80 µm

5 Conclusion

We proposed and demonstrated a synchronous charge-based CMOS VLSI system for parallel analog vector quantization, featuring a mean absolute difference (MAD) metric, and a linear winner-take-all (WTA) structure with globalized positive feedback. By virtue of the MAD metric, a fairly large (34 dB) analog dynamic range of inputs and templates has been obtained in the distance computations through simple charge-based circuitry. Likewise, fast and unambiguous settling of the WTA outputs, using global competition communicated over a single wire, has been obtained by adopting a compact linear circuit structure to implement the positive feedback WTA function. The resulting structure of the VQ chip is highly modular, and the functional characteristics are fairly consistent over a wide range of bias levels, including the MOS weak inversion and subthreshold regions. This allows the circuitry to be tuned to accommodate various speed and power requirements. A summary of the chip features of the 16×16 vector quantizer is presented in Table I.

Acknowledgments

Fabrication of the CMOS chip was provided through the DARPA/NSF MOSIS service. The authors thank Amnon Yariv for stimulating discussions and encouragement.

References

[1] A. Gersho and R.M. Gray, *Vector Quantization and Signal Compression,* Norwell, MA: Kluwer, 1992.

[2] T. Kohonen, *Self-Organisation and Associative Memory,* Berlin: Springer-Verlag, 1984.

[3] Y. He and U. Cilingiroglu, "A Charge-Based On-Chip Adaptation Kohonen Neural Network," *IEEE Transactions on Neural Networks,* vol. **4** (3), pp 462-469, 1993.

[4] J.C. Lee, B.J. Sheu, and W.C. Fang, "VLSI Neuroprocessors for Video Motion Detection," *IEEE Transactions on Neural Networks,* vol. **4** (2), pp 78-191, 1993.

[5] R. Tawel, "Real-Time Focal-Plane Image Compression," in *Proceedings Data Compression Conference,*, Snowbird, Utah, IEEE Computer Society Press, pp 401-409, 1993.

[6] G.T. Tuttle, S. Fallahi, and A.A. Abidi, "An 8b CMOS Vector A/D Converter," in *ISSCC Technical Digest,* IEEE Press, vol. **36**, pp 38-39, 1993.

[7] C.A. Mead, *Analog VLSI and Neural Systems,* Reading, MA: Addison-Wesley, 1989.

[8] J. Lazzaro, S. Ryckebusch, M.A. Mahowald, and C.A. Mead, "Winner-Take-All Networks of O(n) Complexity," in *Advances in Neural Information Processing Systems,* San Mateo, CA: Morgan Kaufman, vol. **1**, pp 703-711, 1989.

[9] A.G. Andreou, K.A. Boahen, P.O. Pouliquen, A. Pavasovic, R.E. Jenkins, and K. Strohbehn, "Current-Mode Subthreshold MOS Circuits for Analog VLSI Neural Systems," *IEEE Transactions on Neural Networks,* vol. **2** (2), pp 205-213, 1991.

An Auditory Localization and Coordinate Transform Chip

Timothy K. Horiuchi
timmer@cns.caltech.edu
Computation and Neural Systems Program
California Institute of Technology
Pasadena, CA 91125

Abstract

The localization and orientation to various novel or interesting events in the environment is a critical sensorimotor ability in all animals, predator or prey. In mammals, the superior colliculus (SC) plays a major role in this behavior, the deeper layers exhibiting topographically mapped responses to visual, auditory, and somatosensory stimuli. Sensory information arriving from different modalities should then be represented in the same coordinate frame. Auditory cues, in particular, are thought to be computed in head-based coordinates which must then be transformed to retinal coordinates. In this paper, an analog VLSI implementation for auditory localization in the azimuthal plane is described which extends the architecture proposed for the barn owl to a primate eye movement system where further transformation is required. This transformation is intended to model the projection in primates from auditory cortical areas to the deeper layers of the primate superior colliculus. This system is interfaced with an analog VLSI-based saccadic eye movement system also being constructed in our laboratory.

Introduction

Auditory localization has been studied in many animals, particularly the barn owl. Most birds have a resolution of only 10 to 20 degrees, but owls are able to orient to sound with an accuracy of 1 to 2 degrees which is comparable with humans. One important cue for localizing sounds is the relative time of arrival of a sound to two spatially separated ears. A neural architecture first described by Jeffress (1948) for measuring this time difference has been shown to exist in the barn owl auditory localization system (Konishi 1986). An analog VLSI implementation of the barn owl system constructed by Lazzaro (1990) is extended here to include a transformation from head coordinates to retinal coordinates.

In comparison to the barn owl, the neurophysiology of auditory localization in cats and primates is not as well understood and a clear map of auditory space does not appear to be present in the inferior colliculus as it is in the owl. It has been suggested that cortical auditory regions may provide the head-based map of auditory space (Groh and Sparks 1992).

In primates, where much of the oculomotor system is based in retinotopic coordinates, head-based information must ultimately be transformed in order to be used. While other models of coordinate transformation have been proposed for visual information (e.g. Zipser and Andersen 1988, Krommenhoek et al. 1993) and for auditory information (Groh and Sparks 1992), the model of coordinate transformation used in this system is a switching network which shifts the entire projection of the head-based map of auditory space onto a retinotopic "colliculus" circuit. This particular model is similar to a basis function approach where intermediate units have compact receptive fields in an eye-position / head-based azimuth space and the output units sum the outputs of a subset of these units.

The auditory localization system described here provides acoustic target information to an analog VLSI-based saccadic eye movement system (Horiuchi, Bishofberger, and Koch 1994) being developed in our laboratory for multimodal operation.

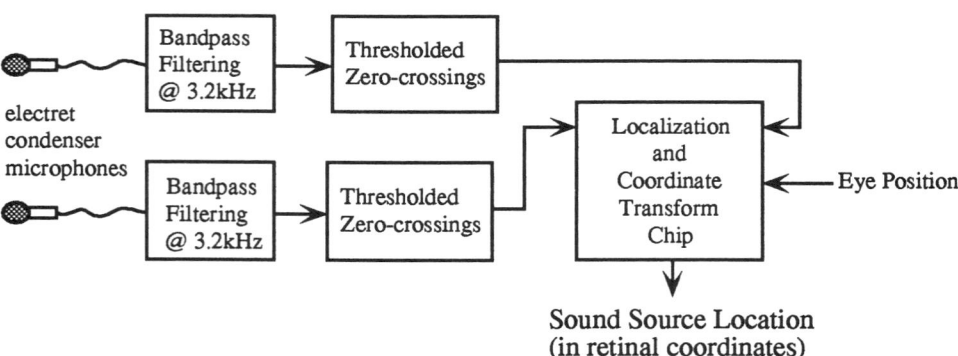

Figure 1: Block diagram of the auditory localization system. The analog front end consists of external discrete analog electronics.

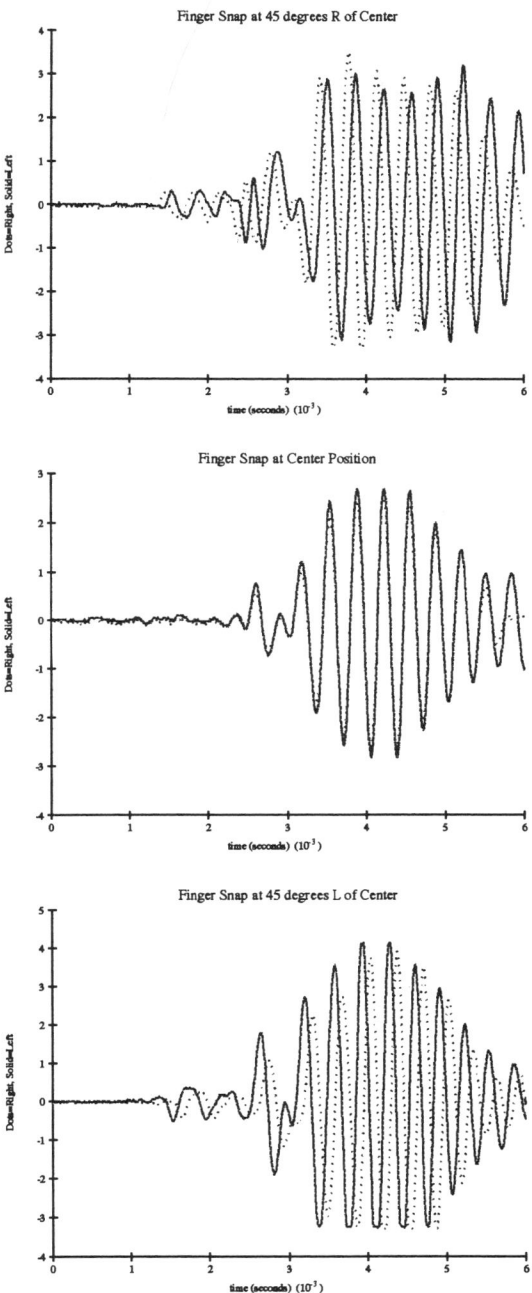

Figure 2: Filtered signals of the left and right microphones from 3 different angles.

The Localization System

The analog front-end of the system (see figure 1) consists of three basic components, the microphones, the filter stage, and the thresholded, zero-crossing stage. Two microphones are placed with their centers about 2 inches apart. For any given time difference in arrival of acoustic stimuli, there are many possible locations from which the sound could have originated. These points describe a hyperbola with the two microphones as the two foci. If the sound source is distant enough, we can estimate the angle since the hyperbola approaches an asymptote. The current system operates on a single frequency and the inter-microphone distance has been chosen to be just under one wavelength apart at the filter frequency. The filter frequency chosen was 3.2 kHz because the author's finger snap, used extensively during development contained a large component at that frequency. The next step in the computation consists of triggering a digital pulse at the moment of zero-crossing if the acoustic signal is large enough.

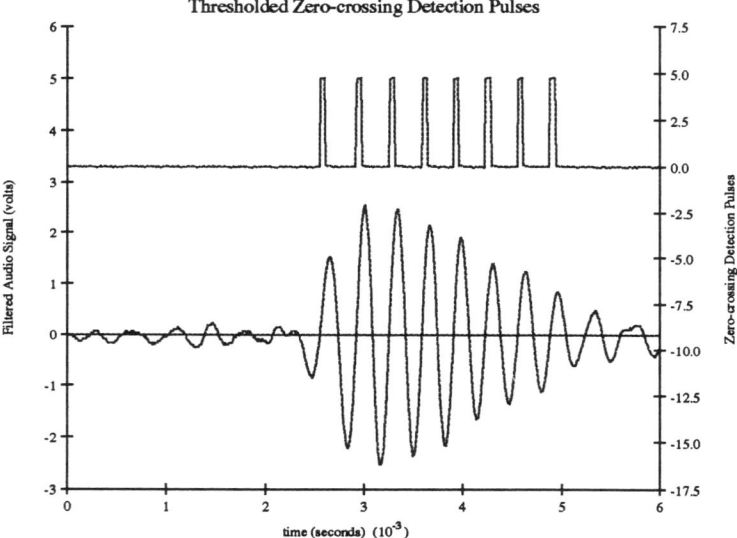

Figure 3: Example of output pulses from the external circuitry. Zero phase is chosen to be the positive-slope zero-crossing. Top: Digital pulses are generated at the time of zero phase for signals whose derivative is larger than a preset threshold. Bottom: 3.2 kHz Bandpass filtered signal for a finger snap.

Phase Detection and Coordinate Transform in Analog VLSI

The analog VLSI component of the system consists of two axon delay lines (Mead 1988) which propagate the left and right microphone pulse signals in opposing directions in order to compute the cross correlation (see Fig 4.) The location of the peak in this correlation technique represents the relative phase of the two signals.

This technique is described in more detail and with more biological justification by Lazzaro (1990). The current implementation contains 15 axon circuits in each delay line. This is shown in figure 4. At each position in the correlation delay line are logical AND circuits which output a logic one when there are two active axon units at that location. Since these units only turn on for specific time delays, they define auditory "receptive fields". The output of this subsystem are 15 digital lines which are passed on to the coordinate transform.

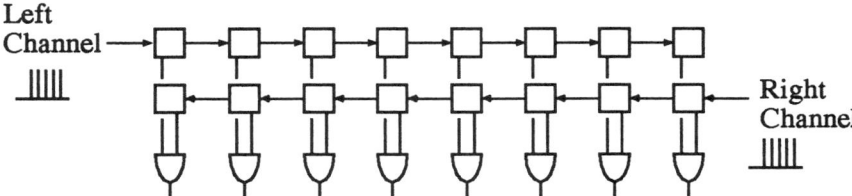

Figure 4: Diagram of the double axon delay line which accepts digital spikes on the inputs and propagates them across the array. Whenever two spikes meet, a pulse is generated on the output AND units. The position of the AND circuit which gets activated indicates the relative time of arrival of the left and right inputs. NOTE: the actual circuit contains 15 axon units.

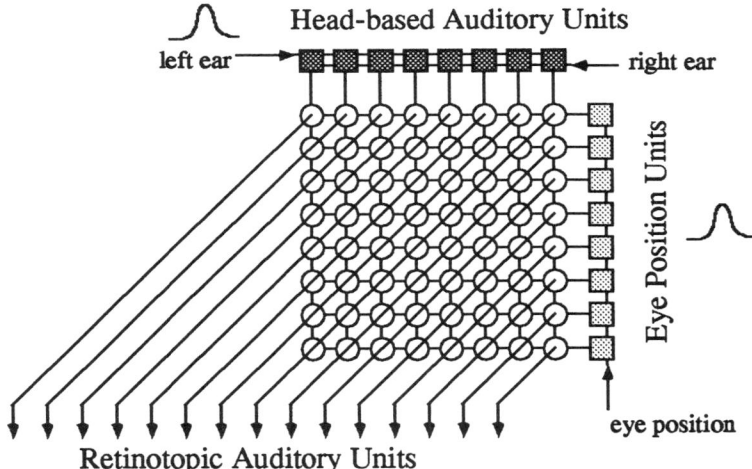

Figure 5:

For the one-dimensional case described in this project, the appropriate transform from head to retinal coordinates is a rotation which subtracts the eye position. The eye position information on the chip is represented as a voltage which activates one of the eye position units. The spatial pattern of activation from the auditory units is then "steered" to the output stage with the appropriate shift. (See figure 5). This is similar to a shift scheme proposed by Pitts and McCulloch (1947) for obtaining pitch invariance for chord recognition. The eye position units are constructed from an array of "bump" circuits (Delbrück 1993) which compare the eye position voltage with its local voltage reference. The two dimensional array of intermediate units take the digital signal from the auditory units and switch the "bump" currents onto the output lines. The output current lines drive the inputs of a centroid circuit.

The current implementation of the shift can be viewed as a basis function approach where a population of intermediate units respond to limited "ball-like" regions in the two-dimensional space of horizontal eye position and sound source azimuth (head-coordinates). The output units then sum the outputs of only those intermediate units which represent the same retinal location. It should be noted that this coordinate transformation is closely related to the "dendrite model" proposed for the projection of cortical auditory information to the deep SC by Groh and Sparks (1992).

The final output stage converts this spatial array of current carrying lines into a single output voltage which represents the centroid of the stimulus in retinal coordinates. This centroid circuit (DeWeerth 1991) is intended to represent the primate SC where a similar computation is believed to occur.

Results and Conclusions

Figure 6 shows three plots of the chip's output voltage as a function of the inter-pulse time interval. Figure 7 shows three plots of the full system's output voltage for different eye position voltages. The output is roughly linear with azimuth and linear with eye position voltage. In operation, the system input consists of a sound entering the two microphones and the output consists of an analog voltage representing the position of the sound source and a digital signal indicating that the analog data is valid.

The auditory localization system described here is currently in use with an analog VLSI-based model of the primate saccadic system to expand its operation into the auditory domain (Horiuchi, Bishofberger, & Koch 1994). In addition to the effort of our laboratory to model and understand biological computing structures in real-time systems, we are exploring the use of these low power integrated sensors in portable applications such as mobile robotics. Analog VLSI provides a compact and efficient implementation for many neuromorphic computing architectures which can potentially be used to provide, small, fast, low power sensors for a wide variety of applications.

Acknowledgements

The author would like to acknowledge Prof. Christof Koch for his academic support and use of laboratory facilities for this project, Brooks Bishofberger for his assistance in constructing some of the discrete electronics and Prof. Carver Mead for running the CNS184 course under which this chip was fabricated.
The author is supported by an AASERT grant from the Office of Naval Research.

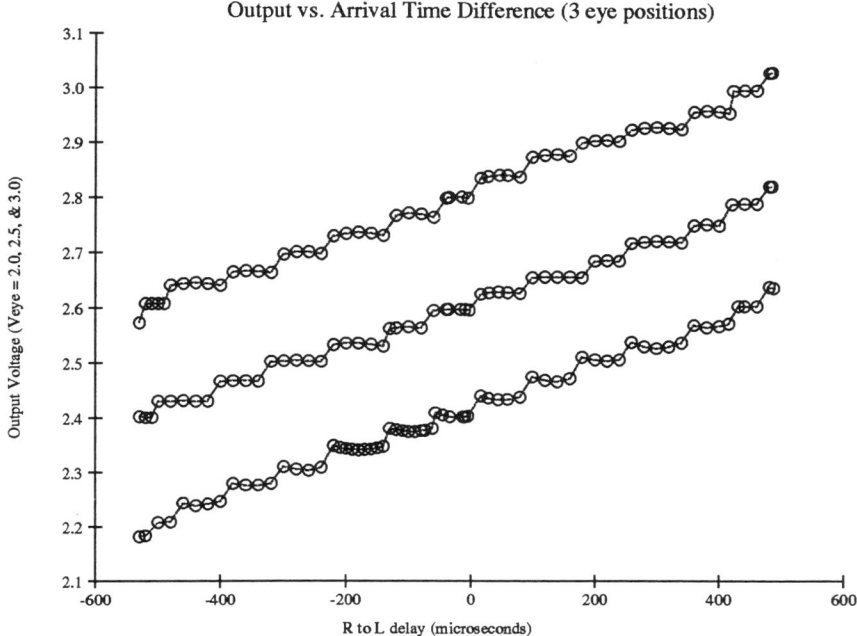

Figure 6: Chip output vs. input pulse timing: The chip was driven with a signal generator and the output voltage was plotted for three different eye position voltages. Due to the discretized nature of the axon, there are only 15 axon locations at which pulses can meet. This creates the staircase response.

References

T. Delbrück (1993) Investigations of Analog VLSI Visual Transduction and Motion Processing, Ph.D. Thesis, California Institute of Technology

J. Groh and D. Sparks (1992) 2 Models for Transforming Auditory Signals from Head-Centered to Eye-Centered Coordinates *Biol. Cybern.* 67(4) 291-302.

T. Horiuchi, B. Bishofberger, & C. Koch, (1994) An Analog VLSI-based Saccadic System, In (ed.), *Advances in Neural Information Processing Systems 6* San Mateo, CA: Morgan Kaufman

L. A. Jeffress (1948) A Place Theory of Sound Localization *J. Comp. Physiol. Psychol.* 41: 35-39.

M. Konishi (1986) Centrally Synthesized Maps of Sensory Space. *TINS* April, pp. 163-168.

K. P. Krommenhoek, A. J. Van Opstal, C. C. A. M. Gielen, J. A. ,M. Van Gisbergen. (1993) Remapping of Neural Activity in the Motor Colliculus: A Neural Network Study. *Vision Research* 33(9):1287-1298.

J. Lazzaro. (1990) Silicon Models of Early Audition, Ph.D. Thesis, California Institute of Technology

C. Mead, (1988) *Analog VLSI and Neural Systems* Menlo Park: Addison-Wesley

W. Pitts and W. S. McCulloch, (1947) How we know universals: the perception of auditory and visual forms. *Bulletin of Mathematical Biophysics* 9:127-147.

D. Zipser and R. A. Andersen (1988) A back-propagation programmed network that simulates response properties of a subset of posterior parietal neurons. *Nature* 331:679-684.

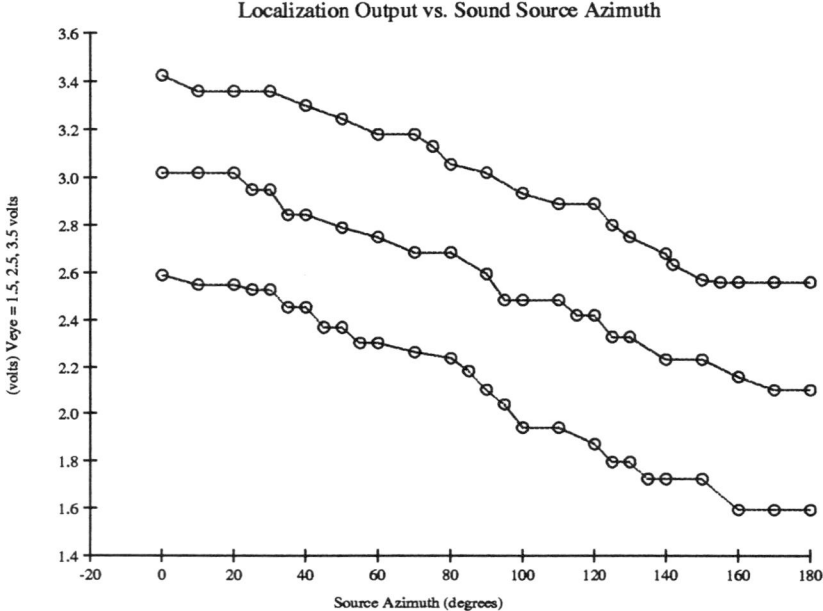

Figure 7: Performance of the full system on continuous input (sinusoidal) delivered by a speaker from different angles. Note that 90 degrees denotes the center position. The three plots are the outputs for three different settings of the eye position input voltage.

An Analog Neural Network Inspired by Fractal Block Coding

Fernando J. Pineda
The Applied Physics Laboratory
The Johns Hopkins University
Johns Hokins Road
Laurel, MD 20723-6099

Andreas G. Andreou
Dept. of Electrical & Computer Engineering
The Johns Hopkins University
34th & Charles St.
Baltimore, MD 21218

Abstract

We consider the problem of decoding block coded data, using a physical dynamical system. We sketch out a decompression algorithm for fractal block codes and then show how to implement a recurrent neural network using physically simple but highly-nonlinear, analog circuit models of neurons and synapses. The nonlinear system has many fixed points, but we have at our disposal a procedure to choose the parameters in such a way that only one solution, the desired solution, is stable. As a partial proof of the concept, we present experimental data from a small system a 16-neuron analog CMOS chip fabricated in a 2m analog p-well process. This chip operates in the subthreshold regime and, for each choice of parameters, converges to a unique stable state. Each state exhibits a qualitatively fractal shape.

1. INTRODUCTION

Sometimes, a nonlinear approach is the simplest way to solve a linear problem. This is true when computing with physical dynamical systems whose natural operations are nonlinear. In such cases it may be expensive, in terms of physical complexity, to linearize the dynamics. For example in neural computation active ion channels have highly non linear input-output behaviour (see Hille 1984). Another example is subthreshold CMOS VLSI technology[1]. In both examples the physics that governs the operation of the active devices, gives rise to gain elements that have exponential transfer characteristics. These exponentials result in computing structures with non-linear dynamics. It is therefore worthwhile, from both scientific and engineering perspectives, to investigate the idea of analog computation by highly non-linear components.

This paper, explores an approach for solving a specific linear problem with analog circuits that have nonlinear transfer functions. The computational task considered here is that of fractal block code decompression (see e.g. Jacquin, 1989).

The conventional approach to decompressing fractal codes is essentially an excercise in solving a high-dimenional sparse linear system of equations by using a relaxation algorithm. The relaxation algorithm is performed by iteratively applying an affine transformation to a state vector. The iteration yields a sequence of state vectors that converges to a vector of decoded data. The approach taken in this paper is based on the observation that one can construct a physically-simple nonlinear dyanmical system whose unique stable fixed point coincides with the solution of the sparse linear system of equations.

In the next section we briefly summarize the basic ideas behind fractal block coding. This is followed by a description of an analog circuit with physically-simple nonlinear neurons. We show how to set the input voltages for the network so that we can program the position of the stable fixed point. Finally , we present experimental results obtained from a test chip fabricated in a 2mm CMOS process.

2. FRACTAL BLOCK CODING IN A NUTSHELL

Let the N-dimensional state vector I represent a one dimensional curve sampled on N points. An *affine* transformation of this vector is simply a transformation of the form $I' = WI+B$, where W is an NxN-element matrix and B is an N-component vector. This transformation can be iterated to produce a sequence of vectors $I^{(0)},...,I^{(n)}$. The sequence converges to a unique final state I^* that is independent of the initial state $I^{(0)}$ if the maximum eigenvalue λ_{max} of the matrix W satisfies $\lambda_{max} <1$. The uniqueness of the final state implies that to transmit the state I^* to a receiver, we can either transmit I^* directly, or we can transmit W and B and let the receiver perform the iteration to generate I^*. In the latter case we say that W and B constitute an *encoding* of the state I^*. For this encoding to be useful, the amount of data needed to transmit W and B must be less than the amount of data needed to transmit I^* This is the case when W and B are sparse and parameterized and when the total number of bits needed to transmit these parameters is less than the total number of bits needed to transmit the uncompressed state I^*

Fractal block coding is a special case of the above approach. It amounts to choosing a

---

[1] We consider subthreshold analog VLSI., (Mead 1989; Andreou and Boahen, 1994). A simple subthreshold model is $I_{ds} = I_o^{(nfet)} \exp(\kappa v_{gb})(\exp(-v_{sb}) - \exp(-v_{db}))$ for NFETS, where $\kappa \sim 0.67$ and $I_o^{(nfet)} = 9.7 \times 10^{-18}$ A. The voltage differences v_{gb}, v_{sb}, and v_{db} are in units of the thermal voltage, $V_{th} = 0.025$V. We use a corresponding expression for PFETs of the from $I_{ds} = I_o^{(pfet)} \exp(-\kappa v_{gb})(\exp(v_{sb}) - \exp(v_{db}))$ where $I_o^{(pfet)} = 3.8 \times 10^{-18}$ A.

blocked structure for the matrix **W**. This structure forces large-scale features to be mapped into small-scale features. The result is a steady state I^* that represents a curve with self similar (actually self affine) features. As a concrete example of such a structure, consider the following transformation of the state I.

$$I'_i = w_L I_{2i+1} + b_L \quad for \quad 0 \leq i \leq \frac{N}{2} - 1$$

$$I'_i = w_R I_{2i-N} + b_R \quad for \quad \frac{N}{2} \leq i \leq N-1 \tag{1}$$

This transformation has two blocks. The transformation of the first N/2 components of I depend on the parameters w_L and b_L while the transformation of the second N/2 components depend on the parameters w_R, and b_R. Consequently just four parameters completely specify this transformation. This transformation can be expressed as a single affine transformation as follows:

$$\begin{pmatrix} I'_0 \\ \cdots \\ I'_{N/2-1} \\ I'_{N/2} \\ \cdots \\ I'_{N-1} \end{pmatrix} = \begin{pmatrix} & w_L & & \\ & & w_L & \\ w_R & & & \\ & w_R & & \end{pmatrix} \begin{pmatrix} I_0 \\ \cdots \\ I_{N/2-1} \\ I_{N/2} \\ \cdots \\ I_{N-1} \end{pmatrix} + \begin{pmatrix} b_L \\ \cdots \\ b_L \\ b_R \\ \cdots \\ b_R \end{pmatrix} \tag{2}$$

The top and bottom halves of I' depend on the odd and even components of I respectively. This subsampling causes features of size l to be mapped into features of size $l/2$. A subsampled copy of the state I with transformed intensities is copied into the top half of I'. Similarly, a subsampled copy of the state I with transformed intensities is copied into the bottom half of I'. If this transformation is iterated, the sequence of transformed vectors will converge provided the eigenvalues determined by w_L and w_R are all less than one (i.e. w_L and $w_R < 1$).

Although this toy example has just four free parameters and is thus too trivial to be useful for actual compression applications, it does suffice to generate state vectors with fractal properties since at steady state, the top and bottom halves of I' differ from the entire curve by an affine transformation.

In this paper we will not describe how to solve the inverse problem which consists of finding a parameterized affine transformation that produces a given final state T. We note, however, that it is a special (and simpler) case of the recurrent network training problem, since the problem is linear, has no hidden units and has only one fixed point. The reader is refered to (Pineda, 1988) or. for a least squares algorithm in the context of neural nets or to (Monroe and Dudbridge, 1992) for a least squares algorithm in the context of coding.

3. A CMOS NEURAL NETWORK MODEL

Now that we have described the salient aspects of the fractal decompression problem, we turn to the problem of implementing an analog neural network whose nonlinear dynamics converges to the same fixed point as the linear system. Nonlinearity arises because we make no special effort to linearize the gain elements (controlled conductances and transconductances) of the implementation medium. In this section we first describe a simple neuron. Then we analyze the dynamics of a network composed of such neurons. Finally we describe how to program the fixed point in the actual physical network.

3.1 The analog Neuron

We would like to create a neuron model that calculates the transformation $I^{(out)} = aI^{(in)} + b$. Consider the circuit shown in figure 1. This has three functional sections which compute by adding and subtracting currents and where voltages are ``log'' coded; this is the essence of the ``current-mode'' aproach in circuit design (Andreou et.al. 1994). The first section, receives an input voltage from a presynaptic neuron, converts it into a current I(in), and multiplies it by a weight a. The second section adds and subtracts the bias current b. The last section converts the output current into an output voltage and transmits it to the next neuron in the network. Since the transistors have exponential transfer characteristics, this voltage is logarithmically coded.

The parameters a and b are set by external voltages. The parameter a, is set by a single external voltage v_a while the bias parameter $b = b^{(-)} - b^{(+)}$ is set by two external voltages $v_{b^{(+)}}$ and $v_{b^{(-)}}$. Two voltages are used for b to account for both positive and negative bias values since $b^{(-)} > 0$ and $b^{(+)} > 0$.

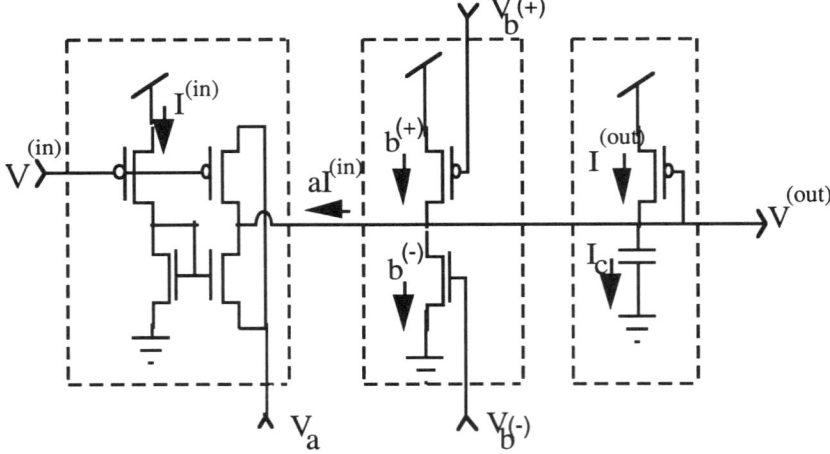

Figure 1. The analog neuron has three sections.

To derive the dynamical equations of the neuron, it is neccesary to add up all the currents and invoke Kirchoff's current law, which requires that

$$I^{(out)} - aI^{(in)} + b^{(+)} - b^{(-)} = I_c. \qquad (3)$$

If we now assume a simple subthreshold model for the behavior of the FET's and PFETs in the neuron, we can obtain the following expression for the current across the capacitor:

$$-\frac{Q}{I^{(out)}} \frac{dI^{(out)}}{dt} = I_c \qquad (4)$$

where $Q = C/\kappa V_{th}$ determines the characteristic time scale of the neuron[2]. It immediately follows from the last two expressions that the dynamics of a single neuron is determined by the equation

$$Q\frac{dI^{(out)}}{dt} = -I^{(out)}(I^{(out)} - aI^{(in)} - b). \tag{5}$$

Where $b = b^{(-)} - b^{(+)}$. This equation appears to have a quadratic nonlinearity on the r.h.s. In fact, the noninearity is even more complicated since, the cooeficients a, $b^{(+)}$ and $b^{(-)}$ are not constants, but depend on $I^{(out)}$ (through $v^{(out)}$). Application of the simple subthreshold model, results in a multiplier gain that is a function of $V^{(out)}$ (and hence $I^{(out)}$) as well as V_a. It is given by

$$a(v_a, v^{(out)}) = 2\exp(-\frac{v_{dd}}{2})\left[\sinh(\frac{v_{dd}}{2} - v_a) - \sinh(\frac{v_{dd}}{2} - v^{(out)})\right]. \tag{6}$$

Similarly, the currents $b^{(+)}$ and $b^{(-)}$ are given by

$$b^{(+)} = I_o^{(fpet)} \exp(\kappa \hat{v}_{b^{(+)}})\left(1 - \exp(-\hat{v}^{(out)})\right) \tag{7.a}$$

and

$$b^{(-)} = I_o^{(nfet)} \exp(\kappa v_{b^{(-)}})\left(1 - \exp(-v^{(out)})\right) \tag{7.b}$$

respectively, where $\hat{v}_\alpha \equiv vdd - v_\alpha$.

3.2 Network dynamics and Stability considerations

With these results we conclude that, a network of neurons, in which each neuron receives input from only one other neuron, would have a dynamical equation of the form

$$Q\frac{dI_i}{dt} = -I_i(I_i - a_i(I_i)I_{j(i)} - b_i) \tag{8}$$

where the connectivity of the network is determined by the function $j(i)$. The fixed points of these highly nonlinear equations occur when the r.h.s. of (8) vanishes. This can only happen if either $I_i = 0$ or if $(I_i - a_i I_{j(i)} - b_i) = 0$ for each i. The local stability of each of these fixed points follows by examining the eigenvalues (λ) of the corresponding jacobian. The expression for the jacobian at a general point I is

$$J_{ik} = \frac{\partial F_i}{\partial I_k} = -Q\left[(I_i - a_i I_{j(i)} - b_i)\delta_{ik} + I_i(1 - a_i' I_{j(i)} - b_i')\delta_{ik} - a_i I_i \delta_{j(i)k}\right]. \tag{9}$$

Where the partial derivatives, a'_i and b'_i are with respect to I_i. At a fixed point the jacobian takes the form

$$J_{ik} = Q\begin{cases} b_i \delta_{ik} & \text{if } I_i = 0 \\ -I_i\left[(1 - a_i' I_{j(i)} - b_i')\delta_{ik} - a_i \delta_{j(i)k}\right] & \text{if } (I_i - a_i I_{j(i)} - b_i) = 0 \end{cases}. \tag{10}$$

---

[2]C represents the total gate capacitance from all the transistors connected to the horizontal line of the neuron. For the 2μ analog process, the gate capacitance is approximately 0.5 fF/μ^2 so a $10\mu \times 10\mu$ FET has a characteristic charge of Q =2.959 x 10^{-14} Coulombs at room temperature.

There are two cases of interest. The first case is when no neurons have zero output. This is the "desired solution." In this case, the jacobian specializes to

$$J_{ik} = -QI_i\left[(1 - a_i'I_{j(i)} - b_i')\delta_{ik} - a_i\delta_{j(i)k}\right]. \quad (11)$$

Where, from (6) and (7), it can be shown that the partial derivatives, a'_i and b'_i are both non-positive. It immediately follows, from Gerschgorin's theorem, that a sufficient condition that the eigenvalues be negative and that the fixed point be stable, is that $|a_i| < 1$. The second case is when at least one of the neurons has zero output. We call these fixed points the "spurious solutions." In this case some of the eigenvalues are very easy to calculate because terms of the form $(b_i - \lambda)$, where $I_i = 0$, can be factored from the expression for $\det(J - \lambda I)$. Thus some eigenvalues can be made positive by making some of the b_i positive. Accordingly, if all the b_i satisfy $b_i > 0$, some of the eigenvalues will necessarily be positive and the spurious solutions will be unstable. To summarize the above discussion, we have shown that by choosing $b_i > 0$ and $|a_i| < 1$ for all i, we can make the desired fixed point <u>stable</u> and the spurious fixed points <u>unstable</u>. Note that a sufficient condition for $b_i > 0$ is if $b_i^{(+)} = 0$.

It remains to show that the system must converge to the desired fixed point, i.e. that the system cannot oscillate or wander chaotically. To do this we consider the connectivity of the network we implemented in our test chip. This is shown schematically in figure 2. The first eight neurons receive input from the odd numbered neurons while the second eight neurons receive input from the even numbered neurons. The neurons on the left-hand side all share the weight, w_L, while the neurons on the right share the weight w_R. By tracing the connections, we find that there are two independent loops of neurons: loop #1 = {0,8,12,14,15,7,3,1} and loop #2 = {2,9,4,10,13,6,11,5}.

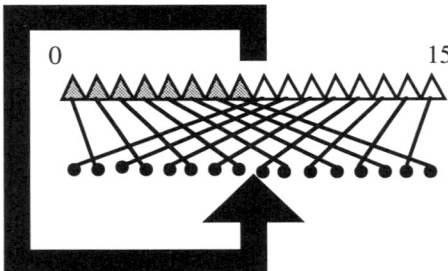

Figure 2. The connection topology for the test chip is determined by the matrix of equation (1). The neurons are labeled 0-15.

By inspecting each loop, we see that it passes through either the left or right hand range an even number of times. Hence, if there are any inhibitory weights in a loop, there must be an even number of them. This is the "even loop criterion", and it suffices to prove that the network is globally asymptotically stable, (Hirsch, 1987).

3.3. Programming the fixed point

The nonlinear circuit of the previous section converges to a fixed point which is the solution of the following system of transcendental equations

$$I_i^* - a_i(I_i^*, v_a)I_{j(i)}^* - b_i^{(-)}(I_i^*, v_{b^{(-)}}) = 0 \quad (12)$$

where the coefficients a_i and b_i are given by equations (6) and (7b) respectively. Similarly, the iterated affine transformations converge to the solution of the following linear equations

$$I_i^* - A_i I_{j(i)}^* - B_i = 0 \qquad (13)$$

where the coefficients $\{A_i, B_i\}$ and the connections $j(i)$ are obtained by solving the approximate inverse problem with the additional constraints that $b_i > 0$ and $|a_i| < 1$ for all i,. The requirement that the fixed points of the two systems be identical results in the conditions

$$\begin{aligned} A_i &= a_i(I_i^*, v_a) \\ B_i &= b_i^{(-)}(I_i^*, v_{b^{(-)}}) \end{aligned} \qquad (14)$$

These equations can be solved for the required input voltages v_a, and $v_{b^{(-)}}$. Thus we are able to construct a nonlinear dynamical system that converges to the same fixed point as a linear system. For this programming method to work, of course, the subthreshold model we have used to characterize the network must accurately model the physical properties of the neural network.

4. PRELIMINARY RESULTS

As a first step towards realizing a working system, we fabricated a Tiny chip containing 16 neurons arranged in two groups of eight. The topology is the same as shown in figure 2. The neurons are similar to those in figure 1 except that the bias term in each block of 8 neurons has the form $b = kb^{(-)} + (7-k)\overline{b}^{(-)}$, where $0 \leq k \leq 7$ is the label of a particular neuron within a block. This form increases the complexity of the neurons, but also allows us to represent ramps more easily (see figure 3).

We fabricated the chip through MOSIS in a 2μm p-well CMOS process. A switching layer allows us to change the connection topology at run-time. One of the four possible configurations corresponds to the toplogy of figure 2. Six external voltages $\{v_{a_L}, v_{b^{(-)}}, v_{\overline{b}^{(-)}}, v_{a_R}, v_{b^{(-)}_R}, v_{\overline{b}^{(-)}_R}\}$ parameterize the fixed points of the network. These are controlled by potentiometers. There is multiplexing circuitry included on the chip that selects which neuron output is to be amplified by a sense-amp and routed off-chip. The neurons can be addressed individually by a 4-bit neuron address. The addressing and analog-to-digital conversion is performed by a Motorolla 68HC11A1 microprocessor.

We have operated the chip at 5volts and at 2.6 volts. Figure 3. shows the scanned steady state output of one of the test chips for a particular choice of input parameters with $v_{dd} = 5$ volts. The curve in figure 3. exhibits the qualitatively self-similar features of a recursively generated object. We are able to see three generations of a ramp. At 2.5 volts we see a very similar curve. We find that the chip draws 16.3 μA at 2.5 volts. This corresponds to a steady state power dissipation of 41μW. Simulations indicate that the chip is operating in the subthreshold regime when $v_{dd} = 2.5$ volts. Simulations also indicate that the chip settles in less than one millisecond. We are unable to perform quantitiative measurements with the first chip because of several layout errors. On the other hand, we have experimentally verified that the network is indeed stable and that network produces qualitative fractals. We explored the parameter space informatlly. At no time did we encounter anything but the desired solutions.

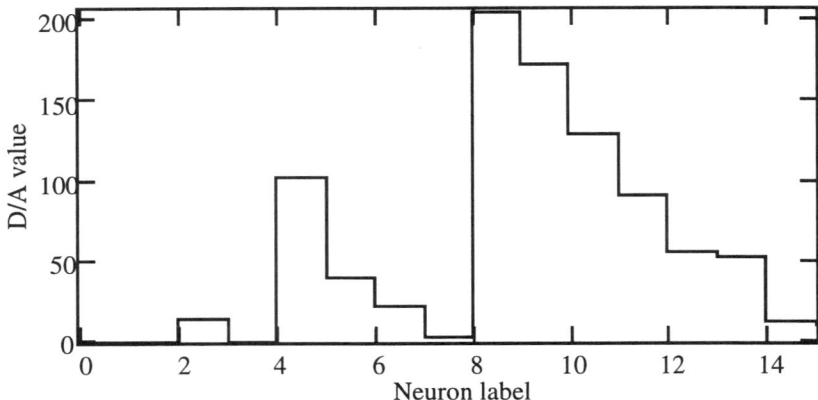

Figure 3 D/A output for chip #3 for a particular set of input voltages.

We have already fabricated a larger design without the layout problems of the prototype. This second design has 32 pixeles and a richer set of permitted topologies. We expect to make quantitative measurements with this second design. In particular we hope to use it to decompress an actual block code.

Acknowledgements

The work described here is funded by APL IR&D as well as a grant from the National Science Foundation ECS9313934, Paul Werbos is the monitor. The authors would like to thank Robert Jenkins , Kim Strohbehn and Paul Furth for many useful conversations and suggestions.

References

Andreou, A.G. and Boahen, K.A. Neural Information Processing I: The Current-Mode approach, *Analog VLSI: Signal and Information Processing,* (eds: M Ismail and T. Fiez) MacGraw-Hill Inc., New York. Chapter 6 (1994).

Hille, B., *Ionic Channels of Excitable Membranes*, Sunderland, MA, Sinauer Associates Inc. (1984).

Hirsch, M. ,Convergence in Neural Nets, *Proceedings of the IEEE ICNN*, San Diego, CA, (1987).

Jacquin , A. E., *A Fractal Theory of iterated Markov operators with applications to digital image coding,* Ph.D. Dissertation, Georgia Institute of Technology (1989).

Mead, C., *Analog VLSI and Neural System*s, Addison Wesley, (1989)

Monroe, D.M. and Dudbridge, F. Fractal block coding of images, *Electronics Letters,* **28**, pp. 1053-1055, (1992).

Pineda, F.J., Dynamics and Architecuture for Neural Computation, *Journal of Complexity,* **4**, 216-245 (1988).

A Study of Parallel Perturbative Gradient Descent

D. Lippe* J. Alspector
Bellcore
Morristown, NJ 07960

Abstract

We have continued our study of a parallel perturbative learning method [Alspector et al., 1993] and implications for its implementation in analog VLSI. Our new results indicate that, in most cases, a single parallel perturbation (per pattern presentation) of the function parameters (weights in a neural network) is theoretically the best course. This is not true, however, for certain problems and may not generally be true when faced with issues of implementation such as limited precision. In these cases, multiple parallel perturbations may be best as indicated in our previous results.

1 INTRODUCTION

Motivated by difficulties in analog VLSI implementation of back-propagation [Rumelhart et al., 1986] and related algorithms that calculate gradients based on detailed knowledge of the neural network model, there were several similar recent papers proposing to use a parallel [Alspector et al., 1993, Cauwenberghs, 1993, Kirk et al., 1993] or a semi-parallel [Flower and Jabri, 1993] perturbative technique which has the property that it measures (with the physical neural network) rather than calculates the gradient. This technique is closely related to methods of stochastic approximation [Kushner and Clark, 1978] which have been investigated recently by workers in fields other than neural networks. [Spall, 1992] showed that averaging multiple parallel perturbations for each pattern presentation may be asymptotically preferable in the presence of noise. Our own results [Alspector et al., 1993] indicated

---

*Present address: Dept. of EECS; MIT; Cambridge, MA 02139; dalippe@mit.edu

that multiple parallel perturbations are also preferable when only limited precision is available in the learning rate which is realistic for a physical implementation. In this work we have investigated whether multiple parallel perturbations for each pattern are non-asymptotically preferable theoretically (without noise). We have also studied this empirically, to the limited degree that simulations allow, by removing the precision constraints of our previous work.

2 GRADIENT ESTIMATION BY PARALLEL WEIGHT PERTURBATION

Following our previous work, one can estimate the gradient of the error, $E(\vec{w})$, with respect to any weight, w_i, by perturbing w_i by δw_i and measuring the change in the output error, δE, as the entire weight vector, $\vec{w}$, except for component w_i is held constant.

$$\frac{\delta E}{\delta w_i} = \frac{E(\vec{w} + \vec{\delta w_i}) - E(\vec{w})}{\delta w_i}$$

We now consider perturbing all weights simultaneously. However, we wish to have the perturbation vector, $\delta \vec{w}$, chosen uniformly on a hypercube. Note that this requires only a random sign multiplying a fixed perturbation and is natural for VLSI using a parallel noise generator [Alspector et al., 1991].

This leads to the approximation (ignoring higher order terms)

$$\frac{\delta E}{\delta w_i} = \frac{\partial E}{\partial w_i} + \sum_{j \neq i}^{W} \left(\frac{\partial E}{\partial w_j} \right) \left(\frac{\delta w_j}{\delta w_i} \right). \qquad (1)$$

The last term has expectation value zero for random and independently distributed δw_i. The weight change rule

$$\Delta w_i = -\eta \frac{\delta E}{\delta w_i},$$

where η is a learning rate, will follow the gradient on the average but with considerable noise.

For each pattern, one can reduce the variance of the noise term in (1) by repeating the random parallel perturbation many times to improve the statistical estimate. If we average over P perturbations, we have

$$\frac{\delta E}{\delta w_i} = \frac{1}{P} \sum_{\rho=1}^{P} \frac{\delta E^{(\rho)}}{\delta w_i^{(\rho)}} = \frac{\partial E}{\partial w_i} + \frac{1}{P} \sum_{\rho=1}^{P} \sum_{j \neq i}^{W} \left(\frac{\partial E}{\partial w_j} \right) \left(\frac{\delta w_j^{(\rho)}}{\delta w_i^{(\rho)}} \right)$$

where ρ indexes the perturbation number.

3 THEORETICAL RELATIVE EFFICIENCY

3.1 BACKGROUND

Spall [Spall, 1992] shows in an asymptotic sense that multiple perturbations may be faster if only a noisy measurement of $E(\vec{w})$ is available, and that one perturbation is superior otherwise. His results are asymptotic in that they compare the rate of convergence to the local minimum if the algorithms run for infinite time. Thus, his results may only indicate that 1 perturbation is superior close to a local minimum. Furthermore, his result implicitly assumes that P perturbations per weight update takes P times as long as 1 perturbation per weight update. Experience shows that the time required to present patterns to the hardware is often the bottleneck in VLSI implementations of neural networks [Brown et al., 1992]. In a hardware implementation of a perturbative learning algorithm, a few perturbations might be performed with no time penalty while waiting for the next pattern presentation.

The remainder of this section sketches an argument that multiple perturbations may be desirable for some problems in a non-asymptotic sense, even in a noise free environment and under the assumption of a multiplicative time penalty for performing multiple perturbations. On the other hand, the argument also shows that there is little reason to believe in practice that any given problem will be learned more quickly by multiple perturbations. Space limitations prevent us from reproducing the full argument and discussion of its relevance which can be found in [Lippe, 1994].

The argument fixes a point in weight space and considers the expectation value of the change in the error induced by one weight update under both the 1 perturbation case and the multiple perturbation case. [Cauwenberghs, 1994] contains a somewhat related analysis of the relative speed of one parallel perturbation and weight perturbation as described in [Jabri and Flower, 1991]. The analysis is only truly relevant far from a local minimum because close to a local minimum the variance of the change of the error is as important as the mean of the change of the error.

3.2 Calculations

If P is the number of perturbations, then our learning rule is

$$\Delta w_i = \frac{-\eta}{P} \sum_{\rho=1}^{P} \frac{\delta E^{(\rho)}}{\delta w_i^{(\rho)}}. \qquad (2)$$

If W is the number of weights, then ΔE, calculated to second order in η, is

$$\Delta E = \sum_{i=1}^{W} \frac{\partial E}{\partial w_i} \Delta w_i + \frac{1}{2} \sum_{i=1}^{W} \sum_{j=1}^{W} \frac{\partial^2 E}{\partial w_i \partial w_j} \Delta w_i \Delta w_j. \qquad (3)$$

Expanding $\delta E^{(\rho)}$ to second order in σ (where $\delta w_i = \pm \sigma$), we obtain

$$\delta E^{(\rho)} = \sum_{j=1}^{W} \frac{\partial E}{\partial w_j} \delta w_j^{(\rho)} + \frac{1}{2} \sum_{j=1}^{W} \sum_{k=1}^{W} \frac{\partial^2 E}{\partial w_j \partial w_k} \delta w_j^{(\rho)} \delta w_k^{(\rho)}. \qquad (4)$$

[Lippe, 1994] shows that combining (2)-(4), retaining only first and second order terms, and taking expectation values gives

$$< \Delta E > = -\eta X + \frac{\eta^2}{P}(Y + PZ) \qquad (5)$$

where

$$X = \sum_{i=1}^{W} \left(\frac{\partial E}{\partial w_i}\right)^2,$$

$$Z = \frac{1}{2} \sum_{i,k=1}^{W} \frac{\partial^2 E}{\partial w_i \partial w_k} \frac{\partial E}{\partial w_i} \frac{\partial E}{\partial w_k},$$

$$Y = Z + \frac{1}{2} \sum_{i,k=1}^{W} \frac{\partial^2 E}{\partial w_i^2} \left(\frac{\partial E}{\partial w_k}\right)^2 - \sum_{i=1}^{W} \frac{\partial^2 E}{\partial w_i^2} \left(\frac{\partial E}{\partial w_i}\right)^2,$$

Note that first term in (5) is strictly less than or equal to 0 since X is a sum of squares[1]. The second term, on the other hand, can be either positive or negative. Clearly then a sufficient condition for learning is that the first term dominates the second term. By making η small enough, we can guarantee that learning occurs. Strictly speaking, this is not a necessary condition for learning. However, it is important to keep in mind that we are only focusing on one point in weight space. If, at this point in weight space, $< \Delta E >$ is negative but the second term's magnitude is close to the first term's magnitude, it is not unlikely that at some other point in weight space $< \Delta E >$ will be positive. Thus, we will assume that for efficient learning to occur, it is necessary that η be small enough to make the first term dominate the second term.

Assume that some problem can be successfully learned with one perturbation, at learning rate $\eta(1)$. Then the first order term in (5) dominates the second order terms. Specifically, at any point in weight space we have, for some large constant μ,

$$\eta(1)X \geq \mu \eta(1)^2 |Y + Z|$$

In order to learn with P perturbations, we apparently need

$$\eta(P)X \geq \mu \frac{\eta(P)^2}{P}|Y + PZ| \qquad (6)$$

The assumption that the first order term of (5) dominates the second order terms implies that convergence time is proportional to $\frac{P}{\eta(P)}$. Thus, learning is more efficient in the multiple perturbation case if

$$\frac{\mu \eta(P)}{P} > \mu \eta(1) \qquad (7)$$

It turns out, as shown in [Lippe, 1994] that the conditions (6) and (7) can be met simultaneously with multiple perturbations if $\frac{-Y}{Z} \geq 2$.

---

[1] If we are at a stationary point then the first term in (5) is 0.

It is shown in [Lippe, 1994], by using the fact that the Hessian of a quadratic function with a minimum is positive semi-definite, that if E is quadratic and has a minimum, then Y and Z have the same sign (and hence $\frac{-Y}{Z} < 2$). Any well behaved function acts quadratically sufficiently close to a stationary point. Thus, we can not get $<\Delta E>$ more than a factor of P larger by using P perturbations near local minima of well behaved functions. Although, as mentioned earlier, we are entirely ignoring the issue of the variance of ΔE, this may be some indication of the asymptotic superiority of 1 perturbation.

3.3 Discussion of Results

The result that multiple perturbations are superior when $\frac{-Y}{Z} \geq 2$ may seem somewhat mysterious. It sheds some light on our answer to rewrite (5) as

$$<\Delta E> = -\eta X + \eta^2(\frac{Y}{P} + Z).$$

For strict gradient descent, the corresponding equation is

$$<\Delta E> = \Delta E = -\eta X + \eta^2 Z.$$

The difference between strict gradient descent and perturbative gradient descent, on average, is the second order term $\eta^2 \frac{Y}{P}$. This is the term which results from not following the gradient exactly, and it obviously goes down as P goes up and the gradient measurement becomes more accurate. Thus, if Z and Y have different signs, P can be used to make the second order term disappear. There is no way to know whether this situation will occur frequently. Furthermore, it is important to keep in mind that if Y is negative and Z is positive, then raising P may make the magnitude of the second order term smaller, but it makes the term itself *larger*. Thus, in general, there is little reason to believe that multiple perturbations will help with a randomly chosen problem.

An example where multiple perturbations help is when we are at a point where the error surface is convex along the gradient direction, and concave in most other directions. Curvature due to second derivative terms in Y and Z help when the gradient direction is followed, but can hurt when we stray from the gradient. In this case, $Z < 0$ and possibly $Y > 0$, so multiple perturbations might be preferable in order to follow the gradient direction very closely.

4 SIMULATIONS OF SINGLE AND MULTIPLE PARALLEL PERTURBATION

4.1 CONSTANT LEARNING RATES

The second order terms in (5) can be reduced either by using a small learning rate, or by using more perturbations, as discussed briefly in [Cauwenberghs, 1993]. Thus, if η is kept constant, we expect a minimum necessary number of perturbations in order to learn. This in itself might be of importance in a limited precision implementation. If there is a non-trivial lower bound on η, then it might be necessary to use multiple perturbations in order to learn. This is the effect that was noticed in [Alspector et al., 1993]. At that time we thought that we had found empirically

Table 1: Running times for the first initial weight vector

P	η	Time for < .1	Time for < .5
1	.0005	1,121,459	32,179
1	.001	831,684	18,534
1	.002	784,768	11,008
1	.003	*494,029*	9,933
1	.004	1,695,974	*9,728*
7	.00625	707,840	23,834
7	.008	*583,654*	16,845
7	.0125	922,880	13,261
7	.025	1,010,355	*12,006*
7	.035	Not tested	17,024

that multiple perturbations were necessary for learning. The problem was that we failed to decrease the learning rate with the number of perturbations.

4.2 EMPIRICAL RELATIVE EFFICIENCY OF SINGLE AND MULTIPLE PERTURBATION ALGORITHMS

Section 3 showed that, in theory, multiple perturbations might be faster than 1 perturbation. We investigated whether or not this is the case for the 7 input hamming error correction problem as described in [Biggs, 1989]. This is basically a nearest neighbor problem. There exist 16 distinct 7 bit binary code words. When presented with an arbitrary 7 bit binary word, the network is to output the code word with the least hamming distance from the input.

After preliminary tests with 50, 25, 7, and 1 perturbation, it seemed that 7 perturbations provided the fastest learning, so we concentrated on running simulations for both the 1 perturbation and the 7 perturbation case. Specifically, we chose two different (randomly generated) initial weight vectors, and five different seeds for the pseudo-random function used to generate the δw_i. For each of these ten cases, we tested both 1 perturbation and 7 perturbations with various learning rates in order to obtain the fastest possible learning.

The 128 possible input patterns were repeatedly presented in order. We investigated how many pattern presentations were necessary to drive the MSE below .1 and how many presentations were necessary to drive it below .5. Recalling the theory developed in section 3, we know that multiple perturbations can be helpful only far away from a stationary point. Thus, we expected that 7 perturbations might be quicker reaching .5 but would be slower reaching .1.

The results are summarized in tables 1 and 2. Each table summarizes information for a different initial weight vector. All of the data presented are averaged over 5 runs, one with each of the different random seeds. The two columns labeled "Time for < .5" and "Time for < .1" are adjusted according to the assumption that one weight update at 7 perturbations takes 7 times as long as one weight update at 1 perturbation. In each table, the following four numbers appear in italics: the shortest time to reach .1 with 1 perturbation, the shortest time to reach .1 with 7 perturbations, the shortest time to reach .5 with 1 perturbation, and the shortest time to reach .5 with 7 perturbations.

7 perturbations were a loss in three out of four of the experiments. Surprisingly,

Table 2: Running times for the second initial weight vector

P	η	Time for < .1	Time for < .5
1	.001	928,236	22,733
1	.002	*719,078*	12,877
1	.003	754,739	*10,675*
1	.004	1,603,354	11,750
7	.00625	629,530	27,059
7	.008	*611,610*	19,712
7	.0125	912,333	15,949
7	.025	1,580,442	*14,515*
7	.035	Not tested	17,741

the one time that multiple perturbations helped was in reaching .1 from the second initial weight vector. There are several possible explanations for this. To begin with, these learning times are averages over only five simulations each, which makes their statistical significance somewhat dubious. Unfortunately, it was impractical to perform too many experiments as the data obtained required 180 computer simulations, each of which sometimes took more than a day to complete.

Another possible explanation is that .1 may not be "asymptotic enough." The numbers .5 and .1 were chosen somewhat arbitrarily to represent non-asymptotic and asymptotic results. However, there is no way of predicting from the theory how close the error must be to its minimum before asymptotic results become relevant.

The fact that 1 perturbation outperformed 7 perturbations in three out of four cases is not surprising. As explained in section 3, there is in general no reason to believe that multiple perturbations will help on a randomly chosen problem.

5 CONCLUSION

Our results show that, under ideal computational conditions, where the learning rate can be adjusted to proper size, that a single parallel perturbation is, except for unusual problems, superior to multiple parallel perturbations. However, under the precision constraints imposed by analog VLSI implementation, where learning rates may not be adjustable and presenting a pattern takes longer than performing a perturbation, multiple parallel perturbations are likely to be the best choice.

Acknowledgment

We thank Gert Cauwenberghs and James Spall for valuable and insightful discussions.

References

[Alspector et al., 1991] Alspector, J., Gannett, J. W., Haber, S., Parker, M. B., and Chu, R. (1991). A VLSI-efficient technique for generating multiple uncorrelated noise sources and its application to stochastic neural networks. *IEEE Transactions on Circuits and Systems*, 38:109–123.

[Alspector et al., 1993] Alspector, J., Meir, R., Yuhas, B., Jayakumar, A., and Lippe, D. (1993). A parallel gradient descent method for learning in analog

VLSI neural networks. In Hanson, S. J., Cowan, J. D., and Giles, C. L., editors, *Advances in Neural Information Processing Systems 5*, pages 836–844, San Mateo, California. Morgan Kaufmann Publishers.

[Biggs, 1989] Biggs, N. L. (1989). *Discrete Math.* Oxford University Press.

[Brown et al., 1992] Brown, T. X., Tran, M. D., Duong, T., and Thakoor, A. P. (1992). Cascaded VLSI neural network chips: Hardware learning for pattern recognition and classification. *Simulation*, 58(5):340–347.

[Cauwenberghs, 1993] Cauwenberghs, G. (1993). A fast stochastic error-descent algorithm for supervised learning and optimization. In Hanson, S. J., Cowan, J. D., and Giles, C. L., editors, *Advances in Neural Information Processing Systems 5*, pages 244–251, San Mateo, California. Morgan Kaufmann Publishers.

[Cauwenberghs, 1994] Cauwenberghs, G. (1994). *Analog VLSI Autonomous Systems for Learning and Optimization*. PhD thesis, California Institute of Technology.

[Flower and Jabri, 1993] Flower, B. and Jabri, M. (1993). Summed weight neuron perturbation: An $o(n)$ improvement over weight perturbation. In Hanson, S. J., Cowan, J. D., and Giles, C. L., editors, *Advances in Neural Information Processing Systems 5*, pages 212–219, San Mateo, California. Morgan Kaufmann Publishers.

[Jabri and Flower, 1991] Jabri, M. and Flower, B. (1991). Weight perturbation: An optimal architecture and learning technique for analog VLSI feedforward and recurrent multilayer networks. In *Neural Computation 3*, pages 546–565.

[Kirk et al., 1993] Kirk, D., Kerns, D., Fleischer, K., and Barr, A. (1993). Analog VLSI implementation of gradient descent. In Hanson, S. J., Cowan, J. D., and Giles, C. L., editors, *Advances in Neural Information Processing Systems 5*, pages 789–796, San Mateo, California. Morgan Kaufmann Publishers.

[Kushner and Clark, 1978] Kushner, H. and Clark, D. (1978). *Stochastic Approximation Methods for Constrained and Unconstrained Systems*. Springer-Verlag, New York.

[Lippe, 1994] Lippe, D. A. (1994). Parallel, perturbative gradient descent methods for learning in analog VLSI neural networks. Master's thesis, Massachusetts Institute of Technology.

[Rumelhart et al., 1986] Rumelhart, D. E., Hinton, G. E., and Williams, R. J. (1986). Learning internal representations by error propogation. In Rumelhart, D. E. and McClelland, J. L., editors, *Parallel Distributed Processing: Explorations in the Microstructure of Cognition*, page 318. MIT Press, Cambridge, MA.

[Spall, 1992] Spall, J. C. (1992). Multivariate stochastic approximation using a simultaneous perturbation gradient approximation. *IEEE Transactions on Automatic Control*, 37(3):332–341.

Implementation of Neural Hardware with the Neural VLSI of URAN in Applications with Reduced Representations

Il-Song Han
Korea Telecom Research Laboratories
17, Woomyun-dong, Suhcho-ku
Seoul 137-140, KOREA

Ki-Chul Kim
Dept. of Info and Comm
KAIST
Seoul, 130-012, Korea

Hwang-Soo Lee
Dept. of Info and Comm
KAIST
Seoul, 130-012, Korea

Abstract

This paper describes a way of neural hardware implementation with the analog-digital mixed mode neural chip. The full custom neural VLSI of Universally Reconstructible Artificial Neural network(URAN) is used to implement Korean speech recognition system. A multi-layer perceptron with linear neurons is trained successfully under the limited accuracy in computations. The network with a large frame input layer is tested to recognize spoken korean words at a forward retrieval. Multichip hardware module is suggested with eight chips or more for the extended performance and capacity.

1 INTRODUCTION

In general, the neural network hardware or VLSI has been preferred in respects of its relatively fast speed, huge network size and effective cost comparing to software simulation. Universally Reconstructible Artificial Neural-network(URAN), the new analog-digital mixed VLSI neural network, can be used for the implementation of the real world neural network applications with digital interface. The basic electronic synapse circuit is based on the electrically controlled MOSFET resistance and is operated with discrete pulses.

The URAN's adaptability is tested for the multi-layer perceptron with the reduced precision of connections and states. The linear neuron function is also designed for the real world applications. The multi-layer network with back propagation learning is designed for the speaker independent digit/word recognition. The other case of application is for the servo control, where the neural input and output are extended to 360 levels for the suitable angle control. With the servo control simulation, the flexibility of URAN is proved to extend the accuracy of input and output from external.

2. Analog-Digital Mixed Chip - URAN

In the past, there have been improvements in analog or analog-digital mixed VLSI chips. Analog neural chips or analog-digital mixed neural chips are still suffered from the lack of accuracy, speed or flexibility. With the proposed analog-digital mixed neural network circuit of URAN, the accuracy is improved by using the voltage-controlled linear MOSFET resistance for the synapse weight emulation. The speed in neural computation is also improved by using the simple switch controlled by the neural input as described in previous works.

The general flexibility is attained by the independent characteristic of each synapse cell and the modular structure of URAN chip. As in Table 1 of URAN chip feature, the chip is operated under the flexible control, that is, the various mode of synaptic connection per neuron or the extendable weight accuracy can be implemented. It is not limited for the asynchronous/direct interchip expansion in size or speed. In fact, 16 fully connected module of URAN is selected from external and independently - it is possible to select either one by one or all at once.

Table 1. URAN Chip Features

Total Synapses	135,424 connections
Computation Speed	200 Giga Connections Per S
Weight Accuracy	8 Bit
Module No.	16
Module Size	92 X 92

As all circuits over the chip except digital decoder unit are operated in analog transistor level, the computation speed is relatively high and even can be improved substantially. The cell size including interconnection area in conventional short-channel technology is reduced less than 900 μ m^2. From its expected and measured linear characteristic, URAN has the accuracy more than 256 linear levels.

The accuracy extendability and flexible modularity are inherent in electrical wired-OR characteristics as each synapse is an independent bipolar current source with switch. No additional clocking or any limited synchronous operation is required in this case, while it is indispensible in most of conventional digital neural hardware or analog-digital neural chip. Therefore, any size of neural network can be integrated in VLSI or module hardware merely by placing the cell in 2 dimensional array without any timing limitation or loading effect.

3. Neural Hardware with URAN - Module Expansion

URAN is the full custom VLSI of analog-digital mixed operation. The prototype of URAN chip is fabricated in 1.0μ digital CMOS technology. The chip contains 135,424 synapses with 8 bit weight accuracy on a 13 X 13 mm^2 die size using single poly double metal technology. As summarized in Table 1 of chip features, the chip allows the variety of configuration. In the prototype chip, 16 fully connected module of 92 X 92 can be selected from external and independently - selecting independent module either one by one, several or all at a time is possible.

With URAN's synapse circuit of linear voltage-controlled bipolar current source, the synaptic multiplication with weight value is done with the switching transistor, in a similar way of analog-sampled data type. The accuracy enhancement and flexible modularity of URAN are inherent in its electrical wired-OR interface from each independent bipolar current source. And the neural network hardware module can be realized in any size with the multi URAN chips.

4. Considerations on the Reduced Precision

URAN chip is applied for the case of Korean speaker independent speech recognition. By changing numbers of hidden units and input accuracy, the result of simulations has not shown any problems in recognition accuracy. It means that the overall performance is not severely affected from the accuracy of weight, input, and output with URAN. Also, it was possible to train with 2 or 1 decimal accuracy for input and output, which is equivalent to 8 bit or 4 bit precisions. With 20 hidden units for the Korean spoken 10 digit recognition, 2 decimal input accuracy yields 99.2% and 1 decimal input accuracy yields 98.6%, while binary 1-bit input results 96.6%.

The following is the condition for the experimentation. The general result is summarized in Table 2.

Conditions for Training and Test
- 2,000 samples from 10 women and 10 men
 (10 times X 10 digits X 20 persons)
▫ Training with 500 spoken samples of 10 digits in Korean from 10 persons
 (5 times X 10 digits X [5 women and 5 men]) from 2,000 samples
▫ Recognition Test with 1,000 spoken samples from the other 10 persons of women and men.

Preprocessing of samples
▫ sampled at 10KHz with 12bit accuracy
▫ preemphasis with 0.95
▫ Hamming window of 20ms
▫ 17 channel critical-band filter bank
▫ noise added for the SNR of 30dB, 20dB, 10dB, 0dB

Table 2. Low Accuracy Connection with Linear Neuron

SNR Ratio	Input / Output Accuracy		
	2 decimal	1 decimal	1 bit
clean	97.5%	97.2%	90.7%
30 dB	96.2%	96.6%	90.5%
20 dB	90.1%	91.3%	86.6%
10 dB	59.8%	59.9%	68.0%
0 dB	30.8%	29.5%	38.5%

In case of servo control, the digital VCR for industrial purpose is modelled for the application. Six inputs are used to minimize the number of hidden units and 20 hidden units are configured for one output. For the adaptation to URAN, the linear neuron function is used during the simulation. The weight accuracy during the learning phase using conventional computer is 4 byte and that in the recall phase using URAN chip is 1 byte. With this limitation, the overall performance is not severely degraded, that is, the reduction of error is attained up to 70% improvement comparing to the conventional method. The nonideal factor of 30% results from the limitation in learning data as well as the limited hardware. Current results are suitable for the digital VCR or compact camcoder in noisy environment

5. Conclusion

In this paper, it is proved to be suitable for the application to the multi-layer perceptron with the use of URAN chip, which is fabricated in conventional digital CMOS technology - 1.0μ single poly double metal. The reduced weight accuracy of 1 byte is proved to be enough to obtain high performance using the linear neuron and URAN.

With 8 test chips of 135,424 connections, it is now under development of the practical module of neural hardware with million connections and tera connections per second - comparable to the power of biological neuro-system of some insects. The size of the hardware is smaller than A4 size and is designed for more general recognition system. The flexible modularity of URAN makes it possible to realize a 1,000,000 connections neural chip in 0.5μ CMOS technology and a general purpose neural hardware of hundreds of tera connections or more.

References

Il Song Han and Ki-Hwan Ahn, "Neural Network VLSI Chip Implementation of Analog-Digital Mixed Operation for more than 100,000 Connections" MicroNeuro'93, pp. 159-162, 1993

M. Brownlow, L. Tarassenko, A. F. Murray, A. Hamilton, I S Han, H. M. Reekie, "Pulse Firing Neural Chips Implementing Hundreds of Neurons," NIPS2, pp. 785-792, 1990

Single Transistor Learning Synapses

Paul Hasler, Chris Diorio, Bradley A. Minch, Carver Mead
California Institute of Technology
Pasadena, CA 91125
(818) 395 - 2812
paul@hobiecat.pcmp.caltech.edu

Abstract

We describe single-transistor silicon synapses that compute, learn, and provide non-volatile memory retention. The single transistor synapses simultaneously perform long term weight storage, compute the product of the input and the weight value, and update the weight value according to a Hebbian or a backpropagation learning rule. Memory is accomplished via charge storage on polysilicon floating gates, providing long-term retention without refresh. The synapses efficiently use the physics of silicon to perform weight updates; the weight value is increased using tunneling and the weight value decreases using hot electron injection. The small size and low power operation of single transistor synapses allows the development of dense synaptic arrays. We describe the design, fabrication, characterization, and modeling of an array of single transistor synapses. When the steady state source current is used as the representation of the weight value, both the incrementing and decrementing functions are proportional to a power of the source current. The synaptic array was fabricated in the standard $2\mu m$ double - poly, analog process available from MOSIS.

1 INTRODUCTION

The past few years have produced a number of efforts to design VLSI chips which "learn from experience." The first step toward this goal is developing a silicon analog for a synapse. We have successfully developed such a synapse using only

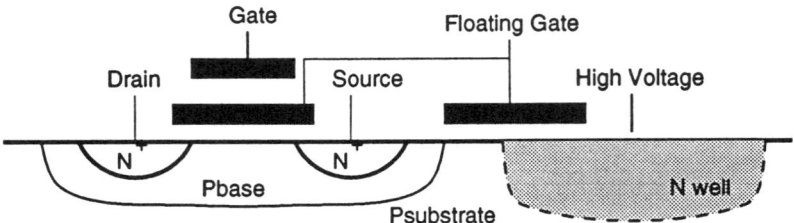

Figure 1: Cross section of the single transistor synapse. Our single transistor synapse uses a separate tunneling voltage terminal The pbase implant results in a larger threshold voltage, which results in all the electrons reaching the top of the SiO_2 barrier to be swept into the floating gate.

a single transistor. A synapse has two functional requirements. First, it must compute the product of the input multiplied by the strength (the weight) of the synapse. Second, the synapse must compute the weight update rule. For a Hebbian synapse, the change in the weight is the time average of the product of the input and output activity. In many supervised algorithms like backpropagation, this weight change is the time average of the product of the input and some fed back error signal. Both of these computations are similar in function. We have developed single transistor synapses which simultaneously perform long term weight storage, compute the product of the input and the weight value, and update the weight value according to a Hebbian or a backpropagation learning rule. The combination of functions has not previously been achieved with floating gate synapses.

There are five requirements for a learning synapse. First, the weight should be stored permanently in the absence of learning. Second, the synapse must compute as an output the product of the input signal with the synaptic weight. Third, each synapse should require minimal area, resulting in the maximum array size for a given area. Fourth, each synapse should operate with low power dissipation so that the synaptic array is not power constrained. And finally, the array should be capable of implementing either Hebbian or Backpropagation learning rule for modifying the weight on the floating gate. We have designed, fabricated, characterized, and modeled an array of single transistor synapses which satisfy these five criteria. We believe this is the first instance of a single transistor learning synapse fabricated in a standard process.

2 OVERVIEW

Figure 1 shows the cross section for the single transistor synapse. Since the floating gate is surrounded by SiO_2, an excellent insulator, charge leakage is negligible resulting in nearly permanent storage of the weight value. An advantage of using floating gate devices for learning rules is the timescales required to add and remove charge from the floating gate are well matched to the learning rates of visual and auditory signals. In addition, these learning rates can be electronically controlled. Typical resolution of charge on the floating gate after ten years is four bits (Holler 89). The FETs are in a moderately doped $(1 \times 10^{17} cm^{-3})$ substrate, to achieve a

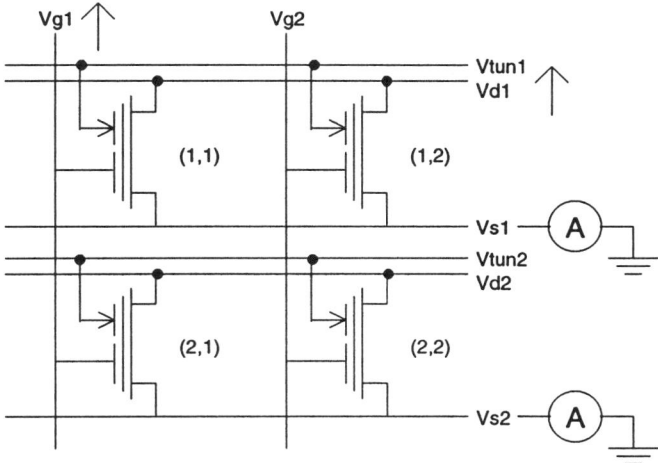

Figure 2: Circuit diagram of the single - transistor synapse array. Each transistor has a floating gate capacitively coupled to an input column line. A tunneling connection (arrow) allows weight increase. Weight decreased is achieved by hot electron injection in the transistor itself. Each synapse is capable of simultaneous feedforward computations and weight updates. A 2 x 2 section of the array allows us to characterize how modifying a single floating gate (such as synapse (1,1)) effects the neighboring floating gate values. The synapse currents are a measure of the synaptic weights, and are summed along each row by the source (V_s) or drain (V_d) lines into some soma circuit.

high threshold voltage. The moderately doped substrate is formed in the $2\mu m$ MOSIS process by the pbase implant. npn transistor. The implant has the additional benefit of increasing the efficiency of the hot electron injection process by increasing the electric field in the channel. Each synapse has an additional tunneling junction for modifying the charge on the floating gate. The tunneling junction is formed with high quality gate oxide separating a well region from the floating gate.

Each synapse in our synaptic array is a single transistor with its weight stored as a charge on a floating silicon gate. Figure 2 shows the circuit diagram of a 2 x 2 array of synapses. The column 'gate' inputs (V_g) are connected to second level polysilicon which capacitively couples to the floating gate. The inputs are shared along a column. The source (V_s), drain (V_d), and tunneling (V_{tun}) terminals are shared along a row. These terminals are involved with computing the output current and feeding back 'error' signal voltages. Many other synapses use floating gates to store the weight value, as in (Holler 89), but none of the earlier approaches update the charge on the floating gate during the multiplication of the input and floating gate value. In these previous approaches one must drive the floating gate over large a voltage range to tunnel electrons onto the floating gate. Synaptic computation must stop for this type of weight update.

The synapse computes as an output current a product of weight and input signal,

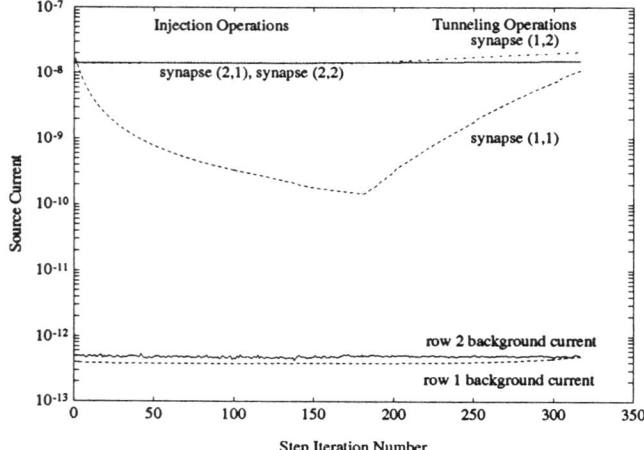

Figure 3: Output currents from a 2 x 2 section of the synapse array, showing 180 injection operations followed by 160 tunneling operations. For the injection operations, the drain ($Vd1$) is pulsed from 2.0 V upto 3.3 V for 0.5s with V_{g1} at $8V$ and V_{g2} at $0V$. For the tunneling operations, the tunneling line ($Vtun1$) is pulsed from 20 V up to 33.5 V with V_{g2} at $0V$ and V_{g1} at $8V$. Because our measurements from the 2 x 2 section come from a larger array, we also display the 'background' current from all other synapses on the row. This background current is several orders of magnitude smaller than the selected synapse current, and therefore negligible.

and can simultaneously increment or decrement the weight as a function of its input and error voltages. The particular learning algorithm depends on the circuitry at the boundaries of the array; in particular the circuitry connected to each of the source, drain, and tunneling lines in a row. With charge Q_{fg} on the floating gate and V_s equal to 0 the subthreshold source current is described by

$$I_{synapse} = I_o e^{\frac{Q_{fg}}{Q_o}} e^{\frac{\delta V_g}{U_T}} \qquad (1)$$

where Q_o is a device dependent parameter, and U_T is the thermal voltage $\frac{kT}{q}$. The coupling coefficient, δ, of the gate input to the transistor surface potential is typically less than 0.1. From (1) We can consider the weight as a current I, defined by

$$I_{synapse} = \left(I_o e^{\frac{Q_{fg}}{Q_o}} e^{\frac{\delta V_{g0}}{U_T}}\right) e^{\frac{\delta \Delta V_g}{U_T}} = I e^{\frac{\delta \Delta V_g}{U_T}} \qquad (2)$$

where V_{g0} is the input voltage bias, and ΔV_g is $V_g - V_{g0}$. The synaptic current is thus the product of the weight, I, and a weak exponential function of the input voltage.

The single transistor learning synapses use a combination of electron tunneling and hot electron injection to adapt the charge on the floating gate, and thereby the weight of the synapse. Hot electron injection adds electrons to the floating gate, thereby decreasing the weight. Injection occurs for large drain voltages; therefore the floating gate charge can be reduced during normal feedforward operation by raising the drain voltage. Electron tunneling removes electrons from the floating gate, thereby increasing the weight. The tunneling line controls the tunneling current; thus the floating gate charge can be increased during normal feedforward operation by raising the tunneling line voltage. The tunneling rate is modulated by both the input voltage and the charge on the floating gate.

Figure 3 shows an example the nature of the weight update process. The source current is used as a measure of the synapse weight. The experiment starts with all four synapses set to the same weight current. Then, synapse (1,1) is injected for 180 cycles to preferentially decrease its weight. Finally, synapse (1,1) is tunneled for 160 cycles to preferentially increase its weight. This experiment shows that a synapse can be incremented by applying a high voltage on tunneling terminals and a low voltage on the input, and can be decremented by applying a high voltage on drain terminals and a high voltage on the input. In the next two sections, we consider the nature of these update functions. In section three we examine the dependence of hot electron injection on the source current of our synapses. In section four we examine the dependence of electron tunneling on the source current of our synapses.

3 Hot Electron Injection

Hot electron injection gives us a method to add electrons to the floating gate. The underlying physics of the injection process is to give some electrons enough energy and direction in the channel to drain depletion region to surmount the SiO_2 energy barrier. A device must satisfy two requirements to inject an electron on a floating gate. First, we need a region where the potential drops more than 3.1 volts in a distance of less than $0.2\mu m$ to allow electrons to gain enough energy to surmount the oxide barrier. Second, we need a field in the oxide in the proper direction to collect electrons after they cross the barrier. The moderate substrate doping level allows us to easily achieve both effects in subthreshold operation. First, the higher substrate doping results in a much higher threshold voltage ($6.1V$), which guarantees that the field in the oxide at the drain edge of the channel will be in the proper direction for collecting electrons over the useful range of drain voltages. Second, the higher substrate doping results in higher electric fields which yield higher injection efficiencies. The higher injection efficiencies allow the device to have a wide range of drain voltages substantially below the threshold voltage. Figure 4 shows measured data on the change in source current during injection vs. source current for several values of drain voltage.

Because the source current, I, is related to the floating gate charge, Q_{fg} as shown in (1) and the charge on the floating gate is related to the tunneling or injection current (I_{fg}) by

$$\frac{dQ_{fg}}{dt} = I_{fg} \qquad (3)$$

an approximate model for the change of the weight current value is

$$\frac{dI}{dt} = \frac{I}{Q_o}I_{fg} \qquad (4)$$

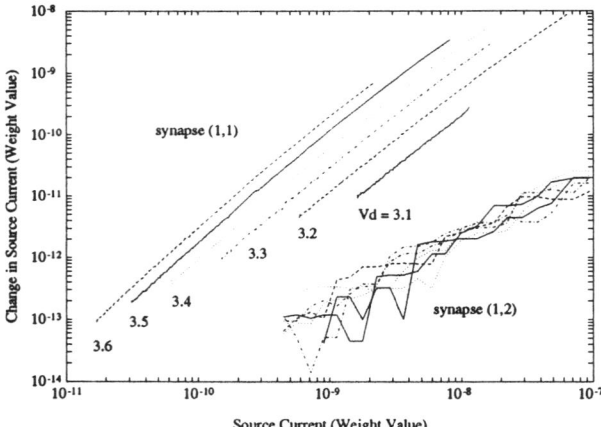

Figure 4: Source Current Decrement during injection vs. Source Current for several values of drain voltage. The injection operation decreases the synaptic weight. $Vg2$ was held at $0V$, and $Vg1$ was at $8V$ during the $0.5s$ injecting pulses. The change in source current is approximately proportional to the source current to the β power, where of β is between 1.7 and 1.85 for the range of drain voltages shown. The change in source current in synapse (1,2) is much less than the corresponding change in synapse (1,1) and is nearly independent of drain voltage. The effect of this injection on synapses (2,1) and (2,2) is negligible.

The injection current can be approximated over the range of drain voltages shown in Fig. 4 by (Hasler 95)

$$I_{fg} = -I_s e^{f(V_{d-c})} = -A I_s^{\beta-1} e^{\frac{V_d}{V_{inj}}} \tag{5}$$

where V_{d-c} is the voltage from the drain to the drain edge of the channel, V_d is the drain voltage, $f()$ is a slowly varying function defined in (Hasler 95), and V_{inj} is in the range of $60mV$ to $100mV$. A is device dependent parameter. Since hot electron injection adds electrons to the floating gate, the current into the floating gate (I_{fg}) is negative, which results in

$$\frac{dI}{dt} = -A \frac{I^\beta}{Q_o} e^{\frac{V_d}{V_{inj}}} \tag{6}$$

The model agrees well with the data in Fig. 4, with β in the range of $1.7 - 1.9$. Injection is very selective along a row with a selectivity coefficient between 10^2 and 10^7 depending upon drain voltage and weight. The injection operations resulted in negligible changes in source current for synapses (2,1) and (2,2).

4 ELECTRON TUNNELING

Electron tunneling gives us a method for removing electrons from the floating gate. Tunneling arises from the fact that an electron wavefunction has finite extent. For a

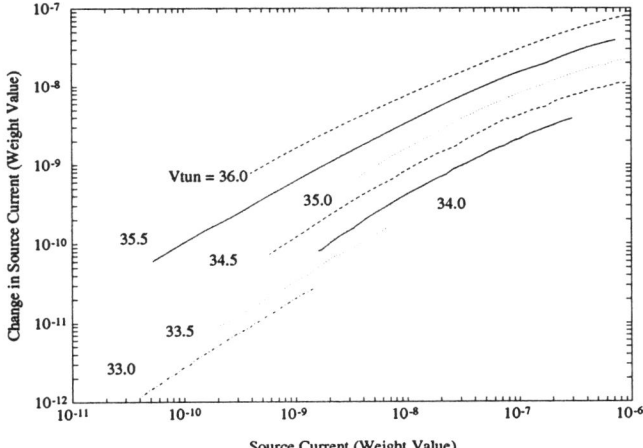

Figure 5: Synapse (1,1) source current increment vs. Source Current for several values of tunneling voltage. The tunneling operation increases the synaptic weight. $Vg1$ was held at $0V$ and $Vg2$ was $8V$ while the tunneling line was pulsed for $0.5s$ from $20V$ to the voltage shown. The change in source current is approximately proportional to the α power of the source current where α is between 0.7 and 0.9 for the range of tunneling voltages shown. The effect of this tunneling procedure on synapse (2,1) and (2,2) are negligible. The selectivity ratio of synapses on the same row is typically between 3-7 for our devices.

thin enough barrier, this extent is sufficient for an electron to penetrate the barrier. An electric field across the oxide will result in a thinner barrier to the electrons on the floating gate. For a high enough electric field, the electrons can tunnel through the oxide.

When traveling through the oxide, some electrons get trapped in the oxide, which changes the barrier profile. To reduce this trapping effect we tunnel through high quality gate oxide, which has far less trapping than interpoly oxide. Both injection and tunneling have very stable and repeatable characteristics. When tunneling at a fixed oxide voltage, the tunneling current decreases only 50 percent after $10nC$ of charge has passed through the oxide. This quantity of charge is orders of magnitude more than we would expect a synapse to experience over a lifetime of operation.

Figure 5 shows measured data on the change in source current during tunneling as a function of source current for several values of tunneling voltage. The functional form of tunneling current is of the form (Lenzlinger 69)

$$I_{fg} = I_{o_{tun}} e^{-\frac{V_o}{V_{tun} - V_{fg}}} \quad (7)$$

where V_o, $I_{o_{tun}}$ are model parameters which roughly correspond with theory. Tunneling removes electrons from the floating gate; therefore the floating gate current is positive. By expanding V_{fg} for fixed V_{tun} as $V_{fg0} + \Delta V_{fg}$ and inserting (1), the

Parameter	Typical Values	Parameter	Typical Values
β	1.7 - 1.9	α	0.7 - 0.9
Q_o	.2 pC	δ	0.02 - 0.1
A	8.6 x 10^{-20}	V_{inj}	78mV

Table 1: Typical measured values of the parameters in the modeling of the single transistor synapse array.

resulting current change is

$$\frac{dI}{dt} = \frac{I_{o_{tun}}}{Q_o} e^{-\frac{V_o}{V_{tun}-V_{fg0}}} I_{s0} \left(\frac{I}{I_{s0}}\right)^\alpha \quad (8)$$

where I_{s0} is the bias current corresponding to V_{fg0}. The model qualitatively agrees with the data in Fig. 5, with α in the range of 0.7 - 0.9. The tunneling selectivity between synapses on different rows is very good, but tunneling selectivity along along a row is poor. We typically measure tunneling selectivity ratios along a row between 3 - 7 for our devices.

5 Model of the Array of Single Transistor Synapses

Finally, we present an approximate model of our array of these single transistor synapses. The learning increment of the synapse at position (i,j) can be modeled as

$$I_{synapse_{ij}} = I_{ij} e^{\frac{\delta \Delta V_g}{U_T}} \equiv I_{s0} W_{ij} x_j$$
$$\frac{dW_{ij}}{dt} = \frac{I_{o_{tun}}}{Q_o} e^{-\frac{V_o}{V_{tun}-V_{fg0}}} W_{ij}^\alpha x_j^{\alpha-1} - \frac{A}{Q_o} e^{\frac{V_{d_j}}{V_{inj}}} W_{ij}^\beta x_j^{\beta-1} \quad (9)$$

for the synapse at position (i,j), where $W_{i,j}$ can be considered the weight value, and x_j are the effective inputs network. Typical values for the parameters in (9) are given in Table 1.

Acknowledgments

The work was supported by the office of Naval Research, the Advanced Research Projects Agency, and the Beckman Foundation.

References

P. Hasler, C. Diorio, B. Minch, and C. Mead (1995) "An Analytic model of Hot Electron Injection from Boltzman Transport", *Tech. Report 123456*

M. Holler, S. Tam, H. Castro, and R. Benson (1989), "An electrically trainable artificial neural network with 10240 'floating gate' synapses", *International Joint Conference on Neural Networks, Washington, D.C., June 1989, pp. II-191 - II-196.*

M. Lenzlinger and E. H. Snow (1969), "Fowler-Nordheim tunneling into thermally grown SiO_2," *J. Appl. Phys., vol. 40, pp. 278-283, 1969.*

PART VII
SPEECH AND SIGNAL PROCESSING

Pattern Playback in the '90s

Malcolm Slaney
Interval Research Corporation
1801-C Page Mill Road,
Palo Alto, CA 94304
malcolm@interval.com

Abstract

Deciding the appropriate representation to use for modeling human auditory processing is a critical issue in auditory science. While engineers have successfully performed many single-speaker tasks with LPC and spectrogram methods, more difficult problems will need a richer representation. This paper describes a powerful auditory representation known as the correlogram and shows how this non-linear representation can be converted back into sound, with no loss of perceptually important information. The correlogram is interesting because it is a neurophysiologically plausible representation of sound. This paper shows improved methods for spectrogram inversion (conventional pattern playback), inversion of a cochlear model, and inversion of the correlogram representation.

1 INTRODUCTION[1]

My interest in auditory models and perceptual displays [2] is motivated by the problem of sound understanding, especially the separation of speech from noisy backgrounds and interfering speakers. The correlogram and related representations are a pattern space within which sounds can be "understood" and "separated" [3][4]. I am therefore interested in resynthesizing sounds from these representations as a way to test and evaluate sound separation algorithms, and as a way to apply sound separation to problems such as speech enhancement. The conversion of sound to a correlogram involves the intermediate representation of a cochleagram, as shown in Figure 1, so cochlear-model inversion is addressed as one piece of the overall problem.

---

1. Much of this work was performed by Malcolm Slaney, Daniel Naar and Richard F. Lyon while all three were employed at Apple Computer. The mathematical details of this work were presented at the 1994 ICASSP[1].

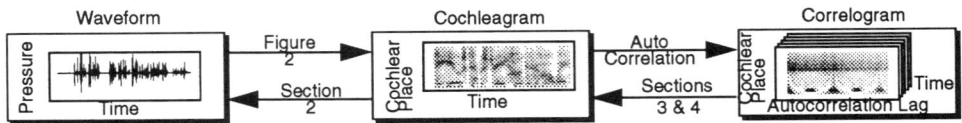

Figure 1. Three stages in low-level auditory perception are shown here. Sound waves are converted into a detailed representation with broad spectral bands, known as cochleagrams. The correlogram then summarizes the periodicities in the cochleagram with short-time autocorrelation. The result is a perceptual movie synchronized to the acoustic signal. The two inversion problems addressed in this work are indicated with arrows from right to left.

There are three factors which can be used to judge the quality of an auditory model: psychoacoustic comparisons, neurophysiological plausibility, and does it represent the perceptually relevant information? First, the correlogram has been shown to simply and accurately predict human pitch perception [5]. The neurophysiological basis for the correlogram has not been found, but there are neural circuits performing the same calculation in the mustached bat's echolocation system [6]. Finally, from an information representation point of view, does the correlogram preserve the salient information? The results of this paper show that no information has been lost. Since the psychoacoustic, neurophysiological, and information representation measures are all positive, perhaps the correlogram is the basis of most auditory processing.

The inversion techniques described here are important because they allow us to readily evaluate the results of sound separation models that "zero out" unwanted portions of the signal in the correlogram domain. This work extends the convex projection approach of Irino [7] and Yang [8] by considering a different cochlear model, and by including the correlogram inversion. The convex projection approach is well suited to "filling in" missing information. While this paper only describes the process for one particular auditory model, the techniques are equally useful for other models.

This paper describes three aspects of the problem: cochleagram inversion, conversion of the correlogram into spectrograms, and spectrogram inversion. A number of reconstruction options are explored in this paper. Some are fast, while other techniques use time-consuming iterations to produce reconstructions perceptually equivalent to the original sound. Fast versions of these algorithms could allow us to separate a speaker's voice from the background noise in real time.

2 COCHLEAGRAM INVERSION

Figure 2 shows a block diagram of the cochlear model [9] that is used in this work. The basis of the model is a bank of filters, implemented as a cascade of low-pass filters, that splits the input signal into broad spectral bands. The output from each filter in the bank is called a channel. The energy in each channel is detected and used to adjust the channel gain, implementing a simple model of auditory sensitivity adaptation, or automatic gain control (AGC). The half-wave rectifier (HWR) detection nonlinearity provides a waveform for each channel that roughly represents the instantaneous neural firing rate at each position along the cochlea.

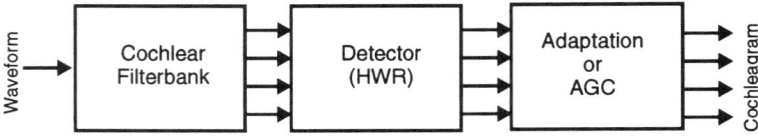

Figure 2. Three stages of the simple cochlear model used in this paper are shown above.

The cochleagram is converted back into sound by reversing the three steps shown in Figure 2. First the AGC is divided out, then the negative portions of each cochlear channel are recovered by using the fact that each channel is spectrally limited. Finally, the cochlear filters are inverted by running the filters backwards, and then correcting the resulting spectral slope.

The AGC stage in this cochlear model is controlled by its own output. It is a combination of a multiplicative gain and a simple first-order filter to track the history of the output signal. Since the controlling signal is directly available, the AGC can be inverted by tracking the output history and then dividing instead of multiplying. The performance of this algorithm is described by Naar [10] and will not be addressed here. It is worth noting that AGC inversion becomes more difficult as the level of the input signal is raised, resulting in more compression in the forward path.

The next stage in the inversion process can be done in one of two ways. After AGC inversion, both the positive values of the signal and the spectral extant of the signal are known. Projections onto convex sets [11], in this case defined by the positive values of the detector output and the spectral extant of the cochlear filters, can be used to find the original signal. This is shown in the left half of Figure 3. Alternatively, the spectral projection filter can be combined with the next stage of processing to make the algorithm more efficient. The increased efficiency is due to better match between the spectral projection and the cochlear filterbank, and due to the simplified computations within each iteration. This is shown in the right half of Figure 3. The result is an algorithm that produces nearly perfect results with no iterations at all.

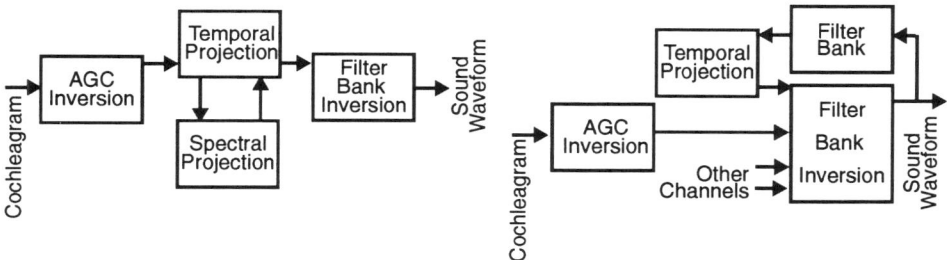

Figure 3. There are two ways to use convex projections to recover the information lost by the detectors. The conventional approach is shown on the left. The right figure shows a more efficient approach where the spectral projection has been combined with the filterbank inversion

Finally, the multiple outputs from the cochlear filterbank are converted back into a single waveform by correcting the phase and summing all channels. In the ideal case, each cochlear channel contains a unique portion of the spectral energy, but with a bit of phase delay and amplitude change. For example, if we run the signal through the same filter the spectral content does not change much but both the phase delay and amplitude change will be doubled. More interestingly, if we run the signal through the filter backwards, the forward and backward phase changes cancel out. After this phase correction, we can sum all channels and get back the original waveform, with a bit of spectral coloration. The spectral coloration or tilt can be fixed with a simple filter. A more efficient approach to correct the spectral tilt is to scale each channel by an appropriate weight before summing, as shown in Figure 4. The result is a perfect reconstruction, over those frequencies where the cochlear filters are non-zero.

Figure 5 shows results from the cochleagram inversion procedure. An impulse is shown on the left, before and after 10 iterations of the HWR inversion (using the algorithm on the right half of Figure 3). With no iterations the result is nearly perfect, except for a bit of noise near the center. The overall curvature of the baseline is due to the fact that informa-

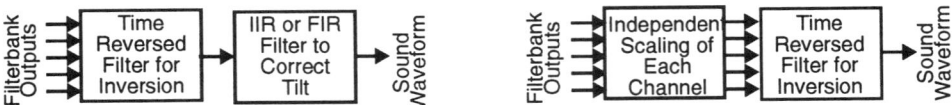

Figure 4. Two approaches are shown here to invert the filterbank. The left diagram shows the normal approach, the right figure shows a more efficient approach where the spectral-tilt filter is converted to a simple multiplication.

tion near DC has been lost as it travels through the auditory system and there is no way to recover it with the information that we have. A more interesting example is shown on the right. Here the word "tap"[1] has been reconstructed, with and without the AGC inversion. With the AGC inversion the result is nearly identical to the original. The auditory system is very sensitive to onsets and quickly adapts to steady state sounds like vowels. It is interesting to compare this to the reconstruction without AGC inversion. Without the AGC, the result is similar to what the ear hears, the onsets are more prominent and the vowels are deemphasized. This is shown in the right half of Figure 5.

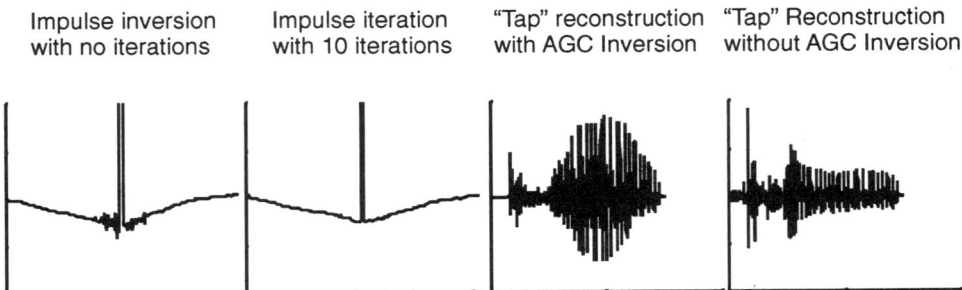

Figure 5. The cochlear reconstructions of an impulse and the word "tap" are shown here. The first and second reconstructions show an impulse reconstruction with and without iterations. The third and fourth waveforms are the word "tap" with and without the AGC inversion.

3 CORRELOGRAM INVERSION

The correlogram is an efficient way to capture the short-time periodicities in the auditory signal. Many mechanical measurements of the cochlea have shown that the response is highly non-linear. As the signal level changes there are large variations in the bandwidth and center frequency of the cochlear response. With these kinds of changes, it is difficult to imagine a system that can make sense of the spectral profile. This is especially true for decisions like pitch determination and sound separation.

But through all these changes in the cochlear filters, the timing information in the signal is preserved. The spectral profile, as measured by the cochlea, might change, but the rate of glottal pulses is preserved. Thus I believe the auditory system is based on a representation of sound that makes short-time periodicities apparent. One such representation is the correlogram. The correlogram measures the temporal correlation within each channel, either using FFTs which are most efficient in computer implementations, or neural delay lines much like those found in the binaural system of the owl.

---

1. The syllable "tap", samples 14000 through 17000 of the "train/dr5/fcdf1/sx106/sx106.adc" utterance on the TIMIT Speech Database, is used in all voiced examples in this paper.

The process of inverting the correlogram is simplified by noting that each autocorrelation is related by the Fourier transform to a power spectrum. By combining many power spectrums into a picture, the result is a spectrogram. This process is shown in Figure 6. In this way, a separate spectrogram is created for each channel. There are known techniques for converting a spectrogram, which has amplitude information but no phase information, back into the original waveform. The process of converting from a spectrogram back into a waveform is described in Section 4. The correlogram inversion process consists of inverting many spectrograms to form an estimate of a cochleagram. The cochleagram is inverted using the techniques described in Section 2.

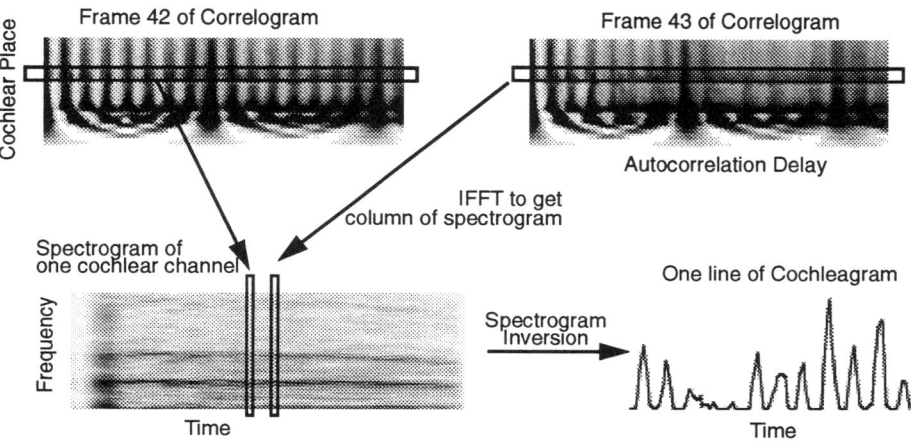

Figure 6. Correlogram inversion is possible by noting that each row of the correlogram contains the same information as a spectrogram of the same row of cochleagram output. By converting the correlogram into many spectrograms, the spectrogram inversion techniques described in Section 4 can be used. The lower horizontal stripe in the spectrogram is due to the narrow passband of the cochlear channel. Half-wave rectification of the cochlear filter output causes the upper horizontal stripes.

One important improvement to the basic method is possible due to the special characteristics of the correlogram. The essence of the spectrogram inversion problem is to recover the phase information that has been thrown away. This is an iterative procedure and would be costly if it had to be performed on each channel. Fortunately, there is quite a bit of overlap between cochlear channels. Thus the phase recovered from one channel can be used to initialize the spectrogram inversion for the next channel. A difficulty with spectrogram inversion is that the absolute phase is lost. By using the phase from one channel to initialize the next, a more consistent set of cochlear channel outputs is recovered.

4 SPECTROGRAM INVERSION

While spectrograms are not an accurate model of human perception, an implementation of a correlogram includes the calculation of many spectrograms. Mathematically, an autocorrelation calculation is similar to a spectrogram or short-time power spectrum. One column of a conventional spectrogram is related to an autocorrelation of a portion of the original waveform by a Fourier transform (see Figure 6). Unfortunately, the final representation of both spectrograms and autocorrelations is missing the phase information. The main task of a spectrogram inversion algorithm is to recover a consistent estimate of the missing phase. This process is not magical, it can only recover a signal that has the same magnitude spectrum as the original spectrogram. But the consistency constraint on the time evolution of the signal power spectrum also constrains the time evolution of the spectral phase.

The basic procedure in spectrogram inversion [12] consists of iterating between the time and the frequency domains. Starting from the frequency domain, the magnitude but not the phase is known. As an initial guess, any phase value can be used. The individual power spectra are inverse Fourier transformed and then summed to arrive at a single waveform. If the original spectrogram used overlapping windows of data, the information from adjacent windows either constructively or destructively interferes to estimate a waveform. A spectrogram of this new data is calculated, and the phase is now retained. We know the original magnitude was correct. Thus we can estimate a better spectrogram by combining the original magnitude information with the new phase information. It can be shown that each iteration will reduce the error.

Figure 7 shows an outline of steps that can be used to improve the consistency of phase estimates during the first iteration. As each portion of the waveform is added to the estimated signal, it is possible to add a linear phase so that each waveform lines up with the proceedings segments. The algorithm described in the paragraph above assumes an initial phase of zero. A more likely phase guess is to choose a phase that is consistent with the existing data. The result with no iterations is a waveform that is often closer to the original than that calculated assuming zero initial phase and ten iterations.

The total computational cost is minimized by combining these improvements with the initial phase estimates from adjacent channels of the correlogram. Thus when inverting the first channel of the correlogram, a cross-correlation is used to pick the initial phase and a few more iterations insure a consistent result. After the first channel, the phase of the proceeding channel is used to initialize the spectrogram inversion and only a few iterations are necessary to fine tune the waveform.

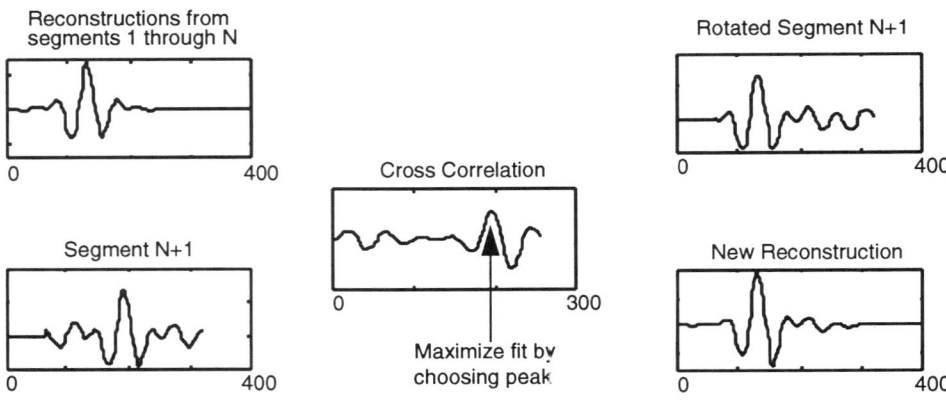

Figure 7. A procedure for adjusting the phase of new segments when inverting a spectrogram is shown above. As each new segment (bottom left) is converted from a power spectrum into a waveform, a linear phase is added to maximize the fit with the existing segments (top left.) The amount of rotation is determined by a cross correlation (middle). Adding the new segment with the proper rotation (top right) produces the new waveform (bottom right.)

5 PUTTING IT TOGETHER

This paper has described two steps to convert a correlogram into a sound. These steps are detailed below:

1) For each row of the correlogram:
   a) Convert the autocorrelation data into power spectrum (Section 3).
   b) Use spectrogram inversion (Section 4) to convert the spectrograms into an estimate of cochlear channel output.
   c) Assemble the results of spectrogram inversion into an estimate of the cochleagram.
2) Invert the cochleagram using the techniques described in Section 2.

This process is diagrammed in Figures 1 and 6.

6 RESULTS

Figure 8 shows the results of the complete reconstruction process for a 200Hz impulse train and the word "tap." In both cases, no iterations were performed for either the spectrogram or filterbank inversion. More iterations reduce the spectral error, but do not make the graphs look better or change the perceptual quality much. It is worth noting that the "tap" reconstruction from a correlogram looks similar to the cochleagram reconstruction without the AGC (see Figure 5.) Reducing the level of the input signal, thus reducing the amount of compression performed by the AGC, results in a correlogram reconstruction similar to the original waveform.

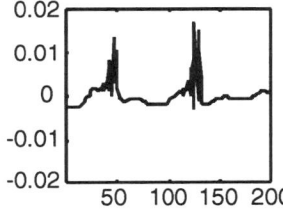
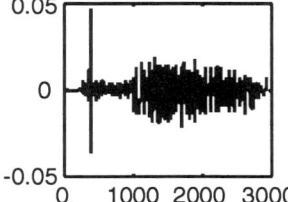

Figure 8. Reconstructions from the correlogram representation of an impulse train and the word "tap" are shown above. Reducing the input signal level, thus minimizing the effect of errors when inverting the AGC, produces results identical to the original "tap."

It is important to note that the algorithms described in this paper are designed to minimize the error in the mean-square sense. This is a convenient mathematical definition, but it doesn't always correlate with human perception. A trivial example of this is possible by comparing a waveform and a copy of the waveform delayed by 10ms. Using the mean-squared error, the numerical error is very high yet the two waveforms are perceptually equivalent. Despite this, the results of these algorithms based on mean-square error do sound good.

7 CONCLUSIONS

This paper has described several techniques that allow several stages of an auditory model to be converted back into sound. By converting each row of the correlogram into a spectrogram, the spectrogram inversion techniques of Section 4 can be used. The special characteristics of a correlogram described in Section 3 are used to make the calculation more efficient. Finally, the cochlear filterbank can be inverted to recover the original waveform. The results are waveforms, perceptually identical to the original waveforms.

These techniques will be especially useful as part of a sound separation system. I do not believe that our auditory system resynthesizes partial waveforms from the auditory scene. Yet, all research systems generate separated sounds so that we can more easily perceive their success. More work is still needed to fine-tune these algorithm and to investigate the ability to reconstruct sounds from partial correlograms.

Acknowledgments

I am grateful for the inspiration provided by Frank Cooper's work in the early 1950's on pattern playback[13][14]. His work demonstrated that it was possible to convert a spectrogram, painted onto clear plastic, into sound.

This work in this paper was performed with Daniel Naar and Richard F. Lyon. We are grateful for the help we have received from Richard Duda (San Jose State), Shihab Shamma (U. of Maryland), Jim Boyles (The MathWorks) and Michele Covell (Interval Research).

References

[1] Malcolm Slaney, D. Naar, R. F. Lyon, "Auditory model inversion for sound separation," *Proc. of IEEE ICASSP*, Volume II, pp. 77-80, 1994.
[2] M. Slaney and R. F. Lyon, "On the importance of time—A temporal representation of sound," in *Visual Representations of Speech Signals*, eds. M. Cooke, S. Beet, and M. Crawford, J. Wiley and Sons, Sussex, England, 1993.
[3] R. F. Lyon, "A computational model of binaural localization and separation," *Proc. of IEEE ICASSP*, 1148-1151, 1983.
[4] M. Weintraub, "The GRASP sound separation system," *Proc. of IEEE ICASSP*, pp. 18A.6.1-18A.6.4, 1984.
[5] D. Hermes, "Pitch analysis," in *Visual Representations of Speech Signals*, eds. M. Cooke, S. Beet, and M. Crawford, J. Wiley and Sons, Sussex, England, 1993.
[6] N. Suga, "Cortical computational maps for auditory imaging," *Neural Networks*, 3, 3-21, 1990.
[7] T. Irino, H. Kawahara, "Signal reconstruction from modified auditory wavelet transform," *IEEE Trans. on Signal Processing*, 41, 3549-3554, Dec. 1993.
[8] X. Yang, K. Wang, and S. Shamma, "Auditory representations of acoustic signals," *IEEE Trans. on Information Theory*, 38, 824-839, 1992.
[9] R. F. Lyon, "A computational model of filtering, detection, and compression in the cochlea," *Proc. of the IEEE ICASSP*, 1282-1285, 1982.
[10] D. Naar, "Sound resynthesis from a correlogram," San Jose State University, Department of Electrical Engineering, Technical Report #3, May 1993.
[11] R. W. Papoulis, "A new algorithm in spectral analysis and band-limited extrapolation," *IEEE Trans. Circuits Sys.*, vol. 22, 735, 1975.
[12] D. Griffin and J. Lim, "Signal estimation from modified short-time Fourier transform," *IEEE Trans. on Acoustics, Speech, and Signal Processing*, 32, 236-242, 1984.
[13] F. S. Cooper, "Some Instrumental Aids to Research on Speech," *Report on the Fourth Annual Round Table Meeting on Linguistics and Language Teaching*, Georgetown University Press, 46-53, 1953.
[14] F. S. Cooper, "Acoustics in human communications: Evolving ideas about the nature of speech," *J. Acoust. Soc. Am.*, 68(1), 18-21, July 1980.

Non-linear Prediction of Acoustic Vectors Using Hierarchical Mixtures of Experts

S.R.Waterhouse   A.J.Robinson
Cambridge University Engineering Department,
Trumpington St., Cambridge, CB2 1PZ, England.
Tel: [+44] 223 332800, Fax: [+44] 223 332662,
Email: srw1001, ajr @eng.cam.ac.uk
URL: http://svr-www.eng.cam.ac.uk/~srw1001

Abstract

In this paper we consider speech coding as a problem of speech modelling. In particular, prediction of parameterised speech over short time segments is performed using the Hierarchical Mixture of Experts (HME) (Jordan & Jacobs 1994). The HME gives two advantages over traditional non-linear function approximators such as the Multi-Layer Perceptron (MLP); a statistical understanding of the operation of the predictor and provision of information about the performance of the predictor in the form of likelihood information and local error bars. These two issues are examined on both toy and real world problems of regression and time series prediction. In the speech coding context, we extend the principle of combining local predictions via the HME to a Vector Quantization scheme in which fixed local codebooks are combined on-line for each observation.

1 INTRODUCTION

We are concerned in this paper with the application of multiple models, specifically the Hierarchical Mixtures of Experts, to time series prediction, specifically the problem of predicting acoustic vectors for use in speech coding. There have been a number of applications of multiple models in time series prediction. A classic example is the *Threshold Autoregressive model* (TAR) which was used by Tong &

Lim (1980) to predict sunspot activity. More recently, Lewis, Kay and Stevens (*in* Weigend & Gershenfeld (1994)) describe the use of Multivariate and Regression Splines (MARS) to the prediction of future values of currency exchange rates. Finally, in speech prediction, Cuperman & Gersho (1985) describe the Switched Inter-frame Vector Prediction (SIVP) method which switches between separate linear predictors trained on different statistical classes of speech. The form of time series prediction we shall consider in this paper is the *single step prediction* $\hat{y}^{(t)}$ of a future quantity $y^{(t)}$, by considering the previous p samples. This may be viewed as a regression problem over input-output pairs $\{x^{(t)}, y^{(t)}\}_{t=0}^{N}$ where $x^{(t)}$ is the *lag vector* $(y^{(t-1)}, y^{(t-2)}, ..., y^{(t-p)})$. We may perform this regression using standard linear models such as the Auto-Regressive (AR) model or via nonlinear models such as connectionist feed-forward or recurrent networks. The HME overcomes a number of problems associated with traditional connectionist models via its architecture and statistical framework. Recently, Jordan & Jacobs (1994) and Waterhouse & Robinson (1994) have shown that via the EM algorithm and a 2nd order optimization scheme known as Iteratively Reweighted Least Squares (IRLS), the HME is faster than standard Multilayer Perceptrons (MLP) by at least an order of magnitude on regression and classification tasks respectively. Jordan & Jacobs also describe various methods to visualise the learnt structure of the HME via 'deviance trees' and histograms of posterior probabilities. In this paper we provide further examples of the structural relationship of the trained HME and the input-output space in the form of *expert activation plots*. In addition we describe how the HME can be extended to give local error bars or measures of confidence in regression and time series prediction problems. Finally, we describe the extension of the HME to acoustic vector prediction, and a VQ coding scheme which utilises likelihood information from the HME.

2 HIERARCHICAL MIXTURES OF EXPERTS

The HME architecture (Figure 1) is based on the principle of 'divide and conquer' in which a large, hard to solve problem is broken up into many, smaller, easier to solve problems. It consists of a series of 'expert networks' which are trained on different parts of the input space. The outputs of the experts are combined by a 'gating network' which is trained to stochastically select the expert which is performing best at solving a particular part of the problem. The operation of the HME is as follows: the gating networks receive the input vectors $x^{(t)}$ and produce as outputs probabilities $P(m_j|x^{(t)}, \eta_j)$ for each local branch m_j of assigning the current input to the different branches, where η_j are the gating network parameters. The expert networks sit at the leaves of the tree and each output a vector $\hat{y}_j^{(t)}$ given input vector $x^{(t)}$ and parameters θ_j. These outputs are combined in a weighted sum by $P(m_j|x^{(t)}, \eta_j)$ to give the overall output vector for this region. This procedure continues recursively upwards to the root node. In time series prediction, each expert j is a linear single layer network with the form:

$$\hat{y}_j^{(t)} = \theta_j x^{(t)}$$

where θ_j is matrix and $x^{(t)}$ is the lag vector discussed earlier, which is identical in form to an AR model.

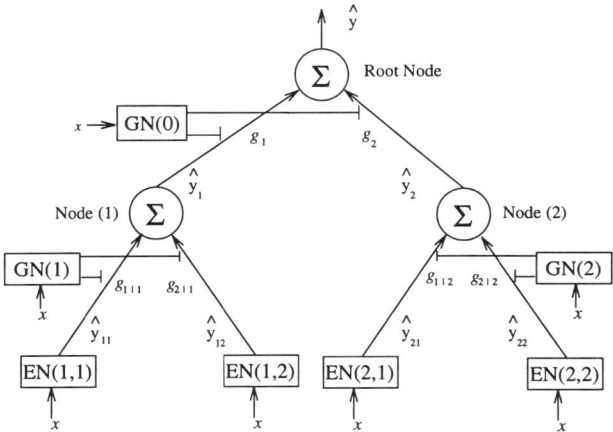

Figure 1: The Hierarchical Mixture of Experts.

2.1 Error bars via HME

Since each expert is an AR model, it follows that the output of each expert $\hat{\boldsymbol{y}}^{(t)}$ is the expected value of the observations $\boldsymbol{y}^{(t)}$ at each time t. The conditional likelihood of $\boldsymbol{y}^{(t)}$ given the input and expert m_j is

$$P(\boldsymbol{y}^{(t)}|\boldsymbol{x}^{(t)}, m_j, \theta_j) = \frac{1}{|2\pi C_j|} \exp\left(-\frac{1}{2}(\boldsymbol{y} - \hat{\boldsymbol{y}}_j^{(t)})^T C_j (\boldsymbol{y} - \hat{\boldsymbol{y}}_j^{(t)})\right)$$

where C_j is the covariance matrix for expert m_j which is updated during training as:

$$C_j = \frac{1}{\sum_t h_j^{(t)}} \sum_t h_j^{(t)} (\boldsymbol{y}^{(t)} - \hat{\boldsymbol{y}}_j^{(t)})^T (\boldsymbol{y}^{(t)} - \hat{\boldsymbol{y}}_j^{(t)})$$

where $h_j^{(t)}$ are the posterior probabilities[1] of each expert m_j. Taking the moments of the overall likelihood of the HME gives the output of the HME as the conditional expected value of the target output $\boldsymbol{y}^{(t)}$,

$$\begin{aligned}\hat{\boldsymbol{y}}^{(t)} &= E(\boldsymbol{y}^{(t)}|\boldsymbol{x}^{(t)}, \Theta, M) \\ &= \sum_j P(m_j|\boldsymbol{x}^{(t)}, \eta_j) E(\boldsymbol{y}^{(t)}|\boldsymbol{x}^{(t)}, \theta_j, m_j) = \sum_j g_j^{(t)} \hat{\boldsymbol{y}}_j^{(t)},\end{aligned}$$

Where M represents the overall HME model and Θ the overall set of parameters. Taking the second central moment of $\boldsymbol{y}^{(t)}$ gives,

$$\begin{aligned}C &= E((\boldsymbol{y}^{(t)} - \hat{\boldsymbol{y}}_j^{(t)})^2|\boldsymbol{x}^{(t)}, \Theta, M) \\ &= \sum_j P(m_j|\boldsymbol{x}^{(t)}, \eta_j) E((\boldsymbol{y}^{(t)} - \hat{\boldsymbol{y}}_j^{(t)})^2|\boldsymbol{x}^{(t)}, \theta_j, m_j) \\ &= \sum_j g_j^{(t)} (C_j + \hat{\boldsymbol{y}}_j^{(t)} \cdot \hat{\boldsymbol{y}}_j^{(t)T}),\end{aligned}$$

---

[1] See (Jordan & Jacobs 1994) for a fuller discussion of posterior probabilities and likelihoods in the context of the HME.

which gives, in a direct fashion, the covariance of the output given the input and the model. If we assume that the observations are generated by an *underlying* model, which generates according to some function $f(x^{(t)})$ and corrupted by zero mean normally distributed noise $n(x)$ with constant covariance Σ, then the covariance of $y^{(t)}$ is given by,

$$V(y^{(t)}) = V(f^{(t)}) + \Sigma,$$

so that the covariance computed by the method above, $V(y^{(t)})$, takes into account the modelling error as well as the uncertainty due to the noise. Weigend & Nix (1994) also calculate error bars using an MLP consisting of a set of tanh hidden units to estimate the conditional mean and an auxiliary set of tanh hidden units to estimate the variance, assuming normally distributed errors. Our work differs in that there is no assumption of normality in the error distribution, rather that the errors of the terminal experts are distributed normally, with the total error distribution being a mixture of normal distributions.

3 SIMULATIONS

In order to demonstrate the utility of our approach to variance estimation we consider one toy regression problem and one time series prediction problem.

3.1 Toy Problem : Computer generated data

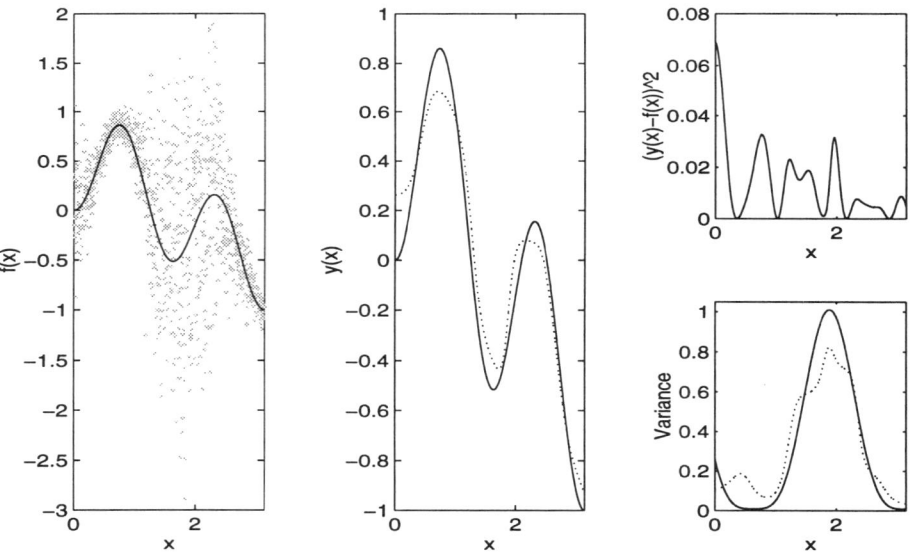

Figure 2: Performance on the toy data set of a 5 level binary HME. (a) training set (dots) and underlying function $f(x)$ (solid), (b) underlying function (solid) and prediction $y(x)$ (dashed), (c) squared deviation of prediction from underlying function, (d) true noise variance (solid) and variance of prediction (dashed).

By way of comparison, we used the same toy problem as Weigend & Nix (1994) which consists of 1000 training points and 10000 separate evaluation points from the function $g(x)$ where $g(x)$ consists of a known underlying function $f(x)$ corrupted by normally distributed noise $N(0, \sigma^2(x))$,

$$f(x) = \sin(2.5x) \times \sin(1.5x), \quad \sigma^2(x) = 0.01 + 0.25 \times [1 - \sin(2.5x)]^2.$$

As can be seen by Figure 2, the HME has learnt to approximate both the underlying function and the additive noise variance. The deviation of the estimated variance from the "true" noise variance may be due to the actual noise variance being lower than the maximum denoted by the solid line at various points.

3.2 Sunspots

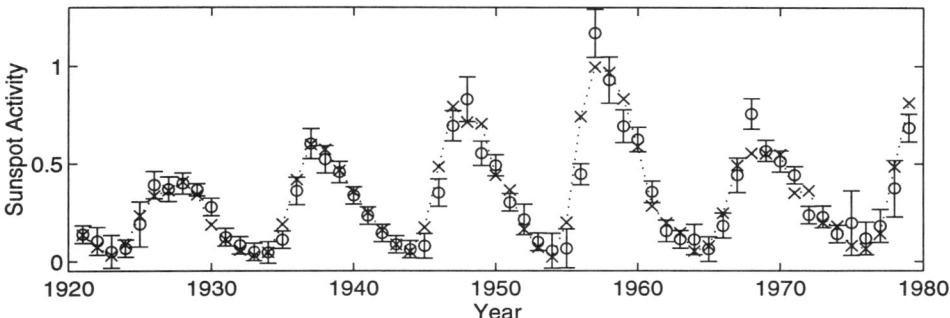

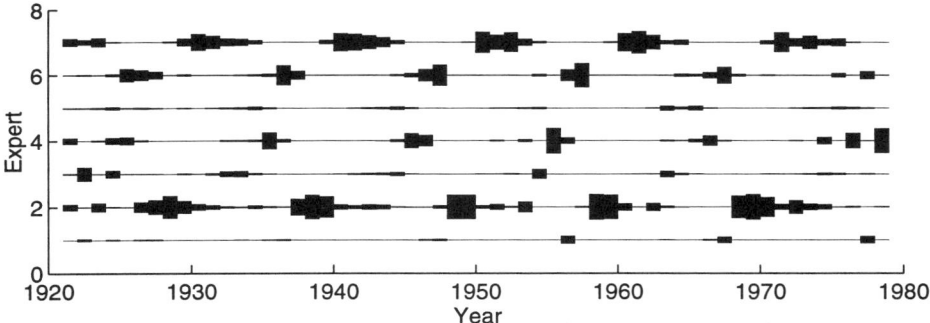

Figure 3: Performance on the **Sunspots** data set. (a) Actual Values (x) and predicted values (o) with error bars. (b) Activation of the expert networks; bars wide in the vertical axis indicate strong activation. Notice how expert 7 concentrates on the lulls in the series while expert 2 deals with the peaks.

METHOD	NMSE'		
	Train	Test	
	1700-1920	1921-1955	1956-1979
MLP	0.082	0.086	0.35
TAR	0.097	0.097	0.28
HME	0.061	0.089	0.27

Table 1: Results of single step prediction on the **Sunspots** data set using a mixture of 7 experts (104 parameters) and a lag vector of 12 years. NMSE' is the NMSE normalised by the variance of the entire record 1700 to 1979.

The **Sunspots**[2] time series consists of yearly sunspot activity from 1700 to 1979 and was first tackled using connectionist models by Weigend, Huberman & Rumelhart (1990) who used a 12-8-1 MLP (113 parameters). Prior to this work, the TAR was used by Tong (1990). Our results, which were obtained using a random leave 10% out cross validation method, are shown in Table 1. We are considering only *single step* prediction on this problem, which involves prediction of the next value based on a set of previous values of the time series. Our results are evaluated in terms of *Normalised Mean Squared Error* (NMSE) (Weigend et al. 1990), which is defined as the ratio of the variance of the prediction on the test set to the variance of the test set itself.

The HME outperforms both the TAR and the MLP on this problem, and additionally provides both information about the structure of the network after training via the expert activation plot and error bars of the predictions, as shown in Figure 3. Further improvements may be possible by using likelihood information during cross validation so that a joint optimisation of overall error and variance is achieved.

4 SPEECH CODING USING HME

In the standard method of Linear Predictive Coding (LPC) (Makhoul 1975), speech is parametrised into a set of vectors of duration one frame (around 10 ms). Whilst simple scalar quantization of the LPC vectors can achieve bit rates of around 2400 bits per second (bps), Yong, Davidson & Gersho (1988) have shown that simple linear prediction of Line Spectral Pairs (LSP) (Soong & Juang 1984) vectors followed by Vector Quantization (VQ) (Abut, Gray & Rebolledo 1984) of the error vectors can yield bit rates of around 800 bps. In this paper we describe a speech coding framework which uses the HME in two stages. Firstly, the HME is used to perform prediction of the acoustic vectors. The error vectors are then quantized efficiently by using a VQ scheme which utilises the likelihood information derived from the HME.

4.1 Mixing VQ codebooks ia Gating networks

In a VQ scheme using a Euclidean distance measure, there is an implicit assumption that the inputs follow a Gaussian probability density function (pdf). This is satisfied if we quantize the residuals from a linear predictor, but not the residuals from an HME which follow a mixture of Gaussians pdf. A more efficient method is therefore to generate separate VQ codebooks for each expert in the HME and combine them via the priors on each expert from the gating networks. The codebook for the overall residual vectors on the test set is then generated at each time dynamically by choosing the first $D \times g_j^{(t)}$ codes, where D is the size of the expert codebooks and $g_j^{(t)}$ is the prior on each expert.

---

[2]Available via anonymous ftp at **ftp.cs.colorado.edu** in **/pub/Time-Series** as **DataSunspots.Yearly**

4.2 Results of Speech Coding Evaluations

Initial experiments were performed using 23 Mel scale log energy frequency bins as acoustic vectors and using single variances $C_j = \sigma_j I$ as expert network covariance matrices. The results of training over 100,000 frames and evaluation over a further 100,000 frames on the Resource Management (RM) corpus are shown in Table 2 and Figure 4 which shows the good specialisation of the HME in this problem.

METHOD	Prediction Gain (dB)	
	Train	Test
Linear	12.07	10.95
1 level HME	18.1	15.55
2 level HME	20.20	16.39

Table 2: Prediction of Acoustic Vectors using linear prediction and binary branching HMEs with 1 and 2 levels. Prediction gain (Cuperman & Gersho 1985) is the ratio of the signal variance to prediction error variance.

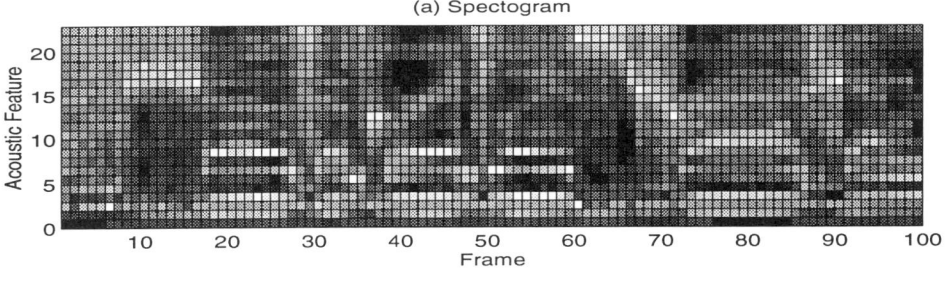

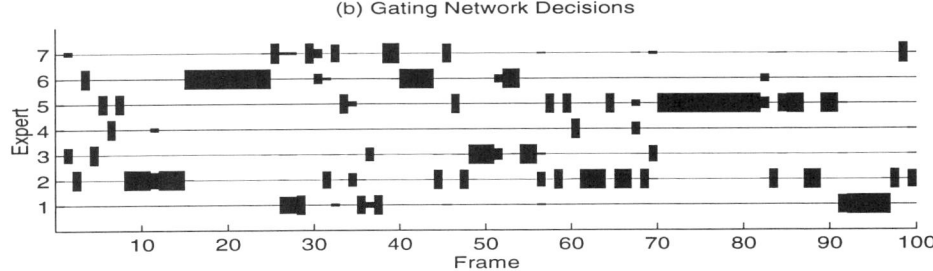

Figure 4: The behaviour of a mixture of 7 experts at predicting Mel-scale log energy frequency bins over 100 16ms frames. The top figure is a spectrogram of the speech and the lower figure is an expert activation plot, showing the gating network decisions.

We have conducted further experiments using LSPs and cepstrals as acoustic vectors, and using diagonal expert network covariance matrices, on a very large speech corpus. However, initial experiments show only a small improvement in gain over a single linear predictor and further investigation is underway. We have also coded acoustic vectors using 8 bits per frame with frame lengths of 12.5 ms, passing power, pitch and degree of voicing as side band information, without appreciable distortion over simple LPC coding. A full system will include prediction of all acoustic parameters and we anticipate further reductions on this initial figure with future developments.

5 CONCLUSION

The aim of speech coding is the efficient coding of the speech signal with little perceptual loss. This paper has described the use of the HME for acoustic vector prediction. We have shown that the HME can provide improved performance over a linear predictor and in addition it provides a time varying variance for the prediction error. The decomposition of the linear prediction problem into a solution via a mixture of experts also allows us to construct a VQ codebook on the fly by mixing the codebooks of the various experts.

We expect that the direct computation of the time varying nature of the prediction accuracy will find many applications. Within the acoustic vector prediction problem we would like to exploit this information by exploring the continuum between the fixed bit rate coder described here and a variable bit rate coder that produces constant spectral distortion.

Acknowledgements

This work was funded in part by Hewlett Packard Laboratories, UK. Steve Waterhouse is supported by an EPSRC Research Studentship and Tony Robinson was supported by a EPSRC Advanced Research Fellowship.

References

Abut, H., Gray, R. M. & Rebolledo, G. (1984), 'Vector quantization of speech and speech-like waveforms', *IEEE Transactions on Acoustics, Speech, and Signal Processing*.

Cuperman, V. & Gersho, A. (1985), 'Vector predictive coding of speech at 16 kbit/s', *IEEE Transactions on Communications* **COM-33**, 685–696.

Jordan, M. I. & Jacobs, R. A. (1994), 'Hierarchical Mixtures of Experts and the EM algorithm', *Neural Computation* **6**, 181–214.

Makhoul, J. (1975), 'Linear prediction: A tutorial review', *Proceedings of the IEEE* **63**(4), 561–580.

Soong, F. K. & Juang, B. H. (1984), Line spectrum pair (LSP) and speech data compression.

Tong, H. (1990), *Non-linear Time Series: a dynamical systems approach*, Oxford University Press.

Tong, H. & Lim, K. (1980), 'Threshold autoregression, limit cycles and cyclical data', *Journal of Royal Statistical Society*.

Waterhouse, S. R. & Robinson, A. J. (1994), Classification using hierarchical mixtures of experts, *in* 'IEEE Workshop on Neural Networks for Signal Processing'.

Weigend, A. S. & Gershenfeld, N. A. (1994), *Time Series Prediction: Forecasting the Future and Understanding the Past*, Addison-Wesley.

Weigend, A. S. & Nix, D. A. (1994), Predictions with confidence intervals (local error bars), Technical Report CU-CS-724-94, Department of Computer Science and Institute of Cognitive Science, University of Colorado, Boulder, CO 80309-0439.

Weigend, A. S., Huberman, B. A. & Rumelhart, D. E. (1990), 'Predicting the future: a connectionist approach', *International Journal of Neural Systems* **1**, 193–209.

Yong, M., Davidson, G. & Gersho, A. (1988), Encoding of LPC spectral parameters using switched-adaptive interframe vector prediction, *in* 'Proceedings of the IEEE International Conference on Acoustics Speech, and Signal Processing', pp. 402–405.

Glove-TalkII: Mapping Hand Gestures to Speech Using Neural Networks

S. Sidney Fels
Department of Computer Science
University of Toronto
Toronto, ON, M5S 1A4
ssfels@ai.toronto.edu

Geoffrey Hinton
Department of Computer Science
University of Toronto
Toronto, ON, M5S 1A4
hinton@ai.toronto.edu

Abstract

Glove-TalkII is a system which translates hand gestures to speech through an adaptive interface. Hand gestures are mapped continuously to 10 control parameters of a parallel formant speech synthesizer. The mapping allows the hand to act as an artificial vocal tract that produces speech in real time. This gives an unlimited vocabulary in addition to direct control of fundamental frequency and volume. Currently, the best version of Glove-TalkII uses several input devices (including a CyberGlove, a ContactGlove, a 3-space tracker, and a foot-pedal), a parallel formant speech synthesizer and 3 neural networks. The gesture-to-speech task is divided into vowel and consonant production by using a gating network to weight the outputs of a vowel and a consonant neural network. The gating network and the consonant network are trained with examples from the user. The vowel network implements a fixed, user-defined relationship between hand-position and vowel sound and does not require any training examples from the user. Volume, fundamental frequency and stop consonants are produced with a fixed mapping from the input devices. One subject has trained to speak intelligibly with Glove-TalkII. He speaks slowly with speech quality similar to a text-to-speech synthesizer but with far more natural-sounding pitch variations.

1 Introduction

There are many different possible schemes for converting hand gestures to speech. The choice of scheme depends on the granularity of the speech that you want to produce. Figure 1 identifies a spectrum defined by possible divisions of speech based on the duration of the sound for each granularity. What is interesting is that in general, the coarser the division of speech, the smaller the bandwidth necessary for the user. In contrast, where the granularity of speech is on the order of articulatory muscle movements (i.e. the artificial vocal tract [AVT]) high bandwidth control is necessary for good speech. Devices which implement this model of speech production are like musical instruments which produce speech sounds. The user must control the timing of sounds to produce speech much as a musician plays notes to produce music. The AVT allows unlimited vocabulary, control of pitch and non-verbal sounds. Glove-TalkII is an adaptive interface that implements an AVT.

Translating gestures to speech using an AVT model has a long history beginning in the late 1700's. Systems developed include a bellows-driven hand-varied resonator tube with auxiliary controls (1790's [9]), a rubber-moulded skull with actuators for manipulating tongue and jaw position (1880's [1]) and a keyboard-footpedal interface controlling a set of linearly spaced bandpass frequency generators called the Voder (1940 [3]). The Voder was demonstrated at the World's Fair in 1939 by operators who had trained continuously for one year to learn to speak with the system. This suggests that the task of speaking with a gestural interface is very difficult and the training times could be significantly decreased with a better interface. Glove-TalkII is implemented with neural networks which allows the system to learn the user's interpretation of an articulatory model of speaking.

This paper begins with an overview of the whole Glove-TalkII system. Then, each neural network is described along with its training and test results. Finally, a qualitative analysis is provided of the speech produced by a single subject after 100 hours of speaking with Glove-TalkII.

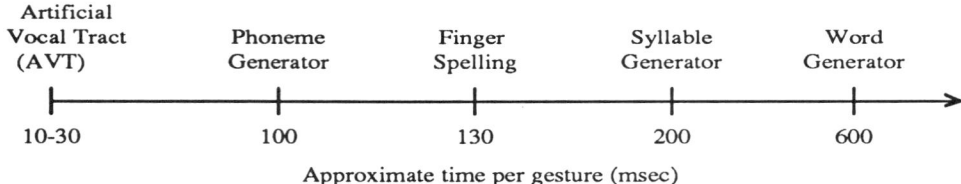

Figure 1: Spectrum of gesture-to-speech mappings based on the granularity of speech.

2 Overview of Glove-TalkII

The Glove-TalkII system converts hand gestures to speech, based on a gesture-to-formant model. The gesture vocabulary is based on a vocal-articulator model of the hand. By dividing the mapping tasks into independent subtasks, a substantial reduction in network size and training time is possible (see [4]).

Figure 2 illustrates the whole Glove-TalkII system. Important features include the

Glove-TalkII

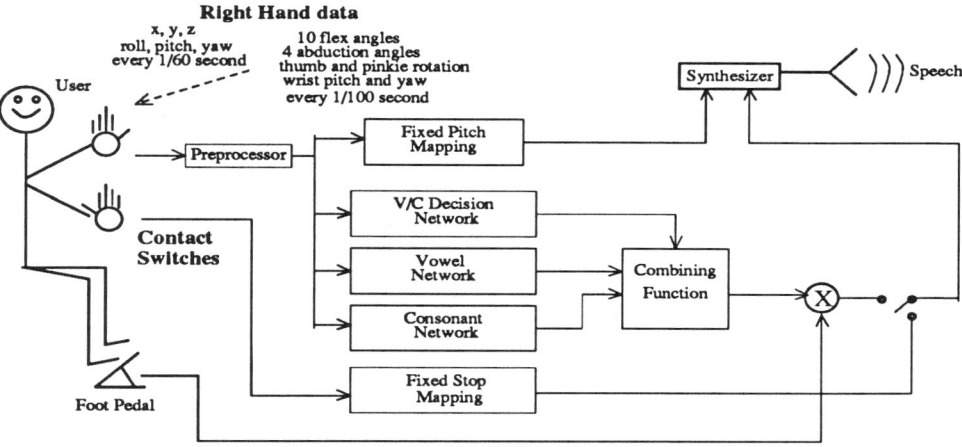

Figure 2: Block diagram of Glove-TalkII: input from the user is measured by the Cyberglove, polhemus, keyboard and foot pedal, then mapped using neural networks and fixed functions to formant parameters which drive the parallel formant synthesizer [8].

three neural networks labeled vowel/consonant decision (V/C), vowel, and consonant. The V/C network is trained on data collected from the user to decide whether he wants to produce a vowel or a consonant sound. Likewise, the consonant network is trained to produce consonant sounds based on user-generated examples based on an initial gesture vocabulary. In contrast, the vowel network implements a fixed mapping between hand-positions and vowel phonemes defined by the user. Nine contact points measured on the user's left hand by a ContactGlove designate the nine stop consonants (B, D, G, J, P, T, K, CH, NG), because the dynamics of such sounds proved too fast to be controlled by the user. The foot pedal provides a volume control by adjusting the speech amplitude and this mapping is fixed. The fundamental frequency, which is related to the pitch of the speech, is determined by a fixed mapping from the user's hand height. The output of the system drives 10 control parameters of a parallel formant speech synthesizer every 10 msec. The 10 control parameters are: nasal amplitude (ALF), first, second and third formant frequency and amplitude (F1, A1, F2, A2, F3, A3), high frequency amplitude (AHF), degree of voicing (V) and fundamental frequency (F0). Each of the control parameters is quantized to 6 bits.

Once trained, Glove-TalkII can be used as follows: to initiate speech, the user forms the hand shape of the first sound she intends to produce. She depresses the foot pedal and the sound comes out of the synthesizer. Vowels and consonants of various qualities are produced in a continuous fashion through the appropriate co-ordination of hand and foot motions. Words are formed by making the correct motions; for example, to say "hello" the user forms the "h" sound, depresses the foot pedal and quickly moves her hand to produce the "e" sound, then the "l" sound and finally the "o" sound. The user has complete control of the timing and quality of the individual sounds. The articulatory mapping between gestures and speech

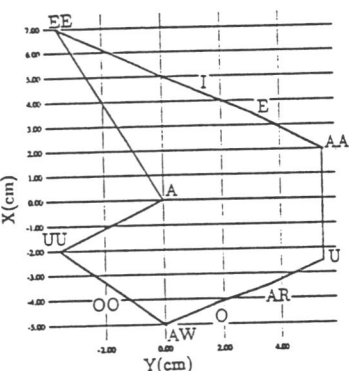

Figure 3: Hand-position to Vowel Sound Mapping. The coordinates are specified relative to the origin at the sound A. The X and Y coordinates form a horizontal plane parallel to the floor when the user is sitting. The 11 cardinal phoneme targets are determined with the text-to-speech synthesizer.

is decided *a priori*. The mapping is based on a simplistic articulatory phonetic description of speech [5]. The X,Y coordinates (measured by the polhemus) are mapped to something like tongue position and height[1] producing vowels when the user's hand is in an open configuration (see figure 2 for the correspondence and table 1 for a typical vowel configuration). Manner and place of articulation for non-stop consonants are determined by opposition of the thumb with the index and middle fingers as described in table 1. The ring finger controls voicing. Only *static* articulatory configurations are used as training points for the neural networks, and the interpolation between them is a result of the learning but is not explicitly trained. Ideally, the transitions should also be learned, but in the text-to-speech formant data we use for training [6] these transitions are poor, and it is very hard to extract formant trajectories from real speech accurately.

2.1 The Vowel/Consonant (V/C) Network

The V/C network decides, on the basis of the current configuration of the user's hand, to emit a vowel or a consonant sound. For the quantitative results reported here, we used a 10-5-1 feed-forward network with sigmoid activations [7]. The 10 inputs are ten scaled hand parameters measured with a Cyberglove: 8 flex angles (knuckle and middle joints of the thumb, index, middle and ring fingers), thumb abduction angle and thumb rotation angle. The output is a single number representing the probability that the hand configuration indicates a vowel. The output of the V/C network is used to gate the outputs of the vowel and consonant networks, which then produce a mixture of vowel and consonant formant parameters. The training data available includes only user-produced vowel or consonant sounds. The network interpolates between hand configurations to create a smooth but fairly rapid transition between vowels and consonants.

For quantitative analysis, typical training data consists of 2600 examples of consonant configurations (350 approximants, 1510 fricatives [and aspirant], and 740 nasals) and 700 examples of vowel configurations. The consonant examples were obtained from training data collected for the consonant network by an expert user. The vowel examples were collected from the user by requiring him to move his hand in vowel configurations for a specified amount of time. This procedure was performed in several sessions. The test set consists of 1614 examples (1380 consonants and 234 vowels). After training,[2] the mean squared error on the training and test

---

[1] In reality, the XY coordinates map more closely to changes in the first two formants, F1 and F2 of vowels. From the user's perspective though, the link to tongue movement is useful.

[2] The V/C network, the vowel network and the consonant network are trained using

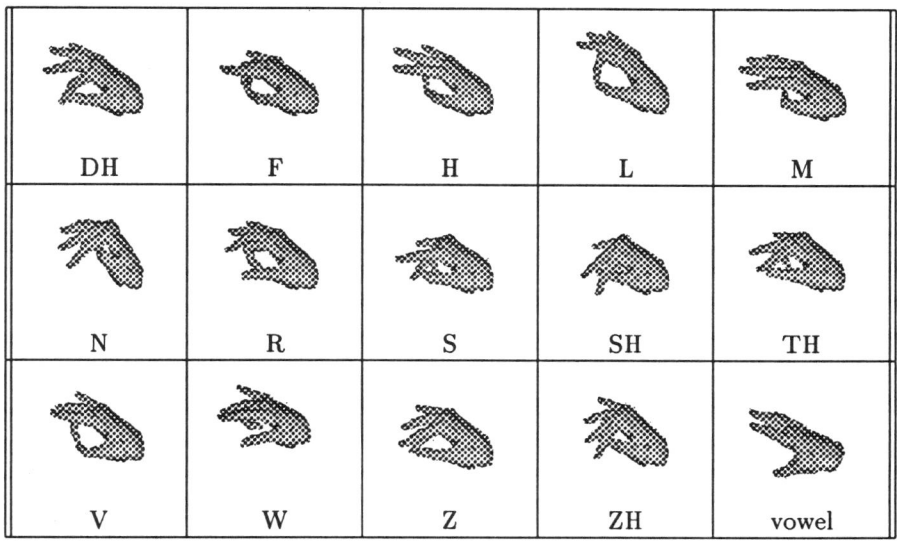

Table 1: Static Gesture-to-Consonant Mapping for all phonemes. Note, each gesture corresponds to a static *non-stop* consonant phoneme generated by the text-to-speech synthesizer.

set was less than 10^{-4}.

During normal speaking neither network made perceptual errors. The decision boundary feels quite sharp, and provides very predictable, quick transitions from vowels to consonants and back. Also, vowel sounds are produced when the user hyperextends his hand. Any unusual configurations that would intuitively be expected to produce consonant sounds do indeed produce consonant sounds.

2.2 The Vowel Network

The vowel network is a 2-11-8 feed forward network. The 11 hidden units are normalized radial basis functions (RBFs) [2] which are centered to respond to one of 11 cardinal vowels. The outputs are sigmoid units representing 8 synthesizer control parameters (ALF, F1, A1, F2, A2, F3, A3, AHF). The radial basis function used is:

$$o_j = e^{-\frac{\sum (w_{ji}-o_i)^2}{\sigma_j^2}} \quad (1)$$

where o_j is the (un-normalized) output of the RBF unit, w_{ji} is the weight from unit i to unit j, o_i is the output of input unit i, and σ_j^2 is the variance of the RBF. The normalization used is:

$$n_j = \frac{o_j}{\sum_{m \in P} o_m} \quad (2)$$

where n_j is the normalized output of unit j and the summation is over all the units in the group of normalized RBF units. The centres of the RBF units are fixed

---

conjugate gradient descent and a line search.

according to the X and Y values of each of the 11 vowels in the predefined mapping (see figure 2). The variances of the 11 RBF's are set to 0.025.

The weights from the RBF units to the output units are trained. For the training data, 100 identical examples of each vowel are generated from their corresponding X and Y positions in the user-defined mapping, providing 1100 examples. Noise is then added to the *scaled* X and Y coordinates for each example. The added noise is uniformly distributed in the range -0.025 to 0.025. In terms of unscaled ranges, these correspond to an X range of approximately $\pm$ 0.5 cm and a Y range of $\pm$ 0.26 cm.

Three different test sets were created. Each test set had 50 examples of each vowel for a total of 550 examples. The first test set used additive uniform noise in the interval $\pm$ 0.025. The second and third test sets used additive uniform noise in the interval $\pm$ 0.05 and $\pm$ 0.1 respectively.

The mean squared error on the training set was 0.0016. The MSE on the additive noise test sets (noise = $\pm$ 0.025, 0.05 and 0.01) was 0.0018, 0.0038, 0.0120 which corresponds to expected errors of 1.1%, 3.1% and 5.5% in the formant parameters, respectively. This network performs well perceptually. The key feature is the normalization of the RBF units. Often, when speaking, the user will overshoot cardinal vowel positions (especially when she is producing dipthongs) and all the RBF units will be quite suppressed. However, the normalization magnifies any slight difference between the activities of the units and the sound produced will be dominated by the cardinal vowel corresponding to the one whose centre is closest in hand space.

2.3 The Consonant Network

The consonant network is a 10-14-9 feed-forward network. The 14 hidden units are normalized RBF units. Each RBF is centred at a hand configuration determined from training data collected from the user corresponding to one of 14 static consonant phonemes. The target consonants are created with a text-to-speech synthesizer. Figure 1 defines the initial mapping for each of the 14 consonants. The 9 sigmoid output units represent 9 control parameters of the formant synthesizer (ALF, F1, A1, F2, A2, F3, A3, AHF, V). The voicing parameter is required since consonant sounds have different degrees of voicing. The inputs are the same as for the manager V/C network.

Training and test data for the consonant network is obtained from the user. Target data is created for each of the 14 consonant sounds using the text-to-speech synthesizer. The scheme to collect data for a single consonant is:

1. The target consonant is played for 100 msec through the speech synthesizer;

2. the user forms a hand configuration corresponding to the consonant;

3. the user depresses the foot pedal to begin recording; the start of recording is indicated by the appearance of a green square;

4. 10-15 time steps of hand data are collected and stored with the corresponding formant parameter targets and phoneme identifier; the end of data collection is indicated by turning the green square red;

5. the user chooses whether to save the data to a file, and whether to redo the current target or move to the next one.

Using this procedure 350 approximants, 1510 fricatives and 700 nasals were collected and scaled for the training data. The hand data were averaged for each consonant sound to form the RBF centres. For the test data, 255 approximants, 960 fricatives and 165 nasals were collected and scaled. The RBF variances were set to 0.05.

The mean square error on the training set was 0.005 and on the testing set was 0.01 corresponding to expected errors of 3.3% and 4.7% in the formant parameters, respectively. Listening to the output of the network reveals that each sound is produced reasonably well when the user's hand is held in a fixed position. The only difficulty is that the R and L sounds are very sensitive to motion of the index finger.

3 Qualitative Performance of Glove-TalkII

One subject, who is an accomplished pianist, has been trained extensively to speak with Glove-TalkII. We expected that his pianistic skill in forming finger patterns and his musical training would help him learn to speak with Glove-TalkII. After 100 hours of training, his speech with Glove-TalkII is intelligible and somewhat natural-sounding. He still finds it difficult to speak quickly, pronounce polysyllabic words, and speak spontaneously.

During his training, Glove-TalkII also adapted to suit changes required by the subject. Initially, good performance of the V/C network is critical for the user to learn to speak. If the V/C network performs poorly the user hears a mixture of vowel and consonant sounds making it difficult to adjust his hand configurations to say different utterances. For this reason, it is important to have the user comfortable with the initial mapping so that the training data collected leads to the V/C network performing well. In the 100 hours of practice, Glove-TalkII was retrained about 10 times. Four significant changes were made from the original system analysed here for the new subject. First, the NG sound was added to the non-stop consonant list by adding an additional hand shape, namely the user touches his pinkie to his thumb on his right hand. To accomodate this change, the consonant and V/C network had two inputs added to represent the two flex angles of the pinkie. Also, the consonant network has an extra hidden unit for the NG sound. Second, the consonant network was trained to allow the RBF centres to change. After the hidden-to-output weights were trained until little improvement was seen, the input-to-hidden weights (i.e. the RBF centres) were also allowed to adapt. This noticeably improved performance for the user. Third, the vowel mapping was altered so that the I was moved closer to the EE sound and the entire mapping was reduced to 75% of its size. Fourth, for this subject, the V/C network needed was a 10-10-1 feed-forward sigmoid unit network. Understanding the interaction between the user's adaptation and Glove-TalkII's adaptation remains an interesting research pursuit.

4 Summary

The initial mapping is loosely based on an articulatory model of speech. An open configuration of the hand corresponds to an unobstructed vocal tract, which in turn generates vowel sounds. Different vowel sounds are produced by movements of the hand in a horizontal X-Y plane that corresponds to movements of the first two formants which are roughly related to tongue position. Consonants other than stops are produced by closing the index, middle, or ring fingers or flexing the thumb, representing constrictions in the vocal tract. Stop consonants are produced by contact switches worn on the user's left hand. F0 is controlled by hand height and speaking intensity by foot pedal depression.

Glove-TalkII learns the user's interpretation of this initial mapping. The V/C network and the consonant network learn the mapping from examples generated by the user during phases of training. The vowel network is trained on examples computed from the user-defined mapping between hand-position and vowels. The F0 and volume mappings are non-adaptive.

One subject was trained to use Glove-TalkII. After 100 hours of practice he is able to speak intelligibly. His speech is fairly slow (1.5 to 3 times slower than normal speech) and somewhat robotic. It sounds similar to speech produced with a text-to-speech synthesizer but has a more natural intonation contour which greatly improves the intelligibility and naturalness of the speech. Reading novel passages intelligibly usually requires several attempts, especially with polysyllabic words. Intelligible spontaneous speech is possible but difficult.

Acknowledgements

We thank Peter Dayan, Sageev Oore and Mike Revow for their contributions. This research was funded by the Institute for Robotics and Intelligent Systems and NSERC. Geoffrey Hinton is the Noranda fellow of the Canadian Institute for Advanced Research.

References

[1] A. G. Bell. Making a talking-machine. In *Beinn Bhreagh Recorder*, pages 61–72, November 1909.

[2] D. Broomhead and D. Lowe. Multivariable functional interpolation and adaptive networks. *Complex Systems*, 2:321–355, 1988.

[3] Homer Dudley, R. R. Riesz, and S. S. A. Watkins. A synthetic speaker. *Journal of the Franklin Institute*, 227(6):739–764, June 1939.

[4] S. S. Fels. Building adaptive interfaces using neural networks: The Glove-Talk pilot study. Technical Report CRG-TR-90-1, University of Toronto, 1990.

[5] P. Ladefoged. *A course in Phonetics (2 ed.)*. Harcourt Brace Javanovich, New York, 1982.

[6] E. Lewis. A 'C' implementation of the JSRU text-to-speech system. Technical report, Computer Science Dept., University of Bristol, 1989.

[7] D. E. Rumelhart, G. E. Hinton, and R. J. Williams. Learning internal representations by back-propagating errors. *Nature*, 323:533–536, 1986.

[8] J. M. Rye and J. N. Holmes. A versatile software parallel-formant speech synthesizer. Technical Report JSRU-RR-1016, Joint Speech Research Unit, Malvern, UK, 1982.

[9] Wolfgang Ritter von Kempelen. *Mechanismus der menschlichen Sprache nebst Beschreibungeiner sprechenden Maschine. Mit einer Einleitung vonHerbert E. Brekle und Wolfgang Wild*. Stuttgart-Bad Cannstatt F. Frommann, Stuttgart, 1970.

Visual Speech Recognition with Stochastic Networks

Javier R. Movellan
Department of Cognitive Science
University of California San Diego
La Jolla, Ca 92093-0515

Abstract

This paper presents ongoing work on a speaker independent visual speech recognition system. The work presented here builds on previous research efforts in this area and explores the potential use of simple hidden Markov models for limited vocabulary, speaker independent visual speech recognition. The task at hand is recognition of the first four English digits, a task with possible applications in car-phone dialing. The images were modeled as mixtures of independent Gaussian distributions, and the temporal dependencies were captured with standard left-to-right hidden Markov models. The results indicate that simple hidden Markov models may be used to successfully recognize relatively unprocessed image sequences. The system achieved performance levels equivalent to untrained humans when asked to recognize the first four English digits.

1 INTRODUCTION

Visual articulation is an important source of information in face to face speech perception. Laboratory studies have shown that visual information allows subjects to tolerate an extra 4-dB of noise in the acoustic signal. This is particularly important considering that each decibel of signal to noise ratio translates into a 10-15% error reduction in the intelligibility of entire sentences (McCleod and Summerfield, 1990). Lip reading alone provides a basis for understanding for a large majority of the hearing impaired and when supplemented by acoustic or electrical signals it allows fluent understanding of speech in highly trained subjects. However visual information plays more than a simple compensatory role in speech perception. From early on humans are predisposed to integrate acoustic and visual information. Sensitivity to correspondences in auditory and visual information for speech events has been shown in 4 month old infants (Spelke, 1976; Kuhl & Meltzoff, 1982). By 6 years of age, humans consistently use audio visual contingencies to understand speech (Massaro, 1987). By adulthood, visual articulation automatically modulates perception of the acoustic signal. Under laboratory conditions it is possible to create powerful illusions in which subjects mistakenly hear sounds which are biased by visual articulations. Subjects in these experiments are typically unaware of

the discrepancy between the visual and auditory tracks and their experience is that of a unified auditory percept (McGurk & McDonnald, 1976).
Recent years have seen a revival of interest in audiovisual speech perception both in psychology and in the pattern recognition literature. There have been isolated efforts to build synthetic models of visual and audio-visual speech recognition (Petahan, 1985; Nishida, 1986; Yuhas, Goldstein, Sejnowski & Jenkins, 1988; Bregler, Manke, Hild & Waibel, 1993; Wolff, Prassad, Stork, & Hennecke, 1994). The main goal of these efforts has been to explore different architectures and visual processing techniques and to illustrate the potential use of visual information to improve the robustness of current speech recognition systems. Cognitive psychologists have also developed high level models of audio-visual speech perception that describe regularities in the way humans integrate visual and acoustic information (Massaro, 1987). In general these studies support the idea that human responses to visual and acoustic stimuli are conditional independent. This regularity has been used in some synthetic systems to simplify the task of integrating visual and acoustic signals (Wolff, Prassad, Stork, & Hennecke, 1994). Overall, multimodal speech perception is still an emerging field in which a lot of exploration needs to be done. The work presented here builds on the previous research efforts in this area and explores the potential use of simple hidden Markov models for limited vocabulary, speaker independent visual speech recognition. The task at hand is recognition of the first four English digits, a task with possible applications in car-phone dialing.

2 TRAINING SAMPLE

The training sample consisted of 96 digitized movies of 12 undergraduate students (9 males, 3 females) from the Cognitive Science Department at UCSD. Video capturing was performed in a windowless room at the Center for Research in Language at UCSD. Subjects were asked to talk into a video camera and to say the first four digits in English twice. Subjects could monitor the digitized images in a small display conveniently located in front of them. They were asked to position themselves so that that their lips be roughly centered in the feed-back display. Gray scale video images were digitized at 30 fps, 100x75 pixels, 8 bits per pixel. The video tracks were hand segmented by selecting a few relevant frames before and after the beginning and end of activity in the acoustic track. Statistics of the entire training sample are shown in table 1.

Table 1: Frame number statistics.

Digit	Average	S.D.
"One"	8.9	2.1
"Two"	9.6	2.1
"Three"	9.7	2.3
"Four"	10.6	2.2

3 IMAGE PREPROCESSING

There are two different approaches to visual preprocessing in the visual speech recognition literature (Bregler, Manke, Hild & Waibel, 1993). The first approach, represented by the work of Wolff and colleagues (Wolff, Prassad, Stork, & Hennecke, 1994) favors sophisticated image preprocessing techniques to extract a limited set of hand-crafted features (e.g., height and width of the lips). The advantage of this approach is that it drastically reduces the number of input dimensions. This translates into lower variability of the signal, potentially improved generalization, and large savings in computing time. The disadvantage is that vital information may be lost when compressing the image into a limited set of hand-crafted features. Variability is reduced at the possible expense of bias. Moreover, tests have shown that subtle holistic features such as the wrinkling and protrusion of the lips may play an important role in human lip-reading (Montgomery & Jackson, 1983). The second approach to visual preprocessing emphasizes preserving the original images as much as possible and letting the recognition engine discover the relevant features in the images. In most cases, images are low-pass filtered and dimension-reduced by using principal component analysis. The results in this papers indicate that good results can be obtained even without the use of principal components. In this investigation image preprocessing consisted of the following phases:

1. Symmetry enforcement: At each time frame the raw images were symmetrized by averaging pixel by pixel the left and right side of each image, using the vertical midline as the axis of symmetry. For convenience from now on we will refer to the raw images as "rho-images" and the symmetrized images as "sigma-images." The potential benefits of sigma-images are robustness, and compression, since the number of relevant pixels is reduced by half.

2. Temporal differentiaion: At each time frame we calculated the pixel by pixel differences between present sigma-images and immediately past sigma-images. For convenience we refer to the resulting images as "delta-images." One of the potential advantages of delta-images in the visual domain is their robustness to changes in illumination and the fact that they emphasize the dynamic aspects of the visual track.

3. Low pass filtering and subsampling: The sigma and delta images were compressed and subsampled using 20x15 equidistant Gaussian filters. Different values of the standard deviation of the Gaussian filters were tested.

4. Logistic thresholding and scaling: The sigma and delta images were independently thresholded by feeding the output of the Gaussian filters through a according to the following equation

$$y = 256 f(K \frac{\pi}{\sqrt{3}\sigma}(x - \mu))$$

where f is the logistic function, and μ, σ, are respectively the average and standard deviation of the gray level distribution of entire image sequences. The constant K controls the sharpness of the logistic function. Assuming an approximately Gaussian distribution of gray levels when K=1 the thresholding function approximates histogram equalization, a standard technique in visual processing. Three different K values were tried: 0.3, 0.6 and 1.2.

5. Composites of the relevant portions of the blurred sigma and delta images were fed to the recognition network. The number of pixels of each processed image was 300 (150 from the blurred sigma images and 150 from the blurred delta images). Figure 1 shows the effect of the different preprocessing stages.

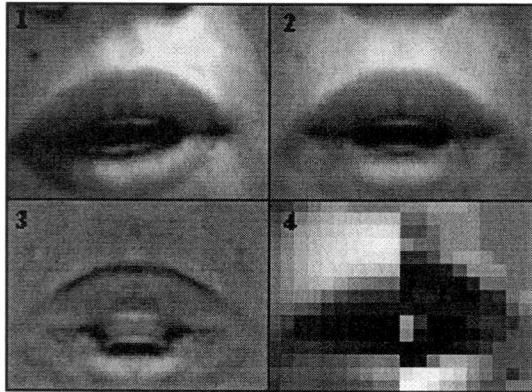

Figure 1: Image Preprocessing. 1) Rho-Image. 2) Sigma-Image. 3) Delta-Image. 4) Filtered and Sharpened Composite.

4 RECOGNITION NETWORK

We used the standard approach in limited vocabulary systems: a bank of hidden Markov models, one per word category, independently trained on the corresponding word categories. The images were modeled as mixtures of continuous probability distributions in pixel space. We tried mixtures of Gaussians and mixtures of Cauchy distributions. The mixtures of Cauchy distributions were very stable numerically but they did perform very poorly when compared to the Gaussian mixtures. We believe the reason for their poor performance is the tendency of Cauchy-based maximum-likelihood estimates to focus on individual exemplars. Gaussian-based estimates are much more prone to blend exemplars that belong to the same cluster. The initial state probabilities, transition probabilities, mixture coefficients, mixture centroids and variance parameters were trained using the E-M algorithm.

We initially encountered severe numerical underflow problems when using the E-M algorithm with Gaussian mixtures. These instabilities were due to the fact that the probability densities of images rapidly went to zero due to the large dimensionality of the images. Trimming the outputs of the Gaussian and using very small Gaussian gains did not work well. We solved the numerical problems in the following way: 1) Constraining all the variance parameters for all the states and mixtures to be equal. This allowed pulling out a constant in the likelihood-function of the mixtures, avoiding most numerical problems. 2) Initializing the mixture centroids using linear segmentation followed by the K-means clustering algorithm. For example, if there were 4 visual frames and 2 states, the first 2 frames were assigned to state 1 and the last 2 frames to state 2. K-means was then used independently on each of the states and their assigned frames. This is a standard initialization method in the acoustic domain (Rabiner & Bing-Hwang, 1993). Since K-means can be trapped in local minima, the algorithm was repeated 20 times with different starting point and the best solution was fed as the starting point for the E-M algorithm.

5 RESULTS

The main purpose of this study was to find simple image preprocessing techniques that would work well with hidden Markov models. We tested a wide variety of architectures and preprocessing parameters. In all cases the results were evaluated in terms of generalization to new speakers. Since the training sample is small, generalization performance was estimated using the jackknife procedure. Models were trained with 11 subjects, leaving one subject out for generalization testing. The entire procedure was repeated 12 times, each time leaving a different subject out for testing. Results are thus based on 96 generalization trials (4 digits x 12 subjects x 2 observations per subject). In all cases we tested several preprocessing techniques using 20 different architectures with different number of states (1,3,5,7,9) and mixtures per state (1,3,5,7). To compare the effect of each processing technique we used the average generalization performance of the best 4 architectures out of the 20 architectures tested.

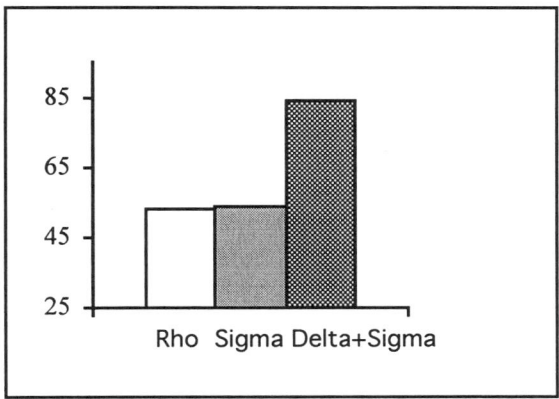

Figure 2: Average performance with the rho, sigma, and delta images.

Figure 2 shows the effects of symmetry enforcement and temporal differentiation. Symmetry enforcement had the benefit of reducing the input dimensionality by half and, as the figure show it did not hinder recognition performance. Using delta images had a very positive effect on recognition performance, as the figure shows. Figure 3 shows the effect of varying the thresholding constant and the standard deviation of the Gaussian filters. Best performance was obtained with blurring windows about 4 pixel wide and with thresholding just about histogram equalization.

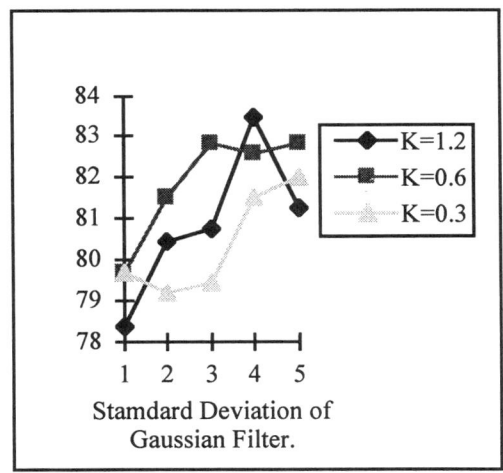

Figure 3: Effect of blurring and sharpening.

Table 2 shows the effects of variations in the number of states (S) and Gaussian mixtures (G) per state. The number within each cell is the percentage of simulations for which a particular combination of states and mixtures performed best out of the 20 architectures tested.

Table 2: Effect of varying the the number of states (S) and Gaussian mixtures (G).

	G1	G3	G5	G7
S1	0.00%	0.00%	0.00%	0.00%
S3	0.00%	21.87%	12.5%	6.25%
S5	3.12%	9.37%	15.62%	0.00%
S7	6.25%	12.5%	0.00%	3.12%
S9	6.25%	0.00%	3.12%	0.00%

Best overall performance was obtained with about 3 states and 3 mixtures per state. Peak performance was also obtained with a 3-state, 3-mixture per state network, with a generalization rate of 89.58% correct.
To compare these results with human performance, 9 subjects were tested on the same sample. Six subjects were normal hearing adults who were not trained in lip-reading. Three were hearing impaired with profound hearing loss and had received training in lip reading at 2 to 8 years of age. The mean correct response for normal subjects was 89.93 % correct, just about the same rate as the best artificial network. The hearing impaired had an average performance of 95.49% correct, significantly better than our network.

Table 3: Confusion matrix of the best artificial system.

	1	2	3	4
"One"	100.00%	0.00%	0.00%	0.00%
"Two"	4.17%	87.50%	4.17%	4.17%
"Three"	12.5%	0.00%	83.33%	4.17%
"Four"	8.33%	4.17%	0.00%	87.50%

Table 4: Average human confusion matrix.

	1	2	3	4
"One"	89.36%	0.46%	8.33%	1.85%
"Two"	1.39%	98.61%	0.00%	0.00%
"Three"	9.25%	3.24%	85.64%	1.87%
"Four"	4.17%	0.46%	1.85%	93.52%

Tables 3 and 4 show the confusion matrices for the best network and the average confusion matrix with all 9 subjects combined. The correlation between these two matrices was 0.99. This means that 98% of the variance in human confusions can be accounted for by the artificial model. This suggests that the representational space learned by the artificial system may be a reasonable model of the representational space used by humans. Figure 5 shows the representations learned by a network with 6 states and 1 mixture per state. Each column is a different digit, starting with "one." Each row is a different temporal state. The two pictures within each cell are sigma and delta image centroids. As the figure shows, the identity of individual exemplars is lost but the underlying dynamics of the digits are preserved. The digits can be easily recognized when played as a movie.

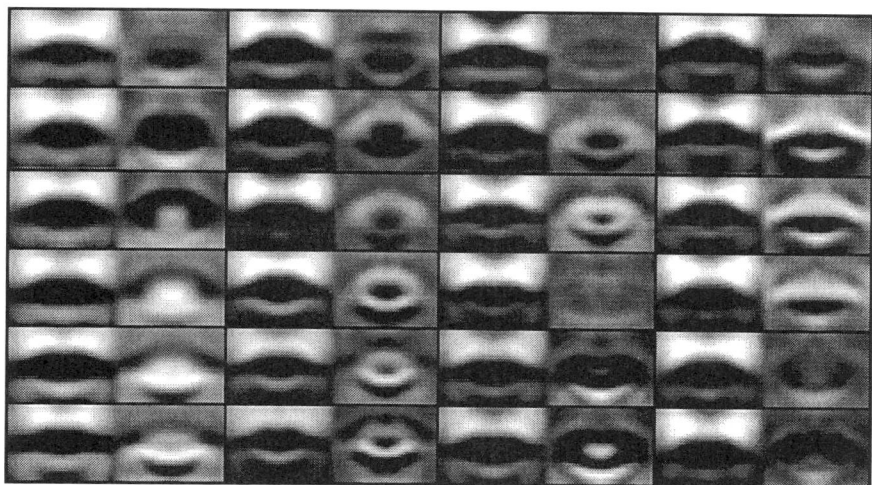

Figure 4: Dynamic representations learned by a simple network.

6   CONCLUSIONS

This paper shows that simple stochastic networks, like hidden Markov models, can be successfully applied for visual speech recognition using relatively unprocessed images. The performance level obtained with these networks roughly matches untrained human performance. Moreover, the representational space learned by these networks may be a reasonable model of the representations used by humans. More research should be done to better understand how humans integrate visual and acoustic information in speech perception and to develop practical models for robust audio-visual speech recognition.

References

Bregler C., Manke S., Hild H. & Waibel A. (1993) Bimodal Sensor Integration on the Example of "Speech-Reading". *Proc ICNN-93*, II, 667-677.

Kuhl P. & Meltzoff A (1982) The Bimodal Development of Speech in Infancy. *Science*, 218, 1138-1141.

MacLeod A. & Summerfield Q. (1990) A Procedure for Measuring Auditory and Audio-visual Speech-Reception Measuring Thresholds for Sentences in Noise: Rationale, Evaluation and Recommendations for Use. *British Journal of Audiology*. 24, 29-43.

Massaro D. (1987) Speech Perception by Ear and Eye. In Dodd B. & Campbell R. (ed.) *Hearing by Eye: The Psychology of Lip-Reading*. London, LEA, 53-83.

Massaro D., Cohen M & Getsi (1993) Long-Term Training, Transfer and Retention in Learning to Lip-read. *Perception and Psychophysics,* 53, 549-562.

McGurk H. & MacDonald J. (1976) Hearing Lips and Seeing Voices. *Nature*, 264, 126-130.

Montgomery A. & Jackson P. (1983) Physical Characteristics of the Lips Underlying Vowel Lipreading Performance. *Journal of the Acoustical Society of America*, 73, 2134-2144.

Nishida S. (1986) Speech Recognition Enhancement by Lip Information. *Proceedings of ACM/CHI 86*, 198-204.

Petajan E. (1985) Automatic Lip Reading to Enhance Speech Recognition. *IEEE CVPR 85*, 40-47.

Rabiner L., Bing-Hwang J. (1993) *Fundamentals of Speech Recognition*. New Jersey, Prentice Hall.

Spelke E. (1976) Infant's Intermodal Perception of Events. *Cognitive Psychology*, 8, 533-560.

Yuhas B., Goldstein T., Sejnowski T., Jenkins R. (1988) Neural Network Models of Sensory Integration for Improved Vowel Recognition. *Proceedings IEEE 78*, 1655-1668.

Wolff G., Prassad L., Stork D., Hennecke M. (1994) Lipreading by Neural Networks: Visual Preprocessing, Learning and Sensory Integration. In J. Cowan, G. Tesauro, J. Alspector (ed.), *Advances in Neural Information Processing Systems 6*, 1027-1035. San Mateo, CA: Morgan Kaufmann.

Hierarchical Mixtures of Experts Methodology Applied to Continuous Speech Recognition

Ying Zhao, Richard Schwartz, Jason Sroka**, John Makhoul
BBN System and Technologies
70 Fawcett Street
Cambridge MA 02138

Abstract

In this paper, we incorporate the Hierarchical Mixtures of Experts (HME) method of probability estimation, developed by Jordan [1], into an HMM-based continuous speech recognition system. The resulting system can be thought of as a continuous-density HMM system, but instead of using gaussian mixtures, the HME system employs a large set of hierarchically organized but relatively small neural networks to perform the probability density estimation. The hierarchical structure is reminiscent of a decision tree except for two important differences: each "expert" or neural net performs a "soft" decision rather than a hard decision, and, unlike ordinary decision trees, the parameters of all the neural nets in the HME are automatically trainable using the EM algorithm. We report results on the ARPA 5,000-word and 40,000-word Wall Street Journal corpus using HME models.

1 Introduction

Recent research has shown that a continuous-density HMM (CD-HMM) system can outperform a more constrained tied-mixture HMM system for large-vocabulary continuous speech recognition (CSR) when a large amount of training data is available [2]. In other work, the utility of decision trees has been demonstrated in classification problems by using the "divide and conquer" paradigm effectively, where a problem is divided into a hierarchical set of simpler problems. We present here a new CD-HMM system which

---
**MIT, Cambridge MA 02139

has similar properties and possesses the same advantages as decision trees, but has the additional important advantage of having automatically trainable "soft" decision boundaries.

2 Hierarchical Mixtures of Experts

The method of Hierarchical Mixtures of Experts (HME) developed recently by Jordan [1] breaks a large scale task into many small ones by partitioning the input space into a nested set of regions, then building a simple but specific model (local expert) in each region. The idea behind this method follows the principle of divide-and-conquer which has been utilized in certain approaches to classification problems, such as decision trees. In the decision tree approach, at each level of the tree, the data are divided explicitly into regions. In contrast, the HME model makes use of "soft" splits of the data, i.e., instead of the data being explicitly divided into regions, the data may lie simultaneously in multiple regions with certain probabilities. Therefore, the variance-increasing effect of lopping off distant data in the decision tree can be ameliorated. Furthermore, the "hard" boundaries in the decision tree are fixed once a decision is made, while the "soft" boundaries in the HME are parameterized with generalized sigmoidal functions, which can be adjusted automatically using the Expectation-Maximization (EM) algorithm during the splitting.

Now we describe how to apply the HME methodology to the CSR problem. For each state of a phonetic HMM, a separate HME is used to estimate the likelihood. The actual HME first computes a posterior probability $P(l|x,s)$, the probability of phoneme class l, given the input feature vector x and state s. That probability is then divided by the *a priori* probability of the phone class l at state s. A one-level HME performs the following computation:

$$P(l|x,s) = \sum_{i=1}^{C} P(l|c_i, x, s) P(c_i|x, s) \qquad (1)$$

where $l = 1, ..., L$ indicates phoneme class, c_i represents a local region in the input space, and C is the number of regions. $P(c_i|x,s)$ can be viewed as a gating network, while $P(l|c_i, x, s)$ can be viewed as a local expert classifier (expert network) in the region c_i [1]. In a two-level HME, each region c_i is divided in turn into C subregions. The term $P(l|c_i, x, s)$ is then computed in a similar manner to equation (1), and so on. If in some of these subregions there are no data available, we back off to the parent network.

3 TECHNICAL DETAILS

As in Jordan's paper, we use a generalized sigmoidal function to parameterize $P(c_i|x)$ as follows:

$$P(c_i|x) = \frac{e^{v_i^T x}}{\sum_j e^{v_j^T x}} \qquad (2)$$

where x can be the direct input (in a one-layer neural net) or the hidden layer vector (in a two-layer neural net), and $v_i, i = 1, ..., C$ are weights which need to train. Similarly, the local phoneme classifier in region c_i, $P(l|c_i, x)$, can be parameterized with a generalized sigmoidal function also:

$$P(l|c_i, x) = \frac{e^{\theta_{li}^T x}}{\sum_j e^{\theta_{ji}^T x}} \quad (3)$$

where $\theta_{ji}, j = 1, ..., L$ are weights. The whole system consists of two set of parameters: $v_i, i = 1, ..., C$ and $\theta_{ji}, j = 1, ..., L, \Theta = \{\theta_{ji}, v_i\}$. All parameters are estimated by using the EM algorithm.

The EM is an iterative approach to maximum likelihood estimation. Each iteration of an EM algorithm is composed of two steps: an Expectation (E) step and a Maximization (M) step. The M step involves the maximization of a likelihood function that is redefined in each iteration by the E step. Using the parameterizations in (2) and (3), we obtain the following iterative procedure for computing parameters $\Theta = \{v_i, \theta_{ji}\}$:

1. initialize $v_i^{(0)}$ and $\theta_{ji}^{(0)}$ for $i = 1, ..., C, j = 1, ..., L$.
2. E-step: In each iteration n, for each data pair $(x(t), l(t)), t = 1, ..., N$, compute

$$\begin{aligned} z_i(t)^{(n)} &= P(c_i|x(t), l(t), \Theta^{(n)}) \\ &= \frac{P(c_i|x(t), v_i^{(n)})P(l(t)|c_i, x(t), \theta_{l(t),i}^{(n)})}{\sum_k P(c_k|x(t), v_k^{(n)})P(l(t)|c_k, x(t), \theta_{l(t),k}^{(n)})} \end{aligned} \quad (4)$$

where $i = 1, ..., C$. $z_i(t)^{(n)}$ represents the probability of the data t lying in the region i, given the current parameter estimation $\Theta^{(n)}$. It will be used as a weight for this data in the region i in the M-step. The idea of "soft" splitting reflects that these weights are probabilities between 0 and 1, instead of a "hard"decision 0 or 1.
3. M-step:

$$\theta_i^{(n+1)} = \max_{\theta_i} \sum_t z_i(t)^{(n)} [\log \frac{e^{\theta_{l(t),i}^T x(t)}}{\sum_j e^{\theta_{ji}^T x(t)}}] \quad (5)$$

$$v_{i=1,...,C}^{(n+1)} = \max_{v_1,...,v_C} \sum_t \sum_k z_k(t)^{(n)} \log \frac{e^{v_i^T x(t)}}{\sum_j e^{v_j^T x(t)}} \quad (6)$$

4. Iterate until θ_{ji}, v_i converge.

The first maximization means fitting a generalized sigmoidal model (3) using the labeled data $(x(t), l(t))$ and weighting $z_i(t)^{(n)}$. The second one means fitting a generalized sigmoidal model (2) using inputs $x(t)$ and outputs $z_i(t)^{(n)}$. The criterion for fitting is the cross-entropy. Typically, the fitting can be solved by the Newton-Raphson method. However, it is quite expensive. Viewing this type of fitting as a multi-class classification task, we developed a technique to invert a generalized sigmoidal function more efficiently, which will be described in the following.

A common method in a multi-class classification is to divide the problem into many 2-class classifications. However, this method results in a positive and negative training unbalance usually. To avoid the positive and negative training unbalance, the following technique can be used to solve multi-class posterior probabilities simultaneously.

Suppose we have a labeled data set, $(x(t), l(t)), t = 1, ..., N$, where $l(t) \in \{1, ..., L\}$ is the label for t-th data. We use a generalized sigmoidal function to model the posterior probability $P(l|x)$, where $l = 1, ..., L$ as follows:

$$P_l(x) = P(l|x) = \frac{e^{\theta_l^T x}}{\sum_k e^{\theta_k^T x}} \tag{7}$$

Obviously, since these probabilities sum up to one, we have

$$P_L(x) = 1 - \sum_{l=1}^{L-1} P_l(x). \tag{8}$$

Now, a training sample $x(t)$ with a class label $l(t)$ can be interpreted as:

$$P_l(x(t)) = \begin{cases} 0.9 & l = l(t) \\ \frac{0.1}{L-1} & l \neq l(t) \end{cases} \tag{9}$$

If we define

$$\theta_l^T x = \log \frac{P_l(x)}{P_L(x)} \tag{10}$$

equation (10) implies that

$$P_l(x) = \frac{e^{\theta_l^T x}}{\sum_l^L e^{\theta_l^T x}} \tag{11}$$

for $l = 1, ..., L$ with $\theta_L^T x = 0$. This expression is the generalized sigmoidal function in (7). This means, we can train parameters in (7) to satisfy Equation (10) from the data. Using a least squares criterion, the objective is

$$\min \sum_t \left[\theta_l^T x(t) - \log \frac{P_l(x(t))}{P_L(x(t))} \right]^2 \tag{12}$$

for $l = 1, ..., L - 1$. Denote a data matrix as

$$X = \begin{bmatrix} x(1) \\ x(2) \\ \cdot \\ \cdot \\ \cdot \\ x(N) \end{bmatrix}$$

A least squares solution to (12) is

$$\theta_l = (\log a)(X^T X)^{-1} \left[\sum_{l(t)=l} x(t) - \sum_{l(t)=L} x(t) \right] \tag{13}$$

for $l = 1, ..., L$, where $a = 9(L - 1)$. Substituting (13) into (11), we get

$$P_l(x) = \frac{a^{x^T (X^T X)^{-1} \sum_{l(t)=l} x(t)}}{\sum_k a^{x^T (X^T X)^{-1} \sum_{l(t)=k} x(t)}} \tag{14}$$

Equation (13) and (14) are very easy to compute. Basically, we only have to accumulate the matrix $X^T X$ and sum $x(t)$ into different classes $l = 1, ..., L$. We can obtain probabilities $P_l(x)$ by a single inversion of matrix $X^T X$ after a pass through the training data.

4 Relation to Other Work

The work reported here is very different from our previous work utilizing neural nets for CSR. There, a single segmental neural network (SNN) is used to model a complete phonetic segment [3]. Here, each HME estimates the probability density for each state of a phonetic HMM. The work here is more similar to that by Cohen *et al.* [4], the major difference being that in [4], a single very large neural net is used to perform the probability density modeling. The training of such a large network requires the use of a specialized parallel processing machine, so that the training can be done in a reasonable amount of time. By using the HME method and dividing the problem into many smaller problems, we are able to perform the needed training computation on regular workstations.

Most of the previous work on CD-HMM work has utilized mixtures of gaussians to estimate the probability densities of an HMM. Since a multilayer feedforward neural network is a universal continuous function approximator, we decided to explore the use of neural nets as an alternative approach for continuous density estimation.

5 Experimental Results

	Word Error Rate
HMM	7.8
SNN	8.5
HMM+SNN	7.1
HME	7.6
HME + HMM	6.8
Prior-modified HME + HMM	6.2

Table 1: Error Rates for the ARPA WSJ 5K Development Test, Trigram Grammar

	Word Error Rate
HMM	9.5
HME + HMM	8.7

Table 2: Error Rates for the ARPA WSJ 40K Test Set, Trigram Grammar

In our initial application of the HME method to large-vocabulary CSR, we used phonetic context-independent HMEs to estimate the likelihoods at each state of 5-state HMMs. We implemented a two-level HME, with the input space divided into 46 regions, and each of those regions is further divided into 46 subregions. The initial divisions were accomplished by supervised training, with each division trained to one of the 46 phonemes in the system. All gating and local expert networks in the HME had identical structures — a two-layer generalized sigmoidal network. The whole HME system was implemented within an N-best paradigm [3], where the recognized sequence was obtained as a result of a rescoring of an N-best list obtained from our baseline BYBLOS system (tied-mixture HMM) with a statistical trigram grammar.

We then built a context-dependent HME system based on the structure of the context-independent HME models described above. For each state, the whole training data was divided into 46 parts according to its left or right context. Then for each context, a separate HME model was built for that context. To be computationally feasible, we used only one-level HMEs here. We first experimented using a left-context and right-context model.

We tested the HME implementation on the ARPA 5,000-word Wall Street Journal corpus (WSJ1, H2 dev set). We report the word error rates on the same test set for a number of different systems. Table 1 shows the word error rates for i) the baseline HMM system; ii) the segment-based neural net system (SNN) iii) the hybrid SNN/HMM system iv) a HME system alone. v) a HME system combined with HMM; vi) a HME +HMM system with modified priors.

From Table 1, The performance of the baseline tied-mixture HMM is 7.8%. The performance of the SNN system (8.5%) is comparable to the HMM alone. We see that the performance of a HME (7.6%) is as good as the HMM system, which is better than the SNN system. When combined with the baseline HMM system, the HME and SNN both improve performance over the HMM alone about 10% from 7.8% to 6.8% and from 7.8% to 7.1% respectively. We found out that the improvement could be made larger for a hybrid HME/HMM by adjusting the context-dependent priors with the context-independent priors, and then smooth context-dependent models with a context-independent model.

More specifically, in a context-dependent HME model, we usually estimate the posterior probability phoneme l, $P(l|c, x, s)$, given left or right context c and the acoustic input x in a particular state s. Because the samples may be sparse for many of context models, it is necessary to regularize (smooth) context-dependent models with a context-independent model, where there is much more data available. However, since the two models have different priors: $P(l|c, s)$ in a context-dependent model and $P(l|s)$ in a context-independent model, a simple interpolation between the two models which is $P(l|c, x, s) = \frac{P(x|l,c,s)P(l|c,s)}{P(x|c,s)}$ in a context-dependent model and $P(l|x, s) = \frac{P(x|l,s)P(l|s)}{P(x|s)}$ in a context-independent model is inconsistent. To scale the context-dependent priors $P(l|c, s)$ with a context-independent prior $P(l|s)$, we weighted each input data point x with the weight $\frac{P(l|s)}{P(l|c,s)}$ for a prior adjusting. After this modification, a context-dependent HME actually estimates $\frac{P(x|l,c,x)P(l|s)}{P(x|s)}$. It combines better with a context-independent model. For the same experiment we showed in Table 1, the word error for the HME (with HMM) dropped from 6.8% to 6.2% when priors were modified. For this 5,000-word development set, we got a total of about 20% word error reduction over the tied-mixture HMM system using a HME-based neural network system.

We then switched our experiment domain from a 5,000-word to 40,000-word the test set. During this year, the BYBLOS system has been improved from a tied-mixture system to a continuous density system. We also switched to using this new continuous density BYBLOS in our hybrid HME/HMM system. The language model used here was a 40,000-word trigram grammar. The result is shown in Table 2.

From Table 2, we see that there is about a 10% word error rate reduction over the continuous density HMM system by combining a context-dependent HME system. Compared with the 20% improvement over the tied-mixture system we made for the 5,000-word development set, the improvement over the continuous density system in this 40,000-word development is less. This may be due to the big improvement of the HMM system itself.

6 CONCLUSIONS

The method of hierarchical mixtures of experts can be used as a continous density estimator to speech recognition. Experimental results showed that estimations from this approach are consistent with the estimations from the HMM system. The frame-based neural net system using hierarchical mixtures of experts improves the performance of both the state-of-the-art tied mixture HMM system and the continuous density HMM system. The HME system itself has the same performance as the state-of-the-art tied mixture HME system.

7 Acknowledgments

This work was funded by the Advanced Research Projects Agency of the Department of Defense.

References

[1] Michael Jordan, "Hierarchical Mixtures of Experts and the EM Algorithm," *Neural Computation*, 1994, in press.

[2] D. Pallett, J. Fiscus, W. Fisher, J. Garofolo, B. Lund, and M. Pryzbocki, "1993 Benchmark Tests for the ARPA Spoken Language Program," *Proc. ARPA Human Language Technology Workshop*, Plainsboro, NJ, Morgan Kaufman Publishers, 1994.

[3] G. Zavaliagkos, Y. Zhao, R. Schwartz and J. Makhoul, "A Hybrid Neural Net System for State-of-the-Art Continuous Speech Recognition," in *Advances in Neural Information Processing Systems 5*, S. J. Hanson, J. D. Cowan and C. L. Giles, eds., Morgan Kaufmann Publishers, 1993.

[4] M. Cohen, H. Franco, N. Morgan, D. Rumelhart and V. Abrash, "Context-Dependent Multiple Distribution Phonetic Modeling with MLPS," in *Advances in Neural Information Processing Systems 5*, S. J. Hanson, J. D. Cowan and C. L. Giles, eds., Morgan Kaufmann Publishers, 1993.

Connectionist Speaker Normalization with Generalized Resource Allocating Networks

Cesare Furlanello
Istituto per La Ricerca
Scientifica e Tecnologica
Povo (Trento), Italy
furlan@irst.it

Diego Giuliani
Istituto per La Ricerca
Scientifica e Tecnologica
Povo (Trento), Italy
giuliani@irst.it

Edmondo Trentin
Istituto per La Ricerca
Scientifica e Tecnologica
Povo (Trento), Italy
trentin@irst.it

Abstract

The paper presents a rapid speaker-normalization technique based on neural network spectral mapping. The neural network is used as a front-end of a continuous speech recognition system (speaker-dependent, HMM-based) to normalize the input acoustic data from a new speaker. The spectral difference between speakers can be reduced using a limited amount of new acoustic data (40 phonetically rich sentences). Recognition error of phone units from the acoustic-phonetic continuous speech corpus APASCI is decreased with an adaptability ratio of 25%. We used local basis networks of elliptical Gaussian kernels, with recursive allocation of units and on-line optimization of parameters ($GRAN$ model). For this application, the model included a linear term. The results compare favorably with multivariate linear mapping based on constrained orthonormal transformations.

1 INTRODUCTION

Speaker normalization methods are designed to minimize inter-speaker variations, one of the principal error sources in automatic speech recognition. Training a speech recognition system on a particular speaker (speaker-dependent or SD mode) generally gives better performance than using a speaker-independent system, which is trained to recognize speech from a generic user by averaging over individual differences. On the other hand, performance may be dramatically worse when a SD system "tailored" on the acoustic characteristics of a speaker (the *reference* speaker) is used by another one (the *new* or *target* speaker). Training a SD system for any new speaker may be unfeasible: collecting a large amount of new training data is time consuming for the speaker and unacceptable in some applications. Given a pre-trained SD speech recognition system, the goal of normalization methods is then to reduce to a few sentences the amount of training data required from a new speaker to achieve acceptable recognition performance. The inter-speaker variation of the acoustic data is reduced by estimating a feature vector transformation between the acoustic parameter space of the new speaker and that of the reference speaker (Montacie et al., 1989; Class et al., 1990; Nakamura and Shikano, 1990; Huang, 1992; Matsukoto and Inoue, 1992). This multivariate transformation, also called *spectral mapping* given the type of features considered in the parameterization of speech data, provides an acoustic front-end to the recognition system. Supervised speaker normalization methods require that the text of the training utterances required from the new speaker is known, while arbitrary utterances can be used by unsupervised methods (Furui and Sondhi, 1991). Good performance have been achieved with spectral mapping techniques based on MSE optimization (Class et al., 1990; Matsukoto and Inoue, 1992). Alternative approaches presented estimation of the spectral normalization mapping with Multi-Layer Perceptron neural networks (Montacie et al., 1989; Nakamura and Shikano, 1990; Huang, 1992; Watrous, 1994).

This paper introduces a supervised speaker normalization method based on neural network regression with a generalized local basis model of elliptical kernels (Generalized Resource Allocating Network: *GRAN* model). Kernels are recursively allocated by introducing the heuristic procedure of (Platt, 1991) within the generalized RBF schema proposed in (Poggio and Girosi, 1989). The model includes a linear term and efficient on-line optimization of parameters is achieved by an automatic differentiation technique. Our results compare favorably with normalization by affine linear transformations based on orthonormal constrained pseudoinverse. In this paper, the normalization module was integrated and tested as an acoustic front-end for speaker-dependent continuous speech recognition systems. Experiments regarded phone units recognition with Hidden Markov Model (HMM) recognition systems.

The diagram in Figure 1 outlines the general structure of the experiment with *GRAN* normalization modules. The architecture is independent from the specific speech recognition system and allows comparisons between different normalization techniques. The *GRAN* model and a general procedure for data standardization are described in Section 2 and 3. After a discussion of the spectral mapping problem in Section 4, the APASCI corpus used in the experiments and the characteristics of the acoustic data are described in Section 5. The recognition system and the experiment set-up are detailed in Sections 6-8. Results are presented and discussed in Section 9.

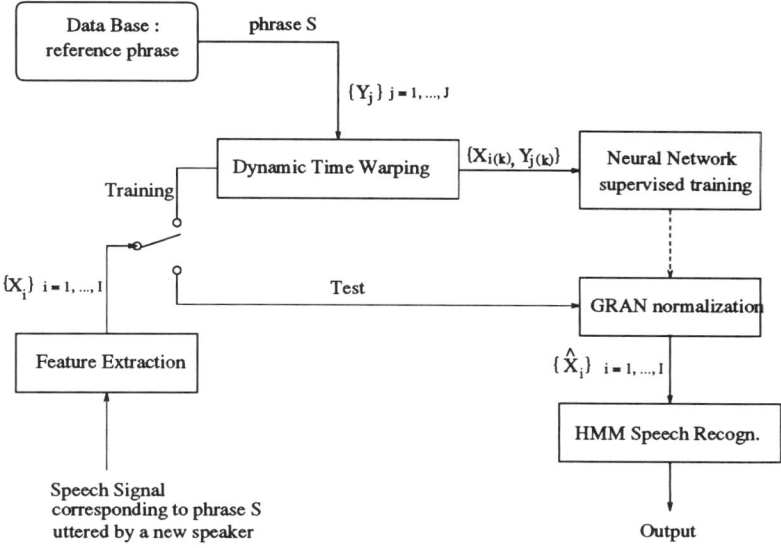

Figure 1: System overview

2 THE GRAN MODEL

Feedforward artificial neural networks can be regarded as a convenient realization of general functional superpositions in terms of simpler kernel functions (Barron and Barron, 1988). With one hidden layer we can implement a multivariate superposition $f(x) = \sum_{j=0}^{N} \alpha_j K_j(x, \omega_j)$ where K_j is a function depending on an input vector x and a parameter vector ω_j, a general structure which allows to realize flexible models for multivariate regression. We are interested in the schema: $\hat{y} = HK(\mathbf{x}) + A\mathbf{x} + \mathbf{b}$ with input vector $\mathbf{x} \in \mathbf{R}^{d_1}$ and estimated output vector $\hat{\mathbf{y}} \in \mathbf{R}^{d_2}$. $K = (K_j)$ is a n-dimensional vector of local kernels, H is the $d_2 \times n$ real matrix of kernel coefficients, $\mathbf{b} \in \mathbf{R}^{d_2}$ is an offset term and A is a $d_2 \times d_1$ linear term. Implemented kernels are Gaussian, Hardy multiquadrics, inverse of Hardy multiquadrics and Epanenchnikov kernels, also in the Nadaraya-Watson normalized form (Härdle, 1990). The kernel allocation is based on a recursive procedure: if appropriate novelty conditions are satisfied for the example $(\mathbf{x}', \mathbf{y}')$, a new kernel K_{n+1} is allocated and the new estimate $\hat{\mathbf{y}}_{n+1}$ becomes $\hat{\mathbf{y}}_{n+1}(\mathbf{x}) = \hat{\mathbf{y}}_n(\mathbf{x}) + K_{n+1}(\|\mathbf{x} - \mathbf{x}'\|_W)(\mathbf{y}' - \hat{\mathbf{y}}_n(\mathbf{x}))$ (Härdle, 1990). Global properties and rates of convergence for recursive kernel regression estimates are given in (Krzyzak, 1992). The heuristic mechanism suggested by (Platt, 1991) has been extended to include the optimization of the weighted metrics as requested in the generalized versions of RBF networks of (Poggio and Girosi, 1989). Optimization regards kernel coefficients, locations and bandwidths, the offset term, the coefficient matrix A if considered, and the W matrix defining the weighted metrics in the input space: $\|\mathbf{x}\|_W^2 = \mathbf{x}^t W^t W \mathbf{x}$. Automatic differentiation is used for efficient on-line gradient-descent procedure w.r.t. different error functions (L_2, L_1, entropy fit), with different learning rates for each type of parameters.

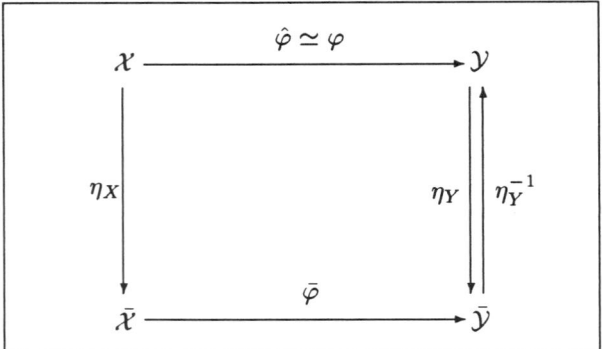

Figure 2: Commutative diagram for the speaker normalization problem. The spectral mapping φ between original spaces $\mathcal{X}$ and $\mathcal{Y}$ is estimated by $\hat{\varphi} = \eta_Y^{-1} \cdot \bar{\varphi} \cdot \eta_X$, obtained by composition of the neural GRAN mapping $\bar{\varphi}$ between PCA spaces $\bar{\mathcal{X}}$ and $\bar{\mathcal{Y}}$ with the two invertible PCA transformations η_X and η_Y.

3 NETWORKS AND PCA TRANSFORMATIONS

The normalization module is designed to estimate a spectral mapping between the acoustic spaces of two different speakers. Inter-speaker variability is reflected by significant differences in data distribution in these multidimensional spaces (we considered 8 dimensions); in particular it is important to take into account *global* data anisotropy. More generally, it is also crucial to decorrelate the features describing the data. A general recipe is to apply the well-known Principal Component Analysis (PCA) to the data, in this case implemented from standard numerical routines based on Singular Value Decomposition of the data covariance matrices. The network was applied to perform a mapping between the new feature spaces obtained from the PCA transformations, mean translation included (Figure 2).

4 THE SPECTRAL MAPPING PROBLEM

A sound uttered by a speaker is generally described by a sequence of feature vectors obtained from the speech signal via short-time spectral analysis (Sec. 5). The spectral representations of the same sequence of sounds uttered by two speakers are subject to significant variations (e.g. differences between male and female speakers, regional accents, ...). To deal with acoustic differences, a suitable transformation (the *spectral mapping*) is sought which performs the "best" mapping between the corresponding spectra of two speakers. Let $Y = (y_1, y_2, ..., y_J)$ and $X = (x_1, x_2, ..., x_I)$ be the spectral feature vector sequences of the same sentence uttered by two speakers, called respectively the *reference* and the *new* speaker. The desired mapping is performed by a function $\varphi(x_i)$ such that the transformed vector sequence obtained from $X = (x_i)$ approximates as close as possible the spectral vector sequence $Y = (y_j)$. To eliminate time differences between the two acoustic realizations, a *time warping* function has to be determined yielding pairs $C(k) = (i(k), j(k))_{k=1...K}$ of corresponding indexes of feature vectors in X and Y, respectively. The desired spectral mapping $\varphi(x_i)$ is the one which minimizes $\sum_{k=1}^{K} d(y_{j(k)}, \varphi(x_{i(k)}))$ where $d(\cdot, \cdot)$ is a distorsion measure in the acoustic feature space. To estimate the transformation, a set of supervised pairs $(x_{i(k)}, y_{j(k)})$ is considered. In summary, the training material considered in the experiments consisted of a set of vector pairs obtained by applying the Dynamic Time Warping (DTW) algorithm (Sakoe and Chiba, 1978) to a set of phrases uttered by the reference and the new speaker.

5 THE APASCI CORPUS

The experiments reported in this paper were performed on a portion of APASCI, an italian acoustic-phonetic continuous speech corpus. For each utterance, text and phonetic transcriptions were automatically generated (Angelini et al., 1994). The corpus consists of two portions. The first part, for the training and validation of speaker independent recognition systems, consists of a training set (2140 utterances), a development set (900 utterances) and a test set (860 utterances). The sets contain, respectively, speech material from 100 speakers (50 males and 50 females), 36 speakers (18 males and 18 females) and 40 speakers (20 males and 20 females). The second portion of the corpus is for training and validation of speaker dependent recognition systems. It consists of speech material from 6 speakers (3 males and 3 females). Each speaker uttered 520 phrases, 400 for training and 120 for test. Speech material in the test set was acquired in different days with respect to the training set. A subset of 40 utterances from the training material forms the adaptation training set, to be used for speaker adaptation/normalization purposes.

For this application, each signal in the corpus was processed to obtain its parametric representation. The signal was preemphasized using a filter with transfer function $H(z) = 1 - 0.95 \times z^{-1}$, and a 20 ms Hamming window is then applied every 10 ms. For each frame, the normalized log-energy as well as 8 Mel Scaled Cepstral Coefficients (MSCC) based on a 24-channel filter-bank were computed. Normalization of log-energy was performed by subtracting the maximum log-energy value in the sentence; for each Mel coefficient, normalization was performed by subtracting the mean value of the whole utterance. For both MSCC and the log-energy, the first order derivatives as well as the second order derivatives were computed. For each frame, all the computed acoustic parameters were combined in a single feature vector with 27 components.

6 THE RECOGNITION SYSTEM

For each of the 6 speakers, a SD HMM recognition system was trained with the 400 utterances available in the APASCI corpus; the systems were bootstrapped with gender dependent models trained on the gender dependent speech material (1000 utterances for male and 1140 utterances for female). A set of 38 context independent acoustic-phonetic units was considered. Left-to-right HMMs with three and four states were adopted for short (i.e. p, t, k, b, d, g) and long (e.g. a, i, u, o, e) sounds respectively. Silence, pause and breath were modeled with a single state ergodic model. The output distribution probabilities were modeled with mixtures of 16 gaussian probability densities, diagonal covariance matrixes. Transitions leaving the same state shared the same output distribution probabilities.

	anco0	bian0	ilco0	dafa0	gisv0	saor0
anco0	82.75	76.89	71.37	69.38	64.99	59.89
bian0	68.80	86.91	65.70	62.77	58.27	50.86
ilco0	62.71	66.32	85.02	64.26	64.53	62.38
dafa0	57.74	56.88	56.84	85.83	68.01	70.21
gisv0	62.43	64.32	68.19	76.20	83.44	71.37
saor0	54.86	53.07	61.77	76.03	69.64	88.21

Table 1: Phone Recognition Rate (Unit Accuracy %) without normalization

7 TRAINING THE NORMALIZATION MODULES

A set of 40 phrases was considered for each pair ($new, reference$) of speakers to train the normalization modules. In order to take into account alternative pronunciation, insertion or deletion of phonemes, pauses between words and other phenomena, the automatic phonetic transcription and segmentation available in APASCI was used for each utterance. Given two utterances corresponding to the same phrase, we considered only their segments having the same phonetic transcription. To determine these segments the DTW algorithm was applied to the phonetic transcription of the two utterances. The DTW algorithm was applied a second time to the obtained segments and the resulting *optimal* alignment paths gave the desired set of vector pairs. The DTW algorithm was applied only to the 8 MSCC and the other acoustic parameters were left unmodified.

We trained networks with 8 inputs and 8 outputs. The model included a linear term: first the linear term was fit to the data, and then the rest of the expansion was estimated by fitting the residuals of the linear regression. The networks grew up to 50 elliptical gaussian kernels using dynamic allocation. Kernel coefficients, locations and bandwidths were optimized using different learning rates for 10 epochs w.r.t the L_1 norm, which proved to be more efficient than the usual L_2 norm.

8 THE RECOGNITION EXPERIMENTS

Experiments concerned continuous phone recognition without any lexical and phonetical constraint (no phone statistic was used). For all the couples ($new, reference$) of speakers in the database, a recognition experiment was performed using 90 (of the 120 available) test utterances from the new speaker with the SD recognition system previously trained for the reference speaker. On average the test sets consisted of 4770 phone units. The experiments were repeated transforming the test data with different normalization modules and performance compared. Results are expressed in terms of insertions (Ins), deletions (Del) and substitutions (Sub) of phone units made by the recognizer. Unit Accuracy (UA) and Percent Correct (PC) performance indicators are respectively defined w.r.t. the total number of units n_{units} as $UA = 100\,(1 - (Ins + Del + Sub)/n_{units})$ and $PC = 100\,(1 - (Del + Sub)/n_{units})$. In Table 1 the baseline speaker dependent performance for the 6 speaker dependent systems is reported. Row labels indicate the speaker reference model while column labels identify whose target acous-

	anco0	bian0	ilco0	dafa0	gisv0	saor0
anco0	–	79.11	73.88	72.57	69.79	69.86
bian0	71.28	–	70.89	71.23	67.04	67.72
ilco0	65.21	70.52	–	67.64	66.56	66.84
dafa0	63.66	66.88	63.85	–	70.54	74.80
gisv0	66.07	69.90	71.29	78.01	–	75.32
saor0	61.88	67.03	66.21	76.89	70.44	–

Table 2: Phone Recognition Rate (Unit Accuracy %) with NN normalization

tic data are used. Thus UA and PC entries in the main diagonal are for the same speaker who trained the system while the remaining entries relate to performance obtained with new speakers. We also considered the *adaptability ratios* for $a = UA$ and $p = PC$ (Montacie et al., 1989): $\rho_a = (a_{RT}^n - a_{RT})/(a_{RR} - a_{RT})$ and $\rho_p = (p_{RT}^n - p_{RT})/(p_{RR} - p_{RT})$ where a_{RT} indicate accuracy for reference speaker R and target T without normalization, a_{RR} is the speaker dependent baseline accuracy and apex n indicates normalization. The same notation applies to the percent correct adaptability ratio ρ_p.

9 RESULTS AND CONCLUSIONS

Normalization experiments have been performed with the set-up described in the previous Section. The phone recognition rates obtained with normalization modules based on the GRAN model are reported in Table 2 in terms of Unit Accuracy (dee Table 1 for the baseline performance). In Table 3 the performance of the GRAN model (NN) and constrained orthonormal linear mapping (LIN) are compared with the baseline performance (SD: no adaptation) in terms of both Unit Accuracy and Percent Correct. The network shows an improvement, as evidenced by the variation in the ρ_a and ρ_p values. Results are reported averaging performance over all the pairs (new,reference) of speakers (Total column), and considering pairs of speakers of the same gender and of different genders (*Female*: only female subjects, *Male*: only males, *Diff*: different genders). An analysis of the adaptability ratios shows that the effect of the network normalization is higher than with the linear network for all the 3 subgroups of pairs: $\rho_a^{NN} = 0.20$ vs $\rho_a^{LIN} = 0.16$ for the Female couples and $\rho_a^{NN} = 0.16$ vs $\rho_a^{LIN} = 0.15$ for the Male couples. The improvement is higher ($\rho_a^{NN} = 0.28, \rho_a^{LIN} = 0.24$) for speaker of different genders. Although these preliminary experiments show only a minor improvement of performance achieved by the network with respect to linear mappings, we expect that the selectivity of the network could be exploited using acoustic contexts and code dependent neural networks.

Acknowledgements

This work has been developed within a grant of the "Programma Nazionale di Ricerca per la Bioelettronica" assigned by the Italian Ministry of University and Technologic Research to Elsag Bailey. The authors would like to thank B. Angelini, F. Brugnara, B. Caprile, R. De Mori, D. Falavigna, G. Lazzari and P. Svaizer.

		Total	Female	Male	Diff	ρ
SD	UA	64.56	68.63	71.91	60.75	-
	PC	70.87	74.35	77.55	67.48	-
LIN	UA	69.04	71.20	73.97	66.67	0.21
	PC	74.97	76.79	79.27	72.93	0.23
NN	UA	69.76	71.81	74.30	67.56	0.25
	PC	75.59	77.27	79.55	73.71	0.28

Table 3: Phone Recognition Rate (%) in terms of both Unit Accuracy, Percent Correct, and adaptability ratio ρ.

References

Angelini, B., Brugnara, F., Falavigna, D., Giuliani, D., Gretter, R., and Omologo, M. (September 1994). Speaker Independent Continuous Speech Recognition Using an Acoustic-Phonetic Italian Corpus. In *Proc. of ICSLP*, pages 1391–1394.

Barron, A. R. and Barron, R. L. (1988). Statistical learning networks: a unifying view. In *Symp. on the Interface: Statistics and Computing Science*, Reston, VI.

Class, F., Kaltenmeier, A., Regel, P., and Troller, K. (1990). Fast speaker adaptation for speech recognition system. In *Proc. of ICASSP 90*, pages I-133-136.

Furui, S. and Sondhi, M. M., editors (1991). *Advances in Speech Signal Processing*. Marcel Dekker and Inc.

Härdle, W. (1990). *Applied nonparametric regression*, volume 19 of *Econometric Society Monographs*. Cambridge University Press, New York.

Huang, X. D. (1992). Speaker normalization for speech recognition. In *Proc. of ICASSP 92*, pages I-465-468.

Krzyzak, A. (1992). Global convergence of the recursive kernel regression estimates with applications in classification and nonlinear system estimation. *IEEE Transactions on Information Theory*, 38(4):1323–1338.

Matsukoto, H. and Inoue, H. (1992). A piecewise linear spectral mapping for supervised speaker adaptation. In *Proc. of ICASSP 92*, pages I-449-452.

Montacie, C., Choukri, K., and Chollet, G. (1989). Speech recognition using temporal decomposition and multi-layer feed-forward automata. In *Proc. of ICASSP 89*, pages I-409-412.

Nakamura, S. and Shikano, K. (1990). A comparative study of spectral mapping for speaker adaptation. In *Proc. of ICASSP 90*, pages I-157-160.

Platt, J. (1991). A resource-allocating network for function interpolation. *Neural Computation*, 3(2):213–225.

Poggio, T. and Girosi, F. (1989). A theory of networks for approximation and learning. A.I. Memo No. 1140, MIT.

Sakoe, H. and Chiba, S. (1978). Dynamic programming algorithm optimization for spoken word recognition. *IEEE-ASSP*, 26(1):43–49.

Watrous, R. (1994). Speaker normalization and adaptation using second-order connectionist networks. *IEEE Trans. on Neural Networks*, 4(1):21–30.

Using Voice Transformations to Create Additional Training Talkers for Word Spotting

Eric I. Chang and Richard P. Lippmann
MIT Lincoln Laboratory
Lexington, MA 02173-0073, USA
eichang@sst.ll.mit.edu and rpl@sst.ll.mit.edu

Abstract

Speech recognizers provide good performance for most users but the error rate often increases dramatically for a small percentage of talkers who are "different" from those talkers used for training. One expensive solution to this problem is to gather more training data in an attempt to sample these outlier users. A second solution, explored in this paper, is to artificially enlarge the number of training talkers by transforming the speech of existing training talkers. This approach is similar to enlarging the training set for OCR digit recognition by warping the training digit images, but is more difficult because continuous speech has a much larger number of dimensions (e.g. linguistic, phonetic, style, temporal, spectral) that differ across talkers. We explored the use of simple linear spectral warping to enlarge a 48-talker training data base used for word spotting. The average detection rate overall was increased by 2.9 percentage points (from 68.3% to 71.2%) for male speakers and 2.5 percentage points (from 64.8% to 67.3%) for female speakers. This increase is small but similar to that obtained by doubling the amount of training data.

1 INTRODUCTION

Speech recognizers, optical character recognizers, and other types of pattern classifiers used for human interface applications often provide good performance for most users. Performance is often, however, low and unacceptable for a small percentage of "outlier" users who are presumably not represented in the training data. One expensive solution to this problem is to obtain more training data in the hope of including users from these outlier classes. Other approaches already used for speech recognition are to use input features and distance metrics that are relatively invariant to linguistically unimportant differences between talkers and to adapt a recognizer for individual talkers. Talker adaptation is difficult for word spotting and with poor outlier users because the recognition error rate is high and talkers often can not be prompted to recite standard phrases that can be used for adaptation. An alternative approach, that has not been fully explored for speech recognition, is to artificially expand the number of training talkers using voice transformations.

Transforming the speech of one talker to make it sound like that of another is difficult because speech varies across many difficult-to-measure dimensions including linguistic, phonetic, duration, spectra, style, and accent. The transformation task is thus more difficult than in optical character recognition where a small set of warping functions can be successfully applied to character images to enlarge the number of training images (Drucker, 1993). This paper demonstrates how a transformation accomplished by warping the spectra of training talkers to create more training data can improve the performance of a whole-word word spotter on a large spontaneous-speech data base.

2 BASELINE WORD SPOTTER

A hybrid radial basis function (RBF) – hidden Markov model (HMM) keyword spotter has been developed over the past few years that provides state-of-the-art performance for a whole-word word spotter on the large spontaneous-speech credit-card speech corpus. This system spots 20 target keywords, includes one general filler class, and uses a Viterbi decoding backtrace as described in (Chang, 1994) to backpropagate errors over a sequence of input speech frames. This neural network word spotter is trained on target and background classes, normalizes target outputs using the background output, and thresholds the resulting score to generate putative hits, as shown in Figure 1. Putative hits in this figure are input patterns which generate normalized scores above a threshold. The performance of this, and other spotting systems, is analyzed by plotting a detection versus false alarm rate curve. This curve is generated by adjusting the classifier output threshold to allow few or many putative hits. The figure of merit (FOM) is defined as the average keyword detection rate when the false alarm rate ranges from 1 to 10 false alarms per keyword per hour. The previous best FOM for this word spotter is 67.8% when trained using 24 male talkers and tested on 11 male talkers, and 65.9% when trained using 24 female talkers and tested on 11 female talkers. The overall FOM for all talkers is 66.3%.

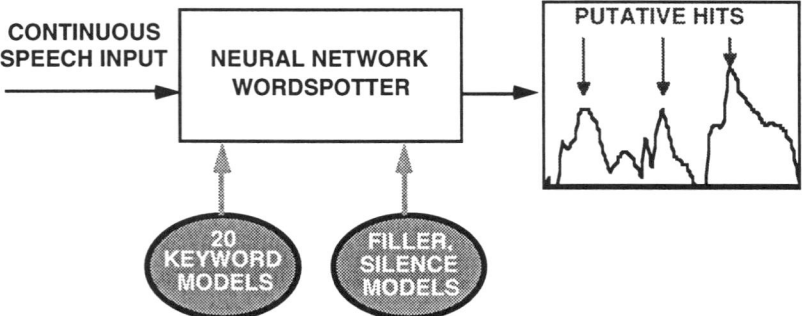

Figure 1:   Block diagram of neural network word spotter.

3 TALKER VARIABILITY

FOM scores of test talkers vary over a wide range. When training on 48 talkers and then performing testing on 22 talkers from the 70 conversations in the NIST Switchboard credit card database, the FOM of the test talkers varies from 16.7% to 100%. Most talkers perform well above 50%, but there are two female talkers with FOM's of 16.7% and 21.4%. The low FOM for individual speakers indicates a lack of training data with voice qualities that are similar to these test speakers.

4 CREATING MORE TRAINING DATA USING VOICE TRANSFORMATIONS

Talker adaptation is difficult for word spotting because error rates are high and talkers often can not be prompted to verify adaptation phrases. Our approach to increasing performance across talkers uses voice transformation techniques to generate more varied training examples of keywords as shown in Figure 2. Other researchers have used talker transformation techniques to produce more natural synthesized speech (Iwahashi, 1994, Mizuno, 1994), but using talker transformation techniques to generate more training data is novel.

We have implemented a new voice transformation technique which utilizes the Sinusoidal Transform Analysis/Synthesis System (STS) described in (Quatieri, 1992). This technique attempts to transform one talker's speech pattern to that of a different talker. The STS generates a 512 point spectral envelope of the input speech 100 times a second and also separates pitch and voicing information. Separation of vocal tract characteristic and pitch information has allowed the implementation of pitch and time transformations in previous work (Quatieri, 1992). The system has been modified to generate and accept a spectral en-

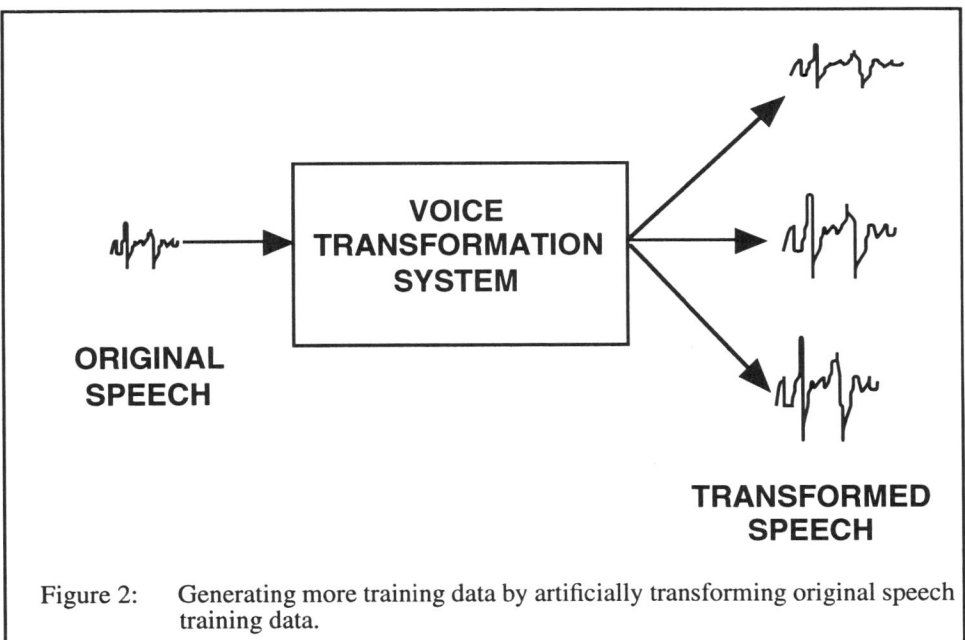

Figure 2: Generating more training data by artificially transforming original speech training data.

velope file from an input speech sample. We informally explored different techniques to transform the spectral envelope to generate more varied training examples by listening to transformed speech. This resulted in the following algorithm that transforms a talker's voice by scaling the spectral envelope of training talkers.

1. Training conversations are upsampled from 8000 Hz to 10,000 Hz to be compatible with existing STS coding software.

2. The STS system processes the upsampled files and generates a 512 point spectral envelope of the input speech waveform at a frame rate of 100 frames a second and with a window length of approximately 2.5 times the length of each pitch period.

3. A new spectral envelope is generated by linearly expanding or compressing the spectral axis. Each spectral point is identified by its index, ranging from 0 to 511. To transform a spectral profile by 2, the new spectral value at frequency f is generated by averaging the spectral values around the original spectral profile at frequency of $0.5 f$. The transformation process is illustrated in Figure 3. In this figure, an original spectral envelope is being expanded by two. The spectral value at index 150 is thus transformed to spectral index 300 in the new envelope and the original spectral information at high frequencies is lost.

4. The transformed spectral value is used to resynthesize a speech waveform using the vocal tract excitation information extracted from the original file.

Voice transformation with the STS coder allows listening to transformed speech but requires long computation. We simplified our approach to one of modifying the spectral scale in the spectral domain directly within a mel-scale filterbank analysis program. The incoming speech sample is processed with an FFT to calculate spectral magnitudes. Then spectral magnitudes are linearly transformed. Lastly mel-scale filtering is performed with 10 linearly spaced filters up to 1000 Hz and logarithmically spaced filters from 1000 Hz up. A cosine transform is then used to generate mel-scaled cepstral values that are used by the wordspotter. Much faster processing can be achieved by applying the spectral transformation as part of the filterbank analysis. For example, while performing spectral transformation using the STS algorithm takes up to approximately 10 times real time, spectral transformation within the mel-scale filterbank program can be accomplished within 1/10 real time on a Sparc 10 workstation. The rapid processing rate allows on-line spectral transformation.

5 WORD SPOTTING EXPERIMENTS

Linear warping in the spectral domain, which is used in the above algorithm, is correct when the vocal tract is modelled as a series of lossless acoustic tubes and the excitation source is at one end of the vocal tract (Wakita, 1977). Wakita showed that if the vocal tract is modelled as a series of equal length, lossless, and concatenated acoustic tubes, then the ratio of the areas between the tubes determines the relative resonant frequencies of the vocal tract, while the overall length of the vocal tract linearly scales formant frequencies. Preliminary research was conducted using linear scaling with spectral ratios ranging from 0.6 to 1.8 to alter test utterances. After listening to the STS transformed speech and also observing

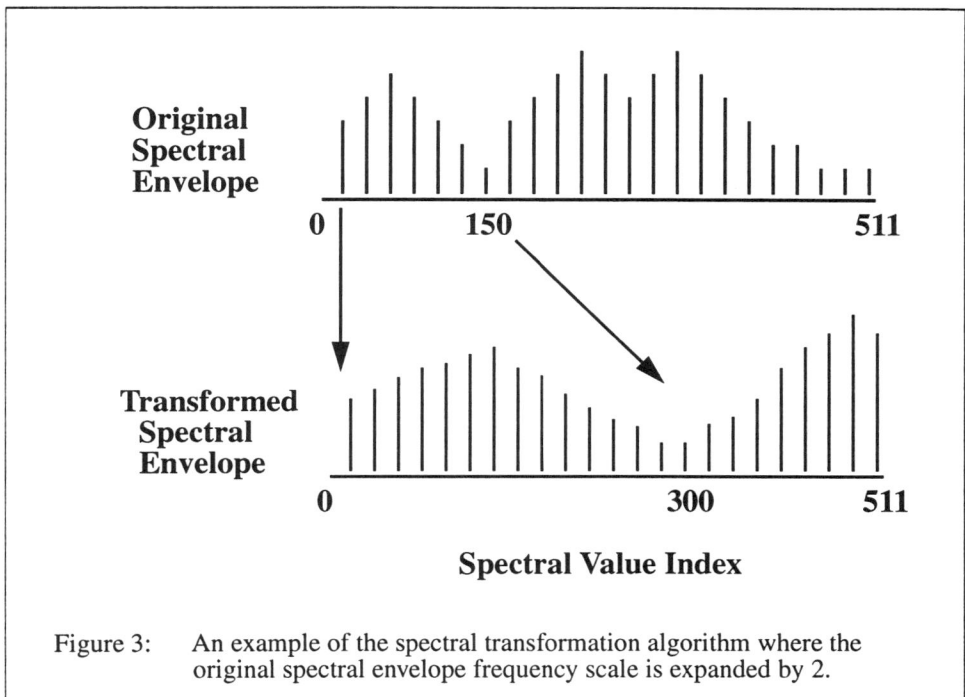

Figure 3: An example of the spectral transformation algorithm where the original spectral envelope frequency scale is expanded by 2.

spectrograms of the transformed speech, it was found that speech transformed using ratios between 0.9 and 1.1 are reasonably natural and can represent speech without introducing artifacts.

Using discriminative training techniques such as FOM training carries the risk of overtraining the wordspotter on the training set and obtaining results that are poor on the testing set. To delay the onset of overtraining, we artificially transformed each training set conversation during each epoch using a different random linear transformation ratio.

The transformation ratio used for each conversation is calculated using the following formula: $ratio \equiv \alpha + N(0, 0.06)$, where α is the transformation ratio that matches each training speaker to the average of the training set speakers, and N is a normally distributed random variable with a mean of 0.0 and standard deviation of 0.06. For each training conversation, the long term averages of formant frequencies for formant 1, 2, and 3 are calculated. A least square estimation is then performed to match the formant frequencies of each training set conversation to the group average formant frequencies. The transformation equation is described below:

$$\begin{bmatrix} \overline{F}_1 \\ \overline{F}_2 \\ \overline{F}_3 \end{bmatrix} = \alpha \bullet \begin{bmatrix} F_1 \\ F_2 \\ F_3 \end{bmatrix}$$

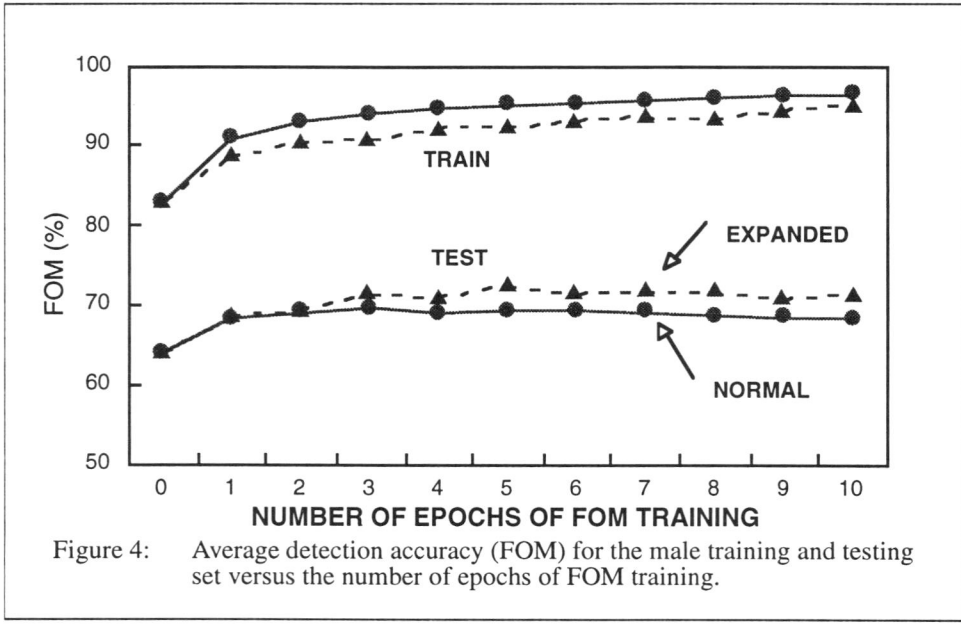

Figure 4: Average detection accuracy (FOM) for the male training and testing set versus the number of epochs of FOM training.

The transform ratio for each individual conversation is calculated to improve the naturalness of the transformed speech. In preliminary experiments, each conversation was transformed with fixed ratios of 0.9, 0.95, 1.05, and 1.1. However, for a speaker with already high formant frequencies, pushing the formant frequencies higher may make the transformed speech sound unnatural. By incorporating the individual formant matching ratio into the transformation ratio, speakers with high formant frequencies are not transformed to very high frequencies and speakers with low formant frequencies are not transformed to even lower formant frequency ranges.

Male and female conversations from the NIST credit card database were used separately to train separate word spotters. Both the male and the female partition of data used 24 conversations for training and 11 conversations for testing. Keyword occurrences were extracted from each training conversation and used as the data for initialization of the neural network word spotter. Also, each training conversation was broken up into sentence length segments to be used for embedded reestimation in which the keyword models are joined with the filler models and the parameters of all the models are jointly estimated. After embedded reestimation, Figure of Merit training as described in (Lippmann, 1994) was performed for up to 10 epochs. During each epoch, each training conversation is transformed using a transform ratio randomly generated as described above. The performance of the word spotter after each iteration of training is evaluated on both the training set and the testing set.

6 WORD SPOTTING RESULTS

Training and testing set FOM scores for the male speakers and the female speakers are shown in Figure 4 and Figure 5 respectively. The x axis plots the number of epochs of FOM training where each epoch represents presenting all 24 training conversations once. The FOM for word spotters trained with the normal training conversations and word spotters

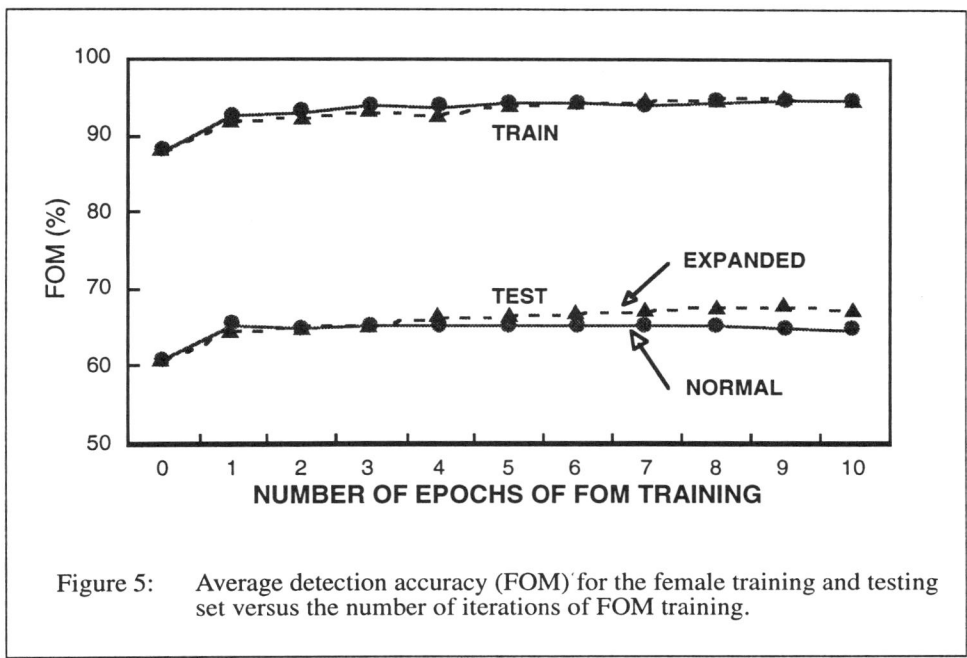

Figure 5: Average detection accuracy (FOM) for the female training and testing set versus the number of iterations of FOM training.

trained with artificially expanded training conversations are shown in each plot. After the first epoch, the FOM improves significantly. With only the original training conversations (normal), the testing set FOM rapidly levels off while the training set FOM keeps on improving.

When the training conversations are artificially expanded, the training set FOM is below the training set FOM from the normal training set due to more difficult training data. However, the testing set FOM continues to improve as more epochs of FOM training are performed. When comparing the FOM of wordspotters trained on the two sets of data after ten epochs of training, the FOM for the expanded set was 2.9 percentage points above the normal FOM for male speakers and 2.5 percentage points above the normal FOM for female speakers. For comparison, Carlson has reported that for a high performance word spotter on this database, doubling the amount of training data typically increases the FOM by 2 to 4 percentage points (Carlson, 1994).

7 SUMMARY

Lack of training data has always been a constraint in training speech recognizers. This research presents a voice transformation technique which increases the variety among training talkers. The resulting more varied training set provided up to 2.9 percentage points of improvement in the figure of merit (average detection rate) of a high performance word spotter. This improvement is similar to the increase in performance provided by doubling the amount of training data (Carlson, 1994). This technique can also be applied to other speech recognition systems such as continuous speech recognition, talker identification, and isolated speech recognition.

ACKNOWLEDGEMENT

This work was sponsored by the Advanced Research Projects Agency. The views expressed are those of the authors and do not reflect the official policy or position of the U.S. Government. We wish to thank Tom Quatieri for providing his sinusoidal transform analysis/synthesis system.

BIBLIOGRAPHY

B. Carlson and D. Seward. (1994) Diagnostic Evaluation and Analysis of Insufficient and Task-Independent Training Data on Speech Recognition. In *Proceedings Speech Research Symposium XIV,* Johns Hopkins University.

E. Chang and R. Lippmann. (1994) Figure of Merit Training for Detection and Spotting. In *Neural Information Processing Systems 6*, G. Tesauro, J. Cohen, and J. Alspector, (Eds.), Morgan Kaufmann: San Mateo, CA.

H. Drucker, R. Schapire, and P. Simard. (1993) Improving Performance in Neural Networks Using a Boosting Algorithm. In *Neural Information Processing Systems 5*, S. Hanson, J. Cowan, and C. L. Giles, (Eds.), Morgan Kaufmann: San Mateo, California.

N. Iwahashi and Y. Sagisaka. (1994) Speech Spectrum Transformation by Speaker Interpolation. In *Proceedings International Conference on Acoustics Speech and Signal Processing*, Vol. 1, 461-464.

R. Lippmann, E. Chang & C. Jankowski. (1994) Wordspotter Training Using Figure-of-Merit Back Propagation. In *Proceedings of International Conference on Acoustics Speech and Signal Processing,* Vol. 1, 389-392.

H. Mizuno and M. Abe. (1994) Voice Conversion Based on Piecewise Linear Conversion Rules of Formant Frequency and Spectrum Tilt. In *Proceedings International Conference on Acoustics Speech and Signal Processing*, Vol. 1, 469-472.

T. Quatieri and R. McAulay. (1992) Shape Invariant Time-Scale and Pitch Modification of Speech. In *IEEE Trans. Signal Processing*, vol 40, no 3. pp. 497-510.

Hisashi Wakita. (1977) Normalization of Vowels by Vocal-Tract Length and Its Application to Vowel Identification. In *IEEE Trans. Acoustics, Speech, and Signal Processing*, vol. ASSP-25, No. 2., pp. 183-192.

A Comparison of Discrete-Time Operator Models for Nonlinear System Identification

Andrew D. Back, Ah Chung Tsoi
Department of Electrical and Computer Engineering,
University of Queensland
St. Lucia, Qld 4072. Australia.
e-mail: {back,act}@elec.uq.oz.au

Abstract

We present a unifying view of discrete-time operator models used in the context of finite word length linear signal processing. Comparisons are made between the recently presented gamma operator model, and the delta and rho operator models for performing nonlinear system identification and prediction using neural networks. A new model based on an adaptive bilinear transformation which generalizes all of the above models is presented.

1 INTRODUCTION

The shift operator, defined as $qx(t) \triangleq x(t+1)$, is frequently used to provide time-domain signals to neural network models. Using the shift operator, a discrete-time model for system identification or time series prediction problems may be constructed. A common method of developing nonlinear system identification models is to use a neural network architecture as an estimator $\mathcal{F}(Y(t), X(t); \theta)$ of $F(Y(t), X(t))$, where θ represents the parameter vector of the network. Shift operators at the input of the network provide the regression vectors $Y(t-1) = [y(t-1), ..., y(t-N)]'$, and $X(t) = [x(t), ..., x(t-M)]'$ in a manner analogous to linear filters, where $[\cdot]'$ represents the vector transpose.

It is known that linear models based on the shift operator q suffer problems when used to model lightly-damped-low-frequency (LDLF) systems, with poles near $(1, 0)$ on the unit circle in the complex plane [5]. As the sampling rate increases, coefficient sensitivity and round-off noise become a problem as the difference between successive sampled inputs becomes smaller and smaller.

A method of overcoming this problem is to use an alternative discrete-time operator. Agarwal and Burrus first proposed the use of the *delta* operator in digital filters to replace the shift operator in an attempt to overcome the problems described above [1]. The delta operator is defined as

$$\delta = \frac{q-1}{\Delta} \tag{1}$$

where Δ is the discrete-time sampling interval. Williamson showed that the delta operator allows better performance in terms of coefficient sensitivity for digital filters derived from the direct form structure [19], and a number of authors have considered using it in linear filtering, estimation and control [5, 7, 8]

More recently, de Vries, Principe at. al. proposed the *gamma* operator [2, 3] as a means of studying neural network models for processing time-varying patterns. This operator is defined by

$$\gamma = \frac{q-(1-c)}{c} \tag{2}$$

It may be observed that it is a generalization of the delta operator with adjustable parameters c. An extension to the basic gamma operator introducing complex poles using a second order operator, was given in [18].

This raises the question, is the gamma operator capable of providing better neural network modelling capabilities for LDLF systems ? Further, are there any other operators which may be better than these for nonlinear modelling and prediction using neural networks ?

In the context of robust adaptive control, Palaniswami has introduced the *rho* operator which has shown useful improvements over the performance of the delta operator [9, 10]. The rho operator is defined as

$$\rho = \frac{q-(1-c_1\Delta)}{c_2\Delta} \tag{3}$$

where c_1, c_2 are adjustable parameters. The rho operator generalizes the delta and gamma operators. For the case where $c_1\Delta = c_2\Delta = 1$, the rho operator reduces to the usual shift operator. When $c_1 = 0$, and $c_2 = 1$, the rho operator reduces to the delta operator [10]. For $c_1\Delta = c_2\Delta = c$, the rho operator is equivalent to the gamma operator.

One advantage of the rho operator over the delta operator is that it is stably invertible, allowing the derivation of simpler algorithms [9]. The ρ operator can be considered as a stable low pass filter, and parameter estimation using the ρ operator is low frequency biased. For adaptive control systems, this gives robustness advantages for systems with unmodelled high frequency characteristics [9].

By defining the bilinear transformation (BLT) as an operator, it is possible to introduce an operator which generalizes all of the above operators. We can therefore define the *pi* operator as

$$\pi = \frac{2}{\Delta}\frac{(c_1 q - c_2)}{(c_3 q + c_4)} \tag{4}$$

with the restriction that $c_1 c_4 \neq c_2 c_3$ (to ensure π is not a constant function [14]). The bilinear mapping produced has a pole at $q = -c_4/c_3$. By appropriate setting of the c_1, c_2, c_3, c_4 parameters each operator, the pi operator can be reduced to each of the previous operators.

In the work reported here, we consider these alternative discrete-time operators in feedforward neural network models for system identification tasks. We compare the popular gamma model [4] with other models based on the shift, delta, rho and pi operators. A framework of models and Gauss-Newton training algorithms is provided, and the models are compared by simulation experiments.

2 OPERATOR MODELS FOR NONLINEAR SIGNAL PROCESSING

A model which generalizes the usual discrete-time linear moving average model, ie, a single layer network is given by

$$\hat{y}(t) = G(\nu, \theta)x(t) \tag{5}$$

$$G(\nu, \theta) = \sum_{i=0}^{M} b_i \nu^{-i}$$

$$\nu^{-i} = \begin{cases} q^{-i} & \text{shift operator} \\ \delta^{-i} & \text{delta operator} \\ \gamma^{-i} & \text{gamma operator} \\ \rho^{-i} & \text{rho operator} \\ \pi^{-i} & \text{pi operator} \end{cases} \tag{6}$$

This general class of moving average model can be termed MA(ν). We define $u_0(t) \triangleq x(t)$, and $u_i(t) \triangleq \nu^{-1} u_{i-1}(t)$ and hence obtain

$$u_i(t) = \begin{cases} x(t-i) & \text{shift operator} \\ \Delta u_{i-1}(t-1) + u_i(t-1) & \text{delta operator} \\ c u_{i-1}(t-1) + (1-c) u_i(t-1) & \text{gamma operator} \\ c_2 \Delta u_{i-1}(t-1) + (1 - c_1 \Delta) u_i(t-1) & \text{rho operator} \\ \frac{\Delta}{2c_1}\left(c_3 u_{i-1}(t) + c_4 u_{i-1}(t-1)\right) - \frac{c_2}{c_1} u_i(t-1) & \text{pi operator} \end{cases} \tag{7}$$

A nonlinear model may be defined using a multilayer perceptron (MLP) with the ν-operator elements at the input stage. The input vector $Z_i^0(t)$ to the network is

$$Z_i^0(t) = [x_i(t), \nu^{-1} x_i(t), ..., \nu^{-M} x_i(t)]' \tag{8}$$

where $x_i(t)$ is the ith input to the system. This model is termed the ν-operator multilayer perceptron or MLP(ν) model.

An MLP(ν) model having L layers with $N_0, N_1, ..., N_L$ nodes per layer, is defined in the same manner as a usual MLP, with

$$z_k^l(t) = f\left(\hat{x}_k^l(t)\right) \tag{9}$$

$$\hat{x}_k^l(t) = \sum_{i=1}^{N_l} w_{ki}^l z_i^{l-1}(t) \tag{10}$$

where each neuron i in layer l has an output of $z_i^l(t)$; a layer consists of N_l neurons ($l = 0$ denotes the input layer, and $l = L$ denotes the output layer, $z_{N_l}^l = 1.0$ may be used for a bias); $f(\cdot)$ is a sigmoid function typically evaluated as $\tanh(\cdot)$, and a synaptic connection between unit i in the previous layer and unit k in the current layer is represented by w_{ki}^l. The notation t may be used to represent a discrete time or pattern instance. While the case we consider employs the ν-operator at the input layer only, it would be feasible to use the operators throughout the network as required.

On-line algorithms to update the operator parameters in the MA(ν) model can be found readily. In the case of the MLP(ν) model, we approach the problem by backpropagating the error information to the input layer and using this to update the operator coefficients. de Vries and Principe et. al., proposed stochastic gradient descent type algorithms for adjusting the c operator coefficient using a least-squares error criterion [2, 12]. For brevity we omit the updating procedures for the MLP network weights; a variety of methods may be applied (see for example [13, 15]).

We define an instantaneous output error criterion $J(t) = \frac{1}{2}e^2(t)$, where $e(t) = y(t) - \hat{y}(t)$.

Defining $\hat{\theta}$ as the estimated operator parameter vector at time t of the parameter vector θ, we have

$$\hat{\theta} = \begin{cases} \hat{c} & \text{gamma operator} \\ [\hat{c}_1, \hat{c}_2]' & \text{rho operator} \\ [\hat{c}_1, \hat{c}_2, \hat{c}_3, \hat{c}_4]' & \text{pi operator} \end{cases} \quad (11)$$

A first order algorithm to update the coefficients is

$$\hat{\theta}_i(t+1) = \hat{\theta}_i(t) + \Delta\hat{\theta}_i(t) \quad (12)$$
$$\Delta\hat{\theta}_i(t) = -\eta \nabla_{\theta_i} J(\theta; t) \quad (13)$$

where the adjustment in weights is found as

$$\Delta\hat{\theta}_i(t) = -\eta \frac{\partial J(t)}{\partial \theta_j}$$
$$= \eta \sum_{i=1}^{M} \psi_i^{j\prime}(t) \delta_j(t) \quad (14)$$

where $\delta_j(t)$ is the backpropagated error at the jth node of input layer, and $\psi_i^{j\prime}(t)$ is the first order sensitivity vector of the model operator parameters, defined by

$$\psi_i^j(t) = \begin{cases} \frac{\partial u_i(t)}{\partial c_j} & \text{gamma operator} \\ \left[\frac{\partial u_i(t)}{\partial c_{j1}}, \frac{\partial u_i(t)}{\partial c_{j2}}\right]' & \text{rho operator} \\ \left[\frac{\partial u_i(t)}{\partial c_{j1}}, \frac{\partial u_i(t)}{\partial c_{j2}}, \frac{\partial u_i(t)}{\partial c_{j3}}, \frac{\partial u_i(t)}{\partial c_{j4}}\right]' & \text{pi operator} \end{cases} \quad (15)$$

Substituting $u_i(t)$ in from (7), the recursive equations for $\psi_i^j(t)$ (noting that $\psi_i^j(t) = \psi_i'(t)$ $\forall j$) are

$$\psi_i(t) = u_{i-1}(t-1) - u_i(t-1) + \hat{c}_i \psi_{i-1}(t-1) + (1-\hat{c})\psi_i(t-1) \quad \text{gamma operator}$$

$$\psi_i(t) = \begin{bmatrix} \hat{c}_2 \Delta \psi_{i-1,1}(t-1) + (1-\hat{c}_1\Delta)\psi_{i,1}(t-1) - \Delta u_i(t-1) \\ \Delta u_{i-1}(t-1) + \hat{c}_2 \Delta \psi_{i-1,2}(t-1) + (1-\hat{c}_1\Delta)\psi_{i,2}(t-1) \end{bmatrix} \quad \text{rho operator}$$

$$\psi_i(t) = \begin{bmatrix} \frac{\Delta}{2\hat{c}_1}\left(\hat{c}_3\psi_{i-1,1}(t) + \hat{c}_4\psi_{i-1,1}(t-1)\right) + \frac{\hat{c}_2}{\hat{c}_1}\psi_{i,1}(t-1) \\ -\frac{\Delta}{2\hat{c}_1^2}\left(\hat{c}_3 u_{i-1}(t) + \hat{c}_4 u_{i-1}(t-1)\right) - \frac{\hat{c}_2}{\hat{c}_1^2}u_i(t-1), \\ \frac{\Delta}{2\hat{c}_1}\left(\hat{c}_3\psi_{i-1,2}(t) + \hat{c}_4\psi_{i-1,2}(t-1)\right) + \frac{\hat{c}_2}{\hat{c}_1}\psi_{i,2}(t-1) + \frac{1}{\hat{c}_1}u_i(t-1), \\ \frac{\Delta}{2\hat{c}_1}\left(u_{i-1}(t) + \hat{c}_3\psi_{i-1,3}(t) + \hat{c}_4\psi_{i-1,3}(t-1)\right) + \frac{\hat{c}_2}{\hat{c}_1}\psi_{i,3}(t-1), \\ \frac{\Delta}{2\hat{c}_1}\left(\hat{c}_3\psi_{i-1,4}(t) + u_{i-1}(t-1) + \hat{c}_4\psi_{i-1,4}(t-1)\right) + \frac{\hat{c}_2}{\hat{c}_1}\psi_{i,4}(t-1) \end{bmatrix} \quad \text{pi operator}$$

for the gamma, rho, and pi operators respectively, and where $\psi_{i,j}(t)$ refers to the jth element of the ith ψ vector, with $\psi_{i,0}(t) = 0$.

A more powerful updating procedure can be obtained by using the Gauss-Newton method [6]. In this case, we replace (14) with (omitting i subscripts for clarity),

$$\hat{\theta}(t+1) = \hat{\theta}(t) + \gamma(t) R^{-1}(t) \psi(t) \Lambda^{-1} \delta(t) \tag{16}$$

where $\gamma(t)$ is the gain sequence (see [6] for details), Λ^{-1} is a weighting matrix which may be replaced by the identity matrix [16], or estimated as [6]

$$\hat{\Lambda}(t) = \hat{\Lambda}(t-1) + \gamma(t) \left(\delta^2(t) - \hat{\Lambda}(t-1) \right) \tag{17}$$

$R(t)$ is an approximate Hessian matrix, defined by

$$R(t+1) = \lambda(t) R(t) + \zeta(t) \psi(t) \psi'(t) \tag{18}$$

where $\lambda(t) = 1 - \zeta(t)$. Efficient computation of R^{-1} may be performed using the matrix inversion lemma [17], factorization methods such as Cholesky decomposition or other fast algorithms. Using the well known matrix inversion lemma [6], we substitute $P(t) = R^{-1}(t)$, where

$$P(t) = \frac{1}{\lambda(t)} P(t) - \frac{\zeta(t)}{\lambda(t)} \left(\frac{P(t) \psi(t) \psi'(t) P(t)}{\lambda(t) + \zeta(t) \psi'(t) P(t) \psi(t)} \right) \tag{19}$$

The initial values of the coefficients are important in determining convergence. Principe et. al. [12] note that setting the coefficients for the gamma operator to unity provided the best approach for certain problems.

3 SIMULATION EXAMPLES

We are primarily interested in the differences between the operators themselves for modelling and prediction, and not the associated difficulties of training multilayer perceptrons (recall that our models will only differ at the input layer). For the purposes of a more direct comparison, in this paper we test the models using a single layer network. Hence these linear system examples are used to provide an indication of the operators' performance.

3.1 EXPERIMENT 1

The first problem considered is a system identification task arising in the context of high bit rate echo cancellation [5]. In this case, the system is described by

$$H(z) = \frac{0.0254 - 0.0296 z^{-1} + 0.00425 z^{-2}}{1 - 1.957 z^{-1} + 0.957 z^{-2}} \tag{20}$$

This system has poles on the real axis at 0.9994, and 0.9577, thus it is an LDLF system. The input signal to the system in each case consisted of uniform white noise with unit variance. A Gauss-Newton algorithm was used to determine all unknown weights. We conducted Monte-Carlo tests using 20 runs of differently seeded training samples each of 2000 points to obtain the results reported. We assessed the performance of the models by using the Signal-to-Noise Ratio (SNR) defined as $10 \log(E[d(t)^2]/E[e(t)^2])$, where $E[\cdot]$ is the expectation operator, and $d(t)$ is the desired signal. For each run, we used the last 500 samples to compute a SNR figure.

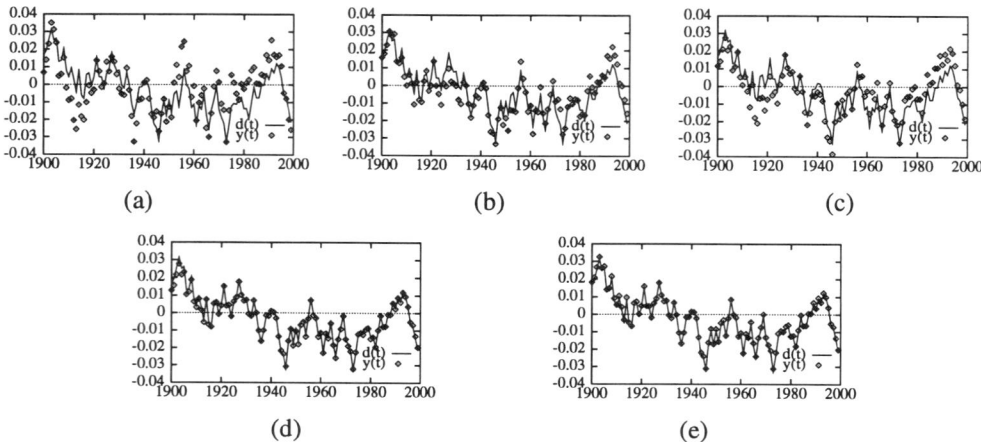

Figure 1: Comparison of typical model output results for Experiment 1 with models based on the following operators: (a) shift, (b) delta (c) gamma, (d) rho, and (e) pi.

Table 1: System Identification Experiment 1 Results

Model Operator	Avg SNR (dB)	Best SNR (dB)
shift	+2.7	+3.6
delta	-7.1	+7.7
gamma	+5.7	+14.1
rho	+9.7	+16.5
pi	+10.0	+16.5

For the purposes of this experiment, we conducted several trials and selected $\theta(0)$ values which provided stable convergence. The values chosen for this experiment were: $\theta(0)$ = $\{0.75, [0.5, 0.75], [0.75, 0.7, 0.35, -0.25]\}$ for the gamma, rho and pi operator models respectively. In each case we used model order $M = 8$.

Results for this experiment are shown in Table 1 and Figure 1. We observe that the pi operator gives the best performance overall. Some difficulties with instability occurring were encountered, thereby requiring a stability correction mechanism to be used on the operator updates. The next best performance was observed in the rho and then gamma models, with fewer instability problems occurring.

3.2 EXPERIMENT 2

The second experiment used a model described by

$$H(z) = \frac{1 - 0.8731z^{-1} - 0.8731z^{-2} + z^{-3}}{1 - 2.8653z^{-1} + 2.7505z^{-2} - 0.8843z^{-3}} \quad (21)$$

This system is a 3rd order lowpass filter tested in [11]. The same experimental procedures as used in Experiment 1 were followed in this case.

For the second experiment (see Table 2), it was found that the pi operator gave the best results

Table 2: System Identification Experiment 2 Results

Model Operator	Avg SNR (dB)	Best SNR (dB)
shift	10.7	12.3
delta	-21.5	10.2
gamma	13.5	15.0
rho	13.3	17.4
pi	14.0	17.9

recorded over all the tests. On average however, the improvement for this identification problem is less. It is observed that that the pi model is only slightly better than the gamma and rho models. Interestingly, the gamma and rho models had no problems with stability, while the pi model still suffered from convergence problems due to instability. As before, the delta model gave a wide variation in results and performed poorly.

From these and other experiments performed it appears that performance advantages can be obtained through the use of the more complex operators. As observed from the best recorded runs, the extra degrees of freedom in the rho and pi operators appear to provide the means to give better performance than the gamma model. The improvements of the more complex operators come at the expense of potential convergence problems due to instabilities occurring in the operators and a potentially multimodal mean square output error surface in the operator parameter space.

Clearly, there is a need for further investigation into the performance of these models on a wider range of tasks. We present these preliminary examples as an indication of how these alternative operators perform on some system identification problems.

4 CONCLUSIONS

Models based on the delta operator, rho operator, and pi operator have been presented and new algorithms derived. Comparisons have been made to the previously presented gamma model introduced by de Vries, Principe et. al. [4] for nonlinear signal processing applications.

While the simulation examples considered show are only linear, it is important to realize that the derivations are applicable for multilayer perceptrons, and that the input stage of these networks is identical to what we have considered here. We treat only the linear case in the examples in order not to complicate our understanding of the results, knowing that what happens in the input layer is important to higher layers in network structures.

The results obtained indicate that the more complex operators provide a potentially more powerful modelling structure, though there is a need for further work into mechanisms of maintaining stability while retaining good convergence properties.

The rho model was able to perform better than the gamma model on the problems tested, and gave similar results in terms of susceptibility to convergence and instability problems. The pi model appears capable of giving the best performance overall, but requires more attention to ensure the stability of the coefficients.

For future work it would be of value to analyse the convergence of the algorithms, in order to design methods which ensure stability can be maintained, while not disrupting the convergence of the model.

Acknowledgements

The first author acknowledges financial support from the Australian Research Council. The second author acknowledges partial support from the Australian Research Council.

References

[1] R.C. Agarwal and C.S. Burrus, "New recursive digital filter structures having very low sensitivity and roundoff noise", IEEE Trans. Circuits and Systems, vol. cas-22, pp. 921-927, Dec. 1975.
[2] de Vries, B. Principe, J.C. "A theory for neural networks with time delays", Advances in Neural Information Processing Systems, 3, R.P. Lippmann (Ed.), pp 162 - 168, 1991.
[3] de Vries, B., Principe, J. and P.G. de Oliveira "Adaline with adaptive recursive memory", Neural Networks for Signal Processing I. Juang, B.H., Kung, S.Y., Kamm, C.A. (Eds) IEEE Press, pp. 101-110, 1991.
[4] de Vries, B. Principe, J. "The Gamma Model – a new neural model for temporal processing". Neural Networks. Vol 5, No 4, pp 565 - 576, 1992.
[5] H. Fan and Q. Li, "A δ operator recursive gradient algorithm for adaptive signal processing", Proc. IEEE Int. Conf. Acoust. Speech and Signal Proc., vol. III, pp. 492-495, 1993.
[6] L. Ljung, and T. Söderström, Theory and Practice of Recursive Identification, Cambridge, Massachusetts: The MIT Press, 1983.
[7] R.H. Middleton, and G.C. Goodwin, Digital Control and Estimation, Englewood Cliffs: Prentice Hall, 1990.
[8] V. Peterka, "Control of Uncertain Processes: Applied Theory and Algorithms", Kybernetika, vol. 22, pp. 1-102, 1986.
[9] M. Palaniswami, "A new discrete-time operator for digital estimation and control". The University of Melbourne, Department of Electrical Engineering, Technical Report No.1, 1989.
[10] M. Palaniswami, "Digital Estimation and Control with a New Discrete Time Operator", Proc. 30th IEEE Conf. Decision and Control, pp. 1631-1632, 1991.
[11] J.C. Principe, B. de Vries, J-M. Kuo and P. Guedes de Oliveira, "Modeling Applications with the Focused Gamma Net", Advances in Neural Information Processing Systems, vol. 4, pp. 143-150, 1991.
[12] J.C. Principe, B. de Vries, and P. Guedes de Oliveira, "The Gamma Filter - a new class of adaptive IIR filters with restricted feedback", IEEE Trans. Signal Processing, vol. 41, pp. 649-656, 1993.
[13] G.V. Puskorius, and L.A. Feldkamp, "Decoupled Extended Kalman Filter Training of Feedforward Layered Networks", Proc. Int Joint Conf. Neural Networks, Seattle, vol I, pp. 771-777, 1991.
[14] E.B. Saff and A.D. Snider, Fundamentals of Complex Analysis for Mathematics, Science and Engineering. Englewood Cliffs, NJ: Prentice-Hall, 1976.
[15] S. Shah and F. Palmieri, "MEKA - A Fast Local Algorithm for Training Feedoward Neural Networks", Proc Int Joint Conf. on Neural Networks, vol III, pp. 41-46, 1990.
[16] J.J. Shynk, "Adaptive IIR filtering using parallel-form realizations", IEEE Trans. Acoust. Speech Signal Proc., vol. 37, pp. 519-533, 1989.
[17] Soderstrom and Stoica, "System Identification", London: Prentice Hall, 1989.
[18] T.O. de Silva, P.G. de Oliveira, J.C. Principe, and B. de Vries, " Generalized feedforward filters with complex poles", Neural Networks for Signal Processing II, S.Y. Kung et. al. (Eds) Piscataway,NJ: IEEE Press, 1992.
[19] D. Williamson, "Delay replacement in direct form structures", IEEE Trans. Acoust., Speech, Signal Processing, vol. ASSP-34, pp. 453-460, April. 1988.

PART VIII
VISUAL PROCESSING

Learning Saccadic Eye Movements Using Multiscale Spatial Filters

Rajesh P.N. Rao and Dana H. Ballard
Department of Computer Science
University of Rochester
Rochester, NY 14627
{rao,dana}@cs.rochester.edu

Abstract

We describe a framework for learning saccadic eye movements using a photometric representation of target points in natural scenes. The representation takes the form of a high-dimensional vector comprised of the responses of spatial filters at different orientations and scales. We first demonstrate the use of this response vector in the task of locating previously foveated points in a scene and subsequently use this property in a multisaccade strategy to derive an adaptive motor map for delivering accurate saccades.

1 Introduction

There has been recent interest in the use of space-variant sensors in active vision systems for tasks such as visual search and object tracking [14]. Such sensors realize the simultaneous need for wide field-of-view and good visual acuity. One popular class of space-variant sensors is formed by *log-polar sensors* which have a small area near the optical axis of greatly increased resolution (the fovea) coupled with a peripheral region that witnesses a gradual logarithmic falloff in resolution as one moves radially outward. These sensors are inspired by similar structures found in the primate retina where one finds both a peripheral region of gradually decreasing acuity and a circularly symmetric *area centralis* characterized by a greater density of receptors and a disproportionate representation in the optic nerve [3]. The peripheral region, though of low visual acuity, is more sensitive to light intensity and movement.

The existence of a region optimized for discrimination and recognition surrounded by a region geared towards detection thus allows the image of an object of interest detected in the outer region to be placed on the more analytic center for closer scrutiny. Such a strategy however necessitates the existence of (a) methods to determine which location in the periphery to foveate next, and (b) fast gaze-shifting mechanisms to achieve this foveation. In the case of humans, the "where-to-look-next" issue is addressed by both bottom-up strategies such as motion or salience clues from the periphery as well as top-down strategies such as search for a particular form or color. Gaze-shifting is accomplished via very rapid eye movements called *saccades*. Due to their high velocities, guidance through visual feedback is not possible and hence, saccadic movement is preprogrammed or ballistic: a pattern of muscle activation is calculated in advance that will direct the fovea almost exactly to the desired position [3].

In this paper, we describe an iconic representation of scene points that facilitates top-down foveal targeting. The representation takes the form of a high-dimensional vector comprised of the responses of different order Gaussian derivative filters, which are known to form the *principal components of natural images* [5], at variety of orientations and scales. Such a representation has been recently shown to be useful for visual tasks ranging from texture segmentation [7] to object indexing using a sparse distributed memory [11]. We describe how this photometric representation of scene points can be used in locating previously foveated points when a log-polar sensor is being used. This property is then used in a simple learning strategy that makes use of multiple corrective saccades to adaptively form a retinotopic motor map similar in spirit to the one known to exist in the deep layers of the primate superior colliculus [13]. Our approach differs from previous strategies for learning motor maps (for instance, [12]) in that we use the visual modality to actively supply the necessary reinforcement signal required during the motor learning step (Section 3.2).

2 The Multiscale Spatial Filter Representation

In the active vision framework, vision is seen as subserving a larger context of the encompassing behaviors that the agent is engaged in. For these behaviors, it is often possible to use temporary, iconic descriptions of the scene which are only relatively insensitive to variations in the view. Iconic scene descriptions can be obtained, for instance, by employing a bank of linear spatial filters at a variety of orientations and scales. In our approach, we use derivative of Gaussian filters since these are known to form the dominant eigenvectors of natural images [5] and can thus be expected to yield reliable results when used as basis functions for indexing[1].

The exact number of Gaussian derivative basis functions used is motivated by the need to make the representations invariant to rotations in the image plane (see [11] for more details). This invariance can be achieved by exploiting the property of *steerability* [4] which allows filter responses at arbitrary orientations to be synthesized from a finite set of basis filters. In particular, our implementation uses a minimal basis set of two first-order directional derivatives at 0° and 90°, three second-order derivatives at 0°, 60° and 120°, and four third-order derivatives oriented at 0°, 45°, 90°, and 135°.

The response of an image patch I centered at (x_0, y_0) to a particular basis filter $G_i^{\theta_j}$ can be obtained by convolving the image patch with the filter :

$$r_{i,j}(x_0, y_0) = (G_i^{\theta_j} * I)(x_0, y_0) = \iint G_i^{\theta_j}(x_0 - x, y_0 - y) I(x, y) dx\, dy \qquad (1)$$

---

[1] In addition, these filters are endorsed by recent physiological studies [15] which show that derivative-of-Gaussians provide the best fit to primate cortical receptive field profiles among the different functions suggested in the literature.

The iconic representation for the local image patch centered at (x_0, y_0) is formed by combining into a single high-dimensional vector the responses from the nine basis filters, each (in our current implementation) at five different scales:

$$\vec{r}(x_0, y_0) = (r_{i,j,s}), \quad i = 1, 2, 3; j = 1, \ldots, i+1; s = s_{min}, \ldots, s_{max} \qquad (2)$$

where i denotes the order of the filter, j denotes the number of filters per order, and s denotes the number of different scales.

The use of multiple scales increases the perspicuity of the representation and allows interpolation strategies for scale invariance (see [9] for more details). The entire representation can be computed using only nine convolutions done at frame-rate within a pipeline image processor with nine constant size 8×8 kernels on a five-level octave-separated low-pass-filtered pyramid of the input image.

The 45-dimensional vector representation described above shares some of the favorable matching properties that accrue to high-dimensional vectors (cf. [6]). In particular, the distribution of distances between points in the 45-dimensional space of these vectors approximates a normal distribution; most of the points in the space lie at approximately the mean distance and are thus relatively uncorrelated to a given point [11]. As a result, the multiscale filter bank tends to generate almost unique location-indexed signatures of image regions which can tolerate considerable noise before they are confused with other image regions.

2.1 Localization

Denote the response vector from an image point as $\vec{r}_i$ and that from a previously foveated model point as $\vec{r}_m$. Then one metric for describing the similarity between the two points is simply the square of the Euclidean distance (or the sum-of-squared-differences) between their response vectors $d_{im} = \|\vec{r}_i - \vec{r}_m\|^2$. The algorithm for locating model points in a new scene can then be described as follows:

1. For the response vector representing a model point m, create a *distance image* I_m defined by
$$I_m(x, y) = min[I_{max} - \beta d_{im}, 0] \qquad (3)$$
where β is a suitably chosen constant (this makes the best match the brightest point in I_m).

2. Find the best match point (x_{b_m}, y_{b_m}) in the image using the relation
$$(x_{b_m}, y_{b_m}) = argmax\{I_m(x, y)\} \qquad (4)$$

Figure 1 shows the use of the localization algorithm for targeting the optical axis of a uniform-resolution sensor in an example scene.

2.2 Extension to Space-Variant Sensing

The localization algorithm as presented above will obviously fail for sensors exhibiting nonuniform resolution characteristics. However, the multiscale structure of the response vectors can be effectively exploited to obtain a modified localization algorithm. Since decreasing radial resolution results in an effective reduction in scale (in addition to some

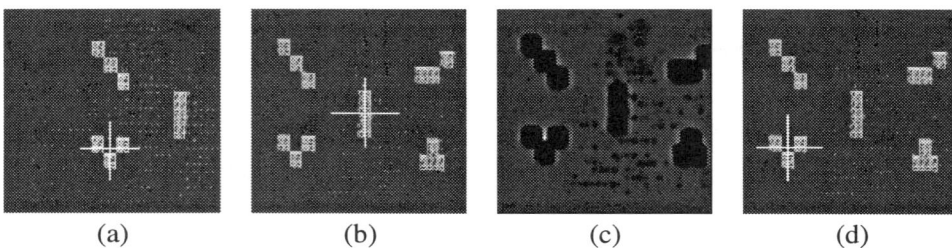

(a) (b) (c) (d)

Figure 1: Using response vectors to saccade to previously foveated positions. (a) Initial gaze point. (b) New gaze point; (c) To get back to the original point, the "distance image" is computed: the brightest spot represents the point whose response vector is closest to that of the original gaze point; (d) Location of best match is marked and an oculomotor command at that location can be executed to foveate that point.

other minor distortions) of previously foveated regions as they move towards the periphery, the filter responses previously occuring at larger scales now occur at smaller scales. Responses usually vary smoothly between scales; it is thus possible to establish a correspondence between the two response vectors of the same point on an object imaged at different scales by using a simple *interpolate-and-compare* scale matching strategy. That is, in addition to comparing an image response vector and a model response vector directly as outlined in the previous section, scale interpolated versions of the image vector are also compared with the original model response vector. In the simplest case, interpolation amounts to shifting image response vectors by one scale and thus, responses from a new image are compared with original model responses at second, third, ... scales, then with model responses at third, fourth, ... scales, and so on upto some threshold scale. This is illustrated in Figure 2 for two discrete movements of a simulated log-polar sensor.

3 The Multisaccade Learning Strategy

Since the high speed of saccades precludes visual guidance, advance knowledge of the precise motor command to be sent to the extraocular muscles for fixation of a desired retinal location is required. Results from neurophysiological and psychophysical studies suggest that in humans, this knowledge is acquired via learning: infants show a gradual increase in saccadic accuracy during their first year [1, 2] and adults can adapt to changes (caused for example by weakening of eye-muscles) in the interrelation between visual input and the saccades needed for centering. An adaptive mechanism for automatically learning the transfer function from retinal image space into motor space is also desirable in the context of active vision systems since an autonomous calibration of the saccadic system would (a) avoid the need for manual calibration, which can sometimes be complicated, and (b) provide resilience amidst changing circumstances caused by, for instance, changes in the camera lens mechanisms or degradation of the motor apparatus.

3.1 Motor Maps

In primates, the *superior colliculus* (SC), a multilayered neuron complex located in the upper regions of the brain stem, is known to play a crucial role in the saccade generation [13]. The upper layers of the SC contain a *retinotopic sensory map* with inputs from

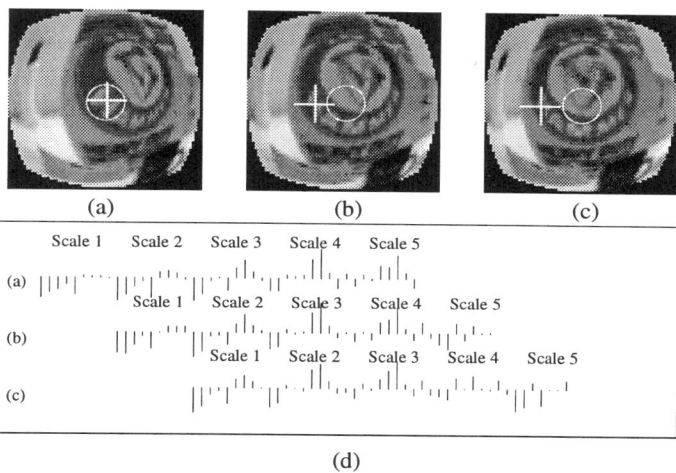

Figure 2: Using response vectors with a log-polar sensor. (a) through (c) represent a sequence of images (in Cartesian coordinates) obtained by movement of a simulated log-polar sensor from an original point (marked by '+') in the foveal region (indicated by a circle) towards the right. (d) depicts the process of interpolating (in this case, shifting) and matching response vectors of the same point as it moves towards the periphery of the sensor (Positive responses are represented by proportional upward bars and negative ones by proportional downward bars with the nine smallest scale responses at the beginning and the nine largest ones at the end).

the retina while the deeper layers contain a *motor map* approximately aligned with the sensory map. The motor map can be visualized as a topologically-organized network of neurons which reacts to a local activation caused by an input signal with a vectorial output quantity that can be transcoded into a saccadic motor command.

The alignment of the sensory and motor maps suggests the following convenient strategy for foveation: an excitation in the sensory layer (signaling a foveal target) is transferred to the underlying neurons in the motor layer which deliver the required saccade. In our framework, the excitation in the sensory layer before a goal-directed saccade corresponds to the brightest spot (most likely match) in the distance image (Figure 1 (c) for example). The formation of sensory map can be achieved using Kohonen's well-known stochastic learning algorithm by using a Gaussian input density function as described in [12]. Our primary interest lies not in the formation of the sensory map but in the development of a learning algorithm that assigns appropriate motor vectors to each location in the corresponding retinotopically-organized motor map. In particular, our algorithm employs a *visual reinforcement signal* obtained using iconic scene representations to determine the error vector during the learning step.

3.2 Learning the Motor Map

Our multisaccade learning strategy is inspired by the following observations in [2]: During the first few weeks after birth, infants appear to fixate randomly. At about 3 months of age, infants are able to fixate stimuli albeit with a number of corrective saccades of relatively large dispersion. There is however a gradual decrease in both the dispersion and the number of saccades required for foveation in subsequent months (Figure 3 (a) depicts a sample set of fixations). After the first year, saccades are generally accurate, requiring at most one corrective saccade[2].

The learning method begins by assigning random values to the motor vectors at each location. The response vector for the current fixation point is first stored and a random saccade is executed to a different point. The goal then is to refixate the original point with the help of the localization algorithm and a limited number of multiple corrective saccades. The algorithm keeps track of the motor vector with minimum error during each run and updates the motor vectors for the neighborhood around the original unit whenever an improvement is observed. The current run ends when either the original point was successfully foveated or the limit MAX for the maximum number of allowable corrective saccades was exceeded. A more detailed outline of the algorithm is as follows:

1. Initialize the motor map by assigning random values (within an appropriate range) to the saccadic motor vectors at each location. Align the optical axis of the sensor so that a suitable salient point falls on the fovea. Initialize the run number to $t := 0$.

2. Store in memory the filter response vector of the point p currently in the center of the foveal region. Let $t := t + 1$.

3. Execute a random saccade to move the fovea to a different location in the scene.

4. Use the localization algorithm described in Section 2.2 and the stored response vector to find the location l of the previously foveated point in the current retinal image. Execute a saccade using the motor vector $\vec{s}_l$ stored in this location in the motor map.

5. If the currently foveated region contains the original point p, return to 2 ($\vec{s}_l$ is accurate); otherwise,

    (a) Initialize the number of corrective saccades $N := 0$ and let $\vec{s} := \vec{s}_l$.

    (b) Determine the new location l' of p in the new image as in (4) and let $\vec{e}_{min}$ be the error vector, i.e. the vector from the foveal center to l', computed from the output of the localization algorithm.

    (c) Execute a saccade using the motor vector $\vec{s}_{l'}$ stored at l' and let $\vec{e}$ be the error vector (computed from the output of the localization algorithm) from the foveal center to the new location l'' of point p found as in 4. Let $N := N + 1$ and let $\vec{s} := \vec{s} + \vec{s}_{l'}$.

    (d) If $\|\vec{e}\| < \|\vec{e}_{min}\|$, then let $\vec{e}_{min} := \vec{e}$ and update the motor vectors for the units k given by the neighborhood function $N(l, t)$ according to the well-known Kohonen rule:
    $$\vec{s}_k := \vec{s}_k + \gamma(t)(\vec{s} - \vec{s}_k) \qquad (5)$$
    where $\gamma(t)$ is an appropriate gain function ($0 < \gamma(t) < 1$).

    (e) If the currently foveated region contains the original point p, return to 2; otherwise, if $N < MAX$, then determine the new location l' of p in the new image as in (4) and go to 5(c) (i.e. execute the next saccade); otherwise, return to 2.

---

[2]Large saccades in adults are usually *hypometric* i.e. they undershoot, necessitating a slightly slower corrective saccade. There is currently no universally accepted explanation for the need for such a two-step strategy.

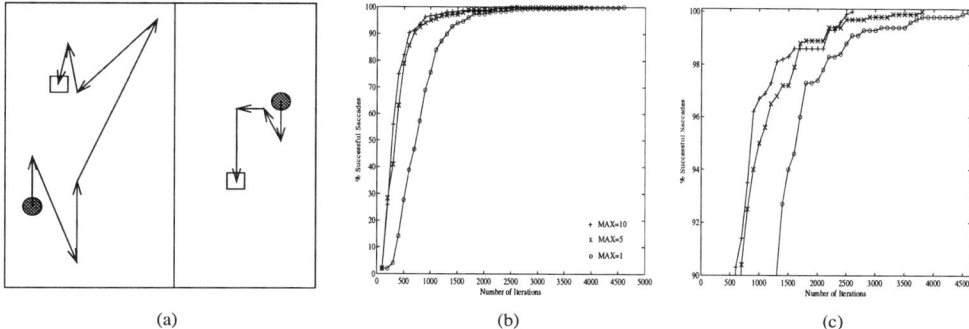

Figure 3: (a) Successive saccades executed by a 3-month old (left) and a 5-month old (right) infant when presented with a single illuminated stimulus (Adapted from [2]). (b) Graph showing % of saccades that end directly in the fovea plotted against the number of iterations of the learning algorithm for different values of MAX. (c) An enlarged portion of the same graph showing points when convergence was achieved.

The algorithm continues typically until convergence or the completion of a maximum number of runs. The gain term $\gamma(t)$ and the neighborhood $N(l,t)$ for any location l are gradually decreased with increasing number of iterations t.

4 Results and Discussion

The simulation results for learning a motor map comprising of 961 units are shown in Figures 3 (b) and (c) which depict the variation in saccadic accuracy with the number of iterations of the algorithm for values of MAX (maximum number of corrective saccades) of 1, 5 and 10. From the graphs, it can be seen that starting with an initially random assignment of vectors, the algorithm eventually assigns accurate saccadic vectors to all units. Fewer iterations seem to be required if more corrective saccades are allowed but then each iteration itself takes more time.

The localization algorithm described in Section 2.1 has been implemented on a *Datacube MaxVideo 200* pipeline image processing system and takes 1-2 seconds for location of points. Current work includes the integration of the multisaccade learning algorithm described above with the Datacube implementation and further evaluation of the learning algorithm. One possible drawback of the proposed algorithm is that for large retinal spaces, learning saccadic motor vectors for every retinal location can be time-consuming and in some cases, even infeasible [1]. In order to address this problem, we have recently proposed a variation of the current learning algorithm which uses a *sparse motor map* in conjunction with *distributed coding* of the saccadic motor vectors. This organization bears some striking similarities to Kanerva's sparse distributed memory model [6] and is in concurrence with recent neurophysiological evidence [8] supporting a distributed population encoding of saccadic movements in the superior colliculus. We refer the interested reader to [10] for more details.

Acknowledgments

We thank the NIPS*94 referees for their helpful comments. This work was supported by NSF research grant no. CDA-8822724, NIH/PHS research grant no. 1 R24 RRO6853, and a grant from the Human Science Frontiers Program.

References

[1] Richard N. Aslin. Perception of visual direction in human infants. In C. Granlund, editor, *Visual Perception and Cognition in Infancy*, pages 91–118. Hillsdale, NJ: Lawrence Erlbaum Associates, 1993.

[2] Gordon W. Bronson. *The Scanning Patterns of Human Infants: Implications for Visual Learning*. Norwood, NJ: Ablex, 1982.

[3] Roger H.S. Carpenter. *Movements of the Eyes*. London: Pion, 1988.

[4] William T. Freeman and Edward H. Adelson. The design and use of steerable filters. *IEEE Transactions on Pattern Analysis and Machine Intelligence*, 13(9):891–906, September 1991.

[5] Peter J.B. Hancock, Roland J. Baddeley, and Leslie S. Smith. The principal components of natural images. *Network*, 3:61–70, 1992.

[6] Pentti Kanerva. *Sparse Distributed Memory*. Bradford Books, Cambridge, MA, 1988.

[7] Jitendra Malik and Pietro Perona. A computational model of texture segmentation. In *IEEE Conference on Computer Vision and Pattern Recognition*, pages 326–332, June 1989.

[8] James T. McIlwain. Distributed spatial coding in the superior colliculus: A review. *Visual Neuroscience*, 6:3–13, 1991.

[9] Rajesh P.N. Rao and Dana H. Ballard. An active vision architecture based on iconic representations. Technical Report 548, Department of Computer Science, University of Rochester, 1995.

[10] Rajesh P.N. Rao and Dana H. Ballard. A computational model for visual learning of saccadic eye movements. Technical Report 558, Department of Computer Science, University of Rochester, January 1995.

[11] Rajesh P.N. Rao and Dana H. Ballard. Object indexing using an iconic sparse distributed memory. Technical Report 559, Department of Computer Science, University of Rochester, January 1995.

[12] Helge Ritter, Thomas Martinetz, and Klaus Schulten. *Neural Computation and Self-Organizing Maps: An Introduction*. Reading, MA: Addison-Wesley, 1992.

[13] David L. Sparks and Rosi Hartwich-Young. The deep layers of the superior colliculus. In R.H. Wurtz and M.E. Goldberg, editors, *The Neurobiology of Saccadic Eye Movements*, pages 213–255. Amsterdam: Elsevier, 1989.

[14] Massimo Tistarelli and Giulio Sandini. Dynamic aspects in active vision. *Computer Vision, Graphics, and Image Processing: Image Understanding*, 56(1):108–129, 1992.

[15] R.A. Young. The Gaussian derivative theory of spatial vision: Analysis of cortical cell receptive field line-weighting profiles. *General Motors Research Publication GMR-4920*, 1985.

A Convolutional Neural Network Hand Tracker

Steven J. Nowlan
Synaptics, Inc.
2698 Orchard Parkway
San Jose, CA 95134
nowlan@synaptics.com

John C. Platt
Synaptics, Inc.
2698 Orchard Parkway
San Jose, CA 95134
platt@synaptics.com

Abstract

We describe a system that can track a hand in a sequence of video frames and recognize hand gestures in a user-independent manner. The system locates the hand in each video frame and determines if the hand is open or closed. The tracking system is able to track the hand to within ±10 pixels of its correct location in 99.7% of the frames from a test set containing video sequences from 18 different individuals captured in 18 different room environments. The gesture recognition network correctly determines if the hand being tracked is open or closed in 99.1% of the frames in this test set. The system has been designed to operate in real time with existing hardware.

1 Introduction

We describe an image processing system that uses convolutional neural networks to locate the position of a (moving) hand in a video frame, and to track the position of this hand across a sequence of video frames. In addition, for each frame, the system determines if the hand is currently open or closed. The input to the system is a sequence of black and white, 320 by 240 pixel digitized video frames. We designed the system to operate in a user-independent manner, using video frames from indoor scenes with natural clutter and variable lighting conditions. For ease of hardware implementation, we have restricted the system to use only convolutional networks and simple image filtering operations, such as smoothing and frame differencing.

Figure 1: Average over all examples of each of the 10 classes of handwritten digits, after first aligning all of the examples in each class before averaging.

Our motivation for investigating the hand tracking problem was to explore the limits of recognition capability for convolutional networks. The structure of convolutional networks makes them naturally good at dealing with translation invariance, and with coarse representations at the upper layers, they are also capable of dealing with some degree of size variation. Convolutional networks have been successfully applied to machine print OCR (Platt *et al*, 1992), machine print address block location (Wolf and Platt, 1994), and hand printed OCR (Le Cun *et al*, 1990; Martin and Rashid, 1992). In each of these problems, convolutional networks perform very well on simultaneously segmenting and recognizing two-dimensional objects.

In these problems, segmentation is often the most difficult step, and once accomplished the classification is simplified. This can be illustrated by examining the average of all of the examples for each class after alignment and scaling. For the case of hand-printed OCR (see Fig. 1), we can see that the average of all of the examples is quite representative of each class, suggesting that the classes are quite compact, once the issue of translation invariance has been dealt with. This compactness makes nearest neighbor and non-linear template matching classifiers reasonable candidates for good performance.

If you perform the same trick of aligning and averaging the open and closed hands from our training database of video sequences, you will see a quite different result (Fig. 2). The extreme variability in hand orientations in both the open and closed cases means that the class averages, even after alignment, are only weakly characteristic of the classes of open and closed hands. This lack of clean structure in the class average images suggested that hand tracking is a challenging recognition problem. This paper examines whether convolutional networks are extendable to hand tracking, and hence possibly to other problems where classification remains difficult even after segmentation and alignment.

2   System Architecture

The overall architecture of the system is shown in Fig. 3. There are separate hand tracking and gesture recognition subsystems. For the hand tracking subsystem, each video frame is first sub-sampled and then the previous video frame (stored) is subtracted from the current video frame to produce a difference frame. These difference frames provide a crude velocity signal to the system, since the largest signals in the difference frames tend to occur near objects that are moving (Fig. 5). Independent predictions of hand locations are made by separate convolutional networks, which look at either the intensity frame or the difference frame. A voting scheme then combines the predictions from the intensity and difference networks along with predictions based on the hand trajectory computed from 3 previous frames.

A Convolutional Neural Network Hand Tracker

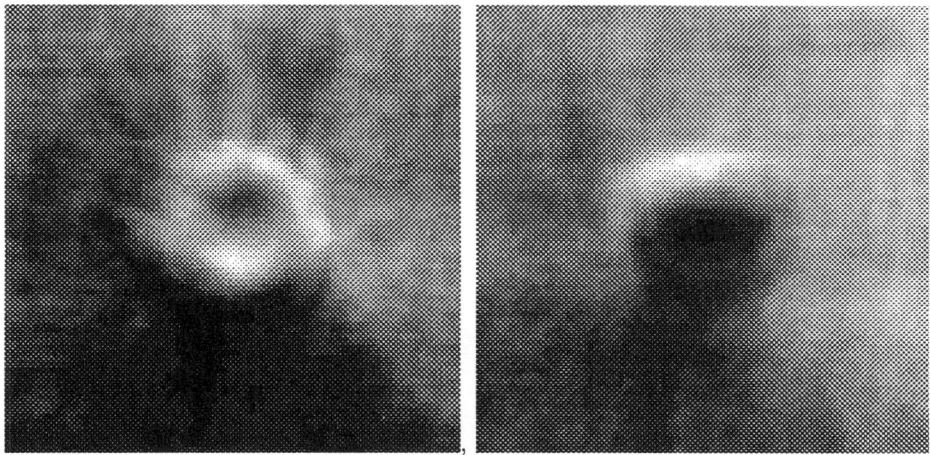

Figure 2: Average over all examples of open and closed hands from the database of training video sequences, after first aligning all of the examples in each class before averaging.

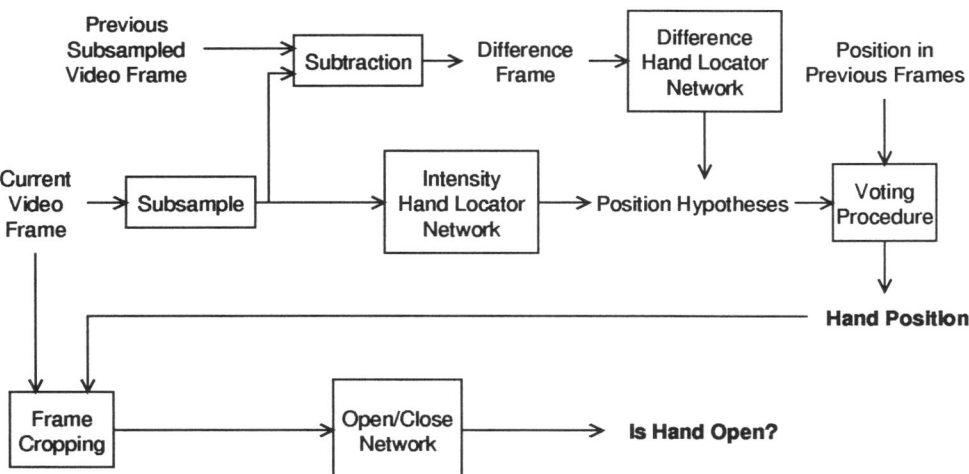

Figure 3: Architecture of object recognition system for hand tracking and open-versus-closed hand identification.

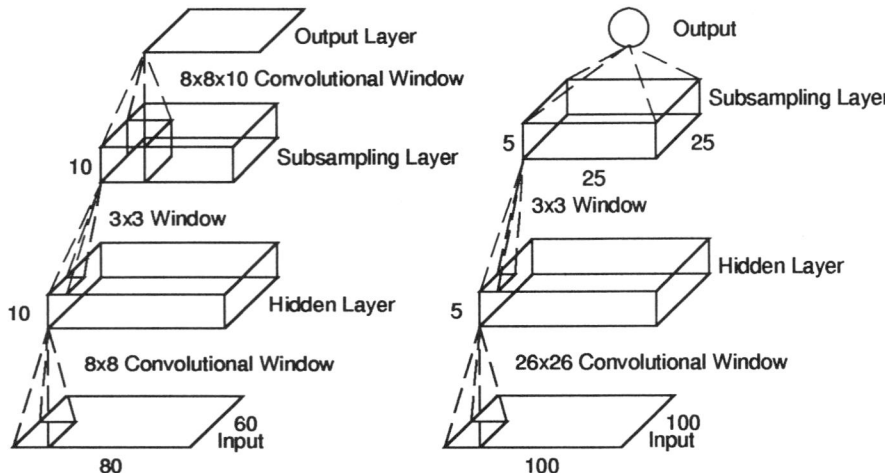

Figure 4: Network architectures. The network on the left will find a hand in either an intensity or difference low-resolution image. The output of the left network is a single convolutional image for encoding the presence of the hand at a location. The network on the right recognizes whether the hand is open or closed in a full resolution image. The output of the right network is a single value that identifies whether the hand is open or closed.

The gesture recognition subsystem takes a 100 by 100 pixel full resolution subimage of the current video frame as input. The position of this subimage is centered around the location output by the hand-tracking subsystem, thus the performance of the gesture recognition subsytem is dependent on the success of the tracking subsystem. A single convolutional network looks at this intensity subimage and indicates if the hand contained in the image is open or closed.

The tracking and gesture recognition subsystems were trained separately, and will be described in detail in the following subsections.

2.1 Hand Tracking

The intensity pathway of the hand tracking subsystem takes the original video images subsampled to 1/4 their original resolution (Fig. 5). The network architecture used to locate the hand position is a fully convolutional network with one hidden layer, a subsampling layer, and an output layer (Fig. 4). The output layer contains a single convolutional unit, which when active above threshold indicates the (possible) presence of the hand at that location.

The difference image pathway of the hand tracking system subtracts the previous subsampled video image from the current subsampled video image, and uses these 1/4 resolution difference images as input (Fig. 5). The network used to locate the hand location in the difference pathway is identical in structure to that used for hand location in the intensity pathway (Fig. 4).

The intensity and difference hand location networks were trained independently to

Figure 5: Sample video frames used by the hand tracking subsystem. The upper frames are used by the intensity pathway. The lower frames are corresponding difference images used by the difference pathway. The white cross indicates the position of the hand predicted by the network.

locate the position of the hand in each training frame to within ±10 pixels (at full resolution). The details of training and the performance of the trained networks is discussed in the following section (see Table 1). In order to provide adequate overall tracking performance, it was necessary to combine information from both hand location networks, using a voting scheme. This voting scheme also takes advantage of the fact that we are attempting to track a smoothly moving object, by using information from the estimated position in previous frames to predict the position of the hand in the current frame.

A simple rule based scheme is used to combine the predictions of hand location from the different sources. We first predict the current position of the hand based on a trajectory computed from 3 previous frames, and construct a plausible bounding box centered at this position. This bounding box represents about one third of the original image. We next find all above threshold network responses from both the intensity and difference networks. If there is a strong response from both of the networks in a similar spatial location, we choose that location. Otherwise, we use the location of the strongest response from the difference network. If there are no above threshold responses from the difference network, we use the response from the intensity network. If there are no above threshold responses from either network, we use the location predicted by the trajectory from previous frames. All thresholds used in this voting scheme are estimated from the training/cross-validation set.

2.2 Recognition of Open versus Closed Hands

The gesture recognition subsystem takes as input a 100 pixel by 100 pixel piece of the original video frame, centered at the location output by the hand tracking subsystem (and usually not centered on the hand itself). This image is only about

50 percent larger than the largest hands in our image database, so the gesture recognition subsystem is dependent on a high quality hand tracking system. The 100 by 100 pixel size chosen for input to the gesture recognition system allows positional errors of up to 25 pixels while still maintaining most of the hand in the input image. The largest positional error made by the hand location subsystem was 11 pixels, well within the tolerance of the gesture recognition subsystem.

The network architecture used to identify if the hand is open or closed is similar to the networks used to track the hand position with a convolutional hidden layer, a subsampling layer, and an output layer (Fig. 4). The primary difference from the hand location networks is that the output layer is non-convolutional and fully connected to the outputs of the subsample layer. The single output unit looks at this entire image at once, and if this unit is active above threshold, it indicates that the hand is open; if the unit is below threshold, the hand is closed.

3 Training and Performance

Our simulations have been conducted on a database of 900 video images from 18 different subjects. These images were captured from a video input in real time, at the rate of 10 frames per second with a resolution of 320 by 240 pixels per image. Each sequence represents a sample of 10 seconds of continuous motion from each subject. Subjects were requested to move one hand about freely, opening and closing the hand as it moved. Video of subjects was taken using a hand-held camcorder under natural lighting conditions in a variety of different rooms containing complex clutter, windows, etc. (Fig. 5). This varied and complicated background greatly increases the difficulty of segmenting the hand from background clutter in many circumstances. Thirty of the frames from each subject were used for training/cross-validation purposes with the remaining nineteen frames reserved for testing. In addition, we obtained a sequence of blind test frames from an individual not part of the original training set, and in a different room environment than any of the original training data.

Both location networks were training using the ISR (Keeler *et al* 1991) training procedure. The gesture network was trained using online back-propagation.

Table 1 summarizes the performance of the two tracking networks individually, as well as the performance of the overall system, on the set of 342 test images. The intensity network alone locates the hand to within ± 10 pixels in 91.8% of the test frames. A large portion of the errors made by this network are due to confusions caused by complex structured backgrounds that can have color and texture very similar to the hand in the intensity image. Another common source of errors are portions of the arms and face, particularly when the hand is closed.

Much of the background complexity can be eliminated by looking at the difference images, which allows the difference network to outperform the intensity network. However, the difference network still has a fairly high error rate. These remaining errors are due to three factors: One cannot move the hand without also moving other parts of the arm and in many cases the head and torso. In addition, when the hand stops, as when reversing direction, it may disappear entirely from the difference frames. Finally, there are instances in our database in which large objects were

Table 1: Summary of test set performance for hand location.

Information Used	Test Error Rate
Intensity	8.2%
Difference	6.4%
Intensity + Difference	3.2%
Intensity + Difference + 3 Frames	0.3%

moving in the background of the scene.

The error rate is improved dramatically when the predictions from the intensity and difference networks are combined. This is a strong indication that the errors made by the intensity and difference networks are only weakly correlated, so a nearly maximal gain is obtained by combining their predictions. The most dramatic performance gain is obtained when the predictions of the network are combined with the trajectory information in the final voting procedure.

The gesture recognition network correctly identifies whether the hand is open or closed in 99.1% of the 342 test images. In contrast, a nearest neighbor classifier using the same training set and using a convolutional euclidean distance metric (*i.e.* the minimum euclidean distance between the training and test pattern allowing up to 10 pixels of misalignment in both x and y directions) could achieve only 43.2% correct classification. This empirically verifies that this is a difficult classification task even if misalignment is taken into account.

To provide a more rigorous test of the generalization ability of the hand tracking and gesture recognition system a second blind performance evaluation was performed, using a sequence of 50 frames from a subject who was not part of the original 18 subjects used for gathering the training and testing images. These frames were shot using a different video camera, and were shot in an open lab area, which was considerably different from the office environments most of the original training data was gathered in.

The hand tracking subsystem performed perfectly on this blind test set, correctly determining the position of the hand within ±10 pixels in all 50 frames. The gesture recognition system correctly classified 94% of the test frames as open or closed, which corresponds to three errors out of 50. For these three frames, the hand was totally blended into the background, and a human observer could not determine from these individual frames whether the hand was open or closed.

4 Discussion and Conclusions

The system we have developed could be extended to recognize a broader range of hand gestures. One problem remaining to be solved is how to deal with relative motion signals in situations which involve moving background or camera.

The speed of the hand tracking and gesture recognition system is dominated by the time required to evaluate the two hand position networks and the gesture recognition network. The evaluation of these three networks requires approximately 25 million operations per frame, which would allow real time operation at video frame rates using existing convolutional hardware (Säckinger, 1992).

We have demonstrated that convolutional neural networks can be used to solve both the hand tracking and gesture recognition problems. The networks can find the hand in 99.7% of the test frames and recognize whether the hand was open or closed in 99.1% of the test frames. The system has demonstrated the ability to generalize to both novel users and novel indoor environments. In addition, the performance requirements of the system allow it to operate at video frame rates with existing hardware.

The high accuracy achieved on the hand tracking and gesture recognition tasks illustrates that convolutional networks can work on very general visual object recognition problems; problems where both segmentation and classification are difficult.

Acknowledgements

This work was carried out under an SBIR Phase I grant (contract N00014-93-C-0101) from the Office of Naval Research. We wish to thank Joel Davis of the ONR for useful suggestions and discussion.

References

J. D. Keeler, D. E. Rumelhart and W-K Leow. (1991) Integrated Segmentation and Recognition of Hand-Printed Numerals. In R. Lippmann, J. Moody, D. Touretzky (eds.), *Advances in Neural Information Processing Systems 3*, 557-563. San Mateo, CA: Morgan Kaufmann.

Y. Le Cun, B. Boser, J. S. Denker, D. Henderson, R. E. Howard, W. Hubbard and L. D. Jackel. (1990) Handwritten Digit Recognition with a Back Propagation Network. In D. S. Touretzky (ed.), *Advances in Neural Information Processing Systems 2*, 396-404. San Mateo, CA: Morgan Kaufmann.

G. Martin, M. Rashid. (1992) Recognizing Overlapping Hand-Printed Characters by Centered-Object Integrated Segmentation and Recognition. In J. Moody, S. Hanson, R. Lippmann (eds.), *Advances in Neural Information Processing Systems, 4*, 504-511. San Mateo, CA: Morgan Kaufmann.

J. Platt, J. Decker, and J. LeMoncheck. (1992) Convolutional Neural Networks for the Combined Segmentation and Recognition of Machine Printed Characters, *USPS 5th Advanced Technology Conference*, **2**, 701-713.

E. Säckinger, B. Boser, J. Bromley, Y. LeCun, L. Jackel. (1992) Application of the ANNA neural network chip to high-speed character recognition, *IEEE Trans. Neural Networks,* **3**, (3), 498-505.

R. Wolf, J. Platt. (1994) Postal Address Block Location Using a Convolutional Locator Network. In J. Cowan, G. Tesauro, J. Alspector (eds.), *Advances in Neural Information Processing Systems 6*, 745-752. San Mateo, CA: Morgan Kaufmann.

Correlation and Interpolation Networks for Real-time Expression Analysis/Synthesis.

Trevor Darrell, Irfan Essa, Alex Pentland
Perceptual Computing Group
MIT Media Lab

Abstract

We describe a framework for real-time tracking of facial expressions that uses neurally-inspired correlation and interpolation methods. A distributed view-based representation is used to characterize facial state, and is computed using a replicated correlation network. The ensemble response of the set of view correlation scores is input to a network based interpolation method, which maps perceptual state to motor control states for a simulated 3-D face model. Activation levels of the motor state correspond to muscle activations in an anatomically derived model. By integrating fast and robust 2-D processing with 3-D models, we obtain a system that is able to quickly track and interpret complex facial motions in real-time.

1 INTRODUCTION

An important task for natural and artificial vision systems is the analysis and interpretation of faces. To be useful in interactive systems and in other settings where the information conveyed is of a time critical nature, analysis of facial expressions must occur quickly, or be of little value. However, many of the traditional computer vision methods for estimating and modeling facial state have proved difficult to perform fast enough for interactive settings. We have therefore investigated neurally inspired mechanisms for the analysis of facial expressions. We use neurally plausible distributed pattern recognition mechanisms to make fast and robust assessments of facial state, and multi-dimensional interpolation networks to connect these measurements to a facial model.

There are many potential applications of a system for facial expression analysis. Personalized interfaces which sense a users emotional state, ultra-low bitrate video conferencing which sends only facial muscle activations, as well as the enhanced recognition systems mentioned above. We have focused on a application in computer graphics which stresses both the analysis and synthesis components of our system: interactive facial animation.

In the next sections we develop a computational framework for neurally plausible expression analysis, and the connection to a physically-based face model using a radial basis function method. Finally we will show the results of these methods applied to the interactive animation task, in which an computer graphics model of a face is rendered in real time, and matches the state of the users face as sensed through a conventional video camera.

2 EXPRESSION MODELING/TRACKING

The modeling and tracking of expressions and faces has been a topic of increasing interest recently. In the neural network field, several successful models of character expression modeling have been developed by Poggio and colleagues. These models apply multi-dimensional interpolation techniques, using the radial basis function method, to the task of interpolating 2D images of different facial expression. Librande [4] and Poggio and Brunelli [9] applied the Radial Basis Function (RBF) method to facial expression modeling, using a line drawing representation of cartoon faces. In this model a small set of canonical expressions is defined, and intermediate expressions constructed via the interpolation technique. The representation used is a generic "feature vector", which in the case of cartoon faces consists of the contour endpoints. Recently, Beymer et al. [1] extended this approach to use real images, relying on optical flow and image warping techniques to solve the correspondence and prediction problems, respectively.

RBF-based techniques have the advantage of allowing for the efficient and fast computation of intermediate states in a representation. Since the representation is simple and the interpolation computation straight-forward, real-time implementations are practical on conventional systems. These methods interpolate between a set of 2D views, so the need for an explicit 3-D representation is sidestepped. For many applications, this is not a problem, and may even be desirable since it allows the extrapolation to "impossible" figures or expressions, which may be of creative value. However, for realistic rendering and recognition tasks, the use of a 3-D model may be desirable since it can detect such impossible states.

In the field of computer graphics, much work has been done on on the 3-D modeling of faces and facial expression. These models focus on the geometric and physical qualities of facial structure. Platt and Badler [7], Pieper [6], Waters [11] and others have developed models of facial structure, skin dynamics, and muscle connections, respectively, based on available anatomical data. These models provide strong constraints for the tracking of feature locations on a face. Williams et. al. [12] developed a method in which explicit feature marks are tracked on a 3-D face by use of two cameras. Terzopoulos and Waters [10] developed a similar method to track linear facial features, estimate corresponding parameters of a three dimensional wireframe face model, and reproduce facial expression. A significant limitation of these systems is that successful tracking requires facial markings. Essa and Pentland [3] applied optical flow methods (see also Mase [5]) for the passive tracking of facial motion, and integrated the flow measurement method into a dynamic system model. Their method allowed for completely passive estimation of facial expressions, using all the constraints provided by a full 3-D model of facial expression.

Both the view based method of Beymer et. al. and the 3-D model of Essa and Pentland rely

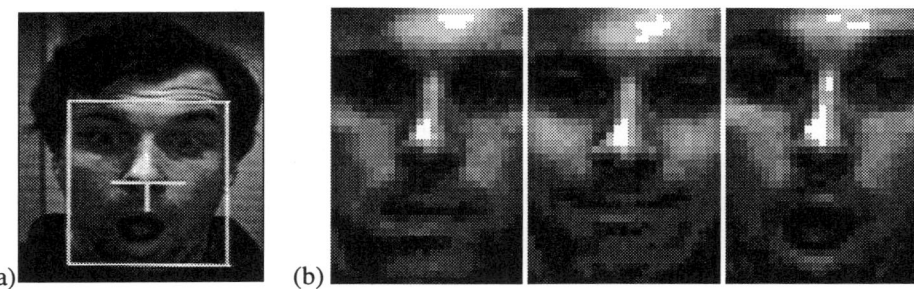

Figure 1: *(a) Frame of video being processed to extract view model. Outlined rectangle indicates area of image used for model. (b) View models found via clustering method on training sequence consisting of neutral, smile, and surprise expressions.*

on estimates of optic flow, which are difficult to compute reliably, especially in real-time. Our approach here is to combine interpolated view-based measurements with physically based models, to take advantage of the fast interpolation capability of the RBF and the powerful constraints imposed by physically based models. We construct a framework in which perceptual states are estimated from real video sequences and are interpolated to control the motor control states of a physically based face model.

3 VIEW-BASED FACE PERCEPTION

To make reliable real-time measurements of a complex dynamic object, we use a distributed representation corresponding to distinct views of that object. Previously, we demonstrated the use of this type of representation for the tracking and recognition of hand gestures [2]. Like faces, hands are complex objects with both non-rigid and rigid dynamics. Direct use of a 3-D model for recognition has proved difficult for such objects, so we developed a view-based method for representation. Here we apply this technique to the problem of facial representation, but extend the scheme to connect to a 3-D model for high-level modeling and generation/animation. With this, we gain the representational power and constraints implied by the 3-D model as a high-level representation; however the 3-D model is only indirectly involved in the perception stage, so we can still have the same speed and reliability afforded by the view-based representation.

In our method each view characterizes a particular aspect or pose of the object being represented. The view is stored iconically, that is, it is a literal image or template (but with some point-wise statistics) of the appearance of the object in that aspect or pose. A match criteria is defined between views and input images; usually a normalized correlation function is used, but other criteria are possible. An input image is represented by the ensemble of match scores from that image to the stored views.

To achieve invariance across a range of transformations, for example translation, rotation and/or scale, units which compute the match score for each view are replicated at different values of each transformation.[1] The unit which has maximal response across all values of the transformation is selected, and the ensemble response of the view units which share the

---

[1]In a computer implementation this exhaustive sampling may be impractical due to the number of units needed, in which case this stage may be approximated by methods which are hybrid sampling/search methods.

same transformation values as the selected unit is stored as the representation for the input image. We set the perceptual state **X** to be a vector containing this ensemble response.

If the object to be represented is fully known a priori, then methods to generate views can be constructed by analysis of the aspect graph if the object is polyhedral, or in general by rendering images of the object at evenly spaced rotations. However, in practice good 3-D models that are useful for describing image intensity values are rare[2], so we look to data-driven methods of acquiring object views.

As described in [2] a simple clustering algorithm can find a set of views that "span" a training sequence of images, in the sense that for each image in the sequence at least one view is within some threshold similarity to that image. The algorithm is as follows. Let $\mathcal{V}$ be the current set of views for an object (initially one view is specified manually). For each frame I of a training sequence, if at least one $v \in \mathcal{V}$ has a match value $M(v, I)$ that is greater than a threshold θ, then no action is performed and the next frame is processed. If no view is close, then I is used to construct a new view which is added to the view set. A view v' is created using a window of I centered at the location in the previous image where the closest view was located. (All views usually share the same window size, determined by the initial view.) The view set is then augmented to include the new view: $\mathcal{V} = \mathcal{V} \cup v'$.

This algorithm will find a set of views which well-characterizes an object across the range of poses or expressions contained in the training sequence. For example, in the domain of hand gestures, inputing a training sequence consisting of a waving hand will yield views which contain images of the hand at several different rotations. In the domain of faces, when input a training sequence consisting of a user performing 3 different expressions, neutral, smile, and surprise, this algorithm (with normalized correlation and $\theta = 0.7$) found three views corresponding to these expressions to represent the face, as shown in Figure 1(b). These 3 views serve as a good representation for the face of this user as long as his expression is similar to one in the training set.

The major advantage of this type of distributed view-based representation lies in the reduction of the dimensionality of the processing that needs to occur for recognition, tracking, or control tasks. In the gesture recognition domain, this dimensionality reduction allowed for conventional recognition strategies to be applied successfully and in real-time, on examples where it would have been infeasible to evaluate the recognition criteria on the full signal. In the domain explored in this paper it makes the interpolation problem of much lower order: rather than interpolate from thousands of input dimensions as would be required when the input is the image domain, the view domain for expression modeling tasks typically has on the order of a dozen dimensions.

4 3-D MODELING/MOTOR CONTROL

To model the structure of the face and the dynamics of expression performance, we use the physically based model of Essa et. al. This model captures how expressions are generated by muscle actuations and the resulting skin and tissue deformations. The model is capable of controlled nonrigid deformations of various facial regions, in a fashion similar to how humans generate facial expressions by muscle actuations attached to facial tissue. Finite Element methods are used to model the dynamics of the system.

---

[2]As opposed to modeling forces and shape deformations, for which 3-D models are useful and indeed are used in the method presented here.

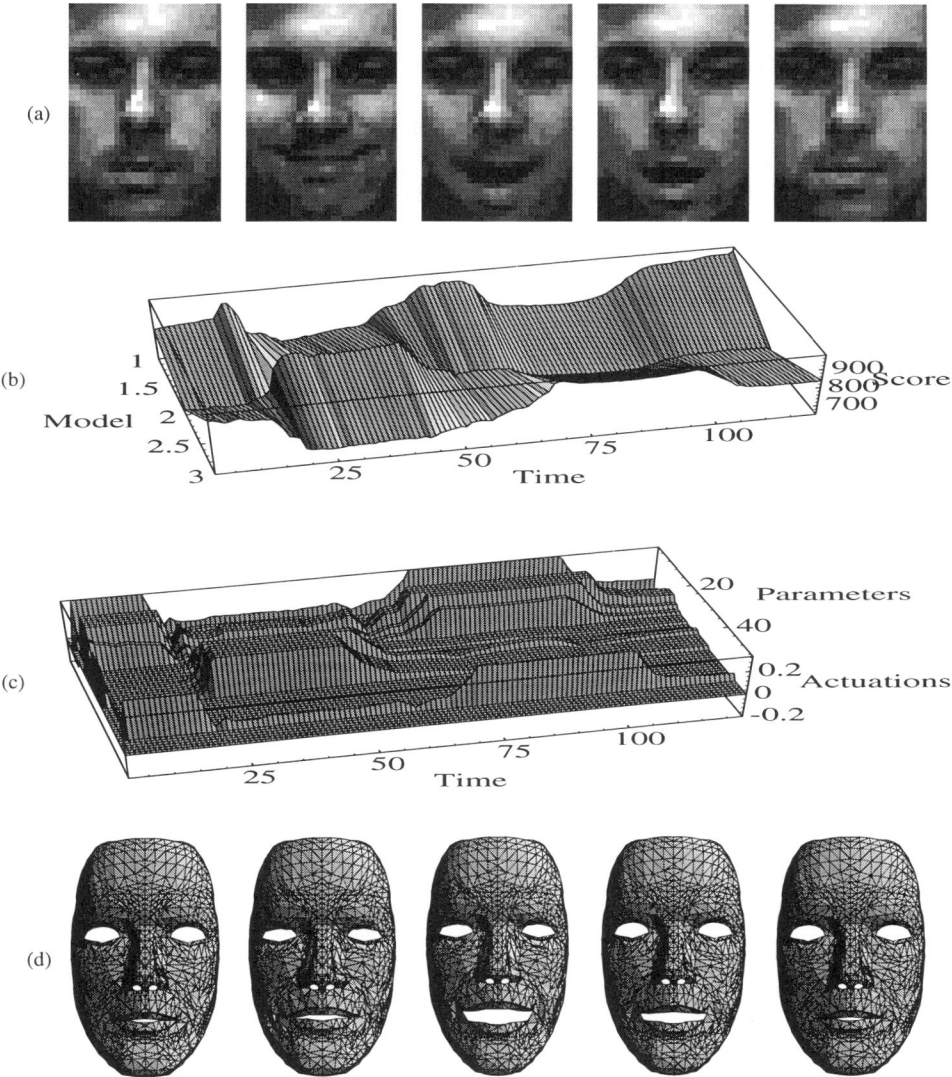

Figure 2: (a) Face images used as input, (b) normalized correlation scores $\mathbf{X}(t)$ for each view model, (c) resulting muscle control parameters $\mathbf{Y}(\mathbf{t})$, (d) rendered images of facial model corresponding to muscle parameters.

This model is based on the mesh developed by Platt and Badler [7], extended into a topologically invariant physics-based model through the addition of a dynamic skin and muscle model [6, 11]. These methods give the facial model an *anatomically-based* facial structure by modeling facial tissue/skin, and muscle actuators, with a geometric model to describe force-based deformations and control parameters.

The muscle model provides us with a set of control knobs to drive the facial state, defined to be a vector $\mathbf{Y}$. These serve to define the motor state of the animated face. Our task now is to connect the perceptual states of the observed face to these motor states.

5 CONNECTING PERCEPTION WITH ACTION

We need to establish a mapping from the perceptual view scores to the appropriate muscle activations on the 3-D face model. To do this, we use multidimensional interpolation strategies implemented in network form.

Interpolation requires a set of control points or exemplars from which to derive the desired mapping. Example pairs of real faces and model faces for different expressions are presented to the interpolation method during a training phase. This can be done in one of two ways, with either a user-driven or model-driven paradigm. In the model-driven case the muscle states are set to generate a particular expression by an animator/programmer and then the user is asked to make the equivalent expression. The resulting perceptual (view-model) scores are then recorded and paired with the muscle activation levels. In the user-driven case, the user makes an expression of his/her own choosing, and the optic flow method of Essa et. al. is used to derive the corresponding muscle activation levels. The model-driven paradigm is simpler and faster, but the user-driven paradigm yields more detailed and authentic facial expressions.

We use the Radial Basis Function (RBF) method presented in [8], and define the interpolated motor controls to be a weighted sum of radial functions centered at each example:

$$\mathbf{Y} = \sum_{i=1}^{n} c_i \mathcal{G}(\mathbf{X} - \mathbf{X_i}) \qquad (1)$$

where $\mathbf{Y}$ are the muscle states, $\mathbf{X}$ are the observed view-model scores, $\mathbf{X_i}$ are the example scores, $\mathcal{G}$ is an RBF (and in our case was simply a linear ramp $\mathcal{G}(\S) = ||\S||$), and the weights c_i are computed from the example motor values $\mathbf{Y_i}$ using the pseudo-inverse method [8].

6 INTERACTIVE ANIMATION SYSTEM

The correlation network, RBF interpolator, and facial model described above have been combined into a single system for interactive animation. The entire system can be updated at over 5 Hz, using a dedicated single board accelerator to compute the correlation network, and an SGI workstation to render the facial mesh. Here we present two examples of the processing performed by the system, using different strategies for coupling perceptual and motor state.

Figure 2 illustrates one example of real-time facial expression tracking using this system, using a full-coupling paradigm. Across the top, labeled (a), are five frames of a video sequence of a user making a smile expression. This was one of the expressions used in the training sequence for the view models shown in Figure 1(b), so they were applicable to be

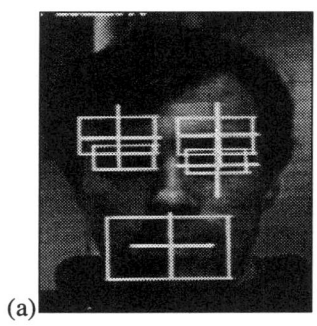 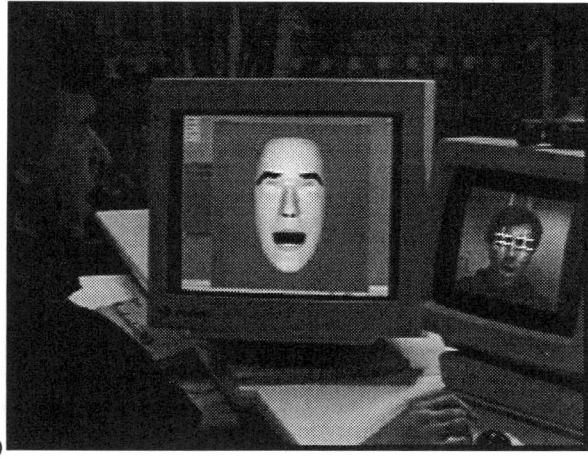

(a) (b)

Figure 3: *(a) Processing of video frame with independent view model regions for eyes, eye-brows, and mouth region. (b) Overview shot of full system. User is on left, vision system and camera is on right, and animated face is in the center of the scene. The animated face matches the state of the users face in real-time, including eye-blinks (as is the case in this shot.)*

used here. Figure 2(b) shows the correlation scores computed for each of the 3 view models for each frame of the sequence. This constituted the perceptual state representation, $\mathbf{X(t)}$.

In this example the full face is coupled with the full suite of motor control parameters. An RBF interpolator was trained using perceptual/motor state pairs for three example full-face expressions (neutral, smile, surprise); the resulting (interpolated) motor control values, $\mathbf{Y(t)}$, for the entire sequence are shown in Figure 2(c). Finally, the rendered facial mesh for five frames of these motor control values is shown in Figure 2(d).

When there are only a few canonical expressions that need be tracked/matched, this full-face template approach is robust and simple. However if the user wishes to exercise independent control of the various regions of the face, then the full coupling paradigm will be overly restrictive. For example, if the user trains two expressions, eyes closed and eyes open, and then runs the system and attempts to blink only one eye, the rendered face will be unable to match it. (In fact closing one eye leads to the rendered face half-closing both eyes.)

A solution to this is to decouple the regions of the face which are independent geometrically (and to some degree, in terms of muscle effect.) Under this paradigm, separate correlation networks are computed for each facial regions, and multiple RBF interpolations are performed for each system. Each interpolator drives a distinct subset of the motor state vector. Figure 3(a) shows the regions used for decoupled local templates. In these examples independent regions were used for each eye, eyebrow, and the mouth region.

Finally, figure 3 (b) shows a picture of the set-up of the system as it is being run in an interactive setting. The animated face mimics the facial state of the user, matching in real time the position of the eyes, eyelids, eyebrows and mouth of the user. In the example shown in this picture, the users eyes are closed, so the animated face's eyes are similarly closed. Realistic performance of animated facial expressions and gestures are are possible through this method, since the timing and levels of the muscle activations react immediately to changes in the users face.

7 CONCLUSION

We have explored the use of correlation networks and Radial Basis Function techniques for the tracking of real faces in video sequences. A distributed view-based representation is computed using a network of replicated normalized correlation units, and offers a fast and robust assesment of perceptual state. 3-D constraints on facial shape are achieved through the use of a an anatomically derived facial model, whose muscle activations are controled via interolated perceptual states using the RBF method.

With this framework we have been able to acheive the fast and robust analysis and synthesis of facial expressions. A modeled face mimics the expression of a user in real-time, using only a conventional video camera sensor and no special marking on the face of the user. This system has promise as a new approach in the interactive animation, video tele-conferencing, and personalized interface domains.

References

[1] D. Beymer, A. Shashua, and T. Poggio, Example Based Image Analysis and Synthesis, MIT AI Lab TR-1431, 1993.

[2] T. Darrell and A. Pentland. Classification of Hand Gestures using a View-Based Distributed Representation In *NIPS-6*, 1993.

[3] I. Essa and A. Pentland. A vision system for observing and extracting facial action parameters. In *Proc. IEEE Conf. Computer Vision and Pattern Recognition*, 1994.

[4] S. Librande. Example-based Character Drawing. S.M. Thesis, Media Arts and Science/Media Lab, MIT. 1992

[5] K. Mase. Recognition of facial expressions for optical flow. *IEICE Transactions, Special Issue on Computer Vision and its Applications*, E 74(10), 1991.

[6] S. Pieper, J. Rosen, and D. Zeltzer. Interactive graphics for plastic surgery: A task level analysis and implementation. *Proc. Siggraph-92*, pages 127–134, 1992.

[7] S. M. Platt and N. I. Badler. Animating facial expression. *ACM SIGGRAPH Conference Proceedings*, 15(3):245–252, 1981.

[8] T. Poggio and F. Girosi. A theory of networks for approximation and learning. MIT AI Lab TR-1140, 1989.

[9] T. Poggio and R. Brunelli, A Novel Approach to Graphics, MIT AI Lab TR- 1354. 1992.

[10] D. Terzopoulus and K. Waters. Analysis and synthesis of facial image sequences using physical and anatomical models. *IEEE Trans. PAMI*, 15(6):569–579, June 1993.

[11] K. Waters and D. Terzopoulos. Modeling and animating faces using scanned data. *The Journal of Visualization and Computer Animation*, 2:123–128, 1991.

[12] L. Williams. Performance-driven facial animation. *ACM SIGGRAPH Conference Proceedings*, 24(4):235–242, 1990.

Learning direction in global motion: two classes of psychophysically-motivated models

V. Sundareswaran   Lucia M. Vaina*
Intelligent Systems Laboratory, College of Engineering,
Boston University
44 Cummington Street, Boston, MA 02215

Abstract

Perceptual learning is defined as fast improvement in performance and retention of the learned ability over a period of time. In a set of psychophysical experiments we demonstrated that perceptual learning occurs for the discrimination of direction in stochastic motion stimuli. Here we model this learning using two approaches: a clustering model that learns to *accommodate* the motion noise, and an averaging model that learns to *ignore* the noise. Simulations of the models show performance similar to the psychophysical results.

1 Introduction

Global motion perception is critical to many visual tasks: to perceive self-motion, to identify objects in motion, to determine the structure of the environment, and to make judgements for safe navigation. In the presence of noise, as in random dot kinematograms, efficient extraction of global motion involves considerable spatial integration. Newsome and Colleagues (1989) showed that neurons in the macaque middle temporal area (MT) are motion direction-selective, and perform global integration of motion in their large receptive fields. Psychophysical studies in humans have characterized the limits of spatial and temporal integration in motion (Watamaniuk et. al, 1984) and the nature of the underlying motion computations (Vaina et. al 1990).

---

*Please address all correspondence to Lucia Vaina

Since the psychophysical and neural substrate of global motion are fairly well understood, we were interested to see whether the perception of direction in such global motion stimuli can improve with practice. Studies specifically addressing this question for other early perceptual tasks have shown that improvements of performance obtained in the first experimental session are preserved in a subsequent session and retained over weeks. This is considered as perceptual learning (Gibson, 1953). Psychophysical studies of perceptual learning show that the beneficial effects of practice are lost if some stimulus parameters are changed significantly, such as orientation, spatial frequency or location in the visual field. Based on the time scale necessary for the improvement to occur, two major learning paradigms have been used in perceptual learning : slow, progressive learning (several thousand trials are required to reach stable performance) and fast learning (improvement occurs and stabilizes in the first 100-200 trials).

The idea of fast learning and the nature of its limits is attractive from a computational point of view because it encourages the exploration of practice-dependent plasticity found in the adult early visual system (Frégnac et. al., 1988, Gilbert and Wiesel 1992). A recent line of research in biologically motivated learning models originated by Poggio (Poggio, 1990) takes perceptual learning as evidence that "the brain may be able to synthesize–possibly in the cortex–appropriate task-specific modules that receive input from retinotopic cells and learn to solve the task after a short training phase in which they are exposed to examples of the task". Poggio and colleagues (1992) have illustrated this approach in learning vernier hyperacuity. Here, we adopted this general framework to study learning of direction in global motion. In contrast to Poggio et. al's supervised learning paradigm, we used unsupervised learning both in the psychophysical experiments and modeling of learning. We designed a set of psychophysical tasks to study whether fast learning occurs in discrimination of opposite directions of global motion and to explore the limits of this learning. To model the learning, we studied two models that differ in the way they deal with noise.

2 Psychophysics

Ball and Sekuler (1982, 1987) showed that discriminability of the direction of motion of two random dot patterns improved with training. In this learning paradigm, more than 2000 trials are required for reaching a stable performance. Such a "slow" learning time scale has been reported for the learning of other perceptual tasks, such as vernier acuity (McKee and Westheimer 1978, Fahle 1994), stereoacuity (Fendick and Westheimer, 1983; Ramachandran and Braddick 1973) and discrimination of line orientation (Vogels and Orban 1985). In contrast to this "slow learning," Fiorentini and Berardi (1981) showed that for learning the discrimination of complex gratings with two harmonics of different spatial phase, 100-200 trials suffice. Similarly Poggio et. al. (1992) show that a small number of trials suffice for significantly improving performance on a vernier hyperacuity task. Both studies discussed the specificity of learning to the stimulus attributes.

In our study, we used a two-alternative, forced-choice psychophysical procedure to measure the subject's ability to discriminate between two opposite directions of motion in dynamic random dot patterns in which 25% of the dots provide a correlated

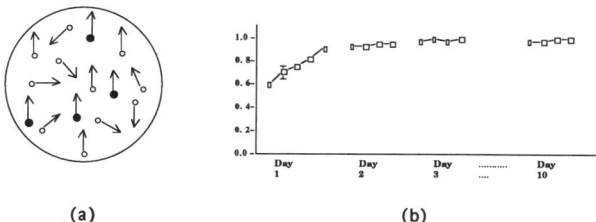

Figure 1: (a) Stimulus: a fraction of the dots (filled circles) move coherently in the signal direction; the rest (open circles) move randomly, (b) Fast improvement is observed on the first day of testing, and retained over a period of time. Each block consisted of 40 trials; data points averaged over 4 subjects, and errorbars show standard error.

motion signal spatially dispersed in a masking motion noise due to random motion of the reminder 75% of dots (Fig. 1(a)). Each trial lasted 90 msec during which two frames were presented (with inter-frame interval equal to zero). A session consisted of 4-6 blocks of 40 trials each. Feedback was not provided during the experimental sessions. Observers were required to maintain fixation on a fixation mark placed at 2° from the imaginary circumference of the stimulus.

To investigate the effects of practice and their retention, the discrimination of leftward vs rightward direction of motion in the display was tested first on each experimental session for 3 consecutive days and repeated 10 days later. The results are presented in Fig. 1(b). For most observers, a fast and dramatic improvement was seen in the first day. Fig. 1(b) shows that learning was maintained in subsequent days, and even ten days later without any training in between. Examination of the individual observers' data revealed that improvement of performance occurred only if they started above chance level. This suggests that this fast learning might imply the improvement of an existing representation of the stimulus.

In additional experiments, we did not find transfer to another direction of motion (up/down), indicating that the learning is selective to specific characteristics of the stimulus. Details of experiments testing the limits of the learning appear in Vaina et. al (1995).

3 Modeling

We propose two paradigms to model the learning found in psychophysics. Both use directionally-tuned units with properties similar to those of neurons found in MT (Maunsell and Van Essen, 1983). Schematic MT neurons used in our modeling integrate global information by summing over localized responses:

$$x_t = \sum_{i=1}^{n} e^{-(\frac{1}{2\sigma_h^2}(\theta_i - \theta_t)^2)}. \qquad (1)$$

where σ_h is the standard deviation of the tuning, and information from n local responses is taken into account. The responses of a collection of such units (each

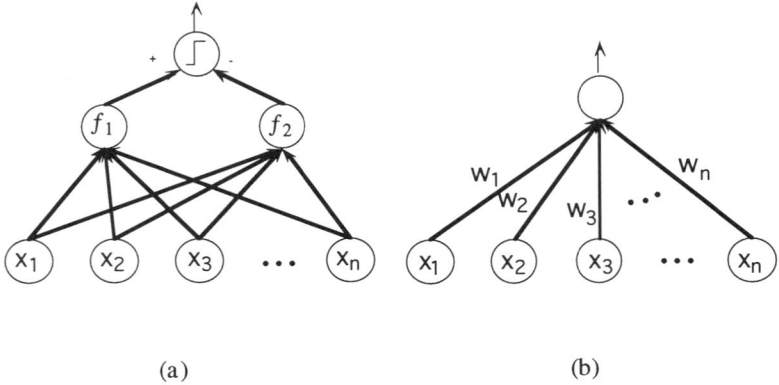

Figure 2: Architectures of the models: (a) Learning to Accommodate: Cluster Gaussians f_1 and f_2 operate on input vector **X** to decide global motion direction, (b) Learning to Ignore: Global motion direction is computed as a weighted combination of units' preferred directions.

tuned to a different direction) form the input vector to the models.

3.1 Learning to accommodate

This model is based on grouping *similar* data. In this paradigm, after learning, the network has an estimate of the contribution of noise, and takes it into account when performing the task of discriminating between two different directions of motion; so, we say that the model "learns to accommodate" the noise.

Fig 2(a) contains a schematic of this model. The representation vector consists of responses $x_1.x_2, \ldots, x_n$ of the directionally-tuned units.. Clustering is done in the space of the representation vectors. The model is a combination of HyperBF-like functions and clustering (Poggio et. al, 1992, Moody and Darken 1989). We use gaussians with mean at the cluster centers, and "move" the cluster centers by a learning algorithm.

A cluster gaussian computes a gaussian function of the representation vector for the current stimulus from the current center of the corresponding cluster. We say "current" because the center is moved as the learning proceeds. At any given point, a center is at the current best estimate of the center of the corresponding data cluster. More precisely, the learning rule to modify the jth coordinate of the center is given by:

$$c_{w,j}^{(t+1)} = c_{w,j}^{(t)} + \eta * (x_j^{(t)} - c_{w,j}^{(t)}), \qquad (2)$$

where w is the index of "winning" cluster and $c_{w,j}$ is the jth coordinate of the center for the wth cluster. This moves the center towards the new data vector X that has been judged to belong to the wth cluster. The parameter η controls the learning rate.

3.2 Learning to ignore

The learning involved in this approach is Hebbian, and is termed "learning to ignore," because in this weighted averaging scheme, as learning occurs, the weights for the noise response are progressively reduced to zero, leaving only the contribution from the signal. In other words, the network learns to ignore the noise (Vaina et. al 1995).

The model's output is a global motion direction. If the weights associated with the responses $x_1, x_2, \ldots x_n$ are $w_1, w_2, \ldots w_n$, the global motion direction is calculated as

$$\theta_o = \tan^{-1}\left(\frac{\sum w_i X_i \sin\theta_i}{\sum w_i X_i \cos\theta_i}\right),$$

where t_i is the tuned direction (angle) of the ith unit. A schematic of the model is shown in Fig. 2(b). The global direction is judged to be rightward if $+\theta_t > \theta_o > -\theta_t$.

We have examined two different learning rules: exposure-based learning, and self-supervised learning.

Exposure-based learning: The weight corresponding to a unit is incremented by an amount proportional to the current weight. Only units whose response values are above a certain threshold are allowed to increase their weights. This learning rule favors units that fire consistently:

$$w_i \leftarrow w_i + \eta w_i, \text{ if } x_i > r_t, \tag{3}$$

where r_t is a threshold, and η is a small fraction that controls the learning rate.

Self-supervised learning: The weight corresponding to a unit is increased by an amount proportional to the product of the current weight and a decreasing function (exponential) of the angular difference between the calculated global motion direction and the direction of tuning of the unit:

$$w_i \leftarrow w_i + \eta w_i e^{(-(\theta_i - \theta_o)^2/2\sigma_t)}, \text{ if } x_i > r_t.$$

In this case, the model uses its own estimate of the global direction as an internal feedback to determine the learning.

An approach similar to this model for learning vernier hyperacuity was proposed by Weiss et. al (1993).

4 Experiments

For the simulations, the input (motion) vectors were represented by their angles relative to the positive horizontal axis (i.e., the magnitude is ignored). The responses of the directionally-tuned units can be directly computed from the angles (see Eqn. 1; alternatively, cosine tuning functions were used, and similar results were obtained). For each trial, the coherent motion direction was randomly decided. In the experiments, σ_h was set to $\frac{\pi}{n_d}$, where n_d is the number of unit preferred directions; the directions θ_t are chosen by uniformly dividing n_d in to 2π. In all the experiments, eight preferred directions were used; each trial contained 40 random dots moving with a correlation of 25% (the same correlation as in the tests with human subjects);

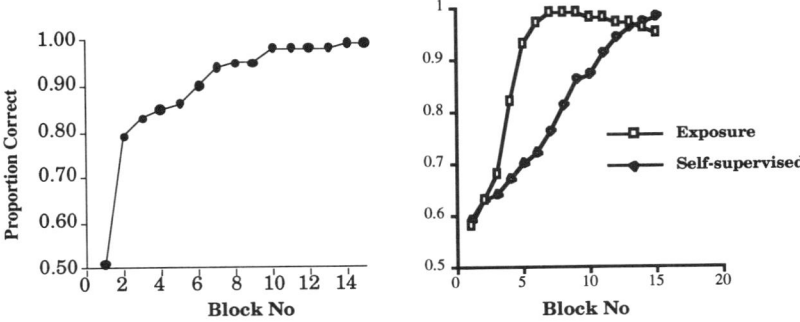

Figure 3: Results from typical simulation runs. On the left is the curve for the *learning to accommodate* model ($\eta = 0.005$; cluster $\sigma = 0.5$) and on the right are the curves for the *learning to ignore* model.

each block consisted of 50 trials. The performance is measured by *fraction correct*, corresponding to the fraction of the inputs that were correctly classified.

For both models, we did simulations to justify the architecture of the models by disabling learning, and studying the performance of the models for increasing correlation. The performance was qualitatively similar to that described in perceptual studies of these stimuli in humans and monkeys.

Learning curves from simulations of both models are shown in Fig. 3. These are results from averaging over the performance in ten simulation runs. As can be seen, the models learn to do the discrimination. While both models successfully learned to do the direction discrimination, there are quantitative differences in the learning curves. The *learning to accommodate* paradigm improved very rapidly (somewhat faster than the human subjects). The *exposure-based* learning rule for the *learning to ignore* paradigm learned at a rate comparable with the human observers. However, the final performance in this case was not very stable, and oscillated (not shown), consistent with the observations of Weiss et. al (1993) in learning vernier hyperacuity. The *self-supervised* rule, on the other hand, reached a stable level of performance, but the learning was slower; the reason is that this learning rule exhibits instability if a high value of learning rate (η) is used.

If either model trained on inputs containing horizontal correlated motion was later presented with inputs containing vertical correlated motion, the performance dropped to pre-training levels. This non-transfer is consistent with psychophysical results mentioned in Section 2.

5 Discussion

In this study, we focused on learning of global motion direction, and not on motion perception. Motion perception is well-understood both physiologically and psychophysically. In a series of studies of neuronal correlates of the perceptual decision of direction of motion in stochastic motion signals like the stimuli used here, together with studies of performance on these stimuli on monkeys with MT lesions, Newsome and his collaborators (for a review, Newsome et. al, 1989) provide strong support for the hypothesis that perceptual judgements of motion direction are by and large based on the directional signals carried by MT neurons.

Salzman and Newsome (1994) reported that in trained monkeys, the perception of motion in stochastic noise is more likely mediated by a winner-take-all mechanism than by a weighted averaging mechanism. Interestingly, our clustering model, after learning, is behaviorally similar to the winner-take-all mechanism: the dominating component of the representation results in the assignment to the closest cluster.

Our psychophysical studies clearly demonstrate that perceptual learning of global motion direction occurs. While significant progress has been made to understand the mechanisms and underlying circuitry of learning (Zohary et. al 1994) as yet there is no satisfactory biologically explanation of how and where this learning may occur (Zohary and Newsome 1994).

Our focus in this paper was on computational models of learning direction in global motion. For this, we proposed two approaches, which differ in the way they deal with noise: one learns to accommodates noise, and the other learns to ignore it. We do not advocate that one or the other of the models we proposed here provides the biologically correct choice for this task. However, together with the psychophysics described here these models suggest new experiments which we are now exploring both psychophysically and computationally.

We hope that by closely connecting models and psychophysics while keeping in mind the aim of neuronal compatibility, we will make progress in understanding how the cortex learns so fast to discriminate direction of motion in extremely noisy situations.

Acknowledgments

This research was conducted at the Intelligent Systems Laboratory of Boston University, College of Engineering. LMV and VS were supported in part by grants from the Office of Naval Research (# N00014-93-1-0381) and the National Institute of Health (EY RO1- 07861) to LMV. VS was in part supported by the Boston University College of Engineering Dean's postdoctoral fellowship. We gratefully acknowledge additional financial support for VS from the Dean's special research fund.

References

[1] K. Ball and R. Sekuler. Direction-specific improvement in motion discrimination. *Vision Research*, 27(6):953–965, 1987.

[2] M. Fahle. Human pattern recognition: parallel processing and perceptual learning. *Perception*, 23:411–427, 1994.

[3] M. Fendick and G. Westheimer. Effects of practice and the separation of test targets on foveal and perifoveal hyperacuity. *Vision Research*, 23:145–150, 1983.

[4] A. Fiorentini and N. Berardi. Perceptual learning specific for orientation and spatial frequency. *Nature*, 287(5777):43–44, September 1980.

[5] Y. Frégnac, D. Shulz, S. Thorpe, and E. Bienstock. A cellular analogue of visual cortical plasticity. *Nature*, 333:367–370, 1988.

[6] E. J. Gibson. Improvements in perceptual judgement as a function of controlled practice of training. *Psychology bulletin*, 50:402–431, 1953.

[7] C. D. Gilbert and T. N. Wiesel. Receptive field dynamics in adult primary visual cortex. *Nature*, 356:150–152, 1992.

[8] A. Karni and D. Sagi. Where practice makes perfect in texture discrimination: Evidence for primary visual cortex plasticity. *Proc. Natl. Acad. Sci. USA*, 88:4966–4970, June 1991.

[9] J. H. R. Maunsell and D. C. Van Essen. Functional properties of neurons in the middle temporal visual area of the macaque monkey i: selectivity for stimulus direction, speed, and orientation. *J. Neurophysiology*, 49:1127–1147, 1983.

[10] S. P. McKee and G. Westheimer. Improvement in venier acuity with practice. *Perception & Psychophysics*, 24:258–262, 1978.

[11] W. T. Newsome, K. H. Britten, and J. A. Movshon. Neuronal correlates of a perceptual decision. *Nature*, 341:52–54, 1989.

[12] T. Poggio. A theory of how the brain might work. In *Cold Spring Harbor Symposia on Quantitative Biology*, pages 899–910. Cold Spring Harbor Laboratory Press, 1990.

[13] T. Poggio, M. Fahle, and S. Edelman. Fast perceptual learning in visual hyperacuity. *Science*, 256:1018–1021, 1992.

[14] T. Poggio and F. Girosi. A theory of networks for approximation and learning. AI Memo 1140, M.I.T, July 1989.

[15] V. S. Ramachandran and O. Braddick. Orientation-specific learning in stereopsis. *Perception*, 2:371–376, 1973.

[16] C. D. Salzman and W. T. Newsome. Neural mechanisms for forming a perceptual decision. *Science*, 264:231–237, 1994.

[17] L. M. Vaina, V. Sundareswaran, and J. Harris. Computational learning and natural learning. Cognitive Brain Research, 1995. (in press).

[18] L. M. Vaina, N. M. Grzywacz, and M. LeMay. Structure from motion with impaired local-speed and global motion-field computations. *Neural Computation*, 2:420–435, 1990.

[19] R. Vogels and G. A. Orban. The effect of practice on the oblique effect in line orientation judgements. *Vision Research*, 25:1679–1687, 1985.

[20] S. Watamaniuk, R. Sekuler, and D. Williams. Direction perception in complex dynamic displays: the integration of direction information. *Vision Research*, 24:55–62, 1984.

[21] Y. Weiss, S. Edelman, and M. Fahle. Models of perceptual learning in vernier hyperacuity. *Neural Computation*, 5:695–718, 1993.

[22] E. Zohary, S. Celebrini, K. H. Britten, and W. T. Newsome. Neuronal plasticity that underlies improvement in perceptual performance. *Science*, 263:1289–1292, March 1994.

[23] E. Zohary and W. T. Newsome. Perceptual learning in a direction discrimination task is not based upon enhanced neuronal sensitivity in the sts. *Investigative Ophthalmology and Visual Science supplement*, page 1663, 1994.

Associative Decorrelation Dynamics: A Theory of Self-Organization and Optimization in Feedback Networks

Dawei W. Dong*
Lawrence Berkeley Laboratory
University of California
Berkeley, CA 94720

Abstract

This paper outlines a dynamic theory of development and adaptation in neural networks with feedback connections. Given input ensemble, the connections change in strength according to an associative learning rule and approach a stable state where the neuronal outputs are decorrelated. We apply this theory to primary visual cortex and examine the implications of the dynamical decorrelation of the activities of orientation selective cells by the intracortical connections. The theory gives a unified and quantitative explanation of the psychophysical experiments on orientation contrast and orientation adaptation. Using only one parameter, we achieve good agreements between the theoretical predictions and the experimental data.

1 Introduction

The mammalian visual system is very effective in detecting the orientations of lines and most neurons in primary visual cortex selectively respond to oriented lines and form orientation columns [1]. Why is the visual system organized as such? We

---

*Present address: Rockefeller University, B272, 1230 York Avenue, NY, NY 10021-6399.

believe that the visual system is self-organized, in both long term development and short term adaptation, to ensure the optimal information processing.

Linsker applied Hebbian learning to model the development of orientation selectivity and later proposed a principle of maximum information preservation in early visual pathways [2]. The focus of his work has been on the feedforward connections and in his model the feedback connections are isotropic and unchanged during the development of orientation columns; but the actual circuitry of visual cortex involves extensive, columnar specified feedback connections which exist even before functional columns appear in cat striate cortex [3].

Our earlier research emphasized the important role of the feedback connections in the development of the columnar structure in visual cortex. We developed a theoretical framework to help understand the dynamics of Hebbian learning in feedback networks and showed how the columnar structure originates from symmetry breaking in the development of the feedback connections (intracortical, or lateral connections within visual cortex) [4].

Figure 1 illustrates our theoretical predictions. The intracortical connections break symmetry and develop strip-like patterns with a characteristic wave length which is comparable to the developed intracortical inhibitory range and the LGN-cortex afferent range (left). The feedforward (LGN-cortex) connections develop under the influence of the symmetry breaking development of the intracortical connections. The developed feedforward connections for each cell form a receptive field which is orientation selective and nearby cells have similar orientation preference (right). Their orientations change in about the same period as the strip-like pattern of the intracortical connections.

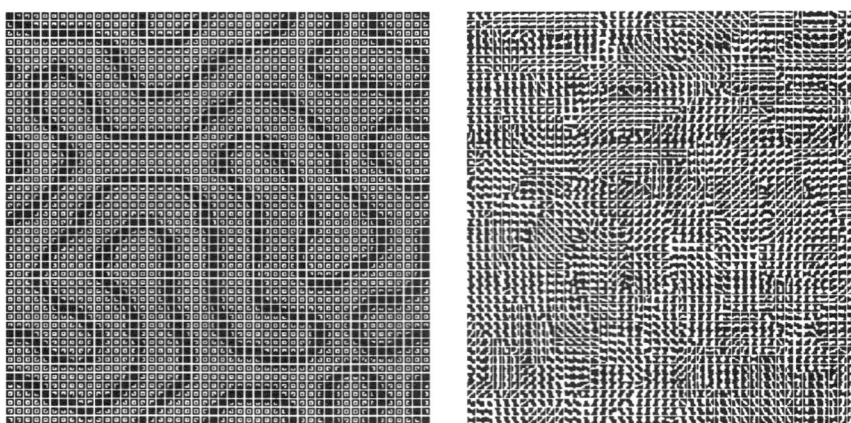

Figure 1: The results of the development of visual cortex with feedback connections. The simulated cortex consists of 48 × 48 neurons, each of which connects to 5 × 5 other cortical neurons (left) and receives inputs from 7 × 7 LGN neurons (right). In this figure, white indicates positive connections and black indicates negative connections. One can see that the change of receptive field's orientation (right) is highly correlated with the strip-like pattern of intracortical connections (left).

Many aspects of our theoretical predictions agree qualitatively with neurobiological observations in primary visual cortex. Another way to test the idea of optimal information processing or any self-organization theory is through quantitative psychophysical studies. The idea is to look for changes in perception following changes in input environments. The psychophysical experiments on orientation illusions offer some opportunities to test our theory on orientation selectivity.

Orientation illusions are the effects that the perceived orientations of lines are affected by the neighboring (in time or space) oriented stimuli, which have been observed in many psychophysical experiments and were attributed to the inhibitory interactions between channels tuned to different orientations [5]. But there is no unified and quantitative explanation. Neurophysiological evidences support our earlier computational model in which intracortical inhibition plays the role of gain-control in orientation selectivity [6]. But in order for the gain-control mechanism to be effective to signals of different statistics, the system has to develop and adapt in different environments.

In this paper we examine the implication of the hypothesis that the intracortical connections dynamically decorrelate the activities of orientation selective cells, i.e., the intracortical connections are actively adapted to the visual environment, such that the output activities of orientation selective cells are decorrelated. The dynamics which ensures such decorrelation through associative learning is outlined in the next section as the theoretical framework for the development and the adaptation of intracortical connections. We only emphasize the feedback connections in the following sections and assume that the feedforward connections developed orientation selectivities based on our earlier works. The quantitative comparisons of the theory and the experiments are presented in section 3.

2   Associative Decorrelation Dynamics

There are two different kinds of variables in neural networks. One class of variables represents the activity of the nerve cells, or neurons. The other class of variables describes the synapses, or connections, between the nerve cells. A complete model of an adaptive neural system requires two sets of dynamical equations, one for each class of variables, to specify the evolution and behavior of the neural system.

The set of equations describing the change of the state of activity of the neurons is

$$a\frac{dV_i}{dt} = -V_i + \sum_j T_{ij} V_j + I_i \tag{1}$$

in which a is a time constant, T_{ij} is the strength of the synaptic connection from neuron j to neuron i, and I_i is the additional feedforward input to the neuron besides those described by the feedback connection matrix T_{ij}. A second set of equations describes the way the synapses change with time due to neuronal activity. The learning rule proposed here is

$$B\frac{dT_{ij}}{dt} = (V_i - V_i')I_j \tag{2}$$

in which B is a time constant and V_i' is the feedback learning signal as described in the following.

The feedback learning signal V_i' is generated by a Hopfield type associative memory network: $V_i' = \sum_j T_{ij}'' V_j$, in which T_{ij}'' is the strength of the associative connection from neuron j to neuron i, which is the recent correlation between the neuronal activities V_i and V_j determined by Hebbian learning with a decay term [4]

$$B' \frac{dT'_{ij}}{dt} = -T'_{ij} + V_i V_j \qquad (3)$$

in which B' is a time constant. The V'_i and T'_{ij} are only involved in learning and do not directly affect the network outputs.

It is straight forward to show that when the time constants $B \gg B' \gg a$, the dynamics reduces to

$$B \frac{d\mathbf{T}}{dt} = (\mathbf{1} - <\mathbf{V}\mathbf{V}^T>) < \mathbf{V}\mathbf{I}^T > \qquad (4)$$

where bold-faced quantities are matrices and vectors and $<>$ denotes ensemble average. It is not difficult to show that this equation has a Lyapunov or "energy" function

$$L = \mathrm{Tr}(\mathbf{1} - <\mathbf{V}\mathbf{V}^T>)(\mathbf{1} - <\mathbf{V}\mathbf{V}^T>)^T \qquad (5)$$

which is lower bounded and satisfies

$$\frac{dL}{dt} \leq 0 \quad \text{and} \quad \frac{dL}{dt} = 0 \;\rightarrow\; \frac{dT_{ij}}{dt} = 0 \quad \text{for all } i,j \qquad (6)$$

Thus the dynamics is stable. When it is stable, the output activities are decorrelated,

$$<\mathbf{V}\mathbf{V}^T> = \mathbf{1} \qquad (7)$$

The above equation shows that this dynamics always leads to a stable state where the neuronal activities are decorrelated and their correlation matrix is orthonormal. Yet the connections change in an associative fashion — equation (2) and (3) are almost Hebbian. That is why we call it associative decorrelation dynamics. From information processing point of view, a network, self-organized to satisfy equation (7), is optimized for Gaussian input ensembles and white output noises [7].

Linear First Order Analysis

In applying our theory of associative decorrelation dynamics to visual cortex to compare with the psychophysical experiments on orientation illusions, the linear first-order approximation is used, which is

$$\begin{array}{ll} \mathbf{T} = \mathbf{T}^0 + \delta\mathbf{T}, & \mathbf{T}^0 = \mathbf{0}, \quad \delta\mathbf{T} \propto - <\mathbf{I}\mathbf{I}^T> \\ \mathbf{V} = \mathbf{V}^0 + \delta\mathbf{V}, & \mathbf{V}^0 = \mathbf{I}, \quad \delta\mathbf{V} = \mathbf{T}\mathbf{I} \end{array} \qquad (8)$$

where it is assumed that the input correlations are small. It is interesting to notice that the linear first-order approximation leads to anti-Hebbian feedback connections: $T_{ij} \propto - <I_i I_j>$ which is guarantteed to be stable around $\mathbf{T} = \mathbf{0}$ [8].

3 Quantitative Predictions of Orientation Illusions

The basic phenomena of orientation illusions are demonstrated in figure 2 (left). On the top, is the effect of orientation contrast (also called tilt illusion): within the two surrounding circles there are tilted lines; the orientation of a center rectangle

Associative Correlation Dynamics

appears rotated to the opposite side of its surrounding tilt. Both the two rectangles and the one without surround (at the left-center of this figure) are, in fact, exactly same. On the bottom, is the effect of orientation adaptation (also called tilt aftereffect): if one fixates at the small circle in one of the two big circles with tilted lines for 20 seconds or so and then look at the rectangle without surround, the orientation of the lines of the rectangle appears tilted to the opposite side.

These two effects of orientation illusions are both in the direction of repulsion: the apparent orientation of a line is changed to increase its difference from the inducing line. Careful experimental measurements also revealed that the angle with the inducing line is $\sim 10°$ for maximum orientation adaptation effect [9] but $\sim 20°$ for orientation contrast [10].

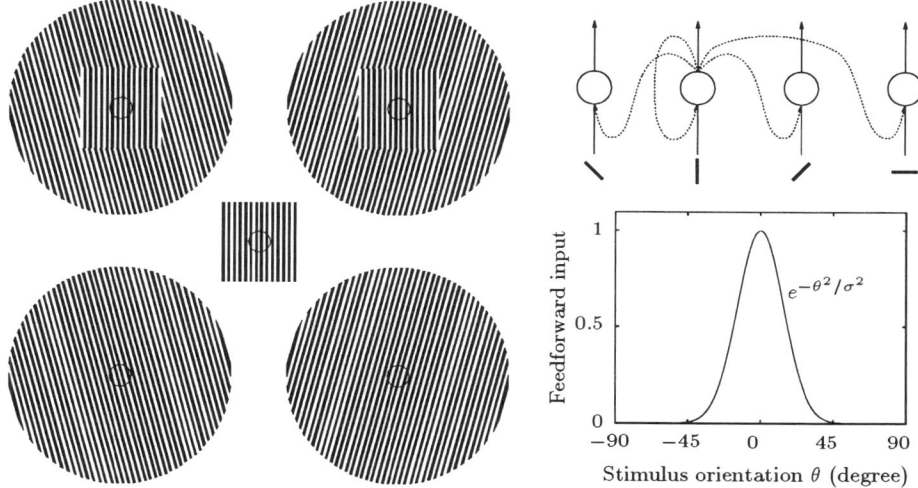

Figure 2: The effects of orientation contrast (upper-left) and orientation adaptation (lower-left) are attributed to feedback connections between cells tuned to different orientations (upper-right, network; lower-right, tuning curve).

Orientation illusions are attributed to the feedback connections between orientation selective cells. This is illustrated in figure 2 (right). On the top is the network of orientation selective cells with feedback connections. Only four cells are shown. From the left, they receive orientation selective feedforward inputs optimal at $-45°$, $0°, 45°$, and $90°$, respectively. The dotted lines represent the feedback connections (only the connections from the second cell are drawn). On the bottom is the orientation tuning curve of the feedforward input for the second cell, optimally tuned to stimulus of $0°$ (vertical), which is assumed to be Gaussian of width $\sigma = 20°$. Because of the feedback connections, the output of the second cell will have different tuning curves from its feedforward input, depending on the activities of other cells.

For primary visual cortex, we suppose that there are orientation selective neurons tuned to all orientations. It is more convenient to use the continuous variable θ instead of the index i to represent neuron which is optimally tuned to the orientation of angle θ. The neuronal activity is represented by $V(\theta)$ and the feedforward input to each neuron is represented by $I(\theta)$. The feedforward input itself is orientation

selective: given a visual stimulus of orientation θ_0, the input is
$$I(\theta) = e^{-(\theta-\theta_0)^2/\sigma^2} \tag{9}$$
This kind of the orientation tuning has been measured by experiments (for references, see [6]). Various experiments give a reasonable tuning width around $20°$ ($\sigma = 20°$ is used for all the predictions).

Predicted Orientation Adaptation

For the orientation adaptation to stimulus of angle θ_0, substituting equation (9) into equation (8), it is not difficult to derive that the network response to stimulus of angle 0 (vertical) is changed to
$$V(\theta) = e^{-\theta^2/\sigma^2} - \alpha e^{-(\theta-\theta_0)^2/\sigma^2} e^{-\theta_0^2/2\sigma^2} \tag{10}$$
in which σ is the feedforward tuning width chosen to be $20°$ and α is the parameter of the strength of decorrelation feedback.

The theoretical curve of perceived orientation $\phi(\theta_0)$ is derived by assuming the maximum likelihood of the the neural population, i.e., the perceived angle ϕ is the angle at which $V(\theta)$ is maximized. It is shown in figure 3 (right). The solid line is the theoretical curve and the experimental data come from [9] (they did not give the errors, the error bars are of our estimation $\sim 0.2°$). The parameter obtained through χ^2 fit is the strength of decorrelation feedback: $\alpha = 0.42$.

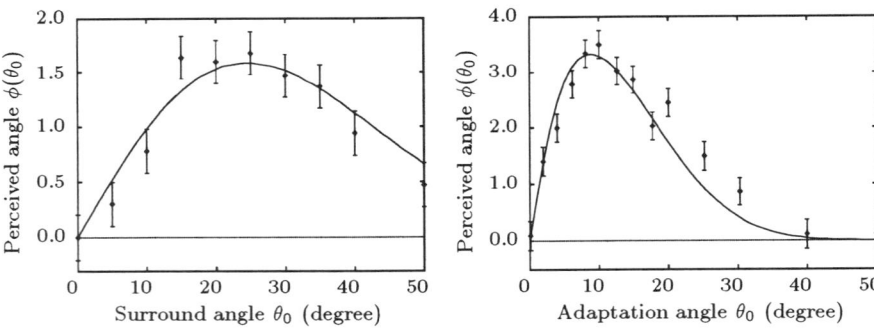

Figure 3: Quantitative comparison of the theoretical predictions with the experimental data of orientation contrast (left) and orientation adaptation (right).

It is very interesting that we can derive a relationship which is independent of the parameter of the strength of decorrelation feedback α,
$$(\theta_0 - \phi_m)(3\theta_0 - 2\phi_m) = \sigma^2 \tag{11}$$
in which θ_0 is the adaptation angle at which the tilt aftereffect is most significant and ϕ_m is the perceived angle.

Predicted Orientation Contrast

For orientation contrast, there is no specific adaptation angle, i.e., the network has developed in an environment of all possible angles. In this case, when the surround is of angle θ_0, the network response to a stimulus of angle θ_1 is
$$V(\theta) = e^{-(\theta-\theta_1)^2/\sigma^2} - \alpha e^{-(\theta-\theta_0)^2/3\sigma^2} \tag{12}$$

in which σ and α has the same meaning as for orientation adaptation. Again assuming the maximum likelihood, $\phi(\theta_0)$, the stimulus angle θ_1 at which it is perceived as angle 0, is derived and shown in figure 3 (left). The solid line is the theoretical curve and the experimental data come from [10] and their estimated error is $\sim 0.2°$. The parameter obtained through χ^2 fit is the strength of decorrelation feedback: $\alpha = 0.32$.

We can derive the peak position θ_0, i.e., the surrounding angle θ_0 at which the orientation contrast is most significant,

$$\frac{2}{3}\theta_0^2 = \sigma^2 \tag{13}$$

For $\sigma = 20°$, one immediately gets $\theta_0 = 24°$. This is in good agreement with experiments, most people experience the maximum effect of orientation contrast around this angle.

Our theory predicts that the peak position of the surround angle for orientation contrast should be constant since the orientation tuning width σ is roughly the same for different human observers and is not going to change much for different experimental setups. But the peak value of the perceived angle is not constant since the decorrelation feedback parameter α is not necessarily same, indeed, it could be quite different for different human observers and different experimental setups.

4 Discussion

First, we want to emphasis that in all the comparisons, the same tuning width σ is used and the strength of decorrelation feedback α is the only fit parameter. It does not take much imagination to see that the quantitative agreements between the theory and the experiments are good. Further more, we derived the relationships for the maximum effects, which are independent of the parameter α and have been partially confirmed by the experiments.

Recent neurophysiological experiments revealed that the surrounding lines did influence the orientation selectivity of cells in primary visual cortex of the cat [11]. Those single cell experiments land further support to our theory. But one should be cautioned that the cells in our theory should be considered as the average over a large population of cells in cortex.

The theory not only explains the first order effects which are dominant in angle range of $0°$ to $50°$, as shown here, but also accounts for the second order effects which can be seen in $50°$ to $90°$ range, where the sign of the effects is reversed. The theory also makes some predictions for which not much experiment has been done yet, for example, the prediction about how orientation contrast depends on the distance of surrounding stimuli from the test stimulus [7].

Finally, this is not merely a theory for the development and the adaptation of orientation selective cells, it can account for effect such as human vision adaptation to colors as well [7]. We can derive the same equation as Atick *etal* [12] which agrees with the experiment on the appearance of color hue after adaptation. We believe that future psychophysical experiments could give us more quantitative results to further test our theory and help our understanding of neural systems in general.

Acknowledgements

This work was supported in part by the Director, Office of Energy Research, Division of Nuclear Physics of the Office of High Energy and Nuclear Physics of the U.S. Department of Energy under Contract No. DE-AC03-76SF00098.

References

[1] Hubel DH, Wiesel TN, 1962 Receptive fields, binocular interactions, and functional architecture in the cat's visual cortex *J Physiol (London)* **160**, 106–54. — 1963 Shape and arrangement of columns in cat's striate cortex *J Physiol (London)* **165**, 559–68.

[2] Linsker R, 1986 From basic network principles to neural architecture ... *Proc Natl Acad Sci USA* **83**, 7508 8390 8779. —, 1989 An application of the principle of maximum information preservation to linear systems *Advances in Neural Information Processing Systems 1, Touretzky DS, ed, Morgan Kaufman, San Mateo, CA* 186–94.

[3] Gilbert C, Wiesel T, 1989 Columnar Specificity of intrinsic horizontal and corticocortical connections in cat visual cortex *J Neurosci* **9(7)**, 2432–42. Luhmann HJ, Martinez L, Singer W, 1986 Development of horizontal intrinsic connections in cat striate cortex *Exp Brain Res* **63**, 443–8.

[4] Dong DW, 1991 Dynamic properties of neural network with adapting synapses *Proc International Joint Conference on Neural Networks, Seattle*, **2**, 255–260. —, 1991 Dynamic Properties of Neural Networks *Ph D thesis, University Microfilms International, Ann Arbor, MI*. Dong DW, Hopfield JJ, 1992 Dynamic properties of neural networks with adapting synapses *Network: Computation in Neural Systems*, **3(3)**, 267–83.

[5] Gibson JJ, Radner M, 1937 Adaptation, after-effect and contrast in the perception of tilted lines *J of Exp Psy* **20**, 453–67. Carpenter RHS, Blakemore C, 1973 Interactions between orientations in human vision *Exp Brain Res* **18**, 287–303. Tolhurst DJ, Thompson PG, 1975 Orientation illusions and after-effects: Inhibition between channels *Vis Res* **15**, 967–72. Barlow HB, Foldiak P, 1989 Adaptation and decorrelation in the cortex *The Computing Neuron, Durbin R, Miall C, Mitchison G, eds, Addison-Wesley, New York, NY*.

[6] Wehmeier U, Dong DW, Koch C, Van Essen DC, 1989 Modeling the mammalian visual system *Methods in Neuronal Modeling: From Synapses to Networks, Koch C, Segev I, eds, MIT Press, Cambridge, MA* 335–60.

[7] Dong DW, 1993 Associative Decorrelation Dynamics in Visual Cortex *Lawrence Berkeley Laboratory Technical Report* LBL-34491.

[8] Dong DW, 1993 Anti-Hebbian dynamics and total recall of associative memory *Proc World Congress on Neural Networks, Portland*, **2**, 275–9.

[9] Campbell FW, Maffei L, 1971 The tilt after-effect: a fresh look *Vis Res* **11**, 833–40.

[10] Westheimer G, 1990 Simultaneous orientation contrast for lines in the human fovea *Vis Res* **30**, 1913–21.

[11] Gilbert CD, Wiesel TN, 1990 The influence of contextual stimuli on the orientation selectivity of cells in primary visual cortex of the cat *Vis Res* **30**, 1689–701.

[12] Atick JJ, Li Z, Redlich AN, 1993 What does post-adaptation color appearance reveal about cortical color representation *Vis Res* **33**, 123–9.

JPMAX: Learning to Recognize Moving Objects as a Model-fitting Problem

Suzanna Becker
Department of Psychology, McMaster University
Hamilton, Ont. L8S 4K1

Abstract

Unsupervised learning procedures have been successful at low-level feature extraction and preprocessing of raw sensor data. So far, however, they have had limited success in learning higher-order representations, e.g., of objects in visual images. A promising approach is to maximize some measure of agreement between the outputs of two groups of units which receive inputs physically separated in space, time or modality, as in (Becker and Hinton, 1992; Becker, 1993; de Sa, 1993). Using the same approach, a much simpler learning procedure is proposed here which discovers features in a single-layer network consisting of several populations of units, and can be applied to multi-layer networks trained one layer at a time. When trained with this algorithm on image sequences of moving geometric objects a two-layer network can learn to perform accurate position-invariant object classification.

1 LEARNING COHERENT CLASSIFICATIONS

A powerful constraint in sensory data is coherence over time, in space, and across different sensory modalities. An unsupervised learning procedure which can capitalize on these constraints may be able to explain much of perceptual self-organization in the mammalian brain. The problem is to derive an appropriate cost function for unsupervised learning which will capture coherence constraints in sensory signals; we would also like it to be applicable to multi-layer nets to train hidden as well as output layers. Our ultimate goal is for the network to discover natural object classes based on these coherence assumptions.

1.1 PREVIOUS WORK

Successive images in continuous visual input are usually views of the same object; thus, although the image pixels may change considerably from frame to frame, the image usually can be described by a small set of consistent object descriptors, or lower-level feature descriptors. We refer to this type of continuity as *temporal coherence*. This sort of structure is ubiquitous in sensory signals, from vision as well as other senses, and can be used by a neural network to derive temporally coherent classifications. This idea has been used, for example, in temporal versions of the Hebbian learning rule to associate items over time (Weinshall, Edelman and Bülthoff, 1990; Földiák, 1991). To capitalize on temporal coherence for higher-order feature extraction and classification, we need a more powerful learning principle.

A promising approach is to maximize some measure of agreement between the outputs of two groups of units which receive inputs physically separated in space, time or modality, as in (Becker and Hinton, 1992; Becker, 1993; de Sa, 1993). This forces the units to extract features which are coherent across the different input sources. Becker and Hinton's (1992) Imax algorithm maximizes the mutual information between the outputs of two modules, $\vec{y_a}$ and $\vec{y_b}$, connected to different parts of the input, a and b. Becker (1993) extended this idea to the problem of classifying temporally varying patterns by applying the discrete case of the mutual information cost function to the outputs of a single module at successive time steps, $\vec{y_a}(t)$ and $\vec{y_a}(t+1)$. However, the success of this method relied upon the back-propagation of derivatives to train the hidden layer and it was found to be extremely susceptible to local optima. de Sa's method (1993) is closely related, and minimizes the probability of disagreement between output classifications, $\vec{y_a}(t)$ and $\vec{y_b}(t)$, produced by two modules having different inputs, e.g., from different sensory modalities. The success of this method hinges upon bootstrapping the first layer by initializing the weights to randomly selected training patterns, so this method too is susceptible to the problem of local optima. If we had a more flexible cost function that could be applied to a multi-layer network, first to each hidden layer in turn, and finally to the output layer for classification, so that the two layers could discover genuinely different structure, we might be able to overcome the problem of getting trapped in local optima, yielding a more powerful and efficient learning procedure.

We can analyze the optimal solutions for both de Sa's and Becker's cost functions (see Figure 1 a) and see that both cost functions are maximized by having perfect one-to-one agreement between the two groups of units over all cases, using a one-of-n encoding, i.e., having only a single output unit on for each case. A major limitation of these methods is that they strive for perfect classifications by the units. While this is desirable at the top layer of a network, it is an unsuitable goal for training intermediate layers to detect low-level features. For example, features like oriented edges would not be perfect predictors across spatially or temporally nearby image patches in images of translating and rotating objects. Instead, we might expect that an oriented edge at one location would predict a small range of similar orientations at nearby locations. So we would prefer a cost function whose optimal solution was more like those shown in Figure 1 b) or c). This would allow a feature i in group a to agree with any of several nearby features, e.g. $i-1$, i, or $i+1$ in group b.

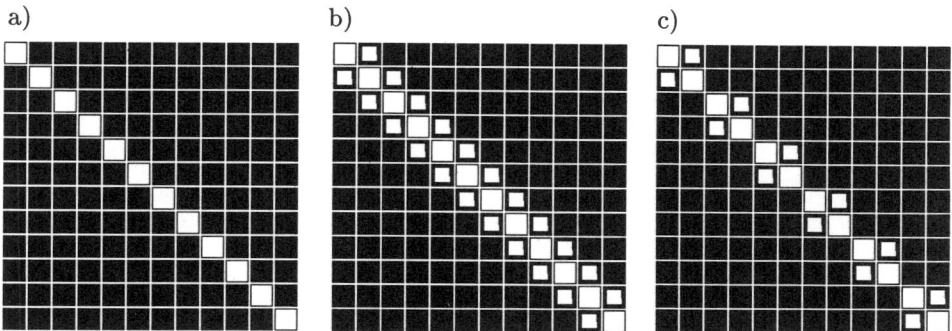

Figure 1: *Three possible joint distributions for the probability that the ith and jth units in two sets of m classification units are both on. White is high density, black is low density. The optimal joint distribution for Becker's and de Sa's algorithms is a matrix with all its density either in the diagonal as in a), or any subset of the diagonal entries for de Sa's method, or a permutation of the diagonal matrix for Becker's algorithm. Alternative distributions are shown in b) and c).*

1.2 THE JPMAX ALGORITHM

One way to achieve an arbitrary configuration of agreement over time between two groups of units (as in Figure 1 b) or c)) is to treat the desired configuration as a prior joint probability distribution over their outputs. We can obtain the actual distribution by observing the temporal correlations between pairs of units' outputs in the two groups over an ensemble of patterns. We can then optimize the actual distribution to fit the prior. We now derive two different cost functions which achieve this result. Interestingly, they result in very similar learning rules.

Suppose we have two groups of m units as shown in Figure 2 a), receiving inputs, $\vec{x_a}$ and $\vec{x_b}$, from the same or nearby parts of the input image. Let $C_a(t)$ and $C_b(t)$ be the classifications of the two input patches produced by the network at time step t; the outputs of the two groups of units, $\vec{y_a}(t)$ and $\vec{y_b}(t)$, represent these classification probabilities:

$$y_{ai}(t) = P(C_a(t) = i) = \frac{e^{net_{ai}(t)}}{\sum_j e^{net_{aj}(t)}}$$

$$y_{bi}(t) = P(C_b(t) = i) = \frac{e^{net_{bi}(t)}}{\sum_j e^{net_{bj}(t)}} \quad (1)$$

(the usual "softmax" output function) where $net_{ai}(t)$ and $net_{bj}(t)$ are the weighted net inputs to units. We could now observe the expected joint probability distribution $q_{ij} = E[y_{ai}(t)y_{bj}(t+1)]_t = E[P(C_a(t) = i, C_b(t+1) = j)]_t$ by computing the temporal covariances between the classification probabilities, averaged over the ensemble of training patterns; this joint probability is an m^2-valued random variable.

Given the above statistics, one possible cost function we could minimize is the $-\log$ probability of the observed temporal covariance between the two sets of units' outputs under some prior distribution (e.g. Figure 1 b) or c)). If we knew the actual *frequency counts* for each (joint) classification $\vec{k} = k_{11}, \ldots, k_{1m}, k_{21}, \ldots, k_{mm}$,

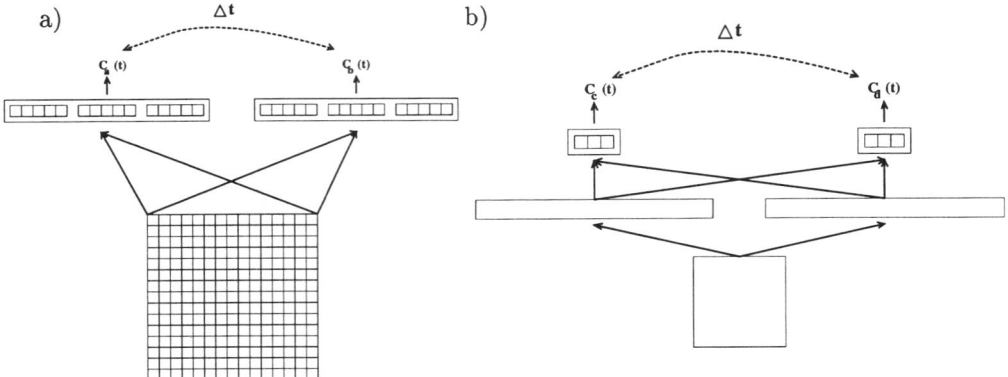

Figure 2: *a) Two groups of 15 units receive inputs from a 2D retina. The groups are able to observe each other's outputs across lateral links with unit time delays. b) A second layer of two groups of 3 units is added to the architecture in a).*

rather than just the observed joint probabilities, $q_{ij} = E\left[\frac{k_{ij}}{n}\right]$, then given our prior model, $p_{11}, \ldots, p_{mm}$, we could compute the probability of the observations under a multinomial distribution:

$$P(\vec{k}) = \frac{n!}{\prod_{i,j} k_{ij}!} \prod_{i,j} p_{ij}^{k_{ij}} \tag{2}$$

Using the de Moivre-Laplace approximation leads to the following:

$$P(\vec{k}) \approx \frac{1}{\sqrt{(2\pi n)^{m^2-1} \prod_{i,j} p_{ij}}} \exp\left(-\frac{1}{2} \sum_{i,j} \frac{(k_{ij} - np_{ij})^2}{np_{ij}}\right) \tag{3}$$

Taking the derivative of the - log probability *wrt* k_{ij} leads to a very simple learning rule which depends only on the observed probabilities q_{ij} and priors p_{ij}:

$$\begin{aligned}\frac{\partial -\log P(\vec{k})}{\partial k_{ij}} &= \frac{np_{ij} - k_{ij}}{np_{ij}} \\ &\approx \frac{p_{ij} - q_{ij}}{p_{ij}}\end{aligned} \tag{4}$$

To obtain the final weight update rule, we just multiply this by $n\frac{\partial q_{ij}}{\partial w_{kl}}$. One problem with the above formulation is that the priors p_{ij} must not be too close to zero for the de Moivre-Laplace approximation to hold. In practice, this cost function works well if we simply ignore the derivative terms where the priors are zero.

An alternative cost function (as suggested by Peter Dayan) which works equally well is the Kullback-Liebler divergence or G-error between the desired joint probabilities p_{ij} and the observed probabilities q_{ij}:

$$G(p,q) = -\sum_i \sum_j (p_{ij} \log p_{ij} - p_{ij} \log q_{ij}) \tag{5}$$

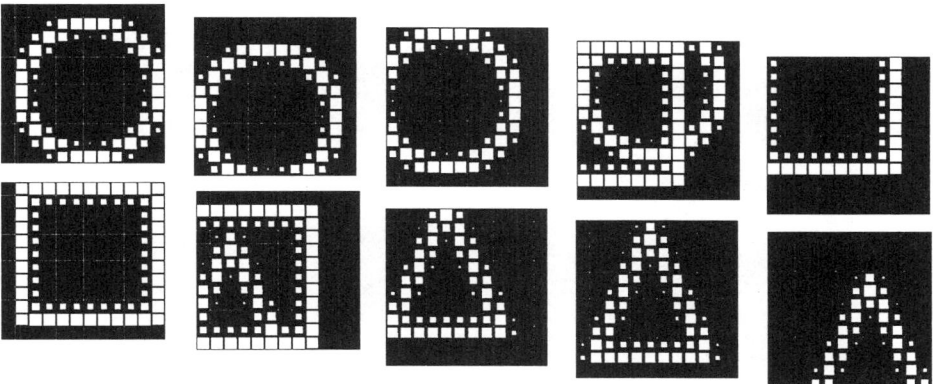

Figure 3: *10 of the 1500 training patterns: geometric objects centered in 36 possible locations on a 12-by-12 pixel grid. Object location varied randomly between patterns.*

The derivative of G wrt q_{ij} is:

$$\frac{\partial G}{\partial q_{ij}} = \frac{p_{ij}}{q_{ij}} \tag{6}$$

subject to $\sum_{ij} q_{ij} = 1$ (enforced by the softmax output function). Note the similarity between the learning rules given by equations 4 and 6.

2 EXPERIMENTS

The network shown in Figure 2 a) was trained to minimize equation 5 on an ensemble of pattern trajectories of circles, squares and triangles (see Figure 3) for five runs starting from different random initial weights, using a gradient-based learning method. For ten successive frames, the same object would appear, but with the centre varying randomly within the central six-by-six patch of pixels. In the last two frames, another randomly selected object would appear, so that object trajectories overlapped by two frames. These images are meant to be a crude approximation to what a moving observer would see while watching multiple moving objects in a scene; at any given time a single object would be approximately centered on the retina but its exact location would always be jittering from moment to moment.

In these simulations, the prior distribution for the temporal covariances between the two groups of units' outputs was a block-diagonal configuration as in Figure 1 c), but with three five-by-five blocks along the diagonal. Our choice of a block-diagonal prior distribution with three blocks encodes the constraint that units in a given block in one group should try to agree with units in the same block in the other group; so each group should discover three classes of features. The number of units within a block was varied in preliminary experiments, and five units was found to be a reasonable number to capture all instances of each object class (although the performance of the algorithm seemed to be robust with respect to the number of units per block). The learning took about 3000 iterations of steepest descent with

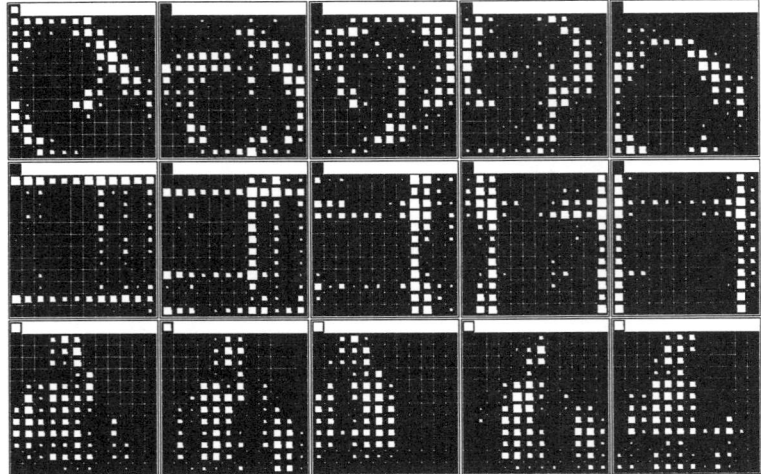

Figure 4: *Weights learned by one of the two groups of 15 units in the first layer. White weights are positive and black are negative.*

momentum to converge, but after about 1000 iterations only very small weight changes were made.

Weights learned on a typical run for one of the two groups of fifteen units are shown in Figure 4. The units' weights are displayed in three rows corresponding to units in the three blocks in the block-diagonal joint prior matrix. Units within the same block each learned different instances of the same pattern class. For example, on this run units in the first block learned to detect circles in specific positions. Units in the second block tended to learn combinations of either horizontal or vertical lines, or sometimes mixtures of the two. In the third block, units learned blurred, roughly triangular shape detectors, which for this training set were adequate to respond specifically to triangles. In all five runs the network converged to equivalent solutions (only the groups' particular shape preferences varied across runs).

Varying the number of units per block from three to five (i.e. three three-by-three blocks versus three five-by-five blocks of units) produced similar results, except that with fewer units per block, each unit tended to capture multiple instances of a particular object class in different positions.

A second layer of two groups of three units was added to the network, as shown in Figure 2 b). While keeping the first layer of weights frozen, this network was trained using exactly the same cost function as the first layer for about 30 iterations using a gradient-based learning method. This time the prior joint distribution for the two classifications was a three-by-three matrix with 80% of the density along the diagonal and 20% evenly distributed across the remainder of the distribution. Units in this layer learned to discriminate fairly well between the three object classes, as shown in Figure 5 a). On a test set with the ambiguous patterns removed (i.e., patterns containing multiple objects), units in the second layer achieved very

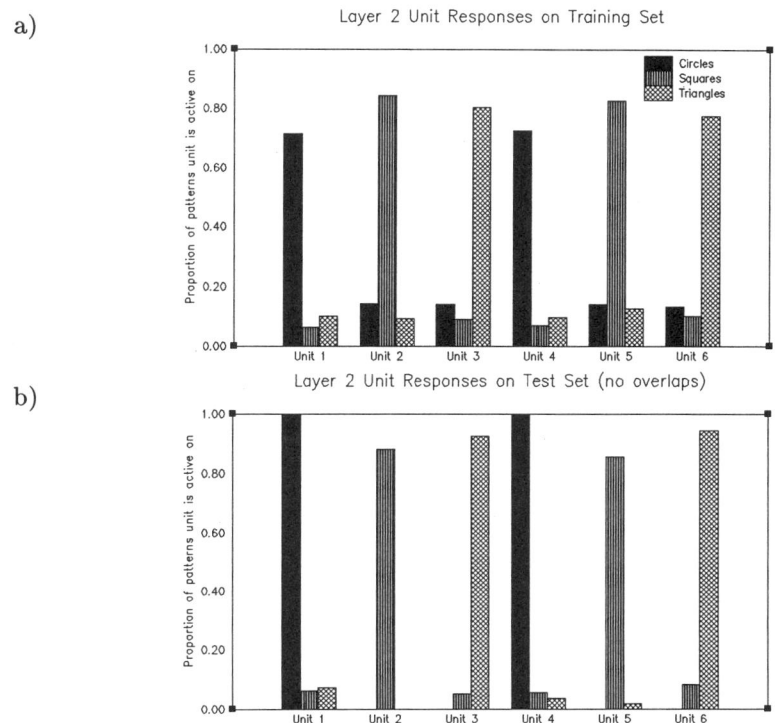

Figure 5: *Response probabilities for the six output units to each of the three shapes.*

accurate object discrimination as shown in Figure 5 b).

On ambiguous patterns containing multiple objects, the network's performance was disappointing. The output units would sometimes produce the "correct" response, i.e., all the units representing the shapes present in the image would be partially active. Most often, however, only one of the correct shapes would be detected, and occasionally the network's response indicated the wrong shape altogether. It was hoped that the diagonally dominant prior mixed with a uniform density would allow units to occasionally disagree, and they would therefore be able to represent cases of multiple objects. It may have helped to use a similar prior for the hidden layer; however, this would increase the complexity of the learning considerably.

3 DISCUSSION

We have shown that the algorithm can learn 2D-translation-invariant shape recognition, but it should handle equally well other types of transformations, such as rotation, scaling or even non-linear transformations. In principle, the algorithm should be applicable to real moving images; this is currently being investigated. Although we have focused here on the temporal coherence constraint, the algorithm could be applied equally well using other types of coherence, such as coherence across space or across different sensory modalities.

Note that the units in the first layer of the network did not learn anything about the geometric transformations between translated versions of the same object; they simply learned to associate different views together. In this respect, the representation learned at the hidden layer is similar to that predicted by the "privileged views" theory of viewpoint-invariant object recognition advocated by Weinshall et al. (1990) (and others). Their algorithm learns a similar representation in a single layer of competing units with temporal Hebbian learning applied to the lateral connections between these units. However, the algorithm proposed here goes further in that it can be applied to subsequent stages of learning to discover higher-order object classes.

Yuille et al. (1994) have previously proposed an algorithm based on similar principles, which also involves maximizing the log probability of the network outputs under a prior; in one special case it is equivalent to Becker and Hinton's Imax algorithm. The algorithm proposed here differs substantially, in that we are dealing with the *ensemble-averaged* joint probabilities of two populations of units, and fitting this quantity to a prior; further, Yuille et al's scheme employs back-propagation.

One challenge for future work is to train a network with smaller receptive fields for the first layer units, on images of objects with common low-level features, such as squares and rectangles. At least three layers of weights would be required to solve this task: units in the first layer would have to learn local object parts such as corners, while units in the next layer could group parts into viewpoint-specific whole objects and in the top layer viewpoint-invariance, in principle, could be achieved.

Acknowledgements

Helpful comments from Geoff Hinton, Peter Dayan, Tony Plate and Chris Williams are gratefully acknowledged.

References

Becker, S. (1993). Learning to categorize objects using temporal coherence. In *Advances in Neural Information Processing Systems 5*, pages 361–368. Morgan Kaufmann.

Becker, S. and Hinton, G. E. (1992). A self-organizing neural network that discovers surfaces in random-dot stereograms. *Nature*, 355:161–163.

de Sa, V. R. (1993). Minimizing disagreement for self-supervised classification. In *Proceedings of the 1993 Connectionist Models Summer School*, pages 300–307. Lawrence Erlbaum associates.

Földiák, P. (1991). Learning invariance from transformation sequences. *Neural Computation*, 3(2):194–200.

Weinshall, D., Edelman, S., and Bülthoff, H. H. (1990). A self-organizing multiple-view representation of 3D objects. In *Advances in Neural Information Processing Systems 2*, pages 274–282. Morgan Kaufmann.

Yuille, A. L., Stelios, M. S., and Xu, L. (1994). Bayesian Self-Organization. Technical Report No. 92-10, Harvard Robotics Laboratory.

PCA-Pyramids for Image Compression*

Horst Bischof
Department for Pattern Recognition
and Image Processing
Technical University Vienna
Treitlstraße 3/1832
A-1040 Vienna, Austria
bis@prip.tuwien.ac.at

Kurt Hornik
Institut für Statistik und
Wahrscheinlichkeitstheorie
Technische Universität Wien
Wiedner Hauptstraße 8–10/1071
A-1040 Vienna, Austria
Kurt.Hornik@ci.tuwien.ac.at

Abstract

This paper presents a new method for image compression by neural networks. First, we show that we can use neural networks in a pyramidal framework, yielding the so-called PCA pyramids. Then we present an image compression method based on the PCA pyramid, which is similar to the Laplace pyramid and wavelet transform. Some experimental results with real images are reported. Finally, we present a method to combine the quantization step with the learning of the PCA pyramid.

1 Introduction

In the past few years, a lot of work has been done on using neural networks for image compression, cf. e.g. (Cottrell et al., 1987; Sanger, 1989; Mougeot et al., 1991; Schweizer et al., 1991)). Typically, networks which perform a Principal Component Analysis (PCA) were employed; for a recent overview of PCA networks, see (Baldi and Hornik, 1995).

A well studied and thoroughly understood PCA network architecture is the linear autoassociative network, see (Baldi and Hornik, 1989; Bourlard and Kamp, 1988). This network consists of N input and output units and $M < N$ hidden units, and is

---

*This work was supported in part by a grant from the Austrian National Fonds zur Förderung der wissenschaftlichen Forschung (No. S7002MAT) to Horst Bischof.

trained (usually by back-propagation) to reproduce the input at the output units. All units are linear. Bourlard & Kamp (Bourlard and Kamp, 1988) have shown that at the minimum of the usual quadratic error function $\mathcal{E}$, the hidden units project the input on the space spanned by the first M principal components of the input distribution. In fact, as long as the output units are linear, nothing is gained by using non-linear hidden units. On average, all hidden units have equal variance.

However, PCA is not the only method for image compression. Among many others, the Laplace Pyramid (Burt and Adelson, 1983) and wavelets (Mallat, 1989) have successfully been used to compress images. Of particular interest is the fact that these techniques provide a hierarchical representation of the image which can be used for progressive image transmission. However, these hierarchical methods are not adaptive.

In this paper, we present a combination of autoassociative networks with hierarchical methods. We propose the so-called PCA pyramids, which can be seen as an extension of image pyramids with a learning algorithm as well as cascaded locally connected autoassociative networks. In other words, we combine the structure of image pyramids and neural network learning algorithms, resulting in learning pyramids.

The structure of this paper is as follows. We first present image pyramids and, in particular, the PCA pyramid. Then, we discuss how these pyramids can be used for image compression, and present some experimental results. Next, we discuss a method to combine the quantization step of compression with the transformation. Finally, we give some conclusions and an outline of further research.

2 The PCA Pyramid

Before we introduce the PCA pyramid, let us describe regular image pyramids. For a discussion of irregular pyramids and their relation to neural networks, see (Bischof, 1993). In the simplest case, each successive level of the pyramid is obtained from the previous level by a filtering operation followed by a sampling operator. More general functions can be used to achieve the desired reduction. We therefore call them *reduction functions*. The structure of a pyramid is determined by the neighbor relations within the levels of the pyramid and by the "father-son" relations between adjacent levels. A cell (if it is not at the base level) has a set of *children (sons)* at the level directly below which provide input to the cell, a set of *neighbors (brothers/sisters)* at the same level, and (if it is not the apex of the pyramid) a set of *parents (fathers)* at the level directly above. We denote the structure of a (regular) pyramid by the expression $n \times n/r$, where $n \times n$ (the number of sons) is the size of the reduction window and r the reduction factor which describes how the number of cells decreases from level to level.

2.1 PCA Pyramids

Since a pyramid reduces the information content of an image level by level, an objective for the reduction function would be to *preserve as much information as possible*, given the restrictions imposed by the structure of the pyramid, or equivalently, to minimize the information loss by the reduction function. This naturally leads to the idea of representing the pyramid by a suitable PCA network. Among the many alternatives for such networks, we have chosen the autoassociative networks for two reasons. First, the analysis of Hornik & Kuan (Hornik and Kuan, 1992) shows that these networks are more stable than competing models. Second, autoassociative networks have the nice feature that they automatically provide us with the expansion function (weights from the hidden layer to output layer).

Since the neural network should have the same connectivity as the pyramid (i.e., the same father-son relations), its topology is determined by the structure of the pyramid. In this paper, we confine ourselves to the $4 \times 4/4$ pyramid for two reasons. First, the $4 \times 4/4$ pyramid has the nice property that every cell has the same number of fathers, which results in homogeneous networks. Second, as experiments have shown (Bischof, 1993) the results achieved with this pyramid are similar to other structures, e.g. the $5 \times 5/4$ pyramid, using fewer weights.

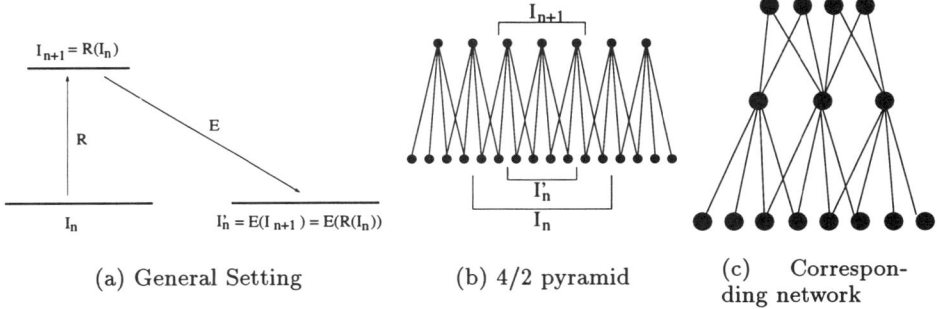

(a) General Setting   (b) 4/2 pyramid   (c) Corresponding network

Figure 1: From the structure of the pyramid to the topology of the network

Figure 1 depicts the one-dimensional situation of a 4/2 pyramid (this is the one-dimensional counterpart of the two-dimensional $4 \times 4/2$ pyramid). Figure 1a shows the general goal to be achieved and the notations employed; Figure 1b shows a 4/2 pyramid. When constructing the corresponding network, we start at the output layer (i.e., I'_n). For an n/r pyramid we typically choose the size of the output layer as n. Next, we have to include all fathers of the cells in the output layer as hidden units. Finally, we have to include all sons of the hidden layer cells in the input layer. For the 4/2 pyramid, this results in an 8-3-4 network as shown in Figure 1c. A similar construction yields an 8×8–3×3–4×4 network for the $4 \times 4/4$ pyramid.

The next thing to consider are the constraints on the network weights due to the overlaps in the pyramid. To completely cover the input image with output units, we can shift the network only by four cells in each direction. Therefore, the hidden units at the borders overlap. For the 4/2 pyramid, the left and right hidden units must have identical weights. In the case of the $4 \times 4/4$ pyramid, the network has four independent units.

The thus constructed network can be trained by some suitable learning algorithm, typically of the back-propagation type, using batches of an image as input for training the first pyramid level. After that, the second level of the pyramid can be trained in the same way using the first pyramid level as training data, and so on.

2.2 PCA-Laplace Pyramid and Image Compression

Thus far, we have introduced a network which can learn the reduction function R and the expansion function E of a pyramid. Analogously to the Laplace pyramid and the wavelet transform we can now introduce the *level* L_i of the PCA-Laplace pyramid, given by

$$L_i = I_i - I'_i = I_i - E(R(I_i))$$

It should be noted that during learning we exactly minimize the squared Laplace

(a) First 2 levels of a Laplace pyramid (upper half) and PCA-Laplace pyramid (lower half) (grey = 0)

(b) Reconstruction error of house image with quantization of 3 bits, 4 bits, 7 bits, and reconstructed image

Figure 2: Results of PCA-Laplace-Pyramid

level. The original image I_0 can be completely recovered from level I_n and the Laplace levels $L_0, \ldots, L_{n-1}$ by

$$I_0 = E(\cdots E(E(I_n) + L_{n-1}) + L_{n-2}) \cdots) + L_0.$$

Since the level I_n is rather small (e.g., 32×32 pixels) and the levels of the PCA-Laplace pyramid are typically sparse (i.e., many pixels are zero, see Figure 2a) and can therefore be compressed considerably by a conventional compression algorithm (e.g. Lempel-Ziv (Ziv and Lempel, 1977)), this image representation results in a lossless image compression algorithm.

In order to achieve higher compression ratios we can quantize the levels of the PCA-Laplace pyramid. In this case, the compression is lossy, because the original image cannot be recovered exactly. The compression ratio and the amount of loss can be controlled by the number of bits used to quantize the levels of the PCA-Laplacian.

To measure the difference between the compressed and the original image, we use the normalized mean squared error (NMSE) as in (Cottrell et al., 1987; Sanger, 1989). The NMSE is given by the mean squared error divided by the average squared intensity of the image, i.e.,

$$\text{NMSE} = \frac{\text{MSE}}{\langle I_0^2 \rangle} = \frac{\langle (I_0 - C(I_0))^2 \rangle}{\langle I_0^2 \rangle},$$

where I_0 and $C(I_0)$ are the original and the compressed image, respectively. The compression ratio is measured by the amount of bits used to store I_0, divided by the amount of bits used to store $C(I_0)$.

2.3 Results

For the results reported here we trained the networks by a conjugate gradient algorithm for 100 steps[1] and used a uniform quantization which is fixed for all levels of the pyramid. As was shown in (Burt and Adelson, 1983; Mayer and Kropatsch, 1989), the results could be improved by gradually increasing the quantization from bottom to top.

Figure 2b shows the error images when the levels of the PCA-Laplacian pyramid are quantized with 3, 4, and 7 bits and the reconstructed image from the 7 bit Laplacian. Note that we used the same lookup-table for the error images. To compress the levels of the PCA-Laplacian pyramid, we employed the standard UNIX compress program which implements a Lempel-Ziv algorithm.

¿From these images one can see that the results with the 4 and 7 bit quantization are very good. Visually, no difference between the reconstructed and the original image can be perceived. Table 1 shows the compression ratios and the NMSEs on these images. We have performed experiments on 20 different images, the results on these images are comparable to the ones reported here.

These results compare favorably with the results in the literature (see Table 1). We have also applied a $5 \times 5/4$ Laplace pyramid to the house image which gave a compression ratio of 3.42 with an NMSE of 0.000087 for quantization with four bits of the Laplace levels. We have also included results achieved with JPEG. One can see that our method gives considerably better results.

We have also demonstrated experimentally what happens if we train a pyramid on one image and then apply this pyramid to another image without retraining. These experiments indicate that the errors are only a little bit larger for images not trained on. With five additional steps of training the errors are almost the same. ¿From

---

[1] In all our experiments the training algorithm converged (i.e. usually after 200 steps, however the improvements between steps 20 and convergence are negligible).

Quant.	Compression ratio	Bits/Pixel	NMSE
3 Bit	37.628	0.212	0.0172
4 Bit	24.773	0.323	0.0019
7 Bit	8.245	0.970	0.0000215
no Quant.	3.511	2.279	0.0
Cottrell (Cottrell et al., 1987)	8.0	1.000	0.0059
Sanger (Sanger, 1989)	22.0	0.360	0.043
5 × 5/4 Laplace	3.420	2.339	0.000087
JPEG	8.290	0.965	0.00139
JPEG	15.774	0.507	0.00348

Table 1: Compression ratios and NMSE for various compression methods

this results we can conclude that we do not need to retrain the pyramid for each new image.

3 Integration of Quantization

For the results reported in the previous section we have used a fixed and uniform quantization scheme which can be improved by using adaptive quantizers like the Lloyd I algorithm, Kohonen's Feature Maps, learning vector quantization, or something similar. Such an approach as taken by Schweizer (Schweizer et al., 1991) who combined a Cottrell-type network with self-organizing feature maps. However, we can go further.

With the PCA network we minimize the squared Laplace level which does not necessarily yield low compression errors. What we really want to minimize are the *quantized* Laplace levels. Usually, the Laplace levels have an unimodally shaped histogram centered at zero. However, for the result of the compression (i.e., compression ratio and NMSE), it is irrelevant if we shift the histogram to the left or the right as long as we shift the quantization intervals in the same way. The best results could be achieved if we have a multimodal histogram with peaks centered at the quantization points.

Using neural networks for both PCA and quantization, this goal could e.g. be achieved by a modular network as in Figure 3 for the 4/2 pyramid. For quantization, we could either apply a vector quantizer to a whole patch of the Laplace level, or use a scalar quantizer (as depicted in Figure 3) for each pixel of the Laplace level. In the second case, we have to constrain the weights of the quantization network to be identical for every Laplace pixel. Since scalar quantization is simpler to analyze and uses less free parameters, we only consider this case.

As each quantization subnetwork can be treated separately (we only have to average the weight changes over all subnetworks), the following only considers the case of one output unit of the PCA network.

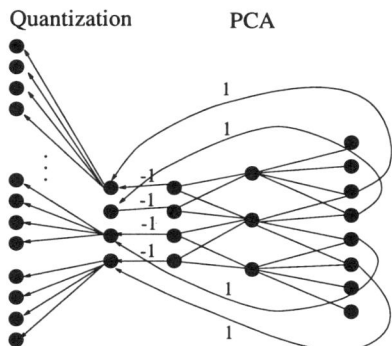

Figure 3: PCA network and Quantization network

The error to be minimized is the squared quantization error

$$E = \sum_p E_p \qquad E_p = \min_k ||c_k - l_p||^2,$$

where p refers to the patterns in the training set, c_k is the kth weight of the quantization network, and l is the output of the PCA-Laplace unit.

Changing the weights of the quantization network by gradient descent leads to the LVQ1 rule of Kohonen

$$\Delta c_k = \begin{cases} 2\alpha(l_p - c_k), & \text{if } k = k_p \text{ is the winning unit,} \\ 0, & \text{otherwise.} \end{cases}$$

For the PCA network we can proceed similarly to back-propagation to obtain the rule

$$\Delta w_{ij} = -K \frac{\partial E_p}{\partial w_{ij}} = -K \frac{\partial E_p}{\partial l_p} \frac{\partial l_p}{\partial w_{ij}} = -K \frac{\partial E_p}{\partial l_p} \frac{\partial l_p}{\partial i'_p} \frac{\partial i'_p}{\partial w_{ij}} = -2K(l_p - c_k) \frac{\partial i'_p}{\partial w_{ij}}.$$

Of course, this is only one out of many possible algorithms. More elaborate minimization techniques than gradient descent could be used; similarly, LVQ1 could be replaced by a different quantization algorithm. But the basic idea of letting the quantization step and the the compression step adapt to each other remains unchanged.

4 Conclusions

In this paper, we presented a new image compression scheme based on neural networks. The PCA and PCA-Laplace pyramids were introduced, which can be seen as both an extension of image pyramids to learning pyramids and as cascaded, locally connected autoassociators. The results achieved are promising and compare favorably to work reported in the literature.

A lot of work remains to be done to analyze these networks analytically. The convergence properties of the PCA pyramid are not known; we expect results similar to the ones (Baldi and Hornik, 1989) for the autoassociative network. Also, for the PCA network it would be desirable to characterize the features which are extracted. Similarly, the integrated network needs to be analyzed. It is clear that for such networks, the usual error function has local minima, but maybe they can be avoided by a proper training regime (i.e. start training the PCA pyramid, then train the vector quantizer, and finally train them together).

References

Baldi, P. and Hornik, K. (1989). Neural Networks and principal component analysis: Learning from examples without local minima. *Neural Networks*, 2:53–58.

Baldi, P. and Hornik, K. (1995). Learning in Linear Neural Networks: a Survey. *IEEE Transactions on Neural Networks, to appear.*

Bischof, H. (1993). *Pyramidal Neural Networks*. PhD thesis, TU-Vienna, Inst. f. Automation, Dept. f. Pattern Recognition and Image Processing.

Bourlard, H. and Kamp, Y. (1988). Auto-Association by Multilayer Perceptrons and Singular Value Decomposition. *Biological Cybernetics*, 59:291–294.

Burt, P. J. and Adelson, E. H. (1983). The Laplacian pyramid as a compact image code. *IEEE Transactions on Communications*, Vol. COM-31(No.4):pp.532–540.

Cottrell, G., Munro, P., and Zipser, D. (1987). Learning Internal Representations from Grey-Scale Images: An Example of Extensional Programming. In *Ninth Annual Conference of the Cognitive Science Society*, pages 462–473. Hillsdale Erlbaum.

Hornik, K. and Kuan, C. (1992). Convergence analysis of local feature extraction algorithms. *Neural Networks*, 5(2):229–240.

Mallat, S. G. (1989). A Theory for Multiresolution Signal Decomposition: The Wavelet Representation. *IEEE Transactions on Pattern Analysis and Machine Intelligence*, Vol. PAMI-11(No. 7):pp. 674–693.

Mayer, H. and Kropatsch, W. G. (1989). Progressive Bildübertragung mit der 3×3/2 Pyramide. In Burkhardt, H., Höhne, K., and Neumann, B., editors, *Informatik Fachberichte 219: Mustererkennung 1989*, pages 160–167, Hamburg. 11.DAGM - Symposium, Springer Verlag.

Mougeot, M., Azencott, R., and Angeniol, B. (1991). Image Compression with Back Propagation: Improvement of the Visual Restoration using different Cost Functions. *Neural Networks*, 4:467–476.

Sanger, T. (1989). Optimal Unsupervised learning in a Single-Layer Linear Feed-forward Neural Network. *Neural Networks*, 2:433–459.

Schweizer, L., Parladori, G., Sicranza, G., and Marsi, S. (1991). A fully neural approach to image compression. In Kohonen, T., Mäkissara, K., Simula, O., and Kangas, J., editors, *Artificial Neural Networks*, volume I, pages 815–820.

Ziv, J. and Lempel, A. (1977). A universal algorithm for sequential data compression. *IEEE Trans. on Information Theory*, 23(5):337 – 343.

Unsupervised Classification of 3D Objects from 2D Views

Satoshi Suzuki   Hiroshi Ando
ATR Human Information Processing Research Laboratories
2-2 Hikaridai, Seika-cho, Soraku-gun, Kyoto 619-02, Japan
satoshi@hip.atr.co.jp, ando@hip.atr.co.jp

Abstract

This paper presents an unsupervised learning scheme for categorizing 3D objects from their 2D projected images. The scheme exploits an auto-associative network's ability to encode each view of a single object into a representation that indicates its view direction. We propose two models that employ different classification mechanisms; the first model selects an auto-associative network whose recovered view best matches the input view, and the second model is based on a modular architecture whose additional network classifies the views by splitting the input space nonlinearly. We demonstrate the effectiveness of the proposed classification models through simulations using 3D wire-frame objects.

1 INTRODUCTION

The human visual system can recognize various 3D (three-dimensional) objects from their 2D (two-dimensional) retinal images although the images vary significantly as the viewpoint changes. Recent computational models have explored how to learn to recognize 3D objects from their projected views (Poggio & Edelman, 1990). Most existing models are, however, based on supervised learning, i.e., during training the teacher tells which object each view belongs to. The model proposed by Weinshall et al. (1990) also requires a signal that segregates different objects during training. This paper, on the other hand, discusses unsupervised aspects of 3D object recognition where the system discovers categories by itself.

This paper presents an unsupervised classification scheme for categorizing 3D objects from their 2D views. The scheme consists of a mixture of 5-layer auto-associative networks, each of which identifies an object by non-linearly encoding the views into a representation that describes transformation of a rigid object. A mixture model with linear networks was also studied by Williams et al. (1993) for classifying objects under affine transformations. We propose two models that employ different classification mechanisms. The first model classifies the given view by selecting an auto-associative network whose recovered view best matches the input view. The second model is based on the modular architecture proposed by Jacobs et al. (1991) in which an additional 3-layer network classifies the views by directly splitting the input space. The simulations using 3D wire-frame objects demonstrate that both models effectively learn to classify each view as a 3D object.

This paper is organized as follows. Section 2 describes in detail the proposed models for unsupervised classification of 3D objects. Section 3 describes the simulation results using 3D wire-frame objects. In these simulations, we test the performance of the proposed models and examine what internal representations are acquired in the hidden layers. Finally, Section 4 concludes this paper.

2 THE NETWORK MODELS

This section describes an unsupervised scheme that classifies 2D views into 3D objects. We initially examined classical unsupervised clustering schemes, such as the k-means method or the vector quantization method, to see whether such methods can solve this problem (Duda & Hart, 1973). Through simulations using the wire-frame objects described in the next section, we found that these methods do not yield satisfactory performance. We, therefore, propose a new unsupervised learning scheme for classifying 3D objects.

The proposed scheme exploits an *auto-associative network* for identifying an object. An auto-associative network finds an identity mapping through a bottleneck in the hidden layer, i.e., the network approximates functions F and F^{-1} such that $\mathbf{R}^n \xrightarrow{F} \mathbf{R}^m \xrightarrow{F^{-1}} \mathbf{R}^n$ where $m < n$. The network, thus, compresses the input into a low dimensional representation by eliminating redundancy. If we use a five-layer perceptron network, the network can perform nonlinear dimensionality reduction, which is a nonlinear analogue to the principal component analysis (Oja, 1991; DeMers & Cottrell, 1993).

The proposed classification scheme consists of a mixture of five-layer auto-associative networks which we call *the identification networks*, or *the I-Nets*. In the case where the inputs are the projected views of a rigid object, the minimum dimension that constrains the input variation is *the degree of freedom* of the rigid object, which is six in the most general case, three for rotation and three for translation. Thus, a single I-Net can compress the views of an object into a representation whose dimension is its degree of freedom. The proposed scheme categorizes each view of a number of 3D objects into its class through selecting an appropriate I-Net. We present the following two models for different selection and learning methods.

Model I: The model I selects an I-Net whose output best fits the input (see Fig. 1). Specifically, we assume a classifier whose output vector is given by the softmax function of a negative squared difference between the input and the output of the I-Nets, i.e.,

$$f_i = \exp\left[-\|y^* - y_i\|^2\right] \Big/ \sum_j \exp\left[-\|y^* - y_j\|^2\right] \tag{1}$$

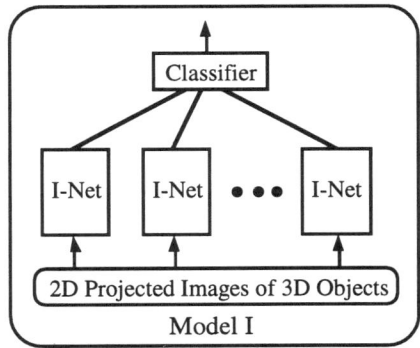 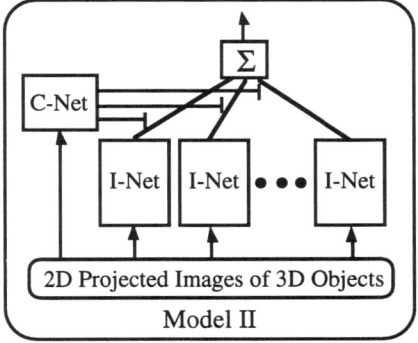

Figure 1: Model I and Model II. Each I-Net (identification net) is a 5-layer auto-associative network and the C-Net (classification net) is a 3-layer network.

where y^* and y_i denote the input and the output of the i th I-Net, respectively. Therefore, if only one of the I-Nets has an output that best matches the input, then the output value of the corresponding unit in the classifier becomes nearly one and the output values of the other units become nearly zero. For training the network, we maximize the following objective function:

$$\ln \frac{\sum_i \exp\left[-\alpha \|y^* - y_i\|^2\right]}{\sum_i \exp\left[-\|y^* - y_i\|^2\right]} \tag{2}$$

where α (>1) denotes a constant. This function forces the output of at least one I-Net to fit the input, and it also forces the rest of I-Nets to increase the error between the input and the output. Since it is difficult for a single I-Net to learn more than one object, we expect that the network will eventually converge to the state where each I-Net identifies only one object.

Model II: The model II, on the other hand, employs an additional network which we call *the classification network* or *the C-Net*, as illustrated in Fig. 1. The C-Net classifies the given views by directly partitioning the input space. This type of modular architecture has been proposed by Jacobs et al. (1991) based on a stochastic model (see also Jordan & Jacobs, 1992). In this architecture, the final output, y, is given by

$$y = \sum_i g_i y_i \tag{3}$$

where y_i denotes the output of the i th I-Net, and g_i is given by the softmax function

$$g_i = \exp[s_i] \Big/ \sum_j \exp[s_j] \tag{4}$$

where s_i is the weighted sum arriving at the i th output unit of the C-Net.

For the C-Net, we use three-layer perceptron, since a simple perceptron with two layers did not provide a good performance for the objects used for our simulations (see Section

3). The results suggest that classification of such objects is not a linearly separable problem. Instead of using MLP (multi-layer perceptron), we could use other types of networks for the C-Net, such as RBF (radial basis function) (Poggio & Edelman, 1990).

We maximize the objective function

$$\ln \sum_i g_i \sigma^{-1} \exp\left[-\|y^* - y_i\|^2 / (2\sigma^2)\right] \quad (5)$$

where σ^2 is the variance. This function forces the C-Net to select only one I-Net, and at the same time, the selected I-Net to encode and decode the input information.

Note that the model I can be interpreted as a modified version of the model II, since maximizing (2) is essentially equivalent to maximizing (5) if we replace s_i of the C-Net in (4) with a negative squared difference between the input and the output of the i th I-Net, i.e., $s_i = -\|y^* - y_i\|^2$. Although the model I is a more direct classification method that exploits auto-associative networks, it is interesting to examine what information can be extracted from the input for classification in the model II (see Section 3.2).

3 SIMULATIONS

We implemented the network models described in the previous section to evaluate their performance. The 3D objects that we used for our simulations are 5-segment wire-frame objects whose six vertices are randomly selected in a unit cube, as shown in Fig. 2 (a) (see also Poggio & Edelman, 1990). Various views of the objects are obtained by orthographically projecting the objects onto an image plane whose position covers a sphere around the object (see Fig. 2 (b)). The view position is defined by the two parameters, θ and ϕ. In the simulations, we used x, y image coordinates of the six vertices of three wire-frame objects for the inputs to the network.

The models contain three I-Nets, whose number is set equal to the number of the objects. The number of units in the third layer of the five-layer I-Nets is set equal to the number of the view parameters, which is two in our simulations. We used twenty units in the second and fourth layers. To train the network efficiently, we initially limited the ranges of θ and ϕ to $\pi/8$ and $\pi/4$ and gradually increased the range until it covered the whole sphere. During the training, objects were randomly selected among the three and their views were randomly selected within the view range. The steepest ascent method was used for maximizing the objective functions (2) and (5) in our simulations, but more efficient methods, such as the conjugate gradient method, can also be used.

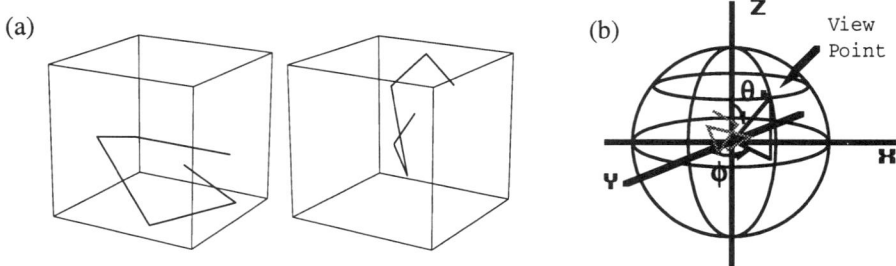

Figure 2: (a) 3D wire-frame objects. (b) Viewpoint defined by two parameters, θ and ϕ.

3.1 SIMULATIONS USING THE MODEL I

This section describes the simulation results using the model I. As described in Section 2, the classifier of this model selects an I-Net that produces minimum error between the output and the input. We test the classification performance of the model and examine internal representations of the I-Nets after training the networks. The constant α in the objective function (2) was set to 50 during the training.

Fig. 3 shows the output of the classifier plotted over the view directions when the views of an object are used for the inputs. The output value of a unit is almost equal to one over the entire range of the view direction, and the outputs of the other two units are nearly zero. This indicates that the network effectively classifies a given view into an object regardless of the view directions. We obtained satisfactory results for classification if more than five units are used in the second and fourth layers of the I-Nets.

Fig. 4 shows examples of the input views of an object and the views recovered by the corresponding I-Net. The recovered views are significantly similar to the input views, indicating that each auto-associative I-Net can successfully compress and recover the views of an object. In fact, as shown in Fig. 5, the squared error between the input and the output of an I-Net is nearly zero for only one of the objects. This indicates that each I-Net can be used for identifying an object for almost entire view range.

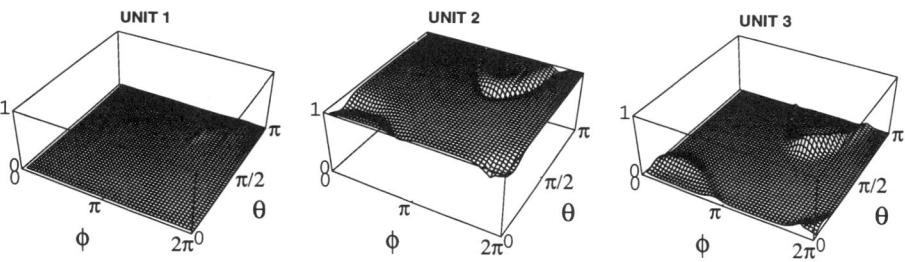

Figure 3: Outputs of the classifier in the model I. The output value of the second unit is almost equal to one over the full view range, and the outputs of the other two units are nearly zero for one of the 3D objects.

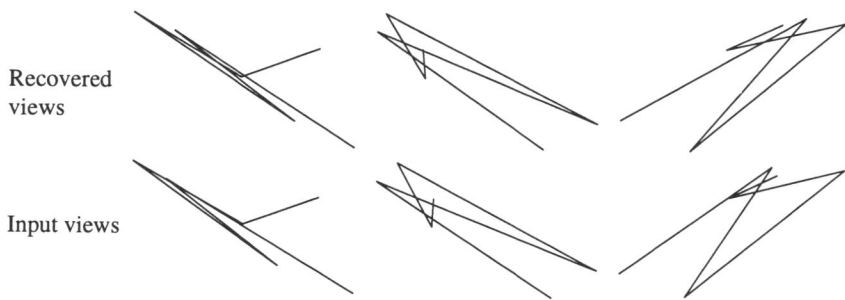

Figure 4: Examples of the input and recovered views of an object. The recovered views are significantly similar to the input views.

We further analyzed what information is encoded in the third layer of the I-Nets. Fig. 6 (a) illustrates the outputs of the third layer units plotted as a function of the view direction (θ, ϕ) of an object. Fig. 6 (b) shows the view direction (θ, ϕ) plotted as a function of the outputs of the third layer units. Both figures exhibit single-valued functions, i.e. the view direction of the object uniquely determines the outputs of the hidden units, and at the same time the outputs of the hidden units uniquely determine the view direction. Thus, each I-Net encodes a given view of an object into a representation that has one-to-one correspondence with the view direction. This result is expected from the condition that the dimension of the third layer is set equal to the degree of freedom of a rigid object.

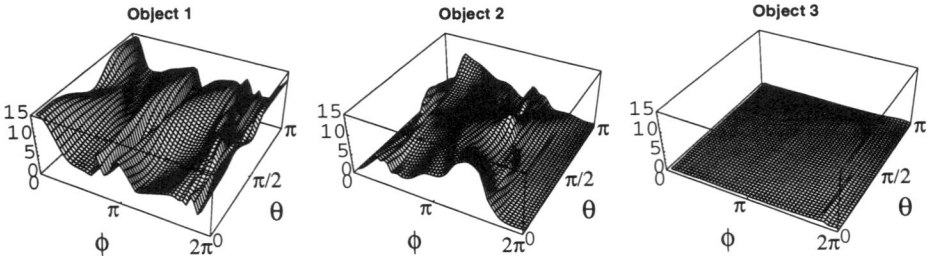

Figure 5: Error between the input view and the recovered view of an I-Net for each object. The figures show that the I-Net recovers only the views of Object 3.

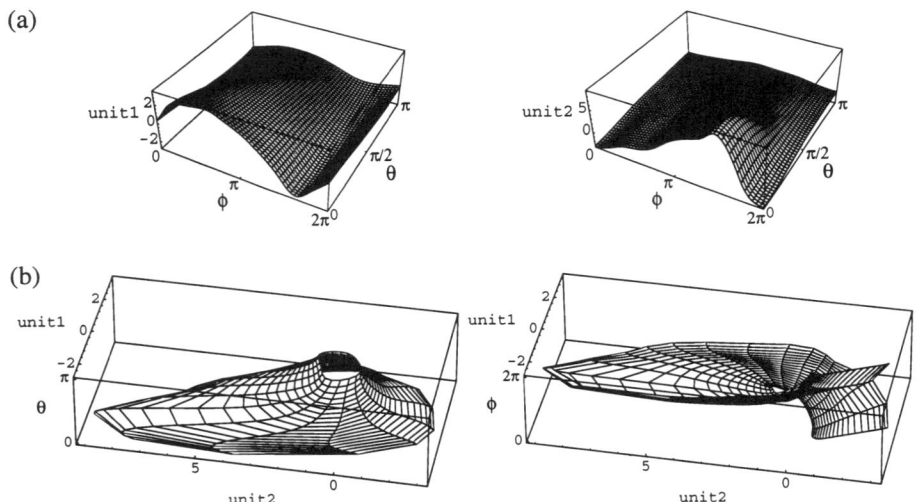

Figure 6: (a) Outputs of the third layer units of an I-Net plotted over the view direction (θ, ϕ) of an object. (b) The view direction plotted over the outputs of the third layer units. Figure (b) was obtained by inversely replotting Figure (a).

3.2 SIMULATIONS USING THE MODEL II

In this section, we show the simulation results using the model II. The C-Net in the model learns to classify the views by splitting the input space nonlinearly. We examine internal representations of the C-Net that lead to view invariant classification in its output.

In the simulations, we used the same 3 wire-frame objects used in the previous simulations. The C-Net contains 20 units in the hidden layer. The parameter σ in the objective function (5) was set to 0.1. Fig. 7 (a) illustrates the values of an output unit in the C-Net for an object. As in the case of the model I, the model correctly classified the views into their original object for almost entire view range. Fig. 7 (b) illustrates the outputs of two of the hidden units as examples, showing that each hidden unit has a limited view range where its output is nearly one. The C-Net, thus, combines these partially invariant representations in the hidden layer to achieve full view invariance at the output layer.

To examine a generalization ability of the model, we limited the view range in the training period and tested the network using the images with the full view range. Fig. 8 (a) and (b) show the values of an output unit of the C-Net and the error of the corresponding I-Net plotted over the entire view range. The region surrounded by a rectangle indicates the range of view directions where the training was done. The figures show that the correct classification and the small recovery error are not restricted within the training range but spread across this range, suggesting that the network exhibits a satisfactory capability of generalization. We obtained similar generalization results for the model I as well. We also trained the networks with a sparse set of views rather than using randomly selected views. The results show that classification is nearly perfect regardless of the viewpoints if we use at least 16 training views evenly spaced within the full view range.

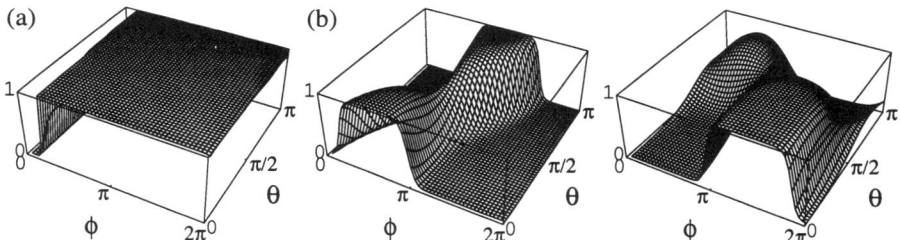

Figure 7: (a) Output values of an output unit of the C-Net when the views of an object are given (cf. Fig.3). (b) Output values of two hidden units of the C-Net for the same object.

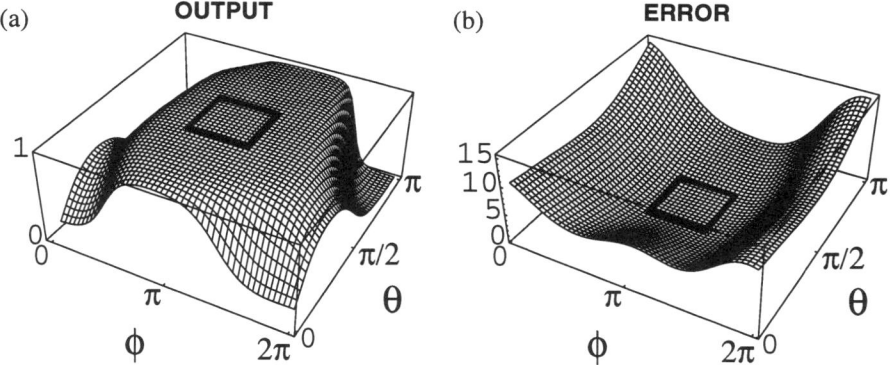

Figure 8: (a) Output values of an output unit of the C-Net. (b) Errors between the input views and the recovered views of the corresponding I-Net. The region surrounded by a rectangle indicates the view range where the training was done.

4 CONCLUSIONS

We have presented an unsupervised classification scheme that classifies 3D objects from their 2D views. The scheme consists of a mixture of non-linear auto-associative networks each of which identifies an object by encoding an input view into a representation that indicates its view direction. The simulations using 3D wire-frame objects demonstrated that the scheme effectively clusters the given views into their original objects with no explicit identification of the object classes being provided to the networks. We presented two models that utilize different classification mechanisms. In particular, the model I employs a novel classification and learning strategy that forces only one network to reconstruct the input view, whereas the model II is based on a conventional modular architecture which requires training of a separate classification network. Although we assumed in the simulations that feature points are already identified in each view and that their correspondence between the views is also established, the scheme does not, in principle, require the identification and correspondence of features, because the scheme is based solely on the existence of non-linear mappings between a set of images of an object and its degree of freedom. Therefore, we are currently investigating how the proposed scheme can be used to classify real gray-level images of 3D objects.

Acknowledgments

We would like to thank Mitsuo Kawato for extensive discussions and continuous encouragement, and Hiroaki Gomi and Yasuharu Koike for helpful comments. We are also grateful to Tommy Poggio for insightful discussions.

References

DeMers, D. and Cottrell, G. (1993). Non-linear dimensionality reduction. In Hanson, S. J., Cowan, J. D. & Giles, C. L., (eds), *Advances in Neural Information Processing Systems 5*. Morgan Kaufmann Publishers, San Mateo, CA. 580-587.

Duda, R. O. and Hart, P. E. (1973). *Pattern Classification and Scene Analysis*. John Wiley & Sons, NY.

Jacobs, R. A., Jordan, M. I., Nowlan, S. J. and Hinton, G. E. (1991). Adaptive mixtures of local experts. *Neural Computation*, 3, 79-87.

Jordan, M. I. and Jacobs, R. A. (1992). Hierarchies of adaptive experts. In Moody, J. E., Hanson, S. J. & Lippmann, R. P., (eds), *Advances in Neural Information Processing Systems 4*. Morgan Kaufmann Publishers, San Mateo, CA. 985-992.

Oja, E. (1991). Data compression, Feature extraction, and autoassociation in feedforward neural networks. In Kohonen, K. et al. (eds), *Artificial Neural Networks*. Elsevier Science publishers B.V., North-Holland.

Poggio, T. and Edelman, S. (1990). A network that learns to recognize three-dimensional objects. *Nature*, 343, 263.

Weinshall, D., Edelman, S. and Bülthoff, H. H. (1990). A self-organizing multiple-view representation of 3D objects. In Touretzky, D. S., (eds), *Advances in Neural Information Processing Systems 2*. Morgan Kaufmann Publishers, San Mateo, CA. 274-281.

Williams, C. K. I., Zemel, R. S. and Mozer, M. C. (1993). Unsupervised learning of object models. *AAAI Fall 1993 Symposium on Machine Learning in Computer Vision*.

New Algorithms for 2D and 3D Point Matching: Pose Estimation and Correspondence

Steven Gold[1], Chien Ping Lu[1], Anand Rangarajan[1],
Suguna Pappu[1] and Eric Mjolsness[2]
Department of Computer Science
Yale University
New Haven, CT 06520-8285

Abstract

A fundamental open problem in computer vision—determining pose and correspondence between two sets of points in space—is solved with a novel, robust and easily implementable algorithm. The technique works on noisy point sets that may be of unequal sizes and may differ by non-rigid transformations. A 2D variation calculates the pose between point sets related by an affine transformation—translation, rotation, scale and shear. A 3D to 3D variation calculates translation and rotation. An objective describing the problem is derived from Mean field theory. The objective is minimized with clocked (EM-like) dynamics. Experiments with both handwritten and synthetic data provide empirical evidence for the method.

1 Introduction

Matching the representations of two images has long been the focus of much research in Computer Vision, forming an essential component of many machine-based ob-

---

[1] E-mail address of authors: lastname-firstname@cs.yale.edu
[2] Department of Computer Science and Engineering, University of California at San Diego (UCSD), La Jolla, CA 92093-0114. E-mail: emj@cs.ucsd.edu

ject recognition systems. Critical to most matching techniques is the determination of correspondence between spatially localized features within each image. This has traditionally been considered a hard problem - especially when the issues of noise, missing or spurious data, and non-rigid transformations are tackled [Grimson, 1990]. Many approaches have been tried, with tree-pruning techniques and generalized Hough transforms being the most common. We introduce a new, robust and easily implementable algorithm to find such poses and correspondences. The algorithm can determine non-rigid transformations between noisy 2D or 3D spatially located unlabeled feature sets despite missing or spurious features. It is derived by minimizing an objective function describing the problem with a combination of optimization techniques, incorporating Mean Field theory, slack variables, iterative projective scaling, and clocked (EM-like) dynamics.

2 2D with Affine Transformations

2.1 Formulating the Objective

Our first algorithm calculates the pose between noisy, 2D point sets of unequal size related by an affine transformation - translation, rotation, scale and shear. Given two sets of points $\{X_j\}$ and $\{Y_k\}$, one can minimize the following objective to find the affine transformation and permutation which best maps Y onto X :

$$E_{2D}(m,t,A) = \sum_{j=1}^{J}\sum_{k=1}^{K} m_{jk}\|X_j - t - AY_k\|^2 + g(A) - \alpha \sum_{j=1}^{J}\sum_{k=1}^{K} m_{jk}$$

with constraints: $\forall j \sum_{k=1}^{K} m_{jk} \leq 1$, $\forall k \sum_{j=1}^{J} m_{jk} \leq 1$, $\forall jk \; m_{jk} \geq 0$ and

$$g(A) = \gamma a^2 + \kappa b^2 + \lambda c^2$$

A is decomposed into scale, rotation, vertical shear and oblique shear as follows:

$$A = s(a)R(\Theta)Sh_1(b)Sh_2(c)$$

where,

$$s(a) = \begin{pmatrix} e^a & 0 \\ 0 & e^a \end{pmatrix} , \; Sh_1(b) = \begin{pmatrix} e^b & 0 \\ 0 & e^{-b} \end{pmatrix} , \; Sh_2(c) = \begin{pmatrix} \cosh(c) & \sinh(c) \\ \sinh(c) & \cosh(c) \end{pmatrix}$$

$R(\Theta)$ is the standard 2x2 rotation matrix. $g(A)$ serves to regularize the affine transformation - bounding the scale and shear components. m is a fuzzy correspondence matrix which matches points in one image with corresponding points in the other image. The constraints on m ensure that each point in each image corresponds to at most one point in the other image. However, partial matches are allowed, in which case the sum of these partial matches may add up to no more than one. The inequality constraint on m permits a null match or multiple partial matches.

The α term biases the objective towards matches. The decomposition of A in the above is not required, since A could be left as a 2x2 matrix and solved for directly in the algorithm that follows. The decomposition just provides for more precise regularization, i.e., specification of the likely kinds of transformations. Also $Sh_2(c)$ could be replaced by another rotation matrix, using the singular value decomposition of A.

We transform the inequality constraints into equality constraints by introducing slack variables, a standard technique from linear programming;

$$\forall j \sum_{k=1}^{K} m_{jk} \leq 1 \quad \rightarrow \quad \forall j \sum_{k=1}^{K+1} m_{jk} = 1$$

and likewise for the column constraints. An extra row and column are added to the matrix m to hold the slack variables. Following the treatment in [Peterson and Soderberg, 1989; Yuille and Kosowsky, 1994] we employ Lagrange multipliers and an $x \log x$ barrier function to enforce the constraints with the following objective:

$$E_{2D}(m, t, A) = \sum_{j=1}^{J} \sum_{k=1}^{K} m_{jk} \|X_j - t - AY_k\|^2 + g(A) - \alpha \sum_{j=1}^{J} \sum_{k=1}^{K} m_{jk}$$
$$+ \frac{1}{\beta} \sum_{j=1}^{J+1} \sum_{k=1}^{K+1} m_{jk}(\log m_{jk} - 1) + \sum_{j=1}^{J} \mu_j (\sum_{k=1}^{K+1} m_{jk} - 1) + \sum_{k=1}^{K} \nu_k (\sum_{j=1}^{J+1} m_{jk} - 1) \quad (1)$$

In this objective we are looking for a saddle point. (1) is minimized with respect to m, t, and A which are the correspondence matrix, translation, and affine transform, and is maximized with respect to μ and ν, the Lagrange multipliers that enforce the row and column constraints for m. m is fuzzy, with the degree of fuzziness dependent upon β.

2.2 The Algorithm

The algorithm to minimize the above objective proceeds in two phases. In phase one, while $\{t, A\}$ are held fixed, m is initialized with a coordinate descent step, described below, and then iteratively normalized across its rows and columns until the procedure converges (iterative projective scaling). This phase is analogous to a softmax update, except that instead of enforcing a one-way, winner-take-all (maximum) constraint, a two-way, assignment constraint is being enforced. Therefore we describe this phase as a softassign. In phase two $\{t, A\}$ are updated using coordinate descent. Then β is increased and the loop repeats. Let $\hat{E}_{2D}$ be the above objective (1) without the terms that enforce the constraints (i.e. the $x \log x$ barrier function and the Lagrange parameters).

In phase one (softassign) m is updated via coordinate descent:

$$m_{jk} = \exp(-\beta \frac{\partial \hat{E}_{2D}}{\partial m_{jk}})$$

Then m is iteratively normalized across j and k until $\sum_{j=1}^{J} \sum_{k=1}^{K} \Delta m_{iajk} < \epsilon$:

$$m_{jk} = \frac{m_{jk}}{\sum_{j'=1}^{J+1} m_{j'k}} \quad ; \quad m_{jk} = \frac{m_{jk}}{\sum_{k'=1}^{K+1} m_{jk'}}$$

Using coordinate descent the $\{t, A\}$ are updated in phase two. If a term of $\{A\}$ cannot be computed analytically (because of its regularization), Newton's method is used to compute the root of the function. So if a is a term of $\{t, A\}$ then in phase two we update a such that $\frac{\partial \hat{E}_{2D}}{\partial a} = 0$. Finally β is increased and the loop repeats.

By setting the partial derivatives of E_{2D} to zero and initializing the Lagrange parameters to zero, the algorithm for phase one may be derived. Beginning with a small β allows minimization over a fuzzy correspondence matrix m, for which a global minimum is easier to find. Raising β drives the m's closer to 0 or 1, as the algorithm approaches a saddle point.

3 3D with Rotation and Translation

The second algorithm solves the 3D-3D pose estimation problem with unknown correspondence. Given two sets of 3D points $\{X_j\}$ and $\{Y_k\}$ find the rotation R, translation T, and correspondence m that minimize

$$E_{3D}(m, T, R) = \sum_{j=1}^{J} \sum_{k=1}^{K} m_{jk} \|RX_j + T - Y_k\|^2 - \alpha \sum_{j=1}^{J} \sum_{k=1}^{K} m_{jk}$$

with the same constraint on the fuzzy correspondence matrix m as in 2D affine matching. Note that there is no regularization term for the $T - R$ parameters.

This algorithm also works in two phases. In the first, m is updated by a softassign as was described for 2D affine matching. In the second phase, m is fixed, and the problem becomes a 3D to 3D pose estimation problem formulated as a weighted least squares problem. The rotation and translation are represented by a dual number quaternion (r, s) which corresponds to a screw coordinate transform [Walker et al., 1991]. The rotation can be written as $R(r) = W(r)^t Q(r)$ and the translation as $W(r)^t s$. Using these representations, the objective function becomes

$$E_{3D} = \sum_{j=1}^{J} \sum_{k=1}^{K} m_{jk} \|W(r)^t Q(r) x_j + W(r)^t s - y_k\|^2$$

where $x_j = (X_j, 0)^t$ and $y_k = (Y_k, 0)^t$ are the quaternion representations of X_j and Y_k, respectively. Using the properties that $Q(a)b = W(b)a$ and $Q(a)^t Q(a) = W(a)^t W(a) = (a^t a)I$, the objective function can be rewritten as

$$E_{3D} = r^t C_1 r + s^t C_2 s + s^t C_3 r + \lambda_1 (r^t r - 1) + \lambda_2 (s^t r), \qquad (2)$$

where

$$C_1 = -\sum_{j=1}^{J} \sum_{k=1}^{K} m_{jk} Q(y_k)^t W(x_j)$$

$$C_2 = \frac{1}{2} \sum_{j=1}^{J} \sum_{k=1}^{K} m_{jk} I$$

$$C_3 = \sum_{j=1}^{J} \sum_{k=1}^{K} m_{jk} (W(x_j) - Q(y_k)).$$

With this new representation, all the information, including the current fuzzy estimate of the correspondence m are absorbed into the three 4-by-4 matrices C_1, C_2, C_3 in (2), which can be minimized in closed-form [Walker et al., 1991].

4 Experimental Results

In this section we provide experimental results for both the 2D and 3D matching problems. As an application of the 2D matching algorithm, we present results in the context of handwritten character recognition.

4.1 Handwritten Character Data

The data were generated using an X-windows tool which enables us to draw an image with the mouse on a writing pad on the screen. The contours of the images are discretized and are expressed as a set of points in the plane. In the experiments below, we generate 70 points per character on average.

The inputs to the point matching algorithm are the x-y coordinates generated by the drawing program. No other pre-processing is done. The output is a correspondence matrix and a pose. In Figures 1 and 2, we show the correspondences found between several images drawn in this fashion.To make the actual point matches easier to see, we have drawn the correspondences only for every other model point.

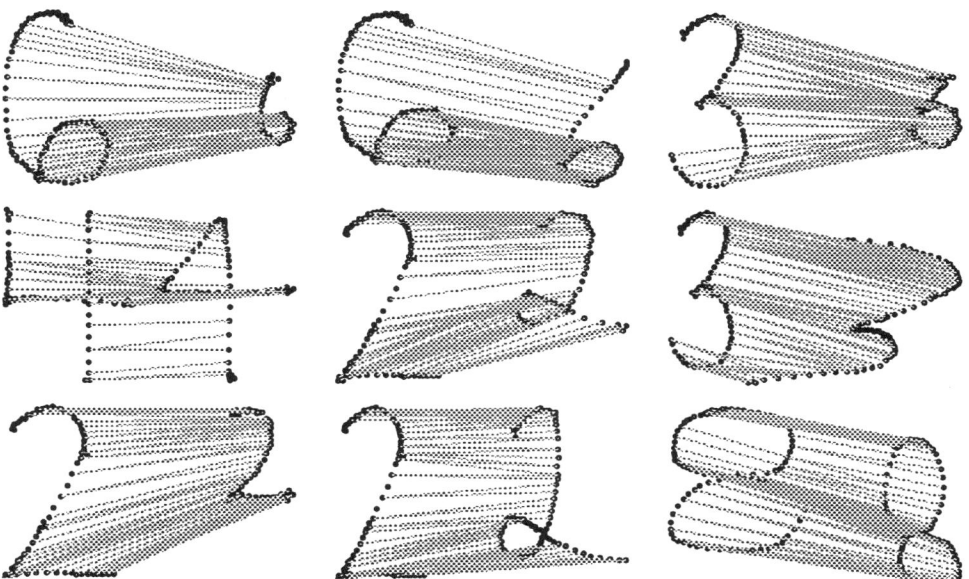

Figure 1: Correspondence of digits

In one experiment, we drew examples of individual digits, one as a model digit and then many different variations of it. In Figure 1, it can be seen that the

Figure 2: Correspondence: "a" found in "cat", "o" found in "song"

correspondences are good for a large variation from the model digit. For example, the correspondence is invariant to scale. Also, the correspondence is good between distorted digits, as in 3 and 6, or between different forms of a digit as in 4, 3, and 2.

In another experiment (Figure 2), individual letters are correctly identified within words. Here, no pre-processing to segment the cursive word into letters is done. The correspondence returned by the point matching algorithm by itself can be good enough for identification. Even similar letters may be differentiated, for example the "a" in "cat" is correctly identified even though the "c" has a similar shape and the "o" is correctly identified in "song", despite the similarity of the "s".

4.2 Randomly generated point sets: 2D

In the second set of experiments, randomly generated dot patterns were used. In each trial a model is created by randomly generating with a uniform distribution, 50 points on a grid of unit area. Independent Gaussian noise $N(0, \sigma)$ is added to each of the points creating a jittered image. Then a fraction, p_d, of points are deleted, and a fraction, p_s, of spurious points are added, randomly on the unit square. Finally, a randomly generated transformation is applied to the set to generate a new image. The objective then is to recover the transformation and correspondence between the transformed image and the original point set.

The transformations we have considered are $\hat{A} \rightarrow$ (Translation, rotation, scale) and the full affine transformation, $A \rightarrow$ (Translation, rotation, scale, vertical shear, oblique shear) The transformation parameters, $\{t_x, t_y, \theta, a, b, c\}$ are bounded in the following way: $-0.5 < t_x, t_y < 0.5$, $-27° < \theta < 27°$, $0.5 \leq e^a \leq 2$ where a is the scale parameter, and $0.7 \leq e^b, e^c \leq 1/0.7$ where b, c are the parameters for the two shears. Each of the parameters is chosen independently and uniformly from the possible ranges.

We use the error measure $e_\alpha = 3|\frac{\alpha^{actual} - \alpha^{estimate}}{width_\alpha}|$ where e_α is the error measure for parameter α and $width_\alpha$ is the range of permissible values for α. Dividing by $width_\alpha$ is preferable to dividing by α^{actual}, which incorrectly weights small α^{actual} values. The reported error (y axes of Figure 3) is the average error over all the parameters.

The time to recover the correspondence and transformation for a problem instance of 50 points is about 50 seconds on a Silicon Graphics workstation with a R4400 processor. By varying parameters such as the annealing rate or stopping criterion, this can be reduced to about 20 seconds with some degradation in accuracy. For each trial combinations of $\sigma \in \{0.01, 0.02, \ldots, 0.08\}$ and $p_d \in \{0\%, 10\%, 30\%, 50\%\}$ and $p_s \in \{0\%, 10\%\}$ were used.

Results are reported separately for transformations $\hat{A}$ and A. For each combination of (σ, p_d, p_s) 500 test instances were generated. Each data point in Figures 3.a and 3.b represents the average error measure for these 500 experiments. The noise and/or deletion-addition factor increases the error measure monotonically. As expected, the transformation $\hat{A}$ has better results than the affine transformation A.

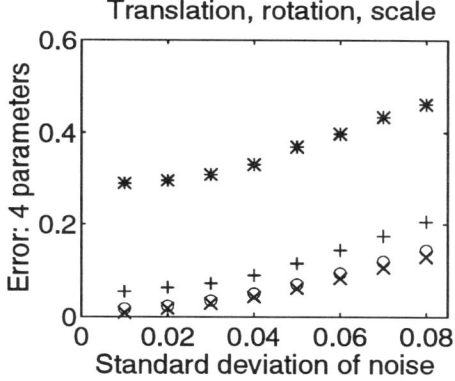
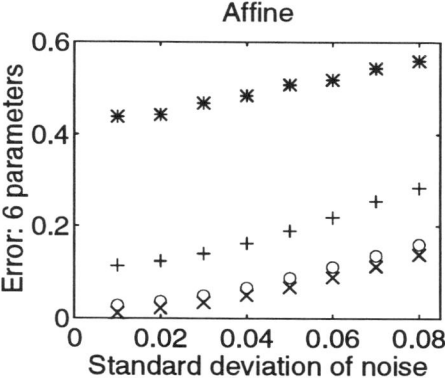

Figure 3: 2D Results for Synthetic Data

x : $p_d = 0.0, p_s = 0.0$,   o : $p_d = 0.1, p_s = 0.1$
\+ : $p_d = 0.3, p_s = 0.1$,   * : $p_d = 0.5, p_s = 0.1$

4.3 Randomly generated point sets: 3D

A test instance for 3D point matching involves generating a random 3D point set as a model image, and then generating a test image by applying a random transformation, adding noise and then randomly deleting points.

20 points are generated uniformly within an unit cube. The parameters for the transformation are generated as follows: The three rotation angles for R are selected from a uniform distribution $U[20, 70]$. Translation parameters T_x, T_y, T_z are selected from a uniform distribution $U[2.5, 7.5]$. Gaussian noise $N(0, \sigma)$ is added to the points. The objective then is to recover the three translation and three rotation parameters and to find the correspondence between this and the original point set. The results are summarized in Figure 4.

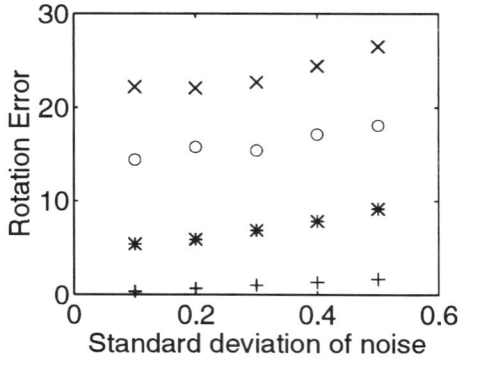 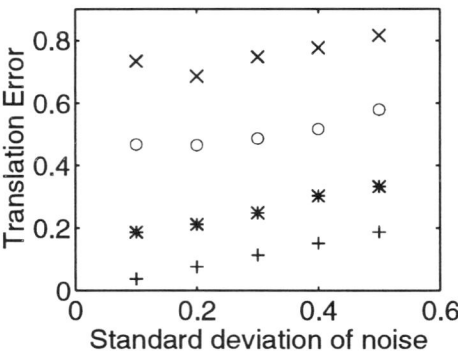

Figure 4: 3D Results for Synthetic Data

x : $p_d = 0.0, p_s = 0.0$, o : $p_d = 0.1, p_s = 0.1$
+ : $p_d = 0.2, p_s = 0.2$, * : $p_d = 0.3, p_s = 0.3$

5 Conclusion

We have developed an algorithm for solving 2D and 3D correspondence problems. The algorithm handles significant noise, missing or spurious features, and non-rigid transformations. Moreover it works with point feature data alone; inclusion of other types of feature information could improve its accuracy and speed. This approach may also be extended to solve multi-level problems. Additionally, the affine transform might be modified to include higher order transformations. It may also be used as a distance measure in learning [Gold et al.,1994].

Acknowledgements

This work has been supported by AFOSR grant F49620-92-J-0465, ONR/DARPA grant N00014-92-J-4048, and the Yale Center for Theoretical and Applied Neuroscience (CTAN). Jing Yan developed the handwriting interface.

References

S. Gold, E. Mjolsness and A. Rangarajan. (1994) Clustering with a domain-specific distance measure. In J.D. Cowan et al., (eds.), *NIPS 6*. Morgan Kaufmann.

E. Grimson, (1990) *Object Recognition by Computer*, Cambridge, MA: MIT Press

C. Peterson and B. Söderberg. (1989) A new method for mapping optimization problems onto neural networks, *Int. Journ. of Neural Sys.*, **1**(1):3:22.

M. W. Walker, L. Shao and R. Volz. (1991) *Estimating 3-D location parameters using dual number quaternions*, CVGIP: Image Understanding *54*(3):358-367.

A. L. Yuille and J. J. Kosowsky. (1994). Statistical physics algorithms that converge. *Neural Computation*, **6**:341-356.

Using a neural net to instantiate a deformable model

Christopher K. I. Williams,[*] Michael D. Revow and Geoffrey E. Hinton
Department of Computer Science, University of Toronto
Toronto, Ontario, Canada M5S 1A4

Abstract

Deformable models are an attractive approach to recognizing non-rigid objects which have considerable within class variability. However, there are severe search problems associated with fitting the models to data. We show that by using neural networks to provide better starting points, the search time can be significantly reduced. The method is demonstrated on a character recognition task.

In previous work we have developed an approach to handwritten character recognition based on the use of deformable models (Hinton, Williams and Revow, 1992a; Revow, Williams and Hinton, 1993). We have obtained good performance with this method, but a major problem is that the search procedure for fitting each model to an image is very computationally intensive, because there is no efficient algorithm (like dynamic programming) for this task. In this paper we demonstrate that it is possible to "compile down" some of the knowledge gained while fitting models to data to obtain better starting points that significantly reduce the search time.

1 DEFORMABLE MODELS FOR DIGIT RECOGNITION

The basic idea in using deformable models for digit recognition is that each digit has a model, and a test image is classified by finding the model which is most likely to have generated it. The quality of the match between model and test image depends on the deformation of the model, the amount of ink that is attributed to noise and the distance of the remaining ink from the deformed model.

---

[*]Current address: Department of Computer Science and Applied Mathematics, Aston University, Birmingham B4 7ET, UK.

More formally, the two important terms in assessing the fit are the prior probability distribution for the instantiation parameters of a model (which penalizes very distorted models), and the imaging model that characterizes the probability distribution over possible images given the instantiated model[1]. Let I be an image, M be a model and z be its instantiation parameters. Then the evidence for model M is given by

$$P(I|M) = \int P(z|M)P(I|M,z)dz \qquad (1)$$

The first term in the integrand is the prior on the instantiation parameters and the second is the imaging model i.e., the likelihood of the data given the instantiated model. $P(M|I)$ is directly proportional to $P(I|M)$, as we assume a uniform prior on each digit.

Equation 1 is formally correct, but if z has more than a few dimensions the evaluation of this integral is very computationally intensive. However, it is often possible to make an approximation based on the assumption that the integrand is strongly peaked around a (global) maximum value z^*. In this case, the evidence can be approximated by the highest peak of the integrand times a volume factor $\Delta(z|I,M)$, which measures the sharpness of the peak[2].

$$P(I|M) \simeq P(z^*|M)P(I|z^*,M)\Delta(z|I,M) \qquad (2)$$

By Taylor expanding around z^* to second order it can be shown that the volume factor depends on the determinant of the Hessian of $\log P(z, I|M)$. Taking logs of equation 2, defining E_{def} as the negative log of $P(z^*|M)$, and E_{fit} as the corresponding term for the imaging model, then the aim of the search is to find the minimum of $E_{tot} = E_{def} + E_{fit}$. Of course the total energy will have many local minima; for the character recognition task we aim to find the global minimum by using a continuation method (see section 1.2).

1.1 SPLINES, AFFINE TRANSFORMS AND IMAGING MODELS

This section presents a brief overview of our work on using deformable models for digit recognition. For a fuller treatment, see Revow, Williams and Hinton (1993).

Each digit is modelled by a cubic B-spline whose shape is determined by the positions of the control points in the object-based frame. The models have eight control points, except for the one model which has three, and the seven model which has five. To generate an ideal example of a digit the control points are positioned at their "home" locations. Deformed characters are produced by perturbing the control points away from their home locations. The home locations and covariance matrix for each model were adapted in order to improve the performance.

The deformation energy only penalizes shape *deformations*. Affine transformations, i.e., translation, rotation, dilation, elongation, and shear, do not change the underlying shape of an object so we want the deformation energy to be invariant under them. We achieve this by giving each model its own "object-based frame" and computing the deformation energy relative to this frame.

---
[1] This framework has been used by many authors, e.g. Grenander *et al* (1991).
[2] The Gaussian approximation has been popularized in the neural net community by MacKay (1992).

The data we used consists of binary-pixel images of segmented handwritten digits. The general flavour of a imaging model for this problem is that there should be a high probability of inked pixels close to the spline, and lower probabilities further away. This can be achieved by spacing out a number of Gaussian "ink generators" uniformly along the contour; we have found that it is also useful to have a uniform background noise process over the area of the image that is able to account for pixels that occur far away from the generators. The ink generators and background process define a mixture model. Using the assumption that each data point is generated independently given the instantiated model, $P(I|z^*, M)$ factors into the product of the probability density of each black pixel under the mixture model.

1.2 RECOGNIZING ISOLATED DIGITS

For each model, the aim of the search is to find the instantiation parameters that minimize E_{tot}. The search starts with zero deformations and an initial guess for the affine parameters which scales the model so as to lie over the data with zero skew and rotation. A small number of generators with the same large variance are placed along the spline, forming a broad, smooth ridge of high ink-probability along the spline. We use a search procedure similar to the (iterative) Expectation Maximization (EM) method of fitting an unconstrained mixture of Gaussians, except that (i) the Gaussians are constrained to lie on the spline (ii) there is a deformation energy term and (iii) the affine transformation must be recalculated on each iteration. During the search the number of generators is gradually increased while their variance decreases according to predetermined "annealing" schedule[3].

After fitting all the models to a particular image, we wish to evaluate which of the models best "explains" the data. The natural measure is the sum of E_{fit}, E_{def} and the volume factor. However, we have found that performance is improved by including four additional terms which are easily obtained from the final fits of the model to the image. These are (i) a measure which penalizes matches in which there are beads far from any inked pixels (the "beads in white space" problem), and (ii) the rotation, shear and elongation of the affine transform. It is hard to decide in a principled way on the correct weightings for all of these terms in the evaluation function. We estimated the weightings from the data by training a simple postprocessing neural network. These inputs are connected directly to the ten output units. The output units compete using the "softmax" function which guarantees that they form a probability distribution, summing to one.

2 PREDICTING THE INSTANTIATION PARAMETERS

The search procedure described above is very time consuming. However, given many examples of images and the corresponding instantiation parameters obtained by the slow method, it is possible to train a neural network to predict the instantiation parameters of novel images. These predictions provide better starting points, so the search time can be reduced.

---

[3]The schedule starts with 8 beads increasing to 60 beads in six steps, with the variance decreasing from 0.04 to 0.0006 (measured in the object frame). The scale is set in the object-based frame so that each model is 1 unit high.

2.1 PREVIOUS WORK

Previous work on hypothesizing instantiation parameters can be placed into two broad classes, correspondence based search and parameter space search. In correspondence based search, the idea is to extract features from the image and identify corresponding features in the model. Using sufficient correspondences the instantiation parameters of the model can be determined. The problem is that simple, easily detectable image features have many possible matches, and more complex features require more computation and are more difficult to detect. Grimson (1990) shows how to search the space of possible correspondences using an interpretation tree.

An alternative approach, which is used in Hough transform techniques, is to directly work in parameter space. The Hough transform was originally designed for the detection of straight lines in images, and has been extended to cover a number of geometric shapes, notably conic sections. Ballard (1981) further extended the approach to arbitrary shapes with the Generalized Hough Transform. The parameter space for each model is divided into cells ("binned"), and then for each image feature a vote is added to each parameter space bin that could have produced that feature. After collecting votes from all image features we then search for peaks in the parameter space accumulator array, and attempt to verify pose. The Hough transform can be viewed as a crude way of approximating the logarithm of the posterior distribution $P(z|I, M)$ (e.g. Hunt *et al*, 1988).

However, these two techniques have only been used on problems involving rigid models, and are not readily applicable to the digit recognition problem. For the Hough space method, binning and vote collection is impractical in the high dimensional parameter space, and for the correspondence based approach there is a lack of easily identified and highly discriminative features. The strengths of these two techniques, namely their ability to deal with arbitrary scalings, rotations and translations of the data, and their tolerance of extraneous features, are not really required for a task where the input data is fairly well segmented and normalized.

Our approach is to use a neural network to predict the instantiation parameters for each model, given an input image. Zemel and Hinton (1991) used a similar method with simple 2-d objects, and more recently, Beymer *et al* (1993) have constructed a network which maps from a face image to a 2-d parameter space spanning head rotations and a smile/no-smile dimension. However, their method does not directly map from images to instantiation parameters; they use a computer vision correspondence algorithm to determine the displacement field of pixels in a novel image relative to a reference image, and then use this field as the input to the network. This step limits the use of the approach to images that are sufficiently similar so that the correspondence algorithm functions well.

2.2 INSTANTIATING DIGIT MODELS USING NEURAL NETWORKS

The network which is used to predict the model instantiation parameters is shown in figure 1. The (unthinned) binary images are normalized to give 16×16 8-bit greyscale images which are fed into the neural network. The network uses a standard three-layer architecture; each hidden unit computes a weighted sum of its inputs, and then feeds this value through a sigmoidal nonlinearity $\sigma(x) = 1/(1+e^{-x})$. The

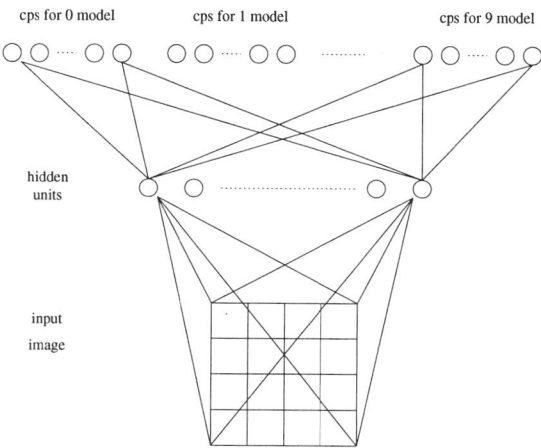

Figure 1: The prediction network architecture. "cps" stands for control points.

output values are a weighted linear combination of the hidden unit activities plus output biases. The targets are the locations of the control points in the normalized image, found from fitting models as described in section 1.2.

The network was trained with backpropagation to minimize the squared error, using 900 training images and 200 validation images of each digit drawn from the *br* set of the CEDAR CDROM 1 database of Cities, States, ZIP Codes, Digits, and Alphabetic Characters[4]. Two test sets were used; one was obtained from data in the *br* dataset, and the other was the (official) *bs* test set. After some experimentation we chose a network with twenty hidden units, which means that the net has over 8,000 weights. With such a large number of weights it is important to regularize the solution obtained by the network by using a complexity penalty; we used a weight penalty $\lambda \sum_j w_j^2$ and optimized λ on a validation set. Targets were only set for the correct digit at the output layer; nothing was backpropagated from the other output units. The net took 440 epochs to train using the default conjugate gradient search method in the Xerion neural network simulator[5]. It would be possible to construct ten separate networks to carry out the same task as the net described above, but this would intensify the danger of overfitting, which is reduced by giving the network a common pool of hidden units which it can use as it decides appropriate.

For comparison with the *prediction net* described above, a trivial network which just consisted of output biases was trained; this network simply learns the average value of the control point locations. On a validation set the squared error of the prediction net was over three times smaller than the trivial net. Although this is encouraging, the acid test is to compare the performance of elastic models settled from the predicted positions using a shortened annealing schedule; if the predictions are good, then only a short amount of settling will be required.

---

[4] Made available by the Unites States Postal Service Office of Advanced Technology.

[5] Xerion was designed and implemented by Drew van Camp, Tony Plate and Geoffrey Hinton at the University of Toronto.

Figure 2: A comparision of the initial instantiations due to the prediction net (top row) and the trivial net (bottom row) on an image of a 2. Notice that for the two model the prediction net is much closer to the data. The other digit models may or may not be greatly affected by the input data; for example, the predictions from both nets seem essentially the same for the zero, but for the seven the prediction net puts the model nearer to the data.

The feedforward net predicts the position of the control points in the normalized image. By inverting the normalization process, the positions of the control points in the un-normalized image are determined. The model deformation and affine transformation corresponding to these image control point locations can then be determined by running a part of one iteration of the search procedure. Experiments were then conducted with a number of shortened annealing schedules; for each one, data obtained from settling on a part of the training data was used to train the postprocessing net. The performance was then evaluated on the *br* test set.

The full annealing schedule has six stages. The shortened annealing schedules are:

1. No settling at all
2. Two iterations at the final variance of 0.0006
3. One iteration at 0.0025 and two at 0.0006
4. The full annealing schedule (for comparison)

The results on the *br* test set are shown in table 1. The general trends are that the performance obtained using the prediction net is consistently better than the trivial net, and that longer annealing schedules lead to better performance. A comparison of schedules 3 and 4 in table 1 indicates that the performance of the prediction net/schedule 3 combination is similar to (or slightly better than) that obtained with the full annealing schedule, and is more than a factor of two faster. The results with the full schedule are almost identical to the results obtained with the default "box" initialization described in section 1.2. Figure 2 compares the outputs of the prediction and trivial nets on a particular example. Judging from the weight

Schedule number	Trivial net	Prediction net	Average time required to settle one model (s)
1	427	200	0.12
2	329	58	0.25
3	160	32	0.49
4	40	36	1.11

Table 1: Errors on the internal test set of 2000 examples for different annealing schedules. The timing trials were carried out on a R-4400 machine.

vectors and activity patterns of the hidden units, it does not seem that some of the units are specialized for a particular digit class.

A run on the *bs* test set using schedule 3 gave an error rate of 4.76 % (129 errors), which is very similar to the 125 errors obtained using the full annealing schedule and the box initialization. A comparison of the errors made on the two runs shows that only 67 out of the 129 errors were common to the two sets. This suggests that it would be very sensible to reject cases where the two methods do not agree.

3 DISCUSSION

The prediction net used above can be viewed as an interpolation scheme in the control point position space of each digit $z(I) = z_0 + \sum_i a_i(I) z_i$, where $z(I)$ is the predicted position in the control point space, z_0 is the contribution due to the biases, a_i is the activity of hidden unit i and z_i is its location in the control point position space (learned from the data). If there are more hidden units than output dimensions, then for any particular image there are an infinite number of ways to make this equation hold exactly. However, the network will tend to find solutions so that the $a_i(I)$'s will vary smoothly as the image is perturbed.

The nets described above output just one set of instantiation parameters for a given model. However, it may be preferable to be able to represent a number of guesses about model instantiation parameters; one way of doing this is to train a network that has multiple sets of output parameters, as in the "mixture of experts" architecture of Jacobs *et al* (1991). The outputs can be interpreted as a mixture distribution in the control point position space, conditioned on the input image. Another approach to providing more information about the posterior distribution is described in (Hinton, Williams and Revow, 1992b), where $P(z|I)$ is approximated using a fixed set of basis functions whose weighting depends on the input image I.

The strategies described above directly predict the instantiation parameters in parameter space. It is also possible to use neural networks to hypothesize correspondences, i.e. to predict an inked pixel's position on the spline given a local window of context in the image. With sufficient matches it is then possible to compute the instantiation parameters of the model. We have conducted some preliminary experiments with this method (described in Williams, 1994), which indicate that good performance can be achieved for the correspondence prediction task.

We have shown that the we can obtain significant speedup using the prediction net. The schemes outlined above which allow multimodal predictions in instantiation parameter space may improve performance and deserve further investigation. We are also interested in improving the performance of the prediction net, for example by outputting a confidence measure which could be used to adjust the length of the elastic models' search appropriately. We believe that using machine learning techniques like neural networks to help reduce the amount of search required to fit complex models to data may be useful for many other problems.

Acknowledgements

This research was funded by Apple and by the Ontario Information Technology Research Centre. We thank Allan Jepson, Richard Durbin, Rich Zemel, Peter Dayan, Rob Tibshirani and Yann Le Cun for helpful discussions. Geoffrey Hinton is the Noranda Fellow of the Canadian Institute for Advanced Research.

References

Ballard, D. H. (1981). Generalizing the Hough transfrom to detect arbitrary shapes. *Pattern Recognition*, 13(2):111–122.

Beymer, D., Shashua, A., and Poggio, T. (1993). Example Based Image Analysis and Synthesis. AI Memo 1431, AI Laboratory, MIT.

Grenander, U., Chow, Y., and Keenan, D. M. (1991). *Hands: A pattern theoretic study of biological shapes*. Springer-Verlag.

Grimson, W. E. L. (1990). *Object recognition by computer*. MIT Press, Cambridge, MA.

Hinton, G. E., Williams, C. K. I., and Revow, M. D. (1992a). Adaptive elastic models for hand-printed character recognition. In Moody, J. E., Hanson, S. J., and Lippmann, R. P., editors, *Advances in Neural Information Processing Systems 4*. Morgan Kauffmann.

Hinton, G. E., Williams, C. K. I., and Revow, M. D. (1992b). Combinining two methods of recognizing hand-printed digits. In Aleksander, I. and Taylor, J., editors, *Artificial Neural Networks 2*. Elsevier Science Publishers.

Hunt, D. J., Nolte, L. W., and Ruedger, W. H. (1988). Performance of the Hough Transform and its Relationship to Statistical Signal Detection Theory. *Computer Vision, Graphics and Image Processing*, 43:221–238.

Jacobs, R. A., Jordan, M. I., Nowlan, S. J., and Hinton, G. E. (1991). Adaptive mixtures of local experts. *Neural Computation*, 3(1).

MacKay, D. J. C. (1992). Bayesian Interpolation. *Neural Computation*, 4(3):415–447.

Revow, M. D., Williams, C. K. I., and Hinton, G. E. (1993). Using mixtures of deformable models to capture variations in hand printed digits. In Srihari, S., editor, *Proceedings of the Third International Workshop on Frontiers in Handwriting Recognition*, pages 142–152, Buffalo, New York, USA.

Williams, C. K. I. (1994). *Combining deformable models and neural networks for handprinted digit recognition*. PhD thesis, Dept. of Computer Science, University of Toronto.

Zemel, R. S. and Hinton, G. E. (1991). Discovering viewpoint-invariant relationships that characterize objects. In Lippmann, R. P., Moody, J. E., and Touretzky, D. S., editors, *Advances In Neural Information Processing Systems 3*, pages 299–305. Morgan Kaufmann Publishers.

Nonlinear Image Interpolation using Manifold Learning

Christoph Bregler
Computer Science Division
University of California
Berkeley, CA 94720
bregler@cs.berkeley.edu

Stephen M. Omohundro[*]
Int. Computer Science Institute
1947 Center Street Suite 600
Berkeley, CA 94704
om@research.nj.nec.com

Abstract

The problem of interpolating between specified images in an image sequence is a simple, but important task in model-based vision. We describe an approach based on the abstract task of "manifold learning" and present results on both synthetic and real image sequences. This problem arose in the development of a combined lip-reading and speech recognition system.

1 Introduction

Perception may be viewed as the task of combining impoverished sensory input with stored world knowledge to predict aspects of the state of the world which are not directly sensed. In this paper we consider the task of *image interpolation* by which we mean hypothesizing the structure of images which occurred between given images in a temporal sequence. This task arose during the development of a combined lip-reading and speech recognition system [3], because the time windows for auditory and visual information are different (30 frames per second for the camera vs. 100 feature vectors per second for the acoustic information). It is an excellent visual test domain in general, however, because it is easy to generate large amounts of test and training data and the performance measure is largely "theory independent". The test consists of simply presenting two frames from a movie and comparing the

---

[*]New address: NEC Research Institute, Inc., 4 Independence Way, Princeton, NJ 08540

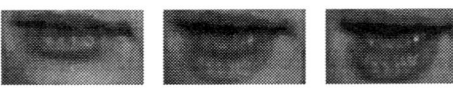

Figure 1: Linear interpolated lips.

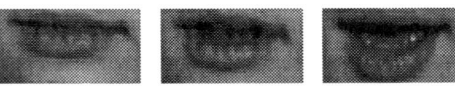

Figure 2: Desired interpolation.

hypothesized intermediate frames to the actual ones. It is easy to use footage of a particular visual domain as training data in the same way.

Most current approaches to model-based vision require hand-constructed CAD-like models. We are developing an alternative approach in which the vision system builds up visual models automatically by learning from examples. One of the central components of this kind of learning is the abstract problem of inducing a smooth nonlinear constraint manifold from a set of examples from the manifold. We call this "manifold learning" and have developed several approaches closely related to neural networks for doing it [2]. In this paper we apply manifold learning to the image interpolation problem and numerically compare the results of this "nonlinear" process with simple linear interpolation. We find that the approach works well when the underlying model space is low-dimensional. In more complex examples, manifold learning cannot be directly applied to images but still is a central component in a more complex system (not discussed here).

We present several approaches to using manifold learning for this task. We compare the performance of these approaches to that of simple linear interpolation. Figure 1 shows the results of linear interpolation of lip images from the lip-reading system. Even in the short period of 33 milliseconds *linear* interpolation can produce an unnatural lip image. The problem is that linear interpolation of two images just averages the two pictures. The interpolated image in Fig. 1 has two lower lip parts instead of just one. The desired interpolated image is shown in Fig. 2, and consists of a single lower lip positioned at a location between the lower lip positions in the two input pictures.

Our interpolation technique is *nonlinear*, and is constrained to produce only images from an abstract manifold in "lip space" induced by learning. Section 2 describes the procedure, Section 4 introduces the interpolation technique based on the induced manifold, and Sections 5 and 6 describe our experiments on artificial and natural images.

2 Manifold Learning

Each $n * m$ graylevel image may be thought of as a point in an $n * m$-dimensional space. A sequence of lip-images produced by a speaker uttering a sentence lie on a

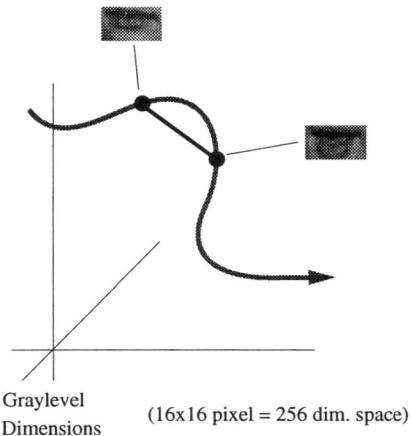

Graylevel Dimensions   (16x16 pixel = 256 dim. space)

Figure 3: Linear vs nonlinear interpolation.

1-dimensional trajectory in this space (figure 3). If the speaker were to move her lips in all possible ways, the images would define a low-dimensional submanifold (or nonlinear surface) embedded in the high-dimensional space of all possible graylevel images.

If we could compute this nonlinear manifold, we could limit any interpolation algorithm to generate only images contained in it. Images not on the manifold cannot be generated by the speaker under normal circumstances. Figure 3 compares a curve of interpolated images lying on this manifold to straight line interpolation which generally leaves the manifold and enters the domain of images which violate the integrity of the model.

To represent this kind of nonlinear manifold embedded in a high-dimensional feature space, we use a mixture model of local linear patches. Any smooth nonlinear manifold can be approximated arbitrarily well in each local neighborhood by a linear "patch". In our representation, local linear patches are "glued" together with smooth "gating" functions to form a globally defined nonlinear manifold [2]. We use the "nearest-point-query" to define the manifold. Given an arbitrary point near the manifold, this returns the closest point on the manifold. We answer such queries with a weighted sum of the linear projections of the point to each local patch. The weights are defined by an "influence function" associated with each linear patch which we usually define by a Gaussian kernel. The weight for each patch is the value of its influence function at the point divided by the sum of all influence functions ("partition of unity"). Figure 4 illustrates the nearest-point-query. Because Gaussian kernels die off quickly, the effect of distant patches may be ignored, improving computational performance. The linear projections themselves consist of a dot product and so are computationally inexpensive.

For learning, we must fit such a mixture of local patches to the training data. An initial estimate of the patch centers is obtained from k-means clustering. We fit a patch to each local cluster using a local principal components analysis. Fine tuning

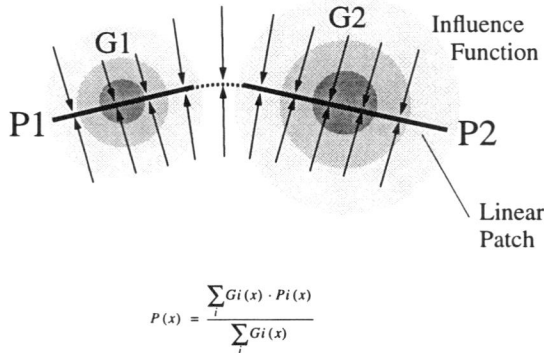

$$P(x) = \frac{\sum_i Gi(x) \cdot Pi(x)}{\sum_i Gi(x)}$$

Figure 4: Local linear patches glued together to a nonlinear manifold.

of the model is done using the EM (expectation-maximization) procedure.

This approach is related to the mixture of expert architecture [4], and to the manifold representation in [6]. Our EM implementation is related to [5], which uses a hierarchical gating function and local experts that compute linear mappings from one space to another space. In contrast, our approach uses a "one-level" gating function and local patches that project a space into itself.

3 Linear Preprocessing

Dealing with very high-dimensional domains (e.g. $256 * 256$ graylevel images) requires large memory and computational resources. Much of this computation is not relevant to the task, however. Even if the space of images is nonlinear, the nonlinearity does not necessarily appear in all of the dimensions. Earlier experiments in the lip domain [3] have shown that images projected onto a 10-dimensional linear subspace still accurately represents all possible lip configurations. We therefore first project the high-dimensional images into such a linear subspace and then induce the nonlinear manifold within this lower dimensional linear subspace. This preprocessing is similar to purely linear techniques [7, 10, 9].

4 Constraint Interpolation

Geometrically, linear interpolation between two points in n-space may be thought of as moving along the straight line joining the two points. In our non-linear approach to interpolation, the point moves along a curve joining the two points which lies in the manifold of legal images. We have studied several algorithms for estimating the shortest manifold trajectory connecting two given points. For the performance results, we studied the point which is halfway along the shortest trajectory.

4.1 "Free-Fall"

The computationally simplest approach is to simply project the linearly interpolated point onto the nonlinear manifold. The projection is accurate when the point is close to the manifold. In cases where the linearly interpolated point is far away (i.e. no weight of the partition of unity dominates all the other weights) the closest-point-query does not result in a good interpolant. For a worst case, consider a point in the middle of a circle or sphere. All local patches have same weight and the weighted sum of all projections is the center point itself, which is not a manifold point. Furthermore, near such "singular" points, the final result is sensitive to small perturbations in the initial position.

4.2 "Manifold-Walk"

A better approach is to "walk" along the manifold itself rather than relying on the linear interpolant. Each step of the walk is linear and in the direction of the target point but the result is immediately projected onto the manifold. This new point is then moved toward the target point and projected onto the manifold, etc. When the target is finally reached, the arc length of the curve is approximated by the accumulated lengths of the individual steps. The point half way along the curve is chosen as the interpolant. This algorithm is far more robust than the first one, because it only uses local projections, even when the two input points are far from each other. Figure 5b illustrates this algorithm.

4.3 "Manifold-Snake"

This approach combines aspects of the first two algorithms. It begins with the linearly interpolated points and iteratively moves the points toward the manifold. The *Manifold-Snake* is a sequence of n points preferentially distributed along a smooth curve with equal distances between them. An energy function is defined on such sequences of points so that the energy minimum tries to satisfy these constraints (smoothness, equidistance, and nearness to the manifold):

$$E = \sum_i \alpha ||v_{i-1} - 2v_i + v_{i+1}||^2 + \beta ||v_i - proj(v_i)||^2 \quad (1)$$

E has value 0 if all v_i are evenly distributed on a straight line and also lie on the manifold. In general E can never be 0 if the manifold is nonlinear, but a minimum for E represents an optimizing solution. We begin with a straight line between the two input points and perform gradient descent in E to find this optimizing solution.

5 Synthetic Examples

To quantify the performance of these approaches to interpolation, we generated a database of $16 * 16$ pixel images consisting of rotated bars. The bars were rotated for each image by a specific angle. The images lie on a one-dimensional nonlinear manifold embedded in a 256 dimensional image space. A nonlinear manifold represented by 16 local linear patches was induced from the 256 images. Figure 6a shows

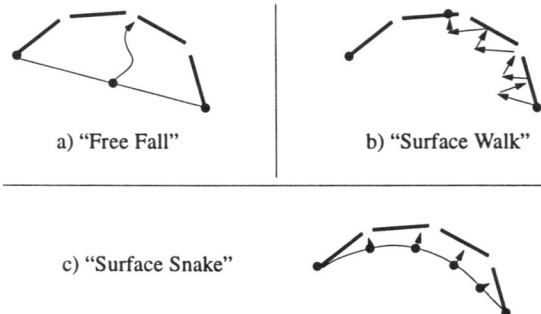

Figure 5: Proposed interpolation algorithms.

Figure 6: a) Linear interpolation, b) nonlinear interpolation.

two bars and their linear interpolation. Figure 6b shows the nonlinear interpolation using the *Manifold-Walk* algorithm.

Figure 7 shows the average pixel mean squared error of linear and nonlinear interpolated bars. The x-axis represents the relative angle between the two input points.

Figure 8 shows some iterations of a *Manifold-Snake* interpolating 7 points along a 1 dimensional manifold embedded in a 2 dimensional space.

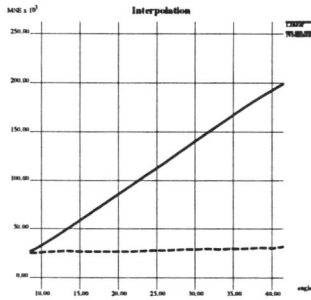

Figure 7: Average pixel mean squared error of linear and nonlinear interpolated bars.

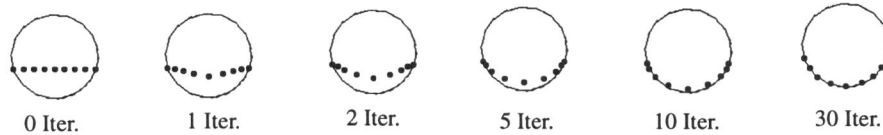

Figure 8: Manifold-Snake iterations on an induced 1 dimensional manifold embedded in 2 dimensions.

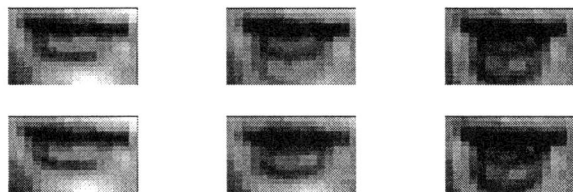

Figure 9: 16x16 images. Top row: linear interpolation. Bottom row: nonlinear "manifold-walk" interpolation.

6 Natural Lip Images

We experimented with two databases of natural lip images taken from two different subjects.

Figure 9 shows a case of linear interpolated and nonlinear interpolated 16 * 16 pixel lip images using the *Manifold-Walk* algorithm. The manifold consists of 16 4-dimensional local linear patches. It was induced from a training set of 1931 lip images recorded with a 30 frames per second camera from a subject uttering various sentences. The nonlinear interpolated image is much closer to a realistic lip configuration than the linear interpolated image.

Figure 10 shows a case of linear interpolated and nonlinear interpolated 45 * 72 pixel lip images using the *Manifold-Snake* algorithm. The images were recorded with a high-speed 100 frames per second camera[1]. Because of the much higher dimensionality of the images, we projected the images into a 16 dimensional linear subspace. Embedded in this subspace we induced a nonlinear manifold consisting of 16 4-dimensional local linear patches, using a training set of 2560 images. The linearly interpolated lip image shows upper and lower teeth, but with smaller contrast, because it is the average image of the open mouth and closed mouth. The nonlinearly interpolated lip images show only the upper teeth and the lips half way closed, which is closer to the real lip configuration.

7 Discussion

We have shown how induced nonlinear manifolds can be used to constrain the interpolation of graylevel images. Several interpolation algorithms were proposed

---
[1] The images were recorded in the UCSD Perceptual Science Lab by Michael Cohen

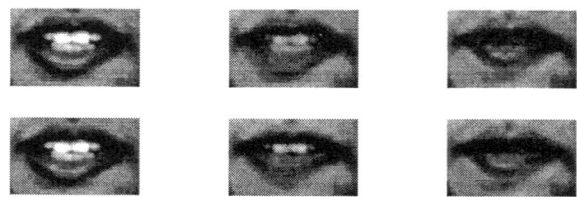

Figure 10: 45x72 images projected into a 16 dimensional subspace. Top row: linear interpolation. Bottom row: nonlinear "manifold-snake" interpolation.

and experimental studies have shown that constrained nonlinear interpolation works well both in artificial domains and natural lip images.

Among various other nonlinear image interpolation techniques, the work of [1] using a Gaussian Radial Basis Function network is most closely related to our approach. Their approach is based on feature locations found by pixelwise correspondence, where our approach directly interpolates graylevel images.

Another related approach is presented in [8]. Their images are also first projected into a linear subspace and then modelled by a nonlinear surface but they require their training examples to lie on a grid in parameter space so that they can use spline methods.

References

[1] D. Beymer, A. Shahsua, and T. Poggio *Example Based Image Analysis and Synthesis* M.I.T. A.I. Memo No. 1431, Nov. 1993.

[2] C. Bregler and S. Omohundro, *Surface Learning with Applications to Lip-Reading*, in Advances in Neural Information Processing Systems 6, Morgan Kaufmann, 1994.

[3] C. Bregler and Y. Konig, *"Eigenlips" for Robust Speech Recognition* in Proc. of IEEE Int. Conf. on Acoustics, Speech, and Signal Processing, Adelaide, Australia, 1994.

[4] R.A. Jacobs, M.I. Jordan, S.J. Nowlan, and G.E. Hinton, *Adaptive mixtures of local experts* in Neural Compuation, 3, 79-87.

[5] M. I. Jordan and R. A. Jacobs, *Hierarchical Mixtures of Experts and the EM Algorithm* Neural Computation, Vol. 6, Issue 2, March 1994.

[6] N. Kambhatla and T.K. Leen, *Fast Non-Linear Dimension Reduction* in Advances in Neural Information Processing Systems 6, Morgan Kaufmann, 1994.

[7] M. Kirby, F. Weisser, and G. Dangelmayr, *A Model Problem in Represetation of Digital Image Sequences*, in Pattern Recgonition, Vol 26, No. 1, 1993.

[8] H. Murase, and S. K. Nayar *Learning and Recognition of 3-D Objects from Brightness Images* Proc. AAAI, Washington D.C., 1993.

[9] P. Simard, Y. Le Cun, J. Denker *Efficient Pattern Recognition Using a New Transformation Distance* Advances in Neural Information Processing Systems 5, Morgan Kaufman, 1993.

[10] M. Turk and A. Pentland, *Eigenfaces for Recognition* Journal of Cognitive Neuroscience, Volume 3, Number 1, MIT 1991.

Coarse-to-Fine Image Search Using Neural Networks

Clay D. Spence, John C. Pearson, and Jim Bergen
National Information Display Laboratory
P.O. Box 8619
Princeton, NJ 08543-8619
cspence@sarnoff.com
John_Pearson@maca.sarnoff.com
jbergen@sarnoff.com

Abstract

The efficiency of image search can be greatly improved by using a coarse-to-fine search strategy with a multi-resolution image representation. However, if the resolution is so low that the objects have few distinguishing features, search becomes difficult. We show that the performance of search at such low resolutions can be improved by using *context* information, i.e., objects visible at low-resolution which are not the objects of interest but are associated with them. The networks can be given explicit context information as inputs, or they can learn to detect the context objects, in which case the user does not have to be aware of their existence. We also use *Integrated Feature Pyramids*, which represent high-frequency information at low resolutions. The use of multi-resolution search techniques allows us to combine information about the appearance of the objects on many scales in an efficient way. A natural form of exemplar selection also arises from these techniques. We illustrate these ideas by training hierarchical systems of neural networks to find clusters of buildings in aerial photographs of farmland.

1 INTRODUCTION

Coarse-to-fine image search is a general technique for improving the efficiency of any search algorithm. (Burt, 1988a and b; Burt et al., 1989). One begins by searching a low-resolution (coarse-scale) version of the image, typically obtained by constructing an image pyramid (Burt and Adelson, 1983). Since this version is smaller than the original, there are far fewer pixels to be processed and the search is correspondingly faster. To improve the certainty of detection and refine the location estimates, the search process is repeated at higher resolution (finer scale), but only in those regions-of-interest (*ROIs*) which were identified at lower resolution as likely to contain one of the objects to be found, thus greatly reducing the actual area to be searched. This process is repeated at successively higher resolutions until sufficient certainty and precision is achieved or the original image has been searched.[1]

These pyramid techniques scale well with image size and can quickly process large images, but the relatively simple, hand-tuned pattern recognition components that are typically used limit their accuracy. Neural networks provide a complementary set of techniques, since they can learn complex patterns, but they don't scale well with image size. We have developed a Hybrid Pyramid/Neural Network (HPNN) system that combines the two techniques so as to leverage their strengths and compensate for their weaknesses.

A novel benefit of combining pyramids and neural networks is the potential for automatically learning to use *context* information, by which we mean any visible characteristics of the object's surroundings which tend to distinguish it from other objects. Examples of context information which might be useful in searching aerial photographs for man-made objects are the proximity of roads and terrain type. Pyramids provide the ability to detect context in a low-resolution image representation, which is necessary for efficient processing of large regions of the image. Neural networks provide the ability to discover context of which we may be unaware, and to learn the relevance of the context to detection, the dependence of detection probability on distance from a context object, etc. Context can help to narrow the search region at low resolutions and improve the detection performance since it is, by definition, relevant information. Of course, the usefulness of the idea will be different for each problem.

Context can be explicitly provided, e.g., in the form of a road map. As mentioned above, a neural net may also learn to exploit some context which is not explicitly provided, but must be inferred from the image data. If there is such context and the network's architecture and input features are capable of exploiting it, it should learn to do so even if we use ordinary training methods that do not explicitly take context into account.

We currently implement these functions in a hierarchical sequence of ordinary feed-forward networks with sigmoidal units, one network at each resolution in an image pyramid (Fig. 1). Each network receives some features extracted from a window in the image, and its output is interpreted as the probability of finding one of the searched-for objects in the center of the window. The network is scanned over all ROIs in this manner. (At the lowest resolution there is one ROI, which is the entire image.)

The networks are trained one at a time, starting at the lowest resolution. Context is made available to networks at higher resolutions by giving them information from the lower-resolution networks as additional inputs, which we will call *context inputs*. These could be

---

[1] Several authors have investigated multi-scale processing of one-dimensional signals with neural networks, e.g., Mozer (1994) and Burr and Miyata (1993) studied music composition. Burr and Miyata use sub-sampling as in a pyramid decomposition. Images differ somewhat from music in that there are primitive features at all scales (limited by the sampling rate and image size), whereas the average frequency spectrum of music over a long time span doesn't seem likely to be meaningful. The original paper on pyramid image representation is (Burt and Adelson, 1983).

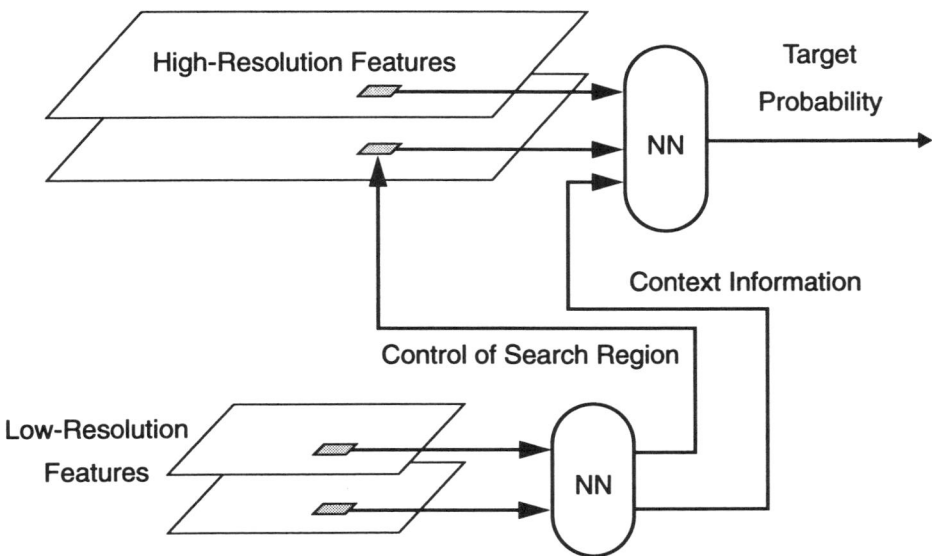

Figure 1. A Hierarchical Search System that Exploits Context.

taken from either the hidden units or output units of the lower-resolution networks. By training the networks in sequence starting at low resolution, we can choose to train the higher-resolution networks in the ROIs selected by the lower-resolution networks, thus providing a simple means of exemplar selection. This *coarse-to-fine training* is often useful, since many problems have relatively few positive examples per image, but because of the size of the image there are an enormous number of more-or-less redundant negative examples.

2 AN EXAMPLE PROBLEM

To demonstrate these ideas we applied them to the problem of finding clusters of buildings in aerial photographs of a rural area. Since buildings are almost always near a road, roads are context objects associated with buildings. We approached the problem in two ways to demonstrate different capabilities. First, we trained systems of networks with explicitly provided context in the form of road maps, in order to demonstrate the possible benefits.[2] Second, we trained systems without explicitly-provided context, in order to show that the context could be learned.

2.1 EXPLICIT CONTEXT

For comparison purposes, we trained one network to search a high-resolution image directly, with no explicit context inputs and no inputs from other networks. To demonstrate the effect of learned context on search we trained a second system with no explicit

---

[2] It would be surprising if this extra information didn't help, since we know it is relevant. For many applications digitized maps will be available, so demonstrating the possible performance benefit is still worth-while.

context provided to the nets, but each received inputs from all of the networks at lower resolutions. These inputs were simply the outputs of those lower-resolution networks. To demonstrate the benefit of explicitly provided context, we trained a third system with both context inputs from lower-resolution networks and explicit context in the form of a road map of the area, which was registered with the image.

2.1.1 Features

To preserve some distinguishing features at a given low resolution, we extracted simple features at various resolutions and represented them at the lower resolution. The low-resolution representations were constructed by reducing the feature images with the usual blur-and-sub-sample procedure used to construct a Gaussian pyramid (Burt and Adelson, 1983). The features should not be too computationally expensive to extract, otherwise the efficiency benefit of coarse-to-fine search would be canceled.

The features used as inputs to the neural nets in the building-search systems were simple measures of the spatial image energy in several frequency bands. We constructed these feature images by building the Laplacian pyramid of the image[3] and then taking the absolute values of the pixels in each image in the pyramid. We then constructed a Gaussian pyramid of each of these images, to provide versions of them at different resolutions. A neural net searching a given resolution received input from each energy image derived from the same resolution and all higher resolutions.[4]

Binary road-map images were constructed from the digitized aerial photographs. They were reduced in resolution by first performing a binary blur of the image and then subsampling it by two in each dimension. In the binary blur procedure each pixel is set to one if any of its nearest neighbors were road pixels before blurring. This is repeated to get road maps at each resolution. To give the networks a rough measure of distance to a road, we gave the nets inputs from linearly-blurred versions of the road maps, which were made by expanding even lower-resolution versions of the road map with the same linear expand operation used in constructing the Laplacian pyramid. These blurred road maps are therefore not binary. The networks at the fifth and third pyramid levels received inputs from the road-maps at their resolution and from the two lower resolutions, while the network at the first pyramid level received input from the road map at its resolution and the next lower resolution.

2.1.2 Training the Networks

To estimate the probability of finding a building cluster at or around a given location in the image, each network received a single pixel from the same location in all of its input images. This should be adequate for search, since a single pixel in a feature image contains information about an extended region of the original. With the features we used, it also makes the system invariant to rotations, so the networks do not have to learn this invariance Also for simplicity, we did not train nets at all resolutions, but only at the fifth, third and first pyramid levels, i.e., on images which were one-thirty-second, one-eighth,

---

[3] The Laplacian pyramid is usually constructed by expanding the lower-resolution levels of a Gaussian pyramid and subtracting each from the next-higher-resolution level. This gives a set of images which are band-passed with one-octave spacing between the bands.

[4] There are many examples of more sophisticated features, e.g., Lane, et al., 1992, Ballard and Wixson, 1993, and Greenspan, et al., 1994. Simple features were adequate for demonstrating the ideas of this paper.

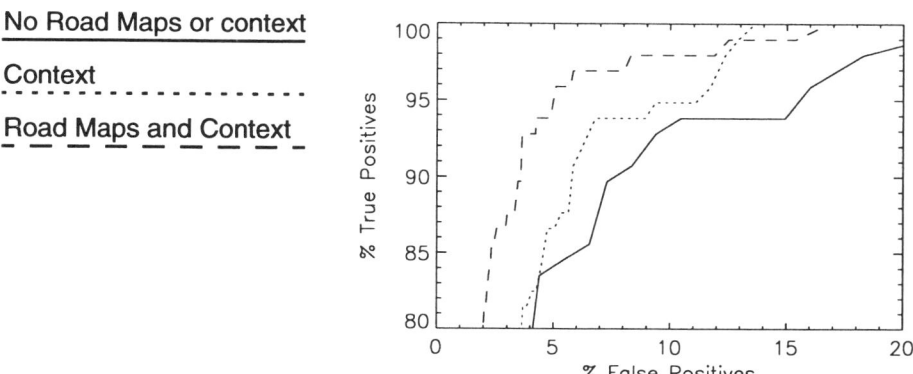

Figure 2. ROC Curves for the Three Network Search Systems.

and one-half the width and height of the original image. A typical building cluster has a linear extent of about 30 pixels in the original images, so in the fifth Gaussian pyramid level they have few distinguishing features. The networks were the usual feed-forward nets with sum-and-sigmoid units and one hidden layer. They were trained using the cross-entropy error measure, with a desired output of one in a hand-chosen polygonal region about each building cluster. The standard quadratic weight-decay term was added to this to get the objective function, and only one regularization constant was used. This was adjusted to give lowest error on a test set. We often found that the weights to two or more hidden units would become identical and/or very small as the regularization term was increased, and in these cases we pruned the extraneous units and began the search for the optimal regularization parameter again. We usually ended up with very small networks, with from two to five hidden units. After training a net at low-resolution, we expanded the image of that net's output in order to use it as a context input for the networks at higher resolution.

2.1.3 Performance

To compare the performance of the three systems, we chose a threshold for the networks' outputs, and considered a building cluster to be detected by a network if the network's output was above the threshold at any pixel within the cluster. The number of detected clusters divided by the total number is the true-positive rate. The false-positive rate is more difficult to define, since we had in mind an application in which the detection system would draw a user's attention to objects which are likely to be of interest. The procedure we used attempts to measure the amount of effort a human would expend in searching regions with false detections by the network. See (Spence, et al., 1994) for details.

The performance figures presented here were measured on a validation set, i.e., an image on which the network was not trained and which was not used to set the regularization parameter. The results presented in Tables 1 and 2 are for a single threshold, chosen for each network so that the true-positive rate was 90%. Figure 2 compares the ROC curves of the three systems, i.e. the parametric curves of the true and false-positive rates as the threshold on the network's output is varied. From Table 1, the features we used would seem adequate for search at very low resolution, although the performance could be better.

Table 1: False-Positive Rates vs. Resolution.
These are results for the system with both road-map and context inputs.

PYRAMID LEVEL	FALSE-POSITIVE RATE
5	16%
3	4.6%
1	3.6%

Table 2: False-Positive Rates of the Search Systems at 90% True-Positive Rate.

NETWORK SYSTEM	FALSE-POSITIVE RATE
No Context or Road-Map Inputs	7.6%
Context Inputs, No Road Maps	5.8%
Context Inputs and Road Maps	3.6%

Table 2 and Figure 2 clearly show the benefits of using the road map and context inputs, although the statistics are somewhat poor at the higher true-positive rates because of the small number of building clusters which are being missed

2.2 LEARNING CONTEXT

Two things were changed to demonstrate that the context could be learned. First, the unoriented spatial energy features are not well suited for distinguishing between roads and other objects with a size similar to a road's width, so we used oriented energies instead. These were the oriented energies derived using steerable filters (Freeman and Adelson, 1991) at four orientations. To force orientation invariance, we sorted the four oriented energies at each pixel for each frequency band. These sorted oriented energy images were then reduced in size as appropriate for the resolution being searched by a network. In this case, we extracted energies only from the first, third, and fifth pyramid levels.

The second change is the use of hidden unit outputs for context inputs, instead of the output unit's outputs. The output units estimate the probability of finding a building cluster. Although this may reflect information about roads, it is very indirect information about the roads. It is more likely to carry some information about the coarse-scale appearance of the potential building clusters. The hidden unit outputs should contain a richer description of the image at a coarser scale.

2.2.1 Performance

The networks were trained in the same way as the networks described in Section 2.1. We trained three networks to search levels five, three, and one. For comparison purposes, we also trained a single-network to search in level one, with the same input features that were used for all of the networks of the hierarchical search system. These include, for example, three versions of each of the oriented energy images from level one (the second highest frequency band). Two of these versions were reduced in size to levels three and five, and then re-expanded to level one, so that they are simply blurred versions of the original energy images. This gives the network a direct source of information on the coarse-scale

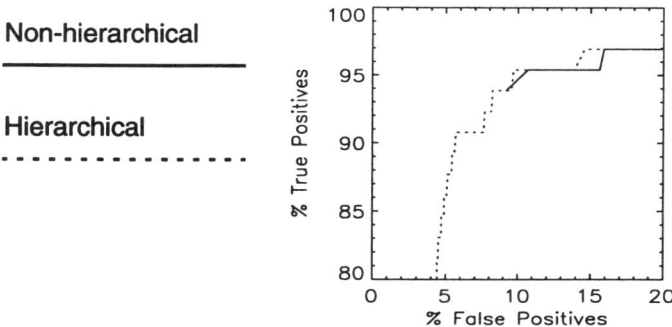

Figure 3. Performance of Hierarchical and Non-hierarchical Algorithms that Learn Context.

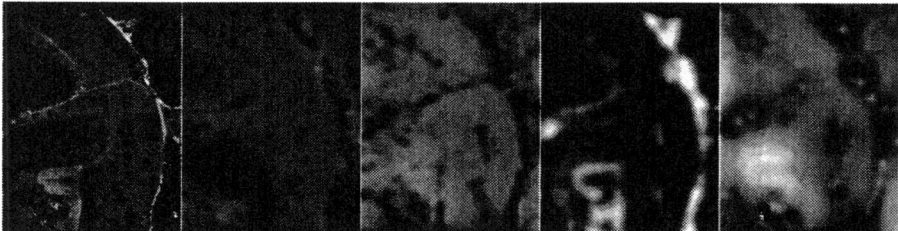

Figure 4. Image and Context Inputs to Highest-Resolution Network.

appearance of the image, although it is an expensive representation in terms of computation and memory, and the network has more inputs so that it takes longer to train.

The ROC curves for the two detection algorithms are shown in Figure 3. Their performance is about the same, suggesting that the coarser-scale networks in the hierarchical system are not performing computations that are useful for the finest-scale network, rather they simply pass on information about the coarse-scale appearance. In this example, the advantage of the hierarchical system is in the efficiency of both the training of the algorithm and its use after training. Figure 4 shows the level-one image and the outputs of several hidden units from the level-three network, expanded to the same size. These outputs suggest that road information is being extracted at coarse scale and passed to the high-resolution network.

3 DISCUSSION

We have performed "proof-of-concept" simulations on a realistic search problem of two of the key concepts of our Hybrid Pyramid/Neural Network (HPNN) approach. We have shown that: 1. The HPNN can learn to utilize explicitly-provided context data to improve object detection; 2. the networks can learn to use context without being explicitly taught to do so. This second point implies that the person training the system does not need to know of the existence of the context objects. The networks at the different scales are trained in sequence, starting at low resolution. A benefit of this *coarse-to-fine training* is a simple form of exemplar selection, since we can choose to train a network only in the regions of interest as detected by the already-trained networks at lower resolution. We could also train all of the networks simultaneously, so that the lower-resolution networks learn to extract the most helpful information from the low-resolution image. The resulting system would probably perform better, but it would also be more expensive to train.

This approach should work quite well for many automatic target recognition problems, since the targets are frequently quite small. For more extended objects like clusters of buildings, our method is an efficient way of examining the objects on several length scales, but the detection at the finest scale is based on a small part of the potential object's appearance. Extended images of real objects typically have many features at each of several resolutions. We are currently working on techniques for discovering several characteristic features at each resolution by training several networks at each resolution, and integrating their responses to compute an overall probability of detection.

Acknowledgments

We would like to thank Peter Burt, P. Anandan, and Paul Sajda for many helpful discussions. This was work was funded by the National Information Display Laboratory and under ARPA contract No. N00014-93-C-0202.

References

D.H. Ballard and L.E. Wixson (1993) Object recognition using steerable filters at multiple scales, *Proceedings of the IEEE Workshop on Qualitative Vision*, New York, NY.

D. Burr and Y. Miyata (1993) Hierarchical recurrent networks for learning musical structure, *Proceedings of the IEEE Conference on Neural Networks for Signal Processing III*, C. Kamm, G. Kuhn, B. Yoon, S.Y. Kung, and R. Chellappa, eds., Piscataway, NJ, pp. 216–225.

P. J. Burt and E. H. Adelson. (1983) The Laplacian pyramid as a compact image code. *IEEE Transactions*, Vol. COM-31:4, April, pp. 532–540.

P.J. Burt (1988a) Smart sensing with a pyramid vision machine, *Proceedings of the IEEE* Vol. 76, pp. 1006–1015.

P.J. Burt (1988b) Attention mechanisms for vision in a dynamic world, *Proceedings of the 9th International Conference on Pattern Recognition*, pp. 977–987.

P.J. Burt, J.R. Bergen, R. Kolczynski, R. Hingorani, W.A. Lee, A. Leung, J. Lubin, and H. Shvayster (1989) Object tracking with a moving camera, *Proceedings of the IEEE Workshop on Motion*, Irvine.

W.T. Freeman and E.H. Adelson (1991) The design and use of steerable filters, *IEEE Trans. PAMI*, **12**:9, pp. 891–906.

S.H. Lane, J.C. Pearson, and R. Sverdlove (1992) Neural networks for classifying image textures, *Proceedings of the Government Applications of Neural Networks Conference*, Dayton, Ohio.

M.C. Mozer (1994) Neural network music composition by prediction: Exploring the benefits of psychoacoustic constraints and multiscale processing, to appear in *Connection Science*.

PART IX
APPLICATIONS

Transformation Invariant Autoassociation with Application to Handwritten Character Recognition

Holger Schwenk **Maurice Milgram**

PARC
Université Pierre et Marie Curie
tour 66-56, boite 164
4, place Jussieu, 75252 Paris cedex 05, France.
e-mail: schwenk@robo.jussieu.fr

Abstract

When training neural networks by the classical backpropagation algorithm the whole problem to learn must be expressed by a set of inputs and desired outputs. However, we often have high-level knowledge about the learning problem. In optical character recognition (OCR), for instance, we know that the classification should be invariant under a set of transformations like rotation or translation. We propose a new modular classification system based on several autoassociative multilayer perceptrons which allows the efficient incorporation of such knowledge. Results are reported on the NIST database of upper case handwritten letters and compared to other approaches to the invariance problem.

1 INCORPORATION OF EXPLICIT KNOWLEDGE

The aim of supervised learning is to learn a mapping between the input and the output space from a set of example pairs (input, desired output). The classical implementation in the domain of neural networks is the backpropagation algorithm. If this learning set is sufficiently representative of the underlying data distributions, one hopes that after learning, the system is able to generalize correctly to other inputs of the same distribution.

It would be better to have more powerful techniques to incorporate knowledge into the learning process than the choice of a set of examples. The use of additional knowledge is often limited to the feature extraction module. Besides simple operations like (size) normalization, we can find more sophisticated approaches like zernike moments in the domain of optical character recognition (OCR). In this paper we will not investigate this possibility, all discussed classifiers work directly on almost non preprocessed data (pixels).

In the context of OCR interest focuses on invariance of the classifier under a number of given transformations (translation, rotation, ...) of the data to classify. In general a neural network could extract those properties of a large enough learning set, but it is very hard to learn and will probably take a lot of time. In the last years two main approaches for this invariance problem have been proposed: *tangent-prop* and *tangent-distance*. An indirect incorporation can be achieved by *boosting* (Drucker, Schapire and Simard, 1993).

In this paper we briefly discuss these approaches and will present a new classification system which allows the efficient incorporation of transformation invariances.

1.1 TANGENT PROPAGATION

The principle of tangent-prop is to specify besides desired outputs also desired changes j^μ of the output vector when transforming the net input x by the transformations t_μ (Simard, Victorri, LeCun and Denker, 1992).

For this, let us define a transformation of pattern p as $t(p, \alpha) : P \to P$ where P is the space of all patterns and α a parameter. Such transformations are in general highly nonlinear operations in the pixel space P and their analytical expressions are seldom known. It is therefore favorable to use a first order approximation:

$$t(p, \alpha) \approx p + \alpha\, t_p \quad \text{with} \quad t_p = \left. \frac{\partial t(p, \alpha)}{\partial \alpha} \right|_{\alpha=0} \tag{1}$$

t_p is called the *tangent vector*. This definition can be generalized to c transformations:

$$t(p, \vec{\alpha}) \approx p + \alpha_1\, t_{p1} + \ldots + \alpha_c\, t_{pc} = p + T_p \vec{\alpha} \tag{2}$$

where T_p is a $n \times c$ matrix, each column corresponding to a tangent vector.

Let us define $R(x)$ the function calculated by the network. The desired behavior of the net outputs can be obtained by adding a regularization term E_r to the objective function:

$$E_r = \sum_{\mu=1}^{c} \left\| j^\mu - \left. \frac{\partial R(t^\mu(x, \vec{\alpha}))}{\partial \vec{\alpha}} \right|_{\vec{\alpha}=0} \right\|^2 \approx \sum_{\mu=1}^{c} \left\| j^\mu - \frac{\partial R(x)}{\partial x} t_x^\mu \right\|^2 \tag{3}$$

t_x^μ is the tangent vector for transformation t^μ of the input vector x and $\partial R(x)/\partial x$ is the gradient of the network with respect to the inputs. Transformation invariance of the outputs is obtained by setting $j^\mu = 0$, so we want that $\partial R(x)/\partial x$ is orthogonal to t_x^μ.

Tangent-prop improved the learning time and the generalization on small databases, but its applicability to highly constraint networks (many shared weights) trained on large databases remains unknown.

1.2 TANGENT DISTANCE

Another class of classifiers are memory based learning methods which rely on distance metrics. The incorporation of knowledge in such classifiers can be done by a distance measure which is (locally) invariant under a set of specified transformations.

(Simard, LeCun and Denker, 1993) define *tangent distance* as the minimal distance between the two hyperplanes spanned up by the tangent vectors T_p in point p and T_q in point q:

$$D_{pq}(p,q) = \min_{\vec{\alpha},\vec{\beta}} \left(p + T_p\vec{\alpha} - q - T_q\vec{\beta}\right)^2 = \left(p + T_p\vec{\alpha}^* - q - T_q\vec{\beta}^*\right)^2 \quad (4)$$

The optimality condition is that the partial derivatives $\partial D_{pq}/\partial \vec{\alpha}^*$ and $\partial D_{pq}/\partial \vec{\beta}^*$ should be zero. The values $\vec{\alpha}^*$ and $\vec{\beta}^*$ minimizing (4) can be computed by solving these two linear systems numerically.

(Simard, LeCun and Denker, 1993) obtained very good results on handwritten digits and letters using tangent distance with a 1-nearest-neighbor classifier (1-nn). A big problem of every nn-classifier, however, is that it uses no compilation of the data and it needs therefore numerous reference vectors resulting in long classification time and high memory usage.

Like reported in (Simard, 1994) and (Sperdutti and Stork, 1995) important improvements are possible, but often a trade-off between speed and memory usage must be made.

2 ARCHITECTURE OF THE CLASSIFIER

The main idea of our approach is to use an *autoassociative multilayer perceptron* with a low dimensional hidden layer for each class to recognize. These networks, called *diabolo network* in the following, are trained only with examples of the corresponding class. This can be seen as supervised learning without counter-examples. Each network learns a hidden layer representation which preserves optimally the information of the examples of *one* class. These learned networks can now be used like discriminant functions: the reconstruction error is in general much lower for examples of the learned class than for the other ones.

In order to build a classifier we use a decision module which interprets the distances between the reconstructed output vectors and the presented example. In our studies we have used until now a simple minimum operator which associates the class of the net with the smallest distance (Fig. 1).

The figure illustrates also typical classification behavior, here when presenting a "D" out of the test set. One can see clearly that the distance of the network "D" is much lower than for the two other ones. The character is therefore correctly classified. It is also interesting to analyze the outputs of the two networks with the next nearest distances: the network "O" tries to output a more round character and the network "B" wants to add a horizontal bar in the middle.

The basic classification architecture can be adapted in two ways to the problem to be solved. One on hand we can imagine different architectures for each diabolo network, e.g. several encoding/decoding layers which allow nonlinear dimension reduction. It is even possible to use shared weights realizing local feature detectors (see (Schwenk and Milgram, 1994) for more details).

One the other hand we can change the underlying distance measure, as long as the derivatives with respect to the weights can be calculated. This offers a powerful and efficient mechanism to introduce explicit knowledge into the learning algorithm of a neural network. In the discussed case, the recognition of characters represented as pixel images, we can use a

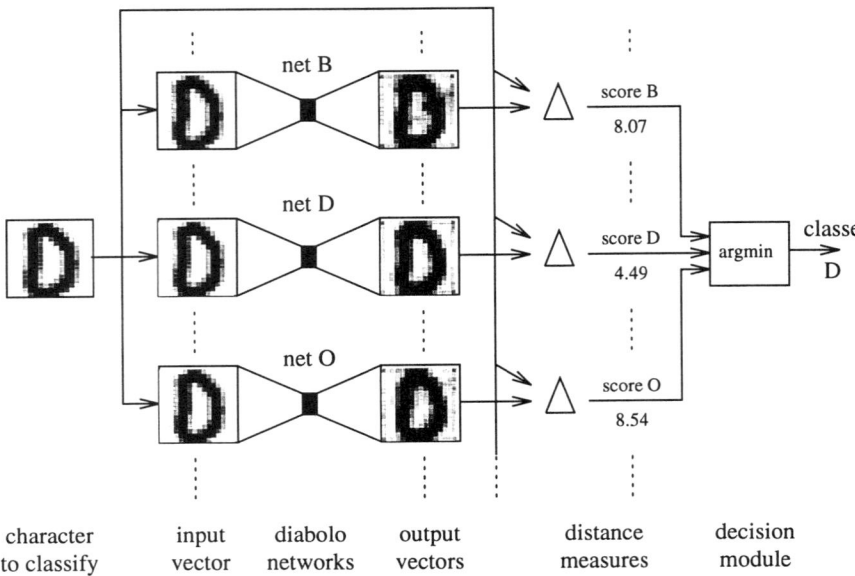

Figure 1: Basic Architecture of a Diabolo Classifier

transformation invariant distance measure between the net output o and the desired output d (that is of course identical with the net input). The networks do not need to learn each example separately any more, but they can use the set of specified transformations in order to find a common *non linear* model of each class.

The advantage of this approach, besides a better expected generalization behavior of course, is a very low additional complexity. In comparison to the original k-nn approach, and supposedly any possible optimization, we need to calculate only one distance measure for each class to recognize, regardless of the number of learning data.

We used two different versions of tangent distance with increasing complexity:

1. **single sided tangent distance:**

$$D_d(d, o) = \min_{\vec{\alpha}} \frac{1}{2} \left(d + T_d \vec{\alpha} - o \right)^2 = \frac{1}{2} \left(d + T_d \vec{\alpha}^* - o \right)^2 \qquad (5)$$

This is the minimal distance between the hyperplane spanned up by the tangent vectors T_d in input vector d and the *untransformed* output vector o.

2. **double sided tangent distance:**

$$D_{do}(d, o) = \min_{\vec{\alpha}, \vec{\beta}} \frac{1}{2} \left(d + T_d \vec{\alpha} - o * g - T_o \vec{\beta} \right)^2 \qquad (6)$$

The convolution of the net output with a Gaussian g is necessary for the computation of the tangent vectors T_o (the net input d is convolved during preprocessing).

Figure 2 shows a graphical comparison of Euclidean distance with the two tangent distances.

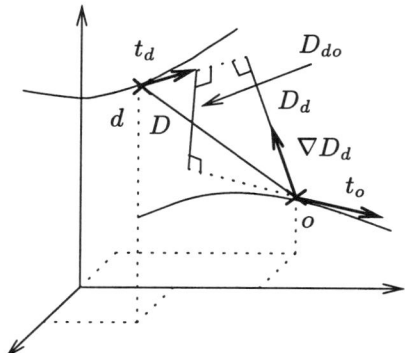

d	: desired output
t_d	: tangent vector in d
o	: net output
t_o	: tangent vector in o
D	: Euclidean distance
D_d	: single sided tangent distance (only d is transformed)
D_{do}	: double sided tangent distance (both points are transformed)
∇D_d	: gradient of D_d

Figure 2: Comparison of Euclidean Distance with the Different Tangent Distances

The major advantage of the single sided version is that we can now calculate easily the optimal multipliers $\vec{\alpha}^*$ and therefore the whole distance (the double sided version demands expensive matrix multiplications and the numerical solution of a system of linear equations). The optimality condition $\partial D_d(d, o)/\partial \vec{\alpha}^* \stackrel{!}{=} 0^T$ gives:

$$\vec{\alpha}^* = T_{dd}^{-1} T_d^T (o - d) \qquad (7)$$

The tangent vectors T_d and the matrix $T_{dd}^{-1} = (T_d^T T_d)^{-1}$ can be precomputed and stored in memory. Note that it is the same for all diabolo networks, regardless of their class.

2.1 LEARNING ALGORITHM

When using a tangent distance with an autoencoder we must calculate its derivatives with respect to the weights, i.e. after application of the chain rule with respect to the output vector o. In the case of the single sided tangent distance we get:

$$-\frac{\partial D_d}{\partial o} = \left(d + T_d \vec{\alpha}^* - o\right)^T \left(T_d \frac{\partial \vec{\alpha}^*}{\partial o} - I\right) = \left(d + T_d \vec{\alpha}^* - o\right)^T \qquad (8)$$

The resulting learning algorithm is therefore barely more complicated than with standard Euclidean error. Furthermore it has a pleasant graphical interpretation: the net output doesn't approach directly the desired output any more, but it takes the shortest way towards the tangent hyperplane (see also fig. 2).

The derivation of the double sided tangent distance with respect to the net output is more complicated. In particular we must derivate the convolution of the net output with a Gaussian as well as the tangent vectors T_o. These equations will be published elsewhere.

Training of the whole system is stopped when the error on the cross validation set reaches a minimum. Using stochastic gradient descent convergence is typically achieved after some ten iterations.

3 APPLICATION TO CHARACTER RECOGNITION

In 1992 the National Institute of Standards and Technology provided a Database of handwritten digits and letters, known under the name NIST Special-Database 3. This database contains about 45 000 upper case segmented characters which we have divided into learning and cross-validation set (60%) and test set (40%) respectively.

We only applied a very simple preprocessing: the binary characters were centered and size-normalized (the aspect-ratio was kept). The net input is 16 × 16 pixels with real-values.

3.1 EXPERIMENTAL RESULTS

All the following results were obtained by fully connected diabolo networks with one low dimensional hidden layer, and a set of eight transformations (x- and y-translation, rotation, scaling, axis-deformation, diagonal-deformation, x- and y-thickness). Figure 3 illustrates how the networks use the transformations.

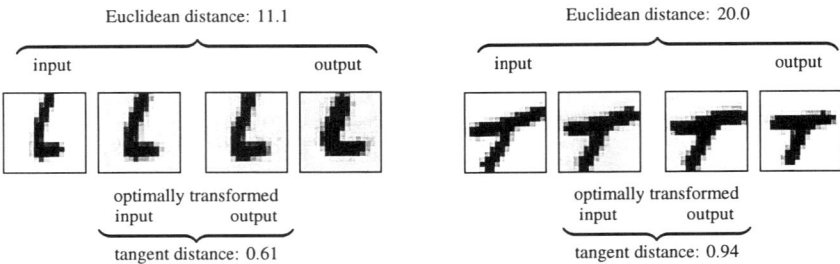

Figure 3: Reconstruction Examples (test set). The left side of each screen dump depicts the input character and the right side the one reconstructed by the network. In the middle, finally, one can see the optimally transformed patterns as calculated when evaluating the double sided tangent distance, i.e. transformed by $\vec{\alpha}^*$ and $\vec{\beta}^*$ respectively.

Although the "L" in the first example has an unusual short horizontal line, the network reconstructs a normally sized character. It is clearly visible how the input transformation lengthens and the output transformation shortens this line in order to get a small tangent distance. The right side shows a very difficult classification problem: a heavily deformed "T". Nevertheless we get a small tangent distance, so that the character is correctly classified. In summary we note a big difference between the Euclidean and the tangent distances, this is a good indicator that the networks really use the transformations.

The performances on the whole test set of about 18 000 characters are summarized in figure 4. For comparison we give also the results of a one nearest neighbor classifier on the same test set. The incorporation of knowledge improved in both cases dramatically the performances. The diabolo classifier, for instance, achieves an error rate of 4.7 % with simple Euclidean distance which goes down to 3.7 % with the single sided and to only 2.6 % with the double sided tangent distance. In order to get the same results with the 1-nn approach, the whole set of 27 000 reference vectors had to be used. It's worth to note the results with less references: when using only 18 000 reference vectors the error rates increased to 3.7% for the single sided and to 2.8% for the double sided version respectively.

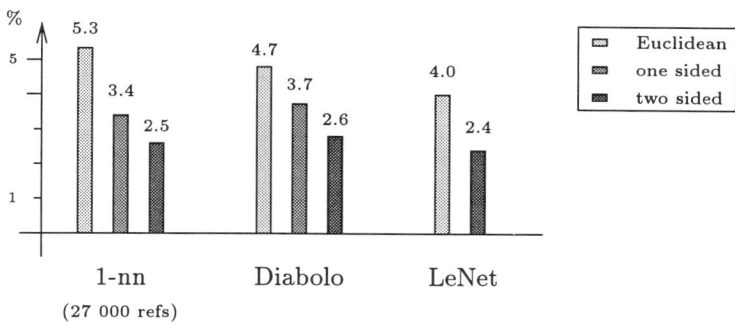

Figure 4: Raw Error Rate with NIST Upper Case Letters (test set)

In practical applications we are not only interested in low error rates, but we need also low computationally costs. An important factor is the recognition speed. The overall processing time of a diabolo classifier using the full tangent distance corresponds to the calculation of about 7 000 Euclidean and to less than 50 tangent distances. This should be less than for any algorithm of the k-nn family. If we assume the precalculation of all the tangent vectors and other expensive matrix multiplications, we could evaluate about 80 tangent distances, but the price would be exploding memory requirements. A diabolo classifier, on the other hand, needs only few memory: the storage of the weights corresponds to about 60 reference vectors per class. On a HP 715/50 workstation we obtained a recognition rate of 7.5 ch/s with the single sided and of more than 2.5 ch/s with the double sided tangent distance. We have also a method to combine both by rejection, resulting in up to 4 ch/s at the same low error rates (corresponds to the calculation of 32 double sided tangent distances).

The table contains also the results of a large multilayer perceptron with extensive use of shared weights, known as LeNet. (Drucker, Schapire and Simard, 1993) give an error rate of 4.0% when used alone and of 2.4% for an ensemble of three such networks trained by boosting. The networks were trained on a basic set of 10 000 examples, the cross validation and test set consisted of 2 000 and 3 000 examples respectively (Drucker, personal communication). Due to the different number of examples, the results are perhaps not exactly comparable, but we can deduce nevertheless that the state of the art on this database seems to be around 2.5 %.

4 DISCUSSION

We have proposed a new classification architecture that allows the efficient incorporation of knowledge into the learning algorithm. The system is easy to train and only one structural parameter must be chosen by the supervisor: the size of the hidden layer. It achieved state of the art recognition rates on the NIST database of handwritten upper case letters at a very low computational complexity.

Furthermore we can say that a hardware implementation seems to be promising. Fully connected networks with only two layers are easy to put into standardized hardware chips. We could even propagate all diabolo networks in parallel. Speedups of several orders of magnitude should therefore be possible.

On this year NIPS conference several authors presented related approaches. A comparable classification architecture was proposed by (Hinton, Revow and Dayan, 1995). Instead of one non-linear global model per class, several local linear models were used by performing separately principal component analysis (PCA) on subsets of each class. Since diabolo networks with one hidden layer and linear activation functions perform PCA, this architecture can be interpreted as an hierarchical diabolo classifier with linear nets and Euclidean distance. Such an hierarchisation could also be done with our classifier, i.e. with tangent distance and sigmoidal units, and might improve the results even further.

(Hastie, Simard and Säckinger, 1995) developed an iterative algorithm that learns optimal reference vectors in the sense of tangent distance. An extension allows also to learn typical invariant transformations, i.e. tangent vectors, of each class. These two algorithms allowed to reduce drastically the number of reference vectors, but the results of the original approach couldn't be achieved no longer.

Acknowledgements

The first author is supported by the German Academic Exchange Service under grant HSP II 516.006.512.3. The simulations were performed with the Aspirin/ MIGRAINES neural network simulator developed by the MITRE Corporation.

References

H. Drucker, R. Schapire, and P. Simard (1993), "Boosting performance in neural networks," *Int. Journal of Pattern Recognition and Artificial Intelligence*, vol. 7, no. 4, pp. 705–719.

T. Hastie, P. Simard and E. Säckinger (1995), "Learning prototype models for tangent distance," in *NIPS 7* (G. Tesauro, D. Touretzky, and T. Leen, eds.), Morgan Kaufmann.

G. Hinton, M. Revow, and P. Dayan (1995), "Recognizing handwritten digits using mixtures of linear models," in *NIPS 7* (G. Tesauro, D. Touretzky, and T. Leen, eds.), Morgan Kaufmann.

H. Schwenk and M. Milgram (1994), "Structured diabolo-networks for handwritten character recognition," in *International Conference on Artificial Neural Networks*, pp. 985–988, Springer-Verlag.

P. Simard, B. Victorri, Y. LeCun, and J. Denker (1992), "Tangent prop - a formalism for specifying selected invariances in an adaptive network," in *NIPS 4* (J. Moody, S. Hanson, and R. Lippmann, eds.), pp. 895–903, Morgan Kaufmann.

P. Simard, Y. LeCun, and J. Denker (1993), "Efficient pattern recognition using a new transformation distance," in *NIPS 5* (S. Hanson, J. Cowan, and C. Giles, eds.), pp. 50–58, Morgan Kaufmann.

P. Simard (1994), "Efficient Computation of complex distance measures using hierarchical filtering," in *NIPS 6* (J.D. Cowan, G. Tesauro, and J. Alspector, eds.), pp. 50–58, Morgan Kaufmann.

A. Sperdutti and D.G. Stork (1995), "A rapid graph-based method for arbitrary transformation invariant pattern classification," in *NIPS 7* (G. Tesauro, D. Touretzky, and T. Leen, eds.), Morgan Kaufmann.

Learning Prototype Models for Tangent Distance

Trevor Hastie*
Statistics Department
Sequoia Hall
Stanford University
Stanford, CA 94305
email: trevor@playfair.stanford.edu

Patrice Simard
AT&T Bell Laboratories
Crawfords Corner Road
Holmdel, NJ 07733
email: patrice@neural.att.com

Eduard Säckinger
AT&T Bell Laboratories
Crawfords Corner Road
Holmdel, NJ 07733
email: edi@neural.att.com

Abstract

Simard, LeCun & Denker (1993) showed that the performance of nearest-neighbor classification schemes for handwritten character recognition can be improved by incorporating invariance to specific transformations in the underlying distance metric — the so called *tangent distance*. The resulting classifier, however, can be prohibitively slow and memory intensive due to the large amount of prototypes that need to be stored and used in the distance comparisons. In this paper we develop rich models for representing large subsets of the prototypes. These models are either used singly per class, or as basic building blocks in conjunction with the K-means clustering algorithm.

---

*This work was performed while Trevor Hastie was a member of the Statistics and Data Analysis Research Group, AT&T Bell Laboratories, Murray Hill, NJ 07974.

1 INTRODUCTION

Local algorithms such as K-nearest neighbor (NN) perform well in pattern recognition, even though they often assume the simplest distance on the pattern space. It has recently been shown (Simard et al. 1993) that the performance can be further improved by incorporating invariance to specific transformations in the underlying distance metric — the so called *tangent distance*. The resulting classifier, however, can be prohibitively slow and memory intensive due to the large amount of prototypes that need to be stored and used in the distance comparisons.

In this paper we address this problem for the tangent distance algorithm, by developing rich models for representing large subsets of the prototypes. Our leading example of prototype model is a low-dimensional (12) hyperplane defined by a point and a set of basis or tangent vectors. The components of these models are learned from the training set, chosen to minimize the average *tangent distance* from a subset of the training images — as such they are similar in flavor to the Singular Value Decomposition (SVD), which finds closest hyperplanes in Euclidean distance. These models are either used singly per class, or as basic building blocks in conjunction with K-means and LVQ. Our results show that not only are the models effective, but they also have meaningful interpretations. In handwritten character recognition, for instance, the main tangent vector learned for the the digit "2" corresponds to addition/removal of the loop at the bottom left corner of the digit; for the 9 the fatness of the circle. We can therefore think of some of these learned tangent vectors as representing additional invariances derived from the training digits themselves. Each learned prototype model therefore represents very compactly a large number of prototypes of the training set.

2 OVERVIEW OF TANGENT DISTANCE

When we look at handwritten characters, we are easily able to allow for simple transformations such as rotations, small scalings, location shifts, and character thickness when identifying the character. Any reasonable automatic scheme should similarly be insensitive to such changes.

Simard et al. (1993) finessed this problem by generating a parametrized 7-dimensional manifold for each image, where each parameter accounts for one such invariance. Consider a single invariance dimension: rotation. If we were to rotate the image by an angle θ prior to digitization, we would see roughly the same picture, just slightly rotated. Our images are 16×16 grey-scale pixelmaps, which can be thought of as points in a 256-dimensional Euclidean space. The rotation operation traces out a smooth one-dimensional curve $X_i(\theta)$ with $X_i(0) = X_i$, the image itself. Instead of measuring the distance between two images as $D(X_i, X_j) = \|X_i - X_j\|$ (for any norm $\|\cdot\|$), the idea is to use instead the rotation-invariant $D^I(X_i, X_j) = \min_{\theta_i, \theta_j} \|X_i(\theta_i) - X_j(\theta_j)\|$. Simard et al. (1993) used 7 dimensions of invariance, accounting for horizontal and vertical location and scale, rotation and shear and character thickness.

Computing the manifold exactly is impossible, given a digitized image, and would be impractical anyway. They approximated the manifold instead by its tangent plane at the image itself, leading to the tangent model $\tilde{X}_i(\theta) = X_i + T_i\theta$, and the *tangent distance* $D^T(X_i, X_j) = \min_{\theta_i, \theta_j} \left\| \tilde{X}_i(\theta_i) - \tilde{X}_j(\theta_j) \right\|$. Here we use θ for the 7-dimensional parameter, and for convenience drop the tilde. The approximation is valid locally, and thus permits local transformations. Non-local transformations are not interesting anyway (we don't want to flip 6s into 9s; shrink all digits down to nothing.) See Säckinger (1992) for further details. If $\|\cdot\|$ is the Euclidean norm, computing the tangent distance is a simple least-squares problem, with solution the square-root of the residual sum-of-squares of the residuals in the regression with response $X_i - X_j$ and predictors $(-T_i : T_j)$.

Simard et al. (1993) used D^T to drive a 1-NN classification rule, and achieved the best rates so far—2.6%—on the official test set (2007 examples) of the USPS data base. Unfortunately, 1-NN is expensive, especially when the distance function is non-trivial to compute; for each new image classified, one has to compute the tangent distance to each of the training images, and then classify as the class of the closest. Our goal in this paper is to reduce the training set dramatically to a small set of prototype models; classification is then performed by finding the closest prototype.

3 PROTOTYPE MODELS

In this section we explore some ideas for generalizing the concept of a mean or centroid for a set of images, taking into account the tangent families. Such a centroid model can be used on its own, or else as a building block in a K-means or LVQ algorithm at a higher level. We will interchangeably refer to the images as points (in 256 space).

The centroid of a set of N points in d dimensions minimizes the average squared norm from the points:

$$M = \frac{1}{N} \sum_{i=1}^{N} X_i = \arg\min_{M} \sum_{i=1}^{N} \|X_i - M\|^2 \tag{1}$$

3.1 TANGENT CENTROID

One could generalize this definition and ask for the point M that minimizes the average squared *tangent distance*:

$$M_T = \arg\min_{M} \sum_{i=1}^{N} D^T(X_i, M)^2 \tag{2}$$

This appears to be a difficult optimization problem, since computation of tangent distance requires not only the image M but also its tangent basis T_M. Thus the criterion to be minimized is

$$C(M) = \sum_{i=1}^{N} \min_{\gamma_i, \theta_i} \|M + T(M)\gamma_i - X_i - T_i\theta_i\|^2$$

where $T(M)$ produces the tangent basis from M. All but the location tangent vectors are nonlinear functionals of M, and even without this nonlinearity, the problem to be solved is a difficult inverse functional. Fortunately a simple iterative procedure is available where we iteratively average the closest points (in tangent distance) to the current guess.

Tangent Centroid Algorithm

Initialize: Set $M = \frac{1}{N}\sum_{i=1}^{N} X_i$, let $T_M = T(M)$ be the derived set of tangent vectors, and $D = \sum_i D^T(X_i, M)$. Denote the current tangent centroid (tangent family) by $M(\gamma) = M + T_M \gamma$.

Iterate: 1. For each i find a $\hat{\gamma}_i$ and $\hat{\theta}_i$ that solves
$\|M + T_M \gamma - X_i(\theta)\| = \min_{\gamma, \theta}$

2. Set $M \leftarrow \frac{1}{N}\sum_{i=1}^{N}(X_i(\hat{\theta}_i) - T_M \hat{\gamma}_i)$ and compute the new tangent subspace $T_M = T(M)$.

3. Compute $D = \sum_i D^T(X_i, M)$

Until: D converges.

Note that the first step in **Iterate** is available from the computations in the third step. The algorithm divides the parameters into two sets: M in the one, and then T_M, γ_i and θ_i for each i in the other. It alternates between the two sets, although the computation of T_M given M is not the solution of an optimization problem. It seems very hard to say anything precise about the convergence or behavior of this algorithm, since the tangent vectors depend on each iterate in a nonlinear way. Our experience has always been that it converges fairly rapidly (< 6 iterations). A potential drawback of this algorithm is that the T_M are not learned, but are implicit in M.

3.2 TANGENT SUBSPACE

Rather than define the model as a point and have it generate its own tangent subspace, we can include the subspace as part of the parametrization: $M(\gamma) = M + V\gamma$. Then we define this *tangent subspace model* as the minimizer of

$$MS(M, V) = \sum_{i=1}^{N} \min_{\gamma_i, \theta_i} \|M + V\gamma_i - X_i(\theta_i)\|^2 \qquad (3)$$

over M and V. Note that V can have an arbitrary number $0 \leq r \leq 256$ of columns, although it does not make sense for r to be too large. An iterative algorithm similar to the tangent centroid algorithm is available, which hinges on the SVD decomposition for fitting affine subspaces to a set of points. We briefly review the SVD in this context.

Let $\mathcal{X}$ be the $N \times 256$ matrix with rows the vectors $X_i - \bar{X}$ where $\bar{X} = \frac{1}{N}\sum_{i=1}^{N} X_i$. Then $SVD(\mathcal{X}) = UDV^T$ is a unique decomposition with $U_{N \times R}$ and $V_{256 \times R}$ the orthonormal *left* and *right* matrices of *singular vectors*, and $R = \text{rank}(\mathcal{X})$. $D_{R \times R}$ is a diagonal matrix of decreasing positive *singular* values. A pertinent property of the SVD is:

> Consider finding the closest affine, rank-r subspace to a set of points, or
> $$\min_{M, V^{(r)}, \{\theta_i\}} \sum_{i=1}^{N} \left\| X_i - M - V^{(r)} \theta_i \right\|^2$$
> where $V^{(r)}$ is $256 \times r$ orthonormal. The solution is given by the SVD above, with $M = \bar{X}$ and $V^{(r)}$ the first r columns of V, and the total squared distance $\sum_{j=1}^{r} D_{jj}^2$.

The $V^{(r)}$ are also the largest r principal components or eigenvectors of the covariance matrix of the X_i. They give in sequence directions of maximum spread, and for a given digit class can be thought of as class specific invariances.

We now present our *Tangent subspace algorithm* for solving (3); for convenience we assume V is rank r for some chosen r, and drop the superscript.

Tangent subspace algorithm

Initialize: Set $M = \frac{1}{N} \sum_{i=1}^{N} X_i$ and let V correspond to the first r right singular vectors of $\mathcal{X}$. Set $D = \sum_{j=1}^{r} D_{jj}^2$, and let the current tangent subspace model be $M(\gamma) = M + V\gamma$.

Iterate:
1. For each i find that $\hat{\theta}_i$ which solves $\|M(\gamma) - X_i(\theta)\| = \min$
2. Set $M \leftarrow \frac{1}{N} \sum_{i=1}^{N} (X_i(\hat{\theta}_i))$ and replace the rows of $\mathcal{X}$ by $X_i(\hat{\theta}_i) - M$. Compute the SVD of $\mathcal{X}$, and replace V by the first r right singular vectors.
3. Compute $D = \sum_{j=1}^{r} D_{jj}^2$

Until: D converges.

The algorithm alternates between i) finding the closest point in the tangent subspace for each image to the current tangent subspace model, and ii) computing the SVD for these closest points. Each step of the alternation decreases the criterion, which is positive and hence converges to a stationary point of the criterion. In all our examples we found that 12 complete iterations were sufficient to achieve a relative convergence ratio of 0.001.

One advantage of this approach is that we need not restrict ourselves to a seven-dimensional V — indeed, we have found 12 dimensions has produced the best results. The basis vectors found for each class are interesting to view as images. Figure 1 shows some examples of the basis vectors found, and what kinds of invariances in the images they account for. These are digit specific features; for example, a prominent basis vector for the family of 2s accounts for big versus small loops.

Each of the examples shown accounts for a similar digit specific invariance. None of these changes are accounted for by the 7-dimensional tangent models, which were chosen to be digit nonspecific.

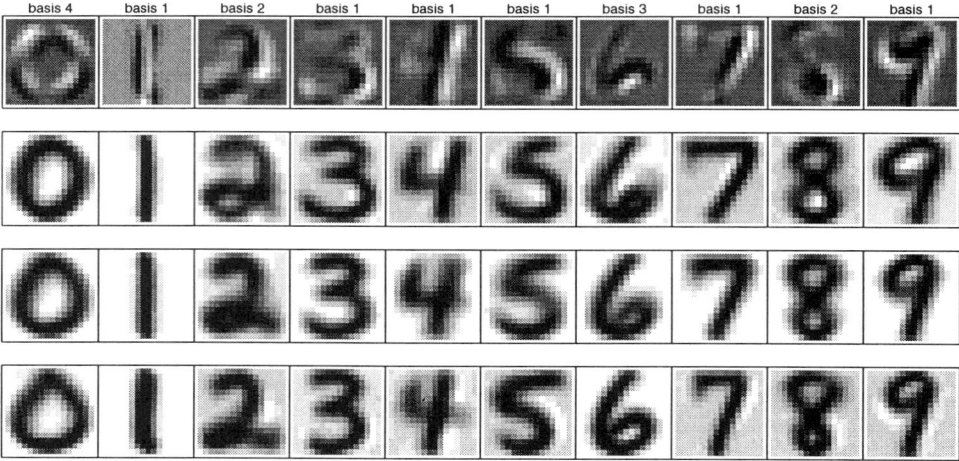

Figure 1: *Each column corresponds to a particular tangent subspace basis vector for the given digit. The top image is the basis vector itself, and the remaining 3 images correspond to the 0.1, 0.5 and 0.9 quantiles for the projection indices for the training data for that basis vector, showing a range of image models for that basis, keeping all the others at 0.*

4   SUBSPACE MODELS AND K-MEANS CLUSTERING

A natural and obvious extension of these single prototype-per-class models, is to use them as centroid modules in a K-means algorithm. The extension is obvious, and space permits only a rough description. Given an initial partition of the images in a class into K sets:

1. Fit a separate prototype model to each of the subsets;
2. Redefine the partition based on closest tangent distance to the prototypes found in step 1.

In a similar way the tangent centroid or subspace models can be used to seed LVQ algorithms (Kohonen 1989), but so far we have not much experience with them.

5   RESULTS

Table 1 summarizes the results for some of these models. The first two lines correspond to a SVD model for the images fit by ordinary least squares rather than least tangent squares. The first line classifies using Euclidean distance to this model, the second using tangent distance. Line 3 fits a single 12-dimensional *tangent subspace* model per class, while lines 4 and 5 use 12-dimensional tangent subspaces as cluster

Table 1: *Test errors for a variety of situations. In all cases the training data were 7291 USPS handwritten digits, and the test data the "official" 2007 USPS test digits. Each entry describes the model used in each class, so for example in row 5 there are 5 models per class, hence 50 in all.*

	Prototype	Metric	# Prototypes/Class	Error Rate
0	1-NN	Euclidean	≈ 700	0.053
1	12 dim SVD subspace	Euclidean	1	0.055
2	12 dim SVD subspace	Tangent	1	0.045
3	12 dim Tangent subspace	Tangent	1	0.041
4	12 dim Tangent subspace	Tangent	3	0.038
5	12 dim Tangent subspace	Tangent	5	0.038
6	Tangent centroid	Tangent	20	0.038
7	(4) ∪ (6)	Tangent	23	0.034
8	1-NN	Tangent	≈ 700	0.026

centers within each class. We tried other dimensions in a variety of settings, but 12 seemed to be generally the best. Line 6 corresponds to the *tangent centroid* model used as the centroid in a 20-means cluster model per class; the performance compares with with K=3 for the subspace model. Line 7 combines 4 and 6, and reduces the error even further. These limited experiments suggest that the tangent subspace model is preferable, since it is more compact and the algorithm for fitting it is on firmer theoretical grounds.

Figure 4 shows some of the misclassified examples in the test set. Despite all the matching, it seems that Euclidean distance still fails us in the end in some of these cases.

6 DISCUSSION

Gold, Mjolsness & Rangarajan (1994) independently had the idea of using "domain specific" distance measures to seed K-means clustering algorithms. Their setting was slightly different from ours, and they did not use subspace models. The idea of classifying points to the closest subspace is found in the work of Oja (1989), but of course not in the context of tangent distance.

We are using Euclidean distance in conjunction with tangent distance. Since neighboring pixels are correlated, one might expect that a metric that accounted for the correlation might do better. We tried several variants using Mahalanobis metrics in different ways, but with no success. We also tried to incorporate information about where the images project in the tangent subspace models into the classification rule. We thus computed two distances: 1) tangent distance to the subspace, and 2) Mahalanobis distance within the subspace to the centroid for the subspace. Again the best performance was attained by ignoring the latter distance.

In conclusion, learning tangent centroid and subspace models is an effective way

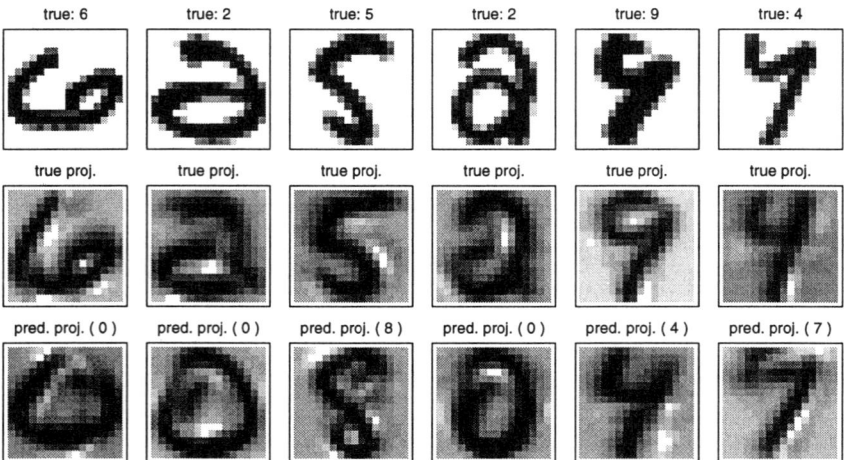

Figure 2: *Some of the errors for the test set corresponding to line (3) of table 4. Each case is displayed as a column of three images. The top is the true image, the middle the tangent projection of the true image onto the subspace model of its class, the bottom image the tangent projection of the image onto the winning class. The models are sufficiently rich to allow distortions that can fool Euclidean distance.*

to reduce the number of prototypes (and thus the cost in speed and memory) at a slight expense in the performance. In the extreme case, as little as one 12 dimensional tangent subspace per class and the tangent distance is enough to outperform classification using $\approx$ 700 prototypes per class and the Euclidean distance (4.1% versus 5.3% on the test data).

References

Gold, S., Mjolsness, E. & Rangarajan, A. (1994), Clustering with a domain specific distance measure, *in* 'Advances in Neural Information Processing Systems', Morgan Kaufman, San Mateo, CA.

Kohonen, T. (1989), *Self-Organization and Associative Memory (3rd edition)*, Springer-Verlag, Berlin.

Oja, E. (1989), 'Neural networks, principal components, and subspaces', *International Journal Of Neural Systems* **1**(1), 61–68.

Säckinger, E. (1992), Recurrent networks for elastic matching in pattern recognition, Technical report, AT&T Bell Laboratories.

Simard, P. Y., LeCun, Y. & Denker, J. (1993), Efficient pattern recognition using a new transformation distance, *in* 'Advances in Neural Information Processing Systems', Morgan Kaufman, San Mateo, CA, pp. 50–58.

Real-Time Control of a Tokamak Plasma Using Neural Networks

Chris M Bishop
Neural Computing Research Group
Department of Computer Science
Aston University
Birmingham, B4 7ET, U.K.
c.m.bishop@aston.ac.uk

**Paul S Haynes, Mike E U Smith, Tom N Todd,
David L Trotman and Colin G Windsor**
AEA Technology, Culham Laboratory,
Oxfordshire OX14 3DB
(Euratom/UKAEA Fusion Association)

Abstract

This paper presents results from the first use of neural networks for the real-time feedback control of high temperature plasmas in a tokamak fusion experiment. The tokamak is currently the principal experimental device for research into the magnetic confinement approach to controlled fusion. In the tokamak, hydrogen plasmas, at temperatures of up to 100 Million K, are confined by strong magnetic fields. Accurate control of the position and shape of the plasma boundary requires real-time feedback control of the magnetic field structure on a time-scale of a few tens of microseconds. Software simulations have demonstrated that a neural network approach can give significantly better performance than the linear technique currently used on most tokamak experiments. The practical application of the neural network approach requires high-speed hardware, for which a fully parallel implementation of the multilayer perceptron, using a hybrid of digital and analogue technology, has been developed.

1 INTRODUCTION

Fusion of the nuclei of hydrogen provides the energy source which powers the sun. It also offers the possibility of a practically limitless terrestrial source of energy. However, the harnessing of this power has proved to be a highly challenging problem. One of the most promising approaches is based on magnetic confinement of a high temperature ($10^7 - 10^8$ Kelvin) plasma in a device called a tokamak (from the Russian for 'toroidal magnetic chamber') as illustrated schematically in Figure 1. At these temperatures the highly ionized plasma is an excellent electrical conductor, and can be confined and shaped by strong magnetic fields. Early tokamaks had plasmas with circular cross-sections, for which feedback control of the plasma position and shape is relatively straightforward. However, recent tokamaks, such as the COMPASS experiment at Culham Laboratory, as well as most next-generation tokamaks, are designed to produce plasmas whose cross-sections are strongly non-circular. Figure 2 illustrates some of the plasma shapes which COMPASS is designed to explore. These novel cross-sections provide substantially improved energy confinement properties and thereby significantly enhance the performance of the tokamak.

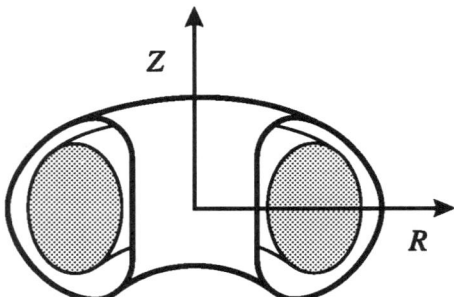

Figure 1: Schematic cross-section of a tokamak experiment showing the toroidal vacuum vessel (outer D-shaped curve) and plasma (shown shaded). Also shown are the radial (R) and vertical (Z) coordinates. To a good approximation, the tokamak can be regarded as axisymmetric about the Z-axis, and so the plasma boundary can be described by its cross-sectional shape at one particular toroidal location.

Unlike circular cross-section plasmas, highly non-circular shapes are more difficult to produce and to control accurately, since currents through several control coils must be adjusted simultaneously. Furthermore, during a typical plasma pulse, the shape must evolve, usually from some initial near-circular shape. Due to uncertainties in the current and pressure distributions within the plasma, the desired accuracy for plasma control can only be achieved by making real-time measurements of the position and shape of the boundary, and using error feedback to adjust the currents in the control coils.

The physics of the plasma equilibrium is determined by force balance between the

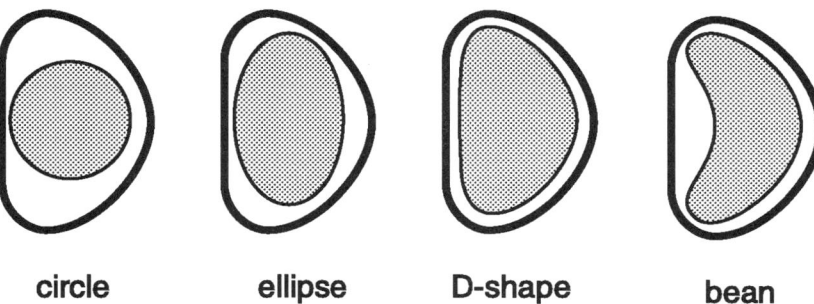

Figure 2: Cross-sections of the COMPASS vacuum vessel showing some examples of potential plasma shapes. The solid curve is the boundary of the vacuum vessel, and the plasma is shown by the shaded regions.

thermal pressure of the plasma and the pressure of the magnetic field, and is relatively well understood. Particular plasma configurations are described in terms of solutions of a non-linear partial differential equation called the Grad-Shafranov (GS) equation. Due to the non-linear nature of this equation, a general analytic solution is not possible. However, the GS equation can be solved by iterative numerical methods, with boundary conditions determined by currents flowing in the external control coils which surround the vacuum vessel. On the tokamak itself it is changes in these currents which are used to alter the position and cross-sectional shape of the plasma. Numerical solution of the GS equation represents the standard technique for post-shot analysis of the plasma, and is also the method used to generate the training dataset for the neural network, as described in the next section. However, this approach is computationally very intensive and is therefore unsuitable for feedback control purposes.

For real-time control it is necessary to have a fast (typically $\leq 50 \mu$sec.) determination of the plasma boundary shape. This information can be extracted from a variety of diagnostic systems, the most important being local magnetic measurements taken at a number of points around the perimeter of the vacuum vessel. Most tokamaks have several tens or hundreds of small pick up coils located at carefully optimized points around the torus for this purpose. We shall represent these magnetic signals collectively as a vector m.

For a large class of equilibria, the plasma boundary can be reasonably well represented in terms of a simple parameterization, governed by an angle-like variable θ, given by

$$\begin{aligned} R(\theta) &= R_0 + a \cos(\theta + \delta \sin \theta) \\ Z(\theta) &= Z_0 + a\kappa \sin \theta \end{aligned} \quad (1)$$

where we have defined the following parameters

R_0 radial distance of the plasma center from the major axis of the torus,
Z_0 vertical distance of the plasma center from the torus midplane,
a minor radius measured in the plane $Z = Z_0$,
κ elongation,
δ triangularity.

We denote these parameters collectively by y_k. The basic problem which has to be addressed, therefore, is to find a representation for the (non-linear) mapping from the magnetic signals m to the values of the geometrical parameters y_k, which can be implemented in suitable hardware for real-time control.

The conventional approach presently in use on many tokamaks involves approximating the mapping between the measured magnetic signals and the geometrical parameters by a single linear transformation. However, the intrinsic non-linearity of the mappings suggests that a representation in terms of feedforward neural networks should give significantly improved results (Lister and Schnurrenberger, 1991; Bishop *et al.*, 1992; Lagin *et al.*, 1993). Figure 3 shows a block diagram of the control loop for the neural network approach to tokamak equilibrium control.

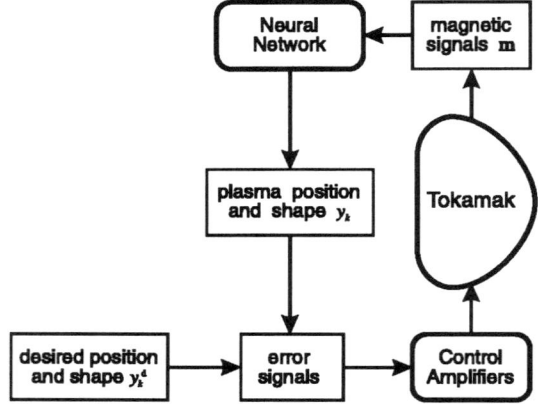

Figure 3: Block diagram of the control loop used for real-time feedback control of plasma position and shape.

2   SOFTWARE SIMULATION RESULTS

The dataset for training and testing the network was generated by numerical solution of the GS equation using a free-boundary equilibrium code. The data base currently consists of over 2,000 equilibria spanning the wide range of plasma positions and shapes available in COMPASS. Each equilibrium configuration takes several minutes to generate on a fast workstation. The boundary of each configuration is then fitted using the form in equation 1, so that the equilibria are labelled with the appropriate values of the shape parameters. Of the 120 magnetic signals available on COMPASS which could be used to provide inputs to the network, a subset of 16 has been chosen using sequential forward selection based on a linear representation for the mapping (discussed below).

It is important to note that the transformation from magnetic signals to flux surface parameters involves an exact linear invariance. This follows from the fact that, if all of the currents are scaled by a constant factor, then the magnetic fields will be scaled by this factor, and the geometry of the plasma boundary will be unchanged. It is important to take advantage of this prior knowledge and to build it into the network structure, rather than force the network to learn it by example. We therefore normalize the vector m of input signals to the network by dividing by a quantity proportional to the total plasma current. Note that this normalization has to be incorporated into the hardware implementation of the network, as will be discussed in Section 3.

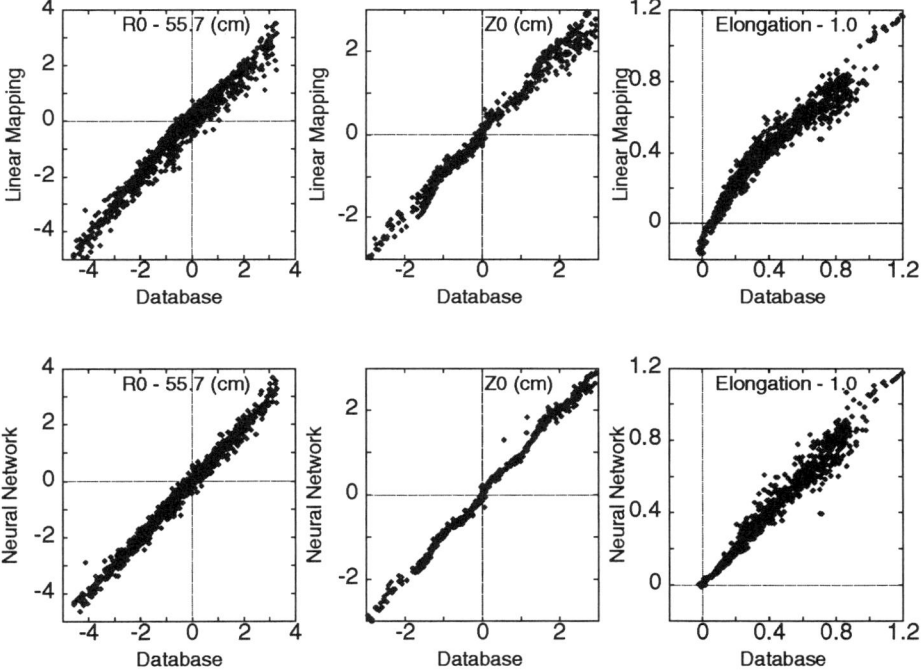

Figure 4: Plots of the values from the test set versus the values predicted by the linear mapping for the 3 equilibrium parameters, together with the corresponding plots for a neural network with 4 hidden units.

The results presented in this paper are based on a multilayer perceptron architecture having a single layer of hidden units with 'tanh' activation functions, and linear output units. Networks are trained by minimization of a sum-of-squares error using a standard conjugate gradients optimization algorithm, and the number of hidden units is optimized by measuring performance with respect to an independent test set. Results from the neural network mapping are compared with those from the optimal linear mapping, that is the single linear transformation which minimizes the same sum-of-squares error as is used in the neural network training algorithm, as this represents the method currently used on a number of present day tokamaks.

Initial results were obtained on networks having 3 output units, corresponding to the values of vertical position Z_0, major radius R_0, and elongation κ; these being parameters which are of interest for real-time feedback control. The smallest normalized test set error of 11.7 is obtained from the network having 16 hidden units. By comparison, the optimal linear mapping gave a normalized test set error of 18.3. This represents a reduction in error of about 30% in going from the linear mapping to the neural network. Such an improvement, in the context of this application, is very significant.

For the experiments on real-time feedback control described in Section 4 the currently available hardware only permitted networks having 4 hidden units, and so we consider the results from this network in more detail. Figure 4 shows plots of the network predictions for various parameters versus the corresponding values from the test set portion of the database. Analogous plots for the optimal linear map predictions versus the database values are also shown. Comparison of the corresponding figures shows the improved predictive capability of the neural network, even for this sub-optimal network topology.

3 HARDWARE IMPLEMENTATION

The hardware implementation of the neural network must have a bandwidth of $\geq$ 20 kHz in order to cope with the fast timescales of the plasma evolution. It must also have an output precision of at least (the the analogue equivalent of) 8 bits in order to ensure that the final accuracy which is attainable will not be limited by the hardware system. We have chosen to develop a fully parallel custom implementation of the multilayer perceptron, based on analogue signal paths with digitally stored synaptic weights (Bishop et al., 1993). A VME-based modular construction has been chosen as this allows flexibility in changing the network architecture, ease of loading network weights, and simplicity of data acquisition. Three separate types of card have been developed as follows:

- Combined 16-input buffer and signal normalizer.

  This provides an analogue hardware implementation of the input normalization described earlier.

- 16×4 matrix multiplier

  The synaptic weights are produced using 12 bit frequency-compensated multiplying DACs (digital to analogue converters) which can be configured to allow 4-quadrant multiplication of analogue signals by a digitally stored number.

- 4-channel sigmoid module

  There are many ways to produce a sigmoidal non-linearity, and we have opted for a solution using two transistors configured as a long-tailed-pair, to generate a 'tanh' sigmoidal transfer characteristic. The principal drawback of such an approach is the strong temperature sensitivity due to the appearance of temperature in the denominator of the exponential transistor transfer characteristic. An elegant solution to this problem has been found by exploiting a chip containing 5 transistors in close thermal contact. Two of the transistors form the long-tailed pair, one of the transistors is used as a heat source, and the remaining two transistors are used to measure temperature. External circuitry provides active thermal feedback control, and stability to changes in ambient temperature over the range 0°C to 50°C is found to be well within the acceptable range.

The complete network is constructed by mounting the appropriate combination of cards in a VME rack and configuring the network topology using front panel interconnections. The system includes extensive diagnostics, allowing voltages at all key points within the network to be monitored as a function of time via a series of multiplexed output channels.

4   RESULTS FROM REAL-TIME FEEDBACK CONTROL

Figure 5 shows the first results obtained from real-time control of the plasma in the COMPASS tokamak using neural networks. The evolution of the plasma elongation, under the control of the neural network, is plotted as a function of time during a plasma pulse. Here the desired elongation has been preprogrammed to follow a series of steps as a function of time. The remaining 2 network outputs (radial position R_0 and vertical position Z_0) were digitized for post-shot diagnosis, but were not used for real-time control. The solid curve shows the value of elongation given by the corresponding network output, and the dashed curve shows the post-shot reconstruction of the elongation obtained from a simple 'filament' code, which gives relatively rapid post-shot plasma shape reconstruction but with limited accuracy. The circles denote the elongation values given by the much more accurate reconstructions obtained from the full equilibrium code. The graph clearly shows the network generating the required elongation signal in close agreement with the reconstructed values. The typical residual error is of order 0.07 on elongation values up to around 1.5. Part of this error is attributable to residual offset in the integrators used to extract magnetic field information from the pick-up coils, and this is currently being corrected through modifications to the integrator design. An additional contribution to the error arises from the restricted number of hidden units available with the initial hardware configuration. While these results represent the first obtained using closed loop control, it is clear from earlier software modelling of larger network architectures (such as 32–16–4) that residual errors of order a few % should be attainable. The implementation of such larger networks is being persued, following the successes with the smaller system.

Acknowledgements

We would like to thank Peter Cox, Jo Lister and Colin Roach for many useful discussions and technical contributions. This work was partially supported by the UK Department of Trade and Industry.

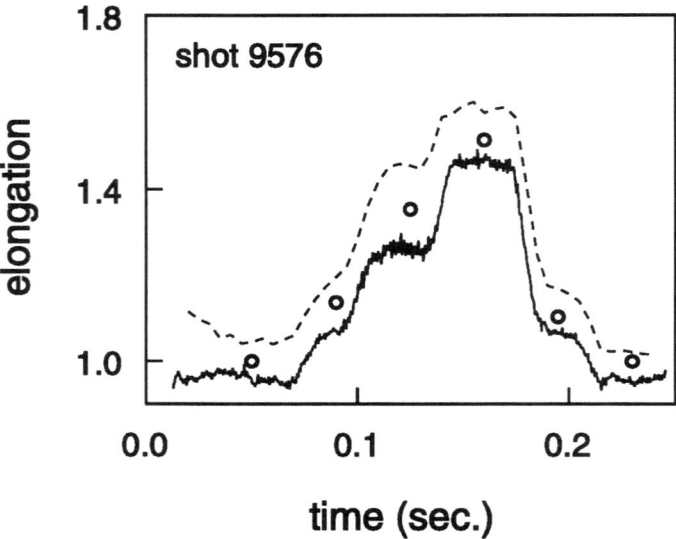

Figure 5: Plot of the plasma elongation κ as a function of time during shot no. 9576 on the COMPASS tokamak, during which the elongation was being controlled in real-time by the neural network.

References

Bishop C M, Cox P, Haynes P S, Roach C M, Smith M E U, Todd T N and Trotman D L, 1992. A neural network approach to tokamak equilibrium control. In *Neural Network Applications*, Ed. J G Taylor, Springer Verlag, 114–128.

Bishop C M, Haynes P S, Roach C M, Smith M E U, Todd T N, and Trotman D L. 1993. Hardware implementation of a neural network for plasma position control in COMPASS-D. In *Proceedings of the 17th. Symposium on Fusion Technology*, Rome, Italy. **2** 997–1001.

Lagin L, Bell R, Davis S, Eck T, Jardin S, Kessel C, Mcenerney J, Okabayashi M, Popyack J and Sauthoff N. 1993. Application of neural networks for real-time calculations of plasma equilibrium parameters for PBX-M, In *Proceedings of the 17th. Symposium on Fusion Technology*, Rome, Italy. **2** 1057–1061.

Lister J B and Schnurrenberger H. 1991. Fast non-linear extraction of plasma parameters using a neural network mapping. *Nuclear Fusion.* **31**, 1291–1300.

Recognizing Handwritten Digits Using Mixtures of Linear Models

Geoffrey E Hinton   Michael Revow   Peter Dayan
Department of Computer Science, University of Toronto
Toronto, Ontario, Canada M5S 1A4

Abstract

We construct a mixture of locally linear generative models of a collection of pixel-based images of digits, and use them for recognition. Different models of a given digit are used to capture different styles of writing, and new images are classified by evaluating their log-likelihoods under each model. We use an EM-based algorithm in which the M-step is computationally straightforward principal components analysis (PCA). Incorporating tangent-plane information [12] about expected local deformations only requires adding tangent vectors into the sample covariance matrices for the PCA, and it demonstrably improves performance.

1 Introduction

The usual way of using a neural network for digit recognition is to train it to output one of the ten classes. When the training data is limited to N examples equally distributed among the classes, there are only $N \log_2 10$ bits of constraint in the class labels so the number of free parameters that can be allowed in a discriminative neural net model is severely limited. An alternative approach, motivated by density estimation, is to train a separate autoencoder network on examples of each digit class and to recognise digits by seeing which autoencoder network gives the best reconstruction of the data. Because the output of each autoencoder has the same dimensionality as the image, each training example provides many more bits of constraint on the parameters. In the example we describe, 7000 training images are sufficient to fit $384,000$ parameters and the training procedure is fast enough to do the fitting overnight on an R4400-based machine.

Auto-encoders can be viewed in terms of minimum description length descriptions of data in which the input-hidden weights produce a code for a particular case and the hidden-output weights embody a generative model which turns this code back into a close approximation of the original example [14, 7]. Code costs (under some prior) and reconstruction error (squared error assuming an isotropic Gaussian misfit model) sum to give the overall code length which can be viewed as a lower bound on the log probability density that the autoencoder assigns to the image. This properly places the emphasis on designing appropriate generative models for the data which will generalise well by assigning high log probabilities to new patterns from the same classes.

We apply this idea to recognising handwritten digits from grey-level pixel images using linear auto-encoders. Linear hidden units for autoencoders are barely worse than non-linear ones when squared reconstruction error is used [1], but have the great computational advantage during training that input-hidden and hidden-output weights can be derived from principal components analysis (PCA) of the training data. In effect a PCA encoder approximates the entire N dimensional distribution of the data with a lower dimensional "Gaussian pancake" [13], choosing, for optimal data compression, to retain just a few of the PCs. One could build a single PCA model for each digit – however the many different styles of writing suggest that more than one Gaussian pancake should be used, by dividing the population of a single digit class into a number of sub-classes and approximating each class by its own model. A similar idea for data compression was used by [9] where vector quantization was used to define sub-classes and PCA was performed within each sub-class (see also [2]). We used an iterative method based on the Expectation Maximisation (EM) algorithm [4] to fit mixtures of linear models.

The *reductio* of the local linear approach would have just one training pattern in each model. This approach would amount to a nearest neighbour method for recognition using a Euclidean metric for error, a technique which is known to be infelicitous. One reason for this poor performance is that characters do not only differ in writing styles, but also can undergo simple transformations such as translations and rotations. These give rise to somewhat non-linear changes as measured in pixel space. Nearest neighbour methods were dramatically improved methods by defining a metric in which locally linearised versions of these transformations cost nothing [12]. In their tangent distance method, each training or test point is represented by a h-dimensional linear subspace, where each of these dimensions corresponds to a linear version of one of the transformations, and distances are measured between subspaces rather than points. The local linear autoencoder method can be seen just like this – variations along one of the h principal component directions are free, while variations along the remaining principal directions cost. However, rather than storing and testing each training pattern, the local models summarise the regularities over a number of patterns. This reduces storage and recognition time, and allows the directions of free variation to be averaged over numbers of patterns and also to be determined by the data rather than being pre-specified. *A priori* knowledge that particular transformations are important can be incorporated using a version of the tangent-prop procedure [12], which is equivalent in this case to adding in slightly transformed versions of the patterns. Also reconstruction error could be assessed either at a test pattern, or, more like tangent distance, between its transformation subspace and the models' principal components subspaces.

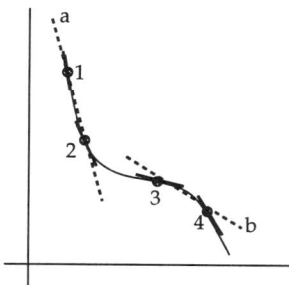

Figure 1: Didactic example of tangent information and local linear models. See text for details.

Figure 1 illustrates the idea. Imagine that the four points 1-4 portray in image space different examples of the same digit, subject to some smooth transformation. As in tangent distance, one could represent this curve using the points and their local tangents (thick lines). However one might do better splitting it into three local linear models rather than four – model 'a' (just a line in this simple case) averages the upper part of the curve more effectively than the combination of the two tangents at '1' and '2'. However, given just the points, one might construct model 'b' for '3' and '4', which would be unfortunate. Incorporating information about the tangents as well would encourage the separation of these segments. Care should be taken in generalising this picture to high dimensional spaces.

The next section develops the theory behind variants of these systems (which is very similar to that in [5, 10]), and section 3 discusses how they perform.

2 Theory

Linear auto-encoders embody a model in which variations from the mean of a population along certain directions are cheaper than along others, as measured by the log-unlikelihood of examples. Creating such a generative model is straightforward. Principal component analysis (PCA) is performed on the training data and the leading h principal components are retained, defining an h-dimensional subspace onto which the n-dimensional inputs are projected. We choose h using cross-validation, although a minimum description length criterion could also be used. We ignore the effect of different variances along the different principal components and use a model in which the code length for example i (the negative log-likelihood) is proportional to the reconstruction error – the squared Euclidean distance between the output of the autoencoder and the pattern itself.

Rather than having just one autoencoder for each digit, there is a whole collection, and therefore we use EM to assign examples to n sub-classes, just as in clustering using a mixture of Gaussians generative model. During the E-step, the responsibility for each pattern is assigned amongst the sub-classes, and in the M-step PCA is performed, altering the parameters of a sub-class appropriately to minimise the reconstruction cost of the data for which it is responsible.

Formally, the algorithm is:
1. Choose initial autoencoder assignments for each example in the training set (typically using a K-means clustering algorithm).
2. Perform PCA separately for each autoencoder;
3. Reassign patterns to the autoencoder that reconstructs them the best;
4. Stop if no patterns have changed sub-class, otherwise return to step 2.

There is a 'soft' version of the algorithm in which the responsibility of autoencoder q for example i is calculated as $r_{iq} = e^{-\|E_{iq}\|^2/2\sigma^2}/(\sum_r e^{-\|E_{ir}\|^2/2\sigma^2})$ where E_{ir} is the reconstruction error. For this, in step 2, the examples are weighted for the PCA by the responsibilities, and convergence is assessed by examining the change in the log-likelihood of the data at each iteration. The soft version requires a choice of σ^2, the assumed variance in the directions orthogonal to the pancake.

The algorithm generates a set of local linear models for each digit. Given a test pattern we evaluate the code length (the log-likelihood) against all the models for all the digits. We use a hard method for classification – determining the identity of the pattern only by the model which reconstructs it best. The absolute quality of the best reconstruction and the relative qualities of slightly sub-optimal reconstructions are available to reject ambiguous cases.

For a given linear model, not counting the code cost implies that deformations of the images along the principal components for the sub-class are free. This is like the metric used by [11] except that they explicitly specified the directions in which deformations should be free, rather than learning them from the data. We wished to incorporate information about the preferred directions without losing the summarisation capacity of the local models, and therefore turned to the tangent prop algorithm [12].

Tangent prop takes into account information about how the output of the system should vary locally with particular distortions of the input by penalising the system for having incorrect derivatives in the relevant directions. In our case, the overall classification process is highly non-linear, making the application of tangent-prop to it computationally unattractive, but it is easy to add a tangent constraint to the reconstruction step because it is linear. Imagine requiring the system $f(\mathbf{p}) = A.\mathbf{p}$ to reconstruct $\mathbf{x} + \lambda \mathbf{t}$ and $\mathbf{x} - \lambda \mathbf{t}$ as well as $\mathbf{x}$, for an input example $\mathbf{x}$, and distortion $\mathbf{t}$ (the tangent vector), and where λ is a weight. Their contribution to the error is proportional to $|\mathbf{x} - A.\mathbf{x}|^2 + \lambda^2 |\mathbf{t} - A.\mathbf{t}|^2$, where the second term is equivalent to the error term that tangent-prop would add. Incorporating this into the PCA is as simple as adding a weighted version of $\mathbf{tt}^\top$ to the covariance matrix – the tangent vectors are never added to the means of the sub-classes.

3 Results

We have evaluated the performance of the system on data from the CEDAR CDROM 1 database containing handwritten digits lifted from mail pieces passing through a United States Post Office [8]. We divided the *br* training set of binary

Clustering	Recognition	Raw Errors
None	None	62 (3.10%)
Heavy	Light	29 (1.45%)
Heavy	None	45 (2.25%)
Heavy	Heavy	90 (4.50%)

Table 1: Classification errors on the validation test when different weightings are used for the tangent vectors during clustering and recognition. No rejections were allowed.

segmented digits into 7,000 training examples, 2,000 validation examples and 2,000 "internal test" examples. All digits were equally represented in these sets. The binary images in the database are all of different sizes, so they were scaled onto a 16 × 16 grid and then smoothed with a Gaussian filter.

The validation set was used to investigate different choices for the Gaussian filter variances, the numbers of sub-classes per digit and principal components per model, and the different weightings on the tangent vectors. Clearly this is a large parameter space and we were only able to perform a very coarse search. In the results reported here all digits have the same number of sub-classes (10) and the number of principal components per model was picked so as to explain 95% of the training set variance assigned to that model. Once a reasonable set of parameter settings had been decided upon, we used all 11,000 images to train a final version which was tested on the official bs set (2711 images).

There are two major steps to the algorithm; defining sub-classes within each digit and reconstructing for recognition. We found that the tangent vectors should be more heavily weighted in the sub-class clustering step than during ultimate recognition. Figure 2 shows the means of the 10 sub-classes for the digit two where the clustering has been done (a) without or (b) with tangent vectors. It is clear that the clusters defined in (b) capture different styles of 2s in a way that those in (a) do not – they are more diverse and less noisy. They also perform better. The raw error rate (no rejections allowed) on the validation set with different amounts of tangent vector weightings are shown in Table 1. The results on the official test set (2711 examples) are shown in Table 2.

4 Discussion and Conclusions

A mixture of local linear models is an effective way to capture the underlying styles of handwritten digits. The first few principal components (less than 20 on 256-dimensional data) extract a significant proportion of the variance in the images within each sub-class. The resulting models classify surprisingly well without requiring large amounts of either storage or computation during recognition. Further, it is computationally easy and demonstrably useful to incorporate tangent information requiring reconstruction to be good for small transformations of the sample patterns in a handful of pre-specified directions. Adding tangent information is exactly equivalent to replacing each digit by a Gaussian cloud of digits perturbed along the tangent plane and is much more efficient than adding extra

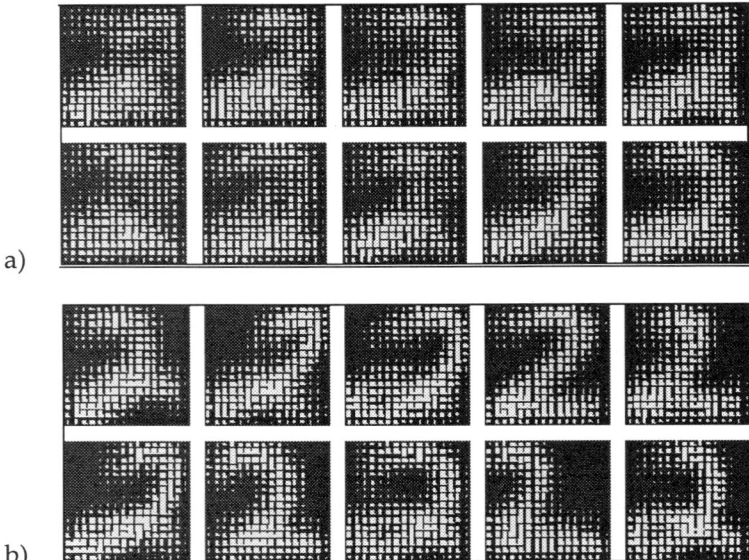

a)

b)

Figure 2: Cluster means for images of twos. (a) Without tangent vectors. (b) Cluster means using translation, rotation and scaling tangent vectors.

stochastically perturbed examples. The weightings applied to reconstruction of the tangent vectors are equivalent to the variances of the cloud.

There is an interesting relationship between mixtures of linear models and mixtures of Gaussians. Fitting a mixture of full-covariance Gaussians is typically infeasible when the dimensionality of the input image space, n, is high and the number of training examples is limited. Each Gaussian requires n parameters to define its mean and $n(n+1)/2$ more parameters to define its covariance matrix. One way to reduce the number of parameters is to use a diagonal covariance matrix but this is a very poor approximation for images because neighbouring pixel intensities are very highly correlated. An alternative way to simplify the covariance matrix is to flatten the Gaussian into a pancake that has h dimensions within the pancake and $n - h$ dimensions orthogonal to the pancake. Within this orthogonal subspace we assume an isotropic Gaussian distribution (*ie* a diagonal covariance matrix with equal, small variances along the diagonal), so we eliminate $(n-h)(n-h+1)/2$ degrees of freedom which is nearly all the degrees of freedom of the full covariance matrix if h is small compared with n. Not counting the mean, this leaves $h(2n-h+1)/2$ degrees of freedom which is exactly the number of parameters required to define the first h principal components.[1] Thus we can view PCA as a way of fiercely constraining a full covariance Gaussian but nevertheless leaving it free to model

---

[1] The hth principal component only requires $n - h + 1$ parameters because it must be orthogonal to all previous components.

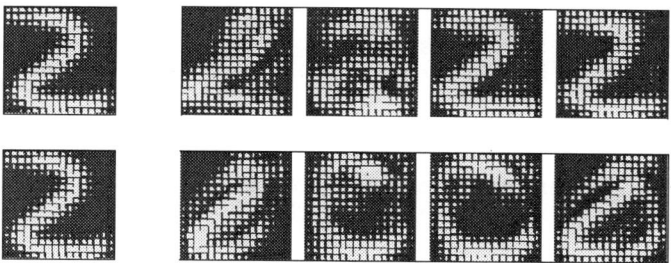

Figure 3: Reconstruction of a 2 (left column) using 2 (upper) and 0 (lower) models.

Method	Raw Error Rate	Memory Requirements
Linear Models	127 (4.68%)	110
Linear Models + Tangent Dist	117 (4.3%)	110
Tangent Distance	97 (3.58%)	1100

Table 2: Classification errors on the official test test when no rejections are allowed. Memory requirements are indicated in terms of the number of 16 × 16 images that need to be stored.

important correlations.

We have investigated a number of extensions to the basic scheme. As only one of these yielded improved results on the validation set, we will only briefly review them. If instead of assuming an isotropic Gaussian within the pancake we use an ellipsoidal subspace, then we can can take into account the different variances along each of the h principal directions. This is akin to incorporating a *code cost* [14]. Similarly, the squared reconstruction error used in the basic scheme also assumes an isotropic distribution. Again a diagonal covariance matrix may be substituted. We surmise that this was not successful because we had insufficient training data to estimate the variances along some dimensions reliably; for example some of the edge pixels were never turned on in the training data for some models.

The Euclidean metric for the reconstruction error is convenient as it authorises the use of a powerful methods such as principal components; however as pointed out in the introduction it is deficient for situations like character recognition. We tried a scheme in which the models were trained as described above, but tangent distance [11] was used during testing. This method yielded marginally improved results on both the validation and test sets (Table 2). More adventurous tangent options, including using them in the clustering phase, were explored by [5, 10].

PCA models are not ideal as *generative* models of the data because they say nothing about how to generate values of components in the directions orthogonal to the pancake. To ameliorate this, the generative model may be formulated as $f(\mathbf{p}) = A.\mathbf{p} + \epsilon$, where the components of ϵ are independent and the *factors* $\mathbf{p}$ have some prior covariance matrix. The generative weights of this autoencoder can be obtained using the technique of maximum likelihood factor analysis (which is closely related to PCA) and the resulting architecture and hierarchical variants of it can be formulated as real valued versions of the Helmholtz machine [3, 6]. The cost of coding the factors relative to their prior is implicitly included in this formulation, as is the possibility that different input pixels are subject to different amounts of noise. Unlike PCA, factor analysis privileges the particular input coordinates (rather than being invariant to rotations of the input covariance matrix).

References

[1] Bourlard, H & Kamp, Y (1988). *Auto-association by Multilayer Perceptrons and Singular Value Decomposition*. Biol. Cybernetics 59, 291-294.

[2] Bregler, C & Omohundro, SM (1995). Non-linear image interpolation using surface learning. This volume.

[3] Dayan, P, Hinton, GE, Neal, RM & Zemel, RS (1995). The Helmholtz machine. *Neural Computation*, in press.

[4] Dempster, AP, Laird, NM & Rubin, DB (1976). Maximum likelihood from incomplete data via the EM algorithm. *Proceedings of the Royal Statistical Society*, 1–38.

[5] Hastie, T, Simard, P & Sackinger, E (1995). Learning prototype models for tangent distance. This volume.

[6] Hinton, GE, Dayan, P, Frey, BJ, Neal, RM (1995). The wake-sleep algorithm for unsupervised neural networks. Submitted for publication.

[7] Hinton, GE & Zemel, RS (1994). Autoencoders, minimum description length and Helmholtz free energy. In JD Cowan, G Tesauro & J Alspector, editors, *Advances in Neural Information Processing Systems 6*. San Mateo, CA: Morgan Kaufmann.

[8] Hull, JJ (1994). A database for handwritten text recognition research. *IEEE Transactions on Pattern Analysis and Machine Intelligence*, 16, 550-554.

[9] Kambhatla, N & Leen, TK (1994). Fast non-linear dimension reduction. In JD Cowan, G Tesauro & J Alspector, editors, *Advances in Neural Information Processing Systems 6*. San Mateo, CA: Morgan Kaufmann.

[10] Schwenk, H & Milgram, M (1995). Transformation invariant autoassociation with application to handwritten character recognition. This volume.

[11] Simard, P, Le Cun, Y & and Denker, J (1993). Efficient pattern recognition using a new transformation distance. In SJ Hanson, JD Cowan & CL Giles, editors, *Advances in Neural Information Processing Systems 5*, 50-58. San Mateo, CA: Morgan Kaufmann.

[12] Simard, P, Victorri, B, LeCun, Y & Denker, J (1992). Tangent Prop - A formalism for specifying selected invariances in an adaptive network. In JE Moody, SJ Hanson & RP Lippmann, editors, *Advances in Neural Information Processing Systems 4*. San Mateo, CA: Morgan Kaufmann.

[13] Williams, CKI, Zemel, RS & Mozer, MC (1993). Unsupervised learning of object models. In *AAAI Fall 1993 Symposium on Machine Learning in Computer Vision*, 20-24.

[14] Zemel, RS (1993). *A Minimum Description Length Framework for Unsupervised Learning*. PhD Dissertation, Computer Science, University of Toronto, Canada.

---

[1]This research was funded by the Ontario Information Technology Research Centre and NSERC. We thank Patrice Simard, Chris Williams, Rob Tibshirani and Yann Le Cun for helpful discussions. Geoffrey Hinton is the Noranda Fellow of the Canadian Institute for Advanced Research.

Optimal Movement Primitives

Terence D. Sanger
Jet Propulsion Laboratory
MS 303-310
4800 Oak Grove Drive
Pasadena, CA 91109
(818) 354-9127 tds@ai.mit.edu

Abstract

The theory of Optimal Unsupervised Motor Learning shows how a network can discover a reduced-order controller for an unknown nonlinear system by representing only the most significant modes. Here, I extend the theory to apply to command sequences, so that the most significant components discovered by the network correspond to motion "primitives". Combinations of these primitives can be used to produce a wide variety of different movements. I demonstrate applications to human handwriting decomposition and synthesis, as well as to the analysis of electrophysiological experiments on movements resulting from stimulation of the frog spinal cord.

1 INTRODUCTION

There is much debate within the neuroscience community concerning the internal representation of movement, and current neurophysiological investigations are aimed at uncovering these representations. In this paper, I propose a different approach that attempts to define the optimal internal representation in terms of "movement primitives", and I compare this representation with the observed behavior. In this way, we can make strong predictions about internal signal processing. Deviations from the predictions can indicate biological constraints or alternative goals that cause the biological system to be suboptimal.

The concept of a motion primitive is not as well defined as that of a sensory primitive

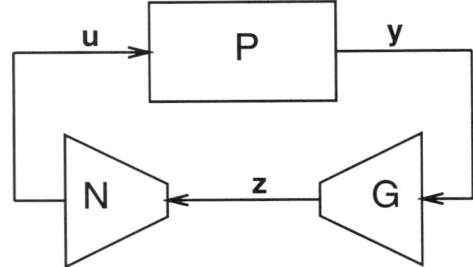

Figure 1: Unsupervised Motor Learning: The plant P takes inputs u and produces outputs y. The sensory map G produces intermediate variables z, which are mapped onto the correct command inputs by the motor network N.

within the visual system, for example. There is no direct equivalent to the "receptive field" concept that has allowed interpretation of sensory recordings. In this paper, I will propose an internal model that involves both motor receptive fields and a set of movement primitives which are combined using a weighted sum to produce a large class of movements. In this way, a small number of well-designed primitives can generate the full range of desired behaviors.

I have previously developed the concept of "optimal unsupervised motor learning" to investigate optimal internal representations for instantaneous motor commands. The optimal representations adaptively discover a reduced-order linearizing controller for an unknown nonlinear plant. The theorems give the optimal solution in general, and can be applied to special cases for which both linear and nonlinear adaptive algorithms exist (Sanger 1994b). In order to apply the theory to complete movements it needs to be extended slightly, since in general movements exist within an infinite-dimensional task space rather than a finite-dimensional control space. The goal is to derive a small number of primitives that optimally encode the full set of observed movements. Generation of the internal movement primitives then becomes a data-compression problem, and I will choose primitives that minimize the resultant mean-squared error.

2 OPTIMAL UNSUPERVISED MOTOR LEARNING

Optimal Unsupervised Motor Learning is based on three principles:

1. Dimensionality Reduction
2. Accurate Reduced-order Control
3. Minimum Sensory error

Consider the system shown in figure 1. At time t, the plant P takes motor inputs u and produces sensory outputs y. A sensory mapping G transforms the raw sensory data y to an intermediate representation z. A motor mapping takes desired values of z and computes the appropriate command u such that $GPu = z$. Note that the loop in the figure is not a feedback-control loop, but is intended to indicate the flow of information. With this diagram in mind, we can write the three principles as:

1. $\dim[z] < \dim[y]$
2. $GPNz = z$
3. $\|PNGy - y\|$ is minimized

We can prove the following theorems (Sanger 1994b):

Theorem 1: For all G there exists an N such that $GPNz = z$. If G is linear and P^{-1} is linear, then N is linear.

Theorem 2: For any G, define an invertible map $\bar{G}$ such that $G\bar{G}^{-1} = I$ on range$[G]$. Then $\|PNGy - y\|$ is minimized when G is chosen such that $\|y - \bar{G}^{-1}G\|$ is minimized. If G and P are linear and the singular value decomposition of P is given by $L^T SR$, then the optimal maps are $G = L$ and $N = R^T S^{-1}$.

For the discussion of movement, the linear case will be the most important since in the nonlinear case we can use unsupervised motor learning to perform dimensionality reduction and linearization of the plant at each time t. The movement problem then becomes an infinite-dimensional linear problem.

Previously, I have developed two iterative algorithms for computing the singular value decomposition from input/output samples (Sanger 1994a). The algorithms are called the "Double Generalized Hebbian Algorithm" (DGHA) and the "Orthogonal Asymmetric Encoder" (OAE). DGHA is given by

$$\Delta G = \gamma(zy^T - \text{LT}[zz^T]G)$$
$$\Delta N^T = \gamma(zu^T - \text{LT}[zz^T]N^T)$$

while OAE is described by:

$$\Delta G = \gamma(\hat{z}y^T - \text{LT}[\hat{z}\hat{z}^T]G)$$
$$\Delta N^T = \gamma(Gy - \text{LT}[GG^T]\hat{z})u^T$$

where LT[ ] is an operator that sets the above diagonal elements of its matrix argument to zero, $y = Pu$, $z = Gy$, $\hat{z} = N^T u$, and γ is a learning rate constant. Both algorithms cause G to converge to the matrix of left singular vectors of P, and N to converge to the matrix of right singular vectors of P (multiplied by a diagonal matrix for DGHA). DGHA is used in the examples below.

3 MOVEMENT

In order to extend the above discussion to allow adaptive discovery of movement primitives, we now consider the plant P to be a mapping from command sequences $u(t)$ to sensory sequences $y(t)$. We will assume that the plant has been feedback linearized (perhaps by unsupervised motor learning). We also assume that the sensory network G is constrained to be linear. In this case, the optimal motor network N will also be linear. The intermediate variables z will be represented by a vector. The sensory mapping consists of a set of sensory "receptive fields" $g_i(t)$

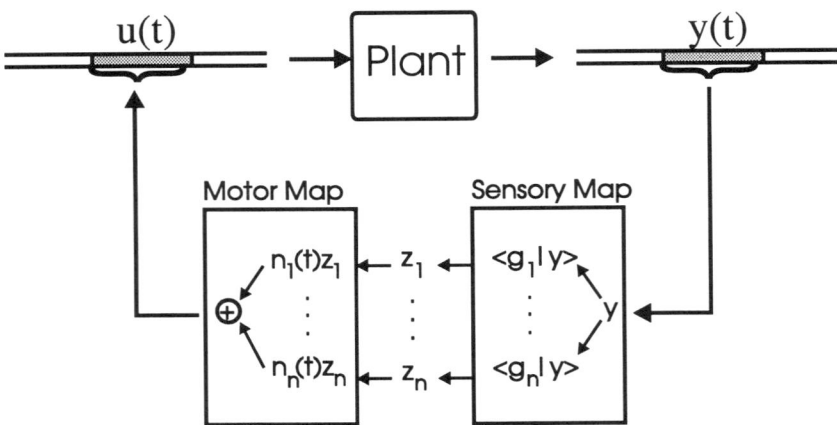

Figure 2: Extension of unsupervised motor learning to the case of trajectories. Plant input and output are time-sequences $u(t)$ and $y(t)$. The sensory and motor maps now consist of sensory primitives $g_i(t)$ and motor primitives $n_i(t)$.

such that
$$z_i = \int g_i(t)y(t)dt = <g_i|y>$$
and the motor mapping consists of a set of "motor primitives" $n_i(t)$ such that
$$u(t) = \sum_i n_i(t)z_i$$
as in figure 2. If the plant is equal to the identity (complete feedback linearization), then $g_i(t) = n_i(t)$. In this case, the optimal sensory-motor primitives are given by the eigenfunctions of the autocorrelation function of $y(t)$. If the autocorrelation is stationary, then the infinite-window eigenfunctions will be sinusoids. Note that the optimal primitives depend both on the plant P as well as the statistical distribution of outputs $y(t)$.

In practice, both $u(t)$ and $y(t)$ are sampled at discrete time-points $\{t_k\}$ over a finite time-window, so that the plant input and output is in actuality a long vector. Since the plant is linear, the optimal solution is given by the singular value decomposition, and either the DGHA or OAE algorithms can be used directly. The resulting sensory primitives map the sensory information $y(t)$ onto the finite-dimensional z, which is usually a significant data compression. The motor primitives map z onto the sequence $u(t)$, and the resulting $\hat{y}(t) = P[u(t)]$ will be a linear projection of $y(t)$ onto the space spanned by the set $\{Pn_i(t)\}$.

4 EXAMPLE 1: HANDWRITING

As a simple illustration, I examine the case of human handwriting. We can consider the plant to be the identity mapping from pen position to pen position, and the

Optimal Movement Primitives

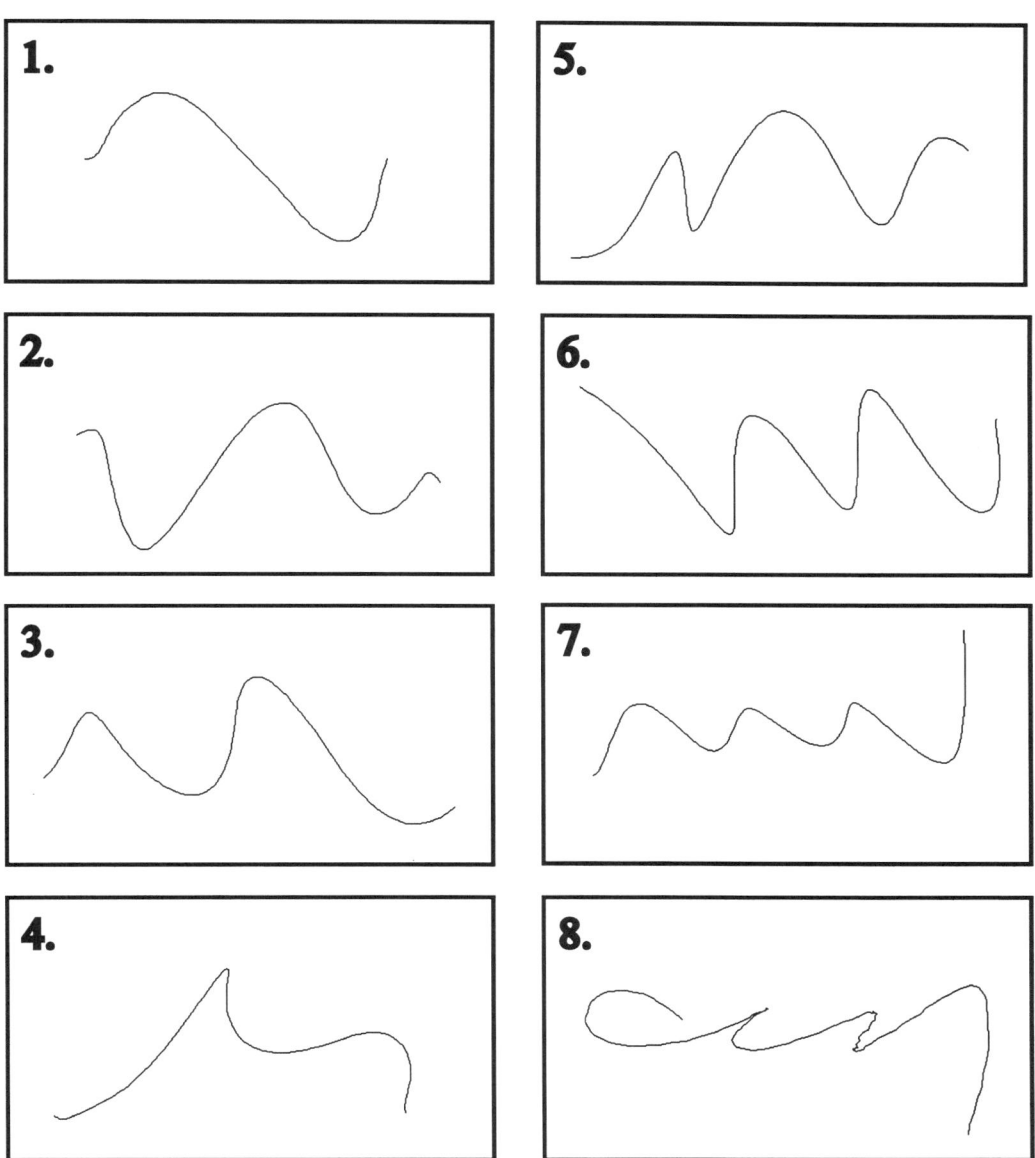

Figure 3: Movement primitives for sampled human handwriting.

human to be taking desired sensory values of pen position and converting them into motor commands to move the pen. The sensory statistics then reflect the set of trajectories used in producing handwritten letters. An optimal reduced-order control system can be designed based on the observed statistics, and its performance can be compared to human performance.

For this example, I chose sampled data from 87 different examples of lower-case letters written by a single person, and represented as horizontal and vertical pen position at each point in time. Blocks of 128 sequential points were used for training, and 8 internal variables z_i were used for each of the two components of pen position. The training set consisted of 5000 randomly chosen samples. Since the plant is the identity, the sensory and motor primitives are the same, and these are shown as "strokes" in figure 3. Linear combinations of these strokes can be used to generate pen paths for drawing lowercase letters. This is shown in figure 4, where the word "hello" (not present in the training set) is written and projected using increasing numbers of intermediate variables z_i. The bottom of figure 4 shows the sequence of values of z_i that was used (horizontal component only).

Good reproduction of the test word was achieved with 5 movement primitives. A total of 7 128-point segments was projected, and these were recombined using smooth 50% overlap. Each segment was encoded by 5 coefficients for each of the horizontal and vertical components, giving a total of 70 coefficients to represent 1792 data points (896 horizontal and vertical components), for a compression ratio of 25:1.

5 EXAMPLE 2: FROG SPINAL CORD

The second example models some interesting and unexplained neurophysiological results from microstimulation of the frog spinal cord. (Bizzi *et al.* 1991) measured the pattern of forces produced by the frog hindlimb at various positions in the workspace during stimulation of spinal interneurons. The resulting force-fields often have a stable "equilibrium point", and in some cases this equilibrium point follows a smooth closed trajectory during tonic stimulation of the interneuron. However, only a small number of different force field shapes have been found, and an even smaller number of different trajectory types. A hypothesis to explain this result is that larger classes of different trajectories can be formed by combining the patterns produced by these cells. This hypothesis can be modelled using the optimal movement primitives described above.

Figure 5a shows a simulation of the frog leg. To train the network, random smooth planar movements were made for 5000 time points. The plant output was considered to be 32 successive cartesian endpoint positions, and the plant input was the time-varying force vector field. Two hidden units z were used. In figure 5b we see an example of the two equilibrium point trajectories (movement primitives) that were learned by DGHA. Linear combinations of these trajectories account for over 96% of the variance of the training data, and they can approximate a large class of smooth movements. Note that many other pairs of orthogonal trajectories can accomplish this, and different trials often produced different orthogonal trajectory shapes.

Figure 4: Projection of test-word "hello" using increasing numbers of intermediate variables z_i.

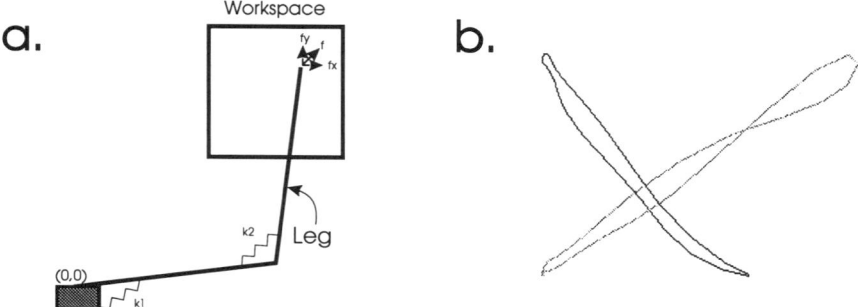

Figure 5: a. Simulation of frog leg configuration. b. An example of learned optimal movement primitives.

6 CONCLUSION

The examples are not meant to provide detailed models of internal processing for human or frog motor control. Rather, they are intended to illustrate the concept of optimal primitives and perhaps guide the search for neurophysiological and psychophysical correlates of these primitives. The first example shows that generation of the lower-case alphabet can be accomplished with approximately 10 coefficients per letter, and that this covers a considerable range of variability in character production. The second example demonstrates that an adaptive algorithm allows the possibility for the frog spinal cord to control movement using a very small number of internal variables.

Optimal unsupervised motor learning thus provides a descriptive model for the generation of a large class of movements using a compressed internal description. A set of fixed movement primitives can be combined linearly to produce the necessary motor commands, and the optimal choice of these primitives assures that the error in the resulting movement will be minimized.

References

Bizzi E., Mussa-Ivaldi F. A., Giszter S., 1991, Computations underlying the execution of movement: A biological perspective, *Science*, 253:287–291.

Sanger T. D., 1994a, Two algorithms for iterative computation of the singular value decomposition from input/output samples, In Touretzky D., ed., *Advances in Neural Information Processing 6*, Morgan Kaufmann, San Mateo, CA, in press.

Sanger T. D., 1994b, Optimal unsupervised motor learning, *IEEE Trans. Neural Networks*, in press.

An Integrated Architecture of Adaptive Neural Network Control for Dynamic Systems

Liu Ke[1,2] Robert L. Tokar[2] Brian D.McVey[2]

[1]Center for Nonlinear Studies, [2]Applied Theoretical Physics Division
Los Alamos National Laboratory, Los Alamos, NM, 87545

Abstract

In this study, an integrated neural network control architecture for nonlinear dynamic systems is presented. Most of the recent emphasis in the neural network control field has no error feedback as the control input, which rises the lack of adaptation problem. The integrated architecture in this paper combines feed forward control and error feedback adaptive control using neural networks. The paper reveals the different internal functionality of these two kinds of neural network controllers for certain input styles, e.g., state feedback and error feedback. With error feedback, neural network controllers learn the slopes or the gains with respect to the error feedback, producing an error driven adaptive control systems. The results demonstrate that the two kinds of control scheme can be combined to realize their individual advantages. Testing with disturbances added to the plant shows good tracking and adaptation with the integrated neural control architecture.

1 INTRODUCTION

Neural networks are used for control systems because of their capability to approximate nonlinear system dynamics. Most neural network control architectures originate from work presented by Narendra[1], Psaltis[2] and Lightbody[3]. In these architectures, an identification neural network is trained to function as a model for the plant. Based on the neural network identification model, a neural network controller is trained by backpropagating the error through the identification network. After training, the identification network is replaced by the real plant. As is illustrated in Figure 1, the controller receives external inputs as well as plant state feedback inputs. Training procedures are employed such that the networks approximate feed forward control surfaces that are functions of external inputs and state feedbacks of the plant (or the identification network during training).

It is worth noting that in this architecture, the error between the plant output and the desired output of the reference model is not fed back to the controller, after the training phase. In other words, this error information is ignored when the neural network applies its control. It is well known in control theory that the error feedback plays a significant role in adaptation. Therefore, when model uncertainty or noise/disturbances are present, a feed forward neural network controller with only state feedback will not adaptively update the control signal. On line training for the neural controller has been proposed to obtain adaptive ability[1][3]. However, the stability for the on line training of the neural network controller is unresolved[1][4].

In this study, an additional nonlinear recurrent network is combined with the feed forward neural network controller to form an adaptive controller. This added neural network uses feedback error between the reference model output and the plant output as an input. In addition, the system's external inputs and the plant states are also input to the feedback network. This architecture is used in the control community, but not with neural network components. The approach differs from a conventional error feedback controller, such as a gain scheduled PID controller, in that the neural network error feedback controller implements a continuous nonlinear gain scheduled hypersurface, and after training, adaptive model reference control for nonlinear dynamic systems is achieved without further parameter computation. The approach is tested on well-known nonlinear control problems in the neural network literature, and good results are obtained.

2 NEURAL NETWORK CONTROL

In this section, several different neural network control architectures are presented. In these structures, identification neural networks, viewed as accurate models for real plants, are used.

2.1 NEURAL NETWORK FEED FORWARD CONTROL

The neural network controllers are trained by backpropagation of errors through a well trained neural identification network. In this architecture, the state variable $y(t)$ of the system is sent back to the neural network, and the external input $x(t)$ also is input to the network. With these inputs, the neural network establishes a feed forward mapping from the external input $x(t)$ to the control signal $u(t)$. This control mapping is expressed as a function of the external input $x(t)$ and the plant state $y(t)$:

$$u(t)=f(x(t), y(t)) \qquad (1)$$

where $x(t)=[x(t), x(t-1), ...]^T$, and $y(t)=[y(t), y(t-1), ...]^T$.
This neural network control architecture is denoted in this study as feed forward neural control even though it includes state feedback . Neural control with error feedback is denoted as feedback neural control.

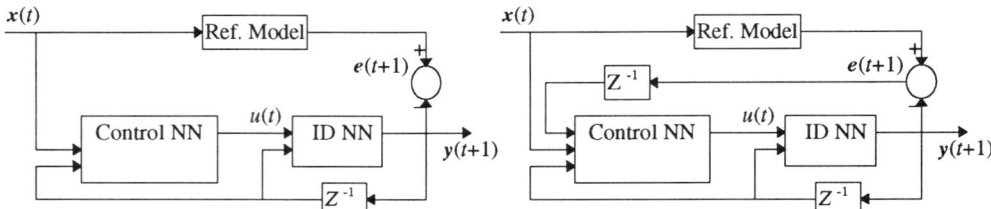

Figure 1 Neural Network Control Architecture. ID NN represents the identification network. Ref. Model means reference model, and NN means neural network.

Figure 2 Neural Network Feedback Control Architecture

During the training phases, based on the assumption that the neural identification network provides a model for the plant, the gradient information needed for error backpropagation is obtained by calculating the Jacobian of the identification network. The following equation describes this process for the control architecture shown in Figure 1. If the cost function is defined as E, then the gradient of the cost function with respect to weight w of the neural controller is

$$\frac{\partial E}{\partial w} = \frac{\partial E}{\partial u}\frac{\partial u}{\partial w} + \left(\frac{\partial E}{\partial u}\frac{\partial u}{\partial y_{t-1}} + \frac{\partial E}{\partial y_{t-1}}\right)\frac{\partial y_{t-1}}{\partial w} \qquad (2)$$

where u is the control signal and y_{t-1} is the plant feedback state.

After the training stage, the neural network supplies a control law. Because neural networks have the ability to approximate any arbitrary nonlinear functions[5], a feed forward neural network can build a nonlinear controller, which is crucial to the use of the neural network in control engineering. Also, since all the parameters of the neural network identification model and the neural network controller are obtained from learning through samples, mathematically untraceable features of the plant can be extracted from the samples and imbedded into the control system.

However, because the feed forward controller has no error feedback, the controller can not adapt to the disturbances occurring in the plant or the reference model. This problem is of substantial importance in the context of adaptive control. In the next subsection, error feedback between the reference models and the plant outputs is introduced into neural network controllers for adaptation.

2.2 NEURAL ADAPTIVE CONTROL WITH ERROR FEEDBACK

It is known that feedback errors from the system are important for adaptation. Due to the flexibility of the neural network architecture, the error between the reference model and the plant can be sent back to the controller as an extra input. In such an architecture, neural networks become nonlinear gain scheduled controllers with smooth continuous gains. Figure 2 shows the architecture for the feedback neural control.

With this architecture, the neural network control surface is not the fixed mapping from the $x(t)$ to $u(t)$ for each state $y(t)$, but instead it learns the *slope* or the *gain* referring to the feedback error $e(t)$ for control. This gain is a continuous nonlinear function of the external input $x(t)$ and the state feedback $y(t)$. Figure 3 shows the recurrent network architecture of the feedback neural controller. The output node needs to be recurrent because the output without the recurrent link from the neural controller is only a correction to the old control signal, and the new control signal should be the combination of old control signal and the correction. The other nodes of the network can be feed forward or recurrent. If we denote the weight for the output node's recurrent link as w_b, then the output from the recurrent link is $w_b u(t-1)$. The following equation describes the feedback network.

$$u(t) = w_b u(t-1) + f(x(t), y(t), e(t)) \qquad (3)$$

where $f(.)$ is a nonlinear function established by the network for which the recurrent link output is not included and $e(t) = [e(t), e(t-1), ...]^T$.

To compare the control gain expression with conventional control theory, consider the Taylor series expansion of the network forward mapping $f(.)$, equation (3) becomes

$$u(t) = w_b u(t-1) + f'(x(t), y(t))\, e(t) + f''(x(t), y(t))\, e^2(t) + ... \qquad (4)$$

where $f'(x(t), y(t)) = [\ \partial f(x(t), y(t), e(t))/\partial e(t),\ \partial f(x(t), y(t), e(t))/\partial e(t-1),\ ...\ ]$. If high order terms are ignored and $g(.)$ represents $f'(.)$, we get

$$u(t) = w_b u(t-1) + g(x(t), y(t))\, e(t) \qquad (5)$$

which is a gain scheduled controller and the gain is the function of external input $x(t)$ and the plant state $y(t)$. It is clear that when $w_b=1.0$, $g(.)$ is a constant vector and $e(t)=[e(t), e(t-1), e(t-2)]^T$, the feedback neural network controller degenerates to a discrete PID controller. Because the neural network can approximate arbitrary nonlinear functions through learning, the neural network feedback controller can generate a nonlinear continuous gain hypersurface.

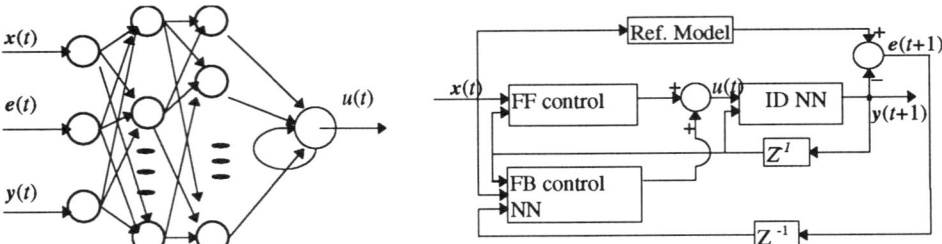

Figure 3 Feedback Neural Network Controller   Figure 4 Integrated NN Control Architeture.

In the training process, error backpropagating through the identification network is used. The process is similar to the training of a feed forward neural controller, but the resulting control surface is completely different due to the different inputs. After training, the neural network is able to provide a nonlinear control law, that is, the desired model following response can be obtained with fixed controller parameters for nonlinear dynamic systems. Traditionally, the control of the nonlinear plant is derived from continuous computing of the controller gains.

This feedback controller is error driven. As long as an error exists, the control signal is updated according to the error and the *gain*. This kind of neural controller is an adaptive controller in principle.

2.3 INTEGRATED NEURAL NETWORK CONTROLLER

The characteristics of feed forward and error feedback neural control networks are described in the previous subsections. In this section, the two controllers are combined. Figure 4 shows the architecture.

In this architecture, we include both feed forward and feedback neural network controllers. The control signal is the combination from these two networks' outputs. In the training stage, it is our experience that the feed forward network should be trained first. The feedback network is not included while training the feed forward network. After training the feed forward controller, the error feedback network is trained with the feed forward network, but the feed forward networks' weights are unchanged. Backpropagating the error through the identification network is applied for the training of both networks.

When training the feedback control network, the feed forward calculation is

$$u(t) = u_{ff}(t)+u_{fb}(t), \qquad (6)$$

$$y(t+1) = P(x(t), y(t), u(t)), \qquad (7)$$

where $u_{ff}(t)$ is the output from the feed forward controller network and $u_{fb}(t)$ is the output from the feedback controller network, $P(.)$ is the identification mapping.

3 CONTROL ON EXAMPLE PROBLEMS

In this section, the control architecture described above is applied to a well-known problem from the literature[1]. The plants and the reference model of the sample problems are described by difference equations

plant:
$$y(t+1) = \frac{y(t)}{1.0 + y^2(t)} + (u(t) - 1.0)u(t)(u(t) + 1.0) \tag{11}$$

reference model:
$$y(t+1) = 0.6y(t) + u(t) \tag{12}$$

This is a nonlinear time varying dynamic system with no analytical inverse.

3.1 FEED FORWARD CONTROL

A feed forward neural network is trained to control the system to follow the reference model. The plant state $y(t)$ and external input $x(t)$ are fed to the controller. During the training, the $x(t)$ is randomly generated. After training, the controller generates a control signal $u(t)$ such that the plant can follow the reference model output. Figure 5 shows the testing result of the reference model output and the controlled plant output. The input function is $x(t)=\sin(2\pi t/25)+\sin(2\pi t/10)$. The controller network architecture is (2, 20, 1).

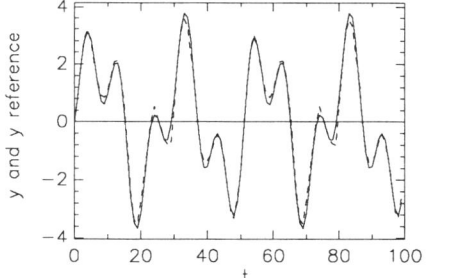
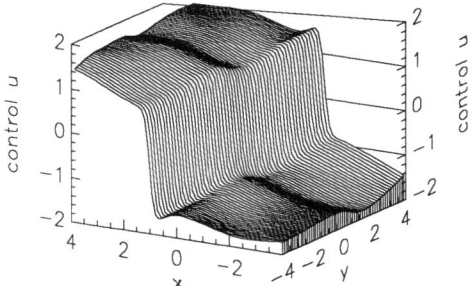

Figure 5 Tracking Result From the Feed Forward NN.
Output of reference (solid line) and plant (dash line).

Figure 6 Feed Forward Control Surface

The output surface of the controller network is shown in Figure 6. By examining the controller output surface, we can see that the neural network builds a feed forward mapping from $x(t)$ to $u(t)$. This feed forward mapping is also a function of the plant state $y(t)$. Under each state, the neural network controller accepts input $x(t)$ to produce control signal $u(t)$ such that the plant follows the reference model reasonably well. In Figure 6, the x axis is the external input $x(t)$ and the y axis is the plant feedback output $y(t)$. The z axis represents the control surface.

The feed forward controller lacks the ability to adapt to plant uncertainty, noise or changes in the reference model. As an example, we apply this feed forward controller to the disturbed plant with a bias 0.5 added to the original plant. The tracking result is shown in Figure 7. With this slight bias, the plant does not follow the reference model. Clearly, the feed forward controller has no adaptive ability to this model bias.

3.2 FEEDBACK CONTROL

First, we compare the neural network feedback controller with fixed gain PID controllers. For many nonlinear systems, the fixed gain PID controllers will give poor tracking and continuous adaptation of the controller parameters is needed. The neural network approach offers an alternative control approach for nonlinear systems. Through the training, control gains, imbedded in the neural network, are established as a continuous function of system external inputs $x(t)$ and plant states $y(t)$.

The sample problem in the above section is now employed to describe how the neural network creates a nonlinear control gain surface with error feedback and additional inputs. First, we show one simple case of neural adaptive feedback controller. This controller can only adapt to the system nonlinearity with a fixed linear input pattern. The reason to show this simple adaptation case first is that its control gain surface can be illustrated graphically.

Figure 8 illustrates, for the system in equations (11) and (12) that a fixed gain PI controller fails to track the reference model, for even one fixed linear input pattern $x(t)=0.2t-2.5$, because the plant nonlinearity. Figure 9 illustrates the result from a recurrent neural network with feedback error $e(t)$ and $x(t)$ as inputs. The neural network is trained by backpropagation error through the identification network. Compared to the fixed gain PI controller, the neural network improves the tracking ability significantly.

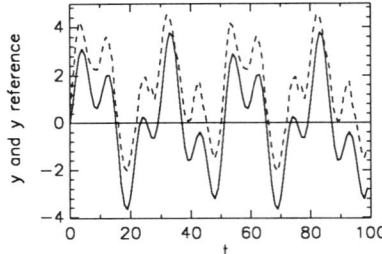
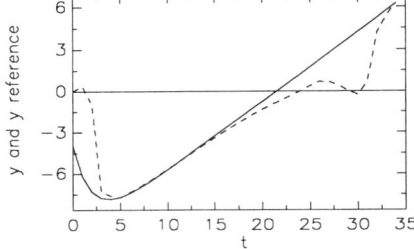

Figure 7 Tracking Result for Shifted Plant, plant output (dash line) and reference output (solid line).

Figure 8 Reference Model Output (solid line) and PID Controlled Plant Output (dashed line)

The control surface of the updating output $f(.)$ is shown in Figure 10, which is the output from the neural network controller without recurrent link (see equation (3)). We plot the surface of the updating output from the controller with respect to input $x(t)$ and error feed back input $e(t)$. The gain of the controller is equivalent to the updating output from the network when error=1.0. As shown in the figure, the gain in the neighborhood about $x(t)=0$ changes largely according to the direction of changes in the plant in the corresponding region. The updating surface for a PID controller is a plane. The neural network implements a nonlinear continuous control gain surface.

For a more complicated case, we add $x(t-1)$ as another input to the neural network as well as $e(t-1)$, and train by error backpropagation through the identification network. These two inputs, $x(t)$ and $x(t-1)$ add difference information to the network. The network can adapt to not only different operating regions indicated by $x(t)$, but also different input patterns. Figure 11 shows the tracking results with two different input patterns. In Figure 11 (a), input pattern is $x(t)=4.0\sin(t/4.0)$. In Figure 11 (b) input pattern is $x(t)=\sin(2\pi t/25)+\sin(2\pi t/10)$.

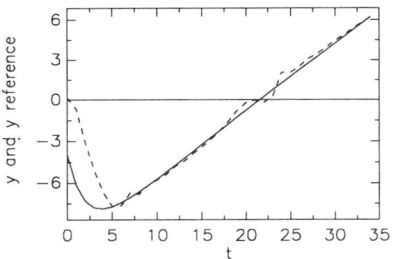
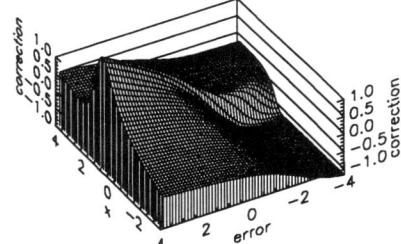

Figure 9 Reference Model Output (solid line) and Neural Network Controled Output (dashed line)

Figure 10 Feedback Neural Controller Updating Surface

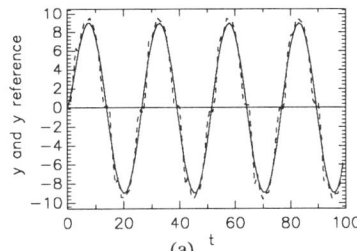
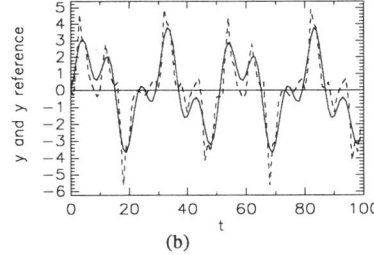

Figure 11 Output of the Reference Model (solid line) and the Plant (dash line)

3.3 INTEGRATED NEURAL CONTROLLER

As shown in the above section, when only error feedback neural controller is used, the control result is not very accurate. Now we combine feed forward and feedback control to realize good tracking and adaptation. Figure 12 shows the control result from the integrated controller when the plant is shifted 0.5. Compared to only feed forward control(Figure 7), the integrated controller has much better adaptation to the shifted plant.

When the plant changes, adding an extra feed back controller can avoid on-line training of feed forward network which may induce potential instability, and the adaptation is achieved. The output from the feedback network controller is driven by the error between the reference model and the plant.

4 DISCUSSIONS

We have emphasized in the above sections that a feed forward controller with only state feedback does not adapt when model uncertainties or noise/disturbance are present. The presence of a feed back controller can make the on line training of the feed forward network unnecessary, thus avoiding potential instability. The main reason for the instability of on-line training is the incompleteness of sample sets, which is referred to as a lack of persistent excitation in control theory[6]. First, it leads to an inaccurate identification network. Training with this network can result in an unstable controller. Second, it makes the training of controller away from global representation. With an error feedback adaptive network, the output from the feedback network controller is driven by the error between the reference model and the plant. In the simplest case when all the activity functions are linear and only the feedback errors are inputs, this kind of neural network is equivalent to a PID controller. However, beyond the scope of PID controllers, the neural networks are capable to approximating nonlinear time variant control gain surfaces corresponding to different operating regions. Also, unlike a PID controller, the coefficients for the neural adaptive controller are obtained through a training procedure.

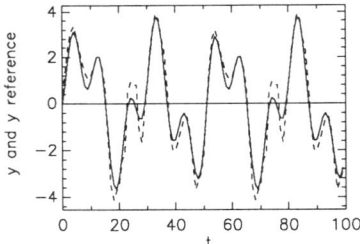

Figure 12 Integrated Network Controller Tracking Result for Shifted Plant,
Plant Output (dash line) and Reference Output (solid line).

The error feedback network behaves as a gain scheduling controller. It has rise time, overshoot consideration and delay problem. Feed forward control can compensate for these problems to some degree. For example, the feed forward network can perform a nonlinear mapping with designed time delay. Therefore with the feed forward network, the delay problem maybe overcame significantly. Also the feed forward controller can help to reduce rise time compare to use only feedback controller.

With the feed forward network, the feedback network controller can have much smaller gains compared to using a feedback network alone. This increases the noise rejection ability. Also this reduces the overshoot as well as settle time.

The neural network control architecture offers an alternative to the conventional approach. It gives a generic model for the broadest class of systems considered in control theory. However this model needs to be configured depending on the details of the control problem. With different inputs, the neural network controllers establish different internal hyperstates. When plant states are fed back to the network, a feed forward mapping is established as a function of the plant states by the neural network controller. When the errors between the reference model and the plant are used as the error feedback inputs to a dynamic neural network controller, the network functions as an associative memory nonlinear gain scheduled controller. The above two kinds of neural controller can be combined and complemented to achieve accurate tracking and adaptation.

References

[1] Kumpati S. Narendra and Kannan Parthasarathy, "Gradient Methods for the Optimization of Dynamical Systems Containing Neural Networks," IEEE Trans. Neural Networks, vol. 2. pp252-262 Mar. 1991
[2] Psaltis, D., Sideris, A. and Yamamura, A., "Neural controllers," Proc. of 1st International Conference on Neural Networks, Vol. 4, pp551-558, San Diego, CA, 1987
[3] G. Lightbody, Q. H. Wu and G. W. Irwin, "Control applications for feed forward networks," Chapter 4, Neural Networks for Control and Systems, Edited by K.warwich, G. W. Irwin and K. J. Hunt 1992
[4] R. Abikowski and P. J. Gawthrop, "A survey of neural networks for control" Chapter 3, Neural Networks for Control and Systems, ISBN 0-86341-279-3, Edited by K.warwich, G. W. Irwin and K. J. Hunt 1992
[5] John Hertz, Anders Krogh and Richard G. Palmer, "Introduction to the Theory of Neural Computation,"
[6] Thomas Miller, Richard S. Sutton and Paul J. Werbos, "Neural Networks for Control"

A Connectionist Technique for Accelerated Textual Input: Letting a Network Do the Typing

Dean A. Pomerleau
pomerlea@cs.cmu.edu
School of Computer Science
Carnegie Mellon University
Pittsburgh, PA 15213

Abstract

Each year people spend a huge amount of time typing. The text people type typically contains a tremendous amount of redundancy due to predictable word usage patterns and the text's structure. This paper describes a neural network system call AutoTypist that monitors a person's typing and predicts what will be entered next. AutoTypist displays the most likely subsequent word to the typist, who can accept it with a single keystroke, instead of typing it in its entirety. The multi-layer perceptron at the heart of AutoTypist adapts its predictions of likely subsequent text to the user's word usage pattern, and to the characteristics of the text currently being typed. Increases in typing speed of 2-3% when typing English prose and 10-20% when typing C code have been demonstrated using the system, suggesting a potential time savings of more than 20 hours per user per year. In addition to increasing typing speed, AutoTypist reduces the number of keystrokes a user must type by a similar amount (2-3% for English, 10-20% for computer programs). This keystroke savings has the potential to significantly reduce the frequency and severity of repeated stress injuries caused by typing, which are the most common injury suffered in today's office environment.

1 Introduction

People in general, and computer professionals in particular, spend a huge amount of time typing. Most of this typing is done sitting in front of a computer display using a keyboard as the primary input device. There are a number of efforts using artificial neural networks and other techniques to improve the comfort and efficiency of human-computer communication using alternative modalities. Speech recognition [Waibel et al., 1988], handwritten character recognition [LeCun et al., 1989], and even gaze tracking [Baluja & Pomerleau, 1993] have the potential to facilitate this communication. But these technologies are still in their infancy, and at this point cannot approach the speed and accuracy of even a moderately skilled typist for textual input.

Is there some way to improve the efficiency of standard keyboard-based human-computer communication? The answer is yes, there are several ways to make typing more efficient. The first, called the Dvorak keyboard, has been around for over 60 years. The Dvorak keyboard has a different arrangement of keys, in which the most common letters, E, T, S, etc., are on the home row right under the typist's fingers. This improved layout requires the typist's fingers to travel 1/16th as far, resulting in an average of 20% increase in typing speed. Unfortunately, the de facto standard in keyboards is the inefficient QWERTY configuration, and people are reluctant to learn a new layout.

This paper describes another approach to improving typing efficiency, which can be used with either the QWERTY or DVORAK keyboards. It takes advantage of the hundreds of thousands of computer cycles between the typist's keystrokes which are typically wasted while the computer idly waits for additional input. By spending those cycles trying to predict what the user will type next, and allowing the typist to accept the prediction with a single keystroke, substantial time and effort can be saved over typing the entire text manually.

There are actually several such systems available today, including a package called "Autocompletion" developed for gnu-emacs by the author, and an application called "Magic Typist" developed for the Apple Macintosh by Olduvai Software. Each of these maintains a database of previously typed words, and suggests completions for the word the user is currently in the middle of typing, which can be accepted with a single keystroke. While reasonable useful, both have substantial drawbacks. These systems use a very naive technique for calculating the best completion, simply the one that was typed most recently. In fact, experiments conducted for this paper indicated that this "most recently used" heuristic is correct only about 40% of the time. In addition, these two systems are annoyingly verbose, always suggesting a completion if a word has been typed previously which matches the prefix typed so far. They interrupt the user's typing to suggest a completion even if the word they suggest hasn't been typed in many days, and there are many other alternative completions for the prefix, making it unlikely that the suggestion will be correct. These drawbacks are so severe that these systems frequently decrease the user's typing speed, rather than increase it.

The AutoTypist system described in this paper employs an artificial neural network during the spare cycles between keystrokes to make more intelligent decisions about which completions to display, and when to display them.

2 The Prediction Task

To operationalize the goal of making more intelligent decisions about which completions to display, we have defined the neural networks task to be the following: Given a list of candidate completions for the word currently being typed, estimate the likelihood that the user is actually typing each of them. For example, if the user has already types the prefix "aut", the word he is trying to typing could any one of a large number of possibilities, including "autonomous", "automatic", "automobile" etc. Given a list of these possibilities taken from a dictionary, the neural network's task is to estimate the probability that each of these is the word the user will type.

A neural network cannot be expected to accurately estimate the probability for a particular completion based on a unique representation for each word, since there are so many words

ATTRIBUTE	DESCRIPTION
absolute age	time since word was last typed
relative age	ratio of the words age to age of the most recently typed alternative
absolute frequency	number of times word has been typed in the past
relative frequency	ratio of the words frequency to that of the most often typed alternative
typed previous	1 if user has typed word previously, 0 otherwise
total length	the word's length, in characters
remaining length	the number of characters left after the prefix to be typed for this word
special character match	the percentage of "special characters" (i.e. not a-z) in this word relative to the percentage of special characters typed recently
capitalization match	1 if the capitalization of the prefix the user has already typed matches the word's usual capitalization, 0 otherwise.

Table 1: Word attributes used as input to the neural network for predicting word probabilities.

in the English language, and there is only very sparse data available to characterize an individual's usage pattern for any single word. Instead, we have chosen to use an input representation that contains only those characteristics of a word that could conceivably have an impact on its probability of being typed. The attributes we employed to characterize each completion are listed in Table 1.

These are not the only possible attributes that could be used to estimate the probability of the user typing a particular word. An additional characteristic that could be helpful is the word's part of speech (i.e. noun, verb, adjective, etc.). However this attribute is not typically available or even meaningful in many typing situations, for instance when typing computer programs. Also, to effectively exploit information regarding a word's part of speech would require the network to have knowledge about the context of the current text. In effect, it would require at least an approximate parse tree of the current sentence. While there are techniques, including connectionist methods [Jain, 1991], for generating parse trees, they are prone to errors and computationally expensive. Since word probability predictions in our system must occur many times between each key the user types, we have chosen to utilize only the easy to compute attributes shown in Table 1 to characterize each completion.

3 Network Processing

The network architecture employed for this system is a feedforward multi-layer perceptron. Each of the networks investigated has nine input units, one for each of the attributes listed in Table 1, and a single output unit. As the user is typing a word, the prefix he has typed so far is used to find candidate completions from a dictionary, which contains 20,000 English words plus all words the user has typed previously. For each of these candidate completions, the nine attributes in Table 1 are calculated, and scaled to the range of 0.0 to 1.0. These values become the activations of the nine units in the input layer. Activation is propagated through the network to produce an activation for the single output unit, representing the probability that this particular candidate completion is the one the user is actually typing. These candidate probabilities are then used to determine which (if any) of the candidates should be displayed to the typist, using a technique described in a later section.

To train the network, the user's typing is again monitored. After the user finishes typing a word, for each prefix of the word a list of candidate completions, and their corresponding attributes, is calculated. These form the input training patterns. The target activation for the single output unit on a pattern is set to 1.0 if the candidate completion represented by that pattern is the word the user was actually typing, and 0.0 if the candidate is incorrect. Note that the target output activation is binary. As will be seen below, the actual output the network learns to produce is an accurate estimate of the completion's probability. Currently, training of the network is conducted off-line, using a fixed training set collected while a user types normally. Training is performed using the standard backpropagation learning algorithm.

4 Experiments

Several tests were conducted to determine the ability of multi-layer perceptrons to perform the mapping from completion attributes to completion probability. In each of the tests, networks were trained on a set of input/output exemplars collected over one week of a single subject's typing. During the training data collection phase, the subject's primary text editing activities involved writing technical papers and composing email, so the training patterns represent the word choice and frequency distributions associated with these activities. This training set contained of 14,302 patterns of the form described above.

The first experiment was designed to determine the most appropriate network architecture for the prediction task. Four architecture were trained on a 10,000 pattern subset of the training data, and the remaining 4,302 patterns were used for cross validation. The first of the four architectures was a perceptron, with the input units connected directly to the single output unit. The remaining three architectures had a single hidden layer, with three, six or twelve hidden units. The networks with hidden units were fully connected without skip connections from inputs to output. Networks of three and six hidden units which included skip connections were tested, but did not exhibit improved performance over the networks without skip connections, so they are not reported.

Each of the network architectures were trained four times, with different initial random weights. The results reported are those produced by the best set of weights from these trials. Note that the variations between trials with a single architecture were small relative to the variations between architectures. The trained networks were tested on a disjoint set of 10,040 collected while the same subject was typing another technical paper.

Three different performance metrics were employed to evaluate the performance of these architectures on the test set. The first was the standard mean squared error (MSE) metric, depicted in Figure 1. The MSE results indicate that the architectures with six and twelve hidden units were better able to learn the task than either the perceptron, or the network with only three hidden units. However the difference appears to be relatively small, on the order of about 10%.

MSE is not a very informative error metric, since the target output is binary (1 if the completion is the one the user was typing, 0 otherwise), but the real goal is to predict the probability that the completion is correct. A more useful measure of performance is shown in Figure 2. For each of the four architectures, it depicts the predicted probability that a completion is correct, as measured by the network's output activation value, vs. the

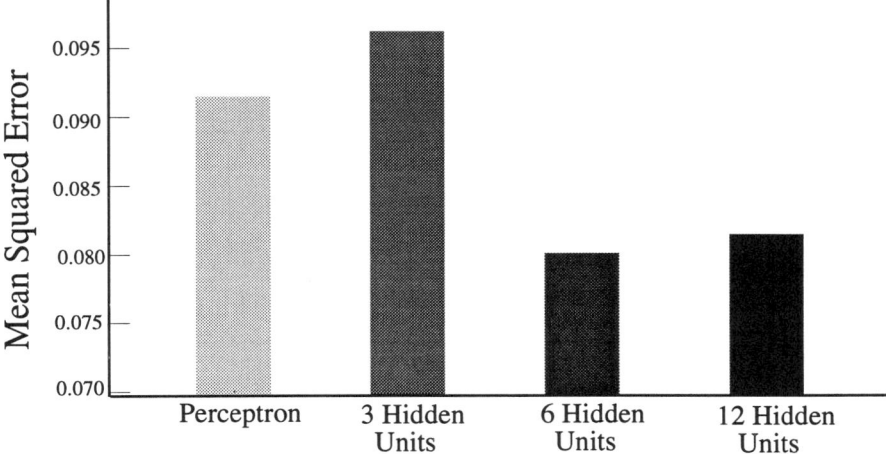

Figure 1: Mean squared error for four networks on the task of predicting completion probability.

actual probability that a completion is correct. The lines for each of the four networks were generated in the following manner. The network's output response on each of the 10,040 test patterns was used to group the test patterns into 10 categories. All the patterns which represented completions that the network predicted to have a probability of between 0 and 10% of being correct (output activations of 0.0-0.1) were placed in one category. Completions that the network predicted to have a 10-20% change of being right were placed in the second category, etc. For each of these 10 categories, the actual likelihood that a completion classified within the category is correct was calculated by determining the percent of the completions within that category that were actually correct.

As a concrete example, the network with 6 hidden units produced an output activation between 0.2 and 0.3 on 861 of the 10,040 test patterns, indicating that on these patterns it considered there to be a 20-30% chance that the completion each pattern represented was the word the user was typing. On 209 of these 861 patterns in this category, the completion was actually the one the user was typing, for a probability of 24.2%. Ideally, the actual probability should be 25%, half way between the minimum and maximum predicted probability thresholds for this category. This ideal classification performance is depicted as the solid 45° line labeled "Target" in Figure 2. The closer the line for a given network matches this 45° line, the more the network's predicted probability matches the actual probability for a completion. Again, the networks with six and twelve hidden units outperformed the networks with zero and three hidden units, as illustrated by their much smaller deviations from the 45° line in Figure 2.

The output activations produced by the networks with six and twelve hidden units reflect the actual probability that the completion is correct quite accurately. However prediction accuracy is only half of what is required to perform the final system goal, which recall was to identify as many high probability completions as possible, so they can be suggested to the user without requiring him to manually type them. If overall accuracy of the probability predictions were the only requirement, a network could score quite highly by classifying

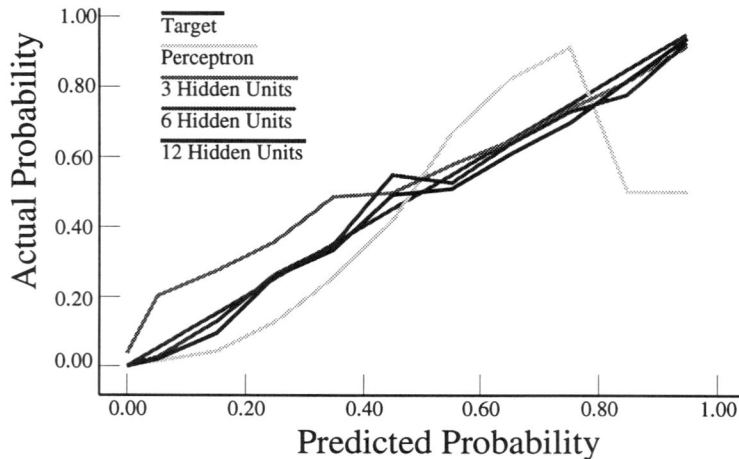

Figure 2: Predicted vs. actual probability of a completion being correct for the four architectures tested.

every pattern into the 10-20% category, since about 15% of the 10,040 completions in the test set represent the word the user was typing at the time. But a constant prediction of 10-20% probability on every alternative completion would not allow the system to identify and suggest to the user those individual completions that are much more likely than the other alternatives.

To achieve the overall system goal, the network must be able to accurately identify as many high probability completions as possible. The ability of each of the four networks to achieve this goal is shown in Figure 3. This figures shows the percent of the 10,040 test patterns each of the four networks classified as having more than a 60% probability of being correct. The 60% probability threshold was selected because it represents a level of support for a single completion that is significantly higher than the support for all the others. As can be seen in Figure 3, the networks with hidden units again significantly outperformed the perceptron, which was able to correctly identify fewer than half as many completions as highly likely.

5 AutoTypist System Architecture and Performance

The networks with six and twelve hidden units are able to accurately identify individual completions that have a high probability of being the word the user is typing. In order to exploit this prediction ability and speed up typing, we have build an X-window based application called AutoTypist around the smaller of the two networks. The application serves as the front end for the network, monitoring the user's typing and identifying likely completions for the current word between each keystroke. If the network at the core of AutoTypist identifies a single completion that it is both significantly more probably than all the rest, and also longer than a couple characters, it will momentarily display the completion after the current cursor location in whatever application the user is currently typing[1]. If the displayed completion is the word the user is typing, he can accept it with a single keystroke

---

[1] The criterion for displaying a completion, and the human interface for AutoTypist, are somewhat more sophisticated than this description. However for the purposes of this paper, a high level description is sufficient.

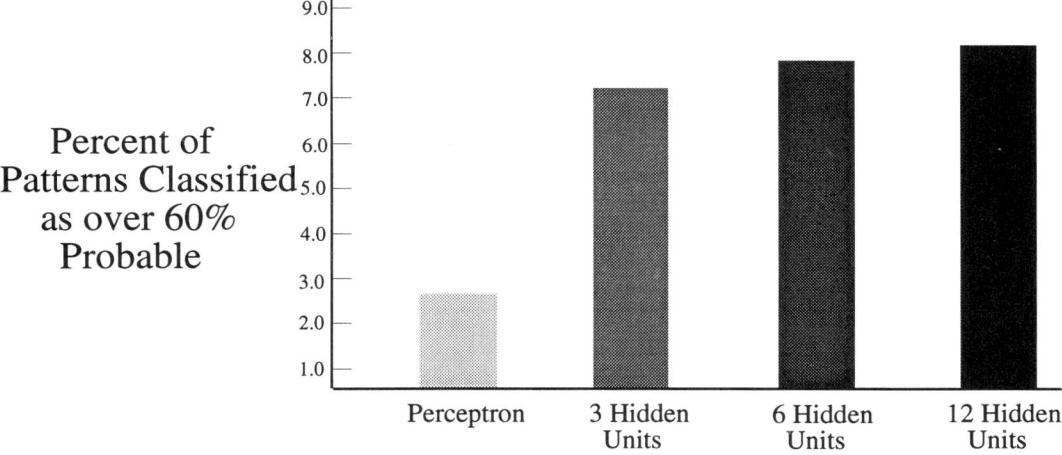

Figure 3: Percent of candidate completions classified as having more than a 60% chance of being correct for the four architectures tested.

and move on to typing the next word. If the displayed completion is incorrect, he can continue typing and the completion will disappear.

Quantitative results with the fully integrated AutoTypist system, while still preliminary, are very encouraging. In a two week trial with two subjects, who could type at 40 and 60 wpm without AutoTypists, their typings speeds were improved by 2.37% and 2.21% respectively when typing English text. Accuracy improvements during these trials were even larger, since spelling mistakes become rare when AutoTypist is doing a significant part of the typing automatically. When writing computer programs, speed improvements of 12.93% and 18.47% were achieved by the two test subjects. This larger speedup was due to the frequent repetition of variable and function names in computer programs, which AutoTypist was able to expedite. Not only is computer code faster to produce with AutoTypist, it is also easier to understand. AutoTypist encourages the programmer to use long, descriptive variable and function names, by making him type them in their entirety only once. On subsequent instances of the same name, the user need only type the first few characters and then exploit AutoTypist's completion mechanism to type the rest. These speed improvements were achieved by subjects who are already relatively proficient typists. Larger gains can be expected for less skilled typists, since typing an entire word with a single keystroke will save more time when each keystroke takes longer.

Perhaps an even more significant benefit results from the reduced number of keystrokes AutoTypist requires the user to type. During the test trials described above, the two test subjects had to strike an average of 2.89% fewer keys on the English text, and 16.42% fewer keys on the computer code than would have been required to type the text out in its entirety. Clearly this keystroke savings has the potential to benefit typists who suffer from repeated stress injuries brought on by typing.

Unfortunately it is impossible to quantitatively compare these results with those of the other completion-based typing aids described in the introduction, since the other systems have not been quantitatively evaluated. Subjectively, AutoTypist is far less disturbing than the alternatives, since it only displays a completion when there is a very good chance it is the correct one.

6 Future Work

Further experiments are required to verify the typing speed improvements possible with AutoTypist, and to compare it with alternative typing improvement systems. Preliminary experiments suggest a network trained on the word usage patterns of one user can generalize to that of other users, but it may be necessary to train a new network for each individual typist. Also, the experiments conducted for this paper indicate that a network trained on one type of text, English prose, can generalize to text with quite different word frequency patterns, C language computer programs. However substantial prediction improvements, and therefore typing speedup, may be possible by training separate networks for different types of text. The question of how to rapidly adapt a single network, or perhaps a mixture of expert networks, to new text types is one which should be investigated.

Even without these extensions, AutoTypist has the potential to greatly improve the comfort and efficiency of the typing tasks. For people who type English text two hours per workday, even the conservative estimate of a 2% speedup translates into 10 hours of savings per year. The potential time savings for computer programming is even more dramatic. A programmer who types code two hours per workday could potentially save between 52 and 104 hours in a single year by using AutoTypist. With such large potential benefits, commercial development of the AutoTypist system is also being investigated.

Acknowledgements

I would like to thank David Simon and Martial Hebert for their helpful suggestions, and for acting as willing test subjects during the development of this system.

References

[Baluja & Pomerleau, 1993] Baluja, S. and Pomerleau, D.A. (1993) Non-Intrusive Gaze Tracking Using Artificial Neural Networks. In *Advances in Neural Information Processing Systems 6*, San Mateo, CA: Morgan Kaufmann Publishers.

[Jain, 1991] Jain, A.N. (1991) PARSEC: A connectionist learning architecture for parsing spoken language. Carnegie Mellon University School of Computer Science Technical Report CMU-CS-91-208.

[LeCun et al., 1989] LeCun, Y., Boser, B., Denker, J.S., Henderson, D., Howard, R.E., Hubbard, W., and Jackel, L.D. (1989) Backpropagation applied to handwritten zip code recognition. *Neural Computation 1(4)*.

[Waibel et al., 1988] Waibel, A., Hanazawa, T., Hinton, G., Shikano, K., Lang, K. (1988) Phoneme recognition: Neural Networks vs. Hidden Markov Models. *Proceedings from Int. Conf. on Acoustics, Speech and Signal Processing,* New York, New York.

PREDICTIVE CODING WITH NEURAL NETS: APPLICATION TO TEXT COMPRESSION

Jürgen Schmidhuber   Stefan Heil

Fakultät für Informatik
Technische Universität München
80290 München, Germany

Abstract

To compress text files, a neural predictor network P is used to approximate the conditional probability distribution of possible "next characters", given n previous characters. P's outputs are fed into standard coding algorithms that generate short codes for characters with high predicted probability and long codes for highly unpredictable characters. Tested on short German newspaper articles, our method outperforms widely used Lempel-Ziv algorithms (used in UNIX functions such as "compress" and "gzip").

1 INTRODUCTION

The method presented in this paper is an instance of a strategy known as "predictive coding" or "model-based coding". To compress text files, a neural predictor network P approximates the conditional probability distribution of possible "next characters", given n previous characters. P's outputs are fed into algorithms that generate short codes for characters with low information content (characters with high predicted probability) and long codes for characters conveying a lot of information (highly unpredictable characters) [5]. Two such standard coding algorithms are employed: Huffman Coding (see e.g. [1]) and Arithmetic Coding (see e.g. [7]).

With the *off-line* variant of the approach, P's training phase is based on a set F of training files. After training, the weights are frozen. Copies of P are installed at all machines functioning as message receivers or senders. From then on, P is used to encode and decode unknown files without being changed any more. The weights become part of the code of the compression algorithm. Note that the storage occupied by the network weights does not have to be taken into account to measure the performance on *unknown* files – just like the code for a conventional data compression algorithm does not have to be taken into account.

The more sophisticated *on-line* variant of our approach will be addressed later.

2 A PREDICTOR OF CONDITIONAL PROBABILITIES

Assume that the alphabet contains k possible characters $z_1, z_2, \ldots, z_k$. The (local) representation of z_i is a binary k-dimensional vector $r(z_i)$ with exactly one non-zero component (at the i-th position). P has nk input units and k output units. n is called the "time-window size". We insert n default characters z_0 at the beginning of each file. The representation of the default character, $r(z_0)$, is the k-dimensional zero-vector. The m-th character of file f (starting from the first default character) is called c_m^f.

For all $f \in F$ and all possible $m > n$, P receives as an input

$$r(c_{m-n}^f) \circ r(c_{m-n+1}^f) \circ \ldots \circ r(c_{m-1}^f), \tag{1}$$

where $\circ$ is the concatenation operator for vectors. P produces as an output P_m^f, a k-dimensional output vector. Using back-propagation [6][2][3][4], P is trained to minimize

$$\frac{1}{2} \sum_{f \in F} \sum_{m > n} \| r(c_m^f) - P_m^f \|^2. \tag{2}$$

Expression (2) is minimal if P_m^f always equals

$$E(r(c_m^f) \mid c_{m-n}^f, \ldots, c_{m-1}^f), \tag{3}$$

the conditional expectation of $r(c_m^f)$, given $r(c_{m-n}^f) \circ r(c_{m-n+1}^f) \circ \ldots \circ r(c_{m-1}^f)$. Due to the local character representation, this is equivalent to $(P_m^f)_i$ being equal to the conditional probability

$$Pr(c_m^f = z_i \mid c_{m-n}^f, \ldots, c_{m-1}^f) \qquad (4)$$

for all f and for all appropriate $m > n$, where $(P_m^f)_j$ denotes the j-th component of the vector P_m^f.

In general, the $(P_m^f)_i$ will not quite match the corresponding conditional probabilities. For normalization purposes, we define

$$P_m^f(i) = \frac{(P_m^f)_i}{\sum_{j=1}^{k}(P_m^f)_j}. \qquad (5)$$

No normalization is used during training, however.

3 HOW TO USE THE PREDICTOR FOR COMPRESSION

We use a standard procedure for predictive coding. With the help of a copy of P, an unknown file f can be compressed as follows: Again, n default characters are inserted at the beginning. For each character c_m^f ($m > n$), the predictor emits its output P_m^f based on the n previous characters. There will be a k such that $c_m^f = z_k$. The estimate of $P(c_m^f = z_k \mid c_{m-n}^f, \ldots, c_{m-1}^f)$ is given by $P_m^f(k)$. The code of c_m^f, $code(c_m^f)$, is generated by feeding $P_m^f(k)$ into the Huffman Coding algorithm (see below), or, alternatively, into the Arithmetic Coding algorithm (see below). $code(c_m^f)$ is written into the compressed file. The basic ideas of both coding algorithms are described next.

3.1 HUFFMAN CODING

With a given probability distribution on a set of possible characters, Huffman Coding (e.g. [1]) encodes characters by bitstrings as follows.

Characters are terminal nodes of a binary tree to be built in an incremental fashion. The probability of a terminal node is defined as the probability of the corresponding character. The probability of a non-terminal node is defined as the sum of the probabilities of its sons. Starting from the terminal nodes, a binary tree is built as follows:

> **Repeat as long as possible:**
> *Among those nodes that are not children of any non-terminal nodes created earlier, pick two with lowest associated probabilities. Make them the two sons of a newly generated non-terminal node.*

The branch to the "left" son of each non-terminal node is labeled by a 0. The branch to its "right" son is labeled by a 1. The code of a character c, $code(c)$, is the bitstring obtained by following the path from the root to the corresponding node. Obviously, if $c \neq d$, then $code(c)$ cannot be the prefix of $code(d)$. This makes the code uniquely decipherable.

Characters with high associated probability are encoded by short bitstrings. Characters with low associated probability are encoded by long bitstrings. Huffman Coding guarantees minimal expected code length, provided all character probabilities are integer powers of $\frac{1}{2}$.

3.2 ARITHMETIC CODING

In general, Arithmetic Coding works slightly better than Huffman Coding. For sufficiently long messages, Arithmetic Coding achieves expected code lenghts arbitrarily close to the information-theoretic lower bound. This is true even if the character probabilities are not powers of $\frac{1}{2}$ (see e.g. [7]).

The basic idea of Arithmetic Coding is: a message is encoded by an interval of real numbers from the unit interval $[0, 1[$. The output of Arithmetic Coding is a binary representation of the boundaries of the corresponding interval. This binary representation is incrementally generated during message processing. Starting with the unit interval, for each observed character the interval is made smaller, essentially in proportion to the probability of the character. A message with low information content (and high corresponding probability) is encoded by a comparatively large interval whose precise boundaries can be specified with comparatively few bits. A message with a lot of information content (and low corresponding probability) is encoded by a comparatively small interval whose boundaries require comparatively many bits to be specified.

Although the basic idea is elegant and simple, additional technical considerations are necessary to make Arithmetic Coding practicable. See [7] for details.

Neither Huffman Coding nor Arithmetic Coding requires that the probability distribution on the characters remains fixed. This allows for using "time-varying" conditional probability distributions as generated by the neural predictor.

3.3 HOW TO "UNCOMPRESS" DATA

The information in the compressed file is sufficient to reconstruct the original file without loss of information. This is done with the "uncompress" algorithm, which works as follows: Again, for each character c_m^f ($m > n$), the predictor (sequentially) emits its output P_m^f based on the n previous characters, where the c_l^f with $n < l < m$ were gained sequentially by feeding the approximations $P_l^f(k)$ of the probabilities $P(c_l^f = z_k \mid c_{l-n}^f, \ldots, c_{l-1}^f)$ into the inverse Huffman Coding procedure (see e.g. [1]), or, alternatively (depending on which coding procedure was used), into the inverse Arithmetic Coding procedure (e.g. [7]). Both variants allow for correct decoding of c_l^f from $code(c_l^f)$. With both variants, to correctly decode some character, we first need to decode all previous characters. Both variants are **guaranteed** to restore the original file from the compressed file.

WHY NOT USE A LOOK-UP TABLE INSTEAD OF A NETWORK?

Because a look-up table would be extremely inefficient. A look-up table requires k^{n+1} entries for all the conditional probabilities corresponding to all possible combinations of n previous characters and possible next characters. In addition, a special procedure is required for dealing with previously unseen combinations of input characters. In contrast, the size of a neural net typically grows in proportion to n^2 (assuming the number of hidden units grows in proportion to the number of input units), and its inherent "generalization capability" is going to take care of previously unseen combinations of input characters (hopefully by coming up with good predicted probabilities).

4 SIMULATIONS

We implemented both alternative variants of the encoding and decoding procedure described above.

Our current computing environment prohibits extensive experimental evaluations of the method. The predictor updates turn out to be quite time consuming, which makes special neural net hardware recommendable. The limited software simulations presented in this section, however, will show that the "neural" compression technique can achieve "excellent" compression ratios. Here the term "excellent" is defined by a statement from [1]:

> "In general, good algorithms can be expected to achieve an average compression ratio of 1.5, while excellent algorithms based upon sophisticated processing techniques will achieve an average compression ratio exceeding 2.0."

Here the average compression ratio is the average ratio between the lengths of original and compressed files.

The method was applied to German newspaper articles. The results were compared to those obtained with standard encoding techniques provided by the operating system UNIX, namely "pack", "compress", and "gzip". The corresponding decoding algorithms are "unpack", "uncompress", and "gunzip", respectively. "pack" is based on Huffman-Coding (e.g. [1]), while "compress" and "gzip" are based on techniques developed by Lempel and Ziv (e.g. [9]). As the file size goes to infinity, Lempel-Ziv becomes *asymptotically optimal* in a certain information theoretic sense [8]. This does not necessarily mean, however, that Lempel-Ziv is optimal for finite file sizes.

The training set for the predictor was given by a set of 40 articles from the newspaper *Münchner Merkur*, each containing between 10000 and 20000 characters. The alphabet consisted of $k = 80$ possible characters, including upper case and lower case letters, digits, interpunction symbols, and special German letters like "ö", "ü", "ä". P had 430 hidden units. A "true" unit with constant activation 1.0 was connected to all hidden and output units. The learning rate was 0.2. The training phase consisted of 25 sweeps through the training set.

The test set consisted of newspaper articles excluded from the training set, each containing between 10000 and 20000 characters. Table 1 lists the average compression ratios. The "neural" method outperformed the strongest conventional competitor, the UNIX "gzip" function based on a Lempel-Ziv algorithm.

Method	Compression Ratio
Huffman Coding (UNIX: pack)	1.74
Lempel-Ziv Coding (UNIX: compress)	1.99
Improved Lempel-Ziv (UNIX: gzip -9)	2.29
Neural predictor + Huffman Coding, $n = 5$	2.70
Neural predictor + Arithmetic Coding, $n = 5$	2.72

Table 1: *Compression ratios of various compression algorithms for short German text files (< 20000 Bytes) from the unknown test set.*

Method	Compression Ratio
Huffman Coding (UNIX: pack)	1.67
Lempel-Ziv Coding (UNIX: compress)	1.71
Improved Lempel-Ziv (UNIX: gzip -9)	2.03
Neural predictor + Huffman Coding, $n = 5$	2.25
Neural predictor + Arithmetic Coding, $n = 5$	2.20

Table 2: *Compression ratios for articles from a different newspaper. The neural predictor was* not *retrained.*

How does a neural net trained on articles from *Münchner Merkur* perform on articles from other sources? *Without retraining the neural predictor*, we applied all competing methods to 10 articles from another German newspaper (the *Frankenpost*). The results are given in table 2.

The *Frankenpost* articles were harder to compress for all algorithms. But relative performance remained comparable.

Note that the time-window was quite small ($n = 5$). In general, larger time windows will make more information available to the predictor. In turn, this will improve the prediction quality and increase the compression ratio. Therefore we expect to obtain even better results for $n > 5$ and for recurrent predictor networks.

5 DISCUSSION / OUTLOOK

Our results show that neural networks are promising tools for loss-free data compression. It was demonstrated that even *off-line* methods based on small time windows can lead to excellent compression ratios – at least with small text files, they can outperform conventional standard algorithms. We have hardly begun, however, to exhaust the potential of the basic approach.

5.1 ON-LINE METHODS

A disadvantage of the off-line technique above is that it is off-line: The predictor does not adapt to the specific text file it sees. This limitation is not essential, however. It is straight-forward to construct an *on-line* variant of the approach.

With the on-line variant, the predictor continues to learn *during* compression. The on-line variant proceeds like this: Both the sender and the receiver start with *exactly the same* initial predictor. Whenever the sender sees a new character, it encodes it using its current predictor. The code is sent to the receiver who decodes it. Both the sender and the receiver use *exactly the same* learning protocol to modify their weights. *This implies that the modified weights need **not** be sent from the sender to the receiver and do not have to be taken into account to compute the average compression ratio.* Of course, the on-line method promises much higher compression ratios than the off-line method.

5.2 LIMITATIONS

The main disadvantage of both on-line and off-line variants is their computational complexity. The current off-line implementation is clearly slower than conventional standard techniques, by about three orders of magnitude (but no attempt was made to optimize the code with respect to speed). And the complexity of the on-line method is even worse (the exact slow-down factor depends on the precise nature of the learning protocol, of course). For this reason, especially the promising on-line variants can be recommended only if special neural net hardware is available. Note, however, that there are *many* commercial data compression applications which rely on specialized electronic chips.

5.3 ONGOING RESEARCH

There are a few obvious directions for *ongoing experimental research:* (1) Use larger time windows – they seem to be promising even for off-line methods (see the last paragraph of section 4). (2) Thoroughly test the potential of on-line methods. Both (1) and (2) should greatly benefit from fast hardware. (3) Compare performance of predictive coding based on neural predictors to the performance of predictive coding based on different kinds of predictors.

6 ACKNOWLEDGEMENTS

Thanks to David MacKay for directing our attention towards Arithmetic Coding. Thanks to Margit Kinder, Martin Eldracher, and Gerhard Weiss for useful comments.

References

[1] G. Held. *Data Compression*. Wiley and Sons LTD, New York, 1991.

[2] Y. LeCun. Une procédure d'apprentissage pour réseau à seuil asymétrique. *Proceedings of Cognitiva 85, Paris*, pages 599–604, 1985.

[3] D. B. Parker. Learning-logic. Technical Report TR-47, Center for Comp. Research in Economics and Management Sci., MIT, 1985.

[4] D. E. Rumelhart, G. E. Hinton, and R. J. Williams. Learning internal representations by error propagation. In *Parallel Distributed Processing*, volume 1, pages 318–362. MIT Press, 1986.

[5] J. H. Schmidhuber and S. Heil. Sequential neural text compression. *IEEE Transactions on Neural Networks*, 1994. Accepted for publication.

[6] P. J. Werbos. *Beyond Regression: New Tools for Prediction and Analysis in the Behavioral Sciences*. PhD thesis, Harvard University, 1974.

[7] I. H. Witten, R. M. Neal, and J. G. Cleary. Arithmetic coding for data compression. *Communications of the ACM*, 30(6):520–540, 1987.

[8] A. Wyner and J. Ziv. Fixed data base version of the Lempel-Ziv data compression algorithm. *IEEE Transactions Information Theory*, 37:878–880, 1991.

[9] J. Ziv and A. Lempel. A universal algorithm for sequential data compression. *IEEE Transactions on Information Theory*, IT-23(5):337–343, 1977.

Predicting the Risk of Complications in Coronary Artery Bypass Operations using Neural Networks

Richard P. Lippmann, Linda Kukolich
MIT Lincoln Laboratory
244 Wood Street
Lexington, MA 02173-0073

Dr. David Shahian
Lahey Clinic
Burlington, MA 01805

Abstract

Experiments demonstrated that sigmoid multilayer perceptron (MLP) networks provide slightly better risk prediction than conventional logistic regression when used to predict the risk of death, stroke, and renal failure on 1257 patients who underwent coronary artery bypass operations at the Lahey Clinic. MLP networks with no hidden layer and networks with one hidden layer were trained using stochastic gradient descent with early stopping. MLP networks and logistic regression used the same input features and were evaluated using bootstrap sampling with 50 replications. ROC areas for predicting mortality using preoperative input features were 70.5% for logistic regression and 76.0% for MLP networks. Regularization provided by early stopping was an important component of improved performance. A simplified approach to generating confidence intervals for MLP risk predictions using an auxiliary "confidence MLP" was developed. The confidence MLP is trained to reproduce confidence intervals that were generated during training using the outputs of 50 MLP networks trained with different bootstrap samples.

1 INTRODUCTION

In 1992 there were roughly 300,000 coronary artery bypass operations performed in the United States at a cost of roughly $44,000 per operation. The $13.2 billion total cost of these operations is a significant fraction of health care spending in the United States. This has led to recent interest in comparing the quality of cardiac surgery across hospitals using risk-adjusted procedures and large patient populations. It has also led to interest in better assessing risks for individual patients and in obtaining improved understanding of the patient and procedural characteristics that affect cardiac surgery outcomes.

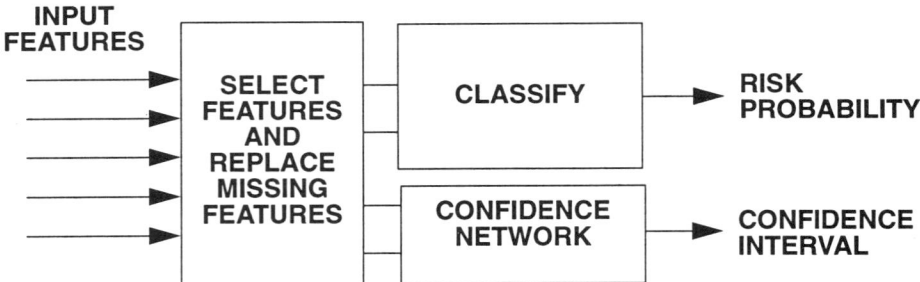

Figure 1. Block diagram of a medical risk predictor.

This paper describes a experiments that explore the use of neural networks to predict the risk of complications in coronary artery bypass graft (CABG) surgery. Previous approaches to risk prediction for bypass surgery used linear or logistic regression or a Bayesian approach which assumes input features used for risk prediction are independent (e.g. Edwards, 1994; Marshall, 1994; Higgins, 1992; O'Conner, 1992). Neural networks have the potential advantages of modeling complex interactions among input features, of allowing both categorical and continuous input features, and of allowing more flexibility in fitting the expected risk than a simple linear or logistic function.

2 RISK PREDICTION AND FEATURE SELECTION

A block diagram of the medical risk prediction system used in these experiments is shown in Figure 1. Input features from a patient's medical record are provided as 105 raw inputs, a smaller subset of these features is selected, missing features in this subset are replaced with their most likely values from training data, and a reduced input feature vector is fed to a classifier and to a "confidence network". The classifier provides outputs that estimate the probability or risk of one type of complication. The confidence network provides upper and lower bounds on these risk estimates. Both logistic regression and multilayer sigmoid neural network (MLP) classifiers were evaluated in this study. Logistic regression is the most common approach to risk prediction. It is structurally equivalent to a feed-forward network with linear inputs and one output unit with a sigmoidal nonlinearity. Weights and offsets are estimated using a maximum likelihood criterion and iterative "batch" training. The reference logistic regression classifier used in these experiments was implemented with the S-Plus glm function (Mathsoft, 1993) which uses iteratively reweighted least squares for training and no extra regularization such as weight decay. Multilayer feed-forward neural networks with no hidden nodes (denoted single-layer MLPs) and with one hidden layer and from 1 to 10 hidden nodes were also evaluated as implemented using LNKnet pattern classification software (Lippmann, 1993). An MLP committee classifier containing eight members trained using different initial random weights was also evaluated.

All classifiers were evaluated using a data base of 1257 patients who underwent coronary artery bypass surgery from 1990 to 1994. Classifiers were used to predict mortality, post-operative strokes, and renal failure. Predictions were made after a patient's medical history was obtained (History), after pre-surgical tests had been performed (Post-test), immediately before the operation (Preop), and immediately after the operation (Postop). Bootstrap sampling (Efron, 1993) was used to assess risk prediction accuracy because there were so few patients with complications in this data base. The number of patients with complications was 33 or 2.6% for mortality, 25 or 2.0% for stroke, and 21 or 1.7% for renal failure. All experiments were performed using 50 bootstrap training sets where a risk prediction technique is trained with a bootstrap training set and evaluated using left-out patterns.

	$\dfrac{NComplications}{NHigh}$	% True Hits
HISTORY		
Age	27/674	4.0%
COPD (Chronic Obs. Pul. Disease)	7/126	5.6%
POST-TEST		
Pulmonary Ventricular Congestion	8/71	11.3%
X-ray Cardiomegaly	6/105	5.7%
X-ray Pulmonary Edema	6/21	26.6%
PREOP		
NTG (Nitroglycerin)	21/447	4.7%
IABP (Intraaortic Balloon Pump)	11/115	6.6%
Urgency Status	10/127	7.9%
MI When	7/64	10.9%
POSTOP		
Blood Used (Packed Cells)	12/113	10.6%
Perfusion Time	9/184	4.9%

Figure 2. Features selected to predict mortality.

The initial set of 105 raw input features included binary (e.g. Male/Female), categorical (e.g. MI When: none, old, recent, evolving), and continuous valued features (e.g. Perfusion Time, Age). There were many missing and irrelevant features and all features were only weakly predictive. Small sets of features were selected for each complication using the following procedures: (1) Select those 10 to 40 features experience and previous studies indicate are related to each complication, (2) Omit features if a univariate contingency table analysis shows the feature is not important, (3) Omit features that are missing for more than 5% of patients, (4) Order features by number of true positives, (5) Omit features that are similar to other features keeping the most predictive, and (7) Add features incrementally as a patient's hospital interaction progresses. This resulted in sets of from 3 to 11 features for the three complications. Figure 2 shows the 11 features selected to predict mortality. The first column lists the features, the second column presents a fraction equal to the number of complications when the feature was "high" divided by the number of times this feature was "high" (A threshold was assigned for continuous and categorical features that provided good separation), and the last column is the second column expressed as a percentage. Classifiers were provided identical sets of input features for all experiments. Continuous inputs to all classifiers were normalized to have zero mean and unit variance, categorical inputs ranged from $-(D-1)/2$ to $(D-1)/2$ in steps of 1.0, where D is the number of categories, and binary inputs were -0.5 or 0.5.

3 PERFORMANCE COMPARISONS

Risk prediction was evaluated by plotting and computing the area under receiver operating characteristic (ROC) curves and also by using chi-square tests to determine how accurately classifiers could stratify subjects into three risk categories. Automated experiments were performed using bootstrap sampling to explore the effect of varying the training step size

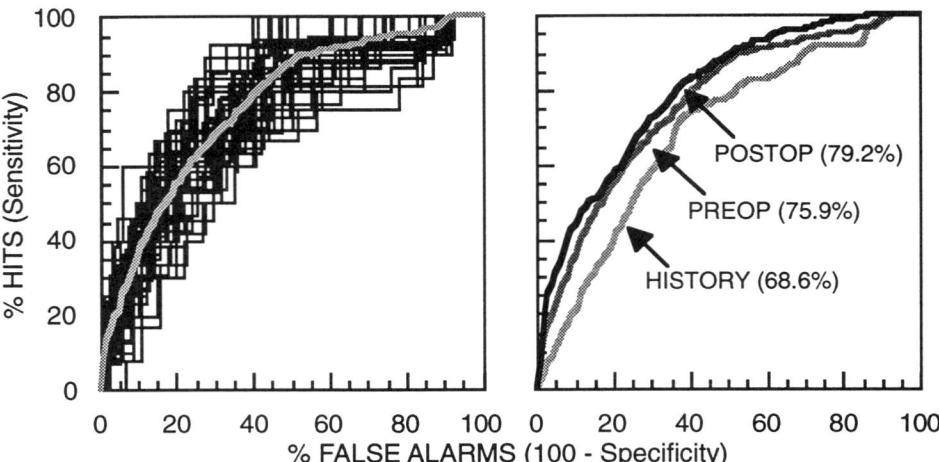

Figure 3. Fifty preoperative bootstrap ROCs predicting mortality using an MLP classifier with two hidden nodes and the average ROC (left), and average ROCS for mortality using history, preoperative, and postoperative features (right).

from 0.005 to 0.1; of using squared-error, cross-entropy, and maximum likelihood cost functions; of varying the number of hidden nodes from 1 to 8; and of stopping training after from 5 to 40 epochs. ROC areas varied little as parameters were varied. Risk stratification, which measures how well classifier outputs approximate posterior probabilities, improved substantially with a cross-entropy cost function (instead of squared error), with a smaller stepsize (0.01 instead of 0.05 or 0.1) and with more training epochs (20 versus 5 or 10). An MLP classifier with two hidden nodes provided good overall performance across complications and patient stages with a cross-entropy cost function, a stepsize of 0.01, momentum of 0.6, and stochastic gradient descent stopping after 20 epochs. A single-layer MLP provided good performance with similar settings, but stopping after 5 epochs. These settings were used for all experiments. The left side of Figure 3 shows the 50 bootstrap ROCs created using these settings for a two-hidden-node MLP when predicting mortality with preoperative features and the ROC created by averaging these curves. There is a large variability in these ROCs due to the small amount of training data. The ROC area varies from 67% to 85% ($\sigma=4.7$) and the sensitivity with 20% false alarms varies from 30% to 79%. Similar variability occurs for other complications. The right side of Figure 3 shows average ROCs for mortality created using this MLP with history, preoperative, and postoperative features. As can be seen, the ROC area and prediction accuracy increases from 68.6% to 79.2% as more input features become available.

Figure 4 shows ROC areas across all complications and patient stages. Only three and two patient stages are shown for stroke and renal failure because no extra features were added at the missing stages for these complications. ROC areas are low for all complications and range from 62% to 80%. ROC areas are highest using postoperative features, lowest using only history features, and increase as more features are added. ROC areas are highest for mortality (68 to 80%) and lower for stroke (62 to 71%) and renal failure (62 to 67%).The MLP classifier with two hidden nodes (MLP) always provided slightly higher ROC areas than logistic regression. The average increase with the MLP classifier was 2.7 percentage

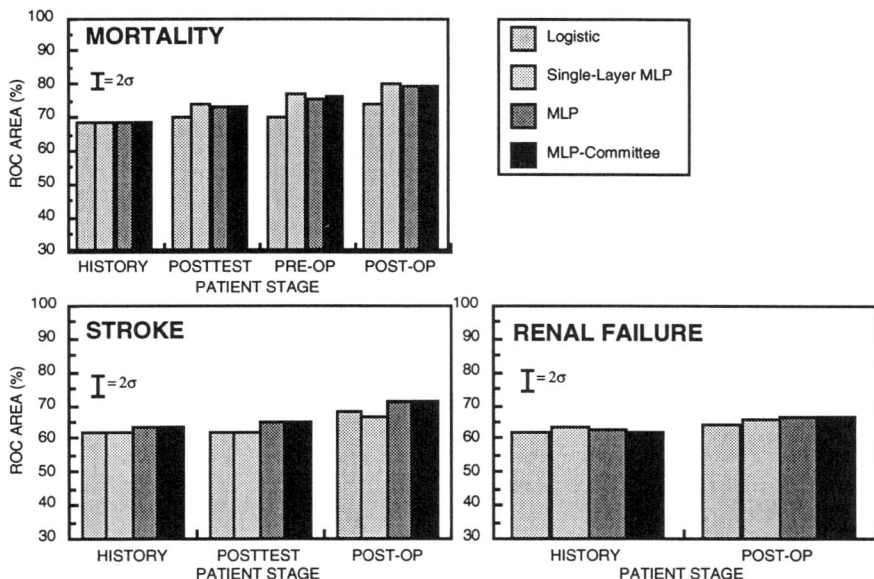

Figure 4. ROC areas across all complications and patient stages for logistic regression, single-layer MLP classifier, two-layer MLP classifier with two hidden nodes, and a committee classifier containing eight two-layer MLP classifiers trained using different random starting weights.

points (the increase ranged from 0.3 to 5.5 points). The single-layer MLP classifier also provided good performance. The average ROC area with the single-layer MLP was only 0.6 percentage points below that of the MLP with two hidden nodes. The committee using eight two-layer MLP classifiers performed no better than an individual two-layer MLP classifier.

Classifier outputs were used to bin or stratify each patient into one of four risk levels (0-5%, 5-10%, and 10-100%) by treating the output as an estimate of the complication posterior probability. Figure 5 shows the accuracy of risk stratification for the MLP classifier for all complications. Each curve was obtained by averaging 50 individual curves obtained using bootstrap sampling as with the ROC curves. Individual curves were obtained by placing each patient into one of the three risk bins based on the MLP output. The x's represent the average MLP output for all patients in each bin. Open squares are the true percentage of patients in each bin who experienced a complication. The bars represent ±2 binomial deviations about the true patient percentages. Risk prediction is accurate if the x's are close to the squares and within the confidence intervals. As can be seen, risk prediction is accurate and close to the actual number of patients who experienced complications. It is difficult, however, to assess risk prediction given the limited numbers of patients in the two highest bins. For example, in Figure 5, the median number of patients with complications was only 2 out of 20 in the middle bin and 2 out of 13 in the upper bin. Good and similar risk stratification, as measured by a chi-square test, was provided by all classifiers. Differences between classifier predictions and true patient percentages were small and not statistically significant.

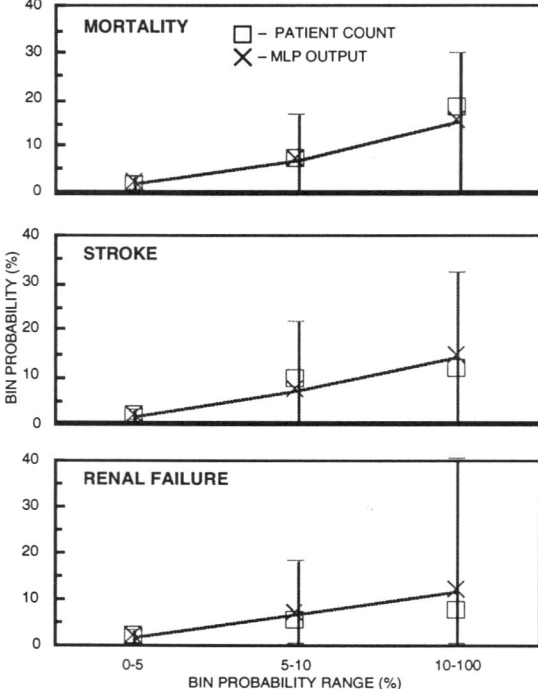

Figure 5. Accuracy of MLP risk stratification for three complications using preoperative features. Open squares are true percentages of patients in each bin with a complication, x's are MLP predictions, bars represent ±2 binomial standard deviation confidence intervals.

4 CONFIDENCE MLP NETWORKS

Estimating the confidence in the classification decision produced by a neural network is a critical issue that has received relatively little study. Not being able to provide a confidence measure makes it difficult for physicians and other professionals to accept the use of complex networks. Bootstrap sampling (Efron, 1993) was selected as an approach to generate confidence intervals for medical risk prediction because 1) It can be applied to any type of classifier, 2) It measures variability due to training algorithms, implementation differences, and limited training data, and 3) It is simple to implement and apply. As shown in the top half of Figure 6, 50 bootstrap sets of training data are created from the original training data by resampling with replacement. These bootstrap training sets are used to train 50 bootstrap MLP classifiers using the same architecture and training procedures that were selected for the risk prediction MLP. When a pattern is fed into these classifiers, their outputs provide an estimate of the distribution of the output of the risk prediction MLP. Lower and upper confidence bounds for any input are obtained by sorting these outputs and selecting the 10% and 90% cumulative levels.

It is computationally expensive to have to maintain and query 50 bootstrap MLPs whenever confidence bounds are desired. A simpler approach is to train a single confidence MLP to replicate the confidence bounds predicted by the 50 bootstrap MLPs, as shown in the bot-

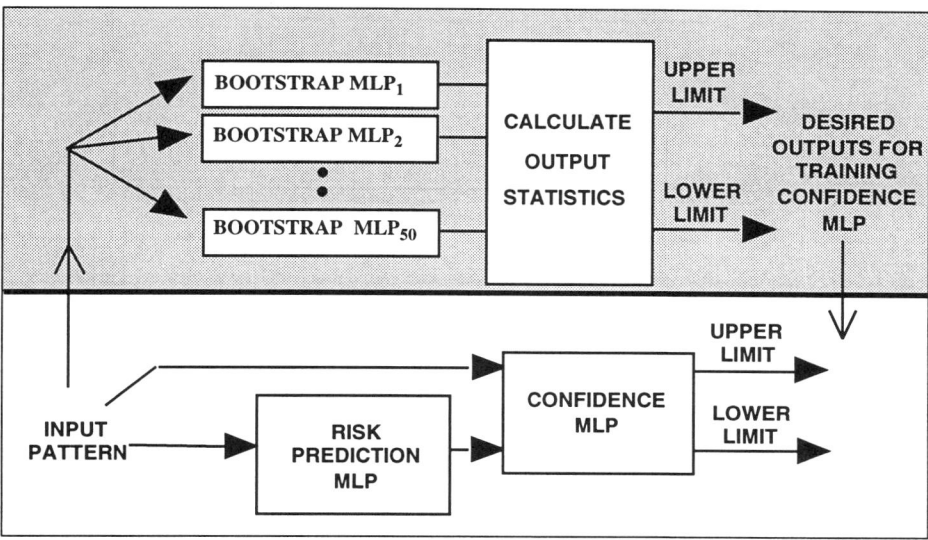

Figure 6. A confidence MLP trained using 50 bootstrap MLPs produces upper and lower confidence bounds for a risk prediction MLP.

tom half of Figure 6. The the confidence MLP is fed the input pattern and the output of the risk prediction MLP and produces at its output the confidence intervals that would have been produced by 50 bootstrap MLPs. The confidence MLP is a mapping or regression network that replaces the 50 bootstrap networks. It was found that confidence networks with one hidden layer, two hidden nodes, and a linear output could accurately reproduce the upper and lower confidence intervals created by 50 bootstrap two-layer MLP networks. The confidence network outputs were almost always within ±15% of the actual bootstrap bounds. Upper and lower bounds produced by these confidence networks for all patients using preoperative features predicting mortality are show in Figure 7. Bounds are high (±10 percentage points) when the complication risk is near 20% and drop to lower values (±0.4 percentage points) when the risk is near 1%. This relatively simple approach makes it possible to create and replicate confidence intervals for many types of classifiers.

5 SUMMARY AND FUTURE PLANS

MLP networks provided slightly better risk prediction than conventional logistic regression when used to predict the risk of death, stroke, and renal failure on 1257 patients who underwent coronary artery bypass operations. Bootstrap sampling was required to compare approaches and regularization provided by early stopping was an important component of improved performance. A simplified approach to generating confidence intervals for MLP risk predictions using an auxiliary "confidence MLP" was also developed. The confidence MLP is trained to reproduce the confidence bounds that were generated during training by 50 MLP networks trained using bootstrap samples. Current research is validating these results using larger data sets, exploring approaches to detect outlier patients who are so different from any training patient that accurate risk prediction is suspect, developing approaches to explaining which input features are important for an individual patient, and determining why MLP networks provide improved performance.

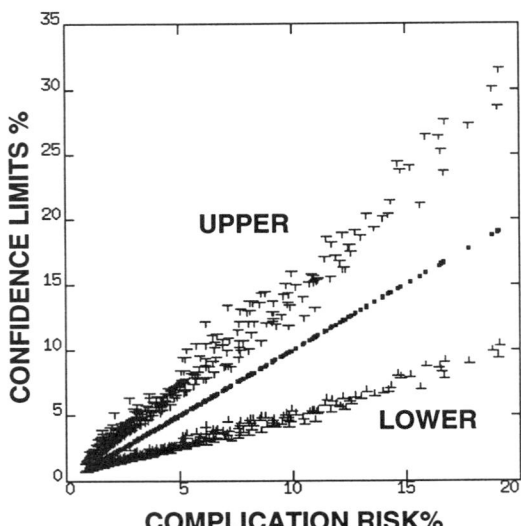

Figure 7. Upper and lower confidence bounds for all patients and preoperative mortality risk predictions calculated using two MLP confidence networks.

ACKNOWLEDGMENT

This work was sponsored by the Department of the Air Force. The views expressed are those of the authors and do not reflect the official policy or position of the U.S. Government. We wish to thank Stephanie Moisakis and Anne Nilson at the Lahey Clinic and Yuchun Lee at Lincoln Laboratory for assistance in organizing and preprocessing the data.

BIBLIOGRAPHY

F. Edwards, R. Clark, and M. Schwartz. (1994) Coronary Artery Bypass Grafting: The Society of Thoracic Surgeons National Database Experience. In *Annals Thoracic Surgery*, Vol. 57, 12-19.

Bradley Efron and Robert J. Tibshirani. (1993) An Introduction to the Bootstrap. Monographs on Statistics and Applied Probability 57, New York: Chapman and Hall (1993).

T. Higgins, F. Estafanous, et. al. (1992) Stratification of Morbidity and Mortality Outcome by Preoperative Risk Factors in Coronary Artery Bypass Patients. In Journal of the American Medical Society, Vol. 267, No. 17, 2344-2348.

R. Lippmann, L. Kukolich, and E. Singer. (1993) LNKnet: Neural Network, Machine Learning, and Statistical Software for Pattern Classification. In *Lincoln Laboratory Journal*, Vol. 6, No. 2, 249-268.

Marshall Guillermo, Laurie W. Shroyer, et al. (1994) Bayesian-Logit Model for Risk Assessment in Coronary Artery Bypass Grafting, In *Annals Thoracic Surgery*, Vol. 57, 1492-5000.

G. O'Conner, S. Plume, et. al. (1992) Multivariate Prediction of In-Hospital Mortality Associated with Coronary Artery Bypass Surgery. In *Circulation*, Vol. 85, No. 6, 2110-2118.

Statistical Sciences. (1993) S-PLUS Guide to Statistical and Mathematical Analyses, Version 3.2, Seattle: StatSci, a division of MathSoft, Inc.

Comparing the prediction accuracy of artificial neural networks and other statistical models for breast cancer survival

Harry B. Burke
Department of Medicine
New York Medical College
Valhalla, NY 10595

David B. Rosen
Department of Medicine
New York Medical College
Valhalla, NY 10595

Philip H. Goodman
Department of Medicine
University of Nevada School of Medicine
Reno, Nevada 89520

Abstract

The TNM staging system has been used since the early 1960's to predict breast cancer patient outcome. In an attempt to increase prognostic accuracy, many putative prognostic factors have been identified. Because the TNM stage model can not accommodate these new factors, the proliferation of factors in breast cancer has lead to clinical confusion. What is required is a new computerized prognostic system that can test putative prognostic factors and integrate the predictive factors with the TNM variables in order to increase prognostic accuracy. Using the area under the curve of the receiver operating characteristic, we compare the accuracy of the following predictive models in terms of five year breast cancer-specific survival: pTNM staging system, principal component analysis, classification and regression trees, logistic regression, cascade correlation neural network, conjugate gradient descent neural, probabilistic neural network, and backpropagation neural network. Several statistical models are significantly more accurate than the TNM staging system. Logistic regression and the backpropagation neural network are the most accurate prediction models for predicting five year breast cancer-specific survival

1 INTRODUCTION

For over thirty years measuring cancer outcome has been based on the TNM staging system (tumor size, number of lymph nodes with metastatic disease, and distant metastases) (Beahr et. al., 1992). There are several problems with this model (Burke and Henson, 1993). First, it is not very accurate, for breast cancer it is 44% accurate. Second its accuracy can not be improved because predictive variables can not be added to the model. Third, it does not apply to all cancers. In this paper we compare computerized prediction models to determine if they can improve prognostic accuracy. Artificial neural networks (ANN) are a class of nonlinear regression and discrimination models. ANNs are being used in many areas of medicine, with several hundred articles published in the last year. Representative areas of research include anesthesiology (Westenskow et. al., 1992), radiology (Tourassi et. al., 1992), cardiology (Leong and Jabri, 1982), psychiatry (Palombo, 1992), and neurology (Gabor and Seyal, 1992). ANNs are being used in cancer research including image processing (Goldberg et. al., 1992), analysis of laboratory data for breast cancer diagnosis (O Leary et. al., 1992), and the discovery of chemotherapeutic agents (Weinstein et. al., 1992). It should be pointed out that the analyses in this paper rely upon previously collected prognostic factors. These factors were selected for collection because they were significant in a generalized linear model such as the linear or logistic models. There is no predictive model that can improve upon linear or logistic prediction models when the predictor variables meet the assumptions of these models and there are no interactions. Therefore he objective of this paper is not to outperform linear or logistic models on these data. Rather, our objective is to show that, with variables selected by generalized linear models, artificial neural networks can perform as well as the best traditional models . There is no a priori reason to believe that future prognostic factors will be binary or linear, and that there will not be complex interactions between prognostic factors. A further objective of this paper is to demonstrate that artificial neural networks are likely to outperform the conventional models when there are unanticipated nonmonotonic factors or complex interactions.

2 METHODS

2.1 DATA

The Patient Care Evaluation (PCE) data set is collected by the Commission on Cancer of the American College of Surgeons (ACS). The ACS, in October 1992, requested cancer information from hospital tumor registries in the United States. The ACS asked for the first 25 cases of breast cancer seen at that institution in 1983, and it asked for follow up information on each of these 25 patients through the date of the request. These are only cases of first breast cancer. Follow-up information included known deaths. The PCE data set contains, at best, eight year follow-up.

We chose to use a five year survival end-point. This analysis is for death due to breast cancer, not all cause mortality.

For this analysis cases with missing data, and cases censored before five years, are not included so that the prediction models can be compared without putting any prediction model at a disadvantage. We randomly divided the data set into training, hold-out, and testing subsets of 3,100, 2,069, and 3,102 cases, respectively.

2.2 MODELS

The TMN stage model used in this analysis is the pathologic model (pTNM) based on the 1992 American Joint Committee on Cancer's Manual for the Staging of Cancer (Beahr et. al., 1992). The pathologic model relies upon pathologically determined tumor size and lymph nodes, this contrasts with clinical staging which relies upon the clinical examination to provide tumor size and lymph node information. To determine the overall accuracy of the TNM stage model we compared the model's prediction for each patient, where the individual patient's prediction is the fraction of all the patients in that stage who survive, to each patient's true outcome.

Principal components analysis, is a data reduction technique based on the linear combinations of predictor variables that minimizes the variance across patients (Jollie, 1982). The logistic regression analysis is performed in a stepwise manner, without interaction terms, using the statistical language S-PLUS (S-PLUS, 1992), with the continuous variable age modeled with a restricted cubic spline to avoid assuming linearity (Harrell et. al., 1988). Two types of Classification and Regression Tree (CART) (Breiman et. al., 1984) analyses are performed using S-PLUS. The first was a 9-node pruned tree (with 10-fold cross validation on the deviance), and the second was a shrunk tree with 13.7 effective nodes.

The multilayer perceptron neural network training in this paper is based on the maximum likelihood function unless otherwise stated, and backpropagation refers to gradient descent. Two neural networks that are not multilayer perceptrons are tested. They are the Fuzzy ARTMAP neural network (Carpenter et. al., 1991) and the probabilistic neural network (Specht, 1990).

2.3 ACCURACY

The measure of comparative accuracy is the area under the curve of the receiver operating characteristic (Az). Generally, the Az is a nonparametric measure of discrimination. Square error summarizes how close each patient's predicted value is to its true outcome. The Az measures the relative goodness of the set of predictions as a whole by comparing the predicted probability of each patient with that of all other patients. The computational approach to the Az that employs the trapezoidal approximation to the area under the receiver operating characteristic curve for binary outcomes was first reported by Bamber (Bamber, 1975), and later in the medical literature by Hanley (Hanley and McNeil, 1982). This was extended by Harrell (Harrell et. al., 1988) to continuous outcomes.

Table 1: PCE 1983 Breast Cancer Data: 5 Year Survival Prediction, 54 Variables.

PREDICTION MODEL	ACCURACY*	SPECIFICATIONS
pTNM Stages	.720	0,I,IIA,IIB,IIIA,IIIB,IV
Principal Components Analysis	.714	one scaling iteration
CART, pruned	.753	9 nodes
CART, shrunk	.762	13.7 nodes
Stepwise Logistic regression	.776	with cubic splines
Fuzzy ARTMAP ANN	.738	54-F2a, 128-1
Cascade correlation ANN	.761	54-21-1
Conjugate gradient descent ANN	.774	54-30-1
Probabilistic ANN	.777	bandwidth = 16s
Backpropagation ANN	.784	54-5-1

* The area under the curve of the receiver operating characteristic.

3 RESULTS

All results are based on the independent variable sample not used for training (i.e., the testing data set), and all analyses employ the same testing data set. Using the PCE breast cancer data set, we can assess the accuracy of several prediction models using the most powerful of the predictor variables available in the data set (See Table 1).

Principal components analysis is not expected to be a very accurate model; with one scaling iteration, its accuracy is .714. Two types of classification and regression trees (CART), pruned and shrunk, demonstrate accuracies of .753 and .762, respectively. Logistic regression with cubic splines for age has an accuracy of .776. In addition to the backpropagation neural network and the probabilistic neural network, three types of neural networks are tested. Fuzzy ARTMAP's accuracy is the poorest at .738. It was too computationally intensive to be a practical model. Cascade-correlation and conjugate gradient descent have the potential to do as well as backpropagation. The PNN accuracy is .777. The PNN has many interesting features, but it also has several drawbacks including its storage requirements. The backpropagation neural network's accuracy is .784.4.

4 DISCUSSION

For predicting five year breast cancer-specific survival, several computerized prediction models are more accurate than the TNM stage system, and artificial neural networks are as good as the best traditional statistical models.

References

Bamber D (1975). The area above the ordinal dominance graph and the area below the receiver operating characteristic. *J Math Psych* 12:387-415.

Beahrs OH, Henson DE, Hutter RVP, Kennedy BJ (1992). *Manual for staging of cancer*, 4th ed. Philadelphia: JB Lippincott.

Burke HB, Henson DE (1993). Criteria for prognostic factors and for an enhanced prognostic system. *Cancer* 72:3131-5.

Breiman L, Friedman JH, Olshen RA (1984). *Classification and Regression Trees.* Pacific Grove, CA: Wadsworth and Brooks/Cole.

Carpenter GA, Grossberg S, Rosen DB (1991). Fuzzy ART: Fast stable learning and categorization of analog patterns by an adaptive resonance system. *Neural Networks* 4:759-771.

Gabor AJ, M. Seyal M (1992) . Automated interictal EEG spike detection using artificial neural networks. *Electroencephalogr Clin Neurophysiology* 83:271-80.

Goldberg V, Manduca A, Ewert DL (1992). Improvement in specificity of ultrasonography for diagnosis of breast tumors by means of artificial intelligence. *Med Phys* 19:1275-81.

Hanley JA, McNeil BJ (1982). The meaning of the use of the area under the receiver operating characteristic (ROC) curve. *Radiology* 143:29-36.

Harrell FE, Lee KL, Pollock BG (1988). Regression models in clinical studies: determining relationships between predictors and response. *J Natl Cancer Instit* 80:1198-1202.

Jollife IT (1986). *Principal Component Analysis.* New York: Springer-Verlag, 1986.

Leong PH, Jabri MA (1982). MATIC - an intracardiac tachycardia classification system. *PACE* 15:1317-31, 1982.

O'Leary TJ, Mikel UV, Becker RL (1992). Computer-assisted image interpretation: use of a neural network to differentiate tubular carcinoma from sclerosing adenosis. *Modern Pathol* 5:402-5.

Palombo SR (1992). Connectivity and condensation in dreaming. *J Am Psychoanal Assoc* 40:1139-59.

S-PLUS (1991), v 3.0. Seattle, WA; Statistical Sciences, Inc.

Specht DF (1990). Probabilistic neural networks. Neural Networks 3:109-18.

Tourassi GD, Floyd CE, Sostman HD, Coleman RE (1993). Acute pulmonary embolism: artificial neural network approach for diagnosis. *Radiology* 189:555-58.

Weinstein JN, Kohn KW, Grever MR et. al. (1992) Neural computing in cancer drug development: predicting mechanism of action. *Science* 258:447-51.

Westenskow DR, Orr JA, Simon FH (1992). Intelligent alarms reduce anesthesiologist's response time to critical faults. *Anesthesiology* 77:1074-9, 1992.

Learning To Play the Game of Chess

Sebastian Thrun
University of Bonn
Department of Computer Science III
Römerstr. 164, D-53117 Bonn, Germany
E-mail: thrun@carbon.informatik.uni-bonn.de

Abstract

This paper presents NeuroChess, a program which learns to play chess from the final outcome of games. NeuroChess learns chess board evaluation functions, represented by artificial neural networks. It integrates inductive neural network learning, temporal differencing, and a variant of explanation-based learning. Performance results illustrate some of the strengths and weaknesses of this approach.

1 Introduction

Throughout the last decades, the game of chess has been a major testbed for research on artificial intelligence and computer science. Most of today's chess programs rely on intensive search to generate moves. To evaluate boards, fast evaluation functions are employed which are usually carefully designed by hand, sometimes augmented by automatic parameter tuning methods [1]. Building a chess machine that learns to play solely from the final outcome of games (win/loss/draw) is a challenging open problem in AI.

In this paper, we are interested in learning to play chess from the final outcome of games. One of the earliest approaches, which learned solely by playing itself, is Samuel's famous checker player program [10]. His approach employed *temporal difference learning* (in short: TD) [14], which is a technique for recursively learning an evaluation function. Recently, Tesauro reported the successful application of TD to the game of Backgammon, using artificial neural network representations [16]. While his TD-Gammon approach plays grandmaster-level backgammon, recent attempts to reproduce these results in the context of Go [12] and chess have been less successful. For example, Schäfer [11] reports a system just like Tesauro's TD-Gammon, applied to learning to play certain chess endgames. Gherrity [6] presented a similar system which he applied to entire chess games. Both approaches learn purely inductively from the final outcome of games. Tadepalli [15] applied a lazy version of explanation-based learning [5, 7] to endgames in chess. His approach learns from the final outcome, too, but unlike the inductive neural network approaches listed above it learns analytically, by analyzing and generalizing experiences in terms of chess-specific knowledge.

The level of play reported for all these approaches is still below the level of GNU-Chess, a publicly available chess tool which has frequently been used as a benchmark. This illustrates the hardness of the problem of learning to play chess from the final outcome of games.

This paper presents NeuroChess, a program that learns to play chess from the final outcome of games. The central learning mechanisms is the explanation-based neural network (EBNN) algorithm [9, 8]. Like Tesauro's TD-Gammon approach, NeuroChess constructs a neural network evaluation function for chess boards using TD. In addition, a neural network version of explanation-based learning is employed, which analyzes games in terms of a previously learned neural network chess model. This paper describes the NeuroChess approach, discusses several training issues in the domain of chess, and presents results which elucidate some of its strengths and weaknesses.

2 Temporal Difference Learning in the Domain of Chess

Temporal difference learning (TD) [14] comprises a family of approaches to prediction in cases where the event to be predicted may be delayed by an unknown number of time steps. In the context of game playing, TD methods have frequently been applied to learn functions which predict the final outcome of games. Such functions are used as board evaluation functions.

The goal of TD(0), a basic variant of TD which is currently employed in the NeuroChess approach, is to find an evaluation function, V, which ranks chess boards according to their goodness: If the board s is more likely to be a winning board than the board s', then $V(s) > V(s')$. To learn such a function, TD transforms entire chess games, denoted by a sequence of chess boards $s_0, s_1, s_2, \ldots, s_{t_{\text{final}}}$, into training patterns for V. The TD(0) learning rule works in the following way. Assume without loss of generality we are learning white's evaluation function. Then the target values for the *final board* is given by

$$V^{\text{target}}(s_{t_{\text{final}}}) = \begin{cases} 1, & \text{if } s_{t_{\text{final}}} \text{ is a win for white} \\ 0, & \text{if } s_{t_{\text{final}}} \text{ is a draw} \\ -1, & \text{if } s_{t_{\text{final}}} \text{ is a loss for white} \end{cases} \quad (1)$$

and the targets for the intermediate chess boards $s_0, s_1, s_2, \ldots, s_{t_{\text{final}}-2}$ are given by

$$V^{\text{target}}(s_t) = \gamma \cdot V(s_{t+2}) \quad (2)$$

This update rule constructs V recursively. At the end of the game, V evaluates the final outcome of the game (Eq. (1)). In between, when the assignment of V-values is less obvious, V is trained based on the evaluation two half-moves later (Eq. (2)). The constant γ (with $0 \leq \gamma \leq 1$) is a so-called *discount factor*. It decays V exponentially in time and hence favors early over late success. Notice that in NeuroChess V is represented by an artificial neural network, which is trained to fit the target values V^{target} obtained via Eqs. (1) and (2) (*cf.* [6, 11, 12, 16]).

3 Explanation-Based Neural Network Learning

In a domain as complex as chess, pure inductive learning techniques, such as neural network Back-Propagation, suffer from enormous training times. To illustrate why, consider the situation of a *knight fork*, in which the opponent's knight attacks our queen and king simultaneously. Suppose in order to save our king we have to move it, and hence sacrifice our queen. To learn the badness of a knight fork, NeuroChess has to discover that certain board features (like the position of the queen relative to the knight) are important, whereas

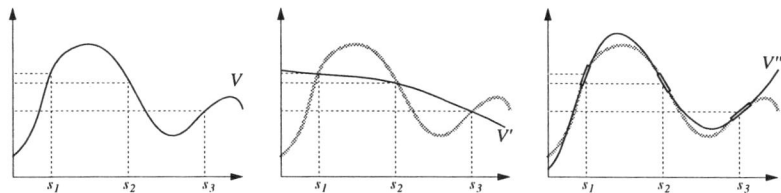

Figure 1: **Fitting values and slopes in EBNN:** Let V be the target function for which three examples $\langle s_1, V(s_1)\rangle$, $\langle s_2, V(s_2)\rangle$, and $\langle s_3, V(s_3)\rangle$ are known. Based on these points the learner might generate the hypothesis V'. If the slopes $\frac{\partial V(s_1)}{\partial s_1}$, $\frac{\partial V}{\partial}(s_2)\partial s_2$, and $\frac{\partial V(s_3)}{\partial s_3}$ are also known, the learner can do much better: V''.

others (like the number of weak pawns) are not. Purely inductive learning algorithms such as Back-propagation figure out the relevance of individual features by observing statistical correlations in the training data. Hence, quite a few versions of a knight fork have to be experienced in order to generalize accurately. In a domain as complex as chess, such an approach might require unreasonably large amounts of training data.

Explanation-based methods (EBL) [5, 7, 15] generalize more accurately from less training data. They rely instead on the availability of domain knowledge, which they use for explaining and generalizing training examples. For example, in the explanation of a knight fork, EBL methods employ knowledge about the game of chess to figure out that the position of the queen is relevant, whereas the number of weak pawns is not. Most current approaches to EBL require that the domain knowledge be represented by a set of symbolic rules. Since NeuroChess relies on neural network representations, it employs a neural network version of EBL, called *explanation-based neural network learning (EBNN)* [9]. In the context of chess, EBNN works in the following way: The domain-specific knowledge is represented by a separate neural network, called the *chess model* M. M maps arbitrary chess boards s_t to the corresponding expected board s_{t+2} two half-moves later. It is trained prior to learning V, using a large database of grand-master chess games. Once trained, M captures important knowledge about temporal dependencies of chess board features in high-quality chess play.

EBNN exploits M to bias the board evaluation function V. It does this by extracting slope constraints for the evaluation function V at all non-final boards, *i.e.*, all boards for which V is updated by Eq. (2). Let

$$\frac{\partial V^{\text{target}}(s_t)}{\partial s_t} \quad \text{with} \quad t \in \{0, 1, 2, \ldots, t_{\text{final}} - 2\} \quad (3)$$

denote the target slope of V at s_t, which, because $V^{\text{target}}(s_t)$ is set to $\gamma V(s_{t+2})$ according Eq. (2), can be rewritten as

$$\frac{\partial V^{\text{target}}(s_t)}{\partial s_t} = \gamma \cdot \frac{\partial V(s_{t+2})}{\partial s_{t+2}} \cdot \frac{\partial s_{t+2}}{\partial s_t} \quad (4)$$

using the chain rule of differentiation. The rightmost term in Eq. (4) measures how infinitesimal small changes of the chess board s_t influence the chess board s_{t+2}. It can be approximated by the chess model M:

$$\frac{\partial V^{\text{target}}(s_t)}{\partial s_t} \approx \gamma \cdot \frac{\partial V(s_{t+2})}{\partial s_{t+2}} \cdot \frac{\partial M(s_t)}{\partial s_t} \quad (5)$$

The right expression is only an approximation to the left side, because M is a trained neural

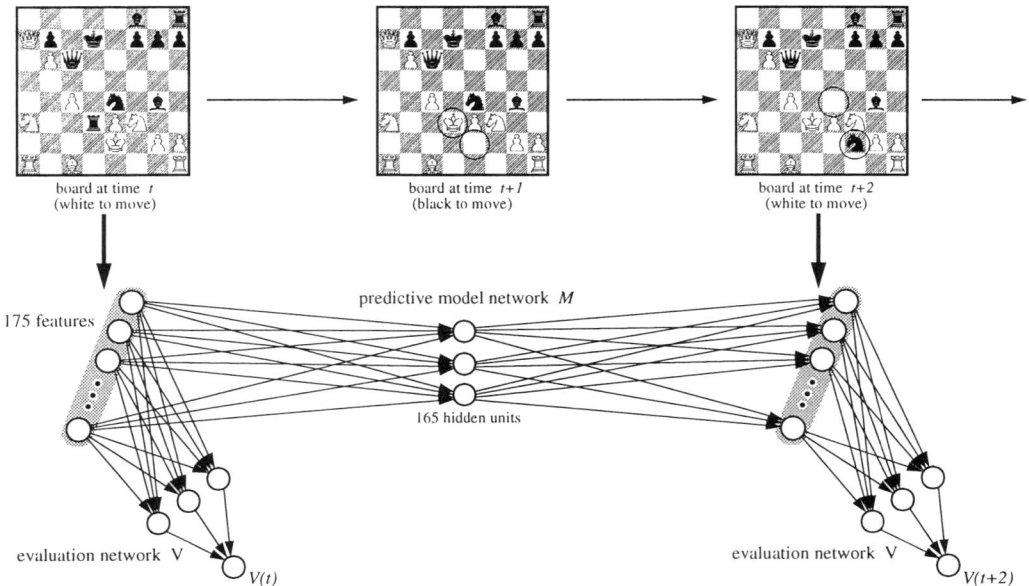

Figure 2: **Learning an evaluation function in NeuroChess.** Boards are mapped into a high-dimensional *feature vector*, which forms the input for both the evaluation network V and the chess model M. The evaluation network is trained by Back-propagation and the TD(0) procedure. Both networks are employed for analyzing training example in order to derive target slopes for V.

network and thus its first derivative might be erroneous. Notice that both expressions on the right hand side of Eq. (5) are derivatives of neural network functions, which are easy to compute since neural networks are differentiable.

The result of Eq. (5) is an estimate of the slope of the target function V at s_t. This slope adds important shape information to the target values constructed via Eq. (2). As depicted in Fig. 1, functions can be fit more accurately if in addition to target values the slopes of these values are known. Hence, instead of just fitting the target values $V^{\text{target}}(s_t)$, NeuroChess also fits these target slopes. This is done using the Tangent-Prop algorithm [13].

The complete NeuroChess learning architecture is depicted in Fig. 2. The target slopes provide a first-order approximation to the relevance of each chess board feature in the goodness of a board position. They can be interpreted as biasing the network V based on chess-specific domain knowledge, embodied in M. For the relation of EBNN and EBL and the accommodation of inaccurate slopes in EBNN see [8].

4 Training Issues

In this section we will briefly discuss some training issues that are essential for learning good evaluation functions in the domain of chess. This list of points has mainly been produced through practical experience with the NeuroChess and related TD approaches. It illustrates the importance of a careful design of the input representation, the sampling rule and the parameter setting in a domain as complex as chess.

Sampling. The vast majority of chess boards are, loosely speaking, not interesting. If, for example, the opponent leads by more than a queen and a rook, one is most likely to loose. Without an appropriate sampling method there is the danger that the learner spends most of its time learning from uninteresting examples. Therefore, NeuroChess interleaves self-play and expert play for guiding the sampling process. More specifically, after presenting a random number of expert moves generated from a large database of grand-master games, NeuroChess completes the game by playing itself. This sampling mechanism has been found to be of major importance to learn a good evaluation function in a reasonable amount of time.

Quiescence. In the domain of chess certain boards are harder to evaluate than others. For example, in the middle of an ongoing material exchange, evaluation functions often fail to produce a good assessment. Thus, most chess programs search selectively. A common criterion for determining the depth of search is called *quiescence*. This criterion basically detects material threats and deepens the search correspondingly. NeuroChess' search engine does the same. Consequently, the evaluation function V is only trained using quiescent boards.

Smoothness. Obviously, using the raw, canonical board description as input representation is a poor choice. This is because small changes on the board can cause a huge difference in value, contrasting the smooth nature of neural network representations. Therefore, NeuroChess maps chess board descriptions into a set of board features. These features were carefully designed by hand.

Discounting. The variable γ in Eq. (2) allows to discount values in time. Discounting has frequently been used to bound otherwise infinite sums of pay-off. One might be inclined to think that in the game of chess no discounting is needed, as values are bounded by definition. Indeed, without discounting the evaluation function predicts the *probability* for winning—in the ideal case. In practice, however, random disturbations of the evaluation function can seriously hurt learning, for reasons given in [4, 17]. Empirically we found that learning failed completely when no discount factor was used. Currently, NeuroChess uses $\gamma = 0.98$.

Learning rate. TD approaches minimize a Bellman equation [2]. In the NeuroChess domain, a close-to-optimal approximation of the Bellman equation is the constant function $V(s) \equiv 0$. This function violates the Bellman equation only at the end of games (Eq. (1)), which is rare if complete games are considered. To prevent this, we amplified the learning rate for final values by a factor of 20, which was experimentally found to produce sufficiently non-constant evaluation functions.

Software architecture. Training is performed completely asynchronously on up to 20 workstations simultaneously. One of the workstations acts as a weight server, keeping track of the most recent weights and biases of the evaluation network. The other workstations can dynamically establish links to the weight server and contribute to the process of weight refinement. The main process also monitors the state of all other workstations and restarts processes when necessary. Training examples are stored in local ring buffers (1000 items per workstation).

5 Results

In this section we will present results obtained with the NeuroChess architecture. Prior to learning an evaluation function, the model M (175 input, 165 hidden, and 175 output units) is trained using a database of 120,000 expert games. NeuroChess then learns an evaluation

1. e2e3 b8c6	16. b2b4 a5a4	31. a3f8 f2e4	46. d1c2 b8h2	61. e4f5 h3g4	65. a8e8 e6d7
2. d1f3 c6e5	17. b5c6 a4c6	32. c3b2 h8f8	47. c2c3 f6b6	62. f5f6 h6h5	66. e8e7 d7d8
3. f3d5 d7d6	18. g1f3 d8d6	33. a4d7 f3f5	48. e7e4 g6h6	63. b7b8q g4f5	67. f4c7
4. f1b5 c7c6	19. d4a7 f5g4	34. d7b7 f5e5	49. d4f5 h6g5	64. b8f4 f5e6	
5. b5a4 g8f6	20. c2c4 c8d7	35. b2c1 f8e8	50. e4e7 g5g4		
6. d5d4 c8f5	21. b4b5 c6c7	36. b7d5 e5h2	51. f5h6 g7h6	**final board**	
7. f2f4 e5d7	22. d2d3 d6d3	37. a1a7 e8e6	52. e7d7 g4h5		
8. e1e2 d8a5	23. b5b6 c7c6	38. d5d8 f6g6	53. d7d1 h5h4		
9. a4b3 d7c5	24. e2d3 e4f2	39. b6b7 e6d6	54. d1d4 h4h3		
10. b1a3 c5b3	25. d3c3 g4f3	40. d8a5 d6c6	55. d4b6 h2e5		
11. a2b3 e7e5	26. g2f3 f2h1	41. a5b4 h2b8	56. b6d4 e5e6		
12. f4e5 f6e4	27. c1b2 c6f3	42. a7a8 e4c3	57. c3d2 e6f5		
13. e5d6 e8c8	28. a7a4 d7e7	43. c2d4 c6f6	58. e3e4 f5g5		
14. b3b4 a5a6	29. a3c2 h1f2	44. b4e7 c3a2	59. d4e3 g5e3		
15. b4b5 a6a5	30. b2a3 e7f6	45. c1d1 a2c3	60. d2e3 f7f5		

Figure 3: **NeuroChess against GNU-Chess.** NeuroChess plays white. Parameters: Both players searched to depth 3, which could be extended by quiescence search to at most 11. The evaluation network had no hidden units. Approximately 90% of the training boards were sampled from expert play.

---

network V (175 input units, 0 to 80 hidden units, and one output units). To evaluate the level of play, NeuroChess plays against GNU-Chess in regular time intervals. Both players employ the same search mechanism which is adopted from GNU-Chess. Thus far, experiments lasted for 2 days to 2 weeks on 1 to 20 SUN Sparc Stations.

A typical game is depicted in Fig. 3. This game has been chosen because it illustrates both the strengths and the shortcomings of the NeuroChess approach. The opening of NeuroChess is rather weak. In the first three moves NeuroChess moves its queen to the center of the board.[1] NeuroChess then escapes an attack on its queen in move 4, gets an early pawn advantage in move 12, attacks black's queen pertinaciously through moves 15 to 23, and successfully exchanges a rook. In move 33, it captures a strategically important pawn, which, after chasing black's king for a while and sacrificing a knight for no apparent reason, finally leads to a new queen (move 63). Four moves later black is mate. This game is prototypical. As can be seen from this and various other games, NeuroChess has learned successfully to protect its material, to trade material, and to protect its king. It has not learned, however, to open a game in a coordinated way, and it also frequently fails to play short endgames even if it has a material advantage (this is due to the short planning horizon). Most importantly, it still plays incredibly poor openings, which are often responsible for a draw or a loss. Poor openings do not surprise, however, as TD propagates values from the end of a game to the beginning.

Table 1 shows a performance comparison of NeuroChess versus GNU-Chess, with and without the explanation-based learning strategy. This table illustrates that NeuroChess wins approximately 13% of all games against GNU-Chess, if both use the same search engine. It

---

[1]This is because in the current version NeuroChess still heavily uses expert games for sampling. Whenever a grand-master moves its queen to the center of the board, the queen is usually safe, and there is indeed a positive correlation between having the queen in the center and winning in the database. NeuroChess falsely deduces that having the queen in the center is good. This effect disappears when the level of self-play is increased, but this comes at the expense of drastically increased training time, since self-play requires search.

| | GNU depth 2, NeuroChess depth 2 | | GNU depth 4, NeuroChess depth 2 | |
# of games	Back-propagation	EBNN	Back-propagation	EBNN
100	1	0	0	0
200	6	2	0	0
500	35	13	1	0
1000	73	85	2	1
1500	130	135	3	3
2000	190	215	3	8
2400	239	316	3	11

Table 1: Performance of NeuroChess vs. GNU-Chess during training. The numbers show the total number of games won against GNU-Chess using the same number of games for testing as for training. This table also shows the importance of the explanation-based learning strategy in EBNN. Parameters: both learners used the original GNU-Chess features, the evaluation network had 80 hidden units and search was cut at depth 2, or 4, respectively (no quiescence extensions).

also illustrates the utility of explanation-based learning in chess.

6 Discussion

This paper presents NeuroChess, an approach for learning to play chess from the final outcomes of games. NeuroChess integrates TD, inductive neural network learning and a neural network version of explanation-based learning. The latter component analyzes games using knowledge that was previously learned from expert play. Particular care has been taken in the design of an appropriate feature representation, sampling methods, and parameter settings. Thus far, NeuroChess has successfully managed to beat GNU-Chess in several hundreds of games. However, the level of play still compares poorly to GNU-Chess and human chess players.

Despite the initial success, NeuroChess faces two fundamental problems which both might well be in the way of excellent chess play. Firstly, training time is limited, and it is to be expected that excellent chess skills develop only with excessive training time. This is particularly the case if only the final outcomes are considered. Secondly, with each step of TD-learning NeuroChess loses information. This is partially because the features used for describing chess boards are incomplete, i.e., knowledge about the feature values alone does not suffice to determine the actual board exactly. But, more importantly, neural networks have not the discriminative power to assign arbitrary values to all possible feature combinations. It is therefore unclear that a TD-like approach will ever, for example, develop good chess openings.

Another problem of the present implementation is related to the trade-off between knowledge and search. It has been well recognized that the ultimate cost in chess is determined by the time it takes to generate a move. Chess programs can generally invest their time in search, or in the evaluation of chess boards (search-knowledge trade-off) [3]. Currently, NeuroChess does a poor job, because it spends most of its time computing board evaluations. Computing a large neural network function takes two orders of magnitude longer than evaluating an optimized linear evaluation function (like that of GNU-Chess). VLSI neural network technology offers a promising perspective to overcome this critical shortcoming of sequential neural network simulations.

Acknowledgment

The author gratefully acknowledges the guidance and advise by Hans Berliner, who provided the features for representing chess boards, and without whom the current level of play would be much worse. He also thanks Tom Mitchell for his suggestion on the learning methods, and Horst Aurisch for his help with GNU-Chess and the database.

References

[1] Thomas S. Anantharaman. *A Statistical Study of Selective Min-Max Search in Computer Chess*. PhD thesis, Carnegie Mellon University, School of Computer Science, Pittsburgh, PA, 1990. Technical Report CMU-CS-90-173.

[2] R. E. Bellman. *Dynamic Programming*. Princeton University Press, Princeton, NJ, 1957.

[3] Hans J. Berliner, Gordon Goetsch, Murray S. Campbell, and Carl Ebeling. Measuring the performance potential of chess programs. *Artificial Intelligence*, 43:7–20, 1990.

[4] Justin A. Boyan. Generalization in reinforcement learning: Safely approximating the value function. In G. Tesauro, D. Touretzky, and T. Leen, editors, *Advances in Neural Information Processing Systems 7*, San Mateo, CA, 1995. Morgan Kaufmann. (to appear).

[5] Gerald DeJong and Raymond Mooney. Explanation-based learning: An alternative view. *Machine Learning*, 1(2):145–176, 1986.

[6] Michael Gherrity. *A Game-Learning Machine*. PhD thesis, University of California, San Diego, 1993.

[7] Tom M. Mitchell, Rich Keller, and Smadar Kedar-Cabelli. Explanation-based generalization: A unifying view. *Machine Learning*, 1(1):47–80, 1986.

[8] Tom M. Mitchell and Sebastian Thrun. Explanation based learning: A comparison of symbolic and neural network approaches. In Paul E. Utgoff, editor, *Proceedings of the Tenth International Conference on Machine Learning*, pages 197–204, San Mateo, CA, 1993. Morgan Kaufmann.

[9] Tom M. Mitchell and Sebastian Thrun. Explanation-based neural network learning for robot control. In S. J. Hanson, J. Cowan, and C. L. Giles, editors, *Advances in Neural Information Processing Systems 5*, pages 287–294, San Mateo, CA, 1993. Morgan Kaufmann.

[10] A. L. Samuel. Some studies in machine learning using the game of checkers. *IBM Journal on research and development*, 3:210–229, 1959.

[11] Johannes Schäfer. Erfolgsorientiertes Lernen mit Tiefensuche in Bauernendspielen. Technical report, Universität Karlsruhe, 1993. (in German).

[12] Nikolaus Schraudolph, Pater Dayan, and Terrence J. Sejnowski. Using the TD(lambda) algorithm to learn an evaluation function for the game of go. In *Advances in Neural Information Processing Systems 6*, San Mateo, CA, 1994. Morgan Kaufmann.

[13] Patrice Simard, Bernard Victorri, Yann LeCun, and John Denker. Tangent prop – a formalism for specifying selected invariances in an adaptive network. In J. E. Moody, S. J. Hanson, and R. P. Lippmann, editors, *Advances in Neural Information Processing Systems 4*, pages 895–903, San Mateo, CA, 1992. Morgan Kaufmann.

[14] Richard S. Sutton. Learning to predict by the methods of temporal differences. *Machine Learning*, 3, 1988.

[15] Prasad Tadepalli. Planning in games using approximately learned macros. In *Proceedings of the Sixth International Workshop on Machine Learning*, pages 221–223, Ithaca, NY, 1989. Morgan Kaufmann.

[16] Gerald J. Tesauro. Practical issues in temporal difference learning. *Machine Learning*, 8, 1992.

[17] Sebastian Thrun and Anton Schwartz. Issues in using function approximation for reinforcement learning. In M. Mozer, P. Smolensky, D. Touretzky, J. Elman, and A. Weigend, editors, *Proceedings of the 1993 Connectionist Models Summer School*, Hillsdale, NJ, 1993. Erlbaum Associates.

A Mixture Model System for Medical and Machine Diagnosis

Magnus Stensmo   Terrence J. Sejnowski

Computational Neurobiology Laboratory
The Salk Institute for Biological Studies
10010 North Torrey Pines Road
La Jolla, CA 92037, U.S.A.
{magnus,terry}@salk.edu

Abstract

Diagnosis of human disease or machine fault is a missing data problem since many variables are initially unknown. Additional information needs to be obtained. The joint probability distribution of the data can be used to solve this problem. We model this with mixture models whose parameters are estimated by the EM algorithm. This gives the benefit that missing data in the database itself can also be handled correctly. The request for new information to refine the diagnosis is performed using the maximum utility principle. Since the system is based on learning it is domain independent and less labor intensive than expert systems or probabilistic networks. An example using a heart disease database is presented.

1 INTRODUCTION

Diagnosis is the process of identifying diseases in patients or disorders in machines by considering history, symptoms and other signs through examination. Diagnosis is a common and important problem that has proven hard to automate and formalize. A procedural description is often hard to attain since experts do not know exactly how they solve a problem.

In this paper we use the information about a specific problem that exists in a database of cases. The disorders or diseases are determined by variables from observations and the goal is to find the probability distribution over the disorders, conditioned on what has been observed. The diagnosis is strong when one or a few of the possible outcomes are differentiated from the others. More information is needed if it is inconclusive. Initially there are only a few clues and the rest of the variables are unknown. Additional information is obtained by asking questions and doing tests. Since tests may be dangerous, time consuming and expensive, it is generally not possible or desirable to find the answer to every question. Unnecessary tests should be avoided.

There have been many attempts to automate diagnosis. Early work [Ledley & Lusted, 1959] realized that the problem is not always tractable due to the large number of influences that can exist between symptoms and diseases. Expert systems, e.g. the INTERNIST system for internal medicine [Miller et al., 1982], have rule-bases which are very hard and time consuming to build. Inconsistencies may arise when new rules are added to an existing database. There is also a strong domain dependence so knowledge bases can rarely be reused for new applications.

Bayesian or probabilistic networks [Pearl, 1988] are a way to model a joint probability distribution by factoring using the chain rule in probability theory. Although the models are very powerful when built, there are presently no general learning methods for their construction. A considerable effort is needed. In the Pathfinder system for lymph node pathology [Heckerman et al., 1992] about 14,000 conditional probabilities had to be assessed by an expert pathologist. It is inevitable that errors will occur when such large numbers of manual assessments are involved.

Approaches to diagnosis that are based on domain-independent machine learning alleviate some of the problems with knowledge engineering. For decision trees [Quinlan, 1986], a piece of information can only be used if the appropriate question comes up when traversing the tree. This means that irrelevant questions can not be avoided. Feedforward multilayer perceptrons for diagnosis [Baxt, 1990] can classify very well, but they need full information about a case. None of these these methods have adequate ways to handle missing data during learning or classification.

The exponentially growing number of probabilities involved can make exact diagnosis intractable. Simple approximations such as independence between all variables and conditional independence given the disease (naive Bayes) introduce errors since there usually are dependencies between the symptoms. Even though systems based on these assumptions work surprisingly well, correct diagnosis is not guaranteed. This paper will avoid these assumptions by using mixture models.

2   MIXTURE MODELS

Diagnosis can be formulated as a probability estimation problem with missing inputs. The probabilities of the disorders are conditioned on what has currently been observed. If we model the *joint probability distribution* it is easy to marginalize to get any conditional probability. This is necessary in order to be able to handle missing data in a principled way [Ahmad & Tresp, 1993]. Using *mixture models* [McLachlan & Basford, 1988], a simple closed form solution to optimal regression with missing data can be formulated. The EM algorithm, a method from parametric statistics for parameter estimation, is especially interesting in this context since it can also be formulated to handle missing data in the training examples [Dempster et al., 1977; Ghahramani & Jordan, 1994].

2.1 THE EM ALGORITHM

The data underlying the model is assumed to be a set of N D-dimensional vectors $X = \{x_1, \ldots, x_N\}$. Each data point is assumed to have been generated independently from a *mixture density* with M components

$$p(x) = \sum_{j=1}^{M} p(x, \omega_j; \theta_j) = \sum_{j=1}^{M} p(\omega_j) p(x|\omega_j; \theta_j), \qquad (1)$$

where each mixture component is denoted by ω_j. $p(\omega_j)$, the a priori probability for mixture ω_j, and $\theta = (\theta_1, \ldots, \theta_M)$ are the model parameters.

To estimate the parameters for the different mixtures so that it is likely that the linear combination of them generated the set of data points, we use *maximum likelihood estimation*. A good method is the iterative *Expectation-Maximization*, or *EM*, algorithm [Dempster et al., 1977].

Two steps are repeated. First a likelihood is formulated and its expectation is computed in the *E-step*. For the type of models that we will use, this step will calculate the probability that a certain mixture component generated the data point in question. The second step is the *M-step* where the parameters that maximize the expectation are found. This can be found analytically for models that can be written in an exponential form, e.g. Gaussian functions. Equations can be derived for both batch and on-line learning. Update equations for Gaussian distributions with and without missing data will be given here, other distributions are possible, e.g. binomial or multinomial [Stensmo & Sejnowski, 1994]. Details and derivations can be found in [Dempster et al., 1977; Nowlan, 1991; Ghahramani & Jordan, 1994; Stensmo & Sejnowski, 1994].

From (1) we form the log likelihood of the data

$$L(\theta|X) = \sum_{i=1}^{N} \log p(x_i; \theta_j) = \sum_{i=1}^{N} \log \sum_{j=1}^{M} p(\omega_j) p(x_i|\omega_j; \theta_j).$$

There is unfortunately no analytic solution to the logarithm of the sum in the right hand side of the equation. However, if we were to know which of the mixtures generated which data point we could compute it. The EM algorithm solves this by introducing a set of binary indicator variables $Z = \{z_{ij}\}$. $z_{ij} = 1$ if and only if the data point x_i was generated by mixture component j. The log likelihood can then be manipulated to a form that does not contain the log of a sum.

The expectation of z_i using the current parameter values θ_k is used since z_i is not known directly. This is the *E-step* of the EM algorithm. The expected value is then maximized in the *M-step*. The two steps are iterated until convergence. The likelihood will never decrease after an iteration [Dempster et al., 1977]. Convergence is fast compared to gradient descent.

One of the main motivations for the EM-algorithm was to be able to handle missing values for variables in a data set in a principled way. In the complete data case we introduced missing indicator variables that helped us solve the problem. With missing data we add the missing components to the Z already missing [Dempster et al., 1977; Ghahramani & Jordan, 1994].

2.2 GAUSSIAN MIXTURES

We specialize here the EM algorithm to the case where the mixture components are radial Gaussian distributions. For mixture component j with mean μ_j and covariance matrix Σ_j this is

$$p(x|\omega_j) = G_j(x) = \left(\frac{1}{\sqrt{2\pi}}\right)^D |\Sigma_j|^{-\frac{1}{2}} \exp\left[-\frac{1}{2}(x-\mu_j)^T \Sigma_j^{-1}(x-\mu_j)\right].$$

The form of the covariance matrix is often constrained to be diagonal or to have the same values on the diagonal, $\Sigma_j = \sigma_j^2 I$. This corresponds to axis-parallel oval-shaped and radially symmetric Gaussians, respectively. Radial and diagonal basis functions can function well in applications [Nowlan, 1991], since several Gaussians together can form complex shapes in the space. With fewer parameters over-fitting is minimized. In the radial case, with variance σ_j^2

$$G_j(x) = \left(\frac{1}{\sqrt{2\pi}\sigma_j}\right)^D \exp\left[-\frac{\|x-\mu_j\|^2}{2\sigma_j^2}\right].$$

In the E-step the expected value of the likelihood is computed. For the Gaussian case this becomes the probability that Gaussian j generated the data point

$$p_j(x) = \frac{p(\omega_j) G_j(x)}{\sum_{k=1}^M p(\omega_k) G_k(x)}.$$

The M-step finds the parameters that maximize the likelihood from the E-step. For complete data the new estimates are

$$\hat{p}(\omega_j) \longleftarrow \frac{S_j}{N}, \qquad \hat{\mu}_j \longleftarrow \frac{1}{S_j}\sum_{i=1}^N p_j(x_i)x_i, \qquad (2)$$

$$\hat{\sigma}_j^2 \longleftarrow \frac{1}{DS_j}\sum_{i=1}^N p_j(x_i)\|x_i - \hat{\mu}_j\|^2, \qquad \text{where } S_j = \sum_{i=1}^N p_j(x_i).$$

When input variables are missing the $G_j(x)$ is only evaluated over the set of observed dimensions O. Missing (unobserved) dimensions are denoted by U. The update equation for $\hat{p}(\omega_j)$ is unchanged. To estimate $\hat{\mu}_j$ we set $x_i^U = \hat{\mu}_j^U$ and use (2). The variance becomes

$$\hat{\sigma}_j^2 \longleftarrow \frac{1}{DS_j}\sum_{i=1}^N p_j^O(x_i)\left[\|x_i^O - \hat{\mu}_j^O\|^2 + |U|\hat{\sigma}_j^2\right].$$

A least squares regression was used to fill in missing data values during classification. For missing variables and Gaussian mixtures this becomes the same approach used by [Ahmad & Tresp, 1993]. The result of the regression when the outcome variables are missing is a probability distribution over the disorders. This can be reduced to a classification for comparison with other systems by picking the outcome with the maximum of the estimated probabilities.

3 REQUESTING MORE INFORMATION

During the diagnosis process, the outcome probabilities are refined at each step based on newly acquired knowledge. It it important to select the questions that lead to the minimal number of necessary tests. There is generally a cost associated with each test and the goal is to minimize the total cost. Early work on automated diagnosis [Ledley & Lusted, 1959] acknowledged the problem of asking as few questions as possible and suggested the use of *decision analysis* for the solution. An important idea from the field of decision theory is the *maximum expected utility principle* [von Neuman & Morgenstern, 1947]: A decision maker should always choose the alternative that maximizes some expected utility of the decision. For diagnosis it is the cost of misclassification. Each pair of outcomes has a utility $u(x, y)$ when the correct diagnosis is x but y has been incorrectly determined. The expectation can be computed when we know the probabilities of the outcomes.

The utility values have to be assessed manually in what can be a lengthy and complicated process. For this reason a simplification of this function has been suggested by [Heckerman et al., 1992]: The utility $u(x, y)$ is 1 when both x and y are benign or both are malign, and 0 otherwise. This simplification has been found to work well in practice. Another complication with maximum expected utility principle can also make it intractable. In the ideal case we would evaluate every possible sequence of future choices to see which is the best. Since the size of the search tree of possibilities grows exponentially this is often not possible. A simplification is to look ahead only one or a few steps at a time. This nearsighted or *myopic* approach has been tested in practice with good results [Gorry & Barnett, 1967; Heckerman et al., 1992].

4 THE DIAGNOSIS SYSTEM

The system we have developed has two phases. First there is a learning phase where a probabilistic model is built. This model is then used for inference in the diagnosis phase.

In the learning phase, the joint probability distribution of the data is modeled using mixture models. Parameters are determined from a database of cases by the EM algorithm. The k-means algorithm is used for initialization. Input and output variables for each case are combined into one vector per case to form the set of training patterns. The outcomes and other nominal variables are coded as *1 of N*. Continuous variables are interval coded.

In the diagnosis phase, myopic one-step look-ahead was used and utilities were simplified as above. The following steps were performed:

1. Initial observations were entered.

2. Conditional expectation regression was used to fill in unknown variables.

3. The maximum expected utility principle was used to recommend the next observation to make. Stop if nothing would be gained by further observations.

4. The user was asked to determine the correct value for the recommended observation. Any other observations could be made, instead of or in addition to this.

5. Continue with step 2.

Table 1: The Cleveland Heart Disease database.

	Observation	Description	Values
1	age	Age in years	continuous
2	sex	Sex of subject	male/female
3	cp	Chest pain	four types
4	trestbps	Resting blood pressure	continuous
5	chol	Serum cholesterol	continuous
6	fbs	Fasting blood sugar	lt or gt 120 mg/dl
7	restecg	Resting electrocardiogr.	five values
8	thalach	Max heart rate achieved	continuous
9	exang	Exercise induced angina	yes/no
10	oldpeak	ST depr. induced by exercise relative to rest	continuous
11	slope	Slope of peak exercise ST segment	up/flat/down
12	ca	# major vess. col. flourosc.	0-3
13	thal	Defect type	normal/fixed/reversible
	Disorder	**Description**	**Values**
14	num	Heart disease	Not present/4 types

5 EXAMPLE

The Cleveland heart disease data set from UC, Irvine has been used to test the system. It contains 303 examples of four types of heart disease and its absence. There are thirteen continuous- or nominally-valued variables (Table 1). The continuous variables were interval coded with one unit per standard deviation away from the mean value. This was chosen since they were approximately normally distributed. Nominal variables were coded with one unit per value. In total the 14 variables were coded with 55 units. The EM steps were repeated until convergence (60–150 iterations). A varying number of mixture components (20–120) were tried.

Previously reported results have used only presence or absence of the heart disease. The best of these has been a classification rate of 78.9% using a system that incrementally built prototypes [Gennari et al., 1989]. We have obtained 78.6% correct classification with 60 radial Gaussian mixtures as described above. Performance increased with the number of mixture components. It was not sensitive to a varying number of mixture components during training unless there were too few of them. Previous investigators have pointed out that there is not enough information in the thirteen variables in this data set to reach 100% [Gennari et al., 1989].

An annotated transcript of a diagnosis session is shown in Figure 1.

6 CONCLUSIONS AND FURTHER WORK

Several properties of this model remain to be investigated. It should be tested on several more databases. Unfortunately databases are typically proprietary and difficult to obtain. Future prospects for medical databases should be good since some hospitals are now using computerized record systems instead of traditional paper-based. It should be fairly easy to

> The leftmost number of the five numbers in a line is the estimated probability for no heart disease, followed by the probabilities for the four types of heart disease. The entropy, defined as $-\sum_i p_i \log p_i$, of the diagnoses are given at the same time as a measure of how decisive the current conclusion is. A completely determined diagnosis has entropy 0. Initially all of the variables are unknown and starting diagnoses are the unconditional prior probabilities.
>
> ```
> Disorders (entropy = 1.85):
>   0.541254  0.181518  0.118812  0.115512  0.042904
> What is cp ? 3
> ```
>
> The first question is *chest pain*, and the answer changes the estimated probabilities. This variable is continuous. The answer is to be interpreted how far from the mean the observation is in standard deviations. As the decision becomes more conclusive, the entropy decreases.
>
> ```
> Disorders (entropy = 0.69):
>   0.888209  0.060963  0.017322  0.021657  0.011848
> What is age ? 0
>
> Disorders (entropy = 0.57):
>   0.91307619  0.00081289  0.02495360  0.03832095  0.02283637
> What is oldpeak ? -2
>
> Disorders (entropy = 0.38):
>   0.94438718  0.00089016  0.02539957  0.02691099  0.00241210
> What is chol ? -1
>
> Disorders (entropy = 0.11):
>   0.98848758  0.00028553  0.00321580  0.00507073  0.00294036
> ```
>
> We have now determined that the probability of no heart disease in this case is 98.8%. The remaining 0.2% is spread out over the other possibilities.

Figure 1: Diagnosis example.

generate data for machine diagnosis.

An alternative way to choose a new question is to evaluate the variance change in the output variables when a variable is changed from missing to observed. The idea is that a variable known with certainty has zero variance. The variable with the largest resulting *conditional variance* could be selected as the query, similar to [Cohn et al., 1995].

One important aspect of automated diagnosis is the accompanying explanation for the conclusion, a factor that is important for user acceptance. Since the basis functions have local support and since we have estimates for the probability of each basis function having generated the observed data, explanations for the conclusions could be generated.

Instead of using the simplified utilities with values 0 and 1 for the expected utility calculations they could be learned by reinforcement learning. A trained expert would evaluate the quality of the diagnosis performed by the system, followed by adjustment of the utilities. The 0 and 1 values can be used as starting values.

Acknowledgements

The heart disease database is from the University of California, Irvine Repository of Machine Learning Databases and originates from R. Detrano, Cleveland Clinic Foundation. Peter Dayan provided helpful comments on an earlier version of this paper.

References

Ahmad, S. & Tresp, V. (1993). Some solutions to the missing feature problem in vision. In *Advances in Neural Information Processing Systems*, vol. 5, pp 393–400. Morgan Kaufmann, San Mateo, CA.

Baxt, W. (1990). Use of an artificial neural network for data analysis in clinical decision-making: The diagnosis of acute coronary occlusion. *Neural Computation*, **2(4)**, 480–489.

Cohn, D. A., Ghahramani, Z. & Jordan, M. I. (1995). Active learning with statistical models. In *Advances in Neural Information Processing Systems*, vol. 7. Morgan Kaufmann, San Mateo, CA.

Dempster, A., Laird, N. & Rubin, D. (1977). Maximum likelihood from incomplete data via the EM algorithm. *Journal of the Royal Statistical Society, Series, B.*, **39**, 1–38.

Gennari, J., Langley, P. & Fisher, D. (1989). Models of incremental concept formation. *Artificial Intelligence*, **40**, 11–62.

Ghahramani, Z. & Jordan, M. (1994). Supervised learning from incomplete data via an EM approach. In *Advances in Neural Information Processing Systems*, vol. 6, pp 120–127. Morgan Kaufmann, San Mateo, CA.

Gorry, G. A. & Barnett, G. O. (1967). Experience with a model of sequential diagnosis. *Computers and Biomedical Research*, **1**, 490–507.

Heckerman, D., Horvitz, E. & Nathwani, B. (1992). Toward normative expert systems: Part I. The Pathfinder project. *Methods of Information in Medicine*, **31**, 90–105.

Ledley, R. S. & Lusted, L. B. (1959). Reasoning foundations of medical diagnosis. *Science*, **130(3366)**, 9–21.

McLachlan, G. J. & Basford, K. E. (1988). *Mixture Models: Inference and Applications to Clustering*. Marcel Dekker, Inc., New York, NY.

Miller, R. A., Pople, H. E. & Myers, J. D. (1982). Internist-1: An experimental computer-based diagnostic consultant for general internal medicine. *New England Journal of Medicine*, **307**, 468–476.

Nowlan, S. J. (1991). *Soft Competitive Adaptation: Neural Network Learning Algorithms based on Fitting Statistical Mixtures*. PhD thesis, School of Computer Science, Carnegie Mellon University, Pittsburgh, PA.

Pearl, J. (1988). *Probabilistic Reasoning in Intelligent Systems: Networks of Plausible Inference*. Morgan Kaufmann, San Mateo, CA.

Quinlan, J. R. (1986). Induction of decision trees. *Machine Learning*, **1**, 81–106.

Stensmo, M. & Sejnowski, T. J. (1994). A mixture model diagnosis system. Tech. Rep. INC-9401, Institute for Neural Computation, University of California, San Diego.

von Neuman, J. & Morgenstern, O. (1947). *Theory of Games and Economic Behavior*. Princeton University Press, Princeton, NJ.

Inferring Ground Truth from Subjective Labelling of Venus Images

Padhraic Smyth, Usama Fayyad
Jet Propulsion Laboratory 525-3660,
Caltech, 4800 Oak Grove Drive,
Pasadena, CA 91109

Michael Burl, Pietro Perona
Department of Electrical Engineering
Caltech, MS 116-81,
Pasadena, CA 91125

Pierre Baldi[*]
Jet Propulsion Laboratory 303-310,
Caltech, 4800 Oak Grove Drive,
Pasadena, CA 91109

Abstract

In remote sensing applications "ground-truth" data is often used as the basis for training pattern recognition algorithms to generate thematic maps or to detect objects of interest. In practical situations, experts may visually examine the images and provide a subjective noisy estimate of the truth. Calibrating the reliability and bias of expert labellers is a non-trivial problem. In this paper we discuss some of our recent work on this topic in the context of detecting small volcanoes in Magellan SAR images of Venus. Empirical results (using the Expectation-Maximization procedure) suggest that accounting for subjective noise can be quite significant in terms of quantifying both human and algorithm detection performance.

1 Introduction

In certain pattern recognition applications, particularly in remote-sensing and medical diagnosis, the standard assumption that the labelling of the data has been

---

[*]and Division of Biology, California Institute of Technology

carried out in a reasonably objective and reliable manner may not be appropriate. Instead of "ground truth" one may only have the subjective opinion(s) of one or more experts. For example, medical data or image data may be collected off-line and some time later a set of experts analyze the data and produce a set of class labels. The central problem is that of trying to infer the "ground truth" given the noisy subjective estimates of the experts. When one wishes to apply a supervised learning algorithm to the data, the problem is primarily twofold: (i) how to evaluate the relative performance of experts and algorithms, and (ii) how to train a pattern recognition system in the absence of absolute ground truth.

In this paper we focus on problem (i), namely the performance evaluation issue, and in particular we discuss the application of a particular modelling technique to the problem of counting volcanoes on the surface of Venus. For problem (ii), in previous work we have shown that when the inferred labels have a probabilistic interpretation, a simple mixture model argument leads to straightforward modifications of various learning algorithms [1].

It should be noted that the issue of inferring ground truth from subjective labels has appeared in the literature under various guises. French [2] provides a Bayesian perspective on the problem of combining multiple opinions. In the field of medical diagnosis there is a significant body of work on latent variable models for inferring hidden "truth" from subjective diagnoses (e.g., see Uebersax [3]). More abstract theoretical models have also been developed under assumptions of specific labelling patterns (e.g., Lugosi [4] and references therein). The contribution of this paper is twofold: (i) this is the first application of latent-variable subjective-rating models to a large-scale *image* analysis problem as far as we are aware, and (ii) the focus of our work is on the pattern recognition aspect of the problem, i.e., comparing human and algorithmic performance as opposed to simply comparing humans to each other.

2 Background: Automated Detection of Volcanoes in Radar Images of Venus

Although modern remote-sensing and sky-telescope technology has made rapid recent advances in terms of data collection capabilities, image analysis often remains a strictly manual process and much investigative work is carried out using hardcopy photographs. The Magellan Venus data set is a typical example: between 1991 and 1994 the Magellan spacecraft transmitted back to earth a data set consisting of over 30,000 high resolution (75m per pixel) synthetic aperture radar (SAR) images of the Venusian surface [5]. This data set is greater than that gathered by all previous planetary missions combined — planetary scientists are literally swamped by data. There are estimated to be on the order of 10^6 small (less than 15km in diameter) visible volcanoes scattered throughout the 30,000 images [6]. It has been estimated that manually locating all of these volcanoes would require on the order of 10 man-years of a planetary geologist's time to carry out — our experience has been that even a few hours of image analysis severely taxes the concentration abilities of human labellers.

From a scientific viewpoint the ability to accurately locate and characterize the many volcanoes is a necessary requirement before more advanced planetary geology studies can be carried out: analysis of spatial clustering patterns, correlation with other geologic features, and so forth. From an engineering viewpoint, automation of the volcano detection task presents a significant challenge to current capabilities in computer vision and pattern recognition due to the variability of the volcanoes and the significant background "clutter" present in most of the images. Figure 1 shows a Magellan subimage of size 30km square containing at least 10 small volcanoes.

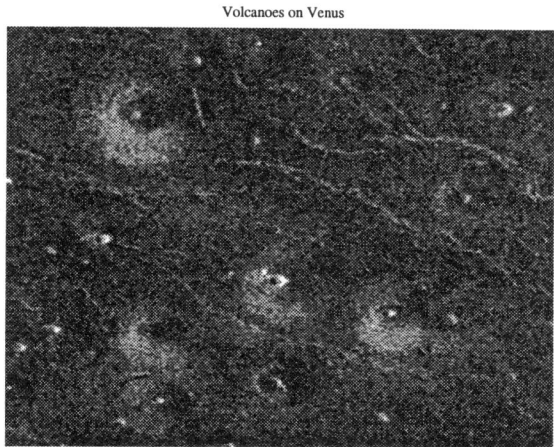

Figure 1: A 30km × 30km region from the Magellan SAR data, which contains a number of small volcanoes.

The purpose of this paper is not to describe pattern recognition methods for volcano detection but rather to discuss some of the issues involved in collecting and calibrating labelled training data from experts. Details of a volcano detection method using matched filtering, SVD projections and a Gaussian classifier are provided in [7].

3 Volcano Labelling

Training examples are collected by having the planetary geologists examine an image on the computer screen and then using a mouse to indicate where they think the volcanoes (if any) are located. Typically it can take from 15 minutes to 1 hour to label an image (depending on how many volcanoes are present), where each image represents a 75km square patch on the surface of Venus. An image may contain on the order of 100 volcanoes, although a more typical number is between 30 and 40.

There can be considerable ambiguity in volcano labelling: for the same image, different scientists can produce different label lists, and even the same scientist can produce different lists over time. To address this problem we introduced the notion of having the scientists label training examples into quantized probability bins or "types", where the probability bins correspond to visually distinguishable sub-categories of volcanoes. In particular, we have used 5 types: (1) summit pits, bright-dark radar pair, and apparent topographic slope, all clearly visible, probability 0.98, (2) only 2 of the 3 criteria of type 1 are visible, probability 0.80, (3) no summit pit visible, evidence of flanks or circular outline, probability 0.60, (4) only a summit pit visible, probability 0.50, (5) no volcano-like features visible, probability 0.0. These subjective probabilities correspond to the mean probability that a volcano exists at a particular location given that it belongs to a particular type and were elicited after considerable discussions with the planetary geologists. Thus, the observed data for each ROI consists of labels $\underline{l}$, which are noisy estimates of true "type" t, which in turn is probabilistically related to the hidden event of interest, v, the presence of a volcano:

$$p(v|\underline{l}) = \sum_{t=1}^{T} p(v|t)p(t|\underline{l}) \tag{1}$$

where T is the number of types (and labels). The subjective probabilities described above correspond to $p(v|t)$: to be able to infer the probability of a volcano given a set of labels $\underline{l}$ it remains to estimate the $p(t|\underline{l})$ terms.

4 Inferring the Label-Type Parameters via the EM Procedure

We follow a general model for subjective labelling originally proposed by Dawid and Skene [8] and apply it to the image labelling problem: more details on this overall approach are provided in [9]. Let N be the number of local regions of interest (ROI's) in the database (these are 15 pixel square image patches for the volcano application). For simplicity we consider the case of just a single labeller who labels a given set of regions of interest (ROIs) a number of times — the extension to multiple labellers is straightforward assuming conditional independence of the labellings given the true type. Let n_{il} be the number of times that ROI i is labelled with label l. Let Y_{it} denote a binary variable which takes value 1 if the true type of volcano i is t^*, and is 0 otherwise. We assume that labels are assigned independently to a given ROI from one labelling to the next, given that the type is known. If the true type t^* is known then

$$p(\text{observed labels}|t^*, i) \propto \prod_{l=1}^{T} p(l|t)^{n_{il}}. \tag{2}$$

Thus, unconditionally, we have

$$p(\text{observed labels}, t^*|i) \propto \prod_{t=1}^{T} \left(p(t) \prod_{l=1}^{T} p(l|t)^{n_{il}} \right)^{Y_{it}}, \tag{3}$$

where $Y_{it} = 1$ if $t = t^*$ and 0 otherwise. Assuming that each ROI is labelled independently of the others (no spatial correlation in terms of labels),

$$p(\text{observed labels}, t^*_i) \propto \prod_{i}^{N} \prod_{t=1}^{T} \left(p(t) \prod_{l=1}^{T} p(l|t)^{n_{il}} \right)^{Y_{it}}. \tag{4}$$

Still assuming that the types t for each ROI are known (the Y_{it}), the maximum likelihood estimators of $p(l|t)$ and $p(t)$ are

$$\hat{p}(l|t) = \frac{\sum_i Y_{it} n_{il}}{\sum_l^T \sum_i Y_{it} n_{il}} \quad (5)$$

and

$$\hat{p}(t) = \frac{1}{N} \sum_i Y_{it}. \quad (6)$$

From Bayes' rule one can then show that

$$p(Y_{it} = 1|\text{observed data}) = \frac{1}{C} \prod_l^T p(l|t)^{n_{il}} p(t) \quad (7)$$

where C is a normalization constant. Thus, given the observed data n_{il} and the parameters $p(l|t)$ and $p(t)$, one can infer the posterior probabilities of each type via Equation 7.

However, without knowing the Y_{it} values we can not infer the parameters $p(l|t)$ and $p(t)$. One can treat the Y_{it} as hidden and thus apply the well-known Expectation-Maximization (EM) procedure to find a local maximum of the likelihood function:

1. Obtain some initial estimates of the expected values of Y_{it}, e.g.,

$$E[Y_{it}] = \frac{n_{il}}{\sum_l n_{il}} \quad (8)$$

2. M-step: choose the values of $p(l|t)$ and $p(t)$ which **maximize** the likelihood function (according to Equations 5 and 6), using $E[Y_{it}]$ in place of Y_{it}.

3. E-step: calculate the conditional **expectation** of Y_{it}, $E[Y_{it}|\text{data}] = p(Y_{it} = 1|\text{data})$ (Equation 7).

4. Repeat Steps 2 and 3 until convergence.

5 Experimental Results

5.1 Combining Multiple Expert Opinions

Labellings from 4 geologists on the 4 images resulted in 269 possible volcanoes (ROIs) being identified. Application of the EM procedure resulted in label-type probability matrices as shown in Table 1 for Labeller C. The diagonal elements provide an indication of the reliability of the labeller. There is significant miscalibration for label 3's: according to the model, a label 3 from Labeller C is most likely to correspond to type 2. The label-type matrices of all 4 labellers (not shown) indicated that the model placed more weight on the conservative labellers (C and D) than the aggressive ones (A and B).

The determination of posterior probabilities for each of the ROIs is a fundamental step in any quantitative analysis of the volcano data: $p(v|\underline{l}) = \sum_{t=1}^T p(v|t) p(t|\underline{l})$ where the $p(t|\underline{l})$ terms are the posterior probabilities of type given labels provided

Table 1: Type-Label Probabilities for Individual Labellers as estimated via the EM Procedure

Marginal Label Probabilities, Labeller C

Label 1	Label 2	Label 3	Label 4	Label 5
0.026	0.056	0.193	0.416	0.309

Probability(type|label), Labeller C

	Type 1	Type 2	Type 3	Type 4	Type 5
Label 1	1.000	0.000	0.000	0.000	0.000
Label 2	0.019	0.977	0.004	0.000	0.000
Label 3	0.000	0.667	0.175	0.065	0.094
Label 4	0.000	0.000	0.042	0.725	0.233
Label 5	0.000	0.000	0.389	0.000	0.611

Table 2: 10 ROIs from the database: original scientist labels shown with posterior probabilities estimated via the EM procedure

ROI	Scientist Labels (l)				Posterior Probabilities (EM), $p(t|l)$					$p(v|l)$
	A	B	C	D	Type 1	Type 2	Type 3	Type 4	Type 5	
1	4	4	4	5	0.000	0.000	0.000	0.816	0.184	0.408
2	1	4	4	2	0.000	0.000	0.000	0.991	0.009	0.496
3	1	1	2	2	0.023	0.977	0.000	0.000	0.000	0.804
4	3	1	5	3	0.000	0.000	1.000	0.000	0.000	0.600
5	3	1	3	3	0.000	0.536	0.452	0.012	0.000	0.706
6	2	2	2	4	0.000	1.000	0.000	0.000	0.000	0.800
7	3	1	5	5	0.000	0.000	1.000	0.000	0.000	0.600
8	2	1	4	4	0.000	0.000	0.000	0.999	0.000	0.500
9	3	2	5	3	0.000	0.000	0.992	0.000	0.008	0.595
10	4	4	4	4	0.000	0.000	0.000	0.996	0.004	0.498

by the EM procedure, and the $p(v|t)$ terms are the subjective volcano-type probabilities discussed in Section 3.2. As shown in Table 2, posterior probabilities for the volcanoes generally are in agreement with intuition and often correspond to taking the majority vote or the "average" of the C and D labels (the conservative labellers). However some $p(v|\underline{l})$ estimates could not easily be derived by any simple averaging or voting scheme, e.g., see ROIs 3, 5 and 7 in the table.

5.2 Experiment on Comparing Human and Algorithm Performance

The standard receiver operating characteristic (ROC) plots detections versus false alarms [10]. The ROCs shown here differ in two significant ways [11]: (1) the false alarm axis is normalized relative to the number of true positives (necessary since the total number of possible false alarms is not well defined for object detection in images), and (2) the reference labels used in scoring are probabilistic: a detection "scores" $p(v)$ on the detection axis and $1 - p(v)$ on the false alarm axis.

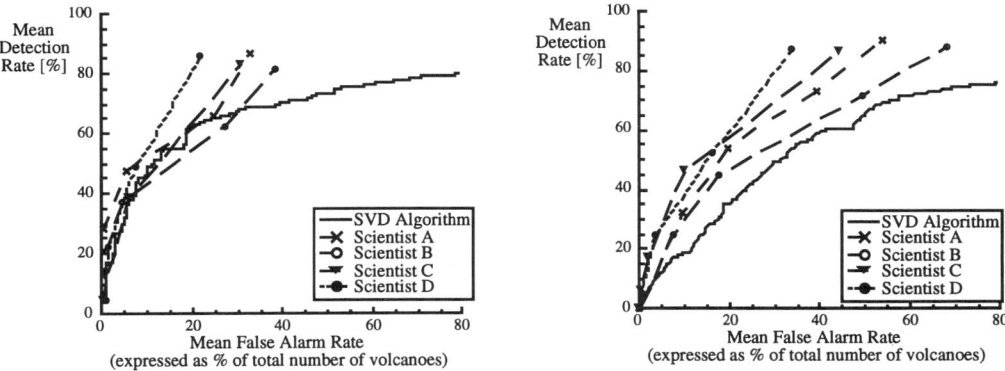

Figure 2: Modified ROCs for both scientists and algorithms: (a) without the labelling or type uncertainty, (b) with full uncertainty model factored in.

As before, data came from 4 images, and there were 269 labelled local regions. The SVD-Gaussian algorithm was evaluated in cross-validation mode (train on 3 images, test on the 4th) and the results combined. The first ROC (Figure 2(a)) does not take into account either label-type or type-volcano probabilities, i.e., the reference list (for algorithm training and overall evaluation) is a consensus list (2 scientists working together) where labels 1,2,3,4 are ignored and all labelled items are counted equally as volcanoes. The individual labellers and algorithm are then scored in the standard "non-weighted" ROC fashion. This curve is optimistic in terms of depicting the accuracy of the detectors since it ignores the underlying probabilistic nature of the labels. Even with this optimistic curve, volcano labelling is relatively inaccurate by either man or machine.

Figure 2(b) shows a weighted ROC: for each of 4 scientists the probabilistic "reference labels" were derived via the EM procedure as in Table 2 from the *other* 3 scientists, and the detections of each scientist were scored according to each such reference set. Performance of the algorithm (the SVD-Gaussian method) was evaluated relative to the EM-derived label estimates of all 4 scientists. Accounting for all of the uncertainty in the data results in a more realistic, if less flattering, set of performance characteristics. The algorithm's performance degrades more than the scientist's performance (for low false alarms rates compared to Figure 2(a)) when the full noise model is used. The algorithm is estimating the posterior probabilities of volcanoes rather poorly and the complete uncertainty model is more sensitive to this fact. This is a function of the SVD feature space rather than the Gaussian classification model.

6 Conclusion

Ignoring subjective uncertainty in image labelling can lead to significant overconfidence in terms of performance estimation (for both humans and machines). For the volcano detection task a simple model for uncertainty in the class labels provided insight into the performance of both human and algorithmic detectors. An obvious extension of the maximum likelihood framework outlined here is a Bayesian approach [12]: accounting for parameter uncertainty in the model given the limited amount of training data available is worth investigating.

Acknowledgements

The research described in this paper was carried out by the Jet Propulsion Laboratory, California Institute of Technology, under a contract with the National Aeronautics and Space Administration and was supported in part by ARPA under grant number N00014-92-J-1860.

References

1. P. Smyth, "Learning with probabilistic supervision," in *Computational Learning Theory and Natural Learning Systems 3*, T. Petcshe, M. Kearns, S. Hanson, R. Rivest (eds), Cambridge, MA: MIT Press, to appear.

2. S. French, "Group consensus probability distributions: a critical survey," in *Bayesian Statistics 2*, J. M. Bernardo, M. H. DeGroot, D. V. Lindley, A. F. M. Smith (eds.), Elsevier Science Publishers, North-Holland, pp.183–202, 1985.

3. J. S. Uebersax, "Statistical modeling of expert ratings on medical treatment appropriateness," *J. Amer. Statist. Assoc.*, vol.88, no.422, pp.421–427, 1993.

4. G. Lugosi, "Learning with an unreliable teacher," *Pattern Recognition*, vol. 25, no.1, pp.79–87. 1992.

5. *Science*, special issue on Magellan data, April 12, 1991.

6. J. C. Aubele and E. N. Slyuta, "Small domes on Venus: characteristics and origins," in *Earth, Moon and Planets*, 50/51, 493–532, 1990.

7. M. C. Burl, U. M. Fayyad, P. Perona, P. Smyth, and M. P. Burl, "Automating the hunt for volcanoes on Venus," in *Proceedings of the 1994 Computer Vision and Pattern Recognition Conference: CVPR-94*, Los Alamitos, CA: IEEE Computer Society Press, pp.302–309, 1994.

8. A. P. Dawid and A. M. Skene, "Maximum likelihood estimation of observer error-rates using the EM algorithm," *Applied Statistics*, vol.28, no.1, pp.20–28, 1979.

9. P. Smyth, M. C. Burl, U. M. Fayyad, P. Perona, 'Knowledge discovery in large image databases: dealing with uncertainties in ground truth,' in *Knowledge Discovery in Databases 2*, U. M. Fayyad, G. Piatetsky-Shapiro, P. Smyth, R. Uthurasamy (eds.), AAAI/MIT Press, to appear, 1995.

10. M. S. Chesters, "Human visual perception and ROC methodology in medical imaging," *Phys. Med. Biol.*, vol.37, no.7, pp.1433-1476, 1992.

11. M. C. Burl, U. M. Fayyad, P. Perona, P. Smyth, "Automated analysis of radar imagery of Venus: handling lack of ground truth," in *Proceedings of the IEEE Conference on Image Processing*, Austin, November 1994.

12. W. Buntine, "Operations for learning with graphical models," *Journal of Artificial Intelligence Research*, 2, pp.159–225, 1994.

The Use of Dynamic Writing Information in a Connectionist On-Line Cursive Handwriting Recognition System

Stefan Manke   Michael Finke   Alex Waibel

University of Karlsruhe
Computer Science Department
D-76128 Karlsruhe, Germany
manke@ira.uka.de, finkem@ira.uka.de

Carnegie Mellon University
School of Computer Science
Pittsburgh, PA 15213-3890, U.S.A.
waibel@cs.cmu.edu

Abstract

In this paper we present **NPen**$^{++}$, a connectionist system for writer independent, large vocabulary on-line cursive handwriting recognition. This system combines a robust input representation, which preserves the dynamic writing information, with a neural network architecture, a so called Multi-State Time Delay Neural Network (MS-TDNN), which integrates recognition and segmentation in a single framework. Our preprocessing transforms the original coordinate sequence into a (still temporal) sequence of feature vectors, which combine strictly local features, like curvature or writing direction, with a bitmap-like representation of the coordinate's proximity. The MS-TDNN architecture is well suited for handling temporal sequences as provided by this input representation. Our system is tested both on writer dependent and writer independent tasks with vocabulary sizes ranging from 400 up to 20,000 words. For example, on a 20,000 word vocabulary we achieve word recognition rates up to 88.9% (writer dependent) and 84.1% (writer independent) without using any language models.

1 INTRODUCTION

Several preprocessing and recognition approaches for on-line handwriting recognition have been developed during the past years. The main advantage of on-line handwriting recognition in comparison to optical character recognition (OCR) is the temporal information of handwriting, which can be recorded and used for recognition. In general this dynamic writing information (i.e. the time-ordered sequence of coordinates) is not available in OCR, where input consists of scanned text. In this paper we present the **NPen**$^{++}$ system, which is designed to preserve the dynamic writing information as long as possible in the preprocessing and recognition process.

During preprocessing a temporal sequence of N-dimensional feature vectors is computed from the original coordinate sequence, which is recorded on the digitizer. These feature vectors combine strictly local features, like curvature and writing direction [4], with so-called context bitmaps, which are bitmap-like representations of a coordinate's proximity.

The recognition component of **NPen**$^{++}$ is well suited for handling temporal sequences of patterns, as provided by this kind of input representation. The recognizer, a so-called Multi-State Time Delay Neural Network (MS-TDNN), integrates recognition and segmentation of words into a single network architecture. The MS-TDNN, which was originally proposed for continuous speech recognition tasks [6, 7], combines shift-invariant, high accuracy pattern recognition capabilities of a TDNN [8, 4] with a non-linear alignment procedure for aligning strokes into character sequences.

Our system is applied both to different writer dependent and writer independent, large vocabulary handwriting recognition tasks with vocabulary sizes up to 20,000 words. Writer independent word recognition rates range from 92.9% with a 400 word vocabulary to 84.1% with a 20,000 word vocabulary. For the writer dependent system, word recognition rates for the same tasks range from 98.6% to 88.9% [1].

In the following section we give a description of our preprocessing performed on the raw coordinate sequence, provided by the digitizer. In section 3 the architecture and training of the recognizer is presented. A description of the experiments to evaluate the system and the results we have achieved on different tasks can be found in section 4. Conclusions and future work is described in section 5.

2 PREPROCESSING

The dynamic writing information, i.e. the temporal order of the data points, is preserved throughout all preprocessing steps. The original coordinate sequence $\{(\bar{x}(t), \bar{y}(t))\}_{t \in \{0...T'\}}$ recorded on the digitizer is transformed into a new temporal sequence $\boldsymbol{x}_0^T = \boldsymbol{x}_0 \ldots \boldsymbol{x}_T$, where each frame $\boldsymbol{x}_t$ consists of an N-dimensional real-valued feature vector $(f_1(t), \ldots, f_N(t)) \in [-1, 1]^N$.

Several normalization methods are applied to remove undesired variability from the original coordinate sequence. To compensate for different sampling rates and varying writing speeds the coordinates originally sampled to be equidistant in time are resampled yielding a new sequence $\{(\tilde{x}(t), \tilde{y}(t))\}_{t \in \{0...T\}}$ which is equidistant in

Dynamic Writing Information in Cursive Handwriting Recognition

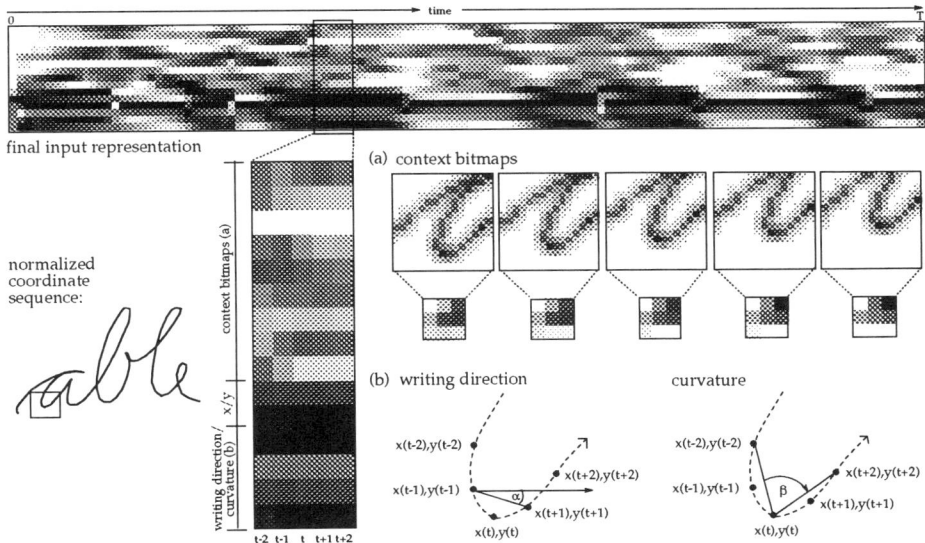

Figure 1: Feature extraction for the normalized word "able". The final input representation is derived by calculating a 15-dimensional feature vector for each data point, which consists of a context bitmap (a) and information about the curvature and writing direction (b).

space. This resampled trajectory is smoothed using a moving average window in order to remove sampling noise. In a final normalization step the goal is to find a representation of the trajectory that is reasonably invariant against rotation and scaling of the input. The idea is to determine the words' baseline using an EM approach similar to that described in [5] and rescale the word such that the center region of the word is assigned to a fixed size.

From the normalized coordinate sequence $\{(x(t), y(t))\}_{t \in \{0...T\}}$ the temporal sequence x_0^T of N-dimensional feature vectors $x_t = (f_1(t), \ldots, f_N(t))$ is computed (Figure 1). Currently the system uses $N = 15$ features for each data point. The first two features $f_1(t) = x(t) - x(t-1)$ and $f_2(t) = y(t) - b$ describe the relative X movement and the Y position relative to the baseline b. The features $f_3(t)$ to $f_6(t)$ are used to describe the curvature and writing direction in the trajectory [4] (Figure 1(b)). Since all these features are strictly local in the sense that they are local both in time and in space they were shown to be inadequate for modeling temporal long range context dependencies typically observed in pen trajectories [2]. Therefore, nine additional features $f_7(t)$ to $f_{15}(t)$ representing 3×3 bitmaps were included in each feature vector (Figure 1(a)). These so-called context bitmaps are basically low resolution, bitmap-like descriptions of the coordinate's proximity, which were originally described in [2].

Thus, the input representation as shown in Figure 1 combines strictly local features like writing direction and curvature with the context bitmaps, which are still local in space but global in time. That means, each point of the trajectory is visible from each other point of the trajectory in a small neighbourhood. By using these context bitmaps in addition to the local features, important information about other parts of the trajectory, which are in a limited neighbourhood of a coordinate, are encoded.

3 THE NPen++ RECOGNIZER

The **NPen++** recognizer integrates recognition and segmentation of words into a single network architecture, the Multi-State Time Delay Neural Network (MS-TDNN). The MS-TDNN, which was originally proposed for continuous speech recognition tasks [6, 7], combines the high accuracy single character recognition capabilities of a TDNN [8, 4] with a non-linear time alignment algorithm (dynamic time warping) for finding stroke and character boundaries in isolated handwritten words.

3.1 MODELING ASSUMPTIONS

Let $W = \{w_1, \ldots w_K\}$ be a vocabulary consisting of K words. Each of these words w_i is represented as a sequence of characters $w_i \equiv c_{i_1} c_{i_2} \ldots c_{i_k}$ where each character c_j itself is modelled by a three state hidden markov model $c_j \equiv q_j^0 q_j^1 q_j^2$. The idea of using three states per character is to model explicitly the initial, middle and final section of the characters. Thus, w_i is modelled by a sequence of states $w_i \equiv q_{i_0} q_{i_1} \ldots q_{j_{3k}}$. In these word HMMs the self-loop probabilities $p(q_{i_j}|q_{i_j})$ and the transition probabilities $p(q_{i_j}|q_{i_{j-1}})$ are both defined to be $\frac{1}{2}$ while all other transition probabilities are set to zero.

During recognition of an unknown sequence of feature vectors $\boldsymbol{x}_0^T = \boldsymbol{x}_0 \ldots \boldsymbol{x}_T$ we have to find the word $w_i \in W$ in the dictionary that maximizes the a-posteriori probability $p(w_i|\boldsymbol{x}_0^T, \theta)$ given a fixed set of parameters θ and the observed coordinate sequence. That means, a written word will be recognized such that

$$w_j = \mathrm{argmax}_{w_i \in W} p(w_i|\boldsymbol{x}_0^T, \theta).$$

In our Multi-State Time Delay Neural Network approach the problem of modeling the word posterior probability $p(w_i|\boldsymbol{x}_0^T, \theta)$ is simplified by using Bayes' rule which expresses that probability as

$$p(w_i|\boldsymbol{x}_0^T, \theta) = \frac{p(\boldsymbol{x}_0^T|w_i, \theta) P(w_i|\theta)}{p(\boldsymbol{x}_0^T|\theta)}.$$

Instead of approximating $p(w_i|\boldsymbol{x}_0^T, \theta)$ directly we define in the following section a network that is supposed to model the likelihood of the feature vector sequence $p(\boldsymbol{x}_0^T|w_i, \theta)$.

3.2 THE MS-TDNN ARCHITECTURE

In Figure 2 the basic MS-TDNN architecture for handwriting recognition is shown. The first three layers constitute a standard TDNN with sliding input windows in each layer. In the current implementation of the system, a TDNN with 15 input

Dynamic Writing Information in Cursive Handwriting Recognition

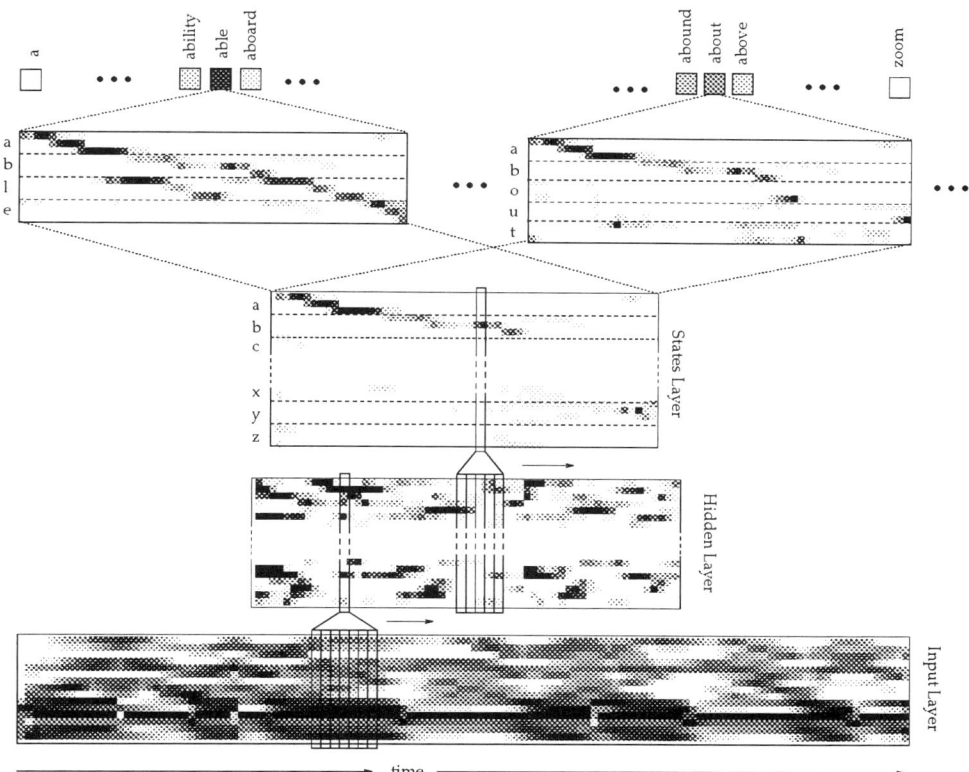

Figure 2: The Multi-State TDNN architecture, consisting of a 3-layer TDNN to estimate the a posteriori probabilities of the character states combined with word units, whose scores are derived from the word models by a Viterbi approximation of the likelihoods $p(x_0^T|w_i)$.

units, 40 units in the hidden layer, and 78 state output units is used. There are 7 time delays both in the input and hidden layer.

The softmax normalized output of the states layer is interpreted as an estimate of the probabilities of the states q_j given the input window $x_{t-d}^{t+d} = x_{t-d} \ldots x_{t+d}$ for each time frame t, i.e.

$$p(q_j|x_{t-d}^{t+d}) \approx \frac{\exp(\eta_j(t))}{\sum_k \exp(\eta_k(t))} \quad (1)$$

where $\eta_j(t)$ represents the weighted sum of inputs to state unit j at time t. Based on these estimates, the output of the word units is defined to be a Viterbi approximation of the log likelihoods of the feature vector sequence given the word model

w_i, i.e.

$$\log p(x_0^T|w_i) \approx \max_{q_0^T} \sum_{t=1}^T \log p(x_{t-d}^{t+d}|q_t, w_i) + \log p(q_t|q_{t-1}, w_i)$$

$$\approx \max_{q_0^T} \sum_{t=1}^T \log p(q_t|x_{t-d}^{t+d}) - \log p(q_t) + \log p(q_t|q_{t-1}, w_i). \quad (2)$$

Here, the maximum is over all possible sequences of states $q_0^T = q_0 \ldots q_T$ given a word model, $p(q_t|x_{t-d}^{t+d})$ refers to the output of the states layer as defined in (1) and $p(q_t)$ is the prior probability of observing a state q_t estimated on the training data.

3.3 TRAINING OF THE RECOGNIZER

During training the goal is to determine a set of parameters θ that will maximize the posterior probability $p(w|x_0^T, \theta)$ for all training input sequences. But in order to make that maximization computationally feasible even for a large vocabulary system we had to simplify that maximum a posteriori approach to a maximum likelihood training procedure that maximizes $p(x_0^T|w, \theta)$ for all words instead.

The first step of our maximum likelihood training is to bootstrap the recognizer using a subset of approximately 2,000 words of the training set that were labeled manually with the character boundaries to adjust the paths in the word layer correctly. After training on this hand-labeled data, the recognizer is used to label another larger set of unlabeled training data. Each pattern in this training set is processed by the recognizer. The boundaries determined automatically by the Viterbi alignment in the target word unit serve as new labels for this pattern. Then, in the second phase, the recognizer is retrained on both data sets to achieve the final performance of the recognizer.

4 EXPERIMENTS AND RESULTS

We have tested our system both on writer dependent and writer independent tasks with vocabulary sizes ranging from 400 up to 20,000 words. The word recognition results are shown in Table 1. The scaling of the recognition rates with respect to the vocabulary size is plotted in Figure 3b.

Table 1: Writer dependent and independent recognition results

Task	Vocabulary Size	Writer Dependent		Writer Independent	
		Test Patterns	Recognition Rate	Test Patterns	Recognition Rate
crt_400	400	800	98.6%	800	92.9%
wsj_1,000	1,000	800	97.8%	-	-
wsj_7,000	7,000	-	-	2,500	89.3%
wsj_10,000	10,000	1,600	92.1%	2,500	87.7%
wsj_20,000	20,000	1,600	88.9%	2,500	84.1%

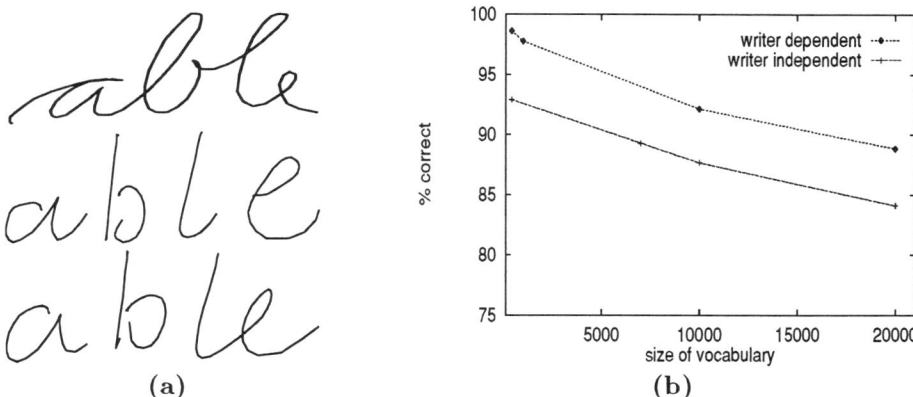

Figure 3: (a) Different writing styles in the database: cursive (top), hand-printed (middle) and a mixture of both (bottom) (b) Recognition results with respect to the vocabulary size

For the writer dependent evaluation, the system was trained on 2,000 patterns from a 400 word vocabulary, written by a single writer, and tested on a disjunct set of patterns from the same writer. In the writer dependent case, the training set consisted of 4,000 patterns from a 7,000 word vocabulary, written by approximately 60 different writers. The test was performed on data from an independent set of 40 writers.

All data used in these experiments was collected at the University of Karlsruhe, Germany. Only minimal instructions were given to the writers. The writers were asked to write as natural as they would normally do on paper, without any restrictions in writing style. The consequence is, that the database is characterized by a high variety of different writing styles, ranging from hand-printed to strictly cursive patterns or a mixture of both writing styles (for example see Figure 3a). Additionally the native language of the writers was german, but the language of the dictionary is english. Therefore, frequent hesitations and corrections can be observed in the patterns of the database. But since this sort of input is typical for real world applications, a robust recognizer should be able to process these distorted patterns, too. From each of the writers a set of 50-100 isolated words, choosen randomly from the 7,000 word vocabulary, was collected.

The used vocabularies CRT (Conference Registration Task) and WSJ (ARPA Wall Street Journal Task) were originally defined for speech recognition evaluations. These vocabularies were chosen to take advantage of the synergy effects between handwriting recognition and speech recognition, since in our case the final goal is to integrate our speech recognizer JANUS [10] and the proposed **NPen^{++}** system into a multi-modal system.

5 CONCLUSIONS

In this paper we have presented the **NPen**$^{++}$ system, a neural recognizer for writer dependent and writer independent on-line cursive handwriting recognition. This system combines a robust input representation, which preserves the dynamic writing information, with a neural network integrating recognition and segmentation in a single framework. This architecture has been shown to be well suited for handling temporal sequences as provided by this kind of input.

Evaluation of the system on different tasks with vocabulary sizes ranging from 400 to 20,000 words has shown recognition rates from 92.9% to 84.1% in the writer independent case and from 98.6% to 88.9% in the writer dependent case. These results are especially promising because they were achieved with a small training set compared to other systems (e.g. [3]). As can be seen in Table 1, the system has proved to be virtually independent of the vocabulary. Though the system was trained on rather small vocabularies (e.g. 400 words in the writer dependent system), it generalizes well to completely different and much larger vocabularies.

References

[1] S. Manke and U. Bodenhausen, "A Connectionist Recognizer for Cursive Handwriting Recognition", *Proceedings of the ICASSP-94*, Adelaide, April 1994.

[2] S. Manke, M. Finke, and A. Waibel, "Combining Bitmaps with Dynamic Writing Information for On-Line Handwriting Recognition", *Proceedings of the ICPR-94*, Jerusalem, October 1994.

[3] M. Schenkel, I. Guyon, and D. Henderson, "On-Line Cursive Script Recognition Using Time Delay Neural Networks and Hidden Markov Models", *Proceedings of the ICASSP-94*, Adelaide, April 1994.

[4] I. Guyon, P. Albrecht, Y. Le Cun, W. Denker, and W. Hubbard, "Design of a Neural Network Character Recognizer for a Touch Terminal", *Pattern Recognition*, 24(2), 1991.

[5] Y. Bengio and Y. LeCun. "Word Normalization for On-Line Handwritten Word Recognition", *Proceedings of the ICPR-94*, Jerusalem, October 1994.

[6] P. Haffner and A. Waibel, "Multi-State Time Delay Neural Networks for Continuous Speech Recognition", *Advances in Neural Information Processing Systems (NIPS-4)*, Morgan Kaufman, 1992.

[7] C. Bregler, H. Hild, S. Manke, and A. Waibel, "Improving Connected Letter Recognition by Lipreading", *Proceedings of the ICASSP-93*, Minneapolis, April 1993.

[8] A. Waibel, T. Hanazawa, G. Hinton, K. Shiano, and K. Lang, "Phoneme Recognition using Time-Delay Neural Networks", *IEEE Transactions on Acoustics, Speech and Signal Processing*, March 1989.

[9] W. Guerfali and R. Plamondon, "Normalizing and Restoring On-Line Handwriting", *Pattern Recognition*, 16(5), 1993.

[10] M. Woszczyna et al., "Janus 94: Towards Spontaneous Speech Translation", *Proceedings of the ICASSP-94*, Adelaide, April 1994.

Adaptive Elastic Input Field for Recognition Improvement

Minoru Asogawa
C&C Research Laboratories, NEC
Miyamae, Miyazaki, Kawasaki Kanagawa 213 Japan
asogawa@csl.cl.nec.co.jp

Abstract

For machines to perform classification tasks, such as speech and character recognition, appropriately handling deformed patterns is a key to achieving high performance. The authors presents a new type of classification system, an Adaptive Input Field Neural Network (AIFNN), which includes a simple pre-trained neural network and an elastic input field attached to an input layer. By using an iterative method, AIFNN can determine an optimal affine translation for an elastic input field to compensate for the original deformations. The convergence of the AIFNN algorithm is shown. AIFNN is applied for handwritten numerals recognition. Consequently, 10.83% of originally misclassified patterns are correctly categorized and total performance is improved, without modifying the neural network.

1 Introduction

For machines to accomplish classification tasks, such as speech and character recognition, appropriately handling deformed patterns is a key to achieving high performance [Simard 92] [Simard 93] [Hinton 92] [Barnard 91]. The number of reasonable deformations of patterns is enormous, since they can be either linear translations (an affine translation or a time shifting) or non-linear deformations (a set of combinations of partial translations), or both.

Although a simple neural network (e.g. a 3-layered neural network) is able to adapt

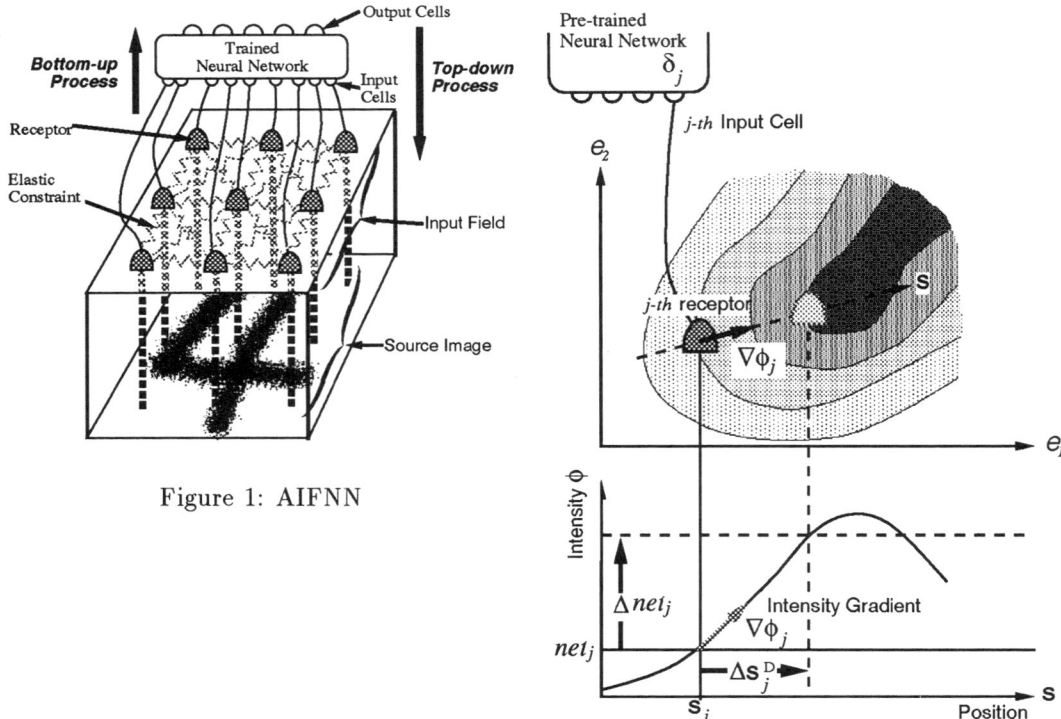

Figure 1: AIFNN

Figure 2: Delta Force

non-linear deformations and to discriminate noises, it is still necessary to have additional methods or data to appropriately process deformations.

This paper presents a new type of classification system, an Adaptive Input Field Neural Network (AIFNN), which includes a simple pre-trained neural network and an elastic input field attached to an input layer. The neural network is applied to non-linear deformation compensations and the elastic input field to linear deformations.

The AIFNN algorithm can determine an optimal affine translation for compensating for the original patterns' deformations, which are misclassified by the pre-trained neural network. As the result, those misclassified patterns are correctly classified and the final classification performance is improved, compared to that for the original neural network, without modifying the neural network.

2 Adaptive Input Field Neural Network (AIFNN)

AIFNN includes a pre-trained neural network and an elastic input field attached to an input layer (Fig. 1). The elastic input field contains receptors sampling input patterns at each location. Each receptor connects to a cell in the input layer. Each receptor links to its adjacent receptors with an elastic constraint and can move over the input pattern independently, as long as its relative elastic constraint is satisfied. The affine translation of the whole receptor (e.g. a shift, rotation, scale and slant translation) satisfies an elastic constraint, since a constraint violation is induced by the receptors' relative locations. [1] Partial deformations are also allowed with a little constraint violation.

This feature of the elastic constraint is similar to that of the Elastic Net method [Durbin 87], which can solve NP-hard problems. Although this elastic net method is directly applicable to the template matching method, the performance is highly dependent on the template selection. Therefore, an elaborated feature space for non-linear deformations is mandatory [Hinton 92]. AIFNN utilizes something like an elastic net constraint, but does not require any prominent templates.

The AIFNN algorithm is a repeated sequence of a bottom-up process (calculating a guess and comparing with the presumption) and a top-down process (modifying receptor's location to decrease the error and to satisfy the input field constraints). For applying AIFNN as a classifier, a parallel search is performed; all categories are chosen as presumption categories and the AIFNN algorithm is executed. After hundreds of repetitions, an L score is calculated, which is the sum of the error and the constraint violation in the elastic input field. A category which produces the lowest L score is chosen as a plausible category. In Section 3, it is proved that all receptors will settle to an equilibrium state. In the following sections, details about the bottom-up and top-down processes are described.

Bottom-Up Process:
When a novel pattern is presented, each receptor samples activation corresponding to a pattern intensity at each location. Each receptor activation is directly transmitted to a corresponding neural network input cell. Those input values are forwarded through a pre-trained neural network and an output guess is obtained.

This guess is compared to the presumption category, and the negative of this error is defined as the presumption certainty. [2] For example, using the mean squared error criterion, the error E^D is defined as follows;

$$E^D = \frac{1}{2}\sum_k (d_k - o_k)^2, \qquad (1)$$

where o_k is the output value, and d_k is the desired value determined by the presumption category. The presumption certainty is defined as $-E^D$.

Top-Down Process:
To minimize the error and to maximize the presumption certainty, each receptor modifies the activation by moving its location over the input pattern. The new location for each receptor is determined by two elements; a direction which yields less error and a direction which satisfies the input field elastic constraint. The former element is called a Delta Force, since it relates to a delta value of an input layer cell. The latter element is named an Address Force. Each receptor moves to

---

[1] In previous papers, [Asogawa 90] and [Asogawa 91], a shift and rotation translation was taken into account. In those models, a scale and slant translation violated the elastic constraint.

[2] Although another category coding schema is also possible, for simplicity, it is presumed that each output cell corresponds to one certain category.

a new location, which is determined by a sum of those two forces. The sum force is called the Combined Force. In the next two sections, details about these forces are described.

Delta Force: The Delta Force, which reduces E^D by altering receptors' locations, is determined by two elements: a partial derivative for the input value to the error, and a local pattern gradient at each receptor location (Fig. 1).

To decrease the error E^D, the value divergence for the j-th cell is computed as,

$$\Delta net_j \equiv -\alpha^D \frac{\partial E^D}{\partial net_j} = \alpha^D \delta_j, \qquad (2)$$

where α^D is small positive number and δ_j is a delta value for the j-th input cell and computed by the back-propagation [Yamada 91]. Δnet_j and a local pattern gradient $\nabla \phi_j$ are utilized to calculate a Delta Force Δs_j^D; a scalar value of Δs_j^D is given as,

$$|\Delta s_j^D| = \frac{\Delta net_j}{|\nabla \phi_j|}. \qquad (3)$$

The direction of the Delta Force Δs_j^D is chosen as being parallel to that of $\nabla \phi_j$. Consequently, Δs_j^D is given as,

$$\Delta s_j^D = \frac{\Delta net_j}{|\nabla \phi_j|} \frac{\nabla \phi_j}{|\nabla \phi_j|} = \alpha^D \frac{\delta_j}{|\nabla \phi_j|^2} \nabla \phi_j. \qquad (4)$$

To avoid Δs_j^D becoming infinity, when $|\nabla \phi_j|$ is almost equal to 0, a small constant $c(=\frac{1}{4})$ is added to the denominator; therefore, Δs_j^D is defined as,

$$\Delta s_j^D = \alpha^D \frac{\delta_j}{|\nabla \phi_j|^2 + c} \nabla \phi_j. \qquad (5)$$

Address Force: If each receptor is moved iteratively following only the Delta Force, the error becomes its minimum. However, receptors may not satisfy the input field constraint and induce a large constraint violation E^A. Here, E^A is defined by a distance between a receptor's lattice $\mathbf{S}$ and a lattice which is derived by an affine translation from the original lattice. Therefore, E^A is defined as follows;

$$\begin{aligned} E^A &\equiv \frac{1}{2} d(\mathbf{S^N}, \mathbf{S}) = \frac{1}{2} \sum_i \|\mathbf{s}_i^N - \mathbf{s}_i\|^2 \\ &= \frac{1}{2} d(\mathcal{T}(\mathbf{S^O}; \mathbf{t}), \mathbf{S}), \end{aligned} \qquad (6)$$

where $d(\cdot, \cdot)$ is a distance measure for two receptor's lattices. $\mathbf{S}$ is a current receptor lattice. $\mathbf{S^N}$ is the receptor lattice given by the affine translation $\mathcal{T}(\cdot)$ with parameters $\mathbf{t}$ and $\mathbf{S^O}$. $\mathbf{S^O}$ is the original receptor lattice.

Therefore, as long as the receptor's lattice can be driven by some affine translation, there is no constraint violation.

The affine parameters $\mathbf{t}$ are estimated so as to minimize E^A;

$$\frac{\partial E^A}{\partial t_i} = 0 \qquad \text{for } i = 1, \cdots, 6. \qquad (7)$$

Since E^A is quadratic with respect to t_i, computing t_i is moderate. The Address Force for the j-th receptor Δs_j^A is defined as the partial derivative to E^A with respect to the receptor's location s_j;

$$\Delta s_j^A \equiv -\alpha^A \frac{\partial E^A}{\partial s_j}, \tag{8}$$

where α^A is a small positive constant.

Combined Force: Here, all receptors are moved by a Combined Force Δs, which is a sum of the Delta Force Δs^D and the Address Force Δs^A.

After one hundred iterations, all receptors are moved to the location which produces the minimum output error and the minimum constraint violation. Final states are evaluated with a new measurement L score, which is the sum of the error E^D and the constraint violation E^A; i.e. $L = E^D + E^A$.

This L score is utilized to choose the correct category in a parallel search. In a parallel search, each category is temporarily chosen as a presumption and converged L scores are calculated. Those scores are compared and the category yielding the smallest L score is chosen as the correct category. This method fully exploits the features of AIFNN, but it requires a large amount of computation, which can fortunately be processed totally in parallel. In the following section, convergence of the AIFNN is shown.

3 Convergence

Convergence is shown by proving that the L is a Lyapunov function. When the L is a Lyapunov function, all receptors converge to some locations after iterations. The necessary and sufficient conditions for a Lyapunov function are (1) L has a lower bound and (2) L monotonically decreases by applying the Combined Forces.

(1) Lower Bound:
E^D is the squared error at the output layer. Therefore, $E^D \geq 0$. E^A is the constraint violation, which is defined with a distance between two lattices. Therefore, $E^A \geq 0$. Since the L is a sum of E^D and E^A, the existence of a lower bound for the L is proved. □

(2) Monotonically Decrease:
The derivative of the L is calculated to show that the L decreases monotonically.

$$\begin{aligned}
\frac{dL}{dt} &= \frac{dE^D}{dt} + \frac{dE^A}{dt} \\
&= \sum_i \left\{ \frac{\partial E^D}{\partial s_i} \frac{ds_i}{dt} \right\} + \sum_i \left\{ \frac{\partial E^A}{\partial s_i} \frac{ds_i}{dt} \right\} \\
&= \sum_i \left\{ \left(\frac{\partial E^D}{\partial s_i} + \frac{\partial E^A}{\partial s_i} \right) \frac{ds_i}{dt} \right\},
\end{aligned} \tag{9}$$

where $\frac{ds_i}{dt}$ is the Combined Force and given as,

$$\frac{ds_i}{dt} = \Delta s^D + \Delta s^A. \tag{10}$$

When a source image is smooth and $|\nabla\phi_i|$ is smaller than c, the following approximation is satisfied;

$$\frac{\nabla\phi_i}{|\nabla\phi_i|^2 + c} \simeq \nabla\phi_i. \tag{11}$$

By using Eq. (11), the Delta Force is approximated as follows;

$$\Delta \mathbf{s}^D = \alpha^D \frac{\nabla\phi_i}{|\nabla\phi_i|^2 + c}\frac{\delta_i}{\nabla\phi_i} \simeq -\alpha^D \frac{\partial E^D}{\partial \mathbf{s}_i}. \tag{12}$$

By using Eqs. (8) and (12), and by letting $\alpha^D = \alpha^A$, the L derivative is computed as follows;

$$\frac{dL}{dt} \simeq -\alpha^A \sum_i \left(\frac{\partial E^D}{\partial \mathbf{s}_i} + \frac{\partial E^A}{\partial \mathbf{s}_i}\right)^2 \leq 0. \tag{13}$$

With Eq. (13), it is proved that L decreases monotonically.□

4   Experiments and Results

Hand-written numerals recognition is chosen as one of the applications of AIFNN, since performance improvement is shown by compensating for deformations [Simard 92] [Simard 93] [Hinton 92]. The numeral inputs are bi-level images of 32×40. They are blurred with a 5×5 Gaussian kernel and resampled to 14×18 pixel gray level images. To calculate an intensity and a local gradient between grids, bi-linear Lagrange interpolation is utilized.

A neural network is 3 layered. The numbers of cells for the input layer, the hidden layer and the output layer are 252, 20 and 10, respectively. To obtain a simpler weight configuration, two techniques are utilized; a constant weight decay [Ishikawa 89] and a small constant addition to output function derivatives [Fahlman 88]. Training is repeated for 180 epochs with 2500 numerals, and tested with another 2500. Since image edges are almost blank, about 2400 connections between the input layer and the hidden layer are equal to 0; therefore, the number of parameters is reduced to 2870.

In this experiment, a simple decision method is used; the maximum output cell is chosen as a guess and patterns are rejected when the error of the guess is greater than a threshold value. Naturally, a low threshold yields a low misclassification rate, but also yields a high rejection rate [Martin 92]. With the maximum threshold, the rates of rejection, correct classification and misclassification are 0.00%(0 patterns), 95.20%(2380 patterns) and 4.80%(120 patterns), respectively. For the 2500 numerals learning data, these rates are 0.00%(0 patterns), 99.40%(2485 patterns) and 0.60%(15 patterns). When a threshold is 0.001, the rates of rejection, correct classification and misclassification are 43.52%(1088 patterns), 56.40%(1410 patterns) and 0.08%(2 patterns), respectively.

AIFNN is applied to these 1088 rejected patterns. and classifies 997 patterns correctly. Therefore, total performances for rejection, correct classification and misclassification become 0.00%(0 patterns), 95.72%(2393 patterns) and 4.28%(107 patterns), respectively. As the classification performance is improved; the number of misclassified patterns reduces from 120 to 107 without modifying the neural network. 10.83% of the originally misclassified patterns are correctly categorized. Fig. 3 shows an input field after one hundred iterations.

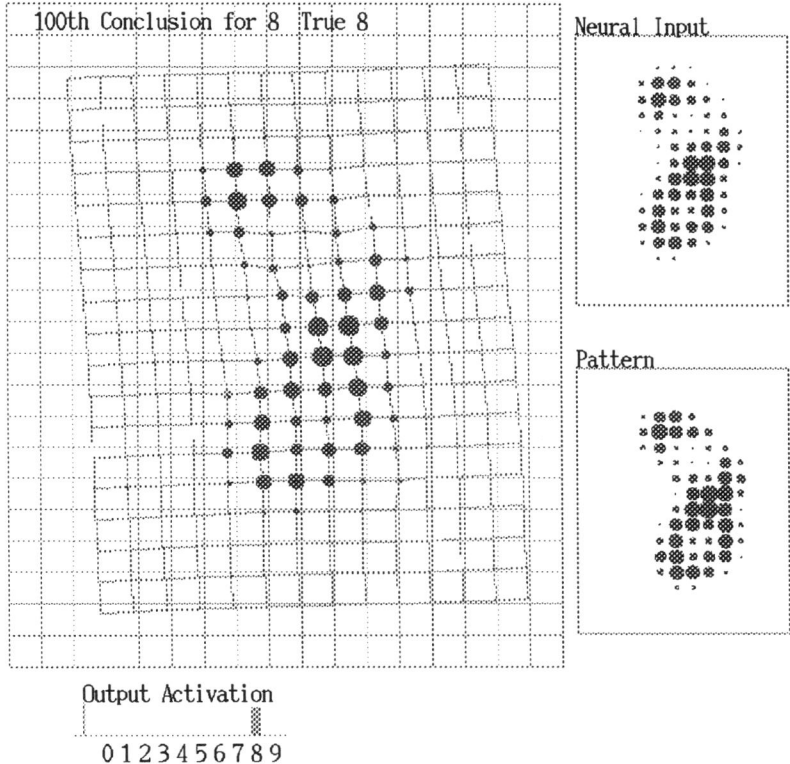

In the figure on the left, receptors are located at each grid point in a gray lattice. The circle diameter corresponds to the pattern intensity at each receptor's location. The bottom right figure indicates the source image, and the top right figure indicates the neural network input. This image was initially misclassified as 3 instead of 8. After iteration with presumption as 8, category 8 gets the highest activation and the receptor's lattice is rotated to compensate for the initial deformation.

Figure 3: Input Field After Adaptation

5 Discussion

It is shown that the AIFNN can improve the classification performance for the original neural network, without modifications. This performance improvement is caused by an optimal affine translations estimation for rejected patterns.

Although an affine translation is discussed in this paper, the algorithm is applicable to any deformation mechanism; such as a gain and offset equalization and 3D perspective deformation.

The requirement for a neural network in AIFNN is the capability of calculating partial derivatives for an input layer, so a layered neural network is utilized in this paper. Since partial derivative can be computed by numerical approximation, practically any neural network is applicable for AIFNN. Moreover, any differentiable error criterion is applicable; such as, a KL information and a likelihood.

To reduce computation, a sequential searching is also possible; a presumption is chosen as the most plausible category, e.g. the smallest error category. If the L score falls behind a threshold, this presumption is regarded as correct. If it's not, another plausible category is chosen as a presumption and tested [Asogawa 91].

References

[Asogawa 90] M. Asogawa, "Adaptive Input Field Neural Network – that can recognize rotated and/or shifted character –", *Proceedings of IJCNN '90 at San Diego*, vol. 3. pp. 733-738. June 1990.

[Asogawa 91] M. Asogawa, "Adaptive Input Field Neural Network", *Proceedings of IJCNN '91 at Singapore*, vol. 1. pp. 83-88. November 1991.

[Barnard 91] E. Barnard et al., "Invariance and Neural Nets", *IEEE trans. on Neural Networks*, vol. 2. no. 5, pp. 498-508. 1992.

[Durbin 87] R. Durbin et al., "An analogue approach to the traveling salesman problem using an elastic net method", *Nature*, vol. 326. pp. 689-691. 1987.

[Fahlman 88] S. Fahlman, "An empirical study of learning speed in back-propagation networks", CMU-CS-88-162, 1988.

[Hinton 92] G.E. Hinton et al., "Adaptive Elastic Models for Hand-Printed Character Recognition", *Advances in Neural Information Processing Systems*, vol. 4. pp. 512-519. 1992.

[Ishikawa 89] M. Ishikawa, "A structural learning algorithm with forgetting of link weights", *Proceedings of IJCNN '89 at Washington DC.*, vol. 2, pp. 626, 1989.

[Martin 92] G. L. Martin et al., "Recognizing Overlapping Hand-Printed Characters by Centered-Object Integrated Segmentation and Recognition", *Advances in Neural Information Processing Systems*, vol. 4. pp. 504-511. 1992.

[Simard 92] P. Simard et al., "Tangent Prop - A Formalism for Specifying Selected Invariances in an Adaptive Network", *Advances in Neural Information Processing Systems*, vol. 4. pp. 895-903. 1992.

[Simard 93] P. Simard et al., "Efficient Pattern Recognition Using a New Transformation Distance", *Advances in Neural Information Processing Systems*, vol. 5. pp. 50-58. 1993.

[Yamada 91] K. Yamada, "Learning of category boundaries based on inverse recall by multilayer neural network", *Proceedings of IJCNN '91 at Seattle*, pp. 7-12 vol.2 1991.

Pairwise Neural Network Classifiers with Probabilistic Outputs

David Price
A2iA and ESPCI
3 Rue de l'Arrivée, BP 59
75749 Paris Cedex 15, France
a2ia@dialup.francenet.fr

Stefan Knerr
ESPCI and CNRS (UPR A0005)
10, Rue Vauquelin, 75005 Paris, France
knerr@neurones.espci.fr

Léon Personnaz, Gérard Dreyfus
ESPCI, Laboratoire d'Electronique
10, Rue Vauquelin, 75005 Paris, France
dreyfus@neurones.espci.fr

Abstract

Multi-class classification problems can be efficiently solved by partitioning the original problem into sub-problems involving only two classes: for each pair of classes, a (potentially small) neural network is trained using only the data of these two classes. We show how to combine the outputs of the two-class neural networks in order to obtain posterior probabilities for the class decisions. The resulting probabilistic pairwise classifier is part of a handwriting recognition system which is currently applied to check reading. We present results on real world data bases and show that, from a practical point of view, these results compare favorably to other neural network approaches.

1 Introduction

Generally, a pattern classifier consists of two main parts: a feature extractor and a classification algorithm. Both parts have the same ultimate goal, namely to transform a given input pattern into a representation that is easily interpretable as a class decision. In the case of feedforward neural networks, the interpretation is particularly easy if each class is represented by one output unit. For many pattern recognition problems, it suffices that the classifier compute the class of the input pattern, in which case it is common practice to associate the pattern to the class corresponding to the maximum output of the classifier. Other problems require graded (soft) decisions, such as probabilities, at the output of the classifier for further use in higher context levels: in speech or character recognition for instance, the probabilistic outputs of the phoneme (character) recognizer are often used by a Hidden-Markov-Model algorithm or by some other dynamic programming algorithm to compute the most probable word hypothesis.

In the context of classification, it has been shown that the minimization of the Mean Square Error (MSE) yields estimates of a posteriori class probabilities [Bourlard & Wellekens, 1990; Duda & Hart, 1973]. The minimization can be performed by a feedforward multilayer perceptrons (MLP's) using the backpropagation algorithm, which is one of the reasons why MLP's are widely used for pattern recognition tasks. However, MLPs have well-known limitations when coping with real-world problems, namely long training times and unknown architecture.

In the present paper, we show that the estimation of posterior probabilities for a K-class problem can be performed efficiently using estimates of posterior probabilities for K(K-1)/2 two-class sub-problems. Since the number of sub-problems increases as K^2, this procedure was originally intended for applications involving a relatively small number of classes, such as the 10 classes for the recognition of handwritten digits [Knerr et al., 1992]. In this paper we show that this approach is also viable for applications with K >> 10.

The probabilistic pairwise classifier presented in this paper is part of a handwriting recognition system, discussed elsewhere [Simon, 1992], which is currently applied to check reading. The purpose of our character recognizer is to classify pre-segmented characters from cursive handwriting. The probabilistic outputs of the recognizer are used to estimate word probabilities. We present results on real world data involving 27 classes, compare these results to other neural network approaches, and show that our probabilistic pairwise classifier is a powerful tool for computing posterior class probabilities in pattern recognition problems.

2 Probabilistic Outputs from Two-class Classifiers

Multi-class classification problems can be efficiently solved by "divide and conquer" strategies which partition the original problem into a set of K(K-1)/2 two-class problems. For each pair of classes ω_i and ω_j, a (potentially small) neural network with a single output unit is trained on the data of the two classes [Knerr et al., 1990, and references therein]. In this section, we show how to obtain probabilistic outputs from each of the two-class classifiers in the pairwise neural network classifier (Figure 1).

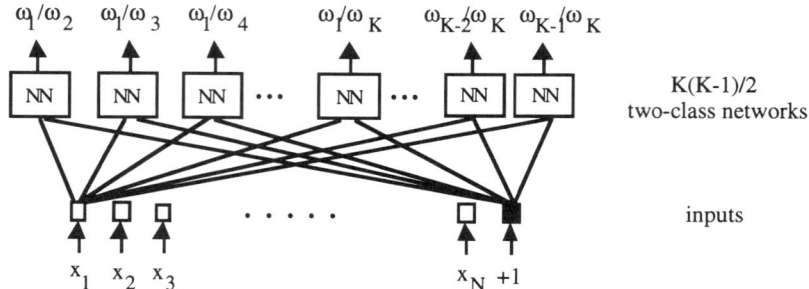

Figure 1: Pairwise neural network classifier.

It has been shown that the minimization of the MSE cost function (or likewise a cost function based on an entropy measure, [Bridle, 1990]) leads to estimates of posterior probabilities. Of course, the quality of the estimates depends on the number and distribution of examples in the training set and on the minimization method used.
In the theoretical case of two classes ω_1 and ω_2, each Gaussian distributed, with means $\mathbf{m}_1$ and $\mathbf{m}_2$, a priori probabilities Pr_1 and Pr_2, and equal covariance matrices Σ, the posterior probability of class ω_1 given the pattern $\mathbf{x}$ is:

$$\text{Pr}(\text{class}=\omega_1 \mid X=\mathbf{x}) = \frac{1}{1 + \frac{\text{Pr}_2}{\text{Pr}_1} \exp\left(-\frac{1}{2}\left(2\mathbf{x}^T\Sigma^{-1}(\mathbf{m}_1-\mathbf{m}_2) + \mathbf{m}_2^T\Sigma^{-1}\mathbf{m}_2 - \mathbf{m}_1^T\Sigma^{-1}\mathbf{m}_1\right)\right)} \quad (1)$$

Thus a single neuron with a sigmoidal transfer function can compute the posterior probabilities for the two classes.
However, in the case of real world data bases, classes are not necessarily Gaussian distributed, and therefore the transformation of the $K(K-1)/2$ outputs of our pairwise neural network classifier to posterior probabilities proceeds in two steps.
In the first step, a class-conditional probability density estimation is performed on the linear output of each two-class neural network: for both classes ω_i and ω_j of a given two-class neural network, we fit the probability density over v_{ij} (the weighted sum of the inputs of the output neuron) to a function. We denote by ω_{ij} the union of classes ω_i and ω_j. The resulting class-conditional densities $p(v_{ij} \mid \omega_i)$ and $p(v_{ij} \mid \omega_j)$ can be transformed to probabilities $\text{Pr}(\omega_i \mid \omega_{ij} \wedge (V_{ij}=v_{ij}))$ and $\text{Pr}(\omega_j \mid \omega_{ij} \wedge (V_{ij}=v_{ij}))$ via the Bayes rule (note that $\text{Pr}(\omega_{ij} \wedge (V_{ij}=v_{ij}) \mid \omega_i) = \text{Pr}((V_{ij}=v_{ij}) \mid \omega_i)$):

$$\text{Pr}(\omega_i \mid \omega_{ij} \wedge (V_{ij}=v_{ij})) = \frac{p(v_{ij} \mid \omega_i)\, \text{Pr}(\omega_i)}{\sum_{k \in \{i,j\}} p(v_{ij} \mid \omega_k)\, \text{Pr}(\omega_k)} \quad (2)$$

It is a central assumption of our approach that the linear classifier output v_{ij} is as informative as the input vector $\mathbf{x}$. Hence, we approximate $\text{Pr}_{ij} = \text{Pr}(\omega_i \mid \omega_{ij} \wedge (X=\mathbf{x}))$ by $\text{Pr}(\omega_i \mid \omega_{ij} \wedge (V=v_{ij}))$. Note that $P_{ji} = 1-P_{ij}$.
In the second step, the probabilities Pr_{ij} are combined to obtain posterior probabilities $\text{Pr}(\omega_i \mid (X=\mathbf{x}))$ for all classes ω_i given a pattern $\mathbf{x}$. Thus, the network can be considered as generating an intermediate data representation in the recognition chain, subject to further processing [Denker & LeCun, 1991]. In other words, the neural network becomes part of the preprocessing and contributes to dimensionality reduction.

3 Combining the Probabilities Pr_{ij} of the Two-class Classifiers to a posteriori Probabilities

The set of two-class neural network classifiers discussed in the previous section results in probabilities Pr_{ij} for all pairs (i, j) with $i \neq j$. Here, the task is to express the posterior probabilities $\text{Pr}(\omega_i \mid (X=\mathbf{x}))$ as functions of the Pr_{ij}.

We assume that each pattern belongs to only one class:

$$\Pr\left(\bigcup_{j=1}^{K} \omega_j \mid (X=x)\right) = 1 \qquad (3)$$

From the definition of ω_{ij}, it follows for any given i:

$$\Pr\left(\bigcup_{j=1}^{K} \omega_j \mid (X=x)\right) = \Pr\left(\bigcup_{j=1, j\neq i}^{K} \omega_{ij} \mid (X=x)\right) = 1 \qquad (4)$$

Using the closed form expression for the probability of the union of N events E_i:

$$\Pr\left(\bigcup_{i=1}^{N} E_i\right) = \sum_{i=1}^{N} \Pr(E_i) + \ldots + (-1)^{k-1} \sum_{i_1<\ldots<i_k}^{N} \Pr(E_{i_1}\wedge\ldots\wedge E_{i_k}) + \ldots + (-1)^{N-1}\Pr(E_1\wedge\ldots\wedge E_N)$$

it follows from (4):

$$\sum_{j=1, j\neq i}^{K} \Pr(\omega_{ij} \mid (X=x)) - (K-2)\Pr(\omega_i \mid (X=x)) = 1 \qquad (5)$$

With

$$\Pr_{ij} = \Pr(\omega_i \mid \omega_{ij}\wedge(X=x)) = \frac{\Pr(\omega_i\wedge\omega_{ij}\wedge(X=x))}{\Pr(\omega_{ij}\wedge(X=x))} = \frac{\Pr(\omega_i \mid (X=x))}{\Pr(\omega_{ij} \mid (X=x))} \qquad (6)$$

one obtains the final expression for the K posterior probabilities given the K(K-1)/2 two-class probabilities $\Pr_{ji}$:

$$\Pr(\omega_i \mid (X=x)) = \frac{1}{\displaystyle\sum_{j=1, j\neq i}^{K} \frac{1}{\Pr_{ij}} - (K-2)} \qquad (7)$$

In [Refregier et al., 1991], a method was derived which allows to compute the K posterior probabilities from only (K-1) two-class probabilities using the following relation between posterior probabilities and two-class probabilities:

$$\frac{\Pr_{ij}}{\Pr_{ji}} = \frac{\Pr(\omega_i \mid (X=x))}{\Pr(\omega_j \mid (X=x))} \qquad (8)$$

However, this approach has several practical drawbacks. For instance, in practice, the quality of the estimation of the posterior probabilities depends critically on the choice of the set of (K-1) two-class probabilities, and finding the optimal subset of (K-1) $\Pr_{ij}$ is costly, since it has to be performed for each pattern at recognition time.

4 Application to Cursive Handwriting Recognition

We applied the concepts described in the previous sections to the classification of pre-segmented characters from cursive words originating from real-world French postal checks. For cursive word recognition it is important to obtain probabilities at the output of the character classifier since it is necessary to establish an ordered list of hypotheses along with a confidence value for further processing at the word recognition level: the probabilities can be passed to an Edit Distance algorithm [Wagner et al., 1974] or to a Hidden-Markov-Model algorithm [Kundu et al., 1989] in order to compute recognition scores for words. For the recognition of the amounts on French postal checks we used an Edit Distance algorithm and made extensive use of the fact that we are dealing with a limited vocabulary (28 words).

The 27 character classes are particularly chosen for this task and include pairs of letters such as "fr", "gt", and "tr" because these combinations of letters are often difficult to pre-segment. Other characters, such as "k" and "y" are not included because they do not appear in the given 28 word vocabulary.

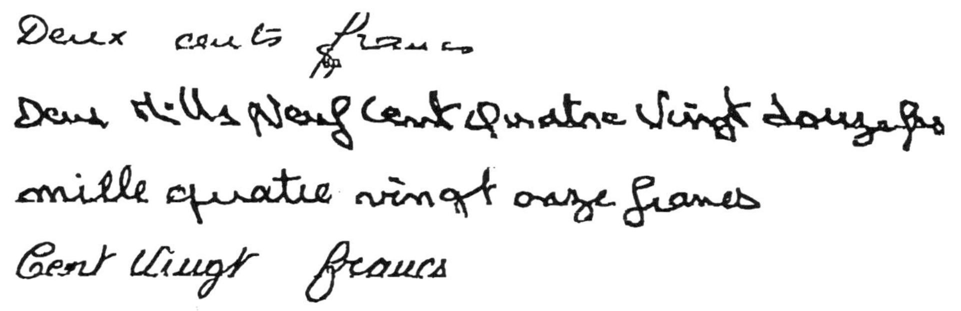

Figure 2: Some examples of literal amounts from live French postal checks.

A data base of about 3,300 literal amounts from postal checks (approximately 16,000 words) was annotated and, based on this annotation, segmented into words and letters using heuristic methods [Simon et al., 1994]. Figure 2 shows some examples of literal amounts. The writing styles vary strongly throughout the data base and many checks are difficult to read even for humans. Note that the images of the pre-segmented letters may still contain some of the ligatures or other extraneous parts and do not in general resemble hand-printed letters. The total of about 55,000 characters was divided into three sets: training set (20,000), validation set (20,000), and test set (15,000). All three sets were used without any further data base cleaning. Therefore, many letters are not only of very bad quality, but they are truly ambiguous: it is not possible to recognize them uniquely without word context.

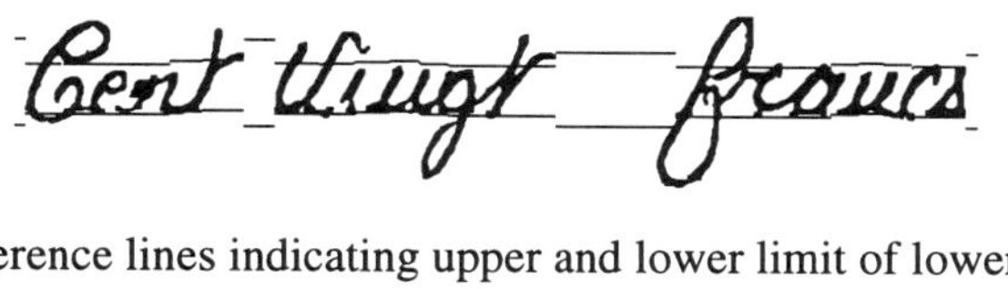

Figure 3: Reference lines indicating upper and lower limit of lower case letters.

Before segmentation, two reference lines were detected for each check (Figure 3). They indicate an estimated upper and lower limit of the lower case letters and are used for normalization of the pre-segmented characters (Figure 4) to 10 by 24 pixel matrices with 16 gray values (Figure 5). This is the representation used as input to the classifiers.

Figure 4: Segmentation of words into isolated letters (ligatures are removed later).

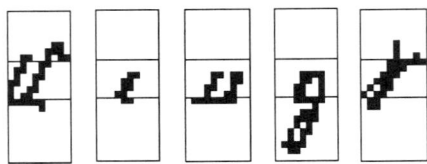

Figure 5: Size normalized letters: 10 by 24 pixel matrices with 16 gray values.

The simplest two-class classifier is a single neuron; thus, 351 neurons of the resulting pairwise classifier were trained on the training data using the generalized delta rule (sigmoidal transfer function). In order to avoid overfitting, training was stopped at the minimum of MSE on the validation set. The probability densities $p(v_{ij} | \omega_i)$ were estimated on the validation set: for both classes ω_i and ω_j of a given neuron, we fitted the probability densities over the linear output v_{ij} to a Gaussian. The two-class probabilities Pr_{ij} and Pr_{ji} were then obtained via Bayes rule. The 351 probabilities Pr_{ij} were combined using equation (7) in order to obtain a posteriori probabilities $Pr(\omega_i | (X=\mathbf{x}))$, $i \in \{1,..,27\}$. However, the a priori probabilities for letters as given by the training set are different from the prior probabilities in a given word context [Bourlard & Morgan, 1994]. Therefore, we computed the posterior probabilities either by using, in Bayes rule, the prior probabilities of the letters in the training set, or by assuming that the prior probabilities are equal. In the first case, many informative letters, for instance those having ascenders or descenders, have little chance to be recognized at all due to small a priori probabilities.

Table 1 gives the recognition performances on the test set for classes assumed to have equal a priori probabilities as well as for the true a priori probabilities of the test set. For each pattern, an ordered list (in descending order) of posterior class probabilities was generated; the recognition performance is given (i) in terms of percentage of true classes found in first position, and (ii) in terms of average position of the true class in the ordered list. As mentioned above, the results of the first column are the most relevant ones, since the classifier outputs are subsequently used for word recognition. Note that the recognition rate (first position) of isolated letters without context for a human reader can be estimated to be around 70% to 80%.

We compared the results of the pairwise classifier to a number of other neural network classification algorithms. First, we trained MLPs with one and two hidden layers and various numbers of hidden units using stochastic backpropagation. Here again, training was stopped based on the minimum MSE on the validation set. Second, we trained MLPs with a single hidden layer using the Softmax training algorithm [Bridle, 1990]. As a third approach, we trained 27 MLPs with 10 hidden units each, each MLP separating one class from all others. Table 1 gives the recognition performances on the test set. The Softmax training algorithm clearly gives the best results in terms of recognition performance. However, the pairwise classifier has three very attractive features for classifier design:

(i) training is faster than for MLP's by more than one order of magnitude; therefore, many different designs (changing pattern representations for instance) can be tested at a small computational cost;

(ii) in the same spirit, adding a new class or modifying the training set of an existing one can be done without retraining all two-class classifiers;

(iii) at least as importantly, the procedure gives more insight into the classification problem than MLP's do.

Classifier	AveragePosition equal prior probs	First Position equal prior probs	AveragePosition true prior probs	First Position true prior probs
Pairwise Classifier	2.9	48.9 %	2.6	52.2 %
MLP (100 hid. units)	3.6	48.9 %	2.7	60.0 %
Softmax (100 hid. units)	2.6	54.9 %	2.2	61.9 %
27 MLPs	3.2	41.6 %	2.4	55.8 %

Table 1: Recognition performances on the test set in terms of average position and recognition rate (first position) for the various neural networks used.

Our pairwise classifier is part of a handwriting recognition system which is currently applied to check reading. The complete system also incorporates other character recognition algorithms as well as a word recognizer which operates without pre-segmentation. The result of the complete check recognition chain on a set of test checks is the following: (i) at the word level, 83.3% of true words are found in first position; (ii) 64.1% of well recognized literal amounts are found in first position [Simon et al., 1994]. Recognizing also the numeral amount, we obtained 80% well recognized checks for 1% error.

5 Conclusion

We have shown how to obtain posterior class probabilities from a set of pairwise classifiers by (i) performing class density estimations on the network outputs and using Bayes rule, and (ii) combining the resulting two-class probabilities. The application of our pairwise classifier to the recognition of real world French postal checks shows that the procedure is a valuable tool for designing a recognizer, experimenting with various data representations at a small computational cost and, generally, getting insight into the classification problem.

Acknowledgments

The authors wish to thank J.C. Simon, N. Gorsky, O. Baret, and J.C. Deledicq for many informative and stimulating discussions.

References

H.A. Bourlard, N. Morgan (1994). *Connectionist Speech Recognition*. Kluwer Academic Publishers.

H.A. Bourlard, C. Wellekens (1990). Links between Markov Models and Multilayer Perceptrons. IEEE Transactions on Pattern Analysis and Machine Intelligence, Vol. 12, No. 12, 1167-1178.

J.S. Bridle (1990). Probabilistic Interpretation of Feedforward Classification Network Outputs, with Relationships to Statistical Pattern Recognition. In *Neurocomputing: Algorithms, Architectures and Applications*, Fogelman-Soulie, and Herault (eds.). NATO ASI Series, Springer.

J.S. Denker, Y.LeCun (1991). Transforming Neural-Net Output Levels to Probability Distributions. In *Advances in Neural Information Processing Systems 3*, Lippmann, Moody, Touretzky (eds.). Morgan Kaufman.

R.O. Duda, P.E. Hart (1973). *Pattern Classification and Scene Analysis*. Wiley.

S. Knerr, L. Personnaz, G. Dreyfus (1990). Single-Layer Learning Revisited: A Stepwise Procedure for Building and Training a Neural Network. In *Neurocomputing: Algorithms, Architectures and Applications*, Fogelman-Soulie and Herault (eds.). NATO ASI Series, Springer.

S. Knerr, L. Personnaz, G. Dreyfus (1992). Handwritten Digit Recognition by Neural Networks with Single-Layer Training. *IEEE Transactions on Neural Networks*, Vol. 3, No. 6, 962-968.

A. Kundu, Y. He, P. Bahl (1989). Recognition of Handwritten Words: First and Second Order Hidden Markov Model Based Approach. *Pattern Recognition*, Vol. 22, No.3.

J.C. Simon (1992). Off-Line Cursive Word Recognition. *Proceedings of the IEEE*, Vol. 80, No. 7, 1150-1161.

Ph. Refregier, F. Vallet (1991). Probabilistic Approach for Multiclass Classification with Neural Networks. *Int. Conference on Artificial Networks*, Vol. 2, 1003-1007.

J.C. Simon, O. Baret, N. Gorski (1994). Reconnaisance d'écriture manuscrite. *Compte Rendu Academie des Sciences*, Paris, t. 318, Serie II, 745-752.

R.A. Wagner, M.J. Fisher (1974). The String to String Correction Problem. J.A.C.M. Vol. 21, No. 5, 168-173.

Interference in Learning Internal Models of Inverse Dynamics in Humans

Reza Shadmehr[*], Tom Brashers-Krug, and Ferdinando Mussa-Ivaldi[†]
Dept. of Brain and Cognitive Sciences
M. I. T., Cambridge, MA 02139
reza@bme.jhu.edu, tbk@ai.mit.edu, sandro@parker.physio.nwu.edu

Abstract

Experiments were performed to reveal some of the computational properties of the human motor memory system. We show that as humans practice reaching movements while interacting with a novel mechanical environment, they learn an *internal model* of the inverse dynamics of that environment. Subjects show recall of this model at testing sessions 24 hours after the initial practice. The representation of the internal model in memory is such that there is interference when there is an attempt to learn a new inverse dynamics map immediately after an anticorrelated mapping was learned. We suggest that this interference is an indication that the same computational elements used to encode the first inverse dynamics map are being used to learn the second mapping. We predict that this leads to a forgetting of the initially learned skill.

1 Introduction

In tasks where we use our hands to interact with a tool, our motor system develops a model of the dynamics of that tool and uses this model to control the coupled dynamics of our arm and the tool (Shadmehr and Mussa-Ivaldi 1994). In physical systems theory, the tool is a mechanical analogue of an admittance, mapping a force as input onto a change in state as output (Hogan 1985). In this framework, the

---

[*]Currently at Dept. Biomedical Eng, Johns Hopkins Univ, Baltimore, MD 21205
[†]Currently at Dept. Physiology, Northwestern Univ Med Sch (M211), Chicago, IL 60611

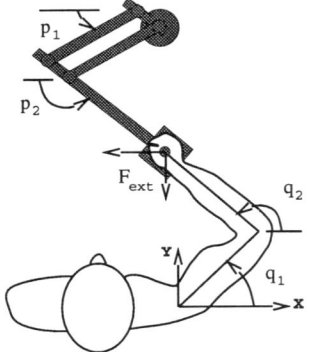

Figure 1: The experimental setup. The robot is a very low friction planar mechanism powered by two torque motors that act on the shoulder and elbow joints. Subject grips the end-point of the robot which houses a force transducer and moves the hand to a series of targets displayed on a monitor facing the subject (not shown). The function of the robot is to produce novel force fields that the subject learns to compensate for during reaching movements.

model developed by the motor control system during the learning process needs to approximate an inverse of this mapping. This inverse dynamics map is called an *internal model* of the tool.

We have been interested in understanding the representations that the nervous system uses in learning and storing such internal models. In a previous work we measured the way a learned internal model extrapolated beyond the training data (Shadmehr and Mussa-Ivaldi 1994). The results suggested that the coordinate system of the learned map was in intrinsic (e.g., joint or muscles based) rather than in extrinsic (e.g., hand based) coordinates. Here we present a mathematical technique to estimate the input–output properties of the learned map. We then explore the issue of how the motor memory might store two maps which have similar inputs but different outputs.

2 Quantifying the internal model

In our paradigm, subjects learn to control an artificial tool: the tool is a robot manipulandum which has torque motors that can be programmed to produce a variety of dynamical environments (Fig. 1). The task for the subject is to grasp the end-effector and make point to point reaching movements to a series of targets. The environments are represented as force fields acting on the subject's hand, and a typical case is shown in Fig. 2A. A typical experiment begins with the robot motors turned off. In this "null" environment subjects move their hand to the targets in a smooth, straight line fashion. When the force field is introduced, the dynamics of the task change and the hand trajectory is significantly altered (Shadmehr and Mussa-Ivaldi 1994). With practice (typically hundreds of movements), hand trajectories return to their straight line path. We have suggested that practice leads to formation of an internal model which functions as an inverse dynamics mapping, i.e., from a desired trajectory (presumably in terms of hand position and velocity, Wolpert et al. 1995) to a prediction of forces that will be encountered along the trajectory. We designed a method to quantify these forces and estimate the output properties of the internal model.

If we position a force transducer at the interaction point between the robot and the subject, we can write the dynamics of the four link system in Fig. 1 in terms of the

following coupled vector differential equations:
$$I_r(p)\ddot{p} + G_r(p,\dot{p})\dot{p} = E(p,\dot{p}) + J_r^T F \qquad (1)$$
$$I_s(q)\ddot{q} + G_s(q,\dot{q})\dot{q} = C(q,\dot{q},q^*(t)) - J_s^T F \qquad (2)$$
where I and G are inertial and Corriolis/centripetal matrix functions, E is the torque field produced by the robot's motors, i.e., the environment, F is the force measured at the handle of the robot, C is the controller implemented by the motor system of the subject, $q^*(t)$ is the reference trajectory planned by the motor system of the subject, J is the Jacobian matrix describing the differential transformation of coordinates from endpoint to joints, q and p are joint positions of the subject and the robot, and the subscripts s and r denote subject or robot matrices.

In the null environment, i.e., $E = 0$ in Eq. (1), a solution to this coupled system is $q = q^*(t)$ and the arm follows the reference trajectory (typically a straight hand path with a Gaussian tangential velocity profile). Let us name the controller which accomplishes this task $C = C_0$ in Eq. (2). When the robot motors are producing a force field $E \neq 0$, it can be shown that the solution is $q = q^*(t)$ if and only if the new controller in Eq. (2) is $C = C_1 = C_0 + J_s^T J_r^{-T} \hat{E}$. The internal model composed by the subject is $C_1 - C_0$, i.e., the change in the controller after some training period. We can estimate this quantity by measuring the change in the interaction force along a given trajectory before and after training. If we call these functions F_0 and F_1, then we have:
$$F_0(q,\dot{q},\ddot{q},q^*(t)) = J_s^{-T}(C_0 - I_s\ddot{q} - G_s\dot{q}) \qquad (3)$$
$$F_1(q,\dot{q},\ddot{q},q^*(t)) = J_s^{-T}(C_0 + J_s^T J_r^{-T}\hat{E} - I_s\ddot{q} - G_s\dot{q}) \qquad (4)$$
The functions F_0 and F_1 are impedances of the subject's arm as viewed from the interaction port. Therefore, by approximating the difference $F_1 - F_0$, we have an estimate of the change in the controller. The crucial assumption is that the reference trajectory $q^*(t)$ does not change during the training process.

In order to measure F_0, we had the subjects make movements in a series of environments. The environments were unpredictable (no opportunity to learn) and their purpose was to perturb the controller about the reference trajectory so we could measure F_0 at neighboring states. Next, the environment in Fig. 2A was presented and the subject given a practice period to adapt. After training, F_1 was estimated in a similar fashion as F_0. The difference between these two functions was calculated along all measured arm trajectories and the results were projected onto the hand velocity space. Due to computer limitations, only 9 trajectories for each target direction were used for this approximation. The resulting pattern of forces were interpolated via a sum of Gaussian radial basis functions, and are shown in Fig. 2B. This is the change in the impedance of the arm and estimates the input–output property of the internal model that was learned by this subject. We found that this subject, which provided some of best results in the test group, learned to change the effective impedance of his arm in a way that approximated the imposed force field. This would be a sufficient condition for the arm to compensate for the force field and allow the hand to follow the desired trajectory. An alternate strategy might have been to simply co-contract arm muscles: this would lead to an increased stiffness and an ability to resist arbitrary environmental forces. Figure 2B suggests that practice led to formation of an internal model specific to the dynamics of the imposed force field.

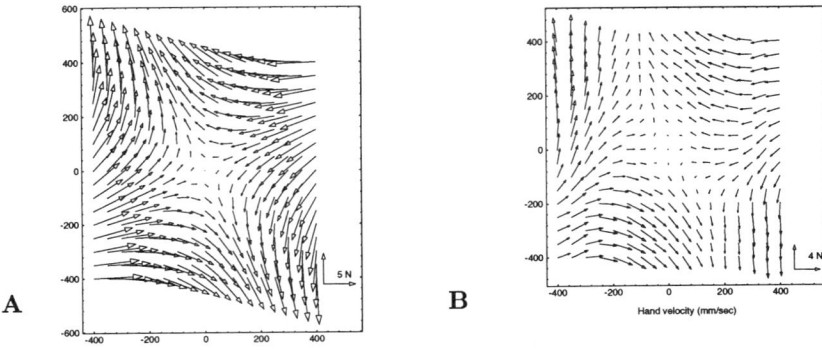

Figure 2: Quantification of the change in impedance of a subject's arm after learning a force field. **A:** The force field produced by the robot during the training period. **B:** The change in the subject's arm impedance after the training period, i.e., the internal model.

2.1 Formation of the internal model in long-term memory

Here we wished to determine whether subjects retained the internal model in long-term motor memory. We tested 16 naive subjects. They were instructed to move the handle of the robot to a sequence of targets in the null environment. Each movement was to last 500 ± 50 msec. They were given visual feedback on the timing of each movement. After 600 movements, subjects were able to consistently reach the targets in proper time. These trajectories constituted a baseline set.

Subjects returned the next day and were re-familiarized with the timing of the task. At this point a force field was introduced and subjects attempted to perform the exact task as before: get to the target in proper time. A sequence of 600 targets was given. When first introduced, the forces perturbed the subject's trajectories, causing them to deviate from the straight line path. As noted in previous work (Shadmehr and Mussa-Ivaldi 1994), these deviations decreased with practice. Eventually, subject's trajectories in the presence of the force field came to resemble those of the baseline, when no forces were present. The convergence of the trajectories to those performed at baseline is shown for all 16 subjects in Fig. 3A. The timing performance of the subjects while moving in the field is shown in Fig. 3B.

In order to determine whether subjects retained the internal model of the force field in long-term memory, we had them return the next day (24 to 30 hours later) and once again be tested on a force field. In half of the subjects, the force field presented was one that they had trained on in the previous day (call this field 1). In the other half, it was a force field which was novel to the subjects, field 2. Field 2 had a correlation value of -1 with respect to field 1 (i.e., each force vector in field 2 was a 180 degree rotation of the respective vector in field 1). Subjects who were tested on a field that they had trained on before performed significantly better ($p < 0.01$) than their initial performance (Fig. 4A), signifying retention. However, those who were given a field that was novel performed at naive levels (Fig. 4B). This result suggested that the internal model formed after practice in a given field was (1) specific to that field: performance on the untrained field was no better than

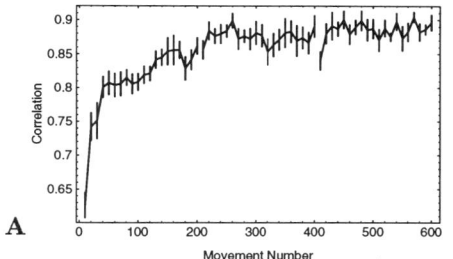
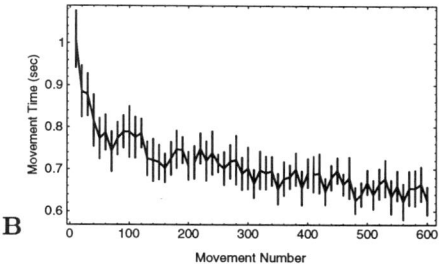

Figure 3: Measures of performance during the training period (600 movements) for 16 naive subjects. Short breaks (2 minutes) were given at intervals of 200 movements. **A:** Mean ± standard error (SE) of the correlation coefficient between hand trajectory in a null environment (called baseline trajectories, measured before exposure to the field), and trajectory in the force field. Hand trajectories in the field converge to that in the null field (i.e., become straight, with a bell shaped velocity profile). **B:** Mean ± SE of the movement period to reach a target. The goal was to reach the target in 0.5 ± 0.05 seconds.

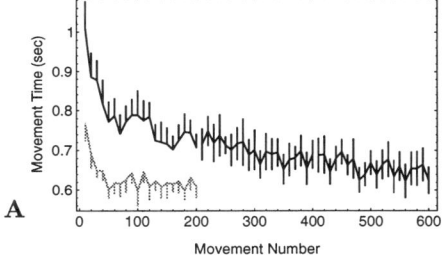
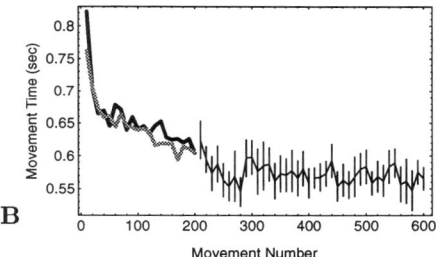

Figure 4: Subjects learned an internal model specific to the field and retained it in long-term memory. **A:** Mean ± standard error (SE) of the movement period in the force field (called field 1) during initial practice session (upper trace) and during a second session 24–30 hours after the initial practice (lower trace). **B:** Movement period in a different group of subjects during initial training (dark line) in field 1 and test in an anti-correlated field (called field 2) 24–30 hours later (gray line).

performance recorded in a separate set of naive subjects who were given than field in their initial training day; and (2) could be retained, as evidenced by performance in the following day.

2.2 Interference effects of the motor memory

In our experiment the "tool" that subjects learn to control is rather unusual, nevertheless, subjects learn its inverse dynamics and the memory is used to enhance performance 24 hours after its initial acquisition. We next asked how formation of this memory affected formation of subsequent internal models. In the previous section we showed that when a subject returns a day after the initial training, although the memory of the learned internal model is present, there is no interference (or decrement in performance) in learning a new, anti-correlated field. Here we show that when this temporal distance is significantly reduced, the just learned

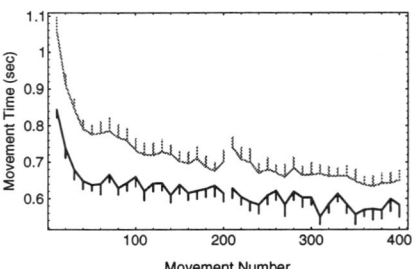

Figure 5: Interference in sequential learning of two uncorrelated force fields: The lower trace is the mean and standard error of the movement periods of a naive group of subjects during initial practice in a force field (called field 1). The upper trace is the movement period of another group of naive subjects in field 1, 5 minutes after practicing 400 movements in field 2, which was anti-correlated with field 1.

model interferes with learning of a new field.

Seven new subjects were recruited. They learned the timing of the task in a null environment and in the following day were given 400 targets in a force field (called field 1). They showed improvement in performance as before. After a short break (5–10 minutes in which they walked about the lab or read a magazine), they were given a new field: this field was called field 2 and was anti-correlated with respect to field 1. We found a significant reduction ($p < 0.01$) in their ability to learn field 2 (Fig. 5) when compared to a subject group which had not initially trained in field 1. In other words, performance in field 2 shortly after having learned field 1 was significantly worse than that of naives. Subjects seemed surprised by their inability to master the task in field 2. In order to demonstrate that field 2 *in isolation* was no more difficult to learn than field 1, we had a new set of subjects ($n = 5$) initially learn field 2, then field 1. Now we found a very large decrement in learnability of field 1.

One way to explain the decrement in performance shown in Fig. 5 is to assume that the same "computational elements" that represented the internal model of the first field were being used to learn the second field.[1] In other words, when the second field was given, because the forces were opposite to the first field, the internal model was badly biased against representing this second field: muscle torque patterns predicted for movement to a given target were in the wrong direction.

In the connectionist literature this is a phenomenon called *temporal interference* (Sutton 1986). As a network is trained, some of its elements acquire large weights and begin to dominate the input–output transformation. When a second task is presented with a new and conflicting map (mapping similar inputs to different outputs), there are large errors and the network performs more poorly than a "naive" network. As the network attempts to learn the new task, the errors are fed to each element (i.e., pre-synaptic input). This causes most activity in those elements that

---

[1] Examples of computational elements used by the nervous system to model inverse dynamics of a mechanical system were found by Shidara et al. (1993), where it was shown that the firing patterns of a set of Purkinje cells in the cerebellum could be reconstructed by an inverse dynamic representation of the eye.

had the largest synaptic weight. If the learning algorithm is Hebbian, i.e., weights change in proportion to co-activation of the pre- and the post-synaptic element, then the largest weights are changed the most, effectively causing a loss of what was learned in the first task. Therefore, from a computational stand point, we would expect that the internal model of field 1 as learned by our subjects should be destroyed by learning of field 2. Evidence for "catastrophic interference" in these subjects is presented elsewhere in this volume (Brashers-Krug et al. 1995).

The phenomenon of interference in sequential learning of two stimulus–response maps has been termed *proactive interference* or negative transfer in the psychological literature. In humans, interference has been observed extensively in verbal tasks involving short–term declarative memory (e.g., tasks involving recognition of words in a list or pairing of non-sense syllables, Bruce 1933, Melton and Irwin 1940, Sears and Hovland 1941). It has been found that interference is a function of the similarity of the stimulus–response maps in the two tasks: if the stimulus in the new learning task requires a response very different than what was recently learned, then there is significant interference. Interestingly, it has been shown that the amount of interference decreases with increased learning (or practice) on the first map (Siipola and Israel 1933).

In tasks involving procedural memory (which includes motor learning, Squire 1986), the question of interference has been controversial: Although Lewis et al. (1949) reported interference in sequential learning of two motor tasks which involved moving levers in response to a set of lights, it has been suggested that the interference that they observed might have been due to cognitive confusion (Schmidt 1988). In another study, Ross (1974) reported little interference in subjects learning her motor tasks.

We designed a task that had little or no cognitive components. We found that shortly after the acquisition of a motor memory, that memory strongly interfered with learning of a new, anti-correlated input–output mapping. However, this interference was not significant 24 hours after the memory was initially acquired. One possible explanation is that the initial learning has taken place in a temporary and vulnerable memory system. With time and/or practice, the information in this memory had transferred to long-term storage (Brashers-Krug et al. 1995).

Brain imaging studies during motor learning suggest that as subjects become more proficient in a motor task, neural fields in the motor cortex display increases in activity (Grafton et al. 1992) and new fields are recruited (Kawashima et al. 1994). It has been reported that when a subject attempts to learn two new motor tasks successively (in this case the tasks consisted of two sequences of finger movements), the neural activity in the motor cortex is lower for the second task, even when the order of the tasks is reversed (Jezzard et al. 1994). It remains to be seen whether this decrement in neural activity in the motor cortex is correlated with the interference observed when subjects attempt to learn two different input–output mappings in succession (Gandolfo et al. 1994).

References

Brashers-Krug T, Shadmehr R, Todorov E (1995) Catastrophic interference in human motor learning. Adv Neural Inform Proc Syst, vol 7, in press.

Bruce RW (1933) Conditions of transfer of training. J Exp Psychol 16:343–361.

French, R. (1992) Semi-distributed Representations and Catastrophic Forgetting in Connectionist Networks, Connection Science 4:365-377.

Grafton ST et al. (1992) Functional anatomy of human procedural learning determined with regional cerebral blood flow and PET. J Neurosci 12:2542–2548.

Gandolfo F, Shadmehr R, Benda B, Bizzi E (1994) Adaptive behavior of the monkey motor system to virtual environments. Soc Neurosci Abs 20(2):1411.

Hogan N (1985) Impedance control: An approach for manipulation: Theory. J Dynam Sys Meas Cont 107:1–7.

Jezzard P et al. (1994) Practice makes perfect: A functional MRI study of long term motor cortex plasticity. 2nd Ann Soc. Magnetic Res., p. 330.

Kawashima R, Roland PE, O'Sullivan BT (1994) Fields in human motor areas involved in preparation for reaching, actual reaching, and visuomotor learning: A PET study. J Neurosci 14:3462–3474.

Lewis D, Shephard AH, Adams JA (1949) Evidences of associative interference in psychomotor performance. Science 110:271–273.

Melton AW, Irwin JM (1940) The influence of degree of interpolated learning on retroactive inhibition and the overt transfer of specific responses. Amer J Psychol 53:173–203.

Ross D (1974) Interference in discrete motor tasks: A test of the theory. PhD dissertation, Dept. Psychology, Univ. Michigan, Ann Arbor.

Schmidt RA (1988) Motor Control and Learning: A Behavioral Emphasis. Human Kinetics Books, Champaign IL, pp. 409–411.

Sears RR, Hovland CI (1941) Experiments on motor conflict. J Exp Psychol 28:280–286.

Shadmehr R, Mussa-Ivaldi FA (1994) Adaptive representation of dynamics during learning of a motor task. *J Neuroscience*, 14(5):3208–3224.

Shidara M, Kawano K, Gomi H, Kawato M (1993) Inverse dynamics model eye movement control by Purkinje cells in the cerebellum. Nature 365:50–52.

Siipola EM, Israel HE (1933) Habit interference as dependent upon stage of training. Amer J Psychol 45:205–227.

Squire LR (1986) Mechanisms of memory. Science 232:1612–1619.

Sutton RS (1986) Two problems with backpropagation and other steepest-descent learning procedures for networks. Proc 8th Cognitive Sci Soc, pp. 823–831.

Wolpert DM, Ghahramani Z, Jordan MI (1995) Are arm trajectories planned in kimenatic or dynamic coordinates? An adaptation study. Exp Brain Res, in press.

Computational structure of coordinate transformations: A generalization study

Zoubin Ghahramani
zoubin@psyche.mit.edu

Daniel M. Wolpert
wolpert@psyche.mit.edu

Michael I. Jordan
jordan@psyche.mit.edu

Department of Brain & Cognitive Sciences
Massachusetts Institute of Technology
Cambridge, MA 02139

Abstract

One of the fundamental properties that both neural networks and the central nervous system share is the ability to learn and generalize from examples. While this property has been studied extensively in the neural network literature it has not been thoroughly explored in human perceptual and motor learning. We have chosen a coordinate transformation system—the visuomotor map which transforms visual coordinates into motor coordinates—to study the generalization effects of learning new input–output pairs. Using a paradigm of computer controlled altered visual feedback, we have studied the generalization of the visuomotor map subsequent to both local and context-dependent remappings. A local remapping of one or two input-output pairs induced a significant global, yet decaying, change in the visuomotor map, suggesting a representation for the map composed of units with large functional receptive fields. Our study of context-dependent remappings indicated that a single point in visual space can be mapped to two different finger locations depending on a context variable—the starting point of the movement. Furthermore, as the context is varied there is a gradual shift between the two remappings, consistent with two visuomotor modules being learned and gated smoothly with the context.

1 Introduction

The human central nervous system (CNS) receives sensory inputs from a multitude of modalities, each tuned to extract different forms of information from the environment. These sensory signals are initially represented in disparate coordinate systems, for example visual information is represented retinotopically whereas auditory information is represented tonotopically. The ability to transform information between coordinate systems is necessary for both perception and action. When we reach to a visually perceived object in space, for example, the location of the object in visual coordinates must be converted into a representation appropriate for movement, such as the configuration of the arm required to reach the object. The computational structure of this coordinate transformation, known as the visuomotor map, is the focus of this paper.

By examining the change in visuomotor coordination under prismatically induced displacement and rotation, Helmholtz (1867/1925) and Stratton (1897a,1897b) pioneered the systematic study of the representation and plasticity of the visuomotor map. Their studies demonstrate both the fine balance between the visual and motor coordinate systems, which is disrupted by such perturbations, and the ability of the visuomotor map to adapt to the displacements induced by the prisms. Subsequently, many studies have further demonstrated the remarkable plasticity of the map in response to a wide variety of alterations in the relationship between the visual and motor system (for reviews see Howard, 1982 and Welch, 1986)—the single prerequisite for adaptation seems to be that the remapping be stable (Welch, 1986). Much less is known, however, about the topological properties of this map.

A coordinate transformation such as the visuomotor map can be regarded as a function relating one set of variables (inputs) to another (outputs). For the visuomotor map the inputs are visual coordinates of a desired target and the outputs are the corresponding motor coordinates representing the arm's configuration (e.g. joint angles). The problem of learning a sensorimotor remapping can then be regarded as a function approximation problem. Using the theory of function approximation one can make explicit the correspondence between the representation used and the patterns of generalization that will emerge. Function approximators can predict patterns of generalization ranging from local (look-up tables), through intermediate (CMACs, Albus, 1975; and radial basis functions, Moody and Darken, 1989) to global (parametric models).

In this paper we examine the representational structure of the visuomotor map through the study of its spatial and contextual generalization properties. In the spatial generalization study we address the question of how pointing changes over the reaching workspace after exposure to a highly localized remapping. Previous work on spatial generalization, in a study restricted to one dimension, has led to the conclusion that the visuomotor map is constrained to generalize linearly (Bedford, 1989). We test this conclusion by mapping out the pattern of generalization induced by one and two remapped points in two dimensions.

In the contextual generalization study we examine the question of whether a single point in visual space can be mapped into two different finger locations depending on the context of a movement—the start point. If this context-dependent remapping occurs, the question arises as to how the mapping will generalize as the context is varied. Studies of contextual remapping have previously shown that variables such as eye position (Kohler, 1950; Hay and Pick, 1966; Shelhamer et al., 1991), the feel of prisms (Kravitz, 1972; Welch, 1971) or an auditory tone (Kravitz and Yaffe, 1972), can induce context-dependent aftereffects. The question of how these context-dependent maps generalize—which has not been previously explored—reflects on the possible representation of multiple visuomotor maps and their mixing with a context variable.

2 Spatial Generalization

To examine the spatial generalization of the visuomotor map we measured the change in pointing behavior subsequent to one- and two-point remappings. In order to measure pointing behavior and to confine subjects to learn limited input-output pairs we used a virtual visual feedback setup consisting of a digitizing tablet to record the finger position on-line and a projection/mirror system to generate a cursor spot image representing the finger position (Figure 1a). By controlling the presence of the cursor spot and its relationship to the finger position, we could both restrict visual feedback of finger position to localized regions of space and introduce perturbations of this feedback.

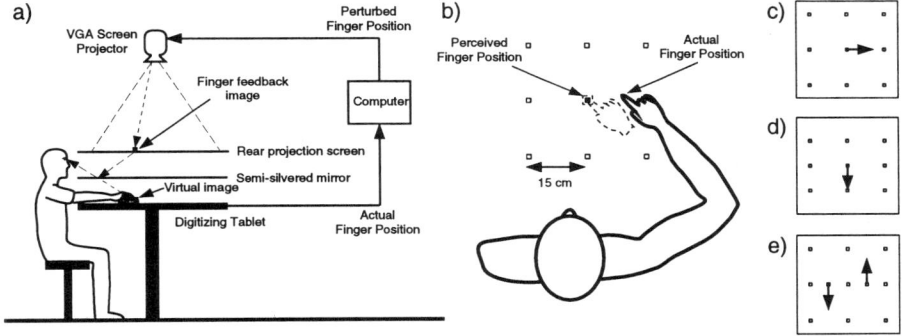

Figure 1. a) Experimental setup. The subjects view the reflected image of the rear projection screen by looking down at the mirror. By matching the screen-mirror distance to the mirror-tablet distance all projected images appeared to be in the plane of the finger (when viewed in the mirror) independent of head position. b) The position of the grid of targets relative to the subject. Also shown, for the x-shift condition, is the perceived and actual finger position when pointing to the central training target. The visually perceived finger position is indicated by a cursor spot which is displaced from the actual finger position. c) A schematic showing the perturbation for the x-shift group. To see the cursor spot on the central target the subjects had to place their finger at the position indicated by the tip of the arrow. d) & e) Schematics similar to c) showing the perturbation for the y-shift and two point groups, respectively.

In the tradition of adaptation studies (e.g. Welch, 1986), each experimental session consisted of three phases: pre-exposure, exposure, and post-exposure. During the pre- and post-exposure phases, designed to assess the visuomotor map, the subject pointed repeatedly, without visual feedback of his finger position, to a grid of targets over the workspace. As no visual input of finger location was given, no learning of the visuomotor map could occur. During the exposure phase subjects pointed repeatedly to one or two visual target locations, at which we introduced a discrepancy between the actual and visually displayed finger location. No visual feedback of finger position was given except when within 0.5 cm of the target, thereby confining any learning to the chosen input-output pairs. Three local perturbations of the visuomotor map were examined: a 10 cm rightward displacement (x-shift group, Figure 1c), 10 cm displacement towards the body (y-shift group, Figure 1d), and a displacement at two points, one 10 cm away from, and one 10 cm towards the body (two point group, Figure 1e). For example, for the x-shift displacement the subject had to place his finger 10 cm to the right of the target to visually perceive his finger as being on target (Figure 1b). Separate control subjects, in which the relationship between the actual and visually displayed finger position was left unaltered, were run for both the one- and two-point displacements, resulting in a total of 5 groups with 8 subjects each.

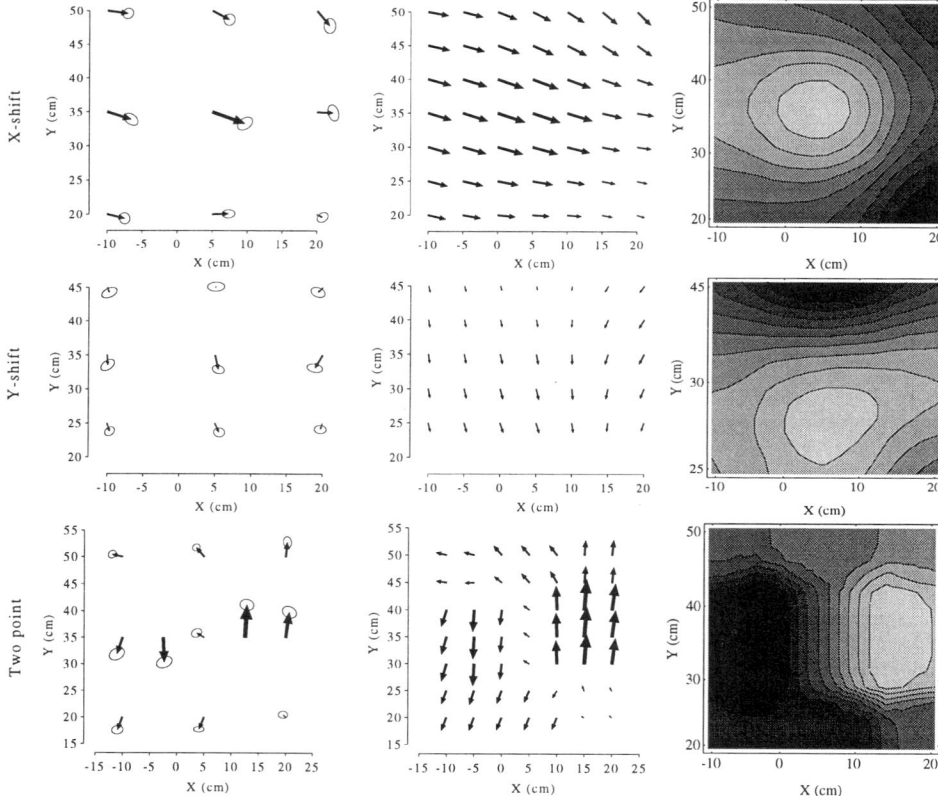

Figure 2. Results of the spatial generalization study. The first column shows the mean change in pointing, along with 95% confidence ellipses, for the x-shift, y-shift and two point groups. The second column displays a vector field of changes obtained from the data by Gaussian kernel smoothing. The third column plots the proportion adaptation in the direction of the perturbation. Note that whereas for the x- and y-shift groups the lighter shading corresponds to greater adaptation, for the two point group lighter shades correspond to adaptation in the positive y direction and darker shades in the negative y direction.

The patterns of spatial generalization subsequent to exposure to the three local remappings are shown in Figure 2. All three perturbation groups displayed both significant adaptation at the trained points, and significant, through decremented, generalization of this learning to other targets. As expected, the control groups (not shown) did not show any significant changes. The extent of spatial generalization, best depicted by the shaded contour plots in Figure 2, shows a pattern of generalization that decreases with distance away from the trained points. Rather than inducing a single global change in the map, such as a rotation or shear, the two point exposure appears to induce two opposite fields of decaying generalization at the intersection of which there is no change in the visuomotor map.

3 Contextual Generalization

The goal of this experiment was first to explore the possibility that multiple visuomotor maps, or modules, could be learned, and if so, to determine how the overall system behaves as the context used in training each module is varied. To achieve this goal, we exposed subjects to context-dependent remappings in which a single visual target location was mapped to two different finger positions depending on the start point of the movement. Pointing to the target from seven different starting points (Figure 3) was assessed before and after an exposure phase. During this exposure phase subjects made repeated movements to the target from starting points 2 and 6 with a different perturbation of the visual feedback depending on the starting point. The form of these context-dependent remappings is shown in Figure 3. For example, for the open x-shift group (Figure 3c), the visual feedback of the finger was displaced to the right for movements from point 2 and to the left from point 6. Therefore the same visual target was mapped to two different finger positions depending on the context of the movement. To test learning of the remapping and generalization to other start points we examined the change in pointing, without visual feedback, to the target from the 7 start points.

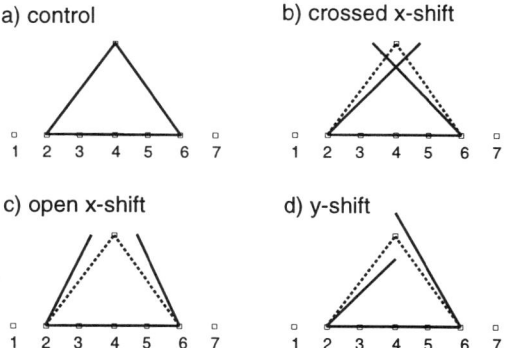

Figure 3. Schematic of the exposure phase in the contextual generalization experiment. Shown are the actual finger path (solid line), the visually displayed finger path (dotted line), the seven start points and the target used in the pre- and post-exposure phases. The perturbation introduced depended on whether the movement started form start point 2 or 6. Note that for the three perturbation groups, although the subjects saw a triangle being traced out, the finger took a different path.

The results are shown in Figure 4. Whereas the controls did not show any significant pattern of change, the three other groups showed adaptive, start point dependent, changes in the direction opposite to the perturbation. Thus, for example, the x-open group displayed a pattern of change in the leftward (negative x) direction for movements from the left start points and rightwards for movements from the right start points. Furthermore, as the start point was varied, the change in pointing varied gradually.

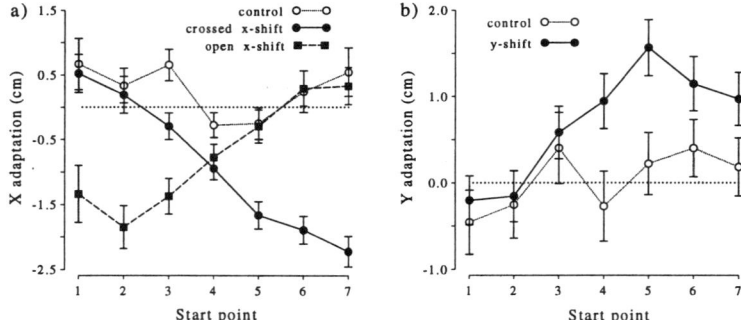

Figure 4. a) Adaptation in the x direction plotted as a function of starting point for the control, crossed x-shift and open x-shift groups (mean and 1 s.e.). b) Adaptation in the y direction for the control and y-shift groups.

4 Discussion

Clearly, from the perspective of function approximation theory, the problem of relearning the visuomotor mapping from exposure to one or two input-output pairs is ill-posed. The mapping learned, as measured by the pattern of generalization to novel inputs, therefore reflects intrinsic constraints on the internal representation used.

The results from the spatial generalization study suggest that the visuomotor coordinate transformation is internally represented with units with large but localized receptive fields. For example, a neural network model with Gaussian radial basis function units (Moody and Darken, 1989), which can be derived by assuming that the internal constraint in the visuomotor system is a smoothness constraint (Poggio and Girosi, 1989), predicts a pattern of generalization very similar the one experimentally observed (e.g. see Figure 5 for a simulation of the two point generalization experiment).[1] In contrast, previously proposed models for the representation of the visuomotor map based on global parametric representations in terms of felt direction of gaze and head position (e.g. Harris, 1965) or linear constraints (Bedford, 1989) do not predict the decaying patterns of Cartesian generalization found.

---

[1] See also Pouget & Sejnowski (this volume) who, based on a related analysis of neurophysiological data from parietal cortex, suggest that a basis function representation may be used in this visuomotor area.

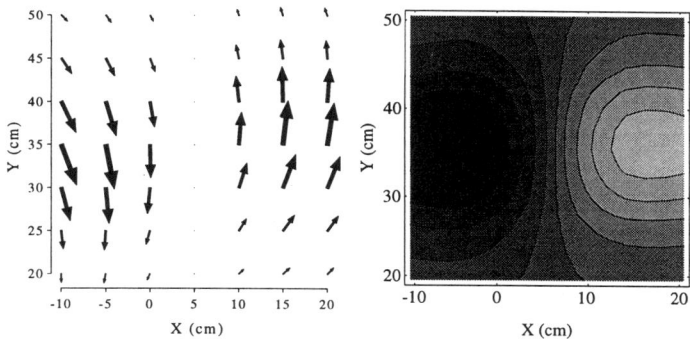

Figure 5. Simulation of the two point spatial generalization experiment using a radial basis function network with 64 units with 5 cm Gaussian receptive fields. The inputs to the network were the visual coordinates of the target and the outputs were the joint angles for a two-link planar arm to reach the target. The network was first trained to point accurately to the targets, and then, after exposure to the perturbation, its pattern of generalization was assessed.

The results from the second study suggest that multiple visuomotor maps can be learned and modulated by a context. A suggestive computational model for how such separate modules can be learned and combined is the mixture-of-experts neural network architecture (Jacobs et al., 1991). Interpreted in this framework, the gradual effect of varying the context seen in Figure 4 could reflect the output of a gating network which uses context to modulate between two visuomotor maps. However, our results do not rule out models in which a single visuomotor map is parametrized by starting location, such as one based on the coding of locations via movement vectors (Georgopoulos, 1990).

5 Conclusions

The goal of these studies has been to infer the internal constraints in the visuomotor system through the study of its patterns of generalization to local remappings. We have found that local perturbations of the visuomotor map produce global changes, suggesting a distributed representation with large receptive fields. Furthermore, context-dependent perturbations induce changes in pointing consistent with a model of visuomotor learning in which separate maps are learned and gated by the context. The approach taken in this paper provides a strong link between neural network theory and the study of learning in biological systems.

Acknowledgements

This project was supported in part by a grant from the McDonnell-Pew Foundation, by a grant from ATR Human Information Processing Research Laboratories, by a grant from Siemens Corporation, and by grant N00014-94-1-0777 from the Office of Naval Research. Zoubin Ghahramani and Daniel M. Wolpert are McDonnell-Pew Fellows in Cognitive Neuroscience. Michael I. Jordan is a NSF Presidential Young Investigator.

References

Albus, J. (1975). A new approach to manipulator control: The cerebellar model articulation controller (CMAC). *J. of Dynamic Systems, Measurement, and Control*, 97:220–227.

Bedford, F. (1989). Constraints on learning new mappings between perceptual dimensions. *J. of Experimental Psychology: Human Perception and Performance*, 15(2):232–248.

Georgopoulos, A. (1990). Neurophysiology of reaching. In Jeannerod, M., editor, *Attention and performance XIII*, pages 227–263. Lawrence Erlbaum, Hillsdale.

Harris, C. (1965). Perceptual adaptation to inverted, reversed, and displaced vision. *Psychological Review*, 72:419–444.

Hay, J. and Pick, H. (1966). Gaze-contingent prism adaptation: Optical and motor factors. *J. of Experimental Psychology*, 72:640–648.

Howard, I. (1982). *Human visual orientation*. Wiley, Chichester, England.

Jacobs, R., Jordan, M., Nowlan, S., and Hinton, G. (1991). Adaptive mixture of local experts. *Neural Computation*, 3:79–87.

Kohler, I. (1950). Development and alterations of the perceptual world: conditioned sensations. *Proceedings of the Austrian Academy of Sciences*, 227.

Kravitz, J. (1972). Conditioned adaptation to prismatic displacement. *Perception and Psychophysics*, 11:38–42.

Kravitz, J. and Yaffe, F. (1972). Conditioned adaptation to prismatic displacement with a tone as the conditional stimulus. *Perception and Psychophysics*, 12:305–308.

Moody, J. and Darken, C. (1989). Fast learning in networks of locally-tuned processing units. *Neural Computation*, 1(2):281–294.

Poggio, T. and Girosi, F. (1989). A theory of networks for approximation and learning. *AI Lab Memo 1140, MIT*.

Pouget, A. and Sejnowski, T. (1994). Spatial representation in the parietal cortex may use basis functions. In Tesauro, G., Touretzky, D., and Alspector, J., editors, *Advances in Neural Information Processing Systems 7*. Morgan Kaufmann.

Shelhamer, M., Robinson, D., and Tan, H. (1991). Context-specific gain switching in the human vestibuloocular reflex. In Cohen, B., Tomko, D., and Guedry, F., editors, *Annals Of The New York Academy Of Sciences*, volume 656, pages 889–891. New York Academy Of Sciences, New York.

Stratton, G. (1897a). Upright vision and the retinal image. *Psychological Review*, 4:182–187.

Stratton, G. (1897b). Vision without inversion of the retinal image. *Psychological Review*, 4:341–360, 463–481.

von Helmholtz, H. (1925). *Treatise on physiological optics (1867)*. Optical Society of America, Rochester, New York.

Welch, R. (1971). Discriminative conditioning of prism adaptation. *Perception and Psychophysics*, 10:90–92.

Welch, R. (1986). Adaptation to space perception. In Boff, K., Kaufman, L., and Thomas, J., editors, *Handbook of perception and performance*, volume 1, pages 24-1–24-45. Wiley-Interscience, New York.

Author Index

Abu-Mostafa, Yaser, 411
Ahmad, Subutai, 689
Alexander, Jay, 609
Alspector, J., 803
Ando, Hiroshi, 949
Andreou, Andreas G., 795
Asogawa, Minoru, 1101

Back, Andrew, 883
Baird, Leemon C., 353
Baldi, Pierre, 1085
Ballard, Dana H., 893
Baluja, Shumeet, 451
Barkai, N., 303
Barto, Andrew G., 401
Becker, Suzanna, 933
Behrman, Elizabeth C., 771
Bell, Anthony, 467
Bengio, Yoshua, 427, 553, 585
Bergen, Jim, 981
Berthold, Michael R., 521
Bischof, Horst, 941
Bishop, Chris M., 641, 1007
Bottou, Léon, 585
Boyan, Justin, 369
Bradtke, Steven, 393
Brashers-Krug, Tom, 19, 1117
Brauer, Wilfried, 247
Braver, Todd S., 141
Bregler, Christoph, 973
Brown, Thomas H., 69
Bruske, Jörg, 497
Buhmann, Joachim, 459
Burgess, Neil, 51
Burke, Harry, 1063
Burl, Michael, 1085

Carnevale, Nicholas, 69
Caruana, Rich, 657
Cauwenberghs, Gert, 779

Chang, Eric, 875
Chiang, Wan-Ping, 239
Churcher, S., 763
Claiborne, Brenda J., 69
Coggins, Richard, 739
Cohen, Jonathan D., 141
Cohn, David, 705
Cooper, Leon N., 747
Cortes, Corinna, 239
Cottrell, Garrison W., 481
Cowan, Jack D., 271
Crites, Robert, 401
Cruz-Cabrara, Alvaro A., 771

Darrell, Trevor, 909
Dayan, Peter, 1015
Deco, Gustavo, 247
Deffayet, Cedric, 125
Diamond, Jay, 521
Diorio, Chris, 739
Dong, Dawei, 925
Douglas, Rodney, 3
Doya, Kenji, 101
Dreyfus, Gérard, 1109
Duff, Michael O., 393

Edelman, Shimon, 117
Erwin, E., 93
Essa, Irfan, 909

Fayyad, Usama, 1085
Fels, S. Sidney, 843
Feng, Jianfeng, 319
Ferra, Herman, 215
Fine, Terrence L., 327, 335
Finke, Michael, 1093
Flower, Barry, 731
Frasconi, Paolo, 427, 553
Fritzke, Bernd, 625
Furlanello, Cesare, 867

Ghahramani, Zoubin, 43, 617, 705, 1125
Giles, C. Lee, 537, 649, 697
Giuliani, Diego, 867
Gold, Steven, 713, 957
Goodman, Philip H., 1063
Graham, Bruce, 513

Hadjifaradji, Saeed, 279
Hajto, J., 763
Hammer, Martin, 61
Han, Il-Song, 811
Hansen, Lars Kai, 673
Harmon, Mance, 353
Hasler, Paul, 739, 817
Hasselmo, Michael E., 77
Hassibi, Babak, 191
Hastie, Trevor, 999
Haynes, Paul S., 1007
Heil, Stefan, 1047
Hinton, Geoffrey, 843, 1015
Hinton, Geoffrey E., 635, 965
Hochreiter, Sepp, 529
Hoffmann, Thomas, 459
Holmes, A.J., 763
Horiuchi, Timothy, 787
Horn, David, 149
Horne, Bill G., 537, 649, 697
Hornik, Kurt, 941
Huertas, J. L., 755

Jaakkola, Tommi, 345, 361
Jabri, Marwan, 537, 731
Jackel, L. D., 239
James, Daniel L., 577
Jim, Kam, 649
Jordan, Michael I., 43, 345, 361, 435, 633, 705, 1125

Kailath, Thomas, 191
Kairiss, Edward W., 85
Kambhatla, Nanda, 681
Kazlas, Peter, 721
Ke, Liu, 1031
Kim, Ki-Chul, 811
Kindermann, Jörg, 443
Klopf, A. Harry, 353
Knerr, Stefan, 1109
Knierim, James J., 173
Koch, Christof, 3
Kowalczyk, Adam, 215
Krogh, Anders, 231

Kudrimoti, Hemant S., 173
Kukolich, Linda, 1055
Kuo, Jyh-Ming, 311

Lee, Hwang-Soo, 811
Leen, Todd K., 223, 681
Leerink, Laurens, 537
Legleye, Claire, 641
Lemmon, Michael, 569
Linares-Barranco, B., 755
Lippe, D., 803
Lippmann, Richard P., 875, 1055
Lu, Chien Ping, 957

Maass, Wolfgang, 183
Makhoul, John, 859
Malach, Rafael, 117
Malaka, Rainer, 61
Malpeli, Joseph G., 133
Manke, Stefan, 1093
Marchand, Mario, 279
Marion, Glenn, 255
Mathis, Donald, 11
McCallum, R. Andrew, 377
McNaughton, Bruce L., 173
McVey, Brian D., 1031
Mead, Carver, 739
Meir, Ronny, 295
Miikkulainen, Risto, 109, 577
Milgram, Maurice, 991
Minch, Bradley A., 739
Mjolsness, Eric, 713, 957
Moore, Andrew W., 369
Movellan, Javier, 851
Mozer, Michael C., 11, 609
Mukherjee, Sayandev, 335
Murphy, Sean D., 85
Murray, A. F., 763
Mussa-Ivaldi, Ferdinando, 1117

Nakano, Ryohei, 545
Negishi, Michiro, 27
Neuneier, Ralph, 689
Nix, David, 489
Niyogi, Partha, 593
Nowlan, Steven, 901

Obermayer, K., 93
Ohira, Toru, 271
Omohundro, Stephen M., 973
Oshima-Takane, Yuriko, 601

Author Index

Paass, Gerhard, 443
Pan, H., 319
Pappu, Suguna, 957
Pearson, John C., 981
Pedersen, Morten, 673
Pedroni, Volnei, 779
Pentland, Alex, 909
Perona, Pietro, 1085
Perrone, Michael P., 747
Personnaz, Léon, 1109
Pickard, Stephen, 731
Pineda, Fernando, 795
Platt, John C., 901
Pomerleau, Dean A., 451, 1039
Pouget, Alexandre, 125, 157
Price, David, 1109
Principe, Jose, 311

Ragg, Thomas, 61
Rangarajan, Anand, 713, 957
Rao, Rajesh, 893
Reggia, James A., 35, 149
Revow, Michael D., 965, 1015
Robinson, A. J., 835
Rose, M. J., 763
Rosen, David B., 1063
Roychowdhury, V. P., 319
Ruppin, Eytan, 35, 149

Saad, David, 255, 287
Säckinger, Eduard, 999
Sanger, Terence, 1023
Saul, Lawrence K., 435
Schmidhuber, Jurgen, 529, 1047
Schnell, Eric, 77
Schraudolph, Nicol, 475
Schulten, K., 93
Schulten, Klaus, 133
Schwartz, Anton, 385
Schwartz, Richard, 859
Schwenk, Holger, 991
Sejnowski, Terrence J., 101, 125, 157, 165, 467, 475, 1077
Serrano-Gotarredona, T., 755
Servan-Schreiber, David, 141
Seung, H. S., 303
Shadmehr, Reza, 19, 1117
Shahian, David, 1055
Shultz, Thomas, 601
Simard, Patrice, 999
Singh, Satinder, P. 345, 361

Sirosh, Joseph, 109
Skaggs, William, 173
Skinner, Steven R., 771
Slaney, Malcolm, 827
Smith, Mike E. U., 1007
Smyth, Padhraic, 1085
Sollich, Peter, 207, 287
Sommer, Gerald, 497
Spector, Kalanit Grill, 117
Spence, Clay D., 981
Sperduti, Alessandro, 665
Sroka, Jason, 859
Steck, James E., 771
Stensmo, Magnus, 1077
Stork, David G., 665
Suarez, Humbert, 3
Sundareswaran, V., 917
Sung, Kah Kay, 593
Suzuki, Satoshi, 949
Szymanski, Peter T., 569

Takane, Yoshio, 601
Taniguchi, Michiaki, 419
Tenenbaum, Joshua, 561
Terman, David, 199
Thrun, Sebastian, 1069
Thrun, Sebastian, 385, 505
Todd, Tom N., 1007
Todorov, Emanual V., 19, 561
Tokar, Robert L., 1031
Trentin, Edmondo, 867
Tresp, Volker, 419, 689
Trotman, David L., 1007
Tsai, Kenneth Y., 69
Tsoi, Ah Chung, 883
Tsung, Fu-Sheng, 481
Turmon, Michael, 327
Tzonev, Svilen, 133

Ueda, Naonori, 545

Vaina, Lucia M., 917
Vedelsby, Jesper, 231
Venkatesh, Santosh S., 263

Waibel, Alex, 1093
Wang, Changfeng, 263
Wang, DeLiang, 199
Waterhouse, S.R., 835
Weigend, Andreas S., 489, 721
Williams, Christopher, 965

Willshaw, David, 513
Windsor, Colin G., 1007
Wolpert, Daniel M., 43, 1125

Xu, Lei, 633

Zemel, Richard, 165
Zhao, Ying, 859

Keyword Index

a-Si:H, 763
abstraction, 385
action hierarchies, 385
activation functions, 279
active example selection, 593
active learning, 231, 287, 385, 443, 593, 705, 1069
active memory, 141
active vision, 451, 893
actor/critic algorithms, 401
adaptive control, 1031
adaptive critic, 401
adaptive interface, 843
adaptive optimal control, 361
advantage updating, 353
affine transformation, 713, 1101
AIFNN, 1101
alternating minimization, 569
amorphous silicon memory, 763
amplification, 3
analog VLSI, 731, 755, 787, 795, 803, 817
analog-digital VLSI, 811
analog VLSI synapses, 763
annealing schedule, 965
approximate dot product, 747
arm movements, 1117
ART 1, 755
articulatory loop, 51
associative memory, 35, 77, 149, 513, 925
associative net, 513
attractor networks, 11, 35, 149
attractors, 173
auditory localization chip, 787
auditory models, 827
auditory system, 125
autoassociative MLP, 991
autoassociative networks, 941
autoencoder networks, 165
autonomous vehicle navigation, 657
averaging, 419

awareness, 11
axon circuit, 739

backpropagation, 191, 1031, 1055
barn owl, 125
basis functions, 157
Bayesian inference, 255
Bellman residual, 353
bias, 295
binary features, 475
biological modeling, 61
biophysical modeling, 3
blind separation, 467
block codes, 795
Boltzmann learning, 435, 617
boosting, 875
bootstrap, 1055
breast cancer, 1063

cable theory, 69
capacity information efficiency, 513
CART, 1063
cascade-correlation, 537, 601
catastrophic forgetting, 419
catastrophic interference, 19
centroid, 999
chaotic time series, 311
character recognition, 747
chemosensory receptors, 69
chess, 1069
circular normal density, 641
City Block multilayer perceptron, 747
classification, 1109
cleanup process, 11
clustering, 361, 459, 585, 625, 681, 713, 779, 999
CMOS, 709, 811
CMOS vector quantizer, 779
coarse-to-fine search, 981
cochlear model, 827

cocktail party, 467
cognitive models, 141
cognitive task, 11
combined estimators, 295, 419
combining sensory modalities, 787
committee, 231, 419
compartmental models, 69
competition, 199
competitive clustering, 561
competitive learning, 85, 475, 497
computational complexity, 183
computational models, 85
conditional densities, 641
conditional probability, 1047
confidence, 1055
confidence intervals, 489
connectionist expert systems, 505
consciousness, 11
consolidation, 19
constrained rank Gaussian mixtures, 681
constructive learning, 537
context, 981
continuous speech recognition, 859
continuous time, 353
control, 19, 361, 1007, 1031
control gain, 1031
convergence, 585, 649
convergence of backpropagation, 335
convergence of stochastic gradient descent, 335
convolution network, 901
cooperation, 199
cooperative vector quantization, 617
coordinate transformations, 1125
coronary artery bypass, 1055
correlation based learning, 93
correlation network, 909
correlogram, 827
cortical columns, 117
cortical plasticity, 109
cosine units, 537
cost functions, 529
credit assignment through time, 427, 553
cross connections, 601
cross-validation, 231, 489
cursive handwriting recognition, 1109

data sampling, 593
data selection, 459
data transformations, 223
decision processes, 345

decision theory, 1077
decoding with dynamics, 795
decorrelation, 475, 925
deformable model, 965
delay line, 739
delusions, 149
dementia, 35
density estimation, 419, 641, 1047
desynchrony, 199
diagnosis, 1077
differential games, 353
direct multi-step prediction, 721
direction selectivity, 3
discrete-time, 883
distance measures, 713
distributed representations, 505, 577
dopamine, 101, 141
dynamic decay adjustment, 521
dynamic modelling, 311
dynamic programming, 345, 369, 393, 401
dynamic writing transformation, 1093
dynamical decorrelation, 925
dynamical systems, 481, 1031

early stopping, 263, 489
effective complexity, 263
effective machine size, 263
electronic transformation, 69
electrontonic space, 69
electrotonus, 69
EM algorithm, 419, 427, 435, 545, 553,
    585, 617, 681, 713, 835, 957, 1077, 1085
ensemble, 231
entropy, 287, 467, 475
error feedback, 1031
ERS-1 satellite, 641
estimation, 295
evidence, 255
example selection, 593
expectation-maximization, 419, 427, 435, 545,
    553, 585, 617, 681, 713, 835, 957, 1077,
    1085
experiment design, 593
explanation-based neural networks, 1069
extra outputs, 657

face recognition, 747
facial expressions, 909
factorial coding, 467
factorial learning, 561, 617
feature maps, 577

feedback, 925
feedback connections, 3
financial markets, 411, 529
finite size effects, 217
finite state machine, 697
fixed point attractors, 319
flat minima, 529
floating gate synapses, 817
focal lesions, 35
forecasting, 721
foreign exchange, 411
forward model, 43
frame of reference, 157
function approximation, 231, 361
fusion, 1007

gain control, 925
games, 1069
Gamma operator, 883
Gauss-Newton, 673
Gaussian mixture models, 1077
generalization, 207, 215, 223, 263, 287, 303,
    327, 361, 489, 529, 649, 657, 1125
generalization dynamics, 263
gesture recognition, 901
gesture-to-speech device, 843
Gibbs sampling, 617
global motion perception, 917
Glove-Talk II, 843
gradient descent, 585, 803
grammar, 27
grammar inference, 427
graph matching, 713
graph searching, 665
ground truth, 1085
grow-support algorithm, 369
growing structures, 497

H-infinity training, 191
hallucinations, 149
hand tracking, 901
handwriting decomposition, 1023
handwriting preprocessing, 1093
handwriting synthesis, 1023
handwritten character recognition, 965,
    1093, 1101
handwritten digit recognition, 999
head direction, 173
heart arrythmia , 731
heart attack, 1055
Hebbian learning, 93, 319

Hebbian synapses, 69
Helmholtz machine, 1015
hidden Markov models, 427, 435, 553, 617,
    851, 859, 867, 875
hidden state, 377
hierarchical mixture of experts, 835
hierarchical representation, 941
hierarchies, 385
high dimensional spaces, 747
hints, 411
hippocampal neurons, 69
hippocampus, 173
hippocampus model, 77
HMM, 427, 435, 553, 617, 851, 859, 867, 875
honey bee, 61
horizontal connections, 109
Hough transform, 965
human-computer interaction, 901, 1039
hybrid digital-analogue network, 1007
hyperparameters, 255
hysteresis, 3

image analysis, 1085
image compression, 941
image interpolation, 973
image model, 965
image processing, 451, 901
image pyramids, 941
image recognition, 657
image search, 981
imperfectly learnable problems, 287
implantable systems, 731
incomplete data, 545
incomplete patterns, 689
information gain, 287, 475
information theory, 467, 925
inhibition, 61, 141
instance-based learning, 377
instantiation parameters, 965
interacardiac electrogram classifier, 731
interference, 1117
interior point method, 569
internal model, 43
invariances, 991, 1007
invariant distance, 999
invariant recognition, 223
inverse dynamics, 19
inverse problems, 101
iterated prediction, 311
iterative projective scaling, 957

joint probability distribution, 1077
JPMAX, 933

k-blocking, 279
k-means, 585, 681
k-nearest neighbor, 377
Kalman filter, 43
Kerr-type materials, 771
keyboard input, 1039
knowledge incorporation, 991
knowledge representations, 601
Kohonen map, 497, 893
Korean speech recognition, 811

Lagrangian, 771
lateral connections, 117
lateral geniculate, 133
lateral inhibition, 109
learning curves, 239, 303, 327
learning dynamics, 207
learning from hints, 411
learning rate, 303
least squares, 295
lesions, 35
LGN organization, 133
Lie groups, 223
limit cycles, 481
limiting performance, 239
linear perceptron, 207
linear programming, 505
Linsker model, 319
lipreading, 851, 973
LISSOM, 109
local error bars, 835
local linear models, 973, 1015
local models, 697
local PCA, 973
locally weighted regression, 705
LOESS, 705
log-polar sensors, 893
logistic regression, 1055, 1063
long-term dependencies, 427
low loss redundancy reduction, 247
low power neural net, 731
LVQ, 681
Lyapunov exponent, 311

macaque monkey, 93
magnetic equilibrium, 1007
manifold learning, 973

Markov decision problems, 345, 393
Markov decision process, 361
Markov distributions, 279
Markov Monte Carlo, 443
master equations, 271
maximum entropy, 459, 545
maximum expected utility, 1077
maximum likelihood, 489, 545, 633
mean field theory, 957
medical risk, 1055
medicine, 1063
memory, 51
memory-based learning, 377
minimax, 353
minimax estimation, 191
minimum description length, 165, 1015
missing data, 459, 545, 689, 1077
mixture models, 419, 459, 585, 641, 681, 689,
    705, 713, 1015, 1077
mixture of experts, 19, 419, 427, 633, 843,
    859, 973, 1125
model selection, 443
model-fitting, 933
modular architecture, 901
modularity, 11
moments, 271
Monte-Carlo, 345
morphogenesis, 133
motion, 933
motion processing, 165
motor control, 43, 1017, 1125
motor learning, 19, 1023, 1117
motor maps, 893
movement primitives, 1023
MST, 165
multi-resolution, 981
multidimensional scaling, 459
multiple attractors, 319
multiple experts, 1085
multiple outputs, 721
multitask learning, 657

n-of-m expressions, 609
natural language, 27
navigation, 173
nearest neighbor, 377, 999
nearest sequence memory, 377
network analysis, 601
network interpretation, 505, 609
neural coding, 165
neural control, 1031

neural development, 93
neural gas, 497, 625
neural predictor, 1047
neuroanatomy, 117
neuro-chess, 1069
neuromodulation, 141
neuromorphic rendering, 69
neuronal modeling, 3
neuroscience, 125
Newton optimization, 585
NMDA synapse, 101
noise, 649
noisy data, 689
noisy neurons, 279
non-equilibrium systems, 271
non-Gaussian limiting behavior, 335
non-Markov environments, 377
nonlinear control, 1031
nonlinear decorrelation, 247
nonlinear dynamics, 319
nonlinear interpolation, 973
nonlinear system identification, 883

object recognition, 901, 933
observer model, 43
OCR, 965, 991, 1015, 1093, 1101, 1109
ocular dominance, 93
ocular dominance wavelength, 109
ocular-motor learning, 1125
olfaction, 61
on-line learning, 303, 335
optic flow, 165
optical back-propagation, 771
optical character recognition, 665, 991, 1015, 1093, 1101, 1109
optical imaging, 93
optical implementation, 771
optimal brain surgeon, 673
optimal stopping, 263
orientation, 173
orientation adaptation, 925
orientation columns, 925
orientation selectivity, 93, 117
oscillator, 199
outcome, 1063
overfitting, 489, 529

PAC learning, 215, 279
pairwise classifier, 1109
pancakes, 1015
parallel implementations of MLP, 747

parameter estimation, 545
parameter fitting, 61
parietal cortex, 157
Parzen windows, 689
patchy projections, 117
pathological attractors, 149
pattern classification, 665
pattern model, 93
pattern recognition, 999
PCA-pyramids, 941
perceptron, 279, 303
perceptual learning, 917
perceptual organization, 165
performance prediction, 239
periodic variables, 641
persistent state, 11
perturbative learning, 803
phase space learning, 481
phonological store, 51
piecewise fits, 633
plasma, 1007
plasticity, 173
plasticity site, 125
plasticity-mediated competition, 475
Poisson clumping heuristic, 327
pose, 957
posterior probabilities, 545, 1109
prediction, 489, 1063
prediction error, 443
predictive coding, 1047
prefrontal cortex, 141
primary visual system, 319
principal component analysis, 601, 941
prior knowledge, 411, 419, 553, 713
probabilistic classifier, 1109
probabilistic interpretation, 489
probabilistic outputs, 1109
product units, 537
protein sequences, 459
pruning, 529, 673
psychophysical models, 917
psychophysics, 19
pulse-based computation, 739

Q-learning, 353, 361, 385, 393, 401
qualitative analysis, 319
quantization, 941
quaternions, 957
queries, 443, 593, 705
query learning, 231, 287
queueing systems, 393

radial basis functions, 497, 521, 569, 1125
rank deficient mixtures, 681
rat, 173
RBF, 521
real-time recurrent learning, 673
real-time control, 1007
receiver operating characteristic, 875, 1085
receptive field formation, 319
receptor-transducer model, 61
recurrent networks, 141, 311, 427, 553, 649, 697
redundancy reduction, 247
refractory effects, 271
regression, 231, 489
regularization, 223, 649
rehearsal, 51
reinforcement learning, 101, 125, 345, 361, 369, 377, 385, 393, 401, 1069
relaxation, 199
remote sensing, 641, 1085
representation, 361
residual gradient algorithms, 353
robot arm kinematics, 505
robustness, 191
ROC , 875, 1085
rotation invariance, 665
rule extraction, 505, 601, 609
rule verification, 505

saccadic eye movements, 893
saliency map, 451
sample complexity, 215, 327
sample size requirements, 327
scene segmentation, 199
schizophrenia, 141, 149
second messenger, 61
second-order methods, 529, 585
second-order optimization, 673
segmentation, 165, 901
selective attention, 451
selective gating, 199
self-organization, 27, 77, 109, 319, 925
semi-Markov decision problems, 393
sense of direction, 173
sensorimotor coordination, 157
sensorimotor integration, 43, 1125
sequence analysis, 933
sequence learning, 427, 553
sequence processing, 577
serial order, 51
shared hidden units, 721

shift operator, 883
short-term memory, 51, 141
signal processing, 883
single transistor synapses, 817
singular value decomposition, 999
skills, 385
smooth value iteration, 369
soft clustering, 957
soft assign, 957
softmax, 51
spatial filters, 893
spatial representations, 157
speaker adaptation, 867
speaker normalization, 867
speaker transformation, 875
spectrogram inversion, 827
speech coding, 835
speech processing, 467
speech reading, 851
speech recognition, 577, 859, 867, 875
speech recognition with mixture of experts, 859
speech reconstruction, 827
speech representation, 827
spikes, 739
spiking neurons, 183
state aggregation, 361
state estimation, 43
state identification, 377
statistical mechanics, 271, 287, 545
statistical physics, 255
statistical properties of high-D spaces, 747
stochastic approximation, 303, 335, 803
stochastic gradient ascent, 101
stochastic learning, 649
stochastic neurodynamics, 271
stochastic perceptrons, 279
strabismus, 109
structure, 385
subjective probability, 1085
subspace models, 999
sun spots, 673
superior colliculus, 893
supervised learning, 255, 657, 721
survival, 1063
symbolic rules, 609
symmetries, 223
symmetry hint, 411
synaptic interactions, 69
synaptic perturbation, 101
synchrony, 199

Keyword Index

system identification, 697, 883

talker transformation, 875
talking machine, 843
tangent distance, 665, 991, 999, 1015, 1101
TD learning, 721
templates, 957
temporal coherence, 933
temporal difference, 401
temporal difference learning, 1069
temporal dynamics, 263
temporal processing, 85, 883
temporal sequences, 51
text compression, 1047
text prediction, 1039, 1047
thalamus, 173
thermodynamic limit, 207
three-dimensional object recognition, 949
three-state neurons, 271
time series, 489
time series prediction, 435, 673, 721, 835
time-delay neural network, 697, 1093
timing precision, 183
TNM staging system, 1063
tokamak, 1007
topological map, 497, 577
trajectory learning, 481
transfer, 19
transformation, 991
transformation invariance, 665
translation invariance, 665
two-dimensional views, 949
two-port analysis, 69
two-spirals problem, 601
typing, 1039

unrealizable rule, 255, 287
unsupervised 3-D object recognition, 949
unsupervised learning, 109, 165, 247, 459, 467, 475, 497, 561, 577, 585, 617, 625, 681, 713, 933, 949
unsupervised motor learning, 1023
URAN, 811

validity interval analysis, 505
value iteration, 369
van der Pol oscillator, 481
variance, 295
variance estimation, 705
VC dimension, 215, 327
VC bounds, 327

vector quantization, 625, 779, 835
vectorial code, 157
velocity tuning, 3
virtual examples, 411
vision, 451, 933, 973
visual attention, 451
visual cortex, 3, 93, 157, 165
visuomotor learning, 1125
VLSI, 731, 811
VLSI algorithms, 747
VLSI dynamical decoder, 795
VLSI synapses, 817
vocabulary acquisition, 51
VQ chip, 779

weight decay, 529, 649
weight perturbation, 803
weight templates, 609
well-formed state, 11
wind vectors, 641
winner-take-all, 51, 513, 681
word spotting, 875
working memory, 1117

zip codes, 999